THE AMERICAN INSTITUTE OF ARCHI

M000210178

The Architecture Student's Handbook of Professional Practice

Fourteenth Edition

WILEY

John Wiley & Sons, Inc.

This book is printed on acid-free paper. ♾

Copyright © 2009 by The American Institute of Architects. All rights reserved. "AIA" and the AIA logo are registered trademarks and service marks of The American Institute of Architects.

Published by John Wiley & Sons, Inc., Hoboken, New Jersey

Published simultaneously in Canada

No part of this publication may be reproduced, stored in a retrieval system, or transmitted in any form or by any means, electronic, mechanical, photocopying, recording, scanning, or otherwise, except as permitted under Section 107 or 108 of the 1976 United States Copyright Act, without either the prior written permission of the Publisher, or authorization through payment of the appropriate per-copy fee to the Copyright Clearance Center, 222 Rosewood Drive, Danvers, MA 01923, (978) 750-8400, fax (978) 646-8600, or on the web at www.copyright.com. Requests to the Publisher for permission should be addressed to the Permissions Department, John Wiley & Sons, Inc., 111 River Street, Hoboken, NJ 07030, (201) 748-6011, fax (201) 748-6008, or online at www.wiley.com/go/permissions.

Limit of Liability/Disclaimer of Warranty: While the publisher and the author have used their best efforts in preparing this book, they make no representations or warranties with respect to the accuracy or completeness of the contents of this book and specifically disclaim any implied warranties of merchantability or fitness for a particular purpose. No warranty may be created or extended by sales representatives or written sales materials. The advice and strategies contained herein may not be suitable for your situation. You should consult with a professional where appropriate. Neither the publisher nor the author shall be liable for any loss of profit or any other commercial damages, including but not limited to special, incidental, consequential, or other damages.

For general information about our other products and services, please contact our Customer Care Department within the United States at (800) 762-2974, outside the United States at (317) 572-3993 or fax (317) 572-4002.

Wiley also publishes its books in a variety of electronic formats. Some content that appears in print may not be available in electronic books. For more information about Wiley products, visit our web site at www.wiley.com.

Library of Congress Cataloging-in-Publication Data:

The architecture student's handbook of professional practice / the American Institute of Architects.
—14th ed.
     p. cm.
   Rev. ed. of: Architect's handbook of professional practice. student ed., 13th ed.
   Includes bibliographical references and index.
   ISBN 978-0-470-08869-2 (alk. paper/cd)
   1. Architectural practice—United States—Handbooks, manuals, etc.   2. Architectural services marketing—United States—Handbooks, manuals, etc.   I. American Institute of Architects.
   II. Architect's handbook of professional practice.
   NA1996.A726 2008b
   720.68—dc22
                                                                          2008018988

Printed in the United States of America

10 9 8 7 6 5 4 3 2

Contents

About The Architecture Student's Handbook
of Professional Practice   vii

PART 1 THE PROFESSION _____ 1

1 Professional Life   2
1.1 Architecture as a Profession   2
1.2 Ethics and Professional Conduct   6
  2004 AIA Code of Ethics & Professional Conduct   15
1.3 Service Leadership in Architecture Practice   19
1.4 Participating in Professional Organizations   23

2 Legal Dimensions of Practice   30
2.1 Architects and the Law   30
  *Copyright and Intellectual Property in the
  Digital Age   37*
2.2 Regulation of Professional Practice   44
  Mandatory Continuing Education   48

3 Professional Development   51
3.1 Developing Leadership Skills   51
3.2 Developing Communication Skills   64

PART 2 PRACTICE _____ 75

4 Developing a Practice   76
4.1 Starting an Architecture Firm   76
4.2 Firm Legal Structure   87
4.3 Firm Identity and Expertise   97
  Establishing a Niche Practice   108
4.4 Team Building   110
4.5 Marketing Strategy and Planning   121
4.6 How Clients Select Architects   133

5 Running a Practice   145
5.1 Financial Planning   145
5.2 Financial Management Systems   155
  Computerized Financial Systems   162
5.3 Maintaining Financial Health   165

5.4 Risk Management Strategies   174
  How to Use Risk Assessment Matrixes   186
5.5 Insurance Coverage   194
5.6 Managing and Avoiding Disputes   208
5.7 Information Management   218
5.8 Computer Technology in Practice   225
  Building Information Modeling   237

PART 3 THE PROJECT _____ 239

6 Project Definition   240
6.1 Defining Project Services   240
6.2 Architectural Services and Compensation   249
6.3 Programming   260
6.4 Research and Analysis   267
6.5 Design Based on Evidence   281
6.6 Integrated vs. Traditional Practice   293

7 Project Development   303
7.1 Sustainable Design   303
7.2 Environmentally Preferable Product
  Selection   318
7.3 Design Phases   330
7.4 Value Analysis   341
7.5 Life Cycle Costing   356

8 Project Delivery   371
8.1 Project Delivery Methods   371
  Construction Management   381
  Design-Build Project Delivery   384
8.2 Integrated Project Delivery   387
8.3 Construction Documentation   391
  The U.S. National CAD Standard   419
  AIA MASTERSPEC   420
8.4 Bidding or Negotiation Phase   422
8.5 Construction Contract Administration   433

9 Project Management   452
9.1 The Effective Project Manager   452
9.2 Managing Architectural Projects   459
9.3 Project Controls   478
  Project Scheduling   491

9.4 Construction Cost Management   495

9.5 Maintaining Design Quality   510

9.6 Project Closeouts   522

10 Building Codes and Regulations   533

10.1 Community Planning Controls   533

10.2 Building Codes and Standards   554

The International Building Code   568

PART 4 CONTRACTS AND AGREEMENTS ———— 575

11 Types of Agreements   576

11.1 Agreements with Owners   576

11.2 Owner-Generated Agreements   585

11.3 Project Design Team Agreements   602

11.4 Construction Contracts   612

12 AIA Contract Documents   622

12.1 The AIA Documents Program   622

2007 AIA Contract Documents   632

12.2 AIA Contract Documents Synopses by Family   634

Appendices   655

A: Resources for Intern Architects   655

B: Allied Professional Organizations   657

C: Schools of Architecture   664

D: State Registration Boards   670

E: Glossary   673

Index   695

Note: Topic backgrounders are shown in italics.

Fourteenth Edition Student Handbook Participants

Student Edition Steering Group
Michael Hricak, FAIA, Chair
Joseph Bilello, FAIA
Jonathan Cohen, FAIA
Ed Friedrichs, FAIA
Richard L. Hayes, AIA
Barbara Jackson, Ph.D., DBIA
Marvin J. Malecha, FAIA, ACSA
Deborah Sweitzer
James B. Atkins, FAIA (ex-officio)

Contributing Authors
AIA California Council
James B. Atkins, FAIA
Phillip G. Bernstein, FAIA
Glenn W. Birx, AIA
Brian Bowen
Christopher Bushnell, AIA
Ann Casso
William Charvat, FAIA
David S. Collins, FAIA
Kenneth C. Crocco, FAIA
Philip R. Croessmann, Esq., AIA
Richard D. Crowell
Dana Cuff, Ph.D.
Jessica L. Darraby, Esq.
Clark Davis, AIA
Michael Dell'Isola, PE
James T. Dunn, Assoc. AIA
George Elvin, Ph.D.
Kristine K. Fallon, FAIA
Scott R. Fradin, Esq., AIA
Phillip H. Gerou, FAIA
Lowell V. Getz
David Greusel, AIA
Dennis J. Hall, FAIA
D. Kirk Hamilton, FAIA
Gregory Hancks, Esq., AIA
Suzanne Harness, Esq., AIA
Douglas C. Hartman, FAIA
Robert G Hershberger, FAIA
Michael M. Hricak, FAIA
Joseph H. Jones Jr., Esq., AIA

Mark Jussaume, PE
David F. Kinzer III
Steven Kirk, FAIA
David Koren, Assoc. AIA
Peggy Lawless
Thom Lowther
John-Paul Lujan, Esq.
Nadav Malin
Nancy Malone, AIA
Paul T. Mendelsohn
Elena Marcheso Moreno
Frank Musica, Esq., Assoc. AIA
Robert Mutchler, FAIA
Bradford Perkins, FAIA
Peter Piven, FAIA
Barry Posner, Ph.D.
Wendy Pound
G. William Quatman, Esq., FAIA
Jack Reigle
Tony Rinella, Assoc. AIA
William C. Ronco
Patricia P. Rosenzweig
Andrea S. Rutledge
Fredric W. Schultz
Henry Siegel, FAIA
Grant Armann Simpson, FAIA
Debra L. Smith, AIA
Frank A. Stasiowski, FAIA
Steven G. M. Stein, Esq.
Larry Strain, FAIA
Timothy R. Twomey, Esq., AIA

AIA Project Staff
Richard L. Hayes, AIA, Ph.D.
Joseph A. Demkin, AIA
Pamela James Blumgart
Jamila Shrestha Yeung

Wiley Project Staff
John Czarnecki, Assoc. AIA
Michael Olivo
Jacqueline Beach

About *The Architecture Student's Handbook of Professional Practice*

This book goes to press at a time when society faces both challenging economic issues and an increasing awareness of the impact of global climate change. In this context, a host of forces are coming together to demand more of the architecture profession, allied design professionals, and the construction industry. We have learned, in unequivocal terms, that everyone everywhere is affected by the built environment and its relationship to, and effect on, the natural environment.

These times call for a wider definition of what is meant by "practice" and "design," both in the profession and in schools of architecture. An end to the estrangement between the core design curriculum and the examination and study of practice is also long overdue. Until now, the focus in architecture schools has been on the end product of the design process. To address mounting demands, architecture practice and education must begin operating with new tools, beliefs, and behaviors. The evolving role of the architect is addressed in this *The Architecture Student's Handbook of Professional Practice*, Fourteenth Edition.

TITLE AND ORGANIZATION OF THE BOOK

In a noted departure, this book is not simply an abridged version of *The Architect's Handbook of Professional Practice*, Fourteenth Edition. Recognizing its use as required reading in professional practice courses and sometimes as a companion in studio courses—along with the fact that the information needs of architecture students are not the same as those of professionals—this book contains knowledge specific to the needs of students and emerging professionals that has been organized to be approachable for them. To reflect this increased focus on the needs of students, the publisher John Wiley & Sons and the American Institute of Architects (AIA), as author, chose to name this book *The Architecture Student's Handbook of Professional Practice*.

Like *The Architect's Handbook of Professional Practice*, 14th edition, published in 2008, *The Architecture Student's Handbook* is presented in four key parts. However, the names of the parts—The Profession, Practice, The Project, and Contracts and Agreements—and the organization of the material within them are different. The progression of material makes the book suitable for use as a professional practice course outline, beginning with consideration of the concepts of professionalism through the construction and closeout of projects, as well as consideration of the legal agreements used for project delivery.

Content Structure

Content from *The Architect's Handbook* has been either included in *The Architecture Student's Handbook* in its entirety or edited or abridged as appropriate for the student reader. Unlike the previous student editions, this volume contains new material prepared specifically for *The Architecture Student's Handbook* that does not appear in *The Architect's Handbook*. This text was written for those beginning to learn about the architecture profession or navigating the beginning of their careers. Conceived as a true handbook, this volume is a resource to be used in the examination of all aspects of architecture practice, including research, programming, professional relationships, the design process, and the intricacies of delivering a project.

In addition, the book contains unique content on changes under way in the design and construction industry that are having a profound impact on the practice of architecture. This material invites readers to explore new possibilities in architecture practice and to redefine both what architects do and how they accomplish their goals. Particular emphasis is given to integrated practice and integrated project delivery and the emerging tools that enable architects to approach practice—in its widest sense—in new, more effective, and more expansive ways. In parallel with the focus of the AIA, new content is included on research and "evidenced-based" design. The variety of subject matter makes *The Architecture Student's Handbook* a useful resource for design studios, seminars, and research efforts, in addition to its use as a professional practice textbook.

A NEW APPROACH TO PRACTICE

A theme running through this edition is the protection of the design integrity of projects, a greater concern as architects increasingly rely on electronic tools. Behaviors and practices necessary to accomplish this goal, which both protects client interests and allows for professional satisfaction and reward, are discussed. In today's design and construction marketplace, architects are called on to consider accepting new risks and responsibilities. Students studying architecture, as well as recent graduates, can use the same creative impulse in use in the studio to design a method of practice that ultimately makes it possible to deliver the projects conceived.

In accepting the 2005 AIA/ACSA Topaz Medallion, Edward Allen, FAIA, spoke to the issue of art versus science in architecture education. He suggested that these two categories have long been inadequate for describing what architecture truly is and offered the following alternate perspective: "Architecture is neither art nor science; it belongs to a realm of intellectual endeavor called design. Its goal is to produce new products to solve human problems."

It is through practice that design becomes useful. Practice provides a framework that enables the architect to progress confidently from concept to completion. *The Architecture Student's Handbook* introduces the concept of professional practice to students so they will enter the profession with a well-rounded education that has readied them for all aspects of architecture practice.

— Michael Hricak, FAIA
The editor of *The Architecture Student's Handbook of Professional Practice*, Fourteenth Edition, Michael Hricak owns his own firm, Michael Hricak Architects, and has taught professional practice courses at the University of Southern California.

PART 1
THE PROFESSION

CHAPTER 1

Professional Life

1.1 Architecture as a Profession

Dana Cuff, Ph.D.

Architecture is in the family of vocations called professions, all of which share certain qualities and collectively occupy a special position in society. Architects' status as professionals provides them with an underlying structure for their everyday activities.

To be a professional means many things today. One can be a professional athlete, student, or electrician. Each of these occupations uses the term in ways distinct from what we mean by the professional who is a doctor, lawyer, or architect.

Typically, we distinguish professionals who do certain work for a living from amateurs who work without compensation. The term *amateur* connotes a dabbler, or someone having less training and expertise than a professional.

We also differentiate between professions and other occupations. Expertise, training, and skill help define those vocations that "profess" to have a specialized territory of knowledge for practice. While many occupations require expertise, training, and skill, professions are based specifically on fields of higher learning. Such learning takes place primarily in institutions of higher education rather than in vocational schools or on the job. Universities introduce prospective professionals to the body of theory or knowledge in their field. Later, this introduction is augmented by some form of internship in which practical skills and techniques are mastered.

A high level of education is expected of professionals because their judgments benefit—or, if incompetently exercised, endanger—the public good. Thus people who are attracted to the professions usually have altruistic concerns for their society.

Dana Cuff is a professor in the Architecture and Urban Design department of the School of the Arts and Architecture at the University of California, Los Angeles.

The status of professions, their internal characteristics, and their relationship to society are constantly, if not always perceptibly, changing. The professions have grown dramatically in recent years, in keeping with the rise of the postindustrial, service economy. Growth in professional employment has accompanied expansion of the service sector of the economy, estimated today to be 70 percent of the labor force. In a service economy, information and knowledge industries become dominant, creating the context in which professions can rise among occupations.

CHARACTERISTICS OF A PROFESSION

Professions are dynamic entities that reflect our society, our economy, and, generally, our times. There is no widely accepted definition or list of features that covers all professions. Nevertheless, they have some characteristics in common, which have appeared throughout history.

Lengthy and Arduous Education

Perhaps the most frequently cited characteristic of a profession is a lengthy and sometimes arduous education. A professional must learn a body of technical knowledge and also develop an ability to exercise judgment in the use of that knowledge. Thus, all established professions incorporate long periods of high-level education.

Professional education is also a form of socialization. Like a rite of passage for initiates, architecture, medical, and law schools are places where future practitioners are introduced to the knowledge, values, and skills of their profession. Students undergo tests of their commitment and ability. In architecture schools, a good example is the charrette (often involving all-nighters), during which students concentrate all their efforts to finish a project. These experiences instill tacit beliefs about the significance of architecture, the work effort required to do a good job, and the commitment needed to become an architect. Through selective admissions, carefully designed curricula, and rigorous graduation standards, schools guide the formation of their professional progeny. Professional schools play a key role in developing the shared worldview that characterizes a professional community.

Expertise and Judgment

Professions traffic in ideas and services rather than in goods or products. Rather than marketing a better widget, professionals sell their expertise. They have knowledge outside the ken of the layperson. Professions are based upon a balance of technical knowledge, reasoned judgment in applying such knowledge, and inexplicable, even mysterious talents that some call artistry. Thus, while doctors need a high degree of scientifically based knowledge, they also need diagnostic ability and a good bedside manner.

Expertise begins with theoretical knowledge taught in universities, but being a competent professional also means knowing how to apply this knowledge. Among practitioners, both expertise and experience contribute to quality performance. While initial skills are taught in school, a large share of professional training comes from the practicum or internship; it then continues in lifelong learning through the gathering of experience and the application of new concepts and technologies.

Registration

Because professional judgments affect the public good, professionals generally are required to be licensed in order to practice. This serves as a means of protecting the public health, safety, and welfare. Professions require sophisticated relationships with people and information. To become licensed, professionals are usually required to meet education and experience standards and to pass a compulsory comprehensive examination.

Relative Autonomy

Because professionals exercise considerable judgment and discretion, professional work is intended to be more autonomous and self-determined than work controlled by owner-managers as in the production of goods.

Other Traits

In addition to these primary characteristics, a number of other traits are typical of professions:

- Because they are well trained to perform complex services, professionals generally command relatively high incomes and high prestige in their communities.
- As a group, professionals attach a large part of their identity to their careers, rarely changing vocations.
- Within each profession, members usually hold a set of common values; they often speak what amounts to a dialect that is not easily understood by outsiders.
- Professionals understand the importance and value of lifetime learning.
- Professions are relatively well organized, and a significant proportion of their members belong to a national professional organization such as the American Medical Association, the American Bar Association, or the American Institute of Architects.

These characteristics are in constant evolution. For example, the prestige of a given profession may suffer under consumer dissatisfaction or be enhanced by significant developments in the field that have positive social repercussions. The professional degree that was once optional becomes a necessity. Professional organizations are periodically strengthened by programs that capture practitioners' attention. Such evolution depends in part upon the participation of professionals themselves—in their schools, professional associations, and communities.

ARCHITECTURE AMONG THE PROFESSIONS

Many of the trends influencing architectural practice have parallels in other professions. For example, the tensions created by complexity and specialization, consumer influences, and divergence of goals among practices can also be seen in the professions of law and medicine.

These common influences notwithstanding, each profession introduces its own variations and idiosyncrasies. Looking at architecture among the professions, we observe the following features.

Relationships with the Arts

The qualities that most clearly set architecture apart from other established professions are its close ties to the arts and its similarities to artistic endeavors. Creativity is crucial to all professions, but for the architect it is of the highest priority. Moreover, architects produce objects that are fixed in space, highly public, and generally long-lasting.

Importance of Design

Although all professions are based on a balance of technical and indeterminate knowledge, some stress one over the other. Architecture emphasizes an artistic, relatively inexplicable domain of expertise—design—as the core of the practitioner's identity. Design requires rational knowledge of how buildings are put together, how they will function, historical models for building types, materials, mechanical systems, structures, and so on. But being a good architect also presumes that the professional possesses something extra—aesthetic sensibility, talent, or creative ability, whatever we choose to call it.

Place in the Social Structure

According to one study that compared a number of professions on a variety of dimensions, architecture ranked high in terms of prestige but in the middle range in average years of education, average income, and proportion of members belonging to professional organizations. This suggests that architecture's respected place in the social structure has been granted by society rather than defined through numbers, dollars, or professional control.

The profession's position in the social structure has been changing. Historically, the church, the state, and powerful individuals were the primary patrons for architectural services. Now, industrial and commercial enterprises have become major clients as well. During the 1960s, when community design emerged as a subdiscipline, architects sought and secured a role in housing and neighborhood revitalization; this activity has evolved into a growing presence in community and urban design.

Architectural practice is developing in new ways that allow architects to intermingle with a broader population. One recent study argues that architecture is more closely connected to a large, relatively affluent middle class than to a small group of the very rich. In a similar vein, the composition of the profession is changing, particularly as more women and ethnic minorities become architects.

Place in the Economic Structure

The well-being of the architectural profession depends upon ties to a healthy building industry. The level of construction activity both nationally and internationally significantly determines the amount and type of services architects will render.

As the United States urbanized and industrialized, the demand for buildings was great and the architectural profession grew rapidly. In more recent times, however, construction has declined proportionately in the national economy. With the evolution from a goods-producing economy to a service economy, there are fewer major new building projects.

At the same time, the demand for architectural services has increased—especially in the predesign and postconstruction phases. This suggests a repositioning of the profession, along with other professions, as part of the service economy. New roles and markets for services have been created. In addition, new roles and specializations mean that more professionals are doing what was once one individual's job.

Internal Social Structure

Within any profession, there are social divisions that complement and compete with one another. Those who study professions call these divisions the rank and file, the administrators, and the intelligentsia.

In the architectural profession, the rank and file might be considered to include drafters and junior design and production people; the administrators to include principals, senior designers, and project managers; and the intelligentsia to include academicians, critics, practitioner-theorists, and those architects who push the parameters of architecture outward and whose work often establishes precedents for others to follow.

The values and objectives of each group are likely to conflict with those of other groups at times. The first two groups have very different convictions, agendas, and knowledge of the way practice operates. These differences become important in a profession where, even though a majority of architecture firms are small, the provision of architectural services has been heavily influenced by larger firms in which many of the architects are wage-earning employees who work not for clients but for their architect-employers. Data from the 2006 AIA Firm Survey confirm this: While only 4 percent of the firms owned by AIA members had fifty or more employees in them, these firms accounted for 52 percent of the operating revenues earned by all AIA member-owned firms.

Initially, an increase in intraprofessional stratification brought a greater need to formalize professional control. Firms created organization charts, personnel policies, and manuals governing project procedures. Many professionals devoted themselves to managing the organization. As firms grew, they dealt with these phenomena in different ways. Compare, for example, the large law firm, which is a collection of relative coequals (the main distinction being seniority among partners), and the hospital, which has a stricter hierarchy of medical administrators, senior physicians, residents, and interns. In recent years, however, there seems to be a general trend away from stratification in architecture firms—even in large firms. The advent of the second generation of digital technology and the maturing of the architectural profession in its use, along with an integrated approach to project delivery, has encouraged firms to be more horizontally organized and much less hierarchical.

PROFESSIONS AND SOCIETY

Professionals possess knowledge and ability not accessible to the public. As a result, the public establishes a special relationship with professional groups, essentially granting each a monopoly in its area of practice. Society thus grants members of professional groups certain rights and privileges:

- A certain level of prestige and respect
- A certain amount of autonomy and authority
- A relatively high level of compensation
- A standard of reasonable care with which to judge the appropriateness of professional actions

In return for these rights and privileges, society expects a profession to assume certain obligations:

- Establishing and maintaining standards for admission and practice
- Protecting public health, safety, and welfare
- Considering the public good when working for an individual client
- Respecting public welfare over personal gain

Every profession participates in a coordinated body of tasks necessary to fulfill its obligations to the public and to manage the profession. These tasks include establishing a body of professional knowledge, regulating entry to the profession, and maintaining standards for practice. Each profession develops mechanisms for accrediting educational programs, licensing professionals to practice, encouraging continuing education, and regulating professional ethics and conduct.

By and large, these mechanisms are designed, staffed, and implemented by professionals. Architects have the major voice in where and how new architects are educated. They sit on registration boards, write and grade the licensing examination, and recommend laws and administrative guidelines for registration. Architects conduct disciplinary hearings and, through the AIA, establish and enforce codes of ethical behavior. Like all professionals, architects have substantial voices in establishing their own destiny.

1.2 Ethics and Professional Conduct

Phillip H. Gerou, FAIA

Architects are confronted daily with moral choices, competing loyalties, and ethical dilemmas. Although such situations can be ambiguous or paradoxical, basic tenets held in common by the profession can help architects determine how to respond to them.

Phillip H. Gerou is a former director and vice president of the American Institute of Architects and served six years as a member and chairman of the AIA National Ethics Council.

The need to articulate and advocate ethical standards has never been more critical. Concern about professional ethics, while not a recent development, has certainly become more conspicuous in recent years. This visibility has led to extensive inquiries into the sources, development, interpretation, and enforcement of ethical codes. Principles guiding professional conduct are based on the core values held by that profession. These core values originate in legal definitions, social mores, moral codes, and common business practices.

Legal systems are based on historical precedent and commonly accepted social interactions between individuals or legal entities. The rights of individuals are protected by mutual acceptance of this legal structure. Contractual and other legal responsibilities and their consequences are generally well defined in law and in written agreements. But when these responsibilities and their consequences are specific to a profession, they may prove difficult to legally enforce.

There are many social conventions, moral beliefs, and ethical dilemmas that are not legislated or enforced by any regulatory agency. These may include widely accepted values but are not part of our legal system because they lack consensus or represent conflicting opinions. These values are often defined by religious doctrine, corporate policies, or societal rules. While morality describes behavior that is generally accepted as either correct or incorrect, ethical situations often present dilemmas in which equally relevant positions compete.

Ethics is traditionally defined as the rules or standards for moral behavior. Often the terms *morality* and *ethics* are used interchangeably, and to many there is no distinction between the two. The definition of ethics has also evolved to express a set of values held by a unique and finite group of individuals, such as a corporation, legislature, industry, or profession. Ethical codes are based on common values and moral laws such as religious doctrine, social conventions, secular beliefs, and traditional philosophies; they may even incorporate the values of courtesy, civility, mutual respect, or equality. Ethical standards for doctors or priests are different in their details from those of architects or engineers, although the core beliefs and the moral guidelines on which they are founded may be nearly identical. The distinction in ethical standards depends on the specific practices of a particular group.

Ethics also define fairness and equity and quite often relate to issues in which two parties may hold opposing but equally valid points of view or an individual may be torn between two compelling positions. For example, an individual may find that speaking the truth could breach a confidence, someone's dedication to a friendship might result in injury to others if an obligation to protect the public is ignored, or a client's goals could be at odds with protection of the environment. In certain situations, ethical standards may take precedence over other important standards. For example, life safety issues are usually perceived as a primary concern in comparison to, for example, obligations to employers. Although a solution that positively addresses each competing issue is preferred, occasionally a choice is necessary. Ethical codes address such situations, but it is often left to an informed and impartial observer to make the final judgment.

ETHICAL STANDARDS FOR ARCHITECTS

In the United States, there are two widely used standards of conduct for architects. In 1977 the National Council of Architectural Registration Boards (NCARB) issued a set of model rules of conduct for use by its member boards. NCARB rules are guided by certain core values as they pertain to the protection of the life, safety, and welfare of the public, issues to which architects are legally bound by individual state licensure laws. NCARB's rules of conduct have been adopted, with modifications, by various NCARB member boards as part of the licensing regulations that apply to individual architects.

The American Institute of Architects (AIA) has established a Code of Ethics and Professional Conduct. This code addresses life safety and public welfare issues, and also includes rules of conduct that deal with professional interactions between architects and their colleagues and their clients. Members of the AIA are also held accountable by the code for such broad issues as seeking aesthetic excellence and respecting the environment.

The first AIA ethical code was established in 1909. By today's standards, some of the original principles seem out-of-date. Under the original code, design-build was a forbidden practice and paid advertising by architects was not allowed. The code also prohibited architects from competing on the basis of fees or entering design competitions that were not in keeping with Institute principles. These restrictions were derived more from the common business practices of the day than universal core values or widely accepted moral principles.

By the late 1970s, the AIA code of ethics had been significantly amended. Design-build became an accepted approach to project delivery, and advertising was no longer the anathema it had been. By 1972 the U.S. Justice Department had determined that the 1890 Sherman Antitrust Act demanded that architects be allowed to compete on the basis of fees and that not doing so constituted an unreasonable restraint of trade. In a 1978 case involving the National Society of Professional Engineers, the Supreme Court ruled that unfettered competition was essential to the health of a free-market economy, and the only lawful way competition could be constrained was through state or federal legislation. In its opinion, the court dismissed arguments stressing the possible negative effects of fee competition on the health, safety, and welfare of the public.

In 1977, an architect sued the Institute for civil damages when his AIA membership was suspended for violating the AIA code of ethics by supplanting another architect on a project. Although the violation was not disputed, in 1978 a federal district court ruled that enforcement of this particular rule in the code violated federal antitrust laws and the accused architect was awarded substantial monetary damages.

In response to these rulings, in 1980 the AIA suspended its code of ethics. The following year a statement of ethical principles was established as a guideline for the voluntary conduct of members. Recognizing a need for mandatory professional guidelines, the AIA Board of Directors subsequently appointed a task force to propose a substitute Code of Ethics and Professional Conduct. In 1986 the membership adopted the new code at the AIA National Convention. Since that time, minor revisions have been made to keep pace with current technologies, economic realities, and changing social demands.

PROFESSIONAL ASPIRATIONS VS. ETHICAL CONDUCT

Some ethical situations are not regulated by the AIA Code of Ethics and Professional Conduct. For example, the profession of architecture as a whole may aspire to contribute to the preservation of historical and cultural resources by helping to develop appropriate building codes or formulating aesthetic guidelines. Nonetheless, some architects are more suited to such tasks than others; for instance, participation in this effort may not be a reasonable requirement for an AIA member whose expertise lies in financial management or graphic design. Similarly, it is not a requirement that all AIA members provide pro bono services, as some may choose to support causes or organizations by other means. A code of ethics cannot embrace every aspiration of a profession. Rather, it must exhibit restraint in defining actions to which all members may reasonably submit.

AIA Code of Ethics and Professional Conduct

The current AIA Code of Ethics and Professional Conduct defines in detail the obligations of AIA members. The code is organized into five canons that describe broad principles of conduct: general obligations, obligations to the public, obligations to the client, obligations to the profession, and obligations to colleagues.

Each canon is defined by a number of ethical standards. These standards provide more defined goals, which members should aspire to in their professional performance and behavior. Individual ethical standards incorporate specific rules of conduct that are mandatory and enforceable. Violation of a rule by an AIA member may be grounds for disciplinary action by the Institute. Commentary, which is offered to clarify or elaborate the intent of the rule, is provided for some of the rules of conduct.

The code applies to the professional activities of all AIA members regardless of their membership category and is enforced by the AIA National Ethics Council. Only AIA members are obligated to comply with these standards.

AIA National Ethics Council

The National Ethics Council (NEC) is made up of seven AIA members selected and appointed according to specific credentials. Each of the seven members represents a diverse constituency. They come from various regions of the country and different types of practice and professional backgrounds, and they are representative of the general membership based on diverse demographic criteria. Prospective NEC members are recommended to the AIA Board of Directors, which makes the final decision and appointment. Appointments are for a three-year term, although members of the NEC may be, and usually are, reappointed for a second three-year term. An NEC member may not serve more than two consecutive full terms.

The full ethics council meets three times per year to hear and consider complaints. The particulars of each case, along with a recommendation for resolving it, are presented to the NEC by one of its members who serves as a hearing officer. This individual is then excused while the remaining NEC members consider the report and recommendation and ultimately decide whether to accept, reject, or modify the hearing officer's recommendation or to return the case for rehearing.

The principal responsibility of the NEC as defined by the AIA Bylaws is enforcement of the AIA Code of Ethics and Professional Conduct. However, the NEC also provides guidelines to the public and within the Institute on a variety of professional topics. In addition, the NEC presents programs at the AIA National Convention, to AIA components, and to schools of architecture throughout the country.

AIA NATIONAL ETHICS COUNCIL PROCEDURES

Local AIA components manage ethical situations in a variety of ways. Some components provide advice and mediation for ethical violations through experienced members or established committees, while others simply refer local inquiries to the national organization. The general counsel's office at the national component is available to answer technical questions concerning the AIA Code of Ethics and Professional Conduct and can provide other information to members and nonmembers.

The AIA National Ethics Council has established strict rules of procedure for considering ethics cases. If it is believed that a member has violated the code of ethics, anyone—a member or nonmember of the AIA—may initiate a formal complaint. The NEC then initiates its review and hearing process.

If the architect is found to have violated the ethics code, the penalties available to the NEC are as follows:

- *Admonition (private).* A letter of the ruling is sent to the parties involved and kept in the respondent's membership file.
- *Censure (public).* A letter is sent and notification of the case and ruling is published to the AIA membership.
- *Suspension of membership.* The respondent's membership is suspended for a period of time, usually one or two years, and the ruling is published.
- *Termination of membership.* The respondent's membership is terminated and the ruling is published.

The respondent may appeal the NEC's decision to the AIA Executive Committee, whose subsequent ruling is final except in cases in which termination of membership is the penalty. Those cases are automatically appealed to the AIA Board of Directors.

Ethics complaints against AIA members should be addressed to:

Chair, National Ethics Council
The American Institute of Architects
1735 New York Avenue NW
Washington, DC 20006

COMMON ETHICS VIOLATIONS

Although the AIA Code of Ethics and Professional Conduct regulates a wide range of professional activities, several issues generate the majority of complaints. These include the following:

- Attribution of credit (i.e., stating or giving proper credit for project involvement)
- Accurate representation of qualifications
- Attainment and provision of examples of work
- Basic honesty

The predominant reason these four issues continually resurface is that each has an identifiable injured party—an angry colleague or an upset client—who is intent on seeing justice served. Also, even if the alleged infraction does not have legal or contractual consequences, it may still indicate an ethical breach. More serious issues, such as misappropriation of a client's or partner's funds, tend to be presented to the NEC less frequently. If a member knowingly violates the law (Rule 2.101) or displays discrimination (Rule 1.401), for instance, other forums with more severe remedies are available to the offended party.

To offer some guidance on issues commonly presented to the NEC, the following detailed illustrations are offered.

Attribution of Credit

Architecture is a profession in which design capability and originality is prized. Intellectual property is the most common proof of worth in terms of talent and experience. However, the collaborative nature of contemporary practice sometimes obscures the individual contributions of each team participant. The more complex the project and the more prolonged the design and construction process, the more individuals may lay valid claim to credit for some part of the work.

The most frequent violation of the code of ethics is improperly taking or not giving appropriate credit and recognition. The NEC recognizes that these infractions are frequently due to an incomplete understanding of the ethical standards and rules of conduct that direct members in this area. The following ethical standards apply to this issue:

> **Ethical Standard 4.2, Dignity and Integrity:** Members should strive, through their actions, to promote the dignity and integrity of the profession, and to ensure that their representatives and employees conform their conduct to this Code.
>
> **Ethical Standard 5.3, Professional Recognition:** Members should build their professional reputation on the merits of their own service and performance and should recognize and give credit to others for the professional work they have performed.

The rules associated with these standards mandate the required professional conduct:

> **Rule 4.201:** Members shall not make misleading, deceptive, or false statements or claims about their professional qualifications, experience, or performance and shall accurately state the scope and nature of their responsibilities in connection with work for which they are claiming credit.
>
> **Rule 5.301:** Members shall recognize and respect the professional contributions of their employees, employers, professional colleagues, and business associates.

Based on these standards and rules, the NEC has adopted guidelines to help AIA members determine how to handle this concern, although individual cases may present circumstances not explicitly covered. These guidelines are recommended for application to any oral, written, or graphic representation of an architect's work, whether it was developed for use in a public or private presentation.

Following are the AIA "Guidelines for the Attribution of Credit" (also published on the AIA Web site) that should be considered when making representations of an architect's work:

- An architectural project, built or unbuilt, involves any of the services provided by or under the direction of an architect.
- In analyzing attribution-of-credit issues, the National Ethics Council typically views the Architect-of-Record as the legal entity that has contracted for and completed the work in question. [The entity] can be a corporation, partnership, or individual architect. If the Architect-of-Record takes credit for a project, there is no further need to define the role or state "Architect-of-Record." Unless specific attribution is noted, it is assumed the Architect-of-Record is making a representation of complete responsibility for a project, including the design, production of construction documents, and construction observation.
- A Member taking credit for a project or a specific role on a project other than as the Architect-of-Record must clearly define that role. In addition to the Member's specific role, the Architect-of-Record must be acknowledged.
- It is not necessary to present a complete or exhaustive list of all the team participants. The acknowledgment of major team participants is recommended.
- Designation of the Member's role and/or the Architect-of-Record must be obvious, plainly visible, and legible at the anticipated viewing distance. The reference text should be no less obvious than the text used to describe the project. The description must be specific enough to make clear the services the Member rendered on this project. In the instance of a mailer/postcard that shows only an image of a project on the front, it is necessary to give the appropriate credit on the other side. The Member shall not overstate, actually or implicitly, his/her involvement in a project.
- If attribution of credit is not previously defined in a written agreement, and to avoid potential conflict, it is recommended that Members open a dialogue between all concerned parties prior to making any representations.

Accurate Representation of Qualifications

It is human nature and good business practice to present professional qualifications in the best light. However, overstatement, even if well-intentioned, can lead to unrealistic expectations on the part of the client or other project participants and thus to subsequent owner dissatisfaction. The architect-of-record must ultimately be responsible for complying with laws and codes as well as with other commitments, such as the project budget, a client's goals, a building's function, or environmental standards.

> **Rule 1.101:** In practicing architecture, Members shall demonstrate a consistent pattern of reasonable care and competence, and shall apply the technical knowledge and skill which is ordinarily applied by architects of good standing practicing in the same locality.
>
> **Rule 3.102:** Members shall undertake to perform professional services only when they, together with those whom they may engage as consultants, are qualified by education, training, or experience in the specific technical areas involved.

As an architecture firm evolves, its expertise may become somewhat different from that stated in promotional materials or in a previous statement of qualifications. Members are obliged to always ensure that the expertise and resources presented match those that are currently available.

Professionals are often compelled to make commitments regarding time, cost, or results based more on the urgency of the moment than on rational evaluation. Too often, architects make changes that affect the scope or budget of a project without presenting viable options or possible ramifications of the proposed changes. Architects may also feel pressure to articulate results by describing the final product of the work in terms that naturally speak well of the process and the architect's capabilities to attain those results. Great care and restraint should be taken in clarifying expectations relating to budget, building function, quality of materials, and other anticipated results of the design process. Project and individual responsibilities should be clearly defined contractually and verbally. Revisiting the following statements of obligation periodically throughout the life of a project is beneficial:

> **Rule 3.103:** Members shall not materially alter the scope or objectives of a project without the client's consent.
>
> **Rule 3.301:** Members shall not intentionally or recklessly mislead existing or prospective clients about the results that can be achieved through the use of the Member's services, nor shall the Members state that they can achieve results by means that violate applicable law or this Code.

Helping the client reach realistic expectations is important. The medical profession characterizes this as informed consent, where a patient must be informed of a situation to the level of understanding that allows an informed decision. Clients in every profession deserve the same consideration.

Attainment and Provision of Samples of Work

In light of current technologies and the variety of roles that architects perform, defining an architect's work is increasingly difficult. For example, should an architect who predominantly created or adapted computer software or developed unique technical details be given copies of that work upon leaving a firm? How can the rights of the firm and of the employee be protected? Ethical Standard 5.3 pertaining to professional recognition provides a framework for guidance (see above). The specific rules that apply to this question are these:

> **Rule 5.302:** Members leaving a firm shall not, without the permission of their employer or partner, take designs, drawings, data, reports, notes, or other materials relating to the firm's work, whether or not performed by the Member.
>
> **Rule 5.303:** A Member shall not unreasonably withhold permission from a departing employee or partner to take copies of designs, drawings, data, reports, notes, or other materials relating to work performed by the employee or partner that are not confidential.

In addition, the code provides the following commentary: "A Member may impose reasonable conditions, such as the payment of copying costs, on the right of departing persons to take copies of their work."

The best advice is that the question of whether and how copies of work will be granted to an employee should be discussed before an employee decides to leave a firm or at least during the departure process. This discussion may help mitigate an awkward, emotional, or volatile termination process. A departing employee should expect to receive reasonable *examples* of work; the employer is not obligated to make the entire volume of work produced by the employee available. The intent is to allow the employee a reasonable opportunity to present qualifications to future employers or potential clients. It is equally important for the firm to retain proprietary or confidential materials and the work products it rightfully owns, such as renderings, photography, or proprietary software.

The AIA has published a Best Practices article titled "Personal Use of Documents: A Sample Firm Policy" to help firms establish policies for the ethical use of documents during and after employment. (AIA Best Practices are available on the Internet.)

COMPETING VALUES

It seems simple enough to be honest, but even well-meaning professionals from time to time are presented with competing obligations, such as family responsibilities or religious convictions. For example, employees may decide to work outside the office to build a client base, take advantage of opportunities to demonstrate design talent, or simply make money. In doing so, they may unwittingly expose the firm to liability and may compromise their own ability to perform adequately for the compensation they are receiving. Or, an employee may use the firm's software for personal use, believing that no harm is done by making a copy of it. Architects have certainly lied, stolen, defrauded, or taken advantage of a situation. Sometimes the individual is well-intentioned, sometimes not, but almost always he or she feels justified in his or her actions.

Architecture is a profession replete with competing values. Within every project are decisions to be made about quality of materials versus budget constraints, owner-prescribed requirements versus building codes or architectural review committees, and confidentiality versus truthfulness. Resolving these conflicts does not require decisions about right and wrong, but rather decisions to resolve situations in which competing principles are equally correct but may be mutually exclusive.

Responsibility for ethics extends to all members of a firm, not just the principals or those in management positions. Members of the firm at all levels are in positions that require a clear understanding of ethical behavior.

Entry-level professionals and interns, as part of their daily responsibilities, make choices and perform tasks that need to be guided by a code of ethics. With the trend toward flattened, less hierarchical professional organizations, these firm members are attending meetings with clients, conducting daily tasks, and issuing project communications. The skills necessary to perform in these situations are seldom discussed, much less taught, within the architectural curriculum. As a result, the young architect is left to learn them on the job. The understanding of ethical behavior that should guide all firm members is thus often introduced in a work situation.

Questions of ethics can arise from examining seemingly routine or common behaviors:

- Discussing details of a proposal or comparing fee structures with colleagues in another firm
- Repeating information gathered within the context of a project or client meeting
- Casually sharing digital files (text, drawings, renderings, objects, and so on) with a colleague in another firm to bring each other up-to-date as to "what are you working on"
- Using the firm's Internet connection for personal instant messaging or other online activities not related to work
- Installing personal software on an office computer to assist in the production of a project, marketing material, or particular task at hand
- Working on personal projects in the workplace after hours using office resources

These examples touch on actions that are often misunderstood or not even considered as issues by those entering the profession and often by those in practice.

Confidentiality

Everyone has a certain expectation of confidentiality. In a work situation, these expectations are formalized and there are often implications if a confidence is breached. Clients have the right to expect that their project, project information (e.g., schedule, budget, legal hurdles, and public reviews and approvals), and communications will be kept confidential. Sending project information over the Internet to a colleague—whether or not the project is in a sensitive stage of the approval process—is a clear violation of this expectation.

The firm has a certain level of expectation of discretion on the part of its employees. While exposing secrets and violating confidences appears to be a part of daily life in the media, office gossip and the sharing of situations within the workplace is seldom useful or appropriate. An architecture firm is not just any job, and firm members are not simply employees. A profession demands more of all those involved, both seasoned practitioners and aspiring professionals.

Employees likewise have certain expectations of their employers. They have a right to assume that personal information, whether health, financial, or behavioral in nature, will be held in trust by the firm.

Ethical practice is not merely a two-way street, but a network of complex relationships and behaviors.

Intellectual Property

Although there may be shades of gray in situations involving ethical behavior, many legal issues are black and white.

Software appropriately acquired while an individual is in school is provided by most software developers with the understanding and explicit agreement that it be used for academic purposes only. Many of these digital products are offered free or at substantial discounts to the student. Even the private, personal use of these products after graduation is questionable. Without question, bringing these products into a work setting, even in an attempt to support the efforts of the firm, exposes the firm to considerable legal liability, undue risk, and the possibility of fines and penalties. Such unauthorized use of software within a firm also exposes the employee to actions by the employer since, once this use is discovered, the firm is obligated to respond appropriately.

As professionals, architects have made considerable progress in protecting their intellectual property. The Architectural Works Copyright Protection Act of 1990 allows for protection of both technical drawings and building designs. Other work products (e.g., specifications, reports, etc.) may be covered under other provisions of copyright law.

(continued)

If, as creative professionals, architects seek legal protection for what they produce, it is appropriate that they respect the efforts of others and equally value their intellectual property. This is not only the ethical response but also the legal one.

Personal Commitment

While the term "multitasking" is used to describe the ability to conduct several operations simultaneously, the work of an architect, or someone who aspires to become one, requires focus, concentration, and commitment to the task at hand. Design issues, buildings, the project delivery process, and the entire construction industry have become increasingly complex. It is essential for architects to use available technology to improve the process and better serve both their firms and their clients. At the same time, the ever-improving digital tools used by architects may make the actual act of design increasingly demanding. Building information modeling (BIM) software gives the members of the project team tremendous power in the creation of the information set necessary to construct a building.

Very unlike years past, there is no "backroom" filled with drafters performing routine and often mindless tasks. The cut-and-paste 2-D world of the last decade is rapidly giving way to operations that require a much more knowledgeable and thoughtful person at the controls, entering and monitoring the quality of the information being contributed to the building information model. For these and countless other reasons, everyone involved in the project delivery process must acknowledge and take responsibility for the quality of the work, since so many hands are involved in its creation.

Personal Projects/Moonlighting

Taking on outside projects, whether for financial reward or professional satisfaction, is often attractive. Pro bono work, which at the outset appears to be a harmless allocation of a person's free time, also falls into this category.

Seldom do individuals involved in such outside projects realize the implications of their actions. In some cases, a person's energy and attention to the work of the firm is compromised. In others, there are conflicts with commitments made and deadlines and agreements that must be met within the firm.

No matter the size and scope of a personal project, it often requires time during the workday to manage issues and attend to problems. This activity compromises both the time available for the firm's work and the quality of service provided to the moonlight job and client.

In addition to distracting an employee from full commitment to the success of the firm, moonlighting can also expose the firm to legal liabilities. Several court cases have held the parent firm responsible for the actions of an employee, even though the firm had not authorized or even known about those actions.

If the firm's work does not provide the personal, professional, and/or financial rewards an architect seeks, the best action is to improve his or her role and responsibilities within the firm, look for new employment, or start a firm.

Michael Hricak, FAIA

THE FUTURE

Defining professional ethics for the architecture profession will remain the duty of the American Institute of Architects and its National Ethics Council. As they have in the past, the AIA Board of Directors and NEC will periodically reevaluate the Code of Ethics and Professional Conduct based on the profession's core values while responding to societal pressures, changing business practices, advancing technologies, and lessons learned from the results of future litigation.

For More Information

The AIA Web site at www.aia.org/about_ethics provides current information and resources. The process for filing a complaint is described. Also posted are the NEC's previous decisions and advisory opinions, the rules of procedure, the AIA Code of Ethics and Professional Conduct, guidelines for attribution of credit, and answers to frequently asked questions. Specific questions may be directed to the Office of the General Counsel at (202) 626-7311. Members of the AIA National Ethics Council may be available to offer programs, which include case studies, at AIA national and local events.

 **THE AMERICAN INSTITUTE OF ARCHITECTS**

FROM THE OFFICE OF GENERAL COUNSEL

2004 Code of Ethics & Professional Conduct

Preamble

Members of The American Institute of Architects are dedicated to the highest standards of professionalism, integrity, and competence. This Code of Ethics and Professional Conduct states guidelines for the conduct of Members in fulfilling those obligations. The Code is arranged in three tiers of statements: Canons, Ethical Standards, and Rules of Conduct:

- Canons are broad principles of conduct.
- Ethical Standards (E.S.) are more specific goals toward which Members should aspire in professional performance and behavior.
- Rules of Conduct (**Rule**) are mandatory; violation of a Rule is grounds for disciplinary action by the Institute. Rules of Conduct, in some instances, implement more than one Canon or Ethical Standard.

The **Code** applies to the professional activities of all classes of Members, wherever they occur. It addresses responsibilities to the public, which the profession serves and enriches; to the clients and users of architecture and in the building industries, who help to shape the built environment; and to the art and science of architecture, that continuum of knowledge and creation which is the heritage and legacy of the profession.

Commentary is provided for some of the Rules of Conduct. That commentary is meant to clarify or elaborate the intent of the rule. The commentary is not part of the **Code**. Enforcement will be determined by application of the Rules of Conduct alone; the commentary will assist those seeking to conform their conduct to the **Code** and those charged with its enforcement.

Statement in Compliance With Antitrust Law

The following practices are not, in themselves, unethical, unprofessional, or contrary to any policy of The American Institute of Architects or any of its components:

(1) submitting, at any time, competitive bids or price quotations, including in circumstances where price is the sole or principal consideration in the selection of an architect;

(2) providing discounts; or

(3) providing free services.

Individual architects or architecture firms, acting alone and not on behalf of the Institute or any of its components, are free to decide for themselves whether or not to engage in any of these practices. Antitrust law permits the Institute, its components, or Members to advocate legislative or other government policies or actions relating to these practices. Finally, architects should continue to consult with state laws or regulations governing the practice of architecture.

CANON I

General Obligations

Members should maintain and advance their knowledge of the art and science of architecture, respect the body of architectural accomplishment, contribute to its growth, thoughtfully consider the social and environmental impact of their professional activities, and exercise learned and uncompromised professional judgment.

E.S. 1.1 Knowledge and Skill: Members should strive to improve their professional knowledge and skill.

Rule In practicing architecture,
1.101 Members shall demonstrate a

consistent pattern of reasonable care and competence, and shall apply the technical knowledge and skill which is ordinarily applied by architects of good standing practicing in the same locality.

Commentary: By requiring a "consistent pattern" of adherence to the common law standard of competence, this rule allows for discipline of a Member who more than infrequently does not achieve that standard. Isolated instances of minor lapses would not provide the basis for discipline.

E.S. 1.2 Standards of Excellence: Members should continually seek to raise the standards of aesthetic excellence, architectural

education, research, training, and practice.

E.S. 1.3 Natural and Cultural Heritage: Members should respect and help conserve their natural and cultural heritage while striving to improve the environment and the quality of life within it.

E.S. 1.4 Human Rights: Members should uphold human rights in all their professional endeavors.

Rule Members shall not discriminate in
1.401 their professional activities on the basis of race, religion, gender, national origin, age, disability, or sexual orientation.

(continued)

E.S. 1.5 Allied Arts & Industries: Members should promote allied arts and contribute to the knowledge and capability of the building industries as a whole.

CANON II

Obligations to the Public

Members should embrace the spirit and letter of the law governing their professional affairs and should promote and serve the public interest in their personal and professional activities.

E.S. 2.1 Conduct: Members should uphold the law in the conduct of their professional activities.

Rule 2.101 Members shall not, in the conduct of their professional practice, knowingly violate the law.
Commentary: The violation of any law, local, state or federal, occurring in the conduct of a Member's professional practice, is made the basis for discipline by this rule. This includes the federal Copyright Act, which prohibits copying architectural works without the permission of the copyright owner. Allegations of violations of this rule must be based on an independent finding of a violation of the law by a court of competent jurisdiction or an administrative or regulatory body.

Rule 2.102 Members shall neither offer nor make any payment or gift to a public official with the intent of influencing the official's judgment in connection with an existing or prospective project in which the Members are interested.
Commentary: This rule does not prohibit campaign contributions made in conformity with applicable campaign financing laws.

Rule 2.103 Members serving in a public capacity shall not accept payments or gifts which are intended to influence their judgment.

Rule 2.104 Members shall not engage in conduct involving fraud or wanton disregard of the rights of others.
Commentary: This rule addresses serious misconduct whether or not related to a Member's professional practice. When an alleged violation of this rule is based on a violation of a law, or of fraud, then its proof must be based on an independent finding of a violation of the law or a finding of fraud by a court of competent jurisdiction or an administrative or regulatory body.

Rule 2.105 If, in the course of their work on a project, the Members become aware of a decision taken by their employer or client which violates any law or regulation and which will, in the Members' judgment, materially affect adversely the safety to the public of the finished project, the Members shall:
(a) advise their employer or client against the decision,
(b) refuse to consent to the decision, and
(c) report the decision to the local building inspector or other public official charged with the enforcement of the applicable laws and regulations, unless the Members are able to cause the matter to be satisfactorily resolved by other means.
Commentary: This rule extends only to violations of the building laws that threaten the public safety. The obligation under this rule applies only to the safety of the finished project, an obligation coextensive with the usual undertaking of an architect.

Rule 2.106 Members shall not counsel or assist a client in conduct that the architect knows, or reasonably should know, is fraudulent or illegal.

E.S. 2.2 Public Interest Services: Members should render public interest professional services and encourage their employees to render such services.

E.S. 2.3 Civic Responsibility: Members should be involved in civic activities as citizens and professionals, and should strive to improve public appreciation and understanding of architecture and the functions and responsibilities of architects.

Rule 2.301 Members making public statements on architectural issues shall disclose when they are being compensated for making such statements or when they have an economic interest in the issue.

CANON III

Obligations to the Client

Members should serve their clients competently and in a professional manner, and should exercise unprejudiced and unbiased judgment when performing all professional services.

E.S. 3.1 Competence: Members should serve their clients in a timely and competent manner.

Rule 3.101 In performing professional services, Members shall take into account applicable laws and regulations. Members may rely on the advice of other qualified persons as to the intent and meaning of such regulations.

Rule 3.102 Members shall undertake to perform professional services only when they, together with those whom they may engage as consultants, are qualified by education, training, or experience in the specific technical areas involved.
Commentary: This rule is meant to ensure that Members not undertake projects that are beyond their professional capacity. Members venturing into areas that require expertise they do not possess may obtain that expertise by additional education, training, or through the retention of consultants with the necessary expertise.

Rule 3.103 Members shall not materially alter the scope or objectives of a project without the client's consent.

E.S. 3.2 Conflict of Interest: Members should avoid conflicts of interest in their professional practices and fully disclose all unavoidable conflicts as they arise.

Rule 3.201 A Member shall not render professional services if the Member's professional judgment could be affected by responsibilities to another project or person, or by the Member's own interests, unless all those who rely on the Member's judgment consent after full disclosure.

Commentary: This rule is intended to embrace the full range of situations that may present a Member with a conflict between his interests or responsibilities and the interest of others. Those who are entitled to disclosure may include a client, owner, employer, contractor, or others who rely on or are affected by the Member's professional decisions. A Member who cannot appropriately communicate about a conflict directly with an affected person must take steps to ensure that disclosure is made by other means.

Rule 3.202 When acting by agreement of the parties as the independent interpreter of building contract documents and the judge of contract performance, Members shall render decisions impartially.

Commentary: This rule applies when the Member, though paid by the owner and owing the owner loyalty, is nonetheless required to act with impartiality in fulfilling the architect's professional responsibilities.

E.S. 3.3 Candor and Truthfulness: Members should be candid and truthful in their professional communications and keep their clients reasonably informed about the clients' projects.

Rule 3.301 Members shall not intentionally or recklessly mislead existing or prospective clients about the results that can be achieved through the use of the Members' services, nor shall the Members state that they can achieve results by means that violate applicable law or this **Code.**

Commentary: This rule is meant to preclude dishonest, reckless, or illegal representations by a Member either in the course of soliciting a client or during performance.

E.S. 3.4 Confidentiality: Members should safeguard the trust placed in them by their clients.

Rule 3.401 Members shall not knowingly disclose information that would adversely affect their client or that they have been asked to maintain in confidence, except as otherwise allowed or required by this **Code** or applicable law.

Commentary: To encourage the full and open exchange of information necessary for a successful professional relationship, Members must recognize and respect the sensitive nature of confidential client communications. Because the law does not recognize an architect-client privilege, however, the rule permits a Member to reveal a confidence when a failure to do so would be unlawful or contrary to another ethical duty imposed by this Code.

CANON IV

Obligations to the Profession

Members should uphold the integrity and dignity of the profession.

E.S. 4.1 Honesty and Fairness: Members should pursue their professional activities with honesty and fairness.

Rule 4.101 Members having substantial information which leads to a reasonable belief that another Member has committed a violation of this **Code** which raises a serious question as to that Member's honesty, trustworthiness, or fitness as a Member, shall file a complaint with the National Ethics Council.

Commentary: Often, only an architect can recognize that the behavior of another architect poses a serious question as to that other's professional integrity. In those circumstances, the duty to the professional's calling requires that a complaint be filed. In most jurisdictions, a complaint that invokes professional standards is protected from a libel or slander action if the complaint was made in good faith. If in doubt, a Member should seek counsel before reporting on another under this rule.

Rule 4.102 Members shall not sign or seal drawings, specifications, reports, or other professional work for which they do not have responsible control.

Commentary: Responsible control means the degree of knowledge and supervision ordinarily required by the professional standard of care. With respect to the work of licensed consultants, Members may sign or seal such work if they have reviewed it, coordinated its preparation, or intend to be responsible for its adequacy.

Rule 4.103 Members speaking in their professional capacity shall not knowingly make false statements of material fact.

Commentary: This rule applies to statements in all professional contexts, including applications for licensure and AIA membership.

E.S. 4.2 Dignity and Integrity: Members should strive, through their actions, to promote the dignity and integrity of the profession, and to ensure that their representatives and employees conform their conduct to this **Code.**

Rule 4.201 Members shall not make misleading, deceptive, or false statements or claims about their professional qualifications, experience, or performance and shall accurately state the scope and nature of their responsibilities in connection with work for which they are claiming credit.

Commentary: This rule is meant to prevent Members from claiming or implying credit for work which they did not do, misleading others, and denying other participants in a project their proper share of credit.

Rule 4.202 Members shall make reasonable efforts to ensure that those over whom they have supervisory authority conform their conduct to this **Code.**

Commentary: What constitutes "reasonable efforts" under this rule is a common sense matter. As it makes sense to ensure that those over whom the architect exercises supervision be made generally aware of the Code, it can also make sense to bring a particular provision to the attention of a particular employee when a situation is present which might give rise to violation.

(continued)

CANON V

Obligations to Colleagues

Members should respect the rights and acknowledge the professional aspirations and contributions of their colleagues.

E.S. 5.1 Professional Environment: Members should provide their associates and employees with a suitable working environment, compensate them fairly, and facilitate their professional development.

E.S. 5.2 Intern and Professional Development: Members should recognize and fulfill their obligation to nurture fellow professionals as they progress through all stages of their career, beginning with professional education in the academy, progressing through internship and continuing throughout their career.

E.S. 5.3 Professional Recognition: Members should build their professional reputation on the merits of their own service and performance and should recognize and give credit to others for the professional work they have performed.

Rule 5.301 Members shall recognize and respect the professional contributions of their employees, employers, professional colleagues, and business associates.

Rule 5.302 Members leaving a firm shall not, without the permission of their employer or partner, take designs, drawings, data, reports, notes, or other materials relating to the firm's work, whether or not performed by the Member.

Rule 5.303 A Member shall not unreasonably withhold permission from a departing employee or partner to take copies of designs, drawings, data, reports, notes, or other materials relating to work performed by the employee or partner that are not confidential.

Commentary: A Member may impose reasonable conditions, such as the payment of copying costs, on the right of departing persons to take copies of their work.

RULES OF APPLICATION, ENFORCEMENT, AND AMENDMENT

Application

The **Code of Ethics and Professional Conduct** applies to the professional activities of all members of the AIA.

Enforcement

The Bylaws of the Institute state procedures for the enforcement of the **Code of Ethics and Professional Conduct.** Such procedures provide that:

(1) Enforcement of the **Code** is administered through a National Ethics Council, appointed by the AIA Board of Directors.

(2) Formal charges are filed directly with the National Ethics Council by Members, components, or anyone directly aggrieved by the conduct of the Members.

(3) Penalties that may be imposed by the National Ethics Council are:
    (a) Admonition
    (b) Censure
    (c) Suspension of membership for a period of time
    (d) Termination of membership

(4) Appeal procedures are available.

(5) All proceedings are confidential, as is the imposition of an admonishment; however, all other penalties shall be made public.

Enforcement of Rules 4.101 and 4.202 refer to and support enforcement of other Rules. A violation of Rules 4.101 or 4.202 cannot be established without proof of a pertinent violation of at least one other Rule.

Amendment

The **Code of Ethics and Professional Conduct** may be amended by the convention of the Institute under the same procedures as are necessary to amend the Institute's Bylaws. The **Code** may also be amended by the AIA Board of Directors upon a two-thirds vote of the entire Board.

*2004 Edition. *This copy of the* Code of Ethics *is current as of September 2004. Contact the General Counsel's Office for further information at (202) 626-7311.*

1.3 Service Leadership in Architecture Practice

Michael M. Hricak, FAIA

"Vocation" is a concept making a comeback these days. While many individuals have the same job title, few actually have the same calling.

A decade of speaking with young people pursuing a career in architecture has demonstrated that most architecture students are involved in design as though there was no other choice: They simply could not imagine doing anything else. This fact suggests that, for many, architecture is not only a professional career path, but a vocation. It is not that prospective architecture students make their decision in an emotional or irrational manner. On the contrary, it is more a situation in which these individuals' skills, talents, interests, and concerns align with the options that life as an architect offers. This observation does not imply that a professional career is necessarily synonymous with a vocation. Rather, it appears that a strong inclination to pursue a certain career in order to serve or address perceived needs can elevate a career choice to another level.

The vocation for you is the one in which your deep gladness and the world's deep need meet.

Frederick Buechner

A common misconception is that a vocation implies something done for little reward or for purely altruistic purposes. In reality, a vocation is less this than the intersection of what makes a person happy and what the world needs to be done.

The roles that architects are called upon to play are many and varied. The popular press uses the word *architect* to mean someone who takes a complex task and breaks it down into its components, all the while keeping the big picture in mind, and who can bring together certain people and have them perform those tasks necessary to accomplish a goal. In newspapers it is not unusual to see phrases like the "architect of the peace plan" or the "architect of the company's turnaround," to cite two examples of the word's common use in the context of political and business-related situations.

With the proliferation of material (books, magazines, network and cable programming, etc.) on design in general and sustainability in particular, and a general renewed appreciation for architecture and its importance in the quality of our lives, it appears the stage is set for architects to have an ever-increasing influence on the built environment and, by extension, the natural one. Although it is tempting to look to technology and related techniques as a means of fostering and directing meaningful change, it is helpful to look beyond the obvious, most touted new products and examine what needs to change for architects to truly benefit from the public's awareness and acceptance and advances in professional knowledge and emerging tools.

As well, it is necessary to acknowledge that not all change is progress. It is clear that new tools and evolving knowledge increase the possibilities and approaches to what gets designed and how it gets built. However, a prerequisite for leveraging the opportunities that present conditions offer is development of a new set of beliefs and behaviors, which also requires a willingness to abandon current patterns and processes. The motivation to strive for this level of change is the essential core belief that by changing what we design and how we build, we can change the world itself.

Michael Hricak is the principal of Michael Hricak Architects and teaches at the University of Southern California School of Architecture. His firm has received numerous awards, and he has served in leadership positions with AIA National and AIA California Council.

Leadership is a reciprocal process between those who choose to lead and those who choose to follow. Any discussion of leadership must attend to the dynamics of this relationship. Strategies, tactics, skills, and practices are empty unless the fundamental human aspirations that connect leaders and their constituents are understood (constituents is used here, as it connotes a greater sense of engagement and commitment in the relationship than followers). What leaders say they do is one thing; what constituents say they want and how well leaders meet these expectations is another. To balance our understanding of leadership, let's take a look at the expectations people have for their leaders. In other words, what do people look for and admire in someone they would willingly follow?

Research about what constituents expect of leaders has yielded fairly consistent results over time and across the globe, transcending a variety of individual, interpersonal, and organizational differences. (For more information on this research, see James M. Kouzes and Barry Z. Posner, The Leadership Challenge, 4th edition.) In general, an individual must pass several essential tests before others are willing to grant that person the title leader. Although numerous potential characteristics, personal values, traits, and attributes could be considered important, what is most striking is that only four continuously receive more than 50 percent of the responses. For people to follow someone willingly, the majority of constituents must believe the leader is honest, forward-looking, competent, and inspiring.

Honesty. Honesty is the single most important ingredient in the leader-constituent relationship. Before people will follow someone, they want to be assured that person is worthy of their trust. Is the leader truthful, ethical, and principled? Focus groups and in-depth interviews have indicated that constituents measure a characteristic as subjective as honesty by observing the leader's behavior. They are looking for consistency between word and deed. Constituents appreciate leaders who take a stand on important principles; they resolutely refuse to follow those who lack confidence in their own beliefs. Constituents simply do not trust people who cannot or will not communicate their values, ethics, and standards.

Vision. The ability to look ahead is one of the most sought-after leadership traits. Leaders are expected to have a sense of direction and a concern for the future of the group or organization. No matter what this ability is called, the message is clear: Leaders must know where they are going if they expect others to follow. This can be as down-to-earth as selecting a desirable goal for the group. Vision is the magnetic north that provides others with the capacity to chart a course toward the future. Constituents ask that a leader have a well-defined orientation toward the future. They want to know what the organization will look like, feel like, and be like when it arrives at its goal in six months or six years.

Competence. Constituents must believe the person they follow is competent to guide them where they are headed. Leaders must be viewed as capable and effective. Competent leadership is reflected in the leader's track record and ability to get things done and guide the entire organization, whether the group is large or small. It does not refer specifically to requiring the leader to have abilities in the core technology of an operation. In fact, the type of competence demanded appears to vary more with the leader's position in the organization and the condition of the organization than with the type of organization it is. While an understanding of the basics and fundamentals of the industry, market, or professional service environment is important, people accept that leaders cannot be expected to be the most technically competent in their fields. Organizations are too complex and multifunctional for that to be the case; this is particularly true as people reach more senior levels.

The ability to inspire. People expect their leaders to be enthusiastic, energetic, and positive about the future. It is not enough for a leader to have a dream about the future. A leader must be able to communicate that vision in ways that encourage people to sign on for the duration. The enthusiasm, energy, and positive attitude of a good leader may not change the context of work, but they certainly can make work more meaningful. A leader who is upbeat, positive, and optimistic about the future can offer people hope. In times of great uncertainty, leading with positive emotions is absolutely essential to moving people upward and forward. When people are worried, discouraged, frightened, and uncertain about the future, they need someone who communicates—in words, demeanor, and actions—that she or he believes the group will overcome its difficulties. Enthusiasm and excitement are contagious, and such positive emotions resonate throughout an organization.

Honesty, vision, competence, and the ability to inspire are leadership characteristics that remain constant over time, and they make up what communications experts refer to as "source credibility." In assessing the believability of sources of information—whether architects, newscasters, salespeople, physicians, politicians, or civic leaders—people rate more highly those they perceive to be trustworthy, dynamic, and accomplished. In the end, people want to follow leaders who are credible. Credibility is the foundation of leadership.

People must be able to believe in the people they follow. They must believe the leader's words can be trusted, they will do what they say, they are personally excited and enthusiastic about the direction in which the group is headed, they have the knowledge and skill to lead, and they have a sense of direction and intentionality that propels others forward.

Appreciating how constituents view leaders is critical to the understanding and practice of leadership, which underscores the fact that leadership is a relationship. This relationship builds upon the character and actions of leaders in meeting and responding to the needs, expectations, and aspirations of their constituents. The most effective leaders cherish this relationship, realizing the work of the organization will ultimately not be done by the leader but by their constituents. Finally, if people do not believe in the messenger, they will not believe the message.

Barry Posner

For centuries, architects have gathered, organized, and distributed information to dozens, if not thousands, of people in order for this army of skilled labor, tradesmen, craftsmen, and specialists to perform and complete the tasks necessary to accomplish the architect's design, and thereby the client's goals. Put simply, architects have long been in the business of providing information.

The immediate product of the design process is information, which is necessary for the eventual product—the building—to be built. Assuming an improvement in the architect's knowledge of construction logistics and the building process, information of increasing effectiveness and value can be prepared. This reversal of the estrangement of the architect from the construction process allows the architect to take part in conversations that involve not only the "what" of the design stages but the "how" of the construction process. The guiding question in this approach becomes, "Does each and every person involved in the process, from supervisor to hands-on constructor, have what he or she needs to accomplish the task at hand?" Or, asked another way, "Does everyone have the information necessary to succeed?"

To engage in professional practice and project delivery in this way requires the architect to shift from a position of misunderstood genius or frustrated artist, or even efficient and effective manager, to one of constant and confident supporter—through the medium of information—of the efforts of everyone involved in a project. Through the use of the evolving and increasingly sophisticated tools available to the design and construction industry, the information provided by the architect has the potential of becoming more understandable, useful, timely, accurate, and responsive.

It is useful to remember that the architect is 100 percent leveraged, in that the architect does little that directly results in the completion of a building project. The architect's medium or communication tool is information, be it 2D images, 3D material, a building information model, or a hand-sketched detail drawn on-site. The architect can only succeed if, through stewardship of the project information, the architect enables all those involved in a project to be successful.

Frank Gehry has described computer technology, and the digital tools that dramatically improve efficiency and accuracy, as a second chance for architects to reclaim the leadership role they were in danger of forfeiting by becoming too effete and unrealistic.

James Steele in *Architecture: Celebrating the Past, Designing the Future* (AIA, 2008)

LEADING FROM THE INSIDE OUT

Authentic leadership does not come from the outside in. It comes from the inside out. Practicing inside-out leadership means becoming the author of your own story and the maker of your own history.

All effective leadership starts from within. What constituents most want from a leader is to genuinely know who that leader is. Imagine this scene. Someone walks into the room right now and announces to you and your colleagues, "Hi, I'm your new leader." What is the first thing you want to know from this person? What are the questions that immediately pop into your mind? Studies have shown that people want to ask the following questions:

Who are you?

What do you stand for and believe in?

(continued)

Where do you want to take us?

Why you?

What qualifies you for this job?

What makes you think you can do this?

Do you really know what you're getting yourself into?

What changes are you planning to make?

Questions like these get to the heart of what leadership is about. People want to know what inspires a leader, what drives you, what informs your decisions, what gives you strength, what makes you who you are. They want to know the person behind the mask. They want to know what gives you the confidence to think the group can succeed.

The quest for leadership, therefore, is first an inner quest to discover who you are. It is through this process of self-examination that an individual can find the awareness and faith in his or her own powers needed to lead. This self-confidence becomes stronger only as you work to identify and develop your skills. Mastery of the art of leadership comes with mastery of the self.

Developing yourself as a leader begins with knowing your own convictions. Clarifying your values and aspirations is a highly personal matter, and no one else can do it for you. To exhibit authentic leadership—leadership in which your words and deeds are consonant—you must be in tune internally. You must know who you are, what's important to you, and what is not so important.

A person's passion is often another factor in an individual's decision to lead. Finding your passion requires a journey through your inner self—a journey that often involves opening doors that are shut, walking in dark places that are frightening, and touching the flame that burns.

Clarity of personal values and dedication to your passion matters greatly to feeling motivated, creative, and committed to the workplace. People who are clear about their personal values feel empowered and prepared to take action—ready to be a leader.

The importance of these factors in leadership development was reflected by a young architect who explained how he had learned "that clarifying one's values and expressing oneself clearly and confidently is an essential first step that leaders must undertake. There are no shortcuts, workarounds, or other easy alternatives to this primal step in the leadership journey." One immediate payoff from developing a clear sense of values and communicating these to others, he told us, is that "it serves to enlist willing constituents and builds a vital support base for the leader."

We have all heard the expression "Leaders stand up for their beliefs." To have a solid platform on which to stand, an individual's beliefs must be clear to him or her as well as to others. When these values are matched by deeds, you have earned the credibility needed for others to put their trust in you.

It is hard to imagine how someone can stand up for his or her beliefs if that individual is not clear about them. How can you speak out if you don't know what's important to you? How can you have the courage of your convictions if you have no convictions? Without core values and with only shifting positions, would-be leaders are judged as inconsistent and derided for being "political" in their behavior.

Developing leadership ability is not about cramming to learn a lot of new information or trying out the latest technique. It is about leading out what is already in your soul. It is about liberating the leader within. Clarity of values is essential, and the clearer you are about your values, the easier it will be to stay on the path you have chosen. In exploring your inner self and finding your voice, you craft an inner compass by which to navigate daily life that will take you on the first steps to making a difference.

Indeed, who is the very first person you have to lead? Who is the first person who must be willing to follow you? The answer is simple: You! Until you believe in something yourself, it is hard to imagine you could ever convince anyone else to do something.

So, back to that leader who walks into the room and says, "Hi. I'm your new leader." If that leader is you, what would be your answer to the questions others would ask about why they should follow you? What would you say when asked, "Who are you?"

Barry Posner

In the context of this approach to project delivery, "service leadership" is defined as follows: The architect leads the effort by serving all those whose work is necessary to meet the goals of the project. This quiet, but ultimately effective leadership is accomplished by leading from within, from a position of support and service.

Based on the idea that having a vocation means finding an alignment between an individual's interests and concerns with the task at hand, the key to redefining the role of the architect is to recognize that by serving—and only by serving—can the architect become an effective and essential leader.

1.4 Participating in Professional Organizations

Andrea S. Rutledge, SDA, CAE

Participating in professional organizations can help architects enrich their careers and contribute to the advancement of the profession.

It seems as though there is an association for everything. Nearly every profession, vocation, avocation, or trade has a society or association organized to meet the specific needs of its members, and the United States has the most fully developed association sector in the world. Even Garrison Keillor spoofed our national proclivity for forming associations, inventing the American Duct Tape Council as a fictitious sponsor of his radio show, *A Prairie Home Companion.*

The most basic function of associations is to distinguish their members from others in similar professions or types of commerce or to bring together individuals with common vocational interests (e.g., the American Industrial Hygiene Association) or avocational interests (e.g., the Road Runners Club of America). Such organizations are most often formed to provide information to the public; to set standards for a profession, system, or service; to represent their members' interests before legislatures or regulatory bodies; or to provide services or products that enable their members to succeed.

EMERGENCE OF ASSOCIATIONS

Groups of people associated by the business they engage in have been around for a long time. The most recognizable precursors of today's professional associations are the guilds of Western Europe. The guild system, with its formalized apprenticeships and protective regulations, has its origins in Roman culture. Guilds established standards for production, set prices, monitored sales, oversaw wages and hours, and maintained training and apprentice programs. Membership was not voluntary, and the competition with similar guilds from other cities could be fierce. In many cities, guilds came to wield substantial political power and were able to influence civic decisions as well as some of those made by the church. For example, in 1418, the Wool Guild in Florence was involved in design and construction of the famous cathedral dome. And in London, the annual election of the Lord Mayor of the City of London was heavily influenced by the guilds.

The guilds lost power and influence as the modern market economy and democratic principles began to spread. Instead of guilds designed to control trade for their members in a specific commodity or trade within a specific city or town, organizations of merchants and other artisans formed to encourage and support common commercial interests. For example, the first chamber of commerce was formed in New York State in 1768, and the New York Stock Exchange was established in 1792.

During the nineteenth-century Industrial Revolution, new trade associations and professional societies began forming in the United States, particularly among business owners. By 1890 many of these were well established and were lobbying Congress, holding regular meetings, and maintaining offices. The American Institute of Architects falls into this category. Founded in 1857, the AIA celebrated its thirty-third anniversary in

---

Andrea Rutledge, **executive director of the National Architectural Accrediting Board in Washington, D.C., was formerly managing director, Alliances, at the AIA.**

1890 and had just elected its third president. Other familiar organizations were founded later: the American Bar Association (1878), the National Society of Professional Engineers (1905), the Associated General Contractors of America (1918), and the American Council of Engineering Companies (1934).

In the twentieth century, associations and professional societies became more organized, hiring staff trained to support activities of the group, codifying rules and procedures for boards, establishing criteria for membership, and developing an expanding range of services for their members. These groups have coalesced into several distinctive types. The following definitions come from *The Association Law Handbook*:

Professional societies are "composed of individuals or members who have acquired knowledge and experience that qualifies them as specialists in performing particular services." These groups can be horizontal, "servicing one functional level of an industry or profession; alternatively they can be vertical, serving all functional levels." Professional societies related to design and construction include the International Facility Management Association, the Building Owners and Managers Association, the American Society of Landscape Architects, the Society for Design Administration (SDA), and the American Institute of Architects, among others.

Trade associations are "composed of individuals or firms concerned with a single product or service or those concerned with a number of related products or services." A number of trade associations represent participants in the design and construction industry, including the Associated General Contractors of America (AGC), the National Association of Home Builders, and the National Manufacturers Association.

Charitable institutions are composed "of members with interests in whatever kind of science, educational area, or charity is represented by the association." Included in this category are the American Architectural Foundation, the Corcoran Museum of Art, and the Smithsonian Institution.

ROLES PROFESSIONAL SOCIETIES PLAY

People often decide to join professional associations because of an invitation from another professional in their field. Members renew their membership over time because they value specific services the association provides. The services commonly provided by professional societies are described in this section.

Bringing People Together to Effect Change

In his 2001 book *Principles of Association Management*, Henry L. Ersthal, CAE, suggests "the uniqueness of associations rests in their members' strong feelings of ownership and involvement in decision making. Members believe they can make themselves heard and effect change within and through their associations." This is a central reason many cite for joining a professional society or trade association. In a 2006 survey of AIA members' needs, 64 percent of respondents indicated they joined the Institute "to show my commitment to the profession." These individuals clearly believe that collectively, under the aegis of a professional society, they have greater control over the elements that shape and influence their work. In addition to contributing to their professions, many join associations to develop professional networks and contacts. Many experienced professionals remark on the value of spending time in the company of other professionals talking about the things that matter, developing lifelong networks and relationships, and learning from one another in informal settings.

Providing Resources to Members

Another reason people join professional societies is to gain access to knowledge and services that will help them address particular problems. These resources take many forms depending on the association. The AIA, for instance, has for many years published contract documents for use in the design and construction industry, as well as a monthly economic report (*Work-on-the-Boards*), which analyzes the economic trends that affect design and construction. The Society for Design Administration has developed a software program for tracking the continuing education requirements of a firm's licensed professionals. Most professional associations today provide members-only Web sites with much information valuable to the everyday life of their members.

It is against the law for associations to deny nonmembers access to products and services they provide to their members if, as cited in the *Association Law Handbook*, those products or services may be considered to "confer important competitive or economic benefit." However, it is considered lawful to charge nonmembers a higher fee for products and services as long as the difference between the member fee and the nonmember fee is not so high it "compels membership." In other words, the member/nonmember price difference for the *2006 AIA Firm Survey* cannot be the same as the current dues rate.

Promoting the Value of Professional Members

Most professional associations aggressively promote their members as better prepared, more knowledgeable, and more likely to serve the public than nonmembers. For example, many associations, through public relations and marketing campaigns, promote their members as providers of the highest degree of professional service to the client.

Connecting Groups of Allied Professionals

In his 1997 book *Professional Practices in Association Management*, John B. Cox, CAE, says, "The fundamental proposition undergirding all coalitions is simple: People who share a common purpose and perspective can accomplish more when they collaborate than when they pursue narrower interests on their own." And while associations are themselves coalitions, they often work institutionally with other, related organizations to achieve common goals. Sometimes associations form coalitions for specific purposes; for example, in 2006 the American Society of Association Executives (ASAE) led a broad-based coalition of associations to lobby for passage of federal legislation that would enable associations to form groups for the purpose of providing health insurance for their members' small businesses (e.g., sole practitioners). Other coalitions are formed for more general purposes, as the AIA/AGC Joint Committee, which has met twice each year for more than fifty years to discuss "issues of mutual interest and concern."

Offering Continuing Education Programs

Licensing of professionals, especially those whose business may affect the health, safety, and welfare of the public, is a state responsibility. Consequently, each state has established requirements for receiving and maintaining a professional license. In many cases, maintaining a license includes a requirement for continuing education. This is especially true in architecture and the law. Professional societies are often the primary provider of continuing education for their members, and because professional societies are precluded by law from excluding nonmembers from the programs they offer, the societies become the primary provider of continuing education for the entire profession.

In some cases, professional societies work together to provide cross-disciplinary training for their members. For example, each year ASAE offers a symposium on association law. The program is open to anyone interested in the issues; however, association executives and attorneys attending the program can earn six of the education units that may be required for certification (in the case of association executives) or maintaining bar memberships (in the case of attorneys).

Conducting Advocacy and Lobbying

Associations lobby for issues of value to their members—including legislation or regulations that affect their ability to conduct business in a state or other jurisdiction.

Lobbying has become a significant effort of many associations. In addition to employing professional lobbyists on staff or retaining a lobbyist to represent the association, many professional societies engage their members as "grassroots advocates."

In grassroots programs, individual members are brought to Washington, D.C., or the state capital, where they are briefed on specific issues or a particular piece of legislation and encouraged to visit their elected representatives to discuss them. Many associations have also established political action committees (PACs). Members can make voluntary contributions to the PAC, which, in turn, makes contributions to candidates for state or federal office who support positions favored by members. Associations are regulated by the same laws that affect other lobbyists. This means they must file reports with state and federal authorities and can be limited in the amount of money they spend on lobbying activities. Similarly, association PACs are subject to the same reporting requirements as other PACs.

Raising Funds for Special Needs

Trade associations and professional societies, generally speaking, receive tax-exempt status under section 501(c)(6) of the U.S. tax code. While this status exempts associations from certain taxes, it does not allow gifts of money or services given by an individual to be designated as tax-deductible. This limits the ability of associations to raise funds for special needs such as scholarships or research. In response, some professional societies and trade associations have formed foundations or charitable organizations (e.g., the American Architectural Foundation, or AAF, and the AGC Educational and Research Foundation) under section 501(c)(3) of the U.S. tax code, which gives these organizations tax-exempt status. Such foundations have specific educational, cultural, or scientific purposes that are directly related to the profession. For example, the AAF supports several scholarship programs for students enrolled in architecture programs (e.g., the Minority and Disadvantaged Scholarship Program). Under special circumstances, related foundations may also establish special funds for disaster relief or other philanthropic activity. Members of the association, and nonmembers as well, are able to make tax-deductible gifts to these foundations in support of specific initiatives.

Providing Insurance and Other Benefits

Most associations provide benefits for their members. In the case of a professional society, many of these are directed toward improvement of the individual member's ability to succeed in his or her profession. For example, the AIA offers architects access to professional liability and health insurance programs. SDA offers a certification program for its members, and the American Council of Engineering Companies offers an organizational peer review program to architecture and engineering firms. In the case of charitable organizations, the benefit often takes the form of reduced prices for subscriptions or tickets to events.

GETTING INVOLVED

Architects may choose to belong to several organizations related to their careers, from a broadly focused organization such as the AIA to groups with a narrower focus such as the Construction Specifications Institute, International Facility Management Association, American College of Healthcare Architects, U.S. Green Building Council, or Design-Build Institute of America. The decision about which organizations to join is personal; each architect must determine which groups will provide the information most likely to advance his or her professional life. One strategy is to begin by joining just one organization and later add memberships in others as your experience broadens and your career matures.

The first step to involvement is to join the organization. Nearly all professional organizations have membership criteria, forms, and other materials available on their

▶ For a list of professional and related trade organizations in the design and construction industry, see Appendix B, Allied Professional Organizations, in the back of the Handbook.

Web sites. Some groups permit individuals to join directly from the Web site; others require additional information and original signatures on the application form.

Members of professional societies of all sorts generally get more from their membership when they become involved in the activities of the organization, whether it is at the national, state, or local level.

For More Information

Information about opportunities to participate in the AIA at national, regional, and local levels can be found on the AIA Web site at www.aia.org. *AIA Public Policies and Position Statements* and the *AIA Member Benefits Guide*, updated annually, are available in PDF at www.aia.org.

THE AMERICAN INSTITUTE OF ARCHITECTS

The AIA was formed, according to its bylaws, to "organize and unite in fellowship the members of the architectural profession of the United States of America; to promote the aesthetic, scientific, and practical efficiency of the profession; to advance the science and art of planning and building by advancing the standards of architectural education, training, and practice; to coordinate the building industry and the profession of architecture to ensure the advancement of living standards through their improved environment; and to make the profession of ever-increasing service to society." The AIA achieves a contemporary expression of its historical vision and mission through its services, products, and support of the architectural profession.

Member Participation

Today, the AIA has more than 80,000 members worldwide in several membership categories, including Architect, Associate, International Associate, Emeritus, and Allied members. The AIA supports its members in the development of their careers in a creative, constantly evolving profession and provides information that helps them sustain the growth and health of their firms. It also offers some benefits, such as insurance, that support the business of architecture.

AIA members can participate at three levels of membership: national, state, and local. In addition to traditional governance roles (e.g., board member, committee chair, or regional director), members can participate in the AIA through knowledge communities organized by type of practice or special interest (e.g., historic preservation, small practice, building science and performance, and architecture for education) and member affinity groups (e.g., the Young Architects Forum), which are organized to a certain extent by length of time in the profession. Across the AIA, there are many possibilities for participation; for example, opportunities to serve include roles such as the following:

- Chair of the state design awards program
- Regional associate director on the National Associates Committee

- Young Architects Forum regional liaison
- Local AIA component board member
- Member of the national Committee on the Environment advisory group
- State vice president
- Regional treasurer
- National regional director
- College of Fellows bursar

Among the AIA's national leaders are architects whose careers have included decades of service in local, state, and national roles.

AIA Programs

The Institute routinely researches what services, products, and other opportunities its members find valuable. In particular, the AIA carries out a member needs assessment every six months, polls members on advocacy issues each year, surveys interns every three years, collects and evaluates comprehensive information on firms every three years, and analyzes economic data and the projected impact on architecture and construction each month. From this information, the Institute develops position statements, products, services, programs, and other resources in formats that most closely meet members' expressed needs. Some items are available on the AIA Web site, while others are in print; still others (especially continuing education) are presented in person. Recognizing that not all products, services, and programs will meet the needs of all members all of the time, the intent is to provide a mix that will meet the needs of most members.

Continuing education. The AIA offers many education programs at the national, state, and local levels and supports a continuing education system (CES) that serves both members and program providers. AIA/CES provides members with access to programs that enable them to meet the continuing education requirement for AIA membership (eighteen units per year, of which eight must be in subjects related to protecting the health, safety, and welfare of the public), as well as state continuing education

(continued)

requirements for licensure. The AIA/CES registered provider program supports learning partnerships with firms, AIA components, and other continuing education providers. In addition, AIA/CES provides a third-party system for recording participation in professional learning activities.

AIA National Convention and Design Exposition. Each year the AIA national convention and expo offers members and others a major educational opportunity. This four-day event features continuing education sessions (seminars, workshops, and tours), networking and socializing events (e.g., regional receptions and alumni gatherings), presentations on significant issues or from well-known architects (e.g., a panel on integrated practice or a presentation by a recent Gold Medal winner), honors and awards presentations, and a trade show. Members can earn all required continuing education units for membership for the year (and for many, state continuing education requirements) while attending the national convention.

Knowledge communities and knowledge resources. Members have access to specialized architecture knowledge through the AIA knowledge communities. These groups comprise members who share a common interest in a given area of practice and collaborate to sponsor educational and networking opportunities with like-minded others. More than twenty knowledge communities address a variety of professional interests in different aspects of professional practice. Groups have formed around such issues as international practice, the concerns of emerging professionals, practice management, historic preservation, leadership for architects, and sustainable design and the environment, as well as specific building types (e.g., architecture for education, health care architecture, religious architecture, interior architecture, housing, and retail and entertainment architecture).

The AIA also provides knowledge resources to its members through its library and archives, Web sites, and publishing partnerships. With John Wiley & Sons, the AIA produces the *Architect's Handbook of Professional Practice* and *Architectural Graphic Standards* and supports the publication of other practice titles such as the *Architect's Essential* series. With Taunton Press, the AIA publishes specialized works on residential architecture intended to familiarize the public with the benefits of working with an architect.

Lobbying. The AIA advocates on legislative, regulatory, and related issues of importance to AIA members before federal, state, and local governments and other policy-making bodies. These efforts include lobbying for legislation that either benefits member practices (e.g., tax cuts for small businesses) or advances issues that architects believe are important (reducing the energy consumption of buildings). Advocacy activities take place in Washington before the U.S. Congress on such matters as federal tax credits for sustainable design and historic preservation,

health insurance for small businesses, transportation studies, and federal grants to ensure that historic properties damaged by catastrophic storms can be restored. AIA components also lobby for members at the state and local level. This often takes the form of advocacy to prevent encroachment on the title "architect" by other design professionals whose professional qualifications do not meet the standards for architecture education, experience, and examination.

Programs for emerging professionals. The AIA supports its younger members as they advance in the profession, encouraging them to complete an internship and the architect registration examination (ARE) process in a timely, rigorous, and respectful manner. To that end, the AIA provides ARE preparation courses, tools to assist in completing the Intern Development Program (IDP), mentoring information, and the *Emerging Professional's Companion*, an online study tool for earning supplemental IDP credit.

AIA Contract Documents program. With their 120-year history, AIA Contract Documents are the "gold standard" for design and construction contract documents in the United States. More than 100 contracts and forms have been developed through a consensus process that involves owners, contractors, attorneys, engineers, and others, as well as architects. The documents establish relationships between architects and other parties that protect the interests of both. The AIA continually updates the documents to stay current with trends and practices in the construction industry.

Honors and awards programs. The Institute recognizes its members for outstanding work and for service to the profession through a number of different programs, including the College of Fellows, AIA Honors and Awards, and the Gold Medal and Architecture Firm awards.

The AIA College of Fellows honors architect members for outstanding service to the profession over time. Nominations can be made in five categories: design, education, service to the profession, service to the community, and technical advancement of the profession. Fellows are permitted to use the designation "FAIA" after their names on business cards and in professional settings.

In addition to its recognition of the contributions of individuals, the College of Fellows is actively engaged in supporting research in the profession through the Latrobe Prize. Awarded biannually in odd-numbered years, this award is granted to an architect or group of architects working in partnership with scientific and/or academic institutions to develop a specific body of scientific knowledge that will be applicable to architecture practice. Past Latrobe recipients have focused on manufacturing methodologies, neuroscience, and health care.

The AIA Honors and Awards Program seeks to recognize the best work in a given year in the categories of Architecture, Interior Architecture, and Regional and Urban Design. Other groups within the Institute recognize excellence in specific project types through juried competitions. For example, the Housing Knowledge Community recognizes excellence in housing design each year and the Committee on the Environment honors designs that meet specific criteria for sustainable design, such as use of recycled products, and other green factors.

The AIA Gold Medal is conferred on an individual architect by the national AIA board of directors in recognition of a significant body of work of lasting influence on the theory and practice of architecture. The Architecture Firm Award is the highest honor the AIA can bestow on an architecture firm to recognize the consistent production of distinguished architecture.

Member Benefits

Some AIA efforts fall more into the category of general member benefits than programs related to the practice of architecture.

The AIA established the AIA Trust in 1952 as a separate entity to develop, and make available at the greatest possible value, insurance and other benefit programs for members and components of the AIA and to serve as a risk management resource for the practice of architecture. The Trust selects member programs in conjunction with independent consultants to meet high standards of quality, value, financial stability, service, and coverage.

Members can also use the services of the AIA's Affinity partners. These are companies and service providers (e.g., computer sellers, special package delivery services, car rental companies) that have agreed to offer their services to AIA members at a discount. Many sole proprietors and small firms are able to save considerably by taking advantage of these programs.

A Consortium of Like-Minded Professionals

For AIA members, many of the issues architects face today are similar to those faced when the Institute was founded. Each year, the AIA and its members look for new solutions to "old" problems, as well as emerging ones, and work with each other and their communities to create healthy, secure, and sustainable places to live and work. More information about the AIA can be found at www.aia.org.

CHAPTER 2

Legal Dimensions of Practice

2.1 Architects and the Law

Joseph H. Jones Jr., Esq., AIA

The architecture profession functions within a body of laws intended to provide a level of consistency and professionalism for all involved in design and construction.

Architects are confronted on a daily basis with legal issues that pertain to many aspects of architecture practice. These issues are defined and governed by a body of laws, regulations, and judicial interpretations that establish requirements for entering the profession, starting firms, providing professional services, and operating in the business world. A rudimentary understanding of a few basic legal concepts is essential to the successful practice of architecture.

LEGAL CONCEPTS

In our system of jurisprudence, law stems from several complementary but distinct sources:

- The Constitution of the United States and the constitutions of the states
- Statutes passed by federal, state, or local legislative bodies under their constitutional authority

Joe Jones is a vice president and director of risk management services at Victor O. Schinnerer & Company, Inc. He practiced architecture for more than ten years and, before joining Schinnerer, was assistant counsel for the contract documents program of the American Institute of Architects. (This topic is adapted from "Legal Dimensions of Practice" in the thirteenth edition of the Handbook.)

- Administrative rules and regulations developed to implement these statutes
- Private legal arrangements based on contracts
- Interpretations of statutes, regulations, and contracts on a case-by-case basis by the courts and administrative agencies

Most of the legal issues regarding the practice of architecture are *civil* rather than *criminal* matters. Civil laws are enacted by state and federal governments and have evolved over the centuries. These laws are used to adjudicate private rights, duties, and obligations. A lawsuit is a civil legal action brought by a party against another party, alleging violation of the rights of the party bringing the lawsuit. Equity, or fairness to all involved, and damages, which involve compensation for injury, are important civil law concepts.

Much of the architect's everyday exposure to the law is through *administrative law*—the regulations developed to implement civil statutes. These statutes often establish only broad contours of public policy. Subsequently, public officials charged with carrying out these laws adopt regulations to address technical details.

Under their statutory authority, state registration boards, code officials, and other administrative agencies are given the power to develop, implement, and enforce regulations needed to do their jobs. Individuals and entities subject to regulation typically have opportunities to seek variances or appeal decisions through administrative channels (e.g., zoning boards of appeal). When administrative avenues have been exhausted, it is possible to seek review of administrative decisions in the courts.

THE ARCHITECT'S LEGAL RESPONSIBILITY

The law does not require perfection in meeting a client's expectations from an architect. As with any complicated human endeavor in which success depends on exercise of reasoned judgment and skill, the law recognizes that perfection in architecture is practically impossible to achieve.

Accordingly, the law does not look to architects to guarantee, warrant, or otherwise insure the results of their efforts unless the architect agrees to do so by conduct or contract. Rather, the law grants architects the same latitude it provides lawyers, doctors, and other professionals—the freedom to exercise their judgment and skill reasonably and prudently, comfortably aware that as long as they act reasonably and prudently, the law will support their endeavors.

The Standard of Reasonable Care

Specifically, the law sets a standard of reasonable care for the performance of architects and, indeed, of all professionals. The architect is required to do what a reasonably prudent architect would do in the same community, in the same time frame, given the same or similar facts and circumstances.

Although this standard can be specifically modified by contract or conduct, it establishes the law's underlying minimum expectation for the performance of professionals. The architect's legal responsibilities to a client are examined in light of what reasonably prudent architects would have known and done at the time services were performed.

The standard of reasonable care is the cornerstone of professional responsibility. All professionals, including architects, attorneys, and physicians, take seriously their professional obligations but are not required by law to warrant their services. For example, physicians are not required to guarantee a return to good health or lawyers an acquittal. Similarly, architects are not legally required, unless they contractually agree, to guarantee that a building will function perfectly or that its roof will not leak.

The professional standard of care is evolutionary in nature. For example, some jurisdictions now interpret "in the same community" to mean in the entire United States. These jurisdictions reason that communication technologies and the high degree of mobility in American society reduce the impact of regional variations. Stated another way, an architect should be aware of reasonable standards of practice nationally as well as locally. In rejecting a national standard, other jurisdictions reason that local services should mirror local needs and that only by enforcing a local standard of care can the jurisdiction ensure that its citizens' needs will be met.

Meeting the relevant standard of care may not protect an architect from litigation; a suit can be brought by anyone, even a party with whom the architect had no contractual relationship. The requirement to be reasonable, however, does provide a guidepost for the everyday practice of architecture.

Expectations of Project Participants

Although the law sets a standard of reasonable care for professionals, project participants often come to the table with different expectations. Many clients do not understand that architects are neither able nor required to perform perfectly. Such clients have high expectations for their projects and want their design professionals to provide guarantees.

Other project participants in and out of the building enterprise may call for a different standard of care, not understanding that architects, like lawyers and doctors, provide their clients with services, not products. These individuals may also fail to realize that professional judgment is required at each step. Architects need to remind these project participants that buildings, unlike automobiles, cannot be pretested. Despite the effort, care, and conscientiousness of the architect, the process of taking a project from drawing to reality has a lot of unknowns.

The Architect's Conduct

Even though the law requires only reasonable and prudent behavior, an architect can expand or raise the standard of care. This may be done either consciously or inadvertently. For example, the standard of care is altered by the architect's actions in the following examples:

- The architect agrees to contractual language "warranting" that the building will be constructed as designed or that it will perform according to the architect's design.
- The architect signs a financial institution's document "certifying" that "to induce the lender, the project has met all codes and standards."
- The architect writes an indignant letter to a client who has expressed concern about a damp basement, stating, "I promise you that my basements do not and will not leak."
- The architect goes to the construction site and instructs the contractor on the means and methods of forming a complicated concrete wall.
- The architect assures the owner the construction contractors will complete their work by a specific date.

It is important to realize that raising the standard of care increases the architect's liability exposure by making the architect responsible for more than the professional standard requires. Sometimes design professionals—under pressure from clients or contractors or propelled by their own drive for perfection—raise the standard of care that will be applied to their services without intending to do so.

Guidance provided in this handbook, as well as by the architect's legal counsel and insurance advisor, is based on the premise that it is inappropriate to raise the standard of care that will be applied to your services as a professional without first considering the consequences.

Measurement of the Standard of Care

Assuming the architect chooses to operate within the professional standard of care, the issue is not what the standard of care is, but rather what is prudent and reasonable given the facts and circumstances facing the architect in a given situation. Ultimately, what is reasonable is decided on a case-by-case basis when the issue is brought to court or arbitration. In a legal action involving a professional's liability, both sides present expert witnesses who testify whether the professional acted as another reasonably prudent architect would have in the same community, in the same time frame, given the same or similar facts and circumstances.

Most architects are not sued. They must decide for themselves, before they act, what is reasonable and prudent given the circumstances facing them. As professionals, they look to themselves and to their colleagues' experiences for insight into these decisions, as well as to the rules and regulations controlling design and practice. Sources for such information include other architects, state licensing laws, case law, codes and standards, the owner-architect agreement controlling the project, publications from the AIA and other organizations, and insurance company publications.

PROFESSIONAL LIABILITY

A professional who fails to meet the standard of reasonable care may be held negligent in the performance of professional duties if injury or damage results because of that failure.

Negligence

For a successful negligence action against an architect, the law requires proof of four elements:

1. *Duty.* The architect must owe a legal duty to the person making the claim. In other words, the architect has a legal obligation to do something or refrain from doing something.
2. *Breach.* The architect fails to perform the duty or does something that should not have been done.
3. *Cause.* The architect's breach of duty is the proximate cause of harm to the person making the claim.
4. *Damage.* Actual harm or damage must have resulted from the breach.

If these elements are proven to exist, the architect may be held liable and made to pay monetary damages. It is important to note that *all four elements* must exist for a negligence claim to be successful. Sometimes an intervening event, rather than the alleged design error, is the actual cause of the damage.

Negligence actions can arise from either the architect's errors (acts of commission) or the architect's omissions (things that should have been done and were not). Examples of situations that can result in injury or damage, and hence in negligence actions, include the following:

- A building structure is inadequate for the wind loads encountered at the site.
- The architect fails to design in accordance with normally applicable statutes, ordinances, zoning regulations, or building codes.
- The architect fails to detect a readily discernible error in a contractor's application for payment or issues a change order without the owner's authorization.
- The architect follows an instruction from the owner knowing (or having reason to believe) that it will result in a code violation.

The bottom line is architects are responsible both for meeting contractual commitments and for performing professional services without negligence.

Third-Party Actions

In addition to their direct contractual responsibilities, architects can be held liable for negligent acts, errors, or omissions that physically injure or damage third parties with whom the architect has no contractual relationship. These third parties include construction workers, passersby, and occupants or users of projects.

Before 1956, the legal concept of *privity* would have barred third-party actions. Privity required the litigating parties to prove they were in a contractual relationship with each other and that the injury occurred in the course of that relationship. Since that time, courts have—with regard to physical injury and, in some cases, property damage—extended the group of individuals to whom architects owe duties to include third parties whom architects can reasonably foresee will depend on them to provide services in a nonnegligent manner.

Statutes of Limitations

Statute of limitations laws relating to breach of contract and professional negligence vary widely from jurisdiction to jurisdiction. The length of time within which a breach-of-contract action can be brought may be as short as one year, while the length of time within which a professional negligence action can be brought may be as short as four years. Some jurisdictions, however, have no defined time limit.

The limitations period may begin at different times. In some jurisdictions, the starting point is tied to completion of construction or occupancy of a project. These statutes are called *statutes of repose*, and it is important to note that, generally speaking, a statute of repose is an absolute time frame in which a legal action can be brought against the architect. In other jurisdictions, the limitations clock begins running only when the injury occurs or the defect is discovered, which may be many years after substantial completion. These are called *statutes of limitations*. Most jurisdictions have both a statute of repose and a statute of limitations applicable to professional services. However, some jurisdictions do not have a statute of repose, in effect indefinitely extending the time frame an architect may be held liable.

Immunities

An architect is not normally liable for damages due to errors and omissions that are not deemed negligent in the eyes of the law. For example, although an architect may feel obligated to correct a deficiency in the contract documents, this change will not make the architect liable for the cost of correcting the construction work itself unless there was a failure to meet the standard of reasonable care in the first place. In another example, under AIA Document A201–2007, General Conditions of the Contract for Construction, the architect administering the construction contract functions as the impartial interpreter of the contract requirements and the judge of performance by owner and contractor. The courts have provided architects a quasi-judicial immunity while performing this role that protects them from professional liability for decisions made in good faith.

An Area of Rapid Change

Professional liability is a very active area of the law. Architects and other professionals therefore engage lawyers and insurance risk managers to advise them in managing their professional affairs. With this advice, and with good training, experience, awareness of recent trends and developments, and plain common sense, architects can manage the inevitable risks in their practices and projects and reduce their exposure to adverse legal entanglements.

AGENCY RELATIONSHIPS

In entering the contractual relationships necessary for professional practice, architects form several agency relationships that define their legal responsibility. As a legal concept, *agency* is the notion that a party, called a *principal*, may authorize another person or entity, called an *agent*, to act on that party's behalf. The concept permits principals to broaden their activities (and possible rewards) by having a number of agents perform in their stead. Agency presents certain risks, especially as principals are bound by the acts of their agents as long as those agents are (or are believed to be) working within the scope of their authority as agents.

Agency relationships are common in everyday practice: An architect's employee acts as an agent of the architect on a project. A corporate officer acts as an agent of a corporation in signing an agreement for professional services. Partners are agents and, under the law, also principals for each other. That is, partners are agents when they act for other partners (principals) and principals when their other partners (as agents) act for them. Under an owner-architect agreement, the architect may have an agency relationship with the owner for certain designated activities.

The central question in agency relationships is the scope of authority the agent has been granted to act on behalf of the principal. Thus, architects acting as agents of the owner need to know the limits of their authority in dealing with the contractor and other third parties. Firms will want every person who can be perceived as acting as the firm's agent to understand the limits of his or her agency authority. Staying within the limits of their authority is the best protection agents can give themselves and the principals they serve.

Owner-Architect Relationships

Architects often act on behalf of owners who retain them for professional services. As in all professional actions, the architect is legally required to employ reasonable care when acting in this capacity.

Under most AIA contract documents, the architect has a limited agency relationship with the owner during construction. In this agency relationship, the architect represents the owner's interests in some communications with the contractor. Under the terms of these documents, the architect is also called on to render impartial decisions affecting both the owner and the construction contractor, favoring neither party. To facilitate this, the AIA documents stipulate that the architect is not to be held liable for the results of interpretations of the contract documents or other decisions rendered in good faith—even if those interpretations go against the client.

It is also possible for architects to enter into agreements in which they are not in an agency relationship with the owner. For example, an architect who has been retained by a construction manager or a design-builder has moved away from a position as the owner's agent during the construction phase. In such roles, the architect's "client" is the construction manager or design-builder who has retained the architect.

Architect-Employee Relationships

Under the agency concept, an architect is responsible for the acts of employees, partners, and associates when they are acting—or are reasonably believed to be acting—within the scope of their relationships with the architecture firm.

Architect-Consultant Relationships

Consultants who perform professional services on behalf of architects under the terms of an architect-consultant agreement are independent consultants. As in the architect-owner relationship, the consultant may sometimes act as an agent of the architect.

While the law will hold these consultants to the standard of reasonable care applicable to their professional expertise, this does not mean the architect will be absolved from liability should something go wrong. Architects assume what the law labels *vicarious liability* for the actions of their consultants. Because the architect is delegating, to the consultant, duties the architect owes the owner, the architect is still responsible for the performance of those duties.

When the architect must coordinate or supervise consultant services for a project to succeed, the architect often retains these consultants. However, when the owner engages a consultant, the terms of engagement should be clearly stated in writing. Architects usually are not responsible for project consultants hired directly by the owner—unless, of course, the architect agrees to this responsibility in the owner-architect agreement or acts in a way that makes the architect responsible.

Joint Ventures

It is common for the courts to consider the parties to a joint venture to be jointly and separately responsible for the actions of the joint venture. That is, if an injury occurs because of the negligence of either party to the joint venture, the joint venture can be sued collectively or the parties to the joint venture can be sued individually. Therefore, professional responsibility and liability should be carefully allocated in contractual agreements between the parties to a joint venture. Because many states qualify how and under what circumstances professional responsibility may be shifted to another party, legal advice should be sought when preparing such agreements.

THE LAW IN PRACTICE

Architects encounter the law in every aspect of daily practice—in conducting themselves as professionals, in operating their firms, and especially in developing, executing, and administering project agreements.

Giving Advice

Design professionals are constantly called upon to suggest and interpret project agreements with clients, consultants, and contractors. It is not practical or appropriate to bring every question to an attorney; many questions and interpretations involve technical rather than legal issues.

Architects may properly provide technical information concerning building codes, zoning laws, and similar matters that do not require expert legal judgments. On the other hand, not every problem has a technical solution. When legal questions arise or waivers or exceptions need to be sought, clients may want to seek their own legal counsel.

Construction agreements are particularly complex in this regard. Both the architectural and legal professions usually participate in preparing an agreement between owner and contractor. The architect typically suggests to the owner the form and content of the owner-contractor agreement and its general conditions. In this advisory role, the architect may provide the owner with sample agreement forms and other documentation. It should be clear to all involved, however, that the architect is only providing information, that the decisions are the owner's, and that these decisions should be made on the advice of the owner's legal counsel.

When legal counsel is needed on a contract or other project matter, one of the parties to the project may be tempted to seek legal advice from the other party's attorney. It is, however, unethical for lawyers to take more than one side in a controversy or represent more than one party when there are potentially opposing interests (unless all parties are so informed and give their consent). If lawyers are shared, it should be made clear at the outset that the interests of the parties may not coincide.

Asking for Counsel

Architects have to decide for themselves when and how often to seek legal counsel. Lawyers who regularly represent architects say those who keep their lawyers up-to-date on their practices will spend less time and resources on legal expenses in the long run than those who call only when a serious problem arises.

When an architect does ask for and receive legal advice, it is a good idea to question your lawyer until it is clear what's being recommended and the reasons for it. This will help you understand the legal concepts involved in the situation and their effect on your practice.

A SOURCE OF UNDERSTANDING

Architects need to remember that they provide services that are governed by law. In addition to helping architects understand their level of obligation to their clients, other project participants, and the public, these laws also help these stakeholders understand what level of care and professionalism they should expect of the architect. Architects must also remember that the laws that govern their professional services change and evolve over time, so it is important to take steps to keep abreast of changes in the law and in professional standards.

For More Information

Legal casebooks that outline legal principles and provide excerpts from important or illustrative opinions handed down by U.S. appellate courts can be instructive for architects' attorneys but are less helpful for an architect developing practice strategies. Best known is Justin Sweet and Mare M. Schneidar, *Legal Aspects of Architecture, Engineerings and the Construction Process*, seventh edition (2004). Other books focus on interpretations and cases associated with AIA standard forms of agreement. Examples include Werner Sabo, FAIA, Esq., *A Legal Guide to AIA Documents*, fourth edition (1998), and its supplements, and Justin Sweet, *Sweet on Construction Industry Contracts: Major AIA Documents*, 2 volumes, fourth edition (1999).

Construction Law, by Steven G. M. Stein, ed. (available on CD and with subscription), is the foremost treatise on the subject published in the United States. Its eight volumes treat legal issues relating to the design and construction process and contain the *AIA Legal Citator*, which identifies cases from all U.S. jurisdictions that interpret, are premised upon, or could assist in interpreting provisions of the AIA standard forms of agreement. Although it is written for lawyers, much of the information in this work, including the *Citator*, is accessible to design professionals.

The professional liability insurance industry offers ongoing practical guidance in understanding and managing risks and legal liabilities. For example, Victor O. Schinnerer & Company publishes "Guidelines for Improving Practice" for architects and engineers and their counsel. See www.schinnerer.com and www.PlanetRiskManagement.com.

BACKGROUNDER

COPYRIGHT AND INTELLECTUAL PROPERTY IN THE DIGITAL AGE

Jessica L. Darraby, Esq.

Copyright is an everyday concern of architectural practice, its recurrence as common as its range is broad. Copyright issues arise whenever work is created, assigned, commissioned, circulated in person (mechanically or electronically), or shown to or seen by others—whether in master classes, during apprenticeships, on the Internet, to employers, or in job applications, juried competitions, or design studios. Students and practitioners can build upon the copyright basics outlined in this backgrounder to manage copyright as an economic asset with clients, partners, employers, and others, and to incorporate it as a creative asset in a career strategy and architectural portfolio.

The Concept of Copyright

Architects work in two and three dimensions; they design, and these designs are often constructed into buildings. The images they fix as stock-in-trade—plans, technical drawings, construction drawings, photographs, renderings, maquettes, models, slides, transparencies—are copyrightable, and have been for some time. In recent years, the Architectural Works

(continued)

Copyright Protection Act of 1990 (AWCPA) added building designs and constructed buildings to the list of copyrightable works. Thus a broad range of architectural *work product* is covered by U.S. copyright law.

A copyright arises from the fixation of a two- or three-dimensional image in a legally specified form. The law provides copyright protection for "original works of authorship fixed in any tangible medium of expression, now known or later developed."

The owner of a copyright is granted exclusive rights of usage in the image for determinate time periods, a monopolistic power that is at the heart of copyright. A copyright arising from the fixed image is classified as an intangible personal property asset. Copyright gives the owner of this powerful intangible asset—the copyrighted work—a monopoly to use and to control use of the exclusive rights in the work.

In short, copyright provides economic benefits to the copyright owner by authorizing control of use and enabling economic exploitation and creative control of the copyright by such use. In sum and substance, this is the essence of copyright law.

Copyright law contains words and phrases that appear to be plain English but in fact are legal terms of art that have specific, and sometimes carefully defined, meanings. These terms of art are italicized to alert the reader that further inquiry or consultation with a lawyer may be advisable.

The term "copyright law" is used for convenience in this primer on copyright, but in fact copyright law is not a singular monolithic law. Copyright law is a combination of federal statute created by codified legislative enactments like AWCPA, periodically amended, supplemented by federal regulations, and interpreted by judicial construction. Copyright law is a complex, synergistic interplay of constitutional underpinnings, codification, and case law. (See Title 17 of the U.S Code: 37 CFR 202.11.)

Creation of Copyright by Authors

Copyright law specifies several issues that determine what materials can be copyrighted:

Fixed in tangible medium. A copyright subsists in a work by operation of law when its expression has been fixed in a tangible medium of expression by the creator, known as the author. In common parlance, this means a copyright springs to legal life upon creation. Fixing occurs when the embodiment of the work is sufficiently permanent or stable to permit it to be perceived, reproduced, or communicated for more than a transitory duration.

Original. Copyright requires *originality*, a legal term of art rather than an aesthetic hurdle. Originality means that the work is an independent creation by the author, the most

minimal level of creativity. In certain instances a work may be copyrightable even when it is an entire combination of unprotectable elements.

Subject matter of copyright. Copyright only arises if the original work created is *subject matter of copyright*, a term of art in copyright law. There are two types of subject matter relevant to architectural practice, and each is defined by statute: (1) pictorial, graphic, sculptural works; and (2) architectural works.

Ideas and concepts excluded. The law is clear that ideas, however original, are not copyrightable: "In no case does copyright protection for an original work of authorship extend to any idea, procedure, process, system . . . , concept, principle, or discovery, regardless of the form in which it is described, explained, illustrated, or embodied in such work."

Ownership of Copyright

Copyright ordinarily originates with the creator who fixes the image—the author of the work. Copyright, as emphasized above, is a property asset, and like other assets, it may be assigned, conveyed, or devised. The author, by a signed writing, may transfer ownership rights in the copyright in part or in full to another person or entity known as the copyright holder. The author of the copyright and the holder of the copyright are thus not necessarily the same. The holder of the copyright is the one who has the exclusive right to control usage.

Subject Matter of Copyright

What work products produced by architects are eligible for copyright protection? As far as the architect or student of architecture is concerned, there are two things that can be protected by copyright: drawings and the design of buildings (as defined within the copyright statute). These two specific work products are covered in the two categories of copyrightable material described below.

Pictorial, graphic, and sculptural works. Section 101 of the Copyright Act defines "pictorial, graphic, and sculptural works" as follows:

"[T]wo-dimensional and three-dimensional works of fine, graphic, and applied art, photographs, prints and art reproductions, maps, globes, charts, diagrams, models, and technical drawings, including architectural plans. Such works shall include works of artistic craftsmanship insofar as their form but not their mechanical or utilitarian aspects are concerned."

The design elements of these works are copyrightable, but excluded from copyright are the mechanical and utilitarian aspects of the work—a copyright concept referred to in various forms as *separability*. There is not a requirement of separability for architectural works. Technical drawings may be protected under the category of pictorial, graphic, and sculptural works, even if they are not complete or detailed enough to support actual construction of a building.

Architectural works. In 1990 AWCPA, for the first time in American law, expressly extended copyright protection to building designs and buildings. Section 101 defines *architectural works* as follows:

> [A]n architectural work is the design of a building as embodied in any tangible medium of expression, including a building [providing that it is erected in a country adhering to the Berne Convention], architectural plans, or drawings. The work includes the overall form as well as the arrangement and composition of spaces and elements in the design, but does not include individual standard features.

The AWCPA describes buildings as "structures that are habitable by humans and intended to be both permanent and stationary." Examples given in the act are "houses and office buildings and other permanent and stationary structures designed for human occupancy, including but not limited to churches, museums, gazebos, and garden pavilions." Structures "other than buildings, such as bridges, cloverleafs, dams, walkways, tents, recreational vehicles, mobile homes and boats" are excluded from coverage and cannot be registered. In addition, it has been determined that a single store in a shopping mall is not considered a "building" for the purposes of the AWCPA.

The arrangement and composition of spaces and elements acknowledges that creativity in architecture involves the following:

1. Selection, coordination, and/or arrangement of unprotectable elements into a protectable whole
2. Incorporation of new design elements into standard unprotectable building features
3. Protectability of certain interior architecture

Building designs and plans may be protected even if preliminary or conceptual, and regardless of whether a building could actually be constructed from them. A significant recent court holding is that "once a design [of an architectural work] includes 'specific expression and realization of . . . ideas,' copying constitutes infringement." For example, a scale model of a twisting tower, although "rough," is considered a distinctive design that surpasses the level of an unprotected idea or concept.

The overall design may be protected as "overall form [and] arrangement" of spaces and elements even where the individual elements such as windows, doors, twists, and setbacks are standard and unprotectable. Elevation sketches of a building, photomontages displaying a building against a skyline, and sketches of a building's exterior design have all been registered by the U.S. Copyright Office (USCO).

Publication of Copyrighted Material

Publication of a pictorial, graphic, or sculptural work occurs, according to the AWCPA, when there is a "distribution of copies of the work to the public by sale or other transfer of ownership or by rental, lease, or lending" or by "offering to distribute copies to a group for purposes of further distribution or public display." A single copy of a work is not published if the single copy is sold or offered for sale at a gallery, through a dealer, or at auction. Publication occurs for multiples of a work when the "reproductions are publicly distributed or offered to a group for further distribution or public display." Publication can affect *registration*, including *deposit requirements* and other aspects of copyright.

According to the AWCPA, "construction of a building does not constitute publication for purposes of *registration*," except in certain circumstances.

Two-dimensional depictions in public places. Copyright protection for buildings is balanced against the societal and cultural importance of public use of urban landscapes and city skylines. Copyright law recognizes the importance of architecture to the community at large, thus limiting the scope of copyright protection for buildings located in specified public places or public vistas. Copyright owners cannot prevent "the making, distributing, or public display of pictures, paintings, photographs, or other pictorial representations of the [architectural] work, if the [constructed] building . . . is located in or ordinarily visible from a public place."

Standard features. Copyright in general does not protect utilitarian aspects or functionality of works. Standard features of buildings are specifically excluded from architectural works: "standard configurations of spaces and individual standard features, such as windows, doors and other staple building components."

Constructed. The term *constructed* is not defined by statute. Architectural works unconstructed before December 1, 1990, embodied in drawings or plans are protected against unauthorized copying on or after that date, as are unconstructed architectural works created after the effective date. A townhouse "substantially constructed" before December 1, 1990, but not actually completed until after December 1 was judicially deemed "constructed" and therefore not copyrightable within the meaning of AWCPA, even though it was not habitable.

Exclusive Rights of Usage

In summary, a copyright—the grant and control of the monopoly of *exclusive rights*—exists if the following conditions occur:

(continued)

1. The creation is an "original *work of authorship.*"
2. The work is *"fixed"* in a "tangible medium of expression."
3. The work satisfies the legal definition of subject matter of copyright: a *"pictorial, graphic, or sculptural work"* or an *"architectural work."*

What are these exclusive rights that form the framework of copyright? They are a divisible bundle of rights that enable owners to control usage during the term of the copyright by dividing the bundle any way they choose. Specifically a copyright owner has the right "to do and to authorize" the following exclusive rights:

- *To reproduce the work,* commonly called "copying"
- *To prepare derivative works,* which are works based upon one or more preexisting works
- *To distribute copies* to the public by sale or other transfer of ownership
- *To display the work publicly,* where display means to show a copy of the work directly or by other means

Term of Copyright

How long does the author or copyright holder retain copyright in a work? The duration of time established for the life of a copyright is a statutory time period that differs for individuals, corporations, and certain special situations like *work made for hire, compilation* copyrights, and others.

The term of copyright for an architectural work created on or after December 1, 1990, by an individual is the life of the author plus 70 years. The term of copyright for an architectural work created as a work for hire created on or after December 1, 1990, is 95 years from the date of publication of the work or 120 years from the date of creation of the unpublished plans, whichever term is less. The term of copyright for a pictorial, graphic, or sculptural work created by an individual is the life of the author plus 70 years.

Once the copyright expires under the statutory formulas, the work enters the *public domain.* At that time, absent any available legal exception, the monopoly terminates and usage of the work is available to all.

Exclusions for Tangible Personal Property and Realty

Since 1978, copyright—the intangible property interest—does not automatically transfer when the tangible property transfers, unless expressly stated by contract or operation of law. Tangible property—be it personal property like photographs, models, maquettes, drawings, or real property like buildings—are beyond the scope of copyright law. Similarly, owners of buildings embodying architectural work under copyright law are expressly permitted to alter or to destroy the building. As a matter of policy, change and adaptation of buildings is such an important practical necessity that the law excludes copyright owners from controlling alteration and destruction. Issues of ownership, possession, custody and control, monies or accounts owed, and construction defects are evaluated by other areas of law. Architects may wish to exploit, utilize, trade, sell, or protect other property interests actionable under other areas of law, but copyright law applies only to acts, conduct, and activity that involve the specified exclusive rights.

Benefits of Exclusive Rights

The copyright holder enjoys a number of exclusive rights in the copyrighted work:

Authorized use: assignment and licensing. Owners of copyright may control usage proactively by transfer, assignment, or licensing the copyright. Licensing occurs when the holder or licensor authorizes others, known as licensees, to use the work, or some form of the work for some or all of the exclusive purposes, in specified markets, in return for which the licensor receives royalties or commissions known as licensing fees. Licenses may be oral or written. Thus, the architect may allow the client, members of the project team, the contractor, subcontractors, and other construction trades to use the copyrighted material without relinquishing control or ownership.

Unauthorized use: infringement. Owners of copyright may prevent others from unauthorized use, known as infringement. An allegation of infringement is the legal way of saying one owns a valid copyright, and someone else is using the copyright without authorization. Infringement may be claimed during the life of the copyright before use commences, as use continues, or even after it terminates, so long as the claim is timely filed within the statute of limitations, which in civil matters is within three years of the time the claim accrued. However, delay in claiming copyright infringement that *unduly prejudices* the infringer may result in the imposition of equitable doctrines to trump the three-year statutory period. Courts have refused to order destruction of infringing architectural works when the registrants waited more than two years during which an infringing building complex was constructed and sold.

Infringement claims require registration. Copyright springs to life upon being *fixed.* But *registration* is a prerequisite for a lawsuit. In common parlance, this means a copyright holder must apply to the USCO for a certificate of registration for the copyright in order to file a copyright infringement action in a federal court, and for practical purposes, to initiate a claim against an infringer. The importance of the registration certificate as a means of protecting copyright usage is paramount in that it is *prima facie* evidence that the copyright is valid and provides benefits like statutory damages, attorneys' fees, and costs.

Registration

Registration is a formal administrative process undertaken by the holder of the copyright to register, or record, ownership of the copyright with the USCO. The application procedure for an architect to register copyright in work product requires completion of Form VA (see the accompanying example). Technical drawings and other works may be registered in the category of pictorial, graphic, and sculptural works. "Where dual copyright claims exist in technical drawings and the architectural work depicted in the drawings," the copyright claims must be registered separately— one registration for the drawings and a separate registration for the architectural work.

The application. Submission of a completed Form VA along with deposit copies of the work, as required by regulation, and payment of a nonrefundable fee to the USCO constitutes a registration application. Registration has powerful evidentiary effects and economic advantages such as access to statutory damages, injunctive relief, and repayment for attorney's fees and other costs.

An application for registration may be submitted at any time during the life of the copyright. However, damages and fees and costs may not be calculated for infringement prior to the registration date. Registration is effective on the date the USCO receives Form VA and all attachments and payments, regardless of the time it takes the office to process the application.

When the USCO has registered a work, it issues a certificate of registration. This certificate is considered *prima facie evidence* that the copyright is *valid* and owned by the registrant. This is a powerful provision that places the registrant in a preferential legal position vis-à-vis challengers and infringers. The certificate creates a *presumption* that the copyright is valid and by operation of law shifts the burden of proof to the challenging party to produce evidence to rebut the presumption. This is termed a *rebuttable presumption*. In short, by shifting the evidentiary burden, the certificate boosts the status of the registrant as a valid holder of an original work of authorship.

The deposit. The USCO has established guidelines for *deposit* submissions of architectural works, which become the property of the government and are not returned to the applicant. *Deposit* is the term used by the USCO for material submitted to describe the work for which a copyright is requested. The deposit becomes the official visual record of the copyright the registrant sought and the evidentiary basis for any copyright action. For buildings, whether constructed or not, registrants must submit one complete copy of a finished presentation architectural drawing. Finished presentation drawings are acceptable providing they show the overall form of the building and any interior arrangement of spaces and design elements in which copyright is claimed. If the building has been constructed, quality photographs in 8×10-inch formats depicting several exterior and interior views are also required. The preference of the USCO in terms of deposit materials is for presentation drawings in the following modes, and in the following order:

1. Original format, or best quality reproduction, offset, or silk screen print
2. Xerographic or photographic copies on quality paper
3. Positive photostat or photodirect positive
4. Blue line copies, diazo or ozalid process

Note that a single deposit of a technical drawing will suffice for both an architectural work and the work's technical drawings if both Form VA applications are submitted together. In other words, although two separate forms must be submitted, when they are submitted together, only one drawing is required to satisfy the *deposit* requirements.

It is also recommended that the name of the architects and drafters and an identification of the building site (by address if available or by parcel number, legal description, plat map, or other description recorded in the local property office if no address has yet been assigned) be included in the *deposit*.

For pictorial, graphic, and sculptural works that are *unpublished*, the general rule is to submit one complete copy of the work. If *first published* in the United States, submit two complete copies of the *best edition*. For three-dimensional works, submit identifying materials such as photographs for published or unpublished works. Actual three-dimensional work (e.g., models, maquettes, mock-ups) is not accepted for deposit and should not be included with Form VA.

Notice

An owner may notify the public of copyright in a work by placing a *notice* on the work at the time the work is presented to others, or at the time of publication. Notice is optional on works published on or since March 1, 1989. Notice is established by a statutory recitation of the name of the copyright owner, the word "copyright," "copr.," or the symbol "©" and the date.

Notice formerly was considered a form of deterrence, but it has become commonplace for dedicated infringers to delete or to destroy—or in some instances of piracy simply to ignore—the copyright notice. The conduct of the bad faith infringer in removing notice may affect infringement defenses and damages, and remains a recommended practice. Notice does not require registration, nor does registration require notice.

(continued)

Limitations on Exclusive Rights

Copyright law does not always give the creator of a work the exclusive rights to it, as explained here.

Work for hire. Two prevalent legal concepts limit the ability to use and exploit exclusive rights of copyright: *work made for hire* and *fair use*. Both concepts are determined by specific detailed legal formulations, subject to various exceptions, and are well beyond the scope of this piece. The architect ought to be aware of the existence of such concepts, however, because they occur with regularity in the practice.

Work for hire, a concept developed in agency law and incorporated into copyright, basically allows employers or contracting or commissioning parties under specified circumstances to "own" the copyrights of employees or contractors. In other words, by operation of law or by contract, the firm, an employer, or contractor is deemed to be the author of the intangible personal property even though another architect or designer created the work. The AIA standard form of owner-architect agreement intends to avoid a work for hire result by designating the architect as "author and owner" retaining all copyright interests.

Fair use. The second major limitation on exclusive rights is known as *fair use*, a defense to infringement, which balances the monopolistic rights of usage by the owner with unauthorized use by others. Daily life offers familiar examples of fair use for purposes of criticism, comment, news reporting, teaching, scholarship, parody, and other uses. The user is not required to ask permission from the copyright owner nor is payment of a fee or acknowledgment required. Note that lawyers and others can assert the defense of fair use against an infringement claim, but whether or not the use is fair is a legal determination made by a judge in a court of law.

Infringing Uses

The copyright holder is protected by copyright law from infringing uses of a copyright work.

Copying. The legal shorthand for the exclusive right to reproduce a work is *copying*, a term that does not appear under exclusive rights. Architects, artists, and others use similar ideas—*copying*—all the time; there are only so many ways to design, depict, and site structures and buildings. Budgetary considerations, building and safety code requirements, and building materials impose additional limitations on how works appear.

At what point is copying actionable? The legal evaluation after the fact may be more compelling than identifying at what point copying is problematic in the architect's creative process. So many preexisting factors, images, memories, and subconscious symbols collide in the creative process. An architect may not even be cognizant at the time of conceiving an image that he or she is conjuring up another's work. *Independent creation* is not actionable if actual copying is absent. There may be no actual copying as a matter of law because the underlying work is not an original work of authorship, or it is in the *public domain*, or the elements are unprotected standard features or are otherwise not copyrightable.

To prove copying for purposes of an infringement claim, one must show *actual copying* and *substantial similarity* of the protected elements of the works. Copying may be shown by direct evidence or by circumstantial evidence. It is difficult if not impossible in many instances to show copying by direct evidence. To establish copying by indirect evidence, one must show *access* to the copyrighted work and an opportunity (or in some instances, a presumption) to have viewed the work, and a sufficient degree of similarity between the infringing work to the protected expression in the copyrighted work. In some jurisdictions, this copying precursor to substantial similarity is known as *probative similarity*. Some courts have found probative similarity exists when "two works, viewed as a whole," are sufficiently similar that it could be inferred the second work did not "arise independently" because of the similarities. Expert testimony is permissible to evaluate actual copying.

Substantial similarity. Substantial similarity is the defining value judgment that a work actually copied has been unlawfully appropriated, known as legally actionable copying. This portion of the copying equation is ordinarily determined by the trier of fact—a judge or jury. The factfinder's task is to predict the probable reaction of the "*ordinary observer*," a fictive legal persona. The evaluation is made according to the view of an ordinary person in the street—the layperson, not the winner—of the Pritzker Prize. The ordinary observer's task, phrased differently in different courts, is whether the observer, by comparing only the protected portions of the copyrighted work with the alleging infringing work, would have a "spontaneous response" that the works are similar. In some jurisdictions, the observer is one who "unless charged with detecting disparities would overlook them in favor of viewing aesthetic appeal" as the same. Some jurisdictions may allow expert testimony to assist the lay observer in evaluating substantial similarity.

There is not yet a clear accepted legal standard for making comparisons of substantial similarities between architectural works. Certain courts use "total concept and feel" as a standard, comparing the individual elements in isolation in conjunction with their overall look and feel. The works do not need to be exact copies to be substantially similar. Differences may have some effect under certain circumstances. Courts recognize that "modest dissimilarities" in architectural plans may have more significance than with other works. However, the existence of differences is insufficient to end the inquiry in the alleged infringer's favor.

Initiating an Infringement Claim

To initiate action on infringement, the work must have been registered prior to the claim. Thereafter, an infringement claim may commence with a "lawyer's letter" identifying the copyrighted work and the allegedly infringing one and reciting the known infringing use[s], demanding cessation, known as enjoining use, and/or disposition or destruction of the infringing copies, and damages, and threatening legal action if demands are unmet. If communications fail to resolve the matter, the recourse is to file a complaint for copyright infringement action in a federal court of law. A claimant may instead seek an alternative means of dispute resolution such as mediation or arbitration.

Public Policy: A Monopoly for Creativity

Monopolies are ordinarily disfavored in the American private market system. Why does copyright empower monopoly? Copyright is a legislated means of encouraging the output of creativity into the marketplace by allowing creators to exploit the use of their work and to prevent others from using the work without paying a price. Copyright law, thus, reflects a discrete public policy exception providing special economic status for specified types of intellectual property, including select architectural work products, available in certain circumstances, and for limited periods of time.

Public Art and Architecture

Local, county, state, and regional planning and development agencies often mandate so-called percent-for-art programs, which among other benefits may provide tax and economic incentives to developers who incorporate art in the building design. Developers in conjunction with redevelopment agencies, commission artists under such programs to produce integrated designs for features appurtenant or contiguous to the building, like parks, street walls, fountains, lighting structures, and benches rather than single sited sculptures or wallworks. The contracts may be negotiated and executed some time after the architect has been hired. Under the complex contractual relationships between agencies, developers, and artists, and the interaction of AWCPA with other areas of copyright law including provisions on the so-called "moral rights" of visual art, the architect's copyright interests may be impacted.

Visual Artists Rights Act

The civil law rights of attribution and integrity for works of visual art were added to copyright law in 1990 by the Visual Artists Rights Act (VARA). Visual art, which is not subject matter of copyright, and excludes all work for hire, technical drawings, diagrams, models, and other specified materials, is expressly defined under Section 101. The only work created by an architect that could qualify for VARA protection is pictorial, graphic, and sculptural work that satisfies the specific and limited definition of visual art. VARA is informative for architects who prepare work for gallery or museum exhibitions or maintain careers as artists or photographers.

Copyrighted Works are Valuable Assets

Property assets—whether tangible like personal property or intangible like copyright—are exploitable, transferable, and devisable. Copyright as economic asset has market value during the time period of the monopoly, a value that may increase over time as the architect gains professional stature. Copyright has an equally important nonmonetary value to architects as a creative asset in which the architect has pride of authorship. Copyright is a portfolio investment and should be managed like other work product. Thus, certificates of registration should be maintained like other important business and legal records.

Jessica Darraby is an attorney in a private practice dedicated to art and architecture. A Fellow of the American Bar Foundation, chair of the Art & Museums Division for the American Bar Association Entertainment and Sports Forum, and vice chair of Intellectual Property in the International Law Section of ABA, she is the author of the legal treatise Art, Artifact and Architecture Law.

FILLING OUT FORM VA

Get a copy of Form VA to apply for copyright of "visual arts" from the U.S. Copyright Office (USCO). This form is available only in paper form; check www.copyright.gov for ordering instructions.

1. Identify the building in #1. If the building does not have a name, assign it a name. The Copyright Office needs a reference title to register the copyright. Next to the name of the building—the "title" for purposes of the form—enter the construction date of the building. No date is required if the building has not been built.

2. Identify yourself in #2 as the author of the work you created, unless it is work for hire. If you are completing the form, designate your nationality, and it is recommended to provide your year of birth. Check the boxes to indicate if your contribution is acknowledged or anonymous. Anonymous in this context means that your name

(continued)

(i.e. the name of the architect) is not recited on the deposit copy. If the work is made for hire, the full legal name of the employer, or person for whom the work was performed, must be provided, and it is recommended that the name of the employee be recited (e.g. *Apex Architects, Inc., employer for hire of ABC Architect.* Consult a lawyer if you are unsure of whether your work, or any portion of it, is work for hire. Ordinarily, the employer will complete Form VA in work-for-hire situations. Leave dates of birth blank for work-for-hire submissions.

3. Identify the creation date of the work in #3a.

4. Repeat in #4 your name, as the author is the copyright claimant unless it is work for hire, in which case the employer is the copyright claimant. Note that if the claimant is different than the author, Form VA requires an explanation of how the copyright was transferred. (e.g. by will, by assignment, by written contract, etc.). Consult a lawyer if you

believe a transfer of copyright has, or may have, occurred.

5. If the work has been changed and you want registration for the additions or revisions, check box #5c, provide the earlier registration number and date, and complete both parts of #6.

6. Consult a lawyer for derivative works or compilations.

7. Deposit accounts in #7a are available for those regularly registering substantial numbers of material. Leave blank unless you maintain such an account. In #7b identify the person to whom queries or correspondence about the registration should be sent; this could be your lawyer's contact information or your own if you intend to handle questions.

8. Form VA must be signed, and the signature must be *handwritten*. Electronic signatures are not acceptable.

9. The Certificate of Registration is mailed to the person and address in #9; it is important that this "window envelope" be complete and accurate.

2.2   Regulation of Professional Practice

Joseph H. Jones Jr., Esq., AIA

Professionals are granted certain rights by society, and in return they are obligated to meet accepted standards of professional behavior.

A combination of laws, statutes, and codes regulates and influences the behavior of practicing architects. Some of these controls are publicly mandated, while others are voluntary. All are important, and often they act together simultaneously. Mandated controls are included in state licensing statutes for the practice of architecture. Federal antitrust statutes that protect against anti-competitive business behavior also apply to the architecture profession. Architects who elect to join professional societies must subscribe to the rules of conduct and ethics established and administered by those societies.

Joe Jones is a vice president and director of risk management services at Victor O. Schinnerer & Company, Inc. He practiced architecture for more than ten years and, before joining Schinnerer, was assistant counsel for the AIA Contract Documents program.

Architects can contribute to how some legal, professional, and ethical regulations that pertain to the practice of architecture are established and governed. For example, architects often participate in professional degree program accreditation, serve on registration boards, examine candidates for registration, establish codes of ethics, and adjudicate professional misconduct cases. One of the obligations a profession accepts within the larger society is to set and administer standards for professional behavior.

REGISTRATION STATUTES AND REGULATIONS

In the American system of government, the authority to enact legislation protecting public health, safety, and welfare—including the authority to regulate the professions—is exercised primarily by the states and other jurisdictional authorities (the District of Columbia and the U.S. territories). The Bill of Rights reserves to the states all powers not specifically granted to the federal government by the Constitution, and protecting the public health, safety, and welfare is generally one of these powers. Thus, the regulation of most aspects of design and construction falls to the states.

Each jurisdiction has enacted legislation governing the registration of architects, which is implemented by administrative rules and regulations. The statutes that govern the registration of architects are usually broad in form and application. Typically, they

- Define the practice of architecture and limit it to those who are registered as architects within that jurisdiction.
- Restrict the use of the title *architect* to those who are licensed as architects.
- Establish, in broad terms, requirements for entry to the profession.
- Empower a registration board to establish rules and regulations.
- Indicate how architects registered in other jurisdictions may become registered to practice in the jurisdiction.
- Define professional conduct and misconduct.
- Outline penalties for those who practice architecture illegally within the jurisdiction.

Registration laws also may exempt certain structures, such as farm or small residential buildings, from their requirements. They may give another professional group (e.g., professional engineers) the right to design buildings. They also may regulate corporate forms of architecture practice.

The administrative regulations implementing a jurisdiction's registration law typically address issues such as acceptable internship activities; details of applying to take the registration examination; and specific requirements for the architect's seal, including its design, information content, and placement on drawings and other technical documents. An administrative regulation, for example, may require placement of the architect's signature as well as the seal on each drawing. These regulations are usually developed and administered by the state registration board.

PROFESSIONAL CONDUCT RULES

As part of their regulations governing architecture practice, the jurisdictions also promulgate rules of professional conduct. These rules deal with issues such as the use of the architect's seal, conflict of interest, disclosure of financial interests in projects, and other aspects of professional behavior.

Each jurisdiction's regulations include provisions for filing complaints, investigating allegations made in these complaints, hearing both sides of an issue, and administering penalties for violation of the regulations. Usually anyone—a citizen, another architect, the state—may file a complaint. Most violations of these regulations are handled as administrative infractions. They are investigated and adjudicated by an administrative agency that typically has the power to admonish or censure an architect and to suspend or revoke an architect's registration to practice in the jurisdiction.

Architects in violation of a jurisdiction's rules of professional conduct may also find themselves subject to a civil suit. For example, architects who falsely represent that a project is in full compliance with a building code may be the subject of a lawsuit alleging breach of contract, breach of warranty, or even negligence. If the architects are also members of the AIA, they could be found in violation of the AIA Code of Ethics and Professional Conduct, which can lead to a hearing and possible penalty.

AIA CODE OF ETHICS

▶ The AIA Code of Ethics and Professional Conduct appears as a backgrounder in Ethics and Professional Conduct (1.2).

To assist its members in meeting the goal of being "dedicated to the highest standards of professionalism, integrity, and competence," the American Institute of Architects has established a code of ethics. This document—the AIA Code of Ethics and Professional Conduct—provides members with guidelines and rules for fulfilling their obligations to the public, clients and users of architecture, the profession and their professional colleagues, and the building industry.

The AIA Code of Ethics and Professional Conduct applies to all professional activities of AIA members (see also topic 1.2). The code is arranged in three tiers:

Canons are broad principles of conduct. The code's five canons are general statements that address professional responsibilities to the discipline, the public, the client, the profession, and professional colleagues.

For AIA members, obligations under the AIA Code of Ethics exist in addition to those required by the rules of professional conduct promulgated by the states and other jurisdictions that regulate architecture practice. AIA members will want to be familiar with the requirements of both types of codes.

Ethical standards are specific goals to which members should aspire in professional practice and conduct. (As an example, the first ethical standard under Canon III, Obligations to the Client, reads, "Members should serve their clients in a timely and competent manner.")

Rules of conduct implement the canons and ethical standards. The canons and ethical standards are stated in aspirational terms. The rules are mandatory and describe the floor below which a member's actions may not fall. Only a violation of a specific rule of conduct can be the basis for disciplinary action by the AIA. (Continuing the example in the last paragraph, one of the rules under Ethical Standard 3.1 states, "Members shall not materially alter the scope or objectives of a project without the client's consent.")

The AIA Code of Ethics and Professional Conduct covers a wide range of issues. A cursory reading of the code makes it clear that even the rules of conduct, when applied to specific practice issues, will not always result in a decisive answer to the question "Is this activity ethical?" The canons, ethical standards, and rules of conduct serve as a continuum against which architects can measure contemplated activity. The AIA ethics code provides a framework to help the architect in that decision-making process.

ANTITRUST CONCERNS

As with all business enterprises, architects are prohibited under federal law from engaging with others in activities that restrain trade or are otherwise anticompetitive. Understanding the basic principles of antitrust law is important to avoid engaging in illegal activities under these laws.

Basic principles. The most fundamental principle of the antitrust laws as they affect architects is that agreements or other joint conduct between two or more competitors that restrain trade are illegal. In general, agreements between competitors risk being held unlawful if their purpose or their effect among others is to

Fix or maintain prices. "Price fixing" broadly includes agreements that tend to raise, lower, or stabilize maximum or minimum prices that competitors charge for products or services, or that fix other price-related terms and conditions of sale such as discounts, allowances, or credit terms. It is no defense that the prices set are reasonable or that there are socially worthy reasons why particular prices or terms should be fixed. A court can infer an agreement to fix prices from conduct even if no express agreement has been reached. Architects and firms must make independent decisions on fees for their products or services.

Boycott a competitor or customer. An agreement or understanding between competing architects that they will not deal with a third party (e.g., an architect, a particular client or category of clients, or a service provider) risks running afoul of the antitrust laws.

Allocate business or customers. Architects or firms acting alone may decide to specialize their practices or to pursue any commission they choose, but an agreement between competing architects to divide or allocate customers or markets by, for example, geographic regions or practice specialty, is unlawful, even if such agreements are informal, unwritten understandings.

Common activities requiring review. Certain subjects of recurring interest to architects such as fees, competitive bidding, design competitions, and information surveys nearly always have potential antitrust implications. It is therefore important for competing architects working collaboratively on a given project to consider the antitrust implications of their actions in such areas.

Fees. No professional organization or group of competing architects is permitted to have a mandatory fee schedule or to issue *recommended* fee guidelines. Setting fee schedules for competing professionals rises to the level of unlawful price-fixing. Subject to certain conditions, architects may collectively provide information about types of fee arrangements (e.g., stipulated sum, hourly rates, etc.). Actual fees, however, are a matter for negotiation between client and architect.

Competitive bidding. The process by which a professional and a client agree on fees is subject to antitrust laws. It is unlawful for competing architects to collectively decide not to submit price quotations for architecture services. Individual architects and firms may decide for themselves their policy toward bidding.

Design competitions. For many years, the AIA has made recommendations on how to conduct design competitions. The profession has collective insight and experience on this subject that could benefit sponsors of design competitions. It is also appropriate for architects to learn how they can better decide for themselves whether to participate in a competition. However, if a group of architects encourages or organizes members to refuse to participate in a particular competition or type of competition, the group risks being challenged for sponsoring an illegal boycott.

Information surveys. Professional societies often collect information from members about their practices. Collecting this information is generally permissible unless it is used to further a restraint of trade. To ensure compliance with antitrust laws and requirements, surveys of competitively sensitive matters such as fees or costs should be confined to historical—not current or future—data and should be reported in an aggregated form that does not identify or permit the identification of individual contributors.

For More Information

The definitive source for each jurisdiction's registration laws and regulations is its registration board. See Appendix D, "State Registration Boards," for names and addresses of registration boards in the United States and its territories.

The National Council of Architectural Registration Boards (NCARB) manages services for interns and architects, including the Intern Development Program (IDP), the Architect Registration Examination (ARE), reciprocity issues, NCARB certification, and continuing education initiatives. Information on these services can be obtained by writing to NCARB at 1801 K Street NW, Suite 1100, Washington, DC 20006 or by calling (202) 783-6500. Services are also described on the NCARB Web site at www.ncarb.org.

MANDATORY CONTINUING EDUCATION

Thom Lowther, EdS, and Paul T. Mendelsohn

During the 1970s, Iowa became the first state to require mandatory continuing education (MCE) for architects. Under Iowa code 272C.1, the state defined continuing education as "that education which is obtained by a professional or occupational licensee in order to maintain, improve, or expand skills and knowledge obtained prior to initial licensure or to develop new and relevant skills and knowledge." In 1994 the membership of the American Institute of Architects implemented continuing professional education as a requirement of membership. By 1995, only three states—Alabama, Florida, and Iowa—had MCE requirements. By 2006, thirty seven states and ten Canadian provinces required MCE as a condition of licensure.

In each state with mandatory continuing education requirements, the state licensing board addresses these key issues:

- Legal practice requirements for architects
- License renewal reporting dates
- Identification of programs that qualify as continuing professional education
- Identification of providers able to offer qualified programs
- Acceptability of continuing education taken elsewhere
- Health, safety, or welfare (HSW) benefits to the general public of qualified programs

How Many Hours of MCE Do States Require?

Each state has the legal right to establish its own MCE requirements. Most states have followed the recommendations of the NCARB model law, which advocates twelve hours of continuing education annually, at least eight hours of which must be in the area of health, safety, and/or welfare. Several states have elected to require that all twelve hours qualify as HSW. Most of the states have biannual requirements, meaning architects must show twenty-four hours every two years rather than twelve hours annually. New York State has a triannual requirement, or thirty-six total hours of continuing professional education every three years.

What Is the Deadline for Reporting Hours Earned?

Renewal dates are significant and vary from states to state. A state's MCE requirements usually coincide with licensure renewal.

What Qualifies for MCE Credit?

What qualifies as MCE credit varies greatly from state to state. Generally, courses given by the following organizations are approved:

- State licensing boards
- Registered providers of the state boards
- NCARB
- Institutions accredited to give degrees in architecture
- AIA
- AIA/CES program registered providers
- Engineering organizations
- Construction Specifications Institute
- State and local governments/agencies

Who Determines Which Courses or Providers Qualify?

The state board (by statute, regulation, and/or practice) has final authority to determine the areas of study applicable for credit and who can provide qualifying courses.

Who Tracks and Administers the MCE in the States?

Most states allow architects to track their own course activities. Documentation is required at time of license renewal or when the state audits the activity of the architect. All state licensing boards accept the AIA/CES transcript as documentation of participation.

Is There Reciprocity Between States?

The average architect holds multiple licenses. Generally, states honor continuing professional education taken in another state as long as the requirement of that state is equal to or higher than the requirements of the state auditing the architect.

What Other Variations Are There Between the States?

The most common variations relate to credit allowed for teaching, committee and community work, self-study, and distance learning. Generally, full-time faculty cannot receive MCE credit if a course is part of their regular faculty workload. Part-time adjunct faculty usually receive MCE credit for the courses they teach. Most states do not allow MCE or HSW credit for community, volunteer, or committee work. Asynchronous distance learning courses (those where participants can log in according to their own schedules) are generally accepted for MCE; however, a few state boards limit the number of distance learning hours they accept.

What Courses Qualify for HSW Credit?

Most state licensing boards require that at least three-quarters of the MCE courses architects take must relate to health, safety, or welfare. Some states require the entire MCE requirement to be met with courses in these subject areas.

For a course to qualify for HSW credit, a minimum of 75 percent of its content must relate to one or more of the subject areas listed in the accompanying sidebar. The definition of HSW is based on the Architect Registration Examination (ARE). The ARE is designed to determine whether applicants for architectural licensure possess sufficient knowledge, skills, and abilities to provide professional services while protecting the health, safety, and welfare of the general public. Each of the nine divisions of the ARE is designed

(continued)

HSW SUBJECT AREAS

To qualify for health, safety, or welfare (HSW) credit, course content must demonstrate how the general public benefits from the architect taking the course and not just how the architect benefits. For example, the business side of construction documents and services would not qualify for HSW, while the legal issues benefiting the public would. As another example, an insurance course benefiting the architect would not qualify for HSW credit unless it can be clearly demonstrated how the public would benefit from the knowledge the architect gained from the course.

Listed here are a number of commonly accepted HSW subject areas. However, individual states may not consider everything on this list to qualify for HSW credit; therefore, architects should check their state licensing board's HSW definition and requirements.

Accessibility

Acoustics

Building design

Code of ethics

Codes, acts, laws, and regulations governing the practice of architecture

Construction administration (nonbusiness aspects)

Construction contract laws, legal aspects that protect the public

Construction documents and services

Construction functions, materials, methods, and systems

Energy efficiency

Environmental analysis and issues of building materials and systems

Environmental concerns—Asbestos, lead-based paint, toxic emissions

Fire: Building fire codes—Flame spread, smoke contribution, explosives

Fire safety systems—Detection and alarm standards

Insurance to protect the owners of property and injured parties

Interior design

Life safety codes

Materials and systems—Roofing/waterproofing, wall systems, etc.

Material use, function, and features

Mechanical, plumbing, electrical—System concepts, materials, and methods

Natural hazards—Earthquake, hurricane, flood; related to building design

Preservation, renovation, restoration, and adaptive reuse

Security of buildings, design of

Site and soils analysis

Site design

Specification writing

Structural issues

Surveying methods and techniques

Sustainable design

to test for minimum competency in a specific area important to the protection of the public.

What Is the Relationship Between HSW Credit and State Mandatory Continuing Education Requirements?

Both the AIA and state licensing boards base their continuing education requirements on the contact hour. A majority of states require eight contact hours of health, safety, or welfare (HSW) training for their mandatory continuing education (MCE) programs. (Exceptions: Kansas requires no HSW; Alabama, Arkansas, Louisiana, Minnesota, North Carolina, Oklahoma, and Vermont require twelve HSW contact hours.) The AIA/CES program requires eight contact hours of HSW content from a structured provider. Some states allow some types of self-reporting. Due to quality assurance issues posed by the states, the AIA does not accept reporting of *self-designed* activities for HSW credit.

Caution! For members who self-report participation in *structured* activities, it has become very important to clearly report and identify all HSW programs and activities separately. Failure to do so could result in a loss of license due to noncompliance with state MCE requirements.

Thom Lowther is senior director, Continuing Education, at the American Institute of Architects. Paul T. Mendelsohn is vice president, AIA Government & Community Relations, at the American Institute of Architects.

CHAPTER 3

Professional Development

3.1 Developing Leadership Skills

William C. Ronco, Ph.D., and Mark Jussaume, PE

Leadership is an essential component of successful architecture practice. Through professional development efforts, firms can help staff members attain the skills they need to become effective leaders.

Many architects are deeply interested in leadership and committed to becoming better leaders. Because there are different and conflicting views about the nature of effective leadership, numerous methods are available to architects who want to improve their leadership skills and performance. This article clarifies the different views on leadership and offers guidelines to help architects hone their leadership effectiveness.

WHY ARCHITECTS MUST CARE ABOUT LEADERSHIP

The profession places architects in a wide range of leadership positions. Beyond managing projects, architects also lead firms, studios, and committees within firms; mentor young professionals; teach in formal and informal settings; and serve in community and civic groups. In small firms and individual practice, architects also lead in their relationships with clients, stakeholders, government officials, and the community.

William C. Ronco is president of Gathering Pace Consulting in Bedford, Massachusetts. He consults on strategic planning and leadership training and is a coauthor of *The Partnering Solution*. Mark Jussaume is vice president of operations for the Ritchie Organization in Newton, Massachusetts. The original version of this topic appeared in Handbook Update 2005.

Leadership is the most important thing we can provide our clients. Lots of people can draw lines on paper, but it takes leadership to draw the right conclusions. . . . We are in the leadership business; design is our medium.

Scott Simpson, FAIA, president, Stubbins Associates

To be successful in these positions, architects must guide and inspire the actions of others. Leading creates the groups, relationships, and organizations that provide the environments that nurture creative design. Leading enables architects to get their designs built and improve their designs in the process.

Serving as a leader is often challenging and difficult, however. "Leadership is not a walk in the park," observes Richard Fitzgerald, director of the Boston Society of Architects. "It's a mind-set born of commitment to ourselves. Although architects clearly are the visionaries who should be leading clients from dream to reality, too often the leadership role is ceded to or usurped by others." Shifting definitions of legal liabilities and changing contract forms have contributed to these changes. Construction managers and client representatives in particular have taken on some of the key decision-making responsibilities formerly assumed only by architects.

RELEVANT LEADERSHIP CONCEPTS

How can architects become better leaders? The first step is to understand what leadership is. Hundreds of articles and books on leadership are published annually, and many are useful for architects, but four leadership concepts have special relevance for architects: behavioral, contingency (or situational), transformational, and Level 5 leadership. An understanding of these concepts can provide the foundation for effective leadership training for architects.

Behavioral Theory

Initially outlined in the late 1940s and widely used through the 1960s, behavioral theory focuses on behaviors demonstrated by leaders, singling out two as essential for leadership: "initiating structure" and "consideration." Initiating structure is developing a plan to get things accomplished in a new situation. Consideration is treating people with respect.

Behavioral theory provides a foundation for leadership training appropriate for architects that incorporates the following concepts:

- Articulating and following a vision and clear goals
- Communicating effectively
- Demonstrating passion and energy
- Demonstrating high standards, morals, and ethics
- Questioning the status quo
- Expecting more from others
- Demonstrating design sensibility

Contingency Theory

Initially outlined in the 1980s and still widely used, contingency theory or situational leadership emphasizes development of a wide repertoire of approaches suited to various situations. Leaders are expected to address each situation based on its contingencies, or requirements. This approach to leadership implies that architects who want to lead must develop both a variety of leadership behaviors and an ability to read and adapt to changing situations. This focus results in leadership training that devotes a good deal of effort to understanding, appreciating, and working with a wide range of different kinds of people.

Contingency theory validates the interest architects have in the multiple leadership roles they must play. Familiar roles that permeate architects' descriptions of leadership include these:

- Theoretician
- Business development hunter
- Project management warrior

- Civic/community advocate
- Coach/counselor
- Teacher
- Marketing director
- Project manager
- Coach/counselor/mentor
- Renaissance person

In young and/or small firms in particular, it is essential that architects fill multiple leadership roles, and fill them at high levels of competence.

Such a variety of leadership roles means there are different paths to leadership success. However, the different roles also provide fodder for ongoing debate about the nature of meaningful leadership in the profession. Many quarrels arise from architects' fervent beliefs regarding which roles are most important for leaders to fulfill. Partnership groups often argue about the roles they want firm leaders to fill, and some architects resist roles others would have them take on. For example, many strong designers shun roles that involve business development and marketing.

Transactional/Transformational Leadership

In his 1978 book, *Leadership*, James MacGregor Burns articulated the notion that leaders both "transact" and "transform." Transactions are trades and deals that leaders make. Transformation is the learning and development that both leader and follower can experience in the process of leadership. Architects relate to this approach because defining and conducting transactions with clients, subordinates, and peers is a fundamental part of professional practice. The "performance" descriptors of leadership are easily applied to many of these transactions.

LEADERSHIP CONCEPTS RELEVANT TO ARCHITECTURE PRACTICE

Concept	Implies That Leadership Training for Architects Should Focus on:
Behavioral Leadership	
• Focuses on leaders' actual behaviors rather than their traits • Identifies "initiating structure" and "consideration" as important leadership behaviors	• Real-world performance and achievement rather than theory • "Initiating structure," forming goals and vision • Appreciation of diversity and people skills
Contingency/Situational Leadership	
• Makes it clear that different kinds of leadership are effective in different situations • Delineates multiple leadership roles and need to know when and how to change among them	• Skills to use in diverse situations • Ability to "read" different situations and people, i.e., awareness roles may differ significantly from each other • Controversial roles
Transactional/Transformational Leadership	
• Identifies "transactions" as one important leadership task • Clarifies meaning and importance of transformational leadership, i.e., the notion that follower and leader are transformed	• Ability to negotiate • Ability to inspire • Willingness to be inspired and to learn
Level 5 Leadership	
• Links Level 5 leadership with high-performing organizations over extended time periods • Points out combination of humility, fierce commitment, and focus on building the organization	• Skills for building the organization • Understanding of management and organizational processes • Coaching, mentoring, and counseling skills (Level 5 is a relevant model for architecture firms)

Burns points out, however, that leadership is more than simply conducting transactions; it has the potential to transform both the follower and the leader. This potential is especially important for architects because it speaks to the inspiration that can take place when architects educate clients, coach and mentor younger professionals, or devote their energies to civic causes. Burns's ideas remind architects of the potential they have as leaders to go beyond simply getting others to do what they want and truly transforming both themselves and others. It's possible, and quite important, for architects to learn from clients and others.

Level 5 Leadership

I would love to be able to give you a list of steps for becoming a Level 5 [leader], but we have no solid research data that would support a credible list.

James Collins, *Good to Great*

Level 5 leadership is an important leadership theory for architects because it adds a dimension to the meaning of leadership beyond the image of someone who fills multiple roles, initiates structure, and is "considerate." Level 5 involves a selfless dedication to the organization that, in many cases, may conflict with an architect's own ego.

The term "Level 5" comes from Jim Collins's 2001 book, *Good to Great*. In it, Collins draws on extensive research conducted over many years to identify key elements that move companies from good to great with sustained business success. He has determined that the single most important element of a company's ability to make the leap is Level 5 leadership. According to Collins, Level 5 leadership is distinguished by its combination of a unique, counterintuitive quality of humility with unwavering perseverance. Level 5 leaders are selfless "servant" leaders.

In an architecture practice, the ascent to leadership is often built upon an individual's business development success, marketing ability, and outstanding skills in practice areas such as design or planning. In other words, initial success is built on the performance aspects of leadership. Collins believes, however, that the skills necessary to achieve success in these essential aspects of practice are significantly different from the skills necessary to achieve Level 5 status. In fact, some traditional leadership skills may actually inhibit leadership development, making it necessary to abandon them to make room for more effective Level 5 skills. Level 5 leaders set aside their own professional goals and developmental needs. They rearrange their priorities to be subservient to the needs of the firm and other team members.

Because selfless Level 5 leadership can directly conflict with professional aspirations for design and peer recognition, it is a somewhat rare commodity in the architecture profession. This explains why many architects struggle with succession. Architects who were effective Level 4 leaders, highly skilled at achieving the performance aspects of leadership, stumble when it comes to involving others, putting the organization first, and building the infrastructure of the firm.

The concept of Level 5 leadership clearly links leadership behaviors with the success of an organization, an important connection for architects to recognize. Level 5 leadership challenges the notion that successful marketers and designers are also inherently good leaders. This style of leadership also strongly emphasizes a leader's need to both produce results and devote time and energy to developing employees.

Leadership Basics

Consideration of the four leadership concepts described above yields five statements that summarize them and can serve as a foundation for leadership training:

Leaders fill different and sometimes conflicting roles. For example, a principal of an architecture firm demonstrates a strong ability to design as well as to bring a project in under budget, mentor younger staff, and build a lasting organization.

Architects need to lead in small firms and individual practice as well as in large firms. Leadership tasks, responsibilities, and opportunities occur in everyday practice with clients, stakeholders, government, and community, as well as in large AE firms.

Both extroverted and introverted leadership styles work. There is a recurring and noticeable tension between extroverted, authoritative styles of leadership and more introverted, reflective servant leadership. More recent leadership theories recognize the power and validity of the more introverted leadership model and question the apparent superficiality of the more traditional extroverted approach. However, for architects, the most effective leadership combines both extroverted (communicating a vision, connecting, building relationships) and introverted (developing concepts, modesty, sharpening focus, refining goals) styles.

Architects must do more than fill multiple roles—they must perform well in them. Architects recognize the need to fill multiple leadership roles, but they also want to see clear evidence of performance in those roles, not mere figureheads.

A concern for "higher" matters is part of leadership. Caring, inspiration, and the transformation of both the follower and the leader are as much a part of leadership for architects as winning design awards, landing big projects, and building strong client relationships. This transformational/inspirational aspect of leadership is especially important for architects because of its link to the learning and growth inherent in the creative process.

LEADERSHIP TRAINING

Many leadership books and training programs earn strong praise from readers and program participants, their managers, employees, and peers. Universities, professional associations, and consulting companies provide a wide range of highly regarded leadership training programs. However, little empirical research exists documenting the ability of any books or programs to create behavioral change of any kind. Creating change and growth that last is even more difficult, challenging, and elusive.

This is not to contend that leadership training is ineffective, but rather to state that it is important to view such training with a critical, objective eye. In particular, it is important to go beyond the ability of leadership training to generate enthusiastic endorsements from participants and purveyors to its ability to generate lasting results. It is useful for leadership books and training to generate insights and inspire readers and participants. It would be much more useful, however, for books and training to generate lasting results.

Contrary to the opinion of many people, leaders are not born. Leaders are made, and they are made by effort and hard work.

Vince Lombardi

PARTICIPATING IN LEADERSHIP TRAINING

Architects who want to participate in leadership training programs need to consider their own learning style, the format and structure of the training program, and how its content is delivered.

Understanding Your Learning Style

Finding leadership training that works is not simply a matter of leafing through program catalogs and comparing one set of topics and instructors with another. It is crucial to place a strong emphasis on understanding one's own learning style when selecting leadership training. Programs run by the most prestigious institutions may not be effective at all for some participants, depending on the participant's learning style.

Learning is a highly individualized experience. Different people learn in different ways, often *very* different ways. For some, lectures and detailed explanations are

most effective. For others, hands-on experiences are better. For still others, a picture or image will do the trick. Some people do better working with groups, they benefit from the dialogue and discussion. Others find such discussions distracting, and benefit more from one-on-one coaching. And for others, it takes a combination of several different learning approaches to produce meaningful results.

Program Format and Structure

A typical leadership-training program involves a group of fifteen to twenty architects participating in a one-time intensive seminar consisting of several days of lectures and discussions. This format and structure is intense and efficient. Three- and four-day leadership retreats, seminars, and boot camps often generate high levels of emotion and energy. However, this typical format does not necessarily produce optimal, lasting results.

(continued)

3.1 Developing Leadership Skills **55**

Architect-only leadership training programs do ensure program relevance, which is important, but they do not engage other members of the industry. Involving clients, engineers, and contractors in architects' leadership training can broaden the architect's perspective.

The one-time-retreat learning model poses a serious problem for achieving lasting results because it assumes that participants will easily use and apply the information provided in their everyday work. This assumption is problematic for several reasons:

- Translating any kind of insight into any kind of action can be difficult.
- Translating an insight into new leadership behaviors that last over time can be extremely difficult, as they may involve changing deeply ingrained habits.
- Developing basic proficiency in a new skill (e.g., a listening skill) can be challenging in itself in the program. Applying that skill in the more complex flow of everyday professional life can be much more difficult.
- Developing, continuing, and refining new skills after a seminar can be difficult.
- Bringing new insights and skills into organizations that have not changed and are not necessarily receptive to change in their members can be daunting.

With these issues in mind, it is useful to consider leadership training that extends over longer periods of time and builds in a learning loop of insight and application. For example, monthly half-day workshops that involve extensive review of participants' experiences in applying new skills and concepts may be more effective in generating lasting results than one-time programs.

Delivery of the Content

In addition to the format and structure of leadership training, it is important to consider the way in which content is delivered. What training methods and tools generate lasting results? Part of the answer depends on the learning style of the participant and part on knowing with some certainty what methods produce what kinds of results.

For example, two popular training ideas often produce only limited results: Reading biographies and autobiographies of noteworthy leaders and evaluating case studies of leadership situations are often interesting to trainees, but it is actually quite difficult for people to translate what they learn from such exercises into new behaviors to apply to their workplace.

Types of Learning

Effective leadership training involves work in four quite different types of learning: increasing awareness of self and others, clarifying goals, building skills, and implementing processes. Working in any one of these areas alone is likely to yield limited results. Understanding each of these types of learning and how they relate to and reinforce each other provides a useful foundation for effective leadership training.

Increasing awareness of self and others. This aspect of leadership training recognizes the importance of understanding real-world behaviors. Leaders can develop an ability to recognize the ways in which they are effective, and how others perceive them. For this kind of learning, leaders can use 360-degree surveys of their communication style and personality profiles such as the Myers-Briggs Type Indicator, DISC, and the Predictive Index®.

Defining vision and goals. This aspect of leadership training is based on situational leadership and contingency theory. For this kind of training, a leader determines which roles are most important for him or her and what performance criteria are appropriate for those roles. Training tools leaders can use for this kind of learning include a personal vision statement, which clarifies overall individual goals, and a goal-based work plan, which specifies job roles, priorities, and expected outcomes. This aspect of leadership training is also inspired by transformational leadership theory, as it suggests goals can transcend mere accomplishment of tasks and reach for higher orders of learning and development.

Improving communication skills. This kind of leadership training reflects the notion, which is part of all four leadership theories, that leaders must be highly proficient

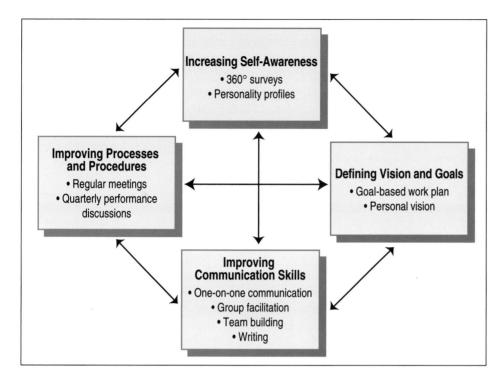

Aspects of Leadership Training. Four different types of training contribute to leadership development. These reinforce and complement each other.

communicators. Leadership in architecture often involves communicating difficult messages—for example, telling clients things they do not want to hear, providing constructive criticism to subordinates and peers, and expressing complex concepts. Architects who want to improve their leadership performance must especially strengthen their skills in collaborative communications as they operate in many collaborative situations with clients, peers, and subordinates.

Improving processes and procedures. This aspect of leadership training stems from the concept of "initiating structure." Architects can learn to apply problem-solving skills they have gained through the design process to the development of processes for carrying out leadership tasks. For example, many architecture firms use outdated methods to conduct design reviews, monthly office meetings, project meetings, and performance appraisals. Leadership development encourages leaders to formulate more effective structures for such tasks.

Leadership training that produces lasting results usually includes all four of these types of training. Increasing awareness without developing skills is not effective. Learning skills with limited understanding and awareness of self and others is also problematic.

Effort in any one training area complements, reinforces, and advances work in the other three. For example, when leaders improve their awareness of how they affect others, it can help them develop more targeted goals for how they communicate. Formulating goals creates a need for skills. Building skills improves a leader's level of performance, changes his or her effect on others, and encourages the leader to formulate goals at a higher level.

Leadership Training Tools

Six tools for leadership training can be applied to the learning categories described above, as explained in the paragraphs that follow.

360-degree performance surveys. A 360-degree survey can provide leaders with valuable data about their leadership performance. Leaders give the survey forms to a select group of people they work with, usually eight to fifteen individuals, including subordinates, peers, and clients. Respondents complete the surveys anonymously, and an objective third party tabulates the results and provides the leader with a report showing anonymous aggregated data to ensure the survey answers of individual respondents are kept confidential.

Scott Simpson comments on the value of such surveys in leadership development programs at Stubbins Associates: "Our work with 360-degree surveys has been instrumental in improving leadership. People can hate it because it clarifies weaknesses they might not want to acknowledge. Until they understand their own weaknesses, though, architects can be poisoned by their own egos."

Often, gaps exist between architects' perceptions of themselves and the perceptions of their staff, clients, and stakeholders. Such gaps are inevitable in professional practice because there are few ways for leaders to get coherent, balanced feedback on the effectiveness of their communications. By providing data that is organized, confidential, and comprehensive, 360-degree surveys can help architects close this perceptions gap.

Although surveys provide more accurate data about communication than informal feedback, they do have some limitations. A firm's organizational successes, failures, and pressures can shape survey responses. Past experience with misuse of 360-degree surveys, even if it occurred at another firm, can inhibit responses to current survey efforts. In addition, concerns about confidentiality can inhibit respondents' comments. No matter the cause, low response rates can yield misleading results.

Despite such limitations, 360-degree surveys provide more valid data than informal feedback, which tends to emphasize high and low spots in communications and neglect the everyday middle ground. Surveys that give respondents the time and structure to assess communications performance thoughtfully can provide more reasoned perceptions and opinions.

Like any tool, however, 360-degree surveys can be misused. To ensure optimal benefit from using them, it is essential to keep several things in mind:

- Respondent confidentiality must be absolute. Even suspected lack of confidentiality can taint the validity of the survey results, not to mention it is unethical to promise something will be confidential and then to reveal the name of a respondent.
- A leader who is the subject of a survey should focus on responses to a handful of questions of particular significance to his or her role. Avoid getting bogged down in responses that reflect your weaknesses.
- Quantitative and open-ended questions elicit different types of information. Responses to quantitative questions provide a framework for the survey results and an overall view of the leader being studied, while responses to open-ended questions add color and nuance to the survey results.
- For a survey to best serve the leader and the firm, the results must lead to action. A leader who has been evaluated can develop goals to address what has been learned from the survey.
- Survey results should be informally linked to performance measures. This will allow architects being surveyed to understand how others' perceptions figure in assessing their leadership performance. On the other hand, attempting to rigidly link survey results with performance metrics often discourages architects from obtaining the feedback they most need to hear and occasionally leads to tampering with the overall survey system.
- Architects receiving survey data can benefit from sharing and discussing their results with peers. Few people can accurately interpret the data they receive or translate their insights into useful action steps on their own.
- Architects receiving survey data may find it helpful to discuss their results with the people who responded to the survey. This does not, of course, mean asking them to comment on their responses. Rather, the idea is to provide a forum in which respondents can provide more data and react to the architect's action plans. Most importantly, this approach lets respondents know the architect is taking the process seriously.

Please mark "x" twice for each question, once for the person's effectiveness and again for the importance of the issue to you	Effectiveness				Importance to Me			
	Very Low			Very High	Very High			Very Low
Informational—This Individual:								
1. Knows what's going on in the firm.								
2. Knows what's going on in the industry.								
3. Provides others with adequate information.								
4. Is accessible.								
5. Is approachable.								
6. Communicates clearly and completely.								
Interpersonal—This Individual:								
7. Treats others with respect.								
8. Initiates relationships appropriately.								
9. Maintains relationships effectively.								
10. Values diversity.								
11. Listens effectively.								
12. Works effectively with others' ideas.								
13. Participates effectively in meetings.								
14. Communicates directly.								
15. Sets a positive tone in communications.								
16. Works effectively with others overall.								
Strategic—This Individual:								
17. Effectively formulates goals and vision.								
18. Effectively communicates goals and vision.								
19. Actively supports the company's goals.								
20. Works effectively with other departments.								
21. Focuses appropriately on the overall firm, not just on his or her projects or department.								
Management—This Individual:								
22. Understands what his or her staff does.								
23. Treats staff fairly, doesn't play "favorites."								
24. Holds employees accountable.								
25. Provides adequate praise and encouragement.								
26. Motivates staff effectively.								
27. Addresses employee development interests.								
28. Manages staff effectively overall.								
Leadership Effectiveness—This Individual:								
29. Works hard.								
30. Manages time effectively.								
31. Manages financial concerns effectively.								
32. Demonstrates strong concern for quality.								
33. Devotes adequate effort to business development.								
34. Maintains a high level of ethics.								
35. Thinks effectively "outside the box."								
36. Strives for continuous improvement.								
37. Overall, leads effectively.								

© William C. Ronco

Personality profiles. Most leadership training and development programs use the Myers-Briggs Type Indicator (MBTI), DISC, the Predictive Index, or other personality profiles, and with good reason. Personality profiles help leaders improve their understanding of themselves and of others. This understanding is an essential foundation for higher leadership performance levels such as transformational leadership and Level 5 leadership.

Personality profiles can improve the awareness of leaders in four primary ways:

- *Clarifying "blind spots."* Personality profiles help architects identify which aspects of their work feel least natural to them.
- *Building a time management agenda.* All respondents tend to spend more time on tasks they feel comfortable with and neglect tasks that come less naturally. As architects progress in their careers, an awareness of their preferences and blind spots can help them manage their time so that tasks they might neglect or undervalue are not ignored.
- *Building on strengths.* As they progress in their careers, it is important for architects to develop a leadership style based on their own deeply seated values and comfort. Working with personality profiles can help an architect rediscover long-standing aspects of his or her personality that may have been neglected while meeting other responsibilities.
- *Understanding others.* Architects who aspire to transformational leadership or Level 5 leadership need tools for understanding others in some depth. No matter which personality profile is employed, valuable detail can be obtained about what makes people tick. Leaders who want to improve their ability to motivate and inspire others will find this information very useful.

Goal-based work plans. What roles should architect leaders fill? How can their performance in these roles be measured? How should effective leaders in architecture spend their time and focus their priorities? The goal-based work plan is a useful tool for architects who want to clarify roles, performance, and priorities. Roles that architects may want to consider as they advance and develop their leadership skills include mentor, business developer, community builder in the firm, relationship builder with clients, design leader, thought leader, and coach.

Architects can use a worksheet to help them clarify and refine an optimal set of roles, job priorities, and deliverables for their job at any given time. Although it is possible to work on this alone, architects will find it much more effective to work on their individual forms in a group. Principals, project managers, or associates often derive optimal insight when they have input into developing each other's goal-based work plans. Completing a goal-based work plan worksheet involves the following steps:

1. Divide your job into seven to ten major task categories in the tasks column. About half the tasks will be technical/quantitative (e.g., managing project schedules, project budgets, or drawing quality). The other half will be more qualitative and communication-based (e.g., building project team, partnering with a customer, or mentoring young designers). On your worksheet, begin each task with a verb (e.g., manage, lead, partner, communicate).

2. Allocate percentage points (totaling 100 percent) among the tasks in a way that reflects what you view as your optimal priorities. This step is meant to help identify the relative importance of the tasks, so do not simply log how you currently spend your time. Rather, focus on the tasks and determine which have the highest priority, without regard to the time they take.

3. For each task, specify several tangible, quantifiable outcomes, results, or measures. This is relatively easy to do for technical tasks but more difficult for qualitative tasks. For example, it is easier to measure the extent to which projects are profitable than it is to assess effectiveness in developing young designers.

GOAL-BASED WORK PLAN WORKSHEET

Current Priority (Allocate 100%)	Priority (next 3 months)	Tasks (Divide your job into 7–10 task categories, half technical/quantitative and half more qualitative.)	Outcomes (For each task, note anticipated outcomes, results. Use numbers and timelines when possible.)

The goal-based work plan form is an excellent tool to use at key moments in an architect's career development: promotion to a new level in the organization, the beginning of a new project, and a change in job priorities. Some firms use the goal-based work plan as an integral part of their regular management of employee performance, enabling all employees to update their plan on a quarterly basis based on feedback.

Personal vision statements. Taking on new leadership roles provides architects with many opportunities for personal growth. However, because such major steps can separate an individual from his or her core sources of motivation and self-understanding, these career advances can sometimes lead to work that is frustrating and empty. Writing a personal vision statement can help architects determine which roles they want to take on and which they want to leave to others.

Leadership roles frequently assumed by architects include managing others, managing budgets and finances, working at marketing and business development, and moving from project manager to principal in the firm, each of which requires them to take on new tasks. Individual architects will respond to these challenges in different ways. Some may find the new roles unpleasant or unnatural. Others may find them more enjoyable than they had anticipated. The latter group may feel the new tasks allow them to play out parts of themselves that were previously untapped.

Writing a personal vision statement clarifies core values, aspirations, sources of energy, motivations, and goals. It can take a variety of forms—a paragraph, a poem, a list, a collage of images; however, it is important for the statement to be recorded and not simply "kept in mind." Several studies suggest the likelihood of achieving personal goals increases dramatically when they are written down.

More important than the format of a personal vision statement is the function it should serve. The statement should work like a divining rod to lead an individual back to core sources of energy and motivation. Many people find it useful to post the statement where they will see it often, for example, on a bathroom mirror or car dashboard or inside an appointment book.

Improved Communication Skills

Successful leaders need a high level of communication skills in both one-on-one and group situations. When an architect formulates goals to motivate young designers, build the office team, or partner with clients, he or she must be able to communicate these goals in an engaging way.

Improving one-on-one communication skills requires a different kind of learning than that needed to build awareness or formulate goals—much more work with practice than with theory. The skills to be acquired are actions, more like golf or tennis than chess. The theories behind the skills are fairly clear and simple. The difficult thing is changing habits and building the skills into an everyday approach.

Communication skills are an aspect of leadership that books and seminars can help leaders improve. Seminars can provide supportive, productive environments for learning these skills, especially when they enable participants to apply and practice them. Numerous books can reinforce the interactive work done in seminars. Two especially useful volumes are Thomas Gordon's *Leader Effectiveness Training* and Robert Bolton's *People Skills*. Both provide excellent explanations of why the skills work and many examples illustrating their use in real situations.

Group communications are also important for architects, who must be able to present convincingly to clients, as well as to firm employees. Many excellent seminars, coaches, and consultants provide assistance for architects who want to hone their presentation skills. Participation in Toastmasters meetings can also help improve group communication skills.

Group discussions require facilitation skills, which are different from those for making presentations. Facilitating a meeting means structuring discussion with carefully prepared questions and breaking the group, even when it is small, into subgroups. Construction partnering facilitators use this approach to ensure that all participants are actively engaged at partnering meetings.

Resources for learning facilitation skills are harder to find. Writing on this subject is often sandwiched into complex texts about group dynamics. Total quality management training programs used by some construction companies may provide a useful perspective on facilitation for architects. Also, human resource professionals in many larger architecture firms have acquired these skills in their training and can provide instruction for members of their firms.

Improved Processes and Procedures

It is useful for leaders to implement a process whereby their new skills can be used most effectively. The ability to define and implement processes is what behavioral leadership theorists call "initiating structure" (i.e., intuiting a process or procedure for addressing a problem or exploring an opportunity).

When architects think of leadership training, they mostly think of the tools mentioned above and overlook the power that initiating new processes can have in improving leadership performance. This is particularly ironic because initiating these processes resembles the design process, giving architects the possibility of tapping into their design skills to improve in this area of leadership.

Like many organizations, architecture firms typically engage in a number of less-than-optimal processes in their everyday work. Architect leaders can substantially enhance the performance of their firms by paying attention to these processes and creating better ones whenever possible. There is significant room for improvement in the following:

Performance appraisals. Few firms are satisfied with the processes they use. There is great potential to enhance leadership performance by replacing outdated, ineffective annual appraisal systems with more agile quarterly coaching and counseling.

"Lessons learned" and design review meetings. Most architects agree it is useful to learn from past experience, but few are able to sustain group discussions on this subject without having them turn defensive and inhibiting. Leaders who can initiate, design, and implement productive lessons-learned discussions advance their own leadership performance as well as the culture of their firm.

Project budgeting and profitability. Few architecture firms derive optimal value from their finance staff. Architects who can devise productive methods for meshing project and finance information, and for financial reporting, are successful leaders.

Streamlining and improving business and practice processes can help enhance leadership performance and thus are legitimately a part of leadership training. However, they are seldom included in leadership training programs. One useful reference that provides both insight and detail into this aspect of leadership training is Donald Schon's book *The Reflective Practitioner*. In it, Schon describes how ongoing reflection and inquiry into their practice can give professionals a fruitful avenue to enhancing leadership and learning.

LEADERSHIP DEVELOPMENT IS ACTION LEARNING

Meaningful leadership development for architects need not be mysterious or all-consuming. However, it does need to be thoughtful and comprehensive if it is to achieve significant results. Like many managers and professionals, some architects work hard at leadership development only to achieve limited results because they concentrate their efforts too narrowly.

Leadership is a lot like golf, tennis, and other action skills. The concepts are pretty simple (keep your eye on the ball, treat others as you would have them treat you, and so on). In leadership as in sports, however, implementing and executing concepts can be excruciating.

Most golfers know that improving your game requires both working with a variety of approaches and continual practice. The same is true for leadership development. Working with a variety of approaches and methods (taking stock, clarifying goals, improving skills, and implementing processes) and practicing consistently over time can produce noticeable gains.

For More Information

Several books on leadership provide a sound background for embarking on a leadership training and development program. In *Good to Great* (Harper Collins, 2001), Jim Collins puts forth his Level 5 leadership theory. Several large A&E firms have successfully used internal reading groups of *Good to Great* to develop increased understanding of leadership and organizational concepts.

Max DePree's books, *Leadership Is an Art* (Currency, 2004) and *Leadership Jazz* (Dell, 1993), provide insight and understanding into the nature of effective leadership.

The MBA text *Organizational Behavior* (Merrill, 1984), by Jerry L. Gray and Frederick A. Starke, provides extensive information about leadership theories and their evolution over time. This approach to leadership contrasts in interesting ways with thinking on leadership by famous architects. For example, Cesar Pelli's *Observations for Young Architects* (Monacelli, 1999) provides another view.

The Reflective Practitioner (Ashgate Publishing, 1995), by Donald Schon, is especially geared to architects. Schon writes eloquently about the nature of personal development in the professions and in architecture in particular. Another book on leadership of value to architects is *The Partnering Solution* (Career Press, 2005), by William and Jean Ronco. It features a chapter on leadership that links partnering methods with leadership approaches.

Books about interpersonal relations can be a good place to learn about improving leadership skills. *People Styles At Work* (AMACOM, 1996), by Robert Bolton, provides useful insights into the nature of effective communication and other interpersonal skills that are especially important for architects. In *Leader Effectiveness Training* (Perigree, 2001), Thomas J. Gordon provides very clear instruction for essential leadership communications skills. Stephen Covey's *Seven Habits of Highly Effective People* (Free Press, 2004) looks at the need for listening: "Seek first to understand before trying to be understood." Covey's *Principle-Centered Leadership* (Free Press, 1992) is also useful.

Laurie Beth Jones provides practical, usable instruction for the complex task of writing a personal vision statement in *The Path: Creating Your Mission Statement for Work and for Life* (Hyperion, 1996).

3.2 Developing Communication Skills

David Greusel, AIA

Generally, architects are better known for their graphic skills than their verbal or writing skills. However, effective oral and written communications benefit a design practice in many ways.

Communication is at the center of architecture practice. An exceptionally gifted designer may not achieve success if he or she is unable to effectively communicate ideas to others. The construction process requires collaboration between many people, and architects must be able to communicate in a clear, concise, and unambiguous manner for a project to be successful.

Of course, architects communicate many ideas visually, but this represents only one of many forms of communication. This topic will focus on common communication problems, describing methods and techniques to help architects listen, speak, and write in a manner that is understandable and useful to clients and others involved in the approval, review, and construction process.

COMMUNICATION BASICS

The purpose of communication is to transmit ideas and facts, from simple social or emotional concepts ("I'm fine, thanks, and you?") to sets of highly complex instructions (e.g., a specification for an escalator). Whatever the idea, if information transferred from one person is not understood by another, communication has not taken place. Communication is, at best, a challenging proposition, but one that can be improved by developing certain skills and techniques.

Because message erosion occurs so easily, the method by which information is communicated is significant. Communication can be casual or formal, polite or terse, clear or muddled—and these variables apply to both spoken and written communication. Because architects communicate so often with so many people in a typical day, they tend to give

David Greusel is a principal with HOK Sport Venue Event, a public assembly design practice with primary offices in Kansas City, London, and Brisbane. He is the author of *Architect's Essentials of Presentation Skills*. The original version of this topic appeared in the 2003 *Update* volume of the Handbook.

little thought to the quality of their communications. However, all players in the project delivery process—officials, manufacturers, fabricators, consultants, engineers, contractors, subcontractors and, particularly, clients—make judgments about the professionalism and effectiveness of architects based on how well they communicate. For example, potential clients may view poorly delivered communications as a sign the architect is a sloppy and inattentive practitioner—not the sort of architect most owners want to hire.

Communication Goals

Professional communication has three basic goals: to inform, to persuade, and to instruct.

Informing. At the outset, much of the communication between architect and client is intended to inform the client about the architecture firm, the services it offers, the design process, the way the firm works, or particular aspects of a design solution. As the project proceeds, the architect is called upon to keep the client and other project participants aware of the status of the activities necessary for the work to proceed, the tasks accomplished, the milestones met, and the overall schedule. When a message is necessary, include a call for action to alert the recipient to its purpose. Even the most mundane memorandum should identify a requested action, such as "Please file this memo for future reference" or "Kindly acknowledge receipt of this memo."

Persuading. Another goal of communication is to encourage the recipient to take action, make a decision, or agree with a particular point of view. Marketing communications come to mind, since the goal of most marketing messages is "hire our firm!" Project communications are also routinely meant to be persuasive, as when an architect asks an owner to release a payment to a contractor, approve a change order, or pay an invoice. In one respect, persuasive messages are simpler to communicate than informative ones because the reason for them is usually more obvious.

Since the purpose of a persuasive communication is more readily grasped, a good first principle of communication is this: Before undertaking any communication, oral or written, determine whether it has a persuasive purpose and identify that purpose. The initial result of consistently applying this principle should be the generation of far fewer unnecessary or competing messages. Bear in mind, however, that keeping someone informed of progress on a project or a task can be a perfectly good reason for sending a message.

Instructing. The last goal of communication is to instruct the recipient on how to proceed. Architects, in the course of a typical project, issue hundreds of sets of instructions. These can appear as drawings, sketches, specifications, product or material literature, details, clarifications, memos, and letters. In fact, it would be fair to say that the main vehicle an architect uses to do his or her work is instructions to those who perform the activities necessary for construction of the project.

The clarity and precision of this category of communication is an important ingredient in the success of any project.

Learning Other Languages

Architects at times are accused of couching their design presentations in obscure academic language or professional jargon that is incomprehensible or confusing to the audience. Clients, too, use terms and jargon particular to their field of expertise or business. These specialized and often competing "languages" can result in misunderstandings and confusion. Thus it is helpful if the architect clarifies the terms and concepts used by all those involved in a project.

If an architect's work involves many projects of a particular type (e.g., laboratories, schools, courthouses, etc.), learning the language of that specialty and learning it well is essential. Here are specific suggestions for speaking a client's language:

Read what your clients read. One of the best ways to improve your client communication skills is to subscribe to and study the trade publications clients read. It does not matter if the publication is *Banker's Week* or *Assisted Living Monthly*, as long as it pertains to a client's field. It is important to be exposed to and familiar with the professional jargon and vocabulary your clients use. As a side benefit, architects can also acquire a better understanding of issues confronting their clients' industries.

One reason trade publications are good for study is that trade journalists usually explain acronyms and jargon in their articles. A story about REITs, for example, will somewhere (usually when it first appears) explain that a REIT is a "real estate investment trust." By reading what your clients read, you can learn their vocabulary.

Attend client events. Attending events sponsored by organizations the client belongs to is also an effective way to learn a specialized language. Attendance at these events is usually not restricted and, more often than not, industry organizations are glad for the architect's interest (and registration fee). Programs, lectures, and conferences by client groups can provide a realistic idea of how clients speak among themselves. Unlike trade journals, however, program speakers do not always take care to explain the terms they are using. So although client events are useful for learning client language, some translation may still be needed. And obviously, this sort of "fieldwork" is more expensive and time-consuming than reading trade publications.

Delve into glossaries and references. It can also be helpful to purchase or download a glossary or reference work pertaining to the client's field. Just as there are dictionaries of architecture terms, there are dictionaries or glossaries for most other professions. Usually, the hardest part is tracking down the publisher, since dictionaries of, say, biochemical research are not likely to be found at a local bookstore. Client trade and professional associations are the best place to start a search for client language references. Often these glossaries can be found online at trade association Web sites.

Learning to speak a client's or specialist's language is an important skill by which an architect can remove potential barriers to good communication. Equally important is the architect's willingness to cultivate listening skills and to improve speaking and writing skills.

LISTENING

You can observe a lot by just watching.

Yogi Berra

We tend to think of communication skills as those skills that help us transmit a message. In fact, the most important communication skill is the means by which we receive messages from others. The most effective and least-used communication tools are the ears. You can learn a lot just by listening.

A Marketing Tool

Listening to clients is perhaps the most effective marketing strategy. Although it is seldom taught in schools, listening is compelling to both current and prospective clients. Clients consistently report selecting an architect because they felt the candidate or firm demonstrated a willingness to listen. Another positive result of listening is that selection committees routinely rank lower those design firms that come into a project interview acting as though they have all the answers.

Why is this? Listening connotes a cooperative and collaborative spirit, which is both effective and persuasive when dealing with clients. Listening implies a willingness to learn and to be fully committed to the client's idea of a successful project. In addition, listening shows respect for the client.

Despite its large and obvious benefits, listening is among the least valued communication skills because it is not glamorous—that is, becoming a better listener does not seem to add much to an architect's professional stature. Indeed, one precondition of good listening is the willingness to learn from clients instead of enlightening them. Humility is rarely the topic of best-sellers, although in *The Seven Habits of Highly Effective People*, author Stephen Covey advises readers to "seek first to understand, then to be understood."

Empathetic Listening

The essence of good listening is to listen with empathy, which requires you to view an interaction from the other person's point of view. Putting yourself in another's shoes will make it much easier to understand that person's message and the motivation behind it. Empathetic listening requires architects to lay aside personal agendas, professional pride, and natural defensiveness in order to enter into a discussion with clients as a person willing to learn.

Keys to empathetic listening. The strategies described below are essential to being an empathetic listener. Architects who learn to cultivate these skills in their interactions with clients should find it much easier to achieve professional and business goals.

- *Check your ego at the door.* Empathetic listening requires a humble attitude. Professional pride is the biggest obstacle to being a good listener. Learn to focus more on what the client wants you to hear and less on what you have to say.
- *Acknowledge your biases.* Everyone has a frame of reference. Yours will always be different from your client's.
- *Establish a "plane of connection."* Attitude is not just a mental disposition. Empathetic listening requires a literal horizontal connection with the speaker, so that communication takes place between equals.
- *Avoid commentary.* Resist the urge to evaluate every statement a client makes for its validity or usefulness. Learn to listen without immediately judging either the speaker or the content of the message.
- *Show interest.* Although it may seem insincere, adopting an interested posture (leaning in, eyes front and not preoccupied) will help you *become* interested.
- *It's not all about you.* Resist the urge to share your own stories, however relevant they may seem. Especially resist the urge to top each point a client makes with an anecdote about how the same thing happened to you.
- *Be affirmative.* Learn to use words and actions that affirm the speaker without necessarily expressing agreement. Affirmation means letting a speaker know his or her message is being received, not that you agree with everything that is said.
- *Take notes.* Taking notes is almost always permissible, unless clients specifically say their comments are "off the record." When you do take notes, you'll be surprised at how much better you remember the conversation later.
- *Be in the moment.* Being in the moment requires full participation in the conversation taking place. This means paying attention to a client while he or she is speaking, not thinking back on something that happened earlier in the day and not anticipating something that might happen later.
- *Respond appropriately.* Reinforce the communication process by restating the speaker's main points, acknowledging expected actions, and asking clarifying questions. Inappropriate responses include reciprocal attacks, defensive posturing, and changing the subject to something of greater interest to you.

Frames of reference. A major consideration when listening empathetically is to remember that architects and clients generally do not share the same frame of reference. In fact, architects are likely to encounter individuals with many different frames of reference within a client organization.

Challenge yourself to think, before a conversation takes place, about how your frame of reference may differ from that of the client. Clues to an individual's frame of reference can be found by observing the following:

- What does he or she seem passionate about?
- What are his or her measures of effective performance?
- To whom does this individual report? What are his or her accountabilities?
- What other constituencies must this person answer to?

> Listen. Listen. Listen better. Understand our culture. Get immersed in what we do, who we are.
>
> Charles Andrews, assistant vice president for space planning and construction, Emory University

COMPARATIVE FRAMES OF REFERENCE

Role in Client Organization	Likely Frame of Reference
Executive	Image, theme, first cost, schedule
Department manager	Functional layout, efficiency, flow
User	Convenience, control, personal space
Facility manager	Standardization, efficiency, life cycle cost
Maintenance staff	Durability, ease of repair, materials, standards

Architects should also be aware of how their own frame of reference filters communications they receive. Are you most passionate about design? About client satisfaction? About profitability? About larger social concerns (e.g., the environment)? The issues an architect cares about most deeply (e.g., design, client satisfaction, profitability, the environment, etc.) define the edges of his or her frame of reference. As a design professional, it is your job to understand both your frame of reference and your client's.

Gender differences. The majority of architects are still male, and some have observed that men do not always model good listening skills. Author Tom Peters points out that women more often exhibit the collaborative skills, like listening, that are needed to succeed in the twenty-first century. As well, women are generally better at entering into a conversation openly, without jockeying for status, and at responding empathetically rather than defensively to what they hear.

Should male architects therefore abandon the quest to become better listeners? Of course not. However, in many instances, men face greater challenges in becoming good listeners. Thus, when opportunities arise, they should observe how women communicate and their sensitivity to context and nuance, and they should seek to cultivate those qualities in their own listening.

Focusing on the Message

One barrier to effective listening is a natural tendency to judge the communication skills of others. The solution is to focus on the *content* of the message and not the person delivering it. Because people can listen much faster than others can talk, the "rate gap"—the difference between the two—can be used to determine what the person speaking is trying to say. Turning listening into a challenging mental game will minimize distractions caused by a client's less-than-perfect delivery.

Avoiding Distractions

Obviously, good listeners avoid distracting themselves. This means not making (or taking) phone calls when speaking with someone, not sending (or reading) e-mails on a wireless device, not doodling, and not looking out the window. For those who are easily distracted, avoiding distraction may take a concerted effort, but the dividends gained in better communication with your clients is well worth it.

PRESENTATION POINTERS

Here are ten good ideas to keep in mind when making a formal presentation to a client:

1. Show up. Be physically prepared for your presentation, recognizing that how you "dance" is part of the message.
2. Know your motivation. Have a clear purpose for your presentation and a call to action. Build your presentation around a story line, rather than just technical facts.
3. Know your lines. Over-preparation (having more to say than you actually say) is the key to confident presenting.
4. Be visible. Know the setting where the presentation will take place, and keep yourself lighted during audiovisual presentations.
5. Face out. Build energy, empathy, engagement, enthusiasm, and entertainment into your talk. Never turn your back to the audience.
6. Keep going. Recognize that things can (and will) go wrong during your presentation. Strategize ahead of time about how to handle them.
7. Project. Speak so you can be heard by the person farthest away from you in the room.
8. Stay in the moment. Concentrate on what you are saying, not on extraneous problems unrelated to your presentation.
9. Remember your props. Think about what sort of visual aids will help you achieve your objective.
10. Know when to stop. Plan generously, so you can finish your presentation before your allotted time runs out.

Adapted from Architect's Essentials of Presentation Skills, *by David Greusel, AIA*

VERBAL COMMUNICATION

Once you have begun to learn a client's language and to practice empathetic listening, you will be well on your way to establishing good communications. The next step is learning to speak to clients in a way that fosters mutual understanding.

Dialogue vs. Monologue

The most practical way architects can improve verbal interactions with clients is to stop making "speeches." In a society where a thirty-second television commercial is considered long, it hardly makes sense for an architect to discourse for an hour or more on a topic before asking for questions. This truth applies to design presentations, marketing efforts, and speeches to clients or public groups.

How can a monologue be turned into a dialogue? By deciding to do it ahead of time. The decision to interact, rather than just talk, is the key to client engagement. Once that decision is made, crafting a dialogue becomes fairly easy.

Darling, for a speech to be immortal, it need not be interminable.

Muriel Humphrey

Asking Questions

A simple way to interact with a client is to ask questions—lots of questions. Begin with a question, either innocuous ("How are you this morning?") or profound ("What adjective best describes your attitude toward this project?"). Continue asking questions throughout the meeting. It is not an exaggeration to say that asking questions is the single most effective way to achieve high-quality communication with clients—assuming you listen to the answers.

Some architects may think, "I've spent a lot of time preparing for this meeting. I have a lot to say! If I'm asking all these questions, how can I make the points I need to make?" The idea is not only to ask questions at the outset, but also to punctuate your presentation with questions throughout. If you find yourself going on about some aspect of a design that particularly interests you, pull yourself up short and say, "It's obvious that I'm having fun. Is any of this making sense to you?" Questions create breathing space in a discussion and allow architects to redirect their remarks to keep the client's interest.

One concern about asking questions is that doing so will make the architect seem weak or tentative, but this is almost never the case. Although asking questions requires a certain level of humility, doing so shows respect for a client's views by inviting him or her into the discussion. Many of the best teachers ask questions of their students, even teachers with vastly superior knowledge. Through the use of questions, teachers engage their students' minds in a discussion. Like the philosopher Socrates, skilled inquisitors can steer a conversation in any direction they want by the questions they ask.

A third objection expresses a basic fear: "What if I ask questions and no one answers? I'm supposed to be making a *presentation*—the panel is there to hear me talk. They don't want to hear themselves talk. What if they simply don't respond?" This fear, as often as it is raised, rarely becomes a reality. All that is needed to get a quiet client to respond to questions is patience. Wait a moment, restate the question, then wait another moment. Eventually someone will break the ice, and more comments will follow.

Crossing Cultural Barriers

As the United States becomes increasingly multicultural, so do architects' clients. It is obvious that the makeup of building committees, architect selection panels, zoning boards, and city councils is far more diverse today than in years past. As a result, it is important for architects to recognize, respect, and be sensitive to cultural differences when communicating with clients and other groups involved in their work.

First—and this should go without saying—avoid potentially offensive jokes or comments altogether. Racial, ethnic, or religious humor has no place in professional communications, no matter how informal.

More to the point, architects should take cultural differences into account as they make presentations. Are all members of the building committee fluent in English? If not, what adjustments should be made to reach them? Are there persons with disabilities needing some type of accommodation? Did everyone in the audience attend college? Considering such questions will help you gear your presentation to the cultural atmosphere of the meeting.

The most important cultural accommodation you can make is to be aware that there will be cultural differences. Following are additional suggestions for addressing such differences.

Communicating with speakers of other languages. One advantage of foreign travel is the empathy it creates for being inexpert in the local language. When communicating with clients or others for whom English is an acquired skill, it may help to remember how you have felt in a non-English-speaking country. Without being patronizing (speaking too loudly, for instance), moderate the pace of conversation to allow listeners less comfortable with English to follow along. Avoid using lofty vocabulary words (e.g., *orientation*) when a plainer expression (such as *facing north*) will suffice. Stopping frequently to ask questions would be helpful as well.

Nonverbal communication. Sometimes nonverbal communication reveals more than is intended. Do you know when to present a business card with one hand and when to use two (as opposed to the American style of flipping it across the conference table like a winning hole card)? Do you understand cross-cultural protocols for handshakes, introductions, and seating locations? These matters are important in dealing with clients of other cultural backgrounds. Remember to be sensitive to nonverbal cues when communicating across cultural boundaries, and take time to do the research that will help prevent a *faux pas*.

Clothing issues. As American business attire veers perennially toward greater casualness, architects should be aware that many cultures (including some American subcultures) view appropriate attire as important. While polo shirts and cotton pants may suffice for many business encounters in the United States, "business attire" often has an entirely different meaning abroad, to foreign clients inside the United States, and even to some American clients whose cultural norms are not in the mainstream. Be aware of cultural expectations, and dress accordingly.

Personal space and other cultural taboos. In dealing with clients from different cultural backgrounds, it is important to avoid actions that are simply unacceptable. For example, failing to reciprocate an "air kiss" or using the left hand may seem innocent to Americans, but these are, in some cultural contexts, major gaffes that can start interactions on a negative footing. Another common cultural difference is the distance deemed appropriate for personal communication. More formal cultures tend to communicate at greater distances as an indication of rank and respect. Other cultures are more comfortable with intimate conversation, and "rubbing shoulders" with the client may be more literal than Americans expect. If you misunderstand your clients' expectations about personal space, you risk being seen as either obnoxious or aloof. To avoid running afoul of these and other cultural taboos, do your homework before dealing with clients from a different culture.

Avoiding jargon and "tech speak." One of the largest barriers in communicating with clients is "architect-ese"—the language of academic architectural criticism. Too easily picked up from lectures, critiques, or professional journals, this transgression is the inverse of "learning a client's language." It's expecting a client to learn the architect's language.

For example, if an architect discusses "the dialectical use of materiality to enhance the phenomenology of the space" during a presentation, clients may wonder if the goal is to inform them or to impress them with an obscurity (and by implication, profundity) of thought. If your goal is truly to inform rather than impress, using obtuse vocabulary is certainly not the way to do it. Avoiding jargon is even more important when a client has a different cultural background.

This [letter] would not be so long had I but the leisure to make it shorter.

Blaise Pascal

Using acronyms (such as HVAC for heating, ventilating, and air conditioning) is another barrier to clear communications. Although using acronyms saves time and effort when architects communicate with similarly trained professionals, they can be a constant source of frustration for clients. Most clients will not stop an architect in mid-sentence and ask him or her to explain an acronym, but the humiliation of not being in the know can have a lasting negative effect.

It is not difficult to talk about design in clear, unornamented English. Just speak plainly, using short sentences, and get to the point. Architects should also use common vocabulary and explain any technical terms necessary to present a project. When you can trust yourself (and your work) enough not to lean on obscure rhetoric to describe it, your communication with clients will improve.

WRITTEN COMMUNICATION

Architects often do not excel at written communication. Perhaps because of their graphic and spatial reasoning skills, architects can find stringing words together into a coherent sentence a daunting task.

Given the opportunity to review other firms' literature, architects will likely be surprised by the sameness in the written communications. The carefully crafted words of your own promotional materials may be echoed in the marketing materials of others. You may also be surprised by numerous grammatical and spelling errors, so visible in others' work but so hard to spot in your own.

Fortunately, good professional writing doesn't require brilliant feats of creativity. In fact, it often is the desire to insert creativity where it does not belong that is the greatest problem. Leave it to novelists to reinvent the English language.

Keep It Simple

In their classic book *The Elements of Style*, authors E. B. White and William Strunk Jr. recommend a prose style that is simple, elegant, and to the point. Architects would do well to follow their advice in most professional communications. Do not mistake convoluted prose for deep thought. If the purpose of written communication is to communicate rather than to dazzle or impress, it is best to write with economy and simplicity. A few simple rules for elegant writing follow.

Trim your train of thought. Run-on sentences are a common problem in architectural prose, even in published writing. It is much easier to write punchy, captivating prose when thoughts don't ramble on for fifty or seventy words.

Deliver just the facts. In most professional communications, it is not necessary to embellish a point beyond the facts. In fact, such embellishment can seem self-serving or patronizing.

Leash your word power. It is one thing to understand long, difficult words; it is quite another to inflict them on

E-MAIL COMMUNICATIONS

Although it is tempting to think of e-mail as a conversational medium, it is a type of written communication and thus the basic rules of written communication apply. Because e-mail is a rapid and seemingly informal medium, a few special rules are worth pointing out:

- Spelling counts. Just because you are responding to a client from a handheld device in an airport does not mean you don't have to correctly spell—or punctuate—your messages. Every message is a reflection of your firm's commitment to quality.

- Context matters. Because e-mail "threads" can be read sequentially from the bottom up, it is tempting to write telegraphic responses like "No problem," or "I agree." While acceptable for internal communications, do your clients the favor of at least restating the question in an e-mail response.

- Don't yell. Typing in all capital letters comes across as shouting.

- Put your name on your paper. It's a good idea to include an automatic signature with basic contact information in every e-mail sent. This allows the recipient to reach you in other ways, if necessary.

- It's on the record. E-mail correspondence is always part of a project's written documentation, and it is acceptable as evidence in court. Architects should bear this in mind before firing off an ill-considered response to a client or a contractor. "Recalling" an inappropriate message does not work; it may still have been received and saved by the recipient. In addition, the firm should retain copies of all work-related e-mail messages and have a method for retrieving them.

- It represents your firm. It bears repeating that e-mail is written communication, despite its apparent informality. Any opinion you express, statements of fact you assert, or project details you clarify are a fixed expression of your professional thought. Rules for more formal, hard-copy written communications apply. The same principle applies for jokes or Internet links architects might forward to clients. A good question to ask before sending an e-mail is, "Would I put this on company letterhead and mail it to my client?"

other people. If your goal is to communicate simple ideas effectively, use commonly understood words.

Give the reader a break. It is possible to write a coherent paragraph that spans several pages, but this doesn't mean that you should. Look at a newspaper: Rare is the paragraph that contains more than one or two sentences. Chopping text into smaller chunks makes it easier for the reader—your client—to digest.

Use vivid language. Most architects use the same dry, professional prose to cover every topic from initial contacts to a final punch list. Although it is possible to overdo it, make an effort to find more lively ways to express your thoughts. For example, *cut* may work better than *reduce*, and *show* can replace *indicate.* Use active instead of passive voice (e.g., "we designed" instead of "was designed by our firm"). Architects need not deviate from the goal of sticking to the facts to make their writing more vivid, and hence, memorable.

Avoid Jargon

We architects demand clarity and rigor in our designs. But we ignore them in our writing as we massacre syntax, chop-shop metaphor, and reach for exactly the wrong polysyllabic word.

Robert Campbell, FAIA

As mentioned above, no one appreciates being spoken to in a foreign language. For many clients, the language that architects use to describe their work seems foreign. As with oral presentations, architects should avoid using jargon in written communications with their clients. If an architecture firm's written materials contain words such as *tectonic* and *morphology*, the firm has a jargon problem.

Jargon can fall into several categories. It's easy to identify (and make fun of) the obtuse academic jargon common in the design press. But other types of jargon can be just as bad. Consider these examples:

Technical jargon. Does your client know what "eefiss" is? Project architects and contractors frequently toss around this word, which has become a common pronunciation for the acronym EIFS (exterior insulation and finish systems). Don't use such shorthand unless you are certain your client understands it.

Process jargon. Process terminology is another source of obscure abbreviations. Rare is the architect who actually spells out "design development" instead of writing "DD." More to the point, clients may not be familiar with the term "design development" at all, let alone its abbreviation. Acquainting clients with such commonly used process terminology can enhance communications.

Academic jargon. Architects may use academic jargon in an attempt to relate their work to books and magazines about architecture. Almost comical in its obscurity, academic jargon includes such words as *Miesian* and *Corbusian, phenomenology,* and *deconstructivism,* as well as obscure references such as *Robie-esque* or *Piranesian.* Unless you are writing a thesis, avoid this type of jargon; it will not usefully address your client's space needs.

Avoid Puffery

Architects who use puffery in written communications can also confound their clients. Puffery refers to the liberties an advertiser takes in describing a product to make it irresistible to consumers. Puffery is easily detectable because it makes vague claims that cannot be substantiated, such as "Best in town!" "Low, low prices!" or "Nothing else like it!"

While architectural puffery may be less shrill, it is no less annoying to clients. This is especially true when, for example, clients wading through their ninth or tenth written proposal read yet another claim to be "uniquely responsive to client needs." If all the architects vying for a project are "uniquely responsive," then what is unique about that?

A better approach to marketing communications is to write about the most distinctive areas of an architecture practice in clear, concise prose. For example, if your firm has won a number of design awards, cite the actual awards instead of a vague phrase such as "commitment to design excellence expressed in our many award-winning projects." To highlight a firm's technical skills, cite its low incidence of change orders (using an actual number or percentage), rather than mentioning a "commitment to quality documentation." If you believe your firm's design process is unusual, state what makes it so, rather than claiming "clients love our collaborative approach to design." Puffery is not always untrue, but it sounds untrue to cynical clients and, as such, it wastes their time and your effort.

RULES TO REMEMBER

This article has dealt briefly with four principal skills integral to good communication with clients: learning a client's language, listening to clients, speaking with clients, and writing for clients. These same skills are applicable and useful in all professional communications. In summary, here are some important principles to keep in mind.

Challenge Your Assumptions

Every client approaches interactions with architects with a different set of assumptions. One of the most effective communication tools architects can use is to constantly challenge their assumptions about what the client knows, what the client expects from the architect or firm, and what the client desires for the project.

Consistently, client surveys show that the goals clients and architects have for construction projects are seldom in perfect alignment. Architects may view each new commission as an opportunity for peer awards or publication. Although clients may have similar aspirations, more often they do not. Rather, they are focused on the practical goals of meeting the budget, finishing on time, and getting a certain quantity and quality of useful space.

Because architects and their clients often enter into projects with different expectations and assumptions, miscommunication is common. One way to counteract this is for architects to spend time with their clients, clarifying expectations early in the relationship. Architects should keep in mind their client's frame of reference, and how it resembles (and differs from) their own, throughout project delivery. This awareness will facilitate communications that flow from a shared understanding rather than divergent goals.

Keep an Empathetic Perspective

Another essential rule for effective client communication is viewing relationships with clients from an empathetic perspective. This means learning to see the world from the perspective of the client. An architect may not agree with a client's worldview, but it is not necessary to endorse the client's view to understand it. When designing libraries, it helps if an architect thinks like a librarian, or at least understands how librarians think. The purpose of viewing projects with empathy is to build a mutual understanding that will result in successful communications and ultimately in a successful project.

It is often said that architects (and other professionals) who reach the top of their profession are not the most skilled practitioners but rather the best communicators. Aspiring to be a successful communicator may not position you to win the Pritzker Prize. However, honing your communication skills with the same intensity you bring to improving your design and technical skills can help you be more effective in all aspects of practice.

For More Information

The following books address the communication elements of writing, listening, and giving presentations. *Writing for Design Professionals*, second edition (W. W. Norton, 2006), by Stephen A. Kliment, discusses how to master the complexities of effective writing in design practice, with a focus on proposals, letters, brochures, portfolios, reports, presentations, and job applications. Madelyn Burley-Allen's *Listening: The Forgotten Skill* (Wiley, 1995) is a guide to learning the techniques for being an effective listener. In *Architect's Essentials of Presentation Skills* (Wiley, 2002), David Greusel covers all aspects of making effective oral presentations.

PART 2

PRACTICE

CHAPTER 4

Developing a Practice

4.1 Starting an Architecture Firm

Elena Marcheso Moreno

Architects may think all they need to go out on their own is experience and a license, but most quickly learn these are just part of what it takes to start a new business. Indeed, time devoted to design competes with time needed to address financial matters, staff direction, marketing, client relations, and the search for new work.

One-third of all firms were started in the last ten years.

2006 AIA Firm Survey

Architects—indeed, all entrepreneurs—must make enough money to stay in business and prosper. The architect who starts a firm must have a clear set of goals, sufficient training, and enough capital to operate for some time. Ideally, a project will be waiting the day after the architect opens his or her office, but many architects begin with no work in hand.

There are as many reasons for starting a new design practice as there are people who start them. Sometimes an architect has a long-held ambition to open his or her own firm. Sometimes the decision is spurred by downsizing at an employer or frustration with the course of a career. Although their reasons vary, many architects of all ages and at most stages of a professional career decide to set up shop on their own.

Architects who make the decision to establish their own firms are immediately confronted with the need to make multiple decisions. While relatively minor ones—where to set up an office—might be readily solved, another tier of items demands careful strategizing and goal setting. A great deal of strategic thinking is required to structure an architecture practice, covering issues that range from the legal structure for the firm to the most promising markets and building types to pursue, the search for clients, and the compensation sought.

Elena Marcheso Moreno writes about architecture, construction, and related business issues from McLean, Virginia.

Careful start-up planning and decision making will pay dividends long into the future. Identify your goals, business plan, target market, capitalization, marketing strategy, and delivery abilities as soon as possible. Thousands of new businesses start up every year, but experts estimate that only 25 percent of all architecture start-ups are still in business three years after their principals first hang out a shingle. Many fail for lack of fee-paying clients and enough capital to see them through slow times.

It is likely that an architect who starts a new architecture firm has the necessary design skills to succeed in the marketplace. However, whether a sole practitioner or the principal of a small firm, an architect starting up a practice will also need some specific business skills or at least access to consultants who can help. It is not enough to know how to put a building together. Architects must also market their services, negotiate contracts, build and maintain client relationships, and hire and manage staff effectively. Finding loans and other financing, entering into leases, and managing cash flow and financial stability are all required skills. The sum of these specific skills is a business that is operated profitably.

MAKING THE DECISION

Is going into business for yourself the right decision for you? Perhaps, but only you can answer that question.

Desire is not the same thing as will. Are you an entrepreneur? Do you understand that to compete with the "big guys" in an industry headed toward increased firm size and consolidation you will need to define your new firm's niche clearly? Do you dream of running your own architecture firm but can't fathom the idea of not getting a paycheck every two weeks? Be realistic about your willingness to put in the work and make the sacrifices needed to start up an architecture practice.

A few common themes emerge among architects who have found the motivation to start a new design firm: a belief in their own talent and a lack of recognition in their current job, an employer's change in philosophy or business activities, downsizing and layoffs at the most recent place of employment, the wish to work closely with specific other architects, and a long-term plan to have a firm of their own. Whatever the driving force behind the desire to head a firm, architects considering a start-up business should ask themselves a few important questions:

What Basic Skills Are Required?

Successful architecture firms have much in common. First, they are owned and operated by entrepreneurs who might be talented designers, but most assuredly are savvy businesspeople. Sometimes the business acumen is obtained along the way, but in virtually all cases, owners of successful new design firms understand that architecture is a business that must be managed.

To run a firm, you—or a partner—will need to have or acquire basic business skills. To obtain work, you need to market your services, negotiate contracts, and reach agreements. Someone needs to build relationships with clients and maintain their trust. To grow, you must hire staff and consultants and then work diligently to build and keep their loyalty. You also need to have the skills to work effectively with contractors and consultants. In addition, finding loans and other financing, entering into leases, and managing cash flow and financial stability all require specific skills, the sum of which is a business that is profitable.

Are You Willing to Work Hard and Long Hours?

A profitable business is not a sure thing. Success requires hard work and long hours. Architects generally have a hand up here—even as students, their time commitments were substantial. When you own the business, however, you will spend a lot of time *and*

Most architects will agree that "God is in the details" when it comes to design, but don't always keep that in mind when it comes to financial matters.

When the start-up approach is aggressive, the start-up capital required can be quite large. Adequate cash flow, which can be difficult to achieve in a thriving business, can be completely unpredictable for a new firm. While start-up capital and loans are often necessary in the first year or two, it is preferable to use personal savings or support from a spouse rather than borrowed funds to pay yourself in the beginning.

Leaving a previous place of employment and starting up on your own is just one path to firm ownership. Buying into a partnership with cash up front or paying over time through deductions from compensation is another. Purchasing an existing firm or buying into the firm where you work are also options, and many firms have transition plans to hand the reins from retiring principals to a new generation of architects.

it will be your money at stake or your loans that must be paid back, and your reputation that will be scrutinized. As well, as employees, architects are responsible for their own jobs, but as employers, they are responsible for everyone else's job, too.

How Will the Business Be Structured?

Once a start-up has been decided on, two further decisions must be made immediately: Will the business be a sole proprietorship, a partnership, or some variation of a corporation? With whom will you go into practice if the business is a partnership or corporation?

▶ See Firm Legal Structure (4.2) for a detailed discussion of the legal forms of business a design firm can use.

Consult an attorney and an accountant when deciding the best way to structure a new business, but first understand your options. There are basically four forms of organization a small business can take: sole proprietorship, partnership, corporation, or limited liability company. Keep in mind that the legal form of existence you select for a fledgling organization may outlive its usefulness as a firm grows and need to be changed.

Do You Like to Work Alone, or Do You Thrive in a More Collegial Atmosphere?

Taking on a partner is a big decision, but it is a relationship many architects gladly enter. If you decide to share the ownership of the firm you are starting, whether it is a partnership, corporation, subchapter S, or limited liability company, work out the specifics with all partners in a legally binding contract. When you and your partners begin with a clear view of who is in charge, how compensation will be paid, and how the work will be divided, misunderstandings are less likely to occur. In addition, the documentation can help resolve differences in the future.

PARTNER AND SHAREHOLDER AGREEMENTS

Fresh beginnings are exciting. The potential for success can seem like a certainty for an enthusiastic new firm starting out. Principals with diverse backgrounds and talents can join forces to create a greater whole, but partners are distinct people who bring their own strengths and weaknesses to a firm. As hard as this can be to envision as you create a new firm, disagreements among partners can ruin a business. Work out the contingencies before you hang out a shingle. In five or ten years, one partner can forget how important the talents of another were to starting a new business, and focus instead on something less positive.

A contract between partners can seem unnecessary when things are going smoothly, but will be a necessity whenever rough spots arise. Avoid conflict before it occurs with a partnership agreement that specifies the following:

- Names of all partners, their legal relationships, and their ownership percentage. Some things that help decide who owns how much of a business include who initiated it, who brings the strongest reputation or expertise, who made financial contributions for start-up, and who does what work.

- How compensation and financial earnings are to be calculated and distributed among partners (or owners, if a corporation).

- Decision making and the pecking order. Determine from the beginning who is in charge. When a partner has a certain skill set or specialized knowledge, responsibility for decisions in those areas can be assigned accordingly.

- Financial responsibilities. How will expenses be divided and paid? Who has the right to financially indebt the firm and its principals?

- Credit for work. Architecture is a creative endeavor. Decide whose name will appear first and any circumstances that might change the order.

- Dispute resolution. If a disagreement does arise, everyone will know in advance whether it will be resolved through arbitration, mediation, or a court of law.

- What happens when a partner is sick or dies.

- How a partner can leave and sell his or her interest to the remaining partners

- The procedure for bringing in new partners or principals.

If the Start-Up Will Involve Others, Who Will They Be?

Assembling a strong team is one of the most important steps for a start-up design firm.

Whether composed of employees or partners, the team does not need to be large, but it does need to be powerful. If the person who starts the firm is a very talented designer, it is unlikely a second high-profile designer will be helpful in the beginning. Rather, an architect with business acumen and management skills could bring more value to a new firm. Also, if the success of the firm hinges on the design talents of the owner, it would be better for the owner to keep designing and to hire someone else to produce construction documents.

When Is the Right Moment to Go Out on Your Own?

Once an architect decides to start a new firm, the question of timing arises. When is the best time to leave a current situation and start out in a new enterprise? According to people who have done it, there is never a good time to leave a job and start a new business. Unless the situation at a current job is really difficult, most architects are likely to have a sense of loyalty to the company they work for and the people they work with. It is really hard to leave a place where you are happy, even to pursue a dream you believe will make you even happier.

An architect who left a prominent firm to start his business explains, "I spent years in gut-wrenching soul-searching, trying to engineer a perfect parting, waiting for large jobs to wind down so there would be a smooth transition. But there never was a perfect time, and it went on for years." So one day he finally decided to just leave.

And leave he did—with no work in hand. "It was scary right up to the minute I left, but once I was on my own, all the fear evaporated," he recalls. And almost by magic, work started coming to him. He was well respected by the firm he left, and the principals there started sending work his way—projects that were too small for a big firm but just right for a one-person business.

Rather than taking business away from a former employer, this architect used his solid relationships with the firm to get referrals for work. His ethical approach helped him bring in work he would not have had otherwise, and it also helped his former firm keep its clients happy by attending to their needs without distracting staff members from the demands of larger projects.

Not all architects starting new firms act so responsibly, however. Unless a designer signs a non-compete clause in an employment contract with a former firm or attempts to undermine an existing design services contract, there are usually no legal consequences for an architect who takes clients from a former firm. Because the ethics of this situation are questionable, it is better to maintain relationships with old clients and pursue their next projects than to take an ongoing project away from a former employer. The AIA code of ethics addresses this issue in detail, but in the end it is really the entrepreneur who must decide between right and wrong. There is, of course, an exception to this—if you are the only one who can do the work on the client's project, you can negotiate an arrangement with your old firm to continue the project when you start your new firm.

PATHS TO FIRM OWNERSHIP

The steps to firm ownership are varied, but some of the most common routes among architects are these:

- Starting a firm of your own
- Taking over a family business
- Actively acquiring stock or percentage interest in an existing firm
- Becoming a partner of the firm where you currently work
- Moving from a position as "in-house" designer at a company that frequently buys design services to a consulting position
- Obtaining specialized training and expertise sought after by other architects
- Freelancing for various architects until you find one to buy into or build a strong enough reputation to start a firm on your own
- Teaming up with a general contractor to establish a design-build firm
- Teaming up with an engineer to start a multidisciplinary firm

ETHICAL MATTERS

Architects starting a new firm will need to show examples of their work, most of which will have been performed as an employee of another firm. According to the AIA code of ethics, architects and architecture firms should "recognize and give credit to others for the professional work they have performed." Thus, departing employees should ask permission to take designs and supporting materials from their old firms, and the old firm should grant reasonable requests related to work performed by the departing employee.

That said, architects who start their own firms still face some ethical dilemmas. For example, how much credit do you take for a team project performed while an employee of another firm? Do you ask your clients to follow you when you leave, or do you wait for their next project to market your expertise and inform them of your availability? Do you take a project for your own firm that a partnering firm had asked you to pursue with them? Do you hire employees from your old firm when you leave? Do you accept payment from clients but not pay subcontractors and consultants for their work on the project?

These are complicated questions, and they have complicated answers. Ethics generally does not involve issues of legality. Rather, ethics is about deciding what is right and what is wrong, and that decision will probably change with the circumstances. However, the advice from people with experience is "take the high road."

▶ Firm Identity and Expertise (4.3) and its backgrounder, Establishing a Niche Practice, address ways to create a distinctive identity.

DESIGNING THE FIRM: PLANNING A PRACTICE

When architects decide to open an office, they generally have a mental image of what they want their firm to be—its size, project types, clients, and perhaps its structure. To turn this image into a reality, they need to meld these components into a single whole that functions well. That means they need strategies for structuring the architecture practice; identifying markets; selecting types of projects; marketing to gain those projects; obtaining clients; pricing projects for profitability; executing projects on time; leading and managing the business; and finding, developing, and retaining staff.

Defining Firm Identity

A firm's identity can be anything you want—a focus on unique aesthetics, providing service and added value, or technological innovations are examples. Take stock of targeted markets and be brutally honest as you evaluate their growth potential for architecture services. Then plan where the firm will concentrate—which building type, which range of services. Don't overextend the firm at this point; it cannot be all things to all people. Clients today are looking for *experts* who can serve not only as their designers but also as their consultants. A firm that finds a niche and specializes in a few areas or even a single one is likely to be more profitable than a firm that can design any building type and offer any type of architectural service.

Preparing a Business Plan

It is important to think through what you want your practice to be and the shape it will take, and then set goals to use as benchmarks down the road. This is done best with a business plan. The business plan should be a formal document if used to secure financing. If used just for your own planning purposes, it can be a few sheets of paper with your plans clearly organized.

Writing a business plan is a challenging task because it requires a clear understanding of the firm you want to create and how you propose to do it. Simple, clear thoughts and descriptions are best. Don't be vague or leave room for more questions than you can answer. Those who will be funding your new architecture firm will review the business plan, and they are looking for a clear outline of how you expect to achieve your goals.

A business plan explains what you plan to do and how you plan to do it. It describes your unique vision for your business. Included are your measurable goals, the approach you expect to take to fulfill them and how they can be successfully verified, a description of your market and competition, and a description of problems likely to pop up along the way and how you plan to solve them. The business plan also needs to include the structure of your organization, listing key personnel and titles (even if one person currently fills all positions).

Most business plans have three main sections. Start with the concept: Discuss the building industry in your location, the demand for the firm's services—and what those services are—and how the firm will bring a unique set of skills to deliver them. In the second section, analyze the firm's client base and describe the market. Don't forget to discuss the competition and how the firm will be positioned. The third section should describe the financial position of the firm, as well as your own. Include income and cash flow projections and a balance sheet. Many financial tools are available to help with this task, but it could be useful to consult with an accountant. This section is also where staffing, operations, and management plans should be discussed, along with the need for physical resources such as equipment and office space.

The last component of your business plan is the amount of capital you will need to finance your new enterprise and keep it running until it is profitable. Include an estimate of how long you expect it will take for the firm to become profitable.

Identifying Staffing Needs

Eventually, most start-ups will need to hire staff to meet the goals of their business plans. Finding the best people may be a challenge because your firm will be competing with larger design firms. Recruiting and hiring can be a full-time job. For a new entrepreneur faced with a long list of start-up responsibilities, this task can be easy to put off—but don't procrastinate. It takes time to find staff with the talents you need and personalities that mesh with yours. Tackle hiring right away, and then as people come on board, they can help with the start-up tasks. One way to attract the people you want is to offer an ownership position, even if the pay is low at first. However, this option may not appeal to entrepreneurs worried about diluting their ownership.

There are a number of ways to advertise for staff besides placing want ads in newspapers. Check with your local AIA chapter, local architecture schools, and friends from your former firm and other firms. Make use of multiple job boards on the Internet, including the Career Center at AIA.org and lists maintained by AIA components. Also, remember to check into community Web sites like CraigsList.org, which are growing exponentially. While on the subject of the Internet, if you do not yet have everything you need to create a Web site for your new firm, at least reserve the business name. You can do this through any one of myriad domain name providers for just a few dollars a month. If you put your address and phone number on the page with a statement that the site is under construction, prospective employees might call you.

If you are hesitant about hiring employees before the firm has work to justify their positions, consider using consultants. You can use drafting services, a bill-paying service to pay invoices in a timely fashion, and research services to help you find and specify products. You can also establish relationships with other small firms and plan on future collaborations.

START-UP TASKS

Business and financial planning are a vital part of getting ready to open a new firm. In addition, it is important to get the word out about the services the firm will be offering as soon as possible.

Acquire Start-Up Funding

To begin a practice, you will need start-up capital. For most new design firms, especially those with an aggressive start-up approach, the sum required can be quite large. Unless a firm has a project—and, therefore, capital coming in—when it opens its doors, start-up capital will be needed to pay for office space (unless a home office is used), phone lines, computers, fax, e-mail, drafting supplies, furniture, and any other equipment needed to begin to design and manage projects. The funds will also need to cover the costs of stationery and business cards. Start-up capital pays your salary if you must have an income to survive and can tide you over while you wait for accounts receivable to be paid into the firm's coffers. Finally, start-up capital can help pay for staff, rent, consultants, and marketing expenses.

After a business plan has been developed and refined, many tasks must be attended to before a firm formally opens its doors. The list below includes most of these, although a firm may omit or modify some or add others, depending on its circumstances.

Legal/Regulatory Issues

- ❑ Engage legal counsel.
- ❑ Register firm (as regular corporation, S-corporation, LLC, etc.).
- ❑ Verify that required professional registrations are current.
- ❑ Obtain required business licenses/permits.
- ❑ Obtain tax ID.

Financial

- ❑ Obtain startup capital (from SBA, bank loans, equity lines, credit cards, etc.).
- ❑ Prepare loan proposal, if required.
- ❑ Establish banking services/accounts.
- ❑ Engage accountant or accounting services (if to be external).

Facilities

- ❑ Obtain office space (purchase, lease, lease to buy, etc.).
- ❑ Arrange for utility service hookups (phones, heat, power, etc.).
- ❑ Get keys/access devices for staff.
- ❑ Obtain office furniture and furnishings.
- ❑ Obtain office signage.
- ❑ Obtain or designate firm automobile.
- ❑ Obtain and set up computers.
- ❑ Obtain and set up copiers, fax machines, scanners, etc.
- ❑ Obtain miscellaneous equipment (camera, measuring devices, etc.).
- ❑ Obtain or arrange for coffee machines, vending, etc.
- ❑ Arrange for staff parking.

Staffing/Consultants

- ❑ Engage professional staff.
- ❑ Engage administrative/support staff.
- ❑ Line up design and technical consultants.

Insurance/Benefits

- ❑ Obtain workers' compensation insurance.
- ❑ Obtain professional liability insurance.
- ❑ Obtain general liability insurance.
- ❑ Obtain property/contents insurance.
- ❑ Obtain key person insurance or officer/director insurance.
- ❑ Obtain auto insurance.
- ❑ Set up employee health care insurance.
- ❑ Set up employee life and disability insurance.
- ❑ Set up employee savings plan (401(k), ESOP, etc.).

Administration/Support

- ❑ Set up office filing systems.
- ❑ Set up bookkeeping/accounting system.
- ❑ Set up tax withholding accounts (federal, state, local).
- ❑ Obtain and set up reference library/resource files.
- ❑ Purchase supplies (for minimum of three months).
- ❑ Purchase software programs.
- ❑ Obtain business stationery, forms, business cards, etc.
- ❑ Obtain printed contract documents (if software is not used).
- ❑ Obtain Internet provider.
- ❑ Set up LAN, Intranet, etc.
- ❑ Design and initiate Web page.
- ❑ Prepare firm policy/procedures manual.
- ❑ Select provider for repro services.

Marketing/Public Relations

- ❑ Develop initial marketing plan (based on business plan).
- ❑ Prepare announcements of firm opening.

Where does start-up capital come from? A number of practitioners receive bank loans during the formative months of the firm and beyond. Designers also use their own savings, borrow from relatives, or convince a new client to pay a hefty retainer.

Banks are in the business of lending money to make money. They like to invest in what they consider to be a good risk. Few start-up or newly formed design firms are recognized as good risks, so you must be well prepared when you approach a bank. Getting a loan is mostly a matter of selling yourself, since your firm does not have a track record. The better prepared you are, the greater your chances for success. It is your responsibility to explain your firm, your track record, and your capabilities to the banker. To start the loan process, you must submit a loan proposal.

Bring Money with You

Typically, banks require that owners of a new firm invest 25 to 50 percent of the capital requirements of their new business. Once a prospective borrower has established an ability to make this investment, banks will consider the character and managerial abilities of the individual and the firm's prospects for making a profit. Generally, a loan to a small business without much of a track record will require a personal guarantee by the owner. Such guarantees can require commitments of personal assets, such as a home, as collateral and should not be entered into lightly. If the business does not generate the necessary income or fails, the loan must be repaid, and the lender can take over assets listed as collateral. Generally, such loans are classified as lines of credit, in which cash is drawn as needed and paid back as funds are generated. The credit line stays open for some period of time, often ten years, as long as the business owner has made timely payments. Be forewarned that some lines of credit require an outstanding balance to be reduced to zero at least once each year, and most credit lines can be called in for untimely payments. Depending on your credit ratings, lines of credit are not always renewable.

A good loan proposal should include the standard financial forms and statements. The proposal should also include a true picture of where you and your start-up are financially, along with a well-thought-out business plan that addresses how the firm will use the loan to prosper and grow and to protect the lender's investment. No matter how good your proposal is, do not be tempted to overburden the new firm with too much debt. Supporting debt can interfere with your ability to hire people, acquire needed equipment, and grow.

When you go to the bank, bring along a preliminary business plan, your current resume, and a projection of your operating budget. Banks want to know where your income will come from, what your expenses will be, and how you plan to handle the firm's cash flow.

Normal operating expenses will drain cash flow. Some new firms take the plunge and rent an office, buy equipment, and otherwise invest at a fairly heavy rate from the very beginning. Unless you have signed contracts for a significant amount of work, a more cautious approach would be to go slowly. To save money, consider setting up a temporary office in your house, leasing a copier for a short period, and buying used equipment until you have a better idea of your actual operating needs. This approach is probably the least risky, yet it is only one option. At this stage, it is a good idea to list the assets you will need and the expenses you expect to incur, along with specific dollar amounts. Then make choices that will immediately help shape the firm identity you have chosen.

Obtain Expert Advice

The services of a lawyer with expertise in starting—and running—a small business are well worth the expense. A good lawyer can help with everything from deciding on a legal business form to filing paperwork with local, state, and federal authorities to

---

COMPONENTS OF A LOAN PROPOSAL

When you approach a bank, be ready to sell them on the viability of your new firm. A loan proposal should include the following:

- *Amount, time, and use of money to be borrowed.* Identify the amount of money you want to borrow, how long you want to pay it back, and how the money will be used. Banks like to collect their money on time, so be sure to mention how you plan to repay the loan, and list anything you can use as collateral.
- *Description of your business.* Explain what you do, your own background and qualifications, and the nature of prospective clients.
- *Current business plan.* Your plan should describe your market, your niche if you have one, your organizational structure, your marketing plans, your approach to financial management, and your profit objectives.
- *Budgets and operation costs.* This information should be organized by project, by month, by year, or by a longer term, as appropriate.
- *Additional financial information.* This may include an income or profit and loss statement, a balance sheet, and personal finances.

STRATEGIES TO COMBAT LACK OF CAPITAL

- Understand that profit is a business expense. Working at break-even leaves nothing for unexpected expenses—and there will be some.
- Do not take loss leaders lightly. Consider the overall benefits to the firm and the likelihood of actually receiving these benefits.
- Ask for retainers. Many clients expect to pay them, but only if you ask.
- Bill on an hourly basis for any portion of the work for which you cannot set extent or duration.
- Bill early and often—at least monthly. Writing small checks routinely is a lot easier than paying large sums less often. Many clients do not mind paying every two weeks if your cash flow requirements are explained to them in advance.
- Never stop marketing, no matter how busy you are right now. When a project is finished, do not overwork it because you have nothing else to do; go out and get another project.

James R. Franklin, FAIA, and Ava J. Abramowitz, Esq.

protecting your interests in the event of a disagreement with a client (or helping to avoid disagreements with carefully crafted contracts).

In addition to finding and working with an attorney who is well versed in corporate law, think ahead and find one who specializes in construction-related matters, including liability issues. Not all lawyers are well versed in both, so develop a relationship with a law firm that is large enough to work in both areas, or consider retaining two lawyers.

In addition to legal expertise, your new firm will need accounting services. Hiring a talented accountant in the formative years of a business will help the owners set financial strategies, optimize their current and future incomes, plan for their retirement, and set the stage for transitioning the business to others at a profit.

Arrange for Office Space

Choosing where to locate a new firm is sometimes difficult. While an office at home could work for a while or for a sole practitioner who plans to remain a firm of one, clients might look askance at this arrangement. Rented or purchased office space implies levels of stability and credibility, whether or not they exist; however, the monthly payments can be quite hefty for a new small business. Many new architecture firms open in space "on the fringe," outside more expensive downtown locations in major cities but near enough to prospective clients to be able to meet with them regularly and service their projects. New firms rarely stay in these first offices for more than a few years. By the time the three-year "make it or break it" milestone has passed, there is usually enough room in the budget for a move to better offices.

Deciding how much office space to acquire at start-up can be difficult. Typically, you must sign a lease for a certain period. If you plan on expanding the staff rapidly, you will need a place for them to work. But if your staffing needs are uncertain, why be saddled with a lot of space you cannot use? One alternative is to share space with another company or to sublet from another occupant for a short time. Alternatively, some new firms bank on their growth plans, and they opt for larger offices that they temporarily sublet to others.

New entrepreneurs may consider purchasing an office facility, although few can afford to both start a new business and purchase real estate at the same time. While both renting and purchasing are deductible business expenses, rent is payment for space you do not own, while a mortgage payment eventually increases your equity and thus your wealth. However, the high rate of failures among start-ups across all industries suggests that rented space is preferable initially. Once the new firm has become successful, you can contemplate purchasing an office facility.

Most commercial space for rent will be leased through a real estate broker. Like accountants and attorneys, a broker can be an asset for your business, helping you find the type of space you desire at a rent you can afford. A good broker will also help you negotiate a few months rent-free while you renovate or build out the space to your own specifications. Try to negotiate for a lease that includes utilities (other than phones or Internet service) to minimize the number of variable expenses the firm will face during the first few years.

Determine Furniture and Equipment Needs

Along with whether to rent or buy office space, decisions must be made about furniture and other capital assets. At a minimum, workers need desks, computers, chairs, lamps, and window coverings. Even in offices with open floor plans, it is a good idea to divide workspaces, perhaps using modular systems. Start-up capital should also cover reception and conference areas with seating. A telephone system, computers, and plotters can cost thousands of dollars.

To keep initial costs down, some assets and equipment can be purchased used rather than new. Look around for firms selling equipment when they upgrade or go out of business or arrange to share equipment with another firm through wireless technology. You can develop relationships with vendors for services such as reprographics and economize on a plotter. Design a nice space for your business without getting caught up in purchasing high-end products until yours is a high-end firm.

Apply for Tax ID Numbers and Business Licenses

To get a loan, open a bank account, rent an office, hire an employee, or engage in business in most localities, you must have a federal tax identification number and often a business license in addition to your architecture license.

Federal tax ID numbers (FEINs) are easy to acquire. Contact the Internal Revenue Service's Business Division at 1-800-829-4933 and fill out the required form with the assistance of an IRS representative. Or apply online at www.IRS.gov. In both cases, you will be given a temporary ID number immediately, which is usually converted to a permanent number. You will need to have a FEIN if you have any employees (including yourself) so that you can acquire an employer identification number (EIN) and file payroll taxes. Either an accountant or an attorney can help with this process, but it is simple enough to do alone. Most states where your firm does business will also require a state tax ID number.

In addition to filing for tax identification numbers, you will want to register the name of your company in the state where it is located. This helps ensure that no one else uses the same name for a similar business. Most states provide information through a state corporation commission, which also registers the companies.

One other government registration is typically required—a local business license. The main purpose for this is to raise revenues for the community where your firm conducts business. Businesses are taxed on their revenues or their expected revenues. Some communities also levy a tax on businesses that occupy space, whether or not they own the space.

Determine Employee Benefits

If you have employees, a benefits package will be required to keep them on staff for any length of time. In addition to holiday and vacation leave policies, a new firm will need to provide some form of health insurance, even on a cost-shared basis. While most health insurance providers will insure individuals directly, they insist that small businesses work through an insurance broker. Check your local chamber of commerce for a list of brokers in your area.

As a business owner, you will probably want to retire at some point, and that means you need a retirement plan. The options are numerous and include SEPs (Simplified Employee Pensions), IRAs (Individual Retirement Accounts), 401(k)s, and defined benefit plans. But if you have employees, there are rules governing how much you must provide for their retirements under certain circumstances if you also provide for your own. Again, an insurance broker or other financial adviser can help you select the best retirement plans for your firm.

Select Financial Systems

Numerous off-the-shelf programs available for small businesses would be suitable for a fledgling architecture firm. Even if an outside accountant is hired to keep your books in order, some familiarity with an industry-specific accounting software program is needed because information must be entered into the program before it is given to the accountant. Many start-up entrepreneurs find that the first employee they really need is one who can provide administrative support such as bookkeeping.

▶ For further information on business financial matters, see Financial Planning (5.1) and Financial Management Systems (5.2).

Develop a Marketing Strategy

Developing an effective marketing strategy is one of the most important activities for a new firm. One way to start marketing is to send a simple letter to prospective clients, previous clients, consultants you have worked with in the past, local business groups, friends, relatives, and just about anyone who might provide a lead. This letter lets people know you are starting a firm and helps establish your identity.

Develop lists of potential clients by checking business directories and company annual reports at your local library. Contact information for associations is arranged by subject, and if you plan to specialize in specific areas, check the reference books for organizations with members who build facilities that match your firm's expertise. Go through publications your potential clients are likely to read, and look for leads. Talk with representatives of specific government agencies and ask about building programs coming up in the near future.

Like image, marketing "happens" with everyday activities as well as those geared toward particular clients. Give a speech, offer a service to a community group, write an article, serve on community organizations, or offer story ideas to the press. The point is to get the name of your firm recognized and to build its image.

▶ Marketing Strategy and Planning (4.5) provides guidance on developing and implementing marketing plans.

Start drafting a marketing strategy after you have pinned down a few points about the firm, including where you want it to go, what are its likely strengths and weaknesses, and what types of projects it will take on. A good marketing plan is clear, to the point, and measurable. The plan can target the steps you want to take to reach a particular market, including the number of calls you will make each day, the meetings you will hold, and the proposals you will submit.

Marketing goals should rely on marketing data—which you can either develop, find in local publications, garner from business publications, or pay a consultant to provide. Avoid committing to a tough marketing challenge unless you have data that prove a need for your services in that market. Statistics show the typical design firm commonly wins only one out of every ten jobs it goes after, so be sure to include the funds and time to go after these jobs in your business planning.

Get the Word Out

Publicity is important to a new firm. Let the world know you've launched your business. Send out announcements. Hold an open house. Contact potential clients and invite them to your office for a lunch meeting to introduce your firm and its credentials. Contact your competitors and turn them into collaborators. All of your marketing efforts should be based on your business plan.

New companies are not likely to be readily recognized, so image alone will not be enough to bring in work. However, when combined with the firm's marketing efforts, the reputation of the principal or other employees and their ability to develop and maintain relationships should help the firm achieve success.

The image you create for your firm should be closely aligned with the vision you have for it. Without consistency between image and vision, it will be difficult to lead your organization to success. The name of the firm, the letterhead and business cards, and the office and location should all reflect your vision. Create an image that is realistic and attainable in the short term, and as the firm grows, its image will grow also.

OPEN FOR BUSINESS

Armed with knowledge about the details of running a business, the new entrepreneur will be ready to focus on architecture. Once start-up capital and business licenses have been obtained, staffing issues addressed, location decisions initialized, and partnership arrangements made, it is time to pursue the dream of creating your kind of architecture in your own space. It is time to start!

For More Information

Architect's Essentials of Starting, Assessing, and Transitioning a Design Firm (Wiley, 2008) by Peter Piven and Bradford Perkins provides specific advice for architects about to launch a start-up design firm. The *Small Business Start-Up Guide* (Information International, 2000) by Robert Sullivan offers practical advice and how-to information for starting businesses of all types.

The Small Business Administration (SBA) provides publications and sometimes offers financial assistance through loans and grants to new firms. The SBA also conducts the SCORE program, which sets up mentoring meetings for new entrepreneurs with experienced business-people. Local colleges offer libraries as well as business departments with many resources for new small businesses, and some include incubator space for students and alumni who start up new endeavors. Software programs for developing business plans can be found on the Internet.

The AIA has business, industry, and technical advice for small firms, and offers training and education through meetings, publications, and other media. (www.aia.org)

WHY DO SOME FIRMS FAIL?

For every new architecture business that succeeds, three others close their doors. They have failed to achieve what they set out to do. Some common threads observed among start-up firms that fail include the following:

- Not paying enough attention to managing growth, finances, and attitudes at a level that can be sustained during a downturn in the building cycle. This is particularly a problem for young firms that are too successful too early.
- Failing to keep abreast of the trends and demands for specific services, thus failing to develop expertise to respond to changing markets.
- Losing key staff due to personality clashes, lack of professional respect, or inadequate training and development.
- Not holding back the reins on spending. A new firm must reinvest in itself on a continual basis, which might mean low salaries, heavy workloads, and less-than-glamorous offices.
- Focusing only on the task at hand, without a plan or strategy for the longer term. This is often the result of inexperienced management.

4.2 Firm Legal Structure

Philip R. Croessmann, AIA, Esq., and David F. Kinzer III, CPA

Regardless of their size and structure, architecture and engineering firms are organized and behave according to certain basic principles established in state and federal law.

An architecture firm may be established as a proprietorship, partnership, corporation, or limited liability company. Although there are important legal, financial, tax, and operational factors to consider when selecting a form of practice, certain legal requirements apply to all forms.

Philip R. Croessmann, an architect and attorney, is a member in the law firm of Westberg Croessmann, P.C., based in Arlington, Virginia. He has extensive experience in construction litigation and contract law and has authored many articles on these and related subjects.
David F. Kinzer III is a licensed CPA in Virginia performing accounting, tax, and consulting services in the Washington, D.C., metropolitan area. His work focuses primarily on the design, architecture, and construction industries.

SOLE PROPRIETORSHIPS

From a legal, compliance, and taxation standpoint, a sole proprietorship is the simplest form of practice. By definition, a *sole proprietor* is an individual conducting business in an unincorporated format. The sole proprietor makes no legal arrangements with other individuals, is not required to file state documents and federal tax forms to conduct the practice, and has full, personal control of the firm. Although a sole proprietorship may have employees, the individual and the unincorporated firm are legally one and the same.

Some of the simplicity inherent in this form of practice can be jeopardized if the proprietor fails to take special efforts to isolate the activities of the architecture practice from personal and unrelated business endeavors. In particular, keeping business and personal finances separate is part of an important management discipline that can contribute to the financial success of a practice. A sole proprietorship does not file a separate federal tax return; rather, relevant information is allocated and included with the proprietor's personal tax return. Preparation of this information for the IRS can be made much easier by keeping personal and business financial matters separate, although there is no legal requirement to do so. For example, the IRS regards business expenses differently—and more favorably—than personal expenses, permitting deductions for certain business expenses. Separate bookkeeping simplifies proper reporting of these expenses.

Two other factors should be considered when determining whether to establish a sole proprietorship: legal liability and the effect of death or retirement on the firm.

Liability. A sole proprietor's liability for professional errors and omissions and for business debts is unlimited. Both a professional liability claimant and a vendor of business services or products can reach all of the assets of the proprietor—except those that may be protected pursuant to state bankruptcy statutes. A professional liability insurance policy will protect the proprietor, to a certain extent, from losses associated with professional liability claims. Nonetheless, the proprietor remains fully liable for all adjudicated business claims.

Death or retirement. The death or retirement of the proprietor terminates the proprietorship. Unless a provision has been made for a successor to purchase the practice or assume the proprietor's projects, the only way to wrap up a sole proprietorship is through an appropriate estate and liquidation plan. Because there are advantages to placing certain assets in trust, such as avoiding probate, a proprietor could consider the use of a trust instrument in conjunction with an estate plan. To determine the best options, a proprietor should seek estate-planning counsel.

PARTNERSHIPS

A *partnership* is an unincorporated association of two or more persons or entities for the purpose of operating a business with the intention of making a profit. The partnership, however, is not a separate legal entity distinct from the partners, and general partnerships are not required to file state organizational documents or federal tax identification forms.

The Partnership Agreement

Partnerships are more complex than proprietorships. A partnership agreement should be in writing and should address issues such as the following:

- Financial (capital) contributions of the partners
- Responsibility and authority of the partners
- Fiduciary duties of the partners
- Liabilities of the partners
- Operation and management of the partnership

▶ Risk Management Strategies (5.4) assesses professional liability insurance as part of a firm's risk management strategy.

▶ Insurance Coverage (5.5) provides details about professional liability coverage for design errors and omissions.

- Distributions of profit and loss
- Transferability of interests
- Admission of new partners
- Resolution of disputes
- Dissolution of the partnership

Nearly all states have enacted some variation of a model statute called the Uniform Partnership Act. The act establishes certain legal requirements to govern relationships between the partners (unless the partners themselves have made other specific arrangements) and between the partnership and other parties.

Establishing a partnership with a specific written agreement is preferable, for several reasons, to relying on state statutes to supply the terms of agreement between partners. For example, partnership statutes presume that all partners share income and losses equally, and do not commonly recognize a partnership's intention to treat certain parties differently with respect to income, losses, or both. Also, the laws do not take into account that certain assets or efforts contributed by the partners should be treated differently if the partnership succeeds or fails. Furthermore, most state statutes do not recognize a partner's contribution of effort in excess of other partners' efforts as the equivalent of making a cash contribution. Thus, if a partnership fails, the state law will allocate the losses according to capital contributions and will ignore the contribution of services.

Partner Liability

Each partner has potential liability for all of the business and professional liability debts of the partnership jointly and severally. Therefore, in the event that a business vendor or a professional liability claimant enforces a judgment against the partnership, each partner's personal assets may be reached to satisfy the full amount of the claim.

What liabilities does an incoming partner assume or an outgoing partner retain? In most states, incoming partners become responsible only for partnership debts incurred after they became partners, except that the new partner's capital is subject to claims by prior claimants or debtors. Departing partners remain liable for all partnership debts incurred by the partnership while they were partners. This is because, technically, when a partner retires or terminates the relationship with a partnership, the partnership is dissolved and a new partnership composed of the remaining partners automatically comes into being. However, a partnership agreement can be drafted to overcome this result.

Another matter to consider before joining a partnership is whether the rules concerning death and disability are addressed to the incoming partner's satisfaction. Often a retiring or deceased partner may be entitled to compensation far beyond what the partnership can or should pay for the partner's contribution. Joining such an arrangement leaves a new partner at risk should the existing partners die or retire.

Architects considering becoming a partner in a firm should carefully weigh the amount of liability they will take on, particularly whether their capital contribution might soon be lost to existing creditors and claimants.

Requirements for Professional Registration

Many states require that all partners be registered architects in the state where the firm is located. Some states specify that a certain percentage of the partners must be registered architects if the firm is to be classified as an architecture partnership. If a partnership consists of practitioners of multiple disciplines, the registered partners must be identified with their respective disciplines—for example, "architects and engineers."

Architects engaged in general contracting—as developers, design-builders, or construction managers—may find it necessary to obtain a contractor's license in states where they intend to engage in construction.

Income Taxes

A partnership files a separate federal tax return (called an information return), but it does not pay federal income tax on profits. A schedule showing each partner's share of the profits or losses and other reportable tax information is filed with the partnership's tax return and is given to each partner. Partners must transfer the information to their individual income tax returns and pay taxes on their share of the partnership's profits, whether or not those profits are distributed. Requirements related to partnership taxes and tax returns vary by state and locality.

CORPORATIONS

Federal, state, and local income tax laws and regulations can be complex. They change frequently and are reinterpreted constantly, making it advisable to have a firm's accountant keep the owners apprised of changes that affect the practice. The table on pages 93–94 in this topic provides a summary of some provisions.

Corporations are separate legal entities that can conduct necessary business operations—including bringing suit and being sued—in their corporate name. Because corporations have "lives" of their own, they are perhaps the most complicated to establish and maintain. Articles of incorporation must be filed with the state to notify the public of the corporation's existence and some of its key characteristics. A federal tax number must also be obtained to identify the entity as a legal taxpayer. There are legal requirements for boards of directors, shareholder meetings, and a variety of other organizational issues. A corporation can be much more stable (in a legal sense) than a sole proprietorship or a partnership because its existence transcends the individuals who own and manage it.

Many states have separate statutes for general business and professional corporations. General business corporations may be formed for any legal purpose and are subject to the requirements of the state's general corporation laws. Every state allows the establishment of general business corporations, although some do not allow stockholders or employees to practice architecture through the general corporation.

Professional corporations, on the other hand, are established specifically to provide professional services and are subject to restrictions enumerated in the professional corporation statute. Professional corporations normally must be owned or at least controlled by professionals licensed to practice in the state. Moreover, the corporate entity usually does not protect individual stockholders or employees from professional liability. Professional corporations may be required to pay income taxes as general business corporations or may be subject to special tax considerations.

Practicing architecture in a corporate form is not permitted in a few states. Some states require architects who want to incorporate to do so as a professional corporation authorized and certified by the secretary of state. Most states permit practice through either a professional corporation or a general business corporation, but some states permit architects to choose either type of entity. The number of principals in the corporation who must be registered architects varies according to the state in which the corporation conducts its practice.

A corporation seeking to practice in a state other than the one in which it is incorporated must register as a foreign corporation in the other state to avoid jeopardizing certain legal rights, including the right to enforce legal claims for fees.

▶ Agreements with Owners (11.1) notes legal issues that partnerships and corporations should be mindful of when entering into project agreements (or any business agreement).

Ownership and Control

A position as shareholder does not necessarily mean an individual's compensation will be proportional to his or her ownership. Compensation in a corporation is based on an oral or written agreement between the corporation and an individual and may or may not be set in relation to the number of shares owned. Such legal differences also apply to management and control of the corporation. It is possible, although uncommon, for ownership of a corporation and its control and management to be in different hands. This is uncommon because most shareholders elect the board of directors, which then appoints the officers. Under most circumstances, the individual or group who owns the majority of shares is able to elect directors who will appoint the individual or group or its designees as officers.

Employees offered shares of a corporation should consider the answers to these questions:

- Is the cost of the shares justified by an increase in compensation?
- Will the value of shares increase over time?
- Will the employee's control over management of the firm increase?

If owning shares does not increase the compensation to which an architect is entitled, there may be no value in purchasing them. This is particularly true if the number of shares to be purchased is small compared with the holdings of others, in which case the new shareholder may have little or no say about the election of directors and appointment of officers. Further, if there is no market for the shares or no buy/sell agreement that will allow the shareholder to sell the stock, the shares may have only minor investment value.

Liabilities

In a corporation, unlike in a proprietorship or a partnership, the personal assets of shareholders cannot be reached to satisfy the corporation's bona fide business debts. If the corporation purchases services or goods in its own name and fails to pay for them, the vendor can look only to the assets of the corporation for payment, not to the assets of individual shareholders.

Professional liability is a different matter. In many states, an architect remains personally liable for his or her professional errors or omissions, even if they were committed while the architect was employed by a corporation. Some states hold the owners of the corporation jointly and severally liable for professional errors and omissions in the same way they would be if they were partners. In other states, practicing architecture as a corporation shields architects from personal liability for errors and omissions.

Because the laws governing the liability of architects practicing in a corporation vary significantly from state to state, professional liability insurance is an important way to manage these risks. Those considering the purchase of shares of a corporation will want to look into how the firm handles professional liability risks. Is the corporation adequately insured against professional errors and omissions? What do the relevant state statutes say about the liability of the new shareholder for such errors and omissions?

Changes in Ownership

As in partnerships, a shareholder who retires or dies may have rights to compensation granted through his or her employment agreement. To determine whether a corporation will be viable into the future, those deciding whether to buy shares should first understand the potential liability the corporation will have to departing shareholders. Similarly, provisions for incoming shareholders' ultimate retirement or termination should be drafted in a way that fairly compensates the existing shareholders for the efforts they have made during their tenure.

Ownership transition in a corporation is, in many respects, easier than in a partnership. Shares of more than one type and variety may be bought and sold under a large number of circumstances to facilitate an orderly ownership transition and to provide severance pay to retiring shareholders.

The usual method for compensating departing shareholders is commonly known as a buy/sell agreement. These agreements require departing shareholders to sell their shares back to the corporation or its shareholders to keep the shares in the "family" of shareholders. This arrangement may be mandated by a state registration statute that requires all shareholders to be licensed architects. An effective buy/sell agreement establishes a purchase price and method of sale for the departing shareholder's shares and may also determine the price to be paid by incoming shareholders. Because such devices affect the long-term viability of a corporation, a prospective shareholder (or his or her counsel) should carefully review the buy/sell agreement to determine the corporation's prospects for viability after the other shareholders depart.

Income Taxes

Unless an "S election" is made under federal tax law, a corporation is a separate taxable entity. Individual shareholders who are employees of the corporation are taxed on their salaries. The corporation itself reports as gross income the professional fees received and deducts salaries and other business expenses. Any amount remaining is taxable at

Architects who plan to establish a corporate form of practice should seek legal counsel and accounting advice to ensure they understand the tax ramifications and conditions of practice in the states where they plan to practice.

the corporate tax rate. The corporation has several options for using the remainder in a way that will make its distribution tax deductible. For example, the earnings may be used to pay bonuses, make contributions to a qualified profit-sharing or pension plan, or, under recent federal tax provisions, be distributed to shareholders as dividends. Under certain circumstances, if earnings are not distributed to shareholders, an accumulated earnings tax may be imposed on the corporation.

COMPARATIVE LEGAL ATTRIBUTES OF LEGAL STRUCTURES

Legal Attribute	Sole Proprietorship	Partnership	S Corporation	Regular Corporation	Limited Liability Company
Liability	Individually liable for all liabilities of business	General partners individually liable for partnership's liabilities; limited partner liable only up to amount of his/her capital contribution	Same as regular corporation	Shareholder's liability in most cases is limited to capital contribution	Shareholder's liability in most cases is limited to capital contribution
Qualified owners	Single individual owner	No limitations; however, need at least two partners (including general partner)	Only individuals, estates, and certain trusts may be shareholders (limited to 75 shareholders)	No limitation	No limitation except for professional LLCs, for which members must conform to the applicable licensing requirement
Type of ownership interests	Individual ownership	More than one class of partner permitted	Only one class of stock permitted	More than one class of stock permitted	One class of member
Transfer of ownership	Assets of business transferable rather than business itself	New partnership may be created; consent of other partners normally required if partnership interest is to be transferred	Shares can only be transferred to individuals, certain types of trusts, or estates; no consent to Subchapter S election is needed; restrictions may be imposed by shareholder agreement	Ready transfer of ownership through the use of stock certificates; restrictions may be imposed by shareholder's agreement	A new limited liability company may be created; consent of other members normally required if partnership interest is to be transferred
Raising capital	Capital raised only by loan or increased contribution by the proprietor	Loans or contributions from partners	Loans or contributions from shareholders; "straight debt" avoids second class of stock	Met by sale of stocks or bonds or other corporate debt	Loans or contributions from members
Business action and management	Sole proprietor makes decisions and can act immediately; proprietor responsible and receives all profits or losses	Action usually depends on unanimous agreement of partners or, at least, general partners. Limited partner actively participating in management may lose limited liability	Same as regular corporation except unanimous consent is required to elect S status; more than 50% of shareholders needed to revoke Subchapter S status	Unity of action based on authority of board of directors	Managed by professional managers or the members
Flexibility	No restrictions	Partnership is contractual agreement, within which members can conduct business subject to the partnership agreement and applicable state laws	Same as regular corporation	Corporation is a legal entity created by the state, functioning within powers granted explicitly or implicitly and subject to judicial construction and decision	Great flexibility is given in management and ownership

COMPARATIVE TAX ATTRIBUTES OF LEGAL STRUCTURES

Tax Attribute	Sole Proprietorship	Partnership	S Corporation	Regular Corporation	Limited Liability Company
Taxable year	Usually calendar year	Generally a calendar year is required, unless §444 or a business purpose test is met	Generally a calendar year is required, unless §444 or a business purpose test is met	Any type of year available; however, personal service corporation has restrictions	Generally a calendar year is required, unless §444 or a business purpose test is met
Ordinary distributions to owners	Drawings from the business are not taxable; net profits are taxable and proprietor is subject to tax on self-employment income	Generally not taxable, but distribution in excess of basis is taxable as capital gain	Payment of salaries deductible by corporation and taxable to recipient; distributions generally not taxable; however, certain distributions can be taxable as dividends; distributions in excess of basis = capital gains	Payments of salaries are deductible by corporation and taxable to recipient; payments of dividends are not deductible by corporation and generally are taxable to recipient shareholders	Generally, not taxable, but distribution in excess of basis is taxable as capital gain
Limitation on losses deductible by owners	Subject to at-risk, hobby loss, and passive activity loss rules.	Subject to basis limitation; partner's investment, plus his or her share of partnership liabilities; at-risk and passive activity loss rules may apply	Subject to shareholder's basis, including loans to the corporation; at-risk and passive activity loss rules may apply	No losses allowed to individual except upon sale of stock or liquidation of corporation. Corporate carryback and carryover rules may apply. Closely held corporations limited by at-risk and modified passive activity rules	Deductible by owners subject to basis limitation; partner's investment, plus his or her share of partnership liabilities; at-risk and passive activity loss rules may apply
Dividends received	Fully taxable	Conduit—fully taxable	Same as partnership	100% dividend-received deduction	Conduit—fully taxable
Former election required to obtain tax status	No	No	Yes	No	Yes
Capital gain	Taxed at individual level	Conduit—taxed at individual level	Conduit—taxed at shareholder level; possible corporate built-in gains tax	Taxed at corporate level	Conduit—taxed at individual level
Capital losses	Carried forward indefinitely; limited to $3,000 per year	Conduit—carried forward indefinitely at partner level; limited to $3,000 per year	Same as partnership	Carry back three years and carryover five years as short-term capital loss offsetting only capital gains	Conduit carried forward indefinitely at partner level; limited to $3,000 per year
Section 1231 gains and losses	Taxed at individual level—combined with other §1231 gains or losses of individual; net gains are capital gains for individual; net losses are ordinary losses for individual	Conduit	Conduit; possible corporate built-in gains tax	Taxable or deductible at the corporate level	Conduit
Basis for allocating income to owners	All income is reported on owner's return	Profit and loss agreement may have "special allowances" of income and deductions if they have substantial economic effect	Pro rata portion of income based on per share, per day allocation	No income allocated to shareholders	Profit and loss agreement may have "special allowances" of income and deductions if they have substantial economic effect

(continued)

Tax Attribute	Sole Proprietorship	Partnership	S Corporation	Regular Corporation	Limited Liability Company
Basis for allocating a net operating loss	All losses flow through to owner's return	Profit and loss agreement may have "special allocation" of income and deductions if they have substantial economic effect	Pro rata portion of income based on per share, per day allocation	No losses allocated to stockholders	Profit and loss agreement may have "special allowances" of income and deductions if they have substantial economic effect
Group hospitalization and life insurance premiums and medical reimbursement plans	100% of self-employed person's health insurance premiums may be deducted from gross income	Cost of partners' benefits generally treated as compensation, deductible by the partnership and includable in the partner's income; 100% self-employment health insurance premiums available as a deduction	Cost of benefits to more than 2% of shareholders treated as compensation, deductible by the corporation and included in shareholders' income; 100% of self-employed health insurance premiums available as a deduction	Cost of shareholder-employee coverage generally deductible as a business expense if plan is "for the benefit of employees"; normally excluded from employee's income	Cost of partners' benefits generally treated as compensation, deductible by the company and includable in partners' income; 100% self-employment health insurance premiums available as a deduction
Retirement benefits	Limitations and restrictions basically same as regular corporations	Limitations and restrictions basically same as regular corporations	Limitations and restrictions basically same as regular corporations	Limitations on benefits from defined benefit plans and from defined contribution plans; special restrictions for top-heavy plans; 401(k) limitation began in 1992	Limitations and restrictions basically same as regular corporations
Organization costs	Not applicable	Amortizable over 60 months	Amortizable over 60 months	Amortizable over 60 months	Amortizable over 60 months
Charitable contributions	Subject to limits for individuals; gifts for use of private foundations, 20% of AGI; gifts to public charity, cash, 50% of AGI; appreciated property, 30% of AGI; other limitations for specific items contributed	Conduit	Conduit	Limited to 10% of taxable income before special deductions	Conduit
Tax preferences (Alternative Minimum Tax)	Graduated from 26% of the first $175,000 of AMTI, 28% of anything over that; applied to minimum taxable income, including tax preferences in excess of $20,000 ($40,000 for joint returns); payable to extent exceeds regular tax	Conduit	Conduit	Taxed at corporate level; 20% on preferences and adjustments in excess of $40,000 or regular tax liability, whichever is greater (does not apply to corp. with < 7,500K gross revenue averaged over 3 years)	Conduit
Character of income and deductions	Taxed at individual level; limitation on investment interest deductions	Conduit	Conduit	Taxed at corporate level	Conduit
Self-employment tax	Half of SE tax paid deductible from gross income	Same as proprietorship	Not applicable	Not applicable	Same as proprietorship

Subchapter S Corporations

A corporation may elect to be treated as an S corporation for federal income tax purposes if it meets certain technical requirements. The shareholders of an S corporation are treated similarly to the partners of a partnership for tax purposes. That is, the shareholders of an S corporation are taxed on their pro rata share of the corporation's income, regardless of whether it is distributed. The S corporation itself, however, is subject to income tax only in special circumstances. Architects who establish an S corporation can avoid or mitigate the double tax that may be imposed on portions of corporate income, or they can take advantage of more favorable tax rates.

TAX CONSIDERATIONS

As suggested so far, the various forms of legal organization are subject to different federal and state income tax methods. Additional income tax considerations follow.

Tax Rates

Under current law, federal income tax rates imposed on individuals are usually lower than the 35 percent corporate income tax rate imposed on architecture and other personal service corporations. As a result, many architecture corporations choose to file for chapter S status.

Tax Year

Sole proprietorships, partnerships, and corporations are generally required to use a calendar taxable year (i.e., January 1 through December 31) unless they can establish sufficient business reasons to adopt a fiscal year. A corporation engaged in architecture or other personal services, whether organized as a professional corporation or a regular business corporation, should consult an accountant to confirm that it is entitled to use a fiscal year for tax planning purposes.

Domestic Production Deduction

A deduction is provided for engineering and architecture firms that perform services in the United States for U.S. construction projects. The deduction is the lowest of the following calculations:

- 6 percent of the gross Domestic Production Activities Deduction (calculated by taking the domestic production gross receipts and subtracting the following from them—the cost of goods sold allocable to those receipts, directly allocable deductions, and the ratable portion of other deductions)
- 6 percent of the firm's taxable income before the Domestic Production Activities Deduction is taken
- 50 percent of W-2 wages

The percentage for the first two calculations was increased from 3 percent in 2005 and 2006 to 6 percent for tax years 2007, 2008, and 2009 and 9 percent thereafter. Architects should consult their tax advisers to discuss a firm's eligibility for the Domestic Production Activities Deduction and to determine its calculation.

Accounting Method

An architecture firm organized as a sole proprietorship, partnership, or S corporation is entitled to compute its taxable income under the cash method of accounting. Under this method, fees are reported as income only when actually received and not when billed. Similarly, expenses are deductible only when actually paid, not in the year in which they accrue. An architecture firm organized as a corporation that has not made an S election may use the cash method only if its gross receipts do not exceed certain amounts and if certain other requirements of the Internal Revenue Code are met.

Pension and Profit-Sharing Plans

Regardless of their form of legal organization, architecture firms may establish pension and profit-sharing plans. If these plans satisfy the requirements of the Internal Revenue Code, contributions to the plans (up to certain limits) are deductible by the plan's sponsor. Corporations are entitled to a deduction for such contributions, as are the partners or the proprietor in partnerships and sole proprietorships. Withdrawals made before the individual participant reaches the age of fifty-nine years and six months may be subject to a penalty.

Substantial differences no longer exist between qualified retirement plans that may be established by corporations and those established by partnerships and proprietorships. Corporations do, however, have some advantages over other forms of organization with respect to certain fringe benefits, such as group term life insurance and medical payment plans (which may be offered on a more favorable tax basis).

Other Taxes

Many states and some cities impose their own income taxes and professional services or gross receipts taxes. Other federal taxes that may affect individual architects and architecture firms include employer and employee Social Security taxes (and the comparable self-employment tax in the case of partnerships and sole proprietorships) and the unemployment tax on compensation paid to employees.

LIMITED LIABILITY COMPANIES

Limited liability companies (LLCs) are complex hybrids of corporations and partnerships. They are separate entities under state law that can conduct business in their own name, and they have many of the characteristics of a corporation. They are, however, classified as partnerships for federal tax purposes. This distinction makes them suitable as investment vehicles and as a business structure for individuals who wish to pass losses through to their personal income while still limiting their liability.

The use of LLCs for architecture practice varies among states. States either permit architecture firms to use general LLCs without any restrictions, prohibit the use of general LLCs for the practice of architecture, or have statutes creating professional LLCs.

Ownership and Control

Under the organizing statutes, the owners of an LLC are called *members*. LLCs do not have to be managed by the members of the company. State statutes generally provide that an LLC may be managed by professional managers, who are afforded limited liability for their acts on behalf of the company yet do not have to be members of it. On the other hand, an LLC that is managed directly by its members or any group of members can provide significant management and ownership flexibility, and can offer creative opportunities for attracting capital. A detailed operating agreement should be developed to tailor management to the needs of the company. Operating agreements, like corporate bylaws and partnership agreements, grant authority to managers and members and establish how the organization will conduct its business.

Liabilities

Like a corporation, the members of an LLC have limited personal liability. In many states, however, architects remain liable for their professional errors or omissions, even if they were committed while the architect was an employee of the company. While laws regarding architect liability vary among the states, design professionals generally cannot avoid professional liability through the use of an LLC.

Changes in Ownership

Like ownership of a corporation, memberships in an LLC may be transferred with the permission of other members. Although many states have limitations on the transferability of membership, the authority to transfer memberships can be specified in the operating agreement. When specifically permitted, a membership may be transferred without terminating the LLC and creating a new company. In addition to including provisions for transfer of membership in the operating agreement, members should enter into buy/sell agreements that will establish a purchase price and methods of sale.

Income Taxes

As previously mentioned, LLCs are generally treated as partnerships under tax laws. However, due to a recent federal statute concerning LLCs, architects should consult with a tax adviser to ensure an LLC meets the requirements for treatment as a partnership for tax purposes in the jurisdiction where they practice.

4.3 Firm Identity and Expertise

Jack Reigle

Clients in all markets seek value from their architects. A firm's distinctive expertise should match what its ideal clients value most.

When all is said and done, the rewards of the architecture profession accrue to value-producing experts. Rather than defining value in the traditional way—as low cost—a deeper look reveals that value is, of course, in the eye of the beholder. Some clients value Sir Norman Foster, while others value the firm that can get things done in town. Some value BSW International and its talent for rollouts, while others value Heery International for its program management expertise.

Large or small, experts build value. In fact, they are the only ones who build sustainable value rather than take advantage of lucky breaks. Just being a responsive and flexible firm that provides service can be a passive approach. Instead, think of your firm in terms of its leadership, mastery, innovation, and contribution.

The new world we function in, marked by global choice, is the era of the expert. So the only important questions are "In what field will a firm build its expertise?" and "How will the firm lead its market?"

The highest responsibility of firm principals is to answer these questions. The answers bring rewards—a successful practice, with good clients, good projects, good people, and a good level of compensation. The answers can evolve for a while, but at some point a commitment to a clear, well-crafted identity, a consciously conceived

Jack Reigle is president of SPARKS: The Center for Strategic Planning, located in Alexandria, Virginia, and Palm Beach Gardens, Florida. The firm counsels architects on company growth and transition strategies. The original version of this topic in the thirteenth edition of the Handbook was written by Ellen Flynn-Heapes, founder of SPARKS.

business design, and a profit model that works must be made. Then you can rivet your attention on making the firm the best it can be.

Like a visit to the doctor, thinking about company design begins with this question: "Where does it hurt?" The answers are where the leaders of an architecture firm can find both ideas and energy for forward motion, but to keep a company focused and to become a recognized expert takes a steadfast commitment.

What frustrates people in the design professions most? The top headaches are competing on price, trying to meet unreasonable client expectations for schedules and budgets, not making the profit deserved, not being able to hire and keep talented people, not having leadership, and handling leadership and ownership transitions. Most of this pain stems directly from poor business design. In their planning, many firms still default to hackneyed mission statements and vague wishes to be "the premier firm in (fill in the blank), providing excellence in service and quality, and meeting or exceeding client expectations." In other words, company leaders plod along as nice people doing good work but do not stand for something special in which the firm can excel.

How can firms begin to design their businesses well, not just tweak their efficiencies or, worse, just go along blindly? Using a comprehensive strategy-mapping tool to develop a framework for analyzing the options can help architecture firm leaders make business design decisions. The result is a detailed road map of the major choices available to a firm—a tool to help principals decide the best direction for the firm, choose the right investments, and build for the future.

POSSIBLE BUSINESS MODELS TO CHOOSE FROM

At its core, the development framework is designed to help firms choose to be great. It offers a way to respond to a simple concept: The firm must become masterful at something—a building type, a client type, a locale, a process. Only then is the firm in a position to create true value for its clients.

To categorize different styles of expertise, which can meet specific client needs, the personality structures of Swiss psychologist Carl Jung's six heroic archetypes have been adapted to correspond to six archetypes for the design professions:

- Innovators
- Project-type specialists
- Full-service client partners
- Community contributors
- Project management experts
- Cost and quality leaders

Virtually every firm, even those that adhere to a single business with great fervor, at times diverges from the area of expertise it has chosen. Such alterations in course may stem from market shifts, the need to experiment, or requests from long-time friends or associates.

It is important to note that these archetypes appear to be universally applicable to the work of design firms. Although there may be hybrids or crossovers and different nomenclature may be used to identify them, these six cover what design professionals commonly accept as options when discussing the design of their firms.

Each archetype has a personality. When you become familiar with the archetypes, you can say, "An innovator would never do *this*," or "Of course they did *that*— we hired them because they're great at PM." In fact, each archetype is a full portrait that includes the underlying driving forces and core values that constitute its identity, a set of best practices that serve as its operating model, and a model for optimizing profit.

See if you can find your firm among the following models. Is it steadfastly seated in one? Is it a well-designed hybrid of two? Or is it straddling the fence—a little of this, a little of that? Too many firms morph from one model to another to "get the next job." How does that hurt the firm's position in the marketplace? When all is said and done, what is the firm *known* for?

Innovators

These firms generate original ideas and new technologies. In architecture, they are the high-profile design firms with original styles or philosophies. In engineering, they're the Ph.D.-owned firms with a strong commitment to research and development. This type of firm often receives research grants or endowments, and its staff members love to experiment as well as to teach and publish. Pritzker Prize–winner Renzo Piano even hosts an online design workshop. (www.rpwf.org)

Norman Foster, Frank Gehry, Michel Virlogeux, Santiago Calatrava, and I. M. Pei all fulfill the innovator definition. They are known for a distinctive set of original ideas, which they can apply across building types and around the world. Their philosophy, however, is singularly focused.

Project-Type Specialists

These experts are specialists, dedicated to a specific type of project or service within a broader market. They watch the experiments of the innovators and adapt them to create state-of-the-art work. They frequently team with a network of other firms to provide full services for a given project and are often national or international in scope.

HOK Sport fits into this category. The firm, which focuses with great success on sports facilities, benefits from its unique reputation relative to its parent company, HOK. At the same time, it benefits from having a separate, descriptive name; a separate location; and separate management.

Other examples of project-type specialists include Duany Plater-Zyberk, a firm with a service niche that focuses on "new urbanism" master planning. Andres Duany and Elizabeth Plater-Zyberk have built a marketplace powerhouse, commanding some of the highest fees in the profession. Beyer Blinder Bell distinguishes itself through its work in historic preservation, the Croxton Collaborative in sustainable design, and Allan Greenberg in neoclassical architecture. The niches of some firms center on an ethnic background, such as Douglas Cardinal, of American Indian descent.

Innovators and project-type experts differ from the other archetypes in that such firms typically invest less effort in cultivating traditional, long-term client relationships.

Full-Service Client Partners

This firm leads in one or a few major markets, such as health care, higher education, the food and beverage industry, or airports. One of the first firms practicing as market partners was Einhorn Yaffee Prescott. When they formed the firm, the principals targeted three markets—academic, corporate, and government—and created an organization around them. M+W Zander is committed to the technology and research-and-development markets. Wimberly Allison Tong & Goo is renowned for its hotel and resort designs. Fanning Howey competes nationally for—and wins— school projects.

Client partners are strong advocates for their clients and their clients' industries, often leading lobbying efforts and crusading at client trade meetings. They share goals and values with their clients, creating a base of personal friendships. They typically serve multiple segments within their industry and benefit from offering a broad range of services to support their chosen market, and to keep their clients coming back for more.

Client partners characteristically incorporate former client-side staff members into the firm. Many firms keyed to federal markets have former employees of the targeted agencies in high-level marketing and project management positions. Many well-known individuals from the transportation and education markets have joined partner firms committed to those markets. Recruiting such seasoned veterans represents a real commitment to the market of choice on the part of the architecture firm.

Community Contributors

These firms aim for a leadership role in their geographic area. They set deep roots in the community, developing close relationships on both social and political levels. They seek premier local project work that ranges across the board in size and type, including public buildings, police and fire stations, recreation centers, schools, shelters, public works, and other municipal facilities. For projects requiring significant technical knowledge, they team with a network of project-type specialists around the country.

Many design professionals begin with a small, local practice. The difference between being a high-performing community firm and an underperforming generalist is the relationship of the firm, particularly its principals, to community organizations and individuals. Community knowledge firms are so woven into the fabric of the community that they open doors that are closed to outsiders. They can expedite decision making by virtue of their professional and personal relationships in the community.

One of the best examples of a community knowledge firm is Carde Ten Architects in Santa Monica, California. Focused on community projects, the firm scouts for funding, arranges real estate opportunities, and organizes the entire project for the potential client. This package of services takes the firm out of the realm of competition and fee-for-time relationships. Besides a healthy design fee, the firm receives part of the development and construction management fees.

Community firms invest heavily in their local networks. Friedl Bohm, president of NBBJ, established his infrastructure in Columbus, Ohio, with the Young Presidents Organization (YPO), local board involvement, and ownership of a successful chain of local restaurants. Harvey Gantt served as mayor of Charlotte, North Carolina, again illustrating a depth of commitment to the community.

Project Management Experts

PM-driven firms focus on outstanding project management, bringing their skills to bear on large, complex projects, including the best design-build jobs. Emphasis is on speed, coordination, and control. Many of these firms are known for their excellent internal management systems and construction management expertise.

Bechtel, Fluor-Daniel, and other large engineer-contractors are classic PM delivery firms. Leading program managers such as Heery International, 3D/International, and CRS Constructors also fall under this classification.

Askew Nixon Ferguson Architects (ANFA) is an example of a smaller organization operating as a PM firm. Early in its history, ANFA started out working for Federal Express, by definition a speed- and logistics-oriented client. ANFA developed a culture to match, full of high-energy people concerned with project management. Today, it still works for FedEx but has added casinos, another fast-paced project type, to its expertise.

Cost and Quality Experts

These firms have the real cost advantage, focusing on prototypes, site adaptations, and multisite project rollouts for retail stores, health maintenance organizations, branch banks, service stations, and large government office projects.

Volume rollouts, a fast and inexpensive way for client organizations to expand into multiple geographic markets, save the costs of individually developed and designed units. Tulsa-based BSW International is a leader here, specializing in multiple-facility building programs for clients such as Wal-Mart, Circuit City, and Marriott. BSW is unabashedly dedicated to improving its clients' financial success, and even casts itself as a real estate development services company that offers program management, real estate, and site development services as well as design and construction. BSW has been featured in the *Wall Street Journal*, *BusinessWeek*, and *Fortune*, not only as a thriving design firm but as a leader among American service firms.

Cost and quality experts have successfully adopted numerous management techniques from the corporate world, unlike other firms in the profession that view speed and cost leadership as unprofessional. Because they are such an integral part of their clients' financial success, these firms must move very quickly. A firm committed to besting time and money challenges needs a serious program that ensures quality—just like their clients have.

▶ Maintaining Design Quality (9.5) addresses managing and controlling quality.

FOCUSING A FIRM

The typology outlined above is based on several major principles. Each of the six archetypes has a bold, clear identity (reflected in its name) that is driven by internal goals and values and matched to complementary client groups. Each has a cohesive, integrated business design—a scaffold of best practices that support its operating model. Although not discussed here, it is worth noting that each of the six archetypes also has a specific profit model that optimizes its financial performance.

Setting company direction begins with the consideration of identity. This is especially true for organizations in the knowledge industry, with no tangible product until after the fact. Can you answer the following questions about your firm?

- What are its most deeply held values?
- What are its driving forces?
- How is it distinctive?
- How is it expert?
- What is its greatest value to the client?
- What does it hope to accomplish in the next 10 to 20 years?

Uncovering and articulating the unique ingredients that make up the essence of an organization is not easy. It is particularly difficult for architects, who in school are trained to have a broader view—virtue lies in the ability to design anything, rather than developing a focused expertise. Doctors, by contrast, are trained with the explicit expectation that they will later choose to focus on a general practice or on a specialty.

Certainly, some firms create wealth in other ways but, like King Midas, if you haven't got your values and purpose right first, you can run into trouble. According to the late management guru Peter Drucker, defining your purpose is especially critical. Since the best and most dedicated people work with passion when they find a purpose that matches their beliefs and interests, they have many lucrative opportunities from which to choose. They have multiple job offers and pick a firm because it is doing something they consider important. In order to attract, motivate, and retain outstanding people, companies need to have a clear understanding of their own identities. This is also true for attracting the best clients.

"Tell us about your firm" is a directive that frequently meets with the following replies: "We were established in 1909/1949/1979. We have 30/300/3,000 people and 3/7/15 offices. We offer these services (laundry list), and work in a wide variety of project types (another laundry list)." Next in the formula is a discussion of their great service and quality. Instead, clients want a firm that can succinctly distinguish itself. For example, a representative from SmithKline said recently, "Please tell us how you're different. We want to hire you. But we can't if you won't tell us how you're the best. Give us real reasons! Give us meat!"

"Understand my problems and deliver to my needs efficiently," project owners tell architects over and over again. In client interviews carried out for design firms, 96 percent of the respondents want the experts, the firms that know what they're doing. Many of the larger firms know that cross-selling services is tough; clients today do not want a firm with experience in a wide variety of project types. They only want to hear about how you relate to their problem. And they don't care about one-stop shopping unless the package gets their current job done most efficiently.

Identifying a Firm's Driving Force

Although many firms operate expediently and reactively, most have a favorite place where they operate—or at least aspire to. They have an array of values, but a single, special one reigns supreme. The firm's supreme business value is called its driving force, and a firm that can capture it is on the way to building the right business model.

For example, the driving force of project management firms is a love of logistics, the chess game. Project management, they believe, is the greatest challenge in the world and the most worthwhile endeavor of all. Professionals in such a firm consider themselves an "elite cadre"—a SWAT team. The business design of such a firm would reveal a very well-organized and planned firm, corporate in feel. Its top staff consists of the best project managers. They have formal training curricula, and they make their highest profit on the most complex projects. All staff members understand what is really important to the firm's success.

Specific driving forces characterize each of the business model archetypes. These are shared gut-level beliefs about what is most essential for firm members to accomplish together. More than any cultural value, such as integrity, collaboration, or "fun," agreement on these driving forces influences the success of a firm. Conflicts on this pivotal point can destroy a firm.

When a firm probes for the deepest elements of identity, fearful protests are often encountered: "We have to be flexible!" "We can't survive without having all these abilities!" "We have to keep looking for new opportunities!"

Flexibility, openness, and responsiveness to clients are always required. But reactivity at a firm's core shows that it has lost its way. Every firm needs a solid baseline of quality, efficiency, creativity, flexibility, openness, and client service in its work. The key is to keep an eye on where the real distinctive value of the firm is and build on this strength. The essential question is not how can a firm respond well but how can it lead well.

Driving forces tend to be discovered rather than invented. Through exercises and models, firms can learn what has been driving them to date. Most likely a hidden structure can be ferreted out that either facilitates or presents obstacles to the full expression of the driver. If you can discover these structures, you can discover the driving forces that have been surreptitiously operating. Then you can work with them.

Rather than seeking simple discovery and refinement, some firms go beyond this to revolutionize things with a brand-new driving force. Sienna Architecture, a midsize firm in Portland, Oregon, is a good example. Over the course of several years, through a well-designed strategic planning process, the firm's owners successfully moved from being a cost/quality-driven firm to being a cutting-edge design leader in the Pacific Northwest.

Once a firm has uncovered its driving force, firm leaders can foster certain values and weed out others, using care and patience. Fine-tune your entire business model, including staffing, marketing, project systems, and perhaps the ownership structure. Once this model is in focus and consensus has been built, you cannot help but bring the more powerful vision to reality. It becomes so clear.

Relating a Firm's Driving Force to Its Client's Hidden Agenda

The beauty of an identity is that it acts like a magnet to attract clients seeking a firm's kind of expertise. In other words, certain client types have typical agendas for which they need certain kinds of firms. Rarely do clients go outside their unspoken agendas, and if they do, they tend not to recognize value.

It is tricky to determine what clients view as most valuable; in fact, some don't consciously know themselves. Sure, they want and need everything it takes to do their project, but certain aspects will be more critical than others. Needless to say, it is wise to spend time on this question and get real answers. Go beyond what the client tells you first. Push beyond the shorthand clichés: "Be faster, be cheaper, and give us good service." Find out whether these are the most important needs or if they are just the outside layer of the onion. Make your firm the ultimate expert in whatever your chosen clients value most—and you find most worthwhile to provide. The accompanying table shows the essential links between driver and typical hidden agenda, by archetype.

A Firm's Driving Force Defines Its Methods

Very specific methodologies characterize each of the archetypes. These are the true centers of excellence for which the firm is valued in the marketplace. They are links on the overall project value chain, but it is a rare customer that considers them all equally valuable. Ask yourself whether you are so busy getting the work in and out that you neglect to nurture the more difficult and risky work that makes you special. When a firm's driving force is clear and its leaders understand what is most valuable to its clients, then its core or "sacred" methods also become clear.

Firm identity (not corporate identity as an advertising statement) is nothing less than the wellspring of value creation. Determining what the firm is—and what it is not—is worth very serious consideration indeed. The process requires experimentation, comparison, and, most of all, the courage to stand for something.

DESIGNING A FIRM

Curiously, many design firms are themselves not designed. They simply do their clients' bidding and react to whatever is needed at the time. Some firms inadvertently build a business design that is dysfunctional, with lots of structural obstacles to success. Perhaps you know a firm that wanted to build deep community relationships, but the leaders were introverted technical folks. Some firms want to build their project management expertise but have a chronic fear of becoming "paper pushers." Some want to master a specialty service but feel they must be flexible.

Beyond choosing a firm identity, the next essential step is a conscious design of the business that will allow a firm to play at its peak. When a firm is "playing the game" well, it is using a scaffold of practices that are both cohesive and aligned. Things are in flow, not in conflict. Although the support for this desired state is not visible, the firm is

WHAT IS YOUR CLIENT'S HIDDEN AGENDA?

Firm Archetype	Hidden Client Agenda
Innovation	Needs to gain prestige, improve image
Project-type specialty	Needs to overcome risky, adverse conditions
Client partnership	Needs to augment client's own skills as full-service "partner"
Community contribution	Needs facilitation through community gatekeepers
Project management challenge	Needs to control project complexity
Cost/quality challenge	Needs to deliver the product while optimizing the budget

WHAT IS SPECIAL ABOUT YOUR WORK?

Firm Operating Model	Sacred Methodology
Innovation	Generating brand-new ideas and technologies
Project-type specialty	Transferring new knowledge to the target niche
Client partnership	Expanding ways to help the sector-specific client
Community connectivity	Nurturing the network of relationships with local leaders
Project management challenge	Pushing sophisticated logistics control on large projects
Cost/quality challenge	Advancing brilliant new production technologies

working with an understood operating model or business design that comprises a very specific web of internal strategies and structures. In a healthy situation, this business model encourages desired behaviors and inhibits less desirable behaviors fairly effortlessly. Although they are largely intangible, business designs reflect culture, aspiration, and even policy—and they are powerful shapers of behavior.

Strategic planning, if done correctly, is the process that helps a firm think through its business design and make deliberate refinements. Some people think the end result of strategic planning is a sequential list of tasks to be implemented, but a list is ineffectual compared with development of a solid business design.

Each of the six archetypes relies on a characteristic business design, and each business design is organized into three distinct strands that form its structural elements:

1. Getting work: markets and marketing
2. Doing work: projects and people
3. Organizing work: money and leadership

These three strands are primary strategic systems that operate in every firm. And each archetype has characteristic strategies and activities that operate within the three systems. Broadly speaking, these strategies and activities can be arrayed along a continuum, ranging from the innovators and project-type specialists at one end to the PM and cost and quality experts at the other. From a macro view only, the accompanying table illustrates the range of these basic practices. By emphasizing the strategies most aligned with their type, firms use their resources most effectively. They can also adopt others as secondary tools if they choose.

For example, when the archetypes shown on the left seek higher visibility, they increase their writing, teaching, and speaking efforts. When the archetypes on the right seek higher visibility, they benefit more from engaging in exhibit development, direct mail, and advertising. When the archetypes on the left seek to improve their work, they try more experimentation and collaboration, while their colleagues on the right focus on greater utilization and productivity. When the archetypes on the left seek to track their performance, they look for design-related statistics, while their colleagues on the right aim for budget and schedule statistics.

A graphic can be used to illustrate each business design in detail. As shown in the sample business model diagram, each corner of the business design model refers to one of the design strands.

Within each of the three strands is a set of subsystems. Of course, many other subsystems operate in any given organization, but those listed are a short list of the most essential.

The business designs shown in the accompanying tables are based on extensive research and practical experience with successful design firms throughout the country.

DIFFERENT PERSPECTIVES ON WORK BY ARCHETYPE

	Innovator	Project-Type Specialist	Client Partner	Community Contributor	Project Management Expert	Cost and Quality Leader
Getting Work	Writing, teaching, and speaking		⟵——————⟶		Exhibits, direct mail, and advertising	
Doing Work	Experiment and collaboration		⟵——————⟶		High utilization and productivity	
Organizing Work	Design performance and statistics		⟵——————⟶		Budget and schedule statistics	

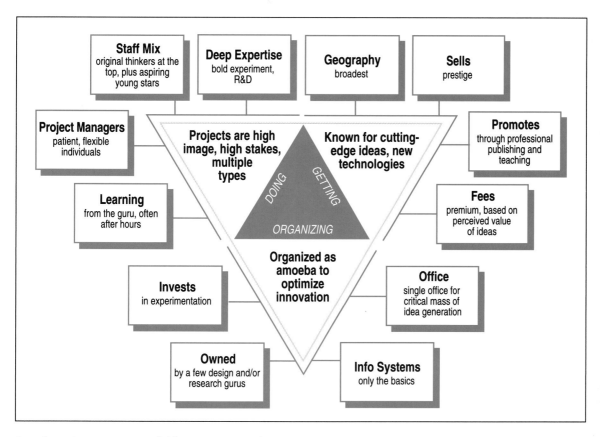

Sample Business Design Model for Innovator Archetype

Organizations are most successful when their strategies are aligned with one model rather than blending elements of various models.

That said, most firms find themselves practicing under several models. Examples of such hybrids are a client partner specialist using a niche strategy or a PM firm using a community knowledge strategy. However, the best choice is to be firmly anchored in one archetype and then cross-fertilize in a deliberately designed way.

The credit belongs to those who, at the best, know the triumph of high achievement; and who, at the worst, if they fail, fail while daring greatly. Their place shall never be with those cold and timid souls who know neither victory nor defeat.

Theodore Roosevelt

BASIC ELEMENTS OF A BUSINESS MODEL

Getting Work: Markets and marketing	What is the firm known for? Sales message Promotional strategy Geographical reach Best fees
Doing Work: Projects and people	What are the firm's targets? Deep expertise Staff mix Project management Learning
Organizing Work: Money and leadership	How does the firm organize for business? Ownership Investments Offices Information systems

FIRM OPERATING MODEL ARCHETYPES

Innovators

Client Agenda	Needs prestige, improved image
Client Value	Cutting-edge ideas or technologies
Getting Work: Known for cutting-edge ideas	Geography: National, international Selling point: Prestige Promotion: Teaching/publishing Fees: Premium, perceived value of ideas
Doing Work: High image, high stakes, multiple types	Deep expertise: Bold experiment, research and development Staff: Original thinkers, aspiring stars Project management: Patient, flexible Learning: From guru, often after hours
Organizing Work: Organized as an amoeba to optimize innovation	Invests in: Experimentation Owned by: One or a few gurus Info systems: Basics Office: Single, critical mass of ideas

Project-Type Specialists

Client Agenda	Needs to overcome project risk, adverse conditions
Client Value	Unsurpassed leadership in a specific area
Getting Work: Known for deep expertise in project or service specialty	Geography: National, international Selling point: Rare knowledge Promotion: Speaking/writing to client groups Fees: Premium, for documented results

Doing Work:
Complex or high-risk, singular type
	Deep expertise: Latest approaches
	Staff: Specialists at top, dedicated youngsters, and
	  stabilizers in middle
	Project management: Dedicated specialists who can
	  also handle the realities of the management
	  process
	Learning: Juniors initiate mentoring

Organizing Work: Organized around specialists to optimize advancement of the niche	Invests in: New applications, depth of network Owned by: Distinguished experts Info systems: Service/design performance Office: Single for critical mass, alliances

Client Partners

Client Agenda	Needs a trusted partner, augment skills
Client Value	Service depth within a market area

Getting Work:
Known for broad experience within
  an industry
	Geography: Regional or national
	Selling points: Market dedication, experience,
	  access
	Promotion: Industry connections, trend setters
	Fees: Improved with patron clients

Doing Work:
Range of types within one or few markets
	Deep expertise: Industry operations, people
	Staff: Stable array of professionals, some from
	  within client industry
	Project management: Well organized, experienced
	  in market
	Learning: Conventions, informal mentors

Organizing Work:
Organized as practice groups to optimize
  market expertise
	Invests in: Bench depth, like-firm acquisitions
	Owned by: Known market players, select
	  technicians
	Info systems: Statistics by market, repeat clients
	Office: Select regional offices

Community Contributors

Client Agenda	Needs access and service
Client Value	Mutual commitment to community
Getting Work: Known for contribution to the community	Geography: Community-based Selling points: Access, service, connectedness Promotion: Community events, PR, network Fees: Improved when "wired in"
Doing Work: Range of types, moderate complexity	Deep expertise: Local relationships, issues Staff: Multidisciplinary groups

Community Contributors (continued)

	Project management: Combined project management/discipline chiefs; if large, firm has strong work-sharing process
	Learning: Networking locally, professionally
Organizing Work: Organized around local leaders to optimize connectivity	Invests in: Local visibility, niche partners, new offices
	Owned by: Broad group, may be employee stock ownership plan
	Info systems: Performance by local office
	Office: One or multiple, for local access

Project Management Experts

Client Agenda	Needs logistical control
Client Value	Skilled project management for larger, complex projects
Getting Work: Known for great project management, organizational skills	Geography: Regional or national
	Selling points: Speed, process control
	Promotion: Through business press
	Fees: Premium fees for project management/ construction management
Doing Work: Highly complex logistically, larger scale, often design-build	Deep expertise: Project management
	Staff: Senior and junior project managers, MBAs
	Project management: Top project management systems, tools, resources
	Learning: Formal training curriculum
Organizing Work: Organized around project managers to optimize systems and technologies	Invests in: Elite corps of project managers, local firm alliances
	Owned by: Current or former project managers, corporate
	Info systems: Project-level statistics
	Office: Corporate headquarters plus satellites; project managers travel

Cost and Quality Leaders

Client Agenda	Needs product delivered, budget optimized
Client Value	Cost, quality, and consistency
Getting Work: Known for quality work at a low cost	Geography: Regional base, broad site alliances
	Selling points: Best quality for price, consistency
	Promotion: Direct mail, ads, sales reps
	Fees: Bid work, clever efficiencies
Doing Work: Mostly prototype/site adaptations	Deep expertise: Replication efficiencies
	Staff: Junior professionals and technicians
	Project management: Accountability, standard procedures
	Learning: Formal training classes
Organizing Work: Organized around production teams to optimize efficiency	Invests in: Production capacity, technology
	Owned by: One or few entrepreneurs, may be family-owned
	Info systems: Production unit costs
	Office: Production center, field offices

THE CHALLENGE

Any firm can go along with conventional growth and diversification tactics, but while the "numbers" side can provide a sense of success, it masks a deeper issue: The better clients with the best projects are seeking out the category experts. What is needed to achieve a spot as a category expert goes much deeper than differentiation—it is a full commitment to becoming identified in the market with a particular knowledge and skill set.

The expert firms delight in seeking mastery. Their work is challenging, and their businesses make meaningful contributions. To create firms of value, company leaders must be the executive designers of their firm's distinctive enterprise. They must treat this responsibility with all the care and passion they bring to just one of their projects. In the age of the expert, the challenge is to look at a fresh reality approach to firm identity:

- Devote your firm to what you care most about achieving.
- Seize the needed resources to fully fund your business design.
- Decisively assert leadership of your market.

For More Information

Recommended works on business strategy and design include the following:

Built to Last: Successful Habits of Visionary Companies (Random House, 1997), by James C. Collins and Jerry I. Porras, examines eighteen world-class companies and the reasons for their success.

In *Focus: The Future of Your Company Depends on It* (Collins, 1996), Al Ries uses the experiences of different companies to show that "focus" on core products or services is the key to success in today's business environment.

In *Positioning: The Battle for Your Mind* (McGraw-Hill, 1993), Al Ries and Jack Trout posit that to become a market leader, a company must choose what kind of customers it wants to serve and design its operating model to fulfill the chosen customers' values, at the same time maintaining appropriate standards in other customer values.

According to Michael Treacy and Fred Wiersema, authors of *The Discipline of Market Leaders* (Perseus Books Group, 1995), there are three kinds of customers, each with a particular idea of what constitutes value in a product or service: (1) high performance, (2) personalized service, or (3) overall cost of the product.

BACKGROUNDER

ESTABLISHING A NICHE PRACTICE

Jack Reigle

Some practitioners look for niche opportunities—ways to differentiate themselves and their practices from others in their marketplace. Drawing on a definition from NicheMarket.com, a niche market is "a narrowly defined group of potential customers." Likewise, a niche practice is a business focused on "addressing a need for a product or service that is not being addressed by mainstream providers."

Most practices aren't niche practices. Some have a niche market focus, though usually not well developed or far-reaching. Typically, firms pursuing a niche market engage in short-term, local opportunities that fade once the competition catches up. Firms that seriously pursue a niche practice, not just a market, find it both more rewarding and more challenging than a general practice. Some of the reasons for this include the following:

- **The firm increases its expertise.** Expertise is highly valued in today's world, and the further away from a commodity a firm's services can be, the better. The challenge is to make a commitment and to staff that commitment in a way that causes your market audience to respond positively. Niche experts are educators and passionate believers who see a path that others learn from and are compelled to follow.

- **The firm invests time and money.** The benefits of operating as a niche practice accrue through investment, not dabbling. The decision to become a niche practice demands much investment in effort and money to reap the rewards.

- **Identity gives the firm credibility.** Once the world has been convinced the firm is serious about succeeding in its chosen niche market, the firm will be identified by what it does and its name will become synonymous with the best in that market, as has been the case with HOK Sport Venue Event.

- **Better projects find the firm.** When a firm's message is clear and consistent, the target audience feels more comfortable coming to it to meet their particular needs.

- **Firm profits are stronger.** Clients with highly specialized needs will pay more to have them met.

A niche practice is a powerful concept. It connotes commitment, depth of knowledge, singular focus, and market positioning as the "go-to" firm for a particular project type. Can a niche be a service? Yes—think Ayers Saint Gross for campus master planning. Can a niche be a technology applied to design? Yes—think CRB Consulting Engineers for clean rooms. Success in its niche will define *who the firm is* to most of the people in its target market or sector.

One element common to all niche practices is *focus*, accompanied by the ability to overcome fear that such focus is too narrow and will create too much risk in an economic downturn. Downturns do happen, but in today's world, who believes that the recognized specialists *will not* get their share of the remaining work when the next crash occurs? Sometimes an entire market segment grinds to a halt; but successful niche firms see it coming and adjust their plans to survive. In the corporate market crash of 2000, the only part of the market that crashed was the commodity side driven by developers. Niche practices were not affected.

Specialization and focus create clarity and help draw a firm's best clients and projects closer. To keep them, though, the firm must perform. A firm that wants to develop a niche practice should take the following actions:

- **Find a source of passion and energy.** You need about three leaders who all want the same thing, share a common vision, and have the verve to move things forward. Any fewer and your efforts become an argument; too many more, and your leadership team becomes a committee.
- **Identify your target market.** Have a clear client set in mind—distinct populations within universities, cities, or corporate markets, or a specific class of end users who will demand recognized expertise from those whose services they engage.
- **Develop corporate autonomy.** A niche practice cannot survive within a general practice with other commitments. If you choose to transition to a niche practice from a general practice, consider creating a studio, division, or other separate entity to insulate the effort from the momentum of the generalist work. Provide staff members with clear direction, then set them free to create, teach, and take risks.
- **Establish point-of-entry services.** Niche experts are ahead of the curve—way ahead. They see the future, develop their own projects, and have an array of useful tools to open client doors well before an RFP is issued or a conceptual design sketch is drawn. Think economic development modeling or supply-chain analysis for an emerging industry. These specialized areas of knowledge can be translated to the needs of users and then to a specific design and feel for a facility.
- **Use research.** There is great power in research, especially when a firm owns it and has created it for others to use. Start small, and do it yourself instead of relying on traditional industry sources. Proprietary research is your first branding opportunity and will establish your identity more quickly than most other actions. Give your research away liberally, and it will turn to gold before your eyes.

Any way you cut it, being a niche practice, having a tightly organized set of focused services, or offering a specialized technology is demanding. A firm will need to continuously refresh its marketing messages, point-of-entry approaches, and client-oriented knowledge base to maintain its niche.

Learn to love travel. The niche world means airplanes, plain and simple. A small (but highly profitable) client base may be spread around the country, continent, and world. If current staff members don't like that lifestyle, you will have to find others who do or forgo the niche practice.

Most clients who hire a niche firm don't come back every year or two for more, so the marketing game changes. While many generalist firms get 50 to 60 percent of their annual revenues from repeat clients, niche firms should forecast only about 10 to 15 percent. Adjust your marketing strategy appropriately.

A good niche opportunity can last about ten years before it becomes commoditized, copied, and otherwise diluted into the mainstream. This means a niche practice needs to create new ideas every five years or so to remain viable. A firm can accomplish this by seeking out or creating new combinations of markets. A recent example is the interest of universities in building retirement communities within their campus complexes or on properties close to traditional campuses. If your firm's niche has been dorms, here's an opportunity to evolve your practice.

A niche practice may have more than one market. If it does, ensure those markets are closely related so as not to dilute the firm's positioning. Practically speaking, it is more effective to have multiple niches in related groups, such as medical complexes or higher education facilities, than to mix niches across unrelated markets. Multiple niches spread among diverse client groups are very difficult to establish or maintain.

One thing is clear: Trying to manage a hybrid firm—half niche, half generalist—is difficult. It can be done as a transitional approach, but not on an ongoing basis. The marketing approaches, fee structures, travel demands, talent needs, and leadership demands, among other things, are too diverse for simultaneous success on both sides. If transitioning from a general practice to a niche practice seems right for your firm, be ready to replace many of your current staff members and begin letting go of the patron clients you have cultivated. Think about establishing a stand-alone firm, division, or studio for the niche practice.

The niche idea has a high threshold. Many firms yearn for such a place, and a small handful make it work over the long term. Is it right for you and for your firm? Many firms will take the chance, put the puzzle pieces together, and attempt to live their particular dream.

4.4 Team Building

William C. Ronco, Ph.D.

Productive teamwork is an essential aspect of professional practice. Architects can improve their ability to work together by employing a set of basic team-building activities that can help architecture teams improve communication, creativity, and performance.

The work of most practicing architects is carried out in teams. Thus, effective teams and teamwork are vital to the success of nearly every architecture firm. Architects may form or work with a variety of teams, including:

- **Project teams.** The work of most projects is carried out in teams that include architects, engineers, contractors, subcontractors, owners, and users. Effective collaboration among teams contributes to project profitability and quality and helps achieve the original design intent.
- **Ownership and leadership teams.** Teams of principals and partners govern many architecture firms. Such teams contribute to achieving firm goals and objectives, producing positive organization cultures, improving information sharing between departments, and increasing productivity and financial performance.
- **Studios, departments, and markets.** Many firms are organized by studios, or departments, that specialize in a building type or serve a specific market or client group. Successful teamwork in these group settings contributes to more optimal personnel assignments, better professional development and mentoring, and higher employee job satisfaction.
- **Teams for special projects.** Firms appoint teams to tackle special issues such as launching marketing initiatives, solving internal matters, or capturing unique opportunities.

Teams often underperform. Projects exceed budgets and schedules. Owners squabble with each other. Some tasks may only be partially completed or achieve low-quality results. To help design professionals cope more effectively with teaming efforts, this topic explores the challenges and rewards of teamwork and provides practical guidance on how to build teams that can achieve high levels of performance.

THE POWER OF TEAMWORK

Research shows that highly effective teams have the following attributes:

- *Synergy.* Most teams have the potential to achieve results that are greater than the sum of results produced by individual team members. In sports, the team tapping its synergistic potential has a strong winning record in spite of average individual player statistics. In architecture, synergy can produce similar results in team settings.
- *Brainstorming/idea generation.* Teams have the capacity to generate useful ideas by tapping into more individual resources. Brainstorming is especially important in architecture because of the scope and complexity of issues involved in any project.

Great people don't equal great teams.

Tom Peters

William C. Ronco is president of Gathering Pace Consulting in Bedford, Massachusetts. He has led hundreds of team-building and partnering programs for architecture, engineering, construction, and real estate organizations. He is author of *The Partnering Solution* and *Partnering Manual for Design and Construction*. (The original version of this topic appeared in Handbook Update 2005.)

- *Motivation.* Teams have the potential to energize and motivate their members. When the group's work is creative, as it is in architecture, this aspect of teamwork is especially strong.
- *Organizational link.* Teamwork can forge strong relationships between individuals within a firm who work together as a team. This outcome of teamwork can occur in firms of any size.

THE CHALLENGES OF TEAMWORK

While research findings show that teamwork offers many inherent benefits, achieving effective teamwork is not without its challenges. Many of these challenges are associated with rather predictable problems frequently encountered with team efforts, and some are specifically associated with the architecture profession.

Predictable Problems

- *Performance slippage.* While all teams have the potential for synergy, many actually suffer from performance slippage. With synergy, 1 + 1 = 3. With slippage, 1 + 1 = 1½. Slippage occurs in architecture teams that enlist talented individual members but fail to produce at the summary level of their talents.
- *Individual negativity and passivity.* People tend to be more critical, negative, and passive in a group than they are in a one-on-one situation. This phenomenon occurs in design reviews, which have the potential to provide useful criticism but often become so negative that their content is lost.
- *Individual focus.* Even when the leader of a team is advocating teamwork, many members are actually thinking, "How does this affect *me*?" This phenomenon occurs in project teams when designers fail to work effectively with other team members. It happens with architecture ownership teams when principals struggle to balance their individual interests with the good of the firm.
- *Groupthink.* Teams may be ineffective not only because they are locked in conflict but also because they do not experience enough conflict. Architecture project teams lapse into groupthink when they conduct project meetings that seem well organized but actually fail to identify and address glaring project problems.
- *Questionable ethics.* Groups and teams of all kinds possess a frightening ability to coerce individuals, even individuals with strong characters, to go along with the group sentiment. This occurs in "old boy" ownership teams that systematically neglect problems in the organization of the firm, career development and advancement issues, and mentoring of younger professionals.
- *Ineffective leadership.* Many of these predictable problems stem from ineffective team leadership. Effective leaders have the skills to manage group discussion, address and control groupthink, and make passive participants more active.

The challenge for architects and for team building is to tap into the strong potential that teams offer while also managing and reducing or eliminating the predictable problems.

Challenges Special to the Profession

Beyond the predictable problems articulated in research literature, architects experience teamwork challenges associated with issues peculiar to the architecture profession:

- *Individual or "loner" focus.* Much of the culture and history of the profession is built around the image of the architect working alone. Teams are vehicles to implement the architect's vision, not groups of peers and collaborators. David Hancock, AIA, a principal at CBT Architects in Boston, explains, "Design schools foster the image that designers are lonely individuals, working alone. Ayn Rand didn't help, and neither does the 'star system' that promotes celebrity designers."

No star playing, just football.

Knute Rockne

- *Ownership of the project.* A second problem architects experience with teamwork occurs when they supplant others and claim a kind of mental ownership of a project. Ed Bond, president of Bond Brothers Construction in Everett, Massachusetts, comments, "Architects can forget that we are all only part of the process, that it's the owner's building, not theirs. They can take a personal kind of ownership for the design that is not in the best interest of the client. Actually, though, all of us can get to think that our part is the most important piece."

Such issues, however, do not dominate the profession. As Hancock also points out, "At the same time that we have one thread of our culture tied up in the individual, we also have some strong traditions in collaboration. There's the Bauhaus movement, and the whole history of The Architects Collaborative." Bond also notes, "Architects are very good at listening to clients and communicating to the rest of the team. They are pretty good at understanding clients and telling the story of the building so that the rest of the team understands it."

In your typical team-building exercise, the employees are subjected to a variety of unpleasant situations until they become either a cohesive team or a ring of carjackers.

Scott Adams, *The Dilbert Principle*

MYTHS AND FACTS ABOUT TEAMWORK AND TEAM BUILDING

Beyond the research literature and recurring problems, many architects hold their own myths that can limit team performance and detract from team building. The facts about how teams and team building actually function belie these myths.

Myths about Teamwork

- **Myth:** *Teams dilute good ideas, especially design ideas.* Architects often worry that working with a team will force them to dilute their design ideas to accommodate other team members. **Fact:** The research pointing out team tendencies to be critical and negative reinforces this worry. However, other research on the creative process shows that teams can stimulate more advanced thinking and strengthen design quality.
- **Myth:** *Working with a team is a sign of weakness.* Some architects fantasize, "The signature architects do not put up with teams. They have it their way." **Fact:** Many of the best designers are also highly skilled at working with teams. The era of the arrogant individual designer who is also successful, if it ever existed, is over.
- **Myth:** *Members of effective teams do not argue; they automatically get along well.* Architects often interpret group conflict as a problem—and it may be. **Fact:** Current research suggests that conflict and disagreement can be important components of effective group performance. A 1997 *Harvard Business Review* article, "How Top Management Teams Can Have a Good Fight," illustrates this point.

- **Myth:** *Teamwork depends on "chemistry."* Some architects comment fatalistically, "If the 'spark' on a team is there, that's fine, but if not, there is little you can do about it." **Fact:** Team building can positively influence the ability of people to get along with each other and work more productively on a team.

Myths about Team Building

- **Myth:** *Team building should never be needed.* If good people are selected, teamwork will follow automatically. **Fact:** Team building is necessary because, especially in the practice of architecture, strong individual performers are often ineffective working in teams. Conflict and miscommunications are inevitable. Team building helps groups understand and manage conflict and miscommunications effectively.
- **Myth:** *Team building cannot accomplish much because people do not really change.* **Fact:** Effective team building does not involve drastic personal change. If teams can simply learn basic skills and run meetings so that all members contribute, listen, and solve problems, team building can be successful.
- **Myth:** *The goal of team building is to get members to like each other.* **Fact:** In effective teams, members may or may not like each other. The goal of team building should be focused on tangible improvements in communications and bottom-line team performance.
- **Myth:** *The goal of team building is to produce insight and awareness.* If team members are aware of the issues, they will take the appropriate actions.

THE TEAM-BUILDING PROCESS

Although effective approaches to team building exist, many architects still struggle with the process of team building. The following list of common and best practices delineates key issues for improving team-building effectiveness.

Common practice: Team building focuses on doing an activity. The goals and outcomes of the activity are unclear.

Best practice: The common practice is to focus on the team-building activity. The best practice is to focus on the outcomes. Team building has a much greater potential to produce lasting outcomes when the people running it clarify what they hope to accomplish. Typical team-building outcomes may include increasing participant awareness of their impacts on others, addressing and resolving old issues, achieving higher levels of group performance and productivity, and so on.

Common practice: Uses a team-building exercise but does not allow enough time for participants to discuss whether the team's actions in the exercise reflect their usual communications and actions.

Best practice: A team-building activity should include time for a group discussion of how the activity relates to everyday team issues. Whatever the team-building activity, it is useful for the group to address questions such as these:

- In what ways were our discussions during the exercise similar to our work every day?
- In what ways were our discussions during the exercise different from our work every day?
- What patterns of discussion in the exercise resemble our everyday work?
- Who did what new things in the exercise? What can the group learn from that?

Common practice: Assumes that discussions of issues themselves and increased awareness of them will lead to change and improvement.

Best practice: Takes time in the exercise to discuss specific action steps specific people will try as a result of their insights.

Common practice: Uses a retreat as a forum for team building.

Best practice: Structures team building into several sessions spread over time, with clear assignments and action steps between sessions.

Construction Partnering

Construction partnering is a form of team building widely used on design and construction projects. When implemented following the best practices above, it can be extremely effective.

People who work with design and construction projects frequently use the term "partnering" to describe a general effort to cooperate, communicate, and work in a reasonable manner with other team members on a project. This general intention is important, but partnering is also a structured method for improving team performance on construction projects.

Construction partnering has demonstrated enough consistent and positive results to earn endorsements from the American Institute of Architects, Associated General

Common Practices

We were a little apprehensive before the team-building session, but by the time it came up on our calendars, most of us new principals were looking forward to it. I got to the retreat site a little early. It was a nice hotel, and I thought I would enjoy a cup of coffee. I met Michele, one of the other new principals, and we talked about our hopes for the firm. Like me, she was willing to participate in the session and was pleased that it would focus on improving our problem-solving skills.

We both sensed that the principals had not been very effective in solving some of the operational problems we have faced with design quality. The firm has the talent to solve this problem, so we assumed that the group had struggled with discussing and addressing it.

The session went very well. The older principals split us into three groups, and we all worked on the same decision-making problems. One exercise was about being lost in the desert, another was about a baseball team, and the last one was some kind of group auction involving Xs, Ys, dimes, and negotiations. It was all very interesting, actually.

We had drinks and snacks afterward, and everybody talked about how much they learned. The discussion was kind of general, no specific plans, but that seemed OK. Everybody seemed to be sincere. People talked about the session for a few weeks afterward, recalling particular moments when others said or did something interesting.

But now it's a month since we had the session, and I just don't think it accomplished anything.

Best Practices

We were a little apprehensive before the team-building session, but by the time it came up on our calendars, most of us new principals were looking forward to it. I got to the retreat site a little early. It was a nice hotel, and I thought I would enjoy a cup of coffee. I met Michele, one of the other new principals, and we talked about our hopes for the firm. Like me, she was willing to participate in the session but unsure of what it was supposed to accomplish.

The session went well enough, I suppose. The older principals split us into three groups, and we all worked on the same decision-making problems. One exercise was about being lost in the desert, another was about a baseball team, and the last one was some kind of auction involving Xs, Ys, dimes, and negotiations.

When we finished each exercise, we discussed in detail how our actions in the exercises reflected what we do or don't do in our everyday work. Although it took a bit of discussion at first, I was amazed at how we apparently replicated all of our work communication patterns in the exercises.

It was all very interesting and detailed. We planned specific action steps. For example, in the exercises, we recognized that we had often shut out our two quietest members, just like we do at work. They contributed valuable information in the exercise, as they do at work. We developed some new processes for the office to make sure we engage these folks.

Now it's a month since the team-building session, and we are planning to have a follow-up in which we discuss what we have tried, what didn't work, and plan new actions. I can't wait to see what we tackle next!

Contractors, and American Consulting Engineers Council. Increasing numbers of government agencies, corporations, and institutional clients require partnering workshops as a condition of project funding.

The Army Corps of Engineers developed the first construction partnering experiments about thirty years ago in its Pacific Northwest region. Frustrated with a growing list of projects that were over budget and off schedule, several Corps managers decided to pilot team building on some of its projects. With their own professional roots in engineering, they developed an approach to team building that differed in key ways from team building rooted in the human resources and organization development fields.

Over the years, various facilitators and managers have adapted and refined the Corps' original material. Still, many current construction partnering efforts share consistent agenda items, content, and structure. Most construction partnering consists of a series of one- or two-day workshops that bring together key project members from each of the entities involved in a project. For a typical $30 million building, a workshop can engage a group of twenty to thirty diverse and usually quite vocal architects, engineers, plumbers, electricians, subcontractors, clients, building users, facility managers, government officers, and others. The meeting usually follows a highly structured agenda:

- *Taking stock.* In the first hour or two, participants list what they think will go well on the project and what they think may cause problems. This part of the workshop identifies the key issues the project will have to address.
- *Building mutual understanding and trust.* Before addressing key issues of the project, most effective partnering workshops work with the Myers-Briggs Type Indicator (MBTI), the DISC Personal Profile System, or another personality profile. Even just an hour or two of this type of introspection accelerates the process of participants getting to know each other and building trust.
- *Writing a goals statement/partnering charter.* After clarifying the key issues, participants develop a project goals statement that addresses the issues. Typically ten to fifteen sentences long, the goals statement includes quantitative performance goals and qualitative goals for the ways people on the project should interact. To give the statement clout, participants sign it. Work on the goals statement takes an hour or two, depending on the number of people in the group and the extent of the differences they attempt to resolve.
- *Refining communication processes and procedures.* Participants develop detailed communication processes and procedures necessary to achieve the goals. These procedures usually include mechanisms for handling changes, clarifying issues likely to arise in the field, resolving disagreements, and ensuring that everyone gets the information they need when they need it.

An external, objective facilitator usually runs the meeting to ensure that everyone participates, no one dominates, and the group stays focused on the agenda. To conclude the workshop, participants plan a follow-up meeting and decide what issues it should address. In follow-ups, people monitor the plans and commitments made in the original workshop, address new problems, and explore new opportunities.

TEAM-BUILDING ACTIVITIES FOR ARCHITECTS

Beyond construction partnering, seven additional team-building activities address especially important issues for architects. Some of these activities draw on parts of the partnering agenda. It is usually most productive for teams to work with all seven activities in this order:

1. Assess team performance.
2. Build mutual understanding and trust (using the MBTI, Predictive Index, or other personality profile).
3. Clarify team goals; write a formal goals statement.
4. Strengthen regular group meetings.
5. Facilitate meetings so that all members participate equally.
6. Clarify individual roles, responsibilities, opportunities, and information needs.
7. Conduct team-building exercises for decision making and problem solving.

Activity 1: Assess Team Performance

Assessing team performance is an essential first step in team building. Teams that skip this step are likely to engage in team-building activities that address minor problems but neglect major issues and opportunities.

Building an objective assessment of how the team is performing can be done with varying degrees of formality, beginning with a simple discussion of the team's major strengths, weaknesses, and opportunities. Or it can take the form of a more empirical survey that lists key performance metrics. Team members can use such surveys to quantify key issues for themselves, and they can survey people outside the team whose perceptions are important to consider.

Simply engaging a team in a brief discussion of its major strengths, weaknesses, and opportunities provides important outcomes. The discussion should

- Highlight key issues the group agrees and disagrees on.
- Identify issues the group can work on in team building.
- Build buy-in, ownership, and a sense of responsibility from team members for the group's success and for the effectiveness of any team-building work to follow.

A productive assessment of a team's performance will strive to ensure that

- All participants contribute equally, with no one either dominating or withdrawing.
- Participants focus on creating a balanced list of strengths, weaknesses, and opportunities, and not on using the discussion simply to vent their problems and complaints.
- The team calibrates the list and separates major issues from minor annoyances.
- The list becomes the agenda for team-building work to follow.

Activity 2: Build Mutual Understanding and Trust with Personality Profiles

"At last, finally, I understand you," one owner of a medium-size architecture firm commented to his partner of eighteen years, after working with a personality profile. "I still don't like you, but at least I understand you!"

Personality profiles enrich the understanding team members have of each other and thus build mutual respect and trust. Having a better understanding of peers makes it possible to understand that they are not trying to provoke but rather are simply acting according to their own preferences.

The MBTI is the most widely used instrument for determining personality profiles. Because many architecture clients also use it, the MBTI can provide valuable insight into client communications. Other useful personality profiles include the Predictive Index, the Strength Finder, and DISC.

Once members of a team better understand each other's personality types, the real work begins. The team discusses in depth what this knowledge explains and what the group should do in response to its particular mix of personalities. For example, the new information might explain why

- The group does some tasks well but struggles with others.
- Miscommunications recur among group members.
- Some people tend to dominate the group and others are ignored.

Given the mix of its personality types, a team can decide to

- Assign some leadership tasks to people it typically neglects.
- Ask two people who often are in conflict (and are probably different types) to collaborate on a project.
- Focus on tasks that are outside the comfort zone of the majority of its personality types.
- Present information in a format that responds to the preferences of team members' personality types.

Activity 3: Clarify Team Goals in a Written Goals Statement

Architecture teams often neglect to clarify goals because the goals seem obvious. With detailed owner contracts and lengthy negotiations, for example, project teams can understandably assume their goals are crystalline. Yet, a discussion of goals often reveals significant disagreements.

Discord on goals often results in other, more tangible problems. Often when high levels of conflict exist on a team, the reason is not a lack of trust or the dominance of strong personalities, as team members suppose, but differing goals. Thus, the most effective way to reduce conflict in a group may not be to work on listening skills or mediation but on clarifying the team goals.

In its work on construction partnering, the Army Corps of Engineers developed a formal, structured approach to writing a goals statement or project charter. Following this method, all the members of a team write a goals statement that specifies eight to ten quantitative performance goals and eight to ten communication goals. After discussing the goals and reaching agreement on their intent, all team members sign the goals statement to confirm they support it.

A team composed of architecture firm owners working on its own goals statement (which would be different from the firm's goals) might include as performance goals such items as "mentor associates so that two new people are ready to become principals in the next quarter" or "motivate all staff so that our multiplier improves by 25 percent in the next month." Communication goals for the same group of partners might include "treat each other with respect" and "communicate our energy for the profession to the whole office." One communication goal many partner groups adopt is "keep our disagreements with each other in the conference room. Always support each other in the office."

It is useful to have all team members sign the completed statement. Signing the statement turns the abstract discussion into a more tangible direction for future actions.

Activity 4: Strengthen Regular Group Meetings

Meetings are the venue in which much teamwork takes place, but many teams lack basic skills for holding successful meetings. Many architects complain that they attend too many meetings, that meetings often accomplish little, and occasionally they cause the team to move backward. Several tactics can help any team improve the productivity of its meetings:

1. Schedule meetings instead of holding them "as needed." If people need to exchange information, they will do so more effectively when they can plan meeting times as part of their ongoing work. As-needed meetings may feel informal, but they make group discussion reactive.
2. Meeting for short periods of time frequently leads to more productive discussion than meeting for long periods of time infrequently. Conflict-ridden, half-day, monthly project review meetings become more productive when they are reformatted as weekly hour-long sessions. Many teams even find that a brief daily meeting (often standing, with no chairs) helps keep them informed.
3. Rotate meeting leadership among team members. The work of planning the meeting agenda and managing the discussion can rotate among team members in most teams. For many teams, rotating meeting leadership increases member accountability to the whole team and a sense of membership in the group.
4. Develop an agenda, circulate it well before the meeting, and review it at the beginning of the meeting. This is a very basic meeting discipline, but it bears repeating because so many architects skip over it. Any meeting that begins with participants asking "Does anyone know what this meeting is about?" is probably going to produce limited results.
5. Use a flip chart to record discussions. Groups that use flip charts to log key points are better able to access ideas than groups in which individuals keep their own notes. Flip charts also can make excellent minutes of meetings, since they can be reduced to 8½- by 11-inch sheets in the graphics departments of many firms. Current technologies, such as the outlining software *Inspiration*, perform the same function as flip charts using laptop computers, but some architects find the new technologies unwieldy.
6. Begin the meeting by posting a flip chart with the heading "Action Steps" and three columns labeled, Who, What, and When. Make sure that discussion of agenda items concludes with an action step that identifies who will do what, and when.

Activity 5: Facilitate All Meetings So That All Team Members Participate

Since a vocal minority tends to dominate any group discussion, it is essential for effective teams to learn to conduct meetings in which all team members participate equally and the tone of the discussion is positive and productive.

Many teams suffer from the myth of open discussion. They believe that if they simply identify a topic and allow a free-flowing discussion, the team will adequately address all the issues and arrive at a reasonable solution. What actually happens is much less productive and can easily become destructive. In an open discussion with a team of nine people, the leader might ask, "What do you think of this design?" Predictably, the discussion that follows will

- Focus on opinions about the design. For example, one person may lead with, "Well for one thing, I don't like the blocking." Another may follow with, "Have you given any thought to alternative site orientation?"
- Be limited to a vocal minority of the group. The majority will remain silent during the meeting. They may voice their opinions later, in one-on-one asides.
- Take on a negative tone. Turning a negative discussion of problems and annoyances to a positive one is difficult.
- Focus on the leader. Often the meeting will consist of one-on-one tangles between team members and the leader. People not directly involved in a tangle wait their turn.
- Produce limited or no results.

The keys to ensuring that all team members participate in a meeting and the discussion remains positive and productive lie in structuring questions posed to the group in a specific format and breaking into subgroups for part of the discussion.

Thinking about questions to ask at meetings is usually new territory for team leaders. People tend to think more about what they are going to present than they do about what they are going to ask. Teams are very literal: They answer whatever question the leader asks. Thus, it is important to word questions carefully. A plus-minus format is the most effective approach for team questions. In the design review, for example, the question would not be "What do you think of the design?" but rather:

- What three aspects of the design do you like the best and the least?
- In what three ways does the design advance the goals of the firm and in what three ways does it detract?
- What three aspects of the design would you keep and what three aspects would you change?

In addition to using the plus-minus question format, it is important to break the group of nine into smaller groups, perhaps three groups of three, for the discussion. Ideally, each group gets its own flip chart. The team leader gives a marker to one person in each small group (preferably to the quietest person in each group) and tells the team it has ten to fifteen minutes to record three pluses and three minuses from each participant.

FACILITATING A MEETING: A FIRSTHAND ACCOUNT

This firsthand account of how the facilitative method works offers some useful insight.

I was looking for ways to get better participation in our project design discussions. People like to discuss design, and it can be a great way to bring the whole firm together. We draw a pretty good crowd, about half the office, and a good mix of senior, middle, and junior staff. The problem was that, very quickly, just a few people would dominate the discussions, always the same three or four people. We would stop the discussion occasionally and ask if anyone else had an opinion, and once in a while, someone else would talk. But then it would quickly go back to the same few people.

It especially bothered me because people who had been quiet during the discussion would come to me afterward and tell me what they were thinking. I asked them why they didn't speak up in the meeting, and they would always say they were not comfortable, even though we asked for their input. When I first learned about facilitating participation by asking plus-minus questions and breaking the group into smaller groups, I was doubtful that these methods would work. I worried about people feeling put on the spot in the small groups, and I just thought people wouldn't like it. Well, I was wrong. I tried it and people were comfortable in the small groups and they liked it.

By breaking the large group into smaller groups, everyone had a chance to offer their thoughts. The quiet people in particular loved it; they were able to express themselves. And they were quite comfortable speaking out because the groups were small. People felt heard and cared for, and we got a lot more accomplished as well.

Audrey O'Hagan, Stubbins Associates, Cambridge, Massachusetts

Activity 6: Clarify Roles, Responsibilities, and Information Needs

Lack of clarity about individual team member roles, responsibilities, and information needs plagues many teams. However, it is relatively easy to address this issue with a basic team-building activity. To prepare for this activity, individual team members write on the top half of a piece of flip-chart paper what they think are their three most important roles and responsibilities on the team. They also make notes about what they think the roles and responsibilities are of each of the other team members.

In the meeting, team members post their own flip charts. Then all team members write what they think the roles and responsibilities of the other team members should be on the open, bottom half of the paper. The group then discusses each team member for ten to fifteen minutes, exploring the gaps between what members thought their roles and responsibilities were and what the rest of the team thought they should be. To log the discussion, it is useful to list three or four tasks the team wants the individual to do more of and the same for tasks the team wants the individual to do fewer of.

Architecture teams often find this discussion useful, as it clarifies major discrepancies with minimal conflict. Project team members often find that their peers want them to do more or less documentation, detail work, or communication of change, among other activities. Ownership teams often use the discussion to clarify expectations about marketing, business development, new initiatives, and office responsibilities.

Activity 7: Conduct Decision-Making Exercises

These are the activities most people think of when they think of team building: group role plays, simulations, skits, problems to solve, exercises, and structured experiences. Several sources provide hundreds of these activities, along with instructions on their use. In addition to these formal team-building activities, other informal activities can also function as team-building activities.

Group exercises can produce insights about team behavior that the team can apply in its everyday work. Teams often find these exercises useful because they bring deep-seated communication patterns to the surface. The process of delineating these patterns is often more successful when the team works on an unfamiliar topic rather than on everyday tasks, where egos are more likely to get in the way of insight.

In classic exercises, such as "Lost At Sea," "NASA Man on the Moon," "Wilderness Survival," and "Hurricane Disaster," for example, the team members individually prioritize a list of items that might be useful in the situation. The team then works together to prioritize the items, after which the team and individual lists are compared to a list ordered by experts in the field. The closer the team list is to the expert list, the more effective the team's communications were. Highly effective teams produce scores that are better than the scores of individual members. Somewhat effective teams still beat their average individual scores. Ineffective and dysfunctional teams perform worse than the worst player on the team.

The key to deriving lasting value from such exercises is the debriefing, discussion, analysis, and action planning the team does after it has completed the exercise. To make exercises worthwhile, it is essential to address questions such as these:

- What three descriptors define the group's communications during the exercise?
- How did the group communicate well during the exercise?
- How did the group not communicate well during the exercise?
- In what ways were the group's patterns of communication during the exercise similar to its everyday communications?
- In what ways were the group's patterns of communication during the exercise different from its everyday communications?
- What should the group do differently in its everyday communications based on insights from this exercise?

These same questions can also be used to debrief informal team-building activities like bowling, sailing, hiking, and golf. Each of these activities can provide useful insight into the effectiveness of team communications. As team members lose themselves in the activity, deep-seated team communication patterns rise to the surface. Often it is easier for teams to see their communication issues when they are communicating about topics that do not involve their professional expertise and egos.

TEAM-BUILDING PRINCIPLES FOR ARCHITECTS

The material covered above can be encapsulated into a set of team-building principles especially relevant for architects. These principles include the following:

- Anticipate the need for team building with all teams involved in architecture practice. Whether you are working on a project team, an owner team, an internal department team, or a special project, the team will benefit from conscious, thoughtful team building.
- Ensure team building involves work with as many of the team-building tasks as possible. Team building that is limited to work in just one of the tasks will produce limited outcomes.
- Be aware of the limitations of retreats. While team-building retreats can generate valuable insights, they can also make it seem that generating the insight is the end of team building.
- Make team building an *ongoing* process. The best sports teams continue to practice all season and often all year. Architecture teams also benefit most from team building when they make it an integral part of their ongoing work.

Teams are the medium for many important activities and tasks of architecture practice. Yet effective teamwork can be elusive because of the challenges of capturing the full power that teamwork offers. If architects make a moderate effort to build teams thoughtfully and conduct their work with care, they should experience noticeable improvements in performance and results.

For More Information
Several resources provide an essential understanding of teamwork and team building:

Marcus Buckingham, *Now, Discover Your Strengths* (Free Press, 2001). A benchmark article addressing many issues that architecture teams confront is presented in "How Management Teams Can Have a Good Fight," *Harvard Business Review* (July–August, 1997) by Kathleen M. Eisenhardt, Jean L. Kahwajy, and L. J. Bourgeois.

An excellent summary of the wisdom of teams can be found in *The Wisdom of Teams* (HarperCollins, 1999) by Jon R. Katzenback and Douglas K. Smith; Patrick Lencioni, *The Five Dysfunctions of a Team* (Jossey-Bass, 2001); and *Death by Meeting* (Jossey-Bass, 2004).

Useful team-building strategies and tips for effective partnering, project management, and communications are presented in *The Partnering Solution* (Career Press, 2005) and *Partnering Manual for Design and Construction* (McGraw-Hill, 1996), both by William C. Ronco and Jean S. Ronco. The *Annual Volumes for Training and Consulting* (Jossey-Bass) contain clearly outlined annual collections of team-building and training activities that enable novices to run their own team-building activities. These are a valuable resource for architecture firms. The "Plan Your Program" link at www.gatheringpace.com provides specific steps to help organizations design team-building programs to achieve lasting results.

4.5 Marketing Strategy and Planning

David Koren, CPSM, Assoc. AIA

A strategic approach to marketing—and a plan to attract new business and retain existing clients—will enable an architecture firm to allocate resources to support the growth of its practice.

Marketing is the process of bringing new business to a firm. Marketing involves everything that helps spread the word about a firm, helps the firm communicate with prospective and existing clients, and gets the work in the door—including correspondence, a Web site, the firm's portfolio, and even how the receptionist answers the phone. It is important to approach marketing strategically to allocate resources efficiently and to be as effective as possible in attracting and retaining clients. Regardless of the firm's size or resources, the basic process of defining a strategy and creating a marketing plan is the same for every firm.

MARKETING ARCHITECTURAL SERVICES

Marketing architectural services is different from marketing other services or marketing a product. Architecture involves a complex mix of creative and technical skills, and marketing architectural services calls for convincing prospective clients that the professionals in a firm offer creative and problem-solving ability, attention to detail and follow-through, and passion for the project. Because the client or potential client is actually buying the individual expertise and ability of team members, the differentiation of one firm from another occurs on an individual and personal level.

Although it is easy to believe that a prospective client's decision about which firm to hire is rational (that the client will hire the firm that has the best experience, capabilities, and fee), the fact is that the prospective client is a person or group of people, and thus, emotional factors will also play a part in which firm they choose. People tend to select people they like and trust, who they believe will be good to work with and help them achieve their desired results.

In building credibility with prospective clients, the portfolio of the firm's prior work is important, but the portfolio will not win the job on its own. The portfolio lets the prospective client know that the firm has completed appropriate work in the past and is capable of doing it again. The client will also generally look at other factors such as quality of work and fee. But from there, the client will make a personal and emotional decision, based on whom he or she likes, trusts, most wants to work with, and, very often, knows best—in other words, "chemistry." All the facts about the firm serve to reinforce and justify the decision, but the decision is at its core an emotional one.

While the marketing efforts of many architecture firms are focused on winning work from new clients, it is important not to forget about existing clients. It is generally much easier and less expensive to win new work from an existing client than from a new one.

David Koren is an associate principal and director of marketing for Perkins Eastman, where he is responsible for developing marketing strategy, leading business development efforts, and supervising marketing staff in the firm's offices in the United States and abroad. He is a past president of the New York Chapter of the Society for Marketing Professional Services, and author of *Architect's Essentials of Marketing*.

Repeat work from existing clients, referrals, and personal or professional contacts are the three most important sources of new projects for 73 percent of U.S. architecture firms.

2006 AIA Firm Survey

Relationships are everything when it comes to marketing architectural services.

If your firm has worked for a client and has done a good job, why wouldn't the client hire your firm again? A first priority in marketing is to make sure the firm is keeping existing clients happy. Established relationships serve as a springboard to move into new relationships and markets. If existing clients are happy, they will not only hire the firm again, they will recommend the firm to other people they know who may be considering an architectural project. No recommendation is more valuable than the endorsement of a satisfied client.

In marketing, relationships are everything—with clients and other third-party influencers in the marketplace like contractors, consultants, and real estate brokers. Relationships will influence the way that others perceive the individual architect and the firm; positive relationships can help, and negative relationships can hurt. When pursuing work with a new client, it is vital to build a relationship with the individuals involved in making the purchase decision. Without some kind of natural affinity between the architect and the prospective client that helps the client to like and trust the firm, it is unlikely that the firm will prevail in a competitive situation. Unfortunately, if you enter the selection process without an existing relationship with the prospective client, it is probably already too late—one of your competitors is probably ahead of you, and now has the "inside track."

One often-overlooked factor that can distinguish one firm from another is passion for the project. In marketing their services, architects are selling the promise of future performance and their ability to deliver on that promise, so enthusiasm for a project can make a huge difference in influencing a potential client to hire a firm. In the selection process, the architect needs to find ways to demonstrate how much he or she wants to do the project, in a way that is natural and proportionate to the project. For example, on a very important project, it may be perfectly appropriate to say, "This is the most exciting project that has happened in this city in years, and we are very excited at the opportunity to work with you on it!" If the project is small or not very exciting, "We really want to work with you!" may be all that is needed. In a close race between competitors, the architect's enthusiasm can be the deciding factor.

MARKETING STRATEGY

Marketing efforts will be most successful when they mesh with the vision and operations of a firm. To create an effective plan for improving marketing and building business, your firm's long-term goals must be clear. This includes setting goals for business growth, as well as goals based on the design aspirations of the firm's principals and staff.

The firm's business plan can provide a good starting point for developing a marketing strategy. A business plan is a high-level discussion of the basis and objectives for beginning a new business venture, and for its overall operations over time. Depending on how your firm has developed its business plan, it may contain some indication of target markets, financial goals, and hiring and staffing strategies.

To begin the marketing planning process, it is advisable to bring key firm leaders together for a strategy meeting. Below are ten key questions that can form the agenda for a productive strategy meeting, one that results in answers that form a basis for the firm's marketing strategy. It will be helpful to do some research before the meeting to have information handy on the firm's markets, competitors, and clients to help facilitate discussion of each question.

1. *Who are we?* Key firm leaders must agree on their vision for the firm and its basic identity. What kind of practice is it? What do the leaders of the firm believe in? What is the firm known for? Is the firm a design-based practice, known for a signature design style that can be applied to many kinds of projects, or is it a specialist practice, expert in the design of a specific facility type?

There are advantages and disadvantages in being either a generalist or a specialist. A strategy of *generalization*, of pursuing work in a number of markets, can enable a firm to grow by pursuing new kinds of work. This strategy is often more stable, as downturns in one market may be offset by opportunities in others. A strategy of *specialization*, of pursuing work in one or just a few markets, can be incredibly profitable while the targeted market is hot but does not usually enable the same long-term stability as the generalist strategy. When a firm "owns" a market—when it becomes the obvious leader in a given area—a lot less time and money are required to bring in new work, and the firm's profitability can soar. In practice, many firms follow a hybrid strategy that involves specializing in several key markets, ideally providing the firm with some of the stability of a general practice and some of the benefits of a specialist practice.

▶ Firm Identity and Expertise (4.3) discusses how architecture firms can create strong firm identities.

2. *What markets do we serve?* Key markets should be defined carefully. Markets can be defined by geography, service, client industry, and facility type. Members of a firm could define its market by saying, "We provide architectural and interior design services for academic institutions in the Midwest, with a special emphasis on dormitory projects." There should be a clear distinction between the markets the firm works in now and the markets the firm would like to move into. It is important to have a clear, realistic picture of the firm's position in each desired market, and to consider the competition in each market. Who is your firm competing against? Which firms are the most successful? Make a list of all major competitors, and briefly discuss the strengths and weaknesses of each.

3. *What are our strengths?* What is your firm really good at? The answer could be design, service, or some special knowledge or expertise. In listing a firm's strengths, it is important to emphasize those that are truly unique to the firm. A generic strength such as "We're responsive to clients" is something any service provider in business today should be able to claim, and therefore would not differentiate a firm from others.

4. *What are our weaknesses?* It is vitally important in the marketing strategy process to be honest about liabilities. What are the things that your firm does not do as well as it could? List everything that might affect the firm's performance, or the perception of the firm's performance—both internally and externally. Establishing an understanding of weaknesses is the first step to overcoming them, and it can minimize the amount of time spent chasing opportunities that will be difficult to capture.

5. *What are our opportunities?* Consider each market in which the firm is active and identify opportunities in those markets for growth or for developing greater depth in existing areas. What's changing in these markets? Are there trends that could be capitalized on to achieve growth? Could the firm offer new services, explore new geographies, or become expert in designing new facility types? It may be helpful to ask, "What will we be doing in ten years that we are not doing now? What opportunities do we need to take advantage of now to get there?"

6. *What threats do we face?* Threats are factors in the marketplace that could hurt a firm's current position. An honest appraisal of threats is invaluable in planning the firm's future direction. What are competitors doing that threatens the firm's position in its existing markets? Is the firm facing new competitors? Are there trends in existing markets that may negatively affect your firm and its business? One way to get at the heart of this subject is to ask, "What keeps us up at night?"

7. *What's our vision for the firm?* A vision statement is a written expression of the firm's highest aspirations. This is the place to use superlatives: best, leading, largest, most, finest. What is your firm all about? Design? Innovation? Efficiency? Service? How does the firm's work improve the lives of its clients? How does the firm change the world for the better with every project? A vision statement could be something like this: "AB&C is a design firm that improves the lives of hospital patients and medical professionals by taking a fresh look at health care design and applying best practices from around the world to our projects." A vision statement should be as concise as possible. When you are crafting one for the first time, it may help to

begin by writing it as long as it needs to be and then to cut out what is not absolutely essential. Try to pare it down to one key idea, if possible. The final statement should be as active and as ambitious as possible.

8. *What's our mission?* A mission statement is much more directed than the vision statement. It describes where the firm is going. It describes how the firm would like to change its practice in the future. It is important to think big, but at the same time a firm must create a mission that is practical and achievable. A sample mission statement might be, "Our mission is to be the most respected laboratory design firm on the West Coast. We intend to accomplish this by hiring the best staff, rigorously improving the quality and accuracy of our design, and delivering on our promises." When developing a mission statement, it helps to ask, "Where do we want to go now?" Is there an existing market the firm ought to penetrate further? Is there an area of existing practice the firm could strengthen? Be as specific and focused as possible.

9. *What are our goals?* The next step is to identify goals that will help your firm accomplish its mission. What does your firm need to do to accomplish its mission? Does the firm need to hire new kinds of staff, modify the design process, look for different kinds of work, or make other significant changes in strategy or operations? Discuss how firm members are going to work to achieve these goals. Who will be responsible for following through with each goal? How soon will firm leaders reconvene to evaluate progress?

10. *How do we communicate our strategy?* Everyone in the firm has a role to play in marketing; therefore, it is vital for everyone to understand and participate in the marketing strategy. Consider creating a one-page marketing strategy summary that includes all ten of these questions with brief summaries of the firm's answers and action plan, and then distributing it to all staff. It is a mistake to have the strategy shared only by the firm's leaders. The marketing strategy will be most effective if everyone is on board with where the firm is headed and if each person understands his or her role in helping the firm move forward.

BRANDING

Branding is a familiar concept in the world of products. Think of a few great product brands—Sony, Nike, Mercedes, Apple, Volvo: These names are closely associated with product attributes or even marketing slogans, such as safety for Volvo or "Just Do It" for Nike. Brands are an incredibly effective means of communication between companies and their customers. If a company has a clear and consistent brand, customers will know what to expect and will associate the company with certain key ideas.

Service companies have brands just like products companies do. Many service providers, however, are more comfortable using the word "reputation" than "brand," but both words have essentially the same meaning: what people have in mind when they think of a given firm. Brand is critical in differentiating one firm from another.

A firm's brand is built by every single interaction that people have with the firm. It is the consistency of experiences with the firm and its work that defines its brand. Once a firm decides on a specific brand message, the message should be conveyed to key audiences in a memorable way. If a firm declares it is all about service, for example, and if the firm's staff delivers on this promise so that everything its clients and the public see supports this, the firm will become known for service.

Once a firm has gone through the strategy development process and carefully considered its vision, mission, and identity, the firm can proceed with spreading the word to existing clients, prospective clients, and other audiences. Building a communications plan around your brand is a five-step process:

1. *Define your audiences.* What specific industries or organizations is the firm focusing on? Who are the people at these organizations that the firm is trying to reach? How do these targeted clients interact with the firm now?

2. *Get a clear picture of how your firm is perceived.* This may require some research—asking people in various audiences what they think of the firm. It may be helpful to periodically take current or former clients to lunch and ask them directly to share what they think the firm's strengths and weaknesses are.

3. *Identify the firm's message.* The message should be as simple and clear as possible, and should be a direct reflection of the firm's vision statement. If possible, summarize the message in one keyword, such as "service," or a short phrase.

4. *Determine how to transmit the firm's message.* A firm's audiences can be reached in many ways. Consider your firm's work, staff, logo, office environment, business cards, advertising, proposals, and marketing materials. How can the firm make use of every contact with potential clients to get its message across?

5. *Make sure your firm "walks the talk."* No matter what, the brand must be backed up with action. A brand is empty and hollow if it is not consistent with the service the firm provides and the quality of the firm's work. If there's any fibbing, the staff will know, and before long the clients will, too.

POSITIONING

Positioning is the application of a firm's brand to a specific market. While branding is the process of trying to influence the perception various audiences have of the firm, positioning is the process of packaging the company for a specific target market and determining how to define it relative to the competition in that market. The brand applies to the entire firm, in all markets, and should originate from the firm's vision statement. The position, however, applies to only one market. When figuring out how to position the firm, you need to ask, "How can we present the firm to this market, and how can we differentiate our firm from the competition?"

The value of market position becomes most apparent when a firm is in pursuit of a specific opportunity. A firm's position is its starting point and consists of what clients and potential clients think of the firm before they open a proposal or grant an interview. What do they know about the firm? What do they think of its work? How is the firm positioned in this particular market? Is it the leader or the underdog?

In their landmark book *Positioning: The Battle for Your Mind* (McGraw-Hill, 2000), Al Ries and Jack Trout describe positioning in terms of ladders in the audience's mind: Each ladder is a market, and each rung is a brand. Where a brand fits on the ladder is its positioning. For example, imagine what the positioning ladder looks like for cola drinks: rung 1: Coca-Cola, rung 2: Pepsi-Cola, rung 3: RC Cola, rung 4: everybody else.

Once the arrangement of a ladder has been set in the mind of the public, it is very tough for a brand to move up the ladder. Even though Pepsi generally wins in blind taste tests, it cannot knock Coke out of its position at the top. In another example, if an architecture firm is competing against HOK Sport in the sports arena market, it may be able to beat the firm on one project, but it will be very difficult to knock it off the top rung of the ladder. HOK is probably the first firm a prospective client thinks of for sports arena design, and there is not much other firms can do about that.

YOUR FIRM NAME

One of the most important tools in a firm's brand communication is its name. It is important to consider the significance a name has to people who hear it, and how it supports the firm's vision and brand. The best names are distinctive and memorable.

Most architecture firms have one of the following types of names:

- *Multiple proper names.* Difficult to remember, and usually shortened to a set of letters that quickly lose their meaning. Examples: HOK, SOM, NBBJ, HLW, KPF, BBB, WATG, P&W.

- *Single name of signature architect or company founder.* Generally calls up the image of a visionary founder. Examples: Polshek, Gensler, Jerde, Rockwell.

- *Anything other than a person's name.* Less ego is implied, but such a name can also seem less personal. Examples: Studios, Morphosis, Pentagram, Arquitectonica.

When choosing a firm name, think about it carefully and objectively. Consider both how it looks on paper and how it sounds when people say it. Is it easy to spell? Is it easy to say? Consider any connotations the name has in your mind and the mind of your audience. Does it sound like anything else? Do you have an emotional response to it? Does it sound like the firm you want to be? If the firm carries a person's name or one combined from several surnames, what associations or connotations do those names have?

The challenge is to define each market (that is, each ladder) as specifically and concisely as possible so that people can accept it as a unique market, remember it, and associate your firm with it. It is vitally important to define your markets carefully. What does your firm offer this market? Why should the firm pursue the market, and how will it become a leader in it? Much as the vision statement describes the firm's aspirations, the positioning statement sums up a specific market and the firm's position in it. For example, a positioning statement might read, "JKL is the leader in the design of intermodal transportation facilities. We are different from the competition because we have a thorough understanding of the complex circulation issues of people, trains, buses, and cars."

Developing a positioning statement is a four-step process that includes considering and answering the following questions:

1. *What is the market?* The market is defined by service, facility type, client industry, and/or geography. It can be any area that could have a marketable specialization and any permutation of those four factors. For example, a market could be the interior design (service) of retail locations (facility type) for fashion companies (industry) in the western United States (geography). Or a market could be only one or two of those factors, for example, real estate developers in Boston.
2. *What does the market need?* An assessment of the needs of the market requires input from clients and prospective clients. Find out what they would like to do differently but so far have not been able to. Find out what their hot issues are. Find out what the trends are. Identify any unsatisfied opportunities in the market. Then determine if your firm can fulfill any of these needs better than your competitors.
3. *Who is the competition?* To position a firm within a market, it is essential to know as much as possible about the competition. What other architects work in this market? How are they perceived? What is their positioning? Is another firm the clear leader in the market? (If so, you may want to redefine the market and try a new "ladder.") Are there any weaknesses in the competition against which a firm could position itself? For example, "We're just as good as RST, but we are cheaper!"
4. *What do we offer?* Most important to determining your firm's positioning is zeroing in on what the firm can bring to this market that none of the competitors can match. What experience, capabilities, or attributes does the firm offer that are truly unique? Why would a prospective client in this market be foolish to hire the competition?

Answers to these questions will help a firm put together a clear positioning statement, such as, "PQR is the leader in designing mini storage facilities in the Midwest. We can design and deliver a mini storage facility faster than anyone." Once the statement has been crafted, the next step is to spread the word in every communication the firm has with the identified market, and to back up the positioning by delivering on its promises.

THE MARKETING PLAN

A marketing plan provides structure to marketing efforts on a continuing basis. Where there is a plan, there is a common understanding of marketing goals and objectives and what actions the firm will take to build its business. It is a measuring stick that guides decision making. When any kind of opportunity arises—whether a project or publicity or joint venture—the marketing plan provides a context for evaluating the opportunity and determining how to proceed.

Most firms create marketing plans in an attempt to expand their practice, whether in overall size, profitability, or the types of opportunities for which the firm can compete. Without a plan, a firm can probably win work and sustain client relationships, but it will be difficult to penetrate new markets or significantly increase market share in existing markets.

Developing a Marketing Plan

A firm should aim to have a marketing plan for each of its markets. If the firm does some retail work, some residential work, and some academic work, it should have a marketing plan for each. A marketing plan should be no more than a page long, if possible. A short and simple plan is most likely to be read and followed. The following is a short outline for what should go into a one-page marketing plan.

The market. Define the market as precisely as possible in terms of geography, service, industry, and facility type.

The mission. What do we want to accomplish? Describe specifically the impact the firm would like to have in this market. What is the major goal of this marketing plan? What do you want your firm's position in this market to be?

Current position and client base. Who are our current clients in this market? Describe where the firm is right now in this market. Is the firm a veteran, an underdog, or a newcomer?

As part of the planning process, consider carefully how much emphasis to place on new clients and how much to place on existing clients. The mix will vary depending on the firm's focus, current position in the market, and goals. Existing clients make great references for potential clients to talk to, and can also recommend your firm to their friends and business associates.

Market size and trends. How big is the market? What is changing? This may be the time to do some research to learn more about the market. How many projects are there each year in this market? How profitable are they? What trends in this market can your firm take advantage of?

Competitors. Which firms is your firm competing against? What are their strengths and weaknesses? Prospective clients will compare your credentials with those of other firms. What other firms will your firm be positioning itself against?

Positioning. Where do you want your firm to stand in this market? Have you defined the market in such a way that your firm can be the leader in it?

Objectives. Break down your firm's mission into smaller pieces. What can you do to achieve your mission? Do you need to do more business development, reach out to existing clients more, or work on media relations? Be as specific as possible here. If there is anywhere in the plan to add additional detail, it is here. This is the heart of the marketing plan—what firm leaders and staff members intend to do to fulfill the identified mission.

Responsibilities. It is important to assign specific responsibilities to individuals to make sure the objectives can be accomplished. Spread around responsibility. Everyone involved in this market should share in the responsibility of fulfilling the plan.

Schedule. Make it very clear in the plan when firm leaders will check on progress. By what date is each person named supposed to have accomplished his or her objective? Give them a time frame. If this is a one-year plan, it may make sense to review the plan every month or two to check progress, update the plan, and make new assignments.

Budget. The budget should quote a specific dollar amount for the firm's marketing efforts in this market. It should include hard costs (printing, networking expenses, etc.) and soft costs (staff time). Consider breaking out big-ticket items, such as a new brochure or attendance at a trade show.

Determining the Marketing Budget

Budgeting can be a difficult process. It is tough to put dollar values on expenses that have not appeared yet and expect to live by them for the lifespan of the budget. It is probably impossible to predict how many award submissions the firm will complete, or how many presentations will be made over the course of a year. This is why a budget is so important—it is a guideline for determining whether an opportunity is reasonable in terms of its cost.

To prepare a budget, start by developing broad categories for expenses. This may include marketing materials, photography, market research, public relations, business

The market: Architectural design of garages for shopping centers in Florida.

The mission: We want to be the leading designer of garages for shopping centers in Florida. We want to double our revenue in this market in the next year.

Current position and client base: We have designed three multistory garages for shopping centers in the last year for three different clients. However, we are often thought of as a designer of garages for corporate offices, not shopping centers.

Market size and trends: Ten to twenty new shopping centers are built in Florida each year. In addition, older shopping centers are being reclaimed as corporate offices (five to ten last year). There may be an opportunity to leverage our corporate office parking garage experience to expertise in shopping centers.

Competitors: VWX designs shopping centers and parking garages. RST designs parking garages and lots, mostly for sports arenas and amusement parks. CDE designs anything, anywhere.

Positioning: We are the leading firm in designing parking garages for shopping centers. Unlike our competitors, we are specialists in this project type. We have deep experience in parking garage design, not only for shopping centers, but also for corporate offices.

Objectives: We intend to

- Build our network of shopping center developers.
- Redesign our marketing materials.
- Conduct a direct mail campaign.
- Get articles placed in trade publications.
- Be more aggressive in closing the deal.

Responsibilities: [Put at least one name next to every item on your objectives list.]

Schedule: The time frame of this plan is one year. We will check on progress next month.

Budget: Our marketing budget for the year is $20,000. Of this, $5,000 will be for printing new marketing materials and the rest for networking and pursuing specific opportunities.

Firms typically spend 9.5 to 11 percent of their fee revenue on marketing, although small firms of two to four people and sole practitioners spend less (8.5 and 5.5 percent, respectively).

2006 AIA Firm Survey

development, proposals, and presentations. Then make a rough guess at a reasonable amount for each category over the course of the next year, using any existing historical data as a benchmark. The first budget will be the most difficult to prepare; in subsequent years, as expenses are tracked, the firm will have more perspective on what is reasonable and which areas require investment of more resources.

A Living Document

The best marketing plans are living documents. The marketing plan should not be filed away, but kept close at hand for reference and revisions. Over the life of the plan, unanticipated opportunities will come up. There may be serious setbacks for one reason or another, or the market may change dramatically. Whenever market conditions change, the plan should be updated accordingly. A plan that is not able to change over time runs the risk of becoming obsolete or irrelevant. When opportunities arise that had not been envisioned, the response should be carefully considered. An opportunity can be outside the parameters of the plan and still serve the mission—the spirit of the plan. The following questions will help determine how to evaluate a new opportunity:

- Does this opportunity serve the mission?
- What is the potential benefit?
- What is the total cost?
- Does it fit the budget?
- What is the risk?
- Is it worth it?

If the opportunity supports the mission, the plan can be changed to encompass the new opportunity. Otherwise, it makes sense to defer to the existing plan and decline the opportunity.

BUDGETING MATRIX

This sample budget matrix has columns for different markets (in this case, academic, labs, and offices) to break down the budget by market sector. The top portion of this budget covers soft costs (principal, staff, and marketing time—probably the biggest dollar-value item on your budget). The bottom portion itemizes specific hard costs, such as project photography, brochure printing, and so on.

SAMPLE BUDGET MATRIX

SOFT COSTS: STAFF TIME	ACADEMIC	LABS	OFFICES
PRINCIPAL TIME			
STAFF TIME			
MARKETING STAFF			

HARD COSTS: EXPENSES			
PHOTOGRAPHY			
BROCHURES			
REPRINTS			
DIRECT MAIL			
AWARD ENTRIES			
PUBLICITY			
TRADE SHOWS			
SHORT-RUN PRINTING			
RESEARCH			
TRAVEL			
NETWORKING			
MEMBERSHIPS			
TRAINING			

BUSINESS DEVELOPMENT AND SALES

The word "sales" can suggest an uphill battle of convincing someone to buy something he or she does not really want or need. Nobody likes to be "sold." Fortunately, the process of winning new business does not have to be about "selling." An architect needs to communicate that his or her firm is the right one for the project by making a personal and compelling case to the client that the firm has the best solution for the client's needs. Professionals win business by being truthful, competent, and personal. People who are hiring an architect generally seek to hire someone they like and trust—not someone who has "sold" them something.

The business development process can be approached in a number of ways. Many established firms are reactive in their approach: Clients and potential clients who know about a firm through prior experience or reputation send requests for proposals (RFPs) to the firm, which responds, hopefully winning a satisfactory portion of work to sustain its business. A proactive approach to business development is one in which a firm carefully selects the individuals and organizations it wants to work for and pursues them. A proactive approach gives a firm more control over whom it works for and the kinds of work it will take on, and can open up significant new opportunities and areas of growth. This approach can require considerable work, but it can also be highly rewarding.

Whatever approach is followed, relationships are critical to the process of winning new work. In an ideal situation, a firm will already have a strong relationship with the project decision makers when they begin the process of selecting an architect. Even if your firm has to compete to satisfy additional stakeholders (a board of directors or a public agency's purchasing policies), if you have a strong relationship, the firm will have an advocate in the decision-making group and will be able to get more accurate information from the potential client as to the real issues guiding the selection process.

If the firm's relationship with the potential client is not strong, or the firm does not have any relationship at all at the start of the process, it can be much harder to compete or even to have a sense of how the competitive process is going to unfold. All you can do is listen carefully to the potential clients and try to figure out who they are and where they are coming from, consider their objectives and priorities carefully, and respond with your qualifications and proposal, tailored to your understanding of the potential client and project.

Networking

Networking is vital to the marketing success of business-to-business services like architecture. A good network can make the difference between a flourishing practice and one that is struggling to survive.

Networking is an ongoing process; it should not happen just when the firm is pursuing work.

Many people think of a network as a set of artificial relationships, a social convention that exists to fulfill a business purpose—sharing and trading information. But a professional network is essentially a circle of friends. The relationships in the network are real; they are based on authentic interpersonal connections.

An architect builds his or her network the same way that an individual looks for new friends. Potentially beneficial contacts can be found in social situations—industry events, parties, and even on projects—or anywhere there are people with whom an individual feels a natural connection and where there is the possibility of a mutually beneficial relationship. What each side offers the other can be almost anything: industry information, connections, a good laugh, knowledge of the local community, gossip. All that is important is that the friendship is real and that each party has something to offer the other.

There are many different ways to build a network. Some people seem as if they want to know everybody, while others try to build tight bonds with a limited number of people. There is not a right or wrong way to build a network; you could build a great network with five friends (if the relationships are strong and they have information and connections) or with 600. Either way, the network needs constant attention to grow and evolve.

If an architect has built a strong network of people in related disciplines (engineers, contractors, real estate brokers, developers, and consultants), they can share information on upcoming projects. Initially, with newer contacts, the sharing may be more guarded and exploratory: "Have you heard anything about this new project?" With more established contacts, professional acquaintances will be thinking of projects for each other: "I heard about a new project that would be perfect for your firm."

Targeting Clients

Firms that are proactive in their business development efforts are much more likely to win projects that members of the firm are truly interested in, from individuals and organizations they want to work for. Being proactive means deciding which organizations you would like to work with, researching them, getting to know the decision makers, building relationships, and eventually pursuing and winning work from them. It can be a long process, but it is very important to building a business and taking it in new directions.

Start by identifying prospective clients with whom you would like to do business. Survey the markets your firm is currently working in (defined by industry, facility type, service, or geography). Are there organizations the firm has not worked for in these markets that would make attractive clients? Make a list of ten to twenty prospective clients to target.

Be realistic. Each potential client on the list must be an achievable target for the firm. Do not consider organizations for which there are serious roadblocks, such as those that only work with firms that are very different from yours, or organizations for whose projects your firm has no relevant experience.

Once you have assembled a list of ideal clients, begin to research them. Go online and find out everything you can. Ask people about them. Most important, try to connect with the key decision makers in these organizations. Who are they? What are their backgrounds? Whom do you know who knows them? How can you meet them? What can be your pretext for approaching them and getting to know them? Pursue the top targets aggressively, and try to make connections and build networks that get you closer to the decision makers.

Of course, you will not be able to get a meeting with every ideal client on the list right away. Simply having a list of target clients, and keeping up-to-date with their businesses and ongoing projects will prepare the firm to act on an opportunity when it appears.

Developing Leads

A lead on a potential project can come from practically anywhere—a friend, a work associate, a client, a family member, or even the newspaper. The more people who are familiar with the work an architecture firm does, the greater the likelihood someone will think of the firm when they hear about appropriate new projects. When a lead to a potential new project comes along, the following questions should be asked:

- *What is the project?* How big is it? Where is it? What is the budget?
- *What is driving the project?* Why is it happening now? What is changing in the potential client's business that necessitates this project? What objective is the potential client trying to achieve by undertaking this project?
- *Is it right for your firm?* Is this project not just something the firm *can* do, but something it is truly qualified to do, experienced in doing, and passionate about?
- *Who is the competition?* Which other firms will be considered for this project? If the answer is "none," great! If the answer is "an open field of 50 or 100 firms," not so great.
- *Does your firm have an existing relationship?* Does the firm have any connection to the people who are involved with this project? Whom can you meet? How can you connect yourself to the decision makers?
- *What is the timing?* If word about the project has hit the street (or if the project has been publicly announced), it may be too late—there are probably other firms already lined up to do the project. If the project is still being planned, there may be time to help the potential client with the process of defining the project and position the firm for the work.

- *Can you win the job?* Realistically, given the potential client and the project, and an assessment of the firm's experience, relationships, and competition, what are the chances of winning this project?
- *What should you do next?* Given everything that is known about the client and the opportunity, what is the best first step to pursuing this project?

Answering these questions puts a firm in a much better position to evaluate the lead and determine the appropriate level of investment. Many people hear about a lead and rush headlong into the pursuit, but it is much better to step back, evaluate the lead objectively, and then determine how high a priority this lead is and the proper course of action.

An important part of the process of pursuing leads is having a system for tracking them. If an architect is working alone to track a few leads, the system can be fairly simple— a notebook or a simple spreadsheet. But if the information needs to be shared with others within an organization, the firm may want to invest in a more robust lead-tracking database system. Generally, there's far more to be gained by sharing, as colleagues can help if they know someone related to the project. There is no one-size-fits-all system for tracking leads in the architecture business, however. Each firm has to find the system that works best.

THE CASE FOR MARKETING STRATEGICALLY

Many leading design firms have achieved success somewhat accidentally, through the personalities, connections, and panache of their founders. It is a rare firm that looks at

COLD CALLS

No matter how hard you try, there are times when you cannot find a connection to the decision makers on a project, or to anyone who knows them. When all other possibilities for contact have been exhausted, your alternatives are reduced to two: Pick up the phone and call "cold," or forget about the lead.

Cold calling is not a particularly effective means for bringing in work, so it should be your absolute last resort, after you have exhausted your network but still want the project and believe it is right for your firm. Relationships, more than any other factor, are what win work, and trying to build a relationship from a cold call is very difficult. In such calls, the person you are calling has no idea who you are—which is why it's called a "cold" call. Any warmth that arises from the situation will have to be your own. Even a warm call is better—when the person you are calling has heard about you or your firm before.

Despite its difficulties, if you are honestly interested in a project and believe your firm is qualified, a cold call may be worth a shot. Following are a few basic rules to follow:

Know whom you are calling. Know as many details as you can about the person you want to talk to. Know his or her name, title, role in the project, history, and anything else you can find out before you pick up the phone. The goal of the call is to get a personal meeting. Personal

relationships are not built over the phone. Have a strong hook (something in your portfolio the person you are calling will want to see) that will get you the meeting.

Rehearse what you are going to say. When you get on the phone with the person, you may not have much time to break through his or her "sales filter" and convince him or her it would be valuable to meet you. Plan it, write it down, and rehearse it.

Be specific and direct. You are calling to talk about a specific project. Ask about it. Do not be shy about why you are on the phone.

Ask questions. Prepare good questions to ask about the project to show you have thought about the project— not just about the selection process. Ask questions the person you are talking to may not have considered.

Be yourself. Your goal is to build a relationship with the person on the other end of the phone line. Strike a balance between being as professional as possible while still letting your energy, enthusiasm, and personality shine through.

Send information, and always follow up. As a follow-up to your call, always send some information about your firm. Make it as specific to the project as possible. It should not be just your standard brochure; it should be specific information that will be interesting to the contact.

marketing as an ongoing strategic process that is integrated into the operations of the firm. For those that do, the benefits are immense, including sustaining the firm, expanding its business, earning higher fees, and gaining access to preferred types of clients and projects.

Professionals who ignore marketing and do not develop their marketing and strategic thinking skills will have the terms of their work life—type of client, type of work, and even compensation—determined by someone else. The better an architect or architecture firm is at marketing, and the more strategically focused, the more likely the sole practitioner or firm will be able to work on truly interesting, profitable projects.

For More Information

In *Selling the Invisible: A Field Guide to Modern Marketing* (Texere, 2001), Harry Beckwith, a leading writer and speaker on marketing for service firms, provides great perspective and insight into marketing services. Also recommended are Beckwith's later books, *The Invisible Touch: The Four Keys to Modern Marketing* (Texere, 2001) and *What Clients Love: A Field Guide to Growing Your Business* (Warner Books, 2003).

Ford Harding's *Rainmaking: The Professional's Guide to Attracting New Clients* (Adams Media Corporation, 1994) is a classic. Even though the book is not specific to architecture firms, Harding's experience as a marketing director for a leading architecture firm gives him a strong grasp of marketing and business development issues for architects.

Architect's Essentials of Marketing (Wiley, 2005) by David Koren is one of the few books on marketing written specifically for architects.

Marketing Professional Services (Prentice Hall Press, 2002) by Philip Kotler, Paul Bloom, and Thomas Hayes is frequently used as a textbook for classes pertaining to marketing services. Although academic in its approach, it covers a broad range of topics in the field of marketing.

Al Ries and Jack Trout's *Positioning: The Battle for Your Mind* (McGraw-Hill, 2001) is a detailed discussion of positioning as a component in the branding and marketing process. The ideas in the book apply to firms of every type in every industry.

The *Marketing Handbook for the Design & Construction Professional* (BNI Publications, 2000) is the authoritative reference on marketing from the Society for Marketing Professional Services (SMPS), the leading source of marketing knowledge and education for architecture, engineering, construction, and related consulting firms. Educational programs offered by SMPS, both at a national level and through local chapters, can be found on its Web site. (www.smps.org)

4.6 How Clients Select Architects

Pat Rosenzweig

The values held by an organization are reflected in its criteria for selecting an architecture firm.

Prospective clients, whether organizations or individuals, select their architects in many ways, but the approaches used can be grouped into four broad categories: cost based, qualifications based, value based, and direct hire. Most often the selection

Pat Rosenzweig is a principal with the Chicago-based architecture firm of OWP/P. She has more than thirty years of experience in marketing architecture, previously as director of marketing for Perkins + Will and owner of Rosenzweig Professional Services Marketing. Her specialty is developing strategies for sales efforts and coaching for interviews.

Across all client types, the selection process criteria are largely the same: cost, chemistry and relationship, and relevant experience.

The Client Experience (AIA, 2002)

criteria are a blend of these categories, but one is likely to dominate. Usually, entities or individuals that seek architectural services do not announce their primary selection criteria. Even when prospective clients share the points they will attribute to each factor, these often allow for subjective judgments.

The architect's challenge is to discern what the selection criteria actually are. How is the prospective client accustomed to working? What are its concerns about this particular project? Many times, when the process is over and a short list is released or selection made, the reason for the selection is "chemistry." Many architects interpret this pejoratively, thinking their competitor's style or salesmanship won the job. In reality, however, jobs are won through the ability of the successful team to convey that it understands the prospect's functional and process issues. Once a prospect becomes a client, the firm can maintain the relationship by recognizing it is always at risk unless the firm maintains the values on which the selection was made throughout the project.

Making a judgment about selection category is not always as easy as it appears. Looking at an RFP, an architect might think, "This is a government office building. This is a QBS [qualifications-based selection] project. We'll show our government office buildings." While experience designing government office buildings is one criterion the architect needs to meet, is it the only one? Are there operational concerns, such as the ability to manage the size of the project or the complex team required? Is the owner concerned about the cost of the project? Is the project going to pursue LEED™ certification at a certain level? In a qualifications-based selection approach, the question is: qualifications for what? At the same time, the architect must determine how to meet the formatting and technical requirements of the solicitation and still show the qualifications that will connect with the client.

The following discussion covers each of the common architect selection approaches and suggests ways to determine what the issues really are, along with suggestions about how to respond to a prospective client.

COST-BASED SELECTION

Cost is always an issue and cost-driven clients base their decisions predominantly on the basis of the architect's proposed fee.

Types of Clients That Tend Toward Cost-Based Selection

Clients that have a complete program, experience with the project type, and explicit design standards usually (but not always) favor cost-based selection. These clients are typically, though not exclusively, from the private sector. However, clients interested in architects who provide innovation and leadership in a collaborative relationship are less likely to rely on cost and more likely to consider other factors. Cost-based selection is often used for branch facilities of restaurants, retail properties, financial services organizations, data or call centers, or industrial processing facilities for which the client or an operations consultant will handle mechanization.

Knowing if the project will require multiple layers of decision making by the client helps the architect determine if the proposed fee is realistic for the effort needed to meet the client's expectations.

Owners rarely make decisions on a pure cost basis. In many cases, the prospect has researched the qualifications of several firms. The short list or final decision then boils down to cost. Similarly, if fees submitted by two firms are very close, other criteria—especially experience—will be decisive. Whether a prospective client reviews qualifications before issuing a request for proposal or in reaction to a submitted proposal, a review of the architect's prior experience is relevant to even the cost-oriented prospect. A lack of similar project experience on the part of the architect could suggest that the client will pay for the architect to learn.

Determining If Cost Is the Most Important Criterion

Clients do not always say their decision will be based on the lowest fee. Therefore, the architect must find ways to judge how strong a role fee will play in client decisions.

Are there questions in the RFP related to cost and cost control, such as enumeration of change order requests and budgeted and final construction costs? An unusual number of such questions may indicate the prospective client was burned on past projects by out-of-control budgets or schedules. On the other hand, such clients may be unsophisticated school boards or municipal clients who did not effectively evaluate earlier project proposals or did not know how to manage their architects and want to ensure they do not make the same mistake again. They ask questions in the RFP and interviews in an attempt, however inappropriate, to find a more responsive architect.

An RFP from either a public or private client may also include information on the status of the project, such as the existence of a developed floor plan, site plan, or elevation and other program details. If a project is to be part of a chain of similar facilities, the architect should ask about the existence and scope of a prototype or design standards.

Sometimes cost- and schedule-based questions that appear in an RFP seem out of place. This may happen when one organization borrows an RFP from another and does not adapt it fully to its own needs. Nothing can resolve conflicts or ambiguities in the language of an RFP better than contacting the prospect directly.

Some prospective clients are unwilling to talk to the architect about the competition and believe they have no obligation to the architect beyond supplying performance standards and specifications. Similarly, a client may not realize that knowing who the competition is can help architects understand what the client is actually seeking, which will help them provide a more meaningful response to the RFP. "After all," this client thinks, "you all do the same thing, so what does it matter?" As well, some facility owners believe that if they talk to the architect, the playing field will not be level—that one architect may have an unfair advantage. There are subtle differences among these attitudes. The former signals a cost- and commodity-based approach to selection, and the latter suggests naiveté or perhaps respect for the architect's contribution to a successful facility.

The objective in talking to prospective clients is to learn as much as possible about their programs and their commitment to existing planning documents, how they will manage their projects, and who will be involved in decision making. For projects in the cost-based selection category, it is vitally important to learn anything that can help the architect create an appropriate fee.

Contacting allied professionals with whom a prospective client has worked, such as contractors and engineers, can provide insight into how the client works. This enables the architect to construct a fee appropriate to the client's work style and to make project cost assumptions consistent with the client's expectations.

Responses to a Cost-Based Prospect

The architect must first adhere to the rules of the RFP. Answer every question thoroughly and with respect. Try to understand the client's point of view. As examples, select projects with stellar references for which budgets and schedules were met. Remember, rigorous responses signal rigorous cost control. Here are a few guidelines:

- Provide budget adherence information, even if it is not requested.
- Respond respectfully to what appear to be "dumb" questions (e.g., those about change orders).
- Provide a schedule as detailed as the information permits. Frequently fee, construction cost, and schedule are closely linked in a prospect's value system. If there is not

WHAT TO ASK A PROSPECTIVE CLIENT

- Who is on the selection committee? Who are the leaders of the selection committee? What particular concerns does each have?
- Who will our firm work with on a day-to-day basis?
- Can you tell us a little about the person/group/committee that makes decisions?
- Can you describe the program? Is it room-by-room, or departmental? Do you know how many people will use the facility? What is this assessment based on?
- Have you identified the site? Where is it? If the site has not been identified, how much control over its location do you have?
- What worries you about this project? What about this project keeps you up at night?
- How do the worries of others on the selection committee differ from yours?
- Why are you doing this project *now*?

enough information to provide a detailed schedule, provide alternative scenarios, thoroughly explaining the assumptions for each.

- Provide an absolutely clear fee for the requested scope only. If the firm strongly believes additional services or a different weighting of activities is required to meet project demands, these should be presented separately. For example, if the architect suspects the program is not as complete as the RFP represents, the primary scenario would assume the level of programming verification the RFP states; in a second scenario, the architect could suggest a reason to do more extensive programming based on other information the client has provided (e.g., appointment of a new board or an acquisition).

- For a planning study (whether a master plan, feasibility study, or other type), determine how the client intends to use the plan. Is it to establish a rough budget or to test site capacity before executing an option? In such cases, only a modest fee suitable for assessing major system requirements is appropriate. Resist the temptation to provide more information than the client needs. However, if a client needs to submit the proposal to a regulatory body, the cost analysis and imagery may need to be more extensive to allow agencies to assess the validity of the cost. These studies will command appropriately higher fees, as will traditional master plans that identify future construction requirements.

- Do not take lightly any requests for elaborate matrixes showing hours-by-phase-by-person and "related experience" of personnel. This information is not necessarily requested to put the architect through the wringer. The request allows sophisticated clients to assess whether the fee is realistic (i.e., a reasonable number of hours); whether they would be getting enough time from the right level of personnel; whether the scope and complexity is over- or under-estimated, and thus whether the fee is realistic; and whether the team assigned really has the same experience as the firm.

- Carry the same awareness of cost into the interview. Bring the schedule. Whether it is formally presented or not, have it available for discussion during Q&A. If it is part of the formal presentation, highlight critical and, if possible, innovative stages that will ensure deadlines are met and perhaps save costs. Highlight cost-saving measures taken in the design or implementation of previous firm projects and have their costs on the tip of your tongue. When an RFP requires the submission of data showing staff hours by project task or discipline, know that information inside out. For many major corporations, the discussion of this information will be the sole issue in the interview.

QUALIFICATIONS-BASED SELECTION

Experience, or qualifications, is the starting point for just about every type of selection, even cost-based selection. Conversely, cost ultimately plays a role in architect selection in nearly every project. Clients using qualifications-based selection (QBS) methods select architects primarily on the basis of the similarity of an architect's prior work with the proposed project, under the assumption the architect's fee will be fair, competitive, negotiable, and consistent with the requirements of the project.

Mandated QBS

▶ Defining Project Services (6.1) describes steps for effectively identifying and defining the scope of project services.

Federal projects, many state and local government projects, and projects from owners that build many projects, such as public or private hospitals and universities, often mandate QBS. These clients usually follow a schedule that dictates fee ranges in accordance with the size and complexity of a project. Thus, once the firm has been selected, the fee negotiation focuses on project scope rather than on team qualifications.

Government agencies using QBS have formal processes with which firms must comply. The selection processes used by the Government Services Administration are

In June 2004, the federal government formally updated its standard forms 254 and 255 to the new, consolidated Standard Form 330, Architect-Engineer Qualifications. The new form is more concise than previous versions, allowing federal clients to assess the qualifications of architects and their consultant teams more easily. (In many cases, the form can be completed using fewer than twenty pages.)

Countless publications and software applications are available to help architects fill out these forms, but common sense should reign. As with previous versions, form 330 rewards firms that highlight work of appropriate size and offer strong references. Form 330 also allows architects to emphasize work that has been designed by the proposed team.

Other federal procurement methods include the highly praised Design Excellence Program, operated through GSA's Public Buildings Service. Started more than a decade ago, this program has afforded firms of all sizes the opportunity to design new federal buildings, major additions, and comprehensive renovations of existing federal architecture. In fact, most projects under $20 million in construction value are set aside for small businesses.

In this program, firms are recognized and selected based on the quality of their design and, in particular, the design skills of the proposed lead designer. Competition for these projects is heated. A five-person panel consisting of government officials and practicing architects selects the lead designer and prime A/E firm, usually from a pool of more than fifty statements of qualifications. At the earliest stage, the exemplary projects of the lead designer do not need to be exactly the same as the project being pursued, which is a significant departure from the practices supported by form 330 and other qualifications-based selection processes. In some cases, the short-listed firms are asked to compete in a single-day charrette or—even more rare—a month-long design competition before a winner is chosen.

The odds of winning these Design Excellence competitions are obviously slim, but successful teams can be rewarded with projects that have solid construction budgets and a broad public profile. These projects may also allow the firm to work with new building types.

The criteria for Design Excellence portfolios are standardized, and brevity is almost always preferred. Design teams should submit a limited number of images (usually no more than three pages per project) and even less text (no section permits more than three pages of description). The Design Excellence Program has been so successful that other public and nonprofit agencies have adopted its standards to structure their requests for qualifications.

For detailed requirements, visit GSA online at www.gsa.gov. Look for the Web page on "New Construction and Modernizations," which outlines design process and related submission requirements and provides information about the Design Excellence Program.

all qualifications based but vary depending upon the scope of the project and its position in a community. More information about these approaches to qualifications-based selection can be found in the accompanying sidebar.

A variation of the federal QBS process is a "task order agreement," commonly used by universities, government agencies, and corporations. Firms compete to be on a list of professionals deemed qualified to perform projects of a specified nature and scope. To be considered for a particular project, prequalified architects may be required to enter a fee competition. In this case, the design firm submits a chart to identify the fee per square foot for various project functions and sizes, whether renovation or new construction. If the client requests this information, further competition may be unnecessary. If provided at the initiative of the firm, it may enable a direct hire without further competition.

Voluntary QBS

Clients using qualifications-based selection approaches generally believe their architects know the fundamental program, materials, and sources for their particular facility or industry type (e.g., hospital casework standards and suppliers or furniture systems

Ordinarily a design competition connotes a selection process independent of traditional questionnaires with their lists of related qualifications. However, it is increasingly common that after creation of a short list, the finalists are expected to present a concept for the project. However the competitive aspect is framed, client goals are the same—they seek design innovation.

Whether a competition is composed of an invited list of competitors or advertised in design publications, the competition process can be fierce. While architects should be compensated for all stages of the competition or at least for a final round, it is the rare firm that stays within the budget suggested by the fee that is offered. Similarly, many competitions do not guarantee the project will go forward or that the winning firm will actually be awarded the project.

So why does a firm enter competitions? They are an excellent way for a firm to gain experience in a market or building type. Participation in competitions provides great team building and can boost staff morale, particularly among younger professionals. Some firms do no marketing except for entries in design competitions because many competition entrants are published.

Design competitions are frequently criticized, however. Complaints include that insufficient program information is provided for the architect to do a responsible job and that the jury is led to believe it can actually have a project at its anticipated cost even when some competitors disregard the stated budget.

The more precise the design program information is, the better firms can assess the risks of participating. A solicitation with a well-developed program, a precise articulation of payment provisions and process, opportunities to meet with the sponsoring organization, a list of jury members, clear and consistent rules on the method of presentation, and a budget will provide more security than one that is vague in any of these respects.

Above all, design solutions for competitions must be inspiring and understandable. If a short list will be made without benefit of an in-person interview, presentation boards and any required models have to be self-explanatory. Make sure text on the boards is concise and large enough to read easily.

For project interviews, the architect should remember that the jury is far more likely to remember a designer's enthusiasm and clarity of thought than a lot of details. Rely on the Q&A period to communicate all but the basic concept, logic, and most significant examples of how the concept is reflected in the design.

Above all, follow the rules.

consistent with a particular client's budget). Use of this approach to selection may also reflect a prospective client's appreciation for an established relationship with an architect or interest in gaining insight into what their peers are doing. QBS is sometimes used for projects in virtually every market segment.

Identifying the Qualifications Wanted

A client's idea of "relevant experience" and other appropriate qualifications varies from market sector to market sector, but several general types of experience are of interest to all clients.

Experience with project type. QBS generally signals the importance of a firm's past experience. Some RFPs may include precise requirements, such as a request for presentations of a certain number of public libraries, middle schools, or law firms completed by the firm in the past decade. They may also request examples of projects of "similar scope and complexity." Firms with deep experience usually can respond easily to these types of requests.

Firms with project type expertise may still be challenged if their experience is not with the same kind of client. For example, firms that have completed swimming pools and emergency departments may not have the experience to compete for a university natatorium or an emergency department of a certain size. Or a firm that has designed a significant number of K–12 schools may not have the experience to tackle a freestanding K–8 school with a small school philosophy.

Experience with project size and complexity. The relative importance of scope, complexity, function, and philosophy may be perceptible if an RFP includes an explanation of the evolution of the project. If a prospect also asks for a fee amount, this does not necessarily signal the selection will be based on fee. Rather, it may be a preliminary screening to eliminate a firm whose fee is way off base. A sophisticated client may eliminate a candidate whose fee is too low because the prospect recognizes the respondent does not understand the client's objectives or the complexity of the project.

Understanding of client needs. Clients may also want to know how a firm will "approach" the work. Usually this question is asked to find out how the firm will interact with the project's stakeholders. The client can learn whether applicants have over- or underestimated the number of meetings that will be required, can meet the schedule, and understand the nature of the client organization and decision-making process. Owners are likely to be interested in who from the architecture firm will lead the various stages of a project. This is particularly true for large projects and those that include associated firms or consultants, such as health care and higher education clients.

Researching the Client's Values

Others with whom a prospective client has worked know the client's values. They know how much stakeholders are involved in project development and delivery; the importance of the facility to the owner's marketing, recruitment, and retention; how the prospect makes decisions and who is involved; and how the prospect approaches risk.

The client's Web site can also provide some insight into the character of a company, government agency, or institution, but much more in-depth and objective information can be gained from other sources, especially direct client contact.

Responses to a Qualifications-Based Prospect

Responding to an RFP in a QBS process is likely to require both a written proposal, with accompanying exhibits, and a project interview.

Written proposal elements. The project proposal should showcase the firm's qualifications and tell what the firm will provide for the project.

USE THE INTERNET CAREFULLY

The Internet can be a useful way to learn about a prospective client, but some caution is required. Here are some things to consider when researching on the Internet:

- The corporate roles of members of the architect selection committee may be available on the company or institutional Web site. Based on these roles, the architect can make some presumptions as to what each person's priorities may be. If HR is involved, workplace environment or growth may be a consideration, while a CFO may be worried about cost. Sometimes architects can leverage existing relationships with board members.

- The Web site may show pictures of various existing facilities, which can indicate the degree of design freedom a prospective client may allow the architect.

- Those sections of a client's Web site directed at recruitment may suggest the importance of facilities, especially of amenities and a firm's priorities with regard to sustainability and workplace comfort. These sections may also reveal locations where the client is growing or where recruitment is difficult. Facility design will need to respond to such concerns.

- The vision, mission statement, or list of programs an organization posts on its Web site can provide information the architect can use to initiate discussion, as well as an idea of what will be involved in programming efforts for this client.

- Be cautious when using the Internet to discern information about a corporate culture. Marketers often prepare Web sites, and their views may not be consistent with the way an organization actually operates.

To begin, the cover letter should never be simply a letter of transmittal. It directs attention to the firm's experience and knowledge that can serve the client's needs. It should be specific: "During the past ten years, we have designed more than fifty emergency departments for community hospitals. Of special note are the ABC and QRS projects highlighted in Section 2 which, like yours, were designed to segregate pediatric and adult trauma areas."

An executive summary allows the architect to present seemingly dissimilar qualifications and can be useful when following the rules does not allow the architect to shine. For example, when an RFP has page limits, an executive summary can give the firm more space to describe the depth of its experience. Similarly, if an RFP does not include questions that address a design or process perspective in which the architect excels, an executive summary will allow the architect to highlight that expertise.

Short narratives can be used to explain the relevance of previous projects and the talents of staff who will be assigned to the client's project. These explanations may allow the use of standard, unedited project description pages or resumes. The tone of such language might read like these examples:

- "We have selected these projects because they exemplify our experience working with banks on new branches and on other projects with highly specific design standards."
- "The team we have selected includes personnel who have managed projects of this scale."

Never leave it to the client to figure out why particular projects and people have been included in your proposal. Obviously, projects listed should include only those that can offer good references.

Explanatory exhibits. Lawyers call these demonstrative exhibits; they are documents that address gaps in the architecture firm's direct qualifications.

A matrix of qualifications (see example in sidebar) can be used to demonstrate how the firm has previously met similar project requirements. The items in the matrix can be highly specialized functional spaces, delivery methods, cost parameters, leadership roles, or geographic or regulatory agency experience—any subjects that communicate the full scope of the firm's strengths to the client. This tactic is particularly useful when a firm has experience with all of the components of a project (e.g., training rooms, open offices, food service, dry labs, and 24/7 building systems) but has not done a project that combines all of them.

A matrix is also useful when a firm wants to propose a staff that includes new hires and associated specialists because it allows the firm to highlight individual staff member experience without improperly suggesting the firm has experience with projects it has not previously delivered. Finally, a matrix is useful when research indicates a key decision maker has a short attention span, as it provides a snapshot of what the firm has to offer.

Concept diagrams or block models are increasingly being used during project interviews. The firm's interview team can employ them to facilitate discussion about the project, which is almost always desirable. In addition, at the RFP stage, a concept diagram can inspire the client and demonstrate knowledge and abilities of the architecture firm that may not be evident in the written part of the proposal.

A diagram may also be useful when the firm's portfolio is dominated by small projects and the proposed project is substantially larger. For example, a diagram of conceptual solutions to parking and access sequences might be effective. Or, if the firm is not known for its design, an inspiring elevation or sketch could be helpful. If the prospect has identified a provocative approach to an operational issue, a drawing of a well-annotated floor plan may be effective.

Qualifications-based interviews. Jobs are won and often lost at the interview stage. Winning at this stage is about connecting with the values and priorities of the client better than the competition does. Thus it is incumbent on the architecture firm to find out from the client or from an architecture network who the competition is. Once the

This qualifications matrix for a proposed regional electronics assembly facility matches the needs of the project with the abilities of the architecture firm. The project is to be located in a suburb of a major city. It will be approximately 100,000 square feet in size and needs to be completed within one year. The company's personnel will be a blend of its own relocated employees and employees of a recently acquired competitor. The architecture firm submitting a proposal specializes in hospital design. The firm is associating with a world-class M/E/P firm for the project and has assigned a new hire with corporate experience to the project.

Prior Projects of Team Members	Experience Needed for Electronics Assembly Facility Project					
	Zoning in Suburb A	Projects of 100,000 s.f.	Dry Labs or Designer-Led Design-Build	Fast-Tracked Merged Organizations	Programming	Clean Rooms
University of Q Physics Addition		■	■			■
ABC Company	■			■	■	
Suburb A Community Hospital Surgicenter	■					■
University of Z Electrical and Mechanical Engineering School		■	■		■	■
Suburb A Community Hospital Parking Structure	■	■		■		
QRS, Inc. Headquarters		■		■	■	

competition is known, the firm can shape its proposal content and interview methods to highlight its winning strengths.

It is equally important to know who will represent the client at the interview, what the role and voting power of those people will be, and how much they have been involved in the selection process to date. In most groups, there is a person who has ultimate decision-making power, knowledge, or persuasiveness. It is critical to know who that person is so the interview can be shaped with that person's interests in mind.

Those determining the short list may not be the same as those making the final selection. This is particularly true in public education, where the superintendent or other senior staff manages the short-list process but the board often chooses the winning firm. If the architecture firm does not already know the opinions of the members of the board of education, researching the local newspapers for their positions on certain issues, as well as their professions, can be helpful. Most firms seeking work with local public bodies make it their business to attend board meetings, not just to be seen, but to learn the issues and positions of the members.

More than a few architects with great strategies have lost in the details. Common mistakes during interviews include the following:

- *The organization chart is not clear.* The client must know and see who is in charge. There should be only one leader.
- *Weak presenters are in key positions.* This error has its roots at the RFP stage. The firm must anticipate the interview when selecting the project team members. If management is a key issue, the project manager or director needs to be assertive and methodical. A designer needs to inspire. Manage the message and the time allotted to each person according to his or her ability to command attention.
- *The interview is not focused.* The interview replicates the RFP response; it is not a catalog. It should address the issues the client deems important, not what the architect believes are the key issues and challenges that should drive the project. To the degree the interview is about design, architects should discuss only those projects that parallel an issue of specific interest to this client, rather than highlighting a laundry list of projects. A rule of thumb is that each visual should deal with no more than two thoughts.
- *The team, especially the project manager, goes into unnecessary detail.* An interview is about making connections with an audience on issues relevant to meeting their objectives. Highlight, don't bore. Show that you respect the time of the client's interviewers and know what is important.
- *During Q&A, the senior manager on the team either does not control the responses or dominates them.* Unless a question is asked directly of a team member, the team leader should grab each question and direct it to the appropriate member of the team. If other team members jump in to respond, it will appear they do not trust the leader, but if the leader answers all the questions, the client may wonder about the strength of the team.
- *Answers to questions wander.* Q&A responses should be treated like a deposition. Answer directly and briefly. Your answer can be followed with, "Did I answer your question?"

VALUE-BASED SELECTION

Qualifications-based selection and value-based selection can look very similar. However, there are two significant differences between clients using QBS and those using value-based selection. The latter group is looking for an architect who is not only qualified to do the job but can take a leadership role in helping the client achieve its goals. The two bulleted paragraphs below illustrate this concept:

- The client has a project that fills a significant strategic role, but the client is inexperienced with the project type. Therefore, the client looks to the architect for ideas gained from working with other innovative clients. Often, a real estate decision has not been made and programming is not complete, giving the architect an opportunity to provide knowledge and recommendations beyond those required when the client is familiar with the project type.

- The client's predominant interest is in design. Government clients using the GSA Design Excellence Program and design competitions in qualifications-based selection of architects are looking for architects who can provide superior innovation, superior aesthetics, and superior sensitivity to context and history—in other words, value.

Client contact is almost mandatory to distinguish value-based criteria from pure qualifications-based criteria. In fact, clients may not be aware that architects could lead a team to meet their strategic needs. For example, a discussion may reveal the prospect does not know whether to lease, buy, develop, or engage in a sale/leaseback to acquire property for a project. An architecture firm knowledgeable about these client challenges can distinguish itself from the competition by submitting a response that includes relevant information from an associated real estate professional.

Responses to a Value-Based Prospect

The value-based RFP response should demonstrate leadership. It is still a qualifications-based response, but project descriptions should be tailored to the primary concern of the client. For example, if the client's priority is to compete with its peers (e.g., to be the best music school or the best trading company work environment), the firm can present past projects that highlight the client's best-in-class competition. The prospect is interested in learning what its competition does and that the proposing architect can provide such information.

If the client is looking for process leadership, on the other hand, the RFP response can include a broad mix of projects. For example, if a proposed project requires programming a science facility that will bring together formerly competing departments, the client may fear it will be difficult to reach an agreement between the departments, resulting in program creep. To address this concern, the RFP response can include project examples highlighting the firm's ability to lead a process with competing interests and accommodate needs in a reasonable time frame, such as design of a project for the merger of two companies with dissimilar cultures.

To communicate the architect's role in a useful way to the prospective client looking for value, standard project pages will have to be tailored for use in the proposal. A cover letter or executive summary is essential to quickly give the selection committee an understanding of why, for example, the architect is using a corporate facility to demonstrate experience relevant to the design of their biology/physics building.

To illustrate process leadership, the proposing firm also needs to identify and describe the steps in its project delivery process, whether or not the client has requested this. Identify which members of the proposing team will lead the process at each stage and their relationships with the client and stakeholders along the way. This can be done with a diagram supported by simple, clearly understandable text.

DIRECT HIRE

An organization often rehires an architect they have worked with before without requiring the architect to compete for the project. However, it is rare for an owner to establish a new relationship with an architect without a traditional selection process.

New Clients

When a firm finds itself in a non-compete situation with a new client, it is likely the client's colleagues have provided laudatory references for the architect. Nonetheless, it is crucial for the architect to understand the requirements, priorities, status, budget, schedule, decision-making process, and relationship the prospective client anticipates having with the architect before entering into even the most superficial agreement. Be prepared to walk away if the client's temperament and expectations suggest a poor

Projects acquired through non-competitive selection reflect a growing share of project revenue, with 48 percent of that revenue from repeat clients and 26 percent from new clients.

2006 AIA Firm Survey

relationship will ensue. Remember, the great advantage of the traditional selection process is that much of this information is revealed during the architect's pursuit of the project.

Existing Clients

Keeping existing clients is a primary way many architects get work. To maintain a good relationship, never take the client for granted. Architects who understand that their relationships with clients are always at risk are likely to keep those clients. Relationships will not survive on client loyalty alone. Thus, it is important for architects to relate to their existing clients with the same enthusiasm, creativity, and attentiveness they bring to establishing new client relationships. The following techniques can help architects maintain these relationships:

- Initiate process or design innovations. Don't wait to be asked.
- Initiate fee reviews. Don't wait to be challenged.
- Keep a stable team and notify the client if the team must change.
- Have senior staff develop personal relationships with clients.

Despite the architect's efforts, an existing client may still ask a familiar firm to interview for a new project. This can happen for a number of reasons, including new leadership in the client organization, a problem on a past project, the client's desire to "keep you honest," or the organization's policy to periodically review relationships. Whatever the client's reason for bidding a project, the architecture firm should use the advantage of inside knowledge to discover why the client is looking for something new and to try to address those issues. For example:

- If the client has had a change in administration, the new leaders may have an existing relationship with another architect. Get to know the new administrators, and let them know your firm's experience and qualifications. Learn the new priorities, especially with regard to process, cost, and management, and find out what internal operational changes the administration wants to make. Shape the proposal or interview to focus on the new people—looking forward and not backward.
- If the administration is not new and nothing else appears to be different, the firm could try to identify something new in the client's situation and use that to suggest change or improvement. This should be handled delicately, however, so as not to criticize the client's actions.
- If the client has already progressed to the interview stage with another architect because of a known problem with your firm, it may be too late to save the relationship, but an effort should still be made. Find out if your firm has advocates on the selection committee. Acknowledge problems, and ask for a trial period to implement solutions. The firm can also consider appointing different staff members to communicate with the client. These latter two suggestions challenge the architect's ability to introduce change without raising the question "Why haven't you done this already."

SUMMING UP

When organizations or individuals seek architecture services, they have certain expectations for their relationships with the architecture firm. These expectations, or values, are reflected in the criteria they use to choose an architect. To connect with the client and stay within the confines of the RFP rules and interview constraints, the firm must accurately assess the client's values by carefully analyzing information obtained during the selection process.

For More Information

In *The Tipping Point* (Little, Brown, 2000), Malcolm Gladwell provides insight into the importance of message clarity and obtaining information directly from clients.

CHAPTER 5

Running a Practice

5.1 Financial Planning

Lowell V. Getz, CPA

Financial planning is the process whereby performance goals are established and reports are prepared to measure whether these goals are being achieved.

The principal task of financial management systems is to help firms achieve their financial goals. Effective financial management requires guideposts that show where a firm is versus where it wants to be next month, next year, and beyond. The guideposts come from firm objectives: profit targets, staffing needs, and the costs of providing the level of service that management deems appropriate.

BUSINESS PLANNING

Business planning enables the principals in an architecture firm to chart its course instead of reacting to situations and opportunities as they arise. Planning begins with "big-picture" strategic thinking and positioning. Goals and strategies are then translated into a business plan—a set of financial projections and operational plans that guide the principals in managing the firm.

Business plans may be prepared with different degrees of formality, from a few ideas and numbers on a single sheet of paper to a carefully prepared document that can be presented to a bank when seeking a loan. Frequency of preparation varies, although the usual approach is to prepare or update the plan before the start of each year.

Annual financial plans typically include four components:

- A *revenue projection* that outlines anticipated revenues from projects under contract, those in the negotiation stages, and estimated revenues from projects not yet obtained

Lowell Getz is a financial consultant to architecture, engineering, planning, and environmental service firms. He has written, taught, and lectured widely on financial management.

- A *staffing plan* that defines the size and cost of the staff required to provide the services outlined in the revenue projection
- An *overhead expense budget* that identifies the indirect costs of supporting the staff as it provides the services outlined in the revenue projection
- A *profit plan* that establishes and budgets the profit required to sustain the firm and allow it to meet its goals

These components are closely interrelated, and decisions made about any one will affect the others, so it is necessary to develop them concurrently. As shown in the accompanying diagram, the planning process can proceed along one of two paths:

- *Path A.* Start with the workload that is expected, and determine what staff and other resources will be needed.
- *Path B.* Start with the staff available, and determine the workload it can support.

It is also possible to begin with an achievable profit margin and determine the relationship of revenue and expenses needed to produce it. All of the approaches set profit goals, help in deciding billing rates, and provide yardsticks for monitoring progress and making course adjustments to keep the firm on track.

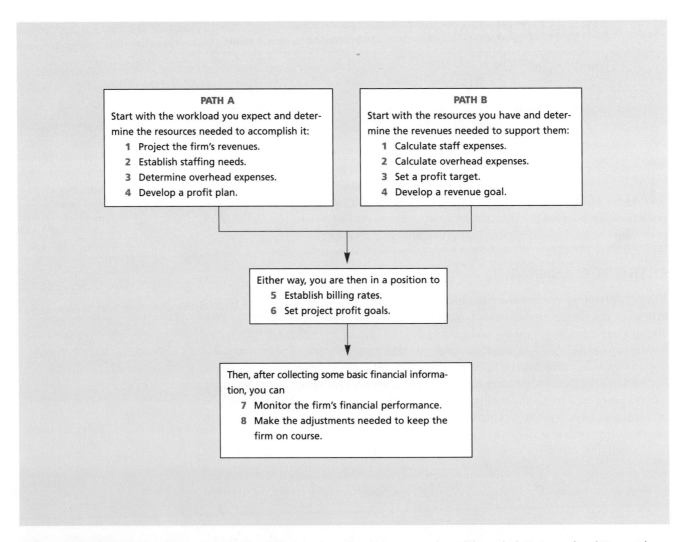

PATH A
Start with the workload you expect and determine the resources needed to accomplish it:
  1 Project the firm's revenues.
  2 Establish staffing needs.
  3 Determine overhead expenses.
  4 Develop a profit plan.

PATH B
Start with the resources you have and determine the revenues needed to support them:
  1 Calculate staff expenses.
  2 Calculate overhead expenses.
  3 Set a profit target.
  4 Develop a revenue goal.

Either way, you are then in a position to
  5 Establish billing rates.
  6 Set project profit goals.

Then, after collecting some basic financial information, you can
  7 Monitor the firm's financial performance.
  8 Make the adjustments needed to keep the firm on course.

Paths to Profit Planning The discussion in the text follows Path A. The discussion in the sidebar titled "A Streamlined Financial Planning Process," at the end of this topic, follows Path B.

REVENUE PROJECTION

The planning process starts with a projection of what revenue management can expect to achieve in the plan year. The projection should be neither too optimistic nor too pessimistic, but should reflect the best estimate based on market conditions over the next twelve months. Beginning with projects in hand and projecting the possibility of acquiring projects from outstanding proposals, this plan establishes marketing goals for the firm over the planning period. The revenue projection covers these categories of projected income:

- Existing projects to be completed
- Proposals that are outstanding
- Unidentified future work

Work to be accomplished on existing projects is budgeted by month for the balance of the year. Work that extends beyond the plan year is budgeted in total for the following year. The sum of these projects is the firm backlog. The backlog figure is an important planning tool and needs to be monitored continually. An early warning sign of impending problems is a shrinking backlog. If the backlog is not replenished at the rate revenue is realized from it, the firm will face a shortfall of work in the months ahead. Likewise, if the backlog is increasing, it is a sign that management may need to hire more staff. The hiring process often takes months to accomplish.

The revenue projection lists includes a section on proposals that are outstanding, with an estimate of the probability of this work being awarded. An estimate is also made regarding when this work is likely to begin. The revenue estimate is then made by month and entered into the plan.

Management knows that some portion of the revenues for the next year will come from projects that have not yet been identified. Using experience to project what is likely to happen, the planner estimates how much new work can be expected. Follow-on work from existing projects is also included in this estimate.

Preparing a monthly projection may seem unnecessary, but this effort will help a firm plan its cash flow. It is as important to know when cash is likely to arrive as how much is expected.

STAFFING EXPENSES

The next step is to develop a staffing plan, starting with a list of firm staff and anticipating salary increases over the next year. In larger firms, staff members are grouped into categories such as junior or senior architects. The plan may be modified through new hires and attrition to coordinate it with the revenue projection.

Certain assumptions need to be made when developing a staffing plan. For example, the percentage of billable time (utilization ratio) for each individual or category of personnel should be estimated. Vacations and holidays need to be considered, as do allowances for training new personnel and continuing professional education for the staff.

Staffing plans require development of billing rates, either for individuals or for categories of staff. This process begins with direct labor costs (hourly salary) and adds payroll burden (payroll taxes and fringe benefits), general and administrative expenses, and a target profit that the firm hopes to achieve.

For example, assume the firm has an architect whose salary is equivalent to $115.00 per hour. The billing rate can be calculated as follows:

▶ Maintaining Financial Health (5.3) describes utilization ratios and their importance in managing a firm.

Architect's hourly rate	$115.00
Indirect expense*	172.50
Subtotal	$287.50
Profit @ 25%	71.75
Hourly billing rate	$359.25

*Includes payroll burden @ 150%

This sidebar and the sidebars titled "Staffing Plan," "Overhead Expense Budget," and "Profit Plan" provide views of the business plan of a hypothetical firm as it appears at the beginning of the year just ended.

An analysis of the revenue projection shows the firm undertakes many projects of short duration. On the date this version of the plan was prepared (January 1), the firm had a backlog of $650,000 in expected revenues over the next nine months. Three outstanding proposals total $300,000 in fees. After applying probability factors for actually receiving these projects, the principal preparing the plan assumed the firm would realize $105,000 in revenues from these proposals beginning in March. (The firm includes outstanding proposals by applying a probability factor to each one. For example, Project Z has an expected fee of $120,000, and the firm estimates it has a 25 percent chance of acquiring the project. Thus only $30,000 is included in the projection.)

The firm estimates that $60,000 to $70,000 in revenue is required each month to sustain its staff and meet its overall goals; this figure is derived from the staffing, overhead expense, and profit plans shown in the next three sidebars, as well as an assessment of how much of the projected revenue will be passed through to consultants. The "unidentified future work" figures, taken from the firm's marketing plan, establish the revenue that must be raised to meet the firm's revenue goals.

Given the nature of the firm's projects, its revenue projection is updated monthly. Both backlog and outstanding proposals are carefully tracked, giving the firm a clear idea of the marketing effort required if it is to meet its goals.

Existing Projects		Total	Jan	Feb	Mar	Apr	May	June	July	Aug	Sept	Oct	Nov	Dec
Project A		$360*	$40	$40	$40	$40	$40	$40	$40	$40	$40			
Project B		120	20	20	20	20	20	20						
Project C		170	45	45	40	40								
Total backlog		$650	105	105	100	100	60	60	40	40	40			
Proposals Outstanding														
Project X	60 @ 25%	15			5	5	5							
Project Y	120 @ 50%	60					20	20	20					
Project Z	120 @ 25%	30					15	15						
Total proposals		$105			5	5	40	35	20					
Unidentified Future Work														
Institutional clients		5											2	3
Planning studies		5											3	2
Total future work		$10											5	5
Grand Totals		$765	105	105	105	105	100	95	60	40	40		5	5

*All figures are in thousands of dollars.

The overhead and profit rates used in this calculation come from other portions of the business plan. Using the figures shown in the example produces a billing rate that is 3.124 times the cost of direct salary. In other words, a multiplier of 3.124 covers the cost of direct labor and overhead and also yields the desired profit in the example. It is important for a firm to calculate the multiplier it requires to meet its goals so it can price its services correctly.

OVERHEAD EXPENSES

The next step is to develop an estimate of overhead or indirect expenses for the coming year. Each element of indirect expense should be listed with the actual expenses for the previous year. Then assumptions are made about what is likely to happen in the plan year.

Known cost increases, such as an increase in rent or insurance, should be factored in at actual amounts. Other expenses should be examined and, where necessary, adjusted to account for inflation and historical trends. It is better to make realistic assumptions based on what is likely to occur rather than to increase all expenses by a flat percentage to account for inflation.

It is now possible to set the projected overhead rate for the coming year. Most architecture firms use the direct salary expense (DSE) approach, in which the total overhead (indirect expense) budget is divided by the total budgeted direct salary expense to arrive at an overhead rate.

Other firms use a direct personnel expense (DPE) approach. Under this method, payroll burden on direct salaries is removed from overhead and added to direct salaries before the overhead rate is calculated.

STAFFING PLAN

The hypothetical firm has a staff of five. For each staff member, the planner first calculates an hourly rate for direct labor (by dividing the individual's annual base salary by the number of hours available to be worked over the year, assumed at 2,080—52 weeks at 40 hours per week—for a full-time person employed for a full year).

Since all staff hours cannot be billed directly to projects, a utilization ratio (percent chargeable) is projected for each staff member. The resulting chargeable hours are translated into direct salary expense (chargeable hours

times hourly rate) and then into total billable revenue (direct salary expense times the firm's multiplier). The last column shows the portion of each staff member's salary that is not expected to be charged to projects and that will become part of the overhead (indirect) expense budget.

This firm must bill approximately $700,000 during the year in net revenues (i.e., exclusive of consultants and reimbursable expenses) to sustain the level of staffing shown, cover its overhead, and meet its profit goal.

	Base Salary	Hours per Year	Hourly Rate	Percent Chargeable[1]	Chargeable Hours	Direct Salary[2]	Billable Revenue[3]	Indirect Salary[4]
Principal	$110,000	2,080	$52.88	60%	1,248	$66,000	$211,000	$44,000
Registered architect	75,000	2,080	36.06	70%	1,456	53,000	170,000	22,000
Technical employee	55,000	2,080	26.44	85%	1,768	47,000	150,000	8,000
Technical employee	55,000	2,080	26.44	85%	1,768	47,000	150,000	8,000
Secretary	40,000	2,080	19.23	12.5%	260	5,000	16,000	35,000
Totals	$335,000				6,500	$218,000	$697,000	$117,000

[1]It is important to recognize the distinction between the terms *billable* and *chargeable* and their implications. Time spent on projects is chargeable and may or may not be billable. If the project fee is anything other than an hourly fee (with or without a maximum), then none of the hours charged to the project are billed. Billing is a percentage of the fee for work completed. Therefore, billable hours are possible only on hourly fee projects.

[2]Direct salary is calculated by multiplying the chargeable hours by the staff member's hourly rate.

[3]Billable revenue is calculated by multiplying direct salary expense by the firm's DSE multiplier (3.20—see "Profit Plan" sidebar).

[4]Indirect salary is calculated by multiplying non-chargeable hours (available hours minus chargeable hours) by each staff member's hourly rate.

OVERHEAD EXPENSE BUDGET

The hypothetical firm anticipates that its overhead expenses will total $341,000 for the planning year. Dividing this figure by the total projected direct salary expense ($218,000, from the staffing plan) yields an overhead rate of 1.56 or 156 percent of direct salary expense (DSE); this rate is used to determine multipliers (for hourly billing rates).

Overhead Expenses	Prior Year	Budget Year	Change
Indirect labor	$115,000	$117,000	$2,000
Payroll burden (on total salary)	96,000	101,000	5,000
Rent	20,000	20,000	0
Utilities	9,000	10,000	1,000
Telephone	3,200	4,000	800
Equipment purchase/maintenance	12,000	10,000	(2,000)
Postage and shipping	3,000	3,000	0
Publications	2,000	2,000	0
Insurance	27,000	25,000	(2,000)
Office supplies	10,600	10,000	(600)
Travel	7,000	8,000	1,000
Printing	7,000	5,000	(2,000)
Marketing tools	9,200	10,000	800
Professional development	6,000	8,000	2,000
Legal and accounting expenses	6,000	6,000	0
Other general/administrative expenses	2,000	2,000	0
Totals	$335,000	$341,000	$6,000

Calculation of Overhead Rate Based on Direct Salary Expense (DSE)

Total overhead	$341,000
Divided by total salary expense (staffing plan)	218,000
Yields overhead rate	1.56 (156%)

Calculation of DSE Break-Even Multiplier*

Total direct salary expense + total overhead	$559,000
Divided by total direct salary expense	218,000
Yields DSE "break-even" multiplier	2.56

Calculation of DPE Break-Even Multiplier*

Total direct personnel expense	
Total direct salary expense	$218,000
Direct payroll burden @ 30%	65,000
Total personnel expense	$283,000
Total overhead (without direct payroll burden)	276,000
Total direct personnel expense + total overhead	$559,000
Divided by total direct personnel expense	$283,000
Yields DPE break-even multiplier	1.97

*These are called break-even multipliers because a profit target has yet to be considered.

THE PROFIT PLAN

Profit is budgeted in the same manner as any other item in the plan. That is, the firm should have an expected level of profit and should budget for it in the same way that it budgets for staffing and overhead expenses.

The profit plan presented here includes the information developed above. To provide a complete picture, it adds the amount the firm expects to pay for outside consultants ($189,000) and for reimbursable expenses ($55,000). The plan shows a profit target of $140,000, or 20 percent of net revenues (gross revenues minus pass-throughs to consultants and reimbursable expenses).

This, and the previous three commentaries, all provide insights into the hypothetical firm's business plan and performance. The information shows how the firm's budget, revenue, staffing, overhead expense, and profit plans relate to and interact with each other.

There is, however, a great deal that we don't know about the hypothetical firm: What are its overall goals, and how is it positioning itself? Are its utilization rates going up or down? Are accounts receivable aging and collection periods lengthening? Is the firm financially healthy over the long run? Is the firm producing quality architecture? Business plans and financial reports can't answer the first and last questions. As they are produced, updated, and compared with past performance, however, these financial plans and reports—and the judgments drawn from them—produce a picture of the firm and its ability to realize its financial goals.

Profit Target

Projected gross revenues	$943,000
Minus reimbursable expenses	(55,000)
Minus outside consultant expenses	(189,000)
Projected net fees	$699,000
Minus projected expenses:	
Direct salary expense	$218,000
Indirect expenses	341,000
Total projected expenses	$559,000
Profit target (20% of projected net fees)	$140,000

Net DSE Multiplier Required to Attain Profit Target

Total projected net fees	$699,000
Divided by direct salary expense	$218,000
Yields net DSE multiplier (rounded)	3.2

Profits are required to provide bonuses to employees, to fund capital expenditures, and to reward the owners for their risk. Some profits are reinvested in the firm. It may not be possible to earn the targeted profit on all projects, but the important point is to establish an overall expectation for the firm that will balance profits and losses on all projects.

The most common method of estimating profit in an architecture firm is to establish it as a percentage of net revenue. Another approach to establishing a profit target is to consider owner investment in the firm, establish a reasonable return on that investment, and then calculate how much must be earned at the expected level of activity both to achieve that return and to provide bonuses or profit-sharing contributions as well.

Once the profit target has been set, each new project should be reviewed in light of this target. Projects that do not achieve the target reduce the overall profit margin of the firm.

INDIVIDUAL PROJECT PLANNING

An architecture firm accomplishes its profit plan one project at a time. Each project is a building block that helps achieve, or detracts from, the firm's practice goals. Following are keys to meeting firm profit targets:

- Acquire clients and projects that are right for the firm.
- Price projects appropriately to the firm and its clients.
- Negotiate contracts that implement the firm's goals.
- Hire staff and consultants with the talent and experience to provide the services offered by the firm.
- Manage projects, relationships, and risks well.

The remaining implementation details involve other aspects of the firm's financial management, such as acquiring and maintaining the proper levels of cash, billing and collecting funds, and keeping a steady hand on the financial tiller. These subjects are addressed in the topic in this chapter, "Maintaining Financial Health."

A STREAMLINED FINANCIAL PLANNING PROCESS

The following is a simplified approach to financial planning and management.

Step 1: Establish a Profit Plan

Financial guideposts come from a profit plan—which is also an estimated operating budget. Here is a bare-bones method for profit planning for the small firm:

- Estimate your expenses. Include salaries of principals and staff (include any planned adjustments), payroll taxes and benefits, and office expenses (use past history as a starting point and estimate anticipated changes over the next year). Do not include pass-throughs such as reimbursables and fees for project-related outside consultants.

- Set a profit goal. Each firm sets its own profit goal. In the case illustrated here, the firm has established a goal of 20 percent of net revenues before any federal income taxes are paid.

- Calculate the net revenue goal by adding estimated expenses and the profit goal. This is called net because you have omitted reimbursables and outside consultant fees.

Sample Profit Plan (Excludes Consultants and Reimbursable Expenses)

Expenses

Salaries		
Principal	(1 @ $110,000)	$110,000
Registered architect	(1 @ $75,000)	75,000
Technical employees	(2 @ $55,000)	110,000
Secretary	(1 @ $40,000)	40,000
Total salaries		$335,000
Payroll taxes and benefits (@ 30%)		$101,000
Office expenses		
Rent		$20,000
Utilities		10,000
Telephone		4,000
Equipment purchase, lease, maintenance		10,000
Postage, shipping		3,000
Publications		2,000
Insurance (auto, office, liability)		25,000
Office supplies		10,000

Travel	8,000
Printing	5,000
Marketing tools	10,000
Professional development costs	8,000
Legal and accounting fees	6,000
Other expenses	2,000
Total office expenses	$123,000
Total expenses	$559,000
Profit goal @ 20% of net revenues	140,000
Net revenue goal	$699,000

Step 2: Restate the Profit Plan to Reflect Efficiency

In architecture firms, revenue (and profit) are generated by direct services labor—people working on projects. The most easily used common denominator for planning and measuring financial performance is direct salary expense:

> Direct salary expense (DSE) = Salary cost of hours charged to projects (billable time)

Financial guideposts in the form of DSE multipliers can easily be calculated from a profit plan that has been restated to isolate expected DSE. This can be done by applying an expected utilization ratio to total salaries:

> Utilization ratio = Direct salary expense ÷ Total salary expense

Stated another way:

> Direct salary expense = Total salary expense × Utilization ratio

Utilization ratios are different for different firms, but statistical surveys indicate that most achieve about 65 percent overall efficiency (averaging all principals and employees) to maintain reasonable profitability. The other 35 percent is spent on nonbillable (indirect) time such as that spent for marketing, staff development, general office administration, vacations, holidays, sick leave, and so on.

The utilization ratio should be monitored because it reflects the firm's ability to generate revenue. A low percentage means low revenue potential, and a high percentage means high revenue potential.

Using the utilization ratio just described, the firm's profit plan can be restated:

Restated Profit Plan (using a 65% utilization ratio)

Direct salaries	($335,000 × 0.65)	$218,000
Indirect expenses		
Indirect salaries	($335,000 × 0.35)	$117,000
Payroll taxes and benefits		101,000
Office expenses		123,000
Total indirect expenses		341,000
Total direct salaries + indirect expenses		$559,000
Profit goal @ 20% of revenues		140,000
Net revenue goal		$699,000

Step 3: Calculate Net Multipliers

The next step is to calculate the planned DSE multipliers for each major item in the restated profit plan. Divide each major item by the direct salary expense amount as shown. The results for the illustrated firm are shown on the following page:

A low utilization ratio increases the necessary break-even multiplier because there are more indirect hours and fewer direct hours, which results in a lower profit margin.

(continued)

To pay for direct salary expenses	$218,000 ÷ $218,000	1.00
To pay for indirect expenses	341,000 ÷ $218,000	1.56
Equals the firm's break-even multiplier		2.56
To add profit	140,000 ÷ $218,000	0.64
Equals the planned net multiplier		3.20

Step 4: Use The Net Multiplier To Set Minimum Hourly Billing Rates

Using the sample firm's 3.20 net multiplier yields the hourly billing rates show (at 2,080 hours in a year, rounded to the nearest dollar). These are the minimum rates needed to meet the profit plan. Actual rates charged may also reflect the value of the services and market considerations.

Principal (@ $110,000)	$52.88 × 3.2 = $169/hour
Registered architect (@ $75,000)	$36.06 × 3.2 = $115/hour
Technical staff (@ $55,000)	$26.44 × 3.2 = $85/hour
Clerical/administrative staff (@ $40,000)	$19.23 × 3.2 = $62/hour

Step 5: Set Project Profit Goals

To meet its profit plan, this firm needs to set aside 20 percent of its net revenues. When a project comes in, 20 percent off the top of the net fee must be set aside as untouchable. The project must be done for the money left if the profit plan is to be met.

Step 6: Use Actual Net Multiplier Earned to Monitor Financial Performance

This can be done quickly, easily, with reasonable accuracy, and without accountants. The only information needed is

- Net revenue earned (derived from fees invoiced)
- Direct salary expense (project hours at hourly salary rate as recorded on time sheets)

Following is a sample current project analysis using the break-even multiplier established as this firm's goal in Step 3. All figures except multipliers are rounded to the nearest $1,000.

The break-even multiplier is the only variable factor in this analysis. It should be recalculated periodically using accrual-based financial information (you will probably need your accountant for this). In the meantime, check your utilization ratio. If it is holding about as planned, your break-even probably hasn't changed much—unless, of course, some large indirect expense has come up unexpectedly.

Although it is not 100 percent accurate (due to possible variations in the break-even multiplier), this method of monitoring provides a simple and timely means of staying abreast of financial performance—and determining if and on which projects corrective action is needed.

Sample Current Project Analysis

	Step 1		Step 2		Step 3		Step 4		Step 5	Step 6
	Net Revenue Earned	÷	Direct Salary Expense (DSE)	=	Net Multiplier Earned	−	Break-Even Multiplier	=	Profit Multi-plier	Approximate Profit or (LOSS)
Project A	$220,000		$75,000		2.93		2.56		0.37	$28,000
Project B	135,000		42,000		3.21		2.56		0.65	27,000
Project C	112,000		53,000		2.11		2.56		(0.45)	(24,000)
Project D	242,000		101,000		2.40		2.56		(0.16)	(17,000)

Adapted from "The Minimalist Financial Manager" by William H. Haire, AIA, Oklahoma State University, in previous Handbook editions.

5.2 Financial Management Systems

Lowell V. Getz, CPA

Managing the finances of a firm and monitoring financial performance on a regular basis are essential for a successful practice.

Architects who understand how to manage the financial operations of a firm can achieve better performance and a higher level of success. People can be hired to perform the accounting function, but the responsibilities of management cannot be delegated.

To manage firm finances, it is necessary to have a financial control system in place. Principals require a clear, timely, and accurate method of monitoring financial performance of individual projects and the firm as a whole to:

- Know if the firm is meeting its financial goals and making a profit. To remain in practice, an architecture firm must earn a profit—an excess of revenue over expenses that sustains the firm and allows it to provide the level of service it aspires to offer.
- Know if there will be cash to cover payroll and other current expenses. Even a profitable firm will have difficulty meeting its obligations if it does not maintain a positive cash flow.
- Plan for capital expenditures. As new and improved technology becomes available, it is necessary to set aside funds for acquiring capital equipment.
- Provide quality professional services priced at competitive levels.

This topic provides basic information on financial systems in architecture firms, including common sources and uses of funds, accounting methods, and financial reports. The remaining topics in this chapter address financial planning, monitoring performance, and acquiring capital equipment. Some firms pursue associated business ventures, such as real estate development or purchasing interior furnishings for clients. These ventures increase the complexity of financial management.

SOURCES AND USES OF FUNDS

To understand the financial aspects of an architecture firm, it is necessary to become familiar with certain terms.

Revenues

Revenues to operate the firm come from projects, that is, from fees received for providing professional services. Additional sources of funds include the following:

- Infusions of capital from the founders when the firm is started and from new principals as ownership is expanded
- Revenue from associated business ventures, such as real estate development
- Income from interest, rents, sale of assets, or other miscellaneous sources

Direct (Project) Expenses

Like revenues, a significant portion of a firm's expenses are incurred in providing project services. These *direct expenses* are identified with specific projects and categorized as:

▶ Financial Planning (5.1) addresses profit planning.

▶ Maintaining Financial Health (5.3) suggests indicators for determining the financial well-being of the firm.

Lowell V. Getz is a financial consultant to architecture, engineering, planning, and environmental service firms. He has written, taught, and lectured widely on financial management.

Government agencies may have their own definitions of what are considered to be direct and indirect expenses, and what indirect expenses are allowed within a firm's overhead rate or multiplier.

- Direct salary expenses, representing time charged by professional and technical staff in providing project services, as well as time spent administering and coordinating consultant services.
- Expenses for outside consultants working on projects.
- Other direct expenses for providing project services, such as travel, telephone, and printing expenses. Such expenses may be nonreimbursable (included in the architect's fee) or reimbursable (paid for separately by the client).

Reimbursable Expenses

Reimbursable expense categories are specified in the owner-architect agreement and may include travel, lodging and meals, telephone, reproduction expenses, and similar project-related costs. Charges are billed to the client and any requested documentation is provided, such as copies of telephone charges. Reimbursable expenses invoiced to the client usually include a markup of approximately 10 percent. A "not-to-exceed" limit on reimbursable expenses is sometimes included in the owner-architect agreement. The architect, therefore, needs to develop a reasonable estimate that includes a contingency amount.

Indirect Expenses

Indirect expenses are those expenses that do not directly support project activities. Indirect expenses are classified as payroll burden or general and administrative expenses.

Payroll burden is the cost of benefits provided to staff members and includes health insurance, workers' compensation insurance, federal and state unemployment insurance, and payroll taxes.

General and administrative expenses consist of salaries and benefits for management and staff members when they are not working on projects. These nonproject activities may include management, marketing, professional development, civic functions, and other activities that are important to the firm but cannot be charged to a billable project. The cost of renting space, office operations, business taxes, liability insurance, and depreciation are also indirect expenses.

Indirect expenses, often called overhead, represent a significant portion of firm expenses. In making a proposal for services, the usual practice is to include overhead either as a percentage of direct salary expense (for example, 150 percent of DSE) or as a break-even multiplier applied to direct salary expense (in the same example, 2.5 times DSE). Adding a 20 percent profit arrives at a multiplier for billing purposes of 3.0 times DSE. Some firms apply overhead rates and multipliers to direct personnel expense (DPE). DPE includes direct salary expense plus associated payroll burden. Payroll burden on direct salaries is therefore removed from overhead.

In the above example, if payroll burden represents 30 percent of direct salaries, a break-even multiplier of 1.9 times DPE equals a break-even multiplier of 2.5 times DSE ($1.3 \times 1.9 = 2.5$). Adding a 20 percent profit results in a multiplier for billing purposes of 2.3 times DPE ($1.3 \times 2.3 = 3.0$).

Profit

Defined as the difference between revenues and expenses, *profit* represents the funds required to sustain the practice in lean times, buy capital equipment, reward staff members for outstanding performance, and allow firm owners to achieve a return on their investment.

ACCOUNTING SYSTEMS

An accounting system consists of a chart of accounts and a coding system.

Chart of Accounts

A *chart of accounts* is a list of the various accounts used by the firm. In a sense, it is a directory that evolves to meet firm needs. The chart of accounts classifies accounts under the following six headings:

- *Assets* (everything owned by the firm or owed to the firm by others)
- *Liabilities* (claims of creditors against these assets; what the firm owes to others)
- *Net worth* (claims of the firm owners against its assets; what the firm owes to its owners)
- *Revenues* (amounts earned by a firm during an accounting period)
- *Expenses* (what it costs the firm to produce its revenue)
- *Profit or loss* (the difference between revenue and expenses)

EXPENSES

Direct Expenses

In addition to the expenses of salaries and outside services, architecture firms incur other expenses that can be charged directly to a specific project. These expenses, which may be nonreimbursable or reimbursable, often include costs for

- Printing, duplication, and plotting, including reproduction of drawings and specifications
- Photography
- Diskettes, tapes, and other electronic media requested by the client
- CAD and other computer services associated with the project
- Items purchased on the client's behalf (e.g., fees, permits, bid advertising, models, renderings)
- Project meeting expenses
- Transportation, including expenses to and from the job site
- Lodging and meals
- Long-distance telephone, fax, telex, etc.
- Postage, courier, and overnight delivery
- Project professional liability insurance premiums
- Additional premiums for project professional liability insurance in excess of basic firm coverage
- Other project-related insurance premiums
- Legal and accounting services related to the project
- Financing and carrying costs of professional services at the client's request

General And Administrative Expenses

Indirect or overhead expenses—expenses that cannot easily be attributed to a specific project in the office—include salaries not charged to a project, payroll burden (fringe benefits), and a wide variety of general and administrative expenses. These G&A expenses may include costs for the following items:

Current Operating Expenses

- Rent (or equivalent), utilities, operation and maintenance, and repair of buildings, equipment, and automobiles
- Printing, duplication, photographs, and similar items for marketing and other nonproject uses
- Printing of in-house check sets and consultant base sheets
- Computer hardware, software, and operating expenses
- Postage and messenger services
- Travel and entertainment for marketing and firm or staff development
- Office supplies
- Library materials, books, periodicals
- Telephone, facsimile, electronic mail, information services
- Taxes (e.g., real estate, personal property)
- Professional dues and licensing fees
- Seminars, conventions, in-house training, and professional development
- Marketing and proposal preparation
- Public relations
- Charitable and civic contributions
- Insurance (e.g., automobile, contents, building, principals' life, valuable papers, comprehensive general liability, equipment, professional liability)
- Interest on loans and credit lines
- Bond premiums

(continued)

Capital Expenditures

- Depreciation (e.g., furniture, equipment, automobiles, buildings)
- Amortization on leasehold improvements

Losses

- Theft or casualty loss not covered by insurance
- Expenses to correct design errors and omissions, including deductibles on insurance payouts
- Uncollectible compensation and bad debts

Prepaid Expenses

Expenses that affect operations beyond the current fiscal year and that the Internal Revenue Service requires to be spread over more than one year (e.g., long-term insurance premiums, certain taxes, equipment leases, licenses/fees, organization expenses)

Accounting Codes

A *coding system* is the shorthand used to record various entries in the proper accounts. Each project is assigned a number. In more complex systems, subcodes may be used for departments, phases, or tasks. Accounting codes are listed in the chart of accounts and identify various types of expenses. Accounting codes allow a firm to track expenses by project, by phase or task, or by type of expenditure to better control costs and to improve budgeting.

The financial management system uses the chart of accounts and coding system to provide reports on individual projects (project accounting), as well as for the firm as a whole (general accounting).

Project Accounting

Reports from the project accounting system contain information on the time and expenses directly assigned to projects. Time sheets are used to record hours spent working on projects and nonproject activities. Other direct expenses are coded to projects either when they are incurred or when they are paid. Overhead expenses are assigned to projects as a percentage of direct labor expense. Project accounting compares project labor spent with revenue earned to determine whether a profit or loss was incurred on the project. Project control systems produce reports that compare actual project expenses with budget to determine whether the project is proceeding in accordance with the work plan.

Accounting systems vary in complexity. A wide range of software is available so that even the smallest firms can obtain timely and accurate information for project control.

General Accounting

General accounting software produces reports needed to prepare financial statements and tax returns. The general accounting system consists of payroll records, receipts and disbursements journals, accounts receivable, accounts payable, and the general ledger. These various records are used to summarize transactions and prepare financial statements and management reports.

ACCOUNTING METHODS

There are two primary methods of accounting: the cash and accrual methods. A firm accounting system may use one, or more likely, both methods.

Cash Method

Cash accounting records entries at the time they impact cash. For example, revenue is recorded when checks are received from clients, and expenses are recorded when cash is paid out. Transactions that do not involve cash are not recorded until they do. When an invoice is sent to a client, it is not recorded as revenue until the check arrives.

Cash accounting is very straightforward. However, revenue is not matched with expenses. Certain cash expenses, such as salaries and vendor invoices, are paid shortly after the obligation is incurred. However, revenue for services provided may not be received until later. Cash accounting statements therefore record only the excess or deficit of cash that occurred.

Accrual Method

For income tax purposes, most professional services firms pay tax on a cash basis, since few want to pay taxes on money that has not been collected. These firms keep accrual records for management purposes, which are then converted to a cash basis for tax purposes at the year's end.

The accrual system of accounting records revenue when it is earned and expenses when they are incurred. For example, if labor and expenses are charged to a project in January, the revenue earned is reported in January as well, even though the cash has not yet been received. The drawback, of course, is that the firm may not collect the cash for the reported revenue. The revenue is then written off when the bad debt is discovered, which may be several months later. However, this should be a rare occurrence.

Similarly, expenses are recorded in the accounting period when they are incurred rather than when paid. For example, a vendor invoice for supplies provided to the firm in January is recorded as an expense in January even though it may not be paid until February. The invoice is recorded as an account payable to match it against the corresponding revenue. Likewise, certain expenses such as insurance premiums that are paid in advance (prepaid) are spread over the entire period to which they apply.

Many firms prefer accrual accounting because it addresses the question of profitability by matching revenue with expenses. Additionally, the revenue earned but not yet billed (work in progress) and its billed revenue (accounts receivable) are recorded as assets on the balance sheet. By reporting these amounts each month, the firm principals can see how much they are owed and can take steps to collect it. Similarly, unpaid expenses are recorded as liabilities, indicating how much the firm owes to others.

The emphasis on accrual accounting does not minimize the importance of cash and the need to monitor the firm's cash position on a regular basis. The reporting system needs to supply both cash and accrual information, but for management purposes, accrual statements give the most pertinent information. Firms that are organized as regular corporations generally are allowed to pay taxes on the cash basis. The outside accountant converts the accrual income statements to cash basis at year-end for purposes of calculating corporate taxes owed.

FINANCIAL REPORTS

Financial control systems produce reports that can be used to keep the firm and its projects on track.

▶ Maintaining Financial Health (5.3) offers a number of ratios and samples of reports that can help assess a firm's financial performance.

Income Statements and Balance Sheets

The most common statements used to describe the financial status of a firm are the income statement and balance sheet. Taken together, these statements present a complete picture of the firm's current financial position. In essence, an income statement is a moving picture, whereas a balance sheet is a snapshot. The income statement presents the results of operations or a summary of revenue, expenses, and profit for a period of time, such as a month, quarter, or year. The balance sheet, on the other hand, is a report of current condition of the firm showing the status of assets, liabilities, and net worth as of a particular date.

The income statement can be used to monitor various key ratios, such as profit margin, multipliers, utilization, revenue per employee, and overhead factors. The balance sheet can be used to monitor working capital and average collection period. These

Accrual accounting provides an accurate picture of the firm's revenues and expenses within a given time frame—in the case of our example, the month of January. This picture is not skewed by cash coming in or going out that does not relate to the month's activities.

Look at this simple example: On a cash basis, this firm recorded a surplus of $16,000 in January. In reality, though, much of the revenue producing this surplus resulted from old invoices not paid by the firm's clients until this month—perhaps as the result of a year-end effort to clean up accounts receivable. In January the firm actually committed to spend $10,000 more than it earned.

January—Cash Basis

Revenues received by the firm:	
October invoices	10,000
November invoices	27,000
December invoices	30,000
Total January revenues	$67,000
Expenses dispersed for salaries, vendors, etc.	$51,000
Net cash revenue for January	$16,000

January—Accrual Basis

Revenues earned from clients	$80,000
Expenses incurred in January	
Billable to clients (project services)	65,000
Not billable (marketing)	15,000
Other expenses	10,000
Total January expenses	$90,000
Net income (or loss) for January	($10,000)

statements provide indicators of the firm's ability to manage debt (leverage), pay current debt (solvency), and convert assets to cash (liquidity).

Management Reports

▶ Project Controls (9.3) discusses and provides samples of project status reports.

The financial management system produces invoices, summaries of amounts owed to and owed by the firm (accounts receivable and accounts payable), reports for tax and regulatory agencies, and other information for management. Project reports track actual expenses against budget. These reports provide detail to help project architects manage the financial aspects of their projects. The reports also provide summary information on project performance for management.

Frequency of Reporting

How often should financial statements be prepared? The answer is a function of the size and complexity of the firm and how often management needs to review financial performance. Many firms operate with weekly summaries of project hours spent and monthly financial statements. Others input timesheets daily online and access information whenever it is needed—sometimes in the form of "flash reports" or summaries of critical information, such as project status or cash on hand. Firms also need to prepare reports for banks, insurance companies, and various governmental agencies. These requirements may influence the frequency of reporting.

Shown here are the income statement and balance sheet for a hypothetical nine-person firm for the year just ended.

As shown in the income statement, the firm took in $1,057,000 in revenues and incurred $969,000 in expenses, ending the year with a profit of $88,000. (This is labeled net profit before taxes because no federal income taxes have been deducted.)

While the principals may have considered this profit level to be adequate, the firm missed its budgeted profit of $154,000.

An analysis of the income statement shows that revenues from fees were below estimates, the firm was able to keep direct labor and other direct expenses within budget, and it was less successful at controlling indirect (overhead) expenses.

In budgeting for the coming year, this firm will need to boost fees, control overhead expenses, or establish a more realistic profit target.

On the balance sheet, the firm ended the year with $510,000 in assets, $300,000 of which represents work billed but not yet paid by clients (accounts receivable) and another $100,000 of which is work in progress.

The firm's liabilities, including a few bills payable and a note to the bank, totaled $45,000. Subtracting this amount from assets produces a net worth (owners' equity) of $465,000.

Note that the balance sheet is only a snapshot. It produces some valuable information (for example, the firm has only $10,000 in cash on hand—not enough to cover its accounts payable of $20,000) and flags significant problems (for example, the need to track and collect accounts receivable). To be most useful, however, this balance sheet would need to be compared with one from the end of the previous period to determine if assets, liabilities, and owner's net worth are increasing or decreasing.

PART 2: PRACTICE

Income Statement (for the period beginning January 1 and ending December 31)

	Budget	Actual	Variance
Revenues			
Fees	$1,200,000	$1,000,000	$200,000
Reimbursable expenses	61,000	57,000	4,000
Total revenues	$1,261,000	$1,057,000	$204,000
Expenses			
Direct expenses			
Direct personnel cost	$321,000	$273,000	$48,000
Outside consultants	212,000	189,000	23,000
Other direct expenses	31,600	24,000	7,000
Total direct expenses	564,000	486,000	78,000
Indirect expenses			
Indirect personnel	222,000	211,000	11,000
Other indirect expenses	188,000	217,000	(29,000)
Total indirect expenses	410,000	428,000	(18,000)
Reimbursable expenses	133,000	55,000	78,000
Total expenses	$1,107,000	$969,000	$138,000
Net profit before taxes	$154,000	$88,000	66,000

Balance Sheet (as of December 31)

	Budget	Actual	Variance
Assets			
Cash	$15,000	$10,000	($5,000)
Accounts receivable	280,000	300,000	20,000
Work in progress	80,000	100,000	20,000
Fixed assets (less depreciation)	75,000	100,000	25,000
Total assets	$450,000	$510,000	60,000
Liabilities and owner's equity			
Accounts payable	$40,000	$20,000	($20,000)
Notes payable	45,000	25,000	(20,000)
Total liabilities	85,000	45,000	(40,000)
Owner's equity	365,000	465,000	100,000
Total liabilities and equity	$450,000	$510,000	$60,000

SELECTING A FINANCIAL CONSULTANT

In several areas of the financial arena, it may be necessary or merely helpful to seek special advice. Types of consultants who can provide financial advice are described below. When looking for someone to advise your firm, however, make sure of the following:

- The consultant has the appropriate credentials.
- The consultant has relevant experience, especially in situations similar to yours.
- The consultant is prepared to listen to and understand your problem, not just give pat answers or prescriptions.
- You feel personally comfortable and believe you can work closely with the consultant.

Accountants

Public accountants and certified public accountants (CPAs) are experts in preparing financial statements, auditing, and preparing and filing tax returns. CPAs are required to undergo additional formal preparation and testing and are licensed by the state. They are experts in tax and audit matters. Accountants can help set up the financial books of a firm and can direct the bookkeeping staff in proper procedures. Depending on their background and experience, accountants may be equipped to provide management advice to architects about their business operations.

Lawyers

Lawyers are knowledgeable in matters such as legal form of practice, business entity registrations, labor and employment, corporate bylaws, securities, pensions, contracts, liability, and litigation. In addition, some lawyers have become adept at various forms of business transactions, relationships, and regulations; such experience may be helpful to architects in areas affecting finances, such as contract and fee negotiations and collections.

Management Consultants

Architecture practice management has emerged as a new and distinct discipline. Such capabilities can be provided by management consultants, some of whom have specialized in working with architects and who may be architects themselves.

Personal Financial Advisers

Financial advisers, analysts, and planners provide advice regarding personal financial matters, including personal income and expense budgeting, insurance, investments, and retirement. Although some of these individuals may represent insurance companies, stockbrokers, or retirement plan administrators, others are independent consultants who provide advice on a fee-for-service basis.

Peter Piven, FAIA

USING FINANCIAL REPORTS

Architects do not have to be accountants to manage the financial aspects of their firms. Architects need to understand the significance of financial information rather than the details of how reports are prepared. They are then in a position to ask questions, seek clarification, and have enough information to make the decisions necessary to maintain a successful practice.

BACKGROUNDER

COMPUTERIZED FINANCIAL SYSTEMS

Lowell Getz, CPA

With the price of hardware and software within reach of even the smallest firms, virtually any architecture firm can use a computerized financial system. The task facing the architect is to identify and select the system that is most appropriate to the firm's current needs and its needs for the foreseeable future.

Getting Started

First-time buyers should begin by talking with colleagues to learn about their experiences with various systems. Attending seminars, subscribing to newsletters, and talking with experienced consultants are other ways of getting the latest information. The point is that research should be conducted before selecting a system.

Selecting The System

Concentrate on finding the most appropriate software for your firm's use. As you become familiar with what is available, the search will narrow to a few software vendors whose financial reports appear to meet your needs. Review the output reports in detail, and evaluate the system for its management aspects. Will you be able to find needed information without hunting through several reports? Are the summary reports valuable and the detail breakdowns appropriate for your use? Try not to get bogged down in the technical aspects of the system, such as maximum capabilities and transaction speed. The following points will prove useful for finding the right system:

- Review your present system. Look for improvements that you would like incorporated into the new system.
- Solicit vendor responses. Develop a list of vendors whose systems interest you, and request additional information.
- Determine finalists. Narrow your choices to two or three systems that best satisfy your needs. Obtain a demonstration disk, and examine samples of the vendor's documentation.
- If possible, view a working demonstration, preferably in the office of a comparable firm, and check references.

Accounting Functions

As you begin to examine the products available, you will be reviewing system modules to accomplish various accounting functions:

Accounts receivable. The system prepares and keeps track of invoices that have been sent out but are not yet paid, as well as unbilled work in progress. Information is posted from time sheet records and reimbursable expense reports into the accounts receivable module. Billing software should provide automatic invoicing of standard AIA contracts such as lump sum, lump sum by phase, labor times multiplier, labor times billing rate, and cost plus fixed fee. Revenue recognition software can produce accurate statements showing amounts earned on projects whether the contract is lump sum or time based, with or without maximums. The financial statements then reflect revenue based on the progress of each project within the firm.

Accounts payable. The system prepares checks and keeps track of the amount of payables owed by the firm. The accounts payable module ensures that materials and services have been charged either to the proper project or to an overhead account. Reimbursable expenses need to be controlled separately so that they can be properly billed to the client.

Payroll. The payroll module is set up to deduct appropriate federal, state, and local taxes, along with insurance payments and any other payroll deductions. Payroll reports are automatically prepared on a quarterly and year-end basis.

General ledger. This module collects all accounting transactions and creates summaries at the end of the month or the close of the accounting period. The summarized information is presented to firm principals in the form of financial statements.

Project control. The project control module collects and reports actual-against-budgeted information, which enables project managers to determine how projects are progressing. The project control software should allow for the allocation of indirect costs to projects so that a full cost can be shown on the project. This module is the most important one to consider in making your selection. The other modules are basic to all businesses, but project control is unique to project-related firms. That is why it is important to select a system specifically designed for architecture firms rather than one adapted from some other source (e.g., a time-and-billing system for lawyers or accountants).

Key System Characteristics

Keep the following points in mind when choosing a computer system:

Integrated systems. Integrated systems allow data to be entered once and automatically posted to all modules. For example, a time sheet entry would be processed in both the project control and payroll modules. Integrated systems are superior to stand-alone systems (which require that data be entered separately into each module) because fewer mistakes are likely to be made.

Experience. How long has the vendor been serving the architecture market, and what is its reputation in the industry? These points are very important because although many excellent systems have been developed, vendors that do not have staying power may not be around later to serve your needs.

References. What firms in your area are using the system? Can you visit them for an on-site demonstration? Checking references is a must before making a decision.

Documentation and training. What kind of documentation is available with the software, and how clearly is it written? What training is available with the system, and what kind of service is available after the sale (e.g., is there an 800 number for help)?

System upgrades. Good software vendors are constantly upgrading and improving their products to stay current with the state of the art. Inquire about the vendor's history of upgrades and on what terms they are made available to customers.

(continued)

Custom programming. If the system does not meet your needs in all respects, what are the possibilities for customization? Does the system allow you to design your own reports? Will the vendor provide custom programming services? Keep in mind that the latter may make the system unable to incorporate later upgrades or require updating of the customization.

Local support. Are there local support people who really know how to operate the system to help in troubleshooting, advise on upgrades, and customize the system if you need it?

Contract terms. Review contract terms with an attorney who is familiar with computer-service contracts. Try to negotiate some holdback payments until the system has been operated using your data; that is the ultimate test. Negotiate as much training time as you can get; this is one area in which the vendor has considerable leeway. Ask the attorney to investigate the contract provisions concerning what happens if the software vendor goes out of business.

User group. Determine whether a local or national user group exists for the system under investigation, and obtain information on the group's activities. Call members of the group and ask about their experience with the system. User groups are formed to help the vendor get feedback about desired system enhancements. Although not an overriding consideration, the existence of a user group is one more sign that the vendor is committed to the long-term development of the system.

Overall service. The vendor's attitude and responsiveness are often good clues about whether the product should be selected. Observe how easy it is to contact the vendor's representatives and get answers to your questions. If the vendor is difficult to reach, the problem will only grow after you become a customer.

You will rarely find one system that clearly stands out among all others. Thus, when making the final decision, weigh the pros and cons and choose based on a few overriding characteristics. By making a careful study and comparing the various systems, you increase the chance of selecting one that meets your needs.

Financial Management Software for Large Architecture Firms

BST
BST Global
5925 Benjamin Center Drive, Suite 110
Tampa, FL 33634
(800) 726-3300 or (813) 886-3300
Fax: (813) 884-8528
www.bstglobal.com

Advantage/Vision
Deltek
13880 Dulles Corner Lane
Herndon, VA 20171
(703) 734-8606
(800) 456-2009
Fax: (703) 734-1146
www.deltek.com

Financial Management Software for Medium-Sized to Large Firms (Ten or More Employees)

AXIUM
XTS Software Corporation
9750 SW Nimbus Avenue
P.O. Box 2208
Beaverton, OR 97008-7172
(800) 637-2727
www.axiumae.com

Deltek Vision
Deltek Systems, Inc.
100 Cambridge Park Drive, 5th Floor
Cambridge, MA 02140-2314
(617) 492-4410
www.deltek.com

Peachtree Software
1505 Pavilion Place
Norcross, GA 30093
(800) 247-3224
www.peachtree.com

Financial Management Software for Small Firms

QuickBooks Pro
Intuit, Inc.
Corporate Headquarters
2632 Marine Way
Mountain View, CA 94043
(800) 433-8810
www.quickbooks.com

QuickBooks is a general small business accounting software program. Some customization is needed to adapt it to the accounting needs of a small architecture practice.

5.3 Maintaining Financial Health

Peter Piven, FAIA

Well-managed firms continually assess their financial health and take appropriate measures to stay on track.

Architects aspire to financial health. The reason is simple—they cannot attain their practice goals unless they do. They must practice at whatever level of profitability is required to stay in business, fulfill promises made to clients, and fulfill their own practice goals, including providing appropriate rewards for performance and risk and a reasonable return on the investment of firm owners.

The glossary in Appendix E defines most of the financial terms used in this topic.

MAJOR FINANCIAL PLANNING FACTORS

Financial health requires understanding, planning, monitoring, and controlling three interrelated aspects of the firm's financial picture:

- *Profitability* (the ability to create an excess of revenue over expenses)
- *Liquidity* (the ability to convert an asset to cash with relative speed and ease and without significant loss in value)
- *Solvency* (the ability to meet financial obligations as they come due)

Profitability

Profitability is required at three levels:

- For the firm, generally in the form of retained or reinvested earnings, so it can provide for capital investment, endure downward economic cycles, and sustain growth
- For those who produce the profit, as a reward for having done so
- For the risk taken by firm owners and as a return on their investment in the firm

▶ Financial Management Systems (5.2) describes the revenue and expenses, as well as cash and accrual accounting methods, of architecture firms.

By attending to profitability, architects ensure that they will not incur more expense than revenue on a project or on a firmwide basis. The normal project cash cycle includes three steps: performing services, invoicing, and collecting cash to cover the costs—both direct and indirect—of performing the services. If the architect manages successfully, this cycle not only yields sufficient cash to cover costs but also returns profit to the firm. Practicing at a loss means two things: There is no profit and, even worse, essential costs are not being covered. Regardless of whether the firm uses the cash method or the accrual method for its accounting, losses eventually result in a cash drain—more is expended than is taken in.

Liquidity

In operating their practices, architects acquire both fixed (long-term) and current (short-term) assets. *Fixed assets* are assets such as real estate, leasehold improvements, furniture, fixtures, equipment, and automobiles that they do not intend to convert to cash in the foreseeable future. *Current assets* include both cash and other assets that

Peter Piven is the Philadelphia-based principal consultant of the Coxe Group, Inc., marketing and management consultants to design professionals. He has written and lectured widely on practice issues including compensation management.

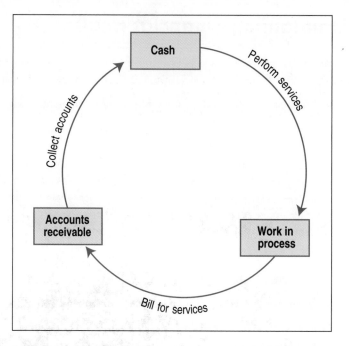

Cash Cycle

▶ Project Controls (9.3) suggests strategies for invoicing and collecting payments.

must be converted to cash, especially *accounts receivable* (the value of services billed but not yet collected) and *work in progress* (the value of services performed but not yet billed).

To keep a practice financially viable, the architect must maintain the liquidity of the firm; this is accomplished by invoicing regularly with the goal of continually converting work in progress to accounts receivable. Then, to convert accounts receivable to cash, the architect must follow up by assiduously maintaining collections.

Solvency

Solvency is the firm's ability to pay its bills. Solvency and profitability are closely related; a firm that is unprofitable will, in the long run, not have enough money to pay its debts. In the extreme, the inability to pay debts when they come due leads to insolvency and bankruptcy.

MANAGING CASH

Keeping solvent requires sound cash management. Solvency is a cash issue: How much cash is needed? For what purposes? When? From what sources?

Cash management is a systematic procedure for forecasting and controlling the cash that flows through the firm. The objective of cash management is to ensure that adequate cash is always on hand and that cash surpluses, when they exist, are invested wisely.

Cash Flow Projections

The best tool for addressing these questions and evaluating firm solvency is *cash budgeting*. This involves forecasting anticipated flows of cash into and out of the firm over time by gathering and reporting information about the amounts, timing, and certainty of future cash receipts and payments. The cash budget predicts cash flow. Its purpose is to provide a plan to indicate when cash receipts and disbursements can be expected. The forecast should indicate needs for short-term borrowing as well as surpluses available for short-term investing.

The steps in developing a cash budget are listed here:

- Forecast billings
- Forecast amounts and timing of cash receipts (collections) from those billings
- Forecast cash receipts from sources other than project revenues, such as investments, rents, and sale of assets
- Forecast cash disbursements, including payroll, consultants, other direct (project) expenses, indirect (overhead) expenses, reimbursable expenses, and capital expenditures
- Combine receipt and disbursement schedules and calculate net monthly cash increases or decreases

Monthly increase or decrease, when combined with the beginning cash balance, indicates the cash position of the firm at the end of each month. The ending cash balance of one month is the beginning balance for the next month.

CASH FLOW PROJECTION PROCESS

This cash projection, made as of March 1, looks at anticipated revenues in terms of when the firm expects to collect them. For example, a total of $72,000 was billed in January; of this, $18,000 was paid in January, an additional $43,200 in February, and the remaining $10,800 is projected for collection in March. Similarly, 25 percent of the anticipated billing for March ($16,500 of $66,000) is expected to be earned in March, another 60 percent ($39,600) in April, and the final 15 percent ($9,900) in May.

Adding receipts from sources other than billings (e.g., interest) provides the total cash figure for each month. Subtracting disbursements leaves the firm with an expected monthly cash gain or loss. Adding the cash balance at the end of each previous month produces the projected cash balance for each month. Adding the actual $3,000 cash balance from February to the projected $7,900 net cash gain from March brings the month-ending cash balance for March to the $10,900 shown.

Cash Flow Projection: March 1	January	February	March	April	May
Total billings					
Actual					
Projected	$72,000	$68,000	$66,000	$76,000	$80,000
Collections on accounts receivable					
First month (25%)	18,000	17,000	16,500	19,000	20,000
Second month (60%)		43,200	40,800	39,600	45,600
Third month (15%)			10,800	10,200	9,900
Other (nonoperating) receipts			2,000	2,000	2,000
Total cash receipts (cash in)			$70,100	$70,800	$77,500
Cash disbursements					
Direct expenses			$29,800	$31,000	$34,000
Indirect expenses			32,000	35,000	30,400
Other (nonoperating disbursements)			400	0	12,000
Total cash disbursements (cash out)			$62,200	$66,000	$76,400
Net cash gain (loss) during month			$7,900	$4,800	$1,100
Cash balance at beginning of month			3,000	10,900	15,700
Cash balance at end of month	$3,000	$10,900	$15,700	$16,800	

Robert F. Mattox, FAIA

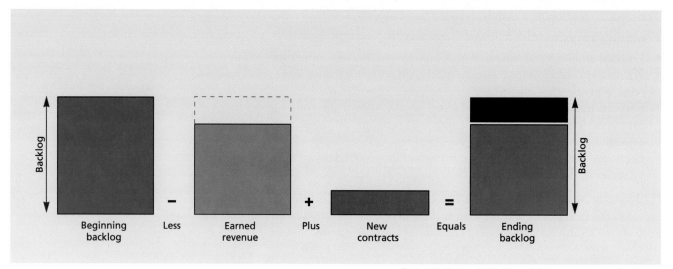

Backlog

Robert F. Mattox, FAIA, Financial Management for Architects

Cash Flow Controls

Cash budgeting is planning in advance for cash that will be required in the future. Controlling cash flow requires measuring actual performance against the budget and taking corrective action as needed. Techniques for managing cash include the following:

- Sustaining backlog by developing a continuing flow of new projects and services
- Billing promptly and correctly, ensuring that clients are aware of the services provided
- Monitoring cash receipts and pursuing collections
- Controlling disbursements
- Preparing cash budgets on a regular basis and using them to monitor actual cash flow

Billing and collection are especially important in managing cash flow. From an overall practice perspective, clients who are slow to pay may be in the process of becoming less satisfied or even dissatisfied with the firm's professional service—or perhaps experiencing other problems that do not bode well for the project.

In managing cash flow, timely billing and collections are only half the problem; the other half involves controlling disbursements. Careful timing of disbursements can be an effective way to control cash outflow. The firm has more ability to control when it makes a disbursement than when it receives a cash payment. It can defer payment to vendors and other payees, reduce the draws or salaries of principals and, if necessary, borrow funds on a short-term basis.

If cash projections indicate a continuing deficit, financing from other, longer-term sources may be needed. Following are some possibilities:

- Refinancing a major asset with a long-term note or mortgage
- Adding capital from existing partners, new partners, or shareholders
- Retaining additional corporate earnings rather than distributing all profits
- Deferring capital or other expenditures

FINANCIAL STRENGTH

There are many indicators of financial performance and financial health. Often these indicators are expressed as simple ratios of numbers created in everyday operations and reflected in the firm's income statement or balance sheet. These ratios can be useful in establishing the need for working capital, assessing productivity, managing overhead and project expenses, establishing fees, and seeking credit.

Working Capital

The architect needs to know not only how much cash will be required to meet expenses in the near term but also the firm's general requirements for working capital. Working capital is the minimum amount of liquid capital needed to sustain the firm in business. More specifically, it is the minimum amount needed to maintain the flow from cash to work in progress to accounts receivable and again to cash. Practically, it is calculated in this way:

$$\text{Working capital} = \text{Current assets} - \text{Current liabilities}$$

Current assets include cash or other assets that are readily convertible into cash (such as work in progress and accounts or notes receivable). Current liabilities are liabilities that come due within the next 12 months.

Receivables

The largest single current asset of an architecture firm is usually its accounts receivable. The liquidity of this asset is extremely important to the firm's financial well-being. It is critical to convert accounts receivable (receivables) to cash in a consistent and timely manner.

If the firm invoices for services at the end of the month in which services are performed and collects two months later, it will need funds to cover three months of operations. This amount represents one-quarter of the firm's annual revenues. Therefore, working capital requirements are closely related to the cycle on which the firm collects its receivables—its average collection period.

Although it is advisable to keep track of individual invoices rendered for collection purposes, it is also valuable to know the rate at which *all* invoices are being collected. The calculation is as follows:

$$\text{Average collection period } (in \; days) = \text{Accounts receivable} \div \text{Average revenue per day}$$

To calculate the average revenue per day, divide gross revenues by the number of days in the period being considered. As a convention, most analysts use 30 days per month and 360 days per year.

Architects are well advised to keep the average collection period as close to 30 days as possible, although this time period will clearly be difficult to meet with certain kinds of clients.

Revenues per Employee

Another measure of financial health is earned revenue per employee. This ratio can be based on gross revenues (total revenues, including consultants and other project expenses) or a net figure (after subtracting all project consultants and other nonsalary expenses). It can also be calculated per *technical* employee or for *all* employees. Gross revenue per total employees is probably a more useful figure in analyzing the firm's overall volume of activity (such as dollars expended for marketing and business development), while net revenue per total employees is most useful in analyzing matters of operational productivity (such as the effectiveness of computer-aided design systems).

Firmwide Profit

As a percentage of net revenue, profit is an important indicator. Average profitability in the profession was low for many years, with some surveys reporting average profits, before taxes and discretionary distributions, in the range of 7 to 8 percent. More recently, profitability as a percentage of net revenue has increased to 11 to 12 percent, with some firms having profitability as high as 25 to 30 percent. A reasonably attainable profit for many firms might be in the 10 to 15 percent range. (Although it is possible to calculate profit as a percentage of gross revenue, profit divided by net revenue is a more useful and appropriate indicator because of the differences in the way firms use consultants and other nonsalary direct expenses, both firm-by-firm and project-by-project.)

MANAGING OVERHEAD

To continue in practice, an architecture firm incurs indirect (overhead) expenses that are necessary to keep the firm in operation and that are not chargeable to any specific project. Indirect expenses can amount to 30 to 40 percent of revenues and 100 to 200 percent of direct salary expense.

Indirect expense must be managed. If it is too high, the firm will probably not be able to produce a profit, regardless of how efficiently projects are being produced. If it is too low, the firm may be spending too little on marketing, management, benefits, administrative services, or other important areas that ultimately affect the quality and quantity of its services.

Indirect Expense Factor

It is important to understand the relationship between indirect expenses and projects. Although there are many ways to view this relationship, the most useful is the indirect expense (or overhead) factor, which is the ratio of all indirect expenses (including payroll burden and general and administrative expenses) to DSE:

Indirect expense factor = Total indirect expense ÷ DSE

An indirect expense factor of 1.75, or 175 percent, indicates that the firm requires $1.75 in indirect expense to support each $1.00 of DSE; conversely, each $1.00 of DSE requires $1.75 in overhead. Although this ratio will fluctuate on a month-to-month basis, it is possible to plan for, monitor, and control overhead to keep the indirect expense factor appropriate for the firm.

If the firm finds its indirect expense factor acceptable (i.e., the firm is operating within its overhead budget), there may be no specific need to examine individual overhead items. If, on the other hand, the factor is higher than planned or desired, the architect should examine individual overhead items to identify areas of excess.

Indirect Salary Expenses

The most important category of indirect expense is likely to be indirect salaries—salaries paid for clerical services, firm management, marketing, education and training, civic activities, downtime between project tasks, and paid time off, including vacation, holiday, sick, and personal time.

Low payroll utilization frequently contributes to excessive overhead. Utilization is the ratio between DSE and total salary expense:

Time utilization ratio = Direct hours (charged to projects) ÷ Total hours

Payroll utilization ratio = DSE ÷ Total salary expense

The most important thing to understand about utilization ratios is this: As the amount of personnel time and expense charged to projects *decreases*, overhead time and expense *increases* (given a stable staff). Under normal circumstances, shifting staff from project assignments to overhead activities will result in reduced project effort and revenues and, at the same time, increased indirect salary expense and increased total overhead.

▶ Financial Planning (5.1) discusses the roles of overhead, direct salary expenses, and direct personnel expense.

SAMPLE TIME ANALYSIS REPORT

This report, an excerpt from a standard report produced from Deltek Vision™ software, looks at the time reported by firm members over the past month, breaks it into direct and indirect hours, indicates the use of indirect hours (vacation, sick time, etc.), and calculates three ratios: (A) direct hours divided by total hours charged, (B) direct hours divided by hours actually worked, and (C) the target ratio negotiated with each employee and entered into the system.

Time Analysis Report: Apple & Bartlett, PC   As of March 31, 2008   1:17:38 PM

Period	Total Hours	Direct Hours	Indirect Hours	Ratio A	Ratio B	Ratio C	Vacation	Sick	Holiday	Bus dev	Mgmt	Acctg	Prof	Mktg
Employee Number: 00001 Apple, William														
Employee Name: Apple, William														
00001			Apple, William											
MTD	578	504	74	87	91	50	18	4	16	21	7			
YTD	2,440	2,187	253	90	91	50	26	4	32	38	81			
Total for Apple, William														
MTD	578	504	74	87	91	50	18	4	16	21	7			
YTD	2,440	2,187	253	90	91	50	26	4	32	38	81			
Total For 00001														
MTD	578	504	74	87	91	50	18	4	16	21	7			
YTD	2,440	2,187	253	90	91	50	26	4	32	38	81			
Employee Number: 00002 Bartlett, James														
Employee Name: Bartlett, James														
00002			Bartlett, James											
MTD	503	441	62	88	94	40	32		8	12				10
YTD	2,438	2,168	270	89	93	40	88	8	24	71	4			75
Total for Bartlett, James														
MTD	503	441	62	88	94	40	32		8	12				10
YTD	2,438	2,168	270	89	93	40	88	8	24	71	4			75
Total for 00002														
MTD	503	441	62	88	94	40	32		8	12				10
YTD	2,438	2,168	270	89	93	40	88	8	24	71	4			75
Employee Number: 00003 Cohen, Grace														
Employee Name: Cohen, Grace														
00003			Cohen, Grace											
MTD	319	307	12	96	99	65	8			4				
YTD	2,000	1,916	84	96	98	65	40			44				
Total for Cohen, Grace														
MTD	319	307	12	96	99	65	8			4				
YTD	2,000	1,916	84	96	98	65	40			44				
Total for 00003														
MTD	319	307	12	96	99	65	8			4				
YTD	2,000	1,916	84	96	98	65	40			44				

Note: Ratios: A = Direct/Total , B = Direct/(Total − Benefit), C = Target.

Two instruments can be used to monitor utilization:

- A time analysis that records individual and cumulative expenditures of staff time
- An income statement that records direct and indirect salary expenses

Note, too, that utilization is a valid measure only to the extent that the firm is *actually paid* for the direct labor. Charged time is not always billable time. Charging time to projects without expecting to bill the client (as in the case of a fixed fee that is already spent) will result in a flawed view of utilization; the utilization ratio will be high, suggesting low overhead and efficient operations, but the profit will be reduced. On the other hand, it is important for staff to report their chargeable time so that the firm has an accurate idea for estimating future projects. Some firms report using a utilization ratio (UR) chart in combination with a project progress report, which compares actual to budgeted time, as an effective way of managing office efficiency.

Other Indirect Expenses

If overhead is excessive and indirect salary is not the cause, a review of the other items on the firm's indirect expense budget is in order.

These items can be budgeted by projecting prior-year expenses forward, by considering specific new needs, or by using a zero-based budgeting technique that requires thoughtful consideration and justification of any item to be included. Individual items (accounts), subtotals, and totals can be planned and monitored either absolutely (i.e., with the specific dollar amounts) or relative to other items, such as total payroll, total expenses, or total revenues. Exceptions or variances from budget should be noted and examined and corrective action taken as appropriate. If it is not possible to modify overhead expenses to bring them within the budget, it is usually necessary to revise the firm's overall financial plan.

MANAGING PROJECT EXPENSES

▶ Financial Planning (5.1) describes methods for calculating net multipliers and break-even multipliers.

Project expenses include DSE, consultants, and other direct expenses, such as project-related travel, reproductions, models and renderings, long-distance telephone calls, and similar expenses. Of these, the largest expense—and the one over which the architect has the most control—is DSE, the salaries of the staff engaged on projects. The two most important principles in managing DSE are as follows:

- *Utilization* (keeping the staff engaged on projects)
- *Productivity* (the degree to which the direct efforts of the firm can generate revenue; this is measured by the net multiplier)

The most common instrument for measuring productivity is the net multiplier, which measures the dollars of revenue generated by the firm overall or on a project basis (net revenue excludes the cost of consultants and other nonsalary direct expenses, such as travel, reproductions, postage, long-distance telephone, and so on, whether reimbursable or not) as a ratio of each dollar of DSE:

$$\text{Net multiplier} = \text{Net revenues} \div \text{DSE}$$

The net multiplier is the best basis for measuring productivity because it eliminates all pass-through expenses, leaving as net revenue only those revenues produced by the firm's own forces. A net multiplier of 3.0, for example, indicates that each $1.00 of DSE is generating $3.00 of revenue for the firm.

As suggested in the "Financial Planning" topic in this chapter, it is possible to look at an architecture firm as a series of DSE multipliers. For example:

To pay for DSE:	$1.00
To pay for indirect expenses:	$1.50 ($1.50 = 1.5)
Break-even:	$2.50 (DSE multiplier = 2.5)
Profit:	$0.50 ($.50 ÷ $1.00 = 0.50)
Revenue:	$3.00 (Net DSE multiplier = 3.0)

Multipliers are useful in project pricing and in overall firm planning—especially in comparing current multipliers with past performance and with those reported by other architecture firms. Architects commonly establish anticipated project expenses by determining the hours (and thus the DSE) needed to perform services and by using the firm's multipliers to be sure indirect expenses and profit are appropriately considered.

Generally speaking, clients do not need to know about a firm's use of multipliers, unless the firm chooses to inform them. Some approaches to compensating architects, for example, involve multiples of DSE or DPE. (The latter approach includes the payroll burden associated with DSEs as part of the base rather than as an indirect expense.)

For architecture firms that do not provide engineering services in-house, consultant expenses may equal or exceed DSE, especially on large, complex projects. Other direct expenses, such as travel, reproductions, models, and renderings, are generally in the range of 20 to 25 percent of DSE.

Sound management of project expenses requires planning these expenses before they are incurred (creating a project budget and work plan), monitoring revenues and expenses as the project proceeds, and taking corrective action when actual performance varies from the plan.

▶ Financial Planning (5.1) describes planning and budgeting in general.

For More Information

In Chapter 4 of *An Architect's Guide to Financial Management* (AIA Press, 1997), Lowell V. Getz describes financial ratios and analytical methods used to measure the financial health of a firm.

The AIA undertakes periodic firm surveys, which include a number of statistics related to firm billings. *The Business of Architecture: 2006 AIA Firm Survey* contains data on billings by firm size and per employee. Other surveys are listed below. Check the AIA Web site (www.aia.org) for availability, coverage, and prices.

The *Deltek Operating Statistics Survey*, published by Deltek Systems, Inc., can be downloaded from www.deltek.com.

PSMJ Financial Statistics Survey, published by PSMJ, is available from Practice Management Associates, 10 Midland Avenue, Newton, MA 02158, (617) 965-0055. PSMJ also publishes surveys on design fees, executive compensation, and human resources practices. Its Web address is www.psmj.com.

ZweigWhite publishes several surveys on financial performance, finance, and accounting for architects, engineers, and environmental consultants. For a complete list, contact ZweigWhite Research at One Apple Hill Drive, Suite 2, Natick, MA 01760; (800) 466-6275; or www.zweigwhite.com/research.

The Institute of Management and Administration (IOMA) publishes monthly newsletters and an extensive series of guides about cost management and control. Contact IOMA at (212) 244-0360 or www.ioma.com.

5.4 Risk Management Strategies

Richard D. Crowell, Hon. AIACC

Effective risk management is a mind-set—a pervasive, daily, affirmative approach to architecture practice that continuously recognizes, assesses, and deals with its inherent risks. The goal is to accept, within reasonable limits, risks the architect can absorb or manage and to lessen, transfer, or reject unacceptable risks.

The word *risk* means possible damage or harm resulting from unpredictable circumstances. *Risk management* may seem a contradictory term, implying we can control the unpredictable. But in many ways, architects can—and indeed, must—take control of the predictors and causes of their professional risks if they desire a profitable and satisfying practice and career. Successful firms have learned that even those risks that cannot be totally controlled can largely be mitigated or transferred to other appropriate parties.

WHY RISK MANAGEMENT?

Society holds architects to a high standard in return for their unique license to practice their profession, and those expectations continue to rise. The competition for most types of building design services puts pressure on fees and schedules. Every project is unique—a complex, multiparty blend of technologies, materials, relationships, and expectations with a largely unknown final outcome. The architect is not in control of the construction, the weather, the labor supply, or the price of materials. Many times such variables can turn a successful project into a disaster overnight.

Claims against architects and consultants continue at a high level, despite monumental efforts by the building professions and their legal and insurance allies to mitigate them. The cost of a claim can be enormous, even if the architect is not at fault. These costs include an insurance deductible payment, legal fees, staff time to prepare a defense, a possible increase in insurance premiums or loss of future coverage, loss of valued clients, and damage to the firm's reputation. In addition, some costs may be harder to quantify, such as lowered employee morale, distracted management, loss of community goodwill, lost marketing opportunities, and difficulty recruiting staff.

In this high-risk environment, architects simply cannot afford *not* to develop and embrace a comprehensive risk management strategy. To ignore this may mean financial disaster. If this sounds overly pessimistic, just talk to architects who have been involved in a claim. They will not be hard to find, since most firms have had the experience at least once.

Richard D. Crowell was formerly senior vice president of marketing for the Design Professionals Insurance Companies. Retired after a thirty-year career in the insurance industry, he served as an insurance adviser on AIA Contract Documents, Engineer's Joint Contract Documents, and the ACEC Risk Management and Business Practices committees. He is principal author of the DPIC *Contract Guide*.

WHERE TO START?

Risk management begins with a plan, tools for identifying and evaluating different kinds of risks, the time and materials needed to control risks identified in each phase of a project, and the allocation of appropriate responsibility to staff at all levels. Architects must learn to deal assertively and skillfully with their own risks if they expect to practice responsibly in today's business environment.

Planning for Risk

Every project has inherent risks, but excessive risk is hazardous to the fiscal, physical, and mental health of an architecture firm and its staff. Once they have recognized this, architects are ready to develop a blueprint for dealing with these risks. For example, many experienced firms have developed a policy regarding what kinds of risks they are willing to accept, procedures for making go/no-go decisions, and ways to communicate to staff how risks will be handled.

Identifying and Evaluating Risk

Most successful firms use a set of tools for identifying and, when possible, quantifying the risks in pursuing a particular project or new client or offering services in a new market. These tools facilitate an objective, systematic, and consistent method for identifying and analyzing risks. Often lists of questions or checklists are answered and evaluated by several firm members and then compared and analyzed when risk decisions are made. Such tools should be tailored to an individual firm's practice, philosophy about accepting risk, and financial ability to accept or absorb losses.

risk—From the French *risqué*, or the Italian *rischio* or *risco*: the possibility that a future event, if it happens, will have an adverse effect; uncertain harmful consequences; potential peril to which one is exposed; probability of a negative event occurring and how harmful that event would be; possible damage due to unpredictable circumstances . . .

RISK MANAGEMENT METHODS

Some risk is inherent in all human endeavors. In the practice of architecture, the risks of injury or loss are substantial and must be dealt with proactively. Insurers and risk managers identify four basic ways to deal with risk:

- *Retain it.* If there is little likelihood an event will happen, the potential for damages is low, and the architect has sufficient control of the circumstances to prevent or minimize it, the architect normally takes responsibility for the risk. The AIA owner-architect agreements describe risks that architects usually retain and risks the owner must normally accept.

- *Reduce it.* Some risks can be managed, limited, or minimized by planning properly, providing increased services (e.g., more frequent job site visits), or using specialized expertise (e.g., hiring an expert to consult on the design of systems requiring advanced technology). In addition, potential liability exposure associated with risk may be contractually limited or otherwise managed through limits of liability and consequential damage waiver provisions.

- *Transfer it.* If a risk cannot be retained or sufficiently minimized, it may be possible to transfer or assign it to a party better able to control or absorb it. Architects can accomplish this by using contractual indemnities, assigning responsibility to other parties by contract, or purchasing professional liability insurance.

- *Avoid it.* Some risks cannot be retained, mitigated, or transferred. When the consequences are too costly and the probabilities too high, architects may have no reasonable alternative other than to turn down certain risks, no matter how high the potential rewards. This is true for individual project risks (e.g., refusing to provide materials inspection services and specifying this in the owner-architect agreement), as well as the risks of taking on certain clients or project types that would simply be too great a burden for the architect.

These basic methods of dealing with risk are used by all parties to a project based on their past experience and willingness to accept risk. Each party must assess the risks of its participation in a project prior to establishing scope, budget, schedule, and contract terms. Then, each party must decide which of these methods—or combination of them—should be used to address project risks.

FIRM ASSESSMENT

The first step in risk management is for the firm to assess its own capabilities. Too often, architects rush headlong after jobs or clients that call for capabilities beyond those they have. They neglect to take the time to ask these questions:

- Does the firm have the experience, knowledge, and skills needed for this particular project? If not, can it acquire them or hire qualified consultants to fill in the gaps?
- Does the firm have sufficient staff time (management, design, production, and construction phase services) available to take on a new project? If not, can enough people be recruited, hired, and trained within the time constraints and at an affordable cost?
- Does the firm have (or can it get) the financial capacity to pursue the project and sustain it until sufficient income is generated?
- Has the firm been successful on projects like this one in the recent past? (Success can be measured by client satisfaction, quality of outcome, profitability, firm reputation, employee morale, and completion on time, on budget, and claims free.)

Architects should assess their firm's strengths and limitations realistically, so they can identify what they are capable of and what the firm can and cannot do. This is not to say a firm cannot grow, develop new markets or different project expertise, or offer expanded services. Rather, the goal should be to make a rational evaluation of where the firm is at the moment.

Architects should also periodically evaluate the firm on a broader strategic basis. This may be part of an annual or long-term plan update or a strategic planning exercise. Many firms routinely undertake this self-analysis to spot areas where the firm needs strengthening so they can take on new projects and develop and grow in a planned way.

CLIENT SELECTION

Rather than pursuing any and all clients who express an interest in hiring them, successful architects take control by selecting the clients they are willing to serve. For firms who employ it consistently, this proactive approach proves well worth the effort, resulting in a satisfying, successful practice.

Client selection is perhaps the most crucial aspect of managing risk. By improving client selection practices, architects can significantly decrease their chances of being sued. If that seems too broad a statement, consider this: At least two-thirds of the time it is the client who files a claim against the architect. If this figure could be reduced by half, or even a third, consider the effect it would have on a firm.

▶ Matrix A in the backgrounder How to Use Risk Assessment Matrixes at the end of this topic can be used as a tool for an assessment of the firm.

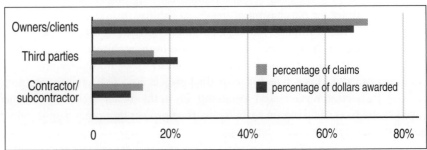

Claims data provided by Design Professional group of XL Insurance companies.

Who Sues Architects? (Based on closed claims 1998 to 2002)

All clients are not created equal. Clients vary in their levels of sophistication and their understanding of the construction process, the role of architects, and the legal responsibilities of each party. Clients also have different financial drivers and financial capabilities. It is critical to evaluate all these issues and more during the selection process.

Architects have control over which clients they choose. Client selection should not be an afterthought or a passive activity. Indeed, client selection should be a serious, deliberate, and conscious decision based on objective, commonsense criteria. But many architects are optimists who think they can get along with anyone, trust almost everyone, and judge a client's character from superficial clues. The reality is that certain discernible facts can help architects decide which prospective clients they should and should not accept.

What Makes a Good Client?

Good clients include those who are willing to openly discuss their project and its objectives in depth and explain how it fits into their business strategy. Although they may have clear expectations about the success of the project, the ideal client is flexible and willing to investigate options and discuss alternatives with the design team. They welcome fresh perspectives and seek new ideas from the architect.

The best clients approach a project as a collaborative process. They understand their roles and responsibilities, as well as the roles of all the other parties involved in the project. They make time to attend meetings, make timely decisions, assign capable people to the project, pay bills on time, and provide the architect with the information and data needed to do the job. They also are willing to accept an equitable contract that does not unduly shift their responsibilities to other parties.

Ideally, clients will want the full service capabilities of the architect and understand how this will add value to their project. Finally, good clients understand that issues and conflicts will arise during the project, and they are willing to work to resolve them quickly and amicably.

Not all clients will possess all of these ideal characteristics. However, if a prospective client is totally lacking in some of them, no amount of additional scope, fee, or schedule can make up for it—and tougher contract terms probably will not help either.

Researching Prospective Clients

Where does the architect start when choosing clients? By asking questions—of prospective clients directly and of people familiar with a prospect's previous experience with the proposed project type, level of knowledge of the construction process, attitude about quality, reputation for honesty and integrity, litigation history, and communication style.

Learning about the client pays off in a variety of ways. The process helps the architect build a relationship with clients, establishes common ground, and improves communication.

Recognizing an Undesirable Client

Knowing what makes a good client is only half the challenge. It is also necessary to identify undesirable clients and to learn to say no if there is a high potential for problems in the future. A client assessment matrix is an excellent tool for determining how well a prospective client matches the characteristics of your firm's ideal client and for helping the firm consider important client selection criteria in an organized and consistent manner.

A review of existing and ongoing clients is an important risk management function, too. Because of experience, familiarity, and the desire to maintain a good relationship, architects may employ looser contracts, less formal communication, and less

▶ Matrix B in the backgrounder at the end of this topic provides a sample client assessment matrix, which a firm can modify based on its own client experience and risk management procedures.

detailed documentation when working with long-term clients. However, even long-term clients may sue the architect. For this reason, some firms review their existing client list annually, assessing them against the same criteria they use to evaluate prospective clients. They identify the lowest-scoring 5 to 10 percent of their clientele, based on the quality of relationships; profitability of work undertaken in the past year; difficulties or problems encountered; ways problems were resolved; claims history; promptness of payment; and sense of mutual respect, confidence, and trust. The results of this assessment can then be considered when the firm is looking at a new project proposed by these clients. Periodically evaluating each client relationship helps architects focus on better serving the clients they value most.

PROJECT SELECTION

Certain types of projects are notorious for generating disputes and claims. Among these are condominiums, facilities with hazardous conditions, asbestos remediation projects, and publicly controversial projects. Understandably, many architects are cautious when considering such projects. Other higher-than-average-risk projects may be less obvious, however. For example, most projects used extensively by the public (e.g., sports, amusement, and convention facilities), projects with difficult site or climatic conditions, or projects that incorporate cutting-edge materials or technology also generate a disproportionate number of claims and greater costs.

Difficult Projects

Much has been written about the claims and problems associated with condominiums, as described in the accompanying sidebar. However, few architects think of prisons, jails, high-tech manufacturing facilities, university or college projects, or projects involving state-of-the-art technology and materials as high risk. Large, highly complex, and long-duration projects derive their higher claims rankings simply because they present more opportunities for claims to occur. Other projects necessitating increased attention to loss prevention include those located in areas of extreme wind, temperature, moisture, earthquake, subsidence zones, or otherwise difficult sites.

If it is anticipated that a project will meet stiff community opposition for environmental or other sensitivities, an architect should consider the risks in becoming involved with demonstrators and appearing on the nightly news, in addition to multiple claims and claimants such projects engender.

Lastly, architects should consider what effect (good or bad) a difficult project will have on the firm's portfolio by determining whether it fits within the firm's short- and long-term marketing goals and whether it will enhance its position or reputation in the community.

HIGHER-RISK PROJECT TYPES

(Based on Closed Claims, 1998–2002*)

Project/Facility Type	% Claims	% of Dollars Awarded
Prison/security/correctional	1.8	3.4
Condominiums (new)	5.1	9.2
Colleges/universities	4.7	7.7
Parking garages	1.6	2.3
Sports/convention/amusement	4.6	6.6
Hospitals	4.1	5.5
Processing/production/manufacturing	2.5	3.0

*Data from the Design Professional group of the XL Insurance companies

Why has the term *condo* become such a red flag in the profession? Why do some insurers refuse to insure architects who do more than just a few of these projects, raise their rates for architects who regularly provide these services, or write dire warning bulletins to their policyholders? The answer to all these questions is *claims*—many, very expensive claims. Yet there are architects who design numerous condominium projects very successfully. What is their secret?

The answer may lie in understanding what factors cause the high frequency and severity of claims on these types of projects. First, let us look at some generalities. Consider the project and its ultimate user/owner. Often, condos are lower-priced housing units purchased largely by first-time buyers, older buyers, or people looking for economical housing. The expectations of these individuals, which are based on the developers' marketing programs, are usually high, sometimes unrealistic, and often unmet. For many, this is probably the first and biggest investment of their lives, and they may have little capital left over to fix problems. There is usually a homeowner or community association, which may have underbudgeted for repairs and underspent on maintenance. The association also has the power to assess owners to instigate and finance litigation against the developers, constructors, and designers of a project that has alleged defects. This expense will probably not be needed, however, because many law firms specialize in this type of defect litigation. (A simple Internet search for "condo litigation attorney" yields more than 1.5 millions hits.) Most of these law firms market their services on a no-risk basis.

Next, consider the client. The client for a condo project is usually a developer, often an entity established solely for the project that will probably disappear when the final unit is sold. The single motivation of this entity is profit from quick sale of the units. Such clients are not concerned with quality design or construction; they will never live in or use the facilities and are not concerned with how well they meet the needs of the buyers. The developers probably do not want the architect to do more than a minimal set of design documents—just enough to get the permits—and they certainly do not want to pay for any construction phase services. The contract for the architect's services is not likely to be based on an AIA model; rather, it is likely to contain numerous indemnities and warranties in favor of the client. Once the project is permitted, the developers may try to find ways to build the condos cheaper and faster. They may build the project using some or most of their own construction labor, or they will hard-bid the project and choose the very lowest bidder.

Does this sound familiar? It probably does if your firm designs many condo projects. Now, look back at the parts of this chapter on project selection, client selection, and contract selection. The checklists are just as useful— perhaps more so—when considering whether to do a condo project. Knowing the substantial claims history associated with condos, evaluate the answers to the questions rigorously. There is no good reason to accept a less-than-ideal condo contract, client, or project.

Nonetheless, a few condominium developers are worthy of consideration. These are developers who have a reputation for standing behind their product, have served the same communities for a substantial period, and will be present if problems develop in the future. They also are interested in quality design, pay an appropriate fee for a full array of design and construction phase services, use a reasonable professional contract, are considerate of the architect's need to manage risks, and are willing to incorporate appropriate protections, such as hold harmless provisions in favor of the architect. Finally, these developers select quality contractors and pay fairly for their work.

If you find an acceptable condo project with an acceptable client and are able to negotiate an acceptable agreement, there are other steps you can take to minimize additional risks, including the following:

- Put your highly qualified staff on the project.
- Produce quality documents.
- Perform site visits with great care and thoroughness.
- Document every aspect of the project, especially design decisions, acceptance of substitutions, client choices, and approved and disapproved changes.

A condo project with these contractual protections in place and a quality-conscious client will still be a gamble— just a less risky one.

Making Project Choices

Firms should select their projects as carefully as they select their clients. Taking the initiative to find projects they want, rather than just accepting what comes their way, will help architects manage risks. Project selection criteria should reflect the firm's expertise and experience with various types of projects, appetite for accepting risk, strategic position relative to the market and client involved, and ability to absorb losses.

A firm's criteria for project selection will change from time to time and may need to be updated frequently. For instance, if a firm has an extensive backlog of work under contract, solid relationships with its key clients, and a strong market position relative to its competition, it might not be as willing to accept a marginal project, such as a prison in an environmentally sensitive location where community protests have already begun. On the other hand, a somewhat risky university lab project might be more attractive if the firm's workload is slack, the university is a good long-term client, and the firm's competitors are trying to compete for business from the university.

The use of project selection assessment matrixes can help ensure a firm identifies, quantifies, and analyzes the risks of a project. In addition, some professional liability insurers consider their use a plus when underwriting a firm's loss prevention practices.

CONTRACT DOCUMENT SELECTION

The careful selection of agreement forms and the contract terms under which the architect agrees to perform services is also vital to the architect's efforts to prevent or minimize risk. Indeed, one of the most overlooked and undervalued risk management tools is the owner-architect agreement and the steps leading to its completion.

Many architects are fortunate to have clients who readily agree to use the AIA family of agreements for all aspects of a construction project. Others struggle to define and negotiate agreements for each project, using custom forms drawn by their own or client attorneys. Still other architects are handed a client's boilerplate standard agreement or, worse, a purchase order and told to "take it or leave it."

Architects must actively identify the risks inherent in using non-standard agreements (e.g., indemnity or warranty provisions) and attempt to eliminate, mitigate, or transfer them. For example, one way for architects to deal with the risks in condominium projects is to insist on contracts that are more protective of the architect. Or, when dealing with a client with limited finances, the contract should include more aggressive billing and collection terms. Architects may also consider the inclusion of limitation of liability provisions for both high- and moderate-risk projects.

It is also worth noting that the process of contract negotiation is an excellent opportunity to observe the client's approach to resolving issues, attitude toward the architect as a trusted adviser, level of respect for the architect's business concerns, and willingness to apportion risk to the party (including the client) best able to control that risk.

While contracts rarely serve to create or prevent a claim, they do establish rules, roles, and risk allocation among the parties to a project. Many firms designate a principal or senior member trained in the nuances of contract development and preparation to review the risk aspects of all nonstandard contracts. These firms also use legal counsel to assist in contract interpretation and negotiation, and insurance representatives to determine the insurability and risk management aspects of unfamiliar contract language. In addition, many firms use a checklist or questionnaire in examination of any nonstandard agreements they are asked to sign.

▶ Matrix C of this topic's backgrounder can be used as a starting point for developing a firm's own project assessment form.

▶ Owner-Generated Agreements (11.2) provides detailed guidance on dealing with agreements prepared by the owner.

▶ Matrix D in this topic's backgrounder includes a sample contract document assessment form.

ORAL AGREEMENTS

In architecture practice today, it is hard to imagine that architects would undertake a project without a written contract of some sort. The results of oral deals can be disastrous for all parties, but especially for architects, as they lead to unknown and undocumented project scope, budget, and payment terms. Such projects have proved fertile ground for lawyers, who must try to prove the terms of an agreement from circumstantial evidence and the actions of the parties. So poor were the results of such efforts to settle disagreements between the parties to an oral agreement that several states have enacted—or are about to enact—laws making it illegal for architects to provide most services without first having a written contract.

LIMITATION OF LIABILITY

A limitation of liability (LOL) is a contractual provision between the architect and the client in which they agree that the architect's maximum liability shall be limited in certain ways. For example, they might agree to limit liability to (1) re-performance of the defective services, (2) a specified dollar amount, (3) the available insurance proceeds, (4) the architect's compensation, (5) certain specified types of damages (e.g., direct damages or change orders over a set contingency), or some other negotiated limit. Although such clauses are usually enforceable in most states, they must be drafted with extreme care. The advice of an attorney experienced in this subject is highly recommended to maximize the effectiveness and enforceability of proposed LOL clauses.

Such clauses do not eliminate all risk from all sources, but they do help cap the exposure of the architect to the amount negotiated. Therefore, LOL clauses are especially useful for high-risk situations in which the probability of claims is substantial, the architect has less-than-optimum control of the risks, and the potential for damages is beyond the potential profits from the project.

The rising tide of claims and litigation has convinced most practitioners that, in many situations, such provisions are not only appropriate but downright necessary to level the playing field of risk between the owner and the architect. Several insurance companies are convinced that LOL reduces not only the severity of claims but also their frequency. Some insurance providers offer premium incentives to encourage policyholders to include these provisions in their client agreements.

Many firms report they are able to obtain LOLs in a significant portion of their agreements, as owners become more accustomed to seeing them and have come to agree with their fairness. Firms also report that although some clients ultimately refused to accept LOL, the negotiations helped generate realistic discussions of project risks and who should bear those risks. These discussions can lead to a more equitable allocation of risks and rewards in other parts of a contract.

The purpose of LOL is simply to allocate the project risks in proportion to the rewards and profits to be gained by each party. The heavy burden of potential risks far outweighs any benefits the architect may hope to derive. For example, suppose an owner wants a factory designed and budgets $5 million for construction. The owner expects a minimum 10 percent rate of return, or $1.5 million, on the facility, which will have a thirty-year useful life. At the end of thirty years, the building will still have some utility and can be sold. The contractor expects to earn a profit of 10 percent, or $500,000. For design services, the architect may bill 6 percent of the construction value, or $300,000. From that $300,000, the architect hopes to earn a profit of 10 percent, or $30,000. With the potential exposure to claims and lawsuits, ever-rising expectations of perfection, shrinking budgets and tightening schedules, a profit of $30,000 is the best this firm can possibly expect to achieve. If there are claims or litigation, even if the architect prevails, legal costs will drain the architect's profits and may render the project a financial loser. It is this inequality that LOL attempts to put back into balance.

AIA Document B103™–2007, Standard Form of Agreement Between Owner and Architect for a Large or Complex Project, contains an LOL in an indemnity provision against third-party claims. This states that the architect's duty to indemnify the owner shall be limited to the available proceeds of insurance coverage. A similar indemnity provision, although not limited to third-party claims, is contained in AIA Document B503™–2007, Guide for Amendments to AIA Owner-Architect Agreements; it is also limited to available insurance proceeds. In addition, B503 contains a section on limitation of liability that provides model language for three different methods of formulating an LOL. Other AIA owner-architect agreements do not contain LOL provisions, except the architect's duty to rectify any deficient services and the waiver of consequential damages.

The important thing is for architects to become comfortable with the reasons for using LOLs in their agreements when the project circumstances and risks merit it. The key element is fully informing the owner about the relative risks and rewards inherent in such projects. By including an LOL, the architect is not attempting to dodge responsibility for actionable errors or omissions, but to establish an equitable upper limit on damages in proportion to the rewards the architect receives.

DESIGN TEAM SELECTION

It's important to choose a design team on the basis of specific expertise in similar projects, rather than on factors such as staff availability and billing rate.

Just as architects should evaluate each project and client, they should also use care when assembling a project team. This is an important step. Many claims can be traced to a lack of sufficient technical knowledge, experience, and understanding of client needs or other project challenges on the part of the project team.

Staff Selection

When assessing a project to determine the most qualified team, architects should consider these key questions:

- What critical skills and special qualifications are needed for this project?
- Are the people with those skills available, or are they involved with other projects in progress?
- If a sufficient number of qualified employees are not available, can they be supplemented by hiring additional employees?
- Can this be done in time to train and integrate additional staff into the project team?
- Are staff members with good nontechnical skills (e.g., communications skills and the ability to resolve disputes) available to work on the project? Project team members with these skills are also important to successful project completion.

Project Manager Selection

▶ The qualifications and skills of project managers are covered in The Effective Project Manager (9.1).

The project manager's performance is critical to project quality, client satisfaction, and the overall success of the firm. Many claims against architecture firms are attributable to the selection and performance of inexperienced or underqualified project managers.

When choosing project managers, consider whether candidates have the following qualifications:

- Leadership skills
- Experience with the same project type of similar scope
- Ability to determine and satisfy the client's needs
- Skills in scheduling, accounting, and documentation
- Ability to anticipate and respond well to obstacles and problems
- Good oral and written communication skills
- Understanding of and ability to use effective risk management practices

Consultant Selection

If a project is large or complex, it is not unusual for architects to require the services of experts in a variety of areas, such as structural, mechanical, and electrical engineering; sustainable design; ADA compliance; vertical transportation; security; communications; acoustics; and lighting. Architects often employ specialists as consultants to address these aspects of a project.

▶ Matrix E of the backgrounder at the end of this topic contains a sample matrix for consultant selection.

In many instances, architects are legally responsible for the conduct and performance of their consultants, just as they are for employees. This concept, known as *vicarious liability*, is the legal responsibility of one party (the architect) for the acts of another party (the consultant). Under this concept, if acts of a consultant cause damage and are found to be negligent, the architect may be held responsible, just as if the architect had actually committed the negligence. For this reason, architects should exercise great caution when selecting consultants. As in other aspects of risk management, a risk selection checklist or matrix can be a useful tool for evaluating consultants before they are engaged.

An important—yet often overlooked—aspect of consultant selection is critical to reducing consultant-related risk for the architect. Although most architects would probably argue that their own services should be retained through qualifications-based selection, many of these same architects hire consultants based strictly on price.

Quality-conscious consultants, just like architects, find it difficult to compete when price is the only criterion. Perhaps some architects and owners do not recognize the risks of using "low bidder" design consultants, who may be forced to cut corners when not paid enough to do a thorough job. Selection of consultants based on qualitative factors is an important step in managing the risk of consultant-related problems and claims.

A good approach to consultant selection is to develop a short list of experienced, high-quality consultants in various disciplines—a favored provider list—with the goal of building long-term relationships with these consultants. Such relationships result in better communication, quicker resolution of disputes, and more effective collaboration.

Whether architects and consultants are involved in one-time or multiple projects, those projects should not be undertaken without a written agreement signed by both parties. The AIA architect-consultant agreements offer an excellent place to start. Both the architect and consultant will benefit from a balanced contract that properly allocates project risks and is integrated with other contracts used on the project.

Lastly, a word about insurance is in order. Since architects are all too frequently held liable in claims caused by faulty consultant services, it is vital that architects select consultants who routinely carry an appropriate level of professional liability insurance. The word "appropriate" is a relative term that can be based on such factors as the overall size of the consultant firm, the size of the projects the firm undertakes, the relative risk of the discipline practiced, and the amount of work performed for the architect. Remember that professional liability policies have an annual aggregate limit of coverage for a policy year, a maximum limit available no matter how many claims they incur.

Architects may want to consult with their own insurance adviser and attorney on the limits of insurance to require of consultants. Generally, consultants should have carried appropriate insurance in the past and should be willing to continue coverage for a reasonable period into the future. These requirements should be spelled out in the architect-consultant contract, along with appropriate indemnity language recommended by the firm's legal counsel and reviewed by the firm's insurance adviser for insurability. Certificates of insurance also can be required of consultants as evidence of their coverage.

▶ Insurance Coverage (5.5) describes various types of professional liability insurance coverage.

WHEN THE CLIENT SELECTS A CONSULTANT

Normally, when an architect selects the design team for a project, the architect chooses the consultants. These selections are based on the architect's prior experience with particular consultants, past successful project outcomes, working relationships, and other factors. Most importantly, the selections are based on the legal reality that the architect may have vicarious liability for the acts and the negligence of subconsultants—just as with employees. Careful selection of consultants is an important factor in managing the risks of any project, and improper choices can have dire consequences.

There are times, however, when a client may want a particular consultant to be part of the design team. This consultant may be unfamiliar to the architect or, worse, someone the architect would not normally hire for a vari-

ety of reasons. If the architect hires the client-selected consultant, the architect will be liable for the consultant's professional services. The risk in this arrangement is obvious.

If the client hires the consultant, this will probably solve the vicarious liability issue, but even this arrangement is more risky than normal. The amount of time needed to coordinate with the client-selected consultant will necessarily be greater, communications will not be optimal, and the arrangement will require more effort and care on the architect's part. The architect should be compensated for this increased effort, and time to accommodate it should be added to the design schedule.

In addition, the architect must be able to rely on the technical accuracy and completeness of the consultant's services—a requirement that should be specifically stated

(continued)

in the owner-architect agreement. The contract should also specify that each of the owner's consultants will provide adequate limits of professional liability insurance and be contractually obligated to maintain such coverage for a reasonable period of time after completion of the project. The client should also be asked to indemnify and hold the architect harmless for any costs, losses, or damages caused by the negligence of the client's consultants, as well as any resulting legal costs.

When the client contracts directly with its chosen consultants, great care must be taken to ensure that all services provided by the consultants are coordinated, both among the consultants and with the architect. In this multi-prime arrangement, it is critical that the scope of work for the architect and the client's consultants be carefully integrated. The possibility for overlaps and conflicts—or worse, gaps in responsibilities—are substantial and the consequences could be devastating. Usually with multiple design professionals under direct contract to the client, each consultant should be obligated to coordinate its instruments of service with the architect and all the other parties. This duty should be spelled out in detail in the owner-architect contract and in all the other multiprime consultant contracts.

CONTRACTOR SELECTION

Although an architect has no control over which contractor a client selects, the client's decision can significantly affect the amount of risk the architect will face on a project. Contractors and their subcontractors account for 10 percent of the claims filed and 13 percent of the dollars expended in claims. Inexperienced contractors selected by clients strictly based on low bids are a significant part of this problem. AIA Document A305, Contractor's Qualification Statement, was developed to help owners assess prospective contractors. Architects should suggest that their clients use this form, which could help them reduce risks for themselves and for their architects.

Matrix F of the backgrounder at the end of this topic can be used as a starting point for developing an evaluation tool to measure risk in contractor selection.

The bidding process itself is also a risk management consideration. Some enlightened owners have discovered that qualifications-based selection of contractors is an attractive alternative to choosing the lowest bidders who, upon starting a job, begin building a case for extras, change orders, and substitutions. Clients who involve architects in the selection process are apt to make better choices, resulting in more successful projects. However, architects cannot participate in selecting contractors on most government projects, which means they may face a higher risk of contractor-related claims in such projects.

SELECTION OF OTHER CONSULTANTS

Clients frequently retain specialists such as geotechnical or environmental consultants and surveyors. In these instances, architects are not vicariously liable for the consultants' services. However, architects must be able to rely on the technical accuracy and sufficiency of the findings and recommendations of any consultants retained by the client.

Matrix G of the backgrounder includes a list of criteria for evaluating the selection of other project parties.

If the client chooses to employ a construction manager, the architect should be made aware of this in advance, as this arrangement will affect the architect's assessment of the project risks. In addition, the duties and responsibilities of the construction manager should be stated in the owner-architect agreement, and the architect should feel confident that the construction manager is well qualified for the project.

MANAGING PROJECT RISKS

Suppose an architect has gone through an intense risk assessment process that included a critical and objective look at the architecture firm's capabilities; the risk potential of the prospective client, project, and contract for services; and the risks associated with the other project participants. Based on all these assessments, summary scores, and risk management strategies, the firm decides to go forward and signs an agreement with the client. It is at this point that the need to increase risk management efforts is greatest. Firms that continuously focus on risk management procedures throughout the life of a project experience fewer claims and less severe losses when claims do occur. This is why professional liability insurance companies evaluate the loss prevention measures that firms follow, and place heavy emphasis on them when setting premium rates.

Several major insurers have developed manuals offering loss prevention guidance based on their claims experiences. Some insurers also present loss prevention seminars throughout the country at AIA state and national conventions and, upon request, may offer in-house training for larger clients or groups of clients. In addition, many specialist insurance brokers are available nationwide to present local and in-house loss prevention training in the states they service. Firms are advised to take advantage of these materials, seminars, and educational opportunities for their ongoing staff training on risk management. (Many of these programs are accredited for AIA-required continuing education credit.)

As a project progresses from planning to design and construction to post-construction services and to other architectural services the firm may offer, each service has its own regimen of loss prevention steps and procedures.

The good news is that most architects practice competently. Few problems arise from strictly technical errors. The vast majority of disputes and claims arise from the following three nontechnical areas:

- Inadequate/improper communication
- A breakdown of relationships
- Poor business practices

Problems happen when architects fail to establish sound procedures or do not follow the procedures they do have. As that famous philosopher Pogo once said, "We have met the enemy, and he is us." Fortunately, architects can do a better job in these areas with sufficient awareness, effort, and willpower. Architects can improve their profitability and career satisfaction by putting more emphasis and effort toward developing and carrying out effective risk management strategies.

For More Information

The AIA Risk Management Resource Center at www.aia.org endeavors to make information available on risk management strategies to help AIA members control the risks inherent in their practice while reducing insurance and associated costs.

The Web site of the AIA Trust provides information on a variety of risk management and insurance topics at www.theAIATrust.com.

Victor O. Schinnerer & Company, Inc., manager of the commended professional liability insurance program for the AIA, is also a source of information on risk management. The following publications and many others are available to non-policyholders at www.schinnerer.com.

- The current issue of *Guidelines for Improving Practice*
- *Concepts in Risk Management*
- *Tips for Reviewing a Contract*

The XL Insurance companies' Web site contains an assortment of papers and discussions about risk management and risk-related issues at www.xldp.com/architects/library.html.

HOW TO USE RISK ASSESSMENT MATRIXES

Richard D. Crowell, Hon. AIACC

The matrixes on the following pages are designed to help architecture firms identify and quantify risks, and describe the techniques available to manage those risks. When properly implemented, they can help individual members of the same firm address risk management from a common perspective.

Adapted from the Victor O. Schinnerer & Company, Inc., "Risk Management Matrix," the matrixes can be helpful tools in managing your firm's risks. You can refine and update them over time to make them most useful to you. Remember, the most successful firms are those that learn to manage their risks most effectively.

Completing the Matrixes

Matrix A provides a form for brief analysis of your firm. Each succeeding matrix (B through G) includes basic factors for risk identification and selection of the client, project, contract, consultants, contractors, and other project team members.

The bold subtitles in each matrix identify specific issues within each broad category. The items under the subtitle contain more detailed questions on the issues. The matrixes can be customized for individual firms and projects by adding or deleting issues or questions as appropriate.

Step 1: Assessment

In the first column of each matrix, the level of risk is assessed. It might be beneficial to rank each risk identified on a scale from 1 to 10, with 1 signifying a very low-risk issue and 10 a very high-risk issue. Numeric scales are used to summarize the level of risk when analyzing the project as a whole because risk "scores" from each category can be combined. However, you can develop your own system—perhaps using a simple "low," "medium," and "high" scale. Over time, you will learn which rating system works best for your firm.

Step 2: Analysis

The second column is used to amplify your response in the first column by ranking the importance of the issue or by adding any notes, questions, or concerns you may have about it. Few issues are simple enough to be categorized effectively using only a numeric scale.

Step 3: Response

The third and last column is probably the most important. It is here where you record how the firm will respond to each of the risks previously identified and assessed. Risk management strategies you might employ include the following:

- Insistence on various contractual provisions to mitigate exposure to certain risks
- Use of special experts to advise on critical technical issues
- Increased number or frequency of project and client meetings to ensure good communications
- Research into alternative insurance solutions, such as project policies, if available

When you are considering a new project, some of the information you will need to complete the matrix may be unavailable in its entirety. However, the matrix is designed to facilitate the fourth step of risk management—control. The matrix can be updated and reassessed as the project progresses.

Step 4: Summary Assessment

At the end of each matrix is a space to record your overall assessment of that broad category of risk, as well as a space to list relevant factors not already included in your entries in the matrix. The overall assessment space can also be used to identify which aspects of a project are most risky. This information can help you devise an overall risk management strategy for the firm.

The final step in completing this series of matrixes to evaluate a project is to carry the content of each overall assessment section down to the "Summary Assessment Matrix" at the end. This will give you a clear, concise picture of the risks associated with the project. Your final analysis can be entered in the line labeled "Overall Result." Based on this, you can complete the "Recommendation" section.

Step 5: Recommendation

The "Recommendation" section is analogous to a traffic signal:

- "Proceed" is a green light. This project should go smoothly as long as you follow the risk management strategies you have defined.
- "Proceed with reservation(s)" is a yellow light. In this case, you have some concerns, but no clear plan yet for addressing them. This may happen because you do not have enough information to effectively complete the matrix. To reach a final conclusion, you can either obtain the needed information or establish appropriate contingencies to assess and manage the risks as the project progresses.
- "Proceed only with change(s)" is a stronger yellow light. In this case, there are issues that concern you, but they can be addressed with appropriate changes. You

can check off these recommended changes right on the matrix as they are made.

- "Do not proceed" is a red light. There are too many risks or not enough strategies to manage the risks to proceed with this project.

Many firms use these kinds of forms regularly, for both new and repeat clients. They usually have several firm members complete them separately and review the results collectively to make decisions about undertaking projects. A senior person is usually designated to make sure the risk management responses are carried through. The firm also maintains files for reference when opportunities arise in the future for similar projects or projects with the same client.

Matrix A: Firm Assessment

Issues	Level of Risk	Importance	Risk Management Response
1. *Capacity* • Does your firm have the capacity to undertake the project? • If you do not have enough qualified employees, can you supplement your existing staff in time by hiring additional employees or consultants? • Will hiring new employees place an unacceptable burden on management or firm staff to recruit, train, and supervise?			
2. *Experience with project type* • Does your firm, and do the available project team members, have sufficient positive experience with the project type? • Under similar conditions? • If past experiences have not been positive, can appropriate steps be taken to correct past problems to make this project successful?			
3. *Other firm factors*			
Overall firm assessment			

Matrix B: Client Assessment

Issues	Level of Risk	Importance	Risk Management Response
1. *Financial strength* • What is the client's financial reputation? • Will the client be able to afford your firm's services? • Can the client afford the project?			
2. *Project objectives* • Are the client's objectives for the project clear? • Is the client able to articulate them?			
3. *Client experience* • Is the client familiar with the construction process in general? • This type of project specifically? • Have prior experiences been positive for the client? • For the previous architect? • If not, does the client realistically understand why?			
4. *Experience with your firm* • Is this a repeat client with whom you have a good rapport and comfort level?			

(continued)

Issues	Level of Risk	Importance	Risk Management Response
5. *Claims history* • Does this client have a reputation for being difficult to work with or for making claims against design professionals? • What is the client's general business reputation? • How does the client handle disputes in the normal course of business?			
6. *Decision makers* • Who are the client representatives to whom your firm would report? • Is there a single decision maker or is it a committee/board? • Are they decisive? • Are they familiar with the building process? • Will they be easily accessible? • Will they have the power to make binding decisions? • Can they be overruled? • By whom?			
7. *Client attitude* • Are the client's project expectations realistic and positive? • Are there open lines of communication between the prospective client and the firm? • If the client is new to the building enterprise, is the client willing and able to learn about it? • What does the client value most: quality, schedule, or budget? • How does that compare to your firm's value system? • Its design and delivery skills?			
8. *Systems compatibility* • What does the client require with respect to the firm's billing, accounting, and design systems? • If data are to be exchanged, are your systems compatible? • If changes or additions are necessary, what are the effects on time, cost, and risk?			
9. *Chemistry* • Does your firm have a good feeling about the client and vice versa? • Are communications open and reliable? • Is there a sense of mutual trust and respect?			
10. *Other client factors*			
Overall client assessment			

Matrix C: Project Assessment

Issues	Level of Risk	Importance	Risk Management Response
1. *Project type* • Is this type of project inherently high-risk?			
2. *Project size and duration* • Does the size or duration of the project pose additional risks?			
3. *Adequate financing* • Does the client have adequate funding for this project? • If not, is adequate funding attainable? • Is the project budget adequate, given the client's expectations? • Given the client's goals and objectives? • How will the client manage cash flow?			

Issues	Level of Risk	Importance	Risk Management Response
4. *Design complexity* • Is your firm capable of managing the required complexity of the design? • How difficult will this project be for your firm? • How much leeway will your firm have in balancing scope, quality, schedule, and budget? • Are the project requirements unique, complex, or challenging the state of the art?			
5. *Construction complexity* • Is the project team capable of managing the complexity of the construction?			
6. *Unique requirements* • Are there unique project requirements that could pose more risk?			
7. *Scope of services* • Will you be hired to provide the full scope of services you think is needed for the project? • Will you be providing at least some construction phase services? • If there is a construction manager or a contractor on the design team, how will your services be affected?			
8. *Schedule* • Are there particular scheduling issues or deadlines that may increase the risk? • Is the overall project timeframe adequate? • Is the schedule for design adequate?			
9. *Adequate fee* • Is the fee adequate for the required services? • Will it cover all costs and provide an acceptable profit? • If not, is the firm willing to absorb the loss? • Has a design contingency been set aside? • Is it adequate?			
10. *New products and technologies* • Will new products and technologies be required or expected in the design and construction of the project? • Have these products or technologies been adequately researched and tested?			
11. *Delivery mode* • Are you comfortable with the mode of project delivery (design-bid-build, design-build, etc.)? • Have the roles and responsibilities of the parties been adequately defined? • Are you satisfied with your assigned role?			
12. *Geographic considerations* • Are there geographic, climatic, or geologic considerations?			
13. *Environmental concerns* • Are there environmental issues that you know or suspect may arise in the course of the project? • Is the project team prepared to address these issues?			
14. *User attributes* • Is this project a type from which subsequent users may generate future claims? • Is there a likelihood of dissatisfied end users? • Are class action lawsuits possible?			

(continued)

Issues	Level of Risk	Importance	Risk Management Response
15. *Community ties* • How does the community view the project? • Is there any perceived opposition or sensitivity in the community that could pose problems? • How does the community view the client? • Will few or many community and government reviews be required? • Will the client be able to help in that process? • What are the client's ties to the community; will the client be around as long as the building?			
16. *Other project factors*			
Overall project assessment			

Matrix D: Agreement Assessment

Issues	Level of Risk	Importance	Risk Management Response
1. *Clear scope of services* • Does the proposed professional services agreement provide a clear and sufficiently detailed scope of services? • Is the scope adequate and appropriate to meet the project requirements?			
2. *Balance of responsibility and authority* • Do all of the proposed contract forms (e.g., owner-architect, architect-consultant, owner-contractor) establish clear and distinct responsibilities balanced by the authority to carry out those responsibilities? • Are the forms compatible and coordinated with each other?			
3. *Clear payment terms* • Are the payment terms clearly delineated? • Are the consequences of nonpayment and slow payment spelled out? • Is there provision for collection expenses, including legal fees?			
4. *Additional services and expenses* • Are there appropriate fee provisions for additional services? • For contingent additional services? • For direct expenses?			
5. *Cash flow* • Do the contract payment provisions (timing/frequency) meet your firm's cash flow needs? • Are the timing and frequency of payments contingent on any outside entity's approval? • Will you be able to bill promptly for all services provided to date? • Any requirement to hold any work in progress?			
6. *Clear, equitable termination provision* • Is there a provision that establishes fair terms for either party terminating the contract should that become necessary?			

Issues	Level of Risk	Importance	Risk Management Response
7. *Equitable dispute resolution provision* • Does the contract contain a fair and balanced dispute resolution provision?			
8. *Balance of risk and reward* • Does the overall contract fairly allocate the risks and rewards? • Do any provisions unduly shift risk or responsibility of others to your firm without commensurate compensation and control?			
9. *Insurance issues* • Are the types of insurance and limits required compatible with coverage carried by your firm? • Are there provisions (e.g., indemnities, warranties, certifications) that create insurance coverage questions or uninsurable professional or general liability exposures?			
10. *Other contract factors*			
Overall contract assessment			

Matrix E: Consultant Assessment

Issues	Level of Risk	Importance	Risk Management Response
1. *Availability of qualified consultants* • Are qualified consultants available who are capable of providing the scope and services required? • Will the consultants have sufficient qualified staff available when you need their services?			
2. *Experience with consultants* • Does your firm have experience with these consultants? • Are these consultants with whom your firm has or can develop compatible working relationships?			
3. *Reputation* • Do these consultants have strong, positive reputations in the design community?			
4. *Adequately insured* • Are these consultants insured for professional liability? • What limits do they presently carry? • Is their coverage adequate? • Are there any pending claims against these consultants?			
5. *Compatible systems* • Are your firm's management and data systems compatible with those of your consultants?			
6. *Shared values* • Do your consultants share the same values (regarding quality, service, reputation, timeliness) as your firm? • How much time will you have to devote to team building?			

(continued)

Issues	Level of Risk	Importance	Risk Management Response
7. *Client-controlled* • Are you being asked to work with consultants selected by and/or working directly for the client? • Will you have coordination responsibilities for consultants not under your control? • Will you be compensated for this coordination?			
8. *Chemistry* • Do you have a positive feeling about the consultants you will retain? • Will they work cooperatively with your firm? • Can you depend on them to identify problems and disputes early and work with you to resolve them?			
9. *Other consultant factors*			
Overall consultants assessment			

Matrix F: Contractor Assessment

Note: If you do not know initially who the contractor is, it is essential to complete this analysis once the contractor is known.

Issues	Level of Risk	Importance	Risk Management Response
1. *Prequalifications list* • Will some contractors be prequalified? • If so, in your professional opinion, are there acceptable considerations in formulating the list of prequalified firms?			
2. *Bidding process* • How will the bidding be conducted? • How will the contract(s) be awarded? • What are the selection criteria and in what order?			
3. *Your involvement in selection* • Will you have sufficient input in the client's review of bids and selection of the contractor?			
4. *Adequate bid* • Is the contractor bidding responsibly?			
5. *Adequate financial strength* • Is the contractor well financed, with adequate financials to procure the necessary bonds and to complete the project?			
6. *Experience with project type* • Does the contractor have positive prior experience with this project type and the anticipated site conditions? • Does it have adequate staff? • Project management?			
7. *Other contractor factors*			
Overall contractor assessment			

Matrix G: Project Team Assessment

Issues	Level of Risk	Importance	Risk Management Response
1. *Construction manager* • Will there be a construction manager involved on this project? • Has the CM been identified? • Has the construction manager's role been adequately defined? • Do you have prior experience on projects with this CM? • Were they positive experiences? • Is the construction manager sufficiently qualified to undertake this role?			
2. *Special consultants* • Are any special (e.g., geotechnical or abatement) consultants required? • Who will select them? • Whom will they work for? • To the best of your knowledge, are these consultants sufficiently qualified? • Are you accepting vicarious liability for these consultants? • If so, will you be appropriately compensated and protected? • Who will coordinate the work of the special consultants?			
3. *Other project team factors*			
Overall project team assessment			

Summary Assessment Matrix

Issues	Level of Risk	Importance	Risk Management Response
A. *Firm assessment*			
B. *Client assessment*			
C. *Project assessment*			
D. *Agreement assessment*			
E. *Consultant assessment*			
F. *Contractor assessment*			
G. *Project team assessment*			
Overall result			

Recommendation:

Proceed _____

Proceed with reservation(s) _____

Proceed only with change(s) _____

Do not proceed _____

Preparer's signature: _____

5.5 Insurance Coverage

Ann Casso and Fredric W. Schultz, CPCU

Architecture firms use insurance as an instrument to help them manage the inherent risks of business and the specific risks associated with projects.

As key players in the highly complex design and construction process, architects must protect their firms against a multitude of risks that can jeopardize the future of their practice, the firm, and the individual financial well-being of themselves and others. Insurance is a means to manage risks by transferring them to an insurance company.

As a firm owner and licensed professional, an architect obtains insurance coverage for professional liability, property loss, and personal loss. As a firm grows, it is useful for staff recruitment and retention to consider providing staff benefits as well, including various insurance and retirement plans.

The AIA Trust is uniquely qualified to offer AIA members the kinds of programs they need to run successful practices. The trustees, who are AIA members, and an AIA component executive work with the staff executive director of the Trust and independent consultants who are experts in their respective fields. Together, they identify and thoroughly evaluate marketplace offerings so the Trust can make the best programs available to AIA members.

The AIA Trust was created to provide life, disability, health, and other important insurance and related benefits, as well as education programs needed for the practice of architecture. The Trust programs are offered to individual members (and their families) and to firms; most programs are also offered to AIA component executives and their staffs. Eligibility for each program, as listed below, is indicated on the AIA Trust Web site at www.TheAIATrust.com:

Firm programs
- Professional liability insurance
- Business owners insurance (may include general liability, property and casualty, valuable documents, workers' compensation, business auto, umbrella, and employment practices)
- Life insurance for firms and components
- Business disability insurance
- Members retirement plan—includes 401(k)s, profit-sharing, SEPs, IRAs
- Practice-related legal information service

Individual programs
- Individual ten-year level term life insurance
- Personal disability insurance
- Short-term and student medical insurance
- Prescription and health care discounts
- Dental insurance
- Accident insurance
- Medicare supplement plan
- Long-term care insurance
- Automobile insurance
- Homeowners/home office/tenant insurance
- A service to identify individual and small group health care plans for members and components, until an endorsed medical plan may be secured in the future.

> Architects may be held liable for design errors and omissions that fall below the professional standard of reasonable care.

Ann Casso is the executive director of the AIA Trust, and Ric Schultz is an adviser to the AIA Trust.

PROFESSIONAL LIABILITY

For architects, the most devastating professional and business risks are almost certainly from litigation alleging negligence in the performance of professional services. Alleged negligent acts, errors, or omissions may cause damage to owners, contractors, or other third parties. As well, the architect's firm may be found liable for these damages. A professional liability insurance policy (sometimes called errors-and-omissions, or E&O, insurance) absorbs a portion of such claims in exchange for the premiums paid to the insurance company.

SELECTING INSURANCE BROKERS AND INSURANCE COMPANIES

Buying insurance is a major business decision. An architecture firm therefore will want to select a broker in much the same way it selects a lawyer and accountant—with care and scrutiny as to the broker's qualifications, independent judgment, offered services, cost, understanding of the profession, and ability to work with the firm. Independent insurance consultants are available to help architects select an insurance broker or decide between the product of an exclusive agent and those offered by an insurance broker.

An independent broker—in contrast to an agent for a specific carrier—will examine the insurance market and obtain premium quotes for specific levels of coverage and service, evaluate the quotes, and provide a professional opinion as to which policies fit the architecture firm's needs. An architect pays for this expertise and service. While some brokers work on a fee basis, most receive a commission—essentially the architect's money—paid to them by the insurance carrier out of the premium. Commission rates vary, and the architect has a right to know the commission level for each quoted premium. In some cases, a broker actually is an agent of a specific company, and while the agent may be able to offer coverage from other carriers, he or she may have a financial incentive to direct the architect to that company. Again, architects have a right to know whether a broker has an agency relationship with a specific company. The architect has the right to request that the broker work on a fee basis instead of for a commission.

A broker can do more than advise in the selection of insurance carriers and policies. Brokers can prepare the application, represent the architect in disputes with the insurer, and send claim notices to the insurer on behalf of the architect. A firm also may rely on a broker to help the firm:

- Communicate with insurance markets regarding all aspects of the firm's insurance needs.
- Evaluate the firm's range of liability exposures and identify of various forms of insurance available to protect it from financial loss.

- Evaluate and recommend a specific insurance program based on criteria such as the company's stability and financial strength; premium cost, limit, and deductible programs; coverage terms; claims management; and risk and practice management techniques.
- Analyze the insurability implications of changes in the organizational structure or nature of the practice.
- Review proposed contractual provisions affecting insurability while the professional services contract is being drafted.
- Monitor claims administration.

Once premium quotes have been obtained, the decision about which policy to accept should not be made on price alone. A number of factors should be scrutinized when considering which carrier best meets a firm's needs:

Policy Considerations

- What is the scope of coverage being offered, what endorsements are available to expand coverage, and what is being excluded from coverage?
- What is the proposed cost of the basic policy and any endorsements?
- Is the firm buying insurance to meet a coverage requirement or as a key component of its financial management program?

Attributes of the Insurer

- How extensive is the insurance company's experience in underwriting professional liability for architects? In particular, what is its track record during hard markets, when few carriers offer insurance?
- How flexible is the company in meeting the firm's needs? Does it offer project insurance and coverage for design-build, prior acts, and retirement?
- How strong is the company? A. M. Best Company rates an insurance company's relative financial strength and ability to meet its contractual obligations based on its

(continued)

profit, cash liquidity, reinsurance quality, adequacy of reserves, and management strength. This rating is part of the annual insurance survey conducted by the AIA and engineering societies, and the rating is also one of the AIA commendation requirements. Standard & Poor's rates a company's ability to pay claims over time. Moody's also rates aspects of an insurer's financial strength.

- Is the company a licensed or admitted carrier? Such a carrier subjects itself to all of a state's insurance rules and regulations. In many states, a state commission reviews and approves company rates and policies before they can be implemented. In all states, having a licensed (admitted) carrier means the insured is covered by guarantee funds, which may provide coverage should the company fail. Coverage for architects under guarantee funds varies by state. Generally, the protection provided by such funds has become more restrictive in terms of limits of liability and eligibility. Nonadmitted (or excess-and-surplus) carriers are not subject to the

same regulation and oversight. The state neither regulates their coverage nor evaluates their rates. This translates into extra flexibility for the carrier, which historically in soft markets has produced low premiums and in hard markets has made insurance less available.

- How extensive is the company's experience in the management of professional liability claims against architects? What claims services will it provide that will benefit the firm?
- How will the legal defense of claims be handled? Against what criteria are the company's defense attorneys evaluated and appointed? How much say will the architect have in the selection of counsel and in the conduct of a legal defense, mediation, arbitration, or in settlement decisions?
- What professional liability risk management services will the insurance company offer? Does it offer reference publications, contract review services, education programs, and risk management updates?

Some firms decide not to purchase professional liability insurance, a business decision usually based on the cost of the coverage. However, not having insurance could ultimately put the firm and its architects in jeopardy. Even firms that buy professional liability insurance retain some risk, such as expenses within their deductible, costs exceeding their policy's limits of liability, or costs for claims excluded from the scope of coverage.

THE AIA-COMMENDED PROFESSIONAL LIABILITY INSURANCE PROGRAM

Since 1957, the AIA has supported a commended professional liability insurance program. The program is continually reviewed by the AIA Risk Management Committee and the AIA Trust. The AIA commends the program because it is national in scope and meets the commendation criteria established by the AIA Board of Directors.

The commendation allows the AIA to set the standard of what a good insurance program is for architects. Further, it affords the AIA the platform to advocate for new and expanded coverage and services as member needs evolve. For example, project insurance, design-build coverage, and asbestos and pollution coverage all were developed with the assistance of the AIA Risk Management Committee. The AIA commendation is reviewed annually by the AIA Trust and the AIA Risk Management Committee to monitor whether criteria are being met.

Professional Liability Coverage

Generally, a professional liability insurance policy covers the insured firm's liability for negligent acts, errors, or omissions resulting from the performance of professional services as an architect, provided these services are performed within the geographical territory defined in the policy. All policies cover the United States, its territories, and its possessions, and many offer worldwide coverage in the basic policy or by specific endorsement.

A basic policy provides legal defense of claims covered by the policy and pays defense costs subject to the policy limit and deductible. Most insurance companies retain attorneys who are experienced in the defense of professional liability claims. When a defense attorney is selected and approved by the policyholder, the policyholder—not the insurance company—is the defense attorney's client. Some companies may allow firms to choose their own defense counsel.

Broad policies insure not only the firm but also any partner, executive officer, director, stockholder, or employee of the insured firm when that individual is acting within the scope of professional duties. Some lower-cost policies may not automatically provide such broad coverage.

Architects should understand that a firm's practice policy covers the firm for negligence in providing services during the life of the policy. They also should know that professional liability claims from all projects can draw on that one policy or on the firm's own resources for indemnification. As a result, owners sometimes ask firms to acquire additional insurance that would not be eroded by claims from other projects. Such insurance can be provided in several ways. For example, the CNA/Schinnerer program offers firms three choices: project insurance, additional liability limits, and split limits.

Project insurance. A separate policy can be purchased for a specific project that covers the entire design team's negligence for that project. Neither the claims nor the billings of the project policy have any effect on a firm's practice policy. The policy can last up to ten years.

Additional liability limits. This arrangement allows firms to purchase an endorsement that can provide up to $5 million of coverage for a specific project in conjunction with their practice policy limit.

Split limits. This choice allows a firm to secure a per-claim limit of liability and a larger term aggregate limit of liability. Although the coverage is not dedicated to any single project, an owner who wants a $1 million dedicated limit might find it acceptable for the firm to have a practice policy with a $1 million limit per claim and a $2 million aggregate limit.

Of course, a firm may always increase its overall practice policy limits. Again, while not dedicated in any way to an owner's project, higher limits give a firm more assets with which to pay all claims on all projects should the need arise.

The lists below highlight the various forms of coverage.

Project Insurance

- Guaranteed term.
- Guaranteed rate.
- Unlimited number of policies.
- Costs easily identifiable to owner.
- Limits up to $30 million available.
- Claims do not affect practice policy.
- Project billings do not affect practice policy.
- Covers entire design team's negligence.
- Dedicated limits.

Additional Liability Limits

- Annual renewal option.
- Annual rate (not guaranteed).
- Only two endorsements per policy.
- Costs easily identifiable to owner.
- Limits up to $5 million available.
- Claims can affect practice policy.
- Project billings affect practice policy.
- Covers only the insured firm's negligence.
- Limits may be shared.

Split Limits

- Annual or multiyear term option.
- Term rate (not guaranteed).
- Per-claim limit available to all projects.
- Must estimate cost for project owner.
- Claims can affect practice policy.
- Project billings affect practice policy.
- Covers only the insured firm's negligence.
- Aggregate limit sharing during policy term.

PART 2: PRACTICE

Policy limits. How much insurance a firm buys is a function of its financial needs (including those of its principals), its tolerance for risk, its risk management abilities, and the demands of its clients. Minimum annual aggregate limits of liability for E&O insurance are usually set at $250,000, with maximum limits running as high as $15 million (even higher limits can be arranged for special circumstances).

Deductibles. To encourage risk management, insurance companies require a deductible amount that a firm must pay to defend each claim or after each determination of negligence. Deductibles as low as $1,000 are available, but many firms increase their deductibles to lower their premium costs. As with most insurance, the higher the level of risk retained by the insured through the deductible, the lower the premium cost.

Costs of insurance. The premium for each firm is calculated individually by an insurer's underwriter, based on such factors as the firm's practice, project mix, claims experience, coverage needs, and resulting risks to the insurer. This makes comparing premiums of different firms difficult at best. Therefore, a firm should work with a broker who can present the firm well to an insurance company. Insurers increase the cost of insurance if risks cannot be clearly delineated, so the more specific and unambiguous the information a firm can provide, the lower the premium will be.

New issues periodically surface that call for specialized risk management techniques, including insurance coverage. Environmental hazards are an example. The AIA Trust and the AIA Risk Management Committee, with the help of other AIA members working in specialized areas, stay abreast of these issues and work with the Commended Program to create coverage for new exposures. The committee also reviews coverage available from other professional liability insurers so that AIA members know what their choices are.

Insurance seems like a simple business. Companies have to collect enough premiums to cover costs, make enough money to stay in business, and keep investors happy. Insurance company costs are many, and most are not apparent to the buyer. They include funds to cover administrative costs, costs of buying reinsurance, broker commission costs, state and federal government taxes, costs associated with insurance commission funds, stockholder dividends, and the investigation, defense, and payment of claims. Insurers operate on the "law of large numbers," which allows pooled premiums to offset individual losses. Over ten years or so, the combined premium collected should approximate these combined costs. In any given year, however, either the insurance company or the insured individuals or firms may benefit more than the other.

The simplicity of insurance, however, often is influenced by the complexity of the financial markets. When interests rates are high, insurance companies try to bring in as much premium as possible to invest. Because there is a lag time between premium payment and the cost of claims, some insurers enter the market, collect premiums for investment, and leave the market before claims mature. When stock prices are increasing, some insurers enter the market offering low premiums to show an increase in their value to stockholders because of the influx of cash. After their stock prices rise and their investments in other stocks increase, they then can abandon the market before claims are brought against their policyholders and enter another venture on a short-term basis.

How does the insurance company calculate the precise premium a firm will pay? Sound underwriting management suggests that the insurer should actually measure the risk posed by the practice. As an example, an insurance company might consider these factors:

- *Billing volume*. Basically, the more services a firm provides, the greater its exposure to claims. This exposure is influenced by the number of projects making up the annual billings. For instance, on an equal-dollar basis, in 1999 small firms were fourteen times more likely to have a claim paid by an insurer than very large firms. Part of this is simply the number of clients and size of each project. The severity (the cost of each claim paid) for small firms, however, was only one-sixth as high as each claim paid on behalf of large firms.

- *Types of services*. On a properly underwritten risk, premium levels mirror claims data. Firms should separate billings for types of services as carefully as possible. If an insurer has less information, the premium will include an "ambiguity cost" to cover the potential effects of unknown risks.

- *Project types*. Firms that do lower-risk projects may pay lower premiums. However, some types of projects, such as condominiums, generate more claims than others because of complexity or number of clients.

- *Firm claims experience*. Premium levels also mirror the firm's claims history. Firms with claims-free histories can get as much as a 25 percent credit off the standard rate charged for similar firms. (State insurance commission regulations generally permit no greater credit.) Firms with bad histories can pay 100 percent higher rates than similar firms with average claims histories; firms with very bad histories may be uninsurable. Each insurance company has its own definition of "bad" and "very bad." In soft markets, when insurers want to write business to bring in cash, the definition loosens. In hard markets, it tightens.

- *Geographic location*. Firms in low-risk states pay lower premiums than those in high-risk states. Again, claims data define high-risk states. In 1999, for example, firms practicing in California or Florida paid significantly higher rates for insurance than firms practicing in Vermont or Kansas.

- *Continuity*. The longer a firm is with a professional liability insurer, the more comfortable the insurer feels in accepting the firm's risk. These clients receive not only better consideration (that is, lower premiums) during tight markets but also the benefit of the doubt should they suffer a series of claims. The value of this "longevity credit" can be substantial.

- *Competition*. The professional liability insurance market is highly competitive. Companies enter and leave the market all the time. The architect should be wary of a quote that looks too good. The history of the industry shows that some companies price their policies lower to bring in premiums and then disappear when the claims roll in, leaving the architect with no coverage. Disappearing or underfunded insurance companies are a key problem with claims-made policies.

- *Coverage.* Based on its assessment of firm risk, an insurer calculates various coverage-deductible-endorsement-exclusion combinations and their premium costs. Firms can exercise some control over their premiums by negotiating these four factors through their broker. For example, agreeing to a higher deductible reduces the insurer's exposure and hence the cost of the insurance premium. Small firms with low deductibles and many small projects create a higher risk of paid claims than firms with higher deductibles. Higher deductibles increase a firm's exposure to claims payments but also provide a greater incentive for careful client selection and practice management.

If you are working with an independent broker who is being paid to represent your interests, give that broker as much information as possible. Your application should accurately reflect your practice. If you have a claim that needs explaining, insist that your broker attach the explanation to your application. If you institute new quality management programs, tell the company about them. If you have continuing clients, make sure that fact is recognized. Anything you and your broker think would help the company evaluate your firm as a risk will be welcomed by insurance companies following sound underwriting procedures. And if you do not understand your premium, have your broker call the insurance company for an explanation.

Insurability issues. Insurability problems arise when owners ask architects in a contract to hold them harmless or otherwise indemnify them for the owner's negligence. Professional liability insurance companies provide coverage only for the insured firm's negligence in performing or furnishing professional services and exclude coverage for express warranties and guarantees. Certificates that have the effect of warranties, without a known fact or qualified professional opinion, are also excluded.

An extension of coverage is needed when an architect agrees by contract, in writing or orally, to indemnify and hold harmless some other person, such as the owner or contractor. However, if the architect is indemnifying the other person for the architect's own negligence, the coverage may be automatic with many policies. In most other contractual liability situations, such coverage may not be possible.

The architect should look for hold-harmless provisions before signing any contract for professional services. A clause that otherwise appears innocuous might contain such a provision. An architect who finds or suspects such a clause should submit the provision to the architect's attorney and insurance adviser. A promise to indemnify may fall within the scope of professional liability insurance coverage, but broad wording may mean that the promise is a contractual obligation that cannot be covered by insurance.

Interprofessional relationships. Architects routinely retain consultants. This relationship means that the architect also has vicarious liability for damage caused by the consultant's negligence. Insured architects will want to review their consultant's insurance status because, ultimately, they will serve as their consultant's insurer if that status is inadequate. Similarly, if an architect agrees by contract to limit the liability of a consultant, the architect may find that the risk of the consultant's negligence has been shifted to the architect and the architect's insurer. At times architects are subconsultants to other professionals or subcontractors to construction contractors. Examining the coverage of the prime design professional or the professional liability coverage of a construction contractor can alert the subconsultant architect to gaps in coverage that could result in the architect becoming the only target of a claim.

Joint ventures. From a legal standpoint, a joint venture is similar to a partnership, except that the joint venture has a more limited scope or purpose. If a professional liability claim is filed against a joint venture, one or all of the members can be held liable for any judgment rendered against it. Broad policies provide automatic joint venture coverage, while others exclude joint ventures from the basic policy and require a special endorsement that will not cover other participating firms in the joint venture.

Each member of a joint venture should obtain evidence from other joint venture partners that their policies have been properly endorsed, if necessary, to cover participation in the joint venture.

Project professional liability insurance. Project insurance covers the design team participants—even those who do not have practice insurance. The policy covers the architect and named professional consultants for the term of the project and for a predetermined discovery period after completion of construction. Depending on the insurance carriers of the firms covered by a project policy, coverage may then revert to the individual firms' professional liability policies.

Project insurance is intended to cover only one project and is usually paid for by an owner who wants coverage beyond that normally carried by architecture firms.

Expanded project delivery approaches. Insurance companies have begun to provide coverage for architects practicing in roles such as design-builder, construction manager, and land developer. While some companies offer endorsements for these services to the basic policy, potential gaps should be investigated to prevent uninsured liability. For example, a construction manager, as adviser to the owner, is covered under most professional liability policies, but the at-risk construction manager, acting as a general contractor, is not.

Claims. In the arena of professional liability insurance, there are two common triggers in a policy that require report of a claim. The first is obvious—receipt of a demand for money or services with an allegation of a wrongful act. This definition produces a clear reference point indicating when the insured and the insurance company should intervene. It also is broad enough to cover not only a lawsuit but also angry calls from clients demanding that the architect "fix it." The second trigger is more subjective— the threat of an action, or just a very troubling circumstance, that requires alerting the insurance company of a potential problem, even though it may not become a formal claim. A careful review of these policy terms is important, as failure to report a claim in a timely manner may jeopardize coverage.

Settlement issues. Most professional liability policies require the insurance company to have the consent of the insured before settling claims. In cases involving a disagreement about settlement between the insured and the insurance carrier, the insured may be liable for any judgment plus the cost of defense above the amount for which the insurance company could have settled the claim. Similarly, the insurance company may be liable for the cost of any judgment above the amount that the insured asked the company to settle for. This check-and-balance approach encourages the insurer and the insured to work together to manage claims.

OTHER LIABILITY INSURANCE

In addition to professional liability, an architecture firm may want to carry general liability and employment practices liability insurance.

Commercial General Liability

Other liability exposures, such as slips and falls, libel and slander claims, and property damage to third parties, can arise from an architect's office operations and nonprofessional activities at the job site. To cover such exposures, architects should carry a commercial general liability policy. The following are elements of protection provided by a general liability policy.

Coverage. A commercial general liability policy provides coverage for claims arising against the insured involving third-party legal liability, but it does not cover professional, automobile, and workers' compensation exposures.

Contractual liability. In addition to professional service contracts, the architect can encounter a variety of business contracts, including office leases, purchase orders, service agreements, and the like, any of which may contain a hold-harmless provision that will contractually transfer another person's legal liability to the architect. The architect must check all contracts, agreements, leases, and purchase orders for hold-harmless agreements. The commercial general liability policy automatically provides contractual liability coverage subject to policy exclusions.

Some policies permit firms to decide whether or not to report an incident and trigger claims assistance. Other policies mandate incident reporting.

Business automobile liability. Business automobile liability protection is an essential part of the architect's insurance program. The insurance should be written with adequate limits of liability to cover the business use of automobiles by the policyholder, by employees, or by others. The policy should name, as insured persons, the individual architect, all partners in a partnership, and all officers and directors of the corporation.

Coordination of liability insurance. Professional, general, automobile, and other liability policies are interrelated. The architect should seek insurance counsel to avoid gaps in protection or duplication of coverage and to correlate limits. Umbrella or excess liability policies may sometimes be needed to provide higher limits than those offered by basic liability coverage.

Excess (umbrella) liability policies. When higher limits of liability are required, certain underlying policy limits can be increased through the purchase of an excess, or umbrella, liability policy. This policy provides higher limits in conjunction with underlying general liability, automobile, and employer's liability policies.

Employment Practices Liability Insurance

No one likes to think that their employees may sue them one day, but employment practices claims are becoming an increasingly common basis of civil litigation. Recent changes in the laws related to employment have dramatically magnified both the complexity and the potential legal dangers inherent in any professional service firm's personnel management function. The number of employee harassment, discrimination, and wrongful termination charges filed has increased correspondingly.

Sound management practices will help deter claims and lawsuits—and will help provide a strong defense when allegations are made against a firm. Employment practices liability insurance is another form of protection.

OTHER BUSINESS INSURANCE

In addition to liability insurance, an architecture firm may choose to purchase insurance for other business risks.

Architect's Property Insurance

The architect's office building or the leasehold improvements where the architect is a tenant should be insured by a standard policy or by a broader all-physical-loss form. Careful attention should be given to establishing an accurate insurable value for the building or improvements. The amount of insurance always should be adequate to meet business requirements, such as purchasing insurance for the building improvements on a replacement cost basis rather than on a depreciated cash value basis. All leases and mortgages should be reviewed, as they frequently stipulate coverage requirements.

Office Contents

The architect's office contents can be insured by a standard policy covering fire, windstorm, and other extended coverage perils. Separate burglary and theft insurance also can be written to cover office contents. However, broader coverage of office contents is generally available to insure them against all risks of direct physical loss except as excluded in the policy.

Such insurance covers drawings that are damaged, but only to the extent of the cost of labor and materials to produce them. It does not cover the cost of the research that went into their preparation, although such coverage may be obtained by purchasing valuable-documents insurance.

Portable equipment that may be used outside the office can be insured under an all-risk floater policy. Money, securities, checks, travel tickets, and other negotiable instruments can be insured under a blanket crime or similar policy.

Valuable Papers and Records

Insurance coverage for valuable papers and media is critical for protection of an architect's property and generally must be specified as part of the overall coverage in a business owners package policy. It covers the total value of documents lost or destroyed by any of the means described in the policy and is generally an all-risk coverage. Coverage also is available for client documents in the custody of the architect.

Business Interruption

Business interruption insurance reimburses the architect for continuing fixed expenses and for loss of profits in the event fire or other insured casualty interrupts normal business operations. This insurance can be written to cover fire, windstorm, computer crashes, and other hazards.

Options are available to reimburse the architect for the expenses of continuing business at another location while the damaged premises are being repaired.

Fidelity Bonds and Loss of Money and Securities Insurance

Usually all persons involved with the custody or disbursement of funds, management of firm finances (receivables and disbursements), authorization of payments to contractors or others, purchasing, and other activities requiring the use of funds or liability for the misuse of funds of others should be bonded. A blanket form of bond covering all employees is typically recommended.

Money, securities, checks, and other negotiable paper may be insured both inside and outside the firm's premises under a broad-form money and securities policy to include loss by robbery, burglary, theft, or disappearance and destruction by fire or other causes.

Comprehensive bonds or blanket crime policies are available. They combine coverage for loss of money, securities, and other property under a blanket fidelity bond. The architect's professional liability policy does not cover claims and losses stemming from the dishonest acts of associates or employees.

EMPLOYER-RELATED INSURANCE

Architects with employees must face the prospect of additional insurance coverage for their employees. Some of this coverage is mandated by statute; some is at the discretion of the firm. This insurance is designed to protect the health and income of the employee and often of the employee's family.

Workers' Compensation

By statute, an employer is required to carry workers' compensation insurance. Sold by commercial insurance companies (or, in some states, available through state-run facilities), workers' compensation policies provide protection for work-related injuries. Benefits are prescribed by statute and include medical expenses, lost wages, and death benefits. These benefits are provided regardless of employer or employee negligence. Employees are precluded from suing their employers for injuries covered by workers' compensation.

A workers' compensation policy is rated, based on the firm's payroll, to cover various classes of employees. A full-time field architect performing construction contract administration services will have a higher rate than an architect who does not perform these services. Care should be exercised in the classification of employees to ensure proper coverage and rates applicable to the hazards involved. Improper classifications can result in much higher premiums.

THE AIA TRUST

The AIA Trust was established in 1952 to develop life, health care, disability, and other insurance programs, as well as benefit and financial planning programs of the greatest-possible value, and to make them available to all AIA members. It is governed by a board of trustees, composed of AIA members and an AIA component executive.

Today the Trust offers comprehensive benefits and services at affordable rates to AIA members. All Trust programs are listed at www.TheAIATrust.com with detailed descriptions and application forms, eligibility requirements, and contact information to obtain personalized quotes. In addition, links to related risk management and health care reports, as well as useful articles for reference from the quarterly newsletter *AIA Trust News,* may be found on the Trust site. The Trust sponsors numerous education seminars at AIA conventions and for AIA components on a wide variety of topics, including risk management, legal issues, and retirement planning.

The following plans are available to AIA members and, as appropriate, to their employees and families; most are also available to component executives and their staff:

- The AIA Commended Professional Liability Insurance.
- Business owners coverage for general liability coverage for firms and optional riders for valuable

documents, workers' compensation, employment practices, and umbrella.
- Health care programs including dental, long-term care, short-term medical, and Medicare supplement insurance, as well as health care discounts. The AIA Trust currently offers a Medical Brokerage Desk service to find individual and small group health care insurance plans for members.
- Life insurance, with ten-year level premiums, for individuals. Group plans for firms are also offered.
- Accidental death and dismemberment insurance.
- Disability insurance for personal and business overhead expenses.
- Auto and homeowners insurance.
- Retirement plans such as 401(k) plans for small firms and component offices.
- LegaLine, a legal information service.

Many of the programs offered by the AIA Trust are aimed at serving the AIA's largest constituency—the small firm. The services the AIA Trust offers AIA members have evolved over the past fifty years and will continue to evolve to meet the future needs and practice requirements of members.

Health Insurance

Health care is a major but costly consideration for employees, the beneficiaries of the coverage, and employers, whose professional livelihood depends on a productive and healthy staff.

The cost of health insurance has been increasing at a rate far higher than that of inflation and wages for the past four decades. As a result of spiraling health care costs, health insurance plans and health care delivery systems have undergone significant changes in recent years, and employers have had to develop strategies to control the increases in their benefits costs.

Medical insurance. The types of health insurance plans available in the marketplace continue to change, and the distinction between plan types has become somewhat blurred. In general, health insurance plans fall under one of the following categories:

- Indemnity plans
- Preferred provider organizations (PPOs)
- Health maintenance organizations (HMOs)
- Point-of-service plans (POS)
- Consumer-directed plans
- Limited medical plans

It is important to keep up-to-date in the fast-moving health insurance arena. The national emphasis on health care reform may produce substantial changes and requirements for both employers and employees.

Indemnity plans, which have become rare except in rural locations or under collective-bargaining agreements, provide the same level of benefits for all providers and generally require an up-front deductible and co-insurance for covered services.

PPO plans provide enhanced benefits if services are rendered by a provider that is part of the vendor's preferred provider network but generally still require some cost sharing through co-payments or co-insurance. A PPO plan also provides benefits when care is obtained through providers that are not part of the PPO network, but requires more patient cost sharing than in-network services.

HMO plans generally limit services to those provided by a network of providers except in emergency situations. In addition, with many HMOs, a primary care physician (PCP) acts as a "gatekeeper" for services, with benefits for non-PCP services being paid only if the PCP provides a referral. Patient cost sharing in an HMO plan is usually lower than a PPO plan.

Similar to HMOs, many POS plans require coordination through a PCP. To receive in-network benefits, care must be recommended and referred by the patient's PCP. Otherwise, out-of-network benefits will apply. However, POS plans frequently have fewer restrictions on the referral process; these are often called "open access" POS plans.

In an attempt to control rising health care costs, new types of account-based medical plans, called consumer-directed plans, have been developed to increase patient awareness of the true cost of health care and provide tools to make patients better health care consumers. The two distinct types of consumer-directed plans available are health reimbursement accounts (HRAs) and health savings accounts (HSAs).

HRAs combine an employer-funded reimbursement account that can be used for qualified medical expenses, with a high-deductible health plan if the funds are exhausted. Unused funds in the HRAs can be rolled over from year to year but are forfeited if the employee leaves the employer plan.

HSAs are generally more uniform than HRAs. For instance, to qualify for an HSA, a participant must be enrolled in a high-deductible health plan with a minimum deductible (indexed, with the following for 2006: $1,050 for individual and $2,100 for family) and a maximum cap on out-of-pocket expenses (indexed, with the following for 2006: $5,250 for individual and $10,500 for family). Enrollees in a qualified high-deductible health plan can set up a separate HSA and accrue tax-free money in this account that can be used for qualified medical expenses. While there is an annual maximum that can be contributed to the HSA, there is no limit to the total amount of money that a participant can accrue in this account. In general, HSAs are funded by the individual, but some employers have chosen to also put money into these accounts for employees who elect high-deductible plans. It is important to note that employer money in an HSA belongs to the employee and remains with the employee, even if the employee terminates employment.

Another new trend is limited medical plans, which offer basic health care coverage with relatively low claim limits and thus maintain reasonable premiums but do not cover catastrophic situations.

When purchasing health insurance, a firm must be aware of state and federal rules and regulations that govern health insurance. A key federal regulation that affects health insurance offerings is the Health Insurance Portability and Accountability Act (HIPAA), which became law in 1996. HIPAA was designed primarily to make health insurance more portable for employees when they change jobs, and to increase availability of health coverage for small employers.

In general, there are three distinct markets within health insurance: individual coverage, small group coverage, and large group coverage. Individual coverage is used when people buy coverage on their own, outside of their employer's coverage (if offered). With individual coverage, insurance companies can request and review medical information and potentially deny individuals who apply for individual coverage. If accepted for coverage, individuals may be required to pay different rates based on their age or health status. The only exception is when an individual switches from a group plan to an individual plan. In this circumstance, there is a special HIPPA protection that requires that the individual be offered a policy with no preexisting limitations; otherwise, HIPAA protections generally do not apply to individual plans.

Small group coverage is an employer-sponsored plan that covers 2 to 49 employees. (Depending on the state, a sole proprietor may qualify for small group coverage.) In the small group market, insurance companies may not turn down employees for coverage, but they can review medical information and adjust their rates based on medical conditions, age, industry, or other factors. Each state regulates how much adjustment insurance companies are allowed to make.

Large group coverage generally refers to groups with fifty or more covered employees. Large group coverage generally has more flexibility in plan design and uses the claims experience of the covered population to establish rates.

The health insurance marketplace has seen significant change and consolidation in the past several years. The number of insurance companies selling health insurance has shrunk to just a handful, and many regional managed care companies have merged with larger national insurance companies.

The small firm owner who lacks buying power may not have access to a great deal of choice in coverage options. Therefore, a key consideration should be selecting a stable insurance provider with a proven track record in offering similar coverage. An employer will also have to weigh the balance between offering a plan with more freedom of choice, such as a PPO, with the cost of a less-managed plan.

Dental insurance. Benefits for dental care required as a result of illness or injury may be provided under a medical insurance plan. Insurance to cover regular dental care can be obtained through either an indemnity plan or a dental HMO or PPO. Typical dental plans provide full coverage for preventive care (cleanings and exams) and require patient cost sharing (deductible and coinsurance) for nonroutine and more expensive treatments.

Vision care. Vision care plans typically provide benefits on the basis of a schedule, paying a flat dollar amount toward the cost of one routine eye examination and a set of appropriate lenses, frames, and contact lenses every twelve to twenty-four months.

Health care flexible spending accounts. These plans, authorized under federal tax laws, allow participants to make pretax contributions to a special employer-managed account and then be reimbursed from this account for eligible, uninsured, out-of-pocket health care costs. Contributions are exempt from FICA, federal, and most state income taxes.

Federal tax laws also authorize similar accounts for dependent care expenses. These accounts permit an employee to pay for work-related child care expenses with pretax dollars. Regulation of such accounts is an especially fast-moving field, and advice from the firm's accountant is essential.

Income Protection and Replacement Benefits

In addition to health benefits, a firm may offer life insurance and long-term disability protection.

Life insurance. These plans provide benefits in the event of the death of the insured. They should be thought of as income protection for the spouse or other employee beneficiaries and also as a potential source of protection for the firm in the event of the death of the owner or a principal. Group term life insurance (such as the product marketed by the AIA Trust) is commonly provided to all employees as a fixed-dollar amount per employee or as a multiple of salary.

Disability benefits. State disability benefit laws provide benefits for employees who are disabled due to non-work-related injury or illness. Not all states require this coverage, but in those that do, minimum benefits are fixed and prescribed by statute. For states where disability benefits are not mandated, or in situations where the architect wishes to increase mandated coverage, voluntary disability coverage is available through a number of commercial insurance companies, as well as through the AIA Trust.

Disability benefits are provided in several forms. Short-term disability benefits protect against absence from work of short duration, typically three to six months. Both small and large employers often self-insure against the risk of short-term disabilities through a sick leave program, although it is possible to buy insurance for this purpose.

Long-term disability benefits protect against extended disabilities, often until the employee recovers or reaches age 65. The cost of this insurance is quite modest, and long-term disability insurance provides greater assurance that the financial resources to pay a claim will be available indefinitely. A third party is often needed to determine the continuance of disability; for architects, it is important that the test of disability be their ability to practice their chosen profession. This is the test used in the AIA Trust policy.

Business overhead expense (BOE). BOE disability benefits are similar to long-term disability benefits except that BOE protects business-related expenses in the event of total disability of a business owner. Benefit periods range from twelve to twenty-four months, and this low-cost insurance helps a business owner cover ongoing business expenses (e.g., rent, mortgage interest, utilities, and employee salaries). This valuable insurance coverage allows a disabled owner to maintain the business viability or avoid a forced sale of the business should the disability condition be long-term or permanent.

Retirement Benefits

In times of increased life expectancy, retirement plans take on added significance. Different retirement plans offer many variations and options. Changing demographics, such as increases in the retirement age and taxing benefits for the growing number of people retiring, have already caused major reductions in Social Security benefits. The key is for firms, as well as individuals, to start planning for retirement early.

Defined contribution plans start with an annual contribution based on earnings. The amount received at retirement is based on total contributions made and the investment strategies employed. Every firm has different needs, goals, and ideas about retirement plans; therefore, there is a choice of several types of defined contribution arrangements that offer flexibility in meeting various goals and needs. Following are some affordable retirement plans offered for employers and their employees:

Pension plan
- Contribution percentage is fixed and can be 3 percent to 25 percent of income
- $44,000 individual cap on contributions (2006)

Profit-sharing plan
- Allows a variable contribution of an annually specified amount
- Only employer may contribute
- Vesting schedules may be adopted to reward long-term employees
- Requires employer to make employee contributions (if an employee wishes to make personal contributions)

Traditional 401(k) plan
- Contribution flexibility
- Increasing contribution limits plus larger "catch up" contributions for workers age 50 or over
- Visible and valuable employee benefit
- Employees manage own investments
- More administrative requirements than SIMPLE or Safe Harbor 401(k) plans

SIMPLE 401(k) plan
- Simple rules: no discrimination testing
- Contribution limits not as high as the traditional 401(k) or Safe Harbor 401(k) (although have increased)

The AIA Trust offers a retirement program with a variety of defined contribution and defined benefit arrangements—as well as IRAs, SEPs, and safe harbors—to assist architects and firms in meeting their retirement savings needs.

- Tax-deductible matching contributions
- Easy to administer

Safe Harbor 401(k) plan
- Defers up to $15,000, regardless of employee participation levels (2006)
- Works with a profit-sharing plan to contribute the maximum
- No discrimination testing
- Higher contribution levels than SIMPLE 401(k)

Owners 401(k) plan
- Designed for one-person businesses
- Contribution limits based on a percentage of income (can be three times higher than other plans)
- Optional yearly funding

New comparability plan
- Age-weighted contributions for participants approaching retirement

Defined benefit plans specify, at the outset, the annual benefit at retirement for each participant. Actuaries then calculate the annual contribution required to reach this goal. These plans can be expensive to maintain but usually allow for larger contributions for older employees than defined contribution plans do. They often are not well suited for sole owners with younger employees, but they can be used to accumulate more retirement savings faster for partners and employees nearing retirement age.

A simplified employee pension plan (SEP) is a type of retirement plan in which the firm sets up individual retirement accounts (IRAs) for its employees. The contributions to the SEP have limits similar to a profit-sharing plan. Firms must cover more employees than in a defined contribution or defined benefit plan, and therefore the SEP may be more costly. However, administration of a SEP may be simpler than defined contribution or defined benefit plans.

IRAs are set up by individuals on their own behalf. Individuals can make relatively low annual contributions ($4,000) to an IRA. These contributions may not be tax-deductible, depending on income and whether the individual participates in a pension plan. Earnings on the IRA accumulate on a tax-deferred basis until withdrawal at age 59½ or later. Withdrawals at an earlier age carry a penalty.

Working within IRS and federal pension plan requirements, firms with retirement plans commonly establish eligibility criteria, vesting schedules, contribution levels, and integration with Social Security benefits.

A PART OF MANAGING RISK

The practice of architecture, like other businesses, requires leaders who can manage risk. Insurance is just a part of that risk management. Yet it is an important vehicle for transferring the risk of financial loss.

For More Information

Each year, the AIA Risk Management Committee, the American Council of Engineering Companies (ACEC), and the PEPP Professional Liability Committee of the National Society of Professional Engineers (NSPE) send a professional liability insurance survey to several of the largest insurance carriers that offer professional liability coverage for architects and engineers in the United States. A number of the companies that respond to the survey are also interviewed by AIA, ACEC, and NSPE/PEPP representatives. A link to the results of the annual survey may be found on the AIA Trust Web site and on the AIA Web site on the Risk Management Resource Center page.

The AIA Trust offers a series of AIA-commended insurance programs for AIA members and their employees. Call (800) 552-1093 for a list of all Trust insurance and financial provider contact information, or call (202) 626-7376 to speak with an AIA Trust representative. The Trust Web site at www.TheAIATrust.com gives comprehensive information about each Trust program, as well as useful articles and links on risk management and health care topics.

For professional liability insurance information, the AIA Trust can provide information on the Small Firm Program, administered by Victor O. Schinnerer & Company, Inc., for the CNA Insurance Companies.

The AIA risk management program publishes information on selecting professional liability insurance and managing professional liability risks. Publications can be ordered from (800) 365-2724.

5.6 Managing and Avoiding Disputes

Frank Musica, Esq., Assoc. AIA

How conflict is managed is key to the success of a project. Differences should be addressed before they become disputes, but if disputes occur, they should be managed before they become demands for money or services. Preventing and mitigating disputes requires knowledge of circumstances that could lead to a dispute and the ability to take appropriate action when a dispute arises.

In recent years, it has become apparent to many in the construction industry that managing the risk and consequences of disputes at the lowest long-term cost to the participants in a project requires the implementation of three essential strategies:

- Preventing disputes from happening in the first place
- Resolving those disputes that cannot be prevented quickly and at the lowest level possible within the project organization
- Resorting to binding adjudication only when voluntary, nonadjudicative procedures fail

Many risk management techniques focus on the strategy of preventing disputes from happening. However, some of these techniques also recognize that disputes arise and should be anticipated and reasonably addressed as part of the project delivery process. This realization is clearly reflected, for example, in the contract forms published by the AIA. While designed to prevent disputes, AIA documents contain mechanisms to deal with disputes and minimize their impact on project progress.

Implicit in the second strategy—to resolve disputes quickly and at the lowest level possible in the project organization—is an emphasis on a continuum of nonadversarial, nonadjudicative methods of dispute resolution. Techniques include various dispute resolution techniques for the project site, negotiation, and mediation. These techniques are nonadjudicative—a resolution of the dispute is not imposed, but voluntarily agreed to by the parties. Sometimes, however, disputes rise to the level where adjudication is needed. Arbitration is an alternative to litigation and is typically faster and less expensive. However, like litigation, arbitration is basically adversarial in nature and results in

Frank Musica is a senior risk management attorney with Victor O. Schinnerer & Company, Inc., where he is responsible for developing practice management information and providing risk management advice for firms in the AIA commended professional liability insurance program. He served as insurance counsel to the AIA contract documents program for fifteen years.

a binding decision imposed by a third party. Therefore, the third strategy—resort to binding adjudication only when voluntary, nonadjudicative procedures fail—generally views both arbitration and litigation as dispute resolution methods of last resort.

DISPUTE ANTICIPATION AND PREVENTION

Professional liability claim statistics indicate that most claims—and most funds spent to resolve claims—are related to client dissatisfaction. Data collected in the past by the AIA Commended Program of professional liability insurance indicates that about two-thirds of all claims (and about three-quarters of all costs) are related to client claims. Therefore, it is highly likely that most disputes arise in this same pattern. Clearly, the process of anticipating and preventing disputes begins at the outset of the architect's relationship with the client. However, success in preventing disputes, and success in mitigating unavoidable disputes, requires both knowledge of the circumstances that could lead to a dispute and the ability to take appropriate action when a dispute occurs.

Parties Bring Differing Expectations to Each Project

Design and construction projects involve stakeholders with differing goals and objectives, skills, and capabilities. With careful attention, these differences are brought into a working balance at the beginning of the project through the negotiation of expectations that results in contracts.

As the project develops, however, the many uncertainties inherent in the building process will accentuate differences among the stakeholders. The client's view of the project and its possibilities is likely to change. Unfulfilled expectations often lead clients to question the process and the architect's role in it. Difficulties during construction lead to further doubts. Contractors often have expectations that are counter to the interests of other stakeholders. And unless expectations are shared, some stakeholders will become dissatisfied with the progress or outcome of the project. It is dissatisfaction and not technical deficiencies that lead to most disputes between architects and their clients.

Disputes Often Arise Because of Changes and Delays

Change is basic to the construction process. But the need for change in the design or the time or cost of construction is sometimes misunderstood, leading to further erosion in the enthusiasm and confidence of the project owner. Change also affects projects—and leads to disputes—in other ways. Conditions in the construction marketplace are likely to change. Energy costs and material availability and pricing often increase. Regulatory, financing, community, and environmental requirements may change. The site and the weather also may add surprises that no one could reasonably predict. These changes, and the climate of uncertainty in which they may emerge, can lead to conflicts among the stakeholders. Regardless of how well initial differences are negotiated, and no matter how well the architecture firm performs its services, something will probably occur during the life of the project to change its course.

Although delay is often unacceptable in our increasingly on-demand world, there can be many reasons for delays in both the design and construction phases of a project. When delays occur, an environment is created in which cost recovery efforts may lead to significant disputes.

Changes, the delays changes cause, and other circumstances that affect the schedule often lead to disputes and conflicts.

Conflict Management Is a Necessary Skill

For the architect, the first and most important differences to manage are those with the client. Poorly managed, these differences can lead to disputes and possibly litigation. The architect-client relationship may deteriorate, jeopardizing the project, future

▶ Agreements with Owners (11.1) explores how parties with disparate interests but a common goal can negotiate effective working arrangements.

▶ Risk Management Strategies (5.4) offers some precepts that should be clearly communicated to clients.

projects with the client, and the architect's reputation, in general. When architects perform the construction contract administration services outlined in the AIA documents, they also play a central role in managing and resolving construction disputes. Thus, conflict management is integral to project management for architects.

MANAGING CLIENT EXPECTATIONS

The internal management and administration of an architecture firm play a critical role in the client education and contracting process, as well as in the process of educating personnel on risk management and dispute prevention principles. The effective performance of that role requires the dedication of time and effort. Management at all levels should encourage identification of potential problems or concerns, both general and project-specific. In addition, management should establish standard contract terms and restrict the contract negotiation and execution role to key personnel.

Contracts Manage Expectations and Can Lessen Disputes

Too often firms enter into contracts for professional services without really understanding how the terms and conditions affect the ability to prevent or manage disputes. With the move to computer-generated contract forms, it becomes easy for firms to agree to contractual terms that greatly increase their risk or take away their abilities to manage disputes. The AIA consensus professional service agreements are careful to keep contractual liability and professional obligations aligned. They also provide the basis for resolving disputes.

Firm employees involved in the actual performance of services should be aware of the dispute resolution specifics of each contract through which they provide their professional services. They also should be aware that contractual liability and professional liability might differ significantly. All professional and managerial employees in a firm should be trained in the importance of educating the client about realistic expectations of the architect's performance and the fair allocation of risk. In addition, these employees should be trained to promptly identify and respond to problems that arise during design, in the field during construction, or as a result of other client contacts. Because field personnel are likely to learn of such problems first, they are in the best position, after consultation with management or supervisors, to address the problems in a timely and professional manner.

Recognizing Danger Signals

Disputes with clients are by far the greatest source of professional liability claims against architects. Certain problems are at the core of many types of client disputes and professional liability claims. Before becoming a dispute or claim, these problems send signals. Dispute avoidance depends on the quick identification of, and effective response to, these signals. Some common and all-too-familiar problems that may give rise to disputes and claims might be headed off by a clear understanding of the client's motivations and actions. During the contract negotiation period, the architect may pick up some of the danger signs. Then, during the project, the architect may be better prepared to react appropriately. Common danger signs include the following situations:

- The client refuses to accept the architect's advice concerning a recommended scope of services or the necessary level of effort required to accomplish the project.
- The client is unwilling to negotiate fair terms and compensation for the architect's services.
- The client insists on holding the architect to a standard of performance that reasonably may be construed as requiring perfection—for example, using superlatives such as "best," "highest," or "most economical."

- The client demands a contractual indemnity agreement that exceeds the normal professional obligation of the architect to correct harm caused by the architect's negligence, such as when the architect is obligated to indemnify the client for all loss or damage, even if the client or some third party causes or contributes to the loss or damage.
- The client mandates that the architect perform services within a certain time frame, even though the architect's ability to meet that schedule is not entirely within the architect's control.
- The client refuses to consider conscientiously the advice of the architect concerning aspects of the contractor's performance.
- The client arbitrarily refuses to pay the architect, particularly when services are complete.

Although these problems and others like them are the basis of many disputes and liability claims, they may often be avoided through client education and problem management. To facilitate the education process, the architect must establish an effective method for timely communication with the client early in their professional relationship. Many professional liability claims arise, to some degree, from communication failures between the architect and the client. In the absence of effective communication, the client may develop unrealistic expectations.

CLAIMS EXPERIENCE

In 2005 about 23,000 architecture, engineering, landscape architecture, and land-surveying firms were covered by the AIA commended professional liability insurance program managed by Victor O. Schinnerer & Company. Nearly 50 percent of the firms were architecture firms. Data from this program provide the AIA with valuable information about the source of claims and resolution costs.

Most Claims Are From Clients

Collectively, almost 2,500 claims were filed against architects insured through the AIA commended program in 2005. About 65 percent of these claims were brought by project owners who experienced some cost, loss, or damage, or were simply dissatisfied and angry. Some of these claims were flow-through claims from contractors. If all contractor and subcontractor claims are included, almost 85 percent of all claims against architects were brought by the owner or other parties in the design and construction process. These claims absorbed over 90 percent of the payments made by the Commended Program to defend insured firms or pay on their behalf.

More than 90 percent of the claims against architects involved property damage or economic loss, with less than 10 percent involving bodily injury to building users or construction workers. Very few injury claims result in any payment to the injured party by the insured architect or by the insurance company on the architect's behalf. Paid injury claims accounted for only 4.5 percent of all payments.

Larger Firms Have More Claims, but Smaller Firms Have More Per-Dollar Volume

Spreading all the claims over all the firms in the program, a total of 22.4 claims were reported for each 100 firms in 2005. Small firms had fewer claims on the average—about 10 per 100 firms—while very large firms averaged over 200 claims per 100 firms. Most claims are resolved without payment. In fact, only about one in four claims ever require a payment on the policyholder's behalf. Still, any dispute increases the cost to architects of providing their services. That is why the Schinnerer statistics have been used to lobby for Certificate of Merit laws and shorter statutes of repose.

Because larger firms retain higher deductible obligations, they tend to have fewer claims that require insurance indemnity payments. Smaller firms, in fact, are about nine times more likely to have a claim that requires an indemnity payment than larger firms if the comparison is made on an equal billings basis. However, the severity of paid claims (the cost of defense and indemnity above the deductible obligation) shows the other side of the claims story. The payment made by the CNA program on behalf of a large firm averages about four times the payment

(continued)

made when a small firm is found liable or settles a claim. In 2005, however, even the architecture firms with less than $500,000 in billings each year had average paid claims levels of about $125,000 above the firm's deductible obligation.

The Frequency of Claims Is Fairly Stable

A fifty-year view of claims frequency shows that claims against architects and engineers grew substantially after 1972, reaching a high of about 44 claims per 100 firms in 1983. Since then, firms have been managing their practices—and selecting their clients—more carefully and with a greater appreciation of the risk management. As a result, the frequency of claims has stabilized at about half the 1983 level and no major rise is anticipated unless the economy once again experiences an "overheated" construction market with higher interest rates, inflated construction costs, and unreasonable project time constraints.

Claims Closely Follow Substantial Completion

As could be expected with property damage and economic loss situations, claims also tend to closely follow substantial completion. Schinnerer studies show that about two-thirds of all claims are filed within three years of substantial completion, 92 percent within five years, and 98 percent within ten years. The AIA has pursued "tort reform" initiatives, such as the requirement of a certificate of merit before a claim can be filed, the elimination of joint and several liability, and realistic statutes of repose to cut off claims after a specific number of years. However, such enacted legislation seems to have little effect on the frequency or severity of claims against architects. Proper contract language—such as the use of AIA standard forms of agreement—and the careful management of projects through quality controls, communications, and documents seems to have the greatest impact on reducing the risk of professional liability claims.

Disputes Require Action

Once aware of an actual or potential problem, the architect should monitor developments and take a proactive role in mitigating the problem. Dispute avoidance includes the exploration of possible avenues of resolution, and dispute management requires the foundation for an effective defense should a claim eventually materialize.

Most architects in senior management positions have had some experience in dealing with client problems and claims situations. They are in a position to give valuable advice to less-experienced project staff handling problems on a day-to-day basis. Maintaining a low profile may be appropriate in some situations, but it is rarely advisable to avoid or ignore a client problem. The interaction between management and professional staff directly involved in the client problem serves to introduce some objectivity into the evaluation and potential resolution of the dispute.

MITIGATING DISPUTES WITH CONTRACTORS

On some projects the early indications of potential problems occur during the contractor bidding or negotiation process. Clients with little experience or financial or legal constraints often end up with a contractor that is a likely source of claims.

Recognizing the enhanced potential for disputes, the architect should assign an experienced, skilled project manager to educate and prepare the client for the possibility of contractor claims. The architect should also clearly articulate project requirements at the preconstruction conference. The preconstruction conference, like the pre-bid conference and pre-award conference (if any) that preceded it, represents an important opportunity to influence and refine owner and contractor expectations.

During project execution, an architect serving as a representative of the project owner should document in a timely manner all pertinent developments and communications with the contractor. Timely responses to the contractor's inquiries or other communications often avoid or reduce the potential for disputes. Finally, the architect

How an architecture firm handles risk is critical to its profitability and is essential to its viability. According to Victor O. Schinnerer & Company, Inc., several techniques are paramount to allowing a firm to pursue its preferred future and to avoid disputes that could generate professional liability or contractual liability claims.

Use a Written Contract to Collect a Reasonable Fee

One of the most valuable proactive risk management tools an architecture practice possesses is the ability to collect fees. Receiving payment for services in a timely manner is essential to the financial health of a business. Establishing and enforcing contractual payment provisions can help a firm avoid disputes that often lead to professional liability claims or to uninsured contractual liability exposures. Professional liability disputes are more easily managed if firms execute written agreements with their clients to clearly define payment terms, a schedule when payments are to be made, and invoicing and collection procedures. Enforcing the contractual right to payment should be considered a key practice management procedure that mitigates the risk of disputes.

Oral agreements create problems. Collecting the appropriate payment for services can be nearly impossible unless a written agreement exists. The agreement should carefully tie the fee to measurements that can be understood by the client and documented by the firm. Unclear or unspecified payment terms and untimely billing and collection often generate disputes. One of the greatest values in using AIA standard forms of agreement is their clarity on payment provisions.

A contract should also clearly state who is authorized to approve payments on behalf of the client and to increase the scope of services. Disputes often occur because of "scope creep" or additional services for which compensation was never properly authorized. While the basis for payment can vary from hourly to value-added, the application of the fee system should be documented.

Retain Control Over Services and Deliverables

Firms should retain the right to their project documentation at least until all fees are paid. If payment is not received according to the contractual obligations of the client, the right to suspend the firm's services is essential. It is good business practice to ask for a sufficient retainer to avoid financing the client. Up-front payments such as this can help minimize disputes as a project is ending. Firms that accept a termination for the client's convenience provision should be careful to negotiate the specifics of such an option, including who has control over the documents in progress and whether lost profits are recoverable.

Avoid Giving the Client the Right to Withhold Payment

Increasingly, firms are faced with clients who want to be able to withhold fees on an arbitrary basis with no independent finding of fault. Fee negotiations can be rendered meaningless if a client can withhold professional fees to a firm at the client's own discretion. Although surrendering a fee to a client whenever the client feels it should recover can minimize disputes, such a practice also can bankrupt professional practices. Remember that any client-written provision that empowers the client to make a unilateral determination of fault or responsibility for damages creates a business risk. The withholding of fees is not the same as a demand for money or services that would trigger professional liability insurance coverage.

should consult with experienced legal or insurance counsel as necessary to obtain timely, preventative advice. The key is to be proactive in anticipating and addressing potential or actual problems.

Procedures for Handling Changes During Construction

The nature, number, and scope of potential changes may be so unpredictable as to frighten the novice to the building enterprise. No one, however, invests the time and money required in design and construction without a reasoned belief in project success.

Unexpected site conditions, construction industry problems, inclement weather, or errors and omissions in the contract documents may suggest or require changes. Client or contractor may demand adjustments in contract amounts or schedule because of untimely submittals, delayed approvals, changes in regulatory procedures, and other administrative problems.

The AIA owner-contractor agreement forms allow the owner and contractor to designate who will render decisions on project claims. If the owner and contractor do not choose to designate an "initial decision maker," the architect assumes that role along with other construction contract administration responsibilities.

The first rule in preventing construction phase disputes is to read and follow the project agreements, which indicate who is responsible for what and when. The parties should live up to their promises. The second rule is to address problems as they arise. Letting them go may have two effects: (1) problems ripen into formal claims, limiting the architect's actions and the timing of those actions to those specified in the project agreements, and (2) the manageable can become unmanageable.

Maintaining open lines of communication and a committed team effort on the part of owner, architect, and contractor can help resolve problems as they arise. The six-step approach outlined below can be effective during construction, when a situation such as change in the time or cost arises that can lead to a dispute.

Step 1: Inform the client. The first step to managing change, as with any aspect of risk management, is to involve the client. It is the client's project, not the firm's, that is at risk. Moreover, informed clients are more likely to be both reasoned and reasonable.

Step 2: Clarify client expectations. Client expectations change during the course of the project. A client who states at the outset that quality is paramount may decide, when presented with a changed circumstance, that budget or time is of greater importance. Clarifying client expectations may lead to viable options.

Step 3: Analyze options. Architects must exercise reasonable care. One way for a firm to act reasonably is to analyze (and then communicate) available options in light of client expectations. Some options may be discarded immediately as too contrary to client wishes to be worthy of consideration; others may require the client to reassess priorities; others may present close-to-perfect solutions to the immediate circumstance but engender even greater changes down the road.

Step 4: Present the options. This step affords the firm the opportunity not only to work with the client to put the project back on course but also the chance to demonstrate visibly the value of architectural services. In reviewing the options with the client, the firm may gain insight into client perception of project progress and client comfort with services rendered to date. The way in which the firm presents the positions and listens as the client weighs and ultimately selects one of them can do much to persuade the client of the firm's commitment to project success and its responsiveness to client need.

Step 5: Document the client's decision. The best way for a firm to secure client commitment to a course of action is to remind the client that he or she selected that course of action. Even if the client tells the architect to decide, not deciding is a client decision and, as such, should be documented. Such documentation need not be written in highly legalistic language. Its purpose is to help the architect and client make reasonable decisions, thus keeping the project on track. It should be written with these purposes in mind. Documentation usually takes one of three forms: If the nature of the change demanded no client involvement, a memo to the file detailing options and the final decision is sufficient. If the client was involved, a memo or letter to the client detailing options and the final decision is appropriate. However, a contract amendment may be called for, outlining the changed services to be provided, the compensation to be rendered for those services, and, if necessary, a schedule for service delivery. In some instances, the firm may choose to document a decision in more than one form—for example, a letter to a client detailing the rationale with the requisite change order attached.

Step 6: Update the client. From time to time, and depending on the nature of the change and its scope and impact, the firm may want to remind the client of his or her decision and the progress being made in implementing it. This dialogue gives a client having second thoughts a chance to state them, which gives the architect the opportunity to reassure the client or to take corrective measures as indicated.

Communication and Documentation Are Essential

An architect-client relationship that includes continual communication fosters an environment in which change and differences can be addressed relatively easily. Noncommunicative clients are problematic. Unstated problems lead to bigger ones, and opportunities for action get lost in the silence. Faced with a noncommunicative client, the firm will have to rely on the client's nonverbal communication to ascertain client satisfaction. In every instance, however, documentation is necessary.

Documentation can help prevent misunderstandings and memory lapses from becoming disputes; it also allows for better, more affirmative project administration and control. Most risk managers agree that more documentation is better. This is based partly on the assumption that most architects conduct their practices properly and perform their services with appropriate professional skill and care and that the records will demonstrate those facts.

Project records should be prepared systematically and contemporaneously as the project proceeds. Such records are much more credible and useful in resolving disputes than ones prepared only after something has gone wrong. Also, although the focus is usually on written records, other types of records, such as audio-or videotapes, photographs, and computer records, can be useful in documenting circumstances and events as the project progresses. All records should be dated, and the author identified.

Records should principally contain facts, not conclusions or opinions, and be written as objectively as possible. At the time when most architects make notes or create other records during the course of a project, they have a limited awareness and understanding of the full range of facts and circumstances existing at the time. Accordingly, conclusions based on such limited facts or understanding may well be incorrect in light of the bigger picture. If the pertinent facts are objectively recorded, however, the author or others will have a chance to draw conclusions when the full set of facts and occurrences is available for review.

Essentially all records, including e-mail and telephone logs, prepared by the architect will be available to adverse parties if a dispute ever reaches litigation. That is all the more reason to be accurate and objective when preparing project records.

Project-Site Dispute Resolution Techniques

An essential strategy for minimizing the effect of disputes is to resolve them quickly and at the lowest-possible level in the project organization. To facilitate this, it is necessary to establish project-site dispute resolution techniques by contract with the client and in the client's contract with the construction entity.

Three common methods of project-site dispute resolution are these: (1) setting up the architect as the initial decision maker, (2) employing a standing neutral, and (3) establishing a dispute review board. These methods are typically built into the project delivery process and are designed to encourage dispute resolution that is contemporaneous with the actual activities on the project. Project-site techniques are often used when initial attempts at direct negotiation fail to resolve a dispute. Their use avoids the need for more formal methods that may require weeks or months to bring to a conclusion.

Architect as initial decision maker. Under the AIA standard documents, the architect serves as the project owner's representative during construction. However, the architect also serves as an impartial interpreter of the requirements of the contract documents and initial arbitrator of disputes between the architect's client—the project owner—and the contractor. When such a dispute arises, the architect's rendering of an initial decision in a quasi-judicial capacity is a condition precedent to the recourse of the owner or contractor to any other rights or remedies provided under the contract documents, such as mediation, arbitration, or litigation.

Some have criticized this project-site technique because the architect is not really neutral, given the architect's conflicting roles not only as the client's representative and initial arbitrator of disputes during construction, but, typically, architect-of-record as well. These conflicts are often pointed out by advocates of other project-site techniques, such as the standing neutral and dispute review board. Notwithstanding these concerns, contractors and project owners commonly accept the architect's decisions under the AIA documents as the final resolution to their disputes.

Standing neutral. A standing neutral is a third party, appointed by the parties to a particular contract, who is ready to resolve disputes on short notice. This standing neutral should be well versed in design and construction issues and involved in the project from the start of construction. The most important attribute of the standing neutral, as well as of the dispute review board, is the ability to garner the respect of the stakeholders. Demonstrated competence, experience, open-mindedness, and ethical integrity are key considerations.

At the outset of the project, the standing neutral is provided copies of the various contract documents and other project documentation as needed. In addition, this individual may attend project meetings to maintain a current understanding of the issues at hand. Opinions issued by the standing neutral may be either binding or nonbinding, depending on the wishes of the parties, but are most often nonbinding. Usually when the standing neutral issues an advisory opinion it is admissible in any subsequent litigation or arbitration concerning that particular issue. The project owner and contractor typically share the expenses of the standing neutral equally.

Dispute review board. Beginning with its application on tunneling contracts in the 1970s, the dispute review board has proven to be one of the most successful applications of nonadjudicative dispute resolution, particularly on larger projects. Like the standing neutral, the dispute review board is established before construction starts, convenes regularly during the project, usually has first-hand and contemporaneous knowledge of the events giving rise to the disputes or claims later submitted to it, and has specialized experience in a particular type of construction. These factors have contributed greatly to the success of this method.

As is the case with the standing neutral, the expenses of a dispute review board are normally shared equally between the project owner and contractor.

WHEN CLAIMS ARE MADE

Unresolved conflicts are likely to result in claims either by the architect's client directly or from the construction contractor, often through the project owner. These demands for additional money, time, or services may be in the form of lawsuits or, more likely, in the form of a letter or other communication to the architect. In the best of all worlds, no client-initiated claim would come as a surprise to the architect. But when the claim is a surprise, lawyers advise that the architect respond to the client's concerns but not admit liability. They suggest this simply because clients whose complaints are ignored become angrier still, and an angry client is often a claim looking for a place to file.

Admitting Responsibility

It is important to note that not once during a dispute resolution process should the architect admit liability or accept blame. There are several reasons for this, and all are equally important:

- The architect may not know what caused the problem or even if there is a problem supporting the client's complaint. To admit liability or accept blame without an investigation of some type is to judge without basis.
- Even if the architect has some sense of causality, that sense will be skewed. Without comprehensive investigation, the architect will place greater emphasis on the strengths or weaknesses of the firm's contribution, if only because that is what the architect knows. This is so even when the contribution of others in the building enterprise may have been the direct cause of the problem.

Timely communication is critical to managing a claim. The sooner you contact your insurance broker or carrier, the better your insurer can respond to your firm's needs and help your claim reach a satisfactory conclusion. Different professional liability insurance carriers have their own procedures. Not all have a staff dedicated to working with architects in the defense of claims. Some insurers simply turn claims over to independent adjusters or attorneys. Some insurers reserve the right to conduct the entire claim resolution process and may have policy language that limits the policyholder's voice regarding accepting or turning down a settlement reached by the insurer. Even if your carrier restricts your firm's participation in defending against a claim, it is important to stay as involved as possible.

You might find the procedures outlined in the checklist below useful when processing a claim. (Note: If your firm is not insured, or if your insurer does not provide claims assistance, it is good advice to contact a lawyer experienced in construction-related professional liability claims and to work closely with your defense counsel.)

What Your Firm Should Do

As policyholder, the firm has the option to report an incident (a situation in which a claim may occur) and is encouraged to do so. By reporting an incident, a firm can often avoid a claim altogether or resolve it in a favorable manner.

Be sure that all principals and staff members involved in the claim are prepared to document the circumstances surrounding the allegation. The preliminary information needed in a written report to the carrier includes the following:

Your firm's name and address
Your firm's policy number
Date, time, and location of the situation
Brief narrative description of the allegation against the firm. (Do not address the merits or your opinion of the claim.)

Name and address of person or entity making the claim
Amount of demand, if known
Any lawsuit papers or legal proceedings
Client/architect agreement for the project
Any other pertinent documents or correspondence, including newspaper accounts

- If the claim or incident involves a traumatic situation (such as the collapse of a structure or bodily injury) and if circumstances permit, take photographs of the claim site. Amateur photographs taken promptly are more valuable than professional photos taken at a later date.
- Consult your firm's claims or legal counsel before agreeing to attend any conferences arranged for the specific purpose of discussing the situation.
- Do not make any admissions, or sign or accept a release from any parties without first obtaining approval from your firm's insurer.
- Keep all pertinent letters of agreement for services, correspondence, and memoranda.
- Accept all letters, memoranda, and suit papers without comment or argument. Do not admit liability and do not attempt to place blame. These are legal concepts; your firm does not have to address them.

What Your Firm's Carrier Should Do

After being notified of your firm's claim (or incident), you should expect the following steps:

- Assignment of a claims specialist to direct, monitor, and assess your case.
- If the situation requires legal counsel, the retention of an attorney specializing in the defense of professional liability claims against architects and engineers so your firm's interests are protected.
- The coordination of the defense of the claim with you.
- An evaluation of your firm's potential liability and advice on the courses of action available, including any recommendations as to the settlement of your firm's claim.

- Liability is a legal concept to be decided by fact finders during arbitration or in a courtroom. The architect was retained to be an architect, not a lawyer. A client's accusation, no matter how vehemently forwarded, does not change that fact. Architects are not trained to make legal determinations. Such an admission or acceptance of blame may adversely affect the ability of a professional liability insurer to provide a defense and may, in some cases, result in the loss of coverage.

MAKING THE CHOICE ON CLAIM RESOLUTION

Once a dispute becomes a formal demand for money or services, a decision on how the claim should be managed must be made. Some insurers have claims specialists who work with the policyholder and defense counsel on claims protocol. For example, how is the decision to negotiate a settlement made? Should mediation, arbitration, or litigation be used? Although some contracts specify mandatory and binding arbitration or litigation, there are often other options.

No hard rules exist for claims resolution. David Perry, who manages claims for CNA, states, "We have claims specialists in every part of the country facing many claims every year. And we know that each claim has to be analyzed and treated individually. The contractual terms and the facts and circumstances of the claim all influence how a claim will be handled." Perry points out that having specialists who know local mediators, arbitrators, and judges is important. In addition to knowing the systems, experienced claims specialists also know the plaintiffs—and their attorneys. Perry states, "Often a client or contractor bringing a claim against [an] insured has been involved in earlier claims. And we usually have a good understanding of their arguments, their interests, and their legal representation. Our goal is always to resolve a claim in a way that minimizes the impact on our policyholder's finances and reputation."

Lawyers have a more difficult time defending a firm that has admitted liability, even if it turns out the firm was not culpable in fact. Also, admitting liability is a violation of most professional liability insurance policies.

Follow-Up Actions

When the architect cannot (or chooses not to) resolve a dispute by claiming either negligence or breach of contract, additional steps are involved. These steps formalize the firm's response and also limit it—again, regardless of the source of the claim. Insurance companies will be informed and defense counsel assigned (or retained directly by the uninsured firm). Records will be collected, explained, and analyzed.

Just as there are various ways to reduce the probability of disputes, there are various approaches that allow and encourage the parties to resolve disputes. For instance, if direct negotiation between the parties is unsuccessful, the next step may be one of several project-site dispute resolution techniques. Beyond that, mediation may be an appropriate option or may even be required as a precondition to arbitration or litigation. Each step represents not only an escalation of the dispute but also an escalation in the time and cost necessary to resolve it.

The key to a sustainable professional practice is avoiding disputes that consume time, money, and a carefully nurtured reputation. Success in preventing disputes requires knowledge of circumstances that could lead to a dispute and action to keep expectations reasonable. Mitigating the cost, loss, or damage of a dispute requires the ability to take appropriate and timely action when a dispute occurs.

5.7 Information Management

Dennis J. Hall, FAIA, FCSI

Although computers and digital technologies have changed almost every aspect of the building design and construction industry, the revolution in design information management has only just begun.

Architects were once primarily concerned with preparing the instruments of service needed to get buildings constructed. Today, however, project documentation is only one part of the body of information needed to create and sustain the

Dennis J. Hall is managing principal of Hall Architects in Charlotte, North Carolina. He is national president of Specifications Consultants in Independent Practice and former chair of the CSI/CSC MasterFormat Expansion Task Team. Hall is also a member of the OmniClass Construction Classification System Development Committee, and the National Institute of Building Sciences' National CAD Standard Project and National Building Information Model Standard committees.

built environment. As members of the architecture profession move from the traditional role of building designers using hand-drawn or CAD-produced construction documents to a broader role in more integrated design processes, more and more building information is stored electronically. Design professionals, owners, facility managers, and A/E/C industry players will use this information not just in new project delivery approaches and team relationships but throughout the life cycle of a facility. This expanded use of building information requires the ability to classify and organize information so it can be used by multiple design disciplines during the planning, design, and construction phases of a project, as well as by owners and facility managers during operation and maintenance of the facility.

▶ See Project Delivery Methods (8.1) for a full description of traditional and emerging methods of project delivery.

INFORMATION MANAGEMENT FOR ARCHITECTS

The ability to understand and locate needed information is critical to any business. For an architecture firm, information management is the classification and structuring of information for storage and retrieval as it flows through the phases of work and later through the facility life cycle. Information management can best be described in the larger context of knowledge management, which is about creating, disseminating, and using information in creative ways to solve problems. Both information management and knowledge management embody more than computer technology, which is simply a tool to support them. Vital to successful information management within the design firm are project delivery expertise and management skills.

Information architecture is the creation of systematic, ordered informational structures for the management of information and knowledge assets. Architects understand the need to create order out of chaos by organizing spatial information, but today we must apply those same skills to the organization of design and building information to create digital information structures.

With design and business information varied in format as well as content, and existing in forms as dissimilar as paper, photographs, film, and digital files, it can seem daunting to organize and integrate a firm's information. Nonetheless, setting up a system so this can be done routinely and consistently will increase firm productivity and provide other benefits, such as strengthening the firm's reputation and improving its performance.

The goal of classifying architectural information is to help produce better buildings more quickly, for less cost, and to allow the owner to easily maintain the finished product.

Approaches to Organizing Architectural Information

Building information in an architecture firm is in a constant state of evolution. Product information becomes design information, which becomes procurement information, which becomes construction information, which becomes operations and maintenance information. Project information may also evolve into marketing or management information for future projects. This fluidity means handling design and building information is not just about classification and organization as much as it is about managing information with respect to time, project phase, or purpose. Today, this often means extracting information from one location or software application and inputting into another application. The goal is to achieve interoperability of the data in this evolving work information management.

In addition to managing building information, architects must organize increasing amounts of information related to the administration of their practices. They use this knowledge to evaluate business opportunities and challenges and to mitigate risk and enhance the firm's profitability.

The information used by most architecture firms can be categorized according to the following uses: business functions, industry resources, project materials, and archives, as outlined below.

Business functions. In addition to the general types listed here, information that falls into this category includes documents developed to give direction to the firm, such as mission statements and strategic plans.

- Accounting records
- Legal records
- Marketing information
- Management information (insurance, human resources, transportation, etc.)

Industry resources. This information category includes materials that support the professional work of the firm, whether general library resources, such as cost databases, or information created by the firm for its specific needs, such as project checklists.

- Product catalogs
- Codes and regulations
- Technical references and publications
- Design publications (books, periodicals, newsletters)
- Cost databases
- Master specifications
- Master contract documents and forms
- Drawing details
- Forms and checklists

Project materials. Project files may include the following:

- Project administration documents (contracts, etc.)
- Drawings
- Specifications
- Design data
- Construction administration records

Archives.

- Business information
- Resource information
- Project information

Developing an Information Management System

Information management begins with organization. In *Information Architects*, Richard Wurman describes five ways to organize information, using the acronym LATCH:

> L—by location
>
> A—by alphabet
>
> T—by time
>
> C—by category
>
> H—by hierarchy

This simple organizational structure provides one way to think about organizing all information, and it illustrates that to be successful (i.e., for firm staff members to actually use it), an information management system must be easily understood by all members of the staff. To ensure the system developed by a firm meets its actual needs, it is best to involve staff in both development and implementation. Once a system has been agreed to, staff and new employees must be educated on its use. Finally, for an information management system to survive over the long term, periodic review and tweaking should be designed into the process. This regular review will ensure that the system evolves with the firm and changes with the technology the firm is using. The most important aspect of any information management system is that it be intuitive, flexible, and adaptable to change.

CLASSIFICATION SYSTEMS FOR ARCHITECTURAL INFORMATION

Classification is the practice of grouping like information together into classes. A class may be divided into a number of subclasses, and this process may be repeated to form a hierarchy. Classes can be simple or compound, analytical or documentary, and they can be organized into systems that are enumerative or faceted.

CLASSIFICATION TERMINOLOGY

Analytical classification (scientific classifications or taxonomies): Classification by physical phenomenon, which provides a basis for explanation, prediction, and understanding.

Classification: Grouping together of like objects and their separation from unlike objects.

Class: A group of objects that share a particular set of properties that no other objects have.

Compound class: A class that reflects more than one principle of division.

Documentary classification: Classification used as an aid to management of documents and other kinds of information, with the aim of making them easy to find. This includes the Dewey Decimal System and the Universal Decimal System.

Enumerative classification: A classification system that attempts to list all possible subclasses of interest in a single hierarchy.

Faceted classification: A classification system that allows assignment of multiple classifications to an object, with each classification considering the object from a different perspective, to permit searching and browsing of related information through several classes.

Hierarchy: A structure that has superordinate classes (classes at a higher level), coordinate classes (classes at the same level), and subordinate classes (classes at a lower level).

Simple class: A class that reflects only one principle of division.

Subclass: A division of a class into subsets of the original class.

Although architects do not need to be expert in classification principles to establish an information management structure for their offices, they should be familiar with the standard classification and organizational structures used in the design and construction industry. The first national information standard for architectural information dates from the early 1960s, when the Construction Specifications Institute (CSI) created the *CSI Format for Construction Specifications* (now known as MasterFormat™) for organizing project specifications. By the early 1980s, standardization of formats for design information was an accepted practice.

Today, the classification of facility information from design through operations is essential to architecture practice. As standard classification systems evolve, applications and tools are developed to use them to their fullest potential. Such tools enable information created by one entity to be easily used by others. For example, information on the Web site of a product manufacturer will be used by architects in the creation of designs, by contractors in the provision of construction services, by fabricators in the creation of products, and by owners for operation and maintenance of facilities. Researchers have conservatively estimated that in 2002, the United States lost $15.8 billion because of the lack of interoperability of construction information, emphasizing the importance of standardizing how architects organize building information.

> The National Institute of Standards and Technology defines interoperability as "the ability to manage and communicate electronic product and project data between collaborating firms and within individual companies' design, construction, maintenance, and business process systems."

MasterFormat

CSI/CSC MasterFormat arranges information by traditional construction practices or "work results"—the way things are put together on the job site. Architects and contractors use the MasterFormat system to organize project manuals, develop detailed cost estimates, and write drawing notations that include reference keynotes. The 2004 edition of MasterFormat is also the source document for the Work Results Table of the OmniClass™ system.

UniFormat

UniFormat, published by CSI in the United States and CSC in Canada, provides a standardized basis for classifying the physical elements of a facility according to function,

Standard/Publication	Typical Uses
U.S. National CAD Standard	Construction drawings Detail libraries
MasterFormat	Specifications Product libraries Detailed cost estimates
UniFormat	Preliminary project descriptions Preliminary cost estimates Detail libraries
Project Resource Manual: CSI Manual of Practice	Construction administration filing
OmniClass Construction Classification System	Building information modeling

without regard to construction practices. UniFormat is most commonly used during the early stages of a project, before particular work results have been determined. It can also be used to organize preliminary project descriptions and reference details and to structure preliminary cost estimates.

U.S. National CAD Standard

▶ A backgrounder following Construction Documentation (8.3) provides more information on the U.S. National CAD Standard.

The U.S. National CAD Standard (NCS) is a compilation of documents by the AIA, CSI, and the National Institute of Building Sciences (NIBS) published as a single standard. Rather than a classification system, the NCS is a standard for practice procedures and printed output from either manually drawn or computer-generated construction documents. Widespread use of this standard helps facilitate the collaboration of design professionals by standardizing layer naming, symbols, drawing sheet layout, file naming, and other graphic display conventions.

OmniClass Classification System

The OmniClass Construction Classification System is an open standard being developed by an industry coalition of public and private U.S. and Canadian organizations. It classifies objects that describe the built environment from various points of view for the entire life cycle of a facility. The National Building Information Model Standard Committee, Specifications Consultants in Independent Practice, and others are using OmniClass as the structure for organizing information in building information models and for specifications standards within BIM systems.

OMNICLASS CONSTRUCTION CLASSIFICATION SYSTEM TABLES

Table 11—Construction entities by function
Table 12—Construction entities by form
Table 13—Spaces by function
Table 14—Spaces by form

Table 21—Elements (including designed elements)
Table 22—Work results
Table 23—Products

Table 31—Phases
Table 32—Services
Table 33—Disciplines
Table 34—Organizational roles
Table 35—Tools
Table 36—Information

Table 41—Materials
Table 49—Properties

Applications of Classification Systems

The classification and organizational systems commonly used in the design and construction industry are excellent starting points for managing project information. However, for them to be useful in practice, they must be used as the basis for the development of an application, which addresses a specific need. A "faceted" application of a classification system is often used because the ability to find needed information is not dependent on where you start a search, but upon having the same components to get to the final answer. Information organized by building type, function and form, material, and work result could be used to identify the building code requirements. For example, the window requirements for schools are different from those for residential structures, office buildings, and hospitals. The code requirements for the height of a window above the floor and the opening of a window are dependent upon the construction entity (building type by function) and the space use by function. Other properties of the window and its installation such as the use of safety glass, thermal performance requirements, and window operation may also be affected by the function of a space as well as building codes. Using a *faceted* search application might allow you to search for code requirements for windows (work results), K–6 schools (construction entity) and classroom (space by function), or for the window manufacturer and model number based upon window sizes, functions, and performance requirements.

Another example of an application of a classification structure is an internal filing system for electronic drawings. Drawing sheets may be organized in a hierarchical structure by project number, project phase, design discipline, drawing view, sequence number, or date. OmniClass tables and the U.S. National CAD Standard provide logical structures for filing, storing, and retrieving electronic project drawing sheets.

STORING AND RETRIEVING INFORMATION

Most architecture firms store information as hard copy (paper) or in electronic computer files. Film, slides, and other media are also used for information storage, but these formats are becoming less common. It is essential that architects develop an intuitive system for storing and retrieving hard-copy and electronic information that is consistent and based on a logical standard.

Paper Records

Paper records may include business, resource, project, and archive information.

Resource information (usually books, journals, product literature, and related matter) is largely stored on bookshelves, and its organizational structure depends on the type of information being stored. For example, product catalogs are usually organized alphabetically or by MasterFormat divisions. Code and regulatory information may be organized by code type or jurisdiction. Many firms find it useful to institute a checkout procedure to ensure that books and other material are returned or can be located if needed by others.

Project information stored in hard-copy format may include drawings in racks or flat files, project manuals on bookshelves, and construction information (e.g., contracts, correspondence, and shop drawings) in file cabinets. The construction administration filing system shown in *The Project Resource Manual: The CSI Manual of Practice* is a good example of a filing system for specific types of information used by architects and other design professionals.

Electronic Files

For ease of use, the filing system a firm employs for electronic files should be similar to the structure used for filing paper materials, although electronic file names must follow an electronic protocol or hierarchy. For example, to create a filing convention for CAD-produced drawing sheets, an architect might begin with a computer drive location, move to a project number, and end with a number following the U.S. National CAD Standard sheet identification system. Project numbers are often a combination of the year the project number was assigned and a sequence number. The National CAD Standard sheet identification system combines a discipline designator, sheet type designator, and sheet sequence number to create a sheet identifier, as follows:

A S	–	1	0 1
Discipline designators		Sheet type designator	Sheet sequence number

Using standard information classification systems makes it easier for firms to develop effective organizational structures for the kinds of information they commonly store.

▶ See Computer Technology in Practice (5.8) for a discussion of digital technologies used by architecture firms.

Architects can also develop templates for standard letters and commonly used forms and other documents. Such templates are normally stored as resource information, whether electronically or in paper form, so they can be retrieved and modified for use on a specific project.

Archives

Business, resource, and project information may be archived when a firm no longer has an immediate need for it. Determining whether to keep or discard information may be a more difficult task than determining how best to archive what should be saved. Some firms have on-site "dead file" storage, while others use off-site commercial file storage. In either case, having an organizational structure that allows easy retrieval of information is essential.

INFORMATION MANAGEMENT: A MUST IN TODAY'S PRACTICE

Effective knowledge management depends on a firm's ability to store information in an integrated fashion that makes it accessible for many applications. In response to the need to manage the proliferation of electronic files, some architects are taking on a new role as project or facility information architects in the project delivery process. These architects ensure that all members of the project team have access to critical information, that relevant project information is maintained throughout the process, and that records of when decisions are made and who makes them are kept.

Project information architects also establish a process and systems that allow owners to incorporate new information into the electronic project information throughout the life cycle of the facility. Project information is, and will certainly continue to be, an extremely valuable asset for clients.

For More Information

The following publications contain information about classification systems and standards used in architecture practice:

- The AIA *CAD Layer Guidelines*, now part of the *U.S. National CAD Standard*, provides a standardized approach to naming layers in electronic building files.
- Version 3.1 of the *U.S. National CAD Standard* was published in 2005 through the efforts of a consensus committee of the National Institute of Building Science, the AIA, the Construction Specifications Institute, and the TriServices CADD/GIS Center.
- *The Architect's Guide to the U.S. National CAD Standard* (Wiley, 2006) by Dennis J. Hall and Charles Rick Green walks architects through the NCS content.

Other classification and organizational documents include the following:

- *MasterFormat* (Construction Specifications Institute and Construction Specifications Canada, 2004)
- *OmniClass Construction Classification System* (OCCS Development Committee, 2006)
- *UniFormat* (Construction Specifications Institute and Construction Specifications Canada, 1998)
- *Uniform Drawing System* (Construction Specifications Institute, 1999–2004)

The Project Resource Manual: The CSI Manual of Practice (Construction Specifications Institute, 2004) provides information about organizing and classifying architectural project information.

If you don't manage the information, it will manage you.

Anonymous

5.8 Computer Technology In Practice

Tony Rinella, AIA

Computer technologies offer architects powerful tools to carry out everyday tasks with greater efficiency. Appropriate application of emerging digital technologies may also help architects leverage their talents and expand their sphere of practice.

Advances in design software and computer hardware are converging with client needs, environmental imperatives, building complexity, and new contract agreements, in ways that promise to transform the practice of architecture. These developments affect the entire range of firms and projects, from small to large, and have been a major theme of recent AIA national conferences. It is clear that the practice of architecture is reaching an inflection point, yet it is still too early to know exactly how this will affect individual firms.

Tangible changes are just beginning to manifest themselves in most architecture offices. Existing computer tools designed to leverage design expertise, support collaboration, organize information, and conduct financial operations are being joined by newer communication, analysis, and building information modeling (BIM) systems. This topic provides an overview of current practice trends, highlights considerations for building a sustainable practice, and provides references to relevant resources.

DESIGN AND VISUALIZATION TOOLS

Many architects incorporate procedures and software into their design process to streamline production and inform design. Some employ technology to extend their artistic reach, realizing new design expressions impossible to achieve by more traditional means.

Design Technologies

Initially introduced as a productivity enhancement to automate traditional drafting processes and provide rudimentary graphics, computer-aided design (CAD) has evolved to provide an organizing structure for information and decisions and a way to visualize a design in three dimensions. Architects are now taking the further step of looking for ways these systems can be leveraged to improve quality and provide superior value for clients. The following are just a few examples of the value-added deliverables that are possible:

- Coordinated technical drawings for consultants that are accurate and do not reflect divergent design alternatives under consideration

DEVELOPING A TECHNOLOGY PLAN FOR YOUR FIRM

Developing strategic plans for selecting and implementing technological systems for an architecture practice requires in-depth understanding of the design and business functions of the office, as well as the operational requirements of consultant, builder, and client project team members who will participate with the architect in an integrated project delivery process. Most firms will benefit from conversation with a wide network of potential project team members to ensure the products and processes they choose will address the full spectrum of technology needs and opportunities of the firm. Broad participation in a firm's planning process also frequently brings the added benefit of confidence, acceptance, and a sense of ownership of the plan among the firm's staff.

The following suggestions should be considered when a firm begins the process of developing a strategic technology plan:

- Form an interdisciplinary team within the firm to research and recommend a plan.
- Hire technology consultants and experts when necessary.
- Share knowledge with similar firms.
- Use AIA publications and knowledge communities as information resources.

Tony Rinella serves on the advisory group of the AIA Technology in Architectural Practice Knowledge Community, and is principal/CIO of Anshen+Allen, Architects. (This topic updates a topic of the same title by Michael Tardif in the thirteenth edition of the Handbook.)

PART 2: PRACTICE

- Presentation drawings (including renderings, animations, videos, and interactive multimedia presentations) for client and internal review
- Presentation drawings that may be ahead of or completely different from the technical development of the project
- Detailed large-scale drawings to facilitate user group meetings

2D computer-aided drafting. Early CAD systems brought automation to traditional drafting processes by providing geometric precision and automatic dimensioning, and enabling reuse of repetitive elements to improve speed and reduce coordination errors. Graphic representation is a primary function of these systems, which provide mechanisms to define and edit geometric elements, display selected combinations of these elements on a computer screen, and draw or print them to paper.

Graphics are based on fairly simple geometric elements: lines, arcs, and circles. Grouping is frequently accomplished through "layers," a concept and term taken from an earlier manual drawing management technique in which related elements were drawn on layers of Mylar and a pin-bar registration mechanism was used to line up the drawings on the different layers. A refinement of CAD technology is more sophisticated element-grouping capabilities, such as the ability to separate collections of graphics into different computer files that can be edited separately then merged in arbitrary combinations for simultaneous display. Another improvement is the ability to create discrete assemblies of graphics to form complex graphic elements (several lines and arcs to represent a door, for example) that can be named and stored for reuse. All CAD systems include some text-handling capabilities, and most support association of database variables with graphic elements to store descriptive information (e.g., door type and hardware group to accompany the graphic element collection representing a door).

While production automation through this kind of system remains an important computer function in project delivery, new capabilities that actually support and inform the design process are now more prominent aspects of computer-aided design.

3D computer modeling. Advances in software and hardware have made three-dimensional depiction practical, making it possible to expand lines and circles into conical sections and spheres. Improved rendering engines and specially developed computer graphics cards have greatly increased the capabilities of relatively inexpensive desktop computers. Stunning visualizations, often with photorealistic detail, enhance communication of design concepts within the design team and to client and public communities.

Many three-dimensional modeling tools support production of the two-dimensional drawings, which are still required as deliverables for most architecture contracts. Provision of 2D drawings from a 3D drawing program has coordination advantages, since the drawings are actually views taken from a single building model.

Physical models generated from computer models are gaining popularity as their cost falls. These physical models, which can be constructed in a wide range of detail and materials, can be extremely useful for conveying characteristics of a design while requiring little additional design team effort once the computer model has been created.

Effective use of computer modeling can complement physical three-dimensional models. Both model types can have a role in studying or communicating a particular aspect of design intent, and they may describe a proposed building more accurately used together than either product can separately.

Virtual building information modeling. When attributes indicating materials, relationships, and function are added to 3D objects in a computer model, the resulting model is frequently called a building information model or a virtual building. While there are many definitions of such models, a succinct and useful definition developed by the National Institute of Building Sciences defines a building information model as a "digital representation of physical and functional characteristics of a facility." As such, the definition continues, the model serves as a "shared knowledge resource for information about a facility, forming a reliable basis for decisions during its life-cycle from

Even though building information modeling is not a new idea, having been floating in the ether since the 1970s, only now has it hit the mainstream, with new complex software tools, new thinking, and new practices.

Charles Eastman, Ph.D., Colleges of Architecture and Computer Science, Georgia Institute of Technology inception onward . . . The [model] is a shared digital representation founded on open standards for interoperability."

Development of a project database as a collection of virtual objects representing real-world building objects, rather than simple geometric elements used to compose drawings, required a conceptual leap that vastly augmented the power of computer-aided design. Changes to an element in the virtual building database are reflected in every subsequent view or report generated from the model; coordination is automatic. The presence of data beyond simple geometry supports various types of analysis as well. Performance analysis of structure, energy use, and environmental comfort are particularly well developed. After design, models are frequently used during building maintenance and operation throughout its life cycle. Use of common language and definitions is important in maximizing the use of building models for interdisciplinary collaboration.

Building information models and virtual buildings support rapid analysis of design options, providing accurate, timely feedback during the design process. Traditional paper or electronic construction documents are diagrams, which must be interpreted by human beings who ascribe meaning to graphics based on representational conventions. A building information model is "machine readable" because it can be interpreted directly by computer software. Direct application of analysis tools to the virtual building reduces preparation for analysis. Turnaround time for energy analysis and cost analysis can be reduced from the two or three weeks typical in traditional processes to one or two days. Architects can quickly explore detailed implications of several design alternatives from many perspectives, balancing aesthetic considerations with function and cost performance to produce a truly balanced design. This is especially important as the effects of diminishing energy supplies and global warming place new physical and economic constraints on the built environment. Buildings are increasingly complex and expensive, and public expectations for improved performance and long-term sustainability are on the rise. Each design decision has myriad consequences, which must be quickly understood and evaluated to ensure architects are providing the best-possible value in terms of both first and life-cycle costs.

Rapid access to reliable design feedback can reduce wasted effort and rework, increase profitability, and speed project delivery. More complete predictions of the outcome each design decision is likely to produce reduce risks for A/E/C firms and clients.

Some building information models include parametric objects, which can change their characteristics, behavior, or location based on variables stored with the object or conditions surrounding the object. For example, a parametric window object may contain specific assembly instructions describing how glass is held in a frame but allow the designer to specify the number of mullions for each installation of the window. In a more complicated example, a parametric door object can be programmed to maintain a minimum clearance from corners of a room. Parametric objects make it possible to encode design logic into virtual building objects, greatly enhancing consistency in application of design principles.

4-D models: moving 3D models through time. When linked with schedules and timelines, virtual building models can be used to unfold the story of development over time. For example, planners may use this method to illustrate the implementation of a campus master plan over time. The technique is also useful for previewing the construction of buildings; builders can rehearse and refine the construction sequence of a building, detecting potential conflicts and arriving at optimal timelines before actually breaking ground.

Detailed Construction Cost Analysis Tools

Simple cost analysis can be achieved by applying standard multipliers to material quantities represented in drawings or in virtual buildings. Advanced cost-estimating tools can support more detailed modeling of work flow patterns, human effort, equipment, and

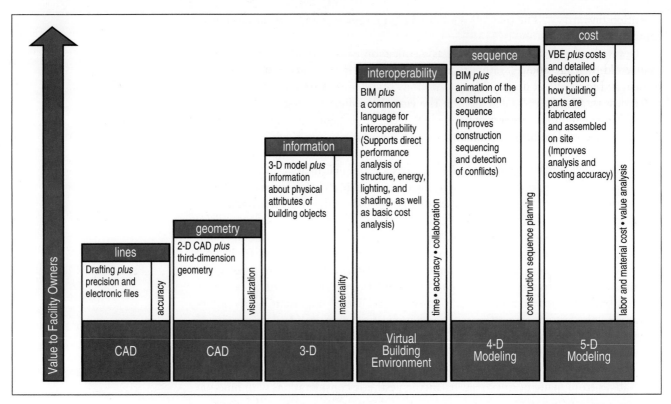

© 2006 Tony Rinella, Anshen+Allen

Virtual Design and Construction Technologies. Technological advances from early CAD systems through "5D" cost modeling made incremental improvements to quality and efficiency possible. These technologies are more significantly leveraged when applied in support of integrated practice, where all stakeholders collaborate to maximize project value.

other resources required for construction. The combination of these tools with virtual buildings and project schedules, sometimes referred to as 5-D modeling, provides extraordinarily powerful cost analysis capabilities.

Support of Integrated Practice

The above-mentioned modeling technologies achieve maximum relevance when used to support integrated practice—free collaboration between experts with diverse competencies working in an environment that encourages rather than inhibits information sharing and value-based decision making.

TOOLS FOR CONSTRUCTION DOCUMENTATION

At the core of an integrated practice are fully collaborative, highly integrated, and productive teams composed of all project life-cycle stakeholders.

Norman Strong, FAIA

Two-dimensional drawings are still a primary deliverable required by the majority of architecture contracts, with detailed specifications still delivered in a text format.

The 2D CAD system can be used to accurately draft traditional construction diagrams and annotations. Most systems provide a separate environment for laying out a set of drawings, and some employ databases to automatically create schedules and maintain appropriate linkages between section and detail drawings and their call-outs throughout the collection of drawings. Coordinating different views of a project (e.g., plans, sections, and elevations) remains the responsibility of those creating the drawings.

BIM systems can also be used to produce traditional annotated diagrams, but the process is quite different from that used with computer-aided design, in which the design team creates a three-dimensional model of the project. As mentioned above, all plotted drawings are reports from this model database, so coordination is automatic.

Like CAD systems, most BIM systems include a drawing layout environment to cartoon and plot drawing sets.

Specifications accompanying construction drawings contain a large body of specialized knowledge about building construction technology, building materials, and means and methods of building assembly. Specification software can manage a large volume of intricately interrelated written construction information.

Software used to create written specifications ranges from simple word processors to custom-built specification systems integrated with CAD and virtual building tools. Sophisticated off-the-shelf software applications are available to simplify the specification-writing process. Architectural Computer Services, Inc. (ARCOM), publishers of the popular AIA MASTERSPEC® specification system, has developed companion software tools that allow rapid, reliable, and accurate editing of the text. For example, appropriate specification sections or paragraphs are linked to references so that deletion or modification of a specific portion of text automatically updates those references.

▶ See the backgrounder AIA MASTERSPEC following Construction Documentation (8.3) for further information about MASTERSPEC software programs.

Interactive tools allow designers to build project-specific specifications by answering a series of questions, rather than actually having to write the text. Other tools manage relationships between specification sections and keynote call-outs used in the drawing set and can automatically construct an outline specification based on assemblies represented in the drawings.

COMMUNICATION AND INFORMATION MANAGEMENT SYSTEMS

Architects traditionally stand at the center of design and construction efforts, integrating, facilitating, and managing the flow of information between client, design team, and construction team. As the volume of information for even the simplest projects increases, more sophisticated tools are necessary to manage data. Downward pressure on schedule and fees has made increased efficiency in communication and leveraging of knowledge essential for the successful operation of architecture firms. Emphasis on collaboration and data sharing creates new information and decision management needs during project delivery. Some architects are leveraging their unique understanding of building propositions to provide new services to facilitate collaboration and to help clients make sense of the complex stream of data they receive.

Fortunately, many communication and information management tools are now mature enough for practical implementation in firms of all sizes. Some of the most popular types are described below. For any of these systems, firms should consider the availability and usefulness of cross-system integration. For example, it may be advantageous to select payroll, HR, and marketing systems that can share a single contact database for employees.

Project Web Sites

A wide selection of software tools and hosted services for project communication and data management are available in the marketplace today. These typically offer document storage and management that support publication of documents and make it possible for users to check out documents for updating and republication, typically with version control and logging features. Work flow routing features allow users to define a specific path for replies, review, and approval of documents. These systems can also track open action items (such as requests for information) and remind responsible parties of deadlines, track progress on various tasks and projects, and display project schedules.

Intranets

Intranets are used to publish information privately within an organization or firm. An intranet may be a simple filing location for phone lists and office policies or a sophisticated knowledge management center containing collected and annotated documentation of experiences from an entire practice. Intranets may include message boards and chat features, site search capabilities, and officewide document retrieval. Some firms distribute project and financial management information via corporate intranets. Most systems provide password-protected access with many levels of security. Off-the-shelf packages are available to create simple or customized intranets, or consulting firms can be hired to craft complete systems.

Financial Systems

► See Financial Management Systems (5.2) for a detailed discussion of bookkeeping, accounting, and financial planning systems.

Good financial systems support efficient financial data entry and powerful business reporting of such information as actual monthly overhead rates, detailed fixed and variable overhead expenses, accounts payable and receivable, and invoice processing.

A number of accounting software applications are available that are designed to meet the specialized accounting needs of design firms of all sizes. They range in price from a few hundred to a few thousand dollars. With a bit of research, architects can easily select a software product that is appropriate for their current needs and will accommodate future growth.

Marketing Software

Contact management systems that track leads, store and track interactions with marketing contacts, and store project history data are widely available and highly useful. High-end systems store staff resumes and project history databases and can assist with proposal development. Some systems can automatically generate standard government forms.

Human Resources Systems

Database systems are available to track and monitor employee information throughout an individual's tenure at the firm. These systems offer a suite of capabilities to track qualifications, performance, promotions, benefits, career objectives, and personnel actions, such as status and compensation adjustments. Many systems provide a Web-based component that can be integrated with the firm's intranet system to give employees easy access to employment information.

Telephone and Message Systems

The traditionally separate services of land phones, mobile phones, and e-mail are rapidly giving way to integrated messaging systems that route unanswered calls from land line to cell phone to a voice mailbox. Many systems collect voice mail as sound files and deliver them to e-mail boxes. Many digital telephone systems support rudimentary video connections at reasonable prices, and high-end video teleconference systems now offer exceptional video and sound fidelity. The concept of "presence" has been added to many systems, which makes it possible to know if someone is available via a particular communication path before attempting contact.

INTEROPERABILITY

Interoperability, based on open, public standards, is a key strategy supporting collaboration between design and construction teams, facility owners, and facility operators. Selection of information management or design systems that adhere to open standards enables seamless integration and communication between all stakeholders. Tools using open standards support faster and better decisions, reduce unplanned changes and rework, and direct effort from clerical functions to value-adding activities. In particular, collaboration supported by interoperable building information models can be an important factor in reaching environmental sustainability and economic goals. Such models provide access to the best-in-class analysis tools that support rapid, frequent, and reliable analysis.

This is just a sampling of hundreds of software packages useful to architects. In addition to products and companies listed below, search for other design, analysis, and information-management tools available from vendors and open-source publishers. Many software publishers offer a wide range of design and information management solutions useful to architects. Be sure to check home pages of parent or umbrella companies for full product lists.

BIM Authoring Tools, CAD, Virtual Building

AllPlan
Allplan Sales and Support
CAD Consulting USA
1777 Saratoga Avenue, #112
San Jose, CA 95129
(866) 277-3355
(408) 873-9979
Fax: (408) 873-9993
www.cadconsulting-usa.com

ArchiCAD
Graphisoft U.S., Inc.
One Gateway Center, Suite 302
Newton, MA 02458-2802
(617) 485-4203
Fax: (617) 641-2801
www.graphisoft.com/

ARRIS
Sigma Design International
5521 Jackson Street
Alexandria, LA 71303
(318) 449-9900
Fax: (318) 449-9901
www.arriscad.com

AutoCAD
Autodesk, Inc.
111 McInnis Parkway
San Rafael, CA 94903
(415) 507-5000
Fax: (415) 507-5100
www.autodesk.com

Bentley Architecture
Bentley Systems, Inc.
685 Stockton Drive
Exton, PA 19341
(800) BENTLEY ([800] 236-8539)
www.bentley.com/architecture

BricsCAD
Bricsys, Inc.
39 Merrimack Drive
Merrimack, NH 03054
(603) 882-5876
Fax (603) 889-6039
www.bricsys.com

BuildersCAD
Sigma Design International
5521 Jackson Street
Alexandria, LA 71303
(318) 449-9900
(318) 449-9901
www.builderscad.com

DataCAD
DataCAD LLC
20 Tower Lane
Avon, CT 06001
(860) 677-4004
www.datacad.com

Digital Project
Gehry Technologies, Inc.
12541-A Beatrice Street
Los Angeles, CA 90066
(877) 487 8877
Fax: (310) 862-1202
www.gehrytechnologies.com

ECOTECT
Square One Research Pty Ltd
P.O. Box 1003
Joondalup, WA 6919, Australia
New York: 347-408-0704
Fax: +61 (0)8 9300 8666
www.squ1.com

U.S. distributor:
Share-It! USA
9625 West 76th Street, Suite 150

(continued)

PART 2: PRACTICE

Eden Prairie, MN 55344

(800) 903-4152

Fax (952) 646-4552

www.ecotect.com

MicroStation

See Bentley Architecture

REVIT

Autodesk, Inc.

111 McInnis Parkway

San Rafael, CA 94903

(415) 507-5000

Fax: (415) 507-5100

www.autodesk.com/revit

SoftCAD.3D Architecture

EdiCAD sarl

Rue des Pinsons

46000 CAHORS

France

+33-(0)5 65 23 91 79

www.softcad.com/english/product/s3dcomp.asp

VectorWorks (formerly MiniCAD)

VectorWorks Sales & Support

Nemetschek N.A., Inc.

7150 Riverwood Drive

Columbia, MD 21046

(410) 290-5114

Fax: (410) 290-8050

www.nemetschek.net/vectorworks

Modeling And Visualization

3ds Max

Autodesk, Inc.

111 McInnis Parkway

San Rafael, CA 94903

(415) 507-5000

Fax: (415) 507-5100

www.autodesk.com

Artlantis

Graphisoft U.S., Inc.

One Gateway Center, Suite 302

Newton, MA 02458-2802

(617) 485-4203

Fax: (617) 641-2801

www.artlantis.com

Canvas X

ACD Systems of America

8550 NW 33rd Street

Miami, FL 33122

(305) 596-5644

Fax: (305) 406-9802

www.acdamerica.com

FormZ

auto·des·sys, Inc.

2011 Riverside Drive

Columbus, OH 43221

(614) 488-8838

Fax: (614) 488-0848

www.autodessys.com

Maxwell Render

Next Limit Technologies

Angel Cavero, 2

28043 – Madrid, Spain

Fax: +34 917 219 464

www.maxwellrender.com

Maya

Autodesk, Inc.

111 McInnis Parkway

San Rafael, CA 94903

(415) 507-5000

Fax: (415) 507-5100

www.autodesk.com/maya

Rhinoceros

McNeel North America

3670 Woodland Park Avenue N

Seattle, WA 98103

(206) 545-7000

Fax: (206) 545-7321

www.rhino3d.com

SketchUp

Google, Inc.

1433 Pearl Street, Suite 100

Boulder, CO 80302

(303) 245-0086

Fax: (303) 245-8562

www.sketchup.com

Content and Work Flow Management

Documentum
EMC Software
6801 Koll Center Parkway
Pleasanton, CA 94566
(888) 362-3367
Fax: (925) 600-6800
http://software.emc.com

Google Desktop
Google, Inc.
1600 Amphitheatre Parkway
Mountain View, CA 94043
(650) 253-0000
Fax: (650) 253-0001
http://desktop.google.com

NewForma Project Center
Newforma, Inc.
1750 Elm Street, 10th Floor
Manchester, NH 03104
(603) 625-6212
Fax: (603) 218-6145
www.newforma.com

Project Management

Microsoft Office Project
Microsoft Corporation

One Microsoft Way
Redmond, WA 98052-6399
(800) 642-7676
Fax: (425) 936-7329
www.office.microsoft.com/project

Primavera
Primavera Systems, Inc.
Three Bala Plaza West, Suite 700
Bala Cynwyd, PA 19004
(800) 423-0245
(610) 667-8600
Fax: (610) 667-7894
www.primavera.com

TurboProject
OfficeWork Software
97 Sandy Creek Way
Novato, CA 94945
(877) 751-8020
(415) 462-1313
Fax: (415) 598-1573
www.officeworksoftware.com

Accounting/HR/Contact Management

For a list of financial management software, see the backgrounder Computerized Financial Systems following the topic Financial Management Systems in 5.2.

Interoperability based on open standards also provides flexibility to select the best software program for the job, rather than choosing a program only because it is compatible with programs used by other team members. Reliable access to effective programs from any software vendor platform is important for all team members, especially those who use programs outside the mainstream of A/E/C applications, and helps overcome barriers between disciplines and firms.

Interoperability supports continuing long-term access to intellectual property by reducing reliance on singular proprietary systems, and contributes to preservation of data integrity as data move from one system to another throughout the life of the project and beyond. Interoperability is particularly important for BIM and other virtual building software systems intended for use throughout the building life cycle. After construction is complete, virtual building models can provide continuing value to facility owners and operators if they are compatible with a variety of facility management packages for space tracking, maintenance scheduling, and heating and cooling system management.

Several organizations develop standards for building models serving the AECOO (architecture, engineering, construction, owning, operating) or AEC/FM (architecture, engineering, construction/facility management) community. The International Alliance for Interoperability (IAI) provides standards for describing virtual building

The most important feature of HTML, a standard language that instructs an Internet browser how to display the text of a Web page, is its near-universal adoption. Any popular Web browsing software can correctly render a Web page described in HTML. Similarly, any virtual building modeling software should be able to correctly render a building described in a standard language.

objects. Industry foundation classes (IFCs) provide a framework for organizing an entire virtual building model for a variety of building design–related applications, including CAD, specification, construction cost estimating, energy analysis, building performance, project management, financial management, and facility management software. The mission of the IAI, and the purpose of the IFCs, is to support the free exchange and preservation of electronic building-design data throughout the life cycle of a building.

The IAI is also spearheading development of aecXML, an A/E/C industry subset of XML (an acronym for eXtensible Markup Language). XML is a standard promulgated by the World Wide Web Consortium (W3C) to support the exchange of data for electronic commerce on the Internet. While IFCs are designed to transfer the complete electronic building information model, aecXML is capable of transferring discrete subsets of nongraphic data in response to narrowly defined queries. This distinction leads to the popular observation that IFCs are used to model a building, whereas aecXML is used to "talk about" building attributes.

The need for standard organization and classification of building design data extends to the user level as well. Many aspects of electronic data classification are user-definable, and a common language to support data exchange is essential.

The National Institute of Building Sciences is leading a multidisciplinary team of designers, builders, facility owners, and operators in the development of a National Building Information Modeling Standard (NBIMS). This is an effort to identify and document useful views of data found in a virtual building and normalize the nomenclature used to describe their attributes. The methodology examines required data exchanges between various parties throughout the life cycle of a building and delineates specific language for each transfer. The NBIMS standard differs from the IFC standard in its level of specificity. The IFC provides an overall structure for building elements, explaining which data each can acquire, whereas the NBIMS will provide specific language to support each required data exchange.

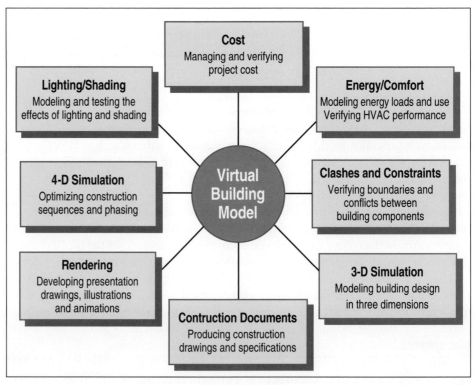

© 2006 Tony Rinella, Anshen+Allen

Uses of Virtual Building Modeling

TEAM COMMUNICATIONS

The means of communication between the members of design and construction teams are highly evolved and formalized, involving standard forms such as addenda, field reports, requests for information, and change orders. Electronic communication via e-mail and the World Wide Web is changing the nature of these communications.

Off-the-shelf computer-based tools designed to automate previously manual tasks are commonly used in firms of all sizes for project management, communication, financial management, contract document preparation, specification writing, bidding, construction administration, graphic design, publishing, and marketing. This type of computer software performs distinct tasks, but the proliferation of such technologies has given rise to an intriguing idea—vertical integration.

Vertically integrated applications share data along a continuum, eliminating repetitive entry of data and allowing data entered for one purpose to be used for another. Vertical integration prompts architects to reconsider and redesign their business and design processes. For example, a project management application, which is designed to forecast the time needed to complete a project, could feed data directly into a financial management application, which would then produce a project budget. Properly linked, a change in the project timeline would automatically update the project budget and vice versa.

FIRMS ADOPT BIM TECHNOLOGY

A number of firms have purchased building information modeling (BIM) software and adapted their project delivery practices to take advantage of it. Two examples are given here:

Improved Quality and Staff Morale

Glenn W. Birx, AIA, a principal at Ayers/Saint/Gross, describes how his firm moved into building information modeling and why it continues to expand its use. "In early 2004," he explains, "our technology committee was exploring new technologies when we first read about BIM technology. We decided it had enough promise to warrant a study. We trained two staffers and purchased one license to use it on a small project as a test case. We came up with a plan to take this project through construction documents, and then to evaluate its effectiveness after one year.

"What actually happened in that one-year period was very different from our thoughtfully conceived plan. I had a line in my office of architects begging me to start their new projects using BIM software. News of this new technology that dramatically aided the design process and was fun to use had spread like wildfire through the office. After one year we had almost all of our staff of forty architects trained on BIM software and had decided that all new projects would use it." As a result, he reports, the firm has seen "dramatic improvements in the quantity and quality of our visual images and are beginning to see time savings in many areas. Most importantly," he continues, staff

morale has improved because staff members love working with the software. This tool allows many man-hours to be shifted "from drafting to design. Architects can spend more time designing and less time drafting."

Boosted Productivity

Oculus, a St. Louis–based firm, is using building information modeling (BIM) software for its services, which include architecture, strategic planning, interior design, and move management. BIM capabilities allow the firm to compete with larger companies, enabling it to accept large corporate clients such as Bank of America and Cingular Wireless. The firm has also found that using BIM technology has facilitated improved relations with clients and contractors, reduced costs to clients and the firm, and boosted productivity and revenue. "I'd say we are 30 to 40 percent more efficient in our processes from design to delivery of construction documents," says Lisa Bell-Reim, president of Oculus. Adds Ron Reim, the firm's executive vice president, "We see up to a 40 percent increase in our productivity across a project. That offers us a whole lot of latitude in the amount of money and time we can spend on a design." The firm's investment in BIM technology has paid off. In the single year that Oculus stepped up its use, the firm's annual revenue and employee base both doubled.

George Elvin (adapted from *Integrated Practice in Architecture: Mastering Design-Build, Fast-Track, and Building Information Modeling* (Wiley, 2007)

THE FUTURE OF COMPUTER TECHNOLOGY IN ARCHITECTURE

The achievement will be in finding balance between the technique we must use, and the artistic vision we must express.

Dr. Ezio Arlati, Politecnico di Milano

Trends toward integrated practice and pressures for higher-quality, sustainable, eco-positive architecture delivered through increasingly more efficient means are likely to continue. At the same time, technological convergence, ubiquitous computer connectivity, escalating computer power, and steadily improving display and visualization systems will open new possibilities for collaboration, knowledge acquisition, and overall practice advancement. Computer interfaces, such as inexpensive "smart" drawing boards in all sizes, along with voice and gesture recognition, are already making interaction with design tools more fluid. Emerging technologies such as "thought" recognition and wearable and implantable computers and interfaces will have an even more profound effect on architecture practice in the near future.

Virtual building modeling is already being used to explore design alternatives and rehearse construction sequences. Digital simulations of the actual use of buildings are increasingly accurate and are being used for real-time assessment of building operation choices for energy and air quality. Computer technology, including that specific to the construction industry, is continually evolving. Architects who want to stay current with changing computer technologies and how they can benefit architecture practice will want to stay on top of improvements in vertical integration and interoperability and the development of industry standards.

For More Information

The AIA Technology in Architectural Practice Knowledge Community advisory group supports the Building Connections Congress, a yearly meeting to coordinate key North American building standards organizations. (www.building-connections.info)

The *Capital Facilities Information Handover Guide* (CFIHG), jointly authored by the National Institute of Standards and Technology, FIATECH, and Uitgebreid Samenwerkingsverband Procesindustrie, Nederland (USPI-NL), outlines methods and specifications for exchange of facility data by all stakeholders throughout the facility life cycle. It is available in PDF at www.fire.nist.gov/bfrlpubs/build06/PDF/b06016.pdf.

The National Institute of Building Sciences publishes the U.S. National CAD Standard (NCS). The NCS defines standards for such things as filenames, layer names, terms and abbreviations, symbols, and notations in order to achieve a consistent format. It also includes standards for the format of printed output, including ways of organizing drawing sets, drawing sheets, and schedules. The AIA *CAD Layer Guidelines* and the Construction Specifications Institute *Uniform Drawing System*™ are key components of the National CAD Standard. Information about other NIBS efforts toward standardization can be found at www.nibs.org.

The Construction Specifications Institute provides a range of nomenclature and organizational standards for building materials and construction documentation, including the UniFormat™ classification system for building components. (www.csinet.org)

The International Alliance for Interoperability is a council of the National Institute of Building Sciences. Its goal is to "develop a standard universal framework to enable and encourage information sharing and interoperability throughout all phases of the whole building life cycle." Information can be founded, including downloads for comment, at www.iai-na.org.

BUILDING INFORMATION MODELING

George Elvin, Ph.D.

Building information modeling (BIM) software combines graphic project data such as 2D and 3D drawings with text information such as specifications, cost data, scope data, and schedules. Most importantly, it enables creation of an object-oriented database, one that it is made up of intelligent objects—representations of doors, windows, and walls, for example—capable of storing both quantitative and qualitative information about a project. For example, while a door represented in a 2D CAD drawing is just a collection of lines, in BIM it is an intelligent object containing information on its size, cost, manufacturer, location, and more. But BIM software goes even further by creating a relational database that facilitates knowledge management. In such a database, all information in the building information model is interconnected, and when a change is made to an object in one portion of the database, all affected areas and objects are immediately updated. For example, if a wall is deleted, doors and windows within the wall are also deleted, and all data on project scope, cost, and schedule are instantly adjusted.

With building information modeling, explains Ben van Berkel of UN Studio, "you have all your parameters, from sound to installations to geometry to light effects in a building, and you can combine certain levels of that information in the computer and read them all at once. An architect right now needs to learn to proportion information more than design."

Because of its comprehensiveness, a building information model offers the project team a comprehensive, dynamic, up-to-date representation of the project with many advantages over more traditional methods of presenting information. Such models can reduce errors dramatically since information can be entered just once, without the redundancy of having each discipline enter the same data in a different location. When specific information needs updating, the change can be made once and the entire model is automatically updated. This fact also reduces questions about which version of a particular drawing is current.

Because when used and managed correctly, the BIM model is always complete and up-to-date, coordination between system installers can be greatly improved and workflow can be accelerated. In addition, because team members spend less time on defensive documentation (phone logs and other records kept in fear of future litigation) and have increased confidence that the documents they are viewing are current, building information modeling increases team efficiency, productivity, and trust. Increased trust in turn helps build a less adversarial and risk-averse culture on the project. Building information modeling has proven so successful among early adopters that the federal General Services Administration now requires its use.

Architects who have learned to manage information with BIM software are also beginning to see its potential as a basis for expanded post-construction services. The rich database of project knowledge in a building information model can be extremely valuable to the owner in operating, maintaining, and redesigning the building. Increasingly, the building model the architect creates serves not only as the basis of design and construction, but also for operation, maintenance, and renovation later in the project life cycle. The architect's position as creator of this dynamic model can offer new long-term service opportunities to the architect, including lease management, energy conservation programming, and operation cost control. Such services can be a great new source of revenue for architects who are interested in them. Even architects interested in building information modeling only as a design tool should consider compensation schemes for the building models they create.

Because BIM creates a comprehensive and dynamic project model, however, it requires intensive collaboration and coordination. Architects, engineers, builders, and owners working in the traditional over-the-wall method, for example, may find building information models hard to create and maintain unless they increase their level of communication. Integrated practice, on the other hand, is ripe for the use of building information modeling because of its collaborative process. "BIM is clearly being applied most quickly on projects where architects and engineers work for the same company," notes architect H. Edward Goldberg, "where a building owner values the building model for proprietary use, and in design/build projects where the liability is shared."

BIM software provides benefits and opportunities, as well as obstacles, to the architects who use it:

Benefits

- Better coordination. Unlike 2D drawings, building information models can instantly highlight interference between building systems and components. Conditions and relationships are clearly understood, and conflicts are readily apparent and easier to resolve.
- Less time to create. Spending fewer labor-hours translates to fewer fee dollars and a higher average billing rate, resulting in greater returns for time invested.
- Greater productivity. Daily input per labor-hour is of higher quality and output is more advanced (i.e., contains more information).
- Better quality design and detailing. Less time spent drafting means more time to think more thoroughly about design and details.

(continued)

- Control of project information. The BIM database is the central source for all project information.
- Opens up new markets. BIM databases give rise to new services for architects, such as cost estimating, scheduling, and imaging.
- Educational opportunity. Proper input requires each user to understand all parameters of the building's parts and systems. This means that less experienced professionals need to carefully consider the quality of their contributions to the building information model and find timely answers to their questions.

Obstacles

- Learning curve. On the "bleeding edge," time must be spent on training.
- Frequent software updates. BIM software is still in development, and some software packages do not include a full complement of MEP, structural, and civil engineering, and other features.
- Shortage of trained staff. Currently, it is difficult to find new employees knowledgeable in design and construction who are already trained to use BIM software.
- Shortage of trainers. Professional software trainers well versed in design and construction are hard to find. Power users may quickly exceed the skills of professional software trainers, leaving further training to the user.
- Industry transition period. Most engineers, contractors, and owners do not currently use BIM software. It will

take some time before the full advantages of building information modeling are seen on construction sites.

Opportunities

- Visualization. Renderings can be done in-house more easily and charged as additional services.
- Fabrication/shop drawings. Full use of a building information model allows continued development and refinement through construction.
- Code reviews. Code officials and other authorities are beginning to see the value of building information models for carrying out their reviews.
- Forensic analysis. A building information model can easily be adapted to graphically illustrate conditions such as potential failures, leaks, evacuation plans, and so on.
- Facility management. Owners and facility managers see the value in using building information models for renovations, space planning, operations, and maintenance.
- Construction information database. The numerous parties involved in providing materials and products, along with those constructing the project, all benefit from having a single source for construction information.
- Cost estimating. Some BIM software has built-in cost estimating features. Material quantities are automatically developed and revised to reflect any change to the model.
- Construction sequencing and logistics. A building information model can be used to create ordering, fabrication, and delivery schedules for all building materials and systems.

The text of this backgrounder has been adapted from material that appears in George Elvin, *Integrated Practice in Architecture: Mastering Design-Build, Fast-Track, and Building Information Modeling* (Wiley, 2007).

PART 3

THE PROJECT

CHAPTER **6**

Project Definition

6.1 Defining Project Services

Glenn W. Birx, AIA

Defining project services carefully is central to developing an agreement that clearly expresses the client's expectations.

To set up a project for success, it is important for the client and the architect to establish a mutual understanding of the project's intent and to define the performance expectations for all project participants. The intent and these expectations are then incorporated into a professional services agreement. Whenever a problem arises on a project concerning architectural and engineering services that is serious enough to include attorneys and a dispute resolution process, the contract for services is the initial document referenced by both sides. All discovery and argument in the resolution process will strive to understand the services performed in the context of those defined in the project agreement. Resolution of the problem will evolve from a determination of the contracted obligations of the parties and whether those obligations were adequately performed.

Building projects are complicated, and architects would all prefer to resolve differences amicably to maintain healthy continuing relationships with clients. Accordingly, a good first step is to establish open communications with a client and to be crystal clear as to the obligations of the parties before beginning work on a project. Because architects and engineers provide many types of services, the client and the architect may have a different understanding of what those services entail. Providing your client with a clear description of services up front will help clarify the client's expectations.

Glenn W. Birx is a principal with the Baltimore-based firm Ayers Saint Gross, Inc. He is responsible for technical services, including proposal generation and design contract development. Ayers Saint Gross provides design services for colleges and universities around the world.

A clear description of services can also serve as an appropriate basis for the architect's response to the owner's programmatic requirements, facilitate the development of an effective work plan, enable negotiation of fair contract terms, and ensure that adequate compensation is agreed to. In addition, it can provide a benchmark for determining when requested services are beyond those specified in the contract and thus require an additional fee.

STEPS FOR DEFINING SERVICES

Proposing and defining services to be provided is a critical part of practice and should not be taken lightly. Thus, the architect should not rely solely on AIA standard forms of agreement or other contracts to perform this task. Each project is unique, with varying code and local requirements and specific client expectations, site conditions, and programmatic requirements.

Communication with the client is a key element in determining what services are required for a particular project. Keep in mind that clients who have worked with more than one architect may have realized they receive different services from each firm even on similar projects. Remember, too, that previous clients can change their expectations or standards.

The following steps can serve as a guide for defining services for a project.

Step 1: Verify the Project Requirements

Many factors can affect the type and quality of an architect's project services and deliverables. Among them are the program, the client's expectations, the client's level of knowledge and experience, the architect's need to retain engineering or specialty consultants, the types of other consultants to be retained by the client, the project budget and schedule, your firm's internal capabilities, and the method of project delivery and construction procurement.

The list in the accompanying sidebar provides a starting point for identifying design factors relevant to a project. Contacting others who may have worked for your client can help uncover potential services that may be expected. Be sure to ask the client in what ways other consultants have not met their expectations. Contact local code and other officials (especially in an unfamiliar locale) to find out about their processes and the extent of required project approvals. Do not skip this last step or assume that you already know these procedures. Intensive research on the factors that could affect the services required for the project will ease project delivery.

Step 2: Prepare a Proposal for the Services to Be Provided

The new AIA series of owner-architect agreements (B101–2007 and its related family of documents) is a good starting point for defining services. Propose the use of these agreements whenever possible. However, be sure the client fully comprehends the scope of proposed services and has reasonable expectations of the project outcome. Many clients do not understand language in professional service

FACTORS AFFECTING THE SCOPE OF SERVICES

The unique nature of most projects requires an understanding of factors that can affect the type, quality, and depth of professional services. Possible factors that can influence the level of professional services include the following:

- Programmatic requirements
- Project budget
- Project schedule
- Inclusion of engineering consultants in basic services
- Requirement for inclusion of specialty consultants under the architect's agreement (those outside your core expertise or different from those usually used with basic services)
- Provision of services by others (consultants or contractors)
- Your firm's own internal capabilities
- Regulatory requirements and public approval processes
- The client's goals, expectations, and values (if you don't know, find out)
- The client's level of knowledge and experience regarding facility development and building construction
- Required use of building information models
- The method of construction procurement (e.g., services for a design-build project will be vastly different from services for a traditional design-bid-build project)
- The form and terms and conditions of the professional services agreement
- The level of risk associated with the project services

agreements with respect to deliverables, requirements for the client to provide information and make timely decisions, and services provided by consultants and contractors. While AIA owner-architect agreements attempt to clarify these items in a thorough manner, direct conversation with the client regarding their extent is always prudent.

A proposal for services, in a letter or other appropriate format, should be prepared in advance of the professional services agreement. The proposal should expand on and clarify the proposed services consistent with the architect's understanding of the project. It can elaborate on specifics such as the schedule (duration of the project), number of design meetings and public presentations, type and quality of renderings, number of site visits and progress meetings during construction, and so on. In some cases, it may be advisable to define the expected number and type of drawings for each phase of the project. If selection of the architect is fee-based, the proposal should include the fee for basic services and for those that are considered additional services.

It may also be useful to provide a list of "services not included" (often termed "exclusions") in the basic services proposal to further clarify what is not included in the basic fee. The proposal should be the starting point for negotiating the professional services agreement, which will more fully describe the scope of services and fees.

Step 3: Negotiate the Final Services and the Fee

▶ See Architectural Services and Compensation (6.2) for further discussion of options for providing professional design services, including value-based approaches.

It is always better to reach agreement on the scope of services before discussing and negotiating fees. Since fees are tied directly to the services provided, it is especially important to have a clear description of services in the proposal. Therefore, if the client should ask you to reduce your fees, it is best to ask which of the proposed services are not needed, since many clients do not fully understand the relationship between fees and services. For hourly based compensation, be prepared to provide an estimate of the required labor hours and other costs associated with each service. Remember that fees can also be based on value provided to the client rather than the hours required to perform them.

Step 4: Prepare the Professional Services Agreement

At the conclusion of negotiations, the proposal should be revised to reflect the final agreed-upon services, schedule, and compensation. Some clients will want the proposal to be included as an exhibit with the professional services agreement. In this case, the final proposal should contain a more complete and detailed description of services whether you are using AIA documents or other contract forms. Keep in mind that AIA documents and other standard contract forms include only general descriptions of services, and that the final proposal will likely incorporate a more detailed description tailored to the unique requirements of the project.

If the client does not accept the detailed description in the final proposal, as with many state or government projects, modify or provide a reference to the proposal so it is represented somewhere in the final agreement or elsewhere in the project records, such as in the client-architect correspondence file. Contracts should be written with the understanding that the signatories to them may not be around, for various reasons, at the time when disputes may arise. Absolutely do not rely on oral agreements. A written record is essential.

Step 5: Monitor and Manage Changes in Scope

A well-written agreement will make clear what services are included and which ones are not. There should be no question as to the legitimacy of a request for additional compensation in the event additional services are requested. There may be times, however, when unanticipated services arise regardless of efforts to include clarifying requirements in the proposal. Thus, members of the project team should be knowledgeable of the scope and the contract language so they can readily identify additional services when they are requested. It is best to raise the issue of additional services prior to beginning work on them. Most professional services agreements require prior client approval for the architect to be paid for additional services.

TYPES AND CATEGORIES OF SERVICES

To make it easier to understand services, it can be helpful to organize them into three groups: predesign services, design through construction phase services, and post-construction services. Typically, most predesign and post-construction services are considered "additional" and those associated with the design through construction phases are considered "basic," although many additional services can be provided during design and construction as well.

Predesign Services

Almost all clients need design consultation prior to the start of schematic design, and through training and experience, architects possess the knowledge to address predesign issues such as site selection and programming. Defining the problem is the first step toward solving it, and architects can assist in the predesign phase in numerous ways, which may include such tasks as scenario planning, strategic planning, facilitation of goal and visioning sessions, campus or master planning, project definition, program management, and related activities. A common predesign task for architects is facilities programming, in which the required spaces proposed for the facility are outlined, along with specific needs for these spaces, such as sizes and number of people they must accommodate, lighting and audiovisual needs, finishes, relationship to other spaces, and other issues. The program becomes an important tool for the design phases and helps the architect design more effectively.

▶ See Programming (6.3) and Research and Analysis (6.4) for information about the processes and methods of architectural programming.

Some clients may require services prior to design to help them with fund-raising activities. These might involve feasibility studies and cost estimating, renderings and models for brochures and fund-raising events, graphic design, return on investment analysis, and other services. The predesign phase offers excellent opportunities for architects to provide "value-added" services for the benefit of the project and to extend relationships with clients.

Design-Through-Construction Phase Services

Most architects and clients are familiar with services traditionally provided during the five phases of design—schematic design, design development, construction documentation, bidding or negotiation, and construction.

▶ Topics in Chapter 8, Project Delivery, cover construction documents production, the bidding or negotiation phase, and construction contract administration.

It is always advisable, however, to review design-through-construction services for each project, because the client's building standards may have changed or the client may be providing some of the services or, conversely, asking for more services than usual. Services can also vary when delivery methods other than design-bid-build are used, such as construction management and design-build. The use of new technologies, such as building information modeling, may also affect the level of project services and how they are carried out.

Most basic architectural services include services for structural engineering and mechanical/electrical/plumbing engineering, and sometimes for civil engineering. However, most other design-through-construction phase services are usually considered "additional." For example, some projects may require use of specialty consultants in connection with food service (kitchen) planning, audiovisual systems, laboratories, libraries, theaters, data/communication systems, security systems, green or sustainable design, and lighting and acoustical design.

Fees for these specialty consultants can be included with the architect's fee proposal, but when this is done, it should be pointed out that such fees are not normally part of basic services. Other "additional" services can include renderings and animations, topographic or furniture and equipment surveys, life cycle cost analysis and energy modeling, additional bid packages and multiple construction phasing, fast-track scheduling, building commissioning, graphic design, assistance with permits and other municipal fees, and many others. Although building owners have traditionally obtained and contracted separately for geotechnical engineering services and utility and boundary surveys, owners are increasingly requesting that these services be packaged with services of the architect. The architect should be aware that providing these site-related services carries considerable risk.

Post-Construction Services

Traditionally, the only post-construction phase services provided by architects have been building commissioning and postoccupancy evaluation. However, architects are increasingly offering more services after construction completion. Such services include maintenance scheduling, space planning, renovations, energy analysis and monitoring, disaster planning, tenant improvements, forensic analysis, code analysis, and space scheduling.

"BASIC" VS. "ADDITIONAL" SERVICES

The importance of distinguishing "basic services" from "additional services" relates to their associated fees. Another way to differentiate services would be to describe them as "services included" versus "services excluded" from the owner-architect agreement. However, over the years, the terms "basic" and "additional" used in AIA documents have become the industry standard for describing architectural services, and the term "basic services" has become the benchmark for comparison of fees by clients. This baseline comes from the AIA description of basic services as something to which the unique requirements of a project are added or subtracted.

A detailed description of the architect's services should be provided with the fee proposal. As well, a description of services that are not included should accompany the proposal. The accompanying sidebar further delineates the distinction between basic and additional services, according to AIA Document B101–2007, Standard Form of Agreement Between Owner and Architect.

BASIC AND ADDITIONAL SERVICES

AIA Document B101–2007, Standard Form of Agreement Between Owner and Architect, identifies and describes both basic and additional services:

Basic Services

B101–2007 categorizes and defines basic services provided by the architect in five discrete phases. The following summarizes what each of these phases includes:

Schematic design phase. The architect makes a preliminary evaluation of the owner's program, schedule, budget, project site, and the proposed method of project delivery. Based on these evaluations, the architect prepares a site plan and preliminary building plans, elevations, and sections; makes preliminary selections of materials and systems; and prepares a preliminary estimate of the cost of the work. (Schematic design documents may also include some combination of study models, perspective sketches, and digital modeling.)

Design development phase. Based on approved schematic design documents, the architect prepares design development documents that fix and describe the character of the project in plans, elevations, sections, typical construction details, diagrammatic layouts of building systems, outline specifications for materials and systems, and an updated estimate for the cost of the work.

Construction documents phase. Based on approved design development documents and any other approved changes, the architect prepares drawings and specifications that establish in detail the requirements for the construction of the project and the quality level of materials and systems required for the project. An updated estimate of the cost of the work is also completed.

Bidding or negotiation phase. In this phase, the architect helps the owner establish a list of prospective contractors. For competitively bid projects, the architect helps organize and conduct a pre-bid conference, prepares addenda to respond to questions from bidders, and assists the owner in analyzing the bid results. For negotiated construction work, the architect helps procure and distribute proposal documents, organize and participate in selection interviews, and prepare a report of negotiation results.

Construction phase. In this phase, the architect administers the contract between the owner and the contractor. Services include responding to requests for information that are consistent with the requirements of the contract documents; interpreting the contract documents; preparing supplemental drawings as appropriate; visiting the site at "intervals appropriate to the stage of construction"; reporting on known deviations from the construction documents and observed defects and deficiencies in the work; rejecting work that does not conform to the construction documents; reviewing and certifying certificates for payment; reviewing and taking appropriate action on the contractor's submittals; preparing orders for minor changes in the work; preparing and issuing change orders and construction change directives, but not for those that require evaluation of the contractor's proposals and supporting data or revisions to the instruments of service; and making inspections for substantial and final completion.

Additional Services

Additional services are addressed in Article 4 of the B101, Standard Form of Agreement Between Owner and Architect. These services are defined and described in two groups.

The first group includes additional services identified in the agreement at its signing. A matrix in the B101 allows these services to be designated along with the party responsible for them. Descriptions of additional services can be inserted into the body of the agreement or attached as exhibits to any AIA owner-architect agreement. At the time the Handbook went to press, the following AIA scope documents for additional services were available:

- B201, Design and Construction Contract Administration
- B203, Site Evaluation and Planning
- B204, Value Analysis (for use when the owner employs a value analysis consultant)
- B205, Historic Preservation
- B206, Security Evaluation and Planning
- B209, Construction Contract Administration (for use when the owner retains another architect for design services)
- B210, Facility Support
- B211, Commissioning
- B214, LEED® Certification
- B252, Architectural Interior Design
- B253, Furniture, Furnishings, and Equipment Design

The second group of additional services includes services that may become necessary during the course of the project. Following are some examples:

- Revisions to architectural documents caused by changes in the initial information, previous instructions, or prior approvals from the owner
- Document revisions due to the enactment of new codes, laws, or regulations after design submissions
- Revisions due to non-timely decisions by the owner
- Material changes to the project size, quality, complexity, schedule, or budget
- Extra work caused by performance failure by owner, contractor, or owner consultants
- Preparation for and attendance at public hearings or dispute resolution proceedings
- Reviews of out-of-sequence submittals from the contractor
- Responses to RFIs when the information requested is in the contract documents or when the RFI is not submitted in conformance with the requirements of the contract documents
- Change orders requiring evaluation of the contractor's proposals and supporting data or requiring revisions to instruments of service
- Services related to fire or other damage to the project
- Reviews for an extensive number of claims
- Evaluation of substitutions and making required revisions to the contract documents for them
- Preparation of design and documentation for alternate bid or proposal requests

(continued)

- Construction administration services occurring more than sixty days after the date of substantial completion, or the date anticipated in the agreement, whichever is earlier
- Assisting the Initial Decision Maker (IDM) in evaluating claims, when the architect is not serving as the IDM
- Assisting the owner in determining the qualifications of specific bidders or persons providing proposals
- Providing services beyond the negotiated number of months from the date of the agreement

- Reviewing shop drawings, product data item, sample and similar submittals that exceed the negotiated number
- Making visits to the site that exceed the negotiated number
- Making inspections that exceed a negotiated number of inspections to determine if the work is substantially complete
- Making inspections that exceed a negotiated number of inspections to determine if final completion is reached

2007 SERIES AIA OWNER-ARCHITECT AGREEMENTS

FORMER NUMBER AND TITLE	2007 NUMBER AND TITLE
B151–1997, Abbreviated Agreement Between Owner and Architect	B101–2007, Agreement Between Owner and Architect
B141–1997 Part 1, Agreement Between Owner and Architect	B102–2007, Agreement Between Owner and Architect Without a Predefined Scope of Architect's Services
B141–1997 Part 2, Scope of Services: Design and Contract Administration	B201–2007, Scope of Services: Design and Construction Contract Administration
N/A	B103–2007, Agreement Between Owner and Architect for a Large or Complex Project
B151–1987, Abbreviated Agreement Between Owner and Architect	B104–2007, Agreement Between Owner and Architect for a Project of Limited Scope
B155–1993, Agreement Between Owner and Architect for a Small Project	B105–2007, Agreement Between Owner and Architect for a Residential or Small Commercial Project

THE PROFESSIONAL SERVICES AGREEMENT

Once the scope of services has been defined and agreed to, it is critical to formalize that agreement in a contract. Regardless of the type of contract form used, the document must include a section outlining and defining the services, and neither party should execute the agreement without thoroughly understanding those services. Three basic types of agreements are used for architectural services: AIA owner-architect agreements, other standard forms of agreement, or owner-generated agreements.

AIA 2007 Owner-Architect Agreements

Part 1 of the B141–1997 agreement was updated and renumbered as B102–2007, and contains terms and conditions. Part 2 of the B141–1997 agreement, which described basic services and allowed for the designation of additional services, was updated and renumbered to become B201–2007, one of the scope series documents.

The B151–1997, Abbreviated Agreement Between Owner and Architect, was updated, renamed, and renumbered as B101–2007, Agreement Between Owner and Architect. No longer an abbreviated agreement, it takes the place of B141–1997 as the primary agreement for design and construction contract administration services. The terms and conditions in B101 are identical to the terms and conditions in B102, and the scope of services in B101 is identical to the scope of services in B201—only the format is different.

The one-part agreement will simplify contracting in most cases. However, the two-part format will be useful for architects who are first retained to perform a unique or specialized service and later retained to perform basic design services. For example, for a project requiring a historic preservation study, scope document B205–2004, Historic Preservation, can be used in combination with B102–2007. Later, design services can be added to the existing B102 agreement using the G606–2000, Amendment to the Professional Services Agreement to add the scope document B201–2007, Design and Construction Contract Administration.

The B101–2007 and its two-part parallel B102/B201 are intended for medium to large projects for which the architect performs traditional services, including cost estimating. In 2007 the AIA also released three other owner-architect agreements for projects of different sizes and levels of complexity:

- The B103–2007, Agreement Between Owner and Architect for a Large or Complex Project, provides an agreement for a large project where the owner will employ fast-track scheduling and will retain a third party to perform cost estimating and scheduling services.
- The B104–2007, Agreement Between Owner and Architect for a Project of Limited Scope, pares down the text of B101–2007 to provide an abbreviated version for smaller, less complex projects.
- The B105–2007, Agreement Between Owner and Architect for a Residential or Small Commercial Project, is the fourth owner-architect agreement. B105 is intended primarily for residential projects or for very small commercial projects. It was rewritten for 2007 to take into consideration comments from the Small Project Practitioners that the document's wording needed to be less legalistic and its format less formal.

Other Standard Agreements

Architects are often presented with other standard types of agreements, such as those produced by the Engineers Joint Contract Documents Committee (EJCDC) and the Construction Management Association of America (CMAA). All of these agreements have sections relating to the scope of services. Be sure to review this language carefully, and do not hesitate to make modifications to accommodate your specific services.

Owner-Generated Agreements

These agreements come in many forms and variations. They could be federal, state, or municipal government contracts and may not have been updated for many years. Unfortunately, some government agencies take the position "Take this contract or leave it," and they will not entertain modifications in spite of out-of-date content.

Some owners have their attorneys prepare professional services agreements. Although some attorneys may not admit it, many have limited experience with the construction process, and the resulting contracts can be dangerous. Therefore, architects are encouraged to read these contracts carefully and have their own attorney and professional liability insurance company provide reviews and advice. These contracts may employ very broad terms (e.g., "as required" or "as necessary"), and they can raise the standard of care of an architect's contracted services to an extent that is not protected by the firm's professional liability insurance policy. As mentioned previously, it is important to be specific in terms of the actual scope of a project and to have definitive scope language placed in the contract.

When dealing with government agencies, request to speak to someone in authority (e.g., the state attorney general) who has the ability to make modifications to the contract. If this is not possible, send a letter to your client carefully outlining the scope of services and deliverables on which you have based your fee proposal. Good documentation will always come in handy should a dispute arise.

CHANGES IN SERVICES

As a general rule, never proceed with services that are considered "additional" without first requesting and receiving written owner approval for further compensation. Although time may be short, a quick e-mail message can inform the owner and document your

▶ See Owner-Generated Agreements (11.2) for guidance in responding to and dealing with agreements presented by the client.

request. Architects who consistently adhere to this rule may encounter fewer disputes about services and payments. Doing the work first and then asking for payment is never received well by clients—and for good reason. Clients want to know ahead of time if additional fees are involved.

Identifying additional services requires careful management. Members of the design team, and especially the project manager, should be intimately aware of services under the project contract. Any proposed changes should be communicated to and discussed with the owner in a timely and professional manner.

Architects could take a lesson from contractors, who typically do not hesitate to submit change orders for work they consider not in their contracts. While professional services are harder to define and quantify than a set of bidding documents, architects should take the same approach to being compensated for additional effort.

Once identified, additional services should be addressed with the same care as any other professional service. Contractual language showing that the work is, in fact, additional should be cited. A reasonable proposal should be submitted in a timely manner, and work should not begin until owner approval has been received. Time spent on additional services should be invoiced separately and a clear distinction made between original contract services and the additional service.

In the event a dispute arises with the owner regarding whether a service was included in the original contract, make every attempt to immediately work out an amicable solution. Set up a meeting or meetings to discuss the issues with parties authorized to make a decision. State your case clearly and professionally, and listen to the owner's position. Architects may find that many disputes about services are caused by misunderstandings that can be cleared up quickly by discussion. Should this approach fail, follow the "dispute resolution" clause that should be contained in your contract. Act quickly, and do not let these issues linger until they become more contentious.

BUILDING INFORMATION MODELING AND PROJECT SERVICES

The use of building information modeling in the A/E/C community is changing the culture of firms and the services they provide. Architecture firms currently using this technology, or planning to do so, must be aware of how it can change the way design services are delivered.

- The approach to project staffing may change. More labor hours may be required of senior architects and more experienced staff assigned earlier in the design process.
- The breakdown and allocation of fees may change, in concert with changes in the approach to project staffing. Because design decisions are moved significantly forward in the process, more labor hours will be expended in early phases and fewer in later phases.
- Renderings and animations are easily achieved using a building information model. Keep in mind that this can bring added value to the client.
- Contractors and subcontractors can use building information models to develop and coordinate fabrication and shop drawings, which can provide added value to them.
- BIM technology makes possible a myriad of facility-related services such as space planning, maintenance planning, energy management, and so on, which can be offered to clients.
- The use of a comprehensive "construction information database" can be offered as a service to the owner, contractor, subcontractors, maintenance personnel, vendors, and others.
- Detailed cost estimating can be facilitated more easily and could be offered as an in-house service.
- Building information modeling can enable the contractor to provide more effective construction staging and sequencing.
- Since building information modeling allows more rapid study of alternate designs, firms must be careful not to offer clients too many options, which can be inefficient and costly to the architect.

STEPS TOWARD SUCCESSFUL PROJECTS

The delivery of successful architectural services begins with determining what work is required, proposing the services to be provided, and negotiating the scope of services and fee. The intent is to achieve a clear description of the project's services that matches the client's expectations with the architect's capabilities. The fee proposal must be clearly linked to the services proposal. Clear definitions and lists of "basic" and "additional" services are essential. The agreement that is ultimately signed between owner and architect must adequately document the understandings reached by the architect and the client. Once the project is under way, remember to monitor and manage the scope of services as carefully as possible. Doing so can substantially reduce potential disputes, go a long way toward establishing a professional and productive client relationship, and help bring the project to a successful conclusion.

6.2 Architectural Services and Compensation

Clark S. Davis, FAIA

Clients are willing to compensate an architect in direct relation to the value they place on that architect's services. Therefore, architects must communicate the full range of their services to their clients as well as the benefits those services provide.

Architects in all types of practice have a common challenge: identifying and receiving appropriate compensation for the services they provide. For most of the twentieth century, project-based fee structures were often calculated as a percentage of construction cost, and the AIA and other industry groups once promoted standard fee percentages. As the practice of architecture has become more complex, however, the challenge of determining appropriate compensation for an architect's work has increased.

By the end of the twentieth century, the complexity, scale, and uniqueness of many building projects had led to the use of cost-based fees for design services. This approach emphasizes the recovery of costs for labor and expenses incurred by architects in performing the work, and invites detailed negotiation of the projected services, staff salaries, overhead rates, fee multipliers, and profit margin the architect will be allowed. While it seems flexible, this cost-based approach to determining fees has some serious limitations. In particular, it evaluates the architect's services solely in terms of hours of effort and does not consider the value of an architect's ideas and results.

Several other trends have emerged in calculating compensation for architectural services as firms work to meet changing client expectations and improve their own economic performance:

- Many architects recognize that maintaining long-term client relationships (rather than focusing on individual projects) is a strong foundation for a successful architecture practice. With this approach, architects can devise flexible compensation terms to cover a wide range of services, project types, and locations.
- More projects today involve delivery methods other than traditional design-bid-build approaches. These may include third-party project management—usually by a developer, construction manager, or program manager—or design-build responsibility. Such approaches require new combinations of architectural services and thus new fee considerations.
- Architects are increasingly sensitive to the business risks imposed by different approaches to delivering their services, and they are seeking appropriate rewards in contract and compensation terms. For example, an architect who shares direct risk for construction cost may negotiate an incentive fee derived if the project comes in under the client's budget.
- Technology has changed the way architects, clients, and consultants around the world work. Significant projects have been completed by "virtual teams" collaborating electronically, and some U.S. firms have explored off-shoring of technical services or documents production to low-cost service providers in other countries. Integrated project delivery supported by building information modeling (BIM) software may change many of the basic rules and practices of the A/E/C industry.

Clark S. Davis is vice chairman of Hellmuth, Obata + Kassabaum (HOK) and managing principal of the firm's regional offices in St. Louis and Chicago. He is past president of the St. Louis and Missouri chapters of the AIA.

- Architects and clients are developing a clearer sense of value based on the contribution architectural services make to the success of a client's project. More clients realize that an architect's ideas can speed business processes, draw and delight customers, attract and retain key employees, and save money through wise choices among facility options.

THE ARCHITECT'S SERVICES

Design remains the architect's focus, and recent iconic buildings have demonstrated the transforming power of design for owners and communities; Frank Gehry's Guggenheim museum in Bilbao, Spain, is a classic example. As well, most corporate clients now understand how well-designed workplaces help attract and retain critical knowledge workers. Leading health care institutions know that well-designed facilities attract increasingly selective patients and contribute to the healing process. Prominent architects have also been commissioned to design popular consumer products. Design matters, and most people know it.

Offering Expanded and Integrated Services

Despite the continued prominence of design services, the last few decades have seen an increase in other services offered by architects, many of whom have expanded their service offerings to meet new client needs and market opportunities. Architects are thinking well beyond the single projects that defined most practices in the past. For example, architects realize that most client needs do not begin with programming and design and end with construction of a facility. Thus, architectural services often address the entire building life cycle: planning, change management (including design and construction), and facility operation. As a result, architects have the opportunity to serve their clients continuously in long-term relationships—from traditional design services to assistance with operational needs and development of strategies that anticipate future facility requirements.

This diversification of services has led to increased specialization among individual architects, firms, and consultants, making the definition and pricing of services more complex. More than ever, firm principals and project leaders must serve as integrators of ideas and information from a variety of team members who have specialized expertise and experience.

The role of architect as integrator can be facilitated by the evolving integrated project delivery approach made possible with object-based building information modeling software. This technology allows architects and engineers to create three-dimensional digital models embedded with a rich body of data about building systems and components. These building information models can become the designer's chief work products, which can then be used by the contractor for construction coordination, fabrication, and assembly. This highly collaborative process, which has all members of a project delivery team employing the same BIM files—often originated by the architect—has the potential to make delivery of architecture services more efficient. At the same time, it would require changes in the legal and business principles underlying most architecture practice, and it remains to be seen whether clients will pay for the enhanced value of this approach or if it will become an expected standard.

Defining Specific Project Services

The first step in structuring architectural services and the compensation appropriate for them is determining the scope and specificity of a client's project requirements. The services may be defined precisely or loosely, depending on the clarity of the client's goals. Understanding and communicating the scope of services can be handled in three basic ways:

▶ For more information about advances in computer technologies and the practice of architecture, see Computer Technology in Practice (5.8).

Client-generated work scope. Some clients may provide detailed service require-ments as part of an RFP soliciting architectural services. This approach is usually employed for repetitive or standard assignments and is managed by the client's person-nel, who compare competing proposals on an equal basis. Detailed RFPs may specify program requirements, site conditions, service expectations, required deliverables, and schedules.

Owner-architect agreements. Standard service agreements are useful in defining architectural services, primarily for traditional design and construction projects. This is particularly true of the 2007 series of AIA standard forms of owner-architect agreement.

Customized work plans and scope descriptions. For a set of special services, the architect creates a customized definition—after extensive consultation with the client—as the basis for a service and compensation agreement. While customized scope docu-ments vary in level of detail, they typically include the following elements:

- Client goals and objectives for the architect's services
- Service tasks and expected work products
- Key review and decision milestones
- Schedules of tasks, phases, and milestone dates
- Requirements for information or services provided by others
- Allowances for changes or events outside the architect's control
- Exclusions and additional services available if needed

Before determining specific compensation options and pricing for the architectural services defined, architects should consider issues of value and risk related to their firm's goals, the particular client, and the project assignment.

▶ For more information about defining the scope of project ser-vices see Defining Project Services (6.1). Many different types of project agreements, including AIA Contract Documents, are discussed in Chapter 11.

Recognizing the Value of Architecture Services

The traditional emphasis on cost-based project compensation has resulted in limited profitability for many architecture firms. Architects have been conditioned to accept marginal rates of return for their businesses, and the cyclical nature of design and con-struction investment has exacerbated this problem. During slow times in the industry, architects and other design professionals often compete vigorously for work performed on a break-even or loss basis just to retain staff and cover overhead costs. However, accepting such low levels of return is not sustainable over the long term, as it hurts a firm's market position and financial performance.

Fortunately, many architects are gaining a new awareness of the value of their ser-vices and the distinct benefits they can provide to clients. Although value is ultimately defined by client perceptions, some successful firms have adopted overall business strategies and market positions based on the benefits their services can provide to clients. The principles are simple: Firms perceived to be the best in a particular arena or to offer unique services will be in demand, and clients will pay a premium for their expertise. Conversely, firms perceived to be "just like everyone else" often will be eval-uated on price alone.

Value in architecture services may be perceived and delivered in a number of ways:

Design preeminence. Firms honored for the signature quality of their design work will be valued and well compensated. This type of recognition can be regional, national, or international in scope and can apply to many different client and building types. For example, a leading designer commanded an up-front fee of more than $250,000 to have his name associated with a major public project, in addition to the fees he charged for the actual design work.

Building type expertise and experience. Most clients seek architects with successful experience in similar projects. Many firms are recognized for their experience in partic-ular building types, such as offices, schools, libraries, hospitals, or housing. For some building types, such as stadiums and airports, just four or five design firms dominate the industry.

In *A Whole New Mind: Moving from the Information Age to the Conceptual Age,* author Daniel Pink identifies design as one of six "senses" required for personal success in the twenty-first century. "It's no longer sufficient," he says, "to create a product, a service, an experience, or a lifestyle that's merely functional. Today it's economically crucial and personally rewarding to cre-ate something that is also beauti-ful, whimsical, or emotionally engaging."

New regard is being given to the architect's creative process as business and industry look for ways to solve complex business and social problems. Several leading MBA programs now include coursework on design methods because of the synthesis in the architect's planning and problem-solving capacity.

[M]any leading professional firms . . . are rated very highly by their clients in terms of . . . expertise, but rather poorly in terms of their capabilities at relationships, including understanding their client's business, communicating effectively, being a pleasure to deal with, and creating broad business outcomes. These same clients indicate that the importance of these relationship factors is increasing . . . . In short, doing great work is not enough.

Ross Dawson, *Developing Knowledge-Based Client Relationships*

Project leadership capability. As clients seek simpler and more efficient ways to manage facility projects, firms that can lead the delivery process through program management, construction management, or design-build services are in demand. Many architects have recognized the need to reclaim this industry leadership position, which has been the purview of construction and engineering firms for the past two decades. Enhanced project management fees can approximate those paid for all of an architect's traditional design services, often with less business risk.

Unique service methods and tools. Many firms offer value through special services that improve quality, speed, and accountability in the planning, construction, and management of client facilities. Some firms also offer guarantees—usually putting their fees at risk—related to technical quality and schedule performance. Still others offer unique computer-aided design and computer-aided facility management (CAFM) capabilities. Such innovations have limited product lives, however, as they become replicated by other firms. For example, facility programming was once a distinctive service that has now become commonplace.

Loyal, long-term client relationships. Many successful architecture firms have built their practices on long-standing partnerships with key clients. These relationships create mutual value, often resulting in better compensation and lower risk for architecture firms.

Every firm should know its own market strategy and value proposition and how they apply to the firm's individual clients and service assignments. The key is what Neil Rackham and John De Vincentis, in *Rethinking the Sales Force: Redefining Selling to Create and Capture Customer Value*, call "consultative selling"—knowing every client well enough to identify key needs and focusing the firm's capabilities to meet them in a way no other firm can.

RISK ASSESSMENT AND PRICING

In addition to creating positive value opportunities, architects must be sensitive to the business risks they assume in providing their services. Technical quality and completeness are considered a given in the provision of architecture services. However, many clients today are demanding unprecedented and sometimes unrealistic levels of perfection in the execution of architecture work. These rising client expectations present architects with new challenges and opportunities.

When anticipating risks associated with a particular client or project, the goal is either to find ways to eliminate sources of risk or to receive fair compensation for conditions that are outside the architect's control. Each project must be evaluated in terms of the risks associated with it as compensation and contract terms are developed.

Architects also face the risk that clients may misunderstand what is included in architectural services, particularly with fixed-fee contracts. For example, if two different clients hire an architect for two identical projects, the clients may have very different expectations about the level of services to be provided, causing one project to require twice the compensation of the other to be consistently profitable. To avoid such misunderstandings, AIA standard owner-architect agreements have become increasingly explicit about the architect's basic and optional responsibilities. The AIA recommends consideration of the following risks when drafting architectural services proposals:

Client decision making and approvals. The architect should know the structure and pace of the client's decision-making process. Will one or two representatives make decisions, or will the architect be required to review options with large groups of people? Will key decisions be reached in days or weeks?

Scope changes. If an assignment is expanded or substantially altered during the design and construction process, the change creates more work and cost for the entire project team. This is a particular issue when clients are experiencing rapid growth or organizational change.

Third-party project management. When a client engages a third-party program or construction manager to lead design and construction of a project, the architect is challenged with responding to direction from two or more parties, which can require more time.

Fast-track and construction-driven delivery schedules. Accelerated construction schedules often drive the demand for design decisions and bidding and construction documents. An architect who plans to produce one or two document packages could be expected to deliver numerous other documents to support a new construction schedule. Producing multiple document packages is inherently more costly and difficult to coordinate than traditional deliverables.

Construction cost responsibility and contingency structure. Architects are usually held accountable for designing to a client's budget based on a budget review and estimation of services. The risk involved is compounded, however, when the architect is asked to rely on estimates by third parties or when construction begins early, based only on partial design and pricing information. At a minimum, the architect should retain parallel estimating capability and ensure that appropriate budget contingencies exist for program uncertainties, design completion, pricing variations, and unforeseen conditions during construction.

Design-build projects also present risks related to construction cost. An architect may be required to make design changes to meet a strict design and construction budget, but may benefit—with the owner's agreement—in savings achieved if the project comes in under the budget or contract amount.

Standard of care for design and technical coordination. As instruments of service, architects' technical documents are never perfect or immune to differences in interpretation. A small percentage of the total cost of any construction project will be related to coordination issues or omissions in technical documents. Some clients and contracts overlook this reality and expect architects to share in additional construction costs attributable to normal coordination issues. This is a subject for serious contract negotiation, as higher fees may need to be charged to offset the architect's risk.

Financial resources and payment terms. Architects should confirm their clients' financial resources and intended payment practices for any project assignment. The carrying costs of unpaid invoices and any at-risk design work can substantively reduce the profitability of a project.

COMPENSATION OPTIONS

Architects can consider several compensation options when structuring a new client relationship or project assignment. The options offer different levels of flexibility, profit potential, and risk protection for the architecture firm.

Fixed (Stipulated Sum) Fees

A fixed fee is a firm compensation amount related to a particular scope of service. Fixed fees are convenient and appropriate when services can be precisely defined, a client understands what is included, and the architect is confident the services can be managed within a fixed budget.

Fixed-fee structures generally offer the greatest profit potential to the firm. Planned profitability is usually not revealed in negotiation, and the architect can increase profitability by completing the required services at lower cost. The risk is that the actual cost of the services will exceed the budget on which the fixed fee is based. To cover this risk, a contingency amount should be included within the fixed fee.

When the entire scope of an assignment is unclear, or when the architect establishes an "umbrella agreement" to include a number of individual project assignments, it is reasonable to propose fixed fees for initial tasks and confirm follow-on fee amounts later. The owner-architect agreement should stipulate how fee adjustments can be made to respond to project changes beyond the architect's control.

Hourly Billing Rates and Fee Multipliers

Hourly billing is the most flexible fee option for architects and clients, and it is generally preferred when no exact service scope can be defined. For this reason, hourly billing is often used for the preliminary phases of project assignments and later converted to fixed fees.

Hourly billing can utilize fixed dollar rates (e.g., $125 per hour) that are calculated to cover direct salary cost, fringe benefits, firm overhead, and profit. This option does not directly reveal actual salaries or the firm's overhead and profit markup. Structuring rates by staff position, rather than by name, allows the architect flexibility in assigning people to roles within the project team.

Some clients prefer to negotiate a fee multiplier, which is applied to salary cost incurred by the project team. Two types of multipliers are commonly used. One is a multiple of direct salary expense (DSE), in which direct salary expenses incurred in performing services are multiplied by a factor that covers fringe benefits, firm overhead, and profit. The other is a multiple of direct personnel expense (DPE), in which staff fringe benefits are part of the DPE base and not part of the multiplier.

The disadvantage of hourly billing structures is their limited profit potential because a planned profit percentage is earned only as staff effort and costs are applied to the work. This problem is compounded when a client imposes a ceiling on hourly service billings. In this instance, an architect bears the risk of any fixed-fee arrangement without the possibility of increasing profit through more efficient work effort. Hourly billings with limits are generally no-win options for architects and should be avoided.

Cost plus Fixed Fee

Cost plus fixed fee is an hourly fee option in which a client is billed for the actual cost of an architect's effort—base salaries, fringe benefits, and firm overhead—on a rate or multiplier basis, and a fixed fee is negotiated as the firm's profit on the assignment. This arrangement can be useful when a client does not want a completely open-ended fee arrangement but there are many unknowns and establishing a stipulated sum at the outset proves difficult. Clients often see the advantage of cost-plus approaches when the uncertainties would force a prudent architect to include substantial contingencies in a fixed-fee proposal. From the architect's perspective, cost-plus approaches limit profit potential but greatly reduce the risk of losses.

Unit Cost Methods

In some cases, clients prefer to compensate professionals based on cost per square foot, room, store, building, or other unit. For example, office planning and interior design are often priced per square foot, which is the same unit used in lease rates and tenant allowances in commercial buildings. Hotel projects are often structured based on cost per room. However, unit cost estimating requires accurate and timely data on the cost of providing the services for each unit and recognition of the fact that earlier units usually require more effort than those that follow.

Percentage of Construction Cost

This method ties the architect's compensation to the budgeted or actual construction cost of a project. While it can be useful to compare or budget fees as percentages based on experience with other projects, this method poses potential inequities for clients and architects and thus is infrequently used.

Disadvantages of a percentage-based contract include the assumption that construction cost is directly proportional to the architect's effort. In fact, though, percentage-based contracts can allow construction market conditions to benefit a client but penalize the architect, or hurt the client and benefit the architect, without any change in the architect's effort. These types of contracts can also penalize architects who invest extra effort in reducing construction costs. Finally, the contracts can lead a client to believe the architect has an incentive to increase rather than decrease construction costs, and could create an adversarial relationship between client and architect.

To avoid these problems, a percentage-based fee agreement can be structured to convert to a fixed fee when the project's scope has been confirmed, often at the end of the schematic design or design development phase. This arrangement allows client and architect to establish an overall fee level, maintain flexibility as the scope and budget are confirmed, and adopt the simplicity of a fixed-fee arrangement for the remainder of the work.

Outcome-Based Value Pricing

Business consultants sometimes tie their compensation to revenue, cost, and profitability results achieved with their assistance. Advertising firms routinely propose "idea fees" and licensing arrangements for ongoing use of their work products. Architects can propose such "value pricing" based on measurable outcomes specific to individual clients and project engagements. Examples of such metrics include sales in retail facilities, leasing successes in housing or commercial office developments, and employee satisfaction or retention in corporate workplaces.

Reimbursable and Nonreimbursable Direct Costs

While staff effort usually represents most of an architect's cost of service, it is also important to anticipate and budget other direct costs that are related to the work but not covered in the firm's overhead structure. These typically include travel, long-distance communications, mail and courier services, printing, photography, computer services and output, and materials or equipment. These direct costs may be reimbursable (billed directly to the client at actual cost or with a markup) or nonreimbursable (covered by an architect's other fees for the assignment). Direct costs are almost always reimbursable under the hourly and cost-plus compensation options.

PUTTING IT ALL TOGETHER: SERVICE AND PRICING STRATEGY

Before proposing services for a new client or project assignment, architects should consider the potential risks and compensation options. There is no single best strategy or approach to determining the compensation for a project; architects must apply professional judgment and experience when considering what terms are appropriate to each new opportunity.

The following process works well for many firms:

Step 1: Consult with the Client About Needs and Priorities

The most important step in forming any new business relationship is knowing the client—understanding the client's needs, expectations, style, and concerns. Architects can achieve this understanding by asking the right questions, listening well, and exploring options for serving the client's organization. This process allows architects to discover a client's "value drivers," or paramount concerns. An architect who addresses these properly in a proposal can improve the chances of being selected for a project and receive a higher level of compensation for the work. It may not always be possible to carry out this step. For example, when an architect is asked for service proposals through a formal RFP process, opportunities to discuss client goals may be limited. However, a successful firm will find some way to determine and respond to the client's needs.

Step 2: Identify Service Strategy, Team, and Work Scope

Once the client's needs are understood, the architect should develop an overall service strategy to address them successfully. Consider questions like these:

- Is the project limited to design and documentation services, or will there be a long-term agreement in which multiple services can be authorized over time?
- Which of the firm's services and key people are appropriate for the assignment?
- What consultants and other outside resources are needed to support the work?
- How will the architect communicate and make decisions with the client, facility users, public agencies, and other team members?

At this point, a description of the architect's services can be prepared using a standard form of agreement or customized work plan. This process should make clear which compensation approach is best for the project.

Step 3: Estimate the Cost of Providing the Services

Unless the architect is proposing an open-ended hourly billing arrangement, it is important to estimate the actual cost of providing the services (including the firm's staff, outside consultants, and direct costs) as the starting point for the compensation proposal. The compensation worksheet that accompanies this topic can be used as a template for this calculation on a fixed-fee assignment.

For an hourly compensation approach, the architect should determine the hourly rate or multiplier that will represent actual costs, including salaries, fringe benefits, and firm overhead. Specific hourly rates should include an allowance for escalation during multiyear contracts, unless the rates will be subject to annual adjustment.

This step requires proposals from engineers and other consultants who will support the architect's work. Architects should use the same criteria to select consultants that clients use to select architects. In other words, cost should be a major factor, but generally not the most important one. Key personnel, experience, work scope, approach, and contract terms should be well understood before an architect relies on consultant proposals.

Step 4: Evaluate Risk Factors and Apply an Appropriate Contingency

The architect should evaluate the potential risks involved in providing proposed services and decide what additional compensation is appropriate to offset them. This may be a specific dollar amount added to the estimated actual cost for a fixed fee, a markup of hourly cost rates, or an increase in the base fee multiplier.

This deliberate approach to potential risks and fee contingencies can be helpful in negotiation of a final compensation agreement because it allows architects and clients to discuss specific risks and associated costs of services without eroding the architect's basic profit expectations.

Step 5: Assess the Firm's Value Position and Add the Appropriate Profit Terms

Architects should assess the special value of their firm's services to a client and determine the most favorable fee and profit structure, based on the following considerations:

- *The firm's minimum profit targets.* With few exceptions, the architect should plan to earn a base level of profit on every project to reward the team and support the firm's overall financial health.
- *The value of the firm's services in the marketplace.* As noted earlier, firms and services that clients perceive as unique or the best can eliminate competition and command higher fees and profits. An architect must know the firm's competitive position and price its services accordingly.

SAMPLE COMPENSATION WORKSHEET

Apple and Bartlett
616 Highland Avenue
Maintown
USA

Phase: Design Development
Proj. No: 1207
Project: Clayton Elementary School
Owner: Maintown School District
Date: 10/23/2007

Project Management/Admin	Hrs	×	Rate	=	Cost
Principal	10		$55		$550
Project Manager	80		$38		$3,000
Architect/Designer III	0		$30		$0
Architect II	0		$25		$0
Architect I	0		$20		$0
Subtotals	90				$3,550

Cost Estimating	Hrs	Rate	Cost
Principal	0	$55	$0
Project Manager	20	$38	$750
Architect/Designer III	40	$30	$1,200
Architect II	20	$25	$500
Architect I	0	$20	$0
Subtotals	80		$2,450

Architectural Design	Hrs	Rate	Cost
Principal	20	$55	$1,100
Project Manager	0	$38	$0
Architect/Designer III	80	$30	$2,400
Architect II	0	$25	$0
Architect I	0	$20	$0
Subtotals	100		$3,500

Documentation	Hrs	Rate	Cost
Principal	0	$55	$0
Project Manager	0	$38	$0
Architect/Designer III	20	$30	$600
Architect II	120	$25	$3,000
Architect I	240	$20	$4,800
Subtotals	380		$8,400

Consultants		Cost
Civil		$7,200
Landscape Design		$3,200
Mechanical		$16,500
Electrical		$13,500
Lighting Design		$5,400
Subtotals		$45,800

	Summary	Total Hrs	Total Cost
1	Principal	30	$1,650
2	Project Manager	100	$3,750
3	Architect III/Designer	140	$4,200
4	Architect II	140	$3,500
5	Architect I	240	$4,800
6	Total in-house salary expense		$17,900
7	Direct personnel expense[1]		0
8	Indirect expense[2] @ 150% of line 6		$26,850
9	Nonreimbursable direct expense[3]		$2,500
10	Total In-house expenses		$47,250
11	Consultants		$45,800
12	Estimated Total		$93,050
13	Contingency		$9,000
14	Proposed compensation		$102,050
15	Estimated reimbursables		$2,400

Alternative Computation

6	Direct in-house salary expense		$17,900
7	Direct personnel expense @ 125% of line (6)		$22,375
8	Indirect expenses @ 20% of line (7)		$4,475

Note: The figures in the above chart are not intended to reflect actual practice, but simply to illustrate the calculation procedure.

[1] Direct personnel expense is defined as the direct salaries of the architect's personnel engaged in the project and the related portion of the cost of their mandatory and customary contributions and benefits (e.g., employment taxes and other statutory employee benefits, insurance, sick leave, holidays, employee retirement plans, and similar contributions).

[2] Indirect expense is defined as all expenses not directly allocated to specific projects and is synonymous with overhead.

[3] Nonreimbursable direct expenses cover expenses not otherwise included in personnel and outside expenses (e.g., reproduction of documents for in-house use, unreimbursed travel, and items paid on behalf of the client without specific reimbursement).

- *The value of the project to the firm.* Occasionally an architect can justify reducing fee and profit levels to help the firm enter a new market, win a strategically important new client, or support the firm's staff and overhead structure during an economic downturn.

At a minimum, the target profit levels will determine the architect's fixed fee, fully loaded hourly rates, or fee multiplier. It is also possible to increase compensation and profit by proposing incentive fees or bonuses to reflect high-value results from the architect's work. For example, an incentive amount might be related to a particularly aggressive schedule, tenant attraction and lease rates, or postoccupancy evaluation of building performance.

Step 6: Compare the Proposal with the Firm's Past Experience

Throughout the pricing process, most firms use previous experience with similar projects to estimate basic design service fees as a percentage of a new project's estimated construction cost. A firm should track its history of fee earnings and profitability to support this process. Given the number of variables, however—even among related projects for the same client—it is wise for several firm principals or project leaders to review proposed compensation terms before the service proposal is completed.

When service scope and compensation terms are finalized, they are normally included in a written proposal document presented to the client. Such proposals may take different forms: letters with attachments, completed owner-architect agreements such as the AIA B102–2007, or more elaborate formats prescribed by a client's RFP. Ultimately, every firm develops its own preferences and standards for proposal documents.

At a minimum, service proposals should contain the following elements:

- A description of the professional services covered by the proposal
- A time schedule for the services proposed
- Identification of the architect's key team members and their relationship to the client's own staff and other project participants
- The proposed compensation terms, including the basis for reimbursable expenses and any additional services required beyond the basic work scope
- Assumptions and qualifications upon which the proposal is based
- The proposed form of agreement for the client's review and approval

This information will provide the architect with a firm basis for negotiating agreements with clients and consultants.

TAKING IT TO THE BANK: BILLING AND COLLECTIONS

It is important to remember that compensation terms don't mean much without the ability to collect payment on a timely basis. Architects can often overlook the importance of collections in negotiating contracts and managing projects and client relationships. Collection usually needs to be addressed by firm principals with their client counterparts. Even the best accounting staff cannot overcome high-level misunderstandings about payment obligations.

Understanding a Client's Administrative and Accounting Practices

An architect should discuss preferred billing and payment terms in early consultations with clients when goals, needs, and service scope are also discussed. Many clients will appreciate this as a sign of good business practice. While the details are prescribed in any owner-architect agreement, a few basic questions should be asked and answered:

- We prefer to bill for services every [state number] weeks. Is that acceptable?
- Is there a particular schedule on which invoices should be submitted?
- What documentation is required with our invoices?
- Who will review our invoices and approve them for payment?
- How quickly will payments be processed once invoices have been approved?

Unfavorable answers to any of these questions pose financial risks that should be addressed when structuring a compensation agreement.

Appropriate Invoicing and Payment Terms

Most architects invoice their clients for services monthly or every four weeks, depending on their internal accounting practices. Collections can be expedited if clients accept more frequent billing, particularly on hourly fee arrangements.

Although thirty days is a general standard for invoice payment, many architecture firms experience average collection periods of sixty days or more. Long collection cycles require the architect to finance the staffing and direct costs of providing services at an increased carrying cost to the firm. Efforts should be made to negotiate a contract provision requiring interest to be paid on payments overdue by more than forty-five days.

Special Risks and Responses

When the following are concerns, they should be addressed before a service agreement is finalized:

Uncertain credit. Like any provider of goods or services, an architect has a right to ask about a client's financial resources to support a specific project assignment. If a client's financial capacity is in doubt, the architect should consider declining the project or requiring an up-front fee and aggressive billing schedule to keep collections ahead of actual project costs.

Fee retainage. Contracts that allow retainage (amounts withheld from professional service fees until the completion of a project or work phase) dilute an architecture firm's financial performance and increase its risk. Retainage provisions should be eliminated from owner-architect agreements whenever possible.

Slow payment. Clients who describe a slow and complex payment process, or decline to commit to any specific process, present serious business risks for architects. This problem is best addressed by principals of the firm with their most senior client counterparts. Charging interest for late payments or requiring prepayment are additional responses.

Payment Patterns as Performance Feedback

Client payment patterns often reflect perceptions about the quality and value of work an architecture firm is providing. Regular invoices provide a natural opportunity for the architect to ask—on paper or in person—for a client's assessment of the firm's performance. If client payment patterns change, it is usually a sign that the perceived value of the service has changed; this is an important time for firm principals to address the client's concerns.

For More Information

Understanding the true needs and values of clients—including the forces that drive client values—is essential to receiving adequate professional compensation. Strategies for understanding and meeting the demands of today's sophisticated clients are presented by Ross Dawson in *Developing Knowledge-Based Client Relationships: Leadership in Professional Services* (Butterworth-Heinemann, 2005) and by Neil Rackham and John De Vincentis in *Rethinking the Sales Force: Redefining Selling to Create and Capture Customer Value* (McGraw-Hill, 1999).

The Professional Pricing Society (PPS) is a global organization that provides full resource support for pricing professionals and executives seeking solutions to pricing challenges. Resources include numerous books and workbooks, a journal, a newsletter, and workshops. Information can be found on the PPS Web site at www.pricingsociety.com.

6.3 Programming

Robert G. Hershberger, FAIA, Ph.D.

Architectural programming is the thorough and systematic evaluation of the inter-related values, goals, facts, and needs of a client's organization, facility users, and the surrounding community. A well-conceived program leads to high-quality design.

Architectural programming has developed as an activity related to, but distinct from, architectural design. It is considered an optional predesign service under AIA Document B141, Standard Form of Agreement Between Owner and Architect. Document B141 states that under "basic services," the architect is required only "to provide a preliminary evaluation of the Owner's program." Presumably after this preliminary evaluation the architect is expected to proceed with normal design services.

An increasing number of architects have found the above approach unsatisfactory and have elected to offer architectural programming as an integral part of their services. In this context, programming has evolved into a far more thorough and systematic endeavor than when it was offered as an incidental part of the architectural design process or when it was conducted by the owner.

Because of the increasing complexity of buildings and building systems, the need for programming services is likely to expand. As well, many clients are becoming much more sophisticated and thus more interested in understanding and managing their physical resources.

Programming led by architects can provide clients with a systematic process for decision making about organizational and project values, goals, and requirements. Many clients have a limited view of the range of physical possibilities for accommodating their operations; architects have the ideal professional background to help them visualize options during programming. The programming process as led by architecture firms can expose clients to a wide range of alternative approaches and help them choose appropriate directions.

CLIENT NEEDS

All types of clients need programming services. Institutional, government, and corporate clients are most likely to recognize this need and be willing to pay for programming services, although in some cases these clients may produce programs in-house or by using other programming consultants before engaging the services of an architect.

Government agencies use programming services extensively because they often base procurement of design services on fully developed programs. Owners of complex institutional facilities such as hospitals and hotels easily recognize the need for careful up-front analysis of design

---

VALUES IN ARCHITECTURAL PROGRAMMING

Human: functional, social, physical, physiological, psychological

Environmental: site, climate, context, resources, waste

Cultural: historical, institutional, political, legal

Technological: materials, systems, processes

Temporal: growth, change, permanence

Economic: finance, construction, operations, maintenance, energy

Aesthetic: form, space, color, meaning

Safety: structural, fire, chemical, personal, criminal

Robert Hershberger, *Architectural Programming and Predesign Manager* (1999).

Robert G. Hershberger is professor and dean emeritus of the College of Architecture at the University of Arizona. He is also a partner in Hershberger and Nickels Architects/Planners of Tucson and Tempe, Arizona. He is the author of *Architectural Programming and Predesign Manager*.

issues and will often employ architecture firms to develop their programs. Owners of owner-occupied office facilities usually want quality programming in order to achieve facilities management objectives. Clients with little experience with the building industry generally appreciate the guidance an architect can provide through the programming process. Developers are the least likely to recognize the need for architectural programming services because many believe they know precisely what is needed in the market and thus see no reason to explore alternatives and weigh potential trade-offs. While some residential clients may not want to pay extra for programming, they need the service, even when they are just remodeling a few rooms.

Discussing the benefits of programming during initial interviews sometimes broadens the vision of resistant clients and helps them understand why they need to contract for these services.

Preliminary Studies

Some clients will need financial feasibility, site suitability, and/or master planning services prior to architectural programming. Financial feasibility studies explore market conditions in relation to specific sites and development plans in order to show whether a particular project will be viable. These studies can be led by architects but often require the expertise of other professionals. Site suitability studies may also be required prior to purchase of a particular property to make certain that the site is properly zoned, has needed services, and is appropriately sized and configured for a proposed project.

Architects are ideally trained to conduct site suitability studies because of their design skills and knowledge of applicable land use and building codes and regulations. Where geotechnical issues are involved, civil engineering consultants may be brought in. Landscape architects should be consulted on projects where there are significant site planning issues.

Clients with a large site and an extensive program that will develop over time should develop a master plan before programming for any particular building or facility. Architects who provide master planning services followed by complete architectural programming services are in an excellent position to prove their value to the client and thus to be assured of obtaining the commission for design services for each phase of master plan implementation.

Architectural Programming

Architectural programming can include all of the above studies but generally commences after they are complete. It tends to focus on specific facilities identified in the master plan and includes all of the areas mentioned in the previous sections: value identification, goal setting, discovery of related facts, and development of specific project requirements. These are all developed in collaboration with the client, user, and community, but depending on the nature of the project, specialists may be required to develop some of the information. Specialists may include kitchen consultants, laboratory consultants, security consultants, data and communications specialists, and transportation and parking specialists.

Some architects specialize in offering programming services, and other professionals, including social and behavioral scientists, systems analysts, interior designers, and building management and operations specialists, have entered the field. Some programming consultants, including architects, specialize in particular building types or functions, such as hospitals, sports complexes, hotels, justice facilities, laboratories, security systems, clean rooms, and kitchens.

Costs of Services

Architects who offer programming services have had increasing success in negotiating fees to cover the cost of these services because owners recognize that the resulting buildings better serve their needs. Indeed, architecture firms that offer programming as a primary service are often recognized by their peers as producing quality architecture. Fees for programming vary. Highly technical buildings such as hospitals or laboratories can command higher figures than commercial and moderate-size institutional buildings. Fees for master planning also vary depending on the expected deliverables and project types.

SKILLS

On smaller projects, one person from the programming firm can usually handle all of the programming tasks. On larger projects, the programming team will generally include a senior architect, who handles sensitive client interviews and work session presentations (or at least introductions); a project programmer, who conducts interviews with key personnel, develops questionnaires (if needed), analyzes data, and oversees development of the programming document; and junior programmers, who do literature searches, conduct user interviews, conduct observational studies including site analysis, and assist the project programmer in developing the program document.

Specialized consultants are used to develop the criteria and parameters for particular spaces or facility types, such as laboratories, airports, prisons, kitchens, and hospitality/entertainment complexes. The involvement of specific personnel should be carefully developed in a programming work plan.

Programmers must be familiar with the fundamentals of the architectural design and building processes and be alert to the design and construction implications of program statements. But they must also have specific knowledge and skill to be effective at programming.

Expertise in information gathering is the heart of the programmer's domain and requires the ability to

- Conduct efficient literature searches.
- Employ active listening skills to conduct diagnostic interviews.
- Record meaningful data during a walk-through study.
- Develop comprehensive space inventories.
- Obtain trace evidence.
- Conduct systematic observations.
- Know when and how to develop and administer questionnaires.

Strong verbal and management skills are necessary for group interviewing and work session leadership. Here again, active listening skills are vital, but the ability to direct the course of the session and to lead people of diverse opinions to consensus is even more important.

Data analysis skills are equally important. Knowing what to collect and then how to convert the raw data to useful information is essential to effective programming. Skilled programmers learn how to avoid "data clog," a favorite term of programming pioneer Willie Peña. The programmer must learn to collect only the needed data and then know how to convert them into meaningful (reliable and valid) information that can influence design of the project.

Knowledge of space size standards for various building types is a fundamental requirement for programmers. Before going into the work session, they must know what the standards are for a building type as well as what space the client actually has, so they can guide the client to agreement on appropriate net space needs for a particular facility. They must also be aware of appropriate efficiencies for various building types and quality levels to be able to apply them to net totals to arrive at gross square footage requirements. Efficiency factors are often less than 70 percent for many building types. But clients rarely understand how much of a building area is consumed by such space as halls, walls, utility chases, and closets. The programmer must have the knowledge and skill to guide the client through this part of program development.

The programmer must be familiar with current construction cost information and with general project delivery timelines. In some cases it may be necessary to consult general contractors or cost estimators in order to develop realistic preliminary costing and project schedules. Where clients require full financial feasibility studies, consultants with backgrounds in real estate development and banking often are used. At this early stage, it is common to provide a contingency budget of 20 or 30 percent of the expected building cost because so many factors (land cost, soils, easements, etc.) are unknown. This percentage will be reduced as the project progresses and more is known, so that a common contingency in the master planning would be 15 percent, dropping to 10 or 12 percent in programming and 5 to 7 percent for construction.

Finally, writing skills are needed to capture and delineate the qualitative and quantitative aspects of the client requirements. An architectural programmer must be able to communicate programming information verbally and visually to the client, the users, the community, and the architect who will design the project.

Equipment

Given that virtually all architects will have a computer that can produce finished drawings and a word-processed report, the only special equipment needed for architectural programming would be a digital or other camera.

No other special equipment is necessary.

PROCESS

Architectural programming is inherently a team process. At a minimum, the programmer and client determine the program, but more often several persons from the programming firm, an array of users, and sometimes community participants are involved. The scale of the project (e.g., a building interior, one building, a building complex) will have a strong effect on team size and composition. Other factors include the type of facilities and level of specialized functions that will be required and possibly constraints on interaction with the client and users.

Client and User Values

Programming is the time to identify, consider, debate, reject, accept, and prioritize values such as institutional purposes, functional efficiency, user comfort, building economics, safety, environmental sustainability, and visual quality. These identified values and concerns can have a profound effect on the ultimate form of a building. If the program is driven primarily by concerns for functional efficiency, as is the case in many owner-produced programs, organizational decisions made during programming will significantly affect the form of the building.

If the program evolves more from the social and psychological needs of the users, prescriptions for form will also be inherent in the identified spaces and their sizes, characteristics, and relationships. If the program responds primarily to economic concerns, it is possible that numerous material and system opportunities as well as potentially unique spaces and places will be eliminated from design consideration during programming. A carefully conceived and comprehensive architectural programming process will help to ensure that all of the appropriate values have been identified and prioritized.

The values identification portion of architectural programming offers the client an opportunity to resolve important questions or make critical decisions about how the client's organization relates to the built environment. As well, consideration should be given to how the client's values relate to the values of the community, the values of the users of the facility, and the values of the design professionals with whom the client is working. Considering these value relationships can help the programmer manage potential conflicts of values and identify opportunities for a fuller expression of common values.

Project Goals

Once the primary values have been identified and prioritized, it is possible to develop specific project goals. What organizational objectives should be accomplished by providing a new, expanded, or renovated facility? Should the resulting building be a statement of the organization's desired image? Should it be a model of efficiency? Or should it be more loosely organized, allowing for serendipitous events or even changes in how operations are conducted? Should it be environmentally sensitive, a showpiece of "green" architecture? What is the target for overall project cost? When should the facility be ready for operation? Goals in these and many other areas need to be set during programming.

Constraints and Opportunities

Achievement of the goals will be made easy or difficult by the characteristics of the organization's operations as well as those of the site. Information must be gathered that identifies the specific nature of the constraints and opportunities. Is there enough land on which to locate the proposed facility? Is it in the right location in terms of visibility, access, service, and the like? Can the existing facilities be easily converted to new uses? Are the organization's cash flow and/or reserves sufficient to ensure that the construction and start-up costs can be managed? Questions of fact must be considered before realistic projections for new and renovated spaces can be made.

Facility Requirements

When the important values and goals of the client, user group, and community and any related facts have been identified, then and only then should the identification of specific space needs begin. Unfortunately, many client-provided programs are developed without adequate consideration of important institutional values and goals. Personnel assigned to prepare the program tend to proceed directly to identification of user needs and space requirements. Those preparing the program may be unaware that their personal value systems are influencing the decisions they are making and that a more conscious identification of institutional values and the setting of specific project goals would have a profound effect on how the specific needs of the project are developed. Often a few known and pressing facts tend to dominate the decision process, while other facts remain uncovered, even though they may be more important relative to the organization's mission.

Steps for identifying the space needs of a specific facility include the following:

- Identify required spaces.
- Establish the size and relationships of these spaces.
- Develop appropriate factors for estimating efficiency.
- Determine project budget and schedule requirements.

When determining factors for estimating efficiency, allow for nonprogrammed areas such as halls, walls, restrooms, service areas, two-story spaces, and the like. Base budget and schedule requirements on previously identified values, goals, and facts in order to get the most accurate guide for the design of proposed new facilities.

Information Gathering

Five types of information gathering are used in architectural programming: literature search/review, interviewing, observation, questionnaire/survey, and group sessions.

Literature search/review. This task comes first in the programming process, beginning even before the commission is awarded, to give the programmer background knowledge of similar facilities and a general familiarity with the client's mission and language. The literature search includes gathering reports on existing facilities, along with site surveys, construction documents, and other relevant documents that the client

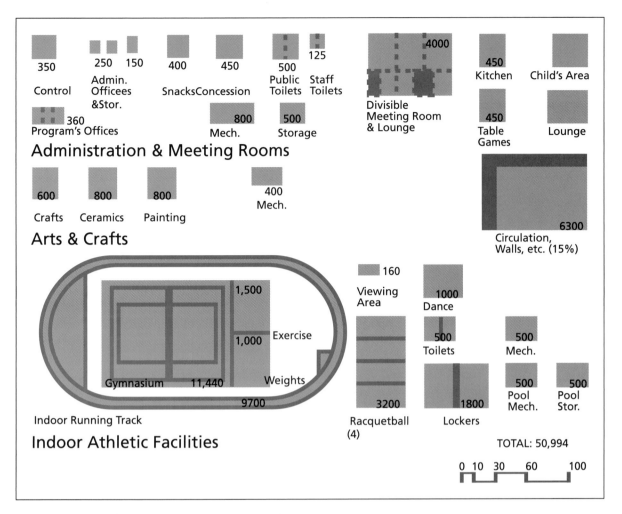

Administration & Meeting Rooms

350 — Control
250, 150 — Admin. Offices & Stor.
360 — Program's Offices
400 — Snacks
450 — Concession
500 — Public Toilets
125 — Staff Toilets
800 — Mech.
500 — Storage
4000 — Divisible Meeting Room & Lounge
450 — Kitchen
Child's Area
450 — Table Games
Lounge
6300 — Circulation, Walls, etc. (15%)

Arts & Crafts

600 — Crafts
800 — Ceramics
800 — Painting
400 — Mech.

Indoor Athletic Facilities

1,500 / 1,000 — Exercise
Gymnasium 11,440
Weights
9700
Indoor Running Track
160 — Viewing Area
1000 — Dance
500 — Toilets
500 — Mech.
3200 — Racquetball (4)
1800 — Lockers
500 — Pool Mech.
500 — Pool Stor.

TOTAL: 50,994

0 10 30 60 100

Revised Space Needs Summary

may possess. It also involves obtaining relevant government documents, including applicable codes and ordinances, as well as recognized building and planning standards, historical documents and archival materials, trade publications, research literature, professional publications, manufacturers' publications, and even sources in popular literature and on the Internet.

Interviewing. In most cases this is the core activity in programming. It begins with the client interview. At this interview, the programmer can learn more about the client's values and goals, refine a work plan and schedule, and ascertain whom to contact within the client organization. Interviews with key personnel, other users (clients, patrons, customers, etc.), and interested community members follow. Successful interviews are carefully planned. The programmer first tries to identify the basic values that will affect the design of the facility—human, cultural, environmental, technological, temporal, economic, aesthetic, and safety-related. In planning interviews, the programmer should consider what data could make a design difference, who could provide the most useful information, who has the authority to make decisions and establish priorities, the amount of time and the size of the budget that are available, and how interviewing will relate to other information-gathering techniques that may be used, such as observations or surveys.

For larger organizations, the programmer usually reviews the organizational chart with the client to identify the key officers, department heads, and other persons likely to be knowledgeable about facility needs or in decision-making positions. Others within the organization who might be interviewed include department managers, members of special committees, maintenance people, a sampling of typical employees, and employees with special needs. Those who use or visit the building but do not work for the client organization, such as suppliers, service people, fire officials, or customers, also may have important input. Interviews may take place in an individual or group setting.

Whoever is interviewed and however the interviews take place, the objective is to obtain complete and reliable information. It helps to conduct the interviews in or near the client's or user's existing environment. This setting tends to make interviewees more comfortable in answering questions, and also makes it easier for them to focus on their own architectural environment. Interviewing techniques vary widely and should match the data-gathering objectives.

Observation. This task is another information-gathering technique that programmers should use. A walk-through observation of the existing facility with the property or facility manager is an excellent way to orient yourself to obvious programming requirements. A space inventory, including plans and annotated photographs of existing spaces, equipment, and furnishings, can provide important baseline information. The programmer photographs and measures existing spaces and documents existing furniture and equipment to better understand the space requirements. Trace observation documents wear and tear on existing facilities (surfaces, furniture, fixtures, and equipment) and may tell an important story about traffic and circulation patterns, use levels, and other factors that should be accounted for in the program. Behavioral observation (time-and-motion studies) can document the functions that the building occupants perform and the adequacy of the space accommodating them. For example, the programmer may observe that a hospital room has an inadequate turning radius for a wheelchair when a visitor chair is placed in the room. Quite often the programmer will be told during client or user interviews that a particular space is a problem, prompting subsequent observational study of the space to determine the cause of the problem.

Questionnaires and surveys. These are yet another information-gathering tool used in programming. Surveys are an efficient way to gather facts and quantitative details in a large organization. Furniture and equipment needs of individual users, for example, can be ascertained through a written survey form. The questions must be carefully developed using a systematic process that includes pretesting, or there is a good chance that the resulting data will be meaningless or at least difficult to analyze.

Group sessions. These are the final way to obtain needed information in architectural programming. It is important to conduct at least one group work session (usually several) as a feedback mechanism to allow the client and users to consider, debate, and eventually resolve and agree upon the true nature of the architecture problem—to reach a consensus as to which values, goals, facts, needs, and ideas should influence the design of the facility. This is a type of group interviewing process that typically involves feedback of information obtained from the other information-gathering methods. Techniques include brainstorming new ideas and rejecting as inappropriate some of the information collected earlier, concluding with prioritizing the goals and needs for the project. It is not only a way of gathering information but also a method of obtaining agreement.

Data Analysis

Throughout the data-gathering process it is important to organize data so that they can be retrieved and analyzed quickly and easily. A key technique is to seek and record only information that will be vital in making design decisions. Based on analysis of all information gathered, the programmer will develop performance and design criteria for the facility. Space requirements, space relationships, circulation, ambient environment, safety and security, needed surfaces, furnishings, flexibility, and site information are among the issues usually addressed. Graphics such as matrices showing space allocations and relationships and bubble diagrams showing adjacency relationships are also developed.

During analysis, the programmer will identify major unresolved programming issues and begin to develop some preliminary ideas about options for their resolution in the final building program. Some writers have referred to these ideas as "precepts" (a term implying a combination of "preliminary" and "concepts," yet still clearly preliminary to conceptual design). Here the programmer's task is to develop options (precepts) for solutions, to help with their evaluation, and to recommend the most effective alternatives. For example, in a residential facility such as a nursing home or a juvenile justice institution, there might be a trade-off between privacy and isolation in residents' bedrooms. Options might be single, double, or multiple-occupancy bedrooms. A recommendation might be to have a mixture of rooms to allow for occupant or staff choice. The programming team presents the various options or precepts to the client and guides the client through evaluation of the alternatives. As with interviewing, there are many different ways to structure these presentations, and the approach should be tailored to the needs of the client organization and the particular project.

Deliverables

The usual deliverable is a written architectural program, which is a comprehensive report that includes documentation of the methodology used, an executive summary, value and goal statements, the relevant facts, data analysis conclusions, and the program requirements, including space listings by function and size, relationship diagrams, space program sheets, stacking plans, precept drawings, and flow diagrams. Photographs or even videos may be used to illustrate space-planning requirements. A comprehensive program will also include project cost estimates and a project schedule.

For More Information

The following titles represent a bookshelf of publications about architectural programming that architects will find useful: Edith Cherry, *Programming for Design: From Theory to Practice* (1998); Donna P. Duerk, *Architectural Programming: Information Management for Design* (1993); Robert Hershberger, *Architectural Programming and Predesign Manager* (1999); Robert R. Kumlin, *Architectural Programming: Creative Techniques for Design Professionals* (1995); Mickey Palmer, ed., *The Architect's Guide to Facility Programming* (1981); William Peña and Steven Parshall, *Problem Seeking: An Architectural Programming Primer*, 4th ed. (2001); Wolfgang F. E. Preiser, ed., *Facility Programming* (1978); Preiser, ed., *Programming the Built Environment* (1985); Preiser, ed., *Professional Practice in Facility Programming* (1993).

6.4 Research and Analysis

Peggy Lawless and Wendy Pound

A thorough understanding of clients and stakeholders can differentiate a firm from competitors and make the firm's architecture more responsive to client needs. From the proposal phase through the postoccupancy phase, architects can use a variety of research methods to identify and assess client needs.

Although not trained as researchers, architects ask questions and evaluate data, particularly during predesign and programming. This experience gives them the skills to carry out research. There *is* a science to client and user research,

Peggy Lawless is a social scientist and the director of Lawless Research, a Denver-based research firm. Wendy Pound is a psychologist and experienced researcher based in Sonora, California.

however. Developing their research skills and expanding their repertoire of research methods can give architects the information they need to design effectively. This topic presents guidelines for seven methods of client and user research. These include business intelligence, in-depth interviews, surveys, behavior observation and mapping, guided walk-throughs, envisioning, and facility performance evaluation.

BUSINESS INTELLIGENCE

The more architects know about their prospective clients, the more successful their proposals and presentations will be. Look beyond the information a prospect provides. Dig deeper to better understand the decision makers, their organization, the industry, and any unique challenges the potential client faces. Insight into a prospect's background helps an architect stand out in an interview. "You have to show us that you know our world; that will get you more points," a library client advises. A county government client agrees: "We select the firm that convinces us they understand our needs."

Business intelligence is information gathered from secondary sources, such as the Internet, newspapers, and journals. All that is needed is access to the Internet and a public library card. The architect's goal is to find information about a prospect that will help him or her respond—better than the competition—to the prospect's situation and values.

Do Your Homework

Begin a search at the prospect's Web site. If the prospective project is a hospital, read the CEO's letter in the annual report, look at the hospital's history, determine what medical services are growing, and identify patterns in employment and inpatient admissions.

Summarize the following about a prospect:

- Organizational values and mission
- Products and services provided by the organization
- Recent events, issues, and changes
- Impetus for proposed building project
- Key decision makers and stakeholders (management, employees, clients, suppliers)
- Unique strengths and challenges
- Financial and budgetary information

Second, explore the outside forces that affect the prospect. Gather information from the Web and library databases to describe the following:

- Characteristics of the population the organization serves
- Industry trends
- Competitive climate
- Technology developments

As an example, if proposing to design a new public school, search for background on bond issues, student demographics, union negotiations, city growth projections, public/private school enrollment trends, student security issues, and developments in educational technology and teaching methods.

Apply the Knowledge

The third step requires analysis and application of the information. Identify the most important findings and decide how to respond to them in your proposal and presentation. Be sure to include key points in the cover letter that accompanies the proposal. For example, in a proposal to design a new community library, you might cite statistics on the number of households without a computer or Internet connection, information on the importance of libraries to immigrant populations, and studies showing how libraries serve as community gathering places.

The objective of research gathered from secondary sources is to find relevant information on a prospect in the shortest amount of time. The following Internet search engines can be useful:

- Google (www.google.com)
- AlltheWeb Advanced (www.alltheweb.com/advanced)
- Ask (www.ask.com)
- AltaVista Advanced (www.altavista.com/web/adv)

METHODS FOR RESEARCHING CLIENTS AND USERS

Method	Value	Proposal and Presentation	Predesign and Programming	Postoccupancy
Business intelligence	• Gives insight into a prospect's organization and industry	X		
In-depth interview	• Uncovers how people experience, understand, and interpret their physical surroundings • Identifies factors that support or inhibit occupants' satisfaction and performance	X	X	X
Survey	• Measures users' satisfaction with the facility and identifies key drivers of effectiveness		X	X
Behavior observation and mapping	• Provides data on how people use space • Shows graphically how a space is used		X	X
Guided walk-through	• Shows the space through users' eyes		X	X
Envisioning	• Gives insight into the daily experience of the building's users • Stimulates user involvement		X	
Facility performance evaluation	• Assesses how well the facility meets the design objectives • Identifies effectiveness of design solutions • Measures user satisfaction with the facility		X	X

EFFECTIVE INTERVIEWING

Architects need to know how building users go about their jobs, how they work, and how they meet customer needs. Interviews are the best way to gather enough data to paint a complete picture of the physical, social, and psychological needs of building users.

Interview Guidelines

Methods of interviewing for ethnographic fieldwork and psychological counseling can be useful for interviewing building users. The seasoned approach used with the informant (anthropology) or client/patient (psychology) builds rapport while increasing the depth of information obtained. Following are guidelines for interviewing clients and users.

Let the informant be the expert. Investigate how people experience, understand, and interpret their physical surroundings. Find out the "what" and the "how" of their perceptions. Often the people who are interviewed are reluctant to be the "expert," particularly when their opinions are seldom sought. Assure them they are the experts of their own experience and use of space.

Mirror the language of the informant. Be sure to use language that has the same flavor as that of the informant. If an informant has a doctorate and wants to talk like a textbook, gear up your vocabulary. If an informant uses simple sentences and asks for definitions, moderate your enthusiasm for technical terms. Keep in mind that the average American's vocabulary stops growing around eighth grade. Be particularly clear when interviewing informants whose first language is not the same as yours.

SOURCES OF FREE PROSPECT AND CLIENT INFORMATION

Source	Description	Location
Databases		
Associations Unlimited	Information about 444,000 international and U.S. nonprofit membership organizations in all fields	Online library database (available to library card holders)
Business & Company Resource Center (Gale)	Broker research reports, trade publications, newspapers, journals, and company directory lists	Online library database (available to library card holders)
Business Source Premier (EBSCO Host)	Full text for nearly 7,400 scholarly business journals across all subject areas. Includes detailed company profiles and country economic reports	Online library database (available to library card holders)
Expanded Academic ASAP (Gale)	Scholarly journals, magazines, and newspapers	Online library database (available to library card holders)
ProQuest	Access to more than 8,000 magazines and newspapers, including the *New York Times* and the *Washington Post*	Online library database (available to library card holders)
Web Resources		
Arts and entertainment	American Association of Museums International Society for Performing Arts National Endowment for the Arts	www.aam-us.org www.ispa.org http://arts.endow.gov
Census data	GlobalEDGE International Business North American Industry Classification System U.S. Census Bureau	http://globaledge.msu.edu www.census.gov/epcd/naics02/ www.census.gov
Corporate	American Productivity & Quality Center Annual reports via the *Wall Street Journal* Business Wire National Association of Manufacturers U.S. Securities & Exchange Commission	www.apqc.org http://wsjie.ar.wilink.com home.businesswire.com www.nam.org www.sec.gov/edgar.shtml
Education	American Association of School Administrators American Association of State Colleges and Universities Association of Higher Education Facilities Officers Design Share National Clearinghouse for Educational Facilities School Building Association School Construction News School Designs U.S. Department of Education	www.aasa.org www.aascu.org www.appa.org www.designshare.com www.edfacilities.org www.cefpi.org www.schoolconstructionnews.com www.schooldesigns.com www.edu.gov
Health care	American Association of Retired Persons American Hospital Association American Medical Association American Nursing Association Assisted Living Federation of America Center for Health Design *Health Facilities Management Journal* Modern Healthcare National Council on Aging	www.aarp.org www.aha.org www.ama-assn.org http://nursingworld.org www.alfa.org www.healthdesign.org www.hospitalconnect.com www.modernhealthcare.com www.ncoa.org
Housing and urban development	Americans with Disabilities Act Fannie Mae Freddie Mac National Apartment Association National Association of Home Builders National Association of Housing and Redevelopment National Multi Housing Council U.S. Department of Housing and Urban Development	www.usdoj.gov/crt/ada/adahom1.htm www.fanniemae.com www.freddiemac.com www.naahq.org www.nahb.org www.nahro.org www.nmhc.org www.hud.gov
Newspapers and magazines	Local business journals Local business journals Internet Public Library (Univ. of Mich.)	www.bizjournals.com http://bibliomaven.com/businessjournals.html www.ipl.org

Source	Description	Location
Web Resources, continued		
Nonprofit organizations	American Society of Association Executives Nonprofit Board The NonProfit Times	www.asaenet.org www.boardsource.org www.nptimes.com
Real estate management and development	Building and Office Management Association Community Associations Institute CoreNet Global Facilities Net FM Link International Facility Management Association National Association of Industrial and Office Properties National Real Estate Investor National Urban League	www.boma.org www.caionline.org www.corenetglobal.org www.facilitiesnet.com www.fmlink.com www.ifma.org www.naiop.org http://nreionline.com www.nul.org
Retail	Institute of Store Planners International Council of Shopping Centers National Retail Federation Retail Industry Leaders Association Retail Source	http://ww3.ispo.org/ www.icsc.org www.nrf.com www.imra.org www.retailsource.com

Use an interview guide, but do not adhere to it rigidly. In-depth interviews help define problems that can be solved through design. Writing a guide before the interview helps focus the exchange on issues relevant to the project at hand. Unlike the fixed questions of a survey, the interview guide merely suggests the course of dialogue with an informant. As the interview progresses, the informant will frequently answer many of the questions before they are asked. The informant's responses will also suggest unanticipated areas of inquiry. As an interview is ending, glance over the guide to make sure all the topic areas have been covered.

Ask open-ended questions. Open-ended questions allow the informant as much freedom as possible to respond. An open-ended question is one that requires more than a yes or no response. For example, ask "What makes it difficult for you to concentrate?" instead of "Do you have trouble concentrating when it is too noisy?" Sometimes an open-ended question is not a question at all: "Describe the worst [or best] workplace you ever worked in."

Avoid asking "why." Informants tend to find "why" questions upsetting. Asking why may cause defensiveness and a loss of rapport. Instead, ask how, in what way, when, and where.

Allow silence. In everyday conversation, silences are filled quickly. Interviewers, however, need to allow longer periods of silence than cultural custom dictates. A period of silence allows an informant to formulate thoughts and indicates that you are listening attentively. This may be uncomfortable for both of you at first, so be sure to offer nonverbal encouragement, such as eye contact. After thirty seconds without a response, restate your question to make sure the informant understands.

Ask for clarification. Be aware of assuming you understand a person's meaning. Be alert for words that could have different meanings. For example, words like "restoration," "green," and "modern" have different meanings to architects than they do in the general population. Ask the informant to describe what is meant by words and phrases that are ambiguous.

Invite stories. One way to clarify meaning is to elicit stories from an informant. As an interview begins, informants may speak in generalities, giving what they think is the expected social response. To get a personal answer, ask a question that will lead to a story. For example, ask a nurse informant who mentions the inaccessibility of emergency equipment, "Could you give me an example of when you could not find the emergency equipment?"

SAMPLE WORKPLACE INTERVIEW GUIDE

Following are questions of the sort that could be used in an interview guide.

I. Your Job

1. What type of work do you do?
2. What activities do you perform most often? Which of them are routine?
3. How often do you need to work alone? In small groups?
4. Which activities or tasks are most important to your job?
5. What barriers do you encounter in doing those tasks?
6. What helps or hinders you when you need to be creative?
7. Describe your most recent day at work. What did you do? Where did you go? With whom did you interact?
8. How often do you meet with customers here? Where do you meet with them? How well does that work?
9. How often do you travel for your job?
10. What technology do you use on the job? How well does it meet your needs?
11. What changes would help you do your job better?

II. Your Work Style

1. What's your style of working?
2. Overall, do you prefer working alone or in groups?
3. What distracts you when you're working?
4. How easy is it for you to ignore distractions?
5. How much privacy do you need? How well is that need met?
6. Under what conditions are you most productive?
7. What do you do when you need to recharge yourself?

III. Your Office or Workspace

1. What is your workspace like?
2. How satisfied are you with the space you have?
3. What do you particularly like about your workspace?
4. What's missing that would help you do your job?
5. Where do you work when you need to concentrate? What makes that space good for concentrating?
6. How comfortable is your office furniture?
7. In what ways have you personalized your office?
8. How convenient is the location of your support services, both administrative assistants and equipment such as photocopiers and printers?

9. What would you change in your current workspace to help you be more productive?
10. Doing the work you do today, what would your ideal work environment be (features, atmosphere, people, interactions, equipment, feel, stimulation)?

IV. Interactions and Communication

1. What people or departments do you work with on a regular basis?
2. How convenient is it for you to reach those people or departments?
3. How do you most often communicate with people? One on one? In groups of two to four people? In meetings? On the phone? Via e-mail? Which method works best for you?
4. How common is it for you to encounter people from other departments? Where does that usually happen?

V. Meeting Space

1. How much of your day do you typically spend in meetings? How productive is that for you?
2. Describe the rooms that work well for meetings.
3. How easy is it for you to schedule a meeting room?

VI. Physical Factors

Do any of these physical factors interfere with your work? If yes, in what way?

- Too much noise
- Too quiet
- Lighting quality
- Too hot or too cold
- Air quality
- Vibration
- Smells

VII. Workplace or Building

1. What is your impression of the building entrance? Lobby?
2. How do you think guests and customers feel when they enter the building?
3. If you were a new employee here, how easy would it be for you to get your bearings?
4. What do you think of how space is laid out here? What changes, if any, would you make?
5. What do you think of the security measures for this building?
6. Are there places for you to get food or refreshments? If so, where? What do you think of those spaces?

Restate. A good way to let an informant know you are listening accurately is to restate a response or to paraphrase a series of responses. Restating accurately builds rapport and trust. If a restatement is not on the mark, you have the opportunity to listen again and add depth to your understanding.

Summarize. Summaries are not just for the end of the interview. At the beginning, summarize the purpose of the interview and the length of time it should take. As the interview progresses, summarize to capture what has been said so far and to refocus the interview. Finally, a good overall summary tells informants the interview is over, and that their viewpoints have been received.

How Many Interviews?

The ideal number of building users and other stakeholders to interview depends on their homogeneity, the project size, the length of the interview, and the skill of the interviewer. Once a number of interviews have been completed, a pattern will begin to appear in the responses. That is, no completely new categories of response will emerge. When you are interviewing homogeneous populations for small to medium-size projects, all the categories of response may appear within ten interviews. From then on, the interviews seek to fill gaps in the previous responses. For larger projects with more diverse stakeholders, a pattern may not appear in the responses until thirty or more interviews have been completed.

SURVEY DESIGN

Surveys are an excellent way to gather information from a large cross section of building users. The survey method is particularly economical for reaching users with known access to e-mail or the Internet, such as employees of an organization or students at a college. Written or telephone surveys may be more appropriate for assessing the needs and perceptions of users whose Web access is less easily identified.

Questionnaire Guidelines

There is a science to writing surveys that yield valid results. The quality of information gathered will be higher if these guidelines are followed:

Select a representative sample. If possible, select a random sample of users to survey. Statistical tests cannot be performed when a research sample is unrepresentative.

Include an introduction. Response rates are significantly higher when an introduction or cover letter invites the recipient's participation and explains the purpose of the survey. Identify the sponsor of the research, and state how the information will be used. Response rates can be greatly enhanced by including a letter on the organization's letterhead from someone such as the CEO. This endorsement sends a message that responding to the survey is important to the organization.

Ensure confidentiality. Participation in surveys (as well as other forms of research) is greater when the respondents are guaranteed confidentiality. Promise confidentiality and honor that pledge. The building owner does not need to know which individuals responded or how they responded.

Make the questionnaire easy to complete. Group similar questions together, and number the questions. Provide directions for answering the questions—for example, "Check all that apply."

Capture and keep the respondent's interest. Stick to topics that respondents care about and know about. Intrigue the respondent with an interesting first question. For example, when surveying teachers about their current facility, ask a question such as, "Overall, how well does the layout of your classroom support your teaching?"

Include a mix of closed-ended and open-ended questions. Closed-ended questions can be answered with a simple yes or no or by choosing a category. They are easily

Interviews may need to be recorded if exact quotations are required or if a summary of the interview must be prepared. Always request permission before recording an interview, and erase the recording once the interview has been summarized. Remember that transcribing a recorded interview takes about three times as long as the interview itself.

QUESTION TYPES

Type	Examples
Multiple-choice	Which statement best describes your opinion?
	What equipment do you have in your laboratory? (check all that apply)
Yes/no	Did you visit the government center in the past week?
Scale	How strongly do you agree or disagree with the following statements?
	On a typical day at work, how often do you interact with people in the following groups?
Open-ended	What gets in the way of doing your best work?
	What factors make finding your way in the airport difficult?

COMMONLY USED SCALE FOR MULTIPLE-CHOICE QUESTIONS

1—Much worse, somewhat worse, stayed about the same, somewhat better, much better

2—Poor, fair, average, good, excellent

3—Very poor, poor, fair, average, good, very good, excellent

4—Disagree strongly, disagree, neither agree nor disagree, agree, agree strongly

5—Disagree strongly, disagree, mildly disagree, neutral, mildly agree, agree, agree strongly

6—Very dissatisfied, dissatisfied, neither satisfied nor dissatisfied, satisfied, very satisfied

quantified, but they can be misleading because of the limited options available to the respondent. Alternatively, open-ended questions ask people to write their responses and require more thought. Although difficult to code and quantify, responses to open-ended questions yield stories, examples, and details that help interpret the quantitative findings. Open-ended questions allow greater freedom of expression and reduce the bias caused by limited response options.

Keep the questionnaire short. Ask only what is needed to meet survey objectives. A questionnaire should take less than fifteen minutes to complete. A rule of thumb is to have thirty or fewer mostly closed-end questions.

Include "not applicable" or "don't know/not sure" in the choice of responses. People are less likely to complete a questionnaire if they are forced to choose responses that are inaccurate. When asking about opinions, behaviors, or preferences, include "other" or "none" as possible answers.

Offer mutually exclusive answer choices. When only one response is allowed in multiple-choice questions, make sure the choices do not overlap. For example, if asked the following question, a respondent who works in Auditing, which is part of Accounting, would be confused about how to respond:

What department do you work in?

a. Accounting
b. Auditing
c. Customer Service
d. Information Technology

Write nonbiased questions. Do not lead the respondent to a particular answer. Ask "How strongly do you agree or disagree with this statement?" rather than "How strongly do you agree with this statement?"

Avoid branching questions. Design the questionnaire so respondents can answer all the questions. Branching questions (e.g., "If yes, skip to question 20.") are confusing and more difficult to interpret.

Avoid double-barreled questions. Double-barreled questions ask two or more things at one time, for example, "Does the new office environment facilitate access to colleagues and equipment?" Correct a double-barreled question by splitting it into separate questions. In the preceding example, write a question about access to colleagues and another question about access to equipment.

Use response scales with five or seven points. Scales with five or seven choices have the highest reliability. Always define each point. It is easier to understand the meaning of "35 percent were very satisfied" than "the average satisfaction level was 5.3 on a seven-point scale." Go from negative to positive, and balance the scale with equal numbers of positive and negative choices and a more neutral choice.

Quantify choices for frequency questions. Define the terms explicitly using relevant time frames. Make ambiguous categories more specific by changing "never, rarely,

WEB SURVEY SOFTWARE

Software Program	Location	Cost (2006)
Hosted on Your Firm's Web Site		
SSI Web (Sawtooth Software)	www.sawtoothsoftware.com	$1,900
Survey Pro (Apian)	www.apian.com	$1,295
Survey Solutions Pro (Perseus)	www.perseus.com	$2,495
Survey System Enterprise Edition	www.surveysystem.com	$1,999
Hosted on a Third-Party Web Site		
SurveyMonkey Professional	www.surveymonkey.com	$19.95/month
WebSurveyor Premium	www.websurveyor.com	$1,995/year
Zoomerang Professional	www.zoomerang.com	$599/year

sometimes, often, or very often" to "never, about once a month, about once a week, two to six times a week, or every day."

Arrange the questions in a logical order. Go from general to particular, easy to difficult, and factual to abstract. Begin with closed-end questions. Put demographic and sensitive questions at the end.

Always pretest the questionnaire and the invitation letter. Ask three to five users to complete the draft survey. Identify questions that are vague or confusing. Ask users what questions especially interest them and what questions you failed to ask.

Make it simple for the respondent to return or submit the questionnaire. If a survey is Web-based, allow the respondent an opportunity to review responses. Include a large "Submit" icon and a message to verify that the survey has been received. For written questionnaires, include a self-addressed stamped envelope and a deadline for submission.

Analyzing Results

Summarize the responses to closed-end questions by showing the percentage of respondents who chose each category of response. Display the findings in tables.

Always state the total number of respondents. Statistical tests (e.g., a comparison of the responses of city and suburban dwellers) require a randomized sample.

Code the responses to open-ended questions. Read through the comments first to identify frequently occurring responses. Read them again to tally the results. Display the results in descending order of occurrence, and use quotations to illustrate the findings (e.g., "Preserve the quaint charm and beautiful old architecture; the friendly, neighborhood atmosphere; the mature trees").

BEHAVIOR OBSERVATION

Usability is the measure of the quality of a user's experience when interacting with a system or a product, such as a Web site or a power tool. Observing people's behavior in

SAMPLE PRESENTATION OF CLOSED-END QUESTION RESULTS

How would you rate the quality of life in your neighborhood?	% of respondents (N = 189)
Excellent	43
Very good	46
Good	10
Fair	1
Poor	0

SAMPLE CODING OF RESPONSES TO AN OPEN-ENDED QUESTION

What do you want to preserve in your neighborhood?	Category Details	No. of Comments (N = 189 Respondents)
1. Housing stock	Unique mix of architecture, historic character	165
2. Urban oasis	Urban forest, green space, quiet streets, peacefulness, village atmosphere, walkability	160
3. Sense of community	Friendliness, involvement, community activities	157
4. Neighborhood institutions	Neighborhood school, community center	46
5. Transportation	Accessibility to both cities, good bus service, bikeways	30

and around a building is one way to evaluate the usability of a facility. The goal of behavior observation is to learn how occupants interact with a building. Being as unobtrusive as possible, the observer watches for what behaviors occur, records where behaviors occur, listens to the sounds that occupants hear, and aims to feel the experience of the occupants.

An architect who uses behavior observation techniques to gather information about building users will stand on a more solid foundation than one who relies solely on intuition and past practice. Two approaches to understanding the interaction between people and their surroundings are detecting traces of human behavior and observing individuals or groups in their natural environments.

Looking for Traces of Behavior

People leave behind physical signs of their presence, often as a result of unconscious or unintentional activity. One kind of trace, called *erosion*, involves things that are worn, trampled, or broken. Grass may be trampled in a direct path from the parking lot to the library, or flooring around the dinosaur exhibit may be worn. An elevator button in an office lobby is rubbed smooth, but the button at the elevator around the corner is like new. Another kind of trace is *accretion*, which is an accumulation of deposits left by human occupation. In building research, accretion could be fingerprints at the level left by preschool children, piles of books on an office floor, or soiled linens outside a hospital room.

Observing an Individual

Observing a single individual is one way to better understand certain aspects of a space. For example, a student in a wheelchair may be observed as he arrives at school, meets his friends, finds his classroom, and changes classes. This would reveal obstacles he encounters and allow the architect to begin seeing the environment from the perspective of universal access. Always request permission before observing an individual.

Observing a Group

For some building types, group behavior is what the architect needs to understand. How do employees interact? How do hotel customers use the lounge area? When designing a city hall, watch community members arrive for a city council meeting, find the chambers, seat themselves, get up to speak, and mingle with others during the break. Or, watch a group of people attending a national convention and record their behavior as they interact with the space. Conventioneers may have difficulty finding rooms because the wayfinding system is confusing, or they may sit on the floor because there is no seating in the hallways.

Systematically select the time and duration of observations. For example, a museum study might record behaviors at 9:00 a.m., 11:30 a.m., and 3:30 p.m. on a weekday and on a Saturday. In a community study, downtown activities might be observed intermittently at midday and evening over the course of a month.

Mapping Behavior

Behavior mapping is a special kind of observation technique used in social psychology. In it, scientists graphically present behavior events over time. When adapted to building research, behavior mapping can reveal patterns of activity not obvious during a single observation. Behavior observation may be used for the following purposes:

- To corroborate information gathered in interviews, surveys, and secondary research
- To identify incompatible activities
- To discover underused or crowded spaces
- To detect inefficient pathways or confusing wayfinding

The procedure for behavior mapping is straightforward but requires practice. Begin by determining the objectives of mapping. For example, the purpose might be to understand how people are using a new coffeehouse. Other steps are outlined here:

Obtain a floor plan or site plan. Make copies on which to record observations.

Develop a simple code for relevant behaviors. Use, for example, W = walking, T = talking, E = eating, P = using a phone, and Q = waiting in a queue.

Select a sampling scheme. An observer using *instantaneous sampling* records behavior at predetermined points in time (e.g., every ten minutes all interactions and behaviors of people in a coffeehouse are recorded). For *set-period sampling*, the observer records behaviors, usually of an individual, over a predetermined period. In the coffeehouse example, the observer might record the activities of the barista in fifteen-minute increments throughout a shift. Set-period sampling works well for measuring events or a sequence of activities. Sampling schedules must be selected before observation begins. The times can be regular (e.g., every hour) or random (e.g., at 2:00, 3:17, and 8:35).

Gather data unobtrusively. As much as possible, try to blend in with the people being observed.

Show the patterns graphically. Create composite maps to show how a particular space is used over time. Scanning and graphics software can be used to make overlays of recorded observations. For example, create a map to show where interactions occur most often or where congestion is a problem.

> Buildings don't enclose space, they enclose behavior.
>
> Robert Bechtel, *Enclosing Behavior*

GUIDED WALK-THROUGHS

A guided walk-through is a walking interview. Users of a facility lead the architect through the spaces they regularly use, making comments as they go. The surroundings and activities stimulate the guides to describe how they use the space and what works or does not work. Walk-throughs conducted during predesign and programming give the architect insight into how people use the building they currently inhabit. They help the architect see the space through the eyes of managers, employees, and customers. Four to twelve months after completion of a building, a guided walk-through can provide useful data on the effectiveness of its design.

The procedure for a walk-through consists of a number of steps:

Select a cross-section of stakeholders. Choose a representative sample. For a major remodeling of a high school, for example, stakeholders might include teachers, support staff, administrators, custodians, students, parents, food-service workers, coaches, and security guards.

Conduct walk-throughs with one person at a time. Ask each guide to give a fifteen- to thirty-minute tour of the areas that he or she most often uses, asking each to describe how he or she uses the space.

Record comments. Record the guide's observations and comments on the left side of a two-column sheet, and write your observations on the right side.

Ask questions. Prompt the guides to talk about the following subjects:

- Who uses the space and how they use it
- What works well and what does not work well
- Ease or difficulty with wayfinding
- Suitability of layout, dimensions, furnishings, lighting, HVAC, sound management, security
- Adjacencies and interactions
- Public image of the facility

Take photographs. Record images for reference and analysis. Photographs should capture images that represent the guide's comments during the tour. Later, these illustrations can be used to elicit commentary from those not on the walk-through.

Summarize your findings. Review and analyze notes from the walk-through to identify patterns and themes. Did all the guides mention being distracted by noise?

SAMPLE GUIDED WALK-THROUGH FORM

Guide:	Design Director	Location:	Branch Office
Date:	July 15, 2004	Time:	2:30 p.m.

Guide's Comments	Interviewer's Observations
Entry	
The entry is crowded. I imagine it's uncomfortable for guests because you're clearly in the receptionist's territory.	Barely room for two chairs and a phone.
Clients say they like the warehouse chic, but I think it looks run-down.	Inadequate lighting in the reception area.
Kitchen	
The 20 people who work here often work through lunch, so we frequently get in each other's way.	Multi-use space. Cleaning supplies and boxes of work samples stored. Toaster, refrigerator, sink, and microwave.
Conference Room	
The conference room is nice, but it's not large enough for big client presentations.	TV, computer hookup, windows into reception area, conference phone. Projects are pinned to the bulletin boards. Room for six, comfortably.
Personal Workspace	
My space isn't too bad. The U-shaped layout works for me.	All surfaces covered with papers and books.
I get light from the windows, but I can't really see anything outside.	Corner, open-plan office, two windows on outside walls. No apparent glare on the computer.
The temperature is highly variable. It can get too hot in the summer and too cold in the winter.	Portable fan blowing on his desk. Sweater on the back of his chair.
I'm not near the people I need to work with (the designers and writers). I do a lot of walking from my corner to the opposite corner.	Circuitous route from his office to where his staff works.
I need more wall space to put up work in progress.	Tape marks on the only open wall.
Shared Space	
We call this area the living room. I like to use this area for informal meetings or brainstorming.	Two leather easy chairs, leather couch, and a coffee table.

Did clients have a different impression of the building than employees? In what ways could the design of the building improve the effectiveness of the organization?

ENVISIONING

Focus group sessions with the stakeholders of an organization, facilitated by an architect or researcher, can elicit a vision for the ideal built environment. The purpose is not to ask the users to design the building, but to ask them to describe the factors that help them achieve their goals. The value of envisioning is twofold: the process gives the architect a deeper layer of knowledge about users before programming begins, and it stimulates support and enthusiasm for the project among the users.

Many studies have demonstrated that involving [building users] in the decision process generates both better solutions and more commitment to carrying them out.

Robert Bechtel, *Workplace by Design*

Who Participates?

Invite stakeholders who are critical to the success of a project to help envision the new facility. If the project is a new arts center, for example, conduct research with groups representing the performing artists, stagehands, adult and youth patrons, instructors and directors, catering staff, and administrative staff. Envisioning for a long-term care facility might involve residents and their families, medical staff, social workers and recreational therapists, volunteers, and dining hall staff.

Guidelines for Envisioning Sessions

The following suggestions will help architects organize sessions that yield useful information.

Build homogeneous groups of eight people. Eight is a magic number for group discussions. Groups of eight people are large enough to represent a variety of opinions and small enough to allow every person to contribute. Keep the groups homogeneous so the participants will have a sense of commonality and freedom to express their opinions.

Schedule ninety-minute sessions. Conduct the sessions at times and locations convenient to the participants. Always serve refreshments or a meal.

Write clear objectives and discussion questions for the session. Arrange the questions in a logical flow, making sure they are open-ended.

Provide confidentiality. Do not allow others from the organization to observe the session.

Introduce the session. Welcome the participants. Explain the purpose and the process for the session. Note that the session will be recorded to facilitate report writing.

Set the tone for a lively discussion. Ask a question and write the group's responses on a flip chart. Encourage people to build on what others have suggested. Individuals are often reluctant to express opinions that are different from those of the majority, so ask participants to write down a few words in response to a question before it is discussed.

Close the session. Thank the participants. Explain how their input will be used in the design process.

FACILITY PERFORMANCE EVALUATION

A facility performance evaluation (FPE), also known as a postoccupancy evaluation (POE), measures how well a building meets the needs of the people who use it and identifies ways to improve building performance and fitness for purpose. An FPE blends quantitative data, such as occupancy rate and revenue generated per employee, with qualitative data, such as "I have to leave my office to concentrate" and "The new meeting rooms are much better for client presentations."

SAMPLE ENVISIONING QUESTIONS

The following questions could be used during an envisioning session for a library project:

- What memories of libraries do you have from when you were a child or a student?
- What words do you associate with public libraries?
- What words would you like to use to describe the new library?
- How, if at all, do you use libraries?
- What limits your use of public libraries?
- What atmosphere would you like the library to have?

SAMPLE FACILITY PERFORMANCE EVALUATION QUESTIONS

Please rate the quality of your primary work space:	Poor	Fair	Average	Good	Excellent
a. Visual privacy	1	2	3	4	5
b. Voice privacy	1	2	3	4	5
c. Access to natural lighting from windows	1	2	3	4	5
d. Temperature comfort	1	2	3	4	5

In the last month, how often did you interact face-to-face with people in the following groups in order to do your work?	Never	Once/ Month	Once/ Week	Once/ Day	Two or More Times/Day
a. Engineering	1	2	3	4	5
b. Customer service	1	2	3	4	5
c. Sales and marketing	1	2	3	4	5

What gets in the way of doing your best work?

Benefits

A formal FPE results in a clearly presented, actionable report delivered to those who can effect the changes suggested. Facility performance evaluations benefit designers, builders, owners, facility managers, and users in the following ways:

- Builds greater understanding of how a design affects behavior and supports organizational objectives
- Establishes good practices and accelerates organizational learning
- Aids communication among stakeholders
- Identifies and resolves problems before they escalate
- Ensures the satisfaction of clients and users
- Evaluates innovative design features
- Links the design with measurable outcomes, such as operating costs, facility flexibility, sustainability, and user productivity and satisfaction

Procedure

Facility performance evaluations are usually conducted for recently completed buildings, buildings experiencing inefficiencies due to outdated or inappropriate design, and buildings undergoing a change in use.

Timing. Timing of an FPE varies with its purpose. For recently completed facilities, an FPE should be done after occupants have settled in but before problems are perceived as chronic. The optimal time is between four months and a year after occupancy. For troubled facilities, an FPE should be done prior to any redesign decisions.

Study populations. Owners, managers, employees, user populations, and visitors to the facility are the subjects of FPEs. Their attitudes, opinions, behavior patterns, satisfaction, and use of the building are the focus of FPEs.

Methods. Incorporating results from three or more research methods will strengthen the FPE findings. For example, an FPE that includes in-depth interviews, a survey, and behavioral observation will build a three-dimensional understanding of how well a space fits the needs of users, how they use the space, and what design solutions worked best. For buildings undergoing remodeling, it is helpful to conduct a baseline FPE before changes are made, and a postoccupancy FPE in the newly designed facility.

STRENGTHENING PROFESSIONAL PRACTICE

From business intelligence to facility performance evaluation, this topic presents a toolbox of research techniques and methods to help architects identify and understand building use issues that can be addressed in a responsive design. With experience, architects who have the temperament, time, and inclination will be able to apply the right tools for the research job at hand. Some architects have no interest in doing client research but will, after studying these methods, be better prepared to supervise in-house research or hire outside researchers. Other architects will find a middle ground, becoming skillful at certain kinds of research and relying on others to do the rest. Client research can help engage stakeholders, generate cooperation and enthusiasm for a project, and reinforce the credibility of the architect. Most importantly, client research results in places and spaces that fulfill both the expressed and unexpressed needs of the client and building users.

For More Information

Twenty-five architects present guidelines on how to assess the design requirements of the people who own, manage, and occupy a building in *Building Evaluation Techniques*, by George Baird, John Gray, Nigel Isaacs, David Kernohan, and Graeme McIndoe (McGraw-Hill, 1996).

In a special issue on postoccupancy evaluation, the British journal *Building Research & Information* describes the Probe (postoccupancy review of buildings and their engineering) methodology and gives detailed examples. See the March–April 2001 issue (no. 29)—Richard Lorch, editor; Taylor & Francis, publisher—at www.tandf.co.uk/journals.

Research experts give an overview and examples of how to evaluate the performance of office buildings in the Federal Facilities Council publication *Learning from Our Buildings: A State-of-the-Practice Summary of Post-Occupancy Evaluation*, Technical Report No. 145 (2001). More information can be found at www.nationalacademies.org/ffc.

Expert advice on why and how to conduct postoccupancy evaluations is given in Research Design Connections, *Building and Place Assessments* (2003). (www.ResearchDesignConnections.com)

6.5 Design Based on Evidence

D. Kirk Hamilton, FAIA, FACHA

Architects make design decisions on the basis of a great deal of knowledge that has accumulated over time. Actively seeking reliable evidence to support design decisions is a model for progressive practice.

The designs of architects are based on evidence both from their own profession and from other fields. Architects have always relied on geometry, mathematics, physics, and engineering science. They have used their knowledge of the strength of materials, moisture protection, soil mechanics, construction law, and real estate economics, among many relevant disciplines founded upon sound evidence. What is different today is that many architects are expected to seek additional sources of evidence in new disciplines and unfamiliar fields. Architects and other designers are finding they need to become knowledgeable about new subjects, most often in the disciplines of their clients or those relevant to specialized building types.

Kirk Hamilton, an associate professor in the College of Architecture at Texas A&M University, practiced for thirty years before joining the faculty. He specializes in health care facility design and researches the relationship of evidence-based design to organizational performance.

The simple phrase "evidence-based design" has begun to appear more often in the architecture and design press. Sessions on evidence-based design have been featured several times at the AIA National Convention. It has been mentioned in articles, in speeches, and on the Internet. Designers using an evidence-based approach are creating classrooms where students' test scores demonstrate that they learn better, hospitals where the building contributes to reductions in staff injuries and in the spread of infection, stores that deliver higher sales per square foot, and community plans that produce fewer vehicular accidents and less obesity among school-age children.

WHAT IS EVIDENCE-BASED DESIGN?

A simple definition of evidence-based design might be the intentional use of credible knowledge to improve design decisions. It is difficult to argue that architects should not use good information. A more formal definition—based on the definition of evidence-based medicine by British physician David L. Sackett and colleagues—reads, "Evidence-based design is a process for the conscientious, explicit, and judicious use of current best evidence from research and practice in making critical decisions, together with an informed client, about the design of each individual and unique project."

According to this definition, the key elements of evidence-based design include the following:

- Commitment to a process for making design decisions
- Design informed by sound evidence from trustworthy sources
- Design influenced by the art of judgment gained through practice
- Collaboration with an educated client
- Recognition of the uniqueness of every project

This approach to project delivery sounds remarkably like a good formula for competent practice: *Make decisions with your client. Base your decisions on credible research or your valuable practical experience. Treat each project as unique.* It is hard to argue that any of these steps should be omitted.

DESIGNERS NEED TO LEARN MORE ABOUT RESEARCH

Basic research skills sufficient for a practicing architect can easily be learned. It doesn't take a Ph.D. to carry out applied research or to understand published research findings. Architects may choose to learn about research at conferences and workshops or through formal education, but practice will make designers more comfortable making critical interpretations of research findings.

Architects can begin to collect information one project at a time, focusing on only a few key decisions. Firms can collect data from their completed projects and perform a variety of before-and-after or comparison studies. Every project thereafter will provide a collection of useful information, and the client will be impressed as the architect demonstrates higher levels of rigor and can demonstrate positive outcomes associated with the firm's designs.

Answer a New Question

The architect who begins by finding answers in the published works of others may be called upon to do some research as part of preparing to design a project. Now the practitioner becomes a researcher. The client may wish to answer a particular question before making an expensive commitment to a particular course of design. It is possible to do field observations, benchmark similar facilities, perform case studies, implement surveys, engage focus groups, do a pilot project, or build a mock-up. Most architects and their firms have engaged in one or more of these types of research. The difference in an evidence-based model is that the practitioner takes the time to learn something about research methods and is more likely to fully and properly document these findings. Adding rigor to the process improves the chances the architect may rely on the findings in the design process. Good data results from proper methodology; poor methods can deliver flawed data that could lead to inappropriate design decisions.

Capture Data on Completed Projects

The need to collect information on completed projects will also make the architect a researcher. Architects have traditionally collected information from completed projects, but not always in a deliberate way. There is a need to get beyond the collection of program material, specifications, square-footage calculations, and documentation of construction cost. The evidence-based practitioner will wish to collect data from the measurement of predicted outcomes that are most relevant to the client.

Report the Findings from Practice

While most architects have long performed some level of applied research in practice, they generally have not publicly reported their results. To achieve a high standard, there must be a commitment to increasing the rigor of practice based on reported hypotheses and measurement of the results that do or do not support them. Open sharing of lessons learned and peer review of research results will make it possible for others to benefit from the contributions of evidence-based practitioners.

Research performed by architects has an important role to play in the development of the field. Although academic research is significant, the practical observations of those involved in the hands-on process of design and construction are equally important.

RISING INTEREST IN EVIDENCE-BASED DESIGN

If architects have consistently used accumulated knowledge and the findings from research in their work, why is so much attention being paid to this concept? There are a number of reasons.

Designers Need Evidence from New Fields

Designing high-tech buildings for the manufacturing of silicon chips requires the architect to have knowledge of the computer industry and a deep understanding of the issues in clean room design. An architect designing elementary schools must be familiar with the latest concepts in pedagogy, along with public, private, and charter school trends. A sustainable design project for which LEED certification is desired requires the architect to know about air quality, consumption of energy in buildings, green building materials, and the ecology of natural systems. A hospital architect is required to learn about medicine, the health care system, and the nurse's role in care delivery. Along with an understanding of kitchen design, food storage, and the role of staff, the restaurant designer could be expected to be familiar with research on the economics of turning tables and the role color plays in stimulating appetite. Architecture students and practitioners using evidence-based design must be prepared to step outside the boundaries of their traditional education to explore information from unfamiliar fields.

Different fields have different definitions and standards of evidence. In the legal world, the admissibility of material as evidence is crucially important and its reliability is relentlessly argued in the courtroom. Medicine recognizes a hierarchy of evidence in which randomized controlled studies are the gold standard and observational studies rank far below. In the context of evidence-based design, evidence refers to information that comes from credible sources the architect can rely upon to make design decisions. There is a range of sources for such information, from scientific studies produced with sound methodology to behavioral observation studies in the field and internal documents recording a firm's evaluation of their own projects.

Evidence-Based Design Is a Process, Not a Product

In this approach to design, the architect and his or her client seek their own answers. Some have expected evidence-based design to provide the definitive response to critical design decisions. They hope that research already performed by others can tell them exactly what color to specify, how to size and shape a technical space, or what types of roof material are most sustainable. Applying ready-made answers to complex problems will lead to disappointment, however. Although the process of turning to credible research and experience from completed projects may offer a path to answer such questions, there will not be many enduring answers in a standards manual. The reason is that new evidence appears almost daily, and relevant evidence must always be evaluated for its impact on an individual project.

The same data may lead to different design concepts for similar projects. A design based on solid research, focus groups with users and the community, and consultation from recognized experts can lead to a clear and obvious outcome. The same combination of data can lead to a very different outcome in another location, where focus groups provide a different context for the decision. Similarly, a project based on research in one time frame may produce different conclusions from a project planned at a later date. New research data is constantly being produced, and new studies are always being published.

Increasing Collaboration Between Architects and Clients

When the designer initiates a new project, the client and users provide important information. Incorporating specialized knowledge associated with the client's activity or business into project decisions will be crucial to the designer's success. It is impossible for the architect to be as knowledgeable about the business as the client, and the client is not as knowledgeable about design and construction as the architect. The two in collaboration can accomplish something neither could have accomplished alone.

Each Project Is Unique

No two projects are exactly alike. Information used to make a design decision on one project may be inappropriate for another. Even when a standard plan is adapted, design should respond to the unique nature of each project. Today's evidence, which will change tomorrow, should rarely be used to justify a rigid standard or regulation for design. Used properly, evidence-based design should lead to both more effective outcomes and greater diversity of successful concepts.

Utilizing a Variety of Information Sources

The range of information potentially relevant to a project is wide. The designer cannot rely on outdated information or ignore new information. Discovering relevant evidence means seeking the most reliable information about any important topic that could influence a key design decision. This requires an understanding of what makes research findings credible. It also means looking for information in places one has not been accustomed to searching, as well as returning to previous reliable sources.

Interpreting the Implications of Research for Design

Designers must interpret the usefulness and value of research findings that come from circumstances other than the building they are designing. In other words, evidence indirectly applicable to the project requires interpretation before it is applied. Critical thinking is used to make a judgment about the quality of the research and the validity of its findings. In this context, critical thinking requires the designer to be disciplined in analyzing, synthesizing, evaluating, and applying information collected or created by observation, experience, reflection, reasoning, or review of communication and literature sources. Thoughtful analysis of the implications of credible findings on a particular project is required.

Designers will come across conflicting findings and implications for their project. Determining the best course of action in the face of contrary information is not easy. Architects and their clients may choose to work with the preponderance of the evidence or a compelling set of the facts. On the other hand, they may choose to go counter to the mainstream. They will need to use a disciplined thought process of deliberate inquiry to form judgments about information in order to arrive at the best decision for their project at that particular moment.

The Chain of Logic from Research to Design

It is important to seek links that run directly from credible research findings, through an interpretation founded on critical analysis, to a design concept based on a hypothesis about expected results. To base a design on evidence, the architect must be able to display the chain of logic that connects specific research findings or credible data to a planned outcome associated with the completed project.

If an architect expects a result from a particular design concept, such as *students will perform better on standardized tests in a particular classroom*, the concept should be directly linked to a body of credible evidence such as findings about the influence of natural light and views. The best logical links will lead to designs whose outcomes can easily be measured to discover whether the design intent was or was not supported. A chain of logic, especially when accompanied by careful measurement of the intended result, can be very convincing to skeptical clients.

An Ethical Obligation to Use Important Information

Architects have the responsibility to protect the public from the collapse of structures, the threat of fire, and other hazardous situations. The means by which the public is protected from these things are based on knowledge that has accumulated over time from research, experimentation, examination of past disasters, and empirical observation in the field. New information from reliable sources encountered by designers, especially regarding the health and safety of building users, is accompanied by an obligation to use it in the best interest of the client, the public, and unknown future users of the structure.

UNDERTAKING EVIDENCE-BASED DESIGN

If significant numbers of architects adopt the model of designing with evidence, a common understanding of such a practice will evolve. At least four escalating levels of rigor differentiate the ways in which architects work with evidence in their practice. Each successive level obliges the practitioner to continue to do everything required by the previous level.

Level One: Follow the Literature; Link Design to Research

A practitioner using evidence at this level believes in the concept of evidence-based design, attempts to stay current with relevant literature or research, and tries to incorporate concepts based on this information in his or her real projects. The architect studies completed projects to discover important lessons. Any success stories are then shared, especially with prospective clients. Some firms collect negative examples and use them internally to improve future designs.

A significant weakness of practicing evidence-based design at level one is the self-assessment of completed projects intended to generate success stories used for marketing. There is a high probability of actual bias in these assessments, and a strong likelihood of perceived bias in such self-serving reports. Another weakness is the absence of a documented connection, or chain of logic, between the research and the observed outcomes.

Level Two: Commit to Hypothesis and Measurement

At level two, the architect adopts the additional commitment to predict intended outcomes associated with proposed design concepts and to confirm whether the outcomes were achieved.

The chain of logic must be developed by explicitly identifying the research on which a specific design concept is based and connecting it to prediction of an outcome. This prediction can be called a hypothesis of how the design will influence an outcome. The design hypothesis or prediction must be accompanied by a commitment to measure the actual outcome to determine if the results support the hypothesis.

Designers have routinely made informal and casual predictions about their design concepts and, without any formal documentation, made unstructured observations to see what has resulted. The difference in level two evidence-based practice is the commitment to carefully document in advance the hypothesis associated with a design concept, and to measure whether the intended results are achieved.

Documentation in advance is important. Scientists consider a hypothesis to have a significantly higher level of validity if the prediction comes to pass. Halley's prediction of the return of the comet that now bears his name, for instance, and Einstein's predictions of phenomena that would finally be observed some years later, are examples of strong science. Similarly, for an architect to predict the expected result of a design concept, and then to confirm the prediction using a reliable measure, significantly elevates the validity of the connection between the design concept and the result.

Designers seeking a connection between their designs and project outcomes are looking to see if their hypotheses are "supported" rather than "proven." Architects should avoid claims that their measurements have proved something in the scientific sense. Observations of architecture in use usually fall into the arena of the social and behavioral sciences, for which causality is more elusive. Serious scientists would readily agree that a hypothesis had been supported, but would remain skeptical about an architect's claims of proof involving small samples of subjects in complex environments containing large numbers of variables.

Level Three: Share Lessons Learned

The next level of rigor in evidence-based practice brings a commitment to share what is learned, and to do so without bias, including sharing negative results. This means that postoccupancy evaluations are best performed by independent third parties, rather than the architect or firm responsible for the project. Even under the best circumstances, the prospect of bias is present in self-assessment.

Practitioners at this level will openly share their results, good and bad, with anyone who asks. They will speak about their experience and the results of their applied research studies at conferences, or publish their stories for all to see. For some architects, this is a new way of thinking. Many have believed that information should be kept within the firm to increase competitive advantage. This tendency runs counter to advancement of the field and may, in fact, be based on an erroneous assumption. In many fields, and most professions, the sharing of knowledge is understood to be an obligation of practice. It is inconceivable that Dr. Jonas Salk might have kept the polio vaccine only for his own patients. He received enormous public acclaim for sharing his discovery. One advantage of open sharing is the reciprocal obligation for those with whom information is shared to return the favor.

Level Four: Submit to the Review of Peers

The final level is reached when the practitioner becomes a serious researcher, independently or in collaboration with academic researchers. The principal obligation of architects at this level of evidence-based practice is to subject their work to the scrutiny of peer review. Subjecting your methods and conclusions to the formal review of experts and qualified peers is the best way to ensure objectivity and to increase the credibility of the findings.

There are several forms of peer review. One of the most important for the practitioner is the independent postoccupancy evaluation by an unbiased third party. Another form occurs when a speaker submits an abstract or proposal to a conference. Competitive selection of speakers by an expert panel increases the credibility of the presentation. The author of a scholarly, peer-reviewed paper will have an obligation to meet an academic standard of documentation, even if he or she is a nonacademic. Scholarly journals require all submitted articles to undergo some form of review by experts with appropriate experience. These panels of blind reviewers have no knowledge of the author as they make their comments.

It would be unethical for an architect to claim to use an evidence-based process, or claim positive evidence-based results, if that architect did not understand how to work in a design process that requires diligent searches, critical interpretation, hypothesized outcomes, and carefully measured results. Architects who believe such a claim could lead to more work may be tempted to exaggerate. However, if too many unsupported claims are made about evidence-based design, the reputation of the profession could be diminished.

SKILLS NEEDED TO PRACTICE EVIDENCE-BASED DESIGN

Architects committed to basing design decisions on evidence will adopt practice models that reinforce their commitment to this rigorous approach. They will begin to read more, especially if they have not been in the habit of following the literature related to their project types. One good idea is to read what the client is reading.

Some architects, far removed from their student days, will be unfamiliar with contemporary search methods and the resources available to scholars. There is more to a serious search than spending a few minutes on Google. An important skill is the ability to convert the description of a key design issue into a researchable question. Properly framing the search question can make the inquiry go more smoothly. The committed designer should get to know a good librarian. For architects who have limited experience reading and evaluating research studies, coaching and practice will be helpful. Experience gained through reading and interpreting the results of research studies will build these skills.

In the moment of creative conception, all designers have probably thought about what their designs will accomplish, mentally predicting an outcome as a result of constructing the concept. What is often lacking is documentation of the intended results in the form of a hypothesis suitable for study. It should only take a moment to record design intent in the format of predicted outcomes. Once the designer has predicted one or more outcomes, the next step is to develop a companion set of measures that will reveal whether their predictions came to pass.

Each skill needed by the evidence-based practitioner can be acquired without returning to the university. Each step of the process is manageable, and the needed skills can be developed with small investments of time and effort.

THE PROCESS OF EVIDENCE-BASED DESIGN

If an architect or firm elects to adopt an evidence-based practice model, a consistent and reliable method for its implementation will be needed. The most effective projects are likely to be delivered in an interdisciplinary context requiring collaboration among several professionals with complementary expertise. The architect should be prepared to lead or participate in a process that could involve representatives of the client, researchers, consultants, engineers, interior designers, contractors, vendors, and representatives of the public.

The best advice for those contemplating a project that features a serious examination of relevant research is to start early. Start the search for information well before design begins. Architects and their clients should spend more time preparing for an evidence-based design than is spent in the predesign phase of a typical project. A great deal of this early preparation occurs in the programming process. Much of what an evidence-based practitioner seeks in the programming phase is precisely what is sought in preparing a traditional program document. The difference is that for key design issues the architect would undertake a more extensive search for relevant information upon which to base a decision, including information about issues that may require search in nontraditional domains of knowledge.

Nine Steps for Designing with Evidence

The model illustrated in the accompanying table is simple and readily understood by design students or professionals. It does not require a deviation from the traditional design process; it simply adds steps to blend the research-based model into a normal process.

Step 1: Establish the client's project goals. Every design student should know how to discover the client's goals and objectives for a project. The architect will need to know a great deal about the client and the client organization. Understanding what the client expects or intends is critical to a successful project. This can be determined by studying the client, including review of mission and vision statements, expressed values, and organizational culture. The most important goals and objectives for guiding the design process, however, are those the client explicitly assigns to the project.

Step 2: List the practitioner's project goals. This is another familiar task. The architect will have an understanding of the firm's mission, vision, and goals, as well as the current project's role in the future of the practice. In addition to guiding the evidence-based design process, the architect must keep in mind his or her goals for the project. The client might be especially important, or the firm may want to emphasize speed of delivery and profitability. The project might be an opportunity to showcase a skill or demonstrate an intended result. Understanding both the architect's and the client's goals and objectives for an evidence-based project is important.

Step 3: Identify the top three to five design issues. Once more, this step should be familiar to every design student or experienced practitioner. Anyone with a design education will have been taught to identify issues crucial to the design problem, and will be accustomed to focusing on these key issues at the beginning of the design process.

EVIDENCE-BASED DESIGN PROCESS

Task	Activity
1 Identify the client's goals.	Note most important facility-related global and project-based goals.
2 Identify consultant goals.	Understand consultants' strategic, project, and evidence-based design objectives.
3 Identify the top three to five key design issues.	Narrow the possible choices; work on high-impact decisions.
4 Convert design issues to research questions.	Reframe statement of design issues to become research topics.
5 Gather information (benchmark examples, literature sources, internal studies).	Narrow infinite possibilities; expand limited perspectives.
6 Use critical thinking to interpret the evidence.	Use open-minded creativity, balance, and critical thinking (there are no direct answers).
7 Create evidence-based design concepts.	Interpret the implications of research findings and apply them to the project design.
8 Develop hypotheses.	Predict the expected results from implementation of your design.
9 Select meaningful metrics to test hypotheses.	Determine whether the hypotheses are supported.

It is impossible to give equal attention to every issue present in a design problem. So, how many issues should be identified as key? There is no best number, and every project may suggest something different. Many "important" issues can be fully addressed on a project, but only a few "key" issues will fundamentally affect the direction of the design. It would be nearly impossible and very time-consuming to use a thorough process to retrieve relevant evidence for fifty or a hundred topics. Current best practice and abbreviated searches should suffice for most issues, reserving an extensive formal search and study process for a manageable number of topics.

Step 4: Convert key design issues into research questions. At this point, the process for evidence-based design begins to require new skills. The typical description of a key design issue is not always in a form that easily lends itself to research. The architect must take each statement of a key design issue and convert it into one or more research questions. It is likely that each design issue will produce several such questions.

The main idea of this step is to break apart the statement of a key design issue into questions that can be researched. The questions need to be specific enough to allow for action on the part of the searcher and to permit the possibility of an answer.

It helps to begin with clear definitions. For example, if the design issue is to generate customer satisfaction in an upscale French restaurant, the architect could start by identifying what specifics constitute "customer satisfaction" in a restaurant as well as what precisely is meant by "upscale." By asking deeper questions, you might begin to research a number of narrow topics such as lighting, music, the scents of French cuisine, distance between tables, and environmental aspects of ambience and image.

Pursuit of the environmental aspects of key issues is particularly important. In a health care practice, a key design issue could be the objective to reduce medication error. A research question to address this might be to find what elements of the physical environment play a role in error. If it were determined that lighting, noise, enclosure, temperature, and air movement were all possible factors associated with error, a series of more specific research questions could be derived to identify specific design improvements.

Step 5: Collect information and gather evidence relevant to the research questions. This is another step that may require skills the designer has seldom used since leaving the university, but it is the heart of an evidence-based process. It builds on the skills used in a traditional programming process, in which decisions are made to define a project's objectives and scope, and expands the search for useful information to sources beyond traditional architectural domains, often to subjects related to the client's field.

There are nearly infinite possibilities for information that could be relevant to a project. The evidence-based process encourages architects to turn to the literature, both academic and nonacademic. In today's world, the library has become a bit less important as electronic sources have increased, but a competent research librarian can help you navigate the available sources, both electronic and printed.

In some cases, a designer believes he or she already knows the answer. The temptation will be to move on to something else, while acting on the basis of the individual's previous understanding of the issue. What may be needed, however, are an open mind and a willingness to expand the search beyond what is already known by the individual or the firm. It is difficult to be open to new ideas when you think you already have the answer. On the other hand, if the designer has no clue about the question, a daunting range of possibilities may lie ahead. In this case, a course of action might be framed around carefully narrowing the places in which to seek information. Knowing when to use each skill—broadening or narrowing the search—is a matter of judgment.

Step 6: Critical interpretation of the evidence. Once information in multiple forms has been gathered, the architect must make judgments about what it means to the specific project. Architects may not have had much experience evaluating evidence, so this step may require development of new skills. The collected evidence must be evaluated through critical thinking. This will require an understanding of the hierarchy of different types of evidence. The designer must be prepared to cope with conflicting findings and know how to judge the preponderance of the evidence.

What is fundamental to this step is the intent to analyze and evaluate research findings that have no direct connection to the project at hand. Even in the case of research on similar projects or topics, the research will not have been about the specific project being planned. The interpretation of what the research means for a particular project may be fairly direct, or it may be extremely speculative and tangential. To be useful, though, the research findings must be plausible and relevant to the key project issues. The judgment required to determine the strength of the connection between the research findings and the project issues makes this step a highly creative moment in the evidence-based design process.

Step 7: Explore design concepts to achieve desired outcomes. The process returns to the familiar at this stage, since every architecture student and design practitioner has learned how to develop design concepts. Each concept is intended to influence some intended result, which can be documented as a hypothesis.

Step 8: Hypothesize outcomes linked to the evidence-based concepts. Documenting design hypotheses may not be a familiar activity, but every designer has intuitively understood the intention of his or her design decisions. Evidence-based design requires that these intentions be documented.

Some have suggested that Steps 7 and 8 might just as easily be reversed. It is certainly possible for the designer to conceive of a design hypothesis in the form of a desired outcome, and then to work to develop one or more design concepts that might lead to the intended outcome. In this case, the hypothesis comes before the design concept.

Step 9: Select measures to answer questions posed by the hypotheses. Once the hypotheses have been thoughtfully described, it is necessary to identify one or more measures by which the hypotheses can be confirmed. It is important for the designer to avoid the presumption that one or more of these measures will "prove" something about the design. The architect should recognize that human behavior in physical environments is influenced by many variable features, making it sufficient to say that a hypothesis was supported or not supported, rather than proven. Scientific proof acceptable to peer review is rarely obtainable for social science and behavioral studies, and should not be a goal of the evidence-based design process.

Document and Construct the Project

If the preceding nine steps result in a design based on interpreted evidence, the rest of the process is already familiar to architects. The design is developed and documented for construction. The contractor uses the documents produced to guide the construction process.

A completed project now becomes the subject for a research study. Evidence-based practitioners will have made a commitment to measure outcomes associated with their projects, so the next obligation is to measure the results. Many architects in traditional practice believe they are not qualified to do research. This is not the case. Other architects believe they have done research anytime they look in a catalog to select a material. This is also a misconception. A large range of practical research efforts lie between casual exploration of information sources and academic research. The data collection and analysis performed in the field by nonacademic practitioners is frequently called "applied" research. Applied research by practitioners can yield important findings that should be shared with other members of the design and construction industry.

DEBUNKING MYTHS ABOUT EVIDENCE-BASED DESIGN

As a relatively new practice model, evidence-based design has been the subject of some misconceptions. The following points respond to concerns some architects have expressed.

Evidence-based design does *not* lead to rigid rules and standards. New information is published continuously, so attempts to codify design based on current knowledge will rapidly be outdated. One example is the requirement for grab bars that came after passage of the Americans with Disabilities Act (ADA). Developed in the 1970s when many injured men returned from Vietnam in a wheelchair, the standards assumed a decent amount of upper-body strength that would allow a person to lift themselves out of the chair and transfer horizontally to a toilet. These assumptions do not serve the infirm elderly with little or no upper-body strength. Research can provide sound reasoning for repealing or updating ineffective regulations.

Evidence-based design does *not* reduce the creativity or the art of architecture. There are some who feel that basing design on research findings reduces opportunities for creativity, but architecture has always been a mix of art and science and will continue to be. The rigorous use of science to answer important questions does not make the design process less creative. It can, in fact, demand higher levels of creativity as the designer responds to the challenges raised by new information.

Evidence-based design does *not* require architects to specialize. While basing design decisions on research may seem more suited to complex or complicated building types, using findings from research can be appropriate for virtually any type of structure. Thus, architects interested in evidence-based design have no obligation to limit their range of practice or adopt a single building type as a specialty. In fact, the ability to make effective use of research in some cases may facilitate expansion beyond a practitioner's current portfolio.

Evidence-based design does *not* mean the client makes all the decisions. Some fear that when decisions are based on hard data, the client will make all of the important ones, reducing the contribution of the architect. On the other hand, acquiring the best current evidence can empower architects to take the lead in the decision-making process. For practitioners, accessing more and better data means making or controlling more decisions, not fewer.

Using research to make better decisions need *not* cost a great deal. Performing the search for information in an evidence-based design process requires a modest expansion of the traditional predesign and programming phases. If the firm or practitioner judiciously limits broader searches to a few key design issues per project, the additional time commitment will not be overwhelming. It is not necessary to collect all the information that might eventually be required for any future project; it is wiser to collect information on a project-by-project basis. Study of postoccupancy results is done less frequently, so this aspect of evidence-based design is likely to require some new investment for a firm. If such data is normally collected by the client (because the topic is important to them), the architect should be able to acquire it at little or no cost. Finally, whatever additional expense is associated with practicing in an evidence-based model should be offset by the volume of new and repeat business attracted by the credibility of the firm's demonstrated results.

ADVANTAGES OF EVIDENCE-BASED DESIGN

From the architect's point of view, evidence-based design can lead to improved competitiveness and quality in a firm's projects. If more design decisions are made on the basis of researched topics, and if the lessons from each project are consistently returned to subsequent projects, the quality of a firm's projects should gradually and measurably improve. There is a potential competitive advantage to linking design to positive client outcomes. Consistently designing on the basis of credible research and delivering believable documentation of positive past results may increase the practitioner's standing in the marketplace. If clients seek to hire those who can demonstrate positive results, architects whose quality improves through diligent and earnest application of an evidence-based process may be more successful than those who do not.

From the client's point of view, evidence-based design can lead to improved project outcomes and sound financial results. The client will appreciate a design process whose end result promises rational decisions based on solid and reliable information, economical solutions, and demonstrated positive outcomes that will affect organizational performance. Clients, after all, are interested in improving overall performance of their businesses. Architects who can deliver evidence of the positive influence of design on organizational performance stand to be favored.

Widespread adoption of evidence-based design can yield increased trust and credibility for the profession. Architects whose practices can demonstrate rigorous research and documented results are likely to be invited back to the decision table in more and more instances. Failure to embrace this approach could erode credibility and diminish the designer's role. To avoid this, architects, in collaboration with their well-informed clients, can consistently make critical decisions about each project on the basis of conscientious, explicit, and judicious use of the best current findings from credible research and lessons from their practical experience. Prospective clients and the larger public will place greater trust in these design professionals. Increasing the rigor in programming, the quality of project design, the performance of buildings, and the trust of the public are noble objectives for the profession.

For More Information

Since evidence-based design is a relatively new concept, information about it is most often found in journal articles rather than in books. Described are a few such articles that will introduce readers to the basic concept and its applications.

In "Four Levels of Evidence-Based Practice: Architecture and Environmental Research," published in the Fall 2004 issue of *AIA/J*, Kirk Hamilton introduces the idea of increasingly rigorous levels of research-informed practice.

An example of the application of research to design solutions is described by Warren Hathaway in "Effects of School Lighting on Physical Development and School Performance," in *Journal of Educational Research*, March/April 1995, vol. 88 (no. 4).

"The Effect of Retail Store Environment on Retailer Performance," by V. Kumar and Kiran Karande, published in the August 2000 issue of the *Journal of Business Research* (49:2), discusses the relationship between the retail environment and sales in grocery stores.

Richard Paul and Linda Elder of the Center for Critical Thinking have written *Critical Thinking: Tools for Taking Charge of Your Professional and Personal Life* (New York: Prentice Hall, 2002), which offers practical advice useful for interpreting research.

Community designs that affect the health of residents by encouraging active living are discussed in *Health and Community Design: The Impact of the Built Environment on Physical Activity* (Washington, DC: Island Press, 2003), by Lawrence Frank and coauthors Peter Engelke and Thomas Schmid.

The Center for Health Design has published much on evidence-based design for health care, including a 2004 research report by Roger Ulrich, Craig Zimring, and their colleagues titled "The Role of the Physical Environment in the Hospital of the Twenty-First Century: A Once-in-a-Lifetime Opportunity." The literature review, funded by the Robert Wood Johnson Foundation, cites more than 650 studies linking design to clinical outcomes and is available on the Web at www.healthdesign.org/research. This is an example of how research relates to designs that impact health and safety of the public.

6.6 Integrated vs. Traditional Practice

George Elvin, Ph.D.

In integrated project delivery, the architect and contractor work together, often as part of the same integrated firm. As a result, project communication and coordination often run more smoothly than in traditional project delivery, which separates designer and builder. This collaboration has many benefits for design and construction practitioners and their clients.

Integrated practice is a holistic approach to building design and construction in which all project stakeholders and participants work in highly collaborative relationships throughout the facility life cycle to achieve effective and efficient buildings. Integrated practice providers include architects, engineers, construction managers, and contractors working together, either as fully integrated firms or in multi-firm partnerships, to offer expanded services to their clients across the full life cycle of the buildings they create.

Integrated practice providers often offer single-source, one-stop shopping for most or all of the major services required to make a building. In addition to uniting design and construction management through design-build contracts, they frequently provide a wide range of services at both the front and back ends of the traditional project life cycle, including feasibility and sustainability studies, procurement, programming, project management, and knowledge management). Integrated practice is facilitated by the use of building information modeling (BIM), building performance evaluation, and facility management. Although firms offering these expanded services rarely provide all aspects of design and construction, the breadth of their skills and experience makes them valuable long-term partners for other project team participants. These long-term strategic alliances often lead to long-term contracts that help ensure the acquisition of future projects and provide a steady income stream.

FOUNDATIONS OF INTEGRATED PRACTICE

Those providing integrated practice frequently cite three primary characteristics that set their work apart from traditional practice: fuller collaboration between disciplines, greater concurrency of design and construction phases, and the opportunity for greater continuity of involvement by the project team over the life cycle of the building. They cultivate continuous involvement in the life cycle through the ability to manage knowledge through the use of building information models, increased building performance evaluation, and sustainable life cycle design.

Collaboration

Integrated practice entities and teams are formed early in the project. They work together to define the scope of the project, its goals, and a plan for achieving them. By working together from the start, these teams build not only a shared vision for the project but also a shared plan for achieving it. Integrated project planning helps team members work more efficiently, saves time and money, and creates better buildings.

George Elvin is an associate professor in the College of Architecture and Planning at Ball State University in Muncie, Indiana. He has operated a firm engaging in integrated practice for ten years. This topic has been adapted from Chapter 2 in George Elvin, *Integrated Practice in Architecture: Mastering Design-Build, Fast-Track, and Building Information Modeling* (Wiley, 2007).

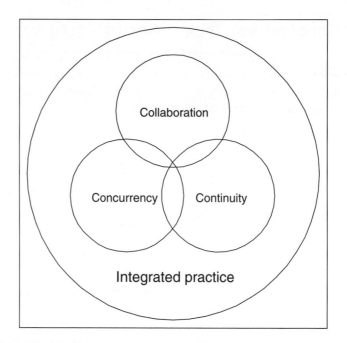

Foundations of Integrated Practice. Greater collaboration between disciplines, concurrency of design and construction, and continuity of involvement by the project team over the entire project life cycle form the foundations of integrated practice.

The integrated project team is typically united by a design-build contract, in which the owner signs a single contract with a design-build entity instead of using separate owner-architect and owner-builder contracts. The design-build entity may be a firm with in-house design and construction capabilities or a joint venture between separate design and construction firms. It may also be a builder who contracts with an architect, or an architect who contracts with a builder.

Because of its team-building advantages, design-build project delivery is used on most projects in Europe and Japan and continues to grow in popularity in the United States.

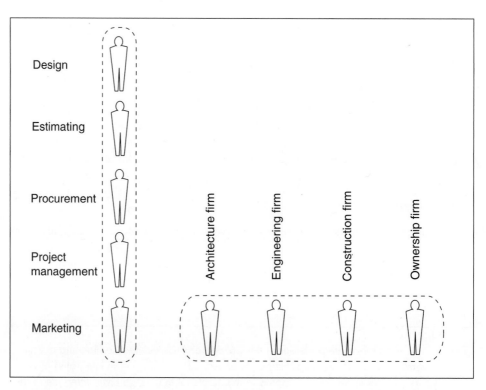

Collaboration. Collaboration can occur both between organizations (right) and within organizations (left).

Regardless of the variation used, the primary advantage of a design-build contract is the single point of responsibility between the owner and the design-build entity. A design-build contract encourages the architect and the builder to resolve conflicts as a team and to present the owner with solutions rather than problems. In contrast, the separate owner-architect and owner-builder contracts that are traditionally used can inhibit teamwork and promote adversarial attitudes.

Although integrated service providers occasionally use project delivery methods other than design-build, many operate as "design-build firms" that offer their clients complete architecture, engineering, and construction management services. Incorporating personnel from all of these disciplines under one roof enables such firms to offer their clients one-stop shopping for all the major services required for a building project from conception through operation. An owner working with a firm using integrated practice principles gains a number of benefits, including a team with experience working together, proven business strategies for combining design and construction, and improved collaboration from having the core project team under one roof.

Concurrency

Because of their team structure and control over the project schedule, integrated firms can often begin construction before design is complete. This overlapping of the design and construction phases facilitates compression of the overall project schedule and

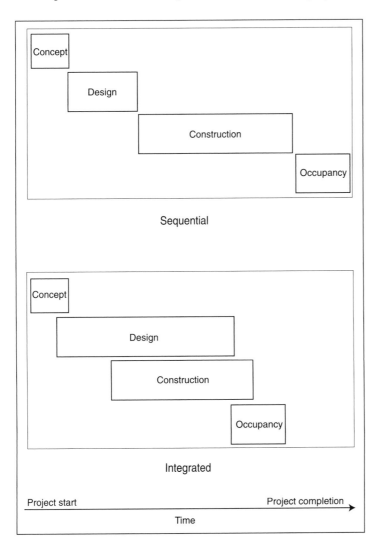

Concurrency. Overlapping design and construction phases allow integrated practice providers to compress the overall project schedule and deliver a building in less time.

delivery of a building in less time than required by more traditional project delivery methods, in which the architect completes the design activities before construction activities can begin.

In traditional project delivery approaches, compressing the project schedule by overlapping design and construction activities is called fast tracking. This approach makes managing concurrency extremely difficult. Because of this, fast-tracked projects are often marred by reduced quality, increased cost, frustration, and delays. Many architects express concern that fast-track production prevents them from delivering the level of quality they and their clients demand, and contractors worry that fast-track can compromise craft quality in the rush to completion.

True integrated practice approaches, in contrast, use specific methods for reducing project schedules without sacrificing project quality; they eliminate much non-value-adding waste, while maintaining the time needed for value-adding design and construction activities. Using flexible planning techniques, communication, and coordination methods, integrated firms can often make concurrent design and construction an opportunity not only to save time and money but to improve quality and owner satisfaction.

Continuity

In integrated practice, the project team is involved, in many cases, throughout the entire lifetime of the buildings it creates. This continuity of involvement grows out of the realization that, to a business owner, issues of design are inseparable from business issues such as personnel, marketing, and management. Design issues are of interest to the client not only during design and construction but for the span of the building's life.

Project team continuity presents firms using integrated approaches with the opportunity to expand their practices and their profits. They can practice life cycle management by offering a broad range of services beyond traditional design and construction, from front-end feasibility studies and site selection to expanded back-end services such as facility management and adaptive reuse. They are able to advise their clients on issues reaching beyond the traditional definition of architectural services because their clients see them as long-term partners advising them to explore and realize a wide range of business strategies.

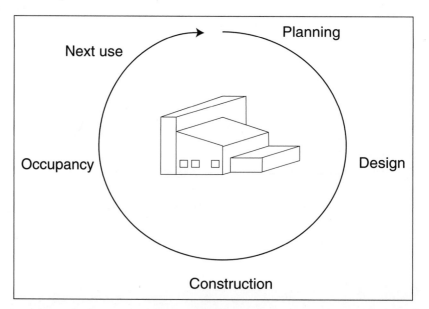

Continuity. Integrated practice providers offer a broad range of services to their clients, stretching from front-end services such as feasibility studies and site selection to back-end services such as facility management and adaptive reuse. Offering their clients services from the broad spectrum included in life cycle management gives a firm many opportunities to expand its practice.

Expanded life cycle services benefit both service providers and their clients. In life cycle knowledge management, for example, knowledge about the client's business, market, and competitors gained in the course of design can be applied to building operations and planning for the future. Through this process, the owner gains the benefit of a data-rich building information model, which can be continuously updated by those who know the building best. The integrated practice firm benefits by taking advantage of the value it has already created in the course of designing a building—value in the form of information about the building—and applying it to the building's operation.

Life cycle knowledge management can expand a firm's services and fees without requiring significant additional effort because the effort to create a building information model is a necessary part of the design process. Through ongoing knowledge management, the integrated firm often gains a foot in the door when the time comes for redesigning, reusing, or recycling the building. Developing strategic alliances with clients can also lead to long-term renewable annual management contracts providing continuous revenues for years to come.

THE EVOLUTION OF TRADITIONAL PROJECT DELIVERY

Many architects, owners, engineers, and contractors find the benefits of integrated practice an attractive alternative to the traditional method of separating design and construction. But why is it becoming so popular? To answer this question, we need to look at the origins of the traditional approach to project delivery.

In the context of architectural history, the separation of design and construction is actually a fairly recent development. The earliest builders did not make a strong distinction between design and construction, as is revealed in the origin of the word architect. In classical Greek, *arki* meant "to oversee" and *tekton* meant "building." This suggests, and historical records verify, that the ancient Greek *arkitekton* oversaw the entire building process from conception to completion.

Like the Greek *arkitekton*, the Gothic master builder wove together a mastery of design, craft, and organization to create architectural wonders. Many early cathedrals of the Middle Ages still contain the full-scale drawings etched into their stone floors by the master builder to guide construction. As the Gothic era progressed, however, the master builders (or architects as they were becoming known) began to distance themselves from the hands-on work on the job site.

During the Enlightenment, architects continued to redefine their role in society, moving further from their craft-based origins and forsaking the job site in favor of the atelier. Architectural education shifted as well, and students who once learned their skills in the guilds of the master builders instead entered the academies, where they focused on the fine art of design. These changes raised the status of architects, but distanced them from the craft of production.

By the end of the nineteenth century, a convergence of social, economic, and technological factors had almost entirely brought an end to the tradition of integrating design and construction in architecture. The Industrial Revolution placed a new urgency on the production of industrial and commercial structures, putting a greater burden of speed on the building professions. Major increases and redistribution of population created a similar demand for the rapid mass production of housing. At the same time, technological advances were reshaping the way Americans built. Steel frame construction enabled the rapid construction of tall buildings in the increasingly dense urban centers, but it required expensive equipment. This put increased pressure on the schedule of production in urban markets. At the same time, the financing of large projects shifted from the tradition of patronage by wealthy individuals to one requiring construction loans from financial institutions, putting additional pressure on the project team to work quickly and avoid costly penalties on their loans. Building regulations establishing standards for public health, safety, and welfare also added to the complexity of production.

Increasing pressure to speed production, incorporate new technologies, and cope with greater regulation resulted in a complete restructuring of the building enterprise by the start of the twentieth century. Gone were the days of the master builder, the single individual responsible for design, construction, and management of the entire building process. Specialization became the key to survival in a changing world. The establishment of professional societies such as the American Society of Civil Engineers (ASCE) in 1852, the American Institute of Architects (AIA) in 1857, and the Associated General Contractors (AGC) of America in 1918 reflected a growing separation of disciplines within the building industry.

An elaborate organizational infrastructure of licensing procedures, standard contracts, laws, and regulations quickly followed, all reinforcing the fragmentation of architecture into a network of interrelated but autonomous disciplines. By 1954 the AIA had barred architects bearing contractors' licenses from its ranks, and the other professional organizations took similar steps to define and defend their territory within the construction industry. The result was a system characterized by islands of expertise and a division of labor in line with the notions of industrial assembly-line production.

FOUR FORCES CHANGING THE MARKETPLACE

At the start of the twenty-first century, dramatic changes are once again transforming the architectural marketplace. Four key forces—speed, complexity, uncertainty, and change—are driving this transformation.

First, the demands of a new economy are forcing building professionals to deliver buildings at greater speed than ever before. Speed to market has become a prime determinant of product success, and quicker time-to-market requirements for their products, a more volatile economy, and increased competition are causing clients to demand faster production of buildings. "Time," as one architect has observed, "has become the most precious element in project delivery."

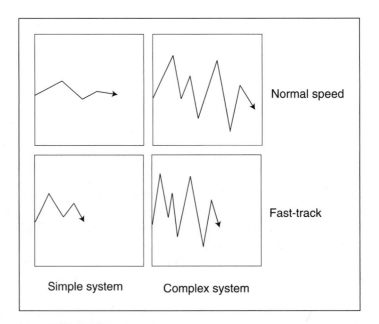

Complexity and Project Speed. In a simple system proceeding at a normal pace (top left), changes may lead to redefinition and redirection of the project. In a simple system proceeding at a fast-track pace (bottom left), those changes in direction are compressed into a shorter time period. In a complex system proceeding at a normal pace (top right), changes of direction are more frequent and of greater magnitude. In a complex system proceeding at a fast-track pace (bottom right), changes of great frequency and magnitude are compressed into a shorter time period, causing considerable uncertainty and risk.

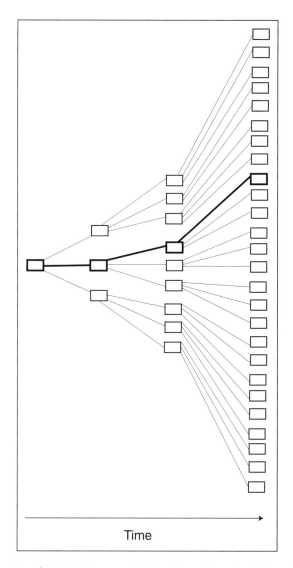

Time

Time and Process Complexity. When considering alternatives, the further into the future outcomes are predicted, the more complex the range of possible outcomes becomes and the less certain it is that any one predicted outcome will occur.

Meanwhile, the complexity of buildings is increasing as are the methods of their production. Growing specialization, globalization, regulation, and activism, as well as expanding technical, legal, and environmental concerns, are creating a level of complexity unimaginable to earlier builders. The 1,600 craftsmen employed in the construction of the thirteenth-century Beaumaris castle in Wales, for example, could hardly have imagined it would take more than 2,400 firms to complete the expansion of the Pittsburgh International Airport in the late 1980s.

Increasing complexity and speed mean greater uncertainty in both the building process and its outcome, and uncertainty in project definition at the start of construction has become the norm. Common matters of uncertainty include the scope of work, activity duration and timing, resource assignment, and quality. Uncertainties particular to the building itself include the definition and configuration of parts, the relationships between parts, and cost and availability of materials.

Finally, greater uncertainty leads to continuous change during production, and the rate of change is increasing every day. As recently as the 1970s, for example, only 5 percent of business leaders saw continuous change coming to their organizations; by the 1990s, 75 percent anticipated continuous change. Building professionals must deal with increasing changes in technology, regulation, globalization, competition, and environmental concerns, as well as project delivery methods, life cycle issues, customer demands, and client organizational structures.

THE COST OF TRADITIONAL PROJECT DELIVERY

Together, the forces of speed, complexity, uncertainty, and change are reshaping the architecture marketplace and revealing some disconcerting cracks in the traditional method of project delivery. For example, as project speed increases, the separation of disciplines makes communication and coordination more difficult. This may help explain why fast-track production so often fails to meet its promise of schedule and cost savings. Also, complexity compounds the flaws in the separation of design and construction, which typically forces project participants to address increasing complexity by defining project scope in greater detail before construction begins. Because increasing complexity creates greater uncertainty, such detailed plans made in advance often yield more change and reworking, adding to project cost and schedule.

Traditional project delivery has also struggled to adapt to increasing change. As reported in 1997, more than $60 billion was spent annually on change during construction in the United States, and more than 12 percent of all construction costs were attributed to the reworking of plans and to work that had to be torn out and redone. The larger number of changes required by design-bid-build projects suggests that using that delivery method may increase project costs.

Consensus estimates suggest that as much as 30 percent of project costs are wasted due to inefficient management, and much of this waste has been attributed to the traditional extreme separation between design and construction. One survey by the Construction Management Association of America found that "during the design phase, 83 percent of owners reported 'a lack of coordination/collaboration among team members.'" The Egan Report by the United Kingdom Construction Task Force similarly concluded that "the fragmented nature of the industry inhibits performance improvement." And when the vice president of a major U.S. mechanical systems firm criticized the "schedule conflicts, time extensions, change orders, and retrofits" that characterize our "suboptimal" building industry, he cited fragmentation as the cause of failure, saying, "Each participant tries to maximize the efficiency of their own system. It's just the way the process is set up. People work to maximize the value of what they are trying to deliver, and nobody looks at things across systems."

By inhibiting collaboration, creating adversarial relationships, reducing the opportunity to improve design during construction, and slowing information exchange and decision making, the traditional method can, along with increasing project costs, extend schedules and reduce building quality. It can impede preconstruction planning because the contractor is rarely brought on board until after the design is complete, thereby reducing the opportunity for feedback on the constructability of the design. Teamwork and trust are often hindered because the team is formed late in the process. In addition, preconstruction communication is limited because project information is transferred between designer and constructor in one large batch (the bid package) rather than in a series of smaller, more efficient batches. And during construction, information exchange is extremely formalized (in written change orders and requests for information), often forcing project participants to focus on communication procedures and defensive documentation rather than on quality.

THE BENEFITS OF INTEGRATION

In addition to addressing speed, complexity, uncertainty, and change, those practicing integrated project delivery today are surmounting the obstacles of traditional delivery by improving collaboration, coordination, and communication. The design-build method of project delivery common to many integrated projects, for example, can reduce project cost by an average of 33 percent and project duration by an average of 6 percent over a project using design-bid-build delivery.

Integrated practice providers are turning the pitfalls of fast-track production into opportunities for project improvement. Fast-track can reduce project duration by up to 25 percent, but only if its simultaneous design and construction activities are carefully coordinated. Traditional project delivery assumes separation of the design and construction phases, which makes coordinating simultaneous design and construction difficult and often undermines fast-track production. Designers working on fast-track projects often find themselves simply reacting to construction activities on site, constantly struggling to stay one step ahead of the construction work. When design is hurried in this way, project quality suffers. Cost and schedule suffer, too: Contractors, for example, have cited waiting for information from designers—an all-too-common occurrence in fast-track projects—as the primary cause of delay in construction.

Integrated practice providers equipped with techniques for coordinating simultaneous design and construction are able to compress project schedules without sacrificing quality. In fact, they are beginning to demonstrate what manufacturers practicing concurrent engineering have known for decades: Properly managed concurrent design and production can actually improve quality. Concurrent engineering is a method for simultaneous design of products and processes that incorporates multidisciplinary teams, shared goals, parallel scheduling of activities, early input from manufacturing to design, and continuous improvement. It has dramatically improved both time-to-market speed and product quality, creating products of consistently superior quality to those made by traditional methods.

Now, through integrated practice, architects, engineers, and contractors are beginning to apply the lessons of concurrent engineering to reduce cost and schedule and improve quality in the building industry. "Integrating services fosters design excellence," says Jan Tasker, AIA, principal and medical planner at Ellerbe Becket. "This approach offers many opportunities to be more creative because as the project evolves I can talk with construction [staff] and get their input or reaction to an idea." Other

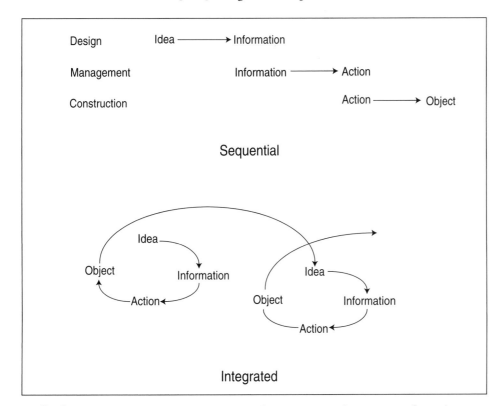

Feedback in Concurrent Engineering. In sequential practice (top), designers transform ideas into information, construction managers transform that information into action, and constructors perform action to create an object. In integrated practice (bottom), these subtransformations occur iteratively rather than sequentially, creating opportunities for feedback and improvement.

6.6 Integrated vs. Traditional Practice **301**

architects find that integrating design and construction gives them greater control over design quality. Spending several hours per day on the job site, for example, enables them to improve design quality by as much as 25 percent during construction.

Integrated practice offers other benefits as well. It can, for example, reduce environmental costs and improve environmental performance. In creating a green building, ecological design pioneer Sim Van der Ryn explained at a conference on concurrent engineering in construction, "The most powerful technique available is an integrated design process that brings together project participants, stakeholders, and outside experts at the earliest practical point in the project to collaborate, co-create, and execute a shared vision."

Integration also builds trust. Trust appears to have reached an all-time low in the 1990s, when one out of every three architects was engaged in some type of litigation. Since that time, however, litigation has declined. Significantly, its decline has mirrored the growth of design-build project delivery, suggesting that integrative approaches may reduce litigation. Because it builds trust and offers many other advantages, integrated practice is growing rapidly, while use of the traditional design-bid-build (increasingly and only half-jokingly referred to as "design-bid-build-sue") method is waning.

IMPLEMENTING INTEGRATED PRACTICE

Although the era of traditional project delivery appears to be passing, it will not pass easily because it is firmly entrenched as our inherited model of the building process. Jeffrey L. Beard, president of the Design-Build Institute of America, fights it every day in advocating for design-build. "The highest hurdle facing design-build advocates," he is quoted as saying in *Legal Aspects of Architecture, Engineering, and the Construction Process*, "is not legislative reluctance but, more simply, historical inertia. Architects learned to design in a vacuum, and engineers and contractors learned to work with 100 percent (complete) drawings. Change is challenging." Change has been slow because, despite its costs, the historical paradigm is entrenched in accepted attitudes and expectations about building projects, as well as in a variety of standard contracts, professional licensing and project procurement laws, and bonding and insurance mechanisms.

By the end of the twentieth century, breaking from these expectations and practices had become difficult and risky because it meant going against others' expectations and assumptions and facing the practical obstacles of finding an off-the-shelf contract or sufficient insurance and bonding mechanisms to adopt alternative methods of practice.

Breaking free of traditional practice has demanded that integrated practice providers put into action Albert Einstein's famous axiom: "You cannot solve a problem with the same mind that created it." Their new way of thinking is beginning to pay off as more and more owners demand integrated project delivery and new forms of standard contracts, bonding and insurance, licensing and procurement laws, and other mechanisms of practice are emerging to support it.

As the demand for integrated practice grows, how do firms grounded in traditional methods enter into it? Reaching the rewards of integrated practice requires vision, training, buy-in from both inside and outside the firm, new reward structures, and a clear plan for what individuals in the organization must do to achieve integration. For integration to flourish, architecture firms must combine new attitudes with new practices and recognize that the degree of change required will be different for every firm. Firms currently practicing design-build, for example, have already taken a major stride toward integration; companies fixed squarely in the traditional approach, however, must take a bigger leap to achieve integrated project delivery.

More and more firms are seeking the rewards of integrated practice. By building on the foundations of collaboration, concurrency, and continuity, they often produce better buildings faster and for less cost than traditional methods—too often characterized by waste, poor quality, and adversarial attitudes—allow.

CHAPTER 7

Project Development

7.1 Sustainable Design

Henry Siegel, FAIA; Larry Strain, FAIA, LEED-AP;
and Nancy Malone, AIA, LEED-AP

Green building combines the best of age-old design traditions with updated construction technology. When current events point to potential environmental and energy crises, the need to understand sustainability becomes increasingly urgent.

Although ecological problems are not a recent development, in the past their results were more immediate and more visible. Today, we live in surroundings that are increasingly removed from nature, making many environmental effects less apparent. Before the Industrial Revolution, environmental problems were caused mostly by concentrated amounts of compounds that occurred naturally and over time. Today, the environment isn't always able to adapt to or assimilate the growing quantity of synthetic materials and compounds or the increased number of waste products.

Henry Siegel is founding principal of Siegel & Strain Architects in Emeryville, California, a firm that has received a number of awards for sustainable design. He has taught sustainable design in the School of Architecture at University of California, Berkeley, and spoken widely on ecological design. Larry Strain, a principal of Siegel & Strain, has a thirty-year background in sustainable design. He cofounded the Solar Center, a solar design and installation company and developed *reSourceful Specifications* for environmentally considered building materials and construction methods, now part of BuildingGreen's *GreenSpec Directory.* Nancy Malone, a principal of Siegel & Strain, has managed many sustainable projects, and she serves on the U.S. Green Building Council's Materials and Resources Technical Advisory Group for the development of the LEED rating system.

The World Watch Institute estimates that population growth and increased consumption are the two leading factors contributing to environmental degradation. This is due in part to a constantly expanding economy, the creation of new markets, and planned obsolescence. Today, we use more resources and produce more waste on a per capita basis than our ancestors did.

The construction and operation of buildings contributes significantly to consumption of resources and generation of waste, and if the rate and manner in which buildings are currently constructed continues, resource consumption will accelerate. In the United States alone, an estimated 300 billion square feet of building area will be either constructed or remodeled by 2035. Unless the rate of construction is managed or changes are made in the way buildings are constructed, this development will place an increased burden on the environment.

According to the U.S. Energy Information Administration, "the architecture and building community is responsible for almost half of all U.S. greenhouse gas emissions annually." That statistic is one reason architect Ed Mazria, AIA, launched the 2030 Challenge initiative in early 2006. This campaign calls upon the building community to drastically reduce fossil fuel energy consumption by designing efficient new buildings or retrofitting existing ones. Most buildings, according to the 2030 Challenge Web site, "can be designed to use only a small amount of energy at little or no additional cost through proper site design, building form, glass properties and location, material selection and by incorporating natural heating, cooling, ventilation and daylighting strategies."

Once, buildings used mostly local sources of materials, water, and energy. However, the twentieth century brought inexpensive fossil fuels; widely distributed electricity and water; widely available mass-produced building components; mechanically operated elevators; heating, cooling, and ventilating systems; and large-scale construction equipment. Combined, these developments made it far easier to quickly construct ever-larger buildings and to operate them comfortably without regard to regional variations in materials or climate. Because the construction and operation of such buildings depend on fossil fuels, a rise in concern about this source of energy consequently increased interest in energy-efficient design. The energy crisis of the 1970s stirred widespread interest in energy efficiency and conservation measures, and experimentation in passive design. Progress slowed in the early 1980s as the oil crisis abated, but interest in ecological issues continued to grow.

In 1992 the United Nations Earth Summit in Rio de Janeiro rekindled broad interest in environmental design issues and inspired a more holistic approach to conservation-minded building design. The practice commonly known as *sustainable design* or *green building* began to include consideration of materials, water use, site design, regional issues, transportation, and human health, in addition to energy conservation. Since then a wider awareness of ecological issues, combined with technological innovation and promotion by government and professional organizations, has increased the importance of sustainable design.

DEFINING SUSTAINABILITY FOR THE BUILT ENVIRONMENT

Reducing environmental impacts is the first step toward sustainable design. True sustainability is more far-reaching, requiring, at a minimum, reduction of environmental impacts to a level the Earth can sustain indefinitely. Almost twenty years ago, the World Commission on the Environment and Development defined sustainability as "meeting the needs of the present without compromising the ability of future generations to meet their own needs."

What's missing from this definition is how we view our relationship to the natural world. Architect and environmental leader William McDonough, FAIA, argues for the need to "recognize interdependence" with the natural world, not merely to use it as a resource, and for the need to "accept responsibility for the consequences of design decisions" so safe buildings of long-term value can be created. Architects need to

A measure of how much land area is required to provide resources for and absorb the wastes of a person, city, or country is the ecological footprint of that individual or community. The City of London, the first major city to map its footprint, was determined to have an ecological footprint the size of Spain.

The number of firms designing projects characterized as "green" (using sustainable principles) is increasing. The share of firms with such projects in the following construction sectors are as follows:

Nonresidential construction	34%
Residential construction	25%
Residential remodeling	22%

2006 AIA Firm Survey

consider stewardship, restorative acts, and regeneration of natural capital, just as nature does.

The definition of sustainability and sustainable design continues to evolve and broaden as more is learned about what it takes to maintain natural systems. Therefore, it is important for architects to recognize that their daily practice is part of a wider web of influence that affects all living systems, and it is important for them to recognize that sustainability is not just a designer's issue but is of concern to many disciplines. Architects will need to find ways to collaborate with new kinds of team members to achieve a sustainable built environment. As author and educator David Orr has stated, "Sustainable design is the careful meshing of human purposes with the larger patterns and flows of the natural world."

MEASURES FOR ACHIEVING SUSTAINABLE DESIGN

The AIA Committee on the Environment (COTE) developed a list of criteria, known as the Top Ten Measures of Sustainable Design, that address both the quantifiable and the intangible aspects of sustainable design. (These measures are also used to choose the winners of COTE's annual Top Ten Green Projects award program.) The following section of this topic uses the Top Ten Measures—quotes from them appear in italics— as a framework for presenting sustainable design strategies available to architects.

Recognize Design Opportunities

Sustainable design embraces the ecological, economic, and social circumstances of a project.

Sustainable building design applies ecological principles and works *with* natural energy flows rather than ignoring them. It creates connections to the natural world and minimizes, or ideally reverses, adverse environmental impacts.

Architect James Wines believes that an ecological approach to design presents an opportunity to change the paradigm for design excellence, to move from "ego-centric to eco-centric." What he proposes is an analysis that reevaluates humanity's evolving relationship with nature and our place in it as the basis for design.

Sustainable design is not a style and is more than a trend. When building orientation or protection of drainage paths or the integration of energy-saving technologies is given equal weight with the classical virtues of symmetry, scale, and proportion, the definition of what constitutes good design will change. Buildings will demonstrate stronger connections to place, and new design solutions may evolve. But it is not enough to design buildings that perform well. The more traditional architectural values apply as well. Buildings that are valued by their communities are the ones that will be maintained and preserved. Ultimately, as David Orr has said, if a building is not beautiful, it is not sustainable.

Strategies for recognizing design opportunities include these:

- Consider ecological models—how nature does it—as models for design.
- Design to strengthen human connections to natural systems.
- Make sustainable design strategies drivers of design aesthetics.

Promote Regional/Community Identity

Sustainable design recognizes the unique cultural and natural character of a given region . . . promotes regional and community identity and an appropriate sense of place . . . reduces automobile travel from home, work, shopping, or other frequent destinations . . . and encourages alternative transportation strategies.

Regional and urban issues lie at the heart of a sustainable future. Buildings and other development fit within the context of local and regional habitat, resources, water, food, transportation, and community. Creating a sense of place grows from analysis and understanding of local circumstances, including cultural and historical patterns as well as local differences in landscape and topography, climate, resources, and habitat. The way architects design affects the health and well-being of natural systems as well as the effectiveness of constructed systems. Designing with an understanding of local factors not only reduces environmental impacts but contributes to the creation of meaningful, memorable places.

American cities are often fragmented by zoning or other use patterns, separating people from jobs, services, and green spaces. Suburban settlements tend to be even more specialized, with housing typically isolated from other uses. The automobile influences development everywhere, but that influence is more dominant in the suburbs. Although suburbs tend to have more open space per capita, the open space often is largely private lawns that require frequent mowing and heavy use of water, fertilizer, and weed killers.

The widespread use of cars has led to sprawl and the infrastructure that goes with it. Development eats up 1 to 1.5 million acres of land every year in the United States. The population of New York City has grown by only 8 percent since the 1960s, but the amount of urbanized land in the New York area has grown by 60 percent in the same period. Sprawl in turn contributes to how much people drive: Studies show that each year U.S. suburban dwellers drive 110 hours—the equivalent of nearly three workweeks—more than city dwellers do.

Resources are increasingly removed from the cities they support. Food is grown far away and shipped great distances. According to the Leopold Center for Sustainable Agriculture at Iowa State University, most food in the United States travels between 1,500 and 2,000 miles before it is eaten. Water is collected and piped from distant watersheds or pumped from diminishing aquifers. Other resources are supplied by global markets to ensure the lowest cost to the consumer, often ignoring proximity to resources, support for the local economy, and other undervalued ecological and social "externalities."

Externalities are costs (sometimes benefits) that are borne by parties "external" to a transaction. For example, air pollution from a power plant can negatively affect people hundreds of miles away and they, rather than the utility company, bear the social and economic costs created by this pollution without necessarily reaping any of the benefits. Traditionally, economists do not account for these external costs, often assuming that negative environmental impacts have little cost. New economic models use a "triple bottom line" method of accounting that considers profit, social equity, and environmental protection.

Similarly, waste is collected and removed from cities, taking problems somewhere else. Garbage goes to landfills or is dumped in the ocean, polluted runoff from roofs and streets is diverted to the nearest body of water, and emissions drift and pollute someone else's air.

Cities and suburbs need to be re-imagined and redesigned to provide economically and socially viable neighborhoods and communities, taking local resources and natural systems into careful consideration. Communities should be pedestrian friendly, have adequate public transportation, and provide connections to nature. Communities should, to the greatest extent possible, draw only from their local resource base, support the local economy, and handle their waste locally. Local control of food, water, and material resources makes people more aware of, and accountable to, the world around them.

Strategies for promoting local identity include these:

- Design from a sense of place.
- Encourage infill development.
- Encourage mixed-use transit development.
- Include nature by providing habitat in yards, on planted roofs and parks, and in wildlife corridors.
- Design buildings and communities in ways that support local food cultivation and suppliers.

- Collect water and protect watersheds.
- Support the local economy and use local materials that do not require transportation over long distances.
- Reuse or recycle urban waste.

Design for the Ecological Context

A project site design should respond to its ecological context. Site selection and design can relate to ecosystems at different scales, from local to regional. Even urban sites relate to ecological issues such as climate, topography, and watershed, as well as transportation and land use.

Sustainable design acknowledges that each site—whether rural, suburban, or urban—is different in resources and context, which can enhance or limit design decisions. Sustainable design requires a level of research and analysis that considers impacts on watersheds, habitats, and other natural systems that intersect a given site. It also includes identification of opportunities for transportation linkages, ways to restore habitat, and use of infill and brownfield sites, the latter defined by the Environmental Protection Agency as a property that may have pollutants or hazardous substances present.

One way to define the extent of the area to be analyzed for a particular project is to identify the site's watershed and determine its water source and its destination for treatment and disposal. It is also essential to consider and analyze wildlife habitat, plant life, topography, and soil conditions, and respond to them in ways that minimize the effects of development and reestablish or strengthen connections to regional ecological systems. What are the important species in the watershed? How can their habitat be protected or restored? Consideration of these factors can make it possible to design landscaping that supports wildlife, while saving water and even helping to store and treat storm water.

Opportunities exist even on most urban sites. Nearly two-thirds of the site footprint of the Solaire, a high-rise apartment building in New York City designed by Cesar Pelli & Associates (now Pelli Clarke Pelli Architects), is green. A roof garden is irrigated with captured rainwater, and some of the captured water is used to help irrigate an adjacent park. The building design has the synergistic effect of providing open space, reducing storm water runoff and reducing the heat island effect—a condition in urban areas where tall buildings retain heat more than the same space would if it were located in an open area.

Strategies for designing in context include these:

- Utilize infill and brownfield sites to reduce development on more pristine habitat areas or productive farmland.
- Retain or restore waterways on or near the site.
- Use native plants or plants that have evolved in similar bioregions to provide and restore biological diversity.
- Use landscape to offset the impacts of the built environment. Plant trees to reduce heat islands created by paving and roofs and to offset carbon dioxide emissions from building operation.
- Use swales, check dams, and storage basins to slow and collect water and keep it on-site to reduce storm water runoff.
- Protect air, water, and soil quality by practicing natural pest control, minimizing use of petroleum-based fertilizers, and conserving and rebuilding topsoil.
- Restore habitat and protect local species.

Engage in Bioclimatic Design

Sustainable design conserves natural resources and maximizes human comfort through an intimate connection with the natural flows and cycles of the surrounding bioclimatic region.

At the turn of the twentieth century the heating, cooling, and lighting of buildings was the domain of the architect. Since then, systems have evolved for lighting, heating,

Pulitzer Prize–winning biologist E. O. Wilson developed the theory of "biophilia"—the innate need of humans to be in close touch with the natural world. He defines biophilia as "the connections that human beings subconsciously seek with the rest of life" and proposes that the deep affiliations we have with nature are rooted in our biology. Designs inspired by biological models that are more strongly connected to nature would be plausible outcomes of applying this theory to architecture.

and cooling that ignore nature and function without regard to whether it is cold or hot, light or dark outdoors. By the 1950s, cheap and abundant energy allowed technology to provide comfort in any climate. One result has been the homogenization of architecture—buildings that look the same regardless of climate or culture. Another result is that architects now work with teams of highly specialized engineers for the design of building systems. In 1973 the first energy shortage revealed our heavy reliance on mechanical conditioning of buildings.

Designing *with* the climate (known as *bioclimatic*, *climate-based*, or *passive design*) is an effective way to reduce a building's dependence on nonrenewable sources of energy. By starting with bioclimatic design principles and considering how buildings will perform when "unplugged," architects can reduce the size of building systems and in some cases even eliminate them. Buildings climatically attuned to their surroundings will also have a stronger sense of place.

Buildings that rely only on locally available resources illustrate sound approaches to climate-based design because they evolved over time as best responses to local conditions. Traditional buildings in similar climate zones around the world illustrate a variety of approaches to comparable climatic conditions. Different cultures demonstrate different approaches to similar climates, and these various approaches are an important resource for design strategies and solutions.

Some understanding of human comfort and strategies for different climate zones is a prerequisite for designing with the climate. This information can be summarized in bioclimatic or psychometric charts that depict local conditions and strategies to accommodate them. These strategies are most effective when addressed at the earliest stages of the design process, when the architect is considering orientation, shape, and building massing.

While the ideal building shape varies from climate to climate, building orientation generally favors maximizing the length of the south side of a building (the north side below the equator) to take advantage of easier sun control, and minimizing eastern and western exposures for the same reason. Buildings can be shaped to aid natural ventilation and daylighting as well as views and connection to the outdoors.

Window shading can help maximize heat gain in winter and minimize it in summer. Windows can be placed to optimize daylight and take advantage of prevailing winds for ventilation. High-mass materials such as concrete or masonry can be optimized to shift absorption of heating and cooling to times of the day or night when it is most needed. These long-standing principles should once again become primary criteria of good design.

Strategies vary by climate zone. Generally, climate zones can be reduced to four: hot and dry, hot and humid, temperate, and cold. A few strategies for each climate zone follow.

Design strategies for hot and dry climates
- Minimize sun exposure; minimize effects of wind.
- Use small windows.
- Optimize thermal mass to take advantage of the large diurnal temperature swing.
- Closely cluster buildings for the shade they offer one another.

Design strategies for hot and humid climates
- Minimize sun exposure; maximize natural ventilation.
- Use lightweight construction to minimize radiation of heat.
- Space buildings far apart to maximize breezes.

Design strategies for temperate climates
- Maximize solar gain in winter, minimize it in summer.
- Maximize breezes in summer; minimize them in winter.
- Take advantage of daylighting opportunities.

Design strategies for cold climates

- Orient buildings and openings for maximum protection from cold winds.
- Use south-facing windows (in the northern hemisphere) to maximize solar gain.
- Use compact shapes and small windows to minimize heat loss.

Create Healthy Indoor Environments

Sustainable design creates and maintains a comfortable interior environment while providing abundant daylight and fresh air.

North Americans spend as much as 90 percent of their time indoors, making buildings the primary locus for health, comfort, well-being, and productivity. Air quality, daylight and views, temperature and humidity, and personal control over the environment contribute to how people experience the indoor environment. While it is difficult to demonstrate which factors are most important, studies have shown that ample daylight and proper ventilation lead to greater satisfaction, an increased sense of comfort, fewer sick days, and increased productivity.

Indoor air can be many times more polluted than outdoor air, especially in poorly ventilated buildings. Illnesses identified with indoor pollutants range from mild allergic symptoms to serious and life-threatening illnesses such as heart disease and cancer. Many chemical and biological pollutants present in indoor air, such as the following, can affect human health:

- Mold, mildew, and other moisture-related contaminants
- Off-gassing from building materials and furnishings
- Maintenance products, including pesticides
- Combustion gases from appliances, automobiles, and tobacco
- Naturally occurring gases such as radon
- Outdoor pollutants that enter the building

An effective supply of fresh outdoor air can dilute the amount of airborne contaminants in a building. Natural and/or mechanical means can provide appropriate ventilation. Passive ventilation has the benefit of being more energy-efficient and less noisy, but it is more difficult to design for larger buildings. "Mixed-mode" systems that use both natural and mechanical ventilation offer a healthier alternative to sealed buildings, which are still the norm for some building types.

Natural light and views to the outdoors can help enhance physical and mental health. Ample daylight increases productivity in the workplace and test scores in schools. Daylight and views can be maximized by coupling a narrow building section with careful window placement, a legal requirement for office buildings in many European countries. Desired amounts of daylight can be achieved with the use of skylights and light shelves, the shape of windows and ceilings, and use of light-colored surfaces. However, care must be taken to avoid excessive heat gain and glare.

Temperature and humidity affect occupant comfort and can be controlled with both passive and mechanical means, depending on the climate and the building type. Postoccupancy studies indicate that building occupants are happier if they have localized or individual control over temperature and air, especially if it includes access to operable windows.

Strategies for creating healthy indoor environments include these:

- Identify potential pollutant sources and eliminate them from the building.
- Separate occupants and any pollutant sources that remain with a barrier.
- Prevent moisture intrusion and buildup.
- Set minimum ventilation rates based on ASHRAE 62–2003.
- For suspected pollutants or health risks that have no verified cause-and-effect relationship, exercise the Precautionary Principle (see following sidebar).
- Optimize daylight and reduce glare.
- Prevent excessive heat gain.
- Provide localized or individual controls for ventilation and light.

Many practitioners make decisions about building materials or systems based on limited evidence that a selection is better for human health or the ecosystem. Sometimes the only available research about new materials is still in development or short of scientific confirmation, yet some evidence indicates a particular material may cause harm. In this situation, the decision-making process should be preventive: Avoid potential harm.

Scientists, environmentalists, and others at a January 1998 Wingspread conference developed the "Precautionary Principle" as a framework for making such decisions. Its main point is this: "When an activity raises threats of harm to human health or the environment, precautionary measures should be taken even if some cause-and-effect relationships are not fully established scientifically."

Conserve Water

Utilize building and site design strategies to conserve water supplies, manage site water and drainage, and capitalize on renewable sources.

Water is becoming a major challenge in the twenty-first century, as issues from overuse to drought to pollution to privatization of sources proliferate. Continued global population growth and industrialization will make water an even more precious commodity.

In most parts of the Untied States—especially the arid West—cities, agriculture, and industry rely on large-scale water distribution systems. In California, water that falls in the Sierras as snow is diverted from rivers and streams and transported over long distances to irrigate Central Valley agribusiness and quench thirsts along the coast. As it travels downslope, this water is used to create electricity, but the system uses more electricity than it creates to pump water and is one of the state's largest consumers of electricity. Other parts of the country tap vast but shrinking aquifers, pumping water from the earth at rates that cause the ground to subside and require deeper wells. According to the *LEED Reference Guide*, Americans extract 3,700 billion gallons more per year than they return to natural systems.

Within the built environment, water is used for drinking, cooking, cleaning, bathing, transporting waste, heating and cooling buildings, and irrigating lawns and gardens. There are established methods of conservation for all of these uses, but such efforts can be further improved. For example, the concept of wastewater must be reconsidered. Gray water—the water collected from sinks and showers—and rainwater can be used to irrigate plants or flush toilets. Even black water—which comes from toilet flushing—can be treated to a level suitable for irrigation. All water and wastewater eventually returns to the natural hydrologic system; it should be returned as clean as possible and treated with the least amount of chemical and energy input possible.

Strategies for conserving water include these:

- Reduce potable water by employing drip irrigation and low-flow water fixtures and appliances.
- Design landscapes that minimize or eliminate the need for irrigation.
- Promote kitchen composting rather than disposal use.
- Catch rainwater for potable water and irrigation.
- Retrieve gray water for uses that do not require potable water, such as flushing toilets.
- Treat black water with biological treatment systems for use in irrigation.
- Return water to the site rather than disposing of it off-site.
- Promote infiltration by minimizing impermeable surfaces.

Minimize Use of Nonrenewable Energy Sources and Maximize Use of Renewable Energy

Good design of building mechanical and electrical systems and integration of those systems with passive design strategies is essential for conserving natural resources and improving building performance . . . . Sustainable design carefully considers the long-term impact of current decisions in order to protect quality of life in the future.

Total operating energy used during the life of a building far surpasses the embodied energy of the materials and the energy use from construction. For green buildings, energy system design starts at the beginning of the design process, when the integrated design team meets to brainstorm best choices for passive and active approaches to energy systems.

Building systems in green buildings can be smaller and more efficient. But they can also be more complex, since they may incorporate more sophisticated control systems and use natural ventilation and daylighting. Whole systems strive to work more like an organism, to maximize opportunities for the building to breathe on its own—to heat and cool itself through good passive design—rather than letting the mechanical or electrical system do all the work. Often, green design requires a change in attitude about how to interact with a building. For example, in accepting wider temperature swings, clients can benefit from more personal control of their environment and have a closer connection to the natural world.

Renewable energy is often an exciting concept to clients—many want to start the discussion of green building with photovoltaic power, wind power, or hydrogen fuels. However, the first and most productive measures for consuming less energy from the grid involve eliminating or reducing the size of systems through good passive design; then the size of renewable energy systems, which often have high first costs, can be reduced. Green technology follows green design.

Renewable energy promises less reliance on the grid, making it possible for buildings to operate better in blackouts and when energy sources change or disappear. Eventually, buildings and communities will need to be energy-independent, producing at a minimum enough energy for their own operation and ideally enough energy for the larger community.

Strategies for reducing energy use from the grid include these:

- At the beginning of the design process, work collaboratively with engineering consultants to optimize systems.
- Design minimal, efficient systems with high-tech and sophisticated controls to improve performance rather than compensate for inefficient design.
- Use energy sources appropriately. Use high-grade energy such as electricity where it is critical, and use lower-grade thermal energy for heating, cooling, and ventilating.
- Once building systems have been optimized, use renewable energy for building operation.

Use Environmentally Preferable Building Materials

The careful selection of materials and products can conserve resources; reduce impacts of harvesting, production, and transportation; improve building performance; and enhance occupant health and comfort.

Buildings are major consumers of materials. Materials affect building performance and user comfort. There are environmental impacts at every stage of a material's life, from extraction, transport, and manufacture to use and final recycling or disposal. Typically, these consequences, generally borne elsewhere, are easily ignored.

Environmental effects must be considered over the complete life cycle of the material. How are materials made, and what are they made from? Selecting durable, regionally appropriate building materials and using them efficiently to enhance the performance of a building are essential elements of sustainable design. For example, engineered lumber can use up to 75 percent more of the wood fiber in a tree than sawn lumber; resource-efficient framing can reduce lumber use by 25 percent or more; and structural slabs can serve as finish floors, eliminating the need for additional finishes.

Individual building materials are typically part of wall, floor, or roof assemblies. It is important to understand how these assemblies work as systems, and how changes in one material can affect other materials in the assembly, the performance of the assembly as a whole, and the building.

Strategies for using environmentally friendly materials include these:

- Do not design buildings larger than needed.
- Select materials and building systems engineered for maximum efficiency, and eliminate unnecessary materials.
- Use durable materials and construction systems. Buildings that last longer use fewer resources over time.
- Avoid irreplaceable and endangered resources. This goes beyond avoiding old-growth redwood; consider irreplaceable habitats as well as individual resources. Consider the forest, not just the trees.
- Use renewable, well-managed resources.
- Use recycled, recyclable resources. Avoid recycled materials that are toxic or cannot themselves be recycled.
- Avoid materials that generate high levels of pollution during manufacturing, extraction, use, or disposal.
- Select materials with low embodied energy. Intensive use of fossil fuels contributes to global warming and other forms of pollution.
- Use materials that help conserve energy. For example, use thermal mass for energy storage, light reflective surfaces for daylighting, and radiant barriers and insulation to conserve heating and cooling energy.

▶ See Environmentally Preferable Product Selection (7.2) for guidance on selecting and specifying building construction products with higher levels of environmental performance.

Plan for the Long Term

Sustainable design seeks to maximize ecological, social, and economic value over time.

Buildings represent a huge investment of capital, resources, and energy, and if they are to be sustainable, they need to last. Buildings last when their inhabitants and communities value them. Aesthetics, suitability of purpose and use, and adaptability to new uses all contribute to long life. Several strategies can help ensure this outcome.

Design new buildings so they can be more easily adapted to accommodate inevitable changes of use. Buildings that are designed too tightly to their programs are often more difficult to adapt. Buildings with longer structural spans and a separation between the structure and the skin and interior walls are generally easier to remodel. Higher ceilings provide more daylight and can make the space more adaptable to new uses.

Designing adaptable buildings does not mean they have to be infinitely flexible or programmatically neutral. Given the rapid rate of change, it may be that buildings, more than most things, can provide some needed sense of permanence and stability. Good design is the key; people will adapt to well-designed, well-built, contextually sound buildings.

Reducing the amount necessary to build is a significant contribution to sustainability. Projects may be "right sized" by, for example, multiplying uses for a space or putting circulation outside when climate and circumstances allow. A good strategy is to design buildings that can be easily expanded.

As well as accommodating changes of program or use, buildings need to be able to adapt to changes in energy, water, and material resources. Buildings that can use future fuels and technologies will last longer than those that rely on limited resources or technologies that will be obsolete long before the building itself. Buildings that perform well "unplugged" will be more likely to stay in use when energy sources change.

When designing for durability, structure is critical. Buildings located where there is a chance of extreme events such as earthquakes or hurricanes need to be designed to withstand such events. Separation of building structure and skin helps make this possible by easing access to finishes so repairs can be made without destroying the structure. The building envelope is also important. Durable materials that age gracefully and are carefully detailed to protect against water or vapor intrusion will extend the life of a building.

Strategies for taking the long view include these:

- Design for adaptability to accommodate future changes in program and use.
- Design for versatility to accommodate future changes in technology.
- Design for durability by using materials, construction methods, and structural systems that will withstand weather, long-term use, and catastrophic events.

Take Advantage of Collective Wisdom and Feedback

Sustainable design recognizes that the most intelligent design strategies evolve over time through shared knowledge within a large community.

Feedback about design and construction processes serves many purposes, from improving building operation to improving construction practice. How well sustainable measures work, or how they could be modified to make them more effective, will be useful information for all practitioners.

It is now widely viewed that commissioning of building systems should be required before building occupancy and use. *Building commissioning* is the process of ensuring that systems are designed, installed, and functionally tested for effective operation and maintenance for an owner's operational needs. *Retrocommissioning* is the systematic investigation process applied to existing buildings to improve and optimize operating and maintenance procedures.

Performance can also be monitored over the life of a building. With baseline data created at commissioning, building performance can continue to be improved as users and uses change. Recent studies by the Pacific Energy Center have shown that performance improves dramatically after commissioning, levels out after two years, and then begins to decline again. It is evident that buildings, especially those with more complicated control systems, need to be recommissioned every two to three years to provide feedback and maintain optimum performance.

Postoccupancy evaluations compare actual building performance to energy models of designs and demonstrate the success or failure of adopted strategies. They can be used to improve building performance and ultimately to improve the analysis tools themselves. Learning how well buildings work for their occupants is a key feedback component rarely utilized by designers. Postoccupancy surveys can gauge satisfaction with many factors, including comfort, lighting, acoustics, and indoor air quality.

Materials and building assemblies can take longer to evaluate, as they are tested against time and climate for durability and longevity. It is worthwhile to visit constructed projects periodically or to contact maintenance staff to see how materials are performing. Architects must also look to studies outside the construction industry for information on whether the extraction and manufacture of materials are harmful to habitats or to human health.

Lessons learned can be disseminated in case studies to establish a body of precedent that future designers can learn from. Professional lectures, conferences, and seminars are also good places to gather and disseminate information and to discuss topics with colleagues.

Strategies for obtaining feedback on the success of design efforts include these:

- Undertake postoccupancy surveys.
- Install equipment to monitor the ongoing performance of building systems.
- Create short feedback loops by designing smaller, simpler buildings and more accessible building systems.
- Develop a common language of building metrics readily understood by designers and laypeople—the equivalent of miles-per-gallon for buildings.
- Disseminate lessons learned. Share with colleagues what does and does not work.
- Create a shared set of precedents by developing a body of case studies.
- Share test results for new materials and methods of construction.

INTEGRATED DESIGN

Traditionally, architects worked closely with builders to design and construct a building and all its systems. Today, architects often develop a concept, then rely on engineers to design the systems and "make it work," and further rely on builders to interpret the design once it is complete. Sustainable design revisits the earlier model, creating a multidisciplinary team of consultants, including builders, to evaluate and identify the best choices for building systems throughout the project delivery process. This team approach is employed from very early in the project, even before programming.

Sustainable design relies on this collaborative approach, now referred to as "integrated design." The process brings the entire design team together at key points in the design process to discuss ways that site design, building form, and mechanical, electrical, and other systems can complement each other to create an effective solution. While not always possible, it is also beneficial to include the construction team in the design process. Synergies and trade-offs occur throughout design and construction, and including the entire team in these discussions allows for educated decisions that benefit the whole project.

Integrated design may require that architects and consultants take on tasks outside their typical roles. Civil engineers design biologically based storm water treatment systems, electrical engineers design daylighting and photovoltaic systems, mechanical engineers consider how thermal mass and glazing affect their system design and model air and heat flows in increasingly sophisticated ways, and architects expand their understanding of all of these systems and how they relate to the building design. Integrated design may also require consultants outside the normal design team. Biologists or ecologists, for example, might participate in planning for a highly sensitive site. Integrated design may also require an unconventional communication process and method. How the design team members share information and ideas among themselves and with other stakeholders can significantly affect the eventual performance of the building and the satisfaction of its users.

SUSTAINABLE ACTIONS IN PROJECT DELIVERY

Outlined below are the typical phases of design and a sampling of strategies related to a sustainable, integrated design process.

Predesign

- Form a multidisciplinary design team.
- Complete a site analysis, including watershed, climate, solar access, views, soils.
- Set and prioritize sustainable design goals.

Schematic Design

- Incorporate considerations for light, air, views, water collection, reduced site disturbance, and so on.
- Reduce demand on M/E/P systems through passive design strategies.
- Create an initial energy model, then respond to the results by adjusting the building design.
- Use a physical or virtual model to analyze daylighting effects.

- Estimate water use based on potential building systems, potential water catchment, and landscape design.
- If proposing unusual systems of any kind (structural, mechanical, water treatment, etc.), visit the local jurisdiction to discuss code requirements.
- Evaluate the schematic design against sustainable design goals.

Design Development

- Refine the design based on information gathered in schematic design.
- Reevaluate the design using computer and physical models.

Construction Documentation

- Thoroughly document all materials, systems, and details that may not be familiar to the plan checker or builder.
- If appropriate, create a narrative of the high-performance systems to enhance understanding by the construction team.

Construction

- Conduct a construction kick-off meeting that includes discussion of the sustainable design goals, strategies, and construction methods.
- Require written plans for erosion control, waste management, indoor air quality, and commissioning.
- Require that the general contractor have an on-site supervisor who is responsible for the sustainable design requirements, including construction waste management and indoor air quality measures.

Occupancy

- Commission all building systems prior to occupancy.
- Provide a building flush-out period prior to occupancy if necessary.

- Incorporate information in the operating manual about environmental aspects of the design and hold a training session for building owners, operators, and if appropriate, occupants.

Postoccupancy

- Evaluate building performance at one-year intervals.
- Recommission systems periodically (e.g., two to three years) to address operational problems and adjust building support systems.
- Learn from the successes and failures of the project, and share this knowledge with others.

EVALUATION TOOLS AND GREEN BUILDING RATING SYSTEMS

Several tools and rating systems have been established to evaluate the performance of green buildings or their particular attributes. Some tools provide qualitative evaluation, some provide quantitative evaluation, and others provide both.

Several computer programs can be used to evaluate energy efficiency, such as DOE-2, Energy–10™, and eQUEST®, which have been widely used to help design buildings and meet energy codes. Programs used to predict daylighting effectiveness include Radiance, Lumen Micro, and the Lightscape visualization system. These tools provide valuable feedback during design and can help designers make decisions about components as diverse as wall assemblies, thermal mass, window size and glazing, and mechanical system size and type. They are particularly helpful in maximizing the use of passive design strategies when used early in design. Physical models can also be used to predict daylighting effectiveness and to help determine building fenestration that will provide effective winter solar gain, summer heat avoidance, and glare control.

Green building rating systems are intended to measure the environmental performance of proposed designs and finished buildings and to help building owners and designers set performance objectives. One of the oldest and most successful rating systems is the Austin Energy Green Building Program®, first used to rate homes and now suitable for commercial projects as well. This program created a rating that measured the environmental performance of a house and created an identifiable brand that became desirable in the Austin, Texas, area.

A number of local, regional, and national rating programs now exist. Nationally, the best-known is the U.S. Green Building Council's LEED Green Building Rating System™. LEED (Leadership in Energy and Environmental Design) rates projects by awarding points in five areas: site design, energy use, water use, materials and resources, and indoor environmental quality. The point total indicates the overall environmental performance of a project. LEED has been a major force for promoting green building and has gained acceptance from a wide range of stakeholders, from designers and clients to manufacturers and construction teams. This acceptance is due in part to the rigor of the certification process and the use of objective national standards and third-party certification to verify that points are given only for what is properly documented once a project is complete.

In the future, rating systems will likely include some form of environmental life cycle assessment (LCA). LCA has been used most widely to evaluate the environmental

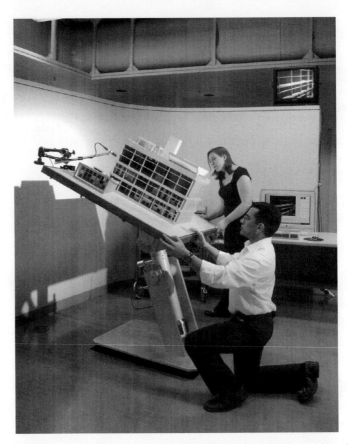

The Heliodon. This device uses a light source and a physical model to simulate the effects of sunlight on a building. This process allows architects to determine during the design phases how a building will function with respect to daylighting, shading, and shadows and to identify opportunities for energy savings.

performance of individual materials and products, but it can also be used to evaluate building assemblies and the entirety of materials in a building. LCA measures all the "inputs" to a finished product, such as raw resources, water, and energy, and all the "outputs" that are the result of manufacturing the product, such as air and water emissions, solid waste, and other by-products. Evaluating the inputs and outputs of like products—different countertop materials, for example—makes educated material selection possible. LCA is, for the most part, still the province of highly specialized consultants, but programs like BEES® (Building for Environmental and Economic Sustainability) and the Athena Institute's software tools—Athena® Impact Estimator for Buildings and Athena® EcoCalculator for Assemblies—are beginning to make such analysis more accessible to architects. BEES software, available free from the National Institute of Standards and Technology, evaluates individual building materials using LCA. The Athena software can provide LCA feedback for whole buildings and for many types of construction assemblies.

Other rating systems and design tools are also available. The widely known Energy Star program of the Environmental Protection Agency rates buildings on energy use. Many utility-sponsored programs across the country, such as the Savings by Design program funded by Pacific Gas & Electric and other California energy companies, also focus on energy use. Another EPA program, Target Finder, helps rate building performance early in the design process for specific building types. State and local agencies across the country have also developed green building guidelines. These programs range from "rule of thumb" suggestions to more sophisticated whole building analyses.

However, none of these rating systems addresses such aspects of building design as aesthetics, comfort, and connection to nature. The Top Ten Measures developed by the AIA Committee on the Environment, outlined earlier, begin to address these intangibles.

AN URGENT CALL

In the last century, the argument that natural resources are "free" capital for human use and the related notion that the natural world has little value until developed were used to justify massive and often thoughtless development and expansion. As the driver of our economic system, growth discounts the value of natural capital and focuses on first cost without consideration of long-term costs or ecological effects. Consequences of this worldview include clear-cut forests, dammed rivers, developed prime agricultural land, and hillsides shaved away in pursuit of stone and ore In addition, cheap and abundant fossil fuels have encouraged wasteful construction and transportation practices. The results of these actions—global warming and a host of other detrimental changes—may damage global environmental systems long before fossil fuels run out.

As society has begun to recognize the urgency of responding to these issues, sustainable design has rapidly grown in importance. The AIA has established ambitious goals to encourage significant reduction of fossil fuel use and emissions in buildings—from 50 percent reduction for all new buildings by 2010 to fully carbon neutral by 2025. Architects have already begun broadening existing planning models and design paradigms, and taking advantage of age-old design strategies and improved building technologies and systems. To reach the goal of sustainability, though, architects can do much to reduce, and eventually reverse, the damages that shortsighted community planning and building design have caused. We urgently need to become stewards of our limited resources and to transform our practices to create a long-term balance between the built environment and nature.

▶ Life cycle cost analysis provides a tool for determining long-term costs for the total building, as well as for building systems and components. See Life Cycle Costing (7.5) for further information.

For More Information

The AIA Committee on the Environment publishes information about sustainable design and its Top Ten Green Projects program on the AIA Web site at www.aia.org/cote. A full version of the Top Ten measures is also available at this address.

In *Sustainable Design: Ecology, Architecture, and Planning* (Wiley, 2007), Dan Williams, FAIA, provides a primer on green building design in which sustainable design concepts are presented along with case study examples.

The 2030 Challenge program links building construction and operation to global warming and proposes a way to reverse the current impact of human development on global warming. For information about how the built environment is specifically related to global warming and the 2030 Challenge, visit www.architecture2030.org.

Natural Capitalism: Creating the Next Industrial Revolution (Back Bay Books, 2000), by Paul Hawken, Amory Lovins, and L. Hunter Lovins, is a good resource for details on the "triple bottom line" and new economic models that consider environmental protection and social equity in addition to profit.

BEES (Building for Environmental and Economic Sustainability) software can be used to evaluate individual building materials using life cycle assessment. The software is free from the National Institute of Standards and Technology. (www.bfrl.nist.gov/oae/software/bees.html)

The Impact Estimator for Buildings and the EcoCalculator for Assemblies, other life cycle assessment tools, are available from the Athena Institute at www.athenasmi.ca.

The Web site of the American Society of Heating, Refrigerating and Air-Conditioning Engineers gives access to the text of the many consensus standards for the design and maintenance of indoor air environments, as well as interpretations of the standards. For example, ASHRAE 62–2003 covers minimum ventilation rates for indoor air quality. ASHRAE created a new technical research group focused on sustainable building guidance and measurements in 2006. (www.ashrae.org)

The U.S. Environmental Protection Agency produces a number of publications on indoor air quality, including information on office buildings, residences, and schools. (www.epa.gov/iaq/pubs)

7.2 Environmentally Preferable Product Selection

Nadav Malin

A comprehensive standard is not yet available for selecting building materials and products according to environmental performance. Building professionals can make more informed choices by becoming familiar with the available information and taking on the challenges associated with this task.

Designers often find themselves trying to assess which products are good for the environment, whether they are trying simply to "do the right thing" or to comply with an agency mandate or company policy. Adding this criterion to the standard list of cost, performance, and aesthetics introduces a whole range of additional issues and considerations for architects to consider.

A variety of programs, initiatives, and tools are available to help architects respond to client requests to use green products. This article provides a general context and some background on many of those tools and initiatives to help architects use them most effectively.

WHAT ARE ENVIRONMENTALLY PREFERABLE PRODUCTS?

Environmentally preferable products (EPPs) are products and materials that—for a given application—represent a better choice than most others from an ecological perspective. The U.S. Environmental Protection Agency, per Executive Order (EO) 13101 (1998), defines environmentally preferable products as "products or services that have a lesser or reduced effect on human health and the environment when compared with competing products or services that serve the same purpose."

In theory, use of these products in a building will result in the lowest ecological burden and/or the highest ecological benefit. In practice, however, the web of relationships between the built and natural environments is so complex that it is not possible to determine with certainty what all those burdens and benefits will be. Despite this uncertainty, some indications based on what we do know suggest which products and materials are better from an environmental perspective.

Green Products in the Context of Green Building

When considering EPPs or green products, it is important to remember they only exist as independent entities until they are used in a building. Once these products and

Although in this article the term "EPP" is used to refer to environmentally preferable products, note that the same initials are sometimes used to describe an environmentally preferable purchasing program rather than a product.

Nadav Malin is vice president of BuildingGreen, Inc., and serves as editor of *Environmental Building News*, executive editor of *GreenSource* magazine, and coeditor of the *GreenSpec* product directory. He is a faculty member and chair of the Materials and Resources Technical Advisory Group for the U.S. Green Building Council LEED Rating System. Nadav has contributed to numerous publications on the environmental aspects of building materials and consults and lectures on sustainable design. (The original version of this topic appeared in Handbook Update 2005.)

PART 3: THE PROJECT

materials have been erected, applied, or installed, they are part of the building. Considered in this way, the environmental performance of an individual product in isolation is less important than the performance of the group of products that form a building. The constellation of products that make up a building inherits the environmental burdens associated with each product. At the same time, how a building is designed, constructed, and used contributes significantly to its environmental impact.

The construction process itself can affect the environment in ways such as habitat disruption, erosion, noise, and pollution emissions from construction equipment. Once a building is occupied, its ongoing operation requires a constant flow of resources (e.g., energy, water, and maintenance supplies) and generates corresponding emissions and waste. These resource demands and waste streams, whether related directly to the facility or more to the activities of the occupants, are influenced by the characteristics of the building in which those activities take place. For example, whether or not facilities are available to help occupants recycle waste materials can determine how much material is separated for recycling.

Finally, when a building no longer serves its intended function and is renovated, altered, or demolished, yet another series of environmental impacts takes place, primarily in the form of disposal or dispersal of the materials. Buildings containing large amounts of hazardous materials, such as asbestos, lead dust, or mercury, may contaminate the local environment.

Many environmental impacts associated with the construction, operation, and decommissioning of a building are at least partially determined by the products and materials initially chosen for the building. In this sense, the environmental impact of a building as a whole is the sum of the environmental burdens each product carries and the impacts associated with assembling, using, and discarding those products and materials.

Varying Definitions of EPP

The initials "EPP" are used differently in different contexts, although these uses are generally closely related. The EPA, many other federal agencies, and state and local governments have programs to promote environmentally preferable purchasing. These EPP programs are intended to promote the use of environmentally preferable products and services, as long as they are available within the cost and performance constraints of the agencies. Unfortunately, most of these programs provide relatively little guidance on what exactly constitutes a preferable product, although that situation is improving.

Some limited EPP guidance is available from the Federal Trade Commission as a result of its effort to manage the claims manufacturers and suppliers make about their products. The FTC has indicated that when manufacturers claim a product is preferable on an environmental basis, they should be able to back up that claim with evidence that the product has a comprehensively lower environmental impact than competing products. Having a lower impact in just one area, such as recycled content, is not sufficient. Therefore, manufacturers should clearly qualify the scope of any claim of environmental preferability.

GREEN ATTRIBUTES OF PRODUCTS AND MATERIALS

For a range of social and cultural reasons, certain characteristics of building materials have been widely adopted as indicators of environmental preferability. These "green attributes" include recycled content, low indoor chemical emissions, and the possibility of using a product in its natural state, in other words, with minimal manufacturing. Because of general familiarity with these attributes, products with any one of them are often selected for use in a building in place of other products, even though the others may, in some cases, have a lower overall environmental impact.

Most existing EPP programs, including purchasing mandates from government agencies and voluntary programs such as the U.S. Green Building Council LEED

Green Building Rating System®, are based on specific green characteristics of products. Sometimes these green attributes are targeted as part of explicit societal agendas. In such cases, the term "EPP" is applied as a way of broadening the appeal of what is fundamentally a narrowly focused initiative. In other instances, an agency or organization may actually intend to promote the use of products that are environmentally preferable in a broader sense, but for practical purposes uses a single green attribute as a preferable environmental indicator.

Recycled Content

Promoting recycled content, as an *overall* preferable environmental indicator, is an example of using a specific societal agenda to make particular products attractive. The recycled content prerogative is a response to the problem that emerged when recycling first became popular—the accumulation of collected material that did not have a viable end use. The federal EPA, many state agencies, and other organizations all have programs that promote or mandate the use of materials with recycled content under the mantra of "closing the loop."

Nearly all recycled-content programs distinguish between post-consumer recycled materials, which have been discarded after fulfilling their intended use, and pre-consumer (or "postindustrial") recycled materials. Pre-consumer materials are those that have entered a waste stream before reaching their intended end use, such as paper trimmings at a printing plant. Most definitions of pre-consumer recycled materials specifically exclude those that are reused within a single manufacturing facility or operation, since those materials have never really become "waste" at all. For example, glass manufacturers routinely break off-spec glass at the end of a processing line and melt it again to make new glass.

Further confusing matters, the EPA uses the term "recovered material" to include both post-consumer and pre-consumer recycled material, but other organizations use that term more broadly to include materials that would not qualify as recycled under most definitions. For example, the Composite Panel Association's EPP specification includes logging slash—tree tops and limbs not usable as lumber—and logs from forest thinning operations in its definition of the "recovered fiber" used in making particleboard and medium-density fiberboard.

Bio-Based Sources

In theory, building materials derived directly from plants are renewable indefinitely and, as such, represent a solution to the problem of products whose manufacture adds to the depletion of finite mineral resources. Plant-based materials tend to be less manufacturing-intensive than materials synthesized from petrochemicals, as well. Their structural qualities are typically provided by the cellular structures of the plants from which they are made. Some agricultural products, however, are grown with extensive use of pesticides and herbicides and in a manner that contributes to the loss of topsoil.

The U.S. government has long promoted the use of agricultural materials as a way of supporting farms, most recently in the 2002 Farm Bill, which mandates that federal agencies establish preferential purchasing programs for certain types of bio-based materials. The Department of Agriculture initiative for implementing this mandate includes a program to label bio-based materials and promote new markets for them. Wood, although obviously bio-based, is excluded from the draft regulation because it is deemed to have a mature market. To address concerns about ecological problems with bio-based materials, the Farm Bill includes a screening process based on environmental life cycle assessment.

Other incentives to promote bio-based materials, such as a credit for using rapidly renewable materials within the LEED rating system, also exclude most wood products on the basis of their relatively long rotation time. This exclusion of wood is at least partly driven by concerns among environmentalists about the impact of logging on sensitive and threatened ecosystems. These concerns are further addressed through the introduction of certification programs for good forestry practices.

Low Chemical Emissions

In response to concerns about indoor air quality in buildings, the off-gassing of chemicals from building materials and furnishings is increasingly being scrutinized. Many of the substances under investigation fall into the category of volatile organic compounds (VOCs), a term that describes carbon-based compounds that occur as gases under ambient temperature and pressure conditions. Some VOCs are known to cause adverse health effects and discomfort, and many contribute to smog. Not all VOCs are harmful, however, and some (both harmful and benign) occur naturally in the environment.

The off-gassing of VOCs and other substances is measured by placing a sample of the product or material in a stainless steel testing chamber and collecting and then analyzing the gases emitted into that chamber. The Carpet and Rug Institute began using this process in the early 1990s as the basis of its Green Label program, which certifies that emissions of total VOCs and certain specific compounds from carpets do not exceed specified thresholds. Beginning in 2004, the Green Label program was replaced with the more robust and stringent Green Label Plus program.

The lab that developed and still implements Green Label Plus for the carpet industry, Atlanta-based Air Quality Sciences, Inc., expanded the program to other industries via the nonprofit Greenguard Environmental Institute. Greenguard establishes allowable chemical emission thresholds for a wide range of materials used indoors and certifies products that do not exceed those thresholds. Greenguard is referenced in the LEED for Commercial Interiors program as an approved certification program for furniture systems. More recently, the furniture manufacturers trade association, BIFMA International, introduced its own similar standards for testing indoor emissions from furniture.

In California, a specification was developed for state office buildings using a similar type of chamber testing for products but with a different list of chemicals and allowable concentrations to determine compliance. This specification is codified in Standard Practice for the Testing of Volatile Organic Emissions from Various Sources Using Small-Scale Environmental Chambers. The California protocol has become the basis

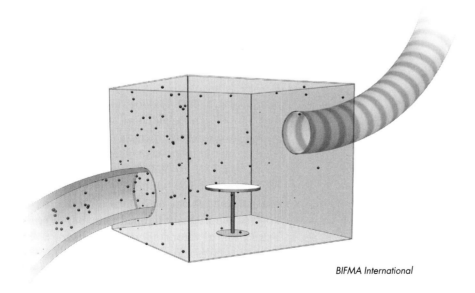

BIFMA International

Off-Gassing Test Chamber. Technicians test for emissions from a product by placing it in a sterile, stainless steel chamber and analyzing air samples from the space.

of the FloorScore certification program for resilient and hard surface flooring and the Indoor Advantage Gold product certification program from Scientific Certification Systems (SCS). SCS also provides the LEED-compliant certification program Indoor Advantage™.

While both Greenguard and the state of California rely on testing methods using stainless steel chambers, their programs differ in other ways. Greenguard requires samples to be collected directly from the manufacturing line and tested immediately to capture the worst-case emissions. California calls for a two-week conditioning period before samples are tested to get a more accurate reflection of conditions when a space is occupied. One explanation for this difference in protocol is that Greenguard emphasizes compounds that have been shown to affect building occupants right away (acute effects), while California is more focused on chemicals associated with long-term health problems and has much stricter limits on those chemicals than Greenguard. However, a new standard from Greenguard—targeted specifically at products for children and schools—incorporates the California thresholds based on long-term health concerns.

Natural and Minimally Processed Materials

Although there are few formal ways to reference or certify natural materials, designers and their clients generally consider natural or minimally processed products to be environmentally preferable. Included in this category are natural fiber carpets and fabrics, natural stone floors, cork, linoleum, and bamboo. The use of wood is omitted from this category, at least in North America. In the United States, concerns about the destruction of domestic old-growth forests and deforestation in the Amazon and other tropical rainforests have discouraged some designers from embracing wood as a green material. In Europe, however, wood is generally considered an ecologically sound material choice.

To assuage concerns about the sustainability of wood, several certification and labeling systems have been developed to provide some assurance that wood from certain sources is a good ecological choice. The most widely accepted system is from the Forest Stewardship Council (FSC). This international organization establishes regional forest management plans based on its "Principles and Criteria for Forest Stewardship" and then accredits third-party organizations to certify forestry operations for conformance with these plans. The FSC also requires certification of every organization in the chain of custody for the wood to ensure that wood from certified well-managed forests is not inadvertently mixed with uncertified wood.

A number of countries, including Malaysia and Indonesia, have developed their own forest certification programs, but these programs have failed to establish credibility among wood buyers, primarily in Europe. In response, the programs have been merged with the FSC system to meet FSC requirements. In North America, the Canadian Standards Association (CSA) and the American Forest & Paper Association (AF&PA) have created other certification programs, which are preferred by most of the forest products industry. Over time, both the CSA National Standard for Sustainable Forest Management and the AF&PA Sustainable Forestry Initiative® have evolved to a level of rigor that seeks to match that of the FSC system. Proponents of the industry-supported systems argue that their programs are now equivalent to those of the FSC, but many environmentalists are unconvinced. Given the complexity of the systems and the ecological and business environments in which they are used, comparing them is not easy.

Low Embodied Energy

Another indicator used to measure environmental impact is the amount of energy used to create a product. This metric is sometimes called "embodied energy," "embedded energy," or the "energy intensity" of a product. Measures of embodied energy include the quantity of fuels and electricity used to mine or harvest raw materials, transport them, and process them into a product ready for delivery to a construction site. The embodied energy of a product is not something that can readily be found on a label or manufacturer's Web site, but some international researchers have estimated embodied energy figures for certain product groups.

Embodied energy is often reported in units of BTUs per pound, or gigajoules per tonne. For these figures to be useful in comparing products, it is necessary to also consider the weight of the material in question and how much of it is needed to perform a given function. For example, concrete may have lower embodied energy than kiln-dried lumber on a per-pound basis, but if it takes many more pounds of concrete to perform the same job, the lumber needed to support a structure will likely have lower embodied energy. The comparison is complicated even further by the question of durability or longevity. If the concrete structure will last significantly longer than the wood structure, that additional longevity should also be factored into the comparison.

LIFE CYCLE ASSESSMENT: A COMPREHENSIVE APPROACH

The environmental product characteristics or attributes described above are widely referenced as preferable indicators, in part because they are often based on relatively accessible information. It is widely acknowledged, however, that they are merely indicators and do not accurately reflect the full environmental performance of a product.

Ideally, EPP claims would be based on comparisons of overall environmental performance. The most common approach to determining the environmental performance of a product is through life cycle assessment (LCA).

Environmental LCA is a science that attempts to quantify the resource and material input, and product and pollution output, over the entire life cycle of a product. Based on this inventory of energy and material flow, LCA characterizes the environmental burdens associated with each type of input and output, thereby quantifying the overall environmental burdens of a product.

Life Cycle Costing vs. Life Cycle Assessment

LCA is not related to life cycle costing (LCC), a methodology commonly used by engineers and financial managers to determine the dollar cost of ownership of a particular item. Life cycle costing accounts for the initial cost of an item, the cost of operating and maintaining the item, the time it will serve, and any costs associated with its eventual disposal. The result of this calculation is what the item will cost the owner throughout its service life. Life cycle assessment, on the other hand, quantifies environmental performance rather than financial cost (although they are often related). LCA also extends the definition of "life cycle" to include where a product comes from (raw materials extraction and manufacturing) and where it ends up after its service life is over.

The resource flows that are quantified in an environmental LCA are typically broken down according to life cycle stage: raw material extraction, manufacturing, transportation, construction, use, and disposal or reuse. In each stage, environmental performance is measured in terms of input (energy, water, resource materials) and output (emissions, effluents, and solid waste and co-products).

Extraction or harvesting of raw materials. The energy used to operate heavy equipment (primarily in the form of diesel or other fossil fuels) is the major input for the extraction and harvesting of raw materials. Output includes pollution associated with burning these fuels, any runoff or erosion into surface waters, and other negative effects on the immediate environment of the operation. The raw material—whether logs, ore, petroleum, or some other material—is also an output.

Manufacturing. Input into a manufacturing process includes all the raw materials and the fuels that provide energy to drive the process. In the case of electricity, the input includes the fuels used to generate the electricity at the power plant. Water is also often used in the manufacturing process.

Output from manufacturing typically includes pollutant emissions to air and effluents to water, as well as any solid waste generated. The desired output is the product itself, along with any usable by-products.

Transportation. Transportation of raw materials and finished products consumes energy and releases pollutants from the use of that energy. Some modes of transportation are more energy-efficient and less polluting than others.

Construction. Construction also consumes energy, and it requires the input of products or materials. The desired output is the completed building. Unwanted output includes air emissions from construction equipment, erosion from the construction site, and job-site waste.

Use. When a product or material is in place in a building, it has become part of a larger whole. It may contribute to reduced (or increased) energy use by the building. Its ongoing maintenance and operation (for example, floor finishes and cleaning supplies, or toner and paper for copiers) will require input. Once put in place, a product or material may release pollutants to the indoor or outdoor environment.

The resource input and pollution output vary significantly depending on the type of product, how it is applied or installed in a building, and how building occupants interact with it. For many materials, these concerns continue over the life of the product. For example, within a few years, the energy used to counteract unwanted solar gain through a window can exceed the energy used to manufacture, transport, and install the window.

Disposal/recycling/reuse. At the end of its useful life, a product or material may become solid waste that must be disposed of, or it may become the raw material for some other product. In some cases, a product may be salvaged and reused intact. If a product has hazardous components, such as the mercury in thermostats or fluorescent lamps, those materials become a potential environmental burden that must be managed appropriately.

Practical Problems and Limitations of LCA

Quantifying all the types of input and output over the entire life cycle of a product is no simple matter, and many assumptions and variables come into play. How broadly to set the boundaries of the study is not always obvious. For example, vehicle fuel is always considered as transportation input, but what about other fluids, such as lubricants and hydraulic fluids? And should the energy and materials used to manufacture and maintain the vehicle or the roads on which it travels be included? If researchers do not address these questions consistently in different studies, the results may not be comparable.

LCA studies have not been performed for many products and materials because so much work is required to produce comprehensive results. Thus it can be hard to interpret good LCA data for a product because of the lack of comparable information for similar products. To further complicate matters, the more comprehensive a study is, the more environmental burdens it is likely to report. As a result, product manufacturers have an incentive to limit the boundaries of their studies.

Translating the Flow of Resources and Waste into Environmental Impacts

When the inventory for a life cycle assessment is available, the next step is to estimate the environmental impacts associated with the use of resources and waste streams created (termed the "flows"). For example, the life cycle of any given product is likely to include emissions of carbon dioxide, nitrous oxides, and methane, all of which are greenhouse gases that contribute to climate change. To estimate the collective impact of emissions from a product on climate change, however, it is not enough to simply add up the quantities of each emission because each gas affects the environment to a different degree. For example, according to EPA figures, methane is 21 times more powerful than CO_2 as a greenhouse gas, and nitrous oxide is 310 times more powerful than CO_2. Thus, the overall climate change impact associated with a product is calculated in units of CO_2 equivalents. CO_2 equivalents are arrived at by multiplying each greenhouse gas by its appropriate factor and then adding the resulting figures together.

A similar process is used to estimate environmental impacts in other categories. In the case of human health and eco-toxicity, however, the list of compounds that can contribute to impacts in each category can be very large, and estimating how much each one contributes is quite complicated. The categories used by the EPA environmental impact assessment protocol—the Tool for the Reduction and Assessment of Chemical Impacts, or TRACI—include ozone depletion, global warming, acidification, eutrophication, photochemical smog, human carcinogenic effects, human noncarcinogenic effects, human health criteria, eco-toxicity, fossil fuel use, land use, and water use.

Interpreting the Results

Aggregating the input and output of the various flows into impact categories is not easy and does not give designers the simple answers they want. When two products or materials are compared, typically one will score lower (better) in some impact categories and the other will score lower in other categories. In other words, a comparison may not make it clear which product or material is preferable. It is tempting to choose the one that is lower in more categories or that appears to be lower overall. However, that solution assumes that all the categories are equally important, which is not likely.

To provide the simple answer designers seek, some tools allow the user to combine the results across all the impact categories to create a single score for each product's environmental impact. Reducing the results to a single score in this way requires a means for comparing unrelated impacts. This is usually done by assigning a level of

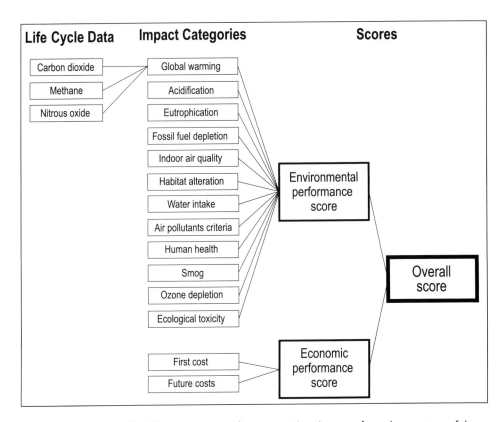

Sample Calculation of Building Product Performance. This diagram from the creators of the BEES LCA software tool illustrates how specific life cycle inventory data (on the left) is consolidated into a limited set of impact categories, then into a single environmental score, and finally into a combined environmental and economic score.

importance or a weighting factor to each category. These factors are then used to combine the category scores into one final score.

This single-score approach makes it easy for someone using the information to compare one product to another, but it requires a great many assumptions and approximations. Unfortunately, unsuspecting users may employ these scores without recognizing their limitations. Not only are the weighting factors highly debatable, but in many cases entire impact categories are omitted from the analysis simply because data was missing or a methodology to make them fit into the calculations was not available. Because of these limitations, any system that claims to reduce LCA results to a single score for each product should be used with caution.

EPP STANDARDS—AN INTERIM SOLUTION

Designers, specification writers, and purchasers are interested in a straightforward indication of which products are environmentally preferable. If LCA data were widely available, consistently developed, and reliable, it would be a relatively simple matter to choose products with the best LCA score, or to provide for preferential purchasing of any product with an LCA score that exceeds the industry average for its product category.

The field of LCA is not yet mature enough for that approach to be practical, however, so a number of organizations have developed EPP standards as an interim solution. These standards are intended to draw from the best available information—including LCA data when it is available—to create a framework for identifying environmentally preferable products.

Using the results of available LCA studies to determine which product attributes are most significant in terms of environmental impact is one way in which LCA benefits EPP standards. The identified attributes can then become an area of focus within the standard. For example, for materials and equipment that directly affect energy use in a building, those impacts usually dominate the life cycle effects associated with the material, making energy use a key aspect of its EPP standard.

Another way products are distinguished in EPP standards is in the difference between materials that are used in large quantities in a building, such as concrete, steel, and wood, and those that are used in relatively small amounts, such as door hardware and wiring. For the materials used in quantity, issues of resource depletion and transportation loom large. For example, even though aggregate used in concrete is considered a relatively low-impact material, in metropolitan areas of the eastern United States, local supplies have been largely depleted and aggregate is sometimes imported by ship from the Caribbean.

For low-volume materials, concerns about by-products, pollution from manufacturing, and hazardous constituents tend to be more significant in an EPP approach. Data cable that is rated for use in plenums (not in conduit), for example, is made with halogenated insulation and sheathing to reduce its susceptibility to fire. Fire codes fail to test for toxic releases from these cables before they ignite, however, and there is evidence these halogenated compounds can release incapacitating acidic gases at temperatures well below their ignition points.

Taking all these variables into account, EPP standards spell out a series of criteria that products in a given category must meet to conform to the standard. Some of these criteria may be absolute requirements, while others may be offered as part of a series of options for achieving conformance.

Different Approaches to EPP Standards

EPA has created a toolkit and spelled out some guidelines for federal agencies and others who are interested in establishing environmental preferences for certain products. Nevertheless, EPP standards are relatively new as a tool for screening products, and organizations developing them have taken different approaches on certain key aspects. Developers face the question of whether the standards should be structured for a simple pass/fail result or provide more nuanced results to be interpreted by end users. The pass/fail approach would be analogous to the UL® designation from Underwriters Laboratories. A product would either be listed or not; the label would have no detailed breakdown of how the product performed in the testing.

A more nuanced approach to standards might be similar to the nutrition labels on food packaging. Most consumers are well-enough informed about nutrition that they prefer to see some detailed information on calories per serving, sodium content, and fat content, as opposed to a simple "healthy" or "unhealthy" label.

Another key question about EPP standards is whether they should require third-party certification or allow companies to self-certify their products. The third-party certification approach is certainly higher in integrity, but it can become quite expensive and thus could limit participation.

Materials and LEED

Since it was first released in 1999, the U.S. Green Building Council LEED Rating System has had a significant effect on the U.S. building industry. To a large degree, it has driven the demand for green buildings. As a result, designers and product manufacturers are particularly interested in the LEED approach to material selection. There are now several different rating systems under the LEED umbrella: LEED for New Construction (LEED-NC), LEED for Existing Buildings, LEED for Commercial Interiors, and LEED for Core & Shell. More rating systems are in a pilot-testing phase or under development.

Each of the LEED rating systems certifies the environmental performance of a building based on conformance with a series of criteria on the LEED checklist. One or more points is assigned to each item on the list, depending on the level of achievement required to conform to that item. A number of the LEED criteria relate directly to the selection of products and materials. Although handled slightly differently in the different LEED rating systems, these criteria all include incentives to use the following types of materials:

- Salvaged materials
- Materials made from recycled content
- Locally harvested and manufactured materials
- Materials made from rapidly renewable resources
- Wood from well-managed forests
- Low-emitting adhesives and sealants
- Low-emitting paints and coatings
- Low-emitting carpet
- Composite wood products made without urea formaldehyde binders

Points are offered based on the use of materials with a specific green attribute. As described earlier, these attributes serve as proxies for a preference based on overall environmental performance. This approach could lead to the use of materials that have certain green attributes, but are not as desirable from a comprehensive life cycle perspective. LEED offsets this limitation, to some extent, by virtue of the fact that designers using LEED are not working with each criterion in isolation, but looking to achieve points over the whole system. Thus, if a carpet has high recycled content but does not meet the low-emissions requirement, it may be avoided in favor of one that meets both criteria.

A great many LEED points do not address material choices explicitly, but their performance requirements indirectly lead to the use of green products. This is especially true in relation to plumbing fixtures, appliances that use water, and energy-related equipment such as chillers, light fixtures, fans, and pumps. The LEED program specifically excludes mechanical, electrical, and plumbing equipment from conformance with the criteria based on material attributes. As a result, there is currently no incentive for designers to select equipment that is both efficient and high in recycled content or locally manufactured. Future versions of the LEED criteria are expected to adopt a more comprehensive LCA approach to product selection, in place of the proxy criteria that are used now.

SOME GUIDING PRINCIPLES

A comprehensive, reliable, and accessible system for choosing environmentally preferable products is not yet a reality. Until LCA-based approaches become more robust and available, architects must base their decisions on less ideal methods. In light of this situation, what options do designers have? Here are some principles to keep in mind:

1. *Think big-picture.* Apply "life cycle thinking" to product choices, even when reliable life cycle data is not available. To do this effectively, learn a bit about where products come from and how they are made. When specifying a product based on certain green characteristics, ask questions about aspects of the product's environmental performance in other areas. A carpet may be low in indoor emissions, for example, but is it also efficient in its use of raw materials? Was it manufactured using renewable energy sources?

2. *Focus on big-ticket items.* Most of a building's materials-related impact on the environment is associated with the materials used in biggest quantities. Therefore, it makes sense to spend time evaluating the structural materials and materials used extensively for cladding or interior finishes. It does not pay to spend a lot of time seeking to optimize the environmental performance of products and materials that are only used in a small area of a project. However, if you are pursuing a LEED point for low-emitting materials, you may have to track down products that conform to the requirements even if they are used in a very limited way.

3. *Remember to look at the usage phase.* With all the information available on recycled content and renewable materials, it is easy to forget that a product's environmental impact once it has been installed in a building can easily overwhelm upstream considerations. Any exterior cladding, insulation, or equipment that can help reduce a building's energy use should be given careful consideration. Interior finish materials that do not require strong cleaning agents and frequent refinishing are also helpful.

4. *Seek life cycle data when comparing dissimilar products.* The environmental impact of two very different materials being considered for the same application may vary in different areas, so it is hard to know which is better overall without good life cycle data. With or without such data, though, the final decision often comes down to a value judgment. For example, an architect may have to choose between agricultural materials with relatively high manufacturing energy requirements and petrochemical-based materials that require less energy to manufacture.

5. *Differentiate products based on specific green attributes.* This technique is useful when products are otherwise quite similar. In the case of ceiling tiles, for example, reflectivity is important because it can lower lighting energy demand. However, if two products are similar in terms of performance characteristics, choosing one with higher recycled content and/or lower indoor emissions makes sense.

6. *Look for reliable resources on which to base decisions.* When reviewing these resources, consider factors such as the stated values of the organization, the methods it uses, the expertise of its personnel, and who pays its bills.

For More Information

Several organizations are working to create and implement standards for environmentally preferable products:

Green Seal is an independent, nonprofit organization that develops standards, certifies products to those standards, and publishes reports with product recommendations. Green Seal employs an open, consensus-based process in the development of its standards. It relies on outside funding to support this process, which limits the number of standards it can develop. (www.greenseal.org)

Scientific Certification Systems, Inc., offers third-party certification services based on systems that range widely in scope, from single-issue claims to comprehensive claims of environmental preferability. (www.scscertified.com)

McDonough Braungart Design Chemistry provides certification of products that conform to its Cradle-to-Cradle protocol for defining environmental preferability. (www.mbdc.com)

The Institute for Market Transformation to Sustainability endorses standards from other organizations and develops its own standards in an effort to provide incentives for companies to pursue sustainable practices. Its SMART© Consensus Sustainable Product Standards provide market definitions and rating systems, as well as other information, for building products, textiles, and flooring, as well as other materials. (www.sustainableproducts.com)

The Healthy Building Network manages the Pharos Project, an open-source collaborative initiative to collect information on building products and materials and score them across multiple performance areas. (www.pharosproject.net)

Other organizations are active in related areas:

The Construction Specifications Institute has developed *GreenFormat: A Reporting Guide for Sustainable Criteria of Products* and is preparing an online database manufacturers can use to publish green information on their products. Information is available at www.csinet.org or www.greenformat.com.

Greenguard Environmental Institute (GEI) certifies products that meet its published standards for low indoor air emissions. Interior furnishings, fixtures, and finishes are well represented in its database of certified products. (www.greenguard.org)

Forest Stewardship Council (FSC) produces guidelines for certifying forest products that originate from forestry operations that are managed in an environmentally and socially responsible manner. FSC also accredits organizations, such as SCS and Smartwood, that can certify compliance with the FSC's guidelines and bestow permission to use the FSC label. (www.fscus.org)

U.S. Life Cycle Inventory Database Project, coordinated by the National Renewable Energy Laboratory and the Athena Sustainable Materials Institute, publishes publicly available and transparent life cycle inventory information on basic industrial processes and materials. This information can be used to improve consistency across life cycle assessments of competing products and reduce the time and effort needed to produce those assessments. (www.nrel.gov/lci)

The Athena Sustainable Materials Institute offers reports and software for performing LCA analyses of building assemblies and whole buildings using generic materials. The Athena software is relatively accessible to professionals with limited LCA training. (www.athenasmi.ca)

Building for Environmental and Economic Sustainability (BEES) is a free software tool from the National Institute for Standards and Technology that facilitates LCA-based comparisons of a range of building materials and furnishings, both by generic category and by brand-specific product. (www.bfrl.nist.gov/oae/software/bees.html)

BuildingGreen Suite is an online resource that includes the full contents of *Environmental Building News* (EBN), *GreenSpec® Directory* of building products, and other resources. The articles from *EBN* apply life cycle thinking to compare material options for specific applications, and include detailed product reviews that address both the functional and environmental performance of green products. *GreenSpec Directory* lists products that have been screened by the editors (manufacturers do not pay for listings). (www.buildinggreen.com)

Green Building Materials, 2nd edition (Wiley, 2006), by Ross Speigel and Dru Meadows, provides guidance on selecting and specifying green products and materials.

AIA MASTERSPEC Section 018113, Sustainable Design Requirements (ARCOM, 2006) provides proposed language for a Division 1 specification section on environmental requirements, including suggested language on criteria for various materials. (www.arcom-net.com)

GreenSource, Environmental Design & Construction, and *eco-structure* are all magazines that cover green building in general, including articles on green materials. (www.greensourcemag.com, www.edcmag.com, www.eco-structure.com)

7.3 Design Phases

Bradford Perkins, FAIA, MRAIC, AICP

Design is the keystone of architecture practice. Translating needs and aspirations into appropriate and exciting places and buildings requires great skill, as well as attention to broader public concerns.

There are many ways of looking at the design process and the design practices in which architects engage. Design decision making can be seen as private and intuitive—for, in many respects, it is—and yet many of the decisions designers make are broadly discussed and rationally analyzed. Design can be seen as complex and inaccessible, and yet it is taught to and practiced by thousands of capable architects—and hundreds of thousands more in a wide array of other disciplines. Design has moments of great inspiration and deep insight—but most of all it requires hours, months, and years of hard work.

Design is a continuous activity. It "begins" somewhere deep in the recesses of the project definition process; somewhere someone has an idea that ultimately takes form. Design never really ends; important design decisions are made at every stage of the process. Even once opened for use, buildings are constantly modified and adapted—redesigned, if you will.

Most projects *do* have beginnings and ends. These points are defined by the contracts written to provide planning, design, construction, and facility management services. Design, however, is the central issue at every step. The design process has been compared to a learning curve on which each step exposes the design team to new opportunities, new problems, and new knowledge about the situation at hand.

DESIGN FACTORS

Every project situation is different. Each presents different requirements, limitations, challenges, and opportunities, as well as a unique set of cultural, environmental, technological, and aesthetic contexts. Design brings to the surface the major considerations inherent in a situation. It is both a problem-seeking and a problem-solving process. Although the particular combination is specific to each project, some of the most important design factors follow.

Architecture is the art of inquiry.

Arthur Ericson

Building design begins with the architect's analysis, understanding, and response to the base of data, intentions, and impressions collected in the process of discovering what there is to know about the project.

Bradford Perkins is the founder and senior partner of Perkins Eastman Architects, a large New York–based architecture, interior design, and planning firm that has won many design awards. He lectures regularly at architecture schools and other institutions, and has published several books and numerous articles on design and architecture management issues.

Program

All building projects have a series of aspirations, requirements, and limitations to be met in design. This information is included in the "program" for the project. The program may be short or long, general or specific, descriptive of needs, or suggestive of solutions. The program may be provided by the client or may be developed as an additional service by the architect.

Community Desires

A growing number of public agency approvals influence design. Many owners and their architects must adjust their designs to satisfy community groups, neighbors, and public officials. These design adjustments are often ad hoc efforts to meet objections or to gain support rather than direct responses to codified requirements.

Codes and Regulations

Regulatory constraints on design have increased steadily. Beginning with simple safety requirements and minimal land use and light-and-air zoning, building codes and regulations have grown into a major force that regulates every aspect of design and construction.

Site and Climate

The site is, of course, a major influence. Physical characteristics (e.g., size, configuration, topography, and geotechnical issues), climate (wind, solar orientation, temperatures, humidity, and precipitation), environmental factors (views, existing vegetation, drainage), access, adjacent land uses, and many other site factors are considered in reaching the final design.

Building Context and Existing Fabric

The surrounding environment has been a site feature of major influence on many buildings. In addition to obvious effects on building configuration, neighboring structures or landscape can influence the materials, fenestration, color, and detailing chosen for the final building design. Of even more importance are any existing structures that may be incorporated into the building being designed. A growing percentage of building design problems call for working within the constraints of an existing structure.

Building Technology

Building configuration, materials, and systems are rarely arbitrarily chosen and are only partially based on aesthetic criteria. For example, the floor-to-floor height required to accommodate structural, mechanical, lighting, and ceiling systems in a cost-effective manner varies significantly from an apartment house to an office building or research facility. Similarly, horizontal divisions are often set to achieve maximum efficiency of layout; thus, office fenestration may be based on one module and housing on another. In still other cases, these dimensions may be dictated largely by mechanical systems or even by the knowledge and preferences of the local construction industry.

Sustainability

In its broadest scope, sustainability refers to the ability of a society, ecosystem, or any ongoing system to continue functioning into the indefinite future without being forced into decline through exhaustion or overloading of the key resources on which that system depends. For architecture, this means design that delivers buildings and communities with lower environmental impacts that also enhance health, productivity, community, and quality of life.

▶ The combination of all data collected and analyzed during programming sets up the decision-making process that leads to the synthesis that is the core of concept design. See Programming (6.3) for a discussion of the programming process.

A building should respond to the order of the city and the order of the land.

Romaldo Giurgola, FAIA

It is becoming increasingly important for us to identify those unique aspects of each project, and explore through design, that will not only result in significant contributions to modern architecture but will also help solve the myriad environmental issues that we now face.

Craig Curtis, AIA of the Miller/Hull Partnership

Special Issues

External factors, such as rapidly rising energy costs or increased security concerns, can also be major design influences. Desire for energy conservation, for example, can be a major determinant in the choice of most major building systems. Security concerns can influence everything from the site plan and entry sequence to the space program and building materials.

Cost

The best things happen when you have to deal with reality.

Robert Venturi, FAIA

Since most projects have limited budgets, cost considerations significantly influence almost all issues from building size and configuration to material selection and detailing. Cost is rarely a simple issue. Budgets may be fixed by the amount of financing available, or they may be flexible and come into focus in the design process. Often a construction budget emerges from an analysis involving the owner and the entire project team. Some owners are willing to increase initial budgets to achieve overall life cycle cost savings, but in most cases, there is a limit to the funds available for construction. Once defined, this limit has a major influence on subsequent design decisions.

Schedule

Because there are so many outside influences on design, it is common for the architect to make design decisions out of sequence or in time frames so compressed that some alternatives cannot be explored. For example, an alternative requiring a time-consuming zoning variance may be discarded in favor of one that can keep the project on schedule. In another project, it may be necessary to commit to a final site plan early in the process—before the building "footprint" drawn on the site plan has been fully designed.

The Client

Designs of purely arbitrary nature cannot be expected to last long.

Kenzo Tange

A central ingredient in most successful design projects is a good client. Some clients have a clear idea of program, budget, and other project objectives, including the final appearance of the building. Others look to their architect to help them define the project objectives, as well as to design a building that meets these goals. In both cases, the effectiveness of the marriage between client and architect is a major factor throughout the design process.

DESIGN PROCESS

Almost every project has a unique set of factors that combine to make each problem different. For their part, individual architects approach design in different ways and with different values and attitudes. While design has a certain linear quality (it involves analysis, synthesis, and evaluation), it is widely acknowledged the process has nonlinear qualities as well. The latter are sometimes described as "flashes of insight" and "creative leaps."

Increasingly, we recognize that the design process works with information and ideas simultaneously on many levels. Thus, the architect can be thinking simultaneously about the overall geometry of the building, the ways in which a wheelchair-bound person might experience the spaces in the building, and the materials of which the building will be constructed.

The challenge is to determine, depending on the circumstances, whether to design the project from the inside out or outside in. Often the constraints of the site, program, or budget will lead to an optimum resolution of these seemingly independent criteria.

Mustafa Abadan, FAIA, of Skidmore Owings & Merrill

At the same time, we view designing as reciprocal action and reflection. Architects process requirements, issues, and variables, and produce tentative design proposals. Examination and criticism of these proposals lead to new proposals. Each proposal reveals more about the problem and suggests an appropriate solution.

Analysis

However nonlinear it may be, design involves analysis. An initial step is to identify, analyze, confirm, and organize the factors that will influence the development of a design concept. Architects typically take available data from the economic feasibility, programming, and site analysis steps and organize them into a form that allows the information to be used in building design. The data may be provided by the owner or developed by the architect in the course of programming or site analysis services. The analyses—often pursued in parallel—are described in the paragraphs that follow.

Program analysis. Many architects translate the words and numbers in the program statement into graphic terms, developing charts, bubble diagrams, and sketches of design concepts. Most architects stress the need to be actively involved in the program as a critical starting point for design. As Herbert McLaughlin of Kaplan McLaughlin Diaz notes, "It is vital to understand that programming is inevitably and necessarily a part of the design process. The ideas of design should be able to influence and often change the size and, inevitably, the shape of spaces as well as their interrelationships and, frequently, their relationships with nature." Even when the owner has prepared a program, it is useful to spend time confirming the program and converting it into understandable and usable design information.

Site analysis. Important site data are typically organized into a graphic record of relevant physical, cultural, and regulatory factors. When organized in a common scale and format, these data often begin to point the way to design solutions. Ideas also present themselves in time spent walking the site, understanding both it and the surrounding community.

Zoning and code analysis. Concurrent with the site analysis, many firms convert zoning and other code issues into graphic form. In the case of complex urban zoning codes, this may include graphic representations of the zoning envelope—height, bulk, setbacks, and other limits imposed by the code. When combined with parking and load requirements, exiting considerations, building area and height limitations, and other code requirements, this analysis can help the architect begin to shape the program into a building mass that fits the site well.

Documentation of existing conditions. Many building design problems must work with or include existing structures in the solution. It is essential, therefore, to establish clear and accurate documentation of existing conditions, either by converting existing drawings into base sheets for use in design or by creating new measured base drawings. In addition to providing basic dimensional data for design, this step typically identifies existing physical and code problems.

Scheduling. The project schedule is a project management tool, but at times, it can also become an important factor in design. Such major scheduling issues as project phasing, the time it takes to seek variances, and the sequencing of design decisions to accommodate fast-track scheduling can all influence the development of a design concept.

Cost. It is important to analyze a project budget to understand its implications for the building design. Virtually all project budgets are limited. The architect must make careful use of funds, directing them to those decisions that appear to be most important to the success of the design solution. An experienced architect can usually identify the size of this discretionary portion of the budget, as well as establish clear guidelines for the basic system selections to take place during the design.

Construction industry practice. Concurrent with schedule and cost analysis, most architects consider the aspects of local construction industry practice relevant to the design assignment. This can range from availability of materials and labor to commonly used materials, systems, and detailing.

Design precedents. In many firms, an important aspect of the initial analysis is the critical assessment of relevant precedents from projects facing similar or related program, site, context, cost, or other design issues. It is common for architects to familiarize themselves with the design of buildings that deal with similar issues to stimulate solutions for their own design problems.

The design process can be summarized in four words: ingenuity, hard work, and talent.

Hugh Stubbins, FAIA

Synthesis

Building design begins with the architect's analysis, understanding, and response to the base data collected and analyzed. The combination of all this into a unified solution is the synthesis that is the core of concept design.

Most architects start with an analysis of the base data and then work through sketches, talking, and thinking—reciprocal action and reflection—until they reach the level of understanding necessary to form a concept. While the particular design stimuli, organizing principles, areas of emphasis, and aesthetic vocabularies may be unique to a particular architect or firm, and while firms may synthesize these in different ways, there are some common tasks in design. These are discussed in the paragraphs that follow.

Establishing design goals. The client and design team have goals for the project, expressed formally or informally. These goals create functional and aesthetic guidelines for judging design decisions, and the project objectives help establish priorities when trade-offs must be accommodated in the design solution. Compromises between budget and quality, appearance and energy efficiency, and hundreds of other decisions have to be made within the context of an understanding of project goals and priorities.

Evolving a design concept. With the design goals in hand, the architect develops a design concept—or perhaps several. This may be a plan concept, the selection of a geometric form, a decision to mass the building vertically or horizontally, or the use of an organizing element (e.g., a central mall for the interior spaces). The concept might be based on a particular image or a historic precedent. It may employ a "design vocabulary" of formal and aesthetic ideas that will govern the development of the design. Whatever the underlying principles, it is common for architects to develop several representations and variations to help them understand and articulate the evolving design concepts.

Evaluating concept alternatives. Working with these possibilities and variations, most architects have developed a process for narrowing them down to a set of workable concepts. In some cases, the selection of alternatives is based on a point-by-point evaluation of the concept against the original project objectives. In other cases, it is an intuitive judgment based on experience. In most instances, it is a combination of both.

Beyond the first conceptual steps, the process becomes more complex. In all but the smallest and simplest projects, the steps that follow development of a concept involve a team of people. As the design team is expanded, most firms begin to involve the engineers, specialist consultants, and cost consultants necessary to help test and develop the selected concepts. Architects generally agree that early participation of other project team participants leads to a more efficient and coordinated design effort. For example, engineers not only guide the selection of many building systems but also define the size, area requirements, and preferred location of these systems. In more complex design problems, engineers often help analyze the feasibility, relative cost, and other critical factors of major design options.

CONTRACTUAL FRAMEWORK

Design is undertaken within a contractual framework that

- Outlines design tasks and requirements.
- Identifies specific responsibilities for design, including those of the architect and the owner, and possibly of third parties.
- Establishes a schedule, including starting and completion dates.
- Often defines design phases with interim milestone dates and owner approvals to proceed.

This contractual framework is established in the agreement between owner and architect. Design activities may be described in detail or, in the case of small or limited-scope projects, in a few sentences. The AIA owner-architect agreements have established five project phases:

In their work and writings, leading design principals express the importance of the nonrational, the indescribable, and the poetic in the creation of successful building design. At key points, judgment, taste, intuition, and creative talent take over.

- Schematic design
- Design development
- Construction documents
- Bidding or negotiation
- Construction

AIA Document B101–2007, Standard Form of Agreement Between Owner and Architect, assumes that a clear definition of the client's program exists. Either the owner brings the program to the start of design or the architect provides the service as part of professional services. It also assumes the process can move ahead in a linear fashion through a series of phases—each of which results in a more complete definition of the design—until the project is sufficiently detailed to go into documentation for bidding (or negotiation) and construction.

Reality is rarely so orderly. Evolving program requirements, budget realities, increased knowledge of site considerations (such as subsoil problems), public agency reviews, and many other factors make it necessary to go back and modify previous steps. Fast-track scheduling—breaking design into "packages" and awarding some before others are completed—further complicates matters. Design moves forward, but rarely in the clear, linear fashion implied by the contractual phases. Building information modeling promises to blur the distinctions between phases even more. As this tool has more architects designing and documenting projects in three dimensions, many of today's later-phase decisions will inevitably become part of the early design process.

Nonetheless, a contractual framework is important. It imposes an order on the process. When there are phases, the architect brings the design to an interim level of development, the owner reviews and approves it, and the project moves forward based on a mutual understanding.

Schematic Design

AIA Document B101–2007 identifies the first phase of services as schematic design. Although the completion of this phase may be defined slightly differently for each project or by different clients and design teams, certain objectives and products are commonly agreed upon.

Schematic design establishes the general scope, conceptual design, and scale and relationships among the components of a project. The primary objective is to arrive at a clearly defined, feasible concept and to present it in a form that achieves client understanding and acceptance. The secondary objectives are to clarify the project program, explore the most promising alternative design solutions, and provide a reasonable basis for analyzing the cost of the project.

Typical documentation at the end of this phase includes the following items:

- A site plan
- Plans for each level
- All elevations
- Key sections
- An outline specification
- A statistical summary of the design area and other characteristics in comparison to the program
- A preliminary construction cost estimate
- Other illustrative materials—renderings, models, computer simulations, or additional drawings—needed to adequately present the concept

Drawings. These are typically presented at the smallest scale that can clearly illustrate the concept, perhaps 1/16" = 1'-0" (1:200 in SI units) for larger buildings and 1/8" = 1"-0" (1:100) or 1/4" = 1'-0" (1:50) for smaller buildings and interiors.

Outline specifications. This is a general description of the work that indicates the major system and material choices for the project and provides the information necessary to communicate the appearance and function of the building.

Preliminary estimate of construction cost. The schematic design estimate usually includes a preliminary area analysis and a preliminary construction cost estimate. The level of detail is necessarily limited; the estimate may be broken down by major trades or by systems (e.g., foundations, structure, exterior closure, interior partitions and finishes, plumbing, mechanical, electrical, site work, and equipment). This may also include a preliminary analysis of the owner's budget, with recommendations for changes based on site, marketplace, or other unusual conditions encountered in schematic design. It is common for preliminary cost estimates made at this stage to include contingencies for further design development, market contingencies, and changes during construction.

AIA Document B101–2007 calls for a preliminary estimate of construction cost based on current area, volume, or other unit costs.

Additional services. As part of schematic design, the architect may agree to provide services such as life cycle cost analyses, energy studies, tenant-related design studies, economic feasibility studies, special renderings, models, brochures, or promotional materials for the owner. These are included as "additional services" in the AIA B201 form of owner-architect agreement (Standard Form of Architect's Services).

Approvals. The final step in schematic design (and, for that matter, in each design phase) is to obtain formal client approval—in writing, if at all possible. If approval is given verbally, it is a good idea to send the client a letter confirming the architect's understanding of the approval. (You may ask the client to initial the letter and return a copy.) The importance of this step cannot be emphasized enough. The schematic design presentation has to be clear enough to gain both the understanding and the approval of the client.

Design Development

Design development is the period in which the approved schematic design receives the refinement and coordination necessary for a really polished work of architecture. The decisions made in schematic design are worked out at a scale that minimizes the possibility of major modifications during the construction documentation phase. Working drawings and specifications are complex and intricately interrelated; changes in those documents are costly and likely to lead to coordination problems during construction. Thus, the primary purpose of design development is to further define and describe all important aspects of the project so that what remains is the final step of creating construction documents.

During design development, the design team works out a clear, coordinated description of all aspects of the design. This typically includes fully developed floor plans, sections, exterior elevations, and, for important areas or aspects of the building, interior elevations, reflected ceiling plans, wall sections, and key details. Often these become the basis for the construction documents. The basic mechanical, electrical, plumbing, and fire protection systems are accurately defined if not fully drawn. No major issues that could cause significant restudy during the construction documentation phase should be left unresolved.

The deliverables of the design development phase are similar to those of schematic design: drawings and specifications that fix and describe the size and character of the project, as well as any recommended adjustments to the preliminary estimate of construction cost. The design development phase usually ends with formal presentation to, and approval by, the owner.

Design development may be a substantial undertaking, or it may be a much briefer transition from schematic design to construction documentation. Some owners require extensive schematic design services, with much of the project "developed" by the time this phase ends. For some straightforward or repetitive projects, the schematic design may be sufficiently clear for both owner and architect to proceed directly to

DESIGN DOCUMENTATION BY PHASE

	Schematic Design	Design Development
Purpose	Drawings and other documents to indicate the scale and relationship of project components.	Drawings, specifications, and other documents fix and describe the project's size and character as to architectural, structural, and M/E/P systems and materials and other elements as appropriate. DD documents can be used to prepare preliminary construction cost estimates.

Drawings

	Schematic Design	Design Development
Title and project data sheet	Not generally required. If provided on larger projects, the project name, owner and team names, location map, possible rendering or other graphic may be included. Rarely includes sheet index, code, standards, etc.	Project name, owner and team names, possible location map, rendering or other graphic. Sheet index all disciplines. Occasionally includes code, standards, etc.
Site plan	Conceptual site plan showing land use, general building location, general parking arrangement, major site features.	Scaled site plan with building locations tied down dimensionally. Street lines, property lines, setbacks and easements shown (survey required). Preliminary grades reviewed with civil engineer. Parking lots with overall dimensions.
Floor plans	Conceptual building plans. Major plan components or departments defined. Departmental blocking and stacking indicated. General structural grid and major M/E/P components indicated. Rarely includes detailed dimensions.	Scaled building plans with building perimeter, structural grid and selected critical areas or elements dimensionally fixed. Major M/E/P systems determined (rooms, shafts, etc.) and indicated. Interior partitions shown at approximate scale. Doors and window systems indicated. Rooms or doors rarely numbered.
Enlarged floor plans	Generally not required except for highly detailed special areas.	Provided only for major typical elements if required (e.g., health care patient room, hotel room, correctional jail cell).
Reflected ceiling plans	Generally not required except for highly detailed special areas.	Occasionally included for major critical elements if required to define major design elements (e.g., health care patient room, major public lobby space). Otherwise, ceiling features indicated by vignette on floor plan.
Exterior elevations	For each major building façade, generally indicating fenestration, entrances, and design vocabulary.	For each major building façade, indicating material, fenestration, entrances, special features, floor levels, and vertical dimensions.
Enlarged elevations	Generally not required except for highly detailed special areas.	Generally not required. Include if needed to define for major critical elements.
Building sections	Conceptual building section to illustrate building shape or spatial features.	Occasionally provided where required to illustrate building shape or spatial features.
Wall sections @ 1/8" or 1/4"	Not applicable.	Not applicable.
Wall sections @ 3/8"	Not applicable.	Full-height sections conveying basic building configuration provided for predominant or typical locations. Indicate materials, structure, foundations, flashings, etc.
Enlarged details @ 1 1/2"	Generally not required.	Generally not required.
Door schedules, door types, frame types	Generally not required.	Not generally required. Specific door types may be shown for some facility types (e.g., correctional facilities, hospitals, etc.). May be generally defined by generic door schedule using matrix or covered by outline spec.
Common door details	Generally not required.	Generally not required.
Room finish schedules	Generally not required. If necessary, generally defined in outline specifications.	Not included as a room-by-room schedule. May be generally defined by generic room type using matrix or covered by outline spec.
Partition types	Generally not required.	Generally not required although some types may be indicated for some facility types. May include standard guide sheet to establish quality, but not referenced on plans.

(continued)

	Schematic Design	Design Development
Elevator sections and details	Generally not required.	Generally not required.
Stair sections and details	Sections generally not required except for highly detailed decorative stairs. Details generally not required	Not required for exit stairs. Occasionally may be needed to define ceremonial or monumental public area stair.
Interior elevations	Rarely included except as a background for other documents (e.g., background in atrium section).	Provided in presentation format for major public spaces. Occasionally provided in sketch format, possibly freehand, for casework, millwork, toilets, elevators, etc.
Interior details	Generally not required. When needed, provide conceptual sketches.	Generally not required. When needed, provide conceptual profile sketches.
Specifications		
	General outline, or bullet point list, briefly describing each primary building system.	Short form specification briefly describing primary materials and building systems. Abbreviated, does not include execution sections.
Optional Documentation		
Renderings and presentation models	Requirements determined by design team. Generally reimbursable.	Requirements determined by design team. Generally reimbursable.

Adapted from a chart created by Grant A. Simpson, FAIA, © HKS, Inc.

construction documents with confidence. In these instances, design development may be brief (or in the most extreme cases, nonexistent).

In some project delivery approaches, the owner may wish to secure construction cost commitments before the design is fully developed—thus reducing or even eliminating the design development phase. This reduces one uncertainty but introduces another, for there is likely to be debate about what was included and not included in a cost estimate made on the basis of preliminary, partial, or "scope" documents.

Design During the Implementation Phases

While most design issues should be resolved by the end of design development, some will continue to be refined, resolved, or modified during the construction documentation, bidding and negotiation, and construction phases of the project.

During construction documentation, additional design issues may emerge as the design team works out the final material and system selections, details, and dimensions. Examples of such issues may clarify this point:

- The final detailing and specification of an exterior wall, including the selection of specific products and manufacturers, inevitably leads to modification of the dimensions, color, transparency, and other aspects of the wall.
- The detailing and specification of interior partitions, openings, and finishes involve a large number of minute design decisions, from the location of joints to the selection of the final materials or acceptable alternates.

Once a contractor or construction manager is selected, the need to make design decisions continues. The bidding and negotiation process inevitably leads to proposed substitutions or modifications in details to achieve cost savings or to simplify the construction process. Usually some of these are accepted and must be successfully integrated with the remainder of the design.

Design continues even through the construction phase. The construction documents require interpretation and elaboration. Field conditions and other problems may force design changes. Confronted with the reality of the project, the owner may request

Design is a continuous process, often broken into phases to gain commitment to more general decisions before they are developed in detail. Here is one view of the level of decision making regarding each of a building's functional subsystems as the project moves through design.

Predesign	Early Schematics	Later Schematics or Early Design Development	Design Development or Early Construction Documents
General			
Project objectives	Program interpretation	Design concept elaboration	Floor plans
Project scope	Basic design concepts	Schematic floor plan	Sections
Program codes and regulations	Siting	Schematic sections	Typical details
Project budget	Building massing		
Project schedule	Blocking and stacking		
Delivery approach	Access and circulation		
	Design vocabulary		
	Style issues and constraints		
	Sustainability		
Site			
Site selection	Siting concepts	Design concept elaboration	Site plan
Site development criteria	Site forms and massing	Initial site plan	Planting plan
Requirements for access, circulation, parking, utilities, landscaping, lighting	Access and circulation	Schematic grading, planting, paving plans	Typical site sections
	Views to/from buildings		Typical site details
	Concepts for grading, planting, paving, etc.		Outline specifications
	Acoustics and other site issues		
Foundation and Substructure			
Performance requirements for foundations, excavations, etc.	Subsurface conditions and requirements	Schematic basement plan	Foundation plan
	Impacts of program, energy on under-ground building	Refinement of special foundation requirements	Basement floor plan
	Exploration of special problems	Selection of foundation system	Sizing of key foundation elements
			Outline specifications
Superstructure			
Performance requirements for floor, roof, stair, other structural elements	Relation of structure to spatial organization, elevations, etc.	Structural system selection	Floor framing plans
	Selection of use modules	Outline framing plan	Roof framing plan
	Basic structural module	Sizes of key elements	Sizing of elements
	Initial system selection		Important details
			Outline specifications
Exterior Closure			
Restrictions on exterior design materials, etc.	Approach to elevations, fenestration	Design concept elaboration	Elevations
Performance requirements for walls, doors, windows, etc.	Views to/from building	Selection of wall systems, materials	Key exterior details
	Initial envelope elements sizing and selection	Schematic elevations fenestration	Outline specifications
Roofing			
Performance requirements for roofing elements	Roof type and pitch	Selection of roof system, materials	Outline specifications
	Initial system selection		
Interior Construction			
Performance requirements for partitions, finishes, specialties	Approach to partitioning built-in furnishings	Room designs	Input to plans and elevations
Flexibility requirements	Interior design vocabulary	Layout of key areas	Key interior elevations
	Layout of key spaces	Selection of partition systems, finishes	Initial finish schedules
		Important fixtures or theme elements	Outline specifications
Vertical Circulation and Conveying Systems			
Performance requirements for conveying systems	Basic organization and circulation scheme	Input to plans, sections and elevations	Input to floor plans, framing plans, sections, elevations
	Need for and types of vertical circulation	Sizing of exits, other circulation areas	Outline specifications
	Need for special conveying systems	Basic elevator and escalator concepts	Detailed systems selection
		Other conveying systems concepts	

(continued)

PART 3: THE PROJECT

Predesign	Early Schematics	Later Schematics or Early Design Development	Design Development or Early Construction Documents
Mechanical Systems			
Performance requirements for conveying systems Performance requirements for plumbing, HVAC, fire protection Need for special mechanical systems	Impact of mechanical concepts on building planning Initial systems selection Initial distribution ideas Space allocation for mechanical areas	Mechanical systems selection Refinement of service, distribution concepts Input to plans, sections, and elevations	Initial system drawings and key details Distribution and riser diagrams Input to floor plans, framing plans, sections, elevations Outline specifications Initial equipment list
Electrical and Lighting Systems			
Performance requirements for lighting systems Performance requirements for electrical systems Need for special systems	Approaches to natural, artificial lighting Lighting quality and character Impact of site, design on electrical systems Space allocation for electrical systems	Window, skylight, and glazing design Selection of lighting, electrical systems Service, power, and distribution concepts Input to plans, sections, and elevations	Detailed systems selection Distribution diagrams Key room lighting layouts, ceiling plans Input to plans, sections, and elevations Outline specifications
Equipment			
Delineation of equipment needs and performance	Impact of key equipment items on siting and design	Impact of key items on room design, framing plans, etc.	Input to plans, sections, and elevations Outline specifications Initial equipment list

David Haviland, Hon. AIA (adapted from *The Architect's Handbook of Professional Practice*, twelfth edition)

changes—reinforcing the elemental idea that design "never really stops" but continues through construction and everyday use of buildings and facilities.

For More Information

The AIA Design Knowledge Community maintains a Web page on the AIA Web site at www.aia.org. The site contains information about the mission, policies, initiatives, and special reports of the Committee on Design.

Numerous books and other resources on the general subject of design, designers, design theory, history, and criticism are available. The following sources include a few selected publications that address the design process, including several about presentation techniques.

In *How Designers Think: The Design Process Demystified*, 4th edition (Architectural Press, 2005), architect and psychologist Bryan Lawson delivers a readable discourse on what design thinking entails and how to understand and apply it. Many architectural examples are used. As noted by the publisher, this book is intended not as an authoritative description of how designers should think but to provide helpful advice on how to develop an understanding of design.

Architect Kenneth Allison meshes design and project management subjects into a single discussion in *Getting There by Design: An Architect's Guide to Design and Project Management* (Architectural Press, 1997). Allison addresses fundamental principles for these dimensions of practice in four major parts: project context, decisions and techniques, managing costs and fees, and cultures as action systems.

C. Thomas Mitchell's *Redefining Designing: From Form to Experience* (Wiley, 1993) contains a provocative discussion about why architects and designers need to elevate the importance of client and user needs in building design. In his *New Thinking in Design* (Wiley, 1996), Mitchell presents a series of interviews with thirteen leading international designers committed to client- and user-centered design approaches.

James Marston Fitch's classic *American Building: The Environmental Forces That Shape It* (originally published in 1947 and updated and expanded in 1999) examines how buildings respond to and control environmental forces through building and system design. Stewart Brand's *How Buildings Learn: What Happens After They're Built* (Penguin, 1995) calls for rethinking the way buildings are designed so they may be more readily adapted to ever-changing user needs. Brand's theses are that buildings adapt best when their occupants constantly refine and reshape them and that architects can mature from being artists of space to becoming artists of time.

Christopher Alexander's two classic titles, *The Timeless Way of Building* (Oxford University Press, 1979) and *A Pattern Language* (Oxford University Press, 1977), deal with design approaches intended to let users participate in the design process. In each of 253 patterns, Alexander explicitly links what takes place in various kinds of spaces to the physical layout of the spaces themselves. Collectively, these patterns represent a "pattern language" that allows designers and nondesigners to communicate with each other.

Design Drawing (Wiley, 1997) by Frank Ching and colleagues describes delineation from several perspectives: drawing from observation, drawing systems, and drawing from imagination. A supplemental CD-ROM contains information and instruction elucidating a broad range of drawing concepts through animation, video, and three-dimensional models. Paul Laseau's *Architectural Representation Handbook: Traditional and Digital Techniques for Graphic Communication* (McGraw-Hill, 2000) provides a guide to traditional, new, hybrid, and emerging representational techniques, along with discussion of the roles of each in the design process. The illustrations are organized in relation to an architectural drawing "vocabulary" that includes the design activities of seeing, thinking, and communicating.

Color Drawing: Design Drawing Skills and Techniques for Architects, Landscape Architects, and Interior Designers, third edition (Wiley, 2006), by Michael E. Doyle, covers drawing techniques, color theory, and presentation drawings and includes step-by-step instructions and in-depth guidance. Discussed are innovative ways to create design drawings with color copiers and the latest computer techniques.

7.4 Value Analysis

Stephen J. Kirk, Ph.D., FAIA, FSAVE, CVS-Life, LEED AP, and Michael D. Dell'Isola, PE, CVS, FRICS

Value analysis provides a method for improved decision making. Focusing on important client issues, value analysis techniques allow the designer to critically examine and evaluate alternatives to make better value decisions.

Clients are increasingly challenging architects to provide greater leadership, accountability, and responsibility. Moreover, clients are beginning to expect their architects to understand the clients' business needs so the architecture

Stephen J. Kirk, president of Kirk Associates, has more than thirty years' experience in value analysis, life cycle costing, and facility economics. He is past president of SAVE International and has authored several books on value analysis. Michael D. Dell'Isola is a senior vice president in the Orlando office of Faithful & Gould. He has more than thirty years' experience in life cycle costing, cost management, value analysis, and technical facilitation/partnering.

firm is better able to help its clients achieve their business goals. Owners may also insist that all "viable" alternatives be considered. To address these expectations, a decision-making process is needed for project team members and stakeholders. Value analysis—a team-based technique that can empower architects and engineers to design *holistically* with the goal of "doing more for less"—is such a process. (Note: While the terms *value analysis* and *value management* carry slight differences of meaning, they are used interchangeably in this topic.)

At the outset, the client, the architect, and other key participants must agree on the scope, the budget, and the expectations for the finished project. The objectives for any specific value analysis effort should be consistent with the overall philosophy and objectives of the owner and the project requirements. To achieve the results desired by the client, cost and function must be kept in balance throughout the design and construction process. This balance is the primary goal of value analysis.

Although value analysis is a team-based technique, it is *not* about designing by committee. Rather, it is about getting effective input into the design process to better address alternative solutions with respect to constructability, as well as about complex issues of sustainability, life cycle cost, operational effectiveness, flexibility, and engineering performance. The process of value analysis is also about maintaining accountability for all decisions. This is true for whatever issues the team (including the owner) agrees to focus on.

A CLOSER LOOK AT VALUE-BASED DECISION MAKING

SAVE International, an international organization devoted to value analysis, defines value methodology as "the systematic application of recognized techniques which identify the functions of the project, establish the worth of those functions, and provide the necessary functions to meet the required performance at the lowest overall cost." For architects, this means facilities of high quality at reasonable cost.

Use of this methodology provides an organized approach to analyzing a project by quickly identifying areas in which value improvement may be possible and selecting alternatives that reduce costs while maintaining quality. It encourages thinking creatively and looking beyond the use of common or standard approaches. The VA process emphasizes total ownership costs (life cycle costs) for a facility, rather than just initial capital costs, and leads to a concise understanding of the purposes and functions of the facility.

In striving to make a design solution more effective at *less cost*, value analysis maintains a focus on *function*, whether it is for a total building, an HVAC system, or a flooring material. This function-oriented optimization can lead to solutions that are significantly different (sometimes radically different) from original solutions. On the other hand, cost-oriented optimization is limited to solutions similar to the component itself.

Owners are responsible for defining quality requirements, and the designer is responsible for delivering a design that meets those requirements. However, owner criteria, standards, and other program requirements usually define only lower limits. Designers, with good intentions, often exceed these minimums because they believe better quality is always better value. This is not necessarily true, since value is cost-dependent and the relationship between cost and quality is not always linear. For example, an incremental improvement in quality may come at an incremental cost two to three times greater. When too many items in a facility design approach a vertical cost curve (large increases in cost are required to achieve modest increases in quality), the budget is exceeded and problems occur. To avoid this, a basic quality cost curve can be applied to most building systems.

Value analysis keeps the quality-cost relationship in the forefront by seeking solutions that provide required quality at minimal life cycle cost. Increasing the quality is certainly desirable, especially when added quality can be obtained at a low incremental cost.

Value analysis can be used to evaluate an array of design and project delivery issues, including these:

- LEED® validation
- Sustainable design
- Cost management
- Project management control
- Document reviews and checking
- Constructability reviews

However, when added quality incurs a large incremental cost, decisions must be made with care. Value analysis proposals therefore present a client with the cost implications associated with improving quality. A sound and desirable goal for the architect is to balance quality and initial cost with the goal of achieving the best life cycle cost for a given design.

Interdisciplinary team building and group dynamics are key ingredients of the value analysis process.

Team Building

Value-based analytical approaches use multidisciplinary teams consisting of the owner, user, architect, engineers, constructor, and facility manager. Some team members may be new to the project to maintain independence and help ensure that all viable ideas are explored. If all project stakeholders are not represented, then role-playing the parts of the missing members can be helpful.

Owners find it to their advantage to bring certified value specialists (CVS) on board early to work with the design team to facilitate exploration of a full range of solution options. Because a value specialist brings skills to the team, such as team building, facilitation, communication, and value-based decision-making methods and techniques, architects find this to their advantage.

Members of the VA team must have good communication skills, particularly an ability to explain technical and management issues to an audience from multiple disciplines and backgrounds. An understanding of basic economic principles and knowledge of construction methods and materials are important. Familiarity with scheduling and an ability to sequence events associated with design and construction are essential. A willingness to collaborate with other team members is also important, as the objectives of the team are more important than individual agendas.

The collection of experts assembled for value-based studies varies from project to project. Therefore, a value specialist must have a large network of experts who can address a variety of projects and who work well on teams. Naturally, a large part of the value specialist's skill set is team-building acumen and an understanding of group dynamics in the facilitation of the team.

Group Dynamics

Ideally, a holistic approach to design can be achieved by involving all stakeholders: the owner, users, facility manager, and constructor, as well as the design team of the architect and engineers.

Owners should be involved from the beginning to define their value expectations and to set priorities. The VA process is conducted in team workshop settings in which real-time decisions can be reached. Some workshops evolve into design charrettes to more fully explore a variety of ideas. The success of these team sessions depends on the skill of the facilitator. A good knowledge of group

VALUE-BASED CONCEPTS

Value: The lowest cost to reliably provide required functions at the desired time and place with the essential quality and other performance factors to meet user requirements.

Value analysis (VA): This is the term originally used by Lawrence D. Miles, the originator of the value process. It consists of forming a team to study a project following a six-phase value process. The purpose is to identify ideas that can be incorporated in a design that will improve the value of the project. The U.S. Office of Management and Budget defines value analysis as "an organized effort directed at analyzing the functions of systems, equipment, facilities, services, and supplies for the purpose of achieving essential functions at the lowest life-cycle cost consistent with the required performance, reliability, quality, and safety."

Value engineering (VE): The systematic application of recognized techniques that identify the functions of the facility, establish the worth of those functions, and provide the necessary functions to meet the required performance at the lowest overall cost. Value engineering is performed by an independent team (not associated with the original design) focusing on ways to lower construction cost during the design phase of a project. (Unfortunately, many VE applications have resulted in ideas that negatively impact functions of the project for the sake of reducing costs. Thus, value engineering came to be identified by many as a cost-cutting exercise.)

Value-enhanced design: The use of value analysis in facility design not only to improve the cost but also to improve functionality (e.g., performance, aesthetics, durability, flexibility, quality, etc.). This can be done by either an independent team (like a peer review) or by the original design team.

Value management (VM): Originally used by the General Services Administration (GSA) of the U.S. government, the term describes the process of applying value-based decision making. It is similar to VA but includes applications to nonconstruction study subjects as well, such as organizational and management processes. Value management is synonymous with value analysis.

dynamics is essential to leading the team through discussions of alternatives to arrive at a selected preferred alternative.

VALUE ANALYSIS METHODOLOGY

The power of team-based value analysis is in its methodology, which centers on a six-step problem-solving process that strives to increase value in terms of cost, quality, and performance. The major activities in these six steps include the following:

1. Information gathering and benchmarking, such as creating cost and quality models
2. Function analysis, which is the exercise of stating the project purpose in a verb/noun form
3. Alternative idea generation, which does not stop with the first workable idea
4. Evaluation of ideas using life cycle cost analysis and cost-benefit comparisons
5. Development of ideas into workable, preferred alternatives
6. Providing recommendations to the decision makers in final report

Prior to convening the workshop, the information identified in Step 1 is gathered, along with the following items, which are usually prepared by the facilitator:

- Cost model(s) using the project cost estimate
- Function analyses for total project and pertinent high-cost systems, as appropriate
- List of key issues and value objectives

To allow for sufficient preparation by the workshop team members, the facilitator should assemble a workbook that includes the items listed above along with workshop logistics and objectives. Obviously, the preparation time will be reduced if design team personnel serve on the VA team.

Step 1: Gather Information

In this initial phase, the VA team gains as much information as possible about the design, background, constraints, and projected costs of the project. The following materials typically are gathered for review prior to the initial workshop, at which time this information is made available for reference:

- Project program and budget development documents
- Drawings for the level of design under study
- Outline or definitive specifications of major construction elements
- Space analysis with respect to the program
- Line-item cost estimates for the level of design under study
- Definition of major systems and subsystems, including architectural, structural, mechanical, electrical, site work, and utilities
- Plot plan, topography, and site planning information (photographs are useful when available)
- Verification of utility (power, sewer, gas, etc.) availability for selected site
- Soil report with response for foundation design concepts indicated on drawings
- Special systems or requirements
- Economic data, budget constraints, discount rate, useful life of facility
- Financial information, including staffing costs and other appropriate figures

Step 2: Conduct Function Analysis

In the VA workshop, after reviewing all project data, the project team prepares a function analysis and the relative cost rankings of systems and subsystems to identify potential high-cost areas and areas where value improvements are most likely. For example, a courthouse function analysis would include identifying the functions of key spaces for the facility. The courtroom is where settlements are reached, so the verb-noun description might be "settle cases." Interesting to note is the function of the corridor, however. Some might think the function is to "connect spaces." But it also serves an important function in "settling cases" because many want to settle their cases out of court. Thus, a corridor has an important role in a courthouse other than connecting spaces. Function analysis, using simple two-word (verb-noun) descriptions, allows participants to agree on the functions of facilities.

Step 3: Identify Alternative Ideas

In a collaborative setting, the VA team identifies alternative ideas for accomplishing the functions of systems or subsystems, improving value, and mitigating key risks. New solutions are proposed in an attempt to achieve the desired functions for less total cost and with improved performance. Participants brainstorm a large number of ideas unconstrained by habit, tradition, negative attitudes, assumed restrictions, and specific criteria. No judgment or discussion occurs during this activity.

Many well-accepted techniques exist for idea generation. The guiding principle is suspension of judgment or evaluation of ideas. Free flow of thoughts and ideas without any criticism is essential. The *quality* aspects of the ideas generated in this *quantity* phase will subsequently be evaluated and developed.

Although this portion of the workshop is relatively short (half a day to a whole day), the ideas generated are the key to success of the process.

Step 4: Evaluate Alternatives

At this point in the process, workshop members screen the ideas generated in the previous activity. Next, selected ideas are evaluated according to project needs, the status of the project budget, and the important objectives identified by the owner. The ideas that show the greatest potential for value improvement are then earmarked for further study.

Step 5: Develop Recommended Changes

Next, the team researches the ideas selected in the previous step, preparing descriptions, sketches, and life cycle cost estimates for each. The resulting proposals consist of a description of each recommended change, the cost of implementing it, sketches, and the advantages and disadvantages of making the change. The included cost data indicates the probable magnitude of cost savings (or added cost). As recommendations are developed, it is important for team members to remember that the aim of value analysis is only to make recommendations. The final selection and implementation of changes are the responsibility of the design team and the owner.

Step 6: Prepare Final Report

Value analysis recommendations may be presented in several stages. At the conclusion of the workshop, the team often makes an informal presentation to the owner, designer, and other consultants. The VA facilitator may also meet with the owner and design team after the workshop to help the designer prepare responses and comments on the workshop results and to clarify any misunderstandings that might arise.

The VA team produces a preliminary written report in collaboration with the designer and the owner's representative. This report summarizes the results of the value analysis to date and assures the owner that the final recommendations will meet the VA program objectives. Emphasis should be placed on innovative recommendations that avoid simple cost cutting and are tailored to fit the project, its objectives, and the overall budget.

Value analysis was first used in traditional design-bid-build projects. As success was gained, it was applied to construction management and design-build projects. While the VA methodology is the same for each of these project delivery methods, there are some differences with respect to objectives, use, and timing.

Delivery Method	VA Objectives, Use, Timing, etc.
Design-bid-build	Value engineering is frequently applied *after* the completion of construction documents, making it difficult and cumbersome to incorporate ideas for improving project performance or lowering life-cycle costs. However, the value analysis process is increasingly being initiated in the crucial decision-making stages of schematic design and design development.
CM at risk	Some construction managers include VA as part of their preconstruction services, where it is applied early in the design process. The CM usually manages the analysis with a focus on cost reduction, since the CM firm is "at risk" if the project overruns the budget. Less emphasis is given to improving performance features such as sustainability, better maintainability, reduced energy, or other facility life cycle issues. Project aesthetics also may be compromised in an attempt to reduce the cost of construction. Some owners include incentives to the CM firm for offering ideas to reduce cost.
Design-build	Prior to the selection of the design-builder, VA can be used during the formation of the project scope and program to help define performance criteria. For example, the National Park Service uses value analysis methods to evaluate cost and benefit impacts of setting specific performance specifications and standards. The design-builder also can use VA to help win the project as well as after the contract award. Working with the owner, the design-builder can conduct VA workshops to improve the value of the project with any cost changes being negotiated with the owner. Some owners include incentives for the design-builder who offers ideas to reduce cost.
Design-build-leaseback	With this relatively new project delivery method, the focus of VA changes from first cost reduction to identifying ideas that offer the best long-term value, since the PPP will be a contractual relationship over an extended period of time. LCC is a particularly important tool for the VA team in this situation.

Value analysis often results in savings of 10 to 15 percent of construction costs. In addition, VA teams usually identify another 10 to 15 percent in life cycle cost savings, as well as quality, performance, and other improvements.

The final report presents the researched recommendations for consideration by the owner and the design team. This should be a concise document that contains enough technical description so that anyone not intimate with the project can understand the major issues. Each recommendation should clearly describe both the original and the proposed design concept and demonstrate the advantages, disadvantages, and economic consequences of accepting the proposed change. Summaries should be presented in a manner that allows for a quick review and provides the designer with a simple means for integrating the proposal into the design.

VALUE ANALYSIS TOOLS

Several tools and techniques have been developed for use in value analysis. Following are two of the significant ones.

Function Analysis

Function definition and analysis is at the heart of value analysis. It is the primary activity that separates value analysis from all other "improvement" practices. The objective

PART 3: THE PROJECT

of function analysis is to develop the most beneficial areas for continuing study. To do this, the team

- Identifies and defines both work (task) and (aesthetic) functions of the facility under study using active verbs and measurable nouns. This is often referred to as Random Function Definition.
- Classifies each function as basic or secondary.
- Expands the functions identified in Step 1.
- Builds a Function Analysis System Technique (FAST) diagram.
- Assigns cost and/or other measurement criteria to functions.
- Establishes worth of functions by assigning the previously established user/customer attitudes to the functions.
- Compares cost to worth of functions to establish the best opportunities for improvement.
- Assesses functions for performance/cost improvement.
- Selects functions for brainstorming ideas.

Life Cycle Costing

Life cycle costing is used to assess the economic consequences of various facility design decisions. It is used for three types of analysis:

1. Deciding whether to renovate, build new, expand, lease, or continue the current situation.
2. Establishing the annual facility budget to cover the life cycle costs of the project.
3. Comparing the life cycle costs of various building system alternatives for the purpose of selecting the best alternative for the design.

Typically, energy and maintenance-related analyses are performed during the schematic and design development stages of a project, while the first two types of LCC studies are completed during early planning and programming.

Active application of life cycle costing for the total facility can provide owners with a return on investment (ROI) in excess of 50 to 1, depending on decisions made during the concept/schematic/design development phase of a project. LCC methodology may be applied at any point in the design process, from early feasibility planning through construction and occupancy. As with any heuristic approach, however, LCC's greatest potential is its use in "early stage" decisions.

▶ Life Cycle Costing (7.5) provides detailed discussions about the concepts and methods for determining costs over the total life cycle of a facility or facility components.

▶ For further discussion of emerging project delivery approaches, see Project Delivery Methods (8.1).

UNDERSTANDING VALUE EXPECTATIONS OF THE CLIENT

The value expectations of building owners depend on their perspectives. Value analysis applications first identify the owner's goals, then use appropriate techniques to achieve those goals. Following are a few examples of how value expectations may vary with the goals and perspective of the client:

- *Long-term value.* Most government agencies will stress long-term value. Of particular concern is a maintainable facility. Quality and environmental sustainability are also important as long as the public's perception of the design solutions is that they are not overindulgent.
- *Profitability.* For private industry, profit is the main incentive for VA. Lowering the capital required for facility investment results in greater opportunity to achieve a higher return on investment. Long-term costs are of less significance to private industry because immediate results are demanded from shareholders.
- *Short-term value.* Developers are most interested in projects that can be quickly built for a low price with a high degree of market appeal. VA can focus on developer goals and improve the bottom line and ROI.

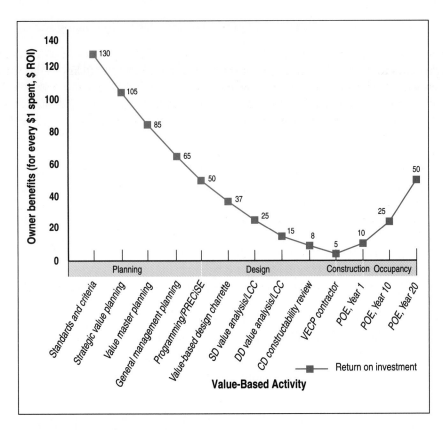

Strategic Value Proposition

VA TRAINING AND CERTIFICATION

Architects should consider joining SAVE International to learn the skills necessary to offer value-based decision-making services. SAVE offers both training and certification in value-based decision making.

TRAINING

Module I, Fundamentals of Value Engineering, workshops provide sufficient information for trainees to be able to participate successfully in future value studies under the guidance of a qualified value specialist, with minimum additional training.

Module II, Advanced Value Engineering, extends the knowledge base of those who wish to become professionals in the value methodology field. Topics include advanced methodology and areas of management. The seminar requires a minimum of twenty-four class hours. Module I is a prerequisite, and it is expected that attendees will have enough practical experience to contribute to the seminar.

Certification

SAVE International maintains a professional certification program to recognize individuals who use value methodology in their principal career and who have met approved education and experience standards. These standards include the following:

- Completion of Module I and Module II training courses
- A minimum of two years of full-time work experience in value analysis or management
- Demonstration of required performance in value studies
- Demonstration of continued growth through learning, teaching, presentations/writing, and contributions to the value management profession
- Submission of an original paper concerning any value-related subject
- Successful completion of the value theory and practice examinations

To assist certification candidates, the SAVE Certification Board has issued a list of topical areas with which qualified value specialists should be familiar.

A PRACTICE OPPORTUNITY

Value-based decision making and value management embody more than traditional approaches to design and can benefit any field of consultation, including architecture. Even when different architects are involved in a project's design and documentation phases, value analysis services can be effectively applied. Such services usually work best with repeat clients, with whom trust and rapport have already been established. An option for providing value analysis services to a first-time client is to come to a project as part of the design or construction management team.

Building owners are recognizing the significant potential returns their facility investments offer, whether for more efficient systems and components, longer-lasting materials, or other sustainable measures. Thus, value analysis represents a growing opportunity for architects seeking to expand their client-oriented practice capabilities. Currently, there are about 200 certified value specialists in the United States. About half of these specialists work in construction. Of those, only about 20 are architects.

Architecture firms that offer value management and analysis services in their project proposals have found this improves their chances of winning commissions and keeping ongoing client involvement. With this true value-added service, architects can demonstrate how project dollars can be effectively reallocated without sacrificing the functional aspects of the project. Often, in fact, the function of a project can be improved through value analysis.

For More Information

SAVE is an international society devoted to the advancement and promotion of value methodology. SAVE offers educational and certification programs as well as a variety of publications on value engineering, value analysis, and value management. Go to their Web site at www.value-eng.org.

The Canadian Society of Value Analysis (www.scav-csva.org) promotes value analysis methodology.

Sustainable Federal Facilities: A Guide to Integrated Value Engineering, Life Cycle Costing, and Sustainable Development (Federal Facilities Council Technical Report No. 142, 2001) provides additional discussion of value-based methods.

VALUE ANALYSIS STUDY EXAMPLE

The following illustrates the process and results of an actual value analysis study that generally follows the methodology previously described in this topic.

Project Description

The facility evaluated in the study was a 77,096 gross-square-foot federal research laboratory adjacent and connected to an existing life sciences center (LSC) on a college campus. The new building is patterned after the existing LSC and is to accommodate long-term research needs.

The facility is to house a maximum of twenty scientists (eighteen in 900 SF wet labs with two spaces for field scientists) and administrative support spaces. Consensus had not yet been reached as to what constitutes a field scientist space, except for having spaces with high computing power and connectivity to broad bandwidth. They had, however, agreed that 900 SF was not required for these

(continued)

areas and that some areas should be reserved with the ability to be partitioned and have exterior windows. This resulted in 2,100 GSF of space being reserved for field scientists along with some open offices for graduate students who cannot be housed on the lab floors.

Laboratory modules. The new lab facility uses structural grid dimensions similar to those in the existing LSC, with the most critical one being the 10'-6" width for each lab. In the other direction, a 30-foot span is used for perimeter laboratory modules and a 25-foot span for core support labs. To gain both structural and functional efficiency, the A/E firm modified the structural span dimensions to permit placement of the 2-foot-by-2-foot interior columns in the corridors so they do not compromise valuable space and usable bench tops in the laboratory spaces. In the office portion, the structural spans are determined by what makes the most sense in relation to the 10-foot width of private offices and system furniture in an open office environment.

Building envelope materials. The building envelope design is similar to the existing exterior of the LSC, which has factory-painted finishes that are relatively easy to match. Matching the masonry material (limestone, brick, and exposed concrete) of the LSC, however, poses a greater challenge. To put a reasonable distance between the existing and new masonry materials to make differences between them less obvious, the portion of the addition that abuts the existing east wing will be clad with metal and glass. The design will also bring daylight into the west end of the addition and provide views to the outside.

Project budget and estimates. The project budget for the construction cost (in FY 2007 dollars) was $24.30 million, and the cost estimate for first quarter of FY 2007 was below the budget at $23.97 million. However, the cost estimate escalates this construction cost to the midpoint of construction at 8 percent per year, resulting in a projected total construction cost of $28.24 million. The budget will also continue to increase at the same rate for cost escalation.

Value Analysis Team and Study Approach

The seven-person study team was composed of representatives from a mix of professional disciplines:

- Architect
- Lab planner
- Civil engineer
- Structural engineer
- Mechanical engineer
- Electrical engineer
- VA facilitator (a certified value specialist)

In a three-day workshop, members of the design A/E team and the client briefed the VA team about the intricacies of the project. The team then used value analysis tools and methods to focus the VA team on the issues, problems, and opportunities presented by the proposed lab project. The objectives for the VA workshop included the following:

- Achieve the basic and secondary functions for the client's facility.
- Generate ideas to increase value for the project (higher performance and quality while seeking lower life cycle costs).
- Improve the flexibility and thus the prospects for long-term use of the facility.
- Identify project risks and mitigation strategies.
- Explore recommendations that ensure an "on budget" response to meeting the basic needs of the facility.
- Identify ideas to facilitate maintenance of the facility.
- Offer suggestions for environmental (LEED) enhancement.

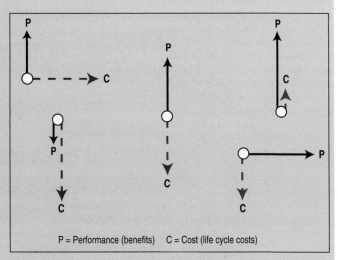

P = Performance (benefits)   C = Cost (life cycle costs)

Value Enhancement. The diagram illustrates five ways a project can enhance value. For example, in the center of the chart an idea might raise performance and also reduce cost. The value analysis team in this example explored ideas in all five categories for value enhancement.

The process for the study consisted of the following VA steps:

- Information gathering
- Function analysis
- Creativity session ("brainstorming")
- Evaluation of ideas
- Development of ideas
- Presentation of recommendations

Information Gathering and Function Analysis

As a basis for this phase of the study, the VA team was provided with the following documents:

- 15 percent submittal: Previous design review findings
- 35 percent submittal: Design binder, project drawings, cost estimate

With the above information and data as references, the VA team developed and used the following to better understand and identify opportunities for value enhancement.

Function logic diagram. Since function analysis is core to any value study, the VA team prepared a function logic diagram to help identify and understand the essential functions of the new facility. This diagram indicates those functions including its core function, which is to support and enable research aimed at discovering new scientific knowledge.

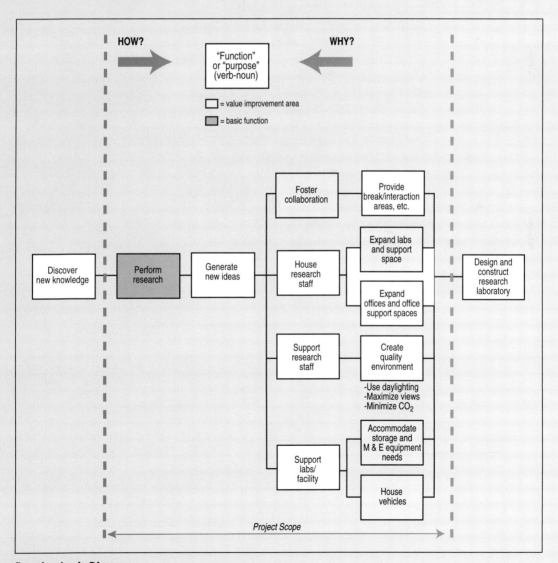

Function Logic Diagram

(continued)

Function Pareto cost model. The VA team prepared a "Function Pareto Cost Model" to profile and evaluate building systems and associated facility functions. The chart describes the item, its function (in parentheses), its associated cost (from the A/E submitted estimate), and VA target worth based on team discussions. This information is shown in a Pareto bar chart (high cost to low cost) to help the team focus on the most expensive functions and target areas for the most significant potential savings.

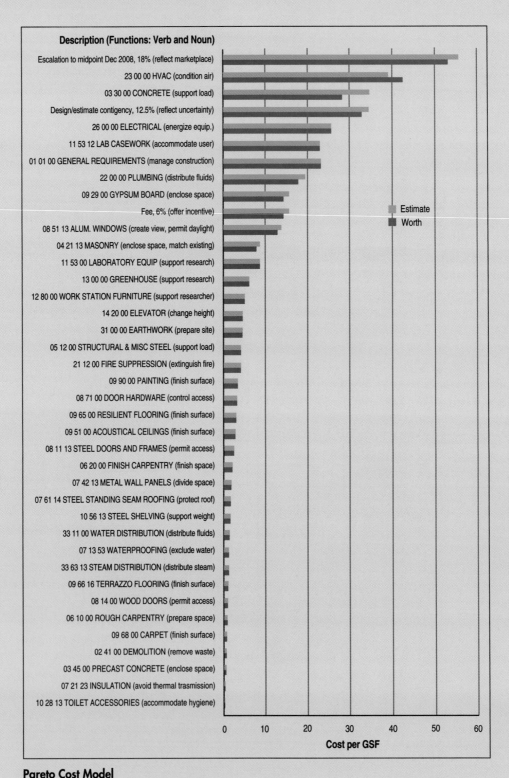

Pareto Cost Model

Life cycle cost model. Overall project life cycle costs were not identified by the A/E, so the VA team relied on historical costs of similar laboratory projects from *Whitestone Building Maintenance and Repair Data 2005–06*. The resulting life cycle cost model is based on this information but adjusted for the project. This pie chart diagram helped the team focus on high-energy, preventive

improving the quality of the project (closing the gaps). The most significant gaps included flexibility/expandability, site planning/image, community values (cultural response), engineering performance, security/safety, operation and maintenance, schedule, and capital cost. A list of issues associated with this analysis is shown in the accompanying figure.

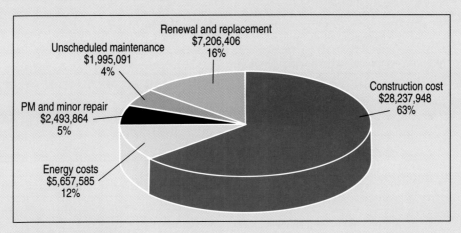

Life Cycle Cost Model

maintenance and minor repair, and renewal and replacement cost items in identifying areas for savings. Largest costs include energy, renewal, and replacement costs. This analysis was based on a twenty-five-year life cycle and a 3 percent discount rate. The costs are shown in present worth values.

Risk model. The client and A/E team prepared a risk model during the workshop to help the VA team identify high project risks and ways to mitigate them. The most significant ones included project schedule, changing government regulations, budget limitations, inadequate subgrade testing, security (visual surveillance of site and building), architectural integration with the existing Bond building, limited site lay-down areas, traffic congestion on site, interference with other work on site, and utility relocations.

Quality model. A quality model helped the VA team identify the elements of quality most important to the success of the project. The model also reflects the client's evaluation of how successfully the quality model elements were satisfied. The differences between the *ideal* and the *current* design were identified as "gaps" for later value improvement. During the brainstorming portion of the VA workshop, the team identified a number of suggestions for

Creativity Phase

In this phase of the value analysis, a "force field analysis" was used to identify both positive aspects of the project and areas to be improved, if possible. The workshop participants prepared a list of the best and weakest features. During the "brainstorming" portion of the VA workshop, they identified and listed 111 creative ideas for improving weak features, reducing risk, improving quality, and lowering initial and life cycle cost. All ideas were to support the functions of the project.

Evaluation Phase

After the brainstorming session, the VA team evaluated the ideas listed to select the most promising ones for development. First, the team members came up with criteria for evaluating the ideas:

- Performance improvements
  —Flexibility
  —Space efficiency
  —Dependability
  —Redundancy
  —Durability

(continued)

RISK MODEL EXCERPT

Risk Areas	Risk Elements	N/A	Low	Medium	High
A. Management, financial, and administrative risks	Schedule (design, bidding, construction, start-up)				
	Changing government regulations				
	Public and political perspectives				
	Budget limitations, approvals process, and other contraints				
	Site acquisition—adjacent site elements				
	Permitting delays				
	Agency jurisdictions and conflicts				
	Project management, organization, decision-making processes, information flow				
	Labor issues				
	Other:				
B. Environmental and geotechnical risks	Inclement weather, storms, floods				
	Hazardous waste disposals, site remediation				
	Environ. restrictions (air quality, noise, toxic mat., etc.)				
	Contaminated soils remediation				
	Groundwater remediation				
	Uncharted undergound testing				
	Inadequate subgrade testing				
	Unanticipated archaeological or historical findings				
	Other:				
C. Technical risks	Systems, processes, and material				
	New, unproven systems, processes, and materials				
	Other: Dependence on university				

- —Environmental enhancement
- —Quality
- Cost savings (all part of life cycle costing)
  - —Capital cost
  - —Energy
  - —Maintenance
  - —Major replacements
- Ease of implementation
  - —Time to modify
  - —Cost to change

Development and Recommendation Phase

The VA team developed the most promising ideas by preparing sketches, performing engineering calculations, estimating initial and life cycle costs, and listing nonmonetary advantages and disadvantages. A report was prepared with a one-page summary of each recommended improvement followed by a complete description of each proposal, including sketches where necessary, and the data used as a basis for initial and life cycle cost estimates.

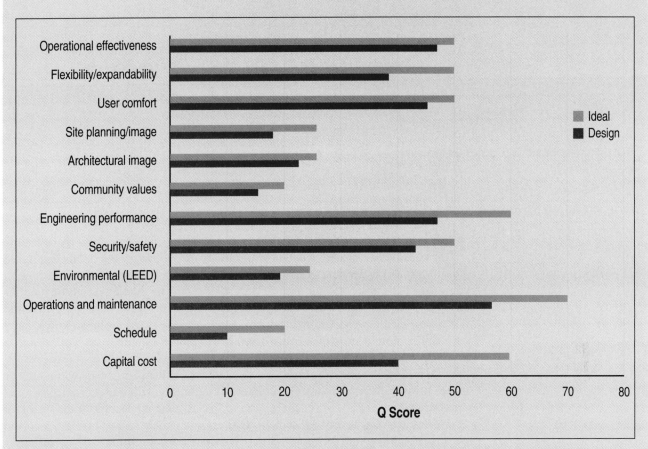

Q Score

Quality Model

Some recommendations would generate significant savings. Others would add costs but improve performance or generate life cycle cost savings. Due to time constraints, some ideas were not developed into proposals, although they may warrant subsequent consideration by the client.

In summary, 111 ideas were identified to maximize value. Some would increase initial costs but are value enhancements because they improve engineering performance, flexibility, maintainability, site planning/image, and energy and other environmental/LEED benefits, while achieving a balance of functional and budget requirements.

Of the 111 ideas identified, the VA team developed 26 into specific recommendations that would result in 83 performance benefits, including improvements to engineer-

ing performance (13), flexibility (15), maintainability (15), site planning/image (6), environmental/ LEED (12), and others (22). In addition, approximately $4.2 to $4.9 million in potential construction cost savings were predicted based on acceptance of all the proposals documented. Although the potential life cycle cost savings were not calculated for every proposal, the team did identify $4.2 to $4.5 million in potential savings (in present worth dollars) over a twenty-five-year period.

Implementation

As work progresses to the next stage, implementation of the value study recommendations rests with the client, the college, and the design team. Further value analysis study may be desired throughout the remaining design phases.

7.5 Life Cycle Costing

Michael D. Dell'Isola, PE, CVS, FRICS, and
Stephen J. Kirk, Ph.D., FAIA, FSAVE, CVS-Life, LEED AP

The expectations of building owners today frequently go beyond good design to include such issues as space effectiveness, systems performance, energy efficiency, sustainability, maintainability, and flexibility. Meeting these expectations competes for limited initial capital, which is dwarfed by long-term facility expenditures. Using life cycle costing, designers can balance competing issues and produce more effective solutions.

Life cycle costing (LCC) is an economic assessment of an item, system, or facility by considering all significant costs of ownership over an economic life, expressed in terms of equivalent costs. In order to ensure that costs are compared on an equivalent basis, the baselines used for initial cost must be the same as those used for all other costs associated with each option, including maintenance, operating cost, and replacement. Life cycle costing is used to compare various options by identifying and assessing economic impacts over the whole life of each alternative.

Why is LCC important to project design and delivery? First, future costs over the life of a facility—operations, maintenance, and replacement—typically will match or exceed the initial cost of facility procurement. If staffing and other use costs are factored into the analysis, the initial procurement may be less than 20 percent of the total cost of ownership. Nearly every decision an architect or engineer makes during design and construction affects project costs. Some decisions are straightforward because they affect building performance or respond to codes and standards and their cost ramifications are apparent. Others are more subtle in their effect on cost. Still other decisions can profoundly affect disciplines and building systems beyond the prime decision maker, such as insulation or glazing choices, which affect building heating and cooling. Design choices have a major effect on life cycle costs.

Second, owners expect their designers to consider future facility expenditures, but at the same time they expect designers to avoid placing an undue burden on initial costs. The move toward sustainable design has highlighted the need for sensitivity to future cost. LCC is an important tool in making more effective design decisions and ultimately for managing costs throughout the life of a facility. This topic discusses methods for defining, estimating, and managing life cycle costs, as well as approaches to procurement that consider life cycle issues and optimizing overall facility costs.

HOW QUALITY AFFECTS LIFE CYCLE COSTS

LCC provides a methodology for comparing competing alternatives over the life of a facility. These alternatives generally reflect the performance of different systems relative to their useful life, required maintenance, and energy consumption. System

Michael D. Dell'Isola is a senior vice president in the Orlando office of Faithful & Gould. He has more than thirty years' experience in life cycle costing, cost management, value analysis, and technical facilitation/partnering. He has lectured and written widely on life cycle costing and cost management. Stephen J. Kirk, president of Kirk Associates, has extensive experience in value analysis, choosing by advantage, life cycle costing, and facility economics. He is past president of SAVE International and has authored several books on value analysis.

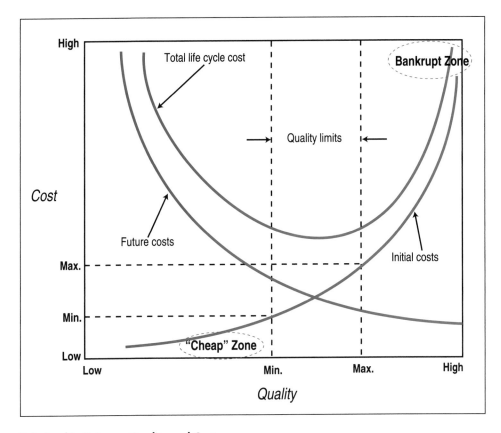

Relationship Between Quality and Cost

performance tends to reflect the quality of the system. In other words, higher-quality systems usually have higher initial costs and lower future costs, while lower-quality systems tend to have lower initial costs but higher future costs.

The diagrammatic relationship between quality and initial costs, future costs, and total life cycle costs is illustrated in the accompanying figure, which demonstrates that there generally is an "optimum life cycle cost" design choice. If the owner's quality expectations are well-founded, this point will occur within the target range of quality called for and will result in optimum life cycle costs.

There is a natural tendency for the design of systems to creep up the quality curve under the premise that better quality is always desirable. However, quality that exceeds actual needs is not necessarily a good investment if the added quality is obtained at a high price. Conversely, cost-cutting, which is often done to maintain capital budget requirements, may reduce quality below needs simply to meet that budget, leading to less than optimum life cycle performance. Achieving a balance between first cost and life cycle cost is the challenge.

ECONOMIC ANALYSIS PRINCIPLES

In making decisions, both present and future costs need to be taken into account and related to one another. A dollar today is not equal to a dollar tomorrow. Money invested in any form has the capacity to earn interest. For example, $100 invested at 10 percent annual interest, compounded annually, will grow to $673 in twenty years. In economic terms, it can be said that $100 today is equivalent to $673 in twenty years' time, provided the money is invested at the rate of 10 percent per year. A current dollar is worth more than the prospect of a dollar at some future time. The exact amount depends on the investment rate (interest or the cost of money) and the length of time. This relationship—that money is always worth money or has the power to earn money—is fundamental to economic analysis and LCC.

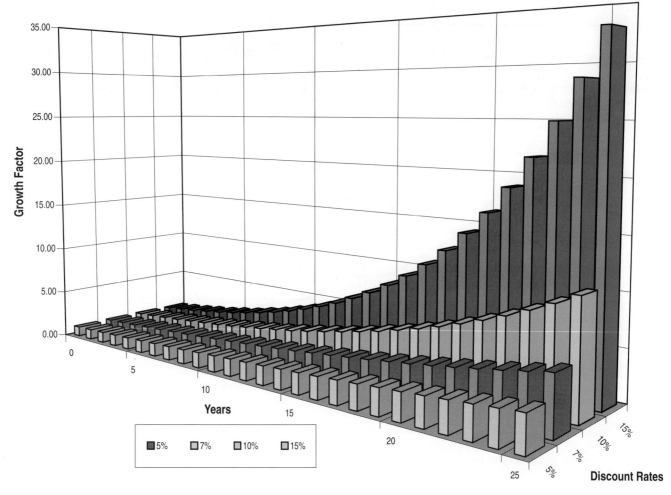

Legend: ■5% □7% □10% □15%

Investment Return on One Dollar—Discount Rates

The terms "interest rate" and "discount rate" are generally used synonymously. "Interest" is more commonly used in financial analyses, while "discount" is more often used in economic studies. Both terms refer to the annual growth rate for the time value of money.

The accompanying figure, "Investment Return on One Dollar," demonstrates the time value of money for various discount rates. Note that at a 5 percent discount rate, a dollar will grow in value by a factor of approximately 3.5 over a twenty-five-year period, while at a 15 percent discount rate, the factor is nearly 35. Even though the discount rates differ by a factor of three, the resulting relationship in value differs by a factor of nearly ten. Obviously, therefore, the selection of a discount rate is important to an LCC analysis.

General inflation does not directly affect the actual time value of money, since, under all circumstances, money must have a time value. Inflation, however, does affect how the time value is calculated and must be accommodated in the calculation. In other words, if the real-time value of money is 7 percent to a particular owner and inflation is predicted to be 3 percent, then any discounting analysis would need to use 10 percent as an interest rate and inflate all future costs by 3 percent. This is called a *current dollars* analysis.

As a simplification, especially in comparative analyses not used for cash flow calculations, *constant dollars* may be used. In this case, a 7 percent discount rate would be used and all future costs would be held at the base date relative cost and not inflated. The one exception would be for any future costs expected to not follow inflation. For example, energy costs have tended to increase at 1 percent to 2 percent above inflation

BASIC ECONOMIC FORMULAS (PRESENT VALUE)

	Constant Dollars			Current Dollars	
Type of Cost	**Typical Applications**	**Formula**	**Type of Cost**	**Typical Applications**	**Formula**
First cost	Initial capital investments	$P = P$ (no conversion)	First cost	Initial capital investments	$P = P$ (no conversion)
Future investment	Replacements Alterations	$P = F \times \dfrac{1}{(1+i)^n}$	Future investment	Replacements Alterations	$P = F \times \dfrac{(1+e)^n}{(1+i)^n}$
Future series	Energy Maintenance	$P = A \times \dfrac{\left[\dfrac{(1+e)^n}{(1+i)^n}\right] - 1}{1 - \left[\dfrac{(1+i)}{(1+e)}\right]}$	Future series	Energy Maintenance	$P = A \times \dfrac{\left[\dfrac{(1+e)^n}{(1+i)^n}\right] - 1}{1 - \left[\dfrac{(1+i)}{(1+e)}\right]}$

i = Real interest rate
e = Escalation rate (portion in excess of general inflation)
n = Number of years to replacement or in series
P = Present value
F = Future value
A = Annual amount

i = Total interest rate (includes real rate plus inflation)
e = Escalation rate (including general inflation)
n = Number of years to replacement or in series
P = Present value
F = Future value
A = Annual amount

PRESENT WORTH CALCULATED AT A DISCOUNT RATE OF 10%

For a Single Escalating Amount

Escalation Rate

Year	0%	1%	2%	3%	4%	5%	6%	7%	8%	9%	10%	11%	12%
1	0.909	0.918	0.927	0.936	0.945	0.955	0.964	0.973	0.982	0.991	1.000	1.009	1.018
2	0.826	0.843	0.860	0.877	0.894	0.911	0.929	0.946	0.964	0.982	1.000	1.018	1.037
3	0.751	0.774	0.797	0.821	0.845	0.870	0.895	0.920	0.946	0.973	1.000	1.028	1.056
4	0.683	0.711	0.739	0.769	0.799	0.830	0.862	0.895	0.929	0.964	1.000	1.037	1.075
5	0.621	0.653	0.686	0.720	0.755	0.792	0.831	0.871	0.912	0.955	1.000	1.046	1.094
6	0.564	0.599	0.636	0.674	0.714	0.756	0.801	0.847	0.896	0.947	1.000	1.056	1.114
7	0.513	0.550	0.589	0.631	0.675	0.722	0.772	0.824	0.879	0.938	1.000	1.065	1.134
8	0.467	0.505	0.547	0.591	0.638	0.689	0.744	0.802	0.863	0.930	1.000	1.075	1.155
9	0.424	0.464	0.507	0.553	0.604	0.658	0.717	0.780	0.848	0.921	1.000	1.085	1.176
10	0.386	0.426	0.470	0.518	0.571	0.628	0.690	0.758	0.832	0.913	1.000	1.095	1.197

For an Annual Escalating Amount

Escalation Rate

Year	0%	1%	2%	3%	4%	5%	6%	7%	8%	9%	10%	11%	12%
1	0.909	0.918	0.927	0.936	0.945	0.955	0.964	0.973	0.982	0.991	1.000	1.009	1.018
2	1.736	1.761	1.787	1.813	1.839	1.866	1.892	1.919	1.946	1.973	2.000	2.027	2.055
3	2.487	2.535	2.584	2.634	2.684	2.735	2.787	2.839	2.892	2.946	3.000	3.055	3.110
4	3.170	3.246	3.324	3.403	3.483	3.566	3.649	3.735	3.821	3.910	4.000	4.092	4.185
5	3.791	3.899	4.009	4.123	4.239	4.358	4.480	4.605	4.734	4.865	5.000	5.138	5.279
6	4.355	4.498	4.645	4.797	4.953	5.115	5.281	5.453	5.630	5.812	6.000	6.194	6.394
7	4.868	5.048	5.234	5.428	5.628	5.837	6.053	6.277	6.509	6.750	7.000	7.259	7.528
8	5.335	5.553	5.781	6.019	6.267	6.526	6.796	7.078	7.372	7.680	8.000	8.334	8.683
9	5.759	6.017	6.288	6.572	6.871	7.184	7.513	7.858	8.220	8.601	9.000	9.419	9.859
10	6.145	6.443	6.758	7.090	7.441	7.812	8.203	8.616	9.053	9.513	10.000	10.514	11.057

over the last ten years. In this case, future energy costs would be inflated differentially (above the general inflation rate) by 1 percent to 2 percent. This effect is referred to in economic analyses as *escalation*.

Economic Formulas

The most common formulas used for present-worth calculations are shown in the accompanying table. Published charts, tables, and spreadsheet programs that provide discounting formulas are available to reduce effort and errors. Illustrated in the accompanying table are sample factors used to calculate the present value of single costs and annual costs at a discount rate of 10 percent at various inflation rates.

Economic Analysis Period

The economic or study period used when comparing alternatives is an important consideration. Generally, predicting future costs for twenty-five to forty years is long enough to capture the most significant costs for economic purposes. In the "Accumulated Present Value" figure, accumulated annual costs are plotted for 100 years discounted to present worth at a 10 percent interest rate. Note that 90 percent of the total equivalent cost is consumed in the first twenty-five years. This result is due to the effect of discounting that makes early-year dollars worth much more than later-year dollars. For this reason, periods longer than forty years generally add little benefit to an LCC analysis unless very low (below 4 percent) interest rates are used.

A time frame must also be identified for each system under analysis. The useful life of each system, component, or item under study may be its physical, technological, or economic life. The useful life of any item depends on such things as the frequency with which it is used, its age when acquired, the policy for repairs and replacements, the climate in which it is used, the state of the art, economic changes, inventions, and other developments within the industry. There may be several periods for component replacement in an overall facility cycle.

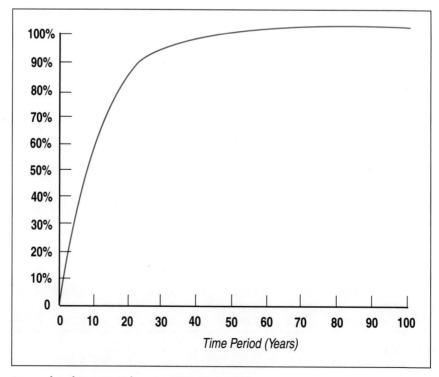

Accumulated Present Value at a 10% Discount Rate

Economic Equivalence

If an item costs $10,000 today and has a life expectancy of twenty years, how much would have to be put aside today to cover its replacement twenty years from now? Inflating the purchase cost at 3 percent per year, the actual replacement cost in year 20 will be just over $18,000. When this cost is discounted back to today, the present value is $2,680 ($10,000 × 0.268). Stated another way, $2,680 placed in the bank today at 10 percent interest rate would grow to provide $18,000 at year 20. This growth would reflect the real discount rate of 7 percent and the inflation rate of 3 percent. In terms of economics, $2,680 today (baseline year) is equivalent to $18,000 at year 20 at a 10 percent discount rate and 3 percent inflation rate. A virtually identical analysis using constant dollars and a 7 percent discount rate results in $2,580 ($10,000 × 0.258).

The example of equivalence shown in the sidebar demonstrates that $1,000 per year for five years is equivalent to $4,123 today at a 10 percent interest rate and 3 percent inflation rate. It also shows that $1,000 per year calculated with no inflation and a 7 percent interest rate yields a virtually equivalent figure.

Categories of Cost

Over the life of a facility, costs will be expended on a broad range of components and for numerous purposes. A life cycle cost analysis is a *comparative analysis* and, therefore, it is important that costs be properly identified and categorized so that common items can be eliminated from the analysis and sufficient effort can be focused on critical items.

The costs of owning a facility can be subdivided as follows:

A. Initial costs
  1. Construction
  2. Fees
  3. Other initial costs

EXAMPLE OF EQUIVALENCE

Year	Expenditure (without Inflation)	Expenditure (with Inflation) @ 3%	Discount Factor @10%	Present Value	Discount Factor @ 10% & 3% Infl.	Discount Factor@ 7%	Present Value
1	$1,000	$1,030	0.909	$936	0.936	0.935	$935
2	$1,000	$1,061	0.826	$877	0.877	0.873	$873
3	$1,000	$1,093	0.751	$821	0.821	0.816	$816
4	$1,000	$1,126	0.683	$769	0.769	0.763	$763
5	$1,000	$1,159	0.621	$720	0.720	0.713	$713
			3.791	$4,123	4.123	4.100	$4,100

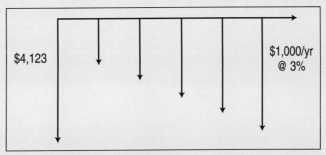

10% interest, 5 years, 3% inflation/escalation
$1,000/year is equivalent to $4,123 today.

B. Future facility one-time costs
   1. Replacements
   2. Alterations
   3. Salvage
   4. Other one-time costs
C. Future facility annual costs
   1. Operations
   2. Maintenance
   3. Financing
   4. Taxes
   5. Insurance
   6. Security
   7. Other annual costs
D. Functional use costs
   1. Staffing
   2. Materials
   3. Denial of use
   4. Other functional use costs

Initial costs include construction, fees, and costs such as land acquisition and moving. These represent up-front costs associated with facility development.

Future one-time costs represent major expenditures that are not annual (although they may be periodic) and include replacement, elective alterations, and salvage.

Facility annual costs include all costs to run the facility itself, exclusive of what the facility produces. These costs include operations, maintenance, and other built environment costs.

Functional use costs are costs associated with using a facility; these include staffing, materials, and any other non-facility costs. Items such as denial of use costs may be necessary during construction, and these may include temporary space, operations, and added security.

In addition to considering life cycle costs, it may be necessary to consider revenue. Eventually, an income stream may offset investments and produce a viable return. While life cycle costing tends to focus on optimizing costs, the process can also be used to optimize income.

The total costs of owning a typical high school are presented in the accompanying pie chart and table. Note that initial costs are only 25 percent of the total costs of owning the facility and construction cost is only 18 percent. Other facility types, such as hospitals, research laboratories, and judicial facilities, may be even more weighted toward future costs. In nearly all cases, the initial costs are 25 percent or less of the total costs of owning a facility.

LIFE CYCLE COSTING PROCEDURES

Life cycle costing focuses on comparing competing alternatives. To compare alternatives, both present and future costs for each alternative must be brought to a common point in time. One of two methods can be used to accomplish this. Costs may be converted into today's costs by the present-worth method, or they may be converted to an annual series of payments by the annualized method. Either method will properly allow comparison between alternatives.

Present-Worth Method

The present-worth method requires conversion of all present and future expenditures to a baseline of today's cost. Initial (present) costs are already expressed in present worth. Future costs are converted to present value by applying the factors presented previously.

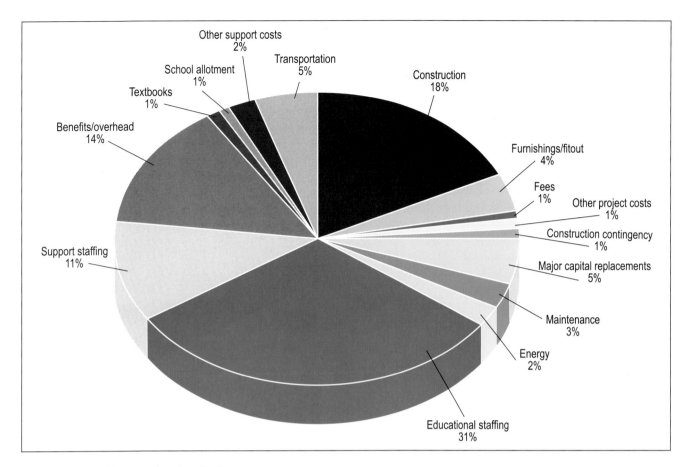

Life Cycle Costs of a Typical High School

A key issue in this process is for the owner to determine the rate of return or the discount rate. The federal government, through OMB Circular A-94, has established 10 percent as the interest rate to be used in government facility studies, excluding the lease or purchase of real property. Normally, a life cycle between twenty-five and forty years is considered adequate for estimating future expenses. Differential escalation (the rate of inflation above the general economy) is taken into account for recurring costs, as necessary.

Annualized Method

The second method converts initial, recurring, and nonrecurring costs to an annual series of payments and may be used to express all life cycle costs as an annual expenditure. Mortgage payments are an example of this procedure; that is, a buyer opts to purchase a home for $1,050 a month (360 equal monthly payments at 10 percent yearly interest) rather than pay $150,000 all at once. Recurring costs are already expressed as annual costs; therefore, no adjustment is necessary. Initial costs, however, require equivalent cost conversion, and nonrecurring costs (future expenditures) must be converted to current cost (present worth) and then to an annual expenditure (annualized cost).

Suggested Format—Present-Worth Analysis

Since the construction industry is capital cost intensive, the present-worth method is recommended. Furthermore, the present-worth method tends to be easier to use and produces results that can be more easily understood.

The sample worksheet shown is used in conducting present-worth life cycle costing studies, as illustrated in the examples at the end of the topic. The worksheet (as a

Statistics

Number of years for period	30			Students		Each	1,600	
Discount rate (interest)	8%			Students per teacher			16.0	
Escalation rate (inflation)	3%			Staff support per teacher			2.3	
Gross area	SF	244,000		Benefits/overhead		%	32%	

Item	Measure	Units	Unit Cost	Current Cost	Factor	Present Value	Percent
Capital Costs							
Construction	$/SF	244,000	$133.00	$32,452,000	1	$32,452,000	18%
Furnishings/fitout	$/SF	244,000	$ 26.50	$ 6,466,000	1	$ 6,466,000	4%
Fees	$/SF	244,000	$ 7.00	$ 1,708,000	1	$ 1,708,000	1%
Other project costs	$/SF	244,000	$ 7.00	$ 1,708,000	1	$ 1,708,000	1%
Construction contingency	$/SF	244,000	$ 6.50	$ 1,586,000	1	$ 1,586,000	1%
Subtotal—Initial capital costs	$/SF	244,000	$180.00	$43,920,000	1	$43,920,000	24%
Major capital replacements	$/SF/yr	244,000	$ 2.50	$ 610,000	$15.63	$ 9,534,894	5%
Grand total capital costs						**$ 53,454,894**	**29%**
Operations and Maintenance							
Maintenance	$/SF/yr	244,000	$1.40	$341,600	$15.63	$5,339,541	3%
Energy	$/SF/yr	244,000	$0.80	$195,200	$15.63	$3,051,166	2%
Subtotal				**$ 536,800**		**$ 8,390,707**	**5%**
Functional Operation							
Educational staffing	Teachers	100	$38,000	$3,800,000	$15.63	$59,397,700	31%
Support staffing	Staff	43	$31,000	$1,333,000	$15.63	$20,836,088	12%
Benefits/overhead	%	32%		$1,642,560	$15.63	$25,674,812	14%
Textbooks	Student	1,600	$ 90	$ 144,000	$15.63	$ 2,250,860	1%
School allotment	Student	1,600	$ 65	$ 104,000	$15.63	$ 1,625,621	1%
Other support costs	Student	1,600	$ 135	$ 216,000	$15.63	$ 3,376,290	2%
Transportation	Student	1,600	$ 360	$ 576,000	$15.63	$ 9,003,441	5%
Subtotal				**$7,514,600**		**$122,164,813**	**66%**
		Present value cost				$184,010,413	
		Equivalent annual cost			0.0640	$ 11,772,166	
		Equivalent annual cost per student			1,600	$ 7,358	
Grand total		*Equivalent annual cost per student(excluding capital)*			1,600	$ 5,220	

spreadsheet) allows input of initial costs, replacement costs, annual costs, and automatic calculation of present worth. Simple and discounted payback periods can also be calculated.

Accuracy Requirements for LCC Analyses

To perform a life cycle cost analysis, certain assumptions must be made. These assumptions concern significant economic variables, including discount rate, study duration, and escalation, as well as data defining cost and performance of competing alternatives. Seldom are clear-cut, obvious, and easy choices available. Invariably, good judgment, experience, and common sense need to be used in making decisions. Here are some guidelines to consider:

- *Issues common to all alternatives can be ignored.* Keep in mind that the objective of LCC analysis is to select between competing alternatives. Therefore, assumptions need to be made, and data sufficient to distinguish performance need to be gathered, only for issues that differ between the alternatives.

- *In general, due to likely margins of error in estimating costs, alternatives would have to exhibit a life cycle cost differential greater than 10 percent to be judged conclusive.* Numeric accuracy should be balanced between the need to differentiate the alternates and

PART 3: THE PROJECT

LIFE CYCLE COSTING—GENERAL PURPOSE WORKSHEET

		Original Design		Option 1		Option 2		Option 3	
		Estimated Costs	Present Worth	Estimated Costs	Present Worth	Estimated Costs	Present Worth	Estimated Costs	Present Worth

Study Title:

Discount Rate :   Date:

Life Cycle (Yrs.)

INITIAL / COLLATERAL COSTS

Initial/Collateral Costs
A.
B.
C.
D.
E.
F.
G.
H.
I.
J.
Total Initial/Collateral Costs
Difference

REPLACEMENT / SALVAGE COSTS

Replacement/Salvage (Single Expenditures) — Occurence Year-or-Cycle | Inflation/ Escal. Rate | PW Factor
A.
B.
C.
D.
E.
F.
G.
H.
I.
J.
Total Replacement/Salvage Costs

ANNUAL COSTS

Annual Costs — Inflation/ Escal. Rate | PW Factor
A.
B.
C.
D.
E.
F.
G.
H.
I.
J.
Total Annual Costs

LIFE CYCLE COSTS

Subtotal Replacement/Salvage + Annual Costs (Present Worth)
Difference

Total Life Cycle Costs (Present Worth)
Life Cycle Cost PW Difference

Payback—Simple Discounted (Added Cost / Annualized Savings)   N/A   N/A   N/A   N/A
Payback—Fully Discounted (Added Cost+Interest / Annualized Savings)   N/A   N/A   N/A   N/A

Total Life Cycle Costs—Annualized   Per Year: Per Year: Per Year: Per Year:

PART 3: THE PROJECT

the dependability of input information. Much of the LCC data available has been gathered from observation and is inherently highly variable, so six digits of accuracy in calculations would imply an unrealistic degree of overall accuracy.

- *A sensitivity analysis should be considered whenever assumptions may be considered questionable.* Even when differentials exceed 10 percent, confidence in major variables in the analysis may limit confidence in the overall conclusions. In these instances, a *sensitivity analysis* may be required. This involves conducting multiple LCC analyses using extremes of the cost parameters in question and evaluating the resulting sensitivity of the analysis to the assumptions. It is not uncommon to still reach the same overall conclusion even when assumptions are significantly varied.
- Under extreme conditions, it may be appropriate to conduct a complete economic risk analysis using probability and Monte Carlo simulation. This is a complicated and challenging subject beyond the scope of this discussion.

Typical Areas of Study

The areas of study for an LCC analysis will vary among facilities and, to some degree, by geographic location. Extracted from "Life Cycle Analysis for State Facilities," published by the state of North Carolina, the accompanying table of components that are typically selected for study provides some general areas for consideration.

Sources of LCC Data

Obtaining life cycle cost data is a challenge. Even when data is available, its applicability to a specific project may be questionable. That said, there are several sources of LCC data. Three are *Cost Planning and Estimating for Facilities Maintenance*, an annual publication of RSMeans; *Life Cycle Costing for Facilities*, an RSMeans/Reed Construction Data publication; and *The Whitestone Building and Repair Cost Reference*, published by Whitestone Research.

Life Cycle Costing Applications in Facility Procurement

Life cycle costing can be a critical component for better analyzing design solutions, providing better-performing facilities, and producing optimum facility financial performance. There are several circumstances in which life cycle costing can influence overall procurement, offering architects opportunities to provide this service:

- Owners emphasize performance in system and facility design, potentially requiring life cycle cost analyses for system selection and even considering life cycle performance in budgeting projects and allocating funds. LCC analysis can help assure owners that investments made in facilities are sound from an overall life cycle perspective. The industry's current move to more "performance specifying" will also likely increase interest in LCC analysis.
- Owners consider life cycle costing capabilities in selecting designers and consultants, and may require provision of life cycle cost estimates for the entire facility throughout the design process. Owners may also tie incentives or penalties to building performance and workspace productivity enhancement.
- Designers can help promote life cycle performance, in general, and especially when presenting competing design solutions to owners. The design team may take this approach in response to project requirements or as a way to gain a competitive advantage and to demonstrate efficiency.
- To produce facilities that are more effective over their life cycles, owners and designers can create value with an acceptable level of initial cost while considering the costs of owning a facility through design and operation and planning for careful investment of initial capital.

TYPICAL COMPONENTS TO BE CONSIDERED IN AN LCC ANALYSIS

Component	Typical Alternatives to Be Analyzed
Predesign	Maintain status quo (do nothing) New acquisition or construction Leasing Renovation, upgrade, or revitalization of an existing facility Use of other state facilities
Site and program	Building shape and orientation on the planned site (including impact on adjacent buildings) Alternative site(s)
Architecture	Substructure ❑ Foundations ❑ Slab on grade ❑ Basement excavation ❑ Basement and retaining walls Superstructure ❑ Floor construction ❑ Roof construction ❑ Stair construction Wall construction ❑ Increased insulation levels, insulation placement, etc. ❑ Mass (passive solar thermal storage) ❑ Daylighting ❑ Building envelope (exterior closure) type Fenestration ❑ Type, amount, and location/orientation of glass ❑ Indoor/outdoor shading devices ❑ Daylighting Interior space plan ❑ Space arrangement ❑ Circulation ❑ Finishes and colors ❑ Ceiling heights Roof construction ❑ Increased insulation levels, type of insulation ❑ Roof membrane type and color ❑ Daylighting Conveyances ❑ Selection of elevators and dumbwaiters ❑ Escalators
HVAC	Secondary HVAC system(s) ❑ System(s) type(s) and zoning ❑ Economizer cycle(s) ❑ Heat recovery (exhaust air, internal source, etc.) ❑ Controls Primary HVAC system(s) ❑ System(s) type(s) and energy sources ❑ Pumping/piping configuration ❑ Heat recovery (waterside economizer cycle, etc.) ❑ Thermal storage (electrical demand shifting) ❑ Controls
Plumbing	Plumbing system(s) ❑ Domestic hot water generation (method and energy source) ❑ Water source—municipal, well, or harvested
Electrical	Lighting ❑ Artificial lighting levels, methods, and control, including general lighting and task lighting ❑ Daylighting ❑ Photovoltaic sources Power ❑ Voltage selection (building and large equipment) ❑ Transformers (quantity, locations, efficiencies)

LCC APPLICATION EXAMPLES

The following examples of life cycle cost analyses are intended to illustrate key aspects of life cycle costing.

Example 1: Storm Window Analysis

The table shows differential investment associated with installing storm windows on a college residence hall. The windows would cost $227,000 to install, but their installation would save $156,500 in added mechanical equipment costs. The annual energy savings from providing storm windows is $12,500, which results in a total present-worth saving of $125,000 over the thirty-year analysis period. The initial added investment is paid back in four years.

LIFE CYCLE COST ANALYSIS—GENERAL PURPOSE WORKSHEET

Residence Hall Renovations

					Alternative 1 Current design storm windows		Alternative 2 No. storm windows	
Study Title: Storm Windows								
Discount Rate: 8.0% Date: 9/4/2007					Estimated Costs	Present Worth	Estimated Costs	Present Worth
Life Cycle (Yrs.)								
INITIAL / COLLATERAL COSTS	**Initial/Collateral Costs**							
	A. Storm windows				227,000	227,000		
	B. Added mechanical equipment						156,500	156,500
	C.							
	D.							
	E.							
	F.							
	G.							
	H.							
	I.							
	Total initial/collateral costs				$227,000	$227,000	$156,500	$156,500
	Difference							$70,500
REPLACEMENT / SALVAGE COSTS	**Replacement/Salvage (Single Expenditures)**	Occurence Year -or- Cycle	Inflation/ Escal. Rate	PW Factor				
	A.							
	B.							
	C.							
	D.							
	E.							
	F.							
	G.							
	H.							
	I.							
	Total replacement/salvage costs							
ANNUAL COSTS	**Annual Costs**		Inflation/ Escal. Rate	PW Factor				
	A. Energy		3%	15.631	15,730	245,875	28,300	442,357
	B.							
	C.							
	D.							
	E.							
	F.							
	G.							
	H.							
	Total annual costs				$15,730	$245,875	$28,300	$442,357
LIFE CYCLE COSTS	**Total life cycle costs (present worth)**					$472,875		$598,857
	Life cycle cost PW difference							($125,981)
	Discounted payback (Alternative 1 vs. Alternative 2)					N/A		4.0 Yrs.
	Total life cycle costs—Annualized				Per year:	$42,004	Per year:	$53,195

Example 2: High School Trade-Off Analysis

An assessment of how much can be saved in staffing costs in the high school example previously presented is shown in the table. This analysis assumes that the student-to-teacher ratio can be increased from 16 to 17 as a result of changes contemplated. Assuming all other issues remain constant, the results indicate that nearly $5 million could be invested initially and the break-even point could be achieved against future savings. In other words, if changes in space efficiency, technology, lighting, or other facility aspects could improve teaching efficiency, as much as $5 million would be available to invest in those changes.

Example 3: HVAC System Analysis

The summary of an owner's independent review of the HVAC system proposed for a school is presented in the third table presenting the results of a sample life cycle cost analysis. It indicates that spending $1.7 million more initially would yield net savings of $3.2 million over the life of the facility and pay back within five years.

EXAMPLE—TYPICAL HIGH SCHOOL TRADE-OFF ANALYSIS

Statistics

Number of years for period	30	Students	Each	1,600	
Discount rate (interest)	8%	Students per teacher		17.0	
Escalation rate (inflation)	3%	Staff support per teacher		2.2	
Gross area	SF	244,000	Benefits/overhead	%	32%

Item	Measure	Units	Unit Cost	Current Cost	Factor	Present Value	Percent
Capital Costs							
Construction	$/SF	244,000	$133.00	$32,452,000	1	$32,452,000	18%
Furnishings/fitout	$/SF	244,000	$ 26.50	$ 6,466,000	1	$ 6,466,000	4%
Fees	$/SF	244,000	$ 7.00	$ 1,708,000	1	$ 1,708,000	1%
Other project costs	$/SF	244,000	$ 7.00	$ 1,708,000	1	$ 1,708,000	1%
Construction contingency	$/SF	244,000	$ 6.50	$ 1,586,000	1	$ 1,586,000	1%
Subtotal—Initial capital costs	$/SF	244,000	$180.00	$43,920,000	1	$43,920,000	24%
Major capital replacements	$/SF/yr	244,000	$ 2.50	$ 610,000	$15.63	$ 9,534,894	5%
Grand total capital costs						$ 53,454,894	30%
Operations and maintenance							
Maintenance	$/SF/yr	244,000	$1.40	$341,600	$15.63	$5,339,541	3%
Energy	$/SF/yr	244,000	$0.80	$195,200	$15.63	$3,051,166	2%
Subtotal				$ 536,800		$ 8,390,707	5%
Functional operation							
Educational staffing	Teachers	94	$38,000	$3,572,000	$15.63	$55,833,838	31%
Support staffing	Staff	43	$31,000	$ 1,333,00	$15.63	$20,836,088	12%
Benefits/overhead	%	32%		$1,569,000	$15.63	$25,534,376	14%
Textbooks	Student	1,600	$ 90	$ 144,000	$15.63	$ 2,250,860	1%
School allotment	Student	1,600	$ 65	$ 104,000	$15.63	$ 1,625,621	1%
Other support costs	Student	1,600	$ 135	$ 216,000	$15.63	$ 3,376,290	2%
Transportation	Student	1,600	$ 360	$ 576,000	$15.63	$ 9,003,441	5%
Subtotal				$ 7,514,600		$117,460,515	66%
	Present value cost					$179,306,115	
	Equivalent annual cost				0.0640	$ 11,471,206	
	Equivalent annual cost per student				1,600	$ 7,170	
Grand total	Equivalent annual cost per student (excluding capital)	1,600 $			5,032		

Original approach = $184,010,413
Investment potential = $ 4,704,298

GENERAL PURPOSE WORKSHEET

					Alternative 1 Individual rooftop units		Alternative 2 Central plan with 4-pipe fan coil units	
Study Title: HVAC System Analysis					Estimated Costs	Present Worth	Estimated Costs	Present Worth
Discount Rate: 8.0% Date: 12/17/07								
Life Cycle (Yrs.)								
INITIAL / COLLATERAL COSTS	**Initial/Collateral Costs**							
	A. Equipment				1,212,354	1,212,354	2,803,000	2,803,000
	B. Screening				55,501	55,501	40,000	40,000
	C. Plant space						128,000	128,000
	D.							
	E.							
	F.							
	G.							
	H.							
	Total initial/collateral costs				$1,267,855	$1,267,855	$2,971,000	$2,971,000
	Difference							($1,703,145)
REPLACEMENT / SALVAGE COSTS	**Replacement/Salvage** **(Single Expenditures)**	Year	Inflation/ Escal. Rate	PW Factor				
	A. Rooftop units (70%)	8		0.540	770,000	416,007		
	B. Rooftop units (70%)	16		0.292	770,000	224,756		
	C. Rooftop units (70%)	24		0.158	770,000	121,428		
	D. Fan coils (100%)	15		0.315			408,888	128,899
	E. Central plant equipment	20		0.215			600,000	128,729
	F.							
	G.							
	H.							
	I.							
	Total replacement/salvage costs					$762,191		$257,627
ANNUAL COSTS	**Annual Costs**		Inflation/ Escal. Rate	PW Factor				
	A. Maintenance–Rooftops		1%	12.496	75,360	941,693		
	B. Maintenance–Fan coils		1%	12.496			37,680	470,847
	C. Maintenance–Central plant & distrib.		1%	12.496			28,800	359,883
	D. Energy		3%	15.631	468,000	7,315,296	192,000	3,001,147
	E.							
	F.							
	G.							
	Total annual costs				$543,360	$8,256,989	$258,480	$3,831,877
	Subtotal-replacement/salvage + annual costs (present worth)					$9,019,180		$4,089,504
	Difference							$4,929,676
LIFE CYCLE COSTS	**Total Life Cycle Costs (Present Worth)**					$10,287,035		$7,060,504
	Life cycle cost PW difference							$3,226,531
	Payback—Simple discounted (added cost/annualized savings)							3.9 Yrs.
	Payback—Fully discounted (added cost+ interest/annualized savings)							4.8 Yrs.
	Total life cycle costs—Annualized				Per year:	$913,771	Per year:	$627,166

AN EFFECTIVE TOOL

Life cycle costing is a valuable tool that owners, architects, engineers, and consultants can use to make more effective decisions, including better building system choices. Focusing on the complete facility life cycle instead of initial capital expenditures can improve the performance of a facility and ultimately benefit facility owners and users.

CHAPTER 8

Project Delivery

8.1 Project Delivery Methods

Phillip G. Bernstein, FAIA, RIBA, LEED AP

The organization, strategy, and responsibilities of the key players in the building process—owner, architect, and contractor—form the project delivery method for a project. The delivery model chosen is based on which project variables—cost, schedule, building quality, risks, and capabilities—drive the project.

A completed building results from a complex sequence of decisions made by the many participants in the design and construction process. For a project to run smoothly, someone must define responsibilities, organize and integrate the work of the participants, and manage the process by which the project is developed and delivered to the owner. The architect, who is deeply involved in most projects from inception to completion, often assumes this role as the first construction professional hired by the owner. The owner relies on the architect's expertise about delivery decisions, and the architect should help determine which delivery method best suits the owner's needs. Since the project delivery model can dramatically affect the results of a building project, an understanding of delivery approach options is central to the successful practice of architecture.

Until recently, delivery methods have evolved primarily in response to different roles assumed by the entity that constructs a building and the relationship of that

Phillip G. Bernstein is vice president for Industry Relations and Strategy at Autodesk, Inc., and a former associate principal with Cesar Pelli & Associates. He teaches professional practice at the Yale School of Architecture and lectures and writes extensively on project delivery and technology issues. Bernstein is a member and former chair of the AIA Contract Documents Committee.

entity to the architect. The roles and responsibilities of this player, variously known as the "contractor," "GC," "construction manager," or "design-builder," can vary greatly in different delivery methods, and the information provided by the design team must be calibrated accordingly. In most project delivery models, the roles and responsibilities of the architect are similar, but the participation of the builder varies greatly.

Through the late 1970s, most projects were built under what was then known as a "traditional" delivery approach. Now termed "design-bid-build," this approach assigns each player a clear, well-defined role. The owner hires and pays the architect to provide design services, and the architect develops and places a set of construction documents into the marketplace for competitive bid. The general contractor assembles a collection of subtrades and submits bids for the project. Generally, the general contractor who submits the lowest bid is awarded the project. The contract for construction between the owner and the contractor incorporates the architect's documents (including drawings and specifications) and an agreement to build the design for the low price, which is the basis for selection of the contractor.

Other project delivery approaches appeared in the design and construction industry in response to the desire of owners to make project decisions based on outcomes beyond lowest first cost. For example, the high cost of borrowed money during the credit crunch of the late 1970s accelerated typical construction schedules, catalyzed the creation of construction management, and gave rise to the increased use of fast-track schedules. The need for speedier project completion replaced the single construction sequence with multiple individual packages that could be bid as their design was completed. This allowed the asynchronous construction of individual project pieces in the field. General contractors thus portrayed themselves as "construction managers" adept at controlling complex projects.

The liability crisis of the 1980s pushed architects further from job site responsibilities and pressed new risks on contractors, who in most cases were willing to assume them in exchange for ever-larger pieces of the overall design and construction fee. As projects became more complex and failures more dangerous and expensive, owners demanded in-depth construction advice during design that architects were unwilling or unable to provide. Frequent and acrimonious disputes between architects and contractors, often fought out in court, led owners to ask if design and construction responsibilities could be consolidated under a single entity. This was particularly appealing for large construction projects such as renovations of hospitals and airports, which needed to continue operating during construction. The sophisticated management and construction planning required for such projects was often beyond the capabilities or interests of architects and created new roles for professional program managers.

Today's building projects, with their increasingly complex building forms, prefabricated construction subassemblies, integrated building control systems, and accelerating interest in sustainable design, include an even broader set of constraints and expectations. Building professionals have also realized that, despite extensive experimentation with delivery approaches, the outcomes of most construction projects remain unpredictable at best. In light of these complications and concerns, the traditional roles and responsibilities of the players bear further scrutiny. A nascent delivery model known today as "integrated project delivery" has emerged, which posits closer collaboration and open sharing of information between the key constituents of the building enterprise, underpinned by the power of building information modeling and Internet-based digital design information.

All in all, projects today are faster, riskier, and involve far more participants than those of even twenty years ago. Choosing an appropriate delivery model is often the key to success—or the source of failure.

The 2006 AIA Firm Survey reported percentages of gross billings for various project delivery methods:

- Design-bid-build: 59.3 percent
- Construction management: 13.6 percent
- Construction management at risk: 10 percent
- Contractor-led design-build: 9.6 percent
- Architect-led design-build: 3.9 percent

Owners may elect to hire a program manager for large, complex projects with multiple building elements and complicated sequencing. Program managers oversee and coordinate the project in support of the owner's interests, in some cases acting as the owner for all practical purposes. Large construction management entities often provide these services, but some architects have begun providing them as well.

Building information modeling (BIM) is not a project delivery method, but rather an enabling technology.

PLAYERS IN THE PROJECT DELIVERY PROCESS

Regardless of how they are structured, all delivery methods involve three elemental parties: owner, architect, and contractor. The distinct roles, expertise, and expectations of each are described below.

The Owner

The client who initiates a building project is usually the eventual owner or operator of the finished facility or interior fit-out. The owner can be an individual, organization, or other entity. For purposes of understanding delivery methods, the owner is the entity that holds one or more contracts with the architect and contractor and is responsible for making payment to them. The owner is also responsible for paying the costs of constructing the building.

An owner's expertise in design and construction can vary widely, usually in proportion to the breadth and complexity of projects the individual or company has previously undertaken. Regardless of their experience, owners of all sorts generally have broad expectations of the other players in the process.

The Architect

The architect is the licensed design professional who provides architecture expertise and generates a design concept for the project. While the specific role of the architect varies greatly according to delivery method, it is the architect who designs, documents, and typically administers the contract(s) for construction of the project. The architect

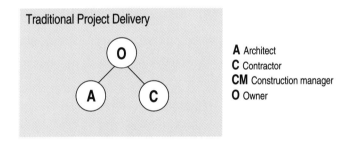

Traditional Project Delivery

A Architect
C Contractor
CM Construction manager
O Owner

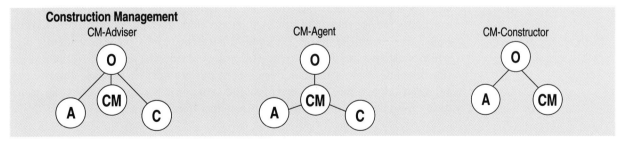

Construction Management

CM-Adviser

CM-Agent

CM-Constructor

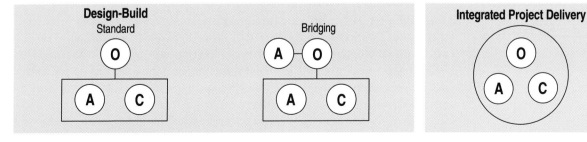

Design-Build

Standard

Bridging

Integrated Project Delivery

Project Delivery Relationships

can be an individual or a firm and may contract with consultants, such as engineers, who augment and support the design effort. In all delivery methods, the architect generates documents that describe the design intent. The contractor uses these documents to build the building.

The Contractor

The contractor is responsible for the actual construction of the project. Typically known as the "contractor" or "general contractor," the contractor's team may include a variety of subcontractors, suppliers, and fabricators who together execute the design intent of the architect's documents. The contractor typically agrees, at a pre-arranged point in the design process, to construct the project for an agreed-upon sum. The decision as to when the contractor agrees to a figure and the resulting responsibilities of the contractor is one of the key differentiators of the various delivery methods.

KEY FACTORS AFFECTING DELIVERY CHOICE

Once only the cost of construction drove the delivery approach of every project, and with few exceptions, the contractor submitting the lowest bid was selected. Today, however, other key variables may affect the selection of a delivery approach. These include construction cost, schedule, quality, risk, and owner capabilities.

Construction Cost

As the owner's greatest financial obligation for a project, construction cost is frequently the central concern of design and construction. Buildings are very expensive, and owners rarely have infinite funds with which to pay for them. Fixed budgets create clear and definite obligations for the architect and the contractor. Meeting those budgets is a high priority for every member of the project team.

Schedule

Most projects include a time frame in which the project must be complete and ready to occupy. When the primary function of a building is critical to an owner's mission, meeting a precise schedule may be the most important consideration in determining how a project will be built. Examples of such situations include academic projects, which must be synchronized with the academic calendar, or performing arts centers that schedule events years in advance. Schedule compliance (and acceleration) is critical when interest rates are very high and capital for building is scarce, as even small delays raise the cost of construction financing dramatically.

Building Quality

The demand for particular standards of performance in systems, finishes, enclosure, or other building elements is directly related to decisions about schedule and construction cost. The architect typically establishes a clear relationship between a project's level of quality, budget, and program, and an increase in one parameter may imply a change in another. An owner may be willing to accept lower levels of quality to save construction cost or to make it possible to complete a project in less time. Conversely, projects with long anticipated life spans (e.g., civic or institutional buildings) may emphasize levels of quality that require construction costs and schedules to be calibrated accordingly. Recently, sustainable design considerations—the relationship of a building to the environment, particularly its long-term use of energy and fresh water—have become a significant component of planned quality for many projects.

Project Scope

Rarely is the project scope completely understood or permanently fixed during the course of a project. The characteristics of a building are never actually resolved until its completion. Until that time, its scope—the combined characteristics of size and quality—may be indeterminate. The project scope is successively refined during design, during preparation of shop drawings, and then during construction. Changing conditions—often caused by changing owner demands, market conditions for materials and construction trades, and unexpected conditions on the project site—will affect the project scope as it unfolds. Delivery models should explicitly acknowledge the degree to which the project scope can or cannot be modified.

Risk

Risk is perhaps the most intractable variable in the building process. Project participants make their best efforts to manage, reduce, or transfer their exposure to liability as the project unfolds. Key risk considerations include the following:

- *For the owner.* Can the project accomplish its goals within the constraints of time and budget? Is the owner able to understand the project and support the decisions necessary to complete it?
- *For the architect.* Can the project be accomplished within the standard of care at an acceptable level of quality that is within the owner's requirements, the architect's capabilities and skill, and the strictures of the fee?
- *For the contractor.* Given market conditions, availability of subcontractors, and the contractor's experience and capabilities, is it possible to complete the project within a contractually stipulated time frame and/or cost?

▶ See Architects and the Law (2.1) for a discussion about the concept of the "standard of care."

Client Capabilities

The internal capabilities of a client organization can significantly affect the roles of the client, architect, and general contractor. The degree to which design, documentation, construction administration, and management are outsourced, as well as the relative importance of each team member's role, frequently depends on the strengths, weaknesses, and preconceived notions of the owner.

CURRENT METHODS OF PROJECT DELIVERY

Project delivery methods are distinguished by the relationships and responsibilities of the players and how they will share information combined with the explicit approach to construction cost, schedule, level of quality, and resulting allocation of risk. Answering questions about the following key issues will help identify a delivery method:

- *Driving factor.* What is the most important outcome driving the project for the owner—cost, risk, quality, or schedule?
- *Architect's role.* What are the responsibilities of the architect, and how do these apply to each successive design and construction phase of the project?
- *Contractor's role.* What entity is responsible for building the project, and when in the process is that player selected?
- *Establishment of construction cost.* When is the actual cost of construction definitively established contractually between the owner and the contractor?
- *Number and type of design and construction contracts.* How many individual contracts for design and construction are necessary to accomplish the approach?

Determining what answers to these questions suit the client and the architect for a particular project will help identify a suitable project delivery approach. Agreeing on a strategy for achieving the project objectives is also helpful.

		Driving Factor					Construction Cost Determined	Number of Construction Contracts
		Cost	Quality	Time	Scope	Risk		
Traditional	**Design-bid-build**	■				□	After design	One
	Negotiated select team	□	■				After design	One
	Cost plux fixed fee				■		At completion	One
Construction Management	**CM-adviser**		□			■	N/A	Many
	CM-agent			□		■	At completion	Many
	CM-constructor	□		■		□	After design	One
Design-Build	**Standard**	□·				■	Before design	One
	Bridging		□			■	After design	One

■ Primary driver
□ Secondary driver

Characteristics of Project Delivery Methods

Delivery models today are typically based on one of three typologies: design-bid-build, construction management, or design-build.

Design-Bid-Build

Once known as the traditional approach, design-bid-build delivery involves a linear design sequence that results in a set of construction documents for which contractors submit fixed-price bids. In this approach, the lowest bidding contractor whose proposal responds to the requirements of the construction documents is usually selected to build the project. Many projects in the United States are constructed under this approach, and many of the business models that drive the construction industry, including contracts, fees, and risk management strategies, are derived from the design-bid-build method.

A variation of design-bid-build is the "negotiated select team" approach, in which the contractor and, in some cases, selected subcontractors are selected early in the design process and certain contract terms (such as overhead and profit multipliers) for the contractor are determined prior to completion of the construction documents. Subcontractors are selected and the final contractor team is assembled once the documents have been completed based on competitive bids. Selected portions of the building that may be particularly difficult to fabricate or construct may be accelerated under the "negotiated select team" approach. The selected contractor may be available for consultation regarding construction issues during design, and in this sense, this approach can be the basis for improved integration and collaboration among members of the delivery team.

Another variation of the design-bid-build method is known as "cost plus fixed fee." In this approach, the contractor is selected at the completion of construction documents, but the scope of construction is unpredictable (due in part to unknown factors such as existing conditions). Under a cost plus fixed fee contract, the contractor is paid actual labor and material costs for construction plus a fee for coordination of trades on the site. Incentives may be added to the fee if the project finishes early or under the original budget.

Construction Management

Owners have increasingly demanded detailed construction and technical advice earlier and earlier in the design process, and the construction community has accommodated this need by creating the field of "construction management" and an associated set of delivery options. The construction manager (CM) can play one of three roles:

- *CM-adviser.* The CM as adviser acts as a constructability and cost management consultant during the design and construction process but does not construct the building. CM-adviser projects can be delivered under any of the methods previously described.
- *CM-agent.* The CM as agent provides early consulting and may act on behalf of the owner in assembling and coordinating the construction trades prior to and during construction. CM-agents typically provide their services for a fixed fee and assume no risk for the actual construction costs but pass on both savings and overruns directly to the owner. The major difference between CM-agent and CM-adviser is that the CM agent is authorized to enter into contracts on behalf of the owner.
- *CM-constructor.* The technical and cost adviser role of the contractor during the project design phase transitions at a predetermined moment to the role of contractor for the project. CM as constructor (CMc) methods of delivery frequently include the use of a guaranteed maximum price, or GMP, which is a commitment by the construction manager to build the project for a specified price developed from design documents (typically those available at the end of design development). An inherent difficulty in CMc arrangements stems from the construction manager's dual role as contractor and estimator, as cost decisions made early in design directly affect the CMc's cost (and profitability) later in construction. Owners considering this approach should be aware of this fact. The apparent conflict of interest may be addressed by requiring the CMc to provide "open book" cost estimates so that all are aware of the details of the cost estimates that eventually become the hard bid cost of the job. The CMc model is also known as "CM-at-risk," since the construction management entity takes responsibility for meeting a fixed cost of construction.

In general, construction management entities present themselves to owners as a central project participant when complexity, schedule, or commitment to budget objectives is critical. Because it is rare when one or more of these issues is not important to project success, construction managers are involved in many large building projects. However, architects with sufficient experience and depth are increasingly offering construction management services.

▶ At the end of this topic, see the backgrounders on construction management and design-build delivery.

Design-Build

The design-build delivery method provides the owner with a single-point responsibility for both design and construction. The approach emerged from the growing dissatisfaction of clients with the inherent tensions and conflicts of delivery methods that place architects and contractors in adversarial roles. In design-build delivery, a consolidated entity provides both design and construction services to the owner. A single contract is established between the owner and the design-build entity, which has both design and construction capabilities. This contract typically includes a fixed price for both design services and construction cost. Design-build delivery requires an explicit determination of the roles and responsibilities of members of the design-build team.

An issue in design-build projects is the mechanism by which the owner establishes and enforces the performance and quality parameters of the project, a role typically assumed by the architect as an agent for the owner separate from the contractor. A variation on the consolidated approach of design-build is "bridged design-build," which

GMP APPROACHES TO CONSTRUCTION COST

Typically, the establishment of a guaranteed maximum price (GMP) suggests a commitment by the owner and the CM-contractor to a construction cost based on a partially complete set of design documents. The price established was understood to account for the "risk" inherent in using these documents.

Many CM-based projects now invoke a GMP as an evolving cost target for the project but sustain it through the completion of construction to maintain flexibility with the owner about the final cost of a project. It might be argued that a GMP, carefully developed and refined based on construction documents, is actually a "hard bid." Care should be taken to understand and define the term GMP when it is used to describe construction cost commitments after design development.

Delivery Type	Option	Project Delivery Phases
Traditional	Design-bid-build	PD · SD · DD · CD · PR · [C] [SC] ($) CA
	Negotiated select team	PD · SD · [C] DD · CD · PR · [SC] ($) CA
	Cost plux fixed fee	PD · SD · [C] DD · CD · PR · [SC] CA
Construction Management	CM-adviser	[CM] PD · SD · DD · CD · PR · [SC] ($) CA
	CM-agent	[CM] PD · SD · DD · CD · PR · [SC] ($) CA
	CM-constructor *	[CM] PD · SD · DD · ($) CD-Pkg 1 · [SC] ($) CA
		GMP · CD-Pkg 2 · [SC] ($) CA
		CD-Pkg 3 · [SC] ($) CA
Design-Build	Standard	[C] [SC] ($) PD · SD · DD · CD · CA
	Bridging	PD · SD · DD · ($) [C] [SC] CD · CA

* Delivery shown with fast-track scheduling

($)	Cost of construction determined	**SD**	Schematic design
[C]	Constructor contract determined	**DD**	Design development
[SC]	Subcontractors selected	**CD**	Contract documentation
[CM]	CM selected	**BN**	Bidding negotiation
PD	Predesign	**CA**	Construction contract administration

Sequences and Key Decisions by Delivery Method

borrows a design approach from architect teams that include both a design architect (who establishes the design concept) and a production architect (who determines technical criteria and generates the construction documents). In bridging, the owner eventually hires two architects, one of which is part of a design-build team. The first architect prepares a preliminary design for a building and establishes, typically through a performance specification, detailed criteria to which the ultimate design must conform. The completed concept and criteria package (typically based on design development drawings and specifications) is then tendered to design-build teams that offer both technical architecture and construction capabilities.

In general, design-build contracts are characterized by a single entity providing consolidated design and construction services. Architects often lead these teams, but firms that undertake "architect-led" design-build should be aware of the business and legal complexities of providing both design and construction services.

EMERGING DELIVERY MODELS

The design and construction community is increasingly coming to grips with the challenges of delivering results with predictable outcomes. Too often projects fail to meet expectations for budget, schedule, or quality—three factors architects must carefully balance as they guide owners through the design and construction process. The project delivery models described above have evolved in part as attempts to address these challenges, each optimizing a different project variable or player capability to yield better results.

CHANGES IN DESIGN SEQUENCE

The typical phasing for project delivery includes standard phases of design (schematic design and design development) resulting in a single package of construction documents. An alternate approach emerged in the 1980s with the advent of fast-track construction scheduling. Most projects today are under significant schedule pressure, and the typical SD-DD-CD sequence is fast giving way to hybrid approaches in which bid packages for individual building components are generated based on their schedule requirements or other market constraints.

Irrespective of delivery model, projects today rarely operate in a strictly linear progression of design, design completion, bidding, and construction. There is some speculation that as integrated methods and digital design technology become more advanced, linear design phasing may change to accommodate new definitions of design deliverables and project phasing.

Currently, a series of alternative models are being examined that do not fit neatly into traditional project delivery typologies. Known generally as integrated practice and delivery, these models cannot yet be categorized as a common approach, except that they attempt to break down barriers to information creation, transmission, and collaboration. Implicit in this new approach to project delivery is acknowledgment that traditional project roles, responsibilities, and risk approaches have contributed to unsatisfactory results. Like industries such as manufacturing in which design and production were integrated years ago, projects using integrated delivery methods look to operate with open collaboration between project participants. In some cases, traditional design-bid-build or CM models are employed, but project participants collaborate closely using digital models and the Internet in lieu of paper drawings. Interesting variants with characteristics of integration are emerging worldwide. Two of the most well-defined approaches include privately financed initiatives and project alliances.

Privately Financed Initiatives

In Great Britain, consolidated design, construction, development, and building operation teams compete to deliver and operate completed buildings for extended periods as long as fifty years. The architect is one member of such teams. Owners pay a yearly fee in exchange for the use of these buildings. Many health care projects in the United Kingdom are using this model, notably when the government does not wish to spend capital on building construction and operation. The build-operate-transfer model in Canada is a similar delivery model.

Project Alliances

In Australia, the industry is experimenting with a radical delivery model in which the entire project team—designers, contractors, and subcontractors—are bound together in a single contract that holds each jointly responsible for the project and rewards all for its success. Of interest in the alliance model is the requirement that each project member fully support the efforts of the others, since their financial success is tied to mutual cooperation. The owner in these projects establishes measurements for success—budget, cost, or quality, for example—and rewards the entire team based on how well these aims are achieved.

In the United States, where standard of care considerations, explicit allocation of responsibility and liability, and entrenched attitudes are the norm, conversations are just beginning about integrated approaches to construction project delivery, and a U.S. integrated model has yet to emerge. The relative advantages of integrated practice and delivery will become more apparent as underlying business structures that define roles and responsibilities, risk, compensation, and contracts are defined.

A CATALYST FOR INTEGRATED PRACTICE

Discussion of integrated practice and project delivery often go hand in hand with explorations of the new digital design technology known as building information modeling. Integrated delivery approaches feature a robust virtual model of a building, rather than physical drawings, which becomes a collaboration platform that allows project participants to share rich building information.

Architecture firms can use building information models as project production tools without affecting relationships between owner, contractor, or consultants. However, the true power and allure of BIM technology lies in its ability to integrate the work of all disciplines, quickly identify coordination issues, speed multiple analyses, support continuous cost estimating, and allow virtual construction of

(continued)

the building, identifying interferences and constructability problems so they can be resolved before physical construction begins.

The AIA has termed this virtual design and construction process "integrated practice." Norman Strong, FAIA, a 2005–2007 Institute vice president and chair of the 2006 Board working group on the subject, suggests, "At the core of an integrated practice are fully collaborative, highly integrated, and productive teams composed of all project life-cycle stakeholders."

The promise of integrated practice is access to construction expertise and facility operations and maintenance experience during early design to inform and improve design decisions in areas such as product availability, construction cost and schedule implications, and facility maintainability. Goals are to minimize revision of completed work in both later design phases and construction and to reduce facility life cycle costs. As suggested by the Architectural/Engineering Productivity Committee of the Construction Users Roundtable (CURT) in an August 2004 report, "The goal of everyone in the industry should be better, faster, more capable project delivery created by fully integrated and collaborative, cross-functional project teams comprised of design, construction, and facility management personnel."

With building information models as cross-organizational tools, new technical and many business issues arise. Standards and procedures must be aligned across all the organizations contributing to and using a model. Whether all team members are using software capable of accessing and updating the model is another issue. Interoperability of BIM systems is discussed further in the Handbook topic "Computer Technology in Practice" in Chapter 5. Production issues are discussed in the sidebar on building information modeling in the Handbook topic "Construction Documentation" (8.3).

In a presentation at Schinnerer's 45th Annual Meeting of Invited Attorneys ("Building Information Modeling: A Great Idea in Conflict with Traditional Concepts of Insurance, Liability, and Professional Responsibility"), attorney Howard W. Ashcraft Jr. outlined six issues pertaining to capturing the fullest potential of integrated practice:

- *Compensation.* Integrated delivery approaches require investments by architecture firms. The greater value of the deliverables to the client suggests an adjustment in compensation for professional services would be appropriate.

- *Risk allocation and reliance.* Increasing the number of parties relying on a building information model increases the architect's potential liability. A project-wide agreement should be negotiated to limit or waive consequential damages due to errors in the model as well as the architect's liability for constructability or means and methods of construction.

- *Design ownership and access.* Ownership of the model should be defined and the project agreement should make clear that sharing it does not waive ownership rights. If the architect cedes ownership of the model, there should be an alternative method of guaranteeing payment for design services.

- *Intellectual property.* Issues include ownership of the design for purposes of reuse or continuation and confidentiality provisions if the model incorporates proprietary information, such as manufacturing process data.

- *Model hosting.* Agreement should be reached as to who will host and manage the model. In its 2005 *Code of Standard Practice for Steel Buildings and Bridges,* the American Institute of Steel Construction has recommended that a single entity be assigned responsibility for managing the official version of the shared model:

"When a project is designed and constructed using EDI [electronic data interchange], it is imperative that an individual entity on the team be responsible for maintaining the LPM [logical product model, or building product model]. This is to assure protection of data through proper backup, storage, and security, and to provide coordination of the flow of information to all team members when information is added to the model. Team members exchange information to revise the model with this Administrator. The Administrator will validate all changes to the LPM. This is to assure proper tracking and control of revisions. This Administrator can be one of the design team members such as an Architect, Structural Engineer, or a separate entity on the design team serving this purpose. The Administrator can also be the Fabricator's detailer or a separate entity on the construction team serving this purpose."

- *Insurance.* Economic losses should be insured to cover all parties if the model is lost or corrupted. In addition, whoever is hosting the model should have additional insurance covering this activity.

Kristine K. Fallon, FAIA

DELIVERY METHODS CONTINUE TO EVOLVE

Like many professionals anticipating the challenges of practice today, architects face increasingly complex decisions that drive the very basis of how projects will be designed and built. Advising owners intelligently about delivery options requires an understanding of the players in the building process and their roles, the key variables that affect the choice of delivery method, and the range of choices available in the current design and construction marketplace. As design, quality, construction, financing, and schedule options evolve, new and unanticipated delivery methods based on principles of integrated practice and delivery are likely to appear. To maintain a central role in the building enterprise, architects must strive to understand, master, fully participate in, and, when necessary, invent these new project delivery methods.

For More Information

The Handbook on Project Delivery, published by the AIA California Council and the Design Professionals Insurance Company (DPIC) in 1996 and revised in 2004, provides a comprehensive look at project delivery methods.

The AIA publishes a series of contract documents to support architect-led CM. These include B801/CMa–1992 (B131–2008), Standard Form of Agreement Between Owner and Construction Manager and A201/CMa–1992 (A232–2008), General Conditions of the Contract for Construction–CM-Adviser Edition. *The CM Contracting System* (Prentice-Hall, Inc., 1998), by C. Edwin Haltenhoff, covers construction management in great detail and is a good source for gaining an overall understanding of construction management. It addresses CM by the architect as well as other CM models.

The Architect's Guide to Design-Build Services (Wiley, 2003), edited by G. William Quatman II and Ranjit Dhar, provides an overview of design-build project delivery for architects considering whether to adopt this approach.

Integrated Practice in Architecture: Mastering Design-Build, Fast-Track, and Building Information Modeling (Wiley, 2007) by George Elvin addresses this emerging project delivery approach around the subjects of team building, project planning, communication, risk management, and implementation.

"Collaboration, Integrated Information, and the Project Lifecycle in Building Design, Construction and Operation," WP-1202 (August 2004), a report of the Construction Users Roundtable, makes recommendations about the roles of owners, architects, and contractors in project delivery. The report is available at www.aia.org/SiteObjects/files/ip_%20productivity.pdf.

BACKGROUNDER

CONSTRUCTION MANAGEMENT

Robert C. Mutchler, FAIA

Construction management (CM) offers a way for architecture firms to expand their services, increase income, and control the construction process while maintaining a professional relationship with their clients. More control of the project schedule, improved integration of design and construction, and daily on-site construction coordination can result in cost savings for the owner and increased profitability for the architect. *The Business of Architecture—2006 AIA Firm Survey* indicates that billings for CM services were 23.6 percent of total billings, second only to those for design-bid-build, the most common method of project delivery.

Construction management got its start in the late 1950s with the advent of scheduling methods such as PERT (project evaluation review technique) and CPM (critical path method)

(continued)

for managing complex projects. The need for construction managers rose during the 1960s and 1970s, when public sector clients began to divide general contracts into multiple packages requiring more coordination. At that time, general construction contractors provided almost all construction management services. In the early 1980s, as architects began looking for ways to expand their practice, construction management and design-build joined the list of professional services offered by architects.

There are two primary models for providing CM services—CM-adviser and CM-constructor. The CM-adviser model can sometimes be limited to consultation for constructability and cost management. CM-agent is a variation of the CM-adviser model in which the construction manager is authorized to enter into contracts on behalf of the owner. CM-constructor model is similar to design-build project delivery.

Firms or individuals providing CM services have a direct contractual relationship with the owner. Architects of record, other architects, independent CM firms, or general construction contractors can provide CM services, with the latter two groups providing most CM services today. Independent CM firms refer to companies that specialize in construction management other than architecture firms or general contractors.

Elements of Construction Management

CM services embody a cluster of activities related to construction scheduling, construction cost estimating, and contractor coordination, among others. Construction managers must be totally familiar with the services included in the owner-construction manager agreement for each project. They must also clearly understand the general conditions of the contract that outline the roles played by the owner, the architect, the contractor, and the construction manager. AIA Document A201/CMa–1992 (A232–2008), General Conditions of the Contract for Construction—CM-Adviser Edition, offers an excellent description of these roles.

Scheduling. Two types of schedules are referenced in owner-architect construction management contracts: the project schedule and the construction schedule.

The project schedule is prepared as early as possible in preconstruction phases of project development. The architect is in the best position to lead in the preparation of this document. Input from all the parties—including the owner, architect, and construction manager—is needed to establish meaningful dates for completing the design, contract documents, and construction work. The construction phase shown in the project schedule can be general in nature, primarily noting construction start and completion dates.

The construction manager prepares the construction schedule during the construction documents phase. This schedule should be included in the specifications so bidders can use it when preparing their bids. The construction man-ager maintains and updates the schedule as it evolves during the construction phase.

Scheduling is one of the most important procedures for a successful CM process. Schedules organize the forces and direct the energies of all project participants toward the successful completion of a project. (See the topic "Project Controls" in Chapter 9 for discussions about various scheduling methods and techniques.)

Preconstruction activities. Preconstruction activities comprise all work done by the architect during the schematic and design development phases. The construction manager works closely with the design architect during this phase to aid in completion of the project design. The construction manager's tasks include estimating costs, advising on materials and equipment, writing specifications, scheduling construction work, and reviewing bidders' qualifications.

As noted in AIA B801/CMa–1992 (B131–2008), Standard Form of Agreement Between Owner and Construction Manager, the construction manager prepares preliminary construction cost estimates based on schematic designs. As the project design progresses, the construction manager updates the estimates and advises the owner and architect if it appears the construction cost may exceed the approved project budget.

Bidding/negotiation activities. A primary difference between a CM-adviser method and a conventional design-bid-build project delivery is the breakdown of the work into a number of bid packages rather than a single prime contract. Depending on the complexity and nature of the work, the actual number of bid packages can vary from as few as four to as many as thirty or more. The CM-constructor method, on the other hand, performs like a negotiated conventional single-prime project, either cost-plus or with a guaranteed maximum price (GMP). In either case, for the best results, open bidding should be pursued, with the owner and architect participating in the selection of the subcontractors.

Construction phase activities. The construction manager's responsibility is to coordinate the efforts of the contractors, while the project architect continues to make all design-related decisions. The construction manager and project architect continue to work closely during construction. General progress, change orders, and contractor applications for payment need review and approval by both the construction manager and architect. Although the construction phase activity centers on the construction manager, the project architect still provides contract administration services as specified in the owner-architect agreement. In projects without a construction manager, architects sometimes provide coordination activities above and beyond basic contract administration services in order to successfully complete the project delivery.

Construction Manager Roles

The CM-adviser delivery method offers an owner a solution to the drawbacks of the conventional design-bid-build method of project delivery (e.g., excessive change orders, cost overruns, and delays in completion). However, while trying to demonstrate their cost-saving value to the owner, independent CM-advisers can sometimes cause adversarial relationships to develop with the design architect. This aside, when administered with an attitude of cooperation and respect, construction management can yield reduced project costs, faster completion time, and a higher quality of construction workmanship.

The CM-constructor method offers the owner a further consolidation of responsibilities. The architect relationship remains much the same as in the CM-adviser method noted above. In addition to providing advice to the owner and architect during the development of the project, the CM-constructor also builds the project. To avoid conflict of interest on the part of a CM-constructor who provides estimates for both the project and final construction cost, it is recommended that all subcontract work be openly bid, with the owner benefiting from any actual cost savings. Construction work is done on either a cost-plus or an "at risk" guaranteed maximum price.

The AIA has prepared contract documents for CM-adviser and CM-constructor methods of project delivery. These documents are similar to conventional design-bid-build documents but are designated "CMa" for CM-adviser services and "CMc" for CM-constructor services. Architects can also contract with clients for CM-adviser work using a B144/ARCH-CM–1993 (B231–2008) amendment to the standard AIA owner-architect agreements. However, care must be taken not to mix documents based on one method of project delivery with those of another method. While the AIA has no specific documents for a CM-as-agent arrangement, the CM-adviser document can be modified by addendum to properly reflect the CM-as-agent relationship.

The Architect as Construction Manager

Why should the architect provide CM services? In traditional project delivery, architects are subject to many forces beyond their control that can greatly affect both design decisions and the financial outcome of the project. In the design-bid-build approach, the contractor drives the construction schedule and, thus, the architect's time during the construction period. The longer a project runs, the more time the architect must spend, resulting in reduced profit. Contractor-led design-build may place the architect under the contractor's control, which can affect both design quality and the architect's income. When a third-party construction manager, separate from the architect for the project, serves as the owner's agent, design challenges and time-consuming reevaluations can sometimes result, placing the architect in a defensive position rather than a position as the owner's trusted agent.

As an integral part of an architecture practice, CM services can often yield the following positive outcomes:

- *Reduced project costs.* Subcontractor prices can be passed directly to the owner without prime contractor markup or general superintendent costs.
- *Substantially reduced construction time.* Proper scheduling and management allows faster construction while high-quality design and construction is maintained.
- *Daily job site representation by the architect.* The architect visits the job site with no additional cost to the project.
- *A single source of responsibility.* When the architect of record also provides CM services, the client has one point of contact for both design and construction.
- *Avoidance of adversarial relationships.* Provision of both design and CM services by the architect promotes collaborative relationships between the architect and prime contractors and independent construction managers.
- *Increased earnings for the architect.* The architect's earnings are greater without the need to increase the number of projects in the office.

Risks and Rewards

Like most professional services, construction management has risks associated with it. An understanding of those risks is important when design firms decide to make construction management part of their services. With this understanding there is a better chance to fully capture the rewards of construction management as reflected in more efficient project delivery, improved client relationships, and greater financial returns.

Risks of CM services. Architect-led CM-adviser services are professional services just as the architect's traditional design work is, and thus they carry similar professional liability risks. Standard professional liability insurance can provide coverage for architects offering CM-adviser services just as it does for design services. However, some additional exposure to job site safety issues could exist even though contractors hold this responsibility as they do in the design-bid-build method.

Job site safety is the greatest concern for the architect engaging in CM-adviser services. The courts might assign responsibility for job site safety to the construction manager, even though the primary duty of the construction manager is coordinating the efforts of the contractors, rather than the means and methods of construction. The general conditions of the contract for CM work very clearly note that responsibility for safety rests with the contractors. Even so, the construction manager may have liability exposure here. Such exposure can be reduced by initiating a

(continued)

proactive job site safety program, and by securing contractor-type liability insurance for CM work. With CM-constructor work, job site risk and construction means and methods must be assumed; however, this increased risk is acknowledged and rewarded with increased income. Again, a proactive job site safety program and the addition of contractor's liability insurance can help the architect address these increased risks.

Rewards of architect-led CM. CM services can yield a high net profit (often about 50 percent of the gross fee) plus increasing the return for design services. Projects can be completed as much as 25 percent sooner using a CM approach, allowing designers to move on to new projects sooner and thus increase production for the firm.

One firm found when it added architect-led CM-adviser services to its service offerings, the net income derived from traditional design-bid-build services increased from 10 percent to as much as 30 percent or more. When the firm used the architect-led CM-constructor method, its net income increased as much as 50 percent. These financial rewards are in addition to the benefit of eliminating adversarial relationships with general contractors and independent CM-advisers and CM-constructors working directly for the owner.

Qualifications for Construction Managers

The primary attribute of an effective construction manager is the ability to see the big picture while coordinating the day-to-day efforts of the construction contractors. Knowledge of construction techniques is important, but the ability to organize and direct the construction process is essential. Candidates for construction managers include those with a bachelor's degree in construction management, graduate architects with a strong interest in construction as well as design, or project architects with experience who could manage both design and CM services. A construction superintendent or a similarly trained person can also do the job, although an architect may be more motivated when it comes to managing and enforcing schedules and controlling costs. In a small firm, the principal architect could provide CM services in addition to designing the project.

Marketing CM Services

Architects can readily incorporate pitches about CM services in such traditional marketing methods involving Web pages, responding to RFPs, participating in interviews, or with the information included in project job site signs. With many clients questioning an architect's construction expertise and ability to control costs, CM services can help allay this concern while demonstrating the strength of total project leadership. Remember, most owners like a single source of responsibility.

Project cost savings for the owner is another positive marketing point for architect-led CM. Prime contractor markups for overhead and profit are seldom less than 5 percent of the construction cost. Negotiated project markups often run as high as 15 percent. The cost for a general superintendent runs about 2.5 percent of the construction cost. These savings to the owner will easily exceed the compensation to the architect for CM services, thus providing an overall project cost reduction.

Perhaps the best marketing message for CM services is the architect's ability to provide an owner a much-desired service: daily job site representation of the owner's interests at no additional cost to the project.

Finally, timing is often everything. The ability to offer construction management with design services at the initial interview for a project can strengthen the profile of the architect and convey to an owner the merits of architect-led construction management before the owner pursues CM services provided by others.

Robert C. Mutchler expanded his architecture practice in 1980 to include CM-adviser and CM-constructor services. He has spoken and written extensively on construction management as an architectural service. He is a past member of the AIA board of directors.

BACKGROUNDER

DESIGN-BUILD PROJECT DELIVERY

G. William Quatman, Esq., FAIA

Design-build is the method of project delivery in which both design services and construction work are bundled together under one contract. While there are many variations on this theme, the one common element that separates true design-build from other methods is a single prime contract. This places all of the responsibility, control, and risk on the design-builder.

The roots of design-build go back to Imhotep, the Egyptian architect and master builder who designed the Step Pyramid. For more than 4,000 years, the design-build approach was used to create most public buildings and civic works. Even as late as the eighteenth and early nineteenth centuries in France, it was very common for the architect to hold all the trade contracts and to serve as the general contractor in order to keep peace among the trade guilds.

Beginning in the nineteenth century, professional and trade organizations began to form in both Europe and America, largely as a means of increasing the professional stature and education of the various occupations. Architects and engineers sought to distinguish themselves from craftsmen and contractors. As the art and science of architecture and engineering began to separate themselves from the building trades, design professionals formed their own associations to promote pure design, separate and distinct from the construction trades, and in protest against so-called "package builders." As building technology developed, builders organized themselves according to trades and the job of managing trade contractors became known as "general contracting."

From this division of work, the "design-bid-build" method of project delivery took hold, and from 1909 until 1978, the AIA forbade its members to engage in design-build work because of a perceived conflict of interest. The 1977 AIA Code of Ethics stated, "Members may not engage in building contracting where compensation, direct or indirect, is derived from profit on labor and materials furnished in the building process except as participating owners. Members may engage in construction management as professionals for professional compensation only."

It was not until September 2005 that the AIA Board of Directors adopted Policy Statement 26 on "Alternative Project Delivery," which states that, regardless of the delivery method used, the AIA "believes that an architect is most qualified to lead" and the AIA "advocates that architects should be retained in that role." From forbidding its members to participate, to encouraging them to lead, the AIA has now embraced this rediscovered delivery process.

The Appeal of Design-Build

In survey after survey, building owners have spoken loud and clear: They are tired of the finger-pointing, litigation, and lack of accountability frequently found in the "traditional," fragmented design-bid-build method of delivery. For this reason, owners have flocked to the concept of one-stop shopping in which general contractors have been quick to take the lead role and sign on as the "prime" design-build provider. Contractors lead more than 50 percent of all design-build projects, with another 25 percent led by "integrated" firms (with in-house design and construction staff); less than 25 percent are "designer-led," mostly by engineers. The balance is led by joint ventures.

Some architects wring their hands about design-build (and design-builders) and complain how it has further reduced the role of the architect. But others recognize that an important choice exists. In fact, good design is still what building owners want, and a designer who can also guarantee the cost, quality, and schedule can dominate the market. Architects who have taken this bold step already say they will never turn back and wonder why they didn't do it years ago. By taking the lead, the architect maintains a close relationship with the owner and has greater control over cost, quality, and schedule. In addition, most architects leading a design-build delivery process report making more money than ever in their careers. They also say they derive more satisfaction from their work by retaining control over the construction process.

Design-build can replace adversarial relationships with true teaming; permits design changes during construction to improve the project, often without fear of a costly change order or delay claim; and supports solving problems on the spot to keep the job moving and reduce the risk of suits or claims over design errors and omissions. Experienced design-builders say, "When you have total control, you have less risk." The traditional method of turning over control of the architect's plans to a group of low-bidding contractors—some of whom may be looking to exploit any error, omission, or ambiguity in the plans and specs—certainly has its risks. Design-build delivery can actually reduce some aspects of risk by giving the architect total project control, from design through project completion.

Risk Factors in Design-Build

Architects deciding to take the lead in design-build should be aware of its risks. These risks, faced daily by contractors but not shared with design professionals, can stem from job site safety, scheduling delays, material cost escalation, equipment breakdowns, nonperforming or defaulting subcontractors and suppliers, delays in fabrication or delivery of materials, mechanics' liens, express warranties and guarantees on workmanship, estimating errors and omissions, unknown site conditions, and labor strikes. While the architect's professional liability insurance covers most types of claims and damages that are made against a design firm, it does not cover much of the risk undertaken by a contractor. Therefore, design-build delivery requires more risk tolerance than designers may be used to.

Start-Up Considerations

Before taking the plunge into the lead design-build role, architects need to consider a number of issues. The most commonly voiced concern is *mandatory bonding* associated with public projects. If a firm does not do public work, this may not be an issue. However, for those in the public market, it is true that substantial assets are needed to attract a surety willing to write bonds for your company. But this con-

(continued)

PART 3: THE PROJECT

8.1 Project Delivery Methods   385

cern is not insurmountable. Many architecture firms have found ways to obtain bonds by teaming with bondable contractors, obtaining "dual obligee" bonds, or retaining enough earnings and providing personal guarantees to qualify for their own bonds. It is not an impasse, as any start-up contractor will tell you; it just takes time and planning.

Another primary concern in taking the lead is risk aversion. Architects have been taught by insurers and lawyers to limit their liability, take on only insurable risks, avoid site safety and "supervision" roles, and never "guarantee" or "warrant" anything. Today's owners want the opposite. They want someone to be responsible and take on risks, which are present in every project. Contractors do it every day, and they are well compensated for it. It is often said, "With risk comes reward." If you talk to firms engaged in the lead role in design-build, you will hear most say the rewards are both personal and financial.

Architects taking on the role of contractor will need a different workers' compensation policy than those traditionally carried by architects, different general liability coverage, and a vehicle insurance policy that covers construction equipment. Workers' compensation is where the premiums will skyrocket from what architects pay now, because architecture firms tend to be fairly safe places to work, while construction sites are one of the most dangerous. However, most architects who have done this say, "Don't worry about the higher premiums. You'll be able to afford them!"

Some architecture firms worry about how the lead role changes the image of the architect. Filippo Brunelleschi (who set precedent with his innovative Duomo in Florence) and Thomas Jefferson (architect of great buildings, a university, and a government) set their minds first and foremost to doing what is right. Taking the lead did not bother them. Leadership creates its own image. When your firm has a menu ranging from pure design to design-assist to design-build services, clients can choose those most appropriate for their particular project needs.

Getting into the Design-Build Market

If you need experience to break into a new market, how do you get that experience in the first place? Here are six ways for those ready to consider participating in design-build delivery, including the ultimate step of leading the design-build process:

1. *Add construction management to your design services.* As a construction manager, the architect is an adviser (or agent) to the owner and manages the trade subcontractors without assuming risk for their work. Construction management is not true design-build because the trade subcontracts are directly with the owner rather than a single contractor. The architect contracts with the owner to manage those subs and provide the design services. This is a way to learn what is involved

in construction management with limited risk. As a CM-adviser, you may want the subs to have "open-book accounting," so you see all of their costs. This will help you learn how subs price work, knowledge you can use in the future when bidding and managing trade subcontractors as the prime design-builder.

2. *Team with a general contractor.* Take on the role of consultant to general contractors with whom you work well, and learn from them for a project or two. Watch them closely. Put one of your staff members in the contractor's office, as the team works together, to observe what they do and how the work is done. You can really get a good start on your education in leading and managing construction this way. The contractor takes the risk as prime, with the architect as a consultant. Use such projects as a learning experience.

3. *Form a true "joint venture" with a contractor.* A joint venture can be a partnership or it could be a new entity—such as a limited-liability company—in which the architect and the contractor are both at risk, but the risk is shared. Subject to state licensing laws, the contractor and the architect may each own a fixed percent of the new company, and the architect is right there in the driver's seat with the contractor—sharing the risks, the control, and the rewards.

4. *Merge corporately with a contractor.* There are many examples nationwide of mergers that have worked successfully. Contractors are looking for ways to bring design services "in-house." So how about you—is your firm for sale? For firms in an ownership transition crisis, merging with a construction company may be the answer you have not considered. It gives the contractor an instant staff, plus a record of project types the company can handle.

5. *Start small with a current client.* A good beginning point for leading the design-build process would be a small project with which your firm has a lot of familiarity, working with a current client. Having the client's trust in you as a designer typically translates to greater willingness to trust you on the construction side as well. Several firms got their start in the lead role with clients who were not comfortable passing off to an unknown contractor. "I know you. Can't you build this, too?" How will your firm answer that question? To reduce risk further, consider starting with small tenant improvements and finish work. What a great way to get experience managing trade subs and build your skills at that level before branching out.

The worst formula is to take on as your first design-build project a building type you've never done before with a client you've never worked with before. It's a formula for disaster. Nonetheless, the big project brings with it a big fee, and some people are determined to plow ahead boldly into the unknown.

6. *Form a design-build firm.* Hire estimators, superintendents, and project managers you do not already have on staff and form a new design-build company with a strong core group. Most firms choose to set up a separate company for the construction—especially when starting out—to minimize the risk to the architecture practice. This works best for private work, since a new company may need several years to get the requisite bonding capacity for public work.

Final Thoughts

The thought of starting a construction company makes many architects shudder. In terms of financial outlay, you don't have to own any equipment at the start—or maybe ever. You can rent most everything you need and charge it to the owner as a cost of the work. Some architects choose to hire temporary labor as needed for manpower to avoid carrying the payroll and overhead burden. For those willing to "staff up" and carry the overhead of construction management personnel until the first job, find staff you can use in your architecture practice for estimating and project administration until that first design-build project comes along. Prepare a strong business plan to present to your banker and secure a line of credit. Look into SBA loans for new small businesses, and consider finding a retired contractor as a "mentor."

Talk to your peers who have already taken the lead in design-build. Get good legal and insurance advice from people who understand design-build. Be prudent and pick familiar projects and clients to start out.

Bill Quatman was 2007 chair of the AIA Design-Build Knowledge Community Advisory Group. He is both a licensed architect and an attorney with Shughart Thomson & Kilroy, P.C., in the law firm's Kansas City, Missouri, office.

8.2 Integrated Project Delivery

Integrated project delivery leverages early contributions of knowledge and expertise through use of new technologies, allowing all team members to better realize their highest potential and expanding the value each provides throughout the project life cycle.

Integrated project delivery (IPD) is a project delivery approach that integrates people, systems, business structures, and practices into a process that collaboratively harnesses the talents and insights of all project participants with the goal of optimizing project results, increasing value to the owner, reducing waste, and maximizing efficiency through all phases of design, fabrication, and construction.

IPD principles can be applied to a variety of contractual arrangements, and IPD teams can include members well beyond the basic triad of owner, architect, and contractor. In all cases, integrated projects are uniquely distinguished by highly effective collaboration among the owner, the prime designer, and the prime constructor, commencing at early design and continuing through the project delivery process until project handover.

CHANGE IS NOW

Technological evolution coupled with ongoing owner demand for more effective processes that result in better, faster, less costly, and less adversarial construction projects are driving significant and rapid change in the construction industry. Envision a new world in which the following statements are true:

- Facility managers, end users, contractors, and suppliers are all involved at the start of the design process.
- Processes are outcome-driven and decisions are not made solely on a first-cost basis.

This topic is excerpted from "Integrated Project Delivery: A Guide," prepared by the American Institute of Architects (AIA National and AIA California Council) and published in 2007.

TRADITIONAL VS. INTEGRATED PROJECT DELIVERY

Traditional Project Delivery		Integrated Project Delivery
Fragmented Assembled on "just-as-needed" or "minimum-necessary" basis Strongly hierarchical, controlled	**Teams**	Integrated team entity composed of key project stakeholders, assembled early in the process Open, collaborative
Linear, distinct, segregated Knowledge gathered "just-as-needed" Information hoarded Silos of knowledge and expertise	**Process**	Concurrent and multilevel Early contributions of knowledge and expertise Information openly shared Stakeholder trust and respect
Individually managed, transferred to the greatest extent possible	**Risk**	Collectively managed, appropriately shared
Individually pursued Minimum effort for maximum return (Usually) first-cost based	**Compensation/Reward**	Team success tied to project success Value-based
Paper-based, 2-dimensional Analog	**Communications/Technology**	Digitally based, virtual Building information modeling (3-, 4-, and 5-dimensional)
Encourage unilateral effort Allocate and transfer risk No sharing	**Agreements**	Encourage, foster, promote, and support multilateral, open sharing and collaboration Risk sharing

- Communications throughout the process are clear, concise, open, transparent, and trusting.
- Designers fully understand the ramifications of their decisions at the time the decisions are made.
- Risk and reward are based on value and appropriately balanced among all team members over the life of a project.
- The industry delivers a higher quality, sustainable built environment.

At the core of an integrated project are collaborative, integrated, and productive teams composed of key project participants. Building upon early contributions of individual expertise, these teams are guided by principles of trust, transparent processes, effective collaboration, open information sharing, team success tied to project success, shared risk and reward, value-based decision making, and use of full technological capabilities and support. The outcome is the opportunity to design, build, and operate as efficiently as possible.

BENEFITS OF INTEGRATED PROJECT DELIVERY

Recent studies document inefficiencies and waste in the construction industry. For example, an *Economist* article from 2000 identifies 30 percent waste in the U.S. construction industry; a 2004 National Institute of Standards and Technology study targets lack of AEC software interoperability as costing the industry $15.8 billion annually; and a U.S. Bureau of Labor Statistics study shows that construction, alone of all nonfarm industries, has decreased in productivity since 1964, while during the same period all other nonfarm industries have increased in productivity by more than 200 percent. New technologies have emerged that, when utilized in conjunction with collaborative processes, demonstrate substantial increases in productivity and decreases in requests for information, field conflicts, waste, and project schedules. Owners are increasingly demanding methodologies that deliver these outcomes.

It has been determined that sustainable results from efforts to meet increasingly aggressive goals for energy and carbon reduction are best achieved through collaborative processes. The AIA experience with the American Society of Heating, Refrigerating and Air-Conditioning Engineers (ASHRAE) Advanced Energy Design Guides suggests that—although some reductions are prescriptively achievable (e.g., through the use of a checklist)—when a 30 percent reduction is exceeded, complex interactions of systems and context must be taken into account. As an example, integrated processes are being acknowledged and encouraged in sustainable ratings systems such as the U.S. Green Building Council's Leadership in Energy and Environmental Design (LEED)® Green Building Rating System™. New energy codes such as ASHRAE Standard 189 also include recommendations regarding integrated processes.

Integrated project delivery results in greater efficiencies. The "Achieving Excellence in Construction Procurement Guide," published in 2007 by the United Kingdom Office of Government Commerce (UKOGC), estimates that savings of up to 30 percent in the cost of construction can be achieved when integrated teams promote continuous improvement over a series of construction projects. UKOGC further estimates that single projects employing integrated supply teams can achieve savings of 2 to 10 percent in the cost of construction.

Beyond the benefits described, IPD provides positive value propositions for the three major stakeholder groups:

- *Owners.* Early and open sharing of project knowledge streamlines project communications and allows owners to effectively balance project options to meet their business goals. Integrated delivery strengthens the project team's understanding of the owner's desired outcomes, thus improving the team's ability to control costs and manage the budget, all of which increase the likelihood that project goals, including schedule, life cycle costs, quality, and sustainability, will be achieved.
- *Constructors.* The integrated delivery process allows constructors to contribute their expertise in construction techniques early in the design process, resulting in improved project quality and financial performance during the construction phase. The constructor's participation during the design phase provides the opportunity for strong preconstruction planning, more timely and informed understanding of the design, anticipation and resolution of design-related issues, visualization of construction sequencing prior to construction start, and improvements in cost control and budget management, all of which increase the likelihood that project goals, including schedule, life cycle costs, quality and sustainability, will be achieved.
- *Designers.* The integrated delivery process allows the designer to benefit from the early contribution of constructors' expertise during the design phase (e.g., accurate budget estimates that can inform design decisions and pre-construction resolution of design-related issues), resulting in improved project quality and financial performance. The IPD process increases the level of effort during early design phases, resulting in reduced documentation time and improved cost control and budget management, all of which increase the likelihood that project goals, including schedule, life cycle costs, quality and sustainability, will be achieved.

PRINCIPLES OF INTEGRATED PROJECT DELIVERY

Integrated project delivery is built on collaboration, which in turn is built on trust. Effectively structured, trust-based collaboration encourages parties to focus on project outcomes rather than individual goals. Without trust-based collaboration, IPD will falter and participants will remain in the adverse and antagonistic relationships that plague the construction industry today. IPD promises better outcomes, but outcomes will not change unless the people responsible for delivering those outcomes change. Thus, achieving the benefits of IPD requires that all project participants embrace the following principles of integrated project delivery.

1. Mutual Respect and Trust

In an integrated project, owner, designer, consultants, constructor, subcontractors, and suppliers understand the value of collaboration and are committed to working as a team in the best interests of the project.

2. Mutual Benefit and Reward

All participants or team members benefit from IPD. Because the integrated process requires early involvement by more parties, IPD compensation structures recognize and reward early involvement. Compensation is based on the value added by an organization and it rewards "what's best for project" behavior. For example, incentives tied to achieving project goals may be offered. Integrated projects use innovative business models to support collaboration and efficiency.

3. Collaborative Innovation and Decision Making

Innovation is stimulated when ideas are freely exchanged among all participants. In an integrated project, ideas are judged on their merits, not on the author's role or status. Key decisions are evaluated by the project team and, to the greatest extent practical, made unanimously.

4. Early Involvement of Key Participants

In an integrated project, the key participants are involved from the earliest practical moment. Decision making is improved by the influx of knowledge and expertise of all key participants. Their combined knowledge and expertise is most powerful during the project's early stages, where informed decisions have the greatest effect.

5. Early Goal Definition

Project goals are developed early and agreed upon and respected by all participants. Insight from each participant is valued in a culture that promotes and drives innovation and outstanding performance, holding project outcomes at the center of a framework of individual participant objectives and values.

6. Intensified Planning

The IPD approach recognizes that increased effort in planning results in increased efficiency and savings during execution. Thus, the thrust of the integrated approach is not to reduce design effort, but rather to greatly improve design results, streamlining and shortening the much more expensive construction effort.

7. Open Communication

IPD's focus on team performance is based on open, direct, and honest communication among all participants. Responsibilities are clearly defined in a no-blame culture, leading to identification and resolution of problems rather than determination of liability. Disputes are recognized as they occur and promptly resolved.

8. Appropriate Technology

Integrated projects often rely on cutting-edge technologies. Technologies are specified at project initiation to maximize functionality, generality, and interoperability. Open and interoperable data exchanges based on disciplined and transparent data structures are essential to support IPD. Because open standards best enable communications among all participants, technology that is compliant with open standards is used whenever available.

9. Organization and Leadership

The project team is an organization in its own right and all team members are committed to the project team's goals and values. Leadership is taken by the team member most capable with regard to specific work and services. Often, design professionals and contractors lead in areas of their traditional competence with support from the entire team; however, specific roles are necessarily determined on a project-by-project basis. Roles are clearly defined, without creating artificial barriers that chill open communication and risk taking.

THOUGH NOT EASY, CHANGE IS ACHIEVABLE

The design and construction industry is changing. Technologies are allowing great advances in efficiency and accuracy, but the changes in process that are resulting in new delivery methods are even more significant. To be successful, integrated project delivery requires the designer, constructor, owner, and other participants in the enterprise to take on new roles and competencies. This is a significant change in culture for all team members. However, the change may not be as daunting as it first appears. A combination of generational skill sets (e.g., the communication skills of baby boomers and the technology skills of the X or Y generation) yield surprising depth in talent within existing firms in all areas of industry. Leveraging those talents by adding effective collaboration with key project participants earlier than is traditional yields a formula for success.

For More Information

"Integrated Project Delivery: A Guide," written and published by the American Institute of Architects and AIA California Council, provides information and guidance on principles and techniques of integrated project delivery. It also explains how to utilize IPD methodologies in designing and constructing projects. A collaborative effort between AIA National and AIACC, the guide suggests a path for transforming the status quo into a collaborative, value-based process that delivers high-outcome results to the entire building team. It includes points to consider when setting up an integrated project, a study of how to implement IPD, and a discussion of how to apply general IPD principles within the framework of new and traditional delivery models currently used in the marketplace.

8.3 Construction Documentation

Kristine K. Fallon, FAIA, and Kenneth C. Crocco, FAIA

Construction documents describe what is to be built, how contractors are to be selected, and how the contracts for construction will be written and administered. The process of producing construction documentation strives for efficiency, comprehensiveness, and quality.

Once a design has been developed and approved, the architect prepares the drawings and specifications that set forth the requirements for construction. The development of the construction documentation is an extension of the

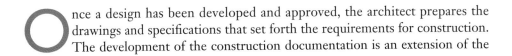

Kristine K. Fallon is a Chicago-based consultant for computer applications in the design and construction industry. Kenneth C. Crocco is vice president of Chicago-based ArchiTech Consulting, Inc., a firm specializing in building specifications and information management. This is an updated version of the "Construction Documents Production" topic in the thirteenth edition of the Handbook.

▶ Bidding or Negotiation Phase (8.4) reviews bidding requirements and addenda.

design process. Decisions on details, materials, products, and finishes all serve to reinforce the design concept—and begin the process of translating the concept into reality. Of all project phases, the preparation of the construction documentation typically takes the most time and resources.

ORGANIZATION AND CONTENT

Construction documentation serves multiple purposes that include the following:

- Communicating to the owner, in detail, what a project involves
- Establishing the contractual obligations the owner and contractor owe each other during a project
- Laying out the responsibilities of the architect or any other party administering or managing construction contracts for the owner
- Communicating to the contractor the quantities, qualities, and configuration of the elements to construct a project

In turn, the contractor uses the documentation to solicit bids or quotations from subcontractors and suppliers, and the construction documents provide the basis for obtaining regulatory and financial approvals needed to proceed with construction.

The project documents typically consist of the project manual and the project drawings. The drawings include architectural, structural, mechanical, electrical, civil, landscape, interior design, and other specialty drawings. The project manual typically includes the following:

- Bidding requirements (advertisement and invitations, instructions, available project information) and procurement forms
- Contract forms and supplements (the form of agreement to be used between owner and contractor, project forms, and certifications)
- Contract conditions (the general conditions of the contract for construction, which outline the rights, responsibilities, and duties of owner and contractor as well as others involved in the construction process, including the architect; supplementary conditions particular to the project)
- Specifications (general requirements, facility construction and facility service specifications, and site work specifications), which describe the level of quality and the standards to be met in the construction of the project

The bidding documents include the project manual and drawings, as well as revisions, clarifications, and modifications to them, including addenda (additions to any of these documents issued by the architect during the bidding or negotiation process).

The contract documents include all of the documents just listed except the bidding requirements. In addition, any contract modifications (orders for minor changes in the work, construction change directives, and change orders) become part of the contract documents.

The construction documents are not intended to be a complete set of instructions on how to construct a building. Construction means, methods, techniques, sequences, procedures, and site safety precautions are customarily assigned as responsibilities of the contractor to give the contractor latitude in preparing bids and carrying out the construction phase. The contractor determines the assignment of work to specific trades and subcontractors. The contractor also manages logistical matters such as the sequence of operations, scheduling, design of temporary supports and facilities, selection of appropriate equipment, and project safety.

Construction documentation contains legal and contractual information, procedural and administrative information (referred to as Division 01 General Requirements of the Project specifications and further expanded in Part 1 of each specification section), architectural and construction information (found in Divisions 02 through 48 of

PROJECT DOCUMENTS

A variety of document types must be produced to accomplish building design and construction.

The *project manual* includes the bidding requirements, contract forms and conditions, and specifications.

Bidding documents are the documents required to bid or negotiate the construction contract.

Construction documents are the drawings and the specifications the architect prepares to set forth the requirements for construction of the project.

Contract documents form the legal agreement between the owner and contractor.

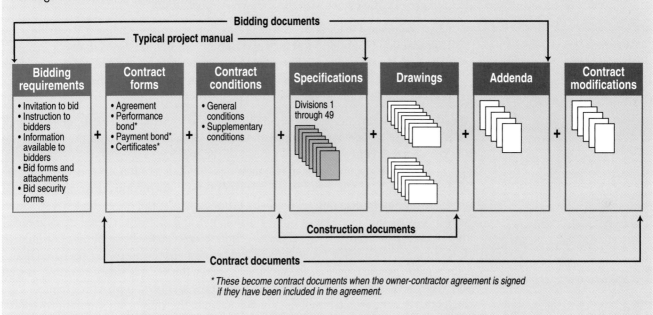

* These become contract documents when the owner-contractor agreement is signed if they have been included in the agreement.

the specifications and in the drawings), and site and infrastructure information, such as topographical surveys and geotechnical investigation data.

Legal and Contractual Information

The contract forms and conditions establish the legal framework of a project by setting forth the rights, duties, and responsibilities of the owner and contractor.

On larger projects, it has been customary to physically separate the contract form from the contract conditions. The *form* is the agreement between owner and contractor enumerating the contract documents, specifying the time of performance, and stating the contractor's compensation. The *conditions* set forth the rights, duties, and responsibilities of owner and contractor and other parties to the construction process (the architect, subcontractors, and possibly the construction manager, the owner's project representative, etc.). Separating the form from the conditions allows the contractor to disclose the contract conditions to subcontractors and suppliers without revealing the contract sum or other items in the agreement that may be privately held between the owner, architect, and contractor.

The architect's responsibility. Several of the AIA owner-architect agreements require the architect to "assist the Owner in the development and preparation of (1) bidding and procurement information that describes the time, place, and conditions of bidding, including bidding or proposal forms; (2) the form of agreement between the Owner and the Contractor; and (3) the Conditions of the Contract for Construction (General, Supplementary, and other Conditions)." The architect is not required to prepare legal and

▶ Construction Contracts (11.4) discusses contract forms and conditions.

contractual information but only to assist in its preparation. The architect is not in the practice of law and is not professionally qualified to give the owner legal or insurance counsel. It is common, however, for architects to assemble the bidding and contractual documents, providing them for review and approval by the owner.

The owner's responsibility. The owner is responsible for furnishing the necessary legal, accounting, and insurance services to accomplish a project. Therefore, the owner, with the advice of the owner's legal counsel, approves the bidding requirements, contract forms, and conditions.

If the owner has little experience with construction projects and contracts, it may help to provide the owner with the following information:

- AIA Document G612–2001, Owner's Instructions to the Architect Regarding the Construction Contract, Insurance and Bonds, and Bidding Procedures
- "You and Your Architect." This brochure, available from the AIA Web site, offers advice to clients on how the owner and architect can work together to keep a project on track throughout the design and construction process.

If used, these documents should be submitted to the owner at or prior to the beginning of construction document development because basic decisions about the handling of the construction contract affect all aspects of the project.

Some owners propose or mandate their own bidding requirements, contract forms, and conditions. Since the contractual agreements for construction are so closely related to the owner-architect contract (and any other contracts the owner may have written with a construction manager or other consultants), and since these agreements are usually already in place, it is essential that all of these agreements be carefully coordinated. It is often worthwhile for the architect's legal counsel to review owner-prepared documents with specific regard to the architect's rights, duties, and responsibilities, as well as to review clauses covering indemnification of the architect, role of the architect during construction, ownership of documents, dispute resolution, and similar provisions.

Procedural and Administrative Information

This information is typically found in three places in the construction documentation: in the conditions of the contract, in Division 01 of the specifications, and in the opening articles (Part 1) of the specifications in Divisions 02 through 48.

The general conditions of the contract for construction contain provisions common to most projects. In addition to legal and contractual information, the general conditions include requirements for a variety of contract administration activities, such as reviewing shop drawings and samples, reviewing contractor's payment requests, approving minor changes in the work, monitoring the progress of the work, issuing site observation reports, and reviewing closeout documents. AIA Document A201, General Conditions of the Contract for Construction, is widely recognized for establishing common general conditions practices.

Division 01 of the specifications expands on information in the general conditions and often includes the following:

- Standard office procedures, such as required format for shop drawing submittals, numbers of sets of submittals required, and procedures for certification of substantial completion
- Procedures required by owners, such as forms for payment requests and waivers of lien
- Procedures that govern the specific project, such as applicable codes, requirements for record documents, temporary facilities, and testing laboratory methods

Division 01 section titles include the following:

011000 Summary

011200 Multiple Contract Summary

012100 Allowances

012200 Unit Prices

012300 Alternates

012600 Contract Modification Procedures

012900 Payment Procedures

013100 Project Management and Coordination

013200 Construction Progress Documentation

013233 Photographic Documentation

013300 Submittal Procedures

013513.16 Special Project Procedures for Detention Facilities

013591 Historic Treatment Procedures

014000 Quality Requirements

014200 References

015000 Temporary Facilities and Controls

015639 Temporary Tree and Plant Protection

016000 Product Requirements

017300 Execution

017329 Cutting and Patching

017419 Construction Waste Management and Disposal

017700 Closeout Procedures

017823 Operation and Maintenance Data

017839 Project Record Documents

017900 Demonstration and Training

018113 Sustainable Design Requirements

019113 General Commissioning Requirements

Part 1 of each of the sections in Divisions 02 through 48 presents administrative and procedural information relating to the elements covered in that section including, for example:

- Definitions
- Delivery, storage, and handling requirements
- Allowance and unit price items
- Alternates
- Site condition requirements
- Submittal requirements
- Warranty requirements
- Quality assurance requirements
- Maintenance requirements

It is worthwhile to develop a consistent approach to placement of procedural and administrative requirements in the documents.

Architectural and Construction Information

Architectural and construction information encompasses the quantities, qualities, and configuration of the elements required for the project. Quantities and relationships are usually best indicated on the drawings; qualities and standards of workmanship are best placed in the specifications. The level of detail provided in the drawings and specifications responds to the needs of the project and of those who will own, regulate, and—most important—build it.

The new millennium has seen the introduction of new software products, including those for building information modeling. The use of BIM software does not preclude the delivery of traditional documentation but does make other methods of communication possible. If there is no specific contractual requirement for the use of BIM software, it is prudent to verify with the contractor in advance the

THE POWER OF INFORMATION MODELS

According to the National Institute of Building Sciences, a building information model is a "digital representation of the physical and functional characteristics of a facility." As such, it serves as "a shared knowledge resource for information about a facility, forming a reliable basis for decisions during its life-cycle, from inception onward." For purposes of discussion, building information modeling is a tool that enables the process of virtual design and construction.

BIM technology is different from first-generation 3D computer modeling used for animation and rendering. In the project depictions created with the first-generation software, data are stored as lines, planes, and surfaces with no other information about the objects represented. Going beyond this basic 3D geometry, a model created using BIM software includes information about material designations, product and equipment specifications, and even performance data. Another important BIM characteristic is that representations are not redundant; in other words, information recorded once then appears in multiple views, ensuring that measurements or properties found in one view are the same in other views of the same design. This is a great improvement over the errors that can be introduced when data must be copied from one drawing to another.

A building information model can be used to check interferences and to extract bills of materials for estimating or procurement purposes. Pioneering project teams have already demonstrated that construction drawings can be bypassed altogether and a building can be constructed directly from a BIM, with any required 2D drawings—plans, sections, elevations, details—extracted from the model as needed. If as-built conditions are documented in the model, the model can then be used for operations and maintenance activities as well.

BIM technology has broad implications for work processes and sequencing, team composition, contractual relationships, and professional liability. It is unlikely the building design and construction industry will transition completely to this way of working in the near term. Nevertheless, the technological tools now exist to reorder the

entire building design and delivery process. BIM tools from multiple vendors have delivered benefits to projects of all types and scales, from K–12 schools to the Beijing National Swimming Center for the 2008 Olympics.

Using an information model as the central design tool, rather than creating and coordinating information in multiple drawings, yields significant production efficiencies, including enhanced productivity, reduced design cycle time, and a better-coordinated work product. The benefit is not that architects draw faster using building information modeling, but that less drawing is required. The traditional documentation approach requires the inclusion of redundant information on multiple drawings, while the building information model is the single authoritative source for building information, and most drawings are extracted directly from it. Changes made to the model can be automatically propagated to all extracted drawings. This has the additional advantage of improving coordination among the drawings, as well as reducing time spent in coordination activities.

Using a BIM approach requires comprehensive rethinking of production techniques, including:

- *Who does what.* Development of a building information model requires more knowledge of architectural technology than production of 2D drawings.
- *CAD and data organization standards.* If a firm wants drawings produced with BIM software to conform to office graphic standards, setup and customization efforts will be required. The firm will also need to rethink how project data is organized and named (i.e., file naming and folder structure).
- *Standard CAD libraries and details.* A firm must determine how much of this information will be needed in the BIM environment and how to get it there.
- *Type and sequence of design activities.* For example, many firms find they need to model the individual components to be used in the building before they develop the building model itself.

- *Effort required in each design phase.* With a building information model, more design decisions must be made early in the design process, while time savings of 50 percent have been reported in construction drawings.
- *Value earned in each project phase.* Design firms should seek a payment schedule that parallels the new level of effort expended and value produced in each design phase.
- *Coordination procedures.* Project coordinators must understand where coordination is automated and where it is not.
- *Checking and other quality assurance procedures.* Because building components are reusable within the same project or across projects, care must be taken to ensure the accuracy and appropriateness of non-graphic attributes that may be used in downstream functions, such as schedules and bills of material.
- *How information is communicated and shared.* A major question is whether to share a particular model with outside team members or simply to provide 2D CAD files. This decision, which depends on the capabilities of the other team members, can raise serious business issues. Although BIM tools inherently produce 2D drawings, many project teams have found that a requirement to produce updated drawing sets on a regular basis becomes a bottleneck. Finally, sharing a building information model requires careful data management techniques.

acceptability of using BIM technology to transmit architectural and construction information.

DRAWINGS

The construction drawings show, in graphic and quantitative form, the extent, configuration, location, relationships, and dimensions of the work to be done. They generally contain site and building plans, elevations, sections, details, diagrams, and schedules. In addition to drawn information, they may include photographs, other imported graphics, and printed schedules.

The U.S. National CAD Standard (NCS) provides comprehensive guidance to users of two-dimensional computer-aided design (CAD) systems on the format, sequencing, and internal organization of CAD drawings. The NCS incorporates the Construction Specifications Institute (CSI) Uniform Drawing System (UDS) and the AIA CAD Layer Guidelines. It covers layer names, plotting guidelines, drawing set organization, drawing sheet layout and organization, schedule formats, drafting conventions, terms and abbreviations, symbols, notations, and code conventions.

NCS is not entirely prescriptive. Firms will find that they need to customize this standard to meet their needs, but NCS does provide guidelines for doing this. It is an excellent starting point for any firm's CAD standard. NCS can be purchased from the National Institute of Building Sciences. An order form is available at www.nibs.org.

Sequence and Sheet Formats

A set of drawings is an organized presentation of the project. To the extent possible, the drawings are organized in the sequence of construction.

Most firms develop office standards for sheet size, layout, and title blocks. Some clients, however, might dictate their own format requirements. In addition to the name, address, and phone number of the architecture firm, the title block may include the following:

- Project title and address, frequently including owner's name and address
- Drawing title and sheet number
- Names and addresses of consultants
- Notation of who worked on the drawing, including checking
- Dates drawings were issued (such as for bid, permit, and construction)
- Dates of revisions

- Architect's seal and, if required, signature
- Engineer's seal and, if required, signature
- Copyright information

The CSI Uniform Drawing System organizes this information according to the following categories:

- Designer identification block
- Project identification block
- Issue block
- Management block
- Sheet title block
- Sheet identification block

Each drawing should include the basic information required to orient the user, such as key plans showing location of partial plans, north arrows, and scales for drawings. Graphic scales are included in the event drawings are reduced. Most firms lay out the drawings early in the project. A cartooning or storyboard process may be used to determine how many and what kinds of plans, sections, elevations, details, schedules, and other graphic elements will be prepared; their scale (and thus size on the sheets); their sequence; and any interrelationships. This helps the architect conceptualize the project and understand what will be involved in developing and communicating it to the owner, regulators, and contractors.

Drawing Scale, Dimensions, and Targets

Appropriate scale, dimensions, and targets (or "keys") are essential communication elements of the drawings. It is common for a firm to establish standard procedures and symbols for dimensions and targets, as well as for lettering size and style. The project manager usually determines the drawing scales to be used, as well as any variations from office standards.

Scale. The smallest scale that clearly presents the required information is chosen for a drawing. The selection of scales and lettering sizes must also take into account whether the drawings will be reduced for distribution.

Dimensions. Necessary dimensions should be numerically indicated on the drawings. Because the contractor is not permitted to scale the drawings for dimensions, drawings should contain sufficient numerical dimensions to construct the building elements shown. The system of dimensioning used in the drawings relates to horizontal and vertical reference planes (such as the structural grid) that, in turn, can be tied to one or more benchmarks established as permanent data points for the project. It is logical to establish a hierarchy of dimensions in the order of construction, using building elements that will be constructed early as dimensional benchmarks for elements constructed later. For example, it is common to first denote the dimensions of structural elements such as a column grid and then measure distances from the columns to nonstructural elements, such as interior partitions.

Dimensions are laid out in lines called *strings*. It is necessary to develop several strings to properly locate a sequence of related building elements. These sets of strings are drawn in a hierarchy of detail, with overall dimensions shown in the outermost string and detailed dimensions shown in the innermost string. To ensure that numbers indicated on the dimension strings correspond to the intended built reality, contractors and others using the drawings will add up strings of dimensions and cross-check them against one another. In some cases, the level of detail of the drawing or the construction method employed makes comprehensive strings, in which every dimension is determined, undesirable. In such cases, the critical dimensions are noted and a noncritical dimension is noted with a plus-or-minus value. This gives the contractor an idea of the desired dimension and further indicates that discrepancies during construction are to be resolved by adjusting this dimension.

Many architects will have "cartooned" the drawings as part of the project pricing and proposal process.

Automatic dimensioning in CAD systems produces accurate dimension annotation. This reduces the need for manual cross-checking of dimensions and has the added benefit of highlighting dimensional discrepancies as the drawings are being completed. When establishing CAD standards and procedures for dimensioning, it is important for firms to thoughtfully select the display precision for their dimensioning—1/32", 1/16" or 1/8"—and to include that parameter in their CAD template or seed file. In the interest of accuracy and coordination, CAD users should not manually override automatically generated dimensions even though CAD systems do permit it.

The drawings should call attention to critical areas where standard construction tolerances are not sufficient or dimensions are tied to specific dimensions of manufactured assemblies. At the same time, the experienced architect recognizes that materials and construction tolerances in the field rarely approach those that can be achieved in manufacturing. For example, some architects regard field-created tolerances of less than 1/8" (1:100 in SI units) or even 1/4" (1:50) as unrealistic.

Targets. Sometimes referred to as "keys," targets are one of the primary methods of establishing the relationships among the drawings. Floor plans use standard symbols to locate (or target) building sections, column grids, door designations, wall types and sections, details, interior elevations, enlarged plans, and similar information. Elevations target building sections, windows, and details. It is also helpful to target details on wall sections and building sections.

Other Drawing Elements

The drawings often include the following:

- *Symbols and abbreviations.* The need to communicate a large amount of information in a limited space commonly dictates the use of symbols and abbreviations. Good practice suggests that these be defined early and used consistently.
- *Drawing/specification coordination.* Designations on the drawings should be coordinated with those used in the specifications. If, for example, only one type of elastomeric sealant is used in the project, the term "elastomeric sealant" is sufficient on the drawings. If more than one sealant type is involved, however, it is necessary to develop and use terminology that clearly differentiates among the various sealants.
- *Notes.* When drawings and specifications are separate, statements on quality and workmanship are made in the specifications. Notes on the drawings should be limited to the minimum needed to convey design intent clearly.
- *Schedules.* Information best presented in tabular form is most commonly shown in a schedule. There may be schedules for doors, windows, hardware, room finishes, paint selections, fixtures and equipment, repetitive structural elements (such as columns, footings, or lintels), and similar items. Schedule formats vary according to office or project requirements. Many schedules can be developed and revised using spreadsheet or word processing software programs. The Uniform Drawing System (UDS) and the U.S. National CAD Standard include a module on schedules. UDS establishes guidelines for creating schedules and complete illustrations of commonly used schedules. The UDS companion CD-ROM includes these schedules in a word-processing format.

Architectural Graphic Standards presents conventions for symbols and abbreviations.

Drawing Production Methods

For hundreds of years architectural drawings were produced manually, making their production one of the most labor-intensive and time-consuming phases of professional service. Technological advances—especially in CAD—have improved productivity in drawing production. This change has also blurred the distinction between design development and construction documentation.

Manual drafting. Some firms continue with manual drafting as the production method of choice. A number of approaches and specific techniques can be used to reduce time and increase the accuracy and utility of manual drafting:

- Standard items such as sheet borders, title blocks, symbols, and common details may be produced ahead of time and incorporated into the drawings as needed. Some firms bind reference information and standard details into the project manual.
- Schedules and other highly organized data sets may be produced using computers and spreadsheet or database programs and incorporated into the drawings or bound into the project manual.
- Photographs of existing conditions may be reproduced directly onto drawing media. Planned renovations can then be drawn directly onto the photographs.
- Individual drawing sheets may be overlays or photographic composites of individual drawings, details, schedules, and notes, allowing flexibility in formatting.

Computer-aided drafting. CAD systems offer the advantages of clarity, easy representation of elements (especially repetitive elements), fast changes, accurate dimensioning, and improved coordination among drawings as well as between drawings and specifications. Computer-produced drawings can be easy to read, with lettering and dimensioning consistent throughout. CAD software packages increasingly incorporate useful ancillary functions such as automatic area and material quantity takeoffs and concurrent development of door, window, and other schedules.

Managing drawing revisions is entirely different in the CAD environment. Telltale erasures, changes in lettering, and other marks that signal changes and revisions to manually drafted drawings are absent. The exchange of computer data files among collaborating design professionals via the Internet has underscored the need for controlling and verifying the integrity of electronically transmitted drawings. Electronic data management (EDM) systems prevent multiple persons from accessing the same drawing simultaneously, track drawing modifications, ensure that changes are not incorporated into the record copy of the drawing until properly approved, and automatically route the pending changes to the party responsible for approvals. However, EDM technology can be too costly and time-consuming to implement in multifirm environments except on large, long-duration projects.

Another CAD approach is for each firm on the project team to manage its own drawing controls internally and post new and revised documents on secure computer bulletin boards or project Web sites called project extranets.

Drawing Standards

There are different approaches to establishing standards or conventions for the uniform production of construction documents. Because the industry lacks comprehensive drawing standards, nearly all firms have developed their own standards as a way of ensuring quality, consistency, and thoroughness in this critical phase of service.

The advent of CAD technology introduces a new level of complexity for construction drawing standards. The manner in which data are created and stored is not readily apparent to the viewer without a detailed examination of the data file. The laborious task of deciphering the organizational system of another person can easily negate any gain in productivity achieved by the use of CAD technology. This underscores the necessity for establishing and adhering to CAD standards, and NCS, discussed above, is a good starting point. It also establishes a common point of reference when exchanging CAD data with consultants or the owner.

The ability to reuse design elements from previous projects is one of the principal benefits of CAD. However, if projects are developed with different layer names, line weights and colors, text fonts, and dimension styles, the reuse of design elements may require extensive editing. This prevents reaping the anticipated productivity benefits of CAD. In a CAD environment, graphic standards for drawing organization must be supplemented by CAD standards for data organization. At a minimum, these standards should address the following subjects:

- Drawing sheet sizes, layout, scales, sequence, and numbering
- Targeting and other references within the documents

- Notes, abbreviations, and graphic conventions
- Dimensioning
- Internal organization of CAD files and the relationships with reference files and drawing sheet layouts
- Where project CAD files and any reusable components should be stored on the firm's file server and how they should be named and organized (i.e., folder structure)
- Procedures for versioning, archiving, and exchanging CAD data with outside organizations

CHRONOLOGY OF STANDARDS DEVELOPMENT FOR CONSTRUCTION DRAWINGS

The development of office standards is a time-consuming overhead task, and the quality of office drawing standards varies greatly from one firm to another. Consequently, even the best of efforts can prove futile if clients and consultants do not share and use the same standards. This situation has prompted a number of independent efforts aimed at bringing industry-wide order to the production of construction documents. The following profiles several of these efforts.

ConDoc Drawing System

ConDoc, developed by Onkal "Duke" Guzey, AIA, and James Freehof, AIA, in the late 1980s, was the first system for organizing construction documents. Based on a simple, uniform arrangement of drawings, a standard sheet format, a sheet identification system, and a keynote system that links drawings and specifications, ConDoc improved quality control, information management, productivity, and bidding results.

Organization of drawings. A uniform arrangement is established for locating project data within a set of drawings and for identifying individual sheets. Drawing sets are divided by disciplines, with each discipline assigned a discipline letter prefix. Discipline drawings are subdivided into groups of like information, with each group assigned a group number. Finally, each sheet within a group is assigned a sequential number. For example, A101 represents the architecture discipline (A), group plan (1), and sheet number (01).

Standard sheet format. Sheets are composed using a standard, modular format that may be subdivided into module blocks. The standard sheet has three zones. The first zone, on the right side of the sheet, contains the sheet title block and drawing keynote legend. Zone 2 is the graphics zone and contains a nonprinting modular grid. Zone 3 is the perimeter or border, with alphanumeric grid coordinates.

Keynote system. This process establishes a connecting link between graphic information shown on the drawings

and the related text in the specifications. Keynotes minimize the amount of text needed on drawings without restricting the notation process. Drawing notations are identified by keynote symbols. In general, notations with their respective keynote symbols are located on each sheet in a keynote legend, while only the keynote symbols are placed in the drawing. Each note may be repeated in the drawing as often as needed by simply repeating the symbol.

The Uniform Drawing System

The creators of ConDoc shared their system widely through seminars and other events, and produced a detailed workshop handbook. In 1994, recognizing the need for a more detailed system fully described in a self-contained publication, the Construction Specifications Institute embarked on a project to create the Uniform Drawing System (UDS).

The first three UDS modules, published in 1997, build upon ConDoc's organizational concepts. The Drawing Set Organization Module (Module 1) establishes consistency between disciplines through the use of standard discipline designators, sheet types, and file names. The Sheet Organization Module (Module 2) establishes graphic layout standards delineating drawing area, title block area, and production data area, as well as a grid system of blocks or modules for organizing drawings and related information on a sheet. The Schedules Module (Module 3) defines a standard format for numerous schedules used in construction documents. In 1999 the UDS was expanded to include Drafting Conventions (Module 4), Terms and Abbreviations (Module 5), and Symbols (Module 6). In 2000 the UDS was completed with the publication of Notations (Module 7) and Code Conventions (Module 8).

CAD Layer Guidelines

Developed and first published by the AIA in 1990, the layer list in *CAD Layer Guidelines* is the only comprehensive system for the standard naming of CAD data file

(continued)

layers. The second edition, published in 1997, contains enhancements and refinements of the original edition. *CAD Layer Guidelines* offers a consistent, comprehensive yet flexible layer-naming system that can be adapted to particular needs while maintaining the integrity of the system.

In 2001 the publication was completely revised and updated and given a new name, *AIA CAD Layer Guidelines: U.S. National CAD Standard, Version 2*. The original layer-naming system has been amended to enable U.S. design firms to conform to ISO Standard 13567, Organization and Naming of Layers for CAD, while largely preserving the integrity of data located according to earlier editions. The layer list has also been expanded for disciplines such as civil, civil works, structural, mechanical, plumbing, telecommunications, survey/mapping, geotechnical, process, and operations.

The U.S. National CAD Standard

The National Institute of Building Sciences recognized a need for a single, comprehensive national standard for electronically produced construction documents. A single standard supports the seamless transfer of building design and construction information among a broad array of users throughout the building life cycle, including architects, planners, engineers, contractors, product manufacturers, building owners, and facility managers.

The NIBS Facility Information Council (formerly the CADD Council) provides an industry-wide forum for the standardization of computer-aided design and drafting. Membership in the council is open to all individuals and organizations with an interest in the subject matter. Components of the CAD standard include the following:

- CAD layering
- Drawing set organization
- Sheet organization
- Schedules
- Drafting conventions
- Terms and abbreviations
- Symbols
- Notations
- Code conventions
- Plotting guidelines

The U.S. National BIM Standard (NBIMS)

NIBS organized the National BIM Standard Project Committee in 2005. The mission of this committee, as defined in its charter, is to improve the performance of facilities over their full life cycle by fostering a common, standard, and integrated life cycle information model for the architecture, engineering, construction, and facility management industries. The basic premise underlying the development of this standard is that the true value of a building information model lies in its accessibility to different stakeholders at different phases of the facility life cycle. The ability of each stakeholder to insert, extract, update, or modify information in the model requires a shared digital representation that can be manipulated by a variety of software applications. This interoperability must be achieved through open standards that allow for the unfettered electronic exchange of graphic and nongraphic information.

SPECIFICATIONS

The specifications present written requirements for materials, equipment, and construction systems, as well as standards for products, workmanship, and the construction services required to produce the work. The specifications are often presented in the project manual, along with the bidding requirements, contract forms, and conditions of the contract.

Organization

In its *Project Resource Manual: CSI Manual of Practice*, CSI publishes a series of widely used conventions for specifications organization, format, and development. Especially important is MasterFormat™, which establishes a master list of section titles and numbers as well as a format for the organization of individual specification sections. This widely used format is incorporated into many industry standards and products, including AIA MASTERSPEC®, which includes fifty divisions. Divisions

00 through 49—the missing division numbers are reserved for future use—are labeled as follows:

Division 00 Procurement and Contracting Requirements

Division 01 General Requirements

Division 02 Existing Conditions

Division 03 Concrete

Division 04 Masonry

Division 05 Metals

Division 06 Wood, Plastics, and Composites

Division 07 Thermal and Moisture Protection

Division 08 Openings

Division 09 Finishes

Division 10 Specialties

Division 11 Equipment

Division 12 Furnishings

Division 13 Special Construction

Division 14 Conveying Equipment

Division 21 Fire Suppression

Division 22 Plumbing

Division 23 Heating, Ventilating, and Air Conditioning

Division 25 Integrated Automation

Division 26 Electrical

Division 27 Communications

Division 28 Electronic Safety and Security

Division 31 Earthwork

Division 32 Exterior Improvements

Division 33 Utilities

Division 34 Transportation

Division 35 Waterway and Marine Construction

Division 40 Process Integration

Division 41 Material Processing and Handling Equipment

Division 42 Process Heating, Cooling, and Drying Equipment

Division 43 Process Gas and Liquid Handling, Purification, and Storage Equipment

Division 44 Pollution Control Equipment

Division 45 Industry-Specific Manufacturing Equipment

Division 48 Electrical Power Generation

Division 01 of MasterFormat presents a series of general procedural and administrative requirements applicable to all portions of the work. Each MasterFormat division contains sections designated by six-digit numbers. Each section, in turn, is organized according to the three-part format with the following article titles: General, Products, and Execution.

▶ The backgrounder at the end of this topic describes AIA MASTER-SPEC programs for specification preparation.

Methods of Specifying

For each specifications section, the architect selects the method of specifying. These methods include descriptive specifying, performance specifying (listing required performance qualities of products and assemblies), specifying by reference standards, and proprietary specifying (listing products and assemblies by one or more manufacturers and trade names). In addition, the architect may use allowances and unit prices for parts of the work that cannot be accurately quantified or qualified at the time of bidding.

Descriptive specifying. Many architects use descriptive specifications, describing exact characteristics of materials and products without listing proprietary names.

Performance specifying. Some architects believe that performance specifications are best in principle because they specify the end result required and allow contractors,

MASTERSPEC® DIVISIONS AND SECTIONS

ARCOM uses the CSI MasterFormat outline for its MASTERSPEC specification system. The outline below is an abridged version of divisions 01 through 14, which include the section titles most frequently used by architects.

Division 00—Procurement & Contracting Requirements

Division 01—General Requirements
010000   General Requirements
011000   Summary

Division 02—Existing Conditions
024116   Structure Demolition
024119   Selective Structure Demolition

Division 03—Concrete
033000   Cast-in-Place Concrete
033300   Architectural Concrete
033816   Unbonded Post-Tensioned Concrete
034100   Precast Structural Concrete
034500   Precast Architectural Concrete
034713   Tilt-Up Concrete
034900   Glass Fiber-Reinforced Concrete
035113   Cementitious Wood Fiber Decks
035216   Lightweight Insulating Concrete
035300   Concrete Topping
035416   Hydraulic Cement Underlayment

Division 04—Masonry
040100   Maintenance of Masonry
040120   Maintenance of Unit Masonry
040140   Maintenance of Stone Assemblies
042000   Unit Masonry
042300   Glass Unit Masonry
044200   Exterior Stone Cladding
044300   Stone Masonry
047200   Cast Stone Masonry

Division 05—Metals
050170   Maintenance of Decorative Metal
051200   Structural Steel Framing
052100   Steel Joist Framing

053100   Steel Decking
054000   Cold-Formed Metal Framing
055000   Metal Fabrications
055100   Metal Stairs
055213   Pipe and Tube Railings
055300   Metal Gratings
057000   Decorative Metal
057113   Fabricated Metal Spiral Stairs

Division 06—Wood, Plastics, and Composites
061000   Rough Carpentry
061323   Heavy Timber Construction
061500   Wood Decking
061600   Sheathing
061753   Shop-Fabricated Wood Trusses
061800   Glued-Laminated Construction
062000   Finish Carpentry
064013   Exterior Architectural Woodwork
064023   Interior Architectural Woodwork
064200   Wood Paneling
066400   Plastic Paneling

Division 07—Thermal and Moisture Protection
071113   Bituminous Dampproofing
071326   Self-Adhering Sheet Waterproofing
071353   Elastomeric Sheet Waterproofing
071354   Thermoplastic Sheet Waterproofing
071413   Hot Fluid-Applied Rubberized Asphalt Waterproofing
071416   Cold Fluid-Applied Waterproofing
071600   Cementitious and Reactive Waterproofing
071613   Polymer Modified Cement Waterproofing
071616   Crystalline Waterproofing
071619   Metal Oxide Waterproofing
071700   Bentonite Waterproofing
071800   Traffic Coatings
071900   Water Repellents
072100   Thermal Insulation
072400   Exterior Insulation and Finish Systems
072413   Polymer-Based Exterior Insulation and Finish System

072419	Water-Drainage Exterior Insulation and Finish System
072700	Air Barriers
073113	Asphalt Shingles
073116	Metal Shingles
073126	Slate Shingles
073129	Wood Shingles and Shakes
073200	Roof Tiles
073213	Clay Roof Tiles
073216	Concrete Roof Tiles
074113	Metal Roof Panels
074213	Metal Wall Panels
074216	Insulated-Core Metal Wall Panels
074243	Composite Wall Panels
074600	Siding
075100	Built-Up Bituminous Roofing
075113	Built-Up Asphalt Roofing
075116	Built-Up Coal Tar Roofing
075200	Modified Bituminous Membrane Roofing
075300	Elastomeric Membrane Roofing
075400	Thermoplastic Membrane Roofing
075556	Fluid-Applied Protected Membrane Roofing
075700	Coated Foamed Roofing
076100	Sheet Metal Roofing
076200	Sheet Metal Flashing and Trim
077100	Roof Specialties
077129	Manufactured Roof Expansion Joints
077200	Roof Accessories
078100	Applied Fireproofing
078200	Board Fireproofing
078413	Penetration Firestopping
078446	Fire-Resistive Joint Systems
079200	Joint Sealants
079500	Expansion Control

Division 08—Openings

081113	Hollow Metal Doors and Frames
081119	Stainless-Steel Doors and Frames
081173	Sliding Metal Fire Doors
081216	Aluminum Frames
081416	Flush Wood Doors
081433	Stile and Rail Wood Doors
083113	Access Doors and Frames
083213	Sliding Aluminum-Framed Glass Doors
083219	Sliding Wood-Framed Glass Doors
083323	Overhead Coiling Doors
083326	Overhead Coiling Grilles
083459	Vault Doors and Day Gates

083463	Detention Doors and Frames
083473	Sound Control Door Assemblies
083513	Folding Doors
083613	Sectional Doors
084113	Aluminum-Framed Entrances and Storefronts
084126	All-Glass Entrances and Storefronts
084229	Automatic Entrances
084233	Revolving Door Entrances
084243	Intensive Care Unit/Critical Care Unit Entrances
084413	Glazed Aluminum Curtain Walls
084423	Structural-Sealant-Glazed Curtain Walls
084433	Sloped Glazing Assemblies
084500	Translucent Wall and Roof Assemblies
084513	Structured-Polycarbonate-Panel Assemblies
084523	Fiberglass-Sandwich-Panel Assemblies
085000	Windows
085113	Aluminum Windows
085123	Steel Windows
085200	Wood Windows
085313	Vinyl Windows
085653	Security Windows
085663	Detention Windows
086100	Roof Windows
086200	Unit Skylights
086300	Metal-Framed Skylights
087100	Door Hardware
087113	Automatic Door Operators
087163	Detention Door Hardware
088000	Glazing
088113	Decorative Glass Glazing
088300	Mirrors
088400	Plastic Glazing
088853	Security Glazing
089000	Louvers and Vents

Division 09—Finishes

090190	Maintenance of Painting and Coating
092216	Non-Structural Metal Framing
092300	Gypsum Plastering
092400	Portland Cement Plastering
092613	Gypsum Veneer Plastering
092713	Glass-Fiber-Reinforced Plaster Fabrications
092900	Gypsum Board
093000	Tiling
093033	Stone Tiling
095113	Acoustical Panel Ceilings
095123	Acoustical Tile Ceilings

(continued)

095133	Acoustical Metal Pan Ceilings
095753	Security Ceiling Assemblies
096229	Cork Flooring
096313	Brick Flooring
096340	Stone Flooring
096400	Wood Flooring
096466	Wood Athletic Flooring
096500	Resilient Flooring
096513	Resilient Base and Accessories
096516	Resilient Sheet Flooring
096519	Resilient Tile Flooring
096536	Static-Control Resilient Flooring
096566	Resilient Athletic Flooring
096600	Terrazzo Flooring
096723	Resinous Flooring
096813	Tile Carpeting
096816	Sheet Carpeting
096900	Access Flooring
097200	Wall Coverings
097500	Stone Facing
097713	Stretched-Fabric Wall Systems
097723	Fabric-Wrapped Panels
098413	Fixed Sound-Absorptive Panels
099100	Painting
099113	Exterior Painting
099123	Interior Painting
099300	Staining and Transparent Finishing
099419	Multicolor Interior Finishing
099600	High-Performance Coatings
099633	High-Temperature-Resistant Coatings
099646	Intumescent Painting
099653	Elastomeric Coatings
099726	Cementitious Coatings

Division 10—Specialties

101100	Visual Display Surfaces
101200	Display Cases
101300	Directories
101400	Signage
101426	Post and Panel/Pylon Signage
101700	Telephone Specialties
102113	Toilet Compartments
102123	Cubicles
102213	Wire Mesh Partitions
102219	Demountable Partitions
102226	Operable Partitions
102600	Wall and Door Protection
102800	Toilet, Bath, and Laundry Accessories

104400	Fire Protection Specialties
104413	Fire Extinguisher Cabinets
104416	Fire Extinguishers
105113	Metal Lockers
105116	Wood Lockers
105500	Postal Specialties
105613	Metal Storage Shelving
107313	Awnings
107500	Flagpoles

Division 11—Equipment

110513	Common Motor Requirements for Equipment
111200	Parking Control Equipment
111300	Loading Dock Equipment
112600	Unit Kitchens
113100	Residential Appliances
114000	Foodservice Equipment
115123	Library Stack Systems
115213	Projection Screens
115313	Laboratory Fume Hoods
116123	Folding and Portable Stages
116143	Stage Curtains
116623	Gymnasium Equipment
116653	Gymnasium Dividers
116800	Play Field Equipment and Structures
118226	Waste Compactors and Destructors

Division 12—Furnishings

122113	Horizontal Louver Blinds
122116	Vertical Louver Blinds
122200	Curtains and Drapes
122413	Roller Window Shades
122416	Pleated Window Shades
123200	Manufactured Wood Casework
123530	Residential Casework
123553	Laboratory Casework
123570	Healthcare Casework
123640	Stone Countertops
124813	Entrance Floor Mats and Frames
124816	Entrance Floor Grilles
125500	Detention Furniture
126100	Fixed Audience Seating
126600	Telescoping Stands
129200	Interior Planters and Artificial Plants
129300	Site Furnishings

Division 13—Special Construction

| 132416 | Saunas |
| 132700 | Vaults |

PART 3: THE PROJECT

133419	Metal Building Systems
133423	Fabricated Structures
134900	Radiation Protection

Division 14—Conveying Equipment
141000	Dumbwaiters
142100	Electric Traction Elevators
149100	Facility Chutes
142400	Hydraulic Elevators
142600	Limited-Use/Limited-Application Elevators
143100	Escalators

| 143200 | Moving Walks |
| 144200 | Wheelchair Lifts |

Division 15–19—RESERVED DIVISIONS
Division 21 Fire Suppression
Division 22 Plumbing
Division 23 Heating, Ventilating, and Air Conditioning
Division 26 Electrical
Division 27 Communications
Division 28 Electronic Safety and Security
Division 31 Earthwork

SECTIONFORMAT™ OUTLINE CSI AND CSC

SectionFormat is used to organize information when specifications are being written. The information is presented in three parts: General, Products, and Execution. A new version of this outline is under consideration.

Part 1 General

Summary

Products supplied but not installed under this section
Products installed but not supplied under this section
Related sections
Allowances
Unit prices
Measurement procedures
Payment procedures
Alternates

References

Definitions

System Description

Design requirements
Performance requirements

Submittals

Product data
Shop drawings
Samples
Quality assurance/control submittals
  Design data
  Test reports
  Certificates
  Manufacturers' instructions
  Manufacturers' field reports
Closeout submittals

Quality Assurance

Qualifications
Regulatory requirements
Certifications
Field samples
Mock-ups
Preinstallation meetings

Delivery, Storage, and Handling

Packing, shipping, handling, and unloading
Acceptance at site
Storage and protection

Project/Site Conditions

Environmental requirements
Existing conditions

Sequencing

Scheduling

Warranty

Special warranty

System Start-Up

Owner's Instructions

Commissioning

Maintenance

Extra materials
Maintenance service

Part 2 Products

Manufacturers

Existing Products

Materials

(continued)

Manufactured Units

Equipment

Components

Accessories

Mixes

Fabrication

Shop assembly

Fabrication tolerances

Finishes

Shop priming

Shop finishing

Source Quality Control

Tests, inspection

Verification of performance

Part 3 Execution

Installers

Examination

Site verification of conditions

Preparation

Protection

Surface preparation

Erection

Installation

Application

Construction

Special techniques

Interface with other work

Sequences of operation

Site tolerances

Repair/Restoration

Reinstallation

Field Quality Control

Site tests

Inspection

Manufacturers' field services

Adjusting

Cleaning

Demonstration

Protection

Schedules

manufacturers, and fabricators the flexibility and creativity to meet the requirements. In practice, however, creating performance specifications can be complicated due to the vast number of factors that can affect the finished result.

Specifying with reference standards. Specifications may also incorporate references to standards published by industry associations and testing organizations. This allows designers, contractors, and suppliers to use industry-accepted standards of practice and performance. The most widely known standards associations are the American National Standards Institute (ANSI), American Society for Testing and Materials (ASTM), and Underwriters Laboratories (UL). These groups either develop and organize performance standards or test material products and assemblies for compliance with published standards.

Proprietary specifying. Many architects use proprietary specifications for their brevity and simplicity and because they are familiar with the qualities of the specific products being specified. These specifications are frequently augmented with reference to standards, narrative descriptions of materials' qualities, and performance requirements.

Some standards, such as those published by the American Society of Heating, Refrigerating, and Air-Conditioning Engineers (ASHRAE), the National Fire Protection Association (NFPA), and the Illuminating Engineering Society (IES), focus on specific aspects of building performance. Industry associations, such as the American Iron and Steel Institute (AISI) and the American Architectural Manufacturers Association (AAMA), write standards for the products and systems produced by their members. For example, AAMA publishes test methods, standards, and guide specifications for aluminum fabrications such as storefronts, curtain walls, and windows.

Restrictive specifying. The architect also determines how restrictive the specifications are to be—whether they will permit only one manufacturer's product, several products, or any product that meets specified criteria. Publicly funded projects require full and open competition. Therefore, several brands of products are specified under the theory that qualified manufacturers should be able to compete equitably for the work. In private work, the architect will typically specify restrictively, unless the owner prefers competition. When there is a choice, the architect should determine which approach best serves the client's interests.

Master Specifications

Most firms employ some form of master specification that is modified for each project. A master specification covers an entire topic, including a range of options. The specifications editor then fills in blanks, deletes options that don't apply, and incorporates special requirements not included in the master.

The most commonly used commercially available master specification is MASTERSPEC, developed by the AIA and available through ARCOM Master Systems. It is distributed on electronic media and is regularly updated by professional staff and an AIA-sponsored review committee of architects and engineers. MASTERSPEC is well suited for use in a variety of architecture offices. It covers most types of projects and is closely coordinated with AIA standard documents and procedures. MASTERSPEC also acts as a specifications-writing tutorial, including overview and reference materials, editorial notes, and specifications and drawing coordination notes.

Other commercially available master specifications include SpecText®, maintained by Construction Sciences Research Foundation Inc., and e-SPECS, created by InterSpec, Inc., which is also available integrated with MASTERSPEC. Master specifications are also available from some government agencies, such as the Veterans Administration and NASA, which developed its own automated system, NASA SpecsIntact. Government agencies that produce master specifications usually require that these be used on their projects.

Specification Production Methods

Specifications are produced using electronic word processing and software developed solely for editing specifications. As a firm finds products and procedures that work well for its markets, it will repeat much of the same information from project to project. Moreover, specifications typically evolve through multiple drafts, and, as in CAD drawings, tracking revisions is increasingly important.

Well-coordinated drawings and specifications are essential in any set of construction documents. In particular, the architect is challenged to ensure that materials and products shown on the drawings are described in the specifications and that the language used is consistent and unambiguous. For small projects, the architect often develops the specifications concurrently with the drawings. These specifications may be included directly on the drawings, perhaps by attaching photocopies to the drawings or importing a word processing file into CAD. For larger projects, however, it is common to include the specifications in a separate project manual. CAD and other automation tools can help architects achieve coordination, and in some cases, they provide new techniques to create more tightly integrated drawings and specifications. One important goal is maintaining consistency between the language used in drawing notations and the language used in the specifications. Inconsistency can be a major source of requests for interpretation and change orders during construction.

In addition to careful review of drawings and specifications, several production techniques are available to help architects achieve this consistency. Numerical keynoting offers one example. Instead of attaching a descriptive note, such as "batt insulation," to a component of a drawing or detail, the architect attaches a keynote number. This number is cross-referenced to a standardized keynote list, which is included on each drawing. It remains the responsibility of the architect to coordinate the keynote list and the specifications, but this technique generally makes it easier to revise drawing notations, and the notations are better coordinated. If a standard material notation changes, for example, only the keynote list needs to be updated—not every plan, section, elevation, or detail in which the material appears.

Keynote-based drawings lend themselves to automation. CAD systems allow the same information to be shared between multiple drawings using reference files. The keynote list, when attached as a reference file to many drawings, can be updated for all drawings simply by changing the master list. This can be especially helpful for international practices. By maintaining the keynote list in multiple languages, the firm's architects can select notes in their own language and output those notes in the language spoken where the building is being constructed.

The ConDoc drawing system that appeared in the late 1980s took the concept of keynotes further by using MasterFormat as the keynote numbering convention. Each material or product notation on a drawing essentially becomes a direct reference to the appropriate specifications section. At any point in the drawing process, the program can scan the drawing and print a keynote legend listing all of the materials on the drawing. Similarly, the user can locate all occurrences of a specific material within the drawings. The keynote list can be used to link drawings and specifications, helping to ensure that each building component drawn is described in the specifications.

CAD provides another mechanism to integrate drawings and specifications by allowing architects to add specifications data directly to the drawing in the form of database attributes. Predrawn standard components in the drawings (metal studs, furring channels, insulation, plumbing fixtures, etc.) can include specifications attributes. Some CAD systems can generate reports based on this information, so the architect can double-check that each component in the drawings is described in the specifications and vice versa. In addition, some systems quantify this information, producing bills of materials. Such systems require that the user know enough about specifications to enter the correct attributes or select the appropriate components.

BIM technology is particularly powerful in this regard. These systems more tightly integrate specifications attributes and permit them to be assigned to assemblies of objects—an insulated masonry wall, for example—as well as to the components of that wall. This allows complete and highly accurate extraction of bills of materials. In addition, these systems may incorporate design rules. In other words, knowledge about how buildings are designed and constructed is programmed into the software. An example might be a rule that a door inserted into a fire-rated wall must be a fire-rated door. The BIM system would prevent the insertion of a nonrated door object into a fire-rated wall.

OTHER CONSTRUCTION DOCUMENTS

Increasingly, contract documents include a code compliance summary—sometimes on the first sheet of documents—for use by the code enforcement official in reviewing the project and issuing the building permit. This and other construction information is usually presented as a combination of documents generated in the architect's office and standard forms supplied by the AIA, the owner, or other sources. AIA documents, with or without modifications, are included in the project manual in their original form; others are commonly developed as word-processed forms that can be used, with appropriate modifications, on future projects.

CONSTRUCTION DOCUMENTATION MANAGEMENT

Planning for this phase includes thinking through the documentation required (usually very early in a project, frequently as part of the proposal to acquire the project in the first place), selecting appropriate production methods, planning the production process, and managing this process to achieve the desired results.

Effective production management of construction documentation is important to meeting both a firm's project goals and its practice goals. Good production management includes these features:

- Careful production planning, scheduling, and oversight.
- Documentation standards.
- A library of construction information and technical references.
- Effective coordination with consultants and others on the project team. (As integrated practice becomes more widespread, this project team will increasingly include contractors and subcontractors during design phases.)
- Thorough review and checking procedures.
- The resources and the desire to produce high-quality construction documentation.
- Approval of the construction documentation by the owner (sometimes at various stages of production).

Firms seeking continuous quality improvement usually consider construction documentation a prime candidate for attention. Creation of the documentation translates design intent into the information needed for approvals and construction. Errors and omissions in the construction documentation inevitably require reworking later and may, in fact, degrade the quality of the service provided and reduce customer satisfaction with that service.

Construction documentation is what its name implies—documentation of decisions made and agreed to in the design development phase. While changes during the construction documentation phase are inevitable, comprehensive design development documentation, carefully coordinated by the design team and approved by the owner, provides a sound foundation for preparing the construction documentation.

It may be necessary to impress upon owners that most design decisions are interrelated. Adding a new door, for example, may require changes in several drawings (floor plans, interior elevations, sections, details, and door and hollow metal schedules). It may also require a new specification section as well as changes in the electrical, mechanical, or structural work. Computers are helpful in coordinating design changes, but professional judgment is involved in even the smallest design decision.

Production Planning

Considering the many interrelationships among the construction documents, most offices identify a single production coordinator. For many projects, this person is the project architect or project manager. For larger projects, production coordination may be delegated to a technical architect, a job captain, or another specially designated individual.

With CAD systems offering the possibility of simultaneous design and production as well as integrated specifications, firms are finding that their project architects and key project staff are doing production as well as design. The traditional distinction between designers and drafters is blurring and, in some offices, disappearing entirely.

As the construction documentation phase approaches, the project manager determines, in detail, the time, staffing, and other resources required to produce the documents. Usually this involves cartooning the drawings, blocking out the specifications (which by now are in outline form), and outlining the remaining content of the project manual. Some, perhaps all, of these decisions may have been made earlier; some firms prepare design development documents in the formats planned for the construction documents.

Production scheduling and budgeting. Many architects have found that the amount of time required to produce working drawings varies greatly, depending on project complexity and the level of detail required. It is good practice to allocate time (based on the previously prepared budget) for each sheet so that each person working on the drawings knows what is expected. Data from past projects will help sharpen these estimates. One of the major challenges in introducing a building modeling approach has been the difficulty in estimating the time and staffing levels required in each design phase.

The time required to produce specifications varies widely, due to a number of factors, including:

- The project delivery approach
- Size and complexity of the project
- Competitive bidding requirements
- Specification scope (broad to narrow)
- Staff knowledge of the specified products and systems
- The level of detail already achieved in the design development phase

Construction documentation is prepared most efficiently if the decision-making process is well structured. With modern production techniques, more time can be spent researching systems and coordinating decisions than producing documents. As might be expected, the time required increases substantially if unfamiliar construction systems are used.

Selection of production methods. As suggested above, each approach to production exerts a discipline on the process. The firm may use the same production approach for all of its projects or mix and match them according to the needs of the project at hand. In a similar vein, the firm must decide how specifications are to be produced, whether separate systems will be used for outline and final specifications, and to what extent specifications are to be integrated with the drawings.

If CAD systems are used, it is especially important that the project manager or production coordinator think through the organization of the CAD data as well as the number of drawings, scales, and sheet layouts. CAD issues include whether a single CAD file or multiple files will be created, the CAD layers to be used, how drawings will be created from the CAD data, and how the data will be presented in drawings of different scales in terms of line weights, text heights, and so forth.

Typically the firm's CAD standards provide guidance on these topics, but almost every project will present some unique requirements. Sharing CAD data with outside consultants or with the client requires additional planning to ensure that all parties can use the data without extensive editing. This highlights the usefulness of industry-wide standards, such as the National CAD Standard discussed above.

If CAD data will be exchanged between different organizations, the team must address the following questions:

- Which organizations are exchanging data?
- What information does each organization need from the others?
- What format data are required?
- What are the project drafting and CAD standards?
- What is the frequency of data exchange?
- How will the data be exchanged (project Web site, bulletin board, e-mail, CD)?
- How much data preparation is required for each exchange and how long does the transfer take?
- Who is the person in each organization responsible for sending and receiving data?
- Who is authorized to request and release electronic data?
- How will data transfers be logged?

▶ Project Delivery Methods (8.1) describes the possible options for the delivery of project services.

ELEMENTS OF PRODUCTION PLANNING

Sound production planning for construction documentation reflects the following:

- *The firm's experience.* Most firms accumulate historical information on which to plan projects and base compensation proposals. Past and present time records are readily adaptable to computerization using spreadsheet programs.
- *The production budget.* A large fraction of the architect's cost is budgeted for the construction documents; it is particularly important that scope, services, and compensation be in balance during this phase of services.
- *Project consultants.* On projects of any size or complexity, the consultants will prepare much of the documentation. It is essential that the architect and consultants agree on both production schedules and documentation standards.
- *Project technology.* CAD and BIM systems require careful planning and management if their potential benefits are to be realized.

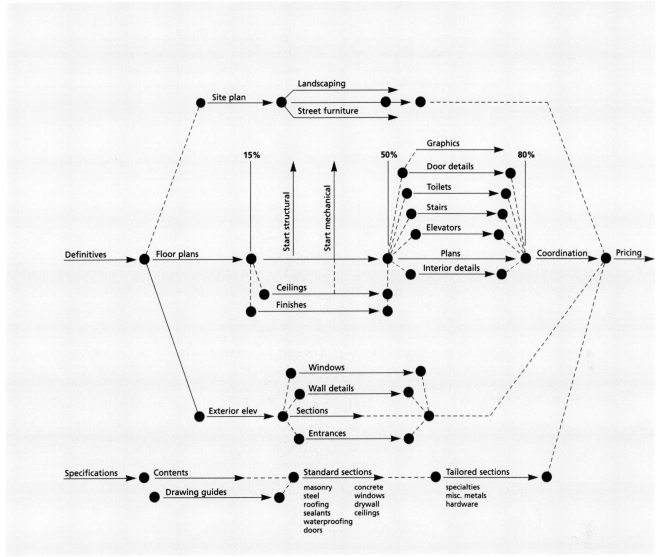

Sample Documents Production Sequence. Here is one firm's production sequence.

Nagle Hartray & Associates, Ltd., Chicago

Archiving procedures are also important and frequently overlooked. Archiving is distinguished from data backup in that it is a complete copy of the project data at a defined point in time, typically at a project milestone. Also, deciding what and when to archive is a project management responsibility, whereas data backup is typically a system management responsibility.

When a BIM is used as the primary communication and coordination vehicle for the project team, all of the issues above must be considered. The American Institute of Steel Construction (AISC) has championed virtual design and construction for several years, including an appendix in the 2005 *Code of Standard Practice for Steel Buildings and Bridges* on what the AISC calls "product models." AISC recommends that a single entity be assigned responsibility for managing the official version of the shared model:

> When a project is designed and constructed using EDI [electronic data interchange], it is imperative that an individual entity on the team be responsible for maintaining the LPM [logical product model, or building product model]. This is to assure protection of data

▶ Computer Technology in Practice (5.8) addresses automated production methods.

through proper backup, storage and security and to provide coordination of the flow of information to all team members when information is added to the model. Team members exchange information to revise the model with this Administrator. The Administrator will validate all changes to the LPM. This is to assure proper tracking and control of revisions. This Administrator can be one of the design team members such as an Architect, Structural Engineer or a separate entity on the design team serving this purpose. The Administrator can also be the Fabricator's detailer or a separate entity on the construction team serving this purpose.

A key aspect of production planning is the search for bottlenecks that may slow down the project and endanger its schedule. Coordination points, where all drawings and specifications need to be brought to a common level of development for checking, are common candidates. Plotting CAD drawings and preparing, translating, and transferring CAD files to outside consultants are other likely bottlenecks. With a BIM, the periodic need to extract and plot full sets of 2D drawings from the model can also be a choke point.

Identifying technical references. Architects increasingly recognize that before new details and construction techniques are formulated, standard approaches should be investigated and understood as part of the design process. To facilitate this research, many valuable references are available to the practitioner. These include the following:

- Building codes and regulations applicable to the project
- Technical references and standards, such as those published by ASTM, ANSI, and professional and industry associations
- Standard references, such as Architectural Graphic Standards
- Journals and other publications of professional societies and industry associations
- Manufacturers' catalogs and trade literature

The above material is available in books, journals, pamphlets, Internet Web sites, or compact disc format. Some of the computerized sources are integrated with product selection, analysis, and detailing routines. Increasingly, product suppliers will be providing technical information in intelligent, 3D digital objects that can be inserted in a BIM.

In addition to working with printed references, most firms find that technical representatives of industry associations, product representatives, consultants, and senior members of architecture firms are valuable resources. Most firms develop a library of technical and reference information. Information on materials and products is often filed by MasterFormat division or section number, making the library easily accessible to all members of the project team.

Documents Coordination

A goal of the construction documentation phase is a fully coordinated building description. When conventional documents are the deliverable, these documents must be internally consistent. Plans, sections, elevations, details, and schedules must agree with each other. Materials shown on the drawings must be specified, the mechanical and electrical systems must fit within the chases and plenums designed for them, and so on. BIM software automates a great deal of this coordination, by extracting drawings as "views" of the single building model. When using a BIM tool, the firm must understand its capabilities and limitations and develop appropriate coordination procedures.

The coordination task is complicated by the reality that more than one person or firm, and usually several, will work on the construction documentation of all but the smallest projects. Staff may be in different groups within the firm or in consultant organizations. For CAD systems, it is necessary to develop protocols for who has access to what layers or drawings, exchange of updated files, and backups for all of the work. When a BIM is to be shared by multiple project team members, it is necessary to establish techniques for partitioning and sharing the model and to establish the responsibility for managing changes to the shared model.

Progress prints or plots of drawings and drafts of project manuals are commonly shared within the project team. Coordination meetings and milestone reviews may be used to achieve ongoing coordination. Projects using a shared BIM have achieved excellent results by scheduling 3D model walk-throughs on a regular basis. Although some projects have used virtual reality environments for these walk-throughs, they can also be conducted on-screen and even include remote sites through Web conferencing techniques. During these walk-throughs, the entire team can see each conflict as it is encountered and discuss possible solutions. For this technique to be most effective, the team should use software that automatically detects and highlights conflicts.

Design changes. Design changes are particularly critical. One of the responsibilities of the project manager or production coordinator is to make sure that when changes occur they are reflected in all appropriate locations in the documents. This includes notification of all disciplines. When overlay drafting or CAD systems are being used, the project manager decides when a new or revised base sheet, layer, or file is created and distributed to each discipline. BIM systems can automatically update all affected drawings when there is a change to the model. When using a building information model as the basis for coordination, the team must develop a procedure for approving design changes and incorporating them into the shared model. However, even with an agreed-upon procedure in place, it is necessary to inform other team members when model updates occur.

As updates are issued, it is good practice to note the date and purpose of the revision on drawing title blocks or on the cover of the project manual. Thus, a record of issue dates and purposes appears on the documents. Some firms note the issue date on each page in the project manual or use a different-colored paper or different binding for subsequent issues. These measures provide effective means of determining whether documents are current. In true virtual design and construction, there may be a main and multiple related submodels produced by the various team members. In those instances, data management systems are needed to track model relationships as well as changes, and apply access controls to ensure that any changes are approved. Similar systems have been used in industries such as aerospace.

Once drawings are issued for contract, it is good practice to number each set of changes, circle and label each change on the documents, and record a new issue date (e.g., "3.24.94, Revision #1").

A number of firms have found that thoughtful organization of CAD data and automation of CAD background updates has yielded significant advantages, both in productivity and in drawing quality and coordination. The key to reaping these benefits is moving beyond the idea that a CAD file is a drawing. It is not—whether the graphics are 2D or 3D, a CAD file should be seen as a model from which many drawings, or "views," can be generated. When setting up a project CAD model, users should follow these guidelines in order to avoid any major operational issues:

- Never draw anything twice.
- Create a primary CAD model and make sure as many drawings as possible reference that model. This is consistent with the sheet file/model file distinction made in the *AIA CAD Layer Guidelines* and incorporated in the NCS.
- Establish CAD standards that permit each drawing to view the appropriate subset of the model information and to plot that information in the correct graphic representation, line weights, and text heights. Consider the needs of all users and all disciplines when setting CAD standards.
- Consider how any irregular geometry or rotated plans will be handled. This may require additional software or customization.
- Consider how data will be transferred to and received from outside consultants. How can the architect ensure that all consultants are referencing the most current version of the model?

1. *Preliminary review*
   a. Quickly make an overview of all sheets, spending no more than one minute per sheet to become familiar with the project.

2. *Specifications check*
   a. Check specs for bid items. Are they coordinated with the drawings?
   b. Check specs for phasing of construction. Are the phases clear?
   c. Compare architectural finish schedule to specification index. Ensure all finish materials are specified.
   d. Check major items of equipment and verify that they are coordinated with contract drawings. Pay particular attention to horsepower ratings and voltage requirements.
   e. Verify that items specified "as indicated" or "where indicated" are in fact indicated on contract drawings.
   f. Verify that cross-referenced specification sections exist.
   g. Try not to indicate thickness of materials or quantities of materials in specifications.

3. *Plan check—civil*
   a. Verify that site plans with new underground utilities (power, telephone, water, sewer, gas, storm drainage, fuel lines, grease traps, fuel tanks) have been checked for interferences.
   b. Verify that existing telephone poles, pole guys, street signs, drainage inlets, valve boxes, manhole castings, and so on do not interfere with new driveways, sidewalks, or other site improvements on architectural site plans.
   c. Verify that limits of clearing, grading, sodding, grass, or mulch are shown and are consistent with architectural or landscaping plans.
   d. Verify fire hydrant and street light pole locations against electrical and architectural plans.
   e. Verify that profile sheets show other underground utilities and avoid conflicts.
   f. Verify that horizontal distances between drainage structures and manholes match with respect to scaled dimensions and stated dimensions on both plan and profile sheets.
   g. Verify that provisions have been included for adjusting valve box and manhole castings (sewer, power, telephone, drainage) to match final or finish grade of pavement, swales, or sidewalks.

   h. Verify that all existing and proposed grades are shown.

4. *Plan check—structural*
   a. Verify column lines on structural and architectural plans.
   b. Verify that all column locations are the same on structural and architectural plans.
   c. Verify that perimeter slab on structural matches architectural plans.
   d. Verify that all depressed or raised slabs are indicated.
   e. Verify slab elevations against architectural plans.
   f. Verify that all foundation piers are identified.
   g. Verify that all foundation beams are identified.
   h. Verify roof framing plan column lines and columns against foundation plan column lines and columns.
   i. Verify perimeter roof line against architectural roof plan.
   j. Verify that all columns and beams are listed in column and beam schedules.
   k. Verify length of all columns in column schedule.
   l. Verify that all sections are properly labeled.
   m. Verify all expansion joint locations against architectural plans.
   n. Verify dimensions.
   o. Verify that drawing notes do not conflict with specifications.

5. *Plan check—architectural*
   a. Verify property line dimensions on site survey plan against architecture.
   b. Verify that building is located behind setback lines.
   c. Verify all concrete columns and walls against structural.
   d. Verify on site plans that all existing and new work is clearly identified.
   e. Verify building elevations against floor plans. Check in particular roof lines, window and door openings, and expansion joints.
   f. Verify building sections against elevations and plans. Check roof lines, windows, and door locations.
   g. Verify wall sections against architectural building sections and structural.
   h. Verify masonry openings for windows and doors.
   i. Verify expansion joints through building.
   j. Verify partial floor plans against small-scale floor plans.

k. Verify reflected ceiling plan against architectural floor plan to ensure no variance with rooms. Check ceiling materials against finish schedule, check light fixture layout against electrical, check ceiling diffusers/registers against mechanical, check soffits and locations of vents.

l. Verify all room finish schedule information including room numbers, names of rooms, finishes, and ceiling heights. Look for omissions, duplications, and inconsistencies.

m. Verify all door schedule information including sizes, types, and labels. Look for omissions, duplications, and inconsistencies.

n. Verify all rated walls.

o. Verify all cabinets will fit.

p. Verify dimensions.

6. *Plan check—mechanical and plumbing*

a. Verify that all new electrical, gas, water, and sewer lines connect to existing.

b. Verify all plumbing fixture locations against architectural plans. Verify all plumbing fixtures against fixture schedule and/or specs.

c. Verify storm drain system against architectural roof plan. Verify that pipes are sized and all drains are connected and do not interfere with foundations. Verify that wall chases are provided on architectural plans to conceal vertical piping.

d. Verify that sanitary drain system pipes are sized and all fixtures are connected.

e. Verify HVAC floor plans against architectural plans.

f. Verify sprinkler heads in all rooms.

g. Verify that all sections are identical to architectural/structural drawings.

h. Verify that adequate ceiling height exists at worst-case duct intersection.

i. Verify that all structural supports required for mechanical equipment are indicated on structural drawings.

j. Verify that dampers are indicated at smoke and fire walls.

k. Verify diffusers against architectural reflected ceiling plan.

l. Verify that all roof penetrations (ducts, fans, etc.) are indicated on roof plans.

m. Verify all ductwork is sized.

n. Verify all notes.

o. Verify all air conditioning units, heaters, and exhaust fans against architectural roof plans and mechanical schedules.

p. Verify that all mechanical equipment will fit in spaces allocated.

7. *Plan check—electrical*

a. Verify that all plans are identical to architectural plans.

b. Verify all light fixtures against architectural reflected ceiling plan.

c. Verify that all major pieces of equipment have electrical connections.

d. Verify location of all panel boards and that they are indicated on the electrical riser diagram.

e. Verify all notes.

f. Verify that there is sufficient space for all electrical panels to fit.

g. Verify that electrical panels are not recessed in fire walls.

h. Verify that electrical equipment locations are coordinated with site paving and grading.

8. *Plan check—kitchen/dietary*

a. Verify equipment layout against architectural plans.

Redicheck (www.redicheck-review.com)

Review and checking. The importance of review and checking cannot be overemphasized, given the extreme time constraints under which construction documentation is often produced. Documents may be produced by individuals who do not fully understand how details fit within the larger context. Therefore, checking goes hand in hand with the ongoing education process that characterizes any professional office.

Lists to help architects check documents are available from many sources. Many offices develop their own guides for document checking—checklists that may be used by the individual in developing the drawing and by the project manager in checking it.

Checking plays a central role in any firm's quality assurance effort. Most firms establish protocols for document checking. Some examples:

- Documents are comprehensively checked at one or more milestones before they are completed.
- A senior person not associated with the project checks all documents before they are issued.
- One person checks all important dimensions.
- The person responsible for the drawings reviews the specifications, and the specifier reviews the drawings.
- Consultants review the documents produced by other contributors for coordination.
- The owner reviews and approves the documents before they are issued for bid or negotiation.

Be sure to document the owner's approval of legal and contractual information, or you may assume liability for it.

The last point is particularly important. The owner issues the construction documentation for bidding or negotiation, and the owner signs the construction agreements with contractors, the construction manager, or the design-build entity. It is the owner's project, and it is critical—and mandated in AIA forms of agreement—for the owner to approve the construction documentation.

Of all project phases, the preparation of the construction documentation typically takes the most time and resources. New technologies, especially computing and computer graphics, are changing the nature of this work, shifting the emphasis from rote production to decision making, coordination, and communication. A sound grasp of design and construction documentation is increasingly central to successful architectural practice.

For More Information

Osamu A. Wakita and Richard M. Linde cover the skills, concepts, and fundamentals for working drawings in *The Professional Practice of Architectural Working Drawings* (Wiley, 2002). *The Working Drawing Manual* (McGraw-Hill, 1998), by Fred A. Stitt, provides systematic checklists for organizing, managing, and coordinating the data needed to prepare accurate construction documents for any building.

With updated and reorganized content, the eleventh edition of *Architectural Graphic Standards* (Wiley, 2007) continues to offer a rich collection of information that provides a basis for designing, developing, and delineating an array of building elements and components.

Several publications address standards for construction drawings. The CSI *Uniform Drawing System* establishes standards for sheet types, sheet organization, and schedules. The AIA's *CAD Layer Guidelines* establishes standard naming of data file layers. Both of these documents have been incorporated, along with plotting standards, into the *U.S. National CAD Standard* (2005). The NCS is available from the AIA Bookstore at (800) 242-3837, the Construction Specifications Institute at www.csinet.org, and the National Institute of Building Sciences at www.nationalcadstandard.org.

In-depth treatment on preparing specifications can be found in *Construction Specifications Writing: Principles and Procedures* (Wiley, 2004) by Harold J. Rosen and John Regener. Specification software is available from ARCOM, including MASTERSPEC master specification system and SPECWARE specification production software. See the AIA MASTERSPEC backgrounder at the end of this section for further descriptions of these practice tools, or contact ARCOM at www.masterspec.com.

RediCheck Associates publishes an overlay checking and interdisciplinary coordination manual as a means for making construction documents more accurate and thorough. For information, call (877) 733-4243 or visit www.redicheck-review.com.

Guidance on the use of BIM tools and the management of BIM data is rapidly emerging. The U.S. National Institute of Standards and Technology published the

Capital Facilities Information Handover Guide in 2006. This publication assists companies in planning for the life cycle capture and use of facility information, starting with a corporate information strategy, defining detailed information handover requirements, and then delivering the required information during design and construction. This publication can be downloaded from the NIST Web site: http://cic.nist.gov/staff/publications.html. Scroll down to Mark Palmer's name to find it.

The National Institute of Building Sciences Web site, www.nibs.org, contains information about the U.S. National CAD Standard and the U.S. National BIM Standard. Search under Facility Information Council or buildingSMART.

Leading-edge research on BIM technology and applications has been undertaken at Stanford University's Center for Facility Engineering (CIFE): http://cife.stanford.edu/Research/index.html, and in the doctoral program at the Georgia Tech College of Architecture: http://bim.arch.gatech.edu.

BACKGROUNDER

THE U.S. NATIONAL CAD STANDARD

Business software applications, including computer-aided design (CAD) applications, allow a high degree of control over the organization and classification of data and the graphic composition of printed output. These user-defined variables allow individual authors to organize and classify CAD data according to their own needs and sense of logic, and to establish their own graphic standards for printed documents. While this freedom to customize is among the benefits of computer technology, the proliferation of customized user-defined settings in the production of CAD documents has eroded the common language for data organization, classification, and communication that evolved over hundreds of years of hand drafting. Even the simplest of CAD software applications can have as many as a hundred user-definable settings. The lack of standards in this arena inhibits the sharing of data even among small design teams. The overhead costs of translating settings between organizations, or developing and enforcing office standards, cut deeply into any productivity gains from adopting CAD software.

Over the years, a number of industry organizations have addressed various aspects of this issue. The AIA published the first edition of *CAD Layer Guidelines* in 1990 to establish a common system of nomenclature for CAD data files and layer names. The second edition, revised and updated, was published in 1997. That same year, the Construction Specifications Institute (CSI) published the first three modules of the *Uniform Drawing System*. This document was intended to serve as an industry standard for the organization of construction documents, whether they are prepared electronically or by hand.

Recognizing the potential for these publications to serve as the foundation of a consensus industry standard, the National Institute of Building Sciences (NIBS) convened a coalition of building design and construction industry organizations in 1997 to explore the development of a national CAD standard.

Under the auspices of the NIBS Facility Information Council (NIBS-FIC), the AIA joined with CSI, the U.S. Coast Guard, the U.S. Department of Defense Tri-Service CADD/GIS Technology Center, the Sheet Metal and Air Conditioning Contractors National Association (SMACNA), and other construction and software industry organizations to prepare the joint publication of the standard. In addition, these groups committed to support the evolution and development of a national CAD standard to keep pace with evolving technology.

The product of a historic and unprecedented cooperative effort, the *U.S. National CAD Standard*™ (NCS) is an important step in streamlining the free flow of building construction and design data throughout the life cycle of buildings, from initial conceptual design through eventual retirement or reuse. The NCS comprises the following items:

- "Uniform Drawing System," published by CSI (a system for the organization of building construction drawings).
- "AIA CAD Layer Guidelines," a system of nomenclature for CAD drawing file names and CAD layer names, published by the AIA. The updated version includes new layer definitions for such disciplines as telecommunications and electronic building systems. It has been revised to improve compatibility with ISO layer standards.
- The Tri-Service "Plotting Guidelines," developed by the U.S. Coast Guard and promulgated by the U.S. Tri-Service CADD/GIS Technology Center of the U.S. Department of Defense (defines colors and line weight assignments for CAD drawings).
- The "U.S. National CAD Standard Foreword, Administration and Amendments," published by NIBS (resolves minor discrepancies between the constituent documents).

(continued)

Several versions of NCS have now been published. Version 1.0 came out in 1999, and version 3.1 was released in January 2005. Version 4.0 is expected to be available in winter 2007. To date, the complete NCS has not yet been incorporated into all CAD software products.

The Benefits of a National CAD Standard

A uniform electronic data classification format establishes a common language for preparing building design and construction documents. It eliminates the need for developing and maintaining office standards. Newly hired employees do not have to be trained or retrained to learn file and layer naming conventions, pen assignments, line weights, drawing set organization, or sheet layout conventions. Project designers and project managers will be able to access design data without having to learn varying arcane organizational systems.

The benefits are better project management, higher-quality construction documents, reduced errors and omissions, and ultimately a better building project. Most important, design firms can provide a higher quality of service to clients by delivering data in an industry-standard format. Savvy design firms will seize the opportunity to let clients know they use the NCS format.

Opportunities to Participate

The NIBS-FIC National CAD Standard Project Committee (NCSPC), with representation from across the twelve NIBS public- and private-interest categories encompassing the entire building construction community, was formed to perform a broad peer review and update of the constituent NCS documents. The NCSPC follows consensus rules approved by the NIBS Board of Direction. Membership is open to industry members. Anyone with an interest in the work of the committee may participate. Most of the committee's work is conducted via the Internet.

All committee members have an equal voice and ballot vote. Details are available at the NCS Web site, www.nationalcadstandard.org. The U.S. National CAD Standard can be ordered by phone from the AIA Bookstore: (202) 626-7541 or (800) 242-3837 (press 4). It can also be purchased from NIBS at www.nationalcadstandard.org and the CSI online bookstore at www.csinet.org. A substantial discount is available to AIA, CSI, and NIBS members.

BACKGROUNDER

AIA MASTERSPEC

MASTERSPEC® is a master guide specification system that offers architects and engineers powerful tools for preparing construction project specifications. MASTERSPEC is a product of the AIA and is exclusively published and supported by ARCOM. Its thirteen libraries are organized by design discipline as follows:

Library	Abbreviation
Architectural/Structural/Civil	A/S/C
Interiors	INT
Roofing	RF
Security & Detention	SD
Structural/Civil/Landscape Architecture	S/C/L
Structural	S
Site Civil	SC
Landscape Architecture	L
Mechanical/Electrical	M/E
Mechanical	M
Fire Protection	FP
Electrical	E
General Requirements	GR

MASTERSPEC libraries are available in four formats—full length, short form, small project, and outline—and in two packages—basic and expanded.

- *Full-length* specifications are comprehensive master specifications that cover a wide range of materials, products, and applications. They include multiple methods of specifying and are the most comprehensive master specifications available in the industry.
- *Short form* specifications are condensed from, and compatible with, full-length sections. They include a limited range of products, streamlined material and quality control requirements, and concise methods of specifying.
- *Small project* specifications are the most abbreviated form of master specifications and are only available in the A/S/C and M/E libraries. These specifications are intended for projects that are limited in scope and complexity.
- *Outline* specifications provide a method for recording product and material decisions early in the documentation process. They can be used as a checklist to help

the project team select products and methods during development of the project manual, to communicate design intent, and to coordinate terminology for use both on the drawings and in the project manual.

- *Basic package* sections, such as concrete and gypsum board, are the most frequently used specifications because they cover the construction products and materials most commonly used for all project sizes and types.
- The *expanded package* includes basic package sections plus more specialized sections, such as laboratory fume hoods.

Section Naming Convention

MASTERSPEC sections come in two complete versions, using assigned numbers and titles according to both the 2004 and 1995 editions of CSI/CSC's MasterFormat™. Each section is organized into one of the CSI/CSC divisions. For example:

MasterFormat 2004
Division 06—Wood, Plastics, and Composites
Section 064023, Interior Architectural Woodwork

MasterFormat 1995
Division 60—Wood and Plastics
Section 06402, Interior Architectural Woodwork

The MASTERSPEC table of contents lists all sections by division and section number and includes issue dates and descriptions of section contents.

Supporting Documents

MASTERSPEC full-length, short form, and small project sections include the following documents:

- *Cover.* This document describes the content of the section text, related products, and work, including products that could be inserted into the section if required. It also describes similar work normally specified elsewhere and closely related work specified in other sections. It includes a summary of changes since the last update.
- *Evaluations.* This document describes characteristics and criteria for specifying the products and materials in the section. Also included are editing instructions, which are referenced in editor's notes in the section text; the scope of the section; a description of product characteristics; special design and detailing considerations, if applicable; environmental considerations; referenced standards; suggested reference materials; and a list of manufacturers. The list of manufacturers provides telephone numbers and Web addresses. Tables of comparative information on products and manufacturers are included in some sections.

- *Section text.* This document is presented in CSI/CSC's three-part *SectionFormat* with editor's notes, alternative text, in-line optional text, and insert notes.
- *Drawing coordination checklist.* This document consists of drawing requirements related to the section content. It indicates items that should be shown on the drawings because they are not in the section text.
- *Specification coordination checklist.* This document includes a list of specification sections and requirements that relate to the section content. Small project sections do not currently include this document.

Editing Assistance

MASTERSPEC is a comprehensive master specification system. The evaluations provide editing instructions for each specification section, as well as product comparisons, a list of national manufacturers, reference standards, references, a discussion of the section topic, and graphics, when appropriate. Each section text includes editor's notes with instructions for editing and selecting alternative text, in-line optional text, and insert notes. All section text is displayed for review and editing. Editor's notes and units of measure appear on screen in color. Editor's notes are formatted as hidden text, which allows them to be toggled on or off. Instructions for editing MASTERSPEC are included in the MASTERSPEC user's guide.

Continuing Education

MASTERSPEC A/S/C Library subscribers receive updates that include specification sections to review for AIA/CES learning unit (LU) credits. MASTERSPEC licensed users complete a test covering each reviewed section to receive one LU credit for each section on which the test score is at least 80 percent. Study materials include the section text, evaluations, and other supporting documents. These LU credits fulfill health, safety, and welfare (HSW) requirements.

SPECWARE

SPECWARE® is a family of ARCOM's specification enhancement software, available to MASTERSPEC licensed users to make editing, formatting, and generating reports more efficient and consistent. SPECWARE includes the following:

- *MASTERWORKS™.* This software, which is provided with each MASTERSPEC license, enhances the capabilities of word-processing programs to simplify the editing of alternative text, to select options, to insert required text, and to add project notes. The multifile capabilities automate spell checking, searching and replacing, reporting, creating headers and footers, generating a table of contents, formatting, and other text appearance functions. Specification output formats include project manual, sheet specification, drawing notes, and outline.

- *e-SPECS® Linx™.* This automated editor, developed in an ARCOM/InterSpec partnership, is available as add-on software and operates on standard full-length, short form, small project, and outline MASTERSPEC sections that are in a database format. Text elements in each section are linked together hierarchically and semantically. Using a checklist, the user selects applicable product and material requirements. All appropriate text elements are marked for deletion when a parent text element is marked for deletion. If a project has no wood decking, for example, deletion of wood decking in Section 061500/06150 would automatically delete all text related to wood decking in all parts of the section text. This software provides an efficient tool for the easy removal of large quantities of text. e-SPECS Linx also allows a user to manually edit the remaining section text, automate spell checking, search and replace text, create headers and footers, generate a table of contents, and create reports. Project collaboration is enhanced through the use of project notes and a shared database in which multiple users can edit the specifications at the same time.

- *e-SPECS for AutoCAD®* and *e-SPECS for Revit®* software, developed by InterSpec, provide the additional capability to extract product and material requirements from CAD drawings and building information models. ARCOM has integrated MASTERSPEC into this software, which allows automatic editing plus better coordination of the drawings and the specifications. Other e-SPECS functions are used to perform final editing and formatting to complete the specifications without exporting or leaving the e-SPECS environment. e-SPECS integrates the entire project team into the specification development process, streamlining the document management process.

Information about MASTERSPEC and ARCOM SPECWARE software is available through ARCOM by phone at (800) 424-5080, on its Web site at www.arcomnet.com, or by e-mail to arcom@arcomnet.com.

PART 3: THE PROJECT

8.4 Bidding or Negotiation Phase

William C. Charvat, AIA

The procurement of construction services brings together the team and resources needed to translate building plans into physical reality.

In the bidding/negotiation phase, the architect assists the client in obtaining competent construction bids or negotiating the construction contract. The architect's services in this phase are most often packaged with other services such as design, construction documentation, or construction administration. However, owners will sometimes choose to treat construction procurement as a discrete service. Traditionally, this choice depended on the project, but today the demand for assistance in procuring construction contracts is increasing with the trend toward alternative delivery methods such as construction management and design-build.

Owners are motivated to seek input from the architect in decisions related to construction procurement when they do not have the experience or resources to perform the task in-house or do not wish to devote in-house resources to the task. Large, complex projects may require the owner to contract with a number of different prime contractors, which requires much coordination of the bid packages. Often such projects

William C. Charvat is executive vice president/chief operating officer of Helman Hurley Charvat Peacock/Architects, Inc., an international architecture, planning, and interior design firm in Maitland, Florida. His practice focuses on project management, construction, and problem solving for large and complex projects.

are on tight time schedules with phased, fast-track work plans, necessitating even greater coordination of the procurement process and a higher level of effort for the construction procurement team.

Construction procurement services require a range of knowledge and skills. Some are developed through practical experience in managing building design and construction and others through previous experience in managing procurement processes. Senior architects with project management experience are most likely to have developed the negotiation skills and the knowledge of construction procedures required to provide advice to the owner with regard to the appropriate procurement and contracting methodology for the project. Most architects possess other, more fundamental skills, including the ability to understand the design intent expressed in construction drawings and specifications and the ability to communicate with vendors and construction contractors.

The increase in construction claims litigation and related trends toward increased control of cost and quality have placed more emphasis on the construction procurement process. Owners want to be reasonably sure that construction contractors are well qualified, their services are obtained for a reasonable cost, and the construction contract minimizes the potential for costly changes and delays. The experienced architect can provide valuable construction procurement advice to the client, but must be mindful of the risk involved.

PREPARATORY STEPS

A decision about the delivery method for a project should be considered no later than the design phase, and ideally prior to signing an agreement with the owner, since the delivery method will affect the professional fees involved. The project delivery approach the owner chooses affects the architect's decision about how project documents will be organized and how construction documents will be developed and packaged. Also, the project team should have staff experienced in the use of the chosen project delivery method. AIA Document B101–2007, Standard Form of Agreement Between Owner and Architect, provides for identification of the construction procurement approach as part of the contract. This allows the architect and the architect's consultants to understand and accept their roles in producing the project deliverables. Each can assist in the timely completion of appropriate, well-coordinated (inter- and intra-disciplinary) construction and bidding documents and construction administration communications.

Negotiating vs. Bidding

Time can be saved by eliminating the bid period when a contract is negotiated directly with a preselected contractor. Only a fee and reimbursable expenses are negotiated using AIA Document A102–2007, Agreement Between Owner and Contractor, Cost Plus a Fee with a Guaranteed Maximum Price. This can be done concurrently with completion of the construction documents. The trade contract work for this approach can be set up in a similar fashion. Under this approach, construction work usually does not start until the construction documents are complete.

Another form of negotiated contract for construction involves construction management (CM) services. Here, the construction manager negotiates to establish a fee for preconstruction services as well as CM overhead during construction. AIA Document A131/CMc–2003, Cost Plus a Fee, No Guarantee of Cost, would be used for this approach. Sometimes when using cost-of-work-plus-a-fee, the construction manager's reimbursable expenses are negotiated as a fixed, or not to exceed, amount. Using such a CM approach is different from a cost-of-work approach in the following ways:

- Inclusion of preconstruction services (cost estimating, constructability review, value analysis)
- Trade contracts bid either as lump sum or with guaranteed maximum limits
- Fast-track or phased construction
- Establishment of a guaranteed maximum cost, with final costs falling under this limit being shared with the owner on an agreed-to percentage basis

With a form of negotiated contract or the lump-sum bidding approach, basic services include documenting the construction procurement process, completing the construction documents, and obtaining responsive, reasonable bids or negotiated prices.

Impact of the Delivery Method on Design Fees

Architects are accustomed to quoting fees based on a traditional design-bid-build delivery method in which the architect and consultants produce a single set of construction documents. Design decisions, including those regarding material, systems, and acceptable manufacturers, are incorporated in the documents. The roles of the architect and consultants during construction, established by AIA Documents B101–2007, Standard Form of Agreement Between Owner and Architect, and A201–2007, General Conditions of the Contract for Construction, include making scheduled site visits to report to the owner known deviations from the contract documents and any defects and deficiencies observed in the work.

Using nontraditional procurement approaches with multiple prime contractors, fast-track phased construction, and/or construction managers can save the owner time and money. However, increased architect's fees are often necessary. The architect needs to do a detailed estimate of the required scope of work, identifying deliverables and related fees, so that proper compensation is paid to the architect and the architect's consultants. Additional fees are required for meetings with the contractor/CM; value analysis (VA, including revisions and updates to the drawings to incorporate VA changes); preparation of multiple document packages; multiple bid periods; administration of multiple construction contracts; and the ability to respond to daily questions from the contractors and/or the construction manager in a timely fashion. Additional fees of 2 to 3 percent above traditional design-bid-build fees may be justified. Architects should not underestimate the additional services required for alternative construction delivery methods.

▶ A detailed discussion of construction contract types is found in Construction Contracts (11.4).

Prequalification of Bidders

Prequalification of the bidders is commonly conducted when bidding will be restricted to a selected list of bidders. Investigation of the general reputation, demonstrated ability and quality of performance, financial integrity, and prior project experience of the bidders can help to determine if each bidder is appropriately qualified for a project. However, before undertaking the process, be sure to review applicable laws to ensure it is permitted. For instance, prequalification is usually prohibited for publicly funded projects. Also, to avoid contractor claims of business interference, it is important for the owner, rather than the architect, to make the final decisions relative to contractor prequalification and selection.

Prequalification of contractors is suggested when a closed bid list is being developed and/or to ensure bidders are qualified in open bidding. AIA Document A305–1986, Contractor's Qualification Statement, is used for this purpose.

Preparation of Bidding Documents

Preparation for bidding and negotiation starts with selection of the project delivery approach and structure of the construction contracts that will be awarded. Ideally, each member of the team should have experience with the method of project delivery being used.

Decisions about the structure of the construction contract must be made prior to procurement. These decisions should address such issues as whether to have

- Combined or separate design and construction services. If they are combined (design-build), the construction contract is usually awarded early in project development. Similarly, when the owner wishes to have a contractor or construction manager involved in preconstruction services, those contracts should be in place early in project development.
- Single or multiple contracts. Who will manage multiple contracts?
- Single or multiple bid packages. Multiple packages require more staffing.
- Traditional or fast-track scheduling. This decision affects the timing of numerous owner and contractor activities, as well as material, equipment, and system procurement issues.
- Open competitive bidding or direct solicitation, such as negotiation.

In addition, these issues should be considered:

- What documents will establish the initial contract sum for construction—scope documents, 50 percent construction documents, or some documents at another percentage of completion?
- What role will the design architect have in bidding and construction? Will the owner also hire a construction manager?
- What will the basis of compensation be for the contractor (e.g., lump sum, cost plus fee, guaranteed maximum price, separate fee for preconstruction services)?

Having advised the owner on decisions such as these concerning contracts and bidding, the architect frequently is requested to assemble bidding documents for the owner. A helpful document is AIA Document D200–1995, Project Checklist. The bidding documents describe the project in detail and indicate the conditions under which it will be bid and built. An experienced architect, in coordination with the owner's attorney, will be able to properly assist in preparation of these documents.

Advertisement for Bids

For public work, the law usually requires placement of an invitation to bid in the classified advertising section of one or more newspapers in the region where the project is located. Additional announcements can be placed in contractor newsletters, magazines, plan rooms, or other media. The ad or announcement should contain, at minimum, the project description, name of the architect, bid date, and information about where bid documents may be reviewed or purchased.

Instructions to Bidders

Use of AIA Document A701–1997, Instructions to Bidders, will establish a consistent understanding of the procedures that bidders should follow in preparing and tendering their bids. The instructions in this document include provisions covering the following:

- Definitions
- Bidder's representations
- Bidding procedures
- Review of bidding documents

The bidding document package includes these items:

- Instruction to bidders
- Notice to bid
- Form of owner-contractor agreement
- Performance bond
- Labor and material bond
- General and supplementary conditions of the contract
- Special contract conditions
- Drawings and specifications
- Addenda issued prior to the receipt of bids

- Consideration of bids
- Post-bid information
- Performance bond and payment bond
- Form of agreement between owner and contractor

Bid Form

For most projects, but particularly for open, publicly funded ones, a bid form should be prepared by either the owner or the architect. Use of a project-specific bid form makes it easier for contractors to submit a complete, responsive, and responsible bid.

The form should indicate the project name, bid date, and location where bids are to be received and include space for entering the name of bidder. Space beside the bidder's name should be provided to record the amount of the bid and any further breakdown of alternates and unit prices. Space for acknowledgment of certificates of insurance, bonds, or other documents (such as certificates regarding prevailing wage standards and other worker employment statute compliance representations required of the contractor) that are required to accompany each sealed bid should also be included. More space may be needed to record additional information required by the instructions to bidders or by the specifications in the project manual. For a contractor's proposal to be considered a qualified bid, it must include all required information, as well as a completed AIA Document A305–1986, Contractor's Qualification Statement.

The bid form ensures that all bids will be submitted in an identical format, which will make the evaluation process easier and help prevent errors in recording multiple base and alternate bid amounts.

Owner-Contractor Agreement Form

The owner-contractor agreement sets forth the respective rights, duties, and obligations of the two parties for the purpose of constructing the project. It may also establish similar conditions for the architect (and possibly a construction manager), who can be retained to administer the construction contract. In addition, it is common for the architect and/or the owner to write supplementary conditions, which cover specific details related to such items as project administrative procedures, bonds, contract time, construction phasing, insurance requirements, site operations, payment procedures, change order markups, and project closeout. It is important for the architect to understand the content, terms, and conditions of the owner-contractor agreement and the general and supplementary conditions. As well, the owner's legal and insurance counsel should be properly consulted in development of these contract documents.

Performance Bond

This bond provides a guarantee that if the contractor defaults or fails to perform, the surety will either complete the contract in accordance with its terms or provide sufficient funds up to the penal amount for such completion. A performance bond also protects against default by subcontractors responsible to the general contractor.

Labor and Material Bond

Sometimes referred to as a payment bond, a labor and material bond constitutes a guarantee that subcontractors, material suppliers, and others providing labor, material goods, and services to the project will be paid. It protects the owner from claims against contract balances by unpaid suppliers and subcontractors in the event of the default of the contractor.

Addenda

Review of the bidding documents during the bidding period by prime bidders, sub-bidders, and material suppliers often reveals items that must be clarified, corrected, or explained. Sometimes the owner or architect will initiate revisions to the bidding documents in response to changes of circumstances or requirements. In these circumstances, written addenda, including drawings or other graphic documents, are issued to modify or interpret the bidding documents before bids are received or the contract is executed.

MANAGEMENT AND CONTROL OF THE BIDDING PROCESS

Management, documentation, and equal treatment of all bidders is important during the bid process to avoid any bid protests. A verbal response should not be given to a single bidder. All responses to bidders need to be in writing and sent to all bidders.

Distribution of the Bidding Documents

Web-based communication offers an expanded level of access to bid documents. Before the digital age, local plan rooms and the architect's office were usually the only places contractors could go to see construction drawings. Today, electronic CAD files of the drawings and the project manual can be sent via e-mail to single or multiple reprographic shops where bidders can order copies anywhere in the world. Password-protected project collaboration Web sites can also receive electronic documents and make them available for bidders to view. With access privileges, a reprographics company can download construction drawings from such Web sites and publish hard copies for use by local bidders.

In any case, a bidder should have access to at least one complete set of drawings and specifications to properly prepare a fully responsive bid. Traditionally, the cost of that set of documents would be paid for either by the owner, the architect (as a reimbursable expense), or the bidder, depending upon the terms of the owner-architect agreement and bidding documents.

To ensure the return of sets of documents sent to unsuccessful bidders, each bidder can be required to provide a security deposit that would be refunded (in whole or in part) upon return of the documents in good condition within an established period of time.

Distribution of Addenda and Notices

A master list (AIA Document G804–2001, Register of Bid Documents) should be maintained showing the name, address (e-mail and physical), and telephone and fax numbers of each contractor who has received complete sets of bidding documents. This list may be maintained by the architect or reprographic shop that is distributing the bidding documents, whichever is more practical. The list is used to issue addenda, track returned sets, and refund deposits during and after the bidding phase. Failure to issue addenda to a bidder can result in a bid protest, causing a potentially costly delay in awarding the contract for construction.

Pre-Bid Conference

The goal of the pre-bid conference is to provide bidders with a clear and consistent understanding of the project requirements and scope. Attendance at this meeting is often required to submit a bid proposal.

Receipt of Bids

In the traditional design-bid-build delivery model, bid proposals are only received from general contractors. The instructions to bidders explain how to submit a proposal and may include a requirement or representation that each bidder identify the major subcontractors (e.g., concrete, steel, mechanical, electrical, plumbing) that will be used to do the work.

Bidding Results

Final selection of the contractor is the owner's decision, made with the architect's assistance. When the qualifications and financial background of the bidders have been determined in the prequalification process, the expectation is that the contract will be awarded to the lowest bidder. However, when bidders have not been prequalified, the expectation is that the contract will be awarded to the lowest responsible and responsive bidder. (Public owners may be required by law to accept the lowest responsible bid.)

Errors, Withdrawals, and Revocations

The bidding documents generally establish a date after which bidders cannot withdraw their bid proposal. This date should allow sufficient time after submission of bids for accurate bid evaluation and authorization of an award.

Bid Bond

Some owners require bidders to provide bid security as part of their bid. The bid security can be in the form of cash, a cashier's check, or a bond. Submittal of bid security guarantees that if a bid is accepted within the specified time, usually thirty to ninety days from the opening of the bids, the bidder will enter into a formal agreement with the owner and will furnish the required construction performance and construction payment bonds.

Evaluation of Bids

The architect usually assists the owner in the selection decision by evaluating the bid proposals received. This assistance commonly includes review and recommendations regarding any alternatives and substitutions the owner has solicited. This evaluation takes on special significance if all bids exceed the owner's budget or if acceptance of alternatives changes the order of the low bidders. The owner's options in such cases include increasing the budget, rebidding, renegotiating, revising the scope, or abandoning the project.

Negotiation of Bids

Even in competitive bidding situations, it is not uncommon for some negotiation to take place after bids have been received. Minor changes required before the contract is signed should be negotiated only with the selected bidder, and then only when permitted by the owner or the awarding authority's regulations. In public work, post-bid negotiations must be consistent with state statutes governing such activity.

Rejection of Bids

The owner customarily includes in the bidding documents the right to reject any or all bids.

Notification of Bidders

After the owner has selected the contractor(s), all bidders should be informed of the results as a matter of courtesy.

Contract Award

The architect (in cooperation with the owner, the owner's attorney, and possibly the owner's insurance consultant) prepares a contract reflecting modifications resulting from negotiations and changes. The owner and contractor(s) sign the agreement(s).

Letter of Intent

When the owner wants to move forward immediately before preparing and executing a formal agreement with the contractor, a written letter of intent may be used to give the successful bidder interim authorization to begin work. Such orders to proceed have legal implications and should be drafted by the owner's attorney for the owner's signature.

A letter of intent is also known as a memorandum of understanding or memorandum of agreement. From a business perspective, a letter of intent is a device to indicate that each party has agreed, through serious negotiations, that a formal agreement can be achieved. The letter or memorandum will set forth a timeline for negotiations, including a deadline for closing the deal and what will occur if the parties fail to meet the deadline.

Preconstruction Conference

Following the contract award and prior to the start of construction, a preconstruction conference should be held that is attended by the owner, contractor, major subcontractors, architect, and engineering consultants. The architect's project manager will work closely with the contractor's project manager to develop the conference agenda. The conference will provide everyone involved with an understanding of project procedures, requirements, due dates, and special characteristics. This meeting will encourage a smooth start to the project.

▶ See Construction Contract Administration (8.5) for suggested agenda items for a preconstruction conference.

AVOIDING BIDDING PROBLEMS

The goal of a bid is to establish a price for the project construction. Deficiencies in the bid documents can result in change orders, which can bring financial risk to the architect as well as the owner. Change order pricing is usually higher than bid pricing due to the small quantity of materials involved and the out-of-sequence nature of the work. An excessive number of change orders may result in the owner bringing a claim against the architect for errors and omissions.

Understanding the Bid

Bidding problems directly expand into cost problems for the owner. Incomplete or inaccurate drawings will result in many bidder questions or inclusion of contingencies in the bids to protect the bidders.

It is accepted in the construction industry that the contractor's bid proposal is only for what is shown on the drawings and written in the specifications. Contractors do not provide a cross-checking and coordination service during the bidding period. This is the design team's responsibility.

When contractors prepare a bid, they only take off quantities from one area of the drawings. Since short bid periods do not allow detailed takeoffs of specific quantities for all items, pricing is commonly established by applying trade contractor square-footage guidelines to the design intent indicated in the drawings. As a practical matter, it is not possible for bidders to detect conflicts between disciplines, incomplete details, dimensional problems, or code violations during a bidding period that is typically only four to six weeks long. Individual drawings that appear complete may have problems that can only be detected when they are compared with other drawings to confirm proper coordination.

Bids Based on Insufficient Construction Documents

If project construction drawings are not complete and have not been given interdisciplinary and intradisciplinary reviews, it is advisable to delay the bid submittal date until this has been done. Failure to take this step is likely to increase the need for addenda during the bidding process and result in cost increases and schedule delays once construction is under way.

If a situation arises in which drawings are not complete and coordinated and the bid date cannot be changed, the following suggestions may be helpful:

- Bid the project as a cost-of-work-plus-a-fee contract. Keep the design team working during the bid period so the documents can be completed early in the construction phase.
- Convert the project to a CM, guaranteed maximum price (GMP) contract, where bidding site work and foundation work can be done to start construction. Concurrently complete the documents for trade bidding by the CM for the balance of the work.
- Bid the site work and possibly the foundation work as early bid packages with the right to assign these contracts to a general contractor. Concurrently with this bidding and construction, complete the drawings for the balance of the project. Bid this work with the assignment of the earlier bid contracts for a total project lump-sum price.

When architects use the bidding period as a time to check and coordinate drawings and issue addenda, this disrupts the bidding process and can cause contractors to increase their bids. In these instances, bidders may be forced to include contingencies in their price, since receiving an addendum within one to two weeks of the bid date does not usually allow enough time for contractors to coordinate the affected work with all previously issued bid documents.

Use of Alternates/Substitutions

When an alternate building feature, material, or system is specified in the construction documents, providing only a simple description of the alternate can cause problems. Drawings, details, and complete specifications illustrating use of the alternate should be prepared to properly coordinate it with adjacent work and to make it possible for the bid to cover the complete scope of work. The number and size of alternates can be disruptive to a short bid period. Therefore, their use should be limited here.

Because voluntary alternates can be disruptive, contractors should avoid using them or substitutions during the bidding phase in most instances. However, many owners find them desirable and may allow their use. In such cases, the contractor should predicate the base bid only on what is on the bid documents, with the alternate or substitution priced separately. A complete description of the contractor's alternate or substitution must accompany the separate bid amount. An alternate should not be accepted until a complete and thorough analysis has been done, which may require the architect to clarify details and/or specification to avoid conflicts with the client's program or adjacent work. This work by the architect should be considered an additional service, which the owner may require the contractor to pay for as part of the alternate bid amount.

Managing Addenda

Addenda need to be dated and sequentially numbered. All drawings, details, and specification sections being changed must be carefully referenced to each other. If large changes result in numerous or significant revisions to the drawings, the affected drawings should be reissued. Large, complicated addenda or numerous addenda may require an extension of the bid period. The last addendum should not be issued fewer than seven calendar days before the bid date.

Keeping the Design Team Involved

Once a project is in the bid phase, it is common for staff of the architect and consultant to be assigned to other projects. However, it is essential for the architect's project manager to provide team leadership during this phase. The architecture staff and consultants who prepared the drawings and specifications must be the same people who respond to questions, especially those that result in addenda. Turning the bidding over to the firm's construction administrator, who had no involvement in preparing the bidding documents, leads to inadequate or incomplete answers.

Responding to Bidder Questions

During bidding, all bidder questions should be submitted to the architect in writing. All answers should be issued to all bidders by written addendum. These requirements must be cited in the instructions to bidders. Despite these requirements, however, suppliers, subcontractors, and contractors often call the architect or engineering consultants associated with work they are questioning. Manufacturers and suppliers also routinely call to ask the architect to list a product as an equal or alternate to what is specified. The architect's best response would be "Thank you for the question; please submit it to me in writing and the answer will be covered by an addendum." The architect must also make it clear that if no answer is issued in an addendum, bidders must apply their best judgment in preparing their bid.

Use of Legal and Insurance Consultants

Terms and conditions in the owner-contractor agreement should be developed in conjunction with the owner's attorney and an insurance agent or consultant to make sure all legal and insurance requirements in the agreement are properly addressed. These advisers also need to review the bonds and insurance certificates issued by the contractor as part of the bid and subsequent contract.

CONTROLLING CONSTRUCTION COST ON BID PROJECTS

Two common causes of construction cost overruns on bid projects are owner program changes and incomplete and uncoordinated documents. To eliminate or minimize untimely program changes, detailed program evaluation in the schematic and design development phases is advisable.

Another obvious way to avoid overruns is to carefully check construction drawings and specifications for completeness and coordinate them with all disciplines. Also, an accurate cost estimate should be prepared during the design phases.

Techniques for Avoiding Construction Cost Problems

Some suggested cost control techniques are explained here:

Detailed programming. Before starting schematic design, the owner should provide a detailed program for all apsects of the project. All design work should be finalized and accepted by the owner by the end of the design development phase; however, this may not occur in all projects. Preparation of the construction drawings before the program is finalized may result in bidding delays and project budget overruns.

Detailed cost estimates. Early project cost estimates should include as much detail as possible. Revisit and update cost estimaes during the design phases. Contingencies and reserves should not be included in the estimates until the design development phase is complete and only with the concurrence of the owner.

Preconstruction services from a general contractor and/or construction manager. Having a contractor or construction manager advise the owner and architect during design and preparation of construction documents can be beneficial. Such advice may include constructability reviews, document reviews for completeness and coordination, value analysis suggestions, construction phasing advice for fast-track scheduling, and detailed cost estimating. The overall goal in having the contractor or CM involved during the design phases is to minimize requests for information (RFIs) and change orders during construction.

Often contractors or CMs are given the opportunity to become prime contractors for a project when they are involved during the design phase. The most commonly used agreements in these situations are the following AIA documents:

▶ See Construction Cost Management (9.4) for a discussion of project budgeting and cost estimating techniques.

- A101–2007, Standard Form of Agreement Between Owner and Contractor where the Basis of Payment is a Stipulated Sum
- A103–2007, Standard Form of Agreement Between Owner and Contractor where the Basis of Payment is the Cost of the Work with a Negotiated GMP
- A121/CMc–2003, Standard Form of Agreement Between Owner and Construction Manager
- A131/CMc–2003, Standard Form of Agreement Between Owner and Construction Manager where the Basis of Payment is Cost Plus a Fee

If the contractor or CM undertakes cost estimating during design, it is advisable for the architect to also provide a detailed cost estimate for comparison with the contractor's numbers, especially if a GMP for construction is involved.

Use of a program manager. A program management firm provides experienced professional staff that may include architects, planners, engineers, and contractors to help the owner manage a project. Program management firms are most often used to manage large, complex projects or to supplement the owner's staff resources in managing a project from programming through building occupancy.

Peer reviews. To verify completeness and accuracy, the owner can hire another design professional (architect or engineer) to review the construction drawings by the architect of record. Peer reviews can also be provided by a program management firm. Such reviews usually occur when the drawings are at least 50 percent complete. The reviews can result in improved bidding documents that will lead to more competitive bids and fewer change orders during construction. If a peer review is planned, the schedule for the construction documents phase must allow adequate time for the review and for making adjustments to the final documents before the project goes to bid.

Regulatory agency or building department reviews. Significant problems with code issues can be avoided when the interpretation of applicable building codes by the architect and engineering consultants is in line with those of the local building official. Meetings to discuss code requirements should be scheduled with the relevant authority having jurisdiction (AHJ) during both the schematic design and the design development phases. A final meeting with the building official to review pre-final construction documents is a must to ensure consensus on all code-related issues.

The architect should prepare and issue a final report on the discussions in these review meetings to document all decisions and commitments agreed to by the AHJ and the architect and consultants.

Design-build cost control. With a design-build delivery approach, careful attention should be given to defining the program and cost of the project in the design-build agreement. Design-build proposals should be based on a detailed program that includes a complete description of project site features (e.g., paving, hardscape, landscape); the quality desired for building features such as exterior walls, roof, windows, doors, hardware, ceiling systems, skylights, and toilet room features and fixtures; desired interior finishes (walls, floors, ceilings, and casework); mechanical and electrical systems and features; and specialty needs (e.g., energy systems, security systems, fire protection systems, graphic systems). Conceptual site, building elevation, and floor plan drawings are also helpful for establishing the design intent.

▶ Design-build delivery is discussed in Project Delivery Methods (8.1), as well as in the accompanying Construction Management backgrounder.

THE CONSTRUCTION TEAM

In the construction procurement process, the architect helps the owner identify, select, and engage a qualified contractor and choose an appropriate project delivery method. The selected contractor joins the architect and the owner on the construction team.

For More Information

Section 5.2 of "Module 5: Construction Documents" in *The Project Resource Manual: CSI Manual of Practice* (McGraw-Hill, 2005) addresses requirements for construction procurement and includes samples of bid invitation and bid forms.

"Module 6: Bidding/Negotiating/Purchasing" of *The Project Resource Manual: CSI Manual of Practice* (McGraw-Hill, 2005) addresses practical aspects of construction procurement including pricing considerations, project information, bidding, negotiating, and award of contract.

Chapter 6 in *A Guide to Successful Construction*, third edition (BNI Publications, 1999), by Arthur F. O'Leary, discusses construction procurement including preparation of bid documents, bid openings, and award of contract.

Chapter 11, "Bidding and Contract Negotiation," of the *Emerging Professional's Companion* addresses all aspects of the construction procurement process including document preparation, pre-bid conferences, and conducting bid openings. The chapter also covers practical and legal safeguards and alternative delivery methods.

8.5 Construction Contract Administration

James B. Atkins, FAIA, KIA

The architect's construction phase services are an important part of the construction process, during which time the building design becomes a physical reality. The architect's successful administration of the construction contract can bring benefits to the owner, contractor, and architect.

The architect's duty to administer the contract for construction (CCA services) begins with the award of the construction contract and ends on the date the architect issues the final certificate for payment to the owner. If requested by the owner, CCA services can extend through the expiration of the contractor's one-year warranty period.

AIA Contract Documents delineate the architect's CCA duties, and the architect has authority to act on the owner's behalf only to the extent stated in the owner-architect agreement. Throughout the construction phase, the architect serves as a representative of, as well as an adviser and consultant to, the owner. During the architect's visits to the job site, CCA duties include the following:

- Becoming generally familiar with the work through site visits
- Keeping the owner informed about the progress and quality of the portions of the completed work
- Reporting observed defects and deficiencies in the work, and deviations from the construction schedule
- Determining in general if the work, when fully completed, will be in accordance with the contract documents

Of course, CCA goes beyond submittal reviews, payment certifications, and field observation reports. Effective project closeouts not only assist owners in obtaining necessary closeout documents and information, they can also leave the owner with positive memories of the architect's services. Following up with the owner prior to the end of the contractor's one-year warranty is also prudent. Owners appreciate being contacted about the performance of their buildings and to see if corrective actions are needed for warranty

Many states have legislated that projects requiring an architect's or engineer's seal must have CCA services provided by a licensed professional.

▶ For information on project closeouts, see Project Closeouts (9.6).

Jim Atkins is a principal with HKS Architects, where he is responsible for construction services, education, people management, and loss prevention activities. Atkins serves on the AIA Documents and Risk Management committees and chaired the steering group for the fourteenth edition of the *Architect's Handbook of Professional Practice*. He has authored numerous articles, including project management topics, for *AIArchitect*.

PROACTIVE VS. REACTIVE CONTRACT ADMINISTRATION

AIA documents require the architect to visit the job site at intervals appropriate to the stage of construction. This leaves it to the discretion of the architect to decide when and how often site visits should be made during the construction phase.

Some architects elect to make visits less frequently, relying on the owner or the contractor to call if a problem or issue arises. This "reactive" approach to contract administration denies the architect opportunities to resolve problems *before* the work is constructed and makes it more difficult for the architect to be fully aware of the overall status of the work as it progresses. For example, when the architect does not attend scheduled site meetings and does not visit the site regularly, change resolution and problem solving may be accomplished without input from the architect.

A "proactive" CCA approach involves initiating steps and measures that can produce greater value for the owner and contractor, as well as for the architect. Such steps and measures include the following:

- Spending adequate time with the owner to build a "trusted adviser" relationship
- Consulting with the contractor and participating in problem resolution and conflicts to influence the final work product
- Making input on scope changes proposed by the owner or the contractor
- Finding opportunities to correct discrepancies or errors or omissions in the contract documents before the work is constructed

The construction phase involves time- and money-induced pressures. To keep your composure while administering the construction contract, keep a professional attitude, look at problems from both sides, and remain calm when dealing with tense situations.

issues. Caring about the owner's experiences with the finished project supports professionalism and greatly reinforces the owner-architect relationship, which, among other benefits, could result in positive recommendations to other potential clients.

ACHIEVING PROACTIVE CCA

A proactive approach to CCA can better capture its potential benefits and can help the architect avoid the pitfalls of a reactive, wait-and-see approach. Proactive CCA can be more easily achieved by pursuing the following objectives prior to and during the construction phase.

Including CCA Services in the Agreement with the Owner

CCA services cannot benefit the owner if they are reduced in scope or omitted from the owner-architect agreement by the owner. Therefore, discussions with some owners may be required to help them understand the importance of CCA services.

For example, the quality of building products and systems established in the specifications cannot be effectively monitored without submittal review. On the other hand, if submittal review is included in the architect's scope of work and site visits are not, installation of specified products and systems cannot be monitored through on-site observations. The determination in general if the work is in conformance with the contract documents is an important part of project delivery.

Staying in the Communication Loop and Being a Team Player

The construction process is not solely an owner-contractor event. Frequent discussions between the owner and the architect on scope and aesthetic matters can benefit the project. As well, the architect participates in and conducts the preconstruction conference and owner-architect-contractor project meetings, which makes it easier for the architect to stay involved in all relevant construction activities. When the contractor comes to view the architect as a resource for resolving issues—which includes providing quick responses—a synergistic and beneficial dynamic is formed.

Maintaining Good Relationships

The construction phase can be challenging, and the pressures of the job can test everyone's self-control. However, much more can be gained through calm and friendly interaction than through hostility. When members of the project team pursue the priority of helping each other, project success can be more easily achieved.

ROLES OF CCA TEAM PARTICIPANTS

Most building design and construction projects include services of the architect and the architect's consultants, the general contractor and the general contractor's

In determining the scope of services for administering the contract on a new project, the architect usually applies historic labor and cost data. However, certain conditions may cause those services to vary from the norm. When estimating fees and labor demands, consider the following factors.

Climate and Weather

Areas with weather conditions such as extreme cold or heat may prevent continuous ongoing construction, and possibly extend total construction time and cause intermittent reassignment of personnel. Areas with heavy seasonal rains can cause acceleration in the dry months to achieve early completion, or they may cause delays in the start of construction to avoid the adverse weather.

Remote and Foreign Locations

Remote locations such as islands may require importing all construction materials in containers. Submittal review must be done before materials are shipped, and time must be allowed to clear customs upon arrival. In most foreign countries, U.S. architects usually cannot legally provide architect-of-record services. Services such as document publication, payment certification, and substantial completion may be deleted from the architect's services and provided by a local architect.

Economic Factors

An inflating economy can cause an increase in work activity, resulting in staffing shortages and limited product availability. The cost of labor and materials increases can cause budget challenges that drive value analysis and substitution efforts in a quest for cheaper materials and systems. As a result, schedules may be protracted, and submittal review and change process activities may increase. A recessive economy increases competition for work, often resulting in unreasonably low bids with low contingency and general conditions amounts and minimum profit margins. The substitution process is frequently used as a vehicle for recovering costs through cheaper materials. As a result, submittal review and RFI activity may increase.

Project Delivery Approach

In contractor-led design-build projects, many of the architect's duties to the owner shift to the contractor. Payment certification services may not be required, and substantial completion may involve additional participants. Submittal review may become more interactive with the contractor, and the RFI process may be more active. When construction manager-advisers, program managers, and contracted owner's representatives are involved, this can add an extra step in many construction phase procedures. Integrated project delivery approaches with the project team using real-time file-sharing could increase or decrease CCA time requirements, depending on the specific interaction of the owner and the contractor. Management of meetings may be more difficult, but submittal reviews, the RFI process, and the change order process may become less demanding due to interactive participation. Multiple prime contracts tend to require additional CCA time due to the lack of a general contractor who controls all of the work.

Multiple Design Contracts

Projects with multiple design contracts can affect payment certification, especially if there is a single contractor who submits one application for payment. The change order process could become more complicated as well, especially if a change affects the work of more than one designer.

Scheduling Approaches

The overlapping phases of fast-track scheduling could require additional time for submittal reviews, change order and RFI processing, site observation, and the determination of substantial completion due to revisions made later in the project.

Renovation Projects

Renovation work or building additions can affect CCA services, especially if the existing facility is occupied or there is limited access to the site. These situations may require additional site observations, additional payment application reviews, and multiple inspections for substantial completion. Buildings that must be occupied during renovation may also require the work to be done at designated times such as at night, on weekends, or during specific hours of the day.

THE ARCHITECT'S CONSTRUCTION PHASE ACTIVITIES

Activities	Representative Tasks	Documentation
For preconstruction conference	Establish administrative procedures. Review contractor schedules. Review general contactor requirements. Review schedule of values. Review quality control procedures. Review allowances/contingencies. Review bond requirements.	Administrative procedures manual
During construction	Conduct scheduled visits. Participate in project meetings. Issue site observation reports. Send/answer RFIs. Review contractor submittals. Review value analysis/substitutions. Prepare change orders. Review applications for payment. Issue work changes proposals. Monitor allowances. Monitor contingencies. Monitor progress and quality of work. Approve minor changes. Review testing and inspection reports. Cooperate with owner consultants. Review change orders.	Site observation reports Change orders Change directives Supplemental instructions Certificates for payment Action item lists Logs
At substantial completion	Inspect project for substantial completion. Review contractor punch lists. Prepare certificate of substantial completion. Qualify owner-accepted nonconforming work. Monitor equipment start-up and commissioning.	Punch lists Certificate of substantial completion
For closeout conference	Review closeout documents. Review record documents.	Closeout lists
At final completion	Receive contractor notice of final completion. Inspect project for final completion. Review final closeout documents. Review final application for payment. Write final change order.	Record drawings for owner Closeout documents Final closeout and final application for payment to owner
For contractor warranty	Review compliance completion items (if requested by owner).	Letter to general contractor citing warranty corrections required
During follow-up review	Review warranty items to be completed or corrected prior to end of warranty (if requested by owner).	List of outstanding warranty items to owner

subcontractors, the owner's representative and its separate contractors, and special consultants hired by the owner, the architect, or the contractor.

- *Architect.* Unless all services are provided in-house, the architect typically engages consultants for the structural, mechanical, electrical and plumbing, and other specialized portions of the work.
- *Contractor.* The general contractor contracts with subcontractors for portions of the work that it cannot provide with its own workforce.
- *Owner.* The owner sometimes retains an "owner's representative" to assist in administering the owner's contracted obligations. A construction manager, program manager, or another architect or engineer may provide this service. The owner may also

have contracts with separate contractors to do interior finishing work or specialty construction not typically provided by a general contractor.

- *Special consultants.* These can include services for quality control testing of materials and the inspection of structural systems. Some states require special inspectors such as the "inspector of record" (California) and the "threshold inspector" (Florida). States require these services in an effort to maintain a higher level of project quality control. Special consultants are sometimes retained to design and engineer special design elements and other critical building components such as roofing and curtain wall systems.

The roles of the owner, architect, and contractor during construction are complementary and interactive. While the architect is contractually obligated to the owner and not to the contractor, AIA Document A201–2007, General Conditions of the Contract for Construction, requires the architect to maintain a neutral position when rendering interpretations concerning the owner's decisions or the contractor's performance.

Although the architect approves submittals illustrating the contractor's work plan and final installation details, the architect cannot stop the work or independently order changes in the work that change the contract sum or contract time. However, the architect can reject work that does not conform to the contract documents.

The contractor's primary role is to supervise and direct the work. The contractor is solely responsible for and has control over means, methods, techniques, sequences, and procedures, and for coordinating all work under the contract, unless designated otherwise in the construction contract. The contractor is also solely responsible for job site safety.

The AIA general conditions require that the contractor provide an express warranty to the owner and the architect that materials and equipment furnished under the contract will be of good quality and new, that the work will be free from defects not inherent in the quality required, and that the work will conform to the requirements of the contract documents.

This warranty of performance and conformance supersedes the actions of the architect, including any observations, inspections, submittal reviews, or certifications; those actions are all expressly qualified in the construction contract so as not to relieve the contractor of its obligation to perform the work in accordance with the contract documents. Moreover, the AIA documents clearly state the architect will not be responsible for the contractor's failure to perform the work in accordance with the requirements of the contract documents. This includes defective work not observed or discovered during the architect's scheduled site observations.

The contractor provides two other warranties in the contractor's application for payment. The first states that title to all work covered by an application for payment will pass to the owner no later than the time of payment. The second states that all work for which certificates for payment have previously been issued and payments received shall be free and clear of liens, claims, security interests, or encumbrances. The bottom line is that the contractor is contractually responsible for the completed work regardless of whether the owner or the architect has approved or failed to observe any nonconforming work.

The owner's role during the construction phase is to furnish descriptive information such as surveys, utility locations, and a legal description of the property. The owner can also stop the work, and should the contractor fail to perform under the contract, the owner can take over and carry out the work. The owner must make payment upon receipt of the architect's certificate for payment within the time stipulated in the contract documents.

The accompanying project authority matrix illustrates the decision-making responsibilities of the owner, architect, and contractor.

Architects in smaller firms frequently have multiple responsibilities and roles, and keeping up with construction phase activities while tending to other duties can be challenging. However, pursuing suggestions covered in this topic can be helpful to architects in firms of all sizes.

The architect is required to endeavor to secure faithful performance by both owner and contractor and not to show partiality to either.

PART 3: THE PROJECT

PROJECT AUTHORITY MATRIX

Owner	Architect	Contractor	Items to Be Approved
•	•		Construction change directives
•	•	•	Change orders
•	•	•	Work conformance
•			Nonconforming work
	•	•	Submittals
	•	•	Application and certificate for payment
•			Special testing
	•		Minor no-cost changes
•	•		Substitutions
	•		Substantial completion
	•		Final completion

• Denotes approval

COMMUNICATIONS IN THE CONSTRUCTION PHASE

Communication is vital for the successful completion of construction phase services. Project team members who communicate well with each other can detect and resolve problems much earlier and much faster. The communications protocol specified in AIA documents requires the owner and contractor to endeavor to communicate with each other through the architect. Communications by and with consultants and subcontractors should occur as follows:

• Architect's consultants: through the architect
• Subcontractors and material suppliers: through the contractor
• Owner's contractors: through the owner

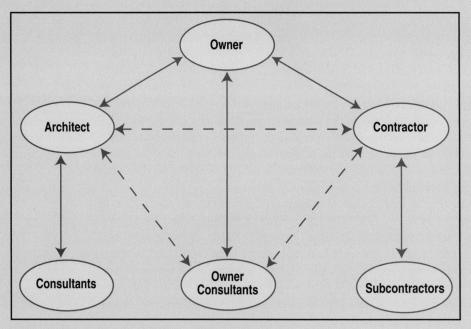

Communications Flow During Construction

PREPARATORY CCA ACTIVITIES

Aggressive schedules and high levels of work coordination associated with construction work can make the architect's CCA activities challenging. By accomplishing the tasks described below, the architect can be better prepared to meet the demands of this challenge.

Review Project Agreements and Documents

The construction contract administrator should assemble sets of drawings and specifications (one for the office and one for use on the project site) and a copy of the owner-architect agreement. After obtaining a copy of the owner-contractor agreement from the owner, the construction administrator reviews this document to identify any conditions that vary from standard AIA language, and to note any atypical conditions. The owner should be advised of conditions or requirements that are or appear to be in conflict with the owner-architect agreement, especially if they prevent the execution of the architect's duties.

▶ See Owner-Generated Agreements (11.2) for advice and guidance on dealing with owner-architect agreements developed by the client.

Set Up the Project Database

A project database is useful for managing the processes and documents associated with the construction phase, and numerous software products on the market are suitable for this purpose. It is important to set up the database in a manner that is not biased against any team member. When the contractor purchases the software, it is often set up to track only the architect's response time on activities such as submittal reviews. Take the initiative and have the software programmed to also track the contractor's response time on activities such as work change proposal requests. As a project tool, the database should benefit all team members equally.

Update the Project Directory

The project directory should be periodically updated to include new team members, such as the contractor's personnel or the owner's consultants. If the project management software is capable, it can be programmed with the project directory to facilitate document distributions to specific team members.

Verify Team Assignments

When construction begins, some members of the team may be assigned to other projects, while others may remain. This is a good time to get everyone together and discuss CCA roles and responsibilities. A project under construction will likely need team members to review designated submittals that are unique to the project. Team members may also need to support the construction contract administrator in scheduled project meetings and to review the work in progress. When construction begins and the pace quickens, team responsibilities should be assigned and understood.

Meet with Consultants

Meet with your consultants *prior* to the start of construction to discuss their roles and to prepare for the preconstruction conference. Issues such as scheduled site visits, site observation report format, project communication protocols, and submittal procedures are among the topics to discuss. Details that can be worked out prior to the start of construction lessen the load when the dirt starts to fly and paper begins to move.

Issue the Notice to Proceed

Construction work typically begins with the notice to proceed. The notice can be given in a variety of ways, but typically it is a letter directing the contractor to begin the work. If initiated by the architect, the notice to proceed should be sent on behalf of the owner and at the owner's direction. The architect does not have the authority to direct the work to proceed.

Conduct Preconstruction Conference

The preconstruction conference is one of the most—if not the most—important meetings during the construction phase. This is the time when construction phase project

▶ AIA Document G612, Owner's Instructions to the Architect Regarding the Construction Contract, Insurance and Bonds, and Bidding Procedures, is useful to the architect during the construction phase. It includes information about insurance and bonds, conditions for releasing retainage funds, and owner separate contractor information.

SAMPLE NOTICE TO PROCEED LETTER

ACE ARCHITECTS

Mr. John Franklin

Millennium Builders
4221 Main Street
Lincoln, Nebraska 24319

Project name: Catenville Place
Project number: 97006
RE: NOTICE TO PROCEED

Dear Mr. Franklin:

The owners, Frontier Developers, have directed me to send this NOTICE TO PROCEED on the referenced project. You are hereby authorized by the owner to proceed with the work of your contract for the construction of Catenville Place. In accordance with your contract with Frontier Developers dated April 15, 2007, you have agreed to complete the contract as stated below.

Contract amount:	$22,860,562
Construction time:	431 calendar days
Start date:	May 15, 2007
Contract completion date:	July 20, 2007

Best Regards,

John H. Williams

John H. Williams, AIA
Principal

cc: Bill Easy, Frontier Developers

SAMPLE PRECONSTRUCTION CONFERENCE AGENDA

I. Introductions

II. Project start-up requirements
   A. List of subcontractors and material suppliers
   B. Schedule of values
   C. Construction schedules
   D. Submittal schedule
   E. Site usage
   F. Quality control

III. Bonds and insurance
   A. Bonding
   B. Insurance

IV. Project procedures
   A. Correspondence
   B. Shop drawings, product data, and samples
   C. Pay applications
   D. Changes in the work
   E. Requests for information
   F. Time extensions
   G. Closeout

V. Site observations
   A. Scheduled visits
   B. Reporting

VI. Miscellaneous items
   A. Separate contracts by owners
   B. Partial occupancy
   C. Field office
   D. Project sign or banner
   E. Owner requirement for certifications

participants meet and get to know each other, and when project procedures for the construction phase are agreed upon. Effective planning prior to the construction work start-up allows for less confusion and lack of coordination after construction begins.

CCA ACTIVITIES DURING CONSTRUCTION

CCA duties during the actual construction of the project include administering change order documents, reviewing submittals, providing supplemental instructions and information, solving problems, reviewing payment applications and stored materials, and appropriately conducting and reporting site visits and on-site observations.

Managing Changes in the Work

It is rare for a project to be constructed without a change in the work. Whether driven by design or by necessity, changes are typically a major part of the construction phase. The design team may cause changes when incorporating what it considers to be "minor touch-ups" to the issued construction drawings. Owners may institute changes as they reexamine their program requirements or when they do not like some aspect of the finished work. Other changes arise due to actual site conditions that are different from those the contractor could have expected from reviewing the contract documents.

After the execution of the owner-contractor agreement, changes in the work can be initiated by change orders, construction change directives, or by minor change instructions. A change order requires the signatures of the owner, the architect, and the contractor. A construction change directive requires the agreement of the owner and architect and may or may not be agreed to by the contractor. The architect may issue an order for a minor change without other signatures; however, it cannot change the contract sum or the construction schedule. If it is subsequently determined that the architect's instructions changed the contract sum or time, a change order will be required to properly document the scope revision.

Changes initiated by the contractor. The contractor can change the work by proposing substitutions during the process of "value analysis," or "value engineering." While some owners request value analysis proposals along with the construction bid, many contractors propose substitutions in an effort to convince the owner they can build the project for less money.

▶ See Value Analysis (7.4) for a complete discussion of the value analysis process and its benefits.

Changes due to nonconforming work. Other changes may occur when the contractor does not build in accordance with the contract documents. This is a common occurrence because construction is not an exact science, and the marriage of building materials and systems during the construction process often yields variations. The architect must determine if the finished work conforms closely enough to the design concept expressed in the documents.

If they wish, owners may choose to accept nonconforming work. Usually, when work is in place and can function, owners tend to want to accept it. However, the owner should not accept nonconforming work without receiving a credit to the contract sum. Because the acceptance of nonconforming work usually represents a change to the contract, any credit must be formalized in an appropriately negotiated change order. The credit may then be processed in the next payment application.

Changes due to errors/omissions. When discovered, errors or omissions in the architect's documents can prompt changes in the work. If the corrective revision changes the project scope, the contractor may be entitled to more money. If the discrepancy is discovered after the work is in place, remediation costs are typically many times greater. Architects strive to produce complete documents before the contract sum is established, but perfection is not always possible and is not required under the legal negligence standard governing the architect's performance. Including CCA services in your contract provides an additional opportunity to find discrepancies before the work is constructed.

▶ See the AIA Contract Documents synopses in Chapter 12 for information on the various types of AIA documents available and their intended use.

Value analysis–induced changes. Value analysis (or value engineering) can be another source for project changes. By definition, value analysis proposals are intended to increase the value of the project. Ideally, this can be accomplished by finding a product or system of higher quality without a cost increase or by finding a product or system of equal quality for less cost. The reality is that you usually get what you pay for, and a product or system of lesser cost may be of lesser quality.

In the value analysis process, owners often expect that the product or system proposed will have the same value as the product or system originally specified. The architect should make efforts to help the owner understand the impact of the substituted item and develop a reasonable expectation of what compromises may be involved. For example, a chiller of lesser cost may have a shorter life cycle or require a higher level of maintenance. Cheaper exterior building materials may have to be repainted or recaulked sooner.

Value analysis proposals that are accepted should be administered as substitutions. However, proposing, reviewing, accepting, and incorporating substitutions into the project take time and effort. Typically, therefore, substitutions are only proposed if they benefit the project in some way—either by lowering the cost or shortening construction time. The specifications set forth the quality of the products to be used in the construction of the work, and acceptable manufacturers are listed under the condition that their product meets the requirements of the specifications. The contractor may propose substituting a product not listed in the specifications, but only the owner can approve substitutions, after the architect evaluates them and gives a recommendation. The Construction Specifications Institute provides two forms for this process: CSI Form 13.1A, Substitution Request Form, and CSI Form 20.3, Substitution Request Checklist.

Product substitutions. Specifications prepared by an architect often reflect years of experience and the observance of product performance. When the architect is unfamiliar with a proposed substitute, caution is advised in accepting it. Because they represent a change to the contract documents, substitutions should be added to the contract by a contract modification, as required by the general conditions.

If a product is added to the contract by a contract modification, the architect could, under certain circumstances, be held responsible for its performance as if it had been specified originally. However, the architect is obligated by its contract to issue change orders and other modifications, and should not try to avoid that duty. For that reason, if the owner accepts a substitution the architect does not recommend, the architect should clarify its position in a letter to the owner and indicate on the face of the modification that the architect does not support or accept responsibility for the performance of the substitution. Such notations will not affect the enforceability of the modification, and—if the modification includes any change in the contract sum or contract time—will formalize those changes to the contract.

Managing Submittals

Submittals include detailed drawings (referred to as "shop drawings") prepared by the contractor, detailed information or data from the product manufacturer, and physical product samples. These submittals serve to illustrate in detail how the contractor plans to construct the work. Until the architect reviews and approves a submittal, the contractor is prohibited by contract from performing portions of the work associated with the submittal.

In submittal reviews, the architect does not verify or determine detailed information such as dimensions, fastening methods, or material gauges. Rather, reviews are made only for the purpose of checking for conformance with the information included in the contract documents. The submittal approval process should be a topic on the pre-construction conference agenda, and the process should be thoroughly discussed, including the required contractual obligations of the team members.

A201–2007 requires that the contractor provide a submittal schedule that is coordinated with the project construction schedule. The architect should review the submittal schedule to determine if it includes the sequence of submitted items and the

▶ See Chapter 12 for AIA documents available for administering changes in the work.

▶ In the event project services are questioned, the architect must be able to easily reference and cite how owner-contractor agreements and owner-architect agreements are applied and used. Chapter 12 addresses AIA agreements and explains their use.

allotted review times. For example, doors, hollow metal door frames, and door hardware should be submitted together to allow for proper coordination. It is also important to verify that all required submittals have been included in the schedule.

MASTERSPEC Section 013300, Submittal Procedures, identifies "action submittals" and "informational submittals" as two submittal types. Action submittals require the approval of the architect, and informational submittals do not. The purpose of receiving them is for the architect to determine if the contractor has met the contracted submittal requirements. Informational submittals, also referenced in A201, can include coordination drawings and contractor-provided engineering calculations.

The architect's contract requires it to take action in reviewing submittals in accordance with the approved submittal schedule, or if there isn't an approved schedule, with reasonable promptness. The contractor is also required to take action on submittals in accordance with the approved schedule.

Allotting review times. Owners sometimes attempt to negotiate short review times in the owner-architect agreement with the notion that it will somehow accelerate project completion. Thus, it is important that architects exercise professional judgment regarding review time. An acceptable minimum review time could be as brief as ten business days after receipt. Some submittal reviews take longer, and if the owner attempts to fix the review time in the contract to a maximum number of days, it is wise to designate the contracted number as an average. This way, the contractor and architect can establish the submittal schedule to allow for less time on less complicated submittals and more time for more complicated ones, while maintaining the "average" review time.

Tracking of submittals. Each submittal should be stamped with the date received, and a letter of transmittal should accompany each submittal sent to another party. Letters of transmittal are important because they document a description of the items sent, the quantity, identifying control numbers, titles, and dates.

Submittals should be recorded in a submittal log. This can be done using AIA Document G712–1972, Shop Drawing and Sample Record, or in a data management system (a variety of software programs are available for this purpose). If the contractor purchases data management software as a job cost item, the contractor can dictate how the data is tracked. In such situations, it is important to communicate to the contractor how you wish the information to be reported. For example, it should indicate the amount of time that all parties, including the contractor, have to process data.

Each submittal should have its own unique control number. A popular system includes the specification number for cross-reference. For example, the first submittal of a shop drawing for metal stairs, which is specified in specifications section 055100, Metal Pan Stairs, would be numbered 055100-01A. This represents the first review of the first submittal in section 055100. The second review would be numbered 055100-01B, and a second submittal from that section would be numbered 055100-02A. Since the submittal number is referenced with the specification section, this system enables quick access to relevant project information if a problem is encountered during building operation.

Review of submittals. AIA documents require the general contractor to review each submittal *prior to submission* to the architect. This is necessary for the contractor to coordinate the work of the construction trades and to fulfill their work plan. Should the contractor choose to accept a submittal that varies from the contract documents, the contractor is required to provide notations in the submittal advising the architect of the deviations. Upon receipt of the submittal, the architect should stamp it received and check to determine that

- The submittal is required by the contract documents.
- A control number is correctly affixed.
- The required routing to a consultant for primary review is indicated.

The architect then proceeds to review submittals in a timely manner, in accordance with the approved submittal schedule. Shop drawings found to be unacceptable must be marked "revise and resubmit" and returned to the contractor. Keep in mind that time can be saved if a subsequent review can be avoided. Adding notations to the submittal with the stamp "approved as noted" can allow the contractor to proceed without resubmitting before construction is begun.

Architects should avoid reviewing submittals that are the responsibility of other design professionals. If the submittal is not in the architect's contract, return it without review. Should the submittal include the work of another contractor, highlight the area and note "not reviewed."

Related issues. In addition to tracking submittal timing and actions taken, it is important to determine if all required submittals have been provided. Equally important is determining if any submitted shop drawings are *not* required. These submittals should be returned without review. There is no need to take time to review submittals that are not part of the contract, and the architect should not review certain types of submittals, such as crane support details, earth retention designs, and temporary handrail safety cables, as those involve construction means and methods and safety procedures for which the contractor is solely responsible under the construction contract.

The fast pace of the workplace today often demands that documents be transmitted as quickly as possible. For this reason, you may choose to allow the contractor to simultaneously submit shop drawings to you, the appropriate consultant, and special consultants or owner's representatives. It is important, however, that such submittals be routed through the architect on their return to the contractor. This is to allow you to review notations from the contractor and consultant, and to check for architectural items included in the submittal that are your responsibility.

While submittals have traditionally been in paper format, electronic submittals are becoming more common. However, sufficient paper documentation of review actions should be maintained. If reviewing digital copies, you should return them in files that cannot be manipulated, such as PDFs or TIFFs.

Responding to Information Needs

Construction documents are typically not an exhaustive set of instructions on how to construct the building. It is therefore important to remember that in the construction phase, the architect can provide supplemental information by responding to requests for information (RFIs) or by issuing Architect's Supplemental Instructions.

The RFI form first appeared in the 1970s as a means for contractors to document questions for design professionals. RFIs were logged, tracked, and used to document time taken for the design professionals to answer questions or to produce drawing clarifications. Today, the RFI is a popular vehicle used by some contractors to allege that the architect's construction documentation is deficient.

The reality is that all parties involved in the construction phase need information. The contractor needs interpretations from the architect, who needs submittal schedules, construction schedules, bond information, and shop drawing submittals from the contractor. The owner needs information from both the contractor and the architect. To meet these needs, the AIA published AIA Document G716–2004, Request for Information. Any team member can send this generic document to another team member. For example, the architect may wish to send an RFI to the contractor requesting the submittal schedule. The architect would log and track its own RFIs in the same way it does the contractor's RFIs.

AIA Document G710–1992, Architect's Supplemental Instructions, is used by the architect to order and record a change in the contract scope that does not affect the contract sum or contract time. It is another form of clarification of the scope that is executed in the process of communicating the design to the contractor.

Problem Solving

Identifying and resolving problematic issues are a valuable part of the construction phase. An important objective here is to identify and resolve a problem before the work is put

The architect's construction documentation sets forth in detail the requirements for the construction work. To carry out the construction, the contractor provides additional information, including shop drawings, product data, samples, and other similar submittals.

in place. In the role of construction administrator, the architect uses problem-solving skills to resolve such issues. The following steps are suggested to resolve a problem.

- *Identify the problem.* Resolution cannot begin until the full scope of the problem has been identified. Take time to document your findings.
- *Analyze the problem.* Research and evaluate what has caused the problem. Gather information from all parties involved. Examine the documents and the construction process to determine how the problem can be avoided in the future.
- *Seek consultation.* Discuss the problem with qualified resources if necessary.
- *Identify solution options.* Review the ways to remedy the problem. Make use of available resources in-house, from the contractor, and from manufacturers.
- *Evaluate solution options.* Prioriti ze the options for resolution. Determine which option presents the best solution to the problems and offers the best benefit to the project.
- *Make a decision.* Decide which option is most beneficial and go with it!
- *Inform the team.* Communicate the chosen solution to the project team.
- *Implement the solution.* Move quickly to implement the solution to the problem. Complete necessary documentation to allow the contractor to proceed.

Site Visits

The architect visits the project site during the construction phase to determine in general if the completed work is installed in accordance with the construction documentation, to report observed defects and deficiencies to the owner, and to monitor and record the general progress of the work. The architect cannot physically be, and is not required to be, in all places at all times. Hundreds, and perhaps thousands, of work activities are occurring on the project simultaneously. Thus the architect may not be able to observe and report all defects and deficiencies in the work. A full-time project representative can do more observations, but likewise cannot physically see all work activities, observe all completed work, or discover all defects and discrepancies.

The design professional determines the number and frequency of site visits as well as when they are appropriate. Obviously, smaller, less complicated projects may require fewer site visits than larger, more complicated projects. For very large projects, a team of design professionals may sometimes reside on the site full-time.

A visit to the site typically presents opportunities to do more than observe the work in progress. Visits can encompass a walk with the contractor to discuss the progress and quality of the work, the scheduled project meeting, payment application reviews, observation of stored materials, and most importantly, time spent with the owner discussing the work and advising on owner decisions.

Adequate preparation helps the architect capture the most benefits from site visits. For example, it can be helpful to discuss unique design conditions with the project team prior to the site visit and to bring a digital camera to record job progress. Having an updated set of drawings during site visits is useful. However, on larger projects with larger quantities of drawings, you may wish to carry just the construction drawings or shop drawings for a specific area that you plan to visit. If the contractor has prepared coordination drawings or clarification sketches, they may come in handy as well.

The best means for documenting a site visit is in a site observation report, which the architect and design consultants issue for each visit. AIA Document G711–1992, Architect's Field Observation Report, is available for this purpose. Digital photo images of completed work may be embedded in the form using the AIA Contract Documents software. Be careful, however, to determine that any nonconforming work discernible in the image is appropriately noted.

Site observation reports should accurately reflect the status of the work, and care should be taken in word usage. For example, the architect may observe a masonry wall that appears to be complete. If the architect reports "the masonry is complete" and there is uncompleted masonry elsewhere on the project, the statement could lead to an

ACE ARCHITECTS

MEETING REPORT
DATE OF MEETING: October 23, 2007
DATE OF ISSUE: October 25, 2007
PROJECT: **Catenville Place**

Project No.   97006

PRESENT: Representing **Frontier Developers (FD)**

Mr. Bill Easy

Representing **Ace Architects (AA)**

Mr. John H. Williams

Representing **Millennium Builders (MB)**

Mr. John Franklin

Representing **Default Mechanical (DM)**

Artie Millsap

LOCATION: Ace Architects

PURPOSE: Project Meeting No. 48

DISCUSSION:

Item No.	Discussion	Action Required By
I.	MAIN BUILDING	
	A. Chiller Sequence The owner has requested a sequence change to allow continuous operation of the system during maintenance operations where the main chillers are offline and the system is run by chiller #4. Default Mechanical will submit recommended sequence changes for review.	DM AA
	B. Handicap Toilet Vanities MM will replaced the toilet room vanities in the North Building with stone countertops as directed by the owner. AA and FD are to select the stone color.	AA FD
	C. Kitchen Makeup Air Diffusers At the owner's request (CW), the general contractor has replaced the egg crate diffusers in the kitchen areas with a perforated type diffuser.	Closed

END OF MEETING

This report is assumed to be a true and accurate account of this meeting, unless written notification to the contrary is received within ten (10) working days of the date of issue of this report.

Respectfully Submitted,

John H. Williams

John H. Williams, AIA
Principal

cc: All present

erroneous conclusion by the reader. It is more prudent to use words like "the masonry in location X appears to be complete" to avoid a misrepresentation.

Site observation reports should be dated, sequentially numbered, and distributed to the appropriate parties. This typically includes the owner, the contractor, and the architect's consultants, but may also include a separate contractor or a special consultant, as requested by the owner.

Project Meetings

When a project meeting is scheduled, the agenda should be distributed in advance when possible. A popular agenda format is the "action item" report format, which lists numbered topics that are carried over from meeting to meeting until they are resolved. The meeting report not only serves as an agenda for the next meeting, but it also provides the attendees with an action item list for their assigned responsibilities.

Either the architect or the contractor can conduct project meetings. Those in attendance should review minutes carefully to verify content accuracy and to respond to assigned action items.

Payment Applications and Certifications

To get paid for their work, contractors submit applications for payment to the architect. AIA Document G702–1992, Application and Certificate for Payment, is a dual form that also includes the architect's certification for payment. AIA Document G703–1992, Continuation Sheet, can be used to list the scheduled values for the work. After comparing the contractor's representations in the application for payment with the completed work and stored materials observed, the architect certifies the amount that he or she believes to be appropriate. The architect then sends the application and certificate for payment to the owner, who makes payment to the contractor.

Application processing. The contractor's application for payment, which includes work by its subcontractors and suppliers, can take substantial time to process. When the contractor receives payment, it distributes funds to subcontractors, who may distribute to sub-subcontractors, who may send payment to suppliers, who may then pay manufacturers. Payment processing, therefore, should be a priority, and contractual time requirements for payment processing should be discussed in the preconstruction conference.

The architect can make processing of the application for payment more efficient by timing site visits to allow for observation of the work in place just before the contractor submits the application for payment. This usually can be accomplished with monthly site visits. While walking the site with the contractor and reviewing a "pencil" copy of the payment application, the architect and contractor can agree on the amount, and the pencil copy can be revised accordingly. The final application copy is prepared from the pencil copy, and when it is sent to the architect, it can be approved quickly and sent on to the owner for payment.

Stored materials. Materials required for the work must be stored either on- or off-site until they can be incorporated into the work. Applications for payment typically include a list of stored materials. Off-site storage must be approved by the owner, and the location should be in a bonded warehouse or secured by other acceptable means. The application allows for payment for the stored materials. Therefore, it may sometimes be necessary for the construction contract administrator to visit off-site locations to observe the materials and confirm delivery. The architect should allow sufficient time for this, and the contractor should make adequate preparations for reviewing stored materials listed in the contractor's application for payment and confirming that bonding or other contract requirements have been met.

Representations of the work. The AIA Application and Certificate for Payment contains a representation by the contractor that the work addressed in the application has been completed in accordance with the contract documents, that all previous amounts paid have been appropriately distributed to the subcontractors, and that the current payment is due. This representation is signed and notarized, if required, by the contractor. The application for payment is further supported by the contractor's warranty to the owner and architect that the materials and equipment furnished under the contract are new, that the work is free from defects, and that it conforms to the requirements of the contract documents. This express warranty that the application is correct and the work is actually in place gives assurance to the owner that it can make payment in good faith.

As stated previously, AIA G702, Application and Certificate for Payment, also contains the architect's certificate for payment. This certification is a representation by the architect that the work has progressed as indicated, that the quality of the work is in accordance with the contract documents, and that the contractor is entitled to the amount certified. This certification is based on site observations and the data included in the application, and is made to the best of the architect's knowledge, information, and belief. The AIA general conditions provide that payment cannot be made without the architect's signed certification, and that the owner must pay the amount the architect certifies.

Related payment information. In addition to the amount applied for payment, AIA Document G702–1992 includes a change order summary, the amount of retainage for both the work in place and stored materials, and the "balance-to-finish" amount, including retainage. The "balance-to-finish" figure helps the architect evaluate whether there are sufficient funds to complete the work. For example, if the project is delayed or the contractor has underbid the work, the funds remaining in the contract sum may be insufficient to complete the construction, and thus the architect cannot certify the application for payment. In fact, if the amount required to complete the work exceeds the contract balance including the current application amount, the architect may have to nullify a previous certification for payment.

Whenever it is determined that funds are insufficient to complete a project, a meeting should be called with the owner and contractor to discuss the actions required for the contractor to complete the work. Certification of the contractor's application for payment is a serious matter, and care should be taken to be fair and reasonable.

When the general contractor is providing work under more than one contract with the owner, multiple contractor applications for payment could be reflected in a single application for payment. If this should occur, care should be taken not to certify work not covered by the architect's contract. The architect should only certify payment for work that is included in the architect's scope of work.

When multiple contracts are included in the payment application, discuss this matter with the owner and contractor, and have the contractor submit a separate application for payment for each design contract. If not desired by the owner, an alternative approach is to have the contractor break out the scheduled values and applied amounts on the form and to add multiple certification signature lines on additional pages. The architect's certification should include a specific cost amount that applies only to the contracted scope.

Substantial Completion

When the work, or a designated portion, is sufficiently complete for the owner to occupy or use for its intended purpose, the project is considered substantially complete. This may not involve final occupancy, as in the case of shell construction with a separate contract for tenant finish-out. Building utilization requirements should be considered when determining substantial completion.

Advance preparation makes the process of substantial completion run more efficiently and smoothly. A list of items still to be completed or corrected, also known as the "punch list," is required from the contractor before the architect determines substantial completion and issues the certificate. Due to the contractor's conflict of

The architect makes "observations" during scheduled site visits but makes only two "inspections"—to determine substantial and final completion toward the end of the project. The word "inspection" connotes a more thorough review and evaluation of the observed work.

interest, the architect sometimes assists in preparing the punch list. However, if the architect prepares the list, it does not relieve the contractor of responsibility for any items not included.

Before preparing the punch list, it can be helpful to walk the project with the owner and contractor to discuss the expected level of finish and quality. This can save time and avoid discord when the list is published. On larger projects, it may be necessary for the construction administrator to assemble additional staff members to assist in reviewing the construction status. In this event, advanced planning and budgeting is recommended. When project completion reviews involve the architect, they should be included in the contractor's construction schedule for planning purposes.

When the contractor considers that the work, or some portion of it, is substantially complete, the contractor submits the punch list to the architect. If the architect has agreed to assist in preparing the contractor's punch list, the contractor should be asked to give notice in writing to the architect when the work is substantially complete. Some architects require a formal certification from the contractor.

Upon receipt of the punch list or such written notification, the architect will conduct an inspection of the work to determine the date or dates of substantial completion. If the architect finds conditions that prevent the owner's occupancy or use of the project, the contractor must complete or correct those conditions before a certificate of substantial completion can be issued. This will require a follow-up inspection to determine if the designated work has been corrected.

The architect can use AIA Document G704–2000, Certificate of Substantial Completion, for certification. This document contains a date of issuance, which is also the date of substantial completion. If the date of issuance is different from the date of substantial completion, it will be necessary to add the date of substantial completion to the form.

Attachments to the certificate include the punch lists. Since few projects are completed without nonconforming work, care should be taken to list known nonconforming items. If the punch lists are voluminous, they can be referenced by project name and date on an attachment in lieu of attaching them to the certificate.

The contractor signs the certificate to agree on the amount of time it will take to complete or correct the punch list items and to agree with the owner regarding responsibilities for security, maintenance, heat, utilities, damage to the work, and insurance coverage. The owner signs the certificate, agreeing with the contractor on the above as well as on the date of substantial completion and the date and time the owner will assume full possession of the project.

Final Completion and Closeout

The contractor provides written notice to the architect indicating the punch list items have been completed. An additional review of the work may be necessary if the architect determines that some punch list items have not been resolved. When the architect is satisfied the items have been completed and all closeout document requirements have been met, the architect certifies payment and submits the final application for payment to the owner for processing.

Final payments. The final application for payment should include a resolution of all change orders and change issues. These can include construction change directives, reconciliation of contingencies and allowances, and resolution of any costs for additional services that resulted from additional substantial or final completion reviews by the architect. If there are varying conditions, such as a cost of the work contract with a shared savings or a completion penalty or bonus, the final contract sum must be resolved to determine the final cost of the work. This can be accomplished with the final change order. The final change order should be prepared by the architect and signed by the contractor and owner prior to submission of the final application for payment to the architect.

Preparations for project closeout should begin prior to substantial completion. It is helpful to conduct a project closeout conference with the contractor and owner to review and discuss closeout activities.

Closeout checklist. Closeout documents and activities can be more easily managed with a checklist, as referenced in "Project Closeouts" (9.6). This checklist serves both as a list of required closeout documents and a means to record receipt and distribution of those documents. The topic also identifies various AIA documents frequently used in the closeout process. Other documents can include the contractor's marked-up drawings, record copies of submittals, warranties, extra materials stored for future use or maintenance, and any other documents required by the project specifications.

Adequate closeout planning and thorough closeout administration can help prevent miscommunications, unreasonable expectations, and disputes over requirements for completing the project. They can also leave the owner with pleasant memories and better satisfaction with how the project was delivered.

Project record keeping. Good record keeping is essential to successful construction administration. Decisions, task assignments, responses, approvals, and the like can be disputed or forgotten if not written down. Remember that if you do not keep good records, your actions will be judged by records kept by others who may not have your best interests in mind.

Primary CA records include the owner-architect agreement and general conditions, architect-consultant agreements, owner-contractor agreement and general conditions, and an up-to-date set of contract drawings and specifications. The contracts are necessary to determine the responsibilities of the parties, and the reference documents are required to determine if the work, when constructed, is in substantial conformance.

- *Transmittal forms* are valuable for transmitting submittals, drawings, and other items that do not contain dates and subject lines as do letters, memoranda, and meeting reports.
- *Memoranda* are useful for documenting events, discussions, and decisions. They can be formal documents distributed to the various team members, or they can be a brief e-mail sent to the project file.
- *Personal journals* are a convenient way to document conversations or to record notes for future reference. Many architects use a journal to document their actions and experiences chronologically throughout the project. A journal can be kept for each project or for multiple projects. A journal with grid pages is useful for sketches or narrative. Some architects prefer using PDAs or other electronic devices to record such notes and activities.

CCA documents should be transportable and easily accessed. Although the laptop computer is today's vehicle of choice for maintaining documents, paper documents still come in handy when walking the site.

An effective filing protocol goes hand in hand with good documentation. For this reason, it is wise to develop a filing system that is consistent for all of your projects. Without a standard system, considerable efficiency can be lost, especially when project personnel change or if a liability claim is made years after project completion. All staff members should understand the project filing system and file documents accordingly. While electronic media is becoming more practical for storage, paper documents will likely remain for the foreseeable future.

Three-Way Win

Although each project is unique, processes and procedures for construction administration are generally consistent. And with thorough planning—along with good communication—CCA services can run smoothly and efficiently. This is especially true when a "proactive" approach is taken in which members of the project team define and agree on activities and procedures in advance. When the team works to the benefit of one another, problems are discovered earlier and claims are less frequent.

▶ See Managing Architectural Projects (9.2) for more information on the use of a journal as a management tool.

▶ A filing system should be simple but comprehensive. If used for all projects, document retrieval can be a brief, routine endeavor. See Information Management (5.7) for discussions about information classification systems and the creation of filing systems.

In providing construction administration services, the architect makes clarifications and interpretations about the construction documentation and helps solve construction problems both before and after they arise—all of which can be valuable to the owner and contractor, as well as to the architect.

Effective construction administration by the architect can result in a three-way win. The owner benefits from the presence of a trusted adviser when construction money is being spent at a high rate. Facing expenses that are time-driven, the contractor benefits from the architect's responses to information requests and assistance in problem solving. Lastly, the architect has the opportunity to resolve problems when they arise, address discrepancies before work is put into place, and be with the owner when the keys are turned over for the completed project.

When the owner, architect, and contractor cross the finish line together, it helps forge stronger, lasting relationships that can lead to future work. A proactive approach to CCA services during the construction phase also increases your chances of pleasing your client, achieving the intended design, and minimizing construction phase problems.

For More Information

In *Why Buildings Fail* (National Council of Architectural Registration Boards, 2001), Kenneth L. Carper investigates "failure" through an enlightening mix of case studies, including failure during the design phase and errors during the construction phase.

Contractor's Guide to Change Orders, third edition (Prentice Hall, 2002), by Andrew M. Civitello Jr. and William D. Locher, includes step-by-step procedures for making change order claims based on the architect's documents and actions during the construction phase. It provides insight into the contractor's strategy for claiming the architect and the high-risk areas of the architect's construction administration services.

The Construction Specifications Institute's *Project Resource Manual: CSI Manual of Practice*, fifth edition (McGraw-Hill, 2005) addresses the requirements of all participants involved in a construction project in a stage-by-stage progression, including owners, A/Es, design-builders, contractors, construction managers, product representatives, financial institutions, regulatory authorities, attorneys, and facility managers. It promotes a team model for successful implementation.

Construction Project Administration, eighth edition (Prentice Hall, 2005), by Edward R. Fisk and Wayne D. Reynolds, provides information needed by design professionals, project managers, contract administrators, and resident engineers or inspectors, and lays out steps for conducting on-site project administration, including the use of digital media.

A Guide to Successful Construction, Effective Contract Administration, third edition (BNI Building News, 1996), by Arthur F. O'Leary, is designed to help construction professionals successfully manage projects through effective contract administration and minimize disputes and litigation. It defines the roles and responsibilities of the contractor, architect, owner/developer, and even the construction attorney, and includes step-by-step procedures for resolving conflicts and handling the threat of legal action.

CHAPTER 9

Project Management

9.1 The Effective Project Manager

Grant A. Simpson, FAIA

The project manager plays a pivotal role in orchestrating and leading the project delivery effort. The effective project manager must possess and apply a variety of skills, which together contribute to achieving desired project goals and objectives.

Most building design and construction projects involve multiple firms and many people. In these endeavors some people *do* the work and others *direct* the work. The latter role—that of project manager—may be assigned to principals of the firm, directors, designers, project architects, or job captains. Regardless of who takes on this role, however, the responsibilities of the project manager must be directed toward accomplishing the goals and objectives of the project.

Project management involves assigning, overseeing, directing, and monitoring the work of members of the project team. It also involves managing employee, client, consultant, and contractor relationships. Although they may vary from firm to firm, project manager to project manager, and project to project, all of these tasks depend on effective communication.

PROJECT MANAGEMENT ACTIVITIES

The management of architectural projects consists of activities that can be grouped into several broad categories for which the project manager is responsible:

- Planning, organizing, and staffing the project
- Facilitating the work

Project management may include different duties for different managers and different projects, but the core activities of project management remain the same.

Grant A. Simpson has served as a project delivery leader for several firms, including RTKL Associates and HKS, where his responsibilities included construction documentation, project management, and loss prevention activities. Simpson served as chair of the 2006 AIA Practice Management Knowledge Community advisory group.

- Monitoring progress
- Concluding the project

Planning, Organizing, and Staffing

The project manager plans when and how the work of the project will be performed, what personnel and resources will be required, and how the people doing the work will be organized. These efforts include determining how the firm's resources will be budgeted, as well as formulating a plan for earning a profit. Some firms also involve the project manager in marketing activities, including the determination of fees. All of these efforts are collectively assembled in the project manager's work plan.

Facilitating the Work

The project manager develops effective working relationships with the client, contractor, and other parties involved in the project. These relationships enable the project manager to foster effective communication among the parties whose decisions are necessary to keep the design services moving forward. Facilitating the work also involves the development and use of effective documentation.

Monitoring Project Progress

Monitoring the progress of the project against the goals and objectives established in the work plan is an essential component of project management. This involves monitoring adherence to the responsibilities established in the owner-architect agreement and those required by the standard of care.

Concluding the Project

Beyond normal closeout activities, concluding the project includes obtaining feedback to determine the quality of the services the architect provided and the opinions of the owner and other participants regarding those services. This information forms the foundation for improving future services.

Execution of the architect's authority falls into two categories: making decisions and giving recommendations. When decisions are being made, the architect is typically in command of the outcome only occasionally; at many other times, the architect can only attempt to influence the outcome by making recommendations.

▶ Project Closeouts (9.6) provides a comprehensive discussion of activities and tasks associated with concluding a project.

THE PROJECT MANAGER'S INVOLVEMENT IN MARKETING

The project manager's first tasks often involve marketing. Usually, project managers would rather have a tooth pulled than participate in the marketing process. This may be due partly to the lack of formal marketing training in architecture school and partly to a bit of stage fright. Most great project managers are extremely detail-oriented and have superb organizational skills and technical knowledge, rather than skills more tailored to making a successful marketing presentation. However, most clients want to meet the person who will manage their project in person, which often means the project manager must make a formal or informal presentation.

The attributes of a successful project manager/marketer include the ability to earn the trust of a client in a very short amount of time, to present management tools and programs in succinct lay terms (without boring the client with unnecessary details), and to express a strong personal vision or management philosophy that will quickly show the client his or her personality. So much of the architect selection process is based on a successful personal connection between the client and project manager that the ability of the manager to connect with the client is usually the most critical aspect of a team presentation.

Some of the personality traits of a successful, experienced project manager that will result in marketing success are confidence, a strong and clear voice, the ability to make direct eye contact, good posture, a pleasant demeanor or ability to use humor in a professional setting, and a take-charge attitude. The project manager is the champion of the project and must exhibit people skills, leadership skills, and management knowledge, all at once, to contribute to the marketing process.

Andrea Cohen Gehring, FAIA

WHERE DO PROJECT MANAGERS COME FROM?

People with good management skills and the ability to lead project teams come from all areas of architecture practice. Many firms seek to identify project management talent from their technical staff, preferring managers with strong technical experience and background. Other firms prefer project managers with design or aesthetic backgrounds. Project managers in small firms may have a wide variety of interests. An individual's primary area of professional expertise and interest may not be a deciding factor in determining who will be an effective project manager.

Project Managers with Technical Backgrounds

Project managers with a strong technical background are generally well equipped to lead projects during construction documentation and construction. These phases represent not only the majority of the work performed but reflect the time when the architect is exposed to the greatest measure of risk. Technically focused managers must be able to collaborate closely with teammates responsible for design or aesthetic leadership. Ideally, a project manager would have both design and technical skills and be able to provide leadership throughout the project. Such dual abilities, more common in the past, are rare in today's practice.

Project Managers with Design Backgrounds

Designers can also be effective project leaders. As a general rule, designers possess excellent communication skills and are accustomed to establishing close working relationships with their clients. Whether called a design principal, a designer, or a project manager, the project leader who is a designer will face the same responsibilities and challenges as any project manager. A project manager with a design background needs to delegate certain technically oriented responsibilities to teammates when those responsibilities lie outside the project manager's area of professional expertise.

Multiple Managers for Complex Projects

As projects have become more complex, many firms have adopted a "project management team" approach. A team of project leaders with appropriate skills to manage all areas and phases of project delivery is assembled. This group might include the firm's principal (proposals and agreements), a project designer (aesthetic leadership), a project manager (planning, facilitating, and monitoring), and possibly a project architect (technical leadership). A project management team can be advantageous for larger projects, for which it is unlikely any one person will have all the needed expertise. A challenge of the project management team approach is that it may be difficult to explain multiple leaders to a client who desires a traditional authority structure with one person "in charge."

Project Managers in Small Firms

In many small firms, the project manager may be the principal, designer, and doer of everything. Indeed, the evolution of the firm may have centered on the unique skills and abilities of the firm leader and/or project manager.

TWO SIDES OF PROJECT MANAGEMENT

Project management has two basic sides, which must operate in unison for success to be achieved in any project management assignment.

The Objective Side

Some project management responsibilities spring from what is objectively defined by the architect's contract for services. These include issuing notices; providing certifications; and reporting findings, decisions, and observations. Other objective responsibilities may be viewed as industry standards, including such things as attending project meetings, preparing meeting agendas, writing meeting reports, and generally attending to correspondence and documentation.

The Subjective Side

Subjective and more intangible responsibilities often require a broader application of judgment than objectively identified responsibilities. This side of project management relies on attitude, personality, behavior, and even personal habits. It involves people skills, such as being a good listener, motivating team members, and leading conflict resolution. For example, project managers are called on to remain calm and function as leaders in times of stress or duress. Project managers must frequently act as teachers to help others understand the decisions required to move the project forward.

Nonetheless, small firms and small projects benefit from effective project management just as larger firms do, even when the activity is not specifically called project management.

WHAT MAKES AN EFFECTIVE PROJECT MANAGER?

Achieving success as a project manager requires more than just performing perfunctory duties associated with the management process. It also calls for a certain frame of mind, the ability to get along with others, and an understanding of what clients expect and appreciate. Perhaps as important as any attribute is the ability to see the big picture and keep problems and issues objectively in context.

Attitude

Project managers must have not only the skills to accomplish activities and responsibilities but also the willingness to bring an appropriate attitude to their role. Most important is dedication to being a strong leader. Project management is not a passive activity. The effective project manager must be willing to make decisions and take action. The project manager cannot do all of the work on a project and must rely on others to do much of it. A willingness to believe in others is necessary. However, the project manager must also frequently look beyond this belief in others in an effort to be prepared for what could go wrong. The project manager must also have the patience to teach others how to view and participate in the project.

> It is the rare project manager who perceives others as doing the work as well as he or she could do it. Yet successful delegation of tasks involves understanding when the work being done is good enough.

Project managers must be willing to see project circumstances from multiple points of view and to maintain a neutral attitude when conflicts inevitably arise. Nearly every aspect of project management requires give-and-take. This give-and-take must be anticipated and embraced. The project manager who finds conflict threatening or frustrating will find successful outcomes difficult when disagreements arise.

Personality and Behavior

The most effective project managers are those who can both deal effectively with conflict and get along well with other people. To a great extent, project management is infused with the need to manage continuing conflict. Problems arise and must be resolved many times throughout the day. The level of conflict may range from simple difficulty in coordinating meeting times to intense, open disagreement among members of the team. Through all of this, the project manager must recognize that his or her behavior sets the tone of leadership for the project team.

WHAT DO PROJECT MANAGERS DO?

In carrying out day-to-day duties and responsibilities, project managers marshal and apply their knowledge and skills to lead, solve problems, motivate others, advocate, measure, document, and communicate.

Project Managers Lead

Project managers are vested with the responsibility and the authority to get the project designed and delivered. They interact with clients to determine the program and verify program compliance. They interact with their firm to determine whether staffing and resources are appropriate.

WHAT CLIENTS APPRECIATE IN PROJECT MANAGERS

Recognizing that some behavior can lead to uncomfortable conflicts between the client, the project manager, and even the project design team itself, it is prudent for the project manager to understand what behaviors clients appreciate. Some of these are

- Careful and objective use of authority
- Reliable performance
- A friendly and approachable demeanor
- Not being defensive
- Promptness in returning phone calls or e-mail
- Prompt arrival at meetings
- Being well-prepared for meetings
- Issuing timely reports and other documentation

In addition, some aspects of a project manager's behavior can make the job run more smoothly. These include

- Being candid and honest
- Being accessible and available
- Being a good listener
- Being responsive to questions
- Using lay terms rather than industry jargon

▶ Developing Leadership Skills (3.1) provides guidance on ways to develop and enhance the leadership capabilities of firm members.

They interact with the project team to help facilitate communication. They interact with contractors to help facilitate construction.

Project Managers Solve Problems

Unexpected issues arise as a part of every project. This makes problem solving a critical part of the management process. Coupled with this is the need for project managers to successfully negotiate solutions to problems, with either the client or the contractor. Problems can be viewed as meat and potatoes for the project manager, served in great helpings on a daily basis. Problems cannot be avoided, nor are they the de facto evidence that someone has done something wrong. For the most part, design, schedule, cost, and quality problems are opportunities to improve the project along the way. Intuition and the ability to research, understand, and resolve problems are important attributes for a project manager.

Project Managers Motivate Others

In overseeing the work of others as the project evolves, it is often necessary for the project manager to be a coach or motivator. This calls for laying the work out in a clear way and setting reasonable goals for what is to be accomplished. If the tasks or time frame are not reasonable, the manager must either revise the work plan until the tasks are more achievable or motivate the team to rise to the occasion. A project manager must realize that most teams can stretch to meet the demands of difficult assignments, but that such assignments should be an exception and not the rule.

Project Managers Serve as Advocates

The project manager must always be an advocate for the project design team. This may include standing by firm employees or the consultants working on the project. However, at times, the project manager is called upon to advocate for the client or for the contractor. Loyalty from clients usually grows from their perception that the architect is doing a good job. The project manager can build this loyalty by understanding that the client, not the project, is the firm's valuable asset. Delivering the project through dedicated service, and taking care to understand and advocate for the client's goals throughout, can help win the client's loyalty. When clients consistently feel the project manager is on their side and has their best interests at heart, success is closer at hand. The project manager also may need to advocate for the contractor, however. For example, contractors frequently make suggestions for improving a project or reducing costs but may require the project manager's assistance to explain these suggestions to the owner.

Project Managers Lead the Project Documentation Effort

The project manager must be the driving force behind creation of the documentary record while the project is ongoing. Documentation includes preparing proposals and agreements, meeting agendas and reports, phase sign-offs, memoranda, and other correspondence that facilitates and explains communications between and among project participants. If a project manager has poor documentation habits, the rest of the team will tend to mimic those habits. In these instances project managers should be encouraged to delegate documentation responsibilities to others.

Project Managers Monitor Progress

When monitoring the progress of a project, the project manager must gauge and measure how well the client, contractor, consultants, and staff are accomplishing the goals established in the work plan. Here, more than in any other activity, the project manager must not adopt a passive stance. If monitoring the progress of the project against the work plan reveals inconsistencies, adjustments in course must be made. The project manager's lines of communication must be energized, and appropriate decisions put in place to bring the project back in line.

Project Managers Communicate Consistently

Communication is the glue that holds all aspects of project delivery together. While the project manager is a distributor of information, a much more important responsibility is facilitating communication among the project participants. Since the project manager is in a position to oversee most of what is happening on a project, he or she is often in the best position to moderate discussions between the client and the design team or between the client and the contractor.

▶ Developing Communication Skills (3.2) provides guidance on how to achieve better communications with clients verbally and in writing.

CLIENT EXPECTATIONS AND PROJECT MANAGEMENT

A significant ingredient for project success involves understanding and meeting client expectations. The foundation of the client's experience is the client's expectation of how the architect is to perform. The project manager who understands the client's expectations has a better chance of successfully guiding the project team's effort to meet them. If client expectations are unreasonably high, the architect may not be able to meet them even if they are fully understood. In such cases, the architect may need to help the client understand the capabilities of the firm and set more relevant and reasonable expectations.

Explaining the Services to Be Provided

The first step toward meeting client expectations is to discuss with the client the services to be provided. The work plan can be an effective tool for doing this. Differences between the services the client expects and the services the architect intends to provide must be resolved as early as possible. Ignoring such differences in hope that conflicts will not occur is shortsighted.

Setting Expectations

An effective way to meet client expectations is to help set them. This is most often accomplished through frank discussion of potentially tough issues, before they become problems.

Tackling difficult issues head on. Architects do not always talk with clients about the services they provide. Often they try to sugarcoat tough issues in an effort to be viewed as nonconfrontational. For example, although errors and omissions are a normal part of professional life, many architects avoid bringing up the subject. However, it is best to discuss difficult issues associated with project expectations directly with the client and other project participants. Determine what each participant believes is true and what is reality. With an understanding of any different perceptions, the issues can be debated in the best interest of both the client and the project. If this communication does not take place, conflicts are definitely on the horizon.

Explaining consequences. Discussing the potential consequences of a decision or a change is important. Clients may not always want to believe what the project manager has to say and, in fact, may disagree. Nonetheless, they usually want to hear the project manager's opinion because it is part of the service they expect. For example, if a client decides to eliminate waterproofing on the basement walls, it is not enough for the architect to simply disagree with the decision. The project manager should go a step further and explain that the decision could result in water leaking into the basement, causing damaged finishes and expensive repair costs. While such consequences may seem obvious to the experienced project manager, they might not be so obvious to the owner. Other client decisions may have less obvious consequences. For instance, a decision to save money on a building system may be likely to increase maintenance expenses. The project manager should tell this to the client in plain language. As long as the potential consequences described represent the project manager's understanding of the truth, the manager is on solid ground.

In all cases, however, the architect's belief should be discussed with the client *when a change is requested* and not after the change has been completed. Even if the architect is overruled, the owner is likely to remember that such concerns were expressed.

A Word About "Absolute" Expectations

Architects frequently do not realize that they may be setting unrealistic expectations for their performance by using jargon that many clients do not understand. The use of "unqualified" language can put the architect in the position of being held to an undefined or unrealistic standard.

Architects tend to state things in absolutes because they want to explain things clearly and without ambiguity. This use of absolute terms may stem from the fact that most owner-architect agreements delineate payment of professional fees in accordance with the percentage of work completed. Thus, the architect may label a set of construction drawings "100% complete" in order to qualify for payment. However, in fact, a single set of construction drawings is unlikely to be 100 percent complete, and labeling them as such can create an expectation of performance that is unintended and even unachievable.

The accompanying table illustrates some common absolute language encountered in project management, along with language that more accurately portrays what may realistically be expected.

RISK MANAGEMENT IN PROJECT MANAGEMENT

More and more, good project management involves good risk management, which can take many forms. Cast in the role of advocate for the client, the project manager may, from time to time, advise the client of risks and consequences that can arise from specific decisions. The project manager must, of course, be vigilant in determining if actions of the owner, the contractor, or the architect may cause elevated risk for the architect. Attentiveness to circumstances that may elevate risk for the owner or contractor is also important. For architectural services, the quality and completeness of the architect's drawings and specifications can be key areas for dispute. Architectural

EXPECTATIONS AND THE WRITTEN WORD

Document	Unqualified Language	Suitable Alternative
Proposal letter	"We look forward to designing a first-class new school for you."	"We look forward to designing your new school project."
Drawing set cover sheet	"100% Complete Construction Documents" "50% Schematic Design Set"	"Issued for Construction" "Interim Schematic Review Set"
Field observation report	"The masonry walls have been completed."	"The masonry walls appear complete."

services provided during construction, such as submittal reviews, answers to requests for information (RFIs), responses to changes, on-site observations, and certifications are also activities that carry elevated levels of risk.

If a project manager becomes an overt advocate only for the architect, he or she risks abandoning and alienating the client. The best approach is to adopt the objective attitude that a good project is a successful project, with ordinary problems and a satisfied client. Clients are likely to be more satisfied when the project runs smoothly, schedule and cost surprises are few, errors and omissions are relatively few, the client is kept informed about the construction process, and the project complies with the client's program. Avoiding unnecessary or unacceptable risks for all parties can go a long way toward achieving success.

▶ Risk Management Strategies (5.4) covers the various dimensions of risk management, including methods for mitigating them.

A PIVOTAL ROLE

The role of the project manager is a pivotal one. The project manager directs the efforts of others to reach desired project goals and objectives. Successfully fulfilling this role calls for the project manager to effectively plan, facilitate, and monitor the work. Whether this role is assigned to a single person or to two or more, the effective project manager must be able to understand and anticipate challenges, work through obstacles and problems as they occur, and negotiate agreement for them—all a routine part of the project management terrain.

9.2 Managing Architectural Projects

Grant A. Simpson, FAIA

When the delivery of services for architectural projects is well managed, those projects are more likely to meet their goals and objectives and fulfill the expectations of their owners.

The design and construction industry is a project-based world. As such, project management is a key component for any architect or architecture firm. Effective project management requires an understanding of project management basics, which are equally applicable to any project, from the development of a large hospital to the design of a one-room addition to a house. Knowing how and when to apply appropriate tools and techniques will make management activities easier, more efficient, and more professional.

Except on the smallest of assignments and in smaller offices, the project manager does not personally produce the major project deliverables. Rather, the project manager must know *who* can produce the required services, *when* those services must be carried out, and *how* those services fit into the overall project delivery scheme. In short, while project managers will do some of the work, their primary role is to direct the work being done by others. In fulfilling this role, the project manager delegates responsibilities to those with the design and technical expertise needed to complete the required work.

▶ This topic covers the process of project management for architectural projects. The Effective Project Manager (9.1) addresses the desirable personal attributes and qualities of project managers.

Grant A. Simpson has served as a project delivery leader for several firms including RTKL Associates and HKS where his responsibilities included construction documentation, project management, and loss prevention activities. Simpson served as chair of the 2006 AIA Practice Management Knowledge Community advisory group.

Project management activities for architectural projects can be clustered in the following groups:

- Planning, organizing, and staffing the project
- Facilitating the work
- Monitoring progress
- Concluding the project

These groups of activities essentially embody the full range of tasks and responsibilities that project managers will encounter in their assignments. The remainder of this topic—organized according to these groups—provides specific guidance and identifies practical methods, tools, and techniques that can be used to carry them out.

Project managers should be actively involved in the development of proposals and agreements. Both small and large offices require a certain discipline when developing these documents, since they set forth the foundation for project success or failure. Ideally, the project manager will be included in both the initial preparation of proposals and agreements as well as in the negotiation of final agreements. Participating in this process will give the project manager an intimate knowledge of both the firm's and the client's goals, and his or her familiarity with the issues will help the firm maintain continuity throughout the delivery process. Encouraging involvement of the project manager during this crucial stage of relationship building with the client also demonstrates the firm's confidence in the leadership and authority of the project manager.

PLANNING, ORGANIZING, AND STAFFING

The project manager usually takes charge of planning, organizing, and staffing a project. This simply means the project manager develops a primary understanding of how and when the project will be worked on and what leadership and staff will be needed to perform the work. The project manager usually interacts with firm leaders, and perhaps with other project managers, as this understanding becomes documented in a work plan.

Development of a work plan for the project begins with consideration of schedules, ways to organize relationships between the parties, the firm's available resources, and perhaps fees. In addition, how the leadership for the project will be organized and what experience and specialty levels will be required are identified.

The Work Plan

The work plan is a key part of effective project management. To be useful, a work plan need not be complicated or lengthy. For most projects, it need only include the elements listed below. Even on large projects, this information may take up no more than a few pages.

1. Project description and client requirements
2. Statement of deliverables
3. Team organization chart
4. Responsibility matrix
5. Preliminary project schedule
6. Preliminary staffing needs
7. Project directory
8. Internal project budget and profit plan
9. Code information (optional)

Maintaining a work plan is an ongoing process. Projections for staffing, schedules, and budgets must be revisited and adjusted as new information becomes available. When carefully prepared, Items 1 through 7 can be presented to clients to illustrate how you plan to approach their projects.

Project description and client requirements. The work plan includes a description of the project, including its scope and the client's budget, as well as a record of what work the client has authorized. The client's primary goals for the scope and quality of the project should also be incorporated into the project description. A project description would read something like this example:

A 300-room four-star luxury hotel, located on the waterfront at 212 Boardwalk Street in Any City, including two restaurants, conference facilities for 500 guests, a full-service spa, a resort-quality swimming pool, and landscaped grounds.

This example demonstrates how the project description can be communicated in a short statement, which can later be expanded in greater detail as the program for the project is developed.

Depending on the project phase, client authorizations may be represented in the work plan by a simple checklist of authorized work keyed to copies of signed owner-architect agreements. Client authorizations can include various kinds of documentation, ranging from letters of agreement to formal contracts to phase-completion sign-offs. The project manager tracks and monitors all of these authorizations.

Statement of deliverables. Projects normally include a work product or deliverable produced by the architect. Such deliverables may include reports, sketches and drawings, specifications, virtual or physical models, and other items. The work plan should include estimates for the types and quantities of deliverables required to complete the work. The format of this estimate can be a simple list or a storyboard or cartoon depiction of the deliverables for each phase of the architect's services. This description and estimate provide a basis for developing the project schedule, staffing needs, and budget for the architect's work.

Team organization. More and more, owners want information on how the architect will organize project staff, and how that staff will relate to other parties involved in the project. A chart is helpful for communicating the relationships between the project team participants.

A team chart typically reflects who the primary project leaders will be, such as the principal-in-charge, the project manager, designers, project architects, and job captains. While there can be many position titles in an architect's office, the basic intent of the team chart is to define the hierarchy of the architect's team, reflect who will be responsible for what assignments, and show primary relationships between members of the project team.

Usually, there will be one or more project leaders, regardless of project size. For a large project, several project leaders may appear on the project management team. For a small firm and a small project, the architect's project team chart may include only the firm principal.

Responsibility matrix. A companion task to defining deliverables is determining who will do what on the project. When a project requires consultants, it is important to have an explicit understanding of what each consultant will do. For example, it is not enough to have a seat-of-the-pants understanding that the M/E/P engineer will "do the M/E/P engineering." A more detailed understanding would distinguish responsibilities such as these: "The electrical engineer will wire and circuit the landscape architect's lighting design" or "The M/E/P engineer will coordinate HVAC equipment selections with the acoustical engineer." The following sidebar illustrates a responsibility matrix, which is a convenient way to communicate project assignments.

"PROJECT AT A GLANCE" WORK PLAN

Some firms formalize the work plan and require that it be maintained throughout the life of the project. At one firm, the work plan is called a "Red File." It includes information that would reasonably be required to give anyone assigned to the project a quick summary of what is going on. In addition to basic project information, the Red File includes a current accounting status printout, an electronic copy of the most current drawings in PDFs, and copies of the owner-architect and owner-contractor agreements and general conditions, if they are available. The file, assembled in a red jacket, is maintained at the project manager's desk and is available for viewing by company leaders or interested employees.

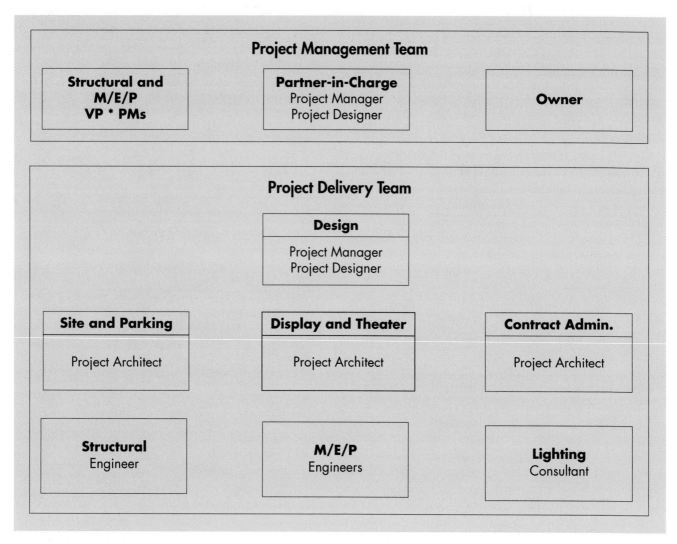

Sample Project Organization Chart (History Museum). The project management team fulfills the need for careful collaboration between managers, designers, consultants, and the owner to effectively address the numerous management decisions associated with a project. Depending on project size, there may be more than one designer, project manager, or project architect on the project delivery team. For smaller projects, these may be the same person wearing different hats.

Preliminary schedule. Most requests for proposals (RFPs) received or tendered by the architect relate in some manner to the project schedule. This means the work plan should delineate the preliminary project schedule as clearly and as accurately as possible. Whether the objective is to complete a retail project in time for the fall shopping season or to open a sports facility for the opening home game, the owner's goals for the project often dictate its major milestones. Into this mix, the architect must project the team's ability to perform the work within the owner's set of key dates. The preliminary schedule is one of the primary drivers of the architect's assessment of staffing needs.

Preliminary staffing needs. Preliminary staffing requirements can be estimated once the project scope has been delineated, the deliverables understood, the consultant's responsibilities defined, and a preliminary schedule developed. The project manager may work with upper management (in a larger firm) to determine what key personnel will be available and what support staff will be required. If available staffing becomes a

SAMPLE PROJECT RESPONSIBILITY MATRIX

	Corporate Office Building	A	TA	S	M/E/P	C	L	SC
1	Site landscape					X	X	
2	Site grading and drainage					X	X	
3	On-grade parking	X		X	X	X	X	
4	Parking structure	X		X	X			
5	Optimize lease depth and floor plate	X	X					
6	Special tenant floor loading requirements			X				
7	Exterior structural plazas			X		X	X	
8	Structural engineering: Core and shell			X				
9	Structural engineering: Tenant specialties			X				
10	Fire exit stairs	X						
11	Stairs: Lobby monumental stair	X	X					
12	Stairs: Special tenant stairs		X	X				
13	Exterior envelope, roofing, and details	X		X				
14	Doors and hardware: Exterior entry doors	X						
15	Doors and hardware: Interior areas		X					
16	Interior: Main lobby, core areas, and toilets	X	X		X			
17	Interior: Tenant areas		X		X			
18	Drywall interior side of exterior wall	X						
19	Interior window treatments		X					
20	Graphics		X					X
21	Cafeteria and kitchen	X	X		X			X
22	Elevator service	X						X
23	HVAC: Equipment/risers	X			X			
24	HVAC: Fixtures and trim		X		X			
25	HVAC: Tenant distribution		X		X			
26	Plumbing: Service and risers	X			X			
27	Plumbing: Fixtures and trim	X			X			
28	Plumbing: Tenant		X		X			
29	Electrical transformers	X			X			
30	Electrical service and risers	X			X	X	X	
31	Emergency generator	X	X		X			
32	Lighting: Exterior and landscape	X			X	X	X	X
33	Voice, PA, and data systems		X		X			X
34	Security systems		X		X			X

Legend

A	Architect
TA	Tenant architect
S	Structural engineer
M/E/P	M/E/P engineer
C	Civil engineer
L	Landscape architect
SC	Special consultant

greater constraint on the firm's ability to deliver the project than the client's scheduling goals, the firm may need to revisit the preliminary schedule with the client and perhaps revise it.

Project directory. A project directory with current listings for all project entities and their key personnel should be included in the work plan. This can be prepared in a format the firm normally uses, or the entries can be printed from an e-mail management

▶ Project Controls (9.3) provides information about managing project budgets.

▶ Building Codes and Standards (10.2) presents the concepts and basic elements of building codes.

▶ See the backgrounder Project Scheduling in Project Controls (9.3) for examples and discussions of different schedules and scheduling software.

program such as Microsoft Outlook. More simply, organized copies of business cards can be used to develop a directory.

Project budget and profit plan. The project manager may sometimes be assigned the duty of apportioning the project fee to the various tasks required to produce the work to help estimate and plan for the firm's profit. Often referred to as a job cost budget or a project budget, a copy of this should be included in the work plan.

Regulatory requirements. Information about the primary building code(s) and local amendments that will apply to the project can be a very useful part of the work plan. This information could range from a simple list of the applicable codes and ordinances to a full building code report prepared by the architect. Including this information gives the project team a close-at-hand opportunity to get an answer to the frequent question, "What code are we using?"

Negotiating and Developing Project Schedules

The greatest prerequisite to negotiating and managing a project schedule is an understanding of what a project schedule is. While many believe a schedule is a list of time periods and deadlines, in reality, it is a series of interrelated commitments agreed upon by all project participants. The owner relies upon the architect and the contractor to understand their duties, obligations, and assignments well enough to predict their performance within a given time frame. The architect and contractor rely upon the owner to understand what actions and decisions will be required to maintain an orderly process for the design and construction phases.

Owners contemplating a project often have definite scheduling goals, and architects often find it difficult to push too hard for a fair and balanced design schedule that conflicts with the owner's goals. Consequently, architects often agree to an owner's schedule on the assumption they can do whatever it takes to complete the project. A more effective approach is to develop a work plan and carefully balance task objectives against available staffing over the project timeline. It is far better to discuss staffing and schedule conflicts before the project begins—or early in the project—than to discuss it after a conflict creates the perception the architect failed to achieve key schedule milestones.

Architectural services take time to provide, and the project schedule should allow adequate time. Negotiating a reasonable schedule that considers how long it will take to perform the work with the architect's available staff is a key precursor to a successful project.

Project Staffing

When project leaders and staff positions have been identified, the project manager reviews the project organization chart and the required tasks to verify that assigned staff have the needed skills and experience for the work they will be doing. In fact, staff experience is rarely evenly matched to the project assignments, so the project manager will always need to make adjustments to effectively use the talents of everyone assigned to a project.

Project managers often face the conundrum of balancing the staff needed to do the work against the project staff the fee can sustain. In this situation, the vulnerability faced by both the firm and the project manager is the temptation to sacrifice quality for profit. The firm principals

SCHEDULING TIPS

Project tasks, which are a set of interrelated project events, should be scheduled to reflect how they are likely to occur. For example, if the M/E/P engineer will require two weeks to coordinate with the structural designs, the schedule should reflect this fact rather than the normally desired alternative that all consultants finish at the same time. Likewise, realistic approval periods for reviews by the authority having jurisdiction (AHJ) should be recognized, even when the time periods seem protracted.

Along similar lines, it is routine to ask the architect and consultants to make changes to the project documentation as selected major suppliers and subcontractors begin to suggest design alternatives and substitutions. Such suggestions are often beneficial but can be disruptive. If time is allowed in the schedule for contractor-initiated document revisions, all parties can anticipate the time that will be required to incorporate those revisions. Time for this activity should also be reflected in the contractor's work plan, since suggested revisions are most commonly generated by the contractor and subcontractors.

A project schedule helps set owner and contractor expectations. When realistic commitments are delineated in the schedule, there are likely to be fewer surprises.

PART 3: THE PROJECT

SAMPLE STAFF SCHEDULE

Proj. No.	Project Name	Phase	Staff	Position	1-Mar	8-Mar	15-Mar	22-Mar	29-Mar	5-Apr	12-Apr
07002	Grandview Condominiums	SD	Anderson	Principal			10	10	10	10	10
07002	Grandview Condominiums	SD	Lombard	Proj Mgr			40	40	40	40	40
07002	Grandview Condominiums	SD	Little	Designer			30	30	30	30	30
07002	Grandview Condominiums	SD	Hill	Arch I						20	40
07002	Grandview Condominiums	SD	Ramos	Arch I					20	40	40
06005	Green Acres CC	DD	Anderson	Principal	10	10	10	10	10	10	10
06005	Green Acres CC	DD	Jordan	Proj Mgr	40	40	40	40	40	40	40
06005	Green Acres CC	DD	Little	Designer	40	40	10	10	10	10	10
06005	Green Acres CC	DD	Garcia	Arch II	40	40	40	40	40	40	40
06005	Green Acres CC	DD	Blanton	Arch I	40	40	40	40	40	40	40
06005	Green Acres CC	DD	Garzoli	Arch I	40	40	40	40	40	40	40
06005	Green Acres CC	DD	Middleton	Arch I	40	40	40	40	40	40	40
06005	Green Acres CC	DD	Li	Intern	20	20	20	20	20	20	20
07001	Midtown Office Complex	SD	Johnson	Principal	10	10	10	10	10	10	10
07001	Midtown Office Complex	SD	Jones	Proj Mgr	30	30	30	30			
07001	Midtown Office Complex	SD	Hickerson	Designer	30	30	30	30	30	30	30
07001	Midtown Office Complex	SD	Kim	Arch II	10	10	20	20			
07001	Midtown Office Complex	SD	Halverson	Arch I	40	40	40	40			
07001	Midtown Office Complex	SD	Jones	Proj Mgr					20	20	40
07001	Midtown Office Complex	DD	Kim	Arch II					20	20	20
07001	Midtown Office Complex	DD	Halverson	Arch I					40	40	40
07001	Midtown Office Complex	DD	Cohen	Arch I					20	20	20
06003	Smith Residence	CA	Anderson	Principal	10	4	4	4	4	4	
06003	Smith Residence	CA	Jones	Proj Mgr	10	10	10	10	20	20	
06001	Valleyview Middle School	CD	Johnson	Principal	20	10	10	10	10	10	10
06001	Valleyview Middle School	CD	Hull	Proj Mgr	40	40	40	40	40	40	40
06001	Valleyview Middle School	CD	Hickerson	Designer	10	10	10	10	10	10	10
06001	Valleyview Middle School	CD	Murphy	Arch I	40	40	40	40	40	40	40
06001	Valleyview Middle School	CD	Kim	Arch II	30	30	20	20	20	20	20
06001	Valleyview Middle School	CD	Minkus	Arch I	40	40	40	40	40	40	40
06001	Valleyview Middle School	CD	Berger	Arch I	40	40	40	40	40	40	40
06001	Valleyview Middle School	CD	Cohen	Arch I	40	40	40	40	20	20	20

This is a sample staff-scheduling chart for a twenty- to twenty-five-person firm showing staff assignments on projects over a seven-week period.

should debate this philosophical question and reach a stance that can be incorporated into the firm's culture so this burden is taken away from the project manager. The project manager must be allowed to focus on the quality of services provided to the client.

FACILITATING THE PROJECT

As the role of the project manager has evolved, what was once thought of as "controlling" the project has come to be more a role of "facilitating" the project. The delivery of design services is facilitated through communicating effectively; developing good working relationships with the client, contractor, and consultants; providing assistance to parties whose decisions are necessary to keep the design services moving forward; and developing and using effective documentation.

Managing the Project Team

Managing the project team? This sounds like an overwhelming responsibility. However, the basic requirement boils down to a few key ideals. The first calls for understanding what the team is to accomplish. The second requires an understanding of who on the team has the skills to do what tasks, and where additional resources may be needed. The third is fostering a communications environment in which all parties are kept informed of what is expected of them and when their assignments are due. The key tools and techniques for accomplishing this are the work plan, effective management of project meetings, and reasonably thorough documentation of key project decisions and actions.

Client Relationships

The project manager's relationship with the client is key to both understanding the client's goals and to communicating with the client. This relationship must be close enough that the project manager can gain a comfortable understanding of the client's expectations. If the client's expectations do not align with the architect's intended services, then either the architect's services must change or the client's expectations must change. Having confidence in each other's abilities and integrity will facilitate resolution when conflicts occur. Candor and honesty are always beneficial for developing a relationship in which news and events can be presented with a neutral, unemotional attitude.

Decision Making

It is commonly understood that there are few occasions when the architect makes a decision. Instead, the architect typically gives a *recommendation* upon which the client may base a decision. For example, the architect makes decisions about substantial completion and final completion, but commonly these decisions are heavily infused with input from the owner and the contractor. In a dispute, the architect—seeking faithful performance by the owner and the contractor—renders a decision about conditions that can reasonably be inferred from the construction documents. The full range of the authority and decision-making responsibilities of the architect are generally delineated in the owner-architect agreements and in the general conditions of the contract for construction.

The architect does not decide on changes in scope, quality, or time except in specifically contracted circumstances. However, although the project manager cannot make decisions for the client, he or she can facilitate needed decisions by providing support and explanations to the client. For example, the project manager may prepare an executive summary of the pros and cons that the client might consider in making a decision. Or the project manager might research alternative materials and costs that reflect the options the client can choose from. Such support from the architect makes the client's work easier, and will inevitably also make the architect's work easier. (The importance of carefully documenting the client's decisions is covered later in this topic.)

Managing Project Meetings

Successful project managers must learn to orchestrate and administrate project meetings. All project managers have faced the frustration of disruptions, lack of preparation on someone's part, or disruptive—even angry—people while trying to run a meeting. It is possible to take an analytical view of managing meetings and look at some ways a project manager can be more effective. A first step is to understand the obstacles to a successful meeting, which include the following:

- Too many people in attendance
- A disruptive participant
- People who don't pay attention
- Unprepared attendees

- Sidebar conversations
- Cell phone or PDA interruptions

You will have to find a way around such obstacles, even if it means bringing a gavel to the meeting. You don't want the meeting so out of control that you have to raise your voice to get attendees to pay attention.

Meetings schedule. Arguably, for any project—but particularly for projects with more than three or four participants—it is important to hold regular meetings. Setting a routine by conducting the meetings on the same day of the week at the same time is advisable. Personal schedules tend to fall into a groove, and the participants will adapt more effectively to regularly set meetings. On smaller projects, it will save time and expense to organize the meeting via conference call if the agenda is short. Remember, it is important not to skip meetings. Missed meetings erode communication, and lack of communication is at the root of most problems on architecture projects.

Meeting management plan. The primary purpose of a meeting management plan is to ensure people attend the meeting when their input is required and stay away when it is not. Decisions cannot be made or obtained without the necessary participants. Conversely, you cannot facilitate decision making as effectively when non–decision makers are debating the issues.

Most projects involve a hierarchy within the client organization, design team, and contractor and subcontractor team. Not every project participant needs to attend every project discussion. Whether the project is large or small, discussions run more smoothly

MEETING MANAGEMENT PLAN

Type	Purpose	Attendees from Firm	Recorded by
Executive Session			
Participants: Principals Owner Contractor/CM A/E team	Executive-level representation Decision making	Principal-in-charge Project manager	Project manager
Design Review Session			
Participants: Owner Contractor/CM A/E team	Design direction Design review and approvals	Principal-in-charge Project manager Project architect	Project manager
Project Meeting			
Participants: Owner Contractor/CM A/E team Special consultants	Project planning and general decision making	Principal-in-charge Project manager Project architect	Project manager and project architect
Coordination Meeting			

Participants:
Project architects
Project engineers
Optional:
    Contractor/CM
    Owner
	Coordination
	Work session
		Project architect
		Job captain
			Project architect

Redline Work Sessions			
Participants: Project architect Job captains Consultants' staff	Coordination Work sessions	Project architect Job captain	Job captain

and time is used more efficiently when meetings are divided into executive sessions, project design meetings, general project meetings, coordination sessions, and redline work sessions. The accompanying chart illustrates a meeting management plan type that can be shared with all parties.

Executive sessions. Critical and formative decisions are made at the highest levels in an owner's organization. Whether the client is a large corporation or a couple desiring a new home, there will be key meetings during which important decisions are made. These meetings are most effective when as few attendees as possible are in the room. Meet with the owner and other key project leaders early on, and develop an understanding of who will make critical decisions about aesthetics, scope, cost, and schedule. Schedule executive sessions separately from other meetings, and invite only key decision makers.

Project design meetings. When design aesthetics are presented and discussed, it may not be necessary to have all the technical leaders present. For example, when lobby floor paving patterns are discussed, input from the mechanical or electrical engineer may not be needed. A generally successful approach is to make design presentations and solicit owner concurrence with the design direction early in a meeting—before most other participants arrive for a general project meeting, or even on a separate day. Owners tend to become more engaged in design issues without the distraction of unnecessary attendees. On smaller projects, owners are more engaged when design issues are kept separate from technical issues.

General project meetings. These are meetings when approved design direction, scope, cost, and schedule are presented and discussed with most or all of the project team members. The agenda should be carefully prepared to keep the meeting as short as possible while accomplishing the purpose of keeping everyone informed. Because general project meetings tend to involve larger groups, it can be difficult to solve detailed or worrisome issues during the meeting. The best use of everyone's time is to designate attendees who will be responsible for resolving and presenting the details of such issues. The discussions required to resolve these details can take place in coordination sessions.

Coordination sessions. Also commonly called consultant work sessions, these meetings are the time to discuss and resolve issues related to building systems and other detailed aspects of the project. For example, the architect and M/E/P engineers could discuss clearances required for lights, sprinklers, and ductwork located in the plenum above the ceiling in an office building. The architect and structural engineers would discuss establishing dimension control for the structural column grid. Depending on their tolerance for long, detailed discussions, owners may or may not choose to attend such meetings. If the client does decide to attend, the project manager must take care that discussion of details is not postponed due to the client's lack of interest or patience.

Redline work sessions. These are the most detailed of all project meetings. In them, basic details for arranging and coordinating the building elements are discussed. For example, the architect and structural engineer might coordinate slab edge and brick ledges, or the architect and lighting consultant might coordinate fixture types and locations. These meetings are most successful when the topic is narrowly focused and the number of attendees is minimized. Often the only agenda items are the drawings and specifications.

The meetings described above encompass most activities that must be managed during the design and documentation phases of most building projects. On larger projects, some of these meetings may actually involve separate groups, and some meetings may be held at separate times. On smaller projects, all of the meeting categories may simply be divisions of the meeting agenda for one meeting. Persons attending and documenting these meetings are assigned and requested to attend based on what the project manager expects to accomplish.

Effective Agendas

Project managers commonly arrive at a meeting with a single sheet of paper titled an agenda. This approach reflects a misunderstanding of what is to be accomplished by

Meetings with authorities having jurisdiction (AHJs) such as zoning or code officials may be considered to be coordination sessions.

using an agenda. The actual purpose of an agenda is to facilitate discussion rather than to remind attendees of what is to be discussed. Therefore, in addition to the typical list of discussion topics, the agenda should be attached to additional pertinent information, such as e-mails, memoranda, schedules, budgets, reports, and the like. While this consumes more paper, attaching pertinent backup information to the agenda removes the risk that an important discussion item will be tabled because a particular attendee cannot recall the details to be discussed.

It is also important to gauge the amount of time to be allocated to each agenda item. To effectively moderate the meeting, the project manager should encourage making a decision and moving on to the next topic after an appropriate amount of discussion. Just as important, however, is the ability to recognize when additional discussion is healthy and to allow the dialogue between attendees to continue without interruption.

The list of agenda topics should be distributed a day or two in advance of the meeting, along with a request for comments. Although some recipients won't bother to read them, at least everyone will have an opportunity to influence the structure of the meeting.

An effective project management tactic is to include an item that may be a sticky issue on the advance copy of the agenda to get attention, even though the item may not appear on the final agenda.

Reporting on Project Meetings

Meeting reports, sometimes called minutes, are a record of the general discussion, decisions made, directions given, and assignments accepted during the course of a project meeting. With time-driven assignments, it is advisable to publish meeting reports as soon as possible after the meeting. A copy of the agenda and any meaningful handouts presented during the meeting, along with copies of drawings or sketches, should be attached to the meeting report. With the advent of digital files and sheet-fed scanners, the entire information package can be distributed quickly and inexpensively via e-mail. Meeting reports may be prepared by the project manager or a team leader appointed by the manager. The primary reporter for each type of meeting should be designated in the meeting management plan.

Although some managers believe meeting reports are primarily prepared for risk management purposes, the effective project manager understands the primary purpose of minutes is to facilitate communication among project participants. Meeting reports should be distributed to all pertinent persons—whether in attendance or not—so they can stay up-to-date on the project status, recent decisions, and what is expected from members of the project team.

Reports should record discussions in enough detail so that decisions and directions given—even if not expressed verbatim—can be reconstructed. The two most popular styles of meeting reports are the narrative report and the action-item report.

- *Narrative meeting report.* During the design and construction documentation phases, issues tend to be a little fuzzier than during the construction phase. While the need for prompt and accurate decision making is not diminished during these phases, the narrative style tends to be less intimidating to clients and thus can actually encourage them to make more timely decisions. Functioning as more of a "history," the narrative meeting report accommodates detailed explanations of issues that may not require follow-up action.
- *Action-item meeting report.* This format consists of a list of items or issues designated with a unique, nonrepetitive number. It is helpful to key each action item to the particular meeting where the issue was raised. For example: Item 21.01 represents the first new report item for meeting 21. The item is assigned to a firm or individual and is not removed from the report until it has been fully addressed or resolved. Each item should be given a due date. This provides a constant reminder to encourage resolution of the action item in a timely fashion.

It does not matter if meeting reports are handwritten or typed, although many architects prefer the formality of the latter. It also does not matter what style of report

Effective managers develop personal documentation habits that become part of their daily work. Documenting key aspects of a project is not drudgery to them because it is essential to the way they manage. Writing a meeting report, making handwritten notes, or sending a client a contract proposal becomes second nature.

From concise contracts that define the obligations of the parties involved in a project to meeting agendas and meeting notes that facilitate effective project meetings, good documentation is the essential fabric of effective project management.

is used. For example, some managers may use a simple list of bullet points to record the meeting discussions. What does matter is that the project manager communicates the discussions to everyone involved as he or she understood them, and that the directions and decisions are recorded as he or she heard them. Sharing this information gives all participants the opportunity to clarify any objections to how any item was perceived and recorded. Sharing the report also gives everyone the information they need to coordinate their efforts.

THE IMPORTANCE OF GENERAL PROJECT DOCUMENTATION

Careful documentation of milestone events and decisions—in some orderly form—is necessary for successful project management. Managers who do not retain at least a brief history of "who told what to whom" and "who decided what when" assume the risk of being unable to prove that such events occurred, a validation that could be critical for resolving any disputes that arise.

Good documentation is more than a defensive procedure to protect the architect in a dispute, however. It provides the basis for effective communication between team members and keeps all parties informed about what has taken place in the past, what is currently taking place, and expectations for what will take place in the future.

Basic Correspondence Rules

There is no industry manual for architects to follow in developing procedures for correspondence and other basic documentation. However, there are some basic principles to follow. For example, all correspondence—e-mail, letters, memos, and transmittals, as well as drawings and sketches—should bear a date and identify the project. Correspondence that cannot be connected to a specific project or cannot be placed in time in all likelihood will be virtually useless.

Memoranda. A memorandum is best used to provide an understanding of the detail of an assignment that has been accepted by a team member. Used in conjunction with a more abbreviated description that might appear in a meeting report, the memorandum provides the necessary level of detail about assignments that team members need to proceed toward delivering the project in the same orderly direction. In today's workplace, e-mail can often serve the purpose of a memorandum. If an e-mail is the preferred platform for sending a memorandum, care must be taken to include the project identifier (name or number); the date will come as a by-product of the medium.

Action items lists. The action items list is used to track the issues recorded in the meeting minutes and memoranda. If an action item-style meeting report is being used, creation of a separate list may be unnecessary, although some clients like the "issues at a glance" convenience afforded by an action items list, which consists of items or issues with brief descriptions given a unique, nonrepetitive number. The list itself might be numbered, or it might be sufficiently tracked by date. It is helpful to key each item to the meeting, memorandum, or other event where the issue was raised. Items may be assigned to a firm or an individual, and they are not removed from the list until they have been resolved.

Documenting conversations. Conversations occur during meetings when others are present. Conversations also occur over the telephone or during chance encounters or in personal meetings. It is probably not necessary for a project manager to keep a record of every conversation that occurs during a project; however, it is necessary to document conversations that can meaningfully affect the project. It is important to keep a record of who generated decisions and direction, as well as when and where these actions were taken.

Important conversations that occur outside of regularly scheduled project meetings can be recorded in several ways. Some firms use a communication record or a telephone memorandum to document them. Whether typed or handwritten, a copy of these documents can be given to the person with whom the conversation took place, as well as to the entire project team, when appropriate. A decision to approve the schematic design submittal or to extend the construction documents schedule might be copied to the entire team, while the record of negotiating the client's approval of an additional service request might be copied only to the client.

E-mail. As a business tool, e-mail is becoming more effective every day. The positive side of e-mail is that it is fast. It does not require direct interaction with a person and can be prepared at any time, without regard to a set schedule. But e-mail also has a negative side. The effective project manager must be aware that the more e-mail he or she sends, the less face-to-face personal communication is undertaken. Everyone has received a seemingly rude e-mail, only to discover after further messages or phone calls that the rudeness was unintentional. Moreover, e-mail can more easily be misunderstood than a phone call or a personal conversation. For this reason, when potentially tense or complex topics requiring in-depth discussion arise, project managers should step away from the keyboard and reach for the telephone.

Personal journal. A valuable tool for the project manager is a personal journal. Kept with the manager at all times, a personal journal provides an excellent opportunity to integrate contemporaneous documentation into the daily routine. Meetings, conversations and casual notes, sketches and business artifacts, such as business cards, can all be recorded or placed in the journal. As project participants become accustomed to seeing the manager with the journal, they will begin to reference it as the project record. The manager will also become dependent on the journal as the key reference

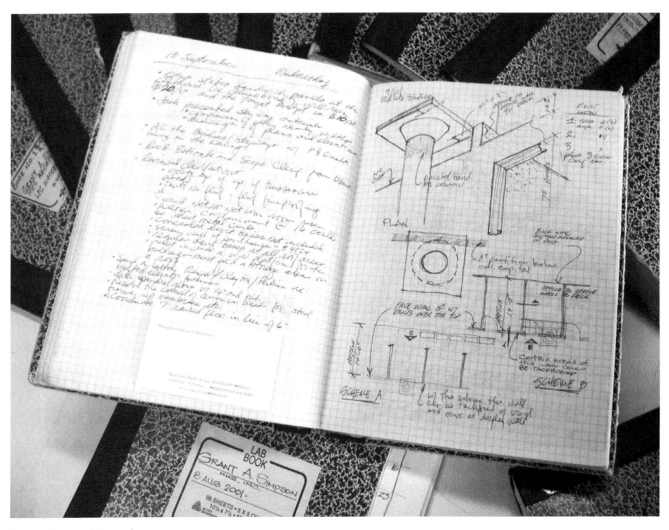

Sample Personal Journal

source for decisions made and direction given and other project experiences. In undertaking to keep a journal of this sort, the project manager must decide whether to keep only one journal for all ongoing projects or to keep a separate journal for each project.

Managing Information

Managing and directing the flow of project information and saving that information in an orderly manner is perhaps the most important responsibility of the project manager. Of course, not all project information is created internally. As information is received from outside sources, such as the owner, consultants, or contractors, it must be processed. Processing includes noting the date the material is received, determining who requires copies, and deciding how the information will be preserved and filed.

Distribution of information. Good project management includes making day-to-day decisions about who on the project team needs to see what. Some of these decisions are predetermined, like sending a plumbing shop drawing to the M/E/P engineer, but others require reasoned judgment. While it is not always possible for the project manager to look at every project document or file that is received, he or she must know who is responsible to look at what and when it must be looked at. The project manager must either decide who will receive what or set up the protocol for others to make that decision. If the firm does not have a central receiving station where mail is received and stamped, the project manager should decide who on the team will receive mail and how it will be dated and distributed.

Project filing system. A project filing system must be flexible and comprehensive enough to accommodate many types of project information. This includes letters,

---

SAMPLE PROJECT FILING SYSTEM

01 Accounting
    01 Agreements
        01 Owner-architect
        02 Owner-contractor, general conditions
        03 Consultants
        XX Other
    02 Invoices
    03 Expenses
    04 Insurance
02 Marketing
03 Correspondence
    01 Owner
    02 Contractor
    03 Consultants
    XX Other
04 Meeting Agendas and Reports
05 Memos and Lists
06 Project Data
    01 Project summary
    02 Project directory
    03 Codes
    04 Estimates
    05 Bids and addenda

06 Schedules
07 Site data
08 Reference
09 Photographs
XX Other
07 Drawings
    01 Architectural
    02 M/E/P
    03 Structural
    04 Consultants
    XX Other
08 Specifications
09 Construction Administration
    01 ASIs, RFIs, CCDs
    02 Observation reports
    03 Submittals
    04 Logs
    05 Certifications and payments
    06 Change orders
    07 Closeout
    XX Other
XX Other

memoranda, e-mail, sketches, drawings and specifications, submittals and shop drawings, test reports, and surveys. Some of these items will be physically filed, some will probably exist only electronically, while others will be drawings, oversized materials, and physical samples. Information, regardless of its type, must be preserved in an orderly manner so it can be easily searched and retrieved. Some firms and managers, not realizing the critical importance of a project filing system, essentially use the "read and stack" method, resulting in waist-high piles of unsorted, though possibly chronologically stacked, information.

When trying to locate information that has been filed, predictability is essential. This is important for the project team as well as others who may need to access and use the project files. To make it easier to find material, most firms—large and small—develop a standard filing structure. As electronic files increasingly replace paper files, the electronic file directory structure should closely track the paper file directory structure. This means whether searching in your metal filing cabinet or on your desktop computer, you will be in familiar territory. A sample directory structure that is effective for both paper and electronic files is shown in the accompanying sidebar. Additional files can be created as project-specific needs arise. For example, if the project is a theater, there will probably be an acoustical consultant file. A firm designing small projects might require fewer file categories. Firms with larger or more complicated projects may develop a more extensive system than the one illustrated.

MONITORING THE PROJECT

The project manager's best efforts will not be sufficient if he or she does not monitor the progress of the project against project goals and objectives, the responsibilities established in the owner-architect agreement, and what is required by the standard of care.

Tracking Required Services

Project services are established by the architect's contract with the owner as well as what is expected by the standard of care for such services.

The agreement. Project managers should keep a copy of the owner-architect agreement in a notebook at their desks at all times. As questions about services arise, the manager can refer to the contract to see if the issue is addressed. The manager should make a checklist of any contract-mandated reports or notices, schedule them, and monitor whether they are being implemented. For example, the contract may require written notice of the architect's awareness of a schedule delay. Effective project managers understand that compliance with contract requirements is *not* optional. Monitoring whether contract provisions are being met is a serious responsibility. For this reason, the project manager should have a copy of the agreement at the ready, and read it often enough that it is dog-eared and annotated to excess when the project is concluded.

Standard of care. Not all activities the architect carries out on a project are described in a contract. Things not described might include, for example, making a subjective judgment as to how complete a set of drawings must be or how often the architect should visit the job site during construction. Such matters relate to the "standard of care" concept, which can be stated in many different ways but essentially boils down to the notion that the architect is required to do what a reasonably prudent architect would do in the same community, in the same time frame, given the same or similar facts and circumstances.

There should be no confusion about the standard of care, which is used in the courts for adjudicating cases involving the work of design professionals. From time to time, the project manager must step back and take an introspective look at the project and the services he or she is managing. If this observation reveals something is missing, or services are not running smoothly, the manager should take corrective action.

If one of the project parameters of scope, cost, or quality is changed, it will affect one or both of the other parameters; thus, a change in one component should not be considered without evaluating the impact on the others. The project manager should keep all issues on the table during change discussions and determine that the owner fully understands these dynamics and the potential result of any change.

James B. Atkins, FAIA

Monitoring Client Objectives

The architect designs a building to accomplish as many of the client's stated goals and objectives as possible. Those objectives are generally focused on the scope of the project, its cost, and its desired quality. Careful attention must therefore be given to how closely the design accommodates these objectives. The project manager should make frequent comparisons of the current design to the client's objectives. If gaps or differences between the design and the client's objectives are found, the manager must take corrective action. This could mean reviewing the differences with the client to determine if the design, the construction budget, or the level of quality should be revised. Small corrective measures could simply require minor revisions to designs or candid discussions with the client.

Project program. Clients establish programs for their project to define project uses, the project size or scope, and the desired quality. The project manager must monitor how well an evolving design addresses each of these programmatic elements. This may include periodically preparing floor-area tabulations to check the project size or obtaining samples of proposed materials and finishes to verify compliance with quality goals. It could also involve checking the detailed program to verify that the design accommodates the intended uses.

Construction budget targets. Although most architects are not construction cost estimators, the project manager should understand the relationship between scope, quality, and cost. The manager should have a good enough grasp of all aspects of the project to be able to make appropriate recommendations for scope or quality adjustments in the event cost estimates or bids exceed target construction budgets.

By far the best approach to meeting client expectations for construction budgets is to carefully monitor the relationship between scope, quality, and cost as a design is being developed. Architects and clients alike are frequently tempted to look past a potential conflict between budget and estimated construction costs, hoping the conflict will be resolved in competitive bidding or subsequent events.

The best practical way to resolve such conflicts—although it may be a painful experience—is to sit with the client and review and adjust one or more of the project parameters of quality, time, and cost before proceeding to the next step in the design process. To help stay on top of this issue, budget compliance or adjustment problems should find their way into meeting agendas and be discussed regularly with the client and the project team. Any statements of probable cost provided by the architect, or required by the contract, should be discussed frequently and provided at required project milestones.

Managing consultants. The way to "do better work" for many projects involves finding a better solution to coordinating with the work of consultants. Architects and consultants face similar problems in project delivery, such as:

- Reaching the finish line at about the same time to avoid disruption when documents are issued for bidding or construction
- Making sure all parties are using the same versions of the plan backgrounds
- Uncovering and coordinating conflicts between the work of different disciplines

Project managers must allot time and resources to attend to challenges such as these.

Quality management. Some project managers believe that quality management and quality control are relegated to the technical guys in the back room. Nothing could be further from the truth. In managing and controlling quality at the project level, quality must be a daily concern of the project manager. As with other management responsibilities, this does not necessarily mean holding a red pencil and constantly marking up the efforts of the people producing the work, any more than the project manager is required to actually prepare the drawings and specifications, although some project managers may choose to do so. It does mean the project manager must know the status of the work at all times and must oversee and direct quality management controls as they are performed.

▶ Project Controls (9.3) provides additional information on monitoring and controlling project budgets.

Responsibility for document reviews. The project manager should consider document reviews as an opportunity to uncover mistakes and other conditions before they create problems during construction. However, many managers are reluctant to invite the criticism that results when documents are reviewed, possibly fearing being perceived as poor managers when scrutiny reveals deficiencies in the work they are directing. The irony of this thinking is that the contractor and subcontractors—through requests for information and change orders—will surely discover deficiencies that make their way into the construction drawings and specifications.

The project manager should schedule both time and resources for internal reviews of the project construction documents, if possible before the project is issued for bidding or negotiation. In small firms, the review might be made directly by the project manager. In large firms, the manager may select a reviewer, often a leader from another project. Specification writers can provide valuable internal peer reviews as their familiarity with the project helps them coordinate terminology between drawings and specifications and identify areas in the drawings where materials or systems have not been correctly represented.

The manager should always be present when review results are presented. Project managers sometimes are tempted to skip these sessions because they are tedious and technical. However, the identification and correction of errors and omissions in the architect's work is an important enough occasion to merit the attention of the primary project leader or leaders. Despite its advantages, peer review checking should not be viewed as a substitute for thorough coordination or creation of a reference set prepared by the project team.

External review of the project documents can also be useful. The project manager should welcome such reviews, whether they are provided by owners, contractors or subcontractors, agencies to which applications have been made for building permits, or architects or engineers specializing in plan checking. Most external reviews provide an excellent opportunity for the project manager to improve the quality of drawings and specifications.

Internal Budget Tracking and Management

Most project managers are asked to allocate portions of the fee to the various project phases in a proportion that matches the anticipated workload for each phase. Referred to as a job cost budget or a project budget, the purpose of these estimates is to budget for the firm's labor and other expenses and profit. Expenses include basic service consultants, unreimbursed expenses, and reimbursable expenses. Producing a realistic project budget requires an understanding of the firm's labor rates and project delivery and staffing practices. As the work progresses, the project manager periodically checks actual costs against the budget plan.

Some firms develop their labor budgets using worker-hour estimates only. When dollar-based estimates are preferred, firms may use actual employee hourly costs or average hourly costs. The advantage of worker-hour-only or average hourly cost methods is that they remove any incentive to reduce costs by choosing only low-priced and/or potentially less experienced staff for the project. Considering that most firms

▶ AIA Document D200–1995, Project Checklist, lists tasks (organized by phase) that architects may perform on projects.

INVOICING TIPS

To avoid billing disputes, a project manager may consider not invoicing for the total of a recently completed phase of work. For example, if the client has "approved" schematic design and authorized design development to proceed, schematic design might be invoiced at 95 percent completion with the remainder billed when design development reaches perhaps 50 percent completion. A client who may be tempted to hold up payment and question whether schematic design is 100 percent complete, may pay the 95 percent, and won't question the 100 percent once design development is 50 percent complete.

Similarly, project managers may consider invoicing reimbursable expenses separately from basic service fees. Doing so may help prevent a hold on a large basic service invoice because of a dispute over a telephone charge or a meal expense.

▶ For information about invoicing clients, see Financial Management Systems (5.2).

calculate profit for distribution at the end of the year based on the firm's total income and expenses, even when employee-specific costs are used, everything averages out by the end of the year. However, for the firm's senior management, having access to and reviewing actual employee-specific costs means the exact financial position of each project can be determined at any time.

Integral to the preparation of the internal budget is reviewing and tracking client invoices and collections. Many firms ask the project manager to review the client invoice before it is sent and to watch over any aging invoices.

Tracking employee time records. Project managers in most firms check the time records of the employees they supervise on an ongoing basis. The time records are approved and sent to the accountants. If corrections are required, they are first returned to the employee.

Consultant invoices. The project manager also reviews invoices from consultants to determine whether the consultant's progress matches the amount invoiced. To simplify this process, some firms pay their primary consultants—such as structural and M/E/P engineers—on the same percentage complete basis as the invoice the architect submits to the client. In this approach, only reimbursable expense invoices are required from these consultants. However, some adjustment of payments is usually required when the consultant's work progress doesn't match the architect's progress, as would be the case with contract administration fees for the structural engineer, who is usually finished before the architect.

Reimbursable expenses. Most architects pass on certain expenses to the client, such as those for out-of-town travel and living, reproduction and printing, photography, postage and shipping, and renderings and models. The way reimbursable expenses will be handled or marked up is typically defined in the owner-architect agreement and must be coordinated and tracked to match the contract requirements.

Client invoices. Invoices should be reviewed before they are sent to the client to determine that the amount billed represents the status of the work that has been completed. This should involve making sure the work being invoiced matches current client work authorizations. Reimbursable expenses should be checked against contract provisions—particularly if there is a limit on the amount to be reimbursed. Some firms believe the close working relationship that project managers have with clients puts them in an ideal position to discuss any overdue invoices. Other firms prefer not to put managers in an adversarial position with clients if there are disputes about amounts due. To reduce or avoid payment disputes, the architect should make sure the client has a clear understanding of the potential ramifications of unpaid and overdue invoices before work commences on the project.

Project status and progress reporting. The project manager tracks all of the project expenses mentioned above through the firm's accounting status and reporting system. Rather than using paper copies of reports, most of today's accounting software for architecture firms can be accessed online via the Internet or a company intranet and checked from time to time at the convenience of the project manager. Developing a routine for checking project status will help prevent unpleasant financial surprises.

CONCLUDING THE PROJECT

This management activity encompasses closeout tasks, such as delivering warranties and operating manuals to the owner, and housekeeping activities such as archiving project files. This activity should also include investigations to determine the quality of the services that were provided and efforts to obtain opinions from the owner, and possibly the contractor, about those services.

Post-Construction Evaluation

The most valuable insight into the effectiveness of the architect's services can come from discussing those services with the owner and contractor immediately after occupancy of the project. At this time, minor irritations and recollection of bumps in the road are still fresh in their minds. While no architect wants to be beat up over minor issues, all want to improve the quality of their services. If a project is successful, the client and contractor may later decide not to mention the little things. The reality of professional service is that what the clients and contractors experience—as users of the architect's services—counts a great deal in determining the quality of the experience. Following are several ways to carry out post-construction evaluation.

Team roundtable and project debriefing. When construction is complete and the architect's services are concluded, the project team may be scattered to the winds. Still, the project manager should gather the remaining troops and share insights gained from discussions with the owner and contractor, as well as detail the degree to which the firm's quality and financial goals were met. An equally important objective of a project debriefing is to allow members of the project team to discuss their experiences, and to offer suggestions and ideas for improving work on future projects.

Year-end review with the client. While it is ordinarily an additional service, many architects make a postoccupancy evaluation part of their normal services, especially with repeat clients. A walk-through or even an inspection is conducted approximately a year after occupancy. This is done with the owner, supervisory personnel, and operations and/or maintenance staff to compare programmed use with actual use, the effectiveness of the design, and the performance of materials and systems. The year-end review allows the architect to reinforce the positive aspects of the relationship with the client. It also provides a heads-up on any problems the owner may be having with the project. While no one enjoys learning of problems that may be brewing, it is certain that bad news—if it is present—does not get better with age.

Mistakes are reality. Although no one likes reliving the mistakes they have made, mistakes are a reality. Architects rarely prepare perfect sets of drawings or provide perfect services. As the project team explores what they did wrong or what they can do differently next time, the project manager should remind them that the purpose of revisiting project experiences is to improve the architect's services—not to castigate participants. Nonetheless, when discussing mistakes, particularly with the owner, an attitude of contrition is preferable to one of defensiveness.

Project Archives

The basic rule to follow in archiving is, "If it is not in your file, it doesn't exist." All firms need an established way for closing projects. Most states have a minimum period during which project records must be stored. Other reasons for archiving records might include providing facility management information down the road, saving information to be used in a future renovation, and, less cheerfully, the potential need to document a defense in the event of a claim or a lawsuit.

LEMONS TO LEMONADE

Reality dictates that mistakes will always occur, no matter how much effort is made to avoid them. An ambitious goal is to strive to eliminate repetitive errors. If that could be done, only original, never-before-experienced mistakes would need to be addressed. Realistically, this may never be achievable; nonetheless, it is a prudent career objective.

There are many approaches to designing and detailing any built condition. Some ways are better than others, some ways are just plain wrong, and no way is absolutely perfect. Experiencing the wrong approach can provide benefits—but only if the correct way is learned as a result. Over time, learning from each misstep helps architects progressively improve their skills and the products of their services.

Every project in architecture is in some way a new adventure because no two projects are exactly the same. Most clients do not wish to commission a building exactly like the one across the street. The quest for originality leads architects to continuously attempt new actions and endeavors, with their concomitant learning curve. However, as Albert Einstein said, "A person who never made a mistake, never tried anything new."

Grant Simpson and Jim Atkins (adapted from AIArchitect, December 2005)

MORE THAN A SERIES OF TASKS

Project management is critical to any architecture firm committed to providing excellent services. While the expansive nature of project management can be challenging to describe, its basic tasks include determining who, when, and how the work will be done; directing and leading those who will do the work; tracking how progress compares to what was planned; taking action to make course adjustments when deviation from the plan is required; and evaluating and communicating how well the work was performed.

Yet project management is more than just a series of tasks. The project manager embodies professionalism, accountability, and integrity. In line with these more subtle and less apparent qualities, project management can also be viewed as an attitude and a way of going about one's work. For these reasons, a wise architect or other design professional will remain a student of project management throughout his or her career.

9.3 Project Controls

Lowell V. Getz, CPA, and Frank A. Stasiowski, FAIA

As the project unfolds, progress is assessed against the owner's project goals—scope, quality, schedule, and budget—as well as the firm's services and compensation requirements.

Project control—tracking progress and comparing it with plans and objectives—is integral to effective project management. Without these activities, it's often not clear whether the project is on track, meeting the expectations—and requirements—established by the client and by the architect.

Project controls do not have to be elaborate, but there are some essentials:

- *Yardsticks.* A series of measuring sticks is necessary. These project objectives (services, scope, schedule, budget, and compensation) are expressed in the project agreements and work plan.
- *Measurements.* The firm periodically takes the pulse of the project, collecting vital signs—information in the form of time spent, costs incurred, and progress made.
- *Comparisons.* Comparing measured progress against the various yardsticks reveals whether expectations are being met.
- *Corrective action.* The will to address variances in progress compared to the plan is essential to keeping projects on track.

SCOPE AND SERVICES CONTROL

The project manager will need to monitor project scope—potential changes at the request of the client or introduced as part of the design process—and the services being performed to evaluate what the architect is doing against the requirements of the owner-architect agreement. Often schedule, budget, and compensation problems are the results of unplanned variations or expansions in scope or services.

Lowell V. Getz is a financial consultant to architecture, engineering, planning, and environmental service firms. He has written, taught, and lectured widely on financial management. Frank Stasiowski is founder and president of PSMJ Resources. He is a consultant to the building and design industry and the author of numerous books and publications about management.

Project Scope

Project scope is made up of the owner's design requirements: program, site, area and volume, and levels of quality. During the course of design, scope can shift—and often grows—as possibilities unfold. Sometimes these shifts are clear and recognized by both owner and architect. More often, the scope of the project creeps under the pressure of owner interests or demands and the architect's enthusiasm for the evolving design.

Scope control involves asking—and answering—these questions:

- Is the scope of the project clear to you and the team?
- Do you and the client have the same view of the project?
- If the scope is changing, are you and the client formalizing those changes—including any that affect the agreement?
- If the scope is changing, are the project budget and schedule also changing as needed? If the schedule and, especially, the budget are not changing, what steps can be taken to keep the project on track?

▶ Construction Cost Management (9.4) addresses "scope creep," which can be a major problem when the construction budget is fixed.

Project Services

In the same vein, it is important to compare the services the project team is actually providing with those in the owner-architect agreement. There is a natural tendency to say yes to additional services in an effort to do the best job. It is also possible that increased scope or an extended schedule is forcing the team to provide more services than contemplated in the agreement. The best advice is to review your agreement and follow its requirements for initiating and seeking owner approval for additional services. This is not something to be left until after the fact.

Milestone Checks

While scope and services review should be ongoing, project submittals provide a handy point for a careful look at both. Frequently the owner-architect agreement sets up design phases or milestones. If this is not the case, the architect may want to establish

Week ending: 6 May 2006

Development AA Project

Activities completed last week

- Submitted draft layout of Parcel 13 to Client X with canal lots option
- Forwarded summary level cost information on canal lot options for Parcel 8
- Internal review of proposal for preparation of 2-B certification documents to reopen airfield
- Reviewed Contractor Y proposal for early clearing/burning and debris removal; scheduled meeting to finalize
- Facilitated videoconference update meeting
- Facilitated Engineering Leads meeting
- Conducted Consultant Z contract status call
- Muck probes received from geotechnical engineer
- Engineering package to support platting sent out for internal QC
- Continued to facilitate progress on early work (burning, debris removal, clearing) permits
- Letters submitted to city summarizing our understanding of the path forward for servicing water and wastewater; also, submitted copy of the "Master Engineering Plan for Water, Wastewater, and Irrigation" for their information

Activities planned this week

- Submit 2-B Certification proposal to Client X for approval.
- Meet with Contractor Y to finalize debris removal proposal.
- Review and approve Consultant Z proposal for additional flushing analysis and surge analysis.
- Coordinate plan for berm with client staff.
- Submit summary level cost information on canal lot options for Parcel 13.
- Submit proposal to prepare next set of required permits, i.e., excavation for inlets, licenses to mine sand, seabed lease, beach restoration.
- Schedule meeting with Client X and Contractor Z on worker housing requirements.

Near-term critical decisions made or to make

- Mike Smith of the city submitted his recommendation for approval of the burn permit.

Information needed from Client X

- Finalize P-8 and P-13 layout.

Issues

- Need to finalize decision on canal lot layout so platting efforts can resume.

interim points to check scope and services. Approaches may include reviews and critiques by people not on the project team.

SCHEDULE AND BUDGET CONTROL

Project schedules are developed to define target completion dates and major milestones. Schedules must be tracked and monitored to ensure that all activities and tasks proceed in an appropriate manner to reach target dates. Various scheduling techniques are used depending on the nature and complexity of the work.

Budget monitoring is usually periodic, with time and expenses charged against the project reviewed and compared to goals on a regular basis. Some firms establish a regular cycle for every project—say, every Monday. Many of these firms report separating these management meetings from design reviews—which may be scheduled on Fridays.

Sophisticated systems are not required to monitor schedules and budgets effectively. What is important is that it be done on a predictable basis so the project manager knows how the project is progressing against expectations.

Account Codes

A coding system is the shorthand used to record various entries into the proper accounts. The project is assigned a number; in more complex systems, various subcodes are used for departments, disciplines, phases, tasks, and staff levels. In addition, account codes (from the chart of accounts) permit identification of specific expenses, categorized by type. Codes are also assigned to the various indirect expense (overhead) categories in the firm's budget.

Accounting codes fine-tune project control. They allow a firm to track its expenses by project, phase or task, or object of expenditure to control costs better and to improve budgeting for future projects. As with many management techniques, there is a trade-off: Detail improves accuracy but can become cumbersome and ineffective. Keep in mind that captured data for multiple account codes will only be as successful as the accuracy reflected on time sheets and expense reports.

Project Charges

Project control begins with recording time and expense charges against the various projects and other accounting codes in the office. Time accounting is the basis of a good reporting system. Most firms require weekly time sheets; to ensure greater accuracy and detail, some firms require them daily. Increasingly, time is entered directly into the firm's financial management software on a computer network.

▶ Financial Management Systems (5.2) looks at the many types of project expenses.

The level of detail on time sheets should to some degree match the level used in project planning. It makes little sense to plan by project task if time is collected by project only. Remember, too, your firm's time and expense records become part of the database used to price upcoming projects.

Employees need to have a clear explanation of how time sheets are used and why accuracy is important. If the staff believes the firm's management values lots of overtime, they may stretch their hours to accommodate. Another employee may believe that being under budget is most important and report fewer hours than worked—essentially putting in extra time for free. Even though such actions may be performed in good faith, both examples distort the project statistics and make them less useful for planning future projects.

Depending on the firm's policy, project managers may review time charges for their projects, either before the time sheets are submitted or after they are recorded. This provides the project manager with an opportunity to make sure the proper accounting codes are charged and the results are commensurate with the work effort.

Nonchargeable or indirect time should also be monitored carefully. Indirect time can be charged to, for example, marketing, administration, new employee orientation, professional development, and civic and professional activities. In addition, time charges for vacation, holidays, and sick leave are generally recorded and monitored. In larger firms, the responsibility for monitoring indirect time generally rests with studio heads or the managing principal.

It is especially important for direct expenses the client will reimburse under the owner-architect agreement to be charged to the project. These expenses are not in the firm's budget; failing to charge them to projects and not billing them to clients means the firm must absorb the charges, which directly affects the bottom line.

Project Reports

Project accounting systems are intended to help project managers exercise proper control over their projects and to take corrective action to prevent unnecessary overruns. The project budget includes hours and dollars for various elements, including labor, consultants, other project expenses, and profits. The accounting system should enable the project manager to compare actual time and expenses charged to a project with the budget to determine any variances.

Managers at various levels in the organization need different kinds of reports. Project managers are likely to want frequent reports on the number of hours worked by individuals on their projects. The firm's management, however, is likely to be more interested in reports that summarize project and non-project activities and flag

SAMPLE PROJECT PROGRESS REPORT

APPLE & BARTLETT, PC

Project Number: 2004013.00 Waterfront Mall of Hull
Phase Number: 03A Feasibility Study

FOR THE PERIOD 5/1/05–5/31/05

Labor

Description	Current Hours	JTD Hours	Budget Hours	Balance Hours	Current Billing	JTD Billing	Budget Billing	Balance Billing	% Exp	% Rpt
AA General										
1 Principal	18.00	42.00	48.00	6.00	1,998.00	4,662.00	5,328.00	666.00	87.50	42.00
2 Senior Architect	30.00	61.00	315.00	254.00	2,040.00	4,148.00	21,420.00	17,272.00	19.37	42.00
A Architect	81.00	196.00	700.00	504.00	4,752.00	12,172.00	35,650.00	23,478.00	34.14	42.00
M Project Manager	12.00	31.00	150.00	119.00	1,044.00	2,697.00	13,050.00	10,353.00	20.67	42.00
Total for AA	141.00	330.00	1,213.00	883.00	9,834.00	23,679.00	75,448.00	51,769.00	31.38	42.00
AB Project Admin.										
1 Principal	23.00	41.00	38.00	-3.00	2,505.00	4,503.00	4,218.00	-285.00	106.76	42.00
2 Senior Architect	17.00	34.00	270.00	236.00	1,496.00	2,992.00	18,360.00	15,368.00	16.30	42.00
A Architect	41.00	95.00	465.00	370.00	2,506.00	5,852.00	23,025.00	17,173.00	25.42	42.00
M Project Manager	13.00	22.00	117.00	95.00	1,131.00	1,914.00	10,179.00	8,265.00	18.80	42.00
Total for AB	94.00	192.00	890.00	698.00	7,638.00	15,261.00	55,782.00	40,521.00	27.36	42.00
AF Site Analysis										
1 Principal	14.00	34.00	34.00		1,554.00	3,774.00	3,774.00		100.00	42.00
2 Senior Architect	50.00	118.00	210.00	92.00	4,350.00	10,266.00	14,070.00	3,804.00	72.96	42.00
A Architect	62.00	123.00	480.00	357.00	4,152.00	8,139.00	24,395.00	16,256.00	33.36	42.00
E Engineer		7.00				504.00				
M Project Manager	9.00	15.00	105.00	90.00	783.00	1,305.00	9,135.00	7,830.00	14.29	42.00
Total for AF	135.00	297.00	829.00	532.00	10,839.00	23,988.00	51,374.00	27,386.00	46.69	42.00
AG Site Develop. Pl										
1 Principal	18.00	18.00	40.00	22.00	1,998.00	1,998.00	4,440.00	2,442.00	45.00	42.00
2 Senior Architect	18.00	33.00	265.00	232.00	1,224.00	2,244.00	18,020.00	15,776.00	12.45	42.00
A Architect	71.00	117.00	580.00	463.00	4,236.00	7,036.00	29,275.00	22,239.00	24.03	42.00
M Project Manager	9.00	15.00	125.00	110.00	783.00	1,305.00	10,875.00	9,570.00	12.00	42.00
Total for AG	116.00	183.00	1,010.00	827.00	8,241.00	12,583.00	62,610.00	50,027.00	20.10	42.00
Total for Labor	**486.00**	**1,002.00**	**3,942.00**	**2,940.00**	**36,552.00**	**75,511.00**	**245,214.00**	**169,703.00**	**30.79**	**42.00**

Expenses

Description	Current Hours	JTD Hours	Budget Hours	Balance Hours	Current Billing	JTD Billing	Budget Billing	Balance Billing	% Exp	% Rpt
Reimbursable Expenses										
521.00 Travel, Meals, and Lodging					6,957.50	12,880.00	14,200.00	1,320.00	90.70	42.00
522.00 Reproductions					2,294.25	3,168.25	7,000.00	3,831.75	45.26	42.00
523.00 Models/Renderings/Photos					2,334.50	4,600.00	9,300.00	4,700.00	49.46	42.00
524.00 Long Distance Telephone					1,035.00	1,957.30	3,800.00	1,842.70	51.51	42.00
529.00 Miscellaneous Reimbursable Expenses					6,900.00	12,391.25	4,600.00	-7,791.25	269.38	42.00
Total for Reimbursable Expenses					**19,521.25**	**34,996.80**	**38,900.00**	**3,903.20**	**89.97**	**42.00**
Total for Expenses					**19,521.25**	**34,996.80**	**38,900.00**	**3,903.20**	**89.97**	**42.00**
Total for 03A	**486.00**	**1,002.00**	**3,942.00**	**2,940.00**	**56,073.25**	**110,507.80**	**284,114.00**	**173,606.20**	**38.90**	**42.00**
Total for 2004013.00	**486.00**	**1,002.00**	**3,942.00**	**2,940.00**	**56,073.25**	**110,507.80**	**284,114.00**	**173,606.20**	**38.90**	**42.00**

Based on an example generated using DelTek software

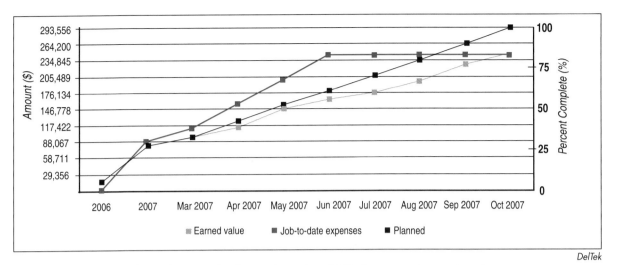

Earned Value Tracking Chart. The earned value tracking chart (EVT) chart is used to track and compare budgeted costs over time with earned costs and actual job-to-date (JTD) expenses.

variances from budgets. The purpose of these reports is to give brief but easy-to-obtain information on a frequent basis so that costs can be controlled accurately.

Increasingly, offices are using financial management software to facilitate timely collection and reporting of results. Sometimes the collecting and reporting cycle is reduced to hours or even real time, providing managers with an instantaneous look at progress and potential problems.

Overruns

Project overruns occur when project expenses exceed their budgets and, ultimately, the amount that the client has agreed to pay. The project thus incurs a loss that must be recovered out of profits on other projects.

Project overruns occur for several reasons, including poor estimating, an unrealistic fee, scope creep, and inadequate project management. Sometimes the client delays providing approvals or requests changes that were not specified in the agreement as requiring additional compensation. When overruns are projected, it is prudent to examine the options:

Additional revenue. Examine the project to determine whether, based on added services or changes in scope, there is justification to ask for additional revenue. If there is, the changes must be documented and a case made for the additional amount. Justifying the case for additional revenue will be easier if the request is made in advance (before the change is accomplished) and the client can see how much it will cost.

Overtime. Staff members may work overtime to complete the project. It is important to account for overtime hours because the firm needs to know the true costs (in both hours and dollars) of all projects in order to price similar new projects correctly.

Review alternatives for completion. Another way to overcome project budgeting problems is to reschedule and reassign the remaining portion of the work. People who can speed up the work might be assigned to the project; part-time people might help. Sometimes it is necessary to renegotiate contracts with clients or consultants.

Take the loss. Occasionally it is necessary to absorb the loss and move on.

BILLING AND COMPENSATION CONTROL

Final project control steps involve billing clients and collecting accounts.

Billing Requirements and Invoices

Requirements for billing—how often invoices are prepared, what they include, the amount of time the owner has to pay them, interest rates on overdue invoices, and

Decisions about reducing overruns must be checked against the terms and conditions of the owner-architect agreement.

Apple & Bartlett, PC | 9:07:38 AM

Billing Status	Date	Labor Code/ Account	Employee/ Reference	Description	Hours/ Units	Billing Rate	Billing Amount
Project Number: 2004005.00 Cambridge YMCA							
Labor							
B	4/18/2005	000	00001	Apple, William	9.00	125.00	1,125.00
B	8/10/2005	000	00001	Apple, William	1.50	125.00	187.50
B	6/13/2005	001	00001	Apple, William	2.00	125.00	250.00
B	4/17/2005	030	00001	Apple, William	7.00	125.00	875.00
B	4/18/2005	030	00001	Apple, William	6.00	125.00	750.00
B	4/17/2005	030	00002	Bartlett, James	6.00	127.00	762.00
B	4/18/2005	060	00002	Bartlett, James	7.00	127.00	889.00
B	6/5/2005	00D	00302	Davidson, Emily	8.00	90.00	720.00
B	6/6/2005	00D	00301	Gonzalez, Luis	4.00	75.00	300.00
					50.50		**5,858.50**
Consultants							
B	4/16/2005	511.00	0000707	Haley Hart Consulting			2,760.00
B	4/16/2005	511.00	0000709	Haley Hart Consulting			5,175.00
B	4/16/2005	511.00	0000709	Haley Hart Consulting			6,095.00
B	6/5/2005	511.00	0009870	Site analysis			862.50
							14,892.50
Expenses							
B	6/10/2005	521.00	0047384	Meeting w/Board of Directors			615.25
B	4/16/2005	522.00	0000708	Blueprints, e+L95tc.			66.70
B	6/3/2005	523.00	0003456	Film			57.50
B	1/9/2006	523.00	0000263	GPI MODELS model #8855			126.50
B	5/27/2005	524.00	0005467	Conference call			40.25
B	4/15/2005	525.00	0000231	FedEx shipping			16.39
							922.59
						Total	**21,673.59**

Based on an example generated using DelTek software

related matters—are included in the owner-architect agreement. As indicated earlier, they are usually captured in some form of project authorization so the project manager (or whoever prepares invoices) has the necessary information on billing cycles, formats, allowable expenses, and other billing requirements.

The firm will not be paid until the client receives an invoice. Therefore, full attention should be given to preparing and mailing invoices as soon as possible after the close of the accounting period. It is good practice for the project manager to review and approve invoices before they are sent to the client. However, a system should be established for approving invoices in the absence of the project manager. If the invoice requires explanation, it may make sense to call the client before it is sent.

Some firms customize their invoices to meet the needs of the client. Some send three invoices: one for regular services, one for any additional services, and one for reimbursable expenses. Some clients require that supporting documentation, such as copies of time records and expense reports, be included with all invoices. Some clients require that billing be submitted on forms prepared by and provided by the client.

Collection

Once an invoice has been sent, the next step is to pursue collection in a timely manner. Many clients establish a payment cycle for invoices. For example, invoices received by the tenth of the month are paid in that month; otherwise, invoices are held for thirty

Apple & Bartlett, PC Architects and Engineers
100 Cambridge Park Drive, 5th Floor
Cambridge, MA 02140

INVOICE

May 30, 2007
Project No: 1999007.00
Invoice No: 0000210

Mr. Charles A. Schwartz
3223 Pali Highway
Honolulu, HI 96817

Project   1999007.00   CAS Residence Design and Planning Services for Luxury Residence

Professional Services from May 1, 2007 to May 31, 2007

Professional Personnel		Hours	Rate ($)	Amount ($)
Principal				
Apple, William	5/1/07	4.00	150.00	600.00
Apple, William	5/2/07	4.00	150.00	600.00
Architect				
Gray, Barbara	5/1/07	4.00	90.00	360.00
Titony, Roberta	5/22/07	4.00	90.00	360.00
Draftsperson				
Gonzalez, Luis	5/20/07	8.00	60.00	480.00
Administrative				
Washington, Thelma	5/23/07	2.00	35.00	70.00
Totals		26.00		2,470.00
Total Labor				**2,470.00**
Reimbursable Expenses				
Structural Consultant		1.35 times	450.00	607.50
Civil & Landscape Consult		1.10 times	150.00	165.00
Travel and Lodging		1.10 times	200.00	220.00
Postage/Shipping/Deliver		1.10 times	73.25	80.58
Total Reimbursables				**1,073.08**
Unit Billing				
Interior Design				
5/7/05 3 Bedrooms	700.0 square ft. @ 1.50			1,050.00
Total Units		**1,050.00**		**1,050.00**
Taxes				
Sales and Use Tax	4.19% of 4,593.08			192.45
Total Taxes				**192.45**
Total This Invoice				**$4,785.53**

Invoices are due when rendered; late payments are subject to late charges.

Deltek

DelTek

days. If your firm knows the client's payment cycle, it is important to comply with the dates established to avoid waiting an extra month for payment.

An aging schedule for accounts receivable helps a firm keep track of how long these accounts have been outstanding. If the firm does not regularly send out invoices at the end of the month for all work accomplished during the month, then the schedule

If interest charges for late payments have been negotiated into the contract, they should be invoiced whenever appropriate.

Apple & Bartlett, PC Architects and Engineers
100 Cambridge Park Drive, 5th Floor
Cambridge, MA 02140

INVOICE

February 28, 2007
Project No: 1998005.00
Invoice No: 970

Department of Public Works
Hampshire Street
Cambridge, MA 02139

Project   1998007.00   Cambridge YMCA

Professional Services from February 1, 2007 to February 28, 2007

Fee

Total Fee				750,000.00

Billing Phase	Percent of Fee	Fee	Percent Complete	Earned
Design	25.00	187,500.00	100.00	187,500.00
Development	25.00	187,500.00	100.00	187,500.00
Construction Documents	50.00	375,000.00	0.00	0.00
Total Earned				375,000.00
Previous Fee Billing				0.00
Current Fee Billing				375,000.00
Total Fee				**375,000.00**
Total this Invoice				**$375,000.00**

Billings to Date

	Current	Prior	Total
Fee	375,000.00	0.00	375,000.00
Totals	**375,000.00**	**0.00**	**375,000.00**

Invoices are due when rendered; late payments are subject to late charge.

DelTek

should also include columns for work in progress. It is customary for the firm's principals to review the report periodically and take action on overdue accounts.

If invoices are not paid within thirty days, the project manager may want to call the client to find out the reason for the delay. Sometimes a delayed payment is an indication of dissatisfaction with the architect's services or an indication of growing owner difficulties that may affect the health of the project, and these need to be addressed. This phone call can be followed by a reminder letter. If the project manager is not a principal in the firm, additional follow-up may best be handled by one of the firm's principals. A tickler file will help bring discipline to this process.

Legal Recourse

Sometimes it becomes necessary to engage the services of an attorney or collection agency when a client does not pay. This decision is usually reached when the firm no longer feels it has a relationship with the client and the firm's only interest is in getting paid for its completed services. The sooner this decision is reached, the more likely the overdue bill will be collected. Statistics show that a claim against the architect often follows a demand for payment for professional services.

Aged as of 6/30/05

Apple & Bartlett, PC							8:55:13 AM
Invoice	Date	Balance	Current	31–60	61–90	91–120	Over 120

Billing Client Name: Atlantic Research Corporation

Project Number: 2004628.92 Faulkner Clinic / Principal-in-Charge: Apple / Project Manager: Anderson

967	1/31/2005	24,000.00					24,000.00

Project Number: 2004009.00 ABC Plaza Study / Principal-in-Charge: Apple / Project Manager: Johnson

196	4/30/2005	3,686.22			3,686.22		
554	3/30/2005	1,007.00				1,007.00	
625	6/30/2005	11,900.00	11,900.00				
955	5/31/2005	3,596.00	3,596.00				
Total for 2004009.00			15,496.00		3,686.22	1,007.00	

Project Number: 2004010.00 Johnson & Johnson Research Center / Principal-in-Charge: Bartlett / Project Manager: Anderson

212	5/30/2005	14,990.43		14,990.43			
1035	6/15/2005	24,137.31	24,137.31				
Total for 2004010.00			24,137.31	14,990.43			

Project Number: 2000250.00 Fox Run Expansion / Principal-in-Charge: Apple / Project Manager: Anderson

979	6/30/2005	410,540.00	410,540.00				

Project Number: 2004002.01 Novvis Headquarters Telecom / Principal-in-Charge: Bartlett / Project Manager: Anderson

953	6/4/2005	381,250.00	381,250.00				
978	5/31/2005	131,250.00	131,250.00				
Total for 2004002.01			512,500.00				
Total for Atlantic Research Corporation			962,673.31	14,990.43	3,686.22	1,007.00	24,000.00

Billing Client Name: City of Cambridge

Project Number: 2004005.00 City Hall Façade Replacement / Project Manager: Johnson

166	5/15/2004	18,079.21					18,079.21
194	4/30/2005	89,093.73				89,093.73	
209	5/30/2005	21,336.05			21,336.05		
972	2/28/2005	610,293.02					610,293.02
976	4/29/2005	361.58				361.58	
Total for 2004005.00					21,336.05	89,455.31	628,372.23
Total for City of Cambridge					21,336.05	89,455.31	628,372.23

DelTek

VARIANCES AND COURSE CORRECTIONS

Periodic monitoring and progress reporting is meant to uncover variances from project plans. Scope and services may shift or expand. Tasks may take too long or cost too much. The client may not render approvals in a timely fashion or pay the bills. Consultants or contractors may not meet their obligations. Given the nature of design and construction and the temporary alliances required to advance projects, variances can occur in many ways.

Each variance represents a decision item for the firm and sometimes for the client. The decision may be to do nothing. Circumstances or actions already made are expected to correct the variance, but the firm may elect to accept the variance, even though it may reduce project profit. For example, a decision to sacrifice quality documents because the design budget is overspent is not taken lightly, and the firm may decide to bite the bullet and move forward.

In other instances, the project manager will need to take corrective action, directing a change in project activity or, in some cases, coordinating the revision of project

Avoiding fee disputes is important in view of the facts that professional service fees do not always provide high profit margins and that firms are often strapped for working capital. As well, the architect's demand for fee payment often results in an allegation that services were not authorized by the client or were negligently performed, causing the client not to pay fees. How can the architect minimize the possibility of a fee dispute? Rely on the basics of good business practices such as the following:

Use a client-evaluation checklist. Before you sign a contract, use due diligence in evaluating the client and the project. Businesses routinely check the financial strength and payment record of their business partners. Architects should ask similar questions, such as these:

- Who are the principals involved in the project?
- What are their business reputations?
- Are they financially secure?
- Is the prospective client a limited liability company with few entity assets, or another entity that could disappear along with an unpaid fee?
- What is the client's track record with other professionals on other projects?
- Is the project financially feasible?
- Are the project scope, quality, schedule, and budget sound?

Answering these questions will inform your decision about whether to work with the client on the project. If you decide to go ahead with the project, these responses will provide insight into special provisions that should be built into the contract to protect your fee.

Make sure your contract is specific as to scope and clear as to compensation. AIA standard documents can help you do just that. Make sure the contract you negotiate addresses the following issues:

- The manner, method, and form in which fees will be paid. This should include a schedule of payment dates and an up-front "mobilization" payment, if appropriate.
- The right to suspend services until delayed payments are received and the right to terminate the contract and pursue legal remedies if the suspension is not effective. Failure by the client to make payments in accordance with the agreement should clearly be identified as "substantial nonperformance" and cause for termination or, at the architect's option, suspension of services.

- The ability of the parties to enforce the contract without the expenditure of extensive time or money. Some architects have been advised to use a prevailing-party provision that requires payment of the victorious party's legal fees by the party found to be at fault. While this may sound good when pursuing payment of a fee, the stronger economic party (the owner) may use the provision as a threat to coerce the weaker economic party (the architect) into a settlement that might not otherwise be justified. Devices such as interest charges on unpaid amounts often are more effective. In addition, some firms attempt to solve fee disputes through the use of arbitration that is specifically authorized only for that purpose. Mediation of fee disputes is a good first-step, good-faith effort.
- The services to be provided, the manner and method in which they are to be delivered, and the time frame for their execution. A clear "meeting of the minds" on scope, timing, and deliverables is vital to preventing the misunderstandings and disappointments that lead to fee disputes.
- The specific responsibilities of the architect and client. In particular, how the parties will handle any questions or problems that might arise during design and construction should be addressed.

Finally, it is recommended that a lawyer review the firm's agreement before it is signed.

Remember the rules of communication and documentation. Clients risk the most on any project. They need to understand what is happening on their project and the value you add to the endeavor. Regular and prompt statements detailing the services provided (with appropriate references to contract clauses) should summarize the progress made since the last billing. By involving your clients in the design process, you make it easier to resolve problems and prevent an argument over fees.

Most disputes arise, in part, when clients become angry over misunderstandings that could have been avoided through good communication. Disputes over fees often become the unsatisfied client's final expression of discontent. However, the refusal to pay a fee—especially a final payment—may reflect an intentional strategy of fee avoidance or an evolution of a cost recovery scheme.

Ongoing communication also serves to keep you aware of your clients' situations. Is a client still enthused about the project, or have you been treated differently? Is something about your services making the client unhappy? Has a client's economic position changed? Delays in payment can also result from a client's internal problems. If your client is encountering financial difficulties, open architect-client communications may help detect these problems early.

Think carefully before escalating a fee dispute into adjudication. Any form of adjudication signals the end of the cooperative working relationship with a client. It probably also signals the end of your opportunity to provide future services to that client. Always consider mediation. While fee disputes are often easily resolved through arbitration, nonbinding mediation affords you and your client a nonthreatening opportunity to find a third party to help you resolve your dispute as soon as you both want it resolved.

Always consider the reasons you want to pursue payment. Are you no longer pleased with the client? Is the amount owed to you substantial? Are you confident that there is no potential liability on your part? Will any judgment you obtain be collectible? Remember, the collection of fees depends on the nature of the architect-client relationship, the soundness of the initial contractual arrangements, and the ability of the architect to reinforce the client's perception of the value of the services being provided.

For a more detailed discussion of avoiding disputes in general, see the topic Managing and Avoiding Disputes (5.6).

Frank Musica, Esq., Assoc. AIA

plans. Actions involving changes in architect, consultant, or client responsibilities may result in amendments to the project agreements among these parties.

Contract Changes

Every project involves changes. The approach to be taken for proposing and approving changes in scope, services, schedule, and compensation should be established (and incorporated into the project agreement) at the outset. Usually the owner's specific authorization is required. Verbal authorizations are best confirmed in writing by the architect.

Some firms issue "zero sum change orders"—that is, proposals for scope changes without added compensation to the architect—for the first one or two small changes. These firms report that this procedure establishes a discipline and reduces surprises when the client authorizes changes that do require compensation adjustments.

Documentation of Changes

The accounting department—or, depending on the firm, the bookkeeper or one of the principals acting in this capacity—maintains project files that contain copies of the project authorization, signed agreements, invoices, and other papers related to the financial aspects of the project. These files are separate from the technical files maintained by the project manager. Whenever any changes are made to the contract, such as increases in project scope or authorizations for additional services, it is important that the accounting department receive a copy of the contract amendments. This can prevent accounting and billing errors.

Suspending Services

If a client is not paying invoices or meeting other contract requirements (such as supplying required information or approvals to the architect), it may be appropriate to suspend services. This act can give the architect leverage and at the same time provide both owner and architect with an opportunity to resolve the problem before additional services (and expenses) pile up.

QUALITY MANAGEMENT AND THE PROJECT NOTEBOOK

The word *quality* doesn't just mean how easily a design can be built, how functional the resulting facility will be, or how attractive it will look. The discussion of quality also includes such issues as how close the project came to its intended schedule and budget, how happy the client is, and how satisfied the firm's employees are. In short, quality embraces every aspect of how a professional service firm conducts its business.

If you are like most design professionals, your first thought in setting up a quality management program is marketing and beyond that is client satisfaction. Because the term *marketing* implies internal processes and actions, a better way to consider the process is as client-focused service. Quality management then becomes an integral part of your firm; the better the job you do at aiming for and providing client service, the better the firm will do for its current clients and in attracting additional projects and clients.

A quality management program requires a systemic response in every aspect of the firm's effort. More than anything, quality management depends on better-than-average project planning and monitoring. A useful tool to help you with both is the client notebook. For each project, set up and keep a three-ring binder with the tabs listed below. This simple binder will provide an at-a-glance view of project progress—for anyone on the project team.

- *Tab 1: Client Expectations.* This is a written list of the client's expectations, reviewed and agreed to by the client. Clients seldom agree to these, but only because they are rarely asked. Make them concentrate, encourage them to let down their guard, and get them to tell you what they really want. Only then will you be prepared to deliver.
- *Tab 2: Schedule.* Place the schedule—and any updates—in this section.
- *Tab 3: Budget.* Break this section into three parts: up-front planning, ongoing project management, and post-project activity. Whenever a new report comes out on the budget, place it here.
- *Tab 4: Contract.* Describe the scope of services and other contract requirements.
- *Tab 5: Team.* Put in a complete list of people working on the project. For each staff member, consultant, contract worker, or other team member, include name, address, telephone, home telephone, fax, cell phone, and any other access number. The goal is to be able to reach everyone at any time of the day. Disasters inevitably happen at eight o'clock on Saturday morning or at nine o'clock at night.
- *Tab 6: Changes.* In this section describe precisely how you will handle design and/or construction changes throughout the project. The client should review and sign off on this section.
- *Tab 7: Communications.* This final section talks about how and when you will communicate with the client. Specify the purpose and frequency of telephone calls and meetings, your mail system, invoice system, and other communications. Get the client to sign off on this section as well.

Frank A. Stasiowski, AIA

The possibility of suspending services should be part of the discussion with clients during negotiation of the owner-architect agreement. At that time the circumstances under which services could be stopped should be described and procedures incorporated into the owner-architect agreement. When negotiating a contract, no one enjoys considering how it might be stopped; yet it may be damaging to both client and architect to allow a project to continue beyond a certain point.

AN EYE ON QUALITY

The overriding purpose of project controls is to help keep the project on track so the client's expectations and the firm's goals can be met. From an attitudinal perspective, architects can view the glass as half empty (projects sometimes veer out of control, and control helps reduce the possibility) or as half full (everyone wants a successful project, and controls provide another set of mechanisms for achieving that).

PROJECT SCHEDULING

Frank A. Stasiowski, FAIA

Over the years, numerous systems have been devised to schedule projects. Each system has advantages and disadvantages, and each project should be scheduled using a method that best suits its scope and complexity. Also, a system must relate to the level of schedule control

The best applications for milestone charts are these:

- Short design projects with few participants and little interrelationship between activities
- Preparation of presentations or proposals
- Summarizing complex schedules containing many tasks

Selecting a Scheduling Method

Evaluation Criteria	Milestone Chart	Bar Chart	Interactive Bar Chart	CPM Schedule
Ease of communication	Good	Good	Excellent	Poor
Cost to prepare	Minimal	Minimal	Moderate	High
Cost to update	Minimal	Minimal	Moderate	High
Degree of control	Fair	Good	Good	Excellent
Applicability to small projects	Excellent	Good	Good	Poor
Applicability to large projects	Poor	Fair	Good	Excellent
Commitment from project team	Fair	Fair	Excellent	Fair
Client appeal	Fair	Good	Excellent	Excellent

needed for the project. Using an overly complex scheduling method requires unnecessary effort and may, in fact, distract the project manager from the task of planning and of keeping things on track once the project begins.

Milestone Charts

Perhaps the simplest scheduling method is the milestone chart. In its most basic form, this method consists of identifying

When using milestone charts, list only key activities to avoid the excessive detail that can defeat the purpose of the chart.

A drawback of the milestone chart is that it only shows completion dates. For complex projects and key interim milestones, this may result in uncertainty about when each activity should begin. Although the tasks are listed in the order in which they are to be undertaken, the completion dates may overlap. Furthermore, comparing actual completion dates with the target dates provides only a general indication of

Sample Milestone Chart

No.	Task	Responsibility	Target	Completed
1	Proposal cover	DB	1/15/07	x
2	Letter of transmittal	AWL	1/22/07	x
3	Introduction	AWL	1/22/07	x
4	Scope of services	MRH	2/19/07	x
5	Project schedule	MRH	2/24/07	
6	Project budget	MRH	2/24/07	x
7	Project organization	DB	2/24/07	
8	Appendix A: Qualifications	DB	2/25/07	
9	Appendix B: Biographical data	DB	3/1/07	
10	Typing and graphics	DB	3/4/07	
11	Final editing	AWL	3/8/07	
12	Printing, binding, mailing	DB	3/10/07	

the target completion date for each activity in the task outline. The chart may also include the name of the person responsible for performing each task and, later, the actual completion date for each task. The two major advantages of milestone charts are their ease of preparation and emphasis on target completion dates.

overall schedule status. Many projects are too complex to be adequately controlled using only a milestone chart.

Bar Charts

Some of the drawbacks of milestone charts can be overcome by using a slightly more complex method—the bar

(continued)

chart, also known as the Gantt chart. Probably the most widely used planning tool among architects, the bar chart consists of a list of tasks along the left side of a page. Horizontal bars along the right side indicate the scheduled start and finish dates for each task. Today there are dozens of computer programs that make this scheduling method both accessible and easy to use.

Some firms create bar chart schedules in an interactive way. They will rough out a bar chart with spreadsheet or project management software before pinning it on the wall for critiques by other team members. During the scheduling meeting, the project manager can obtain commitments from all parties to accomplish their tasks on the schedule

each activity (implicit in the bar chart method) may leave the project manager in a quandary when forced to decide which task should be delayed in the event of a labor shortage. This dilemma may result in assigning priorities to the wrong tasks. Despite these drawbacks, bar charts remain an effective method of controlling straightforward projects.

Critical Path Method (CPM)

A highly mathematical system in which task interrelationships are defined and task schedules analyzed, critical path method scheduling is designed for use in very complex projects with many tasks and complicated logic. CPM is not often used to schedule design projects but is frequently used

BAR CHART SCHEDULE

	Activity Name	Start Date	Finish Date	2006	2007	2008
				A S O N D	J F M A M J J A S O N D	J F M A M J J A S O N
1						
2	**AJAX OFFICE COMPLEX**					
3						
4	**Pre-Design**	**9/11/06**	**10/31/06**			
5	Programming	9/11/06	10/13/06			
6	Site analysis	9/27/06	10/31/06			
7	Code analysis	10/2/06	10/31/06			
8	**Schematic Design**	**11/1/06**	**1/15/07**			
9	Design	11/1/06	1/1/07			
10	Documentation	12/1/06	1/1/07			
11	Preliminary cost estimate	12/1/06	1/1/07			
12	Review/approval	1/1/07	1/15/07			
13	**Design Development**	**1/15/07**	**3/15/07**			
14	Design	1/15/07	3/1/07			
15	Documentation	1/15/07	3/1/07			
16	Specifications	2/1/07	3/1/07			
17	Cost estimate	2/1/07	3/1/07			
18	Review/approaval	3/1/07	3/15/07			
19	**Construction Documents**	**3/15/07**	**6/15/07**			
20	Documentation	3/15/07	5/15/07			
21	Specifications	4/16/07	5/15/07			
22	Cost estimate	4/16/07	5/15/07			
23	Checking/coordination	5/15/07	6/1/07			
24	Review/approval	6/1/07	6/15/07			
25	**Bidding/Negotiation**	**6/15/07**	**8/1/07**			
26	RFPs	6/15/07	7/13/07			
27	Bid analysis and contract awards	7/16/07	8/1/07			
28	**Construction Contract Admin**	**9/3/07**	**10/1/08**			
29	Construction observation	9/3/07	9/1/08			
30	Closeout	9/1/08	10/1/08			
				Aug Sept Oct Nov Dec	Jan Feb Mar Apr May Jun Jul Aug Sept Oct Nov Dec	Jan Feb Mar Apr May Jun Jul Aug Sept Oct Nov

established by the group. Conflicts can be discussed and situations resolved while everyone is still in the room.

The principal drawbacks of bar charts are that they do not show interrelationships among various tasks, nor do they indicate which activities are most crucial for completing the entire project on schedule. Assigning equal importance to

by contractors to schedule construction sequences and projects.

CPM diagrams graphically show the interrelationships among project tasks: which must be started first, which cannot be started until others are completed, and which can be accomplished in parallel. Through calculation, it is possible to develop an early and late starting date (and finish date) for each activity. It is also possible to plot one or more critical paths through the project—sequence(s) of tasks that, if delayed, would delay final completion of the project.

A number of CPM variations have been developed. They include project evaluation and review technique (PERT) and precedence diagramming. While the physical expression and some details vary, the concepts behind these systems are comparable to CPM. Developing a critical path schedule involves these steps:

Step 1: Identify tasks and relationships. The first step is to systematically identify all tasks and the relationships among them. There are three possible relationships between two tasks: Task 1 must be completed before task 2 can begin, task 1 must be partially completed before task 2 can begin, or task 1 must be completed before task 2 can be completed.

Step 2: Construct a precedence (task interface) diagram. The precedence diagram illustrated on the next page shows the relationships described in the first step. Study this diagram to see which of the three types of interrelationships exists between each pair of tasks. Note that in this example there is more than one type of relationship between tasks. Look at tasks C2 and C3; task C3 (cost estimates) cannot begin until task C2 (preliminary design) is partially completed, and task C3 cannot be completed until task C2 has been completed. This double relationship is quite common.

Step 3: Establish optimal task durations. The next step is to establish the length of time required to complete this activity in the most efficient manner possible—assuming that all prerequisite tasks have been completed. A tabulation for the tasks in the sample project is shown in the accompanying task duration list.

Step 4: Prepare the project schedule. Using the precedence diagram and duration list, prepare the project schedule. This requires calculating the earliest each task can start (and finish). When the total duration of the project as depicted in the diagram is known, then work backward to establish the latest possible finish (and start) for each task.

Step 5. Determine the critical path. The last step is to determine which tasks are critical—that is, which tasks will affect the project completion date if any delay occurs. For these tasks, the early start and late start dates are identical (as are the early finish and late finish dates). There is no float time. These tasks are darkened in the CPM schedule shown.

Computer-based project management systems perform all these calculations quickly. They allow the scheduler to easily build, test, and modify various network schedules, and they can provide a series of analyses and reports for the project. Some software also allows the scheduler to allocate resources to each task (to help build budgets) or among multiple projects simultaneously. But use caution. Some software

CPM TASK DURATION LIST

	Activity description	Calendar days
A	Develop background data	180
B1	Select case study sites	30
B2	Prepare briefing documents	30
B3	Develop data management plan	90
B4	Visit case study sites	180
B5	Analyze waste samples	105
C1	Develop computer cost models	90
C2	Perform preliminary case study site designs	135
D	Evaluate treatment, recovery, reuse	90
E	Assess cost impacts	60
F	Evaluate cost impact models	30
G1a	Prepare background data report	60
G1b	Prepare site data report	60
G2	Prepare draft report	60
G3	Prepare final report	60
H	Project management	(completed 60 days after the completion of all other tasks)

(continued)

programs are easier to use than others, and some are designed for specific-size projects. These programs are continually evolving, with new ones being developed. It would be wise to carefully review what is currently available and consider these programs in light of your firm's needs before making a selection.

The principal advantage of a critical path method is that it shows task interrelationships clearly and highlights those activities that could create problems in meeting deadlines. It

gives the project manager the most detailed control of a complex project. The major disadvantages are that CPM diagrams can be time-consuming to prepare, difficult to read, and tedious to update. Even with computers, the time and effort required to maintain a CPM chart can pose a problem for project managers with numerous project responsibilities. Moreover, most design tasks do not require such a precise level of control.

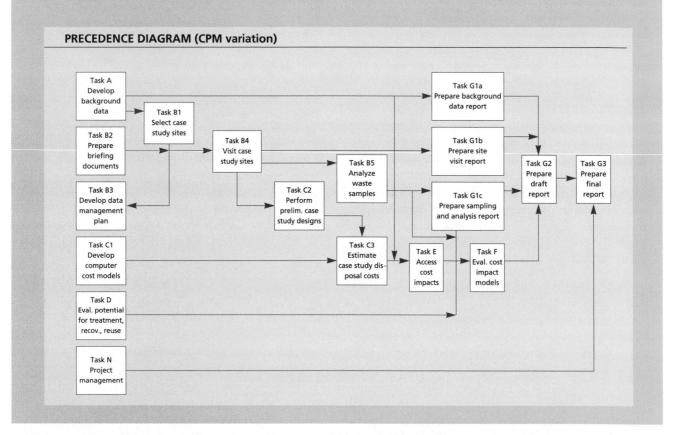

PRECEDENCE DIAGRAM (CPM variation)

PROJECT MANAGEMENT SOFTWARE

Microsoft Corporation
One Microsoft Way
Redmond, WA 98052
Phone: 425-882-8080
www.microsoft.com

Microsoft Project is a planning, scheduling, and tracking program suitable for medium and large projects. It is compatible with Microsoft Office desktop applications and with ODBC-compliant databases. Output in PERT or Gantt formats. (Available for Windows and Macintosh.)

Primavera Systems, Inc.
3 Bala Plaza West, Suite 700
Bala Cynwyd, PA 19004
Phone: 610-667-8600
www.primavera.com

Primavera Project Planner is a program that provides planning, scheduling, and tracking capabilities for sophisticated and multifaceted projects. It allows access by multiple users. Outputs are in PERT or Gantt formats. (Available for Windows.)

Primavera also has a version intended for planning, controlling, and communicating on an enterprise-wide basis with multiuser, multiproject capabilities providing project portfolio management. Outputs are in PERT or Gantt formats. (Available for Windows.)

Many project management books address project controls in conjunction with other facets of project management such as planning, team building, and operations.

Information on the PlanTrax® system is available at the PSMJ/Resources, Inc., Web site at www.psmj.com.

9.4 Construction Cost Management

Brian Bowen, FRICS

Construction cost management is too important to be left to chance. Managing costs requires skill, effort, and continuing discipline throughout design and construction.

Engaging in construction represents a substantial commitment for an owner. The costs of a project, coupled with the effort required to obtain financing, can be daunting. A project whose cost is estimated to exceed the amount borrowed or raised may have to be reevaluated or even abandoned. As a result, clients are very concerned that their projects remain within budget. Given the spotlight on construction cost in most projects, this is an area in which the architect can gain or lose credibility.

THE ARCHITECT'S RESPONSIBILITIES

The architect's responsibilities for estimating and meeting construction costs are detailed in the owner-architect agreement.

Professional Services

If AIA standard forms of agreement are used, the architect's professional services include the following:

- *Budget evaluation.* Project scope, quality, schedule, and construction budget are interrelated, and design generally begins with an evaluation of each in terms of the other.
- *Cost estimates.* AIA Document B101–2007 specifies that the architect provide a preliminary estimate of the cost of the work when the project requirements have been sufficiently identified. The owner must be advised of any adjustments to the previous estimates that result from updates and refinements of the preliminary design.
- *Construction contract administration.* As part of construction contract administration, the architect reviews and certifies amounts due the construction contractor when the contractor requests payment. Change orders are also evaluated and agreed upon.

Depending on the owner's needs and the architect's capabilities, the owner-architect agreement may include other professional services related to construction cost. The architect may agree to provide the following:

Architecture depends on order, arrangement, eurhythmy, symmetry, propriety, and economy . . . economy denotes the proper management of materials and of site, as well as a thrifty balancing of cost and common sense in the construction of works.

Vitruvius, On Architecture, Book 1 (25 BC)

Brian Bowen is a recognized expert in cost management who has written and spoken on the subject to numerous professional societies and technical organizations around the world. Formerly a principal at Hanscomb, Inc., he has now retired.

PART 3: THE PROJECT

- Market research studies
- Economic feasibility studies
- Project financing studies
- Analysis of construction alternatives or substitutions
- Construction contract cost accounting
- Life cycle cost analysis
- Value analysis, engineering, or management
- Bills of materials
- Quantity surveys
- Detailed cost estimating

Detailed construction cost estimates are a separate service that few architects undertake unless they also have specially developed estimating capabilities.

None of these services is included in the basic services package in AIA Document B101-2007. However, the owner and architect may negotiate budgeting, budget evaluation, design analysis, or cost estimating services associated with site selection and development, planning and program options, energy or other special studies, tenant fit-up, and ongoing facility management services.

Not all architects are interested in or able to provide these additional services. Market research, financing, and economic feasibility studies require expertise in specific sales or leasing markets. Detailed construction cost estimating requires the firm to be in touch with the construction marketplace in which the project will be built. Some firms include construction cost consultants, contractors, or construction managers (CMs) on their design teams; others do not.

Budget for the Cost of the Work

In addition to outlining cost-related services, the owner-architect agreement establishes a budget for the cost of the work as a condition of the architect's performance. That is, the agreement may include a statement (usually as part of the project description on the cover page) that reads something like this: "New village town hall of 10,000 gross square feet floor area with a construction cost not to exceed $1,100,000."

Including such a budget in the owner-architect agreement establishes meeting the cost figure as a goal of the architect's performance. This immediately raises a number of questions that, in the interest of both owner and architect, should be addressed in the agreement:

- How is cost of the work defined? What is included and excluded? How will design and marketplace uncertainties be addressed?
- How will the architect achieve the flexibility needed to develop a design within budget?
- What options are available to the owner and architect if bids exceed the fixed limit?
- What happens if there are delays in awarding construction contracts?

These questions are addressed in AIA Document B141 in this way:

- The cost of the work includes the elements of the project designed or specified by the architect and the architect's consultants, excluding their compensation.
- The architect is permitted to include contingencies for design, bidding, and price escalation in statements of construction cost.
- The architect can determine the materials, equipment, components, and types of construction to be included in the project and is permitted to make reasonable adjustments in scope.
- The architect can include alternates that, if necessary, can be used to adjust the construction cost at the time of contract award.

There is nothing absolute about construction prices—as sometimes evidenced by the wide spread among bids on a given project. Pre-contract estimating, therefore, is a hazardous business. An estimator who can bring 60 percent of the projects estimated within 5 percent of the low bid is probably doing better than expected, and it is statistically probable, on average, that one project in five will fall outside a 10 percent range, especially in volatile markets. The architect can avoid some of this hazard by including adequate contingencies and by cooperating with the client in designing contingent features into plans to allow for additions or deletions depending on bid results.

- Several courses of action, including revising scope and quality at no additional cost to the owner but with the owner's cooperation, are listed if the lowest bid or proposal exceeds the budget.
- The budget is to be adjusted if bidding or negotiations have not commenced within 90 days after the architect submits the construction documents.

The Architect's Performance Standard

Unless they agree to a higher standard by contract, architects are expected to use reasonable care in performing all of their professional services, including meeting the owner's construction cost objectives.

It is worth discussing reasonable care here because neither the owner nor the architect can control actual construction cost—the price that one or more contractors will ultimately charge for building the project. That price is a product of competitive market influences associated not just with the bidding contractors but also with their suppliers of materials, products, labor, and construction equipment. Under the standard of reasonable care, professionals do not have to guarantee results; rather, they are obliged to use reasonable care in performing their services.

Many owners, of course, seek guarantees. Construction represents a substantial outlay of funds, and unplanned increases in cost may create very real problems for owners. Because they have no control over the contractor, architects guaranteeing construction cost should understand that this is their choice and that they are offering to perform at a level beyond the standard of reasonable care.

Cost Services and Responsibilities of Others

Some consultants and construction organizations specialize in cost estimating and management, and these specialists may be added to the project team by the owner or the architect. Specialists may include these:

- Cost consultants who provide estimates and advice on constructability, scheduling, and the construction cost implications of functional and design alternatives
- Contractors and CMs who offer cost and constructability expertise during design. These firms may remain as advisers to the owner or architect without competing for the actual construction work, or at a predetermined time they may assume responsibility for construction, including construction cost. Some architects also offer construction management services.
- Design-build entities that assume construction cost responsibility

When construction cost is critical, both the owner and the architect may engage cost consultants, thus building in additional perspectives and problem-solving abilities. For small projects, the nominated contractor (or possibly a contractor engaged on an hourly basis) may provide advice on cost, constructability, and related issues. When responsibilities for providing construction cost services are divided, it is very important that responsibilities and risks be carefully spelled out, allocated among the parties, and incorporated into a series of coordinated project agreements.

COST MANAGEMENT PRINCIPLES

Successful management of construction costs revolves around a set of basic cost management principles.

Set Cost Objectives

It is difficult to manage well without clear intentions and objectives. Depending on the circumstances, cost objectives may include some or all of the following:

. . . neither the Architect nor the Owner has control over the cost of labor, materials or equipment, over the Contractor's methods of determining bid prices, or over competitive bidding, market or negotiating conditions. Accordingly, the Architect cannot and does not warrant or represent that bids or negotiated prices will not vary from the Owner's budget for the Cost of the Work or from any estimate of the Cost of the Work or evaluation prepared or agreed to by the Architect.

AIA Document B101–2007

Some contractors may "force" higher construction costs by deluging architects with requests for information, substitutions, and proposed design changes. Architects' responses that go beyond the construction documents may be treated as "new" requirements and thus as candidates for renegotiating construction cost.

Construction involves too many variables to establish generic cost objectives. These should be decided for each project.

- To complete the project within the capital expenditure limitations established by the owner. These limitations may be included in the owner-architect agreement, or they may be developed by the architect and owner together.
- To provide, within budget limitations, an appropriate use of resources and value for the money
- To optimize longer-term life cycle costs by examining alternatives that provide the best balance between initial capital expenditure and ongoing operating costs
- To provide the owner, during the course of the project, with relevant cost information related to major owner decisions and the status of the construction budget.

Pay Attention Early

The most effective benefits of cost management are gained at the beginning of a project, in establishing scope and levels of quality, making schedule decisions, selecting delivery options, and translating requirements into design concepts. The project's big decisions are made up front, and they lay the groundwork for all the decisions that follow.

PROJECT BUDGETS

There is no easy method for establishing realistic and achievable budgets, because they are usually prepared before there is a definitive project design and before good information regarding construction costs is available. A realistic budget reflects the following:

Project scope. The gross built area and volume, together with occupancy type and numbers of occupants in the building, set the stage for construction cost. Establishing the scope requires accurate identification of the owner's functional space requirements and a reasonable translation of these into gross floor area, including allowances for circulation, mechanical and electrical equipment, custodial space, and other nonusable areas. The statement of project scope should also indicate what is included in the budget for such items as equipment, furnishings, or sitework and also such "soft" costs as fees, financing, and other development costs.

Quality and performance levels. This is perhaps the most challenging set of factors because of the difficulty of adequately defining and describing quality and performance levels expected by the owner or achievable within a given budget limit. Diagrams, comparative projects, and published cost models may be helpful.

Site. The costs of developing the site and accommodating the building to it may be straightforward or complicated.

Schedule. To fix the project in time, it is necessary to establish or assume construction bid and completion dates.

Broad conceptual statement. A statement of key design and budget assumptions (e.g., the number of stories, simple or articulated building form, single or multiple buildings, quantity of above- and below-grade construction, expected levels of renovation of existing structures) is usually helpful.

Contingencies. These may be built into the various budget items, or they may be separately identified. It is common to reduce contingencies as the project moves forward in design.

Realistic figuring. Avoid the temptation to highball the budget figure (protecting yourself but jeopardizing the project) or lowball it (creating what may be unreasonable expectations).

Key assumptions. Note these in the budget statement to reduce the possibility that they will be lost as the budget is communicated, used, and revised.

Remember that the construction budget sets the stage for the project's preliminary design. It provides a framework within which all design decisions will be made. Budgeting, incidentally, provides a good opportunity to help educate the client about scope, quality, time, and cost trade-offs.

Recall, too, that the budget is an estimate. Avoid language that would appear to guarantee or warrant the number. If the owner supplies the first number, do not accept it uncritically but evaluate it against program, site, schedule, and market conditions.

Draft a Realistic Budget

The most important estimate given during the course of a project's life is the first one, for this is the number everyone remembers. The budget may be prepared by the owner and evaluated by the architect or developed jointly based on an analysis of the owner's statement of requirements.

The construction budget can be developed in two fundamentally different ways. It may be a number built up from costing out the project's program and schedule requirements, or it may be a number derived from a project financing study or some other source (e.g., a public referendum). However the number is established, the design usually does not exist, so the budget is typically based on projected function, area, or other general characteristics of the project. Alternatively, it may be based on the actual cost of another, similar project.

Assign Cost Targets

Once a realistic and achievable budget has been drafted, the architect is in a position to assign cost targets to the major categories within the cost framework. The resulting cost plan provides guidance, as design begins, on the funds available for each part of the project. It may also include a cash flow projection to help the owner establish the financing schedule. A cost plan can help avoid the erosive designing/costing/redesigning that characterizes some projects.

A consistent framework for organizing cost data is an important part of the cost plan. This framework allows the architect to correlate data obtained at different stages of the project (reconciliation with original budgets and estimates is always required) and to compare data from different projects.

The most common classification in use within the industry is MasterFormat™, which is used for most specifications and construction documentation. The wide currency of this format makes it useful for cost control, but because it is oriented to construction materials and trade divisions, it is less suitable for cost management at conceptual and early design stages.

▶ The MasterFormat classification system is described in Construction Documentation (8.3).

Recognizing this shortcoming, the AIA, in conjunction with the General Services Administration, developed the UniFormat for design cost management. This format uses functional subsystems (e.g., superstructure, exterior closure, interior construction)

UNIFORMAT CLASSIFICATION OF BUILDING ELEMENTS AND SITEWORK

From UniFormat II (ASTM E-1557-05)

The UniFormat classification system, based on building components, provides a useful framework for developing and organizing cost information and estimates.

Level 1 Major Group Elements		Level 2 Group Elements		Level 3 Individual Elements	
A	SUBSTRUCTURE	A10	Foundations	A1010	Standard foundations
				A1020	Special foundations
				A1030	Slab on grade
		A20	Basement Construction	A2010	Basement excavation
				A2020	Basement walls
B	SHELL	B10	Superstructure	B1010	Floor construction
				B1020	Roof construction
		B20	Exterior Enclosure	B2010	Exterior walls
				B2020	Exterior windows
				B2030	Exterior doors
		B30	Roofing	B3010	Roof coverings
				B3020	Roof openings
C	INTERIORS	C10	Interior Construction	C1010	Partitions
				C1020	Interior doors
				C1030	Fittings
		C20	Stairs	C2010	Stair construction
				C2020	Stair finishes

(continued)

Level 1 Major Group Elements		Level 2 Group Elements		Level 3 Individual Elements	
	INTERIORS (Cont.)	C30	Interior Finishes	C3010	Wall finishes
				C3020	Floor finishes
				C3030	Ceiling finishes
D	SERVICES	D10	Conveying	D1010	Elevators and lifts
				D1020	Escalators and moving walks
				D1090	Other conveying systems
		D20	Plumbing	D2010	Plumbing fixtures
				D2020	Domestic water distribution
				D2030	Sanitary waste
				D2040	Rain water drainage
				D2090	Other plumbing systems
		D30	HVAC	D3010	Energy supply
				D3020	Heat generating systems
				D3030	Cooling generating systems
				D3040	Distribution systems
				D3050	Terminal & package units
				D3060	Controls and instrumentation
				D3070	Systems testing & balancing
				D3090	Other HVAC systems and equipment
		D40	Fire Protection	D4010	Sprinklers
				D4020	Standpipes
				D4030	Fire protection specialties
				D4090	Other fire protection systems
		D50	Electrical	D5010	Electrical service & distribution
				D5020	Lighting and branch wiring
				D5030	Communications & security
				D5090	Other electrical systems
E	EQUIPMENT & FURNISHINGS	E10	Equipment	E1010	Commercial equipment
				E1020	Institutional equipment
				E1030	Vehicular equipment
				E1090	Other equipment
		E20	Furnishings	E2010	Fixed furnishings
				E2020	Movable furnishings
F	SPECIAL CONSTRUCTION & DEMOLITION	F10	Special Construction	F1010	Special structures
				F1020	Integrated construction
				F1030	Special construction systems
				F1040	Special facilities
				F1050	Special controls and instrumentation
		F20	Selective Building Demolition	F2010	Building elements demolition
				F2020	Hazardous components abatement
G	BUILDING SITEWORK	G10	Site Preparation	G1010	Site clearing
				G1020	Site demolition and relocations
				G1030	Site earthwork
				G1040	Hazardous waste remediation
		G20	Site Improvements	G2010	Roadways
				G2020	Parking lots
				G2030	Pedestrian paving
				G2040	Site development
				G2050	Landscaping
		G30	Site Mechanical Utilities	G3010	Water supply
				G3020	Sanitary sewer
				G3030	Storm sewer
				G3040	Heating distribution
				G3050	Cooling distribution
				G3060	Fuel distribution
				G3090	Other site mechanical utilities
		G40	Site Electrical Utilities	G4010	Electrical distribution
				G4020	Site lighting
				G4030	Site communications and security
				G4090	Other site electrical utilities
		G90	Other Site Construction	G9010	Service and pedestrian tunnels
				G9090	Other site systems and equipment

that parallel the way designers think about and ultimately select building components and assemblies. Design cost data are increasingly being published in the UniFormat categories. During the 1990s, an ASTM subcommittee undertook an extensive industry review of UniFormat, which resulted in several changes to the original; this was published as UniFormat II, and it is now ASTM Standard E-1557-05.

Cost as a Design Objective

Controlling cost as a design objective requires an understanding of the factors that affect building costs. A list of geographic, design, and marketplace factors is included in the sidebar "Factors Affecting Building Costs" later in this topic.

▶ Project Controls (9.3) examines approaches for managing project scope.

It is important to recognize that much of a project's cost is built into the project once its location, size, use type, and occupancy load are established; these decisions drive zoning, planning, and building code requirements. Geographic location and site set additional parameters for construction cost. The laws of supply and demand in the construction marketplace can exert great influence. Within these boundaries, the design team influences construction cost through its decisions about form, layout, systems, materials, and finishes.

Scope Control

Clearly, a major cost driver is the scope of the project: how much is to be constructed, and the levels of quality desired in the project. Increasing scope increases construction cost and may add design, financing, and operating costs, as well. Thus, scope control is an essential cost management discipline.

Many projects are subject to "scope creep," an enlargement of scope based on the many good ideas and solutions that arise during design. As the project becomes "real," owners may request changes in program requirements or levels of quality. Often these requests are small but numerous.

Most owners do not see their requests for changes as requiring changes in the budgets they have set. When budgets are fixed, scope creep forces reductions elsewhere: The chiller becomes several rooftop units. The granite facing becomes brick, then split-face block. The atrium becomes a corridor with a skylight (which ends up as an additive alternate).

An important challenge facing architects is to sit down with the owner and talk through changes, especially the small ones. The objective is to secure the client's commitment to the change and its cost implications, or to determine what other owner requirements can be changed to keep the project within budget.

Cost Monitoring and Reporting

Construction cost should be carefully reviewed and, depending on the architect's contractual requirements, reported to the owner at each design submission or at agreed-upon intervals. Cost reports should be reconciled to the cost plan and differences explained. This is a good time to review the status of project cost with the owner and obtain commitments to any budget updates that may be mutually agreed upon.

AIA Document B101–2007 states that the architect's estimate of the cost of the work shall be based on current area, volume, or similar conceptual estimating techniques.

DESIGN COST ESTIMATING

Successful cost management depends on sound estimating skills. Estimating involves two basic steps: quantifying the amount of work to be estimated and applying reasonable unit prices to these quantities.

There is a maxim among estimating professionals that the easier the measurement, the more difficult the pricing, and vice versa. Thus, it is more difficult to prepare accurate estimates at early project stages than later, when complete working drawings are available.

While there are many estimating approaches and systems, they generally fall into one of these basic categories:

- Area, volume, and other single-unit rate methods
- Elemental (assemblies and subsystems) methods
- Quantity survey methods

Area, Volume, and Other Single-Unit Rate Methods

During predesign and even in preliminary design stages, it is usually necessary to develop construction cost estimates on the basis of one or more single units. Whether they are based on units of accommodation or on building area or volume, these estimating methods suffer from oversimplification and can produce widely varying estimates unless buildings of similar character, function, and location are being considered.

Accommodation units. This approach involves counting the units of accommodation to be provided in the proposed building—the number of apartments or dormitory rooms, beds in a hospital or nursing home, parking spaces in a parking garage—and pricing these units at an overall inclusive rate. Selecting the appropriate unit price is usually difficult, even when a reasonable body of historical evidence exists. This is true because there is wide variation in building forms and designs that contain the same units of accommodation.

Area and volume methods. For preliminary estimates, architects often use computations based on the floor area (in square feet) or, less frequently, volume (in cubic feet) of construction. These methods require care in defining and counting area and volume. Basements, balconies, covered walkways, enclosed entries, interstitial spaces, and mechanical spaces may or may not require the same level of construction cost per square or cubic foot as more conventional enclosed and inhabited space. Also, care must be used in selecting the square or cubic foot unit cost factors to be applied. Finally, these methods require skill and experience in adjusting the unit costs to the special conditions of the project.

When using historical cost data for area or volume costs of construction, the architect should ensure that the project or group of projects selected for comparison is similar to the project being estimated. The projects should be compared for similarity of use, size, site, type of construction, finishes, mechanical equipment, and economic climate during construction. The estimator can then compare characteristics and determine the modifications necessary to adjust the unit costs.

It should be noted that published single-rate unit cost figures customarily do not include the following:

- Site improvements and landscaping
- Utilities more than five feet from the building
- Unusual foundation conditions
- Furnishings and movable equipment not normally included in construction contracts
- Other items not normally included in a building of the type reported

Functional area method. This refinement of the simple area method involves separately pricing each functional space type included in the project. Thus, an estimate for a small school might include different square foot cost factors for its classroom, assembly, kitchen, and circulation spaces. This method assumes that the functions performed in the building will have a considerable bearing on its cost—a concept that holds true for interior construction but has less effect on the cost of the basic building shell. Using this method can be difficult because completed projects are rarely analyzed by the cost of individual areas, making it hard to find suitable cost data on which to base estimates.

Elemental (Assemblies and Subsystems) Methods

An approach that falls between single-unit rate methods and the extremely detailed quantity survey method involves measuring basic building systems or elements. This

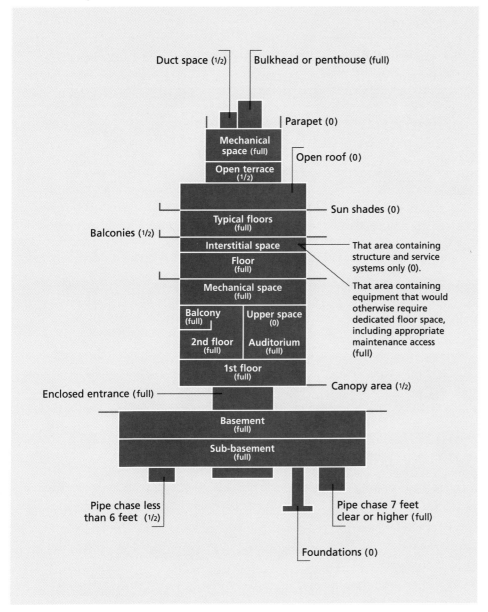

Duct space (1/2)   Bulkhead or penthouse (full)

Parapet (0)

Mechanical space (full)

Open roof (0)

Open terrace (1/2)

Sun shades (0)

Typical floors (full)

Balconies (1/2)

Interstitial space

That area containing structure and service systems only (0).

Floor (full)

Mechanical space (full)

That area containing equipment that would otherwise require dedicated floor space, including appropriate maintenance access (full)

Balcony (full)   Upper space (0)

2nd floor (full)   Auditorium (full)

1st floor (full)

Enclosed entrance (full)

Canopy area (1/2)

Basement (full)

Sub-basement (full)

Pipe chase less than 6 feet (1/2)

Pipe chase 7 feet clear or higher (full)

Foundations (0)

Architectural Area and Volume of Buildings. AIA Document D101–1995, Methods of Calculating the Area and Volume of Buildings, provides a generally accepted set of definitions for establishing building area and volume. For example, an exterior balcony contributes half its floor space to the total net assignable area, while an enclosed entrance is counted at its full floor area.

approach subdivides the building into a series of functional subsystems, perhaps using the UniFormat framework, and establishes a cost target for each subsystem.

The stage of design determines the degree of detail. In early stages, when no layouts have been designed, interior partitions can be priced on the basis of an allowance per square foot of finished area. Once layouts are done, these assemblies can be priced on a cost per linear foot of partition and, further along, on the basis of measured square foot area of the partitions, with doors, frames, and finishes priced separately.

The objective of using elemental methods is to produce an estimate by approaching a building as a sum of its systems and components. Construction cost is related to the configuration and construction of the building rather than just to its area, volume, or quantity of function. These methods require a sophisticated database of information.

Fundamental to the development of sound cost management in design is an understanding of the basic factors that influence building costs. Some of these factors can be controlled in design, and others cannot.

Location Factors

Location factors cover a variety of issues from characteristics of the site to local building regulations.

Geographic location. Costs will be influenced by such factors as climate and comfort requirements, building codes and regulations, ease of access, distances from sources of labor and materials, degree of union influence, and productivity of workers in the area.

Condition of the site. The bearing capacity of the soil, presence of rock, location of groundwater, slope, and existing conditions (such as old foundations or buried hazardous wastes) influence substructure costs and basic building design. Urban sites may require underpinning, extraordinary security, and limitations on access and maneuverability.

Regulations. Building design and construction are affected by a wide range of building codes and standards, as well as planning, zoning, environmental protection, construction labor, and site safety laws and regulations. These requirements, and the regulatory fees the owner must pay, may vary considerably from locality to locality.

Marketplace. Construction prices are subject to change according to the laws of supply and demand. Overstressed and under-stressed construction markets will affect the level and quality of competition, as well as the prices charged.

Design Factors

These are design factors with a direct correlation to the cost of the building.

Plan shape. The plan dictates the amount and complexity of the perimeter required to enclose a given space. Generally, the higher the perimeter-to-floor area ratio, the greater the unit cost. Exterior closure is a high-cost item (often 10 to 20 percent of total cost) and has a secondary effect on lighting and HVAC system capacities and operating costs.

Size. As buildings increase in size, unit costs tend to decrease. This is due to more efficient perimeter ratios, better utilization of high-cost service elements (e.g.,

elevators, toilets, HVAC plant), and the effect of greater quantities on the contractor's purchasing power. As a rule of thumb (and, like all rules of thumb, unworkable in extreme cases), an increase or decrease in size by a given percentage is likely to lead to an increase or decrease in cost of roughly half that percentage.

Building height. Above six or eight stories, unit costs per square foot tend to increase due to the costs of increased loads, wind bracing, elevators, and fire code requirements. Taller buildings also become less efficient in their use of space, requiring more built area to house the same functions.

Story height. The greater the floor-to-floor height, the greater is the cost. The vertical elements in a building may account for 25 to 35 percent of the total cost; thus, a 10 percent reduction in story height might save 2.5 to 3.5 percent overall.

Space utilization and efficiency. To arrive at the gross building area, the architect must add circulation, toilets, mechanical and electrical space, custodial, and other nonusable spaces to the owner's stated net usable square feet requirements. The design task, which may be made more complicated by site or program adjacency requirements, is to minimize these nonusable areas and keep the net-to-gross floor area ratio as high as possible.

Qualitative Factors

There is a direct correlation between qualitative factors, as stated in performance terms, and cost. The more demanding the performance requirements, the higher are the costs. Some owners may have specific performance concerns or aesthetic preferences. Better quality and performance may be needed to justify higher costs on a life cycle basis over a longer term.

Construction Factors

In a marketplace with many available qualified constructors, competitively bid lump-sum contracts are generally expected to produce the best prices. Negotiated lump sums, all things considered, are often most appropriate for smaller projects, and cost-plus contracts may be useful when time or complexity of construction is a factor. Clear and complete documents reduce uncertainties (and possible contingencies) in competitive bidding.

Quantity Survey Method

This method involves detailed calculation of all the components necessary to construct the building, followed by the pricing of each component. For example, the elemental method may base plumbing costs on the number of fixtures, including roughing-in and water and waste connections. The quantity survey method measures each fixture separately, as well as the length of each piece of pipe and the quantities of fittings and trim. It applies prices to the materials involved in each construction operation, including allowances for waste, labor (crew sizes and makeup), installation time, equipment used, and for each trade, appropriate allowances for the contractor's overhead and profit.

Although such approaches to estimating are necessary for contractors, they are of limited value to architects. The designer might elect to do a careful quantity survey of alternative approaches for a given design decision or detail but is unlikely to undertake a quantity survey for an entire project.

Contingencies and Reserves

All estimates should also include reasonable provisions for the following:

Price escalation. This generally is considered from the date of the estimate to the scheduled bidding or negotiation date (if the base estimate includes escalation during the construction period) or to the midpoint of construction (if the base estimate does not include any construction period escalation).

Design contingencies. These may go as high as 20 percent for estimates based on area or volume. The completeness of the documents on which the estimate is based, the complexity of the project, the probable bidding climate, and the accuracy of the information furnished by the owner all must be considered. As design progresses and estimating becomes more detailed, this contingency will be reduced.

Construction contingencies. These generally allow up to 5 percent to provide for unforeseen changes during construction. This figure may be higher for renovation projects.

Sources of Cost Information

Architects providing construction estimates generally rely on published cost information and their own historical information.

COST INDEXES

Construction cost indexes attempt to measure changes in price during a period of time and from place to place. Like the Dow Jones or S&P 500 stock indexes, each construction cost index measures the cost of something specific. The *Engineering News Record Building Cost Index*, for example, is based on a hypothetical unit of construction requiring 1,088 board feet of 2-by-4 lumber, 2,500 pounds of standard structural steel shapes, 1.128 tons of portland cement, and 68.38 hours of skilled labor.

Every index has a base, usually expressed as 100. This may be the value of the index in a given year (e.g., 1990 = 100) or at a given place (e.g., the 30-city index is 100).

Some indexes are segmented to provide additional information. For example, the RSMeans city cost indexes are broken down by trade, revealing that while the overall city construction cost index for, say, Albany, New York, was 97.2 one year, the index for mechanical systems was 96.8 and the index for sitework was 97.4.

Indexes are valuable because they facilitate comparisons. The year that Albany's index was 97.2, the index in New York City (150 miles away) was 131.9, while the index in Charleston, South Carolina, was 75.3. Looking at the change in indexes from year to year provides information on inflation and other changes in the construction marketplace.

Most published construction indexes measure change in the price of inputs to construction, such as labor, materials, and equipment. Very few attempt to modify indexes for changes in productivity, technology, design, or market conditions, so be cautious when using an index.

A number of commercial sources publish cost information at three levels: area and units of accommodation; subsystems and assemblies; and individual components, products, and construction materials. The price levels in these guides represent the general market. Geographic and historical cost indexes may be used to help make the information time- and location-specific. Some guides present variations by building type, size, and general quality level. Some offer models with parameters that can be varied—within limits—to reflect the conditions the architect is facing; it may be possible, for example, to replace a masonry façade with precast concrete and calculate the resulting difference.

Construction cost guides are increasingly available in electronic form, allowing architects to enter cost information (and appropriate modifiers) into their own spreadsheets for what-if analyses and preparation of estimates.

Cost guides, of course, cannot reflect all the variations in the design or the marketplace. Intelligently used, they can help establish ballpark estimates and can assist in the choice of design features and building elements.

To supplement published cost information, many architects maintain cost data files in which their experience accumulated on completed projects is set up in a format that allows for reuse on future projects. Project cost files generally include the following:

- Basic information (e.g., location, owner, names of consultants and contractors)
- Outline project description
- Project statistics (e.g., net and gross floor areas, number of stories above and below grade, story heights, perimeter lengths at each level, exterior closure area, foundation and roof footprint areas)
- Outline specifications and performance criteria
- Cost breakdown (e.g., in UniFormat categories)
- Type and magnitude of change orders

Computer Programs

A number of computer-based estimating programs are available. They range from simple spreadsheet versions to powerful programs linked to databases with plenty of flexibility. They may also have capabilities for interfacing with scheduling and CAD and BIM programs. At this writing, few programs are tailored to the architecture market, so it is wise to treat vendors' claims with caution.

Presentation of Estimates

The method and information used in preparing estimates should be presented to the owner in a clear and concise manner. Depending on the circumstances and the architect's contractual requirements, the following information may be appropriate:

- Project title, location, and date of estimate
- Current project status (e.g., schematics, 50 percent construction documents)
- Estimate summary, with backup as appropriate
- Reconciliation of estimates with budget, previous estimates, or both
- Explanation of any variations and recommendations for action
- Estimating method used
- Assumed bidding and construction schedule
- Assumed delivery approach and procurement method
- Outline of items included and excluded from the estimate
- Assumptions about escalation and any escalation contingency included
- Design and construction contingencies included
- Outline specifications, and assumed performance and quality levels
- List of possible alternates or other considerations
- Comments on special conditions that might affect the accuracy of the estimate

COST ISSUES DURING PROCUREMENT

Even the most assiduous design cost management cannot ensure the marketplace will respond with quotations or bids that exactly match the construction budget. Thus, effective cost management builds in some flexibility at construction contract award time by incorporating an appropriate combination of allowances, alternates, and unit prices into the bidding or negotiation process.

Allowances

Allowances are fixed sums determined by the owner and architect before bidding takes place, and bidders are instructed to include these sums in their bids. Allowances aim to cover the costs of items whose exact character or level of quality cannot be specified at the time of bidding and therefore cannot be accurately bid. Artwork for later selection, special hardware, ornamental lighting, kitchen cabinets, custom carpeting, and similar items may be carried as allowances if the owner or bidding authority permits. If the actual cost exceeds the allowance, the contractor is entitled to additional payment; if the cost is less, the owner receives credit.

Allowances should be priced, identified, and defined in the construction documents. It also should be clear whether allowance figures include overhead, profit, delivery, and sales taxes.

Alternates

The construction documents may require the contractor to provide alternate bids. Alternates may delete work shown, require additional work, or change the level of quality specified. Alternates provide the owner with an opportunity to modify the project to ensure that construction costs fall within a fixed budget. In some cases, alternates are intended to give the owner the opportunity to select specific materials or design features after the actual cost is known. Like changes in construction cost, alternates may increase or decrease the time required for construction.

While deductive alternates are occasionally appropriate, better prices will generally be obtained for additive alternates. It is good practice not to mix the two types of alternates on bid forms. Alternates require extra work by the architect, and especially by bidders, and should be used judiciously.

Decisions about which alternates to accept are usually made by the owner on the architect's recommendation. The base bid plus selected alternates is used to determine the low bid, but the selection of alternates should not be manipulated to favor one bidder over another.

Unit Prices

Unit prices are used to provide a cost basis for changes to the contract, usually to cover unknown conditions and variables that cannot be quantified exactly at the time of bidding. Rock removal, additional excavation, additional concrete for foundations or paving, and additional piping or wiring may be identified as units to be priced by bidders. Unit prices should be specified only when reasonably necessary and when they can be accurately described and estimated. Prices for additional quantities usually exceed credits for reduced quantities, and provision should be made for this fact in the bid form. It is good advice to review unit prices carefully before recommending contract awards.

Bidding Strategies

It is wise to use the bidding process as an opportunity rather than a threat. Do everything you can to "sell" the project to the bidding contractors—provide advanced advice of the forthcoming bid, explain the importance of the work and how it will advance the successful contractor's reputation. It is also advisable to make the process itself as simple as possible:

- Make sure the bidding documents are well coordinated and complete.
- Provide enough time for bid preparation.
- Minimize (or eliminate) addenda.
- Simplify the bid form; avoid requests for cost breakdowns, lists of subcontractors, and so on; and ask for this information to be supplied within 48 hours after bid closing time.

In other words, take charge of the bidding process and make it work to the benefit of your client.

COST CONTROL DURING CONSTRUCTION

There are many opportunities to lose control of construction costs once a project is under way. Assuming the architect is engaged to administer the construction contract under the terms of AIA Document A201, following are some key areas to watch.

Schedule of Values

At the beginning of construction, the contractor submits a schedule of values that lists the various parts of the work and the quantities involved. This information helps the architect assess contractor payment requests and provides feedback for cost data files. It is recommended that a standard schedule of values be specified in the bidding documents that will enable translation between MasterFormat and UniFormat. The chart in "Cost Breakdown Format" would be a good place to start.

Construction Progress Payments

Under AIA standard forms of general conditions, the architect reviews the contractor's requests for payment and certifies them to the owner. To ensure fair value to the owner and fair payment to the contractor, the amounts requested are checked against the schedule of values and actual progress in the field.

Change Orders

As changes take place, the contract sum may be increased (or, rarely, decreased). Each change order is, in effect, an opportunity to renegotiate the contract sum; thus, cost control of changes is essential to effective cost management.

The use of unit prices (noted above) can help in the negotiation of fair cost adjustments, but more often than not, the basis of agreement is reached by negotiation based on estimated cost or actual time and material expended. One contentious item in change order negotiation is the markup for contractor overhead and profit. It is advisable to require bidding contractors to state on the bid form the percentages that will apply, or else to incorporate allowable markups into the specifications.

Claims and Disputes

Claims, too, can lead to higher construction costs. Careful administration of the construction contract, including management of conditions that might lead to disputes, is a key risk management strategy for the architect—on behalf of the project as well as the architect's practice.

Construction Closeout

The closeout process provides an opportunity to wrap up the project in an expeditious way. Cost control here revolves around making inspections and punch lists, handling releases of retainage, and accomplishing the final payments with attendant approvals and releases of liens.

▶ Construction Contract Administration (8.5) discusses changes in the work, contractor payment applications, and project closeout issues.

▶ Managing and Avoiding Disputes (5.6) discusses how to address and resolve differences before they become disputes.

It ain't over 'til it's over.

Yogi Berra

Postproject Review

Astute design professionals learn from their projects, gaining information and insight that helps them better plan and manage the next project. A postproject review can help the architect understand what it cost to construct a project, where the money went, and how the architect's design and project management decisions may have influenced these expenditures.

SPECIAL ESTIMATING CHALLENGES

Some project types offer more estimating challenges than others, particularly renovation or alteration of an existing structure and international projects.

Estimating Renovations and Alterations

This is a particularly challenging aspect of estimating, especially when project definition is just beginning. Renovations entail more unknowns than new construction does. Special issues will arise during renovations and will need to be accounted for with estimates. Some of these issues are as follows:

- Availability of as-built drawings
- Condition assessment
- Impact of building codes and regulations (often upgrades not included in the program are necessary to meet code requirements in older buildings)
- Continued occupancy during alterations (complicating scheduling and staging)
- Need for unforeseen structural changes
- Extent of exterior envelope renovations and alterations
- Contractor access to space and staging areas

Estimating International Projects

Estimating overseas construction costs for international projects adds to the challenge of accurate estimation.

Just as in the United States, construction prices vary from country to country according to competitive and economic factors. Sometimes exchange rates are distorted, and taxes and inflation may vary markedly from those prevailing in the United States. Availability of construction products and systems is different, as well. For example, air-conditioning might be uncommon and expensive at many locations in Europe. Drywall was not available until recently in Brazil, and at most locations, the available choices are extremely limited. Despite these circumstances, it rarely pays to import materials. Design styles and preferences are not uniform—European factory managers prefer open areas and do not like interior columns. Building codes and regulations can be bewildering to navigate—in Germany no office can be placed farther than 6.5 meters from a window, and the windows must be operable even in the presence of air-conditioning.

A common method of early estimating is to calculate the probable cost in the United States and then factor it to the overseas location. However, this is not the best method. Rather, the owner should be asked to fund a proper market survey at the overseas location to ascertain costs and pricing levels and determine other factors likely to influence the cost of the work. Retention of a local cost consultant or contractor is advised.

ORGANIZING FOR COST MANAGEMENT

In small practices, responsibility for cost estimating and management typically falls on the principals and senior staff. Less experienced staff members often do not have knowledge of factors that influence construction prices or an appreciation of current and expected market conditions.

Some practices may develop sufficient volume or depth in a specialty to justify a cost estimator on staff. In recruiting for this position, preference is usually given to candidates with conceptual estimating abilities and all-around construction pricing experience, rather than candidates with work experience in a contractor's office who may be capable of estimating for only a few trades. Cost management personnel are most effective when they are fully integrated into the design team.

The alternative to an in-house cost estimator is an independent cost consultant. It is usually best to bring cost consultants in at an early stage so that their services can be established at the outset and included in the architect's compensation. The cost consultant can provide useful services at all stages, not simply to provide a single estimate. As with all specialist firms, it is best to develop a working relationship with a cost consultant over a period of years.

It is not unusual on construction management projects for the CM to have responsibility for estimating and control, although the architect is rarely entirely relieved of this duty. The architect must be satisfied that the CM's estimates are reasonable and that cost advice is received as expected.

In whatever way the architect arranges to manage construction costs, the challenge is to establish cost as a design discipline and to sustain that discipline from the beginning to the end of the project.

9.5 Maintaining Design Quality

James B. Atkins, FAIA, KIA

In some cases, the quality of design in building projects can be significantly compromised, particularly when substitutions are made during the construction phase. However, management techniques are available to help architects keep the design intent reasonably intact.

Architectural design solutions strive to strike a balance between function, quality, cost, and other project design parameters. However, projects are seldom constructed exactly as they were originally designed. Inadequate or poorly defined budgets, substitution requests based solely on cost, and nonconforming construction can change the performance or the physical appearance of a building. This reality of design and construction often occurs despite diligent efforts by the project team. A properly conducted value analysis (VA) process can help resolve problems that result from exceeded budgets and unavailable materials and thus can help preserve the design quality of a project.

Effective processes and procedures for budget management, substitution control, submittal reviews, and construction nonconformance can help maintain design quality during the delivery of project services. To be successful, these efforts must respond effectively to project objectives and documentation.

Jim Atkins is a principal with HKS Architects, where he is responsible for the firm's organization development and loss prevention activities. He is a member of the AIA Documents committee, previously served on the AIA Risk Management committee, and chaired the steering group for the fourthteenth edition of the Handbook. He has written articles for *AIArchitect* and the *Emerging Professional's Companion*. (This topic originally appeared in the Handbook Update 2004 volume.)

Although complete success may never be realized, much can be done to maintain the intent of the original design. Using the principles, techniques, and tools described in the discussion that follows, architects and other building design professionals can improve the consistency of success of design solutions that influence building performance, thereby optimizing design quality.

MANAGING THE PROJECT BUDGET

A good approach to managing a project budget is to make it a priority in the contract for professional services. The budget amount should be identified as early as possible in the delivery process and confirmed in writing to the owner. Should the owner be reluctant to provide a budget in writing, the architect can document it in a letter. For clarification, the letter can also address costs for services that are not included in the scope.

SAMPLE BUDGET CONFIRMATION LETTER

WILLING • ARCHITECTS
1234 Easy Street, Suite 16
Prosper, Wyoming 78727-1883

Ace Willing, AIA
Senior Principal

June 26, 2008

Mr. Walter Johnson, President
The Johnson Company
6744 Collins Street, Suite 7
Wilbur, OK 67349-7634

RE: Addition to Johnson Company Headquarters
    WA Project No. 5840

Dear Mr. Johnson:

This letter will confirm the project construction budget amount of $7,800,000 as discussed in Project Design Meeting No. 2 held at your office on March 6, 2008.

This budget amount does not include soft costs such as professional fees or land costs.

If this is not the correct amount, please notify us immediately.

Sincerely,

Ace Willing, AIA

AW/

cc: project file 5840

Changing construction markets and increasing labor costs can make budget conformance a challenge. Products and systems specified during construction documentation can prove significantly more expensive due to limited supply, increased production costs, or increased labor costs. AIA Document B101–2007, Standard Form of Agreement Between Owner and Architect, may require the architect to modify the construction documents without additional compensation if the lowest bid or negotiated pricing proposal exceeds the budget.

Document changes late in a project can require the architect to expend extensive additional labor hours. One way to manage this challenge is to include a clause in the owner-architect agreement stating that the architect will absorb the cost of redrawing and revision only if the budget has been exceeded by a specified amount. This margin broadens the budget target to accommodate uncertain market environments. Such a clause was developed by the AIA Large Firm Roundtable Legal Subcommittee (see sidebar) to modify language in AIA owner-architect agreements. Consultation with an attorney is recommended to determine if such a clause suits your firm's needs.

▶ Project Controls (9.3) discusses the management of project schedules and budgets.

To keep from exceeding the budget, it is essential to continually monitor its status. Scope creep is common in the design development process, and scheduled evaluations reconciling the budget and the current scope are critical. When the budget is reviewed in every owner meeting, it is less likely that budget changes caused by scope creep will be overlooked.

Project budgets are initially confirmed by project cost estimates. If in-house estimating services are not available, a consultant should be engaged for this important

BUDGET REDRAW CLAUSE

The Legal Subcommittee of the AIA Large Firm Roundtable developed the following clause and associated language for insertion into the owner-architect agreement to limit how much redrawing and revision the architect will absorb. For example, the following shows language from AIA Document B101–2007, Standard Form of Agreement Between Owner and Architect, as amended by inclusion of this clause:

§ 6.6 If a fixed limit of Construction Cost the Owner's budget for the Cost of the Work at the conclusion of the Construction Document Phase Services is exceeded by the lowest bona fide bid or negotiated proposal, the Owner shall:

.1 Give written approval of an increase in such fixed limit; the budget for the Cost of the Work;

.2 Authorize rebidding or renegotiating of the Project within a reasonable time;

.3 Terminate [the Architect's services] in accordance with [this Agreement];

.4 In consultation with the Architect, revise the Project program, scope, or quality as required to reduce the Cost of the Work; or

.5 Implement any other mutually acceptable alternative.

§ 6.7 If the Owner chooses to proceed under Section 6.6.4, and the lowest bona fide bid or negotiated proposal exceeds the fixed limit of Construction Cost by 10 percent (10%) or more, the Architect, without additional compensation, shall modify the documents for which the Architect is responsible under this Agreement as necessary to comply with the fixed limit, if established as a condition of this Agreement. Owner's current budget for the Cost of the Work. The Architect's modification of the documents for which it is responsible shall be the limit of the Architect's responsibility under this Article 6.

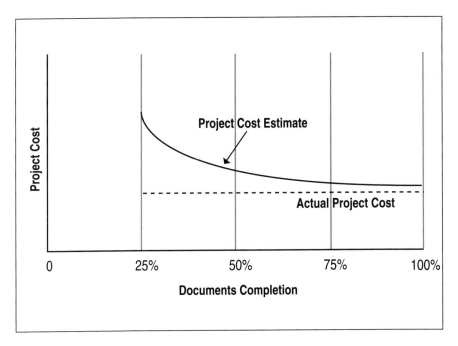

Documents Completion and Project Cost Estimating

task. If an owner retains a contractor to provide preconstruction services, the contractor should be able to provide these estimating services. When such services are provided, the owner should require budget confirmations at each stage of document completion.

When project cost estimates are performed before construction documents are complete, allowances and contingencies sufficient to cover the incomplete work should be included. Initially, an estimate will include "safe" numbers to avoid underestimating costs. As the documents are completed, revised estimates should reflect more accurate numbers, and the overall price may decrease.

Contractors who better understand a firm's documentation methods generally are able to develop more accurate estimates from partially completed drawings than are contractors unfamiliar with a firm's work. When working with a contractor for the first time, architects may find it helpful to show the contractor examples of their drawings from past projects.

It is also important for architects to review pricing issues related to incomplete documents with owners. The goal is to avoid unrealistic expectations on the part of the owner. The accompanying chart showing the relationship between completed documents and project cost estimates can be used to help an owner understand how contractors price partially completed documents.

MANAGING THE SUBMITTAL REVIEW PROCESS

The general conditions require the contractor to provide a submittal schedule coordinated with the construction schedule. The submittal schedule provides a basis for knowing how long substitutions may be proposed. The contractor should submit recommended substitutions no later than the date specified in the schedule.

The contractor can only develop the submittal schedule after the project construction schedule has been completed. The scheduled installation dates in the construction schedule determine when a product must be acquired or fabricated and delivered to the site. Therefore, each submittal needs to be reviewed and processed in a timely fashion. Many contracts include a time limit for submittal review, and a

▶ Construction Contract Administration (8.5) discusses record keeping, document changes, and submittal reviews in further detail.

contractor may intend to submit the product with only the contracted review time remaining, leaving no time for dealing with unforeseen challenges.

The contractor's submittal schedule is an opportunity for the architect to review and comment on whether allocated review times are reasonable. Submittals should be scheduled sufficiently in advance of installation to accommodate reasonable review periods, an acceptable flow of submittals, and if needed, time for resubmitting them. Situations to avoid could include having too many submittals sent at the same time; room finishes submitted too early; or the submittal of doors, frames, and hardware at different times when they obviously need to be reviewed concurrently.

It is helpful to meet with the contractor to discuss plans for preparing the submittal schedule so the contractor is aware of specific review requirements. Be careful not to "approve" contractor schedules, which could mean the architect assumes a responsibility that is not required under the professional services contract.

Sometimes, the architect may not be familiar with a proposed product or be aware of its performance history. As a consequence, architects may find it difficult to accept an unfamiliar product in a short period of time. The research and evaluation of a proposed substitution should be borne by the contractor and approved by the architect. Wording with respect to the performance requirements for substitutions can be added to the general conditions. The following is such an example:

Contractor warrants that substituted material or system will perform the same as the originally specified material or system would have performed. Should accepted substitution fail to perform as required, Contractor shall replace substitute material or system with that originally specified and bear costs incurred thereby.

If project submittals were not required, it would be difficult to determine whether the construction conforms to the design intent until the work is in place. Submittals are the basis for determining work conformance and adherence to design intent. The following is a summary of basic steps that will help architects manage the submittal review process:

1. Provide specifications that include necessary submittal requirements.
2. Review the submittal procedures in the preconstruction conference.
3. Enforce the general conditions requiring the contractor to furnish a submittal schedule coordinated with the construction schedule.
4. Advise the owner and the contractor that if submittals are not provided according to the schedule, additional services may be required to cover additional time for reviewing out-of-sequence submittals. Do not accelerate the review process or review submittals out of phase unless compensation is provided.
5. When a contractor does not follow the submittal schedule, take action as prescribed in the contract documents.

CONTROLLING SUBSTITUTIONS

When design changes are considered early in project delivery (especially prior to the bidding/negotiation and construction phases), the more likely it will be to maintain or even increase the intended quality of the design for the same or at a lower cost. But when design changes are undertaken after completion of the construction documents or after construction has begun, the potential for improving quality or lowering life cycle costs is decreased and becomes more difficult to achieve.

Similarly, the processes of value analysis and value engineering (VE) used to evaluate alternative building products and systems are most effective when applied during the design phases where they can identify alternatives that maintain or increase quality at the same or a lower cost. Value analysis when applied in this way has a rich tradition of increasing design quality. However, when undertaken after completion of the construction documents or after construction has started, the process often results primarily in "cost cutting" with little or no regard to the effects on quality and functional performance. This is especially the case in many design-build, fast-track, and developer-driven projects.

Treat contractor-proposed changes occurring during the phases of bidding/ negotiation or construction as contractor substitutions, since the architect's design has been completed. Be aware that such substitutions may require modification of the construction documents and may require additional coordination efforts.

To help prevent substitutions from diluting quality and lowering performance for the intended design, architects have several options, which are discussed below.

▶ For detailed information on the VA process and an application example, see Value Analysis (7.4).

Establish Performance Criteria

It is important to set performance criteria for proposed products or systems. This is especially so when a proper VA process isn't being used. These criteria will help establish the validity of proposed substitutions and enforce certain contractual obligations of the contractor with respect to the substitution process. MASTERSPEC® recommends that each proposed substitution meet the following criteria:

- Offers the owner a substantial advantage in cost, time, energy conservation, or other considerations, after deducting additional responsibilities the owner may have to assume. Additional responsibilities may include compensation to the architect for redesign and evaluation services or increased cost of other construction by the owner.
- Does not require extensive revisions to the contract documents.
- Is consistent with the contract documents and will produce indicated results.
- Is fully documented and properly submitted.
- Will not adversely affect the contractor's construction schedule.
- Has received necessary approvals from authorities having jurisdiction.
- Is compatible with other portions of the work.
- Has been coordinated with other portions of the work.
- Has a warranty available as the one originally specified.
- Has been coordinated with all trades if it involves more than one.

Review each proposed substitution carefully to determine if the savings to the owner are reasonable and if the change is acceptable from a quality and performance standpoint. Setting benchmarks for cost, quality, and performance may sometimes result in designs that exceed code requirements, but for some projects this level of quality may be desired as a minimum. Keep in mind that owners are often motivated to accept a substitution simply to save money, but the architect is responsible for determining if a product is equivalent to meet the requirements of its intended use.

Use Substitution Request Forms

Use of a substitution request form can make it easier to organize and control the substitution process. This form requires the attaching of supporting catalog data and product specifications for use in evaluating the proposed substitution. It is not the architect's responsibility to research a product and locate the data a second time. This obligation has already been fulfilled in specifying the original item. The contractor, supplier, or subcontractor who proposed the change is responsible for providing supporting research and product data.

The substitution request form includes an affidavit from the contractor stating that the information contained within it is correct. It also states that design changes and their associated costs will be reimbursed from any savings realized. Finally, the form requires a representation by the contractor and a manufacturer's certification of equal

To Contract Manager: ─────────────────────────────────────

Project No.: ──────────────────── Project Name: ─────────────────────

SPECIFIED ITEM:

─────── ─────── ─────── ──────────────────

Section   Page   Paragraph   Description

The undersigned [General Contractor] [Construction Manager] requests consideration of the following:

PROPOSED SUBSTITUTION: ─────────────────────────────────

(Include all product data as indicated in required Specification Section and any supplemental information as requested by the Architect.)

The undersigned [General Contractor] [Construction Manager] warrants to the Architect and Owner that the following paragraphs, unless modified on attachments, are correct.

1. The Proposed Substitution does not affect dimensions shown on Drawings.

2. The cost reduction/increase indicated in item 5 below includes costs for changes to the building design, including engineering, design, detailing and construction costs caused by the requested Substitution. Any additional costs resulting from this substitution will be reimbursed from the cost savings in item 5 or, in its absence, funded as a project cost.

3. The Proposed Substitution will have no adverse effect on other trades, the construction schedule, or specified warranty requirements.

4. Maintenance and service parts will be locally available for the Proposed Substitution.

The [General Contractor] [Construction Manager] further warrants to the Architect and Owner that the function and quality of the Proposed Substitution are equivalent or superior to the Specified Item. The [General Contractor] [Construction Manager] further warrants that the specification section intent has been met.

5. Total Cost Savings/Increase to the Owner: $ ──────────────

Manufacturer's Certification of Equal Quality:

I, ─────────────────────────, represent the manufacturer of the Proposed Substitution item and hereby certify and warrant to the Architect and Owner that the function and quality of the Proposed Substitution are equivalent or superior to the Specified Item.

Manufacturer's Representative   Company:

─────────────────────── Date: ─────────── ───────────────────────

PART 3: THE PROJECT

ACCEPTANCES:

1. [General Contractor] [Construction Manager] Acceptance: Company:

   _____ Date: _____   _____

2. Owner Acceptance: Company:

   _____ Date: _____   _____

3. Architect Acceptance: Company:

   _____ Date: _____   _____

                    RECOMMEND ACCEPTANCE: **YES**   **NO**

HKS, Inc., Dallas, Texas

quality, which must state "the function and quality of the proposed substitution are equivalent or superior to the specified item." Since some substituted products or systems are not equivalent or superior in some cases, this wording will force the issue of providing a credit to the owner for the reduced quality or reduced performance.

Document Accepted Substitutions

Since substitutions may be allowed to continue after construction documents have been issued, accepted substitutions should be exhibited in the owner-contractor agreement. When this list of accepted substitutions is added to the drawings and specifications, it is important to document their substitution status. This can be accomplished by having the contractor provide all supplemental details and data to ensure a substituted product or system will perform as intended. Include with the substitution list the qualification, "All changes are substitutions as defined in the contract documents and all substitution requirements and conditions apply."

A mere list of substitutions exhibited in the contract is usually not, however, sufficient to adequately document the quality and performance requirements of those products. Appropriate specifications must be included. If the contractor does not provide specifications and the architect is asked to provide this information, it may be appropriate to request an additional services fee, since this service is not included in the architect's basic services. Specifying, detailing, and coordinating products for an architectural project are complicated tasks, and reviewing and accepting substitutions is no less complicated.

If the owner pays an additional fee to revise the drawings and specifications to incorporate substituted products and systems, take measures to maintain the "substitution classification" on each substituted item. This can be accomplished by noting each item as a substitution on the drawings, which allows you to issue a certificate of substantial completion without having to list the substitution as owner accepted nonconforming work.

Remember that you have been contracted to determine if the work, when completed, is in substantial conformance to your documents. If an installed product or system does not conform to the contract documents and a certificate of substantial completion is issued without qualification, this could misrepresent the level of project completion. This could expose risks later should the certification be challenged.

When the Owner Overrides Recommendations

Opposing a substitution is not always easy since the specified product often costs more than what is being proposed. In these instances, help the owner understand why the originally specified product was chosen. If the owner fully appreciates the architect's position, there is a greater chance for retaining the originally specified design or product.

When you do not want to make a proposed change because you consider it unsafe or in conflict with code requirements, inform the owner, the contractor, and the building official of this in writing.

In the event the owner is adamant about making a change you firmly disagree with, one option is to refuse to change the drawings unless the owner provides a written indemnity against subsequent failure and damages. While it is unlikely an owner will agree to this, demanding it will firmly communicate your position and help the owner understand why the change is not supported. (This is a bold step that flies in the face of the architect's "service" mentality, so consider it carefully and be sure to consult with your attorney because of potential liability issues.)

Be aware that paragraph 12.3.1 of AIA Document A201–2007, General Conditions of the Contract for Construction, allows the owner to accept work "not in accordance with the requirements of the Contract Documents." If the owner chooses to accept nonconforming work, the architect may help the owner recognize any future implications of that decision.

STEPS FOR AVOIDING CONSTRUCTION NONCONFORMANCE

The determination of nonconforming work can be more difficult when the work has been covered by finish work or subsequent installations. Some aspects of construction provide more opportunity for nonconformance because they are concealed by other work. Examples are listed here:

- Foundation fill materials
- Steel reinforcing
- Concealed fasteners
- Furred enclosures
- Substrates
- Flashing
- Above-ceiling installations
- Below-grade installations
- In-wall installations
- Roofing
- Waterproofing
- Base coatings

It is impossible to observe all work conditions before they are covered up. However, adhering to the steps suggested in the following list may improve the chance of avoiding concealed, nonconforming work:

- During the preconstruction conference, review with the contractor the specification requirements for notifying the architect prior to covering up the work.
- In buildings with modular ceilings, have the contractor include in the project schedule an "above-the-ceiling punch list" review before the ceiling tiles are installed. This is especially helpful in medical facilities, where above-ceiling mechanical, electrical, and plumbing systems are concentrated and extensive.

- Recommend to the owner that services include special reviews, such as observations of reinforcing steel, roofing installation reviews, and soil placement monitoring. These services may require special consultants.
- Require preinstallation conferences for systems that must be coordinated among multiple trades, such as roofing, brick walls and flashing, and exterior cement plaster stucco. Systems related to the building envelope fall within this category.
- If work has been covered and you have questions about the concealed installation, have the contractor uncover the work as provided for in the contract documents. Remember that if the contractor notified you before covering the work and the work is correctly installed, the owner will be required to pay for the uncovering and replacement. Additional contract time for both architect and contractor may also be required if the investigation extends project completion.
- If the project scope warrants, recommend that the owner include a full-time project representative in the scope of services.

IMPROVING THE OUTCOME

Cost-motivated actions that can chip away at the intent and quality of design are all too common in the A/E/C industry. However, it is unlikely that efforts by some owners and contractors to aggressively improve the bottom line will cease. While better-funded projects may escape such pressures, many projects will be confronted with compromises wrought by the economic climate and market competition.

Design changes that result in reduced product and system performance, finishes of lesser quality, materials of lower durability, and similar changes can be hard for design professionals to accept, but there is comfort in knowing there are management techniques for maintaining the integrity of design. Budget control, value analysis, construction observation, and careful attention to substitution requests and submittal reviews offer a greater chance of realizing what the designer intended.

For More Information
Michael D. Dell'Isola addresses all aspects of managing project costs, including budgeting, estimating, monitoring, and the role of value analysis (value engineering)

EXAMPLES OF DESIGN COMPROMISE

The two examples that follow illustrate project design compromises. The first example involves substituting a stock skylight system for a custom-designed system. The second example involves a change in a detail that was considered a substitution.

Manipulation of the Submittal Process

In this example, the architect's design was compromised when a contractor attempted to reduce costs by manipulating the submittal process. The contractor waited until there was insufficient time to fabricate the specified product and submitted a lesser-quality, stock model under the premise that fabrication of the specified item would adversely impact project completion.

The specified product was a custom skylight system for a group of connected, low-rise suburban corporate office buildings in a campus configuration. The design included four three-story brick buildings with standing-seam metal roofs and an extensive skylight system over an interior landscaped area that ran through each building. The skylight design was a custom powder-coated profile to complement the highly finished interior. The specifications called for the submittal schedule to be incorporated into the project construction schedule. The contractor, however, did not provide the specified submittal schedule and waited to submit the skylight shop drawings until just before the installation was scheduled to begin. The contractor submitted a stock, off-the-shelf skylight product, along with a

(continued)

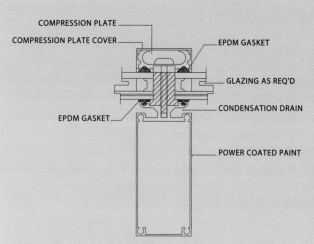

The originally specified custom-designed skylight allows for drainage of condensation and would require cleaning less often.

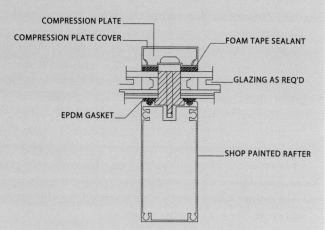

The proposed product substitution uses a stock profile without condensation drainage and would require a higher level of maintenance.

request that the submittal be reviewed and returned within ten working days.

The architect immediately rejected the submittal and directed the contractor to submit the specified product. The contractor responded that there was insufficient time to fabricate the custom profile without delaying installation, which would delay scheduled project completion. A meeting was called immediately with the owner, architect, and contractor to discuss the matter. The contractor offered a credit amount that was a fraction of the value of the specified profile with the caveat that the project would not be delayed if immediate approval of the stock profile was given. Although the architect recommended against the change, the owner accepted the offer. The owner then directed the architect to prepare a change order to reduce the contract amount by the credit amount offered by the contractor. The architect refused to change the drawings to reflect the cheaper profile and directed the contractor to submit a substitution request as a condition of accepting the stock profile. The architect explained to the owner that administering the change as a substitution would provide greater protection against failure of the cheaper product to perform. The architect received and accepted the substitution request, and the original shop drawings were approved with the qualification that the stock profile was considered to be a substitution.

A change order was issued to reduce the contract amount by the accepted credit amount, and "substituted skylight system by contractor" was noted on the drawings where the skylight was indicated. This way of recording the substitution made it possible for the architect to issue the certificate of substantial completion without having to note the stock skylight system as nonconforming work.

The architect managed risk by not changing the drawings. However, the intended design of the new facility was compromised and the owner received a standard skylight system at a cost exceeding its true value. The submittal schedule required by the architect would have served as a tool to force the contractor to plan for and delineate the submittal sequence, duration, and fabrication times. Because the contractor did not provide the required schedule, the contractor was able to use time as a lever to force acceptance of the cheaper solution.

Use of Alternative Construction Detail

This example involves a negotiated cost-plus-a-fee contract for a two-story suburban office building. The building contained an HVAC duct designed to supply air to a large atrium at the building entry. The original design called for the duct to be installed below grade in a concrete trench. The building had a perimeter subsurface drain at an elevation approximately fifteen feet below the trench and the drain from the trench was routed to the storm drainage system.

Pricing on the project was substantially over budget, and the contractor initiated an aggressive process to identify alternatives. A resulting proposal suggested replacing the concrete trench with a membrane and foam pellets around the duct, an assumption being that the subsurface drain around the basement at the lower elevation would catch any groundwater near the duct. The mechanical engineer and the geotechnical engineer reviewed the proposal and accepted it under the condition that a mixture of sand and cement was to be used around the duct in lieu of the foam pellets and that the duct was to be sealed from moisture intrusion. The change was designated as a substitution, and the contractor provided a detail of the new duct design. The substitution was accepted for a credit of $30,000.

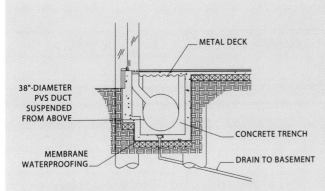

The original design locates the HVAC ductwork below grade in a concrete trench that isolates the duct from water intrusion.

Soon after the project was completed, high humidity levels were experienced in the atrium, along with odors of mildew. An investigation revealed that the duct had filled with water as a result of landscape irrigation and seasonal rain. Even after the water was removed from the duct, subsequent irrigation and rainstorms again filled the duct with water.

The owner notified the contractor of the condition, and the contractor responded that because the architect and engineer approved the change to the design, they were responsible for correcting the problem. The designers responded that the change was a substitution and the contractor would be responsible for the problem under the specification requirements for substitutions.

Because the change was designated as a substitution, the contractor was required to replace the system with the one as originally designed and specified. However, since the architect accepted the substitution, the firm was not off the hook and participated in the repair costs. Nonetheless, this example shows why an accepted change from the contractor should be designated as a substitution. When processed as a substitution, the language in the contract documents regarding substitutions will provide relief—at no additional cost to the owner—should the change not perform as represented.

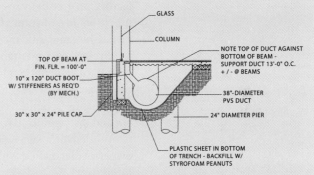

The proposed design substitution locates the HVAC ductwork in a membrane-lined trench with Styrofoam fill.

in controlling project costs in *Architect's Essentials of Cost Management* (Wiley, 2002).

A Guide to Successful Construction: Effective Contract Administration (BNi Publications, 1999), by Arthur F. O'Leary, covers the roles, responsibilities, and tasks of the design professional for construction phase services. Chapter 12 contains an in-depth discussion of shop drawing and submittal procedures.

Additional information about value analysis can be found on the Web sites of SAVE International (www.value-eng.org), an international society devoted to the advancement and promotion of value methodology, and the Canadian Society of Value Analysis (www.scav-csva.org), which promotes the value analysis methodology.

9.6 Project Closeouts

Douglas C. Hartman, FAIA, FCSI, CCS, CCCA, SCIP, LEED AP

Clients value the closeout increment of a construction project. Effective project closeout enables completion of unfinished work, results in a completed building delivered in acceptable condition, and facilitates provision of essential postconstruction documentation to the client.

Ask most building owners who have recently completed a construction project and they will say that one of the most important aspects of the architect's services (aside from the obvious need for a functional design) is effective project closeout. Although architects tend to view the construction documents they prepare as their primary work product, most clients also consider other services essential to satisfactory project delivery. These include successful construction administration, determination of substantial and final completion of construction, orderly transfer of ownership, and guidance on operations and maintenance issues.

Project documentation that remains incomplete or work that does not meet contract requirements can lurk beneath the surface of what otherwise appears to be a successful project. Should incomplete requirements or documentation cause or contribute to problems in building function or maintenance, the situation can vary from unpleasant and disappointing to disastrous and litigious. It would be unfortunate for an architect to deliver a successful design in a timely fashion within budget only to find the owner is dissatisfied with project closeout and will not recommend the architect for future work.

Defining and clearly documenting project closeout tasks in Division 01—General Requirements of the specifications can help foster an efficient and successful closeout process. Keeping project closeout in mind during the construction phase is very important as well, and it should be a regular agenda item in scheduled project meetings.

Tools and processes have been developed to guide the project closeout process and, if effectively utilized and implemented, these can result in project completion that meets the expectations of everyone involved. Diligence and focus on achieving a successful project and facilitating initial owner occupancy are necessary to coordinate the activities and responsibilities of all project participants.

Successful project closeout means different things to each participant. To the contractor, it means resolving the punch list, reconciling the job cost, and collecting the final payment. To the architect, it is the satisfaction of seeing the design result in a completed project that substantially conforms to the construction documents and functions as intended to meet the client's needs. To owners, however, closeout can bring nervous anticipation and anxiety as the operation and ownership of the facility are transferred into their hands. A process for an orderly project closeout, the roles of each participant in the process, and a means of measuring the relative success of project closeout accomplishments are identified in this topic.

Douglas C. Hartman is president of INSPEC, a Dallas-based specialty firm providing specifications, sustainable design, and accessibility consulting services. He regularly teaches courses in contract administration and contributed to the Construction Administration module of a previous edition of *The Project Resource Manual—CSI Manual of Practice.*

RESULTS OF POOR CLOSEOUT

Adverse effects of incomplete project closeout can range from the inconsequential to the disastrous. The following examples illustrate pitfalls that could be experienced by failing to comply with closeout requirements.

Owner Occupancy Date Omitted

AIA G704–2000, Certificate of Substantial Completion, specifies a date and time when the owner may take beneficial occupancy of a project. In this example, the author of the document (the architect) fails to obtain and fill in this important information, and the other signers of the document do not notice this omission. Consequently, the date on which all project warranties commence is not identified, a potentially serious problem when the owner attempts to obtain subsequent warranty work. Potentially more serious is the lack of a specific date on which the owner's obligations for operation, maintenance, security, insurance, and utilities begin. If damage should occur, this omission increases the chance of a period without insurance coverage or of disputes over coverage between the property insurance companies of the owner and contractor. Attention to this detail is extremely important.

Final Change Order Omitted

The general conditions of a contract for construction require that when the cost of the work is more or less than a specified allowance, the architect will prepare and execute a change order to adjust the contract sum accordingly. In this example, the architect failed to prepare and execute a final change order at the end of the project to reconcile project allowances and cost contingencies. The contractor's final application for payment included the total allowance and contingency costs, although the actual cost of the work in each category was less. The owner was not aware of the cost difference, and the contractor apparently overlooked it when preparing the final payment application. Months after the project was closed out, the owner discovered the error during an audit. The owner was not successful at recovering the money from the contractor, and subsequently legal action was initiated against the contractor alleging fraud and against the architect alleging improper certification of the final application for payment.

Maintenance Training Omitted

Requirements for demonstration of the HVAC, electrical, fire protection, communication, and other systems and training of the owner's staff are clearly defined in the contract documents in this example. While the architect's role is simply to confirm that the training was provided, the content of the training was never clearly defined or executed by the contractor. Because the owner's staff had limited knowledge of high-tech controls and instrumentation, and never grasped the complexity of the instructions being communicated, they began operation of critical building systems with inadequate preparation. Operation and maintenance manuals were not submitted during closeout, and the owner's staff failed to de-energize critical electrical systems before HVAC systems were shut down. The resulting damage to the HVAC system required fabrication of new equipment, which took more than a month. The owner was forced to obtain expensive temporary cooling equipment until the problem was resolved, which prompted the owner to take legal action against the architect.

INTEGRATING CLOSEOUT INTO THE PROJECT DELIVERY PROCESS

Thought should be given to project closeout before the owner-architect agreement is signed. Convincing the owner to retain an architect during the construction administration phase not only makes good sense but is mandated by law in many states (in those states, construction administration is deemed an integral part of architectural services and must be provided by a registered architect on projects that require an architect's seal). Nonetheless, the inclusion of construction administration in design services can sometimes be a hard sell, especially with owner-builder and design-builder arrangements and on projects that generally do not enlist full architect services during construction, such as residential and interior tenant improvements. Due to the serious legal implications associated with certifying substantial completion, it is not advisable for architects to agree to issue a certificate unless they periodically review the construction, review submittals and substitutions, and have the authority to reject nonconforming work.

Decisions about project closeout procedures need to be confirmed and documented during the design phase. Closeout procedures include clearly defined requirements written into Division 01–General Requirements of the specifications, including the owner's desires for items such as record documents, demonstration and training, and operations and maintenance information. Determining the owner's need for closeout documentation is no less important than determining the owner's requirements for items such as bonding, insurance, and method of contracting, as solicited in AIA Document G612–2001, Owner's Instructions to the Architect Regarding the Construction Contract, Insurance and Bonds, and Bidding Procedures. Addressing questions such as the following will help the architect learn what project closeout services the client expects:

- Is there a need for multiple substantial completion certificates?
- Does the owner wish to be involved in reviewing or administering punch lists?
- What amount of retainage is preferred, and what formula will be used to determine how it will be released?
- Is there a surety involved that may require notification when retainage is released?
- What are the owner's preferences for submission of record documents: electronic files (i.e., changes are input electronically), reproducible copies of hard-copy markups, or hard-copy markups only?
- What is the preferred extent of record documents? Are only drawings required, or should record specifications (including a list of materials incorporated into the work), record submittals, or color boards and material samples also be included?
- How should warranties and certifications be organized?
- What are the owner's preferences for demonstration and training? What level of demonstration and training is needed for each specific system? Is video documentation of the demonstration and training required? What follow-up mechanical services are required at the first seasonal change?
- Does the owner want the architect to include building commissioning services?
- What are the owner's preferences for operation and maintenance manuals? How many copies are required? How should the manuals be organized?
- What are the owner's preferences for maintenance materials? What products should be included? What percentage of extra products or "attic stock" should be provided?

AIA Document D200–1995, Project Checklist, provides an opportunity to identify and plan for closeout early in the project delivery process. It contains references to closeout in Section 7, Construction Contract Administration, and Section 8, Post-Construction Services. The document can serve not only as a checklist of tasks to be decided with the owner but also as a permanent record of the decisions and actions of the owner, contractor, and architect.

Project closeout tasks continue during the construction documentation phase, as the specific requirements agreed to by the owner and the architect begin to be incorporated into a project manual. AIA Document A201–2007, General Conditions of the Contract for Construction, is a good starting point for identifying contract closeout requirements. Similar provisions are included in the engineer's version (EJCDC C-700), which is commonly used by consulting engineers on projects that consist primarily of

Contractor

- Inspects the project and prepares the punch list (outstanding items to be completed or corrected)
- Submits notice of substantial completion to architect
- Obtains agreement for the owner's acceptance of responsibility for security, maintenance, heat, utilities, damage to the work, and insurance
- Signs certificate of substantial completion
- Completes punch list items as stipulated in the certificate of substantial completion
- Submits required closeout documents and materials
- Submits notice of final completion
- Submits final application for payment and signs final change order
- Warrants to the owner and architect that the work is new, free from defects, and in accordance with the contract documents

Architect

- Reviews the contractor's punch list and supplements it as needed
- Inspects the project to determine substantial completion
- Confirms owner-accepted nonconforming work
- Prepares and issues a certificate of substantial completion with specified date, with attached punch list, if appropriate, and notes any owner-accepted nonconforming work
- Reviews closeout materials to determine contract compliance for submittals
- Prepares final change order
- Inspects project to determine final completion
- Advises contractor to submit final application for payment
- Processes final application for payment

Owner

- Agrees to accept responsibility for security, maintenance, heat, utilities, damage to the work, and insurance
- Signs certificate of substantial completion
- Signs final change order and makes final payment

engineering services. The provisions in these standard general conditions identify the responsibilities for action of each party, as shown in the accompanying sidebar.

These required actions should be clearly described in the general requirements sections of the specifications. In addition, the list of responsibilities should be expanded to include requirements for the following:

- Punch list procedures
- Insurance changeover requirements
- Start-up of systems
- Testing, adjusting, and balancing of systems, including commissioning reports
- Systems demonstration
- Operation and maintenance manuals
- Project record documents
- Spare parts and maintenance materials
- Warranties, workmanship bonds, maintenance service agreements, and final certifications
- Final pest control inspection and warranty
- Final construction completion photographs
- Certified survey, final property survey and survey record log
- Delivery of tools and extra stock materials to the owner
- Changeover of permanent locks and delivery of keys to the owner

Implementation and Enforcement

It may become necessary to encourage the contractor to sustain focus on closeout procedures by enforcing any specified remedies for failure to comply with contract requirements. Such remedies can take several forms:

- Withholding a portion of periodic payments for failure to keep record documents current
- Withholding a portion of periodic payments for nonconforming work
- Refusing to release retainage until closeout documents, testing and adjusting, demonstration and training, operation and maintenance manuals, spare parts and maintenance materials, and warranties and bonds are submitted
- Assessing the contractor for time and expenses of the architect (by way of additional services billing to the owner who then assesses the contractor by means of a deduct change order) when substantial completion inspections are requested before the work is ready or when the architect must repeatedly return to the site only to find that punch list work continues to be incomplete

One way to maintain everyone's focus on the importance of the closeout process is to conduct a project closeout conference before substantial completion. Such a conference can be appended to a regularly scheduled progress meeting and should include a review of all contract closeout requirements, timing requirements for each, and an identification of the party responsible for preparing, conducting, or submitting the specific requirement. A project closeout checklist that identifies the required closeout documents and activities can be distributed to the attendees.

Substantial Completion

Substantial completion is the stage in the progress of the work when the work, or a designated portion thereof, is sufficiently complete, according to the contract documents, for the owner to occupy or use the work for the intended purpose. Before requesting an inspection for substantial completion, the contractor should be required, through amendment of the appropriate portions of Division 01 of the specifications, to perform the following tasks:

1. Prepare a list of items to be completed and corrected (commonly known as a punch list), as required in AIA Document A201–2007, General Conditions of the Contract for Construction. (It is not uncommon for the architect to make major amendments to the punch list.)
2. Coordinate with the owner regarding pending insurance, maintenance, security, and utility changeover requirements, and inform the architect.
3. Submit evidence of final, continuing insurance coverage that complies with insurance requirements.
4. Instruct the owner's personnel in operation, adjustment, and maintenance of products, equipment, and systems.
5. Inform the architect of the time required to resolve punch list items.
6. Obtain and submit occupancy permits from authorities having jurisdiction (AHJs), if applicable. These can include permits from the local building official and from local and state health departments (in the case of restaurants and health care facilities), as well as reviews for accessibility compliance, among others.
7. Deliver spare parts and extra stock materials to a location designated by the owner.
8. Change to permanent lock cylinders and deliver the keys to the owner.
9. Complete start-up testing of systems for operating equipment.
10. Submit test/adjust/balance records for HVAC air and hydronic systems.
11. Terminate and remove temporary facilities, mock-ups, and construction tools from the project site.
12. Complete final cleaning requirements.

Once the above tasks are complete, the architect conducts an inspection of the work to determine the date or dates of substantial completion. The date of substantial completion is the date when the work (or a portion thereof) is in a condition to be occupied or utilized. This date is not determined by the owner or contractor, and it is not necessarily the date on which the owner actually occupies the project. This distinction is very important, and it is critical that it be determined independently by the architect and appropriate consultants, without the influence of any other party, particularly if the contractor is being assessed for liquidated damages for late completion.

The Construction Specifications Institute has developed a form for the punch list to be attached to the certificate of substantial completion. Form 14.1a, available electronically from CSI, can be used to organize punch list items for subcontractor assignment and status determination. When the architect's inspection to determine substantial completion has been completed, items found to be incomplete or uncorrected should be attached to the certificate. This amended punch list should reference the certificate to which it is attached.

It is also important to append a list of all owner-accepted nonconforming work to the certificate of substantial completion. Very few projects conform to contract requirements in total. If latent nonconforming work is discovered that is not noted on the certificate, the architect could be at risk for misrepresenting the completed condition. As another precaution, it is also recommended that the architect obtain written confirmation from all consultants that their portions of the work are substantially complete. These written confirmations can be attached to the architect's certificate.

Final Change Order

The final application for payment cannot be processed until the final cost of the work has been determined. To accomplish this, all variables in the value of the work must be reconciled through a final change order. Examples of such variables include the following:

- Allowances, including contingency allowances
- Alternates
- Construction change directives
- Owner-accepted nonconforming work
- Extension of the one-year correction period for work not performed until after substantial completion
- Extension of the one-year correction period for work not corrected until after substantial completion

The final change order must be executed by the architect, owner, and contractor before submission of the final application for payment, which will include cost adjustments that result from the final change order.

Final Completion

Before final completion, the contractor should be required to perform the following tasks:

- Submit a final application for payment.
- Submit a copy of the architect's substantial completion punch list, with confirmation that each item has been completed or otherwise resolved for acceptance.
- Obtain consent of sureties to final payment if required.

Upon confirmation of the above and receipt of a written request from the contractor for final inspection, the architect proceeds with a final inspection or notifies the contractor of existing unfulfilled requirements. If the architect finds the work acceptable

While AIA Document A201 requires the architect to observe the work during scheduled site visits, the architect must perform inspections for substantial and final completion. Inspections require a greater degree of in-depth review and verification of the work.

under the terms of the contract documents and the contract is fully performed, the architect may issue a final certificate for payment.

PROJECT RECORD DOCUMENTS

Typically, the contractor is required to maintain a separate set of contract documents and shop drawings at the project site. These are to be marked to show actual installations that vary from what is shown on the original contract documents. Project record documentation requirements should be reviewed in detail during the preconstruction conference. The contractor should record the data as soon as possible after obtaining it. Either the contract drawings or shop drawings may be marked, whichever most completely and accurately show actual physical conditions. If shop drawings are marked, they should be cross-referenced on the record drawings.

Preferably, the contractor will mark record sets with erasable colored pencils, using different colors to distinguish between changes for different categories of the work at the same location. When applicable, these notations should include construction change directive numbers, change order numbers, alternate numbers, and similar identification.

In addition, it is important for the contractor to submit record specifications, including addenda and contract modifications. In particular, the actual products installed should be indicated to update the list of several acceptable options included in most specifications. As well, the appropriate proprietary name and model number should be marked in the specifications for the products, materials, and equipment furnished.

Record product data submittals should be marked to indicate the actual product installed when it varies substantially from that indicated in the original product data submittal. Particular attention should be given to information about concealed products and installations that cannot be readily identified. Significant changes in the product delivered to the project site and changes in the manufacturer's written instructions for installation should also be included.

Remember that the architect checks the contractor's marked-up record drawings not for accuracy but to determine if the contractor has complied with the record-keeping and submittal requirements of the contract. The architect should discuss this activity with the owner to be sure the owner understands this distinction. In addition, the architect should affix a stamp on the record drawings that explains the source of the marked-up information.

In addition to printed copies of these documents, electronic copies should be specified and required to be provided by the contractor. Also, providing record drawings in editable digital files is invaluable to an owner when the need arises for renovation, remodeling, and additions to the facility.

OPERATION AND MAINTENANCE MANUALS

All operation and maintenance data should be assembled in manuals, bound and indexed, and placed in heavy-duty binders. This material should include a complete set of specific data for each system and piece of equipment installed in the project. Electronic format (PDF is almost universally preferred) should also be required for these manuals to serve as a permanent record in the event the printed copies are lost.

Maintenance data should include information not only for operating systems but also for building products and applied materials and finishes. Product data should include catalog number and designations as to size, composition, and color and texture of the product. Particularly important for interior finishes are instructions for care and maintenance, including the manufacturer's recommendations for cleaning agents and methods, precautions against detrimental agents and methods, and the recommended schedule for cleaning and maintenance. Moisture-control and weather-exposed products should include recommendations for inspection, maintenance, and repair.

Warranties

Copies of required warranties and bonds for each system, component, and finish specified to comply with a particular warranty period in excess of the correction period should be assembled for easy access by the owner. If the owner takes partial occupancy, warranties should be submitted within fifteen days of completion of the portions of the work occupied by the owner. Warranties should be organized into an orderly sequence based on the table of contents in the project manual and bound in heavy-duty three-ring binders.

Each warranty should be marked to identify the product or installation, complete with a typed description, including the name of the product and the name, address, and telephone number of the installer.

Demonstration and Training

The owner's personnel need to be properly trained to adjust, operate, and maintain systems and equipment. The contractor must provide instructors experienced in operation and maintenance procedures, especially for HVAC and control systems. Instruction should occur at mutually agreed-upon times, and similar instruction at the start of each season should be required for equipment that requires seasonal operation. Scheduling for training, including notification of dates, times, length of instruction, and course content, should be coordinated by the architect.

The contractor should develop an instruction program that includes individual training modules for each system and for equipment that is not part of a system, provided this requirement is clearly specified in Division 01 of the specifications. For each training module, the contractor should be required to develop a learning objective and teaching outline. Instruction may occur in the following areas:

- Review of documentation
- Operations
- Adjustments
- Troubleshooting
- Maintenance
- Repair

FINAL CLEANING

Prior to final completion, the contractor is required to conduct cleaning and waste removal operations. Final cleaning should be performed by experienced workers who know and understand the substrates to be cleaned and the methods that will not damage them. Unless indicated otherwise, cleaning should result in a condition one would expect in a commercial building cleaning and maintenance program, complying with the product manufacturer's written instructions.

Cleaning that occurs prior to substantial completion should include the following:

- Removal of rubbish, waste material, litter, and other foreign substances from project site and grounds in areas disturbed by construction activities, including landscape development areas
- Broom-clean sweeping of paved and unoccupied spaces and removal of spills, stains, and other foreign deposits

- Raking of grounds that are neither planted nor paved to a smooth, even-textured surface
- Removal from project site of tools, construction equipment, machinery, and surplus material
- Cleaning of exposed exterior and interior hard-surfaced finishes to a dirt-free condition, free of stains, films, and similar foreign substances
- Removal of debris from roofs, plenums, shafts, trenches, vaults, manholes, attics, and similar spaces
- Vacuuming of carpet, removal of debris and stains
- Cleaning of mirrors and glass in doors and windows; removal of glazing compounds and other noticeable, vision-obscuring materials; replacement of chipped or broken glass and other damaged transparent materials; polishing of mirrors and glass, taking care not to scratch surfaces
- Removal of labels that are not permanent
- Touch-up and other repair and restoration of marred, exposed finishes and surfaces, including replacement of finishes and surfaces that cannot be satisfactorily repaired or restored or that already show evidence of unsuccessful repair or restoration
- Replacement of parts subject to unusual operating conditions
- Cleaning of plumbing fixtures to a sanitary condition
- Replacement of disposable filters and cleaning of permanent air filters
- Cleaning of exposed surfaces of diffusers, registers, and grills
- Cleaning of ducts, blowers, and coils if units were operated without filters during construction
- Cleaning of light fixtures, lamps, globes, and reflectors to function with full efficiency, including replacement of burned-out lamps and defective or noisy starters in fluorescent and mercury vapor fixtures to comply with requirements for new fixtures

Final cleaning requirements should include a prohibition against discharge of volatile, harmful, or dangerous materials into the drainage systems.

SUSTAINABLE DESIGN DOCUMENTATION

As the movement toward designing and constructing our built environment with an emphasis on minimizing the impact on the natural environment continues to build momentum, an important component of project closeout documentation may include assembly of documentation in support of LEED® (Leadership in Energy and Environmental Design) certification. The LEED program was developed by the U.S. Green Building Council (USGBC) to help determine how "green" a project is by assigning credits for achievement of various sustainable features in the design, construction, and operation of a facility. Documentation in support of these credits can include items such as:

- MSDS (material safety data sheets) in support of VOC levels for paints, sealants, and adhesives
- Certifications from manufacturers demonstrating recycled content, VOC content, chain of custody, and other features
- Certification letters from the owner, architect, and consultants
- Calculations in support of reduced energy and water consumption
- Certification letters in support of construction waste recycling, resource reuse, and building reuse

Since documentation must come from a variety of project team members (owner, contractor, and design consultants), it is important to request this as early as possible in the submittal process to ensure credits are not lost. Although documentation may initially be assembled in print and electronic formats, the USGBC requires all formal submissions to be made in electronic files.

PROJECT FEEDBACK

The objective behind project feedback is to help design and construction teams duplicate successes and minimize future mistakes, failures, and design deficiencies. Feedback is as important to the architect as it is to the contractor, especially when an architect works with clients with prototypical needs who want to improve on the design and construction process with each project.

Mistakes do not always manifest themselves in the form of problems in need of repair or replacement. A "mistake" can simply be a poor detail or something that turns out to be difficult to construct. If recognized in a completed project, such an item can be modified in the future. The architect can focus on the outcomes from using specific materials or details in an effort to improve "corporate memory" and reinforce successful detailing and material applications.

The benefits of constructive feedback are numerous. The perspective will help architects delineate design intent more clearly on future projects, as well as reduce the need for extensive interpretation of documents and costly change orders.

CSI 16.0A, Project Feedback Form, can be used to facilitate provision of project feedback. In addition to written comments, periodic in-house seminars and field visits by design firm staff are an invaluable way to transfer knowledge to those who do not normally have a chance to be involved with construction administration duties.

POSTOCCUPANCY SERVICES

Although not part of the architect's basic services as defined in the AIA series of owner-architect agreements, services provided by the architect during the one-year correction period can greatly benefit the owner and cement a continuing relationship between the architect and the client that may lead to future work.

Systems, finishes, and other components that fail to perform during the first year of building occupancy are always a source of frustration to owners. This is usually the period when the contractor fine-tunes systems and when products and finishes that were installed incorrectly or failed prematurely are repaired or replaced. Timely response on the part of the contractor (and assistance from the architect in prompting this timely response), coupled with postoccupancy reviews at six- and twelve-month intervals, is a valuable service to the owner. Through this interaction, the architect gains a sense of ownership in the project along with the owner and may learn firsthand of valuable feedback that will improve future designs. Such postoccupancy work is beyond the scope of traditional basic services, however, and the architect must decide if a service agreement should be pursued or if the assistance will be provided through goodwill.

For More Information

Various aspects of project closeout activities, procedures, and requirements are addressed in AIA Document A201–2007, General Conditions of the Contract for Construction; Sections 017700, 017823, 017839, 017900, and 019113 of the AIA MASTERSPEC® (ARCOM) master specification; and Module 7.12–Project Closeout of *The Project Resource Manual: CSI Manual of Practice*.

The following forms can also be useful for project closeout:

- AIA Document D200–1995, Project Checklist
- AIA Document G701–2001, Change Order
- AIA Document G707A–1994, Consent of Surety to Reduction in or Partial Release of Retainage
- AIA Document G707–1994, Consent of Surety to Final Payment

- AIA Document G706A–1994, Contractor's Affidavit of Release of Liens
- AIA Document G706–1994, Contractor's Affidavit of Payment of Debts and Claims
- AIA Document G704–2000, Certificate of Substantial Completion
- CSI Form 14.1A, Punch List
- CSI Form 16.0A, Feedback

CHAPTER **10**

Building Codes and Regulations

10.1 Community Planning Controls

Debra L. Smith, AIA, AICP

Zoning regulations have traditionally shaped the form and function of communities. Now form, function, and design reviews—along with sustainable design concepts—are beginning to shape community regulations.

Zoning, subdivision regulations, and building codes play major roles in shaping towns and cities of all sizes. Zoning is perhaps the most influential of the three because it is created at a large scale to show the big-picture interrelationships of land uses and activities throughout a community. It is the general framework used to guide decision making and interpretation of proposed new community development and redevelopment.

Zoning typically addresses issues of land use; density; floor area ratios (FAR); building envelope and massing; parking; building setbacks; signage; lighting; buffers between adjacent uses of different classifications, such as residential and commercial; and similar factors that guide community development.

Subdivision regulations generally apply to a parcel of land within the area addressed by the zoning ordinance and the division of that parcel into lots, tracts, or other divisions of land for sale or development. Many such regulations include design controls for improvements to the property.

> *Growth is inevitable and desirable, but destruction of community character is not. The question is not whether your part of the world is going to change. The question is how.*
>
> Edward T. McMahon
> Quoted in *Aesthetics, Community Character and the Law* by Christopher J. Duerksen and R. Matthew Goebel

Debra L. Smith is the principal urban designer for the city of Kansas City, Missouri. She entered the public sector more than a decade ago after ten years in private architecture practice. She chaired the 2006 and 2007 AIA Center for Communities by Design Committee and the 2003 Regional and Urban Design Committee Advisory Group.

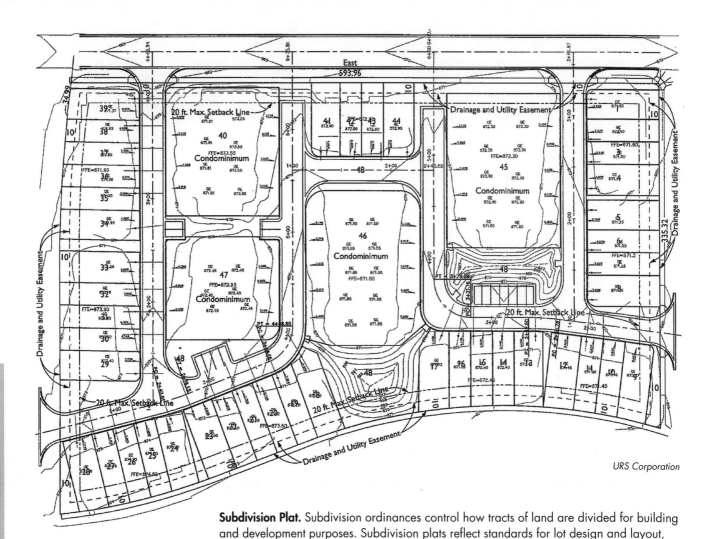

URS Corporation

Subdivision Plat. Subdivision ordinances control how tracts of land are divided for building and development purposes. Subdivision plats reflect standards for lot design and layout, streets, utilities, and other elements to ensure that these improvements are available when construction on the lots begins.

▶ See Building Codes and Standards (10.2) for a detailed discussion of building codes and their use.

Building codes establish minimum requirements for the construction of buildings to ensure public health, safety, and welfare (e.g., appropriate fire separations and exiting requirements).

Demographic changes across the country are causing many communities to reevaluate existing zoning ordinances and to explore new strategies to support the quality of life, character, and types of development desired by their populations. The discussion below describes these strategies along with basic zoning concepts. However, it is advisable to obtain specific information from state or local jurisdictions with respect to their zoning requirements. Regulations and their interpretation differ significantly from community to community.

LONG-RANGE PLANNING

A zoning ordinance, or zoning code, typically is a companion document to a long-range or comprehensive plan. Such plans generally articulate a twenty-year vision for a community and are intended to target locations for land use, development density, services, infrastructure, and amenities. Since planners and others involved in creating long-range plans cannot accurately predict the future, the plan provides a basic framework for development and guides public investment to support that development. Such plans may address scheduling for the installation of streets, sewers, water, and other utilities in areas where development that supports community goals and policies has been approved. Coordination of such infrastructure improve-ments is important to minimize demolition of recent work for new installations.

Zoning Commissions or Boards

Communities typically have a planning and zoning com-mission or board composed of citizens appointed by the mayor and/or the local governing body. The commission-ers or board members review any comprehensive revisions to plans and zoning maps, as well as any proposed devel-opment that varies from the zoning ordinance. They make recommendations to the city council about whether pro-posed variations from the zoning ordinance are in the best interest of the community. Unfortunately, over time, many planning commissions have become more focused on reviewing specific project proposals rather than long-range planning initiatives.

The role and authority of planning and zoning com-missions varies greatly from jurisdiction to jurisdiction. However, a common problem on these boards is lack of participation from the architecture community. As unglam-orous as this type of service may appear, it can be one of the most influential arenas in which architects can help guide the shape, image, identity, and quality of life in a com-munity.

ZONING AS A REGULATORY TOOL
Zoning has existed in the United States since colonial times, when colonies regulated the location of uses such as slaughterhouses and gunpowder mills. Although the rationale to separate different and potentially incompati-ble land uses still serves as the basic premise for zoning today, the forces that brought about assigning the responsibility for zoning by local government occurred in 1916 when New York City adopted citywide regula-tions to address the quality of life issues—to reduce overcrowding and provide access to natural daylight and ventilation to building tenants and residents. These regulations became the essential "blueprint" for cities across the country for establishing their own zoning ordinances, which were tailored to meet location-specific needs and issues.

Long-Range Plans

Most cities have adopted long-range plans to manage the preferred physical develop-ment of the municipality. These plans, in some states referred to as general plans, typ-ically address land use, community goals, housing, transportation and infrastructure, economic development, environmentally critical and sensitive areas, agricultural land, general quality of life, implementation strategies, and related planning issues. Such documents are expected to address the effect the plan will have on neighboring com-munities as well.

Many communities adjust their long-range plans periodically to accommodate changing markets, needs, opportunities, and economic and social climates. For exam-ple, sustainable design is now becoming an important planning consideration for many communities.

Most states require each municipality to adopt a comprehensive plan on which to base decisions on development proposals and public investments. A long-range plan offers a general road map and goals for maintaining quality of life, supporting eco-nomic development, improving shortcomings, preserving community character, and improving public amenities, and directing investment of public monies in a community.

Ideally, a long-range plan also offers consistency, despite changing political administrations and stakeholders, for pursuit of the goals stated in the plan and for strategic investment of public dollars in public infrastructure and services over time. In addition, the plan provides defensible grounds for public figures making deci-sions and protects property owners by providing them with advance knowledge about what may occur on their property, on adjacent property, and in the larger community.

In addition to long-range plans, many communities also prepare plans for specific geographic areas within the community or to address topics of concern. Such docu-ments include plans for neighborhoods, corridors, special districts, urban and regional design, redevelopment areas, housing, transportation, economic development, parks and open space, and environmentally sensitive areas. It is important for these plans,

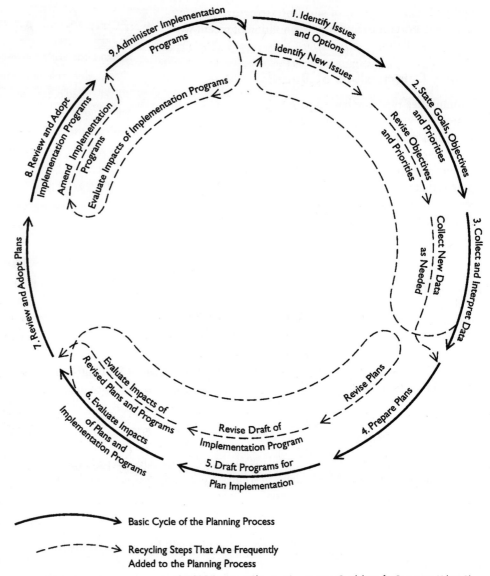

The Planning Process. The process of plan making should be viewed as a continuous cycle, with interrelationships among its phases. Information gained at a later phase can inform the outcome of an earlier phase. It is important to recognize the iterative nature of planning and to allow for continuous cycling to occur.

When designing a project and preparing for the public review process, architects and their clients should search for relevant information in comprehensive plans, plans for specific geographic areas, and any plans that address specific issues of concern in the locale.

which usually cover at least a five-year period, to be compatible with the goals and implementation techniques identified in long-range plans.

A major advantage of preparing plans for specific geographic areas or topics is that issues and goals particular to a given stakeholder group can be addressed at a more detailed level. When decisions are being made about development, the criteria and directions in a more specific plan are usually followed, especially when they are consistent with the comprehensive plan.

Traditionally, city planners often created long-range plans with little input from the general public. However, citizens across the country have become increasingly involved in the planning process, which typically includes town-hall-style meetings, citizen advisory committees, and other ways for the general public to participate.

Long-range plans and zoning ordinances are intended to complement each other. The plan provides the community vision and goals, and the zoning ordinance provides the tools for the local government to implement the plan.

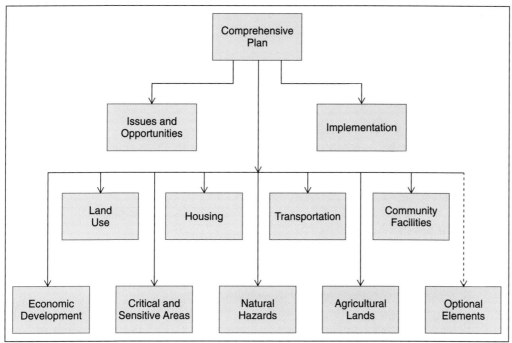

Planning and Urban Design Standards *(Wiley, 2006)*

Comprehensive Plan Elements

City planning departments now often use consultants to prepare long-range plans, and those consultants typically assemble multidisciplinary teams of planners, urban designers, architects, landscape architects, traffic engineers, environmental engineers, financial specialists, public relations advisers, and attorneys. The consultant team offers expertise in various areas affected by a large-scale community plan. The staff of the city planning department brings valuable knowledge about the following:

- Technical information about city projects
- The history, status, and priorities of various policies
- The public review process
- The political climate
- Who's who among citizen and business leaders
- Similar insights that may influence the outcome of the plan

Local governments and civic leaders have realized that planning with public participation is more likely to establish buy-in and generate the civic will necessary to commit to the measures—such as approving bonds or raising taxes—required to make the plan a reality.

Environmental Plans

In recent years, increasing attention has been paid to the protection of environmentally sensitive areas, such as land or bodies of water. Plans to address these areas may be independent documents that identify wetlands, mature woodlands, prairies, steep slopes, streams or rivers with water quality to be maintained or improved, or similar susceptible environmental features. Incorporation of these features as key elements in long-range plans is becoming more common, and many communities see this step as an effective approach to ensure that long-range plans strike a balance with environmental quality and stewardship.

Also, communities are starting to see the cost benefits of planning, designing, and building in ways that use more sustainable methods, such as the reduction of storm water run-off and improved land conservation. To truly be effective, however, environmental plans should include a statement of the local government's goals, policies, and guidelines for the protection of critically sensitive areas and other environmental issues the community chooses to address.

ZONING CONCEPTS

Zoning has evolved over decades to address changing needs, issues, and community expectations. As communities have grown and evolved, so have the types of zoning regulations. This section discusses both traditional zoning concepts and several that are emerging and gaining wider acceptance.

Euclidean Zoning

Euclidean zoning is the most prevalent form of zoning in the United States, and thus is most familiar to planners and design professionals. It has a prescriptive nature; offers objective, easy, and consistent interpretation; and has the benefit of long-established legal precedence. The U.S. Supreme Court upheld this form of zoning in 1926 in the case of *Village of Euclid (Ohio) v. the Ambler Realty Co.* for the purpose of protecting public health, safety, and welfare.

Euclidean zoning is typically characterized by a clear separation of land uses according to specific geographic districts. Typical uses include single-family residential, multifamily residential, commercial, and industrial. Limitations are often imposed on development that affects lots within each district.

In recent years, however, Euclidean zoning has received increasing criticism. Its detractors consider it inflexible and institutionalized. Much of its theory has not kept up with current trends and preferred development patterns. For instance, mixed-use development, which promotes walkability and transit-oriented development, has grown in popularity, but the basic premise of mixed-use zoning contradicts the Euclidean approach. Hence, the exploration of alternative zoning strategies has blossomed.

There is also increasing concern that highly prescriptive zoning approaches, such as Euclidean zoning, lead to lowest common denominator results for aesthetics and development amenities. Limitations on creative solutions may simply institutionalize poor design and continue the status quo.

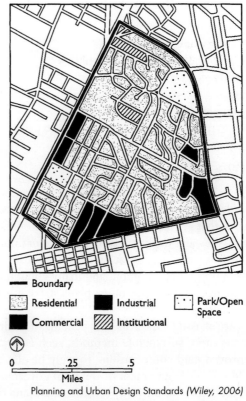

Boundary

Residential   Industrial   Park/Open Space

Commercial   Institutional

0   .25   .5
Miles

Planning and Urban Design Standards *(Wiley, 2006)*

Generalized Neighborhood Land Use Map

In the past several decades, a variety of new concepts and tools have emerged to improve flexibility in interpreting zoning codes and make it possible to achieve better zoning results. These concepts have included planned unit development (PUD), cluster zoning, overlay zoning, incentive zoning, flexible zoning, inclusionary zoning, and transferable (or transfer of) development rights (TOD).

More recently, smart growth, design review, and sustainability concepts have begun influencing how planning controls are created and used. As defined by the American Planning Association, smart growth uses comprehensive planning to develop communities that

- Have a sense of community and place
- Preserve and enhance valuable natural and cultural resources
- Equitably distribute the costs and benefits of development
- Expand the range of transportation, employment, and housing choices in a fiscally responsible manner
- Value long-range, regional considerations of sustainability over short-term, incremental, geographically isolated actions
- Promote public health and healthy communities

Some communities prefer to use the term "growth management" or a similar phrase to expand the goals in the smart-growth description. However, these communities typically have a similar goal in mind—to look at the needs and opportunities of the community through a larger lens and make decisions that benefit the greater good rather than a single project.

Design review has become a common tool to control the community planning process. Communities increasingly receive support from the courts for aesthetic-based regulations, provided the regulations are grounded in enabling authority and based on clear objective standards. Design review and aesthetic-based regulations in planning controls have been established largely in response to the insistence of local governments and the general public, who want a greater say in how their communities develop and what they look like.

Initially applied in historic preservation cases, design reviews are being employed in a much broader context,

including new construction. Some communities are creating conservation districts, typically with design guidelines, to maintain the basic fabric and character of many existing areas. These guidelines apply to remodeling of structures, building additions, and new construction.

Design guidelines and design reviews can be applied to all-new construction if community goals, the review process, and design standards are clearly identified from the beginning. For example, New Urbanism projects typically include a pattern book to guide building forms, massing, orientation, materials, and the relationship to public spaces and adjacent buildings.

Aesthetics-based regulations are particularly effective when incorporated into and consistent with broader community goals, such as economic development and community revitalization. The extensive use of graphics, tables, and similar visual aids are valuable tools for facilitating consistent, defensible, and fair interpretations of the regulations.

Sustainability is an issue on the verge of becoming a major factor in community planning. While some communities are advocating more walkable communities along with denser, more transit-oriented development, these efforts only touch on the much larger issues of sustainable design. If governments, the general public, and the building industry decide to take on this issue aggressively, the following changes can be expected:

- Community development patterns will change to promote effective stewardship of more natural resources.
- Building designs will use environmentally preferable products and will incorporate daylighting, cross-ventilation, and energy-efficient heating and cooling systems.
- Manufacturing processes for fabricating building materials will become better balanced with maintenance and stewardship of the natural environment.

While smart growth, design review, aesthetic regulations, and sustainable design measures are becoming more common, the greatest change in zoning processes is likely to come from local governments and citizens who expect to have a stronger voice in shaping the character of their communities and a greater opportunity to create a sense of place.

Flexible Zoning

As early as the 1950s, planners and communities started seeking zoning that allowed relief from the rigid methodology created by Euclidean zoning. The result was the establishment of "flexible zoning." In this approach, planners modified traditional zoning regulations to allow communities to use techniques that tie approval of unconventional uses to the review of special development plans.

Performance Zoning

The basic concept of performance zoning is regulation of land use based on consideration of the actual physical characteristics and functions of a proposed development when measured against predetermined criteria and standards. This is a significant shift from the Euclidean approach of assigning a land use and limiting development to only the types of uses identified as appropriate for that specific zoning district.

Performance zoning evaluates criteria such as traffic generation, noise, lighting levels, loss of wildlife or natural habitat, storm water runoff, and flood control measures. In theory, if the criteria and standards are met, any type of land use could be located adjacent to any other type of land use. However, many elements of a development—such as site planning, building design, and facility operation—must be strictly controlled to ensure there is no damage to adjacent properties.

Performance zoning typically involves a point-based system. This allows the developer to be awarded points for meeting listed standards and criteria. Examples include the incorporation of affordable housing into a project, providing public amenities such as a new park, or mitigating environmental impacts the development may cause. If a prescribed score is reached, the project may be approved. If the score is not reached, the developer can make modifications or add special features to obtain more points.

Performance zoning offers a high level of flexibility but is often very subjective and difficult to interpret. Consequently, a high level of expertise is required to guide its review and implementation process. For this reason, performance zoning is not widely adopted as a citywide tool but is more commonly used for specifically designated areas.

Incentive Zoning

Incentive zoning was first implemented in Chicago and New York forty years ago. Since then, it has become more common across the country. Incentive zoning uses a reward-based system to encourage development that meets certain community goals. In return for the inclusion of provisions such as public art, public parks or plazas, or affordable housing, the developer may be awarded development incentives such as increased density, building height bonuses, a faster review process, or other bonuses. The improvements required of the developer vary from one community to another, but the above-mentioned ones tend to be the most common.

In incentive zoning, the developer must meet baseline prescriptive limitations for such things as land use, setbacks, floor area ratios, and building heights. The developer may then elect to meet any of the incentive criteria for preestablished bonuses. This form of zoning offers a significant degree of flexibility but can be complex to administer, since the level of discretionary review is proportional to the level of incentives offered. It is also important to ensure that a justifiable balance is maintained between the magnitude of the incentive given and the benefit the community receives for the developer's contribution. Following are examples of incentives used in this form of zoning:

Conditional use or special-use permits provide a way to allow a land use that normally would not be permitted in a particular zoning district, but might be allowed if additional standards and discretionary review are incorporated into the process.

Overlay zoning districts are superimposed on top of portions of one or more underlying general use zoning districts. For example, additional standards may be

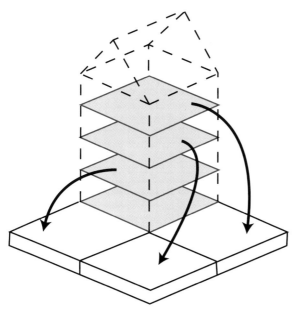

© Joel Crawford

Floor-Area Ratio. The floor-area ratio (FAR) is defined as the gross floor area of a building compared to the total area of the site. The diagram illustrates a four-story building in which each floor contains 25,000 square feet that is built on a site of 100,000 square feet. The building covers a quarter of the site, which is an FAR of 1.0.

applied within the overlay district. These standards typically might address environmental issues, mandate a specific type of design character, or focus on a special purpose, such as historic preservation.

Floating zones are quite subjective as these areas are unmapped and the standards are described only in the zoning ordinance text. However, these zones may be applied through a rezoning process for a development that meets the district's stated standards and policies.

Planned unit developments (PUD) are typically used for large tracts of land that are planned and developed as a whole through a single development operation, or through a coordinated series of development phases consistent with a preestablished and approved master plan.

Cluster development or conservation design provides considerable flexibility in locating building sites, associated roads, utilities, and similar infrastructure so as to encourage the concentration of buildings on parts of a site. This allows a greater amount of land to be used for agriculture, recreation, preservation of environmentally sensitive areas, and other similar open-space uses.

Performance standards were originally used to control industrial uses. They are used to regulate the external effects of development through measurable standards directly related to the operation of the development or facility, such as noise, odor, smoke, noxious gases, vibration, heat, and glare. This strategy may be used for all types of development to address a variety of measurable standards, such as physical appearance, fiscal impacts, traffic level, and hours of operation.

Point rating systems evaluate and rate proposed development according to preset criteria. Each characteristic has a specific number of points assigned to it. A development is required to meet minimum point thresholds, which may vary according to density. The intention is that by achieving adequate points (which are typically performance-based in nature) development will support compatibility with surrounding land uses and development.

The Uniform Development Code (UDC) consolidates the traditionally separated sections of the zoning ordinance and the subdivision regulations into a single, unified development code that provides a more consistent and efficient means of controlling

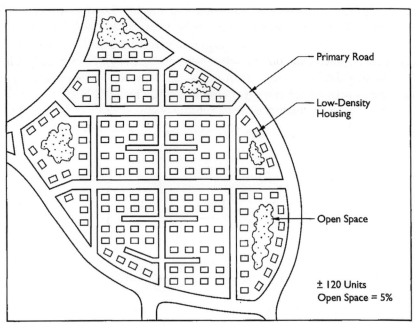

Noncluster Development

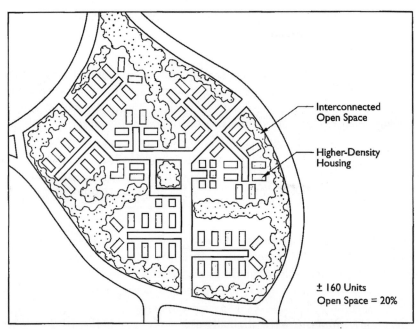

Cluster Development

Planning and Urban Design Standards *(Wiley, 2006)*

development. The UDC also offers greater predictability for all involved in the development process because all stakeholders are involved throughout the process. UDC development standards often include standards for circulation, utilities, and storm water management.

Form-Based Zoning

Form-based zoning, primarily a product of the New Urbanism movement of the late 1980s and early 1990s, is gaining momentum nationwide—largely in response to growing dissatisfaction with the perceived effects of conventional (Euclidean) zoning. Form-based zoning promotes compact, pedestrian-friendly, mixed-use communities, typically similar to pre-World War II-era development patterns. It is a regulatory approach designed to shape the physical *form* of development while setting only broad parameters for land use.

Many communities have well-maintained older neighborhoods that cannot be replicated by the current zoning ordinance for that community. Nonconforming elements typically include smaller lot sizes, insufficient setbacks, mixed-use development, a higher density of development, and other attributes characteristic of older, walkable neighborhoods. Also, neighborhoods may be considered obsolete and require variances for renovation projects because the current zoning ordinance may not offer the flexibility to approve projects that maintain the original character and integrity of the neighborhood.

In large part, the purpose of form-based zoning is to counteract two things in particular:

1. The excessive consumption of land caused by what has become the status quo—separation of land uses and limits on density
2. The erosion of the original character and sense of place in traditional neighborhoods and districts caused by the intrusion of incompatible development types allowed when a one-size-fits-all zoning ordinance is used

The general concept of form-based zoning is to focus on what is desirable, not what is forbidden. The belief is that if a development is physically compatible with its neighbors, the uses that can occur within its structure will also be compatible. The goal is to integrate private development with the public realm to optimize the mutual benefit to both public and private interests.

The sense of place in communities is decreased as formulaic, iconic stores (also known as "big boxes" and commercial strip malls) move in, cookie-cutter subdivisions spread across the landscape, and cars increasingly dominate our communities.

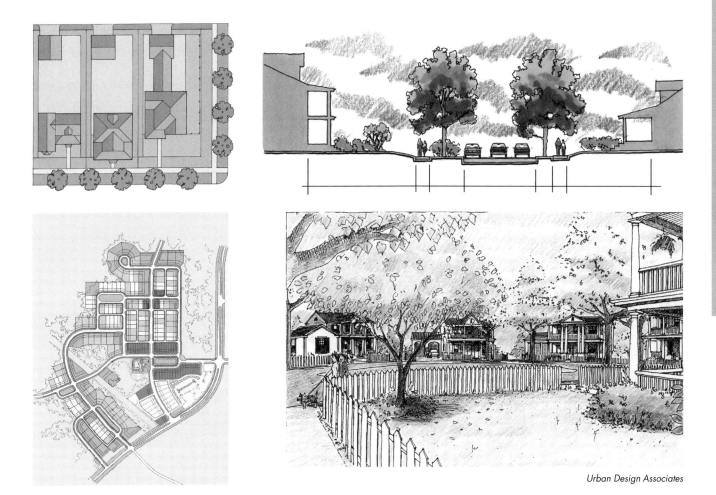

Urban Design Associates

Pattern books provide a shared vision by which neighborhoods, towns, and cities can be developed or renewed. They typically describe the overall character and image of the intended development; the essential qualities of public spaces, including building types; the way buildings are placed on their lots; and the architectural styles and elements for the project.

PART 3: THE PROJECT

Form-based zoning is intended to be a community-wide approach to achieving more attractive physical development throughout a region. Form-based zoning ordinances typically include pattern books, which clearly illustrate the variety of styles and design features considered appropriate to the community.

In practice, form-based zoning does not address many secondary impacts generated by uses on neighboring properties. These include traffic, noise, hours of operation, and possible negative effects on property values. Moreover, the use of form-based zoning tends to be limited to specified geographic areas for several reasons. First, the newness of the concept needs further testing to determine how to effectively apply it in a wider variety of cases (e.g., proximity to transit, topography, market needs and trends in a given area, and population patterns, including whether an area is growing, shrinking, or "graying"). Second, considerable effort is required to develop a form-based code. For instance, steps must be taken to develop a regulating plan to define which building envelope standards are to be applied where and to create a pattern book to set basic design parameters. Third, the public and policy makers are slow to accept change and invest in the time and training required to shift to form-based zoning.

To address these difficulties, more communities are exploring ways to create a hybrid zoning approach that combines form-based zoning with conventional zoning. The goals for such an approach are to balance control, enhance design quality and community character, and improve flexibility of interpretation so the ordinance can accommodate projects that meet the spirit of the zoning requirements, if not the letter of the ordinance.

Variations of Form-Based Zoning

Several variations of form-based zoning have been developed around the country. They include the following:

Smart Code zoning. The Smart Code is a zoning ordinance for an area from the center of the city to the rural edge that is based on the assumption that a mix of uses is the norm. The Smart Code allows for special-use districts where needed. This type of zoning has had limited adoption to date but is gaining momentum.

A key component of the Smart Code is the use of a transect, or transect-based zoning, which is based on a continuum of habitats, or eco-zones, from the rural to urban core. There are seven levels on this continuum, although not all may apply to every project. Each eco-levels is distinguished by varying density and character for the built environment. Similar to form-based zoning, regulations are applied to building design standards, street design, parking requirements, and creation of a high-quality public realm; however, in this type of code the regulations on land use are limited to promote mixed-use development.

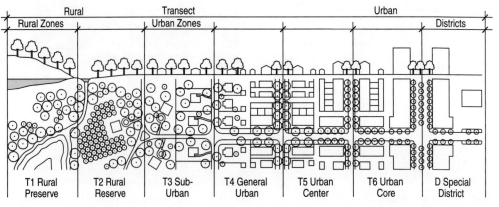

© American Planning Association

Diagram of the Transect System

Traditional neighborhood development. Also known as neo-traditional neighborhood development, this approach to zoning refers to models of urban neighborhoods from the early-to mid-twentieth century in which many of the following characteristics were common:

- Smaller lot sizes that supported a walkable scale for the neighborhood
- Access to garages from an alley
- Neighborhood parks and commercial nodes within walking distance of many houses
- Houses of varying size and price, promoting a greater diversity of age groups and income levels
- Commercial and civic functions as integral elements of the neighborhood

Transit-oriented development (TOD). This type of development focuses on planning and implementing compact development around transit, especially rail transit, stops. The goal is to offer convenience to riders by promoting the location of medium- to high-density, multifamily residential development close to retail services and offices. Such interrelationships make the choice of transit efficient and attractive. TOD designs follow many of the same principles as traditional neighborhood development, incorporating walkable scale, mixed uses, and higher density. They often use overlay zoning districts to ensure the regulations are flexible enough to create a level of density and mix of uses appropriate for supporting transit.

THE IMPORTANCE OF THE REGULATORY ENVIRONMENT

While our system of law establishes the basic framework within which an architect lives and practices, the reality is that the regulatory environment governs many of our everyday actions.

Regulations are developed and promulgated as part of what is called administrative law. The idea is that individual statutes, however well conceived by the legislative bodies that pass them, cannot possibly include all the technical and procedural provisions necessary to implement and enforce them. Thus, under the concept of administrative law, the executive branches of federal, state, and local governments draft and promulgate regulations that apply laws to everyday situations.

Consider building codes, for example. A state legislature may decide it is time to adopt a uniform statewide building code. It passes a law mandating such a code and requires that the executive branch write it. In drafting the code, a department of the executive branch (which, in this case, may be a state building code commission) follows the specific directives included in the law, as well as any legislative intent expressed in the law or in the hearings and proceedings leading to its passage. The resulting building code is very specific and detailed in its technical provisions. It also includes all of the details

necessary to enforce it. Once promulgated as a regulation, it has the force of law.

Because they address complex subjects, most regulations include ways for users to seek variances, exceptions, or other forms of dispensation from the provisions. In the case of building codes, architects may find that a code does not cover their specific situation or, alternatively, that they have a better way to fulfill the intent of the code. Most codes anticipate this by setting up a variance procedure, with decisions on variances made by individuals or panels of people who represent the community and who often have some technical expertise in design and building. This administrative relief from the provisions of regulations is generally easy to access and decisions can be made in a matter of days or weeks rather than months or years.

Once a user has exhausted all administrative avenues, judicial relief (going into the courts) is still possible but rarely successful. Courts generally give great deference to administrative agencies, which have developed significant expertise in their realm of regulation.

Ava J. Abramowitz, Esq.

From *The Architect's Handbook of Professional Practice,* thirteenth edition

ZONING TOOLS

Zoning codes are often in place for years, even decades. This means that numerous people are involved over time in developing projects, interpreting the codes, and deciding how the codes apply to changing community needs and market forces. The tools described below offer some flexible strategies for using zoning codes to serve the interests of a community.

Long-Range Plans

Long-range plans are typically twenty-year documents intended to provide broad goals, principles, and policies that create a vision for the future of a community. These plans provide a framework for evaluating proposed development projects. Zoning ordinances are the regulatory documents used to enforce long-range plans. When a proposed development differs from the zoning ordinance, it is considered a variance. A plan requesting a variance follows a different track in the review process, and different actions are required to bring it into conformity, either granting the variance or rezoning the property.

Variances

Variances typically involve only minor deviations from the specific requirements of a zoning district. It may be as simple as allowing a setback of fifteen feet instead of the required twenty feet for a specific case, or allowing an extra two feet in building height to accommodate an auxiliary unit above a garage in an area where auxiliary units are considered appropriate to the neighborhood character, form, and density.

In order for a request for a variance to be valid, there must be an unnecessary hardship inherent in the physical characteristics of the property. Financial hardship does not constitute a valid unnecessary hardship.

Rezoning

Rezoning is the most important and most common zoning action of a local government. It involves changing the land use map to reclassify land to allow an alternate use. Because plans can only anticipate future changes in demographics and lifestyle patterns, they sometimes do not accurately predict future market trends. Sometimes unforeseen but desirable opportunities arise, and the zoning commission is asked to accommodate them.

In 1922 the U.S. Department of Commerce published the Standard State Zoning Enabling Act, and this model has been adopted by most of the states. This legislation was followed in 1928 by the Standard City Planning Enabling Act, a similar model act also published by the Department of Commerce. These model acts did not provide any effective administrative methods for amending an adopted long-range plan. Therefore, any amendment to a plan must go through the same adoption process as the original plan. This is typically a ten-step process:

1. Submission of application
2. Staff review
3. Public notice of planning commission hearing
4. Preparation of staff report to the planning commission
5. Public planning commission hearing
6. Planning commission action
7. Initial governing body action; includes setting for hearing
8. Public notice of governing body hearing
9. Public hearing of governing body
10. Governing body action

Because a rezoning or map amendment changes the law, it is a serious action. However, the governing body—typically a planning and zoning commission that offers recommendations to the county or city council for final action—has much more latitude in the degree of change it makes, as long as it stays within the broad constitutional and state legislative limitations.

ZONING BOARDS AND COMMISSIONS

City and county planners are key players in reviewing and interpreting how zoning codes are applied. However, in our democratic society, it is important to ensure that the voices of citizens are heard as well. For this reason, communities establish boards and/or commissions composed of volunteer citizens to oversee city zoning and planning goals and policies and to listen to the concerns of citizens.

City or County Planning Commissions

Most communities throughout the United States have planning and zoning commissions. These bodies typically comprise five to nine volunteer members appointed by the local governing body, such as the city council or mayor, or county council or county executive. The structure of the commission is generally governed by the state planning act or, in some cases, by the local government charter.

The role of the commission is to review and act on all planning-related matters, including master plans for a city- or county-wide comprehensive plan, neighborhoods plans, and corridor plans. In these cases, the commission often has direct authority to adopt a plan or approve a subdivision. The commission may also be responsible for reviewing zoning-related matters, but typically it advises the local governing body.

Board of Zoning Appeals

The board of zoning appeals (or board of adjustment) may be a separate entity, or its responsibilities may be assigned to the planning commission. A board of zoning appeals is often the final authority in cases regarding appeals. The board hears primarily two types of cases: those requesting a variance, and those requesting a reconsideration of an earlier decision.

To approve a variance, the board must agree that a departure from the standard rules is justified because of a hardship tied to the physical characteristics of the land. To grant an appeal, the board must agree that an applicant was wrongly deprived of the opportunity to develop land due to an error in the zoning process involving a requirement, decision, or interpretation by an administrative official involved in reviewing and acting on the project application. The board may also address and rule on ambiguous provisions in the zoning ordinance.

Other Citizen Review Boards and Commissions

Communities sometimes create other types of entities to address important local issues as well. The roles of such entities may include review of projects for issues dealing with historic preservation, architectural design, urban design, landscape design, and public art. The reviews are often design-related because design matters are generally more flexible, allowing communities a greater role. Community boards may also review projects requesting TIF (tax increment financing) funds, tax abatements, or similar financing assistance using public dollars.

Governing Body

The governing body, such as the city or county council, has most of the power and responsibility for zoning decisions. The Standard State Zoning Enabling Act, which serves as the model code for most states, anticipates the local governing body will pass zoning as a local law, with the majority of the work administered by staff and interpreted by the board of appeals or adjustments. However, over time, rezoning has become necessary to accommodate development. Since rezoning is a change in the local law, involvement of the governing body is required to hear cases and make decisions.

Other government agencies also may need to be involved, such as a department of transportation, but this will become apparent during the process of working with local government and staff.

The governing body typically has three options for making a decision—to refuse a project, to approve a project as it is presented, or to approve a project subject to specific conditions or revisions. The latter decision may require a follow-up presentation to verify that revisions have been made according to the direction given.

FACTORS INTEGRAL TO ZONING REVIEW

Zoning should reflect the goals and policies of the community, and allow flexible interpretation for projects that meet the intent, if not the actual regulations, of the code. Specific factors are used to determine whether a project is in compliance with zoning regulations. The factors may vary by community, but they must be clearly stated and followed for a community to subsidize development and invest public dollars consistently and fairly.

Land Use Classifications

Land use classification is a legal term that defines permitted uses for a parcel of land. However, most communities have taken the broad categories of land use type and broken them down into very specific uses, which may result in hundreds of identified land uses in the zoning ordinance. For instance, numerous identified and acceptable uses may appear under the heading "retail sales and service," including antique shops, clothing or ready-to-wear stores, confectionery shops, and stationery stores. Even at this level of distinction, new and changing uses will arise that are not identified and therefore hard to classify, such as a live-work art studio. As well, obsolete uses, such as "ice delivery stations" and "livery stables," are still listed in the land use classifications of many states.

Many communities are revising their zoning ordinances to condense hundreds of use types into a single table that identifies broader and more inclusive categories, avoids listing obsolete uses, and ensures flexibility to accommodate new uses that evolve over time.

Contextual Infill

Many older neighborhoods experience a resurgence of interest in new development. Often these neighborhoods offer charm and convenience (including proximity to downtown and cultural hubs) and a sense of place. Over the years, however, the needs and interests of residents have changed and the original housing stock no longer meets their expectations. This usually results in demolition of older housing stock to make way for new homes.

Communities facing teardowns express concern about the effect on community character and affordable housing for working-class people. One strategy for addressing such trends is to promote contextual infill through regulatory measures such as requirements for setback, building coverage, floor area ratio, building height, and building volume ratio. Such strategies can help maintain neighborhood character, while enabling property owners to make changes that accommodate modern amenities, such as upgraded kitchens and baths, and larger bedrooms and closets.

Creating design guidelines for development—whether for renovation or new construction—can also be effective in helping preserve community character. Such design guidelines should address neighborhood context, including building materials, site orientation, building height and setbacks, roof form, and windows, as well as particular neighborhood features, such as front porches or garage placement behind the house.

From a regulatory perspective, it is important for planners to know that the economic conditions leading to a teardown result from social issues unrelated to design. Teardowns often occur in desirable neighborhoods where the housing stock is sound, but dated.

From APA's Zoning Practice Series (June 2005), "Practice Contextual Infill" by Lane Kendig

While keeping older building stock in communities viable for housing, local retail and business operations, and civic uses is important, the structures must also comply with local building code and related regulations. To address this issue, some states have created adjustments (or overlays) to their building codes that allow renovation of older and/or historic buildings without full compliance with requirements of the Americans with Disabilities Act (ADA) or the latest seismic codes. This allowance makes renovation of these structures more practical and financially feasible for developers and property owners, and helps maintain the original community character and building stock.

Sustainable Design and Development Patterns

Planning with regard to sustainable design and development issues promotes clustering of new development to ensure the conservation of natural resources such as wetlands, woodlands, stream and riverbanks, and steep slopes, as well as the preservation of historic resources, such as landmarks, architecturally significant buildings and districts, and the character associated with these areas. Sustainable development also includes reinvesting in existing, walkable neighborhoods, where an initial investment has already been made in streets, sewers, and other utilities. These neighborhoods often provide a density that supports public transit, thereby reducing dependence on automobiles.

Another facet of sustainable design and development is the establishment of guidelines to promote better water quality and use. Among the goals of such guidelines are a reduction in storm water runoff to reduce pollution to bodies of water and an increase in water conservation by reducing the use of potable water for lawns and landscapes.

Communities interested in using a more formal approach to incorporating sustainable standards into local zoning ordinances should start with a review of existing ordinances to determine areas for improvement and create strategies to achieve desired results.

When establishing an ordinance that considers issues of sustainable design, the following should be addressed:

Sustainability is meeting the needs of the present without compromising the ability of future generations to meet their own needs.

United Nations Commission on Environment and Development, 1987

- Landscaping needs, such as watering and fertilizer requirements
- Storm water runoff and related pollution and its impact on water treatment facility capacity
- Wastewater treatment demands and costs
- Stream and wetland preservation
- Floodplain protection
- Soil erosion and sediment control
- Weed control
- Tree preservation
- Building code requirements
- Pedestrian amenities to support walkability
- Street design
- Parking requirements and opportunities for more flexible standards
- Access to multiple modes of transportation, including walking, biking, and public transit

Parking

Parking is a complex zoning issue. According to Donald Shoup, FAICP, author of the 2006 American Planning Association report *Practice Smart Parking*, there are three steps in establishing parking requirements for a specific land use:

1. Identify the land use.
2. Define the factors expected to predict peak parking demand.
3. Use the information from steps one and two to specify the number of parking spaces required to meet the anticipated need of the development.

In a 2002 survey of parking requirements, the Planning Advisory Service of the APA discovered nearly 700 land uses, each with distinct parking requirements. In addition, more than 200 factors were used to determine parking needs in various conditions and for different uses. The need for parking in different communities varied as well, often due to availability of public transit.

In the past, it was common practice to err on the side of caution to ensure an abundance of parking, rather than risk a shortage. However, as cities become more concerned about urban sprawl, storm water management, dependence on cars, and rising gas prices, many of them are exploring strategies to reduce the amount of parking required. Following are descriptions of some of their approaches:

Implementing an effective public transit system. For example, Dallas, St. Louis, Los Angeles, and Denver are automobile-oriented cities achieving success with the relatively recent addition of transit systems.

Using shared parking opportunities. Known in some areas as a "park once" strategy, this approach facilitates the sharing of parking spaces for daytime and evening businesses and residences in mixed-use areas. Where developments provide a sufficient density of uses and a comfortable pedestrian environment, this approach encourages people to park vehicles once and walk to more than one destination without having to move their cars.

Creating strategic parking plans at a district scale. This is similar to the shared-parking plan, but on a larger scale. The general concept is to look at the land use of an area, typically no more than a half mile in diameter, estimate the parking required for that area, and target preferred locations for parking to accommodate the anticipated needs of the buildings. This allows more land to be developed and creates a walkable character to the area because each land use is not required to fully provide its own parking on-site. More density, mixed uses, and opportunities to create more inviting pedestrian zones can be achieved.

Transportation Patterns, Modes, and Design

Today the United States faces rising fuel prices and related transportation costs, increasing public health concerns like obesity and type 2 diabetes, and a growing underemployed population. In light of this situation, transportation investment must be expanded from its emphasis on roads and systems that primarily support privately owned vehicles. Increasing the means of travel available to citizens in communities across the country—including walking, biking, and public transit—can serve young and elderly populations, disabled citizens unable to drive, low-income residents without cars, and those who desire alternative means of transportation. These modes of transportation also promote improved air and water quality and help maintain community character.

Community planning and design can support transportation options that encourage walkable destinations for residents, workers, and visitors by strategically increasing densities around intermodal transportation hubs; increasing desirable amenities such as parks and plazas, libraries, and shops; and encouraging mixed-use development.

Water Conservation

Water usage is becoming a pressing issue around the country and is not limited to times of drought. Older cities face an aging infrastructure that needs significant repairs or complete replacement. Newer communities are struggling with finding sources of water to meet growing demand.

Several strategies commonly employed to address these issues are the use of impact fees, creation of community development districts responsible for providing infrastructure, and institution of pricing policies to cover the cost of providing water and create incentives for reducing water consumption. However, the role zoning and development patterns play in community water use is rarely addressed.

Three general categories of zoning pertain to water use: lot size, landscaping material, and leakage. Lot size relates to the amount of lawn to maintain, car washing, and similar outdoor uses. A variety of studies consistently show that these outdoor water uses can constitute up to 50 to 70 percent of overall household water use. (The statistics are similar for office uses, with the water requirements for maintaining associated landscaping.)

The plants chosen for landscaping can have a dramatic effect on the amount of water required. Plants native to an area typically require less water, and several water utilities are offering tips to homeowners who plant native vegetation. Some cities are also offering incentives to developers and property owners who landscape with plants that need minimal irrigation.

Leakage through pipes and joints occurs with all water systems. The amount of water lost to leaks is difficult to estimate because of variations in such factors as infrastructure age and condition, length of distribution systems, and water pressure. According to the May 2005 issue of the APA publication *Zoning Practice* (a special report on water conservation titled "How Thirsty Is Your Community"), a range of typical leakage is considered to be 6 to 25 percent or more. As water becomes scarce, lost water is

APPROACHING A COMMUNITY BOARD

Probably the best advice is to do your homework. Here are some guidelines to flesh out this simple maxim:

Understand what it takes to get on the agenda of a planning board meeting, zoning hearing, or other hearing. What applications need to be made? What information is required? Does the owner's request need to be denied before the owner or the owner's representative can appear in person? How much time is required to file an appeal from a negative decision? How long does it take to get on the agenda?

Sit down with the public official enforcing the regulations or the secretary of the board and learn the process. Get technical questions about the process answered, as well as an indication of how the board likes to be approached.

Find out who is on the board, what they do when they are not providing this public service, and whether there are specific personal agendas on the table. Most regulatory boards are appointed citizen boards, intended to represent community interests, as well as the law. Find out what those interests are.

Attend a meeting before the one at which you are scheduled to appear. Observe how the board works, how formal or informal the proceedings are, and what the important issues are. While boards operate within a carefully defined regulatory framework, they have considerable latitude in how they approach their responsibilities.

Review the law as it is applicable to your case. In constructing the case to be made, work with the owner, and perhaps the owner's attorney, to review the applicable law

(for example, the conditions under which a zoning board can vote a special-use permit). Address these points.

Consider who, besides the board, will be in the room. By law, hearings and commission meetings are usually open. Public notice is given in the local newspaper, and frequently the law requires that adjacent landowners be notified. Who will come and what will be on their minds? Will the media be interested? It is one thing to present to a five-person zoning board and another to speak to a roomful of angry neighbors.

For controversial projects, suggest that the owner hold informational meetings in the community before the hearing is held. In addition to providing information, these meetings can bring concerns to the surface—concerns the owner may want to address before taking the project to the hearing where a decision will be made.

Be organized. Arrive at the hearing on time, bring the necessary materials, and make sure that everyone involved in the presentation understands their roles.

Keep your presentation short and professional. Make sure visuals are legible. When discussion begins, listen carefully to what is being said, and address concerns as directly as possible.

Be sure the owner knows what to fight for and what to give up in negotiation. Do not state a contrary position during the discussion without first huddling with the owner. Remember, this is the owner's project, not yours.

David Haviland, Hon. AIA

From *The Architect's Handbook of Professional Practice,* thirteenth edition treated as lost money. It is predicted that curbing large water losses from leaks may save some towns or districts the cost of finding additional water sources.

THE ZONING REVIEW PROCESS

Each community has its own zoning review process. For example, some communities offer incentives, such as streamlining the process, if the applicant complies with such community goals as design character, public amenities, or the mitigation of environmental impacts. The following describes a basic review process, based on one used by Blaine County, Idaho. While it serves as an example for discussion, architects should contact the local government where a project is located to confirm the process in that particular community.

Purpose of the Review

All building permits receive zoning review as part of the building permit process. The purpose of the zoning review is to determine if the development proposal complies with the zoning requirements. If a property is located within a subdivision, compliance with the subdivision plat and plat notes will also be determined.

Review by Planning Staff

During the zoning review process, the zoning administrator or other designated planning staff member will make the following determinations:

- Whether the property is a valid "lot of record" as defined in the zoning regulations—either a lot that is part of a recorded subdivision or a lot or parcel described by metes and bounds. If the development involves an unplatted parcel, the developer should contact the planning department and request a parcel determination early in the planning process.
- Whether the proposed use is allowed as a permitted, accessory, or conditional use in the designated zoning district, such as a single-family residence in a residential zone.
- Whether the project meets the minimum building setback requirements or is located within a platted building envelope on a subdivision lot. Building setbacks are measured from the property line to the foundation wall.
- Whether the building height is within the maximum allowed, typically thirty-five feet as measured from existing natural grade to the highest portion of the structure for residential structures.
- Whether the subject property is located in an environmentally sensitive area such as a floodplain, wetlands, avalanche-prone area, or hillside. If so, further information will likely be necessary and a special use permit issued by the Planning and Zoning Commission may be required before a building permit can be issued. Special use permits and variance applications typically take a minimum of six weeks to process. It may take longer depending on the time of year, proposed use, and backlog of other applications awaiting public hearing.
- Whether the project complies with the subdivision plat and plat notes. If there is an active homeowners' association, it will be necessary to acquire its written approval before a building permit can be issued.
- Whether the conditions of approval attached to special zoning permits, such as conditional use and variances, have been satisfied.

Structural Review and Building Permit

Once it has been determined a development proposal complies with applicable zoning regulations, the plans will be referred to the county building department for structural review and issuance of the building permit as appropriate. If the development proposal does not comply with one or more of the zoning requirements, the applicant will be informed of what steps can be taken to bring the project into compliance.

Locally Specific Review Processes

Most communities include all of the steps and order of activities in the description above. However, in larger cities or municipalities with many departments, the process can be more complicated. For example, the New York City Uniform Land Use Review Procedure requires an 11-by-17-inch sheet of paper to accommodate the numerous diagrams and small type needed to outline the wide variety of issues and participants in what can be a lengthy review process.

SATISFYING DEVELOPMENT SOLUTIONS

In the last few decades, housing development has followed a trend where houses are geographically separated by price category. This has the effect of segregating people by socioeconomic groups and by age. It also contrasts with historic patterns in which smaller, affordable housing and larger, more expensive housing were found in the same neighborhood. Recent trends indicate that healthy, sustainable neighborhoods offer a range of housing options, allowing residents to move from apartments or small houses to larger houses and back to smaller housing as income and life cycle needs require. When people stay in their neighborhoods by choice, they can maintain their social networks, shopping patterns, civic involvement, and other important relationships. These connections are often lost when people must move to different neighborhoods to accommodate changing housing needs.

Architects are well positioned to help communities achieve satisfying development solutions. As visual thinkers, architects can help members of the community see the possibilities in creating more livable environments with the potential to support larger community goals for health, safety, and sustainability, as well as the wants and needs of its citizens.

For More Information

Part Six of *Planning and Urban Design Standards* (Wiley, 2006), authored by the American Planning Association (APA), addresses a variety of zoning issues, including its legal foundations. The APA Web site at www.planning.org also provides information about community planning controls.

The Planning Advisory Service regularly publishes booklets addressing a broad range of planning issues. Its Web site is www.pas.gov.uk. Another Web site of interest is Campaign for Sensible Growth at www.growingsensibly.org, which includes an article titled "Zoning for Environmental Sustainability."

The Centers for Disease Control Web site, www.cdc.gov, has a wealth of valuable information addressing urban sprawl, density, and overall community development patterns and their relationship to public health.

The Institute for Transportation Engineers recently published a report titled "Context Sensitive Solutions in Designing Major Thoroughfares for Walkable Communities." It is available as a PDF file on their Web site at www.ite.org.

The American City: What Works, What Doesn't (McGraw-Hill, 1996), by Alexander Garvin, analyzes 250 projects in 100 cities with respect to public/private partnerships, neighborhood revitalization, zoning, and historic preservation.

Additional useful material on zoning and planning can be found in the following publications:

- *The Practice of Local Government Planning*, third edition (International City/County Management Association, 2000)
- *Planning and Control of Land Development: Cases and Materials*, sixth edition, by Daniel Mandelker et al. (Matthew Bender, 2005)

- *Aesthetics, Community Character, and the Law*, by Christopher J. Duerksen and R. Matthew Goebel, cosponsored by Scenic America and APA (2000); available from the APA as Planning Advisory Service Report 489/490
- *Planning and Environmental Law*, a monthly journal of abstracts published by the APA

10.2 Building Codes and Standards

David S. Collins, FAIA

To provide for the public welfare, government at all levels establishes and enforces building codes and regulations. The design of buildings must comply with applicable codes and regulations unless variances or alternative solutions are allowed.

As part of the police powers granted to the states by the U.S. Constitution, each jurisdiction has the legal option to establish minimum standards for safety and health in that community. States either take the authority or permit local communities to take responsibility for the adoption and enforcement of codes, and for years a variety of codes was used around the country. Today, the United States is close to having a single set of adopted codes.

As with many laws, communities have the opportunity to create their own codes or to choose a model code. Generally, a package of model codes provides guidance for communities seeking to comprehensively address how the design and construction of buildings and other facilities affect the health and safety of occupants. Model codes and standards are based on the broadest thinking about how an acceptable level of safety can be achieved and how regulations should be applied. However, in adopting model codes, a community must understand what is expected in administering the codes.

Architects, engineers, designers, and even contractors in many communities are part of the effort to regulate construction by establishing minimum levels of performance and practice. The National Council of Architectural Registration Boards (NCARB) includes several items associated with building code compliance in the Architect Registration Examination. State licensure laws often include criteria for licensure such as preparing construction documents that conform to local law.

Many states use these types of requirements to reinforce the need for architects to be aware that local laws and regulations are an integral part of building design. In the first decade of the twenty-first century, the process of maintaining a library of regulations and standards has become increasingly difficult as the number of regulations—not to mention their complexity—increases each year. This volume is magnified by the continuous evolution of model codes and standards, many of which are modified on a three-year cycle.

To ensure that registered architects remain up-to-date on building codes, a system of mandatory continuing education is now the policy of many states and is also a membership requirement of the AIA. In general, training and education requirements call for at least eighteen hours of continuing education activities, eight hours of which are related to the protection of the health, safety, and welfare of the public.

David S. Collins is president of The Preview Group, Inc., a building regulatory consulting firm with offices in Cincinnati and Berkeley, California. He has served as secretary of the AIA and currently manages the AIA Codes Advocacy Program. Collins serves on the NIST Construction Safety Advisory Committee investigating the World Trade Center collapse, the Underwriters Laboratories (UL) Fire Council, and numerous ICC and NFPA committees.

HISTORY OF U.S. CODE DOCUMENTS

Development of modern building codes began around the turn of the twentieth century, and model codes began to appear soon thereafter. The rise of industrial cities in the United States brought many people to urban areas, resulting in the construction of housing in close proximity to industries. Responding to the hazards that could result from this juxtaposition, communities and insurance companies began writing building codes. Later, communities began sharing their knowledge and understanding of construction regulations and created regional codes.

Standards for building systems began to undergo significant changes in tandem with the development of building codes. The National Fire Protection Association traces the beginnings of NFPA 13, Standard for Installation of Sprinkler Systems, to 1895 when a group of insurers and sprinkler system installers began the process of systematizing the installation of these systems.

Committees for the development of standards typically include industry interests that are close to, and have financial interests in, the materials or systems controlled by the standard. As part of their participation, these industry representatives vote for criteria to encourage appropriate use of those materials or systems. Most model codes, on the other hand, are developed with input from industry interests, although those representing such interests are not allowed to vote on provisions included in the codes. Limiting industry involvement is intended to prevent undue influence on the codes from those with a financial interest in them.

Prior to 1994, model building codes were published in the United States by the Building Officials and Code Administrators International (BOCA), Southern Building Code Congress International (SBCCI), and the International Conference of Building Officials (ICBO). These organizations generated parallel documents and each endorsed a "common code format" that allowed users of the codes who worked in multiple jurisdictions to easily find criteria on the same subject in the same part of the three codes. It also facilitated comparisons and identification of commonalities and differences in the text of the three documents.

In 1975 the AIA Codes and Standards Committee published a white paper titled "One Code: A Program of Regulatory Reform for the United States." This document was the impetus for the consolidation of the three model codes. In 1994, BOCA, SBCCI, and ICBO officially joined together to create the International Code Council (ICC), which began producing the International family of building codes. In 1995 the new code family began with the first edition of the mechanical and plumbing codes. The 2000 edition of the International Building Code was the first publication to include all the major ICC codes.

▶ The backgrounder The International Building Code at the end of this topic describes the basic steps involved in using the IBC.

AIA POLICY ON BUILDING CODES

Policy Statement

Regulation of the construction industry shapes the built environment. As stakeholders, architects must participate in the development and application of appropriate regulations and standards.

Supporting Position Statements

22. Building Codes and Standards

The AIA supports regulation by a single set of comprehensive, coordinated, and contemporary codes and standards, which establish sound threshold values of health, safety, and the protection of the public welfare throughout the United States.

To that end, the AIA espouses the development and adoption of model building codes that:

- Include participation by architects and the public in a consensus process;
- Are the product of informed education and research;
- Are without favoritism or bias to any special interest;
- Include provision for a prompt appeals procedure for all that might be aggrieved;
- Are cost-effective in relation to public benefit; and
- Promote building code provisions that set performance rather than prescriptive criteria.

23. Building Permits

The AIA supports governmental policies, regulatory procedures, and administration that eliminate unnecessary time delays in the construction permitting process.

Today, the ICC publishes the only family of model building codes used in the United States. The complete package of codes currently published by the ICC includes the following:

- International Building Code (IBC)
- International Residential Code for One- and Two-Family Dwellings (IRC)
- International Mechanical Code (IMC)
- International Plumbing Code (IPC)
- International Fire Code (IFC)
- International Fuel Gas Code (IFGC)
- International Energy Conservation Code (IECC)
- International Existing Building Code (IEBC)
- International Private Sewage Disposal Code (IPSC)
- International Wildland-Urban Interface Code (IWUIC)
- ICC Performance Code for Buildings and Facilities (ICCPC)
- International Property Maintenance Code (IPMC)
- International Zoning Code (IZC)
- ICC Electrical Code Administrative Provisions (IEC)

These ICC codes, along with the NFPA National Electrical Code, provide a complete bookshelf of codes appropriate for adoption and enforcement in communities throughout the United States.

In 1999 the National Fire Protection Association (NFPA) announced its intent to develop a model building code despite objections from many groups in the construction industry. Although NFPA has long published several documents, including codes and standards, none included limitations on structural loads and materials specifications. The NFPA product closest to a building code was NFPA 101, Life Safety Code, and NFPA chose that document as a model for its development of NFPA 5000, Building Construction and Safety Code™. NFPA 5000 was published in 2003 and has since undergone one revision cycle, resulting in the 2006 edition.

In marketing its building code, the NFPA partnered with several other organizations to provide expertise that NFPA did not have. They included the International Association of Plumbing and Mechanical Officials (IAPMO) to provide plumbing and mechanical codes, as well as the American Society of Heating, Refrigerating and Air-Conditioning Engineers (ASHRAE) and the Western Fire Chiefs Association (WFCA) for the consolidation of its fire code with NFPA 1.

As this volume went to press, forty-seven states and the District of Columbia were using the International Building Code. As well, forty-five states and the District were using the International Residential Code, and forty-two states and the District were using the International Fire Code. No state, however, had adopted the NFPA building code. However, virtually all of the ICC codes reference NFPA standards, such as NFPA 13 for sprinkler systems, as well as the National Electrical Code, which is used internationally as the standard for design and installation of electrical equipment.

Some government projects or projects that use government funding require adherence to codes and standards other than the model codes just described. A prime example is the Americans with Disabilities Act. Federal legislation established that rules were to be created to afford access to buildings by the disabled, and granted the U.S. Access Board the authority to write guidelines and the Department of Justice the authority to adopt and enforce them.

A difficulty has arisen for architects who want to know which accessibility rules to follow because the Department of Justice has not yet adopted the 2004 guidelines issued by the Access Board. Nonetheless, the guidelines are useful tools, providing designers with information regarding solutions to particular accessibility issues. The fact that they are more lenient in some ways than the current rules (ADAAG) adopted by the Department of Justice puts the designer in the awkward position of wanting

It is incumbent upon architects to know and understand the breadth of regulations that apply to their projects.

to provide the most appropriate solution but knowing it is not endorsed as part of the actual regulations.

The model code organizations have taken different approaches to building accessibility. The ICC has tried to mainstream accessible features into the general requirements of the IBC. NFPA, on the other hand, has simply incorporated the "ADA and ABA Accessibility Guidelines for Buildings and Facilities," as recommended by the U.S. Access Board in its 2004 rules, into the 2006 edition of NFPA 5000, referencing ICC/ANSI A117.1, Standard on Accessible and Usable Buildings and Facilities.

The Access Board guidelines and A117.1 are prime examples of specification requirements. The family of ICC codes and NFPA 5000 and NFPA 101 includes both specification-oriented (minimum requirements and maximum limitations) and performance options. Generally, the specification-oriented codes provide a direct response to the majority of design issues and safety concerns. However, both code groups are aware that despite efforts to be comprehensive in their documents, issues may arise that are not currently addressed or that are so far from the scope of a typical building that they require a different approach to determine what is appropriate for life safety. The performance options within the codes are intended to provide guidelines for designers and their clients looking for a means to resolve a particular problem.

While sections of NFPA 5000 are titled "performance," they actually provide very specific limits for what is to be done in the process. For example, Section 5.3 is titled "retained prescriptive requirements" and covers means of egress and all prescriptive requirements for fire protection systems and features. The ICC Performance Code provides a format for how to take a project through the performance code and indicates what considerations must be followed, but it does not establish any specific prescriptive limits. The ICC's prescriptive codes serve as the measuring stick for the performance of a design, but they do not establish absolute limits for performance.

Performance code provisions were developed to allow innovative solutions that do not fall within the typical design. The fact that the performance approach has been formalized is recognition that the codes are not able to anticipate every circumstance and every possible solution.

Choosing whether to use a prescriptive code or a performance code is a decision that must be made carefully and with the input of the client. In particular, the code choice must be supported by the authorities having jurisdiction (AHJs) that will approve the project. This may mean officials representing virtually every enforcement agency within a community who will regulate the project. According to the ICC documents, this group at least includes building and fire enforcement officials.

IBC AND IFC CODE FUNDAMENTALS

A common thread in both ICC and NFPA documents is the true integration of the building and fire codes and the standards they reference. In previous codes, the approach to code enforcement was often insulated by the document in which the requirements were located. In current codes, the fire and building requirements are totally integrated so the full understanding of what is required can only be ascertained by going to multiple documents. Reference to at least the building and fire codes is necessary to find minimum design requirements, and most often several additional referenced documents (e.g., mechanical and plumbing codes) must be checked to grasp the full impact of the codes on a given building design.

The architect, in conjunction with the client, typically makes the initial decision on occupancy or construction type appropriate for a project, while code officials (AHJs) analyze documents presented for their review. Thus, the following overview of code fundamentals, based on the 2006 edition of the International Building Code, approaches code analysis from the designer's perspective.

To determine the minimum type of construction needed to meet the code, several pieces of information are required. These include the use for the space (occupancy), the combined need for space (height and area) and, because of its occupancy classification, whether the building requires a sprinkler system (fire protection). The code also contains requirements for means of egress with respect to travel distances, paths of travel, and the design of stairs, corridors, and exits.

Occupancy

Every structure must be classified in a specific occupancy, and most buildings will require more than one occupancy classification. For example, a conference room or cafeteria within a business facility would probably be designated as an "assembly" occupancy. In the same type of structure, some supply and storage areas may be appropriately classified as "storage" use occupancies. The IBC requires identification of all the different occupancies in a space or building as part of the design process.

Because the IBC is structured to address the characteristics of the activities in a building, it is critical to understand the various occupancy categories in the code and how to distinguish among them. The categories are as follows:

- Assembly: Groups A-1, A-2, A-3, A-4, and A-5
- Business: Group B
- Educational: Group E
- Factory and Industrial: Groups F-1 and F-2
- High Hazard: Groups H-1, H-2, H-3, H-4, and H-5
- Institutional: Groups I-1, I-2, I-3, and I-4
- Mercantile: Group M
- Residential: Groups R-1, R-2, R-3, and R-4
- Storage: Groups S-1 and S-2
- Utility and Miscellaneous: Group U

Note that several of the categories are divided into subgroups to more clearly differentiate among them. For example, the "assembly" occupancy is subdivided into five different subgroups. Traditional stage theaters and motion picture theaters are classified as A-1, while an outdoor athletic stadium is classified as A-5. Although these facilities share the purpose of accommodating large groups of people watching a common demonstration, they are divided into subgroups because their needs are sufficiently different to require different approaches in a code.

NFPA 5000 has similar occupancy classifications, which are described in Chapter 6 of that code. The differences between the occupancy classifications in the IBC and NFPA 5000 are significant in some details associated with how specific conditions are to be addressed, but the major categories remain the same.

Fire Protection

Chapter 9 of both the IBC and the IFC includes limits, or thresholds, for the size and type of building that must have a sprinkler system. These limits are based on the building size or the area of an occupancy (fire area) that is enclosed by exterior walls, firewalls, or fire barriers. If the threshold for fire suppression for an occupancy classification is based on the building area, a fire area would not be part of the consideration for fire suppression. If the threshold is limited to the area of the occupancy, then the building can be subdivided into fire areas that are less than the specified threshold and not be required to have a sprinkler system.

A fire area is defined by the encompassing walls, roof, and floor that are either exterior walls, fire walls, or fire barriers. Any floor area within such enclosure is part of the fire area. For example, if a building is of Type IIB construction, the floors have zero fire resistance. If the building were three floors, all three floors would be added into the calculation of the fire area.

The ICC codes do not currently require one- and two-family dwellings and utility occupancy buildings to have sprinkler systems. However, all hospitals, nursing homes, and other institutional occupancies, as well as hotels, motels, apartments, and town-houses, are required to be protected with an automatic sprinkler system under all circumstances. Each of the other occupancies included in the IBC has a threshold after which sprinklers are mandatory; these figures are based on the size of the building, the area of the occupancy, or the number of persons the space accommodates.

Two additional conditions, which do not depend on the building occupancy classification determine whether a structure must have a sprinkler system. Floors with no openings (the IBC sets up minimum size and spacing for openings), as well as any building with an occupied floor more than fifty-five feet above the lowest level that fire apparatus responding to the building can reach, must have a sprinkler system, no matter what the occupancy classification.

In NFPA 5000, thresholds for fire suppression are established in the occupancy chapter criteria. For example, an "assembly" occupancy classification in the IBC is required to have fire suppression when the occupant load exceeds 300 or the threshold of a specific occupancy area. The same 300-occupant threshold is found in NFPA 5000.

Additional fire protection thresholds for installation of automatic detection and alarm notification devices are also part of the IBC and NFPA 5000. Requirements for smoke detectors in dwelling units and the installation of pull boxes and the sound level of fire alarms are also repeated in each code.

Height and Area

The means for determining limits on height and area for a building are tied to several factors. Particularly critical are building occupancies and whether the building will be fully protected with sprinklers. Once the building height has been estimated and a concept for the layout of the floors and the location of the building on the site has been determined, the architect can easily determine the minimum type of construction for the project.

Table 503 of the IBC prescribes the base area for calculating the maximum area of a building. The base areas were derived from the area sizes permitted in the three model building codes that preceded the ICC codes. The IBC drafting committee agreed to accept the largest height and largest area of any building that would have been permitted by any of those codes. To accomplish this, the staff of each code organization was asked to determine what the largest area and height of a building would be for any given occupancy and type of construction.

Because the three previous model codes used a different method for calculating the maximum height and area, the committee chose to use the process for determining area included in the report on height and area from the Board for the Coordination of the Model Codes (BCMC). Applying that method in reverse, the values in Table 503 were developed. The formula for determining the maximum area of a building per the IBC is prescribed as follows:

$$A_a = A_t + \left[\frac{A_t I_f}{100} + \frac{A_t I_s}{100} \right]$$

where:

A_a is the allowable area for any single floor in the building,

A_t is the base area in Table 503,

I_f is the increase permitted for frontage, and

I_s is the increase for fire suppression.

In addition, the IBC limits the total area of the building to three times the allowable area calculated from this formula.

Although architects may begin designing a building without knowing what construction type is required, they will have a good idea of what the building configuration will be based on the program, the site and its limits, and site factors such as development and zoning requirements, drainage retention, utility easements, and so on. Given that information, a designer would be able to use the formula to solve the problem in reverse, with the actual area being known and the minimum type of construction being calculated. For example, if the program for an office building calls for 300,000 square feet of office space and supporting areas, the formula can be modified to solve for the area required for the construction type:

$$A_t = \left[\frac{A_a}{1 + I_f + I_s} \right]$$

As long as the type of construction in Table 503 has a larger area than that required for A_t, the building would be permitted for that occupancy. For example, assume a three-story office building without a sprinkler system and frontage around the building providing the minimum separation allowed to consider the building 100 percent open. The area permitted by Table 503 (A_t) would be determined by dividing the actual area (100,000 square feet) by the number of stories, and the frontage increase would be 75 percent. Thus, the formula would be

$$A_t = \left[\frac{100,000}{1 + 0.75 + 0} \right] = 57,143$$

It is then a simple matter to go to Table 503 and determine that the type of construction would have to be either Type IA or IB. However, if it was determined that installation of a sprinkler system was appropriate, the calculation would change to include the 200 percent factor and the formula would be

$$A_t = \left[\frac{100,000}{1 + 0.75 + 2} \right] = 26,600$$

The difference between the results of the two calculations indicates the effect the presence of a sprinkler system has on the construction type. The 57,143 square feet of the original required tabular area would limit the building to Type IA or IB, which is a rather unusual construction type for a low-rise business; with sprinklers, however, Type IIA or IIIA would be permitted.

Note that this example uses a building with a single occupancy (business) with accessory areas of other occupancies (assembly or storage) typically found in office buildings. A mixed-use building (one with more than one principal occupancy) would require further analysis.

Additional considerations that affect the determination of construction type are requirements for fire alarms, standpipes, and means of egress. Thresholds for the installation of fire alarms are based on the use of sprinklers in the building and on the occupancy. For example, the office building just discussed would require a fire alarm if there were 100 occupants above the lowest level of exit discharge. With a total area per floor of 100,000 square feet, the occupant load would exceed 100 (100,000 SF ÷ 100 SF/occupant = 1,000 occupants). However, if the building has a sprinkler system and the alarm is activated by sprinkler flow, the manual pull boxes that would otherwise be a part of an alarm system are not required.

Means of Egress

Exiting, or means of egress, is one of the major code criteria that directly affect building design. Limitations are established in the code for how far a person must travel to reach an exit within a given space in a particular occupancy. These limitations include the distance when only a single path to an exit is available (common path of travel), dead-end corridor distances, and the total distance from any occupied

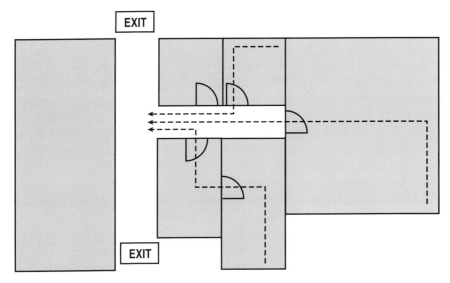

Travel Distance to Exits

location within the building to the exit or stairway or exit enclosure (exit access travel distance).

The allowed distance for each of these limitations is based on the specific occupancy the means of egress is serving. The common path of travel is the initial concern for any space or layout of spaces within a building. This distance is based on the risk of not being able to access an area. The typical distance limit is 75 feet before occupants must be able to access a second route. In a suite of rooms that all discharge through a common lobby or corridor, this would apply to every space within the suite.

For example, a dead-end corridor in the area of a hospital where patients are sleeping is limited to 20 feet of travel in a direction where there is no exit. In the same building, but in areas where administrative offices are located, the dead-end corridor is limited to 50 feet of travel, assuming the entire building is protected by a sprinkler system. This difference in the dead-end limits reflects the difference in hazard to the occupants. The difference is calculated by comparing the potential response times of patients who are asleep or somehow incapacitated and people in an office area who presumably are awake and alert to an emergency.

The required overall travel distance will prescribe the location of the exits from a floor or the building. The typical distance to an exit for most occupancy classifications is 250 feet, which means that from any given point the distance to any exit cannot exceed that distance. Discounting any distance that would be required to travel to a central exit corridor, the exits would have to be located no more than 500 feet apart. However, the reality is that occupants would have to travel an additional distance from within a space to any such central corridor. Thus, the actual distance between the exits would have to be shorter than the optimum distance.

THE RELATIONSHIP BETWEEN STANDARDS AND CODES

Model building codes have always incorporated standards, and within the construction industry, different types of standards serve various purposes in relation to how a building is designed. Some standards regulate specific types of systems or processes. Some provide methods for testing a product in a particular application. Standards for a particular product or material include criteria as a minimum level of quality. Typically, standards are expected to parallel the building or fire code that references them and to be written in language that can easily be incorporated as an enforceable part of a code. Standards that are simply advisory, which are not written in mandatory language, are not included in model building codes.

Most NFPA standards are regulatory, the classic example being NFPA 13 for sprinklers. This standard explains the means and methods necessary to design and install a sprinkler system in a building. Its requirements are based on an industry-wide understanding of the level of hazard in various occupancies and the means needed to actively prevent the spread of a fire. NFPA 13 is considered a consensus standard because the representation of interests on the committee that reviews it and votes on revisions to its content is so broad. The group reaches consensus by balancing conflicting interests.

Standards for testing such as those promulgated by ASTM International or Underwriters Laboratories are used to describe ways in which a material or an assembly of materials can be tested to determine a relative level of performance. ASTM E119, for example, is the fire test for floors and walls that is used to determine their ability to limit the spread of fire. The test prescribes the methods for construction of the test sample, the process of exposing it to the "standard time-temperature curve," and the levels of performance and how they are to be measured and reported. The classic measurement for a wall or floor assembly being tested using ASTM E119 is the length of time an assembly will remain in place before smoke or hot gases on the unexposed side will ignite cotton waste when exposed to these gases. The time duration is reported in hours, although the performance of an assembly in an actual fire is likely to be different from the text in the listing.

The curves for various "standard fires" rise in temperature very quickly. The ASTM E119 test goes up to almost 800°C in less than thirty minutes. At that point, a fire no longer increases at the same rate, although it does continue to increase in intensity until the test has been completed. A real fire may grow as rapidly as shown on these curves and may become even higher in intensity if the materials support rapid rates of combustion. However, a real fire typically dies down after the initial growth. This decrease is either caused by exhaustion of fuel or insufficient oxygen to feed the fire.

The purpose of standards like ASTM E119 is to establish a constant level of performance against which all tested materials can be measured. The use of the "hourly" rating is unfortunate because, as people become familiar with these ratings, the measurements become part of the lexicon of construction and an expected measure of the performance in a real fire.

There are industry standards for the production of various materials that are similar to NFPA standards and are developed using ASTM procedures. Wood, steel, concrete, and similar building products are brought to the marketplace under conventions

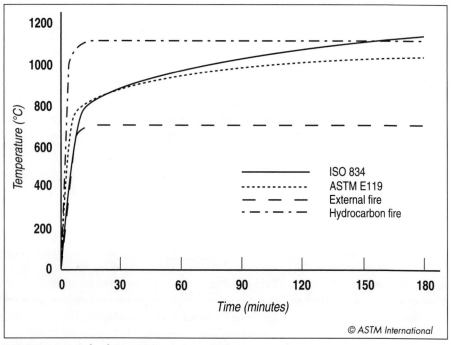

ASTM E119 Standard Time–Temperature Curve

developed using these types of standards. The American Lumber Standard for wood, ACI 318 for concrete, and AISC 360 for steel, are the standards for these major building materials; they are used in combination with building codes and various engineering standards such as ASCE 7, Minimum Design Loads for Buildings and Other Structures, for the design of structures using these particular materials.

When a standard is not developed so it can be used to regulate or enforce a minimum or dictate a means and method for construction, it is considered to be advisory. Such standards may be useful to a designer dealing with a special application, but they are not required and often are not written in a way that allows their use as law.

PERFORMANCE CODES

Recently, the ICC added a performance code option to the standard specification codes that have been used for years. This code is designed to address special needs for a limited number of projects that do not fit within the norm of a typical construction and may require a level of design, investigation, and controls beyond the scope of current model codes. The concept behind a performance code is to support development of unique solutions with the acceptance of the entire project team, which could include as many players as the owner, designer, developer, and contractor, as well as building, fire, and local regulators and development officials, bankers, and so on.

This team sets the goals and objectives for the project within the parameters established in accordance with the performance code. The parameters for a particular project

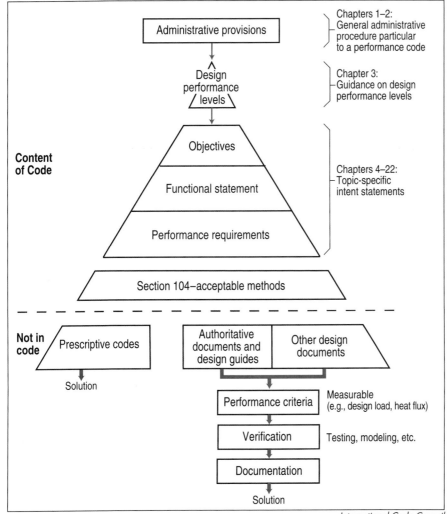

ICC Performance Code

International Code Council

PART 3: THE PROJECT

are determined based on the potential risk associated with the activities and an assessment of the needs of the owner and the community in which the facility will be constructed. By encouraging evaluation of risk and the effect the facility will have on identified risks, the performance code permits alternative methods for compliance.

Often, special testing or modeling tools to analyze specific risks are needed to more accurately define project parameters. For example, computer models can be used to determine egress times based on occupancy conditions. Similarly, there are models for determining how smoke would develop within a space given a specific type of fire. The type of fire is based on detailed analysis of the fire loading likely to be found in the space and includes consideration of factors such as the natural and mechanical ventilation available. By combining these two models, the time associated with evacuation of a given occupancy and the time associated with loss of a tenable environment can be compared and the risks evaluated.

The ICC codes include the risk of tenability for a typical environment, but often have been caught short of addressing special conditions. For instance, at one time, the IBC did not have specific criteria for a covered mall building; the use of a performance code would have been appropriate in that circumstance.

In addition, the performance codes are designed to facilitate solutions beyond those prescribed by the model codes. Typically, the codes are written as specifications and use performance options to achieve specified goals. Performance codes do not specify goals, but allow stakeholders to establish the methods and means to achieve the desired level of safety.

Evaluating risk and probable effect is key to developing appropriate performance solutions, as is being able to identify an appropriate means of testing and justifying the solutions. Often, technical specialists will be added to the design team to bring needed resources to bear on the subject.

INTERNATIONAL BUILDING CODE

Maximum Level of Damage to Be Tolerated

INCREASING LEVEL OF PERFORMANCE →

MAGNITUDE OF DESIGN EVENT		PERFORMANCE GROUP 1	PERFORMANCE GROUP II	PERFORMANCE GROUP III	PERFORMANCE GROUP IV
	VERY LARGE (very rare)	SEVERE	SEVERE	HIGH	MODERATE
	LARGE (rare)	SEVERE	HIGH	MODERATE	MILD
	MEDIUM (less frequent)	HIGH	MODERATE	MILD	MILD
	SMALL (frequent)	MODERATE	MILD	MILD	MILD

International Code Council

Testing and Verification

The National Institute for Standards and Technology has developed many computer software programs for evaluating building performance. Such programs are useful for determining design methods that may fall out of the standard specification for compliance. Following is a list of such programs:

- ALOFT-FT™—A Large Outdoor Fire-Plume Trajectory Model—Flat Terrain
- ASCOS—Analysis of Smoke Control Systems
- ASET-B—Available Safe Egress Time-Basic
- ASMET—Atria Smoke Management Engineering Tools
- BREAK1—Berkeley Algorithm for Breaking Window Glass in a Compartment Fire
- CCFM—Consolidated Compartment Fire Model version VENTS
- CFAST—Consolidated Fire and Smoke Transport Model
- DETACT-QS—Detector Actuation—Quasi Steady
- DETACT-T2—Detector Actuation—Time Squared
- ELVAC—Elevator Evacuation
- FASTLite—A collection of procedures that builds on the core routines of FIRE-FORM and the computer model CFAST to provide engineering calculations of various fire phenomena
- FIRDEMND—Handheld Hosestream Suppression Model
- FIRST—FIRe Simulation Technique
- FPETool—Fire Protection Engineering Tools (equations and fire simulation scenarios)
- Jet—A model for the prediction of detector activation and gas temperature in the presence of a smoke layer
- LAVENT—Response of sprinkler links in compartment fires with curtains and ceiling vents
- NIST Fire Dynamics Simulator and Smokeview: The Fire Dynamics Simulator predicts smoke and/or air flow movement caused by fire, wind, ventilation systems, etc. Smokeview visualizes the predictions generated by NIST FDS.

These programs are free and are available at the NIST Web site at www.bfrl.nist.gov/info/software.html. Used alone, they cannot ensure that the designed level of performance will be acceptable, but the information will provide additional guidance for designs that do not fall within the specifications in the codes. Additional sources of information for performance designs are included in the reference sections of the performance codes.

PRACTICE ISSUES

As a fundamental part of any design, building codes form an important framework for developing a program to achieve the owner's objectives. Consideration of the code criteria for a particular occupancy is critical to preliminary design decisions that will affect safety and health.

Checklists

For many years, model code groups produced code checklists intended to aid in the determination of code compliance. Although these were relatively useful tools for reviewing plans from an AHJ plan examiner's point of view, they did not provide enough information for those making design decisions.

Local Adoption of Current Codes

Building codes adopted by the vast majority of jurisdictions in the United States are now or soon will be based on the ICC family of codes. While many communities make changes to portions of the building code they have adopted for local political or geographic reasons, the use of a single national code appears to be the way of the future. A list of jurisdictions and the codes they have adopted can be obtained from either the National Conference of States on Building Codes and Standards (NCSBCS) or the ICC. Both organizations publish lists of communities and the codes they have adopted. NCSBCS information is available only to members, but the ICC lists are available to anyone on the ICC Web page.

Each of the ICC model codes includes basic directions on how to use them in the form of a sample ordinance for adoption. The ICC identifies sections that must be modified because of local conditions in the sample ordinance. However, most states that adopt the model codes delete the requirements in Chapter 1 and replace them with their own legislatively mandated administrative criteria. This can work well if careful consideration is given to the requirements in Chapter 1 of each code during the adoption process. If care is not taken, however, some unfortunate conflicts can be created either between different codes or between various code enforcing agencies within a jurisdiction.

One of the most important features of the new ICC codes is the level of coordination among them. These codes are meant to be used together to comprehensively address the various elements of construction that affect life safety and health. Without appropriate integration of the code enforcement package these codes provide, a community may miss some important safety features.

For example, as parallel documents, the IBC, IMC, IPC, IECC, and IFC codes are intended to be used in a coordinated fashion. Nonetheless, the IBC and IFC include duplicate criteria for such requirements as sprinklers, means of egress, and occupancies. This duplication is meant to reduce confusion among community enforcement officials. However, the IFC establishes minimum standards for existing buildings whether or not work is being performed or occupancies are being changed. These minimum standards are only enforceable through the IFC. If a community expects to apply such standards to all buildings, adoption of the fire code and a mechanism for enforcement is critical. Similarly, requirements for alterations to an existing structure are found in two documents— the IBC and the IEBC. Although these codes are parallel in many ways, the IBC lacks several specification requirements included in the IEBC. Both codes, however, include an alternative compliance method for evaluating the safety of an existing building.

Property maintenance issues involving handrails and guardrails, addressed in the International Property Maintenance Code, are intended to be applied through adoption of the IPMC. Mechanical and plumbing requirements are referenced in the IBC, and the code includes specific designs for ventilation of an atrium or an open mall. IBC references and the IMC both include general requirements for HVAC systems, including required amounts of fresh air. The IMC and IPC provide specific criteria for plumbing and mechanical systems, which the IBC includes many of the minimum design requirements. For example, the minimum number of plumbing fixtures for an occupancy classification is described in Chapter 29 of the IBC, while the details on materials and installation of the plumbing systems are in the IPC.

The lack of coordination between code documents in the past resulted in disjointed enforcement. To address this confusion, the ICC codes were designed to be applied uniformly by any part of an enforcement team. The building and fire codes are both applicable to the design of new structures, and projects should be designed and reviewed using both documents, thus preventing subsequent conflicts. This arrangement can fall apart, however, when communities fail to recognize this structure within the model codes and adopt different codes for different aspects of code enforcement. This saddles the owner with conflicts that the designer will be forced to resolve.

CODE ENFORCEMENT

Building code enforcement typically includes review of construction plans for proposed projects followed by inspection of the built work to ensure it conforms to the approved plans. State or local building departments operate within legislated authority to determine the acceptable means of designing and constructing the buildings submitted to them. Most often it is illegal to begin construction of a building without approvals or permits from the responsible AHJs. Completion of the construction process is typically marked by the issuance of a certificate of occupancy, which means the project can be used for the purpose indicated.

Some communities have a mandatory certification process that requires the design professional to take responsibility for substantial completion in accordance with the codes. This additional level of responsibility for the designer is unusual and may lead to unnecessary liability if not handled properly.

Planning and Zoning

Planning and zoning regulations are generally found in more developed areas of the country where the land available to be developed is limited. These types of regulations are also part of a model code process, but they are not generally adopted very widely. The ICC has a model zoning code that outlines the major subjects commonly included in zoning codes, such as use districts, limitations on activities and density, location on a lot, and so on. Generally, zoning is strictly local, although planning often can be regional. It is critical during the early stages of any design project to examine the zoning limitations for the site to determine if the use is allowed and what additional requirements, such as height and setback, might affect the design.

▶ Community Planning Controls (10.1) addresses regulations used to shape the form and function of communities.

Water/Plumbing Codes

Criteria for water supply to a building and the plumbing fixtures required for it are established in local plumbing codes. The International Plumbing Code is designed to work closely with the IBC and IMC to specify the proper type of water supply and appropriate number of fixtures for a particular type of facility compatible with those described in the ICC codes. Some local jurisdictions maintain a local plumbing and mechanical code, and the International Association of Plumbers and Mechanical Officials (IAPMO) continues to produce the Uniform Plumbing and Mechanical Code, still in wide use in the western United States.

Controls for the design of storm and sanitary drainage systems are tied to the methods used to design and locate a structure and its site features (e.g., parking lots, sidewalks, etc.). Sites where storm drainage systems are overtaxed commonly retain storm water.

Code Appeals

When the inevitable disagreement occurs about how a code applies, or should apply, to a particular design, the dispute can be resolved through an appeal process. Although most legal disputes are resolved in the courts, the planning and zoning and construction processes require additional opportunities for administrative review in which specific expertise can be employed to resolve a dispute. Most communities establish boards of appeal to facilitate these reviews or hearings.

Variances or equivalent means of achieving compliance to zoning codes are usually allowed under local zoning regulations. However, the ICC has limits on its appeal board as their rules state they have no authority to "waive requirements of this code." Various state laws may or may not permit adjustments to codes. For example, under the Ohio Revised Code, local appeal boards are certified and given the following specific authority:

112.4 Powers, local boards of building appeals. Certified municipal and county boards of building appeals shall hear and decide the adjudication hearings referred to in section 113.1 within the jurisdiction of and arising from orders of the local building official in the enforcement of Chapters 3781 and 3791 of the Revised Code and rules adopted thereunder. The orders may be reversed or modified by the board if it finds:

1. The order contrary to such laws or rules;
2. The order contrary to a fair interpretation or application thereof; or,

3. That a variance from the provisions of such laws or rules, in a specific case, will not be contrary to the public interest where literal enforcement of such provisions will result in unnecessary hardship.

Specific laws that allow variances may exist in other jurisdictions as well.

PARTICIPATION IN CODE DEVELOPMENT

Code development is a process that depends on people who take the time and make the effort to participate. Participation does not necessarily mean serving on a committee or even attending hearings on a subject. It means simply being aware of the codes and being able and willing to suggest ways in which they can better address technical issues. Web sites include forms for proposing changes to the codes, but often no more than a phone call to a staff person at the model code agency responsible for the code will begin the process of change. Many local building officials are part of a local ICC chapter that develops changes to the code, and architects can approach them about ways to fix problems or discrepancies in the model code.

Associations such as the National Association of Home Builders (NAHB), Building Owners and Managers Association (BOMA), and the AIA have resources available to help forward changes to the codes as well, and interested architects should approach them about promoting development of needed changes. In addition, staff members of the code organizations can be an invaluable resource in preparing material to enact a code change. Architects are typically the first to realize a problem with a particular provision, or to develop a unique solution to a problem not recognized in the code. By bringing forward changes that reflect a heightened awareness of what is in the code and what can work within the framework of the codes, an architect can have a profound effect on design and construction throughout the country.

For More Information

The International Code Council Web site provides a lot of information about the development and adoption of codes and standards. In particular, a list of jurisdictions and the ICC building codes they have adopted can be found at www.iccsafe.org/government/adoption.html.

Two heavily illustrated publications offer interpretive guidance on the 2006 International Building Code: *2006 Building Code Handbook* (McGraw-Hill, 2007), by Terry L. Patterson, and *Building Codes Illustrated: A Guide to Understanding the 2006 International Building Code*, second edition (Wiley, 2007), by Francis D. K. Ching and Steven R. Winkel.

BACKGROUNDER

THE INTERNATIONAL BUILDING CODE

David S. Collins, FAIA

Working with a client to solve a particular design problem is the fundamental essence of what an architect does. Critical to the process of solving the problem is understanding the client's needs and the constraints under which the designer will be working to meet them. These constraints include the resources available for a project, such as the means available to cover the costs of construction, fees, and other expenses. The application of building regulations is simply one more constraint on the development of a solution that must be at the forefront of the designer's mind.

Step 1: Determine Occupancy

Codes require establishment of one or more occupancy categories for a building. The terminology used in the various model codes to describe these building uses has evolved in the IBC format to titles such as "Group A-1 Occupancy" for a theater or "Group B Occupancy" for an office building. Since most buildings have more than one occupancy classification, it is important to understand how the code treats different configurations and the relationship between different occupancies.

The IBC treats the relationship between two or more occupancies in three ways—as incidental, accessory, or mixed. The mixed category is further divided into separated and unseparated areas. Areas within a building classified as incidental or accessory are not controlling factors on the building height and area, but they are still considered separately for purposes of specific characteristics, such as egress. For example, although a storeroom in an office building is considered incidental to a Group B business occupancy, the floor loading must still conform to the requirements for storage.

Incidental use areas. Earlier model codes contained a set of requirements for "specific occupancies." Most of these requirements were developed specifically for institutional occupancies and reflected the requirements for separation originally created in the *Life Safety Code*. Now, the IBC requires that areas treated as incidental must be separated by a one-hour fire barrier that have self-closing doors with no air transfer openings and/or have a fire suppression system installed.

Accessory use areas. To be considered accessory to another occupancy, an area cannot exceed 10 percent of the total floor area or the allowed tabular values for height and area for the accessory occupancy as determined by the height and area table.

Mixed occupancy. If the occupancies in a building are too large to be considered either incidental or accessory, the building is considered to have mixed occupancies. The distinction between mixed separated and mixed unseparated affects only how the code is applied to the height and area limits for the type of construction; all other aspects of the code are applied to each occupancy separately.

An unseparated mixed-use building is controlled in height and area by the more restrictive of the occupancies it houses. For a separated mixed occupancy, a comparative ratio can be used to address the limits established by each occupancy classification compared to the actual area. As long as the sum of the ratios of the fractions is equal to or less than 1.0, the areas are permitted to be of that type of construction as determined in Chapter 6 of the IBC.

However, to determine whether a building should be considered a separated or unseparated mixed use, the occupan-

cies must be identified and their characteristics understood. The occupancies listed in the IBC are as follows:

- Assembly: Groups A-1, A-2, A-3, A-4, and A-5
- Business: Group B
- Educational: Group E
- Factory and Industrial: Groups F-1 and F-2
- High Hazard: Groups H-1, H-2, H-3, H-4, and H-5
- Institutional: Groups I-1, I-2, I-3, and I-4
- Mercantile: Group M
- Residential: Groups R-1, R-2, R-3, and R-4
- Storage: Groups S-1 and S-2
- Utility and Miscellaneous: Group U

The subdivisions within the A, F, H, I, R, and S groups are used to differentiate between different hazards within these general classifications. For example, the assembly groups are subdivided into these categories:

- A-1: Traditional stage theaters and motion picture theaters
- A-2: Restaurants and night clubs
- A-3: Churches, dance halls, and small gymnasiums that do not have spectator seating
- A-4: Arenas and gymnasiums with spectator seating
- A-5: Outdoor places of assembly

Any assembly occupancy that is not an accessory space and has an occupant load of less than fifty is classified in the B Group.

Step 2: Identify Thresholds and Fire Areas

Because of the importance the model codes place on the installation of an automatic fire suppression system, once the occupancy of a building is known, it is fairly simple to determine whether the code will require it to be protected by a sprinkler system. The threshold limits for fire suppression are based on one or more of the following:

- The fire area or building area in which the occupancy is located
- Where the occupancy is located in the building
- The number of occupants in a building or fire area

Fire areas are enclosures that provide a particular fire resistance based on the risk associated with the occupancy:

H-1, H-2	4 hrs.
F-1, H-3, S-1	3 hrs.
A, B, E, F-2, H-4, H-5, I, M, R, S-2	2 hrs.
U	1 hr.

Each fire area must be surrounded by firewalls, fire barriers (floors or walls), or exterior walls or roof. Only portions of the enclosure inside the structure are required to provide the fire resistance rating.

(continued)

IBC Threshold Limits for Fire Suppression

Use Group	Threshold
Assembly	
A-1	Fire area >12,000 SF, or >299 occupants, or not on level of exit discharge (contains a multi-theater complex)
A-2	Fire area >5,000 SF, or >99 occupants, or not on level of exit discharge
A-3	Fire area >12,000 SF, or >299 occupants, or not on level of exit discharge
A-4	Fire area >12,000 SF, or >299 occupants, or not on level of exit discharge
A-5	Concession stands, retail, press boxes >1,000 SF in area
Business	
B	No threshold
Educational	
E	Fire area >20,000 SF, or located below the level of exit discharge
Factory and Industrial	
F-1	Fire area >12,000 SF, or > three stories above grade plane, or combined areas on all floors >24,000 SF
High Hazard	
H	All
Institutional	
I	All
Mercantile	
M	Fire area >12,000 SF, or > three stories above grade plane, or combined areas of all floors >24,000 SF
Residential	
R	All
Storage	
S-1	Fire area > 12,000 SF, or > three stories above grade plane, or combined areas of all floors > 24,000 SF
S-2	All enclosed parking garages
Utility and Miscellaneous	
U	No threshold

In the IBC, threshold limits for fire suppression of a building or fire area are as shown in the accompanying table.

To avoid having to install fire suppression within a space, a fire area separation can be used to subdivide a single occupancy. As long as all the fire areas within a building individually fall below the limits, no fire suppression system is required.

In addition to spaces above the area thresholds for a fire area, sprinkler systems are required throughout any windowless stories, any building with a height exceeding fifty-five feet, and underground structures more than thirty feet below the lowest level of exit discharge.

Step 3: Identify Type of Construction Permitted

The accompanying chart compares the types of construction listed in the IBC to those included in previous model codes:

Comparison of Types of Construction by Code

International Building Code (IBC)	National Building Code (BOCA)	Standard Building Code (SBCCI)	Uniform Building Code (UBC)
	1A	1	
IA	1B	II	I FR
IB	2A	—	II FR
IIA	2B	IV 1-hr.	II 1 hr.
IIB	2C	IV unpro.	III N
IIIA	3A	V 1-hr	III 1-hr.
IIIB	3B	V unpro.	III N
IV	4	III	IV HT
VA	5A	VI 1-hr.	V 1 hr.
VB	5B	VI unpro.	V N

Reductions. Tables 601 and 602 in the IBC prescribe minimum fire resistance requirements for building elements based on their function and their location in a building. Significant exceptions are located in the sections regarding use of various materials in both the text of and in footnotes outlining permitted reductions in the required fire resistance.

The UBC had allowed a reduction in the fire resistance of building elements if the building was sprinklered. However, that reduction was permitted only if the fire sprinklers were not required for any other reason in the code. The IBC includes this identical provision.

The means to determine the limits on building height and area are tied to several factors. As noted, the occupancy and whether or not the building is fully sprinklered are critical. Given some idea of what the building height

decided to use the report from the Board for the Coordination of the Model Codes (BCMC). Applying that method in reverse, the values in Table 503 were developed. (See the adjacent excerpt from Table 503, which shows a portion of the base areas.

Height modifications. Buildings are permitted to have a one-story and 20'-0" height increase if the building is protected throughout by a sprinkler system. This increase applies to both NFPA 13 and 13R sprinkler systems (13R is limited to a maximum of four stories and can be used only on residential structures). Group H hazardous occupancies are not permitted to get the increase. Group I-2 occupancies are not permitted the height modification when in buildings of Type IIB, III, IV, or V construction.

Area determination. The overall area of a building is not permitted to exceed three different limits: a one-story

Allowable Height and Building Areas from Table 503, International Building Code

Type of Construction

		I A	B	II A	B	III A	B	IV HT	V A	B
Feet		UL	160	65	55	65	55	65	50	40
Stories										
A-2	S	UL	11	3	2	3	2	3	2	1
	A	UL	UL	15,500	9,500	14,000	9,500	15,000	11,500	6,000
B	S	UL	11	5	4	5	4	5	3	2
	A	UL	UL	37,500	23,000	28,500	19,000	36,000	18,000	9,000
E	S	UL	5	3	2	3	2	3	1	1
	A	UL	UL	26,500	14,500	23,500	14,500	25,500	18,500	9,500
R-1	S	UL	11	4	4	4	4	4	3	2
	A	UL	UL	24,000	16,000	24,000	16,000	20,500	12,000	7,000

Notes:
1. Height limitations shown as stories and feet above grade plane.
2. Area limitations as determined by the definition of "Area, building," per floor.

needs to be and a concept for the layout of the floors and the location of the building, the type of construction can be easily determined.

Table 503 of the IBC is derived from methods for determining height used in the three model building codes. The concept used by the drafting committee was to accept the largest height and area of any building that would have been permitted by any of the codes. To accomplish this, the staff of each code organization was asked to determine the largest area and height of a building given an occupancy and a type of construction.

Because all three model codes used a different method for determining maximum height and area, the committee

building cannot exceed the maximum allowable area, a two-story building cannot exceed the maximum allowable area multiplied by two, and a building with three stories or more is limited to a maximum of three times the allowable area. In addition, the largest floor in any building may not exceed the maximum allowable area per floor. This means that when you calculate the maximum allowable floor for the occupancies, the total building is permitted to only be three times that amount. As a building design gets taller, the maximum area for the occupancy and type of construction does not change, nor does the three-times-the-allowable-area change. So, a four-story building would only be permitted to have floors that were three-quarters of the allowable area.

(continued)

A five-story building would only be allowed three-fifths. These conclusions are based on the assumption that all floors remain the same size.

The code will permit a bit more creativity as long as the total does not exceed three times the allowable area. For example, a five-story building can have one floor that is equal to one allowable area, and the other four floors only have one-half an allowable area $(1 + [4 \times \sim 1/2]) = 3$. Other combinations are also permitted as long as the total does not exceed the magic number of three times the allowable area.

Allowable area. The formula for determining allowable area involves three variables; the tabular area (A_t) from Table 503 for the type of construction, an increase for frontage (I_f) and an increase for fire suppression (I_s). As noted earlier, a designer should know what the actual area of the building is going to be and be able to solve for the minimum tabular area. Thus, the formula is revised to solve for A_t.

$$A_t = \left[\frac{A_a}{1 + I_f + I_s} \right]$$

Frontage increase. The building code provides up to 150 percent credit for additional open space around a building allowing additional protection for spread of fire and allowing access for fire fighting. Most buildings will not be allowed a frontage increase of more than 75 percent. The minimum distance between a building and a property line, or the imaginary line between two buildings on the same lot, in order to gain any credit is 20'-0". Once that distance is achieved, there are two factors; W/30 and a 1 percent increase in building area for each 1 percent of building perimeter that faces on such open space around the building that exceeds a minimum of 25 percent of the building perimeter. W/30 uses the space around the building of between twenty and sixty feet, so a twenty-foot frontage would have a two-thirds factor and a thirty-foot frontage would have a factor of one. For example, if a building has twenty feet of open space around the entire building, the maximum frontage increase would be 50 percent $[(1 \times 100 \text{ percent}) - 25 \text{ percent} = 75 \text{ percent} \times 20/30]$. If the same building had ten feet of open space around 50 percent of the building and twenty feet of open space around 50 percent of the building, the increase would be 16.7 percent $[(1 \times 50 \text{ percent}) - 25 \text{ percent} \times 20/30]$.

An additional consideration for frontage design is the code requirement for fire department vehicular access to the building. An approved route to within 150 feet of the entire perimeter of the first floor of all buildings is required.

Sprinkler increases. A one-story building is permitted a 300 percent increase, and a building of two stories or more is permitted a 200 percent increase when the building has an NFPA 13 sprinkler installed throughout. A building with an NFPA 13R system will add one story and twenty feet to the allowable height of a residential building. NFPA 13D systems, which are permitted in limited residential applications, do not provide area or height increases.

Basement. As long as the area of a single basement does not exceed the area permitted for a single story building, it is not included in the determination of the overall area of the building.

Buildings on same lot. Multiple buildings on the same lot can be considered as a single building as long as the cumulative floor areas and their heights do not exceed the limitations that would be allowed if they were one building.

Unlimited area buildings. Table 503 includes combinations of building types and occupancies that are not limited in height or area. These are different from an unlimited-area building that is controlled by occupancy, a minimum open frontage around the building, fire suppression, and the use of the building. Both one- and two-story buildings can be unlimited in area.

For example, a single-story building that is not Type V construction and used for low-hazard storage or manufacturing can be unlimited in area as long as there is a sixty-foot open space completely around the building. Fire suppression is not required in that type of building, despite the size of it. A two-story building is allowed to be of any construction type and is considered an unlimited area building if it is protected by an NFPA 13 sprinkler system throughout, has a sixty-foot open space around the building, and is used for any combination of B, M, F, or S occupancies. Other occupancies are also permitted in some variations of these extremes and using different combinations of open space, suppression, and types of construction. Even hazardous materials are permitted in unlimited area buildings with the proper location and separation.

Step 4: Means of Egress

The means of egress from a space and subsequently from a building will be very influential in determining the building configuration. Means of egress includes the path from any occupied space in a building to the public way. It is broken down into three elements—exit access, exit, and exit discharge.

Fundamentally, exit access is the path from within any occupied space in the building to the entrance to an exit. The exit is either a door that opens directly to the outside or a protected stair or ramp, and the exit discharge is the path between the exit door and the public way.

The constraints for exit access and exit will be important to the final configuration of a building. There are two fundamental aspects of exit access—travel distance within a space and travel distance to an exit.

For most occupancies, the travel distance within a space will be limited to seventy-five feet before two distinct paths to leave the space are required. In some instances, the maximum travel distance may be shorter due to high occupant loads. In others, if sprinklers are installed, the distance can be increased. Determination of the required travel distance is highly dependent upon the occupancy of the space.

Once out of a space, the exit access continues to the exit. The travel distance to an exit overlaps the travel distance allowed in a space. For example, in an office environment, a suite of offices is not required to have more than one means of egress until the travel distance within the space exceeds 75 feet. However, the overall travel distance from any space within the suite of offices to an exit is 250 feet. The 75 feet of travel is part of the 250 feet of travel; it is not permitted to be added to the overall travel distance to an exit.

When a building requires two exits, the travel distance is only measured to one of the exits, not both. In the office example above, all the spaces within the office would be required to have at least one exit within the 250-foot distance. If the office building is protected by an NFPA 13 sprinkler system, the travel distance is allowed to increase to 300 feet.

Exits. Generally, an exit is a door opening directly to the outside or an enclosed exit stair. There are several exceptions for specific occupancies, and there are some general ones that allow an exit stair to be either an enclosed or unenclosed exit. Unenclosed exits are limited to two-story buildings or to stairs serving only two floors.

Exit travel distance is measured to the entrance of the enclosed stair or door. If an unenclosed stair is used, the distance continues along the stair until the point where an exit door is reached. Enclosed stairs are required to provide a fire-rated enclosure of either one hour or two hours. Two-hour stair enclosures are required when the stair connects four or more floors.

There is no limit on the distance traveled within an enclosed exit. Exits are typically required to discharge to the outside. Up to 50 percent of the exits can discharge through a lobby space on the level of exit discharge as long as it affords protection from any levels below and has a sprinkler system.

Exit discharge. Exit discharge is the aspect of the means of egress that is most often overlooked. With the recommended guidelines for accessibility issued by the Access Board, designing exterior elements to conform to the codes will become even more critical. There are no dimensional limits on the travel distance once outside the building, except if exits discharge onto an exit balcony.

Step 5: Systems

Once the building configuration is generally understood, other elements of the code will have additional influence on the design of a building. These include the ventilation systems, plumbing systems, the structural design, materials used, and so on.

Ventilation. HVAC limits are established first in the IBC with minimum natural ventilation criteria based on the operating features of the windows and openings between spaces. Mechanical ventilation is not required in any building except when the requirements for natural ventilation are not met. For buildings using a mechanical system, the IMC establishes the standard based on the occupancy of the space for the amount of air and the required fresh air. This includes limits on the ability to recirculate the air from various locations within a building, which reduces problems with unhealthy air in large occupant areas but may increase costs for management of the air within a building.

Environmental issues such as mold are not specifically addressed in the building code or mechanical code. The IMC and IBC require either mechanical or natural ventilation of crawl spaces and attic spaces to prevent unwanted stagnation of air, which can promote unacceptable conditions in such spaces.

Structural design. The structural design requirements prescribe the minimum loads under various construction and load conditions. Obviously, the structure must support itself and the load of the building materials that depend on it to remain in place. Occupancy loads are based on the activity within the space, and they determine the "live loads." Environmental loads account for the wind, snow, rain, earthquake, and flood loads that may impact a building.

Special local conditions. The building codes are designed to include the most up-to-date information available from the best resources available; however, there may be local conditions so specialized they cannot be included in any standard set of building safety guidelines. In developing a building design, it is important to understand any such conditions, whether they are known and part of local regulations or unknown and discovered as part of a soils investigation or other means.

Material limits. The code includes specifications for materials, including minimum quality standards, as well as various means for determining the strength of a member to resist a given load. In particular, standards for concrete, masonry, steel, wood, glass, aluminum, and gypsum are specified in the building code. Other materials are permitted by the code if their ability to perform to a level equivalent to those referenced in the code can be demonstrated. This is often a difficult process for new materials, but the level of assurance required to determine conformance with safety standards is very high.

Plumbing fixtures. Sanitation is fundamental to the first element of the "health, safety, and welfare" mantra. The IBC references the International Plumbing Code, which mandates the types and number of fixtures and the systems necessary to support minimum sanitary conditions within buildings.

PART 4

CONTRACTS AND AGREEMENTS

CHAPTER 11

Types of Agreements

11.1 Agreements with Owners

James Dunn, Assoc. AIA, CPA

The architect's agreement with the client should reflect the goals and expectations of both parties and establish the conditions under which services will be rendered.

The architect's agreement or contract (these terms are used interchangeably in this chapter) with the owner should be written to reflect the goals and expectations of each and to establish the conditions for working together in a professional relationship. Normally, architects think of the contract as the primary legal document recording the promises parties make about their responsibilities for the creation of a project. The contract delineates services and compensation, typically allocates risk, helps each party cope with change, and provides a method for resolving disputes.

Contracts can also be an excellent way to communicate and educate. They can make explicit what might otherwise be unsaid and make clear what might be misunderstood. Unstated expectations can be time bombs that explode in misunderstandings and hard feelings, potentially damaging an otherwise good working relationship. On the other hand, clearly stated goals and assumptions are more likely to be mutually understood and confirmed as a basis for a good working and professional relationship. Think of a

---

Jim Dunn, executive vice president of the Boston Architectural College, was formerly general manager for Goody Clancy, a Boston-based firm specializing in architecture, planning, and preservation, where he was responsible for overseeing contracts, technology, and client negotiations. He has been a member of the AIA Contract Documents Committee. (This topic is an updated version of "Agreements with Clients" by Edward T. M. Choi, FAIA, for the thirteenth edition of the Handbook.)

contract as a means of communicating explicitly and as a way to achieve a meeting of minds between parties.

Contracts allocate rights and rewards, and responsibilities and risks, thus aiding architects in managing their exposure to legal liability and business risks. Projects tend to run smoothly and parties tend to perform properly when they know what is expected at the outset of the work. Architects must understand that every owner represents a unique entity with specific project goals and constraints. The unique characteristics of the owner and/or of the project should be taken into consideration when negotiating and drafting the owner-architect agreement.

Experience teaches us that circumstances change over time; through contracts, architects can anticipate and prepare for future possibilities. For example, architects are commonly asked to perform services outside what are considered normal and customary basic services for construction-related projects. When writing an agreement, parties to the contract can anticipate other services and include them in the contract to create a comprehensive package of architectural services that meet the owner's needs. Because not all services can be anticipated, contracts may also need to be amended after the agreement is signed.

Finally, contracts can provide a means of resolving disputes. All contracts begin by assuming each party is operating in good faith and creating a mutually advantageous agreement. However, misunderstandings or differences of opinion are sometimes unavoidable. No contract can prescribe the resolution of every possible problem, but good contracts can specify a mechanism for resolving disputes and for maintaining a working relationship between architect and owner while problems are resolved.

RESPONDING TO REQUESTS FOR PROPOSALS

Architects often get work by responding to a request for proposals. The AIA recommends that this type of solicitation process be based on qualifications and free from price comparison. In other words, owners should examine the talent and experience of the architect and make a selection on the basis of merit before discussing compensation. In some cases, however, and sometimes after making a short list of candidates, the owner may ask for a proposed fee to help distinguish one candidate from another. Architects may be asked first to propose the services they believe necessary along with the services requested by the owner, and then to propose compensation for performing those services. Architects should give careful consideration to the content and wording of the fee proposal.

Every fee proposal for services and compensation should cover the following: what the owner and architect will and will not do, the timing of services, and the compensation for those services. Before preparing a response to a request for proposal, the architect should be satisfied that these three issues can be adequately addressed in the proposal. In addition, the architect should consider the following questions:

▶ Architectural Services and Compensation (6.2) addresses fees for professional services.

- Is what is expected of the parties clear? Are the scope, program, site, and budget for the project complete enough to serve as a basis for agreement? Should the architect propose a two-phase process, in which the first step is a simple contract of short duration to establish the program for the project? Will other professionals work on the project? Are there special legal, approval, or permitting issues the owner or architect should be aware of?
- Is the schedule clearly understood? Would a different project delivery method provide a timelier project? Might the project be fast-tracked? Will multiple contract document packages be required?
- Is the architect being paid appropriately? What if the owner plans to pay only if the construction loan is closed? Will a construction manager be involved? Who will engage special consultants, the architect or the owner? What if the budget is impossible to meet or the owner proposes terms and conditions that require the

architect to provide an unattainable (and uninsurable) level of performance? Is the amount of reward commensurate with the amount of risk the architect is accepting?

Proposals as Offers

A proposal that includes a scope of services and proposed compensation may be considered an offer to provide services. If the owner accepts the offer, a binding agreement is established.

Proposals that become agreements may be problematic, both for what they include and for what they omit. For example, statements included for marketing purposes can create problems if they use superlative descriptions that induce the owner to expect a level of service that exceeds the architect's standard of care. Other problems may arise if the proposal fails to include the terms and conditions under which the architect will perform services. To avoid the latter problem, the architect should complete and incorporate into the proposal the terms and conditions of AIA Document B101–2007, Standard Form of Agreement Between Owner and Architect, or B102–2007, Standard Form of Agreement Between Owner and Architect Without a Predefined Scope of Architect's Services. A statement should be included specifying that the proposal is based on provision of services in accordance with the terms and conditions set forth in the attached agreement, which should be edited to include the particular terms of the proposal to which it is attached.

Oral Agreements and Letters of Intent

Many times, architects feel compelled to begin work before a contract is finalized. Performing services without a written agreement can be quite risky. If things do not proceed as planned, a court or arbiter may find that the parties did not intend to be bound until the formal agreement was signed. In that case, the architect may be considered a "volunteer" to whom no compensation is owed. Clearly, without a signed agreement, the architect is at risk and will remain so until the agreement is finalized and signed.

What about oral agreements? Are they valid? They may be, but it is not the validity of these agreements that is a problem; rather, it is the proof of their terms. What was the intent of the parties? What was agreed upon? Was there really an agreement at all? These questions are usually asked when each party has a vested interest in the answer. Later, architects and owners can each be accused of remembering only what is in their best interests—and that is likely to be different from what the other party wants to remember. So, what can be done?

Always performing work pursuant to an executed written agreement will help architects avoid these issues. If an architect is unable, in certain circumstances, to withhold services until a formal written agreement is signed, the architect may consider using a letter of intent. Such a letter would state that the architect has begun to perform services on the basis outlined in the proposal pending execution of the formal written agreement. The letter of intent should reference the proposed contract terms and preferred contract form, such as the AIA B101–2007, if it has not already been incorporated into the written proposal.

Once the architect is performing services, the owner is likely to feel no urgency to sign a formal agreement, especially if the owner is making payments to the architect. The architect may also feel that given the choice between having a contract and being paid, being paid is the better choice. This may be true to a point, but being without a contract that protects the architect's legal rights puts the architect at considerable risk. The architect should always strive to obtain a comprehensive and fully executed written agreement as promptly as possible.

WHAT TYPE OF AGREEMENT MAKES SENSE?

Architects are generally faced with three types of owner-architect agreements. The first is an owner-generated contract. Often public agencies, large institutions, or major commercial owners who have repeated and ongoing building programs and many years of experience will create a highly specific owner-architect agreement that suits their particular needs. The second source of owner-architect agreements is professional organizations other than the AIA. The third, and most often used form of agreement, is one of the AIA standard form agreements.

The AIA has published standard agreements for more than 120 years, providing the building industry with unbiased documents that represent contractual links between owners, architects, contractors, subcontractors, and consultants. AIA standard documents are periodically updated to reflect the broad changes that affect the building industry as a whole, as well as specific changes in the practice of architecture. Current AIA standard documents include revisions based on legal precedents and recommendations from national organizations representing legal, construction, engineering, and owner interests.

Characteristics of the Owner

For an architect, owners are often considered the hardest-to-understand participant in the contract equation. Unlike the legal and engineering professions, the construction industry and other design professions, owners do not subscribe to one set of tenets. Even owners that focus on building specialties, such as public schools, hospitals, or housing, usually want to see language in their contracts tailored to reflect their special interests and requirements.

Less experienced owners. These owners may not actually understand the role of an architect and thus have unrealistic expectations about the services architects can provide. The architect may need to educate such owners during contract negotiations as well as throughout the project. In a relationship with an inexperienced owner, the architect can use the contract to help keep owners' expectations and goals in line with reality.

Underfunded owners. These owners also require special attention during contract negotiations. Owners may want more building than they can afford, or they may not have the financial resources to do the project at all. Some owners may be dependent on arrangements that are conditional upon a financial closing to fund the construction and to pay for the development costs, including the architect's compensation. In such situations, architects may be at risk of not receiving all or a portion of their compensation until the closing occurs. In any case, a project budget should be established at the beginning of a relationship, especially if the contract requires the architect to design within the budget. Seeing a budget at the outset will also allow the architect to understand how the compensation will be paid. Architects should make every effort to communicate to owners the importance of having a budget, including how the budget affects the project scope. Do not assume an owner has the funds for the project or fully understands the true cost of seeing the project to completion.

Owners represented by boards or committees. School boards, church building committees, and condominium boards—as well as all groups using public monies or funds from members or foundations—operate under the assumption that they function as custodians of their organizations and thus their actions should be available for all to see. Legally, some owners work under "sunshine laws," legal requirements that require public disclosure. Reporting requirements sometimes make it difficult for these groups to develop and maintain consensus on goals, schedules, and budgets. As with project decisions, it may take some time to develop an owner-architect agreement, as it will have to undergo close scrutiny by many people.

This brings us to an important point in all contracts: It is helpful to both parties if the owner designates a representative authorized to deal directly with the architect. The contract should specify a person on the owner's team on whom the architect can rely for decisions in a timely manner. In this particular case, this person may be the board or committee chair, whose job it will be to synthesize input from various sources and give the architect instructions on which the architect can depend.

Litigious owners. Some people and organizations are simply more litigious than others. Researching suspected litigious owners before accepting a commission is always a good idea. Architects should check with the local design community if they have any suspicions about an owner in this regard. In addition, architects may want to consult with their lawyers or check into court records. The mere fact of past litigation should not prejudice an architect against a given owner, but architects will be better able to address potential problems and provide for their solution in their agreement if they are well informed.

How owners select their architects reveals something about their fundamental values and priorities. Some owners investigate and compare the scope and quality of services of different architects to determine what will be in their best interests. Some owners proceed with the idea that price is a consideration when professionals compete for owners and projects. Architects should ask themselves some basic questions: Does the owner understand all the services required to accomplish the project? Does a bidding requirement indicate that the prospective owner is inadequately funded and is trying to make up some of the shortfall by skimping on professional compensation? Does it indicate that the owner does not understand the nature of professional services? Is there a clear chain of command?

Some owners believe that all architecture services are identical. For them, price is the only difference. When that is the case, there may be problems ahead. Owners who see the architect as the provider of a product and not as a provider of professional services will likely be disappointed and dissatisfied if the "product" isn't perfect. The core of an architectural contract is the "fee for services" concept. As with lawyers and accountants, the documents the architect produces (drawings and specifications) are a mere representation of the services that are contracted for. The relationship between owner and architect is better if they are able to negotiate a level of compensation that they both believe reflects the owner's aspirations, the architect's qualifications, the nature of the project, and the type and extent of services required.

Owners who do not have the experience or staff to manage a building project may hire a project manager. In such situations, owners may outsource to a consultant, either a single individual or a company, to act as an owner's representative and manage the project on behalf of the owner. Project managers, who may also be architects, help owners make decisions about projects and help to make communications among the parties timely and adequate.

Characteristics of the Project

Just as types of owners influence contractual matters, types of projects do as well. Relevant project characteristics include the litigation history of the project type, jurisdictional factors, design and construction characteristics, adequacy of the construction and project budgets, and design and construction schedules.

Litigation history. Claims data from insurance companies show condominium, school, and hospital projects are involved in a relatively large number of claims. This may stem from the fact that owners and users of buildings often are not the same, and it may be difficult for architects to meet the expectations of both parties. When an owner will not be the end user of a project, the architect should take steps to add language to the agreement that protects the architecture firm from third-party claims. This language should be based on consultations with a professional liability insurance carrier and an attorney familiar with this type of agreement.

Jurisdictional factors. Each state has different requirements for professional services agreements. Generally, the architect of record for the project must be legally registered in the state where the project is located. For an architecture firm to practice in a state, it must meet the requirements both for running a business in that state and for practicing professionally in the state. Architects are advised to seek legal counsel when they consider practicing in an unfamiliar jurisdiction.

One way to approach a new business opportunity in another jurisdiction is to collaborate with a local architect. Anticipating this arrangement, the AIA has created standard form documents for two types of relationships between architects. The first is a joint venture agreement, AIA Document C101–1993, Joint Venture Agreement for Professional Services, which creates a third, new entity to undertake the project. The second is AIA Document C404–2007, Standard Form of Agreement Between Architect and Consulting Architect. This agreement provides for one architect to work in an associated role under a prime architect who holds the agreement with the project owner.

Design and construction characteristics. When new, cutting-edge design or construction techniques or unusual site conditions will be part of the project, contracts should be flexible enough to reflect the possibility of design changes and a longer-than-normal design period. On the construction side, such conditions may increase construction problems, change order requests, delays, and construction costs. These occurrences are natural outgrowths of this type of project. It is important to use the contract to inform the owner about what to expect and to record the allocation of risks between owner and architect.

Budgets and schedules. Budgets and schedules can be a major source of confusion and misunderstanding. For this reason, AIA Document B101–2007 requires inclusion of budget information in the initial information recorded in a project agreement. For example, owners often confuse the construction budget with the project budget. In fact, there are many costs associated with delivering a project, and construction cost is only one of them. The architect should be prepared to discuss the entire project budget with the owner when providing the initial information. The architect should also discuss cost contingencies with an owner, as actual costs can be affected by market conditions and refinements in design.

Architects should also be realistic when discussing schedule requirements with owners and not allow unrealistic expectations to go unchallenged. Schedules included in contracts should recognize those factors that architects can control. For example, if the architect expects municipal approval of a zoning variance for the project on June 1 and it will take sixty days from that date to complete a phase of services, the contract should not state the work will be completed by August 1. Since the timeliness of municipal approval is a factor beyond the architect's control, the contract should state that services on the phase will be completed sixty days after municipal approval is granted. Owners whose projects are late are usually disappointed and unhappy. Therefore, architects should use the contract to communicate realistic expectations.

Architects are frequently involved with construction budgets—evaluating them and sometimes providing professional services that help owners set them.

▶ Construction Cost Management (9.4) discusses budgets and budgeting.

Selecting the Delivery System

Architects are often among the first members of the design and construction team selected by owners. This position allows architects to have some influence over selection of the project delivery method, the other types of professionals to be involved, the scope of services provided by others, and how these factors will mesh with the architect's services.

In today's building industry, an increasing number of delivery systems are available to owners, including design-bid-build, design-negotiate-build, design-build, turnkey, or one of several other hybrid methods of project delivery. Contract documents can be significantly influenced by the delivery system chosen, and it is important for the owner, with the architect's assistance, to decide early which delivery method to use.

Many owners may rely on a tried-and-true delivery system without being aware of the advantages of using an alternative. Thus, the architect can play a valuable role in discussing the pros and cons of alternative delivery systems. Depending on whether a project has a well-defined scope, fixed and unchangeable budget, or fixed timetable, a customized delivery system may be more economical or efficient than a standard delivery method. Likewise, when architects are involved in the planning stages of a project, they can suggest alternative methods for procurement of construction services.

▶ Project Delivery Methods (8.1) describes various contractual approaches for the delivery of design and construction services.

Early involvement in a project gives the architect an opportunity to provide comprehensive counsel to owners regarding both design and construction. This is a strategic service that architects should contract for separately or in addition to basic architectural services.

Understanding Risk

Two potential causes of increased risk and liability for architects are poor communication with the owner and negligence in the performance of professional services provided to the owner. Effective communication with owners is vital. From the proposal to provide services, to the draft contract stage, to discussions and negotiations that culminate in a formal agreement, and then throughout the life of the contract, architects must strive to stay in close communication with the owner. When owners participate in essential decision making, have realistic expectations, and are kept informed of what is happening, the possibility that problems will result in claims or disagreements is reduced.

The second cause of increased risk is real or perceived shortcomings in the provision of professional services. Common examples include problems with coordination of the architect's and engineer's construction documents, design details that must be modified when prices exceed the owner's construction budget, delays in professional services according to an agreed-upon schedule, and features of a design that may conflict with the most current code or other relevant regulations.

While it is generally not possible to obtain absolution from negligent performance through the owner-architect agreement, when properly drafted, such agreements can go a long way toward minimizing areas of misunderstanding about the owner's or architect's responsibilities. Agreements that include clear descriptions of the architect's services and the owner's responsibilities can minimize risk and liability. Absent a contract provision establishing a different standard of care or level of performance, an architect is normally held to a common law standard. The common law standard of care typically requires the architect to exercise the degree of skill and care ordinarily exercised by other architects providing the same or similar types of services, under the same or similar circumstances, at the same time and in the same location. Sometimes clauses in the owner-architect agreement seek to reallocate or redefine the risks or standards associated with professional liability. The following examples illustrate how this might be viewed from the owner's and the architect's perspectives:

- Some owners—or their lenders—take an extreme position, asking architects to provide "warranties" or to "guarantee" their work. Architects have neither a legal nor a professional obligation to do perfect work, so accepting such language is unwise at best and generally considered uninsurable.
- Some architects take a position at the other extreme, asking owners to hold them harmless from any liability claim that may arise. An owner may reject this position, arguing that while an architect may not be expected to be perfect, the owner is entitled to some measure of protection from shoddy work and lack of professionalism.

Extreme risk-shifting clauses are usually met with resistance from the party to whom risk is shifted or for whom the burden of performance is increased. The contracting parties are more likely to agree to contract provisions that allocate risk fairly to the party in the best position either to manage and control the risk or to obtain insurance to cover it. AIA Contract Documents implement this balanced approach.

Under the common law standard of care, the level of documentation required for a particular project relates to what would be expected of other architects under similar circumstances. The complexity of the project, the delivery method the owner selects, the timetable the owner provides, and the compensation the owner and architect agree upon will all influence the level of documentation needed for the project. For example, an owner using a single contractor to build repetitive retail facilities in many locations

Competition often puts pressure on architects to minimize their fees and to be overly optimistic about what can be accomplished within a given time frame and budget. Though never easy, it's necessary to be coldly analytical at a time when you are excited and enthusiastic.

Paragraph 2.2 of AIA B101–2007 states, "The Architect shall perform its services consistent with the professional skill and care ordinarily provided by architects practicing in the same or similar locality under the same or similar circumstances. The Architect shall perform its services as expeditiously as is consistent with professional skill and care and the orderly progress of the Project."

may request a less detailed set of construction documents from the architect than an owner constructing a one-of-a-kind museum that requires extensive and detailed documentation for unique components. Before executing the agreement, the owner and architect should discuss the issue of performance levels and the level of documentation required for the building type.

Indemnification (hold-harmless) provisions. Construction disputes are usually multiparty disputes. In the early stages of problem analysis, it is often not clear to disinterested parties whether, or to what extent, design defects, construction defects, or operation and maintenance defects have caused the problem. Therefore, all parties involved in the construction process—owner, architect, and contractor—are typically brought into any resulting claim or lawsuit. Even when it may be clear there is no fault or judgment against the architect, significant expense and effort may be incurred. In response, many architects and owners have asked the other party to indemnify and hold them harmless in cases where a third party has filed a claim in which the allegations are based on something other than the negligence of the party seeking indemnity. Some states have special requirements to make hold-harmless clauses enforceable, while others prohibit them. If asked to sign an indemnity provision, architects should seek the advice of insurance counsel.

Limitation of liability. Many AIA owner-architect agreements include mutual waivers of consequential damages because these damages place an unbalanced risk on the architect. Consequential damages, such as the owner's lost rent, could substantially exceed the architect's insurance limits, as well as business and personal assets. When the architect is performing services in an agreement that does not contain a consequential damages waiver, architects often seek to limit to a specific sum the amount of their exposure for all claims that might arise on a project. Limitation of liability clauses used to set these monetary caps usually seek to limit the architect's monetary exposure to the amount of the architect's fees on the project, a stipulated dollar amount, or the limits of the architect's insurance coverage. The architect's ability to enforce these limitations on liability varies from jurisdiction to jurisdiction.

Intellectual property. Some owners will view drawings and specifications as complete products and may try to reuse them for other projects in other locations and circumstances—without the architect's knowledge or consent. Drawings and specifications are instruments of the architect's services, however, and are normally intended for use only on a specific project in specific circumstances. In AIA agreements, standard contract language protects an architect from misappropriation of their drawings and specifications or other instruments of service.

Other Contract Issues

As previously discussed, AIA B101–2007 provides for incorporation of initial information for a proposed project into the owner-architect agreement. This information allows the owner and architect to define the use, size, location, program, budget, and delivery method proposed for a specific project. It also identifies the key individuals who will represent the owner, the architect, and the architect's consultants. This information can be provided in an attachment to the agreement or written into Article 1. It is strongly advised that the owner and architect discuss the initial information requested and come to an understanding of the requirements for the project and that those understandings become part of the agreement.

Additional services. In its simplest definition, an additional service is any service not included in the basic services enumerated in the B101–207 agreement. Further, additional services can be identified in the owner-architect agreement or added after the contract is signed. B101–2007 covers additional services in Article 4.

In Section 4.1, AIA B101–2007 provides a simple table listing possible additional services that an owner might choose to incorporate into the agreement depending on their applicability to a specific project. The architect identifies those services and

Paragraph 3.1 of AIA B101–2007 states that "the Architect's Basic Services consist of those described in Article 3 and include usual and customary structural, mechanical, electrical, and plumbing engineering services."

indicates whether the architect or the owner is responsible for them. If the architect is responsible for a particular additional service, an expanded description of that service may be placed in the space below the table or in an exhibit attached to the agreement.

Construction administration services that exceed limits stated in the owner-architect agreement are also additional services. AIA B101–2007 provides places for quantifying shop drawing, product data, sample, and similar submittal reviews; visits to the site; punch-list preparation; and final inspections.

Designing to the owner's budget. AIA B101–2007 contains language in Article 6 that describes the architect's obligation to design within the owner's budget for the cost of the work. If the cost of constructing the architect's design does not fall within the agreed-upon budget, the architect must redesign at his or her own cost—but with flexibility to revise the project scope and/or quality as required. This obligation varies little from the requirements of AIA B141–1997. It is important to note that the architect is obligated to meet the owner's budget for the cost of the work as identified in the initial information. Once a budget has been accepted and identified as adequate for the program and quality as understood, the architect accepts responsibility for designing within it. Thus, an architect should not agree to design to the owner's budget if the budget seems unrealistic for achieving the owner's objectives.

Dealing with changes. It is likely that both the architect and the owner will modify the standard form of agreement, deleting clauses that are inapplicable or otherwise unnecessary. Removing or adding clauses to reflect the concerns of either party that are not addressed by the standard agreement is always an acceptable way of negotiating. However, architects should be mindful that language in the B101–2007 document is time-tested, coordinated with the text in A201–2007, and crafted to balance the risks between owner and architect. For these reasons, even minor changes can have large implications. It is always best to get legal advice before making changes to these documents.

COPING WITH NONSTANDARD AGREEMENT FORMS

By choice or by regulatory requirement, some owners draft their own agreement forms. Whether they are custom documents or extensive modifications of AIA standard forms, architects presented with nonstandard agreements should approach them with care:

- Be sure you understand the services to be performed, the duties being created, and the compensation being offered.
- If a proposed agreement includes provisions that appear to redefine the architect's liability, suggest exclusions from coverage under the firm's liability insurance, or require indemnification of the owner. Have the agreement reviewed by an insurance adviser.
- Do not be afraid to modify a nonstandard agreement based on terms and condition in AIA documents, and be sure to have an attorney review the proposed agreement. This review can be facilitated by carefully comparing the proposed agreement to AIA Document B101–2007 or to a checklist developed by the architecture firm or an attorney.
- Be sure nonstandard documents are coordinated with the requirements of other project agreements, such as architect-consultant and owner-contractor agreements.

MODIFYING AN AGREEMENT AFTER SIGNING

Initial definitions of the project scope, program, site, schedule, and budget may change as the design gives shape and substance to a project. Regulatory and financing review may require design changes, and the process of bidding or negotiation may suggest or even require substitutions. In addition, detailed information from the contractor during construction—in the form of shop drawings and material and product submittals—will refine the project. Conditions encountered in the field may also require changes. For these reasons, it is important to think of owner-architect agreements as being flexible. They will be interpreted and, if necessary, modified as projects move forward.

▶ The architect needs to carefully review and evaluate the terms and conditions of agreements prepared by the client. Owner-Generated Agreements (11.2) provides guidance on this matter.

The AIA has created documents to assist recording changes as they occur. Just as change orders record changes to a construction contract, AIA G802–2007 can be used to record owner-architect agreement changes with respect to performance period and the contract amount. While some changes may not materially affect the scope, cost, or time of performance of the architect's services, most changes will. Recording these changes and notifying the owner as they occur is the safest way to avoid conflict and misunderstandings. Waiting to communicate makes it harder to get time extensions or additional fees.

EFFECTIVE OWNER-ARCHITECT AGREEMENTS

Carefully delineating the terms of the owner-architect agreement is important to any project. When the agreement fully express the goals and expectations of both the owner and the architect, it provides a better basis for the successful delivery of the design services and offers a greater chance for avoiding misunderstandings during the course of the project.

For More Information

Most general law books addressing architecture practice include treatises and cases relating to owner-architect agreements. To research or investigate legal rulings and interpretations regarding the application of AIA documents, refer to the *AIA Legal Citator*, edited by Steven G. M. Stein and published by the Matthew Bender Company. The *Citator* contains charts and summaries of appellate court decisions that reference AIA series A, B, and C documents.

11.2 Owner-Generated Agreements

Steven G. M. Stein, Esq., Scott R. Fradin, Esq., AIA, and John-Paul Lujan, Esq.

Owner-generated agreements often create unreasonable legal and business risk exposures that the architect must appropriately identify and address during the contract negotiation phase.

The legitimate purpose of any agreement for the provision of design services is to allocate risk commensurate with the services and rewards promised. The standard forms of agreement published by the American Institute of Architects are generally thought to achieve this balance in a fair and equitable manner. However, agreements generated by owners do not always meet that ideal. Taking advantage of their substantial bargaining power, owners sometimes suggest contracts that allocate unacceptable risks to architects and blur the lines between the architect's responsibility, the contractor's responsibility, and the responsibilities of other participants in the

▶ Agreements with Owners (11.1) addresses the types of agreements entered into by owners and architects and issues for architects to consider in their development.

Steven Stein is a leading authority in construction law and specializes in the trial and arbitration of complex design and construction matters. He is editor-in-chief of the *American Institute of Architects Legal Citator*. Scott R. Fradin specializes in construction and design law and has extensive experience negotiating and drafting contracts for architects, engineers, and general contractors. John-Paul Lujan is an attorney and former architect with extensive experience negotiating and drafting contracts for architects, engineers, general contractors, and owners. The authors are partners in the Chicago law firm Stein, Ray & Harris LLP.

project. In addition, owner-generated agreements frequently create liability exposures for architects in relation to other parties, most notably lenders. The guiding principle of this topic is to identify provisions often included in owner agreements that require architects to take responsibility for risks they cannot control or that create risk exposures for the architect that are not commensurate with the professional standard of care or ordinary fees.

KEY CONCERNS IN OWNER-GENERATED AGREEMENTS

The first section of this topic focuses on the key provisions and concepts typical of owner-generated agreements that potentially present the architect with the most far-reaching implications. Recognizing these provisions when they appear in an agreement and negotiating deletion, revision, or the addition of supplements to them should be the main focus of architects seeking to minimize and manage risks and potential liability exposure.

Indemnities

Indemnities or "hold harmless" provisions are consistently the most controversial and heavily negotiated provisions in an owner-generated agreement. An indemnity is simply an agreement for one party to assume the liability of another in the event of a loss. Most, if not all, owner-generated agreements will allocate or transfer risks associated with the architect's services through the use of indemnities. In many cases, an owner-generated indemnification provision will transfer more risk and liability exposure to the architect than the law or industry standards require. Further, such provisions transfer more exposure for risks beyond either the architect's control or the scope of the architect's professional liability insurance. Consider this typical owner-generated indemnification provision:

> To the fullest extent permitted by law, Architect shall *defend*, indemnify and hold *Owner and its officers, directors, members, shareholders, employees, lender, agents, nominees, successors and assigns, and anyone acting for or on behalf of any of them* (collectively, the "Indemnified Parties") harmless from any liabilities, damages, costs, expenses, suits, losses, claims, demands, actions, fines and penalties or other liability, including, without limitation, all costs and reasonable attorneys' fees (hereinafter collectively, the "Claims") *arising out of, or in connection with the Architect's performance of the Services of this Agreement or the breach of any term or condition of this Agreement*; provided, however, the Architect shall not be required to indemnify the Owner from Claims caused *by the sole negligence of the Owner*.

The architect's main objective in responding to an owner's indemnity provision like the one above should be to negotiate a reasonable indemnity that transfers risks the design professional can control in a manner that maximizes available insurance coverage. Because the wording of indemnities is often complex and confusing, it is recommended that the architect break down the indemnity into its most critical components. The architect should consider, at least, the following four basic questions:

- What event will trigger the indemnification obligation?
- Who is the owner asking the architect to indemnify?
- Does the indemnity include a "duty to defend"?
- Is the owner asking the architect to indemnify the owner from claims that arise from the owner's own negligence?

What event will trigger the indemnification obligation? Perhaps the most important component of an indemnification agreement relates to the circumstances that will trigger liability and the architect's obligation to indemnify in the event of a loss on the part of the owner. Generally, to establish liability against an architect for damages, the law requires reasonable proof that the architect failed to provide the usual and customary professional care. Because this is generally the limit of the architect's obligations under the law, an architect's professional liability insurance will only cover the architect for the consequences of the architect's "negligent" acts or omissions. Accordingly, the architect should endeavor to limit exposure under an indemnity to only those claims that arise from the architect's negligent professional performance, thereby maximizing the availability of professional liability insurance. It should be noted, however, that some risks may be appropriate to allocate to an architect even though they may not be insurable, such as violation of copyright or violation of contract provisions that do not relate to adequacy.

An owner-generated agreement will seek to broaden the circumstances under which the architect's obligation to indemnify the owner will be triggered. These agreements generally attempt to provide the owner with the greatest amount of protection, often creating scenarios that are outside the control of the architect or outside the scope of losses covered under the architect's liability policy.

As in the sample indemnification provision above, an owner will most commonly seek to be indemnified by the architect from claims in connection with "the performance of the Services of the Agreement." Such a request may be unreasonably broad in that it arguably includes losses arising out of anything that might be related to the services performed by the architect, without any requirement of fault or negligence on the part of the architect. Such losses, as set forth above, may not be within the control of the architect or may not be insurable. The architect can address this issue simply by inserting the word "negligent" in front of the word "performance" in the sample owner-generated indemnity provision.

The sample provision above also requires an indemnification from claims arising from the "breach of any term or condition of the Agreement." Owners have successfully used such language as a fee-shifting provision entitling the owner to attorney fees and costs under a breach of contract suit brought directly by the owner against the architect, as opposed to by a third party. Essentially, this means the architect will be funding the client's lawsuit against the architect for breach of the agreement. The owner already has a separate remedy for breach of contract, so it would be unfair, unnecessary, and excessive to award attorney fees to the owner, especially if there is no mutual corresponding obligation on the part of the owner. Accordingly, the architect should delete this language and/or, at minimum, add language that will expressly prevent the use of the indemnification as a way to shift responsibility for the attorneys' fee. For example, the foregoing problem may be addressed by adding the following after the words "attorneys' fees" in the sample provision: "excluding any attorneys' fees or costs associated with claims brought directly by Owner."

Who is the owner asking the architect to indemnify? The entity being indemnified by the architect is not always limited to the owner. In the sample indemnification provision above, the parties the architect will be indemnifying include the owner "and its officers, directors, shareholders, employees, lender, agents, nominees, and anyone acting for or on behalf of any of them." Generally, it is appropriate for the architect to indemnify the owner and any party directly part of, or related to, the owner entity, including the owner's officers, directors, shareholders, and employees. By the same token, it is generally not appropriate for the architect to indemnify parties not directly a part of the owner entity or that are otherwise not clearly defined, such as the owner's lender, agents, nominees, or anyone acting for or on behalf of owner. The architect has no contract with these "other" parties. By including such other parties in the indemnification, a contractual right is granted to such parties at the architect's expense, often without a reciprocal obligation, or any consideration, on the part of such other parties. Their inclusion may significantly broaden the architect's risks, may not be covered by insurance and, therefore, should be deleted from the provision.

Does the indemnity include a "duty to defend"? In addition to an indemnification, an owner-generated agreement will commonly request that the architect "defend" the owner from claims arising from the acts of the architect. This will usually be achieved by adding the word "defend" to the existing indemnity provision of the agreement (as seen above), or the duty to defend may be set forth in a separate provision.

The architect should understand that the duty to indemnify and the duty to defend are separate obligations. When an architect agrees to defend the owner, the architect has an obligation to essentially mount and/or fund the owner's defense against any claims under the scope of the indemnification. Without such a defense obligation, the architect may still be required to reimburse the owner for any attorney fees and costs incurred by the owner to defend against such claims. The difference is that this will only occur after a determination of liability against the architect (and, potentially, after several years of litigation). Professional liability insurance carriers, absent certain endorsements, will typically refuse to accommodate the architect's agreement to defend the owner.

Because the defense obligation is not something the architect's professional liability insurance ordinarily covers, the costs and expense of the defense obligation will, at least initially, be paid by the architect. Such an uninsured risk, therefore, should be avoided by deleting the word "defend" from the owner's indemnity provision or by the deletion of any separate provision requiring a defense obligation in the owner-generated agreement.

Is the owner asking the architect for indemnity against the owner's own negligence? Owner-generated agreements often contain language requiring the architect to take responsibility for claims that result not only from the negligence of the architect, but also from the negligence of the owner. The sample provision above provides a typical example of an owner's request to be indemnified for all claims, *except* those claims ". . . caused by the *sole* negligence of the Owner." In other words, under circumstances in which the owner and architect jointly cause the loss or claim for which the owner seeks an indemnification, the owner will be entitled to payment from the architect for the entire loss, even if the architect is found to have been only 1 percent negligent and the owner 99 percent negligent.

Most states place strict limitations on contractual indemnity agreements, particularly those that indemnify a party against the consequences of its own negligence, and place statutory prohibitions against such agreements in certain circumstances. The indemnity language set forth above, therefore, may or may not be enforceable, depending on the state laws that govern the provision. However, regardless of the laws that govern the indemnity in question, it is not reasonable—nor insurable, for that matter—for an architect to take on all liability for losses for which the architect may only be partially responsible. Accordingly, the architect should modify the indemnity language so that the owner takes on a requisite share of responsibility. In the provision above, this can be accomplished by deleting the word "sole" from the last sentence.

The following illustrates the deletions and additions that an architect could propose for the sample owner-generated indemnification provision provided at the beginning of this section:

> To the fullest extent permitted by law, Architect shall ~~defend,~~ indemnify and hold Owner and its officers, directors, members, shareholders, employees, ~~lender, agents, nominees,~~ successors and assigns~~, and anyone acting for or on behalf of any of them~~ (collectively, the "Indemnified Parties") harmless from any liabilities, damages, costs, expenses, suits, losses, claims, demands, actions, fines and penalties or other liability, including, without limitation, all costs and reasonable attorneys' fees (hereinafter collectively, the "Claims") arising out of, or in connection with the Architect's <u>negligent</u> performance of the Services of this Agreement ~~or the breach of any term or condition of this Agreement~~; provided, however, the Architect shall not be required to indemnify the Owner from Claims caused by the ~~sole~~ negligence of the Owner.

Unreasonable Risk Exposure

In addition to indemnities, other concepts in owner-generated agreements are controversial and serve as a direct source of increased risk and liability exposure for the architect. These concepts include "consequential damages" and the architect's "standard of care."

Consequential damages. Consequential damages are such damages, loss, or injury that do not flow directly and immediately from the act of the party but only from the consequences or results of such an act. In the context of construction projects, this refers to an owner's economic losses, such as lost profits, loss of use of a facility, or lost opportunity resulting from delays to the project that were the result of an act, error, or omission of the architect. These losses can be significant, especially when the project being constructed is a profit-generating center. For example, delays in the completion of a production plant could result in an inability to meet orders, which, in turn, could translate into lost profits and loss of valuable customers. In the case of a condominium project, delays could result in huge financial carrying costs and the inability to sell units. Such damages may be difficult to define or calculate. Accordingly, consequential damages present the architect with the greatest exposure to potential damages on construction projects.

► See Risk Management Strategies (5.4) for further discussion of approaches to and ways for minimizing risk.

Owner-generated contracts usually do not address the applicability of consequential damages. Under the law, unless a contract expressly waives the right to seek consequential damages, a party who breaches a contract will be responsible for the consequential damages resulting from its breach. Therefore, when presented with an owner-generated contract, an architect should diligently search for language in the contract that expressly waives the owner's right to seek consequential damages against the architect. If no such language is present, then a provision (similar to the following example) should be added that clearly states that the architect is not responsible for any consequential damages as a result of any alleged breach:

> The Owner and Architect waive and release all claims for, or right to, any consequential, incidental, exemplary, punitive or special damages, including, but not limited to, any damages related to loss of use, lost profits, lost rent, diminution in value, or lost opportunity.

Of all concepts that must be addressed when negotiating an owner-generated agreement, the issue of consequential damages has the greatest potential to be a deal breaker for either party. Though an owner traditionally has more bargaining power, an architect should stand firm and insist on an express mutual waiver of consequential damages. When confronted and advised properly, a knowledgeable and reasonable owner will often agree that it is not fair to expose an architect to such potentially limitless liability, especially if the architect's fee is not commensurate with the potential risk. If the owner will not agree to waive rights to consequential damages, an architect may request a compromise from the owner in the form of a limitation of liability provision, either to a negotiated amount or to the extent of the architect's then-available insurance proceeds.

Standard of care. Needless to say, architects are not perfect. Unfortunately, owners often believe they are paying for perfection and they expect the drawings and specifications prepared by the architect to be free of errors. These unrealistic expectations manifest themselves in the owner's form agreements and need to be appropriately addressed by the architect.

Liability for an architect alleged to have been professionally negligent will depend on whether the architect met the agreed-upon standard of care. Under the common law and absent language in the architect's agreement to the contrary, a professional providing service is expected to do so in a reasonable and prudent manner. Therefore, a design professional should avoid agreeing to a higher standard than required by common law.

An owner-generated agreement will typically include language that attempts to raise the architect's standard of care, which can be accomplished by the owner in various ways. The most common method is to include language that requires the architect to perform services in accordance with "a high" or "the highest" standard of care. Although it is difficult to define what "high" or "highest" means in relation to the architect's services, clearly this language requires more than ordinary or typical care, and progressively moves the architect's services toward a requirement of perfection.

In other instances (sometimes in the same agreement), an owner will ask that the architect "warrant" services, or certain aspects of services. A "warranty" has an established meaning under the law and connotes an assurance or guarantee that the architect's services will be absolutely free of defects. Moreover, an architect should be wary of other, less obvious, or indirect language scattered throughout the owner's agreement that also may raise the architect's standard of care. For example, such language as "the architect represents that its employees have the expertise and experience in the design of first class facilities similar to the Project necessary to properly perform the services of this Agreement" may be argued to be an acknowledgment on the part of the architect that agreed-upon services will be better than those provided by the typical design professional.

Agreeing to any such language will expose the architect to increased risk, as its services will have to meet a standard greater than for the ordinary or reasonably prudent design professional. Moreover, the architect's professional liability insurance carrier may argue that such increase in exposure is not covered. All such language should be deleted or modified appropriately, or, alternatively, the architect should add a "catch-all" provision that will address this matter without having to find every instance of language in the agreement that arguably raises the architect's standard of care. The provision could state the following:

> The Architect, its employees and consultants agree to perform the services of this Agreement in a manner consistent with that degree of skill and care ordinarily exercised by similar professionals, currently practicing in the same geographic location and under similar circumstances. The Architect's services will be rendered without any warranty, express or implied. In no event shall any other term, language or provision contained in this Agreement be deemed to, in any way, alter, modify or otherwise increase the Standard of Care set forth in this Paragraph.

Ownership of Documents

▶ See the Copyright and Intellectual Property in the Digital Age backgrounder with Architects and the Law (2.1) for a further discussion of document ownership and related issues about intellectual property.

Fundamentally, an architect is hired to prepare plans and specifications for the construction of a building. This is clearly the most valuable aspect of the owner-architect relationship. As such, the drawings and specifications become part of a tug-of-war. Architects—for both risk and artistic reasons—do not want to see their designs replicated, and owners believe that since they paid for the designs, they own them.

Most owner-generated agreements contain an ownership of documents provision that vests the owner with ownership of the architect's drawings and specifications. Generally, the decision to transfer ownership of the drawings and specifications to the owner is a business decision. However, if the architect agrees to transfer ownership of the plans and specifications to the owner, the following concepts must be addressed in order to protect the architect from future liability:

- Ownership of the drawings and specifications transfers upon payment.
- The architect retains the right to use standard design elements and architectural details.
- The owner is entitled to transfer ownership of the drawings and specifications to another entity provided that the transferee agrees to be bound by the terms of the ownership of documents provision.
- The owner must indemnify the architect for re-use of the drawings and specifications when the architect is not involved.
- Ownership does not transfer if there is a payment dispute.
- The owner must indemnify the architect if the drawings and specifications are completed by others.

In some instances, an owner-generated agreement may not contain any provisions addressing the ownership of the architect's drawings and specifications. This omission can have serious consequences if the architect is terminated before the project is completed. Although ownership of the document remains with the architect by virtue of both common-law copyright and federal statutory copyright, the architect may lose the right to prevent the owner from using the documents after termination. This situation is exemplified by the federal court case of *I.A.E., Inc. v. Shaver*. In this case, the owner was an entity that had a design-build contract for the construction of an airport cargo hangar and subcontracted with Shaver, an architecture firm, for preparation of schematic drawings pursuant to a letter agreement. Critically, nothing more was said to Shaver about providing services for the remainder of the project. Shaver delivered the drawings to the owner under the belief that, once the drawings were approved, the firm would perform the architecture work for the remaining phases of the project. The owner, however, employed another architect to complete the remaining services. Shaver objected to the owner's use of the drawings and the owner brought an action in court to determine whether it had a right to use the drawings and whether it had infringed on Shaver's copyright.

To determine whether Shaver granted I.A.E. an implied nonexclusive license, the court considered various factors, including the language of the copyright registration certificate, the letter agreement, the deposition testimony, and the delivery of the copyrighted material without warning that its further use would constitute copyright infringement. Applying these factors, the court held that the evidence supported the existence of a license running in favor of the owner to use Shaver's drawings to construct the air cargo building. According to the court, Shaver clearly did not have a contract for any portion of the overall project beyond the initial design phase drawings. Rather, the firm had a mere expectation that it would get further contracts for additional phases once the initial drawings were approved.

Pitfalls Within Basic Services Provisions

When it comes to a legal analysis of the design agreement, architects often gloss over the business terms of a contract, including those provisions affecting scope, fee, and schedule. However, unlike industry form agreements, such as the AIA Contract Documents, owner-generated agreements couch potentially harmful language in such provisions that increase the architect's liability exposure and affect profits. The following are examples of business terms the architect should carefully scrutinize.

Time and scheduling provisions. As set forth earlier in this chapter, an owner's profits are generally tied to how fast a new plant is up and running, or how quickly an owner can remove carrying costs and begin to sell individual residential units of a condominium project. Therefore, to an owner, time is a critical factor that often results in owner-agreements that contain very stringent and unreasonable schedule requirements and limitations that are imposed on the architect. If the architect does not address these provisions, then failure to meet these schedule requirements, no matter what the cause, may result in exposure to significant damages, including consequential damages and damages associated with delays that may have been caused by others. Consider the following owner-drafted provision:

> Time limits on the Architect's services agreed upon by Owner and Architect are of the essence. If, in performing the services, the Architect: (i) fails to complete the services in compliance with the design schedule; or (ii) impedes or prevents achievement of the Contractor's schedule, then the Architect shall be liable for and reimburse the Owner for all damages and sums the Owner incurs resulting therefrom.

Delays not only affect the owner's bottom line, they can also have an adverse effect on the architect's compensation and profits. This is the case when language in the owner-generated agreement protects the owner's profits by limiting the architect's ability to recover damages incurred as a result of any delays to the project, even if not the fault of the architect. Typical examples of such provisions are as follows:

- If the Architect fails to meet the design schedule for any reason, then Architect shall provide such services, including any additional services, to the extent necessary to cure or recover the delay with no additional compensation or reimbursement hereunder.

- The Architect's only recourse for delay, hindrance or obstruction of or to performance hereunder shall be a modification of the design schedule.

As discussed earlier in this chapter, the most effective way that an architect can limit exposure to the excessive damages incurred by owner that can arise from project delays is to include a mutual waiver of consequential damages provision. In addition to such a waiver, the architect should ensure further protection by including a provision that clearly excuses the architect from delays caused by acts of god, the owner, contractor, or causes outside the architect's control. The provision should also entitle the architect to additional compensation in the event of increased costs resulting from delays not the fault of the architect. Such a clause might read like this:

> If the Architect is delayed at any time in the progress of the Architect's services due to: the acts or omissions of Owner, Owner's consultants, Owner's cost consultant, Contractor or anyone for whom any of them are legally responsible; strikes; war; fire; abnormal weather conditions; unavoidable casualties; acts of terror; unanticipated delays by applicable governmental authorities having jurisdiction over the Project in the issuance of approvals, permits and the conducting of inspections of the Work; or other causes beyond the Architect's control, then the design schedule shall, as agreed to by the Owner and Architect, be extended by the additional time caused by such delay and the Architect's compensation shall be equitably increased.

Cost-estimating provisions. Due to the complexity of today's construction environment, the wide variety of materials available, employment of various construction techniques, and instability of prices, estimating the total costs of construction is difficult. Few architects have any training in the area of cost estimating, yet many owners look to the architect to evaluate project budgets and provide cost estimating services as part of the architect's overall scope of basic services. Other owners prefer to separately retain the services of a professional cost consultant (or even a general contractor) during the preconstruction phase. Under either scenario, the architect should ensure that the owner's agreement incorporates the necessary protective language for the benefit of the architect.

If the owner requires cost-estimating services from the architect, the architect should first consider the possibility of avoiding such responsibility in the first place, as agreeing to perform such services may result in significant risk to the architect. For example, failure to design the project within the owner's budget may result in the provision of free design services to bring the costs of construction back into conformance with the owner's budget. In addition, when actual costs of construction have greatly exceeded the architect's estimate, certain courts have held the architect responsible for the difference in construction costs. It should also be noted that not all professional liability insurance carriers cover risks associated with mistakes in cost estimation.

If the architect agrees to provide such services, the architect at least should supplement the owner-generated agreement with the following language (similar to that found in the AIA documents):

> An opinion of probable construction cost, if included in Architect's services, represents Architect's best judgment as a design professional familiar with the construction industry. It is recognized, however, that the Architect does not have control over the cost of labor, materials, or equipment, over the Contractor's methods of determining bid prices, or over competitive bidding, market, or negotiating conditions. Accordingly, Architect cannot and does not warrant or represent that bids or negotiated prices will not vary from any opinion of probable construction cost prepared by the Architect.

Such language effectively limits the owner's ability to rely on the architect's estimate or evaluation as a guarantee by qualifying the architect's services as a professional opinion, based only on the architect's experience and on uncertain market conditions. Use of the term "opinion of probable construction cost" rather than "estimate" is also preferable in conveying the intended limits on such services.

Despite such protective language, however, there is no guarantee that an architect will be completely insulated from liability when performing such services. Therefore, the architect also should consider including language that will limit the extent of liability for errors when providing an opinion of probable costs. Furthermore, as no estimate or opinion on cost can ever be perfect, the architect should also negotiate a permissible variation in actual versus estimated costs prior to the incurrence of any liability, such as the following:

> In the event the Contractor's bids or negotiated proposal exceeds the Architect's opinion of probable construction cost by _____ percent (___%) (the "Permitted Variation"), the Owner's sole and exclusive remedy shall be the no cost performance by the Architect of those design services necessary to conform the Architect's design (or applicable portions of the design) to a cost within the Permitted Variation of the Owner-approved opinion of probable construction cost.

Finally, in the event the owner separately retains a cost consultant, the architect should request the insertion of protective language that appropriately defines and separates the obligations of the owner's cost consultant from that of the architect. The architect should also negotiate an adjustment in the architect's compensation for any redesign services required by the owner to lower the owner's estimates or to bring the design into conformance with the owner-provided estimates. To accomplish this, the following sample language can be added to the owner's provisions regarding cost estimating services:

> Owner agrees to retain the services of a professional cost consultant to provide all necessary cost estimating services for the Project. The Architect shall be entitled to rely on such cost estimating services in the performance of the Architect's obligations hereunder. To the extent the Architect is required to redesign the Project for the purpose of reducing the Owner's approved estimate of construction cost for any reason, or for the purpose of conforming the Architect's existing design to the Owner's approved estimate of construction cost in the event exceeded by the contractors' bids or negotiated proposals, the Architect shall be entitled to an equitable increase in compensation therefor.

Submittal review. Submittals, particularly shop drawings, represent an aspect of construction where the duties of all parties involved (e.g., owner, contractor, and architect) often overlap with no clear boundaries as to where responsibilities of the parties begin and end. The result is that submittal review is a significant source of litigation against architects, as even construction-related errors committed by the contractor can readily be imputed to the architect simply based on the fact that a particular submittal was reviewed and approved by the architect. The typical owner submittal review provision may look like this:

> The Architect shall review and approve upon the Contractor's submittals such as Shop Drawings, Product Data and Samples. The Architect's action shall be taken with such promptness as to cause no delay in the Work or in the activities of the owner, Contractor or separate contractors, while allowing sufficient time to permit adequate review.

Some of the issues affecting the architect's liability exposure with respect to submittal review relate to (1) delays in the handling of a submittal by the architect, thereby exposing the architect to a claim for contractor delays in the construction; (2) the failure of the provision to limit the purpose of the architect's review to matters relating to the design as opposed to other matters that are the responsibility of the contractor, exposing the architect to the acts, errors, or omissions of the contractor or other party; and (3) the architect's approval of a submittal containing an error, which provides the potential for an argument that the design professional has personally adopted the contractor's submittal and, therefore, is liable for the error.

Consequently, precise contractual terms are necessary to ensure that the architect does not assume responsibility beyond that which is reasonable or that which is rightfully the obligation of others. Therefore, if one of the architect's services on a project is the review of submittals, the owner-generated agreement should be modified or supplemented with a provision that (1) permits the architect to handle the submittal within a reasonable time; (2) limits and defines the purpose of the architect's review; and (3) only allows for a review of the submittal, not an approval. The following provision is appropriate:

> Upon Contractor's approval of Shop Drawings, Product Data and Samples, the Architect shall review such submittals for the limited purpose of checking conformance with information given and the design concept expressed in the Contract Documents. The Architect shall have no less than __ days upon receipt of the submittal to complete the review. Review of such submittals is not conducted for the purpose of determining the accuracy and/or completeness of details such as dimensions and quantities, or for substantiating instructions for installation or performance of equipment or systems, all of which remain the responsibility of the Contractor as required by the Contract Documents. Architect's review of a Submittal shall not constitute approval of safety precautions or of construction means, methods, techniques, sequences, or procedures. The review does not constitute an approval of a specific item or the assembly of which the item is a component.

Payment provisions/disputed amounts. From the owner's perspective, controlling payments to the architect is the owner's most convenient form of protection from damages associated with design errors. Accordingly, owner-generated agreements often contain provisions permitting an owner to withhold from the architect's invoices any amounts the owner deems appropriate or necessary. The following is a typical provision that permits the owner to withhold amounts due the architect:

> The Owner reserves the right to reject all or any portion of the Architect's invoice. If the Owner disputes the Architect's entitlement to payment for the Architect's services for any reason (the "Disputed Amount"), Owner may withhold the Disputed Amount until the dispute is resolved by the dispute resolution procedures provided in this Agreement.

From the architect's perspective, however, prompt and full payment is essential. Contractually permitting the owner to withhold sums puts the owner, at least initially, in the potentially abusive position of determining the quality of the performance of the architect's services. Ideally, this provision should be deleted. However, the architect will not always be in a position to obtain such a concession from the owner. Nevertheless, the architect can request certain changes to such a provision that an owner will have a difficult time contesting with any reasonable basis and that will afford some protection to the architect.

For example, the architect can add language to the owner's provision that requires any, all, or a combination of the following concepts: (1) written notice from the owner providing the reason(s) the owner is withholding any amounts claimed due by the architect; (2) a requirement that only an amount be withheld from the architect's invoice that is reasonably necessary to protect the owner's interest; (3) that any amounts not in dispute be released and paid in accordance with the existing requirements of the agreement; and (4) for projects with relatively significant fees, an agreement that any amounts withheld by owner be placed in an interest-bearing escrow account mutually funded by the parties.

Other concepts that may be considered by architects when addressing such a payment provision include (1) an interest penalty placed on any amounts withheld from the architect to the extent any court, arbitrator, or other entity determines that the owner wrongfully withheld such funds and (2) the insertion of language requiring the owner to waive any right to withhold any amount from the architect's invoices in the event the owner fails to provide written notice of such disputed amount within a negotiated time period. It should be recognized that these concessions may be more difficult to obtain from an owner.

Finally, the architect should also include a statement that, despite any permission to withhold amounts from the architect's invoices, the architect's continued performance under the agreement shall not act as a waiver of any claims to any such amounts wrongfully withheld by owner.

Owner's "Boiler-Plate" Provisions

Most owner-generated agreements contain provisions that appear to be harmless but, in reality, can result in the architect undertaking greater liability, losing valuable rights, or both. It is critical for the architect to first identify the provision, recognize the risk, and then address the risk with appropriate modifications that protect the architect.

Lender's requirements. Generally speaking, if the architect is presented with an owner-generated agreement, it is likely that the owner is a business entity rather than an individual. If the owner is a business entity, it is also likely that a commercial lender will be involved in the project. It is understandable that in such cases the lender wants as much protection from a default by the owner under the loan agreement as possible. Accordingly, the owner may attempt to insert provisions into the owner-architect agreement that are designed to protect the interest of the lender. The problem is these provisions are designed to change the rights and liabilities that the architect has under the owner-architect agreement when the owner defaults under the loan agreement.

A typical provision that an architect will encounter states that "the Architect shall comply with all Lender requirements." While this provision may seem innocuous, the fact is there is no way for the architect to know what the lender will require. For example, will the lender require the architect to subordinate a lien right to that of the lender? Will the lender require the architect to complete the project even though the architect has not been paid? Will the lender require the architect to guarantee that the designs are complete and in full compliance with all laws? Will the lender require the architect to relinquish rights to drawings and specifications? Since the architect is usually retained before the owner obtains the loan, the answers to these questions are unknown. Therefore, the following concepts should be incorporated into the Lender's Requirements provision:

- The architect shall only be required to comply with the lender's "reasonable" requirements.
- The architect shall not be required to subordinate lien rights to those of the lender.
- The architect's rights under the owner-architect agreement shall not be diminished.
- The architect's obligations under the owner-architect agreement shall not be increased.
- The architect's liabilities under the owner-architect agreement shall not be increased.

Consent to assignment. It is not unusual for the parties to a business transaction to reserve their right to assign the agreement. The standard form AIA documents address this issue as follows:

Neither the Owner nor the Architect shall assign this Agreement without the written consent of the other, except that the Owner may assign this Agreement to an institutional lender providing financing for the Project. In such event, the lender shall assume the Owner's rights and obligations under this Agreement. The Architect shall execute all consents reasonably required to facilitate such assignment.

On the whole, this provision properly balances the interests of the owner and architect. However, most assignment provisions contained in owner-generated agreements are not as fair. Instead, they usually state the following:

The Architect shall not assign this Agreement without the express written consent of the Owner, which consent may be withheld in the Owner's sole and absolute discretion. The Owner, in its sole and absolute discretion, shall have the right to assign this Agreement. The Architect shall execute all consents required to facilitate such assignment.

Such a provision is problematic for the architect for the following reasons:

- The owner has the absolute right to act unreasonably in precluding the architect from assigning the owner-architect agreement in the event there is a change in the architect's business form (e.g., a merger, a purchase by another firm, or a change in corporate structure).
- The owner has the unfettered right to assign the agreement to whomever it wants— even if it is to someone the architect objects to.
- The architect is contractually required to execute whatever consents the owner requires regardless of what the consents require.
- There is no requirement that the assignee assume any of the owner obligations under the owner/architect agreement (e.g., payment of past due amounts, indemnifications, and liability for owner-supplied information).

When confronted with such a provision, the architect has three options: (1) do nothing, (2) recommend using the standard AIA formulation, or (3) modify the owner's language to create a more balanced provision that does not expose the architect to additional risk. For the third option, the above provision could be appropriately modified as follows to address the most critical concerns:

The Architect shall not assign this Agreement without the express written consent of the Owner, which consent ~~may~~shall not be unreasonably withheld ~~in the Owner's sole and absolute discretion~~. The Owner~~, in its sole and absolute discretion,~~ shall have the right to assign this Agreement <u>upon the written consent of the Architect, which consent shall not be unreasonably withheld, provided that the assignee agrees to undertake all Owner obligations under this Agreement and cure all prior Owner defaults.</u> The Architect shall execute all consents required to facilitate such assignment <u>provided that such consents do not adversely affect the Architect's rights or increase the Architect's obligations under this Agreement. Notwithstanding Owner's assignment of this Agreement, the Owner shall remain fully liable under the Agreement.</u>

Certifications. The standard form AIA documents assume that the architect will certify various matters that arise during the construction process. Typically, the architect will issue certifications concerning contractor payment applications, substantial completion, and final completion. These standard form agreements also assume that the owner may require the architect to certify matters not specifically addressed in the agreement. To limit the architect's potential exposure for providing such certifications, the standard form documents state the following:

If the Owner requests the Architect to execute certificates, the proposed language of such certificates shall be submitted to the Architect for review at least 14 days prior to the requested dates of execution. The Architect shall not be required to execute certificates that would require knowledge, services or responsibilities beyond the scope of this Agreement.

Most owner-generated agreements, however, provide only that "the Architect shall execute such certifications as the Owner requests." This type of language, while seemingly harmless, has the potential to expose the architect to greater liability than would otherwise exist under the owner-architect agreement. More often than not, the liability concern arises when the owner is financing the project through a lender or the owner is leasing the project site. Regardless of whether a lender or a landlord is involved, the issue is generally the same—the architect is asked to make certain representations to entities that are not parties to the owner- architect agreement.

A classic example is where the owner requests that the architect certify to the lender or landlord that the plans are in accordance with all laws, codes, and ordinances. If it turns out that the plans were not in accordance with all laws, codes, and ordinances, the architect will not only be liable to the owner, but also to the lender or landlord who was the intended beneficiary of the architect's certification.

As with consents to assignments discussed above, the architect, when confronted with an overly broad certification provision, has three options: (1) do nothing, (2) recommend using the standard AIA formulation, or (3) modify the owner's language to create a more balanced provision that does not expose the architect to additional risk. With regard to the third option, the following provision can be used:

> Any certification by the Architect shall be issued only for those Contract Documents prepared by the Architect or Architect's Consultants. Such certifications shall be to Architect's best knowledge and belief and only to such matters for which Architect would have knowledge by reason of its performance of this Agreement.

Confidentiality provisions. A common provision found in most owner-generated agreements deals with confidentiality of owner-provided information. Typically, these types of provisions are designed to protect an owner's confidential and/or proprietary information from being disseminated to the owner's competition. While the owner's intention is reasonable, often such provisions fail to take into account that the architect will necessarily disclose confidential owner information when issuing the drawings and specifications to regulatory authorities during the permitting process. Similarly, the architect may be required to disclose confidential owner information when meeting with manufacturer representatives or potential contractors. In essence, a provision that does not address these issues will subject the architect to liability for breach of the contract terms.

Additionally, the scope of the typical owner-generated confidentiality provision is usually overly broad; in other words, the provision defines any information supplied by the owner to the architect as confidential. Similarly, the typical confidentiality provision either does not contain a time period or contains a time period that is so long (five or ten years) that it is per se unreasonable, particularly given the transient nature of the architecture profession. Lastly, this type of provision fails to address what happens in the event of litigation between the parties.

The following is a reasonable approach to dealing with a confidentiality provision:

> The Architect acknowledges and agrees that confidential information relating to the Owner including, but not limited to, the operation, management, or business thereof (collectively, "Owner Confidential Information") may be disclosed to the Architect in connection with its provision of services under this Agreement. All such Owner Confidential Information shall be clearly marked as being confidential. The Architect agrees that all Owner Confidential Information disclosed to the Architect shall not be disclosed to third parties without the Owner's prior written consent, whether during or for a period of one (1) year after the expiration or termination of this Agreement. The Architect shall require anyone directly employed by it or anyone for whose acts it may be liable to comply with this Section. Notwithstanding the foregoing, the Architect may disclose Owner Confidential Information if such disclosure is required by applicable law or by legal, judicial, administrative, or regulatory process, provided that the Architect promptly notifies the Owner so that the Owner may, if it so elects, seek appropriate remedies, or to the Architect's financial and legal advisers in the ordinary course of the Architect's business. Notwithstanding anything contained herein to the contrary, the Drawings and Specifications shall not be considered Owner Confidential Information.

Non-recourse provisions. It is common in today's marketplace for commercial owners—most commonly developers—to set up a single-purpose entity to have a project constructed. The reason is clear: The owner wants to limit its exposure to any potential losses. Typically, the only asset of this single-purpose entity is the property the project will be constructed on. Thus, consistent with the owner's goal of limiting its exposure, the owner will likely include a "non-recourse" provision in the owner-architect agreement. As the title of such a provision makes clear, a non-recourse provision expressly provides that in the event of a claim by the architect against the owner, the architect will not go after the assets of the owner's officers, directors, shareholders, or members (which is done through a legal action referred to as "piercing the corporate veil"). Instead, the architect's only recourse will be against the assets of the entity. The following is a typical example of a non-recourse provision:

> If Owner defaults in the performance of any of Owner's obligations under the Agreement and if, as a consequence of such default, Architect recovers a money judgment against Owner, that judgment shall be satisfied only out of the right, title and interest of Owner in the Project, including the Site, as such right, title and interest may from time to time be encumbered. Architect expressly agrees that under no circumstances will any partner, member, shareholder, officer, director, or employee of Owner be personally liable for the performance of any of Owner's obligations hereunder. Additionally, none of Owner, any of its agents, or employees shall have any liability for performance of Owner's obligations under the Agreement.

Unfortunately, it is almost impossible to have a non-recourse provision stricken from the owner-generated agreement. However, there are two things that the architect should try to do when confronted with this type of provision. First, the architect should attempt to modify the provision so that it is symmetrical—that is, if the architect must agree not to seek recourse against the owner's officers, directors, shareholders, or members, the owner must agree not to seek recourse against the architect's officers, directors, shareholders, or members. Second, the architect should attempt to carve out an exception for the intentional misconduct of an officer, director, shareholder, or member of the owner. For example, if the president of the owner engages in fraudulent conduct, the architect should be entitled to seek recourse directly against the officer.

While the architect may not be able to avoid a non-recourse provision, the architect should carefully review the agreement for a no lien provision or a provision requiring the architect to subordinate lien rights to the lender, as discussed earlier. If the architect unwittingly executes an agreement with these types of contractual provisions, the architect is not likely to recover much, if any, outstanding fee in the event of owner default.

Insurance. Generally, owner-generated agreements contain detailed insurance sections specifying not only the types of insurance the architect is required to maintain but also the limits of such insurance. Commentary on the various types of insurance that owner typically require is beyond the scope of this chapter. Architects are advised to submit any owner-drafted insurance section to their insurance adviser to confirm that the owner's insurance requirements are compatible with the architect's insurance program.

There are, however, three provisions typically contained in the owner-drafted insurance section that the architect should be aware of and avoid. The first provision requires the architect to name the owner as an additional insured on the architect's professional liability policy. It is impossible for the architect to comply with this requirement. The reason lies in the nature of professional liability insurance. Professional liability insurance covers design errors and omissions. Since the owner is usually not an architect, and therefore incapable of making design mistakes, there can be no coverage for the owner. Simply put, professional liability practice policies are not written to provide for additional insured status.

The second provision the architect should avoid requires the architect's consultants to carry insurance with the same limits as those required for the architect. This requirement fails to recognize that many of the architect's consultants, including code, acoustical, audiovisual, signage, and landscape consultants, generally do not carry high limits of insurance. To avoid the risk of being exposed due to a consultant's failure to carry the same limits, the architect should modify the provision to provide that (1) the architect's consultants carry insurance at limits customarily maintained by similarly situated consultants practicing in the same locale and (2) if the owner requires higher limits, the owner will pay the cost for the increase in the cost of insurance as a reimbursable expense. The architect should bear in mind that the architect and consultants should have the minimum insurance coverage appropriate for the type of work they are involved in. The architect should consult an insurance adviser to determine that amount.

The third provision requires that the architect maintain professional liability insurance at the same limits for a specified number of years after completion of the project. With such a provision, the owner is seeking to protect losses arising from design defects that may not manifest until many years after the completion of the project. The problem for the architect is that due to economic conditions, the architect may not be able to bear the cost of maintaining the same limit for professional liability insurance. The most effective way to deal with this requirement is to include language that states that the architect's best efforts will be used to maintain professional liability insurance with the same limits for a reasonable duration (such as three years) provided such insurance is available at reasonable commercial rates.

ADDITIONAL CONSIDERATIONS—MISSING PROVISIONS

The last section of this chapter focuses on key provisions and concepts that are typically omitted from owner-generated agreements. As the reader is undoubtedly aware, the standard form AIA documents have been developed over many years with input from both design and construction professionals. Thus, these standard forms contain provisions that design and construction professionals recognize are unique to the way architecture services are delivered and the role of the architect in the construction process. Unfortunately, most owner-generated agreements are not developed through such a considered approach. Instead, it is likely that the owner-generated agreement was cobbled together from various service agreements used previously by the owner. Thus, most owner-generated agreements are missing provisions that are essential to any owner-architect agreement.

No Responsibility for Construction Means, Methods, Techniques, and Safety

Because the architect does not construct the project, it is reasonable for the architect to disclaim responsibility for the contractor's job site activities. This disclaimer is stated in standard-form AIA owner-architect agreements and AIA owner-contractor agreements. Having a provision that clearly provides that the architect is not responsible for the contractor's construction means, methods, techniques, and safety procedures is crucial, particularly if a lawsuit results from worker injury. Often the architect is able to use this provision to be protected from a lawsuit brought by an injured worker because the provision states that the architect did not have "active control" of the job site.

Most owners fail to incorporate this type of provision in the owner-architect agreement due to lack of familiarity with the construction process. It is, therefore, reasonable for the architect to request inclusion of a disclaimer similar to that found in the standard-form AIA owner-architect agreements in an owner-generated owner-architect agreement.

No Responsibility for Hazardous Materials

One of the downsides of the Industrial Revolution is the introduction and dispersal of toxic substances into our surroundings. As owners develop projects on sites that once housed manufacturing facilities or renovate existing buildings constructed before 1972, architects are encountering these pollutants on a more regular basis.

Without question, the definition of what constitutes a hazardous substance is extremely broad. Most architects recognize that PCBs and asbestos are hazardous materials, but hazardous material means any substance, pollutant, or contaminant listed as hazardous under the Comprehensive Environmental Response, Compensation, and Liability Act (CERCLA) of 1980 and its regulations. Regardless of what a hazardous material is, however, it is not the architect's job to identify it and clean it up.

Thus, no matter how unlikely it seems that a project will involve the presence and handling of hazardous materials, it is critical that the owner-architect agreement address this possibility. The standard-form AIA owner-architect agreements make a reasonable attempt to deal with the architect's responsibility for hazardous materials. However, there are other provisions that the architect should consider negotiating into the agreement. First, there should be a clear definition of what constitutes a hazardous material. Second, in the event that a hazardous material is encountered, there should be a provision that allows the architect to suspend services while the owner abates the material. Third, there should be a clause providing that the owner agrees to indemnify and hold the architect harmless from any loss, cost, or damage resulting from the presence of a hazardous material at the job site. Lastly, the architect should attempt to include a provision providing that the owner agrees not to bring any claim against the architect because of the presence of hazardous material at the project site.

Termination and Suspension of Services

Invariably, the owner-generated agreement will contain a provision allowing the owner to terminate the agreement with or without cause. Just as often, the same agreement will make no reference to the architect's right to terminate the agreement in the event of the owner's breach. Although an unjustified failure by the owner to pay is considered to be a material breach of the contract that entitles the architect to terminate the agreement, it is strongly recommended that the agreement contain a termination provision defining the circumstances under which the architect is entitled to terminate the contract and the architect's remedies for such a termination. For example, an appropriate termination provision would allow for termination in the event of: (1) a substantial failure on the part of the owner to perform in accordance with the terms of the agreement, (2) assignment of the agreement without the architect's written consent, (3) suspension of the project or the architect's services for a specified length of time, (4) material changes in the scope of the architect's services or the scope of the project, and (5) failure of the parties to reach agreement on adjustments to the architect's compensation as the result of delays or requested additional services.

Additionally, the owner's right to terminate without cause, also referred to as a termination for convenience, should be carefully reviewed. Architects should pay particular attention to their rights to drawings and specifications and their ability to recover costs due to early termination. If the termination provision does not address these concerns, the architect should endeavor to negotiate modifications to the termination provision covering these issues.

As noted above, the unjustified failure by the owner to pay entitles the architect to terminate the agreement. In many instances, however, the architect may not want to terminate the agreement; the architect instead may want to suspend providing services until the owner cures the breach. There is a critical difference between suspending and terminating a contract. Suspension keeps the agreement in full force and effect while the duty to perform is held in abeyance. By allowing for suspension rather than termination, the architect's performance can be resumed once the reason for suspension has been abated. However, unless the agreement specifically provides the architect with this right, the only option that the architect has is to terminate the agreement. Thus, if the architect wants the right to suspend, this right has to be provided for expressly in the agreement. Further, the right to suspend should be coupled with an express waiver of any liability resulting from the suspension, a right to recover the reasonable costs the architect incurs as a result of the disruption in services, and a right to an equitable adjustment in the architect's fee and schedule of performance.

Owner-Provided Information

A fundamental concept that most owner-generated agreements fail to address is the fact that the owner is providing the architect with certain information that the architect is to use in developing plans and specifications. Such information can consist of the owner's program, budget, schedule, technical information and plans, reports, and surveys prepared by the owner's consultants. These agreements also fail to recognize that the architect is relying on that information because the architect does not have the time, the fee, or the resources to verify the accuracy or completeness of such owner-provided information. Thus, it is unfair for the owner to hold the architect liable for errors or omissions in the architect's services that result from errors or omissions in such owner-provided information.

The solution to this problem, which is the approach taken by the AIA in the standard form owner-architect agreements, is to insert a provision expressly into the agreement that states (1) what information the owner is to provide and (2) that the architect has the right to rely on the accuracy and completeness of the owner-supplied information.

The AIA Document A201 Indemnity Clause

It is a virtual certainty that if the owner has generated the owner-architect agreement, the owner is also going to generate the owner-contractor agreement. As a result, there is a high likelihood that these two agreements may not be coordinated with one another. This may cause the architect to lose certain protections afforded through the reference to AIA Document A201–2007, General Conditions of the Contract for Construction, found in the standard form owner-architect agreements.

Of particular note are two provisions found in A201–2007. The first provision is an express promise from the contractor to the architect to indemnify the architect for losses, including attorneys' fees, resulting from the performance of the construction work, provided that such loss is attributable to bodily injury, sickness, disease, or death, or to injury to or destruction of tangible property (other than the construction work itself), but only to the extent caused by the negligent acts or omissions of the general contractor, its subcontractor, anyone directly or indirectly employed by them, or anyone for whose acts they may be liable. The second provision is an express waiver by the contractor of any protection afforded contractors under workers' compensation acts, disability benefit acts, or other employee benefit acts. Generally speaking, these types of acts provide that a contractor's liability to an injured employee is limited to the amount that the employee receives by virtue of the act. In other words, if an employee brings a workers' compensation claim against the employer/contractor and the employee receives a payment from the workers' compensation insurer, the contractor's liability to its employee for any damages suffered by the employee is limited to the amount paid by the insurer. However, most courts have held that the protection afforded to the contractor by virtue of these acts can be waived. This is the purpose of the second provision.

From the architect's perspective, these two provisions are critical. This is particularly true in the context of a personal injury lawsuit brought by an employee of the contractor that was injured on the project site. In all likelihood, the employee will bring a lawsuit naming the architect as a defendant. In response, the architect, by virtue of the indemnity provision, will be able to seek indemnification from the contractor for any damages, including attorneys' fees that the architect incurs as the result of the lawsuit (provided, of course, that the architect was not legally responsible for the employee's injuries). Further, these provisions prevent the contractor from avoiding indemnification obligation, notwithstanding the limitations contained in workers' compensation acts, disability benefit acts, or other employee benefit acts.

To alleviate the risk that the architect will lose the protections afforded by the indemnity provisions to AIA Document A201–2007, the architect has two options. The first option is to make sure the owner incorporates the A201–2007 document into the owner-contractor agreement. This option, however, assumes the architect will be involved in the drafting of the owner-contractor agreement. However, some owners may have their own form general conditions. In this situation, the architect should negotiate a provision into the owner-architect agreement stating that the owner agrees to include provisions substantially similar to those discussed above in any agreement it enters into with a contractor.

11.3 Project Design Team Agreements

Timothy R. Twomey, Esq., AIA

When architects engage consultants or establish joint ventures with other firms, additional agreements result.

The project design team may be a very small group—even a single architect who has the necessary expertise and performs all of the professional services required. Often, however, the team includes other design firms with special expertise in building engineering systems, special design issues, a particular building type, or other aspects of the project.

When other design professionals are required on a project, it is common for architects to select them and add them to the project team. These design professionals act as consultants to the architect, and the architect is responsible to the client for their professional services. The architect-consultant relationship may be established just for the project at hand, it may be a strategic alliance developed between the participants, or the two firms may have a long-standing working relationship.

Increasingly, owners are "unbundling" and structuring their own project teams. In these circumstances, the owner may (1) provide overall coordination of the multiple prime design professionals (including the architect) through in-house staff, (2) assign this coordination to an outside project or program manager with whom the owner has contracted, or (3) allocate this coordination to one of the design professionals (perhaps the architect). As a result of the owner's choice, design professionals may hold independent prime agreements directly with the owner, or they may have agreements with the owner's project or program manager.

In each of the above cases, the liability and risk management implications to the architect are varied and different from what they would be in a traditionally structured project. For example, under scenarios 1 and 2, old habits and expectations may die hard for both owners and architects, each of whom may expect and act as if the architect will provide the typical coordination services. This expectation may become especially problematic should the owner's in-house staff or the owner-retained program or project manager prove ineffective at coordination. Pressure for the architect to step in may become tremendous.

Under scenario 3, while the architect may perform in a traditional role, the architect may not have the clout with other design professionals to effectively facilitate—let alone enforce—the needed coordination among the parties, since they are not contractually tied to the architect. In this case, the architect may have coordination responsibility but may lack the tools necessary to carry out this responsibility.

Whether a project is traditionally structured or organized in one of the other scenarios discussed above, the architect's coordination responsibilities should be limited to coordinating services with those of consultants or other design professionals retained by the owner or the owner's project or program manager. In turn, all such design professionals should be contractually obligated to coordinate their services with the other consultants on the team, regardless of their contractual relationships. The architect should never assume the responsibility for the internal coordination of any other design professional's documents.

▶ Project Delivery Methods (8.1) addresses multiple prime construction contracts and other arrangements for the delivery of project services.

Combine appropriate AIA standard forms of agreement to improve coordination of prime and consultant agreements.

Timothy R. Twomey is principal and chief administrative officer for Shepley Bulfinch Richardson and Abbott Incorporated. He is responsible for providing legal, management, and administrative support for the Boston-based architectural firm.

ARCHITECT-CONSULTANT RELATIONSHIPS

The architect may seek consulting arrangements with a wide variety of design professionals and specialists—even with other architects. The most common interprofessional relationship is that between the architect and the professional engineer

SPECIAL EXPERTISE AND CONSULTANTS

Depending on the project, a wide range of special expertise may be needed to provide professional services. Some examples of such expertise are listed here:

Building Types

Airports
Athletics/sports facilities
Computer facilities
Convention centers/public assembly facilities
Criminal justice/corrections facilities
Educational facilities
Health care facilities
Hotels
Laboratories
Libraries
Recreational facilities
Residential facilities
Theater/performing arts facilities

Design/Practice Issues

Accessibility
Acoustics
Audiovisual technology
Building envelope
Building information modeling
Civil engineering
Cladding/curtain wall
Clean room
Code interpretation
Communications
Computer technology
Concrete
Construction
Construction management
Cost estimating
Demography
Digital imaging
Display
Drawing review/quality assurance
Ecology
Economics
Editorial issues
Electrical engineering
Elevators/escalators
Energy systems
Environmental analysis
Equipment

Facilities management
Financial issues
Fire protection
Food service/kitchen
Graphic design
Historic preservation
Insurance
Interior design
Landscape architecture
Legal issues
Life safety
Lighting
Lightning
Management
Market analysis
Materials handling
Mechanical engineering
Model builder
Power support systems
Process engineering
Programming
Project marketing
Psychology
Public relations
Radiation shielding
Real estate
Record retention
Reprographics
Safety
Sanitary engineering
Scheduling
Security
Sociology
Soils/foundations/earth retention
Space planning
Specifications
Structural engineering
Telecommunications
Traffic/parking
Transportation
Urban planning
Value engineering
Window washing/exterior envelope maintenance

responsible for the detailed design and engineering of one or more of the building's systems. Most large, complex projects need special expertise in civil, structural, mechanical, and electrical design. Some architecture firms include one or more of these engineering disciplines in-house; many, however, do not.

Consultant Services and Responsibilities

Consultant services to the architect are outlined in the architect-consultant agreement. These services, and other contract terms and conditions, should be carefully coordinated with those in the architect-owner agreement.

FORMAT FOR ALLOCATING RESPONSIBILITIES

Agreements should carefully and clearly spell out who is going to do what and how the fee will be allocated among the associated firms or within the joint venture. Here is one format for doing this for projects that are more or less conventionally delivered. For less conventional project delivery methods, such as fast-track with multiple construction packages, multiple prime construction contracts, and design-build projects, the format would have to be adjusted to account for services and deliverables typically associated with those delivery approaches. Use the Comments column, as appropriate, to assist in this regard.

Architectural and Engineering Services by Phase	Responsibility		Fee Split		Comments
Firms	A	B	A	B	
Schematic Design Phase					
1. Conferences with the owner	X	O			
2. Analysis of project requirements: program analysis and concepts, site analysis, space and cost analysis, climatic studies	X	O			
3. Building code information	O	X			
4. Diagram studies of space requirements	X	O			
5. Assembly of utility and survey data	O	X			
6. Schematic design studies and recommended solution	X	O			
7. Schematic design plans	X	O			
8. Sketches and study models	X	O			
9. General project description	X	O			
10. Engineering system concepts	X	O			
11. Preliminary cost estimate	X	O			
12. Presentation of SD documents to owner	X	O	1%	5%	
Design Development Phase					
1. Conferences with the owner	X	O			
2. Refinement of project requirements	X	O			
3. Formulation of civil engineering systems	X	O			
4. Formulation of structural systems	X	O			
5. Formulation of mechanical and electrical systems	X	O			
6. Selection of major building materials	X	O			
7. Preparation of DD documents: plans; elevations; building profile sections; outline specifications; description of electrical, mechanical, civil, and structural systems	X	O			
8. Perspectives, sketches, or models	X	O			
9. Preliminary cost estimate	X	O			
10. Equipment schedule	X	O			
11. Reviewing plans with applicable agencies	O	X			
12. Presentation of DD documents to owner	X	O	15%	5%	
Construction Documents Phase					
1. Conferences with the owner	O	X			
2. Development of major detail conditions	O	X			
3. Diagram study of major mechanical and electrical systems	O	X			
4. Diagram study of major civil and structural systems	O	X			

Firms	Responsibility		Fee Split		Comments
	A	B	A	B	
Construction Documents Phase (Cont.)					
5. Architectural working drawings, specifications	O	X			
6. Civil working drawings, specifications	O	X			
7. Structural working drawings, specifications	O	X			
8. Mechanical working drawings, specifications	O	X			
9. Electrical working drawings, specifications	O	X			
10. Built-in equipment working drawings, specifications	O	X			
11. Cost of special consultants	O	X			
12. Update construction cost estimate	O	X			
13. Submission of construction documents to applicable agencies	O	X			
14. Presentation of CD documents to owner	O	X	5%	35%	
Bidding/Negotiation Phase					
1. Conferences with the owner	O	X			
2. Advertising for bids	O	X			
3. Drafting of bid proposals	O	X			
4. Reproduction and distribution of plans and specifications	O	X			
5. Drafting of addenda	O	X			
6. Contractors' questions and information during bidding	O	X			
7. Bid opening procedure and forms	O	X			
8. Preparation of construction contracts	O	X	1%	4%	
Construction Phase					
1. Preconstruction conference	O	X			
2. Architectural construction administration	O	X			
3. Civil construction administration	O	X			
4. Structural construction administration	O	X			
5. Mechanical and electrical construction administration	O	X			
6. Equipment construction administration	O	X			
7. Shop drawing checking and approval	O	X			
8. Material substitutions, architectural	X	O			
9. Material substitutions, engineering systems	O	X			
10. Material color selection	X	O			
11. Change order procedure	O	X			
12. Verifying and approving periodic estimates	O	X			
13. Progress reports to owner	O	X			
14. Pre-final inspection	O	X			
15. Final acceptance procedure and reports	O	X			
16. Final inspection	O	X			
17. Post-final guarantee period administration	O	X	4%	16%	

"X" denotes primary responsibility for performing the service or providing deliverables.

"O" denotes minor responsibility for assisting in the performance of the service or provision of deliverables.

Services. As the architect and owner establish the services to be included in the architect's agreement, both parties may consider the need for the services of other design professionals. It is advisable to review the list of services required to accomplish the project and establish who will be responsible for each. Each professional service identified may be provided by any of the following:

- The architecture firm, through its own staff.
- A design professional subcontracted to the architecture firm. The design professional may be another architect, an alliance partner, or another firm acting as a consultant to the architect.
- A consultant to the owner. This arrangement may include a construction manager, a project or program manager, an independent design professional for another portion

of the project, or another architecture firm performing a portion of the architecture services—with or without coordination by the architect.

- The owner. The owner's staff may provide services themselves or by some other arrangement—with or without coordination by the architect.

Clarifying responsibilities between the owner and the architect accomplishes at least two things: It helps the architect identify the services for which other design consultants will be sought, and it begins to allocate project risks among the owner, architect, and others on the project team.

Role in project planning. When the architect-consultant relationship is formed early in the project—or before the project begins, in a strategic alliance or a team put together to acquire the project—the consultant can be involved in project planning. The consultant then is in a position to commit to services, scope, schedule, and fee before the architect makes these commitments to the owner.

Often it is effective to assemble the project team as part of the marketing effort when attempting to acquire a project. Owners, especially those whose facilities require sophisticated engineering or other special expertise, are often acutely aware of the need for competent consultants and well-founded architect-consultant relationships. For these owners, consultants become an important part of the interview and selection process.

The responsibilities of the architect. As the prime design professional, the architect assumes primary contractual responsibility to the owner for the accuracy and completeness of the work of the architect's consultants. If something goes wrong, the architect can be held contractually liable to the owner for services improperly performed by the architect's consultant. As design professionals, these consultants are required to perform their services in accordance with applicable standards of professional practice, and failure to do so may result in their direct liability to injured parties. However, their failure to meet the standard of care may also make the architect contractually liable to the owner.

This discussion underscores the importance of careful consultant selection and the need for clear agreement between architect and consultant. It is also important for the architect to understand the impact of a consultant's recommendations and to be prepared to accept initial responsibility and liability for these recommendations. This, in turn, explains why insured architects increasingly seek to retain insured consultants and request a certificate of insurance from them.

AIA ARCHITECT-CONSULTANT AGREEMENT FORM

AIA Document C401–2007, Standard Form of Agreement between Architect and Consultant, is intended for use in conjunction with a prime agreement such as AIA Document B101–2007, Standard Form of Agreement between Owner and Architect. C401–2007 covers engineering services, such as structural, mechanical, or electrical engineering, that begin at the schematic design phase and parallel the architect's basic-services package throughout the course of the project. It also establishes the responsibilities the architect and engineer owe to each other and their mutual rights under the agreement. Although most applicable to engineers, C401–2007 may also be used when contracting with other consultants (e.g., landscape architects, lighting consultants, etc.). Its provisions are in accord with those of B101–2007 and AIA Document A201, General Conditions of the Contract for Construction.

Architect-Consultant Agreements

Two major issues are covered in architect-consultant agreements: passing to the consultant the architect's rights and responsibilities to the owner and sharing risks and rewards. Once these key points have been worked out, it is not difficult to prepare an architect-consultant agreement that parallels the owner-architect agreement.

Legal rights and responsibilities. Usually architects want to give their consultants the same legal rights the architect has from the owner. At the same time, with respect to the consultant's professional discipline, a consultant should owe the same responsibilities to the architect that the architect owes to the owner.

Rather than restate all of these rights and responsibilities from the owner-architect agreement—and run the risk of omitting some—it is common to incorporate the owner-architect agreement (often without specifics of the architect's compensation) into the architect-consultant agreement. This binds the consultant to provide all of the services in its discipline and to be subject to the same terms and conditions the architect owes to the owner.

It may be prudent for the architect to clarify with consultants which design services each consultant will provide and what design services, if any, each consultant will delegate to the contractor or others. These specifics should be defined in and coordinated with AIA Document B101–2007, paragraph 2.2, and AIA Document A201–2007, paragraph 3.12.10; reviewed and determined to be in accordance with applicable state law; and discussed by the architect with the owner.

Risks and rewards. In assessing the risks associated with a project, the architect should assess how risks will be shared with consultants. The best advice is for the architect and the consultant to make each other aware of the risks associated with their aspects of the project. Providing a copy of the owner-architect agreement facilitates this process. With this information, the negotiation can proceed openly.

Compensation issues. Consultant compensation is a matter for negotiation between the parties. Consultants who understand the risks and responsibilities they are assuming will be in a position to negotiate compensation with the architect. In considering compensation, architects will want to address two additional issues:

- *What level of coordination is required for consultant services?* Because consultant services must be fully integrated with those of the architect, coordination should not be casual. The architect will commit time and money to coordination, and these factors should be considered in establishing the architect's compensation. Some firms budget coordination services directly; others budget a multiple or markup of consultant costs to reflect the need for coordination as well as the costs of administration and liability.
- *What will happen if the architect is not paid by the owner or if the project is delayed beyond reason?* Typically, the architect will not want to be obligated to pay the consultant until the architect has first been paid by the owner for the consultant's services.

Education is when you read the fine print. Experience is what you get if you don't.

Pete Seeger

Some state laws require that the architect coordinate owner-retained consultants. Check applicable law and take this into account when negotiating the owner-architect agreement.

CONSULTANT COMPENSATION

In most contracts, when the client does not pay the architect, the consultant faces the risk of not being paid even when services have been rendered. The consultant's protection against that risk rests in questioning the architect about the client's solvency and business practices before the project begins. If the answers are not satisfactory, the consultant can reject the commission. Should payments not materialize once a project has been undertaken, the consultant's protection rests in the architect's making reasonable efforts to collect the money owed.

Therefore, when architects develop agreements with consultants, it is important to address this question: How will the consultant be paid if the owner does not pay the architect? If nonpayment is caused by something that is the consultant's responsibility, the consultant understands when payment is not forthcoming. When this is not the case, however, the consultant may not be as understanding. It is a business risk that should be addressed by the parties in their contract.

Assuming the architect-consultant agreement does not state what happens if the architect is not paid, the architect will have to explain that it is the custom in the design profession and construction industry for the consultant's compensation to be contingent on payment being made to the party holding the prime agreement with the owner.

This would be so even if the consultant was the prime contractor with the owner and the architect was the subcontracting consultant.

The reasons for this custom are compelling:

- The prime contractor absorbs the costs—and risks—associated with project acquisition.
- The prime contractor will have to absorb the costs of collecting the fee should payment be tardy or otherwise not forthcoming.
- In the time between marketing and closeout, the prime contractor is directly responsible to the owner for the vagaries and tensions of the design process.

In most jurisdictions, if the consultant agreement does not state when the consultant is to be paid for satisfactory performance of services, the law requires that payment be made within a reasonable period. The fact that the architect has not been paid by the client would be no defense for not paying the consultant unless the architect-consultant agreement states that receipt of payment from the client is a condition for payment to the consultant. Even then, in some states, such a contractual provision may not be enforceable, so caution and an understanding of applicable state law is necessary when drafting such provisions.

Architects seldom have adequate financial resources to fund such payments, which can average between 20 and 40 percent or more of the architect's total fees on a project. Architect-consultant agreements often include a "pay-when-paid" clause for this purpose, sometimes including an agreement and release on the part of the consultant not to pursue the architect until the architect receives such funds. Consultants typically understand and accept the architect's dilemma, but in return would expect the architect to seek prompt payment from the owner. Care has to be taken in drafting such clauses, however, since state laws vary on the enforceability of such provisions.

Forms of agreement. Architect-consultant agreement forms with major consultants such as engineers should parallel the owner-architect agreement. (This is normally less critical for consultants for limited purposes such as specifications, kitchens, elevators, security systems, etc.) Statements of service as well as terms and conditions should be carried consistently throughout the prime agreement and consultant agreements. Using the AIA standard forms achieves this goal. However, if the forms are modified, it is important to verify that the modification is reflected in all the documents. This is particularly important if the scope of services portion of the owner-architect agreement is changed; in this case, the consultant agreement should be modified as well.

Digital practice protocols and BIM management issues. Architect-consultant agreements establish protocols for e-mail, Internet, Web-based, and FTP site communications, information sharing, and document storage and transfer. Protocols should also be established for building information modeling (BIM) requirements with respect to design integration among the project team members, and possibly with respect to vertical integration issues with owners, contractors, subcontractors, fabricators, suppliers, erectors, and others involved in the construction process. Along with the significant potential benefits and opportunities such digital practices can introduce to a project, they also bring new risks, possible liabilities, and some uncertainties. Such concerns can include responsibility for the integrity of the model or its constituent parts, ownership of and use rights with respect to the model and its outputs (drawings, specifications, schedules, energy analyses, cost estimates, etc.), protocols for modifications to the model, and responsibility for errors or omissions in the data included in the model. The architect-consultant agreement offers an excellent opportunity for the parties to determine and agree upon how to handle these issues.

Owner-Retained Consultants

An owner may directly retain project consultants. The architect may or may not have any contractual responsibility for these consultants. If the architect is to have any contractual responsibility, then the architect must be able to review and negotiate those responsibilities.

An owner may decide to write a prime agreement with another consultant in addition to the architect for a number of reasons:

- Services may be substantially different and not overlap.
- The owner may have a long-standing relationship with the consultant.
- The owner may seek the benefit of direct and independent advice.
- The owner may prefer to structure the project team and then assume the responsibilities for its coordination, either through the owner's in-house staff or through a program manager.

On occasion, an owner may have motives that benefit the owner but not necessarily the project. For instance, the owner may want to save money by (usually unwisely) eliminating coordination services during design or construction, or the owner may want to keep total control of the project by retaining overall coordination responsibilities.

In some cases, it is to the architect's advantage to have the owner directly retain a consultant. This is especially true when the architect must rely on a consultant's work but is not—and does not want to be—in a position to review that work independently and take responsibility for it (e.g., in connection with land surveying and geotechnical engineering). For this reason, AIA Document B101–2007 specifies that it is the owner's responsibility to provide any necessary land surveying and geotechnical engineering data to the architect. These consultants are engaged by the owner, and the architect is entitled to rely on the survey and geotechnical information supplied by the owner.

Whatever motivations an owner has for directly retaining consultants, someone must coordinate the services of these professionals. The owner must either assume this responsibility and the risks associated with it, or assign it to a program manager or to one of the prime professionals on the project.

Coordination is especially important from the point of view of the architect. Because architects are the generalist design professionals on building projects, others on the project team may expect them to coordinate professional services even though they might not have contractual responsibility or authority to do so. An architect who acts on that expectation and coordinates activities for other consultants may be held responsible for the results of that coordination, even though the owner has engaged project consultants directly and has not made the architect responsible for them.

This situation poses unique dilemmas for the architect. As a generalist, the architect is usually in the best position to coordinate the activities of other design professionals on the project. If the architect is not assigned these responsibilities and the owner is unable or unwilling to provide them, the architect should inform the owner about potential increased costs and schedule impacts that may result from uncoordinated design services. The architect may also want to negotiate to assume these responsibilities and to be compensated for them. When the architect is assigned coordination responsibilities, owner-retained consultants should be required, by contract, to coordinate their efforts with the architect, to submit to the architect's authority, and to look to the owner only if they have claims with respect to the architect as the owner's agent. And, as discussed earlier in this topic, whether or not the architect is to coordinate the *activities* of owner-retained consultants, the architect should never assume responsibility to coordinate the *documents* of such consultants. Consultants should be obligated to coordinate their own documents with those of the architect; the architect's responsibility should be limited to coordinating the architect's documents with those of such consultants.

However, the architect may choose to select the consultant team but have them contract directly with the owner. In this situation, the architect can work with trusted consultants without being financially responsible for consultant fees. Many clients who want a higher level of control in the project prefer this arrangement. In this case, the architect would assume customary responsibility for the coordination of the work of the consultants.

JOINT VENTURES

A joint venture is a contractual union between two or more firms for one or more specific projects. The joint venture arrangement enables firms to combine key resources, expertise, and experience to perform professional services on a specific project while allowing each participating firm to pursue other projects.

A joint venture functions essentially like a partnership. There is an agreement detailing who brings what to the venture, who will do what, and how the compensation or profit will be shared. The agreement also details how responsibilities and risks are allocated internally. Typically a joint venture retains no profits and pays no income taxes; it passes profits (or losses) and tax liabilities along to its participating members. Participating firms are individually and jointly liable to the client and others for the services offered by the joint venture.

Generally speaking, a joint venture is formed only for the purpose of seeking and executing a specific project. After a successful project, some firms feel there is enough value in the collaboration to seek further projects that require the unique talents represented in the venture. Some joint ventures have been so successful that they have resulted in permanent mergers of the participating firms.

There is always an element of risk in joint ventures. Every design and building project involves a temporary "multi-organization"—a condition that raises its own problems and adds to the risks inherent in the building enterprise. If the design entity itself is a joint venture (another such multi-organization), then it stands to reason there is added risk. The basic concept behind joint ventures is that the potential rewards outweigh the inherent risks.

It is imperative that the joint venture parties have and exhibit a high degree of trust and confidence in one another. It is also essential, before the project moves forward, for the joint venture parties to clearly agree on a division of responsibilities for both the professional services the joint venture will provide to the client and the business responsibilities of managing the joint venture itself. This includes decisions about who will handle the finances and banking arrangements, how key decisions will be made and by whom, and how risk for profit and loss will be allocated. Leaving any of these key decisions to be resolved in "real time," when emotions may be running high and the consequences significant, is not recommended.

Reasons for Forming a Venture

A successful joint venture begins with a clear understanding of why the venture has been formed in the first place. The initiative to form a joint venture is usually taken by the architect, although it may also come from the owner. The reasons for it may be technical or political. For example, a national firm from outside the owner's geographic area may enter a joint venture with a respected local firm.

Each primary participant in a venture must make an independent decision that the venture makes sense, but the participants must make a similar decision collectively. A firm that discovers it is being used in some unexpected and undesired way—by the owner or by another firm—may have trouble remaining content and performing at its best. Finally, it is important to understand that some owners are innately suspicious of joint ventures. They may see the advantages for the firms but may not want *their* project to be the testing ground for the relationship.

Process

The process of forming a joint venture begins with asking these questions: What does the project require? What are your firm's strengths and weaknesses relative to these requirements? Stated another way, what does your firm bring to the project, and what does your firm need to obtain through a joint venture? One approach is to examine these key issues:

- *Required skills.* What skills does the project require, and what does your firm have in-house (or through capable consultants)? Are other disciplines required? Is the owner expecting construction management, financing, or other specific services?
- *Background and knowledge.* What special requirements does the project have? How much expertise or experience does your firm have in accomplishing projects like the one under consideration?
- *Staffing.* Does your firm have the people with the right expertise and experience available to work on the project? If these people are committed to the project, can your firm meet its other commitments?
- *Geography.* Does the location of one or both of the venture partners bring an advantage to the project?
- *Financing.* If the joint venture needs resources your firm does not have (e.g., expanded computer-aided design or building information modeling capability), is your firm in a position to make the investment?
- *Insurance.* Is the scope of each firm's professional liability insurance acceptable to the others—and to the client?

- *Licensing and registration.* While each joint venture member is likely to be properly licensed and registered as a corporation, partnership, or other appropriate legal entity in its home state, will each member and/or the joint venture itself be required to be licensed or registered under the local laws of the state where the project is located?
- *Management.* Does your firm have the leadership and management capabilities to take on the project, service the client, and manage the people, processes, and risks involved?
- *Contacts.* Does your firm have the necessary contacts to secure the commission?

A careful and honest appraisal of what you bring to the project does two things: It helps you decide whether to pursue the opportunity, and it creates a profile of characteristics to seek in your joint ventures.

Joint Venture Agreements

There are many business issues, some related to the project and others related to the ways the two firms will work together, that must be addressed in forming a joint venture. The best advice is to be aware of the full range of issues and to negotiate them before the joint venture offers to provide professional services. Occasionally, whether based on an owner's request, the architect's realization that more expertise is needed, or other demands of the project, the joint venture may not be formed until after professional services have commenced. In such circumstances, though there will be pressure to move quickly, it is just as imperative that these issues be sorted out and agreed upon before entering into the joint venture.

Associated Professional Firms

Sometimes two professional firms choose to represent themselves as "associated" with each other to undertake a project. From a legal standpoint, these firms have two choices: They may form a joint venture, or they may establish a consultant-subconsultant relationship, with one of the firms acting as a prime consultant to the other.

Whatever arrangement is chosen, the issues discussed above should be addressed. Roles, responsibilities, risks, and rewards should be defined and delineated in a written agreement between the parties. Once an agreement has been signed, the associating firms should act with that agreement in mind. For example, two architects with a prime consultant–subconsultant arrangement may act so that a third party sees them as participants in a joint venture, jointly and severally liable for any resulting problems. In other words, each entity is responsible not only for its own actions but also for the actions of the other. This could result in unintended liability for one or both of the parties that would not otherwise exist if it were clear from the parties' actions that a prime consultant–subconsultant arrangement existed.

Architects should approach design team agreements with the same careful attention they pay to arrangements with owners. Both have similar purposes: to put in place an outstanding design team and a framework of arrangements that serve the client and the project well.

For More Information
Most general law books addressing the practice of architecture include treatises and cases about design team agreements. AIA C-series documents relate to the agreement between the architect and consultant for professional services. This series includes standard forms of agreement between the architect and engineer or other consultants, as well as a standard form that may be used for joint ventures among design professionals to provide professional services.

11.4 Construction Contracts

Gregory Hancks, Esq., AIA

The construction agreement, general conditions, and other parts of the construction contract set out what the owner, contractor, and architect are expected to do during the construction phase.

A construction contract is the formal agreement for the purchase of labor, materials, equipment, and services for building work. The construction contract

- Sets forth the rights and obligations of the owner and contractor with respect to each other and to the work
- Details the contractor's scope of work by incorporating the construction documents prepared by the architect
- Determines the total amount that the owner will pay the contractor and when payments are to be made
- Describes procedures that are to be followed in carrying out the work, including information the owner and contractor are to provide
- May set out how each party can assert a claim against the other and how disputes are to be resolved

Many owners request the architect's assistance in selecting and preparing the construction agreement, general conditions, and other parts of the contract—in addition to preparing the construction drawings and specifications. The architect is well positioned to provide the owner with practical and technical information on these matters and to identify standard form documents that are generally consistent with the owner's goals. It is always appropriate, however, to recommend that the owner also obtain the advice of legal and insurance professionals to meet the requirements of the particular project. It also should be remembered that the owner (not the architect) is entering into the contract. Decisions on contract terms are ultimately the owner's responsibility.

At the same time, the construction contract affects the services that the architect will provide during the construction phase of a project. In many projects, the architect provides administration of the construction contract. In the role of construction contract administrator, the architect acts as the owner's representative to the extent agreed upon by the owner and architect. When a construction contract is selected or drafted, the architect should ensure that its provisions for contract administration are coordinated with the provisions of the owner-architect agreement.

For all of these reasons, the architect needs to be familiar with each part of a construction contract and understand alternative approaches that are available in drafting and administering such contracts. This knowledge will enable the architect to contribute to a successful project as well as manage the architect's own services more effectively.

THE EFFECT OF THE PROJECT DELIVERY METHOD ON A CONSTRUCTION CONTRACT

The term "project delivery method" refers to the way that relationships are structured among the primary participants in the design and construction process. A successful construction contract provides an accurate description of those relationships, including their legal, administrative, procedural, and technical aspects.

The party who purchases the construction work is commonly referred to as the "owner." In some instances, this party may be the tenant or lessee of the property where the work is to be performed even though the contract documents use the word "owner." When the tenant enters into the construction contract, the landlord's interests should also be taken into account.

▶ See Construction Contract Administration (8.5) for a discussion of those services provided by the architect.

Gregory Hancks is an associate general counsel in the AIA General Counsel office.

As a result, the initial selection of a standard form agreement and general conditions for a particular project primarily depends on the project delivery method to be used. This selection also depends on the method for determining the amount the contractor will be paid, a subject discussed in detail later in this topic. The project delivery method is critical because the agreement and general conditions contain more than just abstract legal provisions—these documents also describe the basic administrative procedures by which the project will be built. In other words, these documents provide the framework for what the owner, contractor, and architect will do during the construction process.

This topic focuses on construction contracts for projects that follow the traditional design-award-build project delivery method. This method encompasses projects in which the construction contract is negotiated following completion of the design (design-negotiate-build), as well as projects that are competitively bid (design-bid-build). It is common for an owner to enter into a single contract for the general construction work on a project. For some projects, however, the owner may find it advantageous to divide the work into more than one prime contract. When the owner enters into multiple prime construction contracts, each of those contracts will likely follow the design-award-build project delivery method.

This will typically be the case, for example, when the owner enters into multiple prime construction contracts after retaining a construction manager–adviser (i.e., a construction manager who does not perform any of the construction work but serves solely as the owner's consultant). The AIA Construction Manager–Adviser (CMa) family of contract documents, including the CMa construction agreement and general conditions, fits this model and follows the design-award-build project delivery method.

When construction management services are to be provided by a construction company that will also serve as the construction contractor, the owner will normally retain those services during the pre-design or design phase of the project. The AIA Construction Manager–Constructor (CMc) family of contract documents describes this project delivery method. A CMc project is not design-award-build because the owner awards the prime construction contract to the construction manager–constructor *before* the design and construction documents are completed. Once a CMc project enters the construction phase, however, the project relationships mirror the relationships in a design-award-build project. As a result, the information presented in this topic generally applies to the construction phase of an owner-CMc contract. For example, the construction phase provisions in the AIA standard form CMc agreements (A121/CMc–2003 and A131/CMc–2003) are based on the corresponding design-award-build contract documents.

In design-build projects, the relationship between a design-builder and a construction contractor bears many similarities to the owner-contractor relationship in a traditional design-award-build project. For possible ways to structure construction contracts in the design-build context, refer to AIA Document A142–2004, Agreement Between Design-Builder and Contractor, in the AIA Design-Build family of documents. When an architect contracts with a design-builder to provide architecture services in a design-build project, the architect should keep in mind that the scope of architecture services during construction will depend on how construction contract administration will be handled and may differ markedly from an architect's conventional role.

THE PARTS OF A CONSTRUCTION CONTRACT

In the traditional language of the construction industry, the owner-contractor *agreement* is the document that the owner and contractor sign and that sets out the most fundamental or essential terms of their understanding, such as payment terms. The construction *contract*, by contrast, consists of the owner-contractor agreement and everything that is incorporated into that agreement, whether those additional documents are physically attached as exhibits to the agreement or are simply incorporated into the agreement by reference.

Fast-track is a project scheduling technique. Project delivery methods such as construction manager-adviser, construction manager-constructor, and design-build are commonly associated with fast-track scheduling, as are design-award-build projects, especially where multiple prime contracts are awarded.

A contract is an agreed-upon set of mutual promises that gives each party a legal duty to the other and the right to seek a remedy for the other party's breach of its duties. A "letter of intent" or "memorandum of understanding" may not contain actual mutual promises. In that case, it may not be legally enforceable and therefore not a contract.

A construction contract normally includes the following essential documents: owner-contractor agreement, general conditions, supplementary or other conditions, drawings, and specifications. A construction contract also includes any authorized changes to the provisions in these documents. Changes made before the agreement is signed are typically made by addendum. Modifications made after the agreement is signed can be made in whatever way the construction contract itself provides or permits; alternatives include change orders, construction change directives, and minor changes in the work typically issued as architects' supplemental instructions.

Not all documents that are prepared and distributed by the architect are part of the construction contract. Documents prepared solely to describe bidding procedures or bidding requirements do not need to be incorporated into the contract, and confusion can be avoided by omitting them from the list of documents incorporated into the contract. When construction work is procured by negotiation instead of bidding, the request for proposals does not need to be part of the contract if the contractor's proposal or other contract documents set out all of the duties of the contracting parties. Similarly, shop drawings and other contractor submittals, even when approved by the architect, typically should not be incorporated into the construction contract. Incorporating approved submittals would alter the contractor's work requirements when a submittal varies from the original contract documents.

The fact that a construction contract may contain at least four initial written documents (agreement, general conditions, supplementary conditions, and specifications) naturally leads to the question: What subject matter goes where? The answer lies partly in practicality and partly in industry practice and tradition. One factor to consider is who is responsible for the content of the document. The agreement and conditions (general, supplementary, and any other) are ultimately the responsibility of the owner as they contain those matters that should be decided by the owner, such as insurance coverage or the amount of any liquidated damages. The specifications (Division 01 and higher), on the other hand, are the architect's responsibility and generally contain information that is within an architect's expertise. More detailed answers to "what goes where" are available in AIA Document A521–1993, Uniform Location of Subject Matter. Additional guidance may be found in MasterFormat section numbers and titles published by the Construction Specifications Institute.

Owner-Contractor Agreement

The construction agreement typically identifies the parties and the architect, defines the contractor's scope of work by incorporating the construction drawings and specifications, states when the work will begin and when it is to be completed, states the amount the contractor will be paid or describes how that amount will be determined, and describes payment procedures. The agreement incorporates into the contract the conditions (general, supplementary, etc.) and any addenda or other documents. This may be done either by reference or by attaching the documents to the agreement.

General Conditions

As a general rule, the meaning or enforceability of a contract is not affected when a document is incorporated by reference rather than physically attaching it to the agreement. However, attaching a copy of the incorporated document has the practical benefit of better communication between the parties and decreases the chance of disputes resulting from misunderstanding.

This document, which may also be called terms and conditions or general provisions, describes in detail the relationship between owner and contractor. A set of general conditions is designed to apply generically to a project delivery method or other project type. Although the architect is not a party to the construction contract, the general conditions describe responsibilities the architect has during construction; these provisions may be incorporated by reference into the owner-architect agreement as well. Structuring a construction contract with a separate general conditions document instead of including those provisions within the construction agreement itself normally has no effect on the meaning or enforceability of the provisions. An exception occurs when a precedence clause is included that states which document will override in the event of a conflict among the documents.

Supplementary Conditions

General conditions typically must be adapted to suit the particular requirements of a specific project. Supplementary conditions list such additions, deletions, or other changes to the general conditions. AIA Document A503–2007, Guide for Supplementary Conditions, is a resource for drafting them. The practice of making changes to general conditions in a separate set of supplementary conditions originated in the pre-computer age and is likely to decline as computers are increasingly used to generate contract documents. When general conditions are adapted by making changes directly in the general conditions document itself, a separate supplementary conditions document is unnecessary.

Special Conditions or Other Conditions

Other documents that modify the general conditions may be used. For example, some owners have standard modifications, or special conditions, to be used for their projects. In such instances, project contract documents may include both special conditions (describing the owner's typical requirements) and supplementary conditions (describing project-specific requirements).

Drawings

These are the graphic and pictorial portions of the contract documents that show the design, location, configuration, and dimensions of the work. Drawings typically include plans, elevations, sections, details, schedules, and diagrams.

Specifications

These are the written requirements for materials, equipment, systems, standards, and workmanship for the work. Specifications include both technical requirements and administrative or procedural requirements.

Addenda

An addendum is issued before the construction agreement is signed to change or interpret provisions of the proposed contract. An addendum may include graphic as well as written material and can change or interpret the conditions of the contract as well as the drawings and specifications.

Change Orders

A change order is a document signed by the owner and contractor (and by the architect when required by the general conditions) after the contract is signed to modify the work requirements. A change order may also change the amount the contractor is to be paid and the time allowed to complete the work.

Construction Change Directives

When provided for by the construction contract, a construction change directive permits the owner to direct a change in the work when the owner and contractor are initially unable to agree on the cost or time required for a change in the work. Typically, the architect prepares and signs a construction change directive, which the owner also signs.

Minor Change in the Work

The construction contract may authorize the architect to order a minor change in the work that does not involve a change either in the amount the contractor is to be paid or in the time to complete the work. Such orders are to be issued in writing and are binding on the owner and contractor.

AIA contract documents intentionally do not establish an order of precedence among contract documents that would apply in the event of an inconsistency. They require the contractor to consult the architect or owner when a discrepancy is encountered, allowing them to decide on the best course of action rather than leaving the resolution to the contractor.

Other Contract Modifications

The owner and contractor can also agree to modify their contract by signing a written amendment.

BASIS OF PAYMENT

The method used to determine how much the contractor will be paid has a significant effect on the construction contract. Relatively brief contract provisions are required to describe the contract sum when the contractor is to be paid a predetermined fixed amount or "stipulated sum." When the contractor is instead to be paid the actual amounts the contractor expends to do the work ("cost plus fee" or "time and materials"), defining exactly what categories of costs the contractor is allowed to charge to the owner requires considerable detail. Even further provisions are required when the contractor guarantees a maximum price for a project done on a cost-plus basis.

Stipulated Sum

In this type of contract, the contractor agrees to do the entire scope of work for a stated or fixed amount. Under this arrangement, the owner has the advantage of knowing the cost of the work at the time the contract is signed. A stipulated sum contract is almost always used when the work is competitively bid and may also be used in negotiated contracts. The contractor's profit (or loss) is determined by how the contractor's actual costs incurred compare to the amounts assumed in the bid or proposal.

Cost plus Fee

Under this arrangement, the owner reimburses the contractor for the cost of all labor, materials, subcontracts, and other items required to complete the work (referred to as the "cost of the work" in AIA contract documents). The owner also pays the contractor a fee to allow for overhead and profit. The fee may be a fixed sum or may be a percentage of the cost of the work. Establishing the fee as a fixed sum enables the contractor to reduce the cost of the work without reducing its profit. But even in a cost-plus contract with a fixed fee, the owner does not know what the cost of the work will be when the contract is signed. This disadvantage may be outweighed by other considerations, as in the following situations:

- To meet the owner's desired completion schedule, construction must be started before the design is completed, and the design-award-build project delivery method cannot be used.
- Other factors prevent the owner from knowing at the outset of construction what the exact scope of work will be, for example, when the owner will provide the interior finish work for office space to be leased to tenants.
- Construction quality or special construction requirements are more important than cost, such as in defense projects or research facilities.

Particularly in larger cost-plus contracts, a control estimate or target price may be established based on a preliminary cost estimate. This control estimate can be used to monitor costs as they are incurred and billed to the owner.

Guaranteed Maximum Price

This is a variation of the cost-plus-fee arrangement, in which the contractor assumes the risk that the construction cost will not exceed a stated amount. Unlike other cost-plus contracts, a contract with a guaranteed maximum price must include a defined scope of work; without a measurable scope of work, the GMP serves no purpose. Contractors commonly commit to a GMP when construction documents are only 60 to 70 percent complete; larger contingencies can be expected when the construction documents are less complete. In a GMP contract, the contractor is entitled to an increase in the GMP for changes in the scope of work.

When a GMP contract contains a percentage (not fixed) fee, the contractor has a financial incentive to incur the maximum allowable cost and thereby receive the maximum fee. One way to counter this tendency is for the owner and contractor to share the savings, that is, to split the difference between the allowed GMP and the actual cost-plus-fee amount. The proportion of the split can be in whatever percentages the parties agree.

A GMP contract can be adapted in other ways to adjust the cost risks carried by the owner and contractor. For example, the contractor may be able to obtain fixed prices from some subcontractors for their scopes of work; these fixed prices, along with the contractor's associated fee, can be included in the general construction contract, thereby reducing the scope of work that is subject to cost variation.

Unit Price

A unit price is a fixed amount the contractor will be paid for a specified unit of a material or service. Unit prices are used when the quantity of work the contractor will perform cannot be known at the outset, for example, to set the cost for rock excavation or other types of earthwork. Unit prices are used more extensively in construction of civil engineering work than in construction of buildings, although they are often used in building renovation projects and to obtain prices for tenant construction. The unit price method requires a specific description of the work (for example, types of rock excavation may need to be defined) and, during construction, a measurement of the amount of work actually performed (for example, volume of rock excavated). The contractor's cost in performing some kinds of work is dependent on the volume, so care should be taken in estimating how much work will be required on a unit price basis. If the actual amount of work varies significantly from the estimated amount, an adjustment in the unit price may be required to be fair to one party or the other.

OTHER SPECIFIC PROVISIONS

Following is a brief discussion of selected provisions commonly found in construction contracts.

Project and Work

As used in standard form AIA Contract Documents, the term "work" refers to what the contractor provides under a particular contract. The term "project" refers to the owner's entire undertaking and, along with the contractor's work, generally includes such things as professional services; land acquisition; and furniture, furnishings, and equipment (FF&E). The project can be identified in the construction contract by name or other brief description. A description of the work is generally unnecessary because its scope is defined by the entire set of contract documents, including the construction drawings and specifications, which are incorporated by reference into the agreement. A short description of the work may be useful, however, when the project includes work to be performed by more than one prime contractor.

Date of Commencement and Notice to Proceed

The owner may not be ready for construction to begin on the date the contract is signed. The contract can provide that work is to begin on another specified date or on a date to be established later in a notice to proceed that the owner will issue. A notice to proceed may be a letter or other document that states the date when the contractor may begin work and is signed by the owner (or by the architect, if authorized by the owner). A significant delay in issuing a notice to proceed may have an adverse effect on the contractor and give rise to a claim for increased costs or for additional time.

A construction manager doing construction work under a cost-plus contract with a GMP is sometimes referred to as a CM "at risk." Correspondingly, if no GMP is established in the cost-plus contract, the CM may be described as "not at risk." However, the terms "at risk" and "not at risk" are ambiguous and should be used with caution. Even if there is no GMP, a construction manager-constructor performs the construction work (directly or through subcontracts) and may incur a loss if the fee does not cover expenses.

▶ Construction contracts typically contain definitions of key terms. When the definition of a term is not provided in the contract itself, the term should be given its ordinary and customary meaning in the construction industry. The glossary in Appendix E contains meanings of some frequently used terms.

Contract parties: Each party to a contract should be identified by its full legal name. This is particularly important when the party is an incorporated entity. Failure to accurately state a party's name in the agreement may complicate the resolution of any disputes.

Contract Sum

Sometimes referred to as the contract price, this is the total amount that the owner will be required to pay the contractor. If the contract is for a stipulated sum, that fixed amount will be stated in the contract. At completion, the contract sum may be different because of change orders or other contract modifications. In a cost-plus-fee contract, however, the contract sum cannot be stated in the contract as a dollar amount; instead, the contract defines how the cost of the work will be determined and states the contractor's fee amount or percentage.

Progress Payments

Because of the length of time required to perform construction work, the contract typically requires the owner to make partial or progress payments as the work proceeds. Most standard-form construction contracts contain at least basic provisions for how and when such progress payments are to be made. Commonly, applications for payment are submitted monthly. The agreement may list the calendar date deadline for the contractor to make its applications. That date may be based on practical considerations, such as coordination with regularly scheduled project meetings where issues involving progress payments can be discussed and resolved. Other progress payment procedural requirements are typically described in the agreement and in the general conditions. They can be further detailed in the supplementary conditions and in Division 1 of the specifications. Cost-plus-fee contracts generally require more detailed payment provisions than stipulated sum contracts because the contractor is required to justify each of the costs charged to the owner.

Schedule of Values

To certify to the owner the amount to be paid, the architect must evaluate the contractor's application in light of both the scope of work described in the contract and the work completed. A schedule of values breaks down the entire scope of work into categories (such as by subcontract or specification division), which are each assigned a dollar value prior to work beginning. A schedule of values is indispensable for contracts that contain either a stipulated sum or a GMP. (A schedule of values is not required for cost-plus-fee contracts without a GMP, but its use may be considered as a tool for monitoring costs.) The schedule of values enables the architect to certify progress payments with some assurance that the total amount paid corresponds to the completion percentage of the work. To this end, the amount requested in each application for payment must reflect the quantity of work completed by category. In addition, the initial schedule of values must reflect the contractor's anticipated costs with reasonable accuracy. If work to be performed early in the construction process, such as site or foundation work, were assigned excessively high values, the contractor could be overpaid during the early phases of the work.

Retainage

Under traditional industry practice, some percentage of the value of the work completed may be deducted from the amount of each progress payment. This amount or retainage provides some additional assurance that the work can be completed for the unpaid contract amount, thus protecting the owner. The amount of retainage may vary by locale and custom, by project type, and by stage of completion of the work, but the details for any retainage and for any reduction or release of retainage funds must be spelled out in the contract. The amount of retainage on materials stored off-site may be set at a separate percentage. Some states have enacted statutes that affect when retainage must be paid or deposited for subsequent release, so any retainage provisions should be drafted with appropriate legal advice.

When the federal government is the owner, the government will determine the form of contract to be used. When the federal government is providing funding for construction work but is not the owner, applicable federal regulations need to be incorporated into whatever contract forms are used. AIA Document A201/SC–1999, Federal Supplementary Conditions of the Contract for Construction, may be used to adapt the A201 general conditions in this situation.

Substantial Completion

Requiring the contractor to complete the work by a stated date enables the owner to plan for occupancy and use of the project. The contractor's failure to meet that deadline generally constitutes a breach of contract. The standard for judging the contactor's performance for this purpose is "substantial completion" (that is, the project can be used for its intended purpose) instead of full or final completion (every contract requirement has been met). The concept of substantial completion is consistent with the way the common law resolves breach of contract claims. Even when the contract does not fix a required completion date, substantial completion still triggers other contract events. When substantial completion is reached, for example, the architect may be required to perform an inspection, or the method of calculating payments owed to the contractor may change.

Final Completion and Final Payment

The requirements and procedures for final completion and final payment are distributed among the agreement, general and supplemental conditions, and Division 1 of the specifications. Unlike substantial completion, however, a required date for final completion is frequently not stated in the construction contract.

Warranties and the Period for Correction of Work

Three separate mechanisms may be found in construction contracts to ensure the contractor's responsibility for the quality of completed work. First, the contractor has a continuing contractual obligation to have performed the work in accordance with the contract documents. This obligation includes a general warranty against defective work (see, e.g., Section 3.5 of AIA Document A201–2007, General Conditions of the Contract for Construction). This warranty lasts until the expiration of the statute of limitations or statute of repose. Second, the contractor must comply with the specific terms of any product warranty that has been provided, for example, a fifteen-year warranty on a roofing system. These product-specific warranties are in addition to the general warranty and may be enforced for a longer time. Third, some construction contracts, such as those based on the A201, require the contractor to return to the site to correct defective work discovered within a year after substantial completion. This one-year period may sometimes be referred to, informally, as a "one-year warranty period," but that term is misleading because the contractor's warranty and other contractual responsibilities for defective work do not end one year after substantial completion.

Governing law: Construction contracts are typically interpreted under the law of a particular state, except in the case of federal government projects where federal contract law applies. Contracts designate the governing state law in order to avoid disputes over that issue and to increase the predictability of how contract provisions will be applied.

Alternative Dispute Resolution

Unless a construction contract provides otherwise, the owner and contractor generally have a right to resolve contract disputes by litigating them in court with a trial by jury. With limited exceptions, this right can be waived by agreeing in the contract that disputes will be decided in another manner, such as mediation and arbitration. Most such arbitration agreements in construction contracts can be enforced under current law including the Federal Arbitration Act. Arbitration agreements may also contain procedural details regarding how arbitration is to be conducted. When the contract does not contain those details, they will be determined by the laws governing the arbitration procedure, which differ substantially among the states.

Consequential Damages

A party who breaches a contract is ordinarily liable to the other party for all damages that are the result of the breach, including both "direct" damages and "indirect" or "consequential" damages. In construction, an example of direct damages is the cost to repair defective work or to complete work left unfinished by the contractor. Consequential damages are losses that are not the immediate result of the breach, but are losses that the breaching party has reason to know the other party will likely incur when the contract is breached. In the construction of a hotel, for example, lost room rentals are consequential damages incurred by the owner when the contractor fails to complete the work by the date stated in the contract, provided that the contractor knew when the agreement was signed that the owner would suffer lost rent if the work was not completed on time. Contracts such as those based on the A201may contain a waiver of consequential damages. When consequential damages are waived, only direct damages can be recovered when the contract is breached.

Liquidated Damages

Because it may be burdensome to determine the precise amount of damages that a party incurs when a contract is breached, the amount of damages may be predetermined or fixed as "liquidated damages" in the contract. The governing law restricts the ways that liquidated damages provisions can be applied, however, so legal advice is always recommended when including a liquidated damages provision. In construction, liquidated damages are most frequently used to set the amount of damages owed to the owner for delay in completion of the work, generally on a per-day basis. Because such delay damages are typically consequential damages, any provision that waives consequential damages should specifically state that liquidated damages are not precluded. Care must be taken to ensure that a liquidated damages provision does not conflict with any waiver of consequential damages.

Statute of Limitations and Statute of Repose

The governing law restricts the length of time that lawsuits (or arbitrations) may be filed after damages are incurred or after a defect occurs or is discovered. This time period is established by a statute of limitations. Most states have also adopted another type of time restriction on claims against construction contractors (and architects), established by a statute of repose. Unlike a statute of limitations, a statute of repose begins to run at the end of construction or whenever services were last provided. Construction contracts may contain provisions that modify or further define these statutory time restrictions.

SUBCONTRACTS

An architect may have little or no direct communication with subcontractors when administering a construction contract. As a result, architects have less need to be familiar with construction subcontracts than with prime or general construction contracts. Subcontractors nevertheless perform a substantial percentage of construction work, and project success commonly depends on their performance.

The prime construction contract should provide the owner and architect the opportunity to review the qualifications of the subcontractors proposed for the principal portions of the work and, if necessary, the right to request that other subcontractors be used. In competitive bid situations, the contractor has likely relied on the bids submitted by the contractor's initially proposed subcontractors. As a result, substituting alternative subcontractors will frequently increase the contractor's costs. If an objection is made to a proposed subcontractor and another subcontractor is substituted, the owner should expect to pay the contractor for the increased cost unless the subcontractor initially proposed is demonstrably not capable of performing. When the prime contract is awarded by negotiation or when the prime contractor is a construction manager–constructor, the owner has additional opportunity to control the selection of subcontractors, and the contract should describe that process.

The prime construction contract should also require that subcontracts be governed by the same terms as the owner-contractor relationship. This flow-down serves to ensure that the responsibilities of subcontractors for their particular portions of the

The information in this topic applies to general construction contracts, including those limited to interior construction work. Contracts for furniture, furnishings, and equipment fall into a separate category, however. Generally speaking, the purchase of FF&E is governed by Article 2 of the Uniform Commercial Code. This law differs markedly from general construction law, and only contract documents specifically intended for the purchase of FF&E, such as the AIA Interiors family of contract documents, should be used for that purpose.

work match the responsibilities that the contractor has toward the owner. In addition, the prime contract should provide a means for the owner to require subcontractors to continue work in the event the contractor defaults on the prime contract. For example, the A201–2007 General Conditions requires that each subcontract be assigned to the owner, contingent on the contractor's default and on the owner's decision to accept the assignment.

In general, the law does not require a contractor to enter into a subcontract with any particular sub-bidder—even if its sub-bid is the lowest submitted and even if the contractor relied on that sub-bid to make its own bid. At the same time, the contractor can generally require a sub-bidder to honor its bid and enter into a subcontract based on that bid. This lack of symmetry is emblematic of the subcontractor's difficult position within the construction process. The subcontractor is affected by actions of the owner and other subcontractors but has no contract with those parties. Moreover, the subcontractor has no formal direct line of communication with the architect or engineering consultants. Depending on the terms of the subcontract, the subcontractor may have limited control over progress payments to be received from the contractor.

State laws provide some help to subcontractors to ensure they get paid for their work. Some states have enacted prompt payment statutes that may affect when progress payments and retainage must be paid. In addition, mechanic's lien statutes provide a way for subcontractors (as well as contractors) to enforce their rights to payment directly against owners that are not government entities. Under such statutes, a subcontractor providing labor or materials for construction work may assert the right to payment by filing a notice within a certain time. This filing begins a process that can result in a lien similar to a mortgage being placed on the construction site property. If the payment dispute is not resolved, the mechanic's lien can be foreclosed through litigation and the property sold to satisfy the payment. Using the mechanic's lien process, a subcontractor may be able to obtain payment from an owner even though the owner also paid the prime contractor in full. Faced with this risk, many owners seek to ensure subcontractors get paid by requiring that each application for payment be accompanied by subcontractors' lien waivers covering work paid for under prior applications for payment. Mechanic's lien statutes may, however, limit the enforceability of such lien waivers. Statutes governing mechanic's liens and prompt payment vary widely among the states, so legal counsel should be relied on for these matters.

For More Information

Smith, Currie & Hancock LLP's Common Sense Construction Law, edited by Thomas J. Kelleher Jr. (Wiley, 2005), provides further explanation of construction contracts as well as other areas of construction law.

CHAPTER	12

AIA Contract Documents

12.1 The AIA Documents Program

Suzanne H. Harness, Esq., AIA

AIA documents capture and convey the expectations, relationships, responsibilities, and rules that bring parties together for the design and construction of buildings.

The AIA was founded in 1857 by twenty-nine architects who shared the goal of creating an organization that would recognize architects as professionals, as distinguished from the trade contractors who constructed buildings at that time, and that would "promote the scientific and practical perfection of its members." Although the AIA mission statement has changed over the years, and its opinion of design-build has come full circle, the AIA remains committed to serving as (1) the voice of the architecture profession and (2) the resource of choice for its members as they develop the knowledge needed to provide unsurpassed professional services. One important way the AIA speaks for its members, and provides a valuable resource to them, is through AIA Contract Documents®. In 2006, when the AIA asked its members to rate the importance to them of more than twenty AIA programs, members gave AIA Contract Documents the highest rating.

AIA CONTRACT DOCUMENTS DEVELOPMENT

The AIA has published standard form construction agreements for more than 120 years. Early in its history, the Institute recognized the need for a standard system of construction contracting. Working with the Western Association of Architects (which later merged

Suzanne Harness has been managing director and counsel for the AIA Contract Documents program since 2002. She has thirty years of experience in the design and construction industry.

into the AIA) and the National Association of Builders (which later became the Associated General Contractors of America), the AIA published its first standard form document in 1888. Entitled the Uniform Contract, this three-page agreement between owner and contractor contained many concepts that were carried forward into the first General Conditions of the Contract, published in 1911. The successor to that 1911 document is published today as A201–2007, General Conditions of the Contract for Construction.

In publishing the Uniform Contract, the AIA accomplished more than merely filling the need for a standardized construction contracting process. The document clarified, for the first time in American society, the AIA view of the appropriate roles of the owner, architect, and contractor during the construction process. It also firmly established, for nearly 100 years, the bright line separating the responsibilities of the architect and those of the construction contractor.

Benefits of Standard Forms

The industry's acceptance of the Uniform Contract marked the beginning of regulation of the construction process. The Uniform Contract established the steps the owner and contractor would take when entering an agreement to construct a building. The contract also established the most important benefit of standard forms: to ensure nationwide consistency and predictability in contracting and in the construction process. Predictability in the process controls the expectations of the parties and reduces their risks. Reducing the contractor's risk substantially benefits the owner because it results in lower bids that are not padded with contingencies to cover unknowns.

Another significant benefit of standard forms is the savings they achieve in transactional costs, when compared to custom-made contracts. One hour of an attorney's time is easily ten or twenty times the cost of a paper document and is equivalent to the price of a license to use AIA Contract Documents software for an entire year. Standard forms also provide assurances that nothing important is left out of the contract and that the text is internally consistent. Attorneys appreciate these benefits and see the advantage in using a standard form, modifying it liberally to suit a particular project and their clients' needs, instead of incurring the legal malpractice risks inherent in creating a custom contract.

Today, AIA standard forms are not as inflexible as they once were. For example, the 2004 Design-Build family of documents introduced choices for dispute resolution method and for the services the architect will provide. Some 2004 and 2005 standard forms of agreement provide menus for designating those services.

Following the model of the 2004 Design-Build family of agreements, the 2007 owner-contractor agreements and some owner-architect agreements provide check boxes for choosing a binding dispute resolution method. A101–2007, Agreement Between Owner and Contractor, additionally allows the parties to choose whether the architect will be the initial decision maker on claims between the owner and contractor.

The AIA also publishes some model, or alternative, language that can be added to standard forms to modify them to suit particular circumstances. The model language is available in A503–2007, Guide for Supplementary Conditions, and B503–2007, Guide for Amendments to AIA Owner-Architect Agreements, which are provided in AIA Contract Documents software and can be downloaded free from the AIA Web site.

The Documents Committee

Since its early days, the AIA has maintained a committee of its members dedicated to the creation and revision of AIA Contract Documents. The AIA Documents Committee must be drawn from practicing architects representing diverse geographic locations, size and type of practice, and specialized expertise. Committee appointments are made annually, although members are frequently reappointed for ten years or more, based on their ongoing contributions, to ensure continuity in document drafting. The Documents Committee meets at least four times annually and works with AIA staff attorneys and writers, as well as legal and insurance counsel, to draft and revise AIA documents. The Committee revises documents on a ten-year cycle to accommodate changes in practice and to respond to any relevant judicial decisions affecting interpretation of a document.

Guiding Principles

Over a number of years, the AIA has developed what are called the Documents Drafting Principles, which guide the Documents Committee and AIA staff in preparing and revising AIA documents. These principles are as follows:

1. Establish and maintain, for nationwide application, standardized legal forms to enhance the stability of legal transactions in the design and construction industry.
2. Provide assistance to users who otherwise could not obtain knowledgeable legal counsel in a timely or economical fashion by
   - Providing standard documents as an alternative to expensive, custom-drafted documents.
   - Promoting flexible use through the publication of supplemental guides that demonstrate, with model language and instructions, the adaptability of the standard documents to particular circumstances.
   - Providing continuing education on the proper use of the documents.
3. Strive for balanced and fair documents by
   - Conforming to common law and statutory precepts adopted in the majority of jurisdictions.
   - Allocating risks and responsibilities to the party best able to control them; to the party best able to protect against unexpected cost; or to the owner, when no other party can control the risk or prevent the loss.
   - Seeking industry consensus among all parties whose interests may be significantly affected by individual documents.
4. Publish documents that are subject to uniform legal interpretations so as to be predictably enforceable and, thus, reliable.
5. Use language that is unambiguous and comprehensible to users and interpreters (courts and lawyers) of the documents.
6. Where practices are consistent among regions, reflect industry customs and practices, rather than impose new ones; where practices are inconsistent or no guidelines for practice exist, provide a consensus-based model for practitioners to follow.

Allocation of Risk

The AIA intends that its agreements avoid unreasonable bias by first allocating risks and responsibilities to the party with the most knowledge of the risk and in the best position to control it. The agreements then allocate risk to the party best able to protect against unexpected cost by, for example, purchasing insurance. Risk is assigned to the owner, as the ultimate beneficiary of the project, only when no other party can control the risk or prevent the loss. The design and construction of buildings is a risky undertaking so—to prevent an undue burden for any party, and to prevent any one interest (including that of architects) from being overrepresented—the Documents Committee strives to equitably balance risks.

Building Consensus

Starting with the Uniform Contract, the AIA has striven to produce documents that represent the consensus of the design and construction community. For that reason, the AIA seeks comment from industry liaison organizations representing contractors, subcontractors, owners, lenders, engineers, insurance and surety interests, and others when drafting any new document or revising an existing one. Some of those organizations may endorse these documents, which sends a message to the organization's members—and to other users—that the organization's leadership has confidence in the overall fairness of the document.

To ensure that no industry comment is overlooked, the AIA records all the comments it receives, and the Documents Committee reviews and discusses them thoroughly before agreeing to any changes in the existing text. The committee frequently meets in person with those who submit comments so committee members can gain a full understanding of the issue being presented. Through this process, the AIA intends to ensure that its documents fully and fairly represent the interests of those stakeholders significantly affected by a particular document.

In preparing documents for 2007 release, the Documents Committee sought comment from more than a dozen industry groups, including the Associated General Contractors of America, American Subcontractors Association, National Association of State Facilities Administrators, Commercial Owners Association of America, Associated Specialty Contractors, Council of American Structural Engineers, American Council of Construction Lawyers, the American Bar Association's Forum on the Construction Industry, and the American Arbitration Association.

The committee also sought input from outside experts in property, general liability, and errors and omissions insurance. Several AIA knowledge communities, including Technology in Practice, the Committee on the Environment, Small Project Practitioners, and Practice Management, as well as the Integrated Practice Board Discussion Group and the Large Firm Round Table, also provided guidance.

KEEPING PACE WITH THE INDUSTRY

In creating and revising documents, the AIA strives both to reflect and to anticipate the needs of the design and construction industry and to provide agreements that will serve the major delivery methods being used to construct building projects. Design and construction practices are always changing and documents must change to remain relevant to industry needs.

Construction Contracts

Throughout the nineteenth, and most of the twentieth centuries, design-bid/negotiate-build was the most common way to design and construct a project. Today it is still the

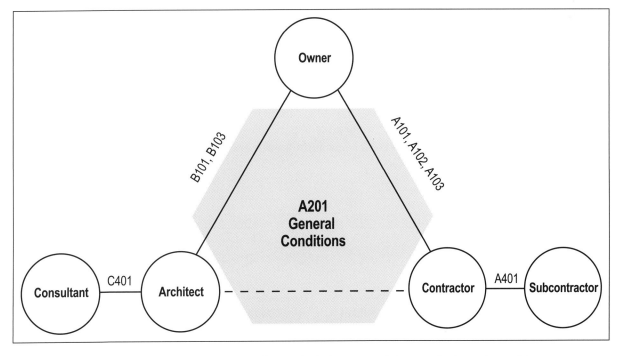

A201 Family of Documents. A201–2007 generally sets forth the responsibilities and relationships of the owner, architect, and contractor for the construction phase. (All documents shown in this diagram were released in 2007.)

dominant project delivery method in the United States. The *2006 AIA Firm Survey* reported that 60 percent of firm billings are derived from projects using the design-bid/negotiate-build delivery method.

This method involves a sequential process whereby the architect completes the construction drawings and specifications and delivers them to the owner for approval. The owner then uses the architect's construction documents to obtain bids or proposals from construction contractors. Documents in the A201 (conventional) family serve the design-bid/negotiate-build delivery method. Since 1967, the AIA has revised the A201 document and associated agreements and forms that rely on it every ten years to keep it current with industry trends.

Construction management emerged in the 1970s, and the AIA responded with its Construction Manager as Adviser (CMa) family of documents in 1974. The AIA revised the CMa family most recently in 1992. The construction manager is an adviser to the owner and does not hold or assume any risk for the construction contracts. The owner holds construction contracts for each trade (multiple prime contracting) or may retain one general contractor. This model works well in some cases, but most owners look for a contractor to assume construction risk. To respond to that concern, Construction Manager as Constructor (CMc) agreements were developed in 1992 and revised in 2003. CMc can be thought of as a hybrid of CMa and design-bid-build because the construction manager serves as an adviser to the owner during the design phase (providing cost estimates and constructability reviews) and as a construction contractor during the construction phase. The construction manager may build the project at risk, by guaranteeing a maximum price, or on a cost-plus-fee basis. The CMc approach in which the construction manager guarantees a maximum price to the owner (using A121 CMc–2003, Standard Form of Agreement Between Owner and Construction Manager Where the Construction Manager is also the Constructor) is a popular delivery method that now rivals design-build delivery.

In 1985 the AIA was the first organization to publish standard form design-build documents. The AIA revised these documents in 1996 and 2004 to keep pace with industry changes. Revisions to the 2004 Design-Build family were not a simple update; rather, they presented an entirely new approach to design-build delivery. The new documents replaced the two-part A191, A491, and B901 agreements first published in 1985 and 1996 with one-part agreements, renumbered A141–2004, A142–2004, and B143–2004, respectively. The AIA made these changes in response to industry rejection of the two-part process, in which the design-builder first entered into a contract with the owner for design services and, upon completion of the design, into a subsequent contract for construction. The industry preference was for one integrated contract for both design and construction.

In addition, the AIA added two new design-build documents. These were B142–2004, an agreement between the owner and a design-build consultant, and G704/DB–2004, a new form for acknowledging substantial completion of the design-build project.

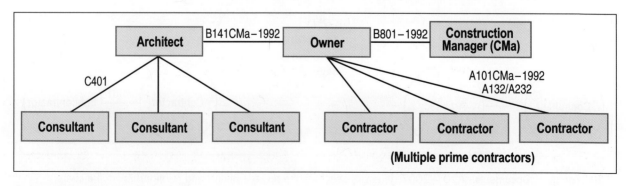

Documents for CMa Projects. Unless otherwise noted, documents shown in this diagram were released in 2007.

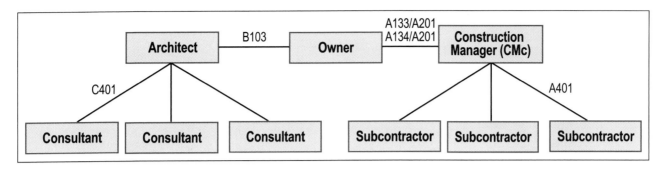

Documents for CMc Projects. Documents shown in this diagram were released in 2007, except A133 and A134, planned for release in 2009.

In the late 1990s, the AIA recognized that the practice of sending requests for information (RFIs) seemed to be creating as many problems as it solved. Contractors complained that due to inadequate contract documents, they were compelled to generate numerous RFIs. Architects protested that contractors frequently requested information they could easily find in the contract documents. Taking these concerns into account, the AIA published its first RFI form, G716–2004. Architects, owners, and contractors can use G716–2004 to request information from each other. The form requires the requesting party to list the relevant drawing, specification, or submittal reviewed when the party attempted to find the requested information.

Design Contracts

The design process is also continually changing. In 1997 the AIA revised the format of B141, the primary AIA owner-architect agreement, by separating the agreement into two parts: B141–1997 Part 1, the agreement terms, and B141–1997 Part 2, the scope of the architect's services. The AIA made this change to recognize, in a very prominent way, the change that had been taking place in the architecture profession over the previous ten years. Many architects found they could practice more successfully by developing specialties, such as providing historic preservation studies and reports. These architects seldom needed an agreement to provide services for the design and construction of buildings; instead, they needed a contract form that would allow for a specialized scope of services. By separating the agreement from the scope of services, the AIA allowed architects to achieve infinite flexibility in contracting for their services. By introducing B141–1997 as a two-part document, the AIA did more than satisfy a need; it made a statement to the industry about the appropriate role of the architect in 1997, just as it had done with the first AIA agreement, the Uniform Contract, in 1888.

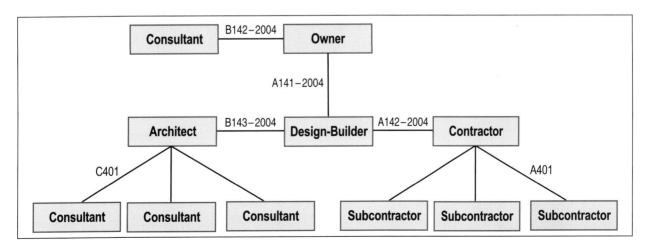

Documents for Design-Build Projects. Unless otherwise noted, documents shown in this diagram were released in 2007.

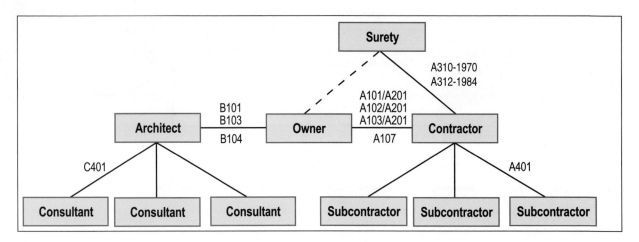

Documents for Design-Bid/Negotiate-Build Projects. Agreements for the design-bid/negotiate-build approach to project delivery are the forms of agreement most widely used in the United States for building projects. (Unless otherwise noted, documents shown in this diagram were released in 2007.)

Standard form of architect's services documents are versatile and may be used to provide the scope of services in any owner-architect agreement at the time of contracting, or combined with G802™-2007, Amendment to the Professional Services Agreement, to create a modification to any existing owner-architect agreement. Appropriately modified, standard form services documents may be used to provide the consultant's scope of services in an architect-consultant agreement such as C401™-2007, Agreement between Architect and Consultant.

With the introduction of B141-1997, the AIA provided only one standard form for traditional design and contract administration services by the architect. In the paper document, the two parts were sold together. The document instructions advised architects not needing Part 2 to remove and replace it with their own unique, specialized scope of services. After releasing B141-1997, the Documents Committee continued working to develop scopes for architect's services in a number of popular, but specialized areas.

In December 2004, the AIA introduced six standard scope documents for these architect's services: Value Analysis, Historic Preservation, Security Evaluation and Planning, Facility Support, Commissioning, and LEED® Certification. These were followed in 2005 by scope documents for Architectural Interior Design; Furniture, Furnishings and Equipment Design; Site Evaluation and Planning; and Construction Contract Administration (for an architect not providing design services). As this book neared completion, the AIA was working on additional standard scope forms for programming and program management.

When revising B141-1997 for release in 2007, the Documents Committee took a hard look at the success of the two-part agreement. They found that while it served the interests of the specialist architect, it created undue complexity for the architect providing traditional design and contract administration services. Those architects and their clients had gravitated toward using B151-1997, a one-part agreement for traditional services, modeled after B141-1987. Recognizing the validity of that choice, the Documents Committee developed B101™-2007, a one-part document that follows the format of B151-1997 but uses text copied and edited from both B141-1997 and B151-1997. B101-2007, titled Standard Form of Agreement Between Owner and Architect, is intended for use as a stand-alone document.

To provide an agreement for the specialist architect, or the architect who may initially provide services for a special scope of work (e.g., a security evaluation) and then provide traditional design and contract administration services, the AIA divided the text of B101-2007 into two parts: the agreement portion (per B141-1997 Part 1) and the services portion (per B141-1997 Part 2). These two new documents are, respectively, B102™-2007, Standard Form of Agreement Between Owner and Architect Without a Predefined Scope of Architect's Services, and B201™-2007, Standard Form of Architect's Services: Design and Construction Contract Administration. B102-2007 may also be combined with other scope of service descriptions, such as the following AIA Contract Document scopes, to create an agreement.

- B203™-2007, Site Evaluation and Planning
- B204™-2007, Value Analysis

- B205–2007, Historic Preservation
- B206–2007, Security Evaluation and Planning
- B209–2007, Construction Contract Administration
- B210–2007, Facility Support
- B211–2007, Commissioning
- B214–2007, LEED Certification
- B252–2007, Architectural Interior Design
- B253–2007, Furniture, Furnishings, and Equipment Design

2007 AIA CONTRACT DOCUMENTS PROGRAM

Today, the AIA publishes more than 100 standard form documents for use in the design and construction industry. These documents include agreements for design services, construction, construction management, and design-build. They also include general conditions documents to establish the terms and conditions of the contract for construction; instructions to bidders; qualification statements for architects and contractors; bonding forms; payment and change order forms; and a request for information form. These standard forms may be modified to insert project-specific information, or may be edited further to change the standard text.

Document Series

Documents are organized by series using a letter prefix to represent the type of agreement or document. For example, owner-contractor agreements are found in the A series and contract administration forms are found in the G series.

- A-series: Owner-contractor documents
- B-series: Owner-architect documents
- C-series: Architect-consultant documents
- D-series: Architect-industry documents
- E-series: Exhibits
- G-series: Contract administration and project management forms

Document Families

A family of documents is a type of classification that refers to the type of project or project delivery method addressed by the documents. The documents within each family provide a consistent structure and text base to support the major relationships on a design and construction project. Understanding these family groupings helps architects select the most appropriate agreements and forms for a project. These classifications include:

- Conventional (A201)
- Small Project
- Construction Manager–Adviser (CMa)
- Construction Manager–Constructor (CMc)
- Interiors
- Design-Build
- Digital Practice
- International
- Contract Administration and Project Management Forms

New Document Numbering

In 2003 the Documents Committee undertook an analysis of the numbering system used to identify AIA documents. The committee hoped to find some logic to the system but was unable to. The committee members then agreed to develop an internally consistent numbering system in which a document's number would have significance

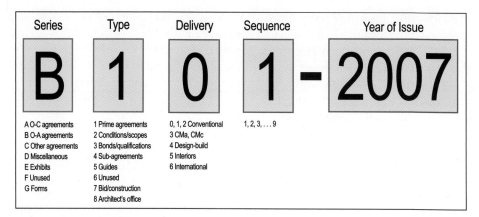

Series	Type	Delivery	Sequence	Year of Issue
B	**1**	**0**	**1**	**-2007**

A O-C agreements	1 Prime agreements	0, 1, 2 Conventional	1, 2, 3, . . . 9
B O-A agreements	2 Conditions/scopes	3 CMa, CMc	
C Other agreements	3 Bonds/qualifications	4 Design-build	
D Miscellaneous	4 Sub-agreements	5 Interiors	
E Exhibits	5 Guides	6 International	
F Unused	6 Unused		
G Forms	7 Bid/construction		
	8 Architect's office		

New AIA Document Numbering System

to its purpose. The committee approved the new system in early 2004, and the AIA used it to number new agreements issued in 2004 and 2005. Many documents revised in 2007 were also assigned new numbers consistent with the new system.

The Documents Committee recognized that introducing a new numbering system could be somewhat confusing at first, but hoped the logic of the system would help users understand it and keep the learning curve from being unduly steep. In developing the system, the committee did not change certain well-known numbers, such as A101, A201, G701, G702, and G703. However, the members could not devise a system that would accommodate the numbers B141, B151, and B155 and still remain internally consistent. Therefore, by unanimous vote, the Documents Committee agreed to retire those numbers and to replace them with sequential numbers for owner-architect agreements beginning with the number B101.

Significant Changes from 1997 Documents

Before the Documents Committee began making revisions to existing 1997 documents, the AIA contacted its industry partners, seeking feedback on the existing 1997 agreements. The AIA wanted to know what its document users thought about the existing text—what they liked, and what they thought had to be changed. Hundreds of comments revealed the following significant issues in A201, General Conditions: the architect as initial decision maker, arbitration, time limit on claims, consolidation and joinder, and consequential damages. For owner-architect agreements, the industry and AIA internal groups shared these concerns: B141 two-part format, phases versus services, basic services and additional services, errors and omissions insurance, standard of care, green design, the architect as initial decision maker, ownership of instruments of service, and design to cost.

The Documents Committee and AIA staff thoroughly addressed the comments received and, in several cases, met in person with industry representatives to clarify their positions. First drafts of B101–2007 and A201–2007 were sent out for review by the same organizations that had earlier provided comments. After reviewing and discussing the comments received on the first drafts, the AIA sent out a second set of drafts and repeated the process. In early 2007, the Documents Committee approved final language for A201–2007 and B101–2007. The approval of these two documents paved the way for revisions to the remainder of the owner-contractor, owner-architect, and architect-consultant agreements in the Conventional (A201) family of documents.

The revised A201–2007 family allows the owner and contractor to designate an optional third-party decision maker to make initial decisions on claims between them, and to name that initial decision maker (IDM) in the owner-contractor agreement. If the owner and contractor fail to appoint an optional IDM, the role will default to the architect, who will make those decisions in the traditional manner. The A201 family also eliminates mandatory arbitration, which AIA documents have required since 1888.

Agreements in the A201 family provide check boxes where the parties may choose arbitration, litigation, or another method of binding dispute resolution for resolving disputes. In addition, the 2007 documents are less restrictive regarding consolidation of arbitration and the joinder of third parties, when arbitration is the selected method of binding dispute resolution. Also, provisions relating to statutory limitation periods in the 2007 documents were substantially revised to follow state law more closely. The waiver of consequential damages clause, added to the A201 family in 1997, remains in the 2007 family as a barrier to "runaway" claims.

B101–2007 is a one-part agreement that consolidates and replaces B141–1997 and B151–1997. B101–2007 sets forth the architect's services during five phases: schematic design, design development, construction documents, bidding/negotiation, and construction contract administration. It also contains a number of novel additions, including a specifically defined professional standard of care, an explicit requirement that the architect carry insurance, and a recognition that environmentally responsible design must be a part of every design project. B101–2007 returns to the concept of "basic" and "additional" services and explicitly sets forth basic services in Article 3. Additional services, listed in Article 4, may be simply thought of as any service that is not a basic service. Additional services may be included in the agreement when it is executed, or added as the project proceeds. Also, B101–2007 substantially revises the instruments of service provisions. The new provisions clarify the architect's ownership rights, while more liberally granting licenses to the owner for use of the instruments of service upon project completion or the agreement's termination. B101–2007 retains the B141–1997 requirement that the architect design the project to the owner's budget, but strengthens the owner's obligation to identify the budget in the agreement and to modify it appropriately as the project proceeds.

USING AIA CONTRACT DOCUMENTS

AIA Contract Documents are available in paper and digital formats. A group of the most frequently used documents is also available via the Internet. In 2003, AIA Contract Documents software was introduced using Microsoft® Word to allow users to easily modify AIA documents using the "track changes" feature and to e-mail them in Word or PDF formats. AIA software is currently available with an annual subscription that provides access to all AIA Contract Documents through a number of different license models.

The AIA registers copyrights in nearly all of its standard form contract documents, claims trademark protection in its document numbers, and has registered the trademark AIA Contract Documents®. The AIA provides notice to document users that documents may not be reproduced or excerpted without express written permission from the AIA. For documents purchased in paper format, the AIA grants written permission in the footers of most documents to reproduce a maximum number of ten copies of the completed document for use in connection with a particular project. Some documents purchased in paper format, such as General Conditions documents, may not be reproduced.

AIA software users may reproduce an unlimited number of copies of the documents they generate, but only for use on their own projects, and only for use on the project for which the document was created. Software users must comply with the End User License Agreement (EULA) provided for review and acceptance prior to purchasing the software.

The AIA registers copyrights and enforces copyright violations in order to protect the integrity of its valuable intellectual property, but copyright registration protects document users as well. Because AIA documents have a reputation for fairness, some parties attempt to take advantage of that reputation by scanning or copying an AIA document, deleting some or all of the AIA standard text, changing the content to suit their own interests, and then passing on the completed work as an AIA document with the AIA trademarked logo and copyright notice still intact. While these abuses do occur, copyright and trademark protection minimize their frequency and give the AIA the legal right to take action against the infringing parties. To report copyright or trademark violations of AIA Contract Documents, e-mail AIA legal counsel at copyright@aia.org.

LOOKING AHEAD

Over the next few years, the AIA will issue additional scope of service documents and new agreements and forms. As this handbook went to press, the Documents Committee was exploring the creation of a new family of documents to provide agreements for integrated practice. To reap the full potential of integrated practice, architects will need to change the way they deliver information to the owner and contractor. Contracts among the project participants will also need to change to allow for more collaboration and sharing of risks and rewards. To assist in this effort, the Documents Committee will collaborate with industry groups, including the Associated General Contractors of America, the Construction Users Roundtable, the AIA Technology in Practice Knowledge Community, and the AIA Integrated Practice Board Discussion Group. New documents and revisions to existing ones will reflect input from industry stakeholders, changes in design and construction industry practices, and judicial decisions affecting owners, architects, consultants, and contractors. The Documents Committee will sift through the data and use its best efforts to develop the consensus required to produce documents that will admirably serve their intended purposes. The committee will continually seek new members who are willing to commit significant hours of volunteer time to ensure that AIA documents retain their stature as the industry standard. If you would like more information about serving as a member of the AIA Documents Committee, please send a message to docinfo@aia.org.

BACKGROUNDER

2007 AIA CONTRACT DOCUMENTS

In 2007 the AIA Contract Documents program implemented a new numbering system, which is described in The AIA Documents Program (12.1). In documents in which content was revised, the suffix "2007" appears after the new document number. In instances where the content of the document did not change, the original date appears after the new document number. As well, three new documents and new commentaries were introduced. Three documents were eliminated; these are listed at the end of the table below.

The table lists the 2007 documents in numerical order by their new numbers, with the corresponding former numbers in the first column. For a list of all AIA documents available when this book went to press, see the Documents Finder (12.2) or the Documents Synopses on the accompanying CD. At any time, a list of current AIA documents is available on the AIA Web site.

2007 AIA Contract Documents Release

Former Number	Revised 2007 Number	Document Name
A101–1997	A101–2007	Standard Form of Agreement Between Owner and Contractor Where the Basis of Payment Is a Stipulated Sum
A111–1997	A102–2007	Standard Form of Agreement Between Owner and Contractor Where the Basis of Payment Is the Cost of the Work Plus a Fee, with a Guaranteed Maximum Price
A114–2001	A103–2007	Standard Form of Agreement Between Owner and Contractor Where the Basis of Payment Is the Cost of the Work Plus a Fee Without a Guaranteed Maximum Price
A105/205–1993	A105–2007	Standard Form of Agreement Between Owner and Contractor for a Residential or Small Commercial Project
A107–1997	A107–2007	Standard Form of Agreement Between Owner and Contractor for a Project of Limited Scope

(continued)

2007 AIA Contract Documents Release *(continued)*

Former Number	Revised 2007 Number	Document Name
A175ID–2003	A151–2007	Standard Form of Agreement Between Owner and Vendor for Furniture, Furnishings, and Equipment Where the Basis of Payment Is a Stipulated Sum
A201–1997	A201–2007	General Conditions of the Contract for Construction
A275ID–2003	A251–2007	General Conditions of the Contract for Furniture, Furnishings, and Equipment
A401–1997	A401–2007	Standard Form of Agreement Between Contractor and Subcontractor
A511–1999	A503–2007	Guide for Supplementary Conditions
A775ID–2003	A751–2007	Invitation and Instructions for Quotation for Furniture, Furnishings, and Equipment
B151–1997	B101–2007	Standard Form of Agreement Between Owner and Architect
B141–1997 Part 1	B102–2007	Standard Form of Agreement Between Owner and Architect Without a Predefined Scope of Architect's Services
(New)	B103–2007	Standard Form of Agreement Between Owner and Architect for a Large or Complex Project
B151–1987	B104–2007	Standard Form of Agreement Between Owner and Architect for a Project of Limited Scope
B155–1993	B105–2007	Standard Form of Agreement Between Owner and Architect for a Residential or Small Commercial Project
B171ID–2003	B152–2007	Standard Form of Agreement Between Owner and Architect for Architectural Interior Design Services
B175ID–2003	B153–2007	Standard Form of Agreement Between Owner and Architect for Furniture, Furnishings, and Equipment Design Services
B611INT–2002	B161–2002	Standard Form of Agreement Between Client and Consultant for Use Where the Project is Located Outside the United States
B621INT–2002	B162–2002	Abbreviated Form of Agreement Between Client and Consultant for Use Where the Project is Located Outside the United States
B141–1997 Part 2	B201–2007	Standard Form of Architect's Services: Design and Construction Contract Administration
B203–2005	B203–2007	Standard Form of Architect's Services: Site Evaluation and Planning
B204–2004	B204–2007	Standard Form of Architect's Services: Value Analysis, for Use Where the Owner Employs a Value Analysis Consultant
B205–2004	B205–2007	Standard Form of Architect's Services: Historic Preservation
B206–2004	B206–2007	Standard Form of Architect's Services: Security Evaluation and Planning
B209–2005	B209–2007	Standard Form of Architect's Services: Construction Contract Administration, for Use Where the Owner Has Retained Another Architect for Design Services
B210–2004	B210–2007	Standard Form of Architect's Services: Facility Support
B211–2004	B211–2007	Standard Form of Architect's Services: Commissioning
B214–2004	B214–2007	Standard Form of Architect's Services: LEED® Certification
B252–2005	B252–2007	Standard Form of Architect's Services: Architectural Interior Design
B253–2005	B253–2007	Standard Form of Architect's Services: Furniture, Furnishings, and Equipment Design
B431–1993	B305–1993	Architect's Qualification Statement
B511–2001	B503–2007	Guide for Amendments to AIA Owner-Architect Agreements
C801–1993	C101–1993	Joint Venture Agreement for Professional Services
(New)	C106–2007	Digital Data Licensing Agreement
C141–1997	C401–2007	Standard Form of Agreement Between Architect and Consultant
(New)	E201–2007	Digital Data Protocol Exhibit
G805–2001	G705–2001	List of Subcontractors
G714–2001	G714–2007	Construction Change Directive
G605–2000	G801–2007	Notification of Amendment to the Professional Services Agreement
G606–2000	G802–2007	Amendment to the Professional Services Agreement
G607–2000	G803–2007	Amendment to the Consultant Services Agreement
B163–1993	Discontinued	Standard Form of Agreement Between Owner and Architect with Description of Designated Services
C105–2005	Discontinued	Standard Form of Agreement Between Architect and Consulting Architect
C142–1997	Discontinued	Abbreviated Standard Form of Agreement Between Architect and Consultant

(continued)

12.2 AIA Contract Documents Synopses by Family

AIA® Contract Documents can be classified by document family, based on project type or project delivery method:

Conventional (A201™)
Small Project
CM Adviser
CM Constructor
Interiors
Design-Build
Digital Practice
International

In addition to these, the AIA offers a series of contract administration and project management forms.

The document families reflect the various legal and working relationships in similar project types. Documents for the same family are linked by common terminology and procedures and may adopt one another by reference. The relevant terms of A201–2007, for example, are adopted by reference in several agreements including A101–2007, A102–2007, A103–2007, A401–2007, B101–2007, and B103–2007.

More than 100 AIA contract and administrative forms are in print today. The precursor of these documents was the Uniform Contract, an owner-contractor agreement first published in 1888. This was followed, in 1911, by the AIA's first standardized general conditions for construction. The 2007 edition of AIA Document A201 is the sixteenth edition of those general conditions.

Many practices common in the construction industry today became established through their inclusion in the AIA's general conditions for construction and its other standardized documents. While the AIA documents have had a profound influence on the industry, the influence also runs the other way. The AIA regularly revises its documents to take into account developments in the construction industry and the law. Standardized documents for design-build, different types of construction management, and international practice have been published in recent years. Because AIA documents are frequently updated, users should consult an AIA component or www.aia.org to confirm current editions.

The AIA documents are intended for nationwide use and thus are not drafted to conform to the law of any one state. With that caveat, however, AIA contract documents provide a solid basis of contract provisions that are enforceable under existing law at the time of publication. Case law on contracts for design and construction has, for the past century, been based largely on the language in AIA standardized documents. These court cases are presented in *The American Institute of Architects Legal Citator*, published by Matthew Bender & Company, Inc. of the LexisNexis Group. Recent cases are summarized, and all cases are keyed to the specific provisions in the AIA documents to which they relate.

Synopses of current AIA Documents grouped by series and sample copies of the documents can be found on a CD-ROM that accompanies this *Handbook*.

A201 FAMILY

A101™–2007 (formerly A101™–1997) Standard Form of Agreement Between Owner and Contractor Where the Basis of Payment Is a Stipulated Sum

A101–2007 is a standard form of agreement between owner and contractor for use where the basis of payment is a stipulated sum (fixed price). A101 adopts by reference and is designed for use with A201™–2007, General Conditions of the Contract for Construction. A101 is suitable for large or complex projects. For projects of a more limited scope, A107™–2007, Agreement Between Owner and Contractor for a Project of Limited Scope, should be considered. For even smaller projects, consider A105™–2007, Agreement Between Owner and Contractor for a Residential or Small Commercial Project.

A102™–2007 (formerly A111™–1997) Standard Form of Agreement Between Owner and Contractor Where the Basis of Payment Is the Cost of the Work Plus a Fee with a Negotiated Guaranteed Maximum Price

This standard form of agreement between owner and contractor is appropriate for use on large projects requiring a negotiated guaranteed maximum price, when the basis of payment to the contractor is the cost of the work plus a fee. A102–2007 is not intended for use in competitive bidding. A102–2007 adopts by reference and is intended for use with A201™–2007, General Conditions of the Contract for Construction.

A103™–2007 (formerly A114™–2001) Standard Form of Agreement Between Owner and Contractor Where the Basis of Payment Is the Cost of the Work Plus a Fee Without a Guaranteed Maximum Price

A103–2007 is appropriate for use on large projects when the basis of payment to the contractor is the cost of the work plus a fee and the cost is not fully known at the commencement of construction. A103–2007 is not intended for use in competitive bidding. A103–2007 adopts by reference, and is intended for use with, A201™–2007, General Conditions of the Contract for Construction.

A107™–2007 (formerly A107™–1997) Standard Form of Agreement Between Owner and Contractor for a Project of Limited Scope

A107–2007 is a stand-alone agreement with its own internal general conditions and is intended for use on construction projects of limited scope. It is intended for use on medium- to large-sized projects where payment is based on either a stipulated sum or the cost of the work plus a fee, with or without a guaranteed maximum price. Parties using A107–2007 will also use A107, Exhibit A, if using a cost-plus payment method. B104™–2007, Standard Form of Agreement Between Owner and Architect for a Project of Limited Scope, coordinates with A107–2007 and incorporates it by reference.

For more complex projects, parties should consider using one of the following other owner-contractor agreements: AIA Documents A101–2007, A102–2007, or A103–2007. These agreements are written for a stipulated sum, cost of the work with a guaranteed maximum price, and cost of the work without a guaranteed maximum price, respectively. Each of them incorporates by reference A201™–2007, General Conditions of the Contract for Construction. For single-family residential projects or smaller and less complex commercial projects, parties may wish to consider A105™–2007, Agreement Between Owner and Contractor for a Residential or Small Commercial Project.

A201™–2007 (formerly A201™–1997) General Conditions of the Contract for Construction

The General Conditions are an integral part of the contract for construction for a large project, and they are incorporated by reference into the owner-contractor agreement. They set forth the rights, responsibilities, and relationships of the owner, contractor, and architect. Though not a party to the contract for construction between owner and contractor, the architect participates in the preparation of the contract documents and performs construction phase duties and responsibilities described in detail in the general conditions. A201–2007 is adopted by reference in owner-architect, owner-contractor, and contractor-subcontractor agreements in the A201 family of documents; thus, it is often called the "keystone" document.

A201™SC–1999 Federal Supplementary Conditions of the Contract for Construction

A201SC–1999 is intended for use on certain federally assisted construction projects. For such projects, A201SC–1999 adapts A201–1997 by providing (1) necessary modifications of the General Conditions, (2) additional conditions, and (3) insurance requirements for federally assisted construction projects.

A401™–2007 (formerly A401™–1997) Standard Form of Agreement Between Contractor and Subcontractor

This agreement establishes the contractual relationship between the contractor and subcontractor. It sets forth the responsibilities of both parties and lists their respective obligations, which are written to parallel A201™–2007, General Conditions of the Contract for Construction, which A401–2007 incorporates by reference. A401–2007 may be modified for use as an agreement between the subcontractor and a sub-subcontractor, and must be modified if used where A107–2007 or A105–2007 serves as the owner-contractor agreement.

A503™–2007 (formerly A511™–1999) Guide for Supplementary Conditions

A503–2007 is not an agreement, but is a guide containing model provisions for modifying and supplementing A201™–2007, General Conditions of the Contract for Construction. It provides model language with explanatory notes to assist users in adapting A201–2007 to specific circumstances. A201–2007, as a standard form document, cannot cover all the particulars of a project. Thus, A503–2007 is provided to assist A201–2007 users either in modifying it, or developing a separate supplementary conditions document to attach to it.

A701™–1997 Instructions to Bidders

This document is used when competitive bids are to be solicited for construction of the project. Coordinated with A201™–2007, General Conditions of the Contract for Construction, and its related documents, A701–1997 provides instructions on procedures, including bonding requirements, for bidders to follow in preparing and submitting their bids. Specific instructions or special requirements, such as the amount and type of bonding, are to be attached to or inserted into A701–1997.

B101™–2007 (formerly B151™–1997) Standard Form of Agreement Between Owner and Architect

B101–2007 is a one-part standard form of agreement between owner and architect for building design and construction contract administration. B101–2007 was developed to replace AIA Documents B141–1997, Parts 1 and 2, and B151–1997, but it more closely follows the format of B151–1997. Services are divided traditionally into basic and additional services. Basic services are performed in five phases: Schematic Design, Design Development, Construction Documents, Bidding and Negotiation, and Construction. This agreement may be used with a variety of compensation methods, including percentage of construction cost and stipulated sum. B101–2007 is intended for use with A201™–2007, General Conditions of the Contract for Construction, which it incorporates by reference.

B102™–2007 (formerly B141™–1997 Part 1) Standard Form of Agreement Between Owner and Architect Without a Predefined Scope of Architect's Services

B102–2007 replaces and serves the same purpose as B141–1997, Part 1. B102–2007 is a standard form of agreement between owner and architect that contains terms and conditions and compensation details. B102–2007 does not include a scope of architect's services, which must be inserted in Article 1 or attached as an exhibit. The separation of the scope of services from the owner-architect agreement allows users the flexibility to append alternative scopes of services. AIA standard form scopes of services documents that may be paired with B102–2007 include B203™–2007, Site Evaluation and Planning; B204™–2007, Value Analysis; B205™–2007, Historic Preservation; B206™–2007, Security Evaluation and Planning; B209™–2007, Construction Contract Administration; B210™–2007, Facility Support Services; B211™–2007, Commissioning; B214™–2007, LEED® Certification; B252™–2007, Architectural Interior Design; and B253™–2007, Furniture, Furnishings, and Equipment Design.

B103™–2007 Standard Form of Agreement Between Owner and Architect for a Large or Complex Project

B103–2007 is a standard form of agreement between owner and architect intended for use on large or complex projects. B103–2007 was developed to replace AIA Documents B141–1997, Parts 1 and 2, and B151–2007 specifically with respect to large or complex projects. B103–2007 assumes that the owner will retain third parties to provide cost estimates and project schedules, and may implement fast-track, phased, or accelerated scheduling. Services are divided along the traditional lines of basic and additional services. Basic services are based on five phases: Schematic Design, Design Development, Construction Documents, Bidding and Negotiation, and Construction. The architect does not prepare cost estimates, but designs the project to meet the owner's budget for the cost of the work at the conclusion of the Design Development Phase Services. This document may be used with a variety of compensation methods. B103–2007 is intended for use with A201™–2007, General Conditions of the Contract for Construction, which it incorporates by reference.

B104™–2007 Standard Form of Agreement Between Owner and Architect for a Project of Limited Scope

B104–2007 is a standard form of agreement between owner and architect intended for use on medium-size projects. B104–2007 is an abbreviated version of B101–2007. B104–2007 contains a compressed form of basic services with three phases: Design, Construction Documents, and Construction. This document may be used with a variety of compensation methods. B104–2007 is intended for use with A107™–2007, Standard Form of Agreement Between Owner and Contractor for a Project of Limited Scope, and A201™–2007, General Conditions of the Contract for Construction, both of which it incorporates by reference.

B144™ARCH-CM-1993 Standard Form of Amendment to the Agreement Between Owner and Architect Where the Architect Provides Construction Management Services as an Adviser to the Owner

B144ARCH–CM-1993 is an amendment to B141–1997 for use in circumstances where the architect, already under contract to perform architectural services for the owner, agrees to provide the owner with a package of construction management services to expand upon, blend with, and supplement the architect's design and construction contract administration services described in B141–1997.

B163™–1993 Standard Form of Agreement Between Owner and Architect for Designated Services

B163-1993 will be discontinued after May 31, 2009. This three-part document contains a list of eighty-three possible services divided among nine phases, covering predesign through supplemental services. This detailed classification allows the architect to estimate more accurately the time and personnel costs required for a particular project. Owner and architect benefit from the ability to establish clearly the scope of services required for the project as responsibilities and compensation issues are negotiated and defined. The architect's compensation may be calculated on a time/cost basis through use of the worksheet provided in the instructions to B163–1993.

B181™-1994 Standard Form of Agreement Between Owner and Architect for Housing Services

This document, developed with the assistance of the U.S. Department of Housing and Urban Development and other federal housing agencies, is primarily intended for use in multiunit housing design. B181–1994 requires that the owner (and not the architect) furnish cost-estimating services. B181–1994 is coordinated with and adopts by reference A201™–1997, General Conditions of the Contract for Construction.

B188™–1996 Standard Form of Agreement Between Owner and Architect for Limited Architectural Services for Housing Projects

B188–1996 is intended for use in situations where the architect will provide limited architectural services for a development housing project. It anticipates that the owner will have extensive control over the management of the project, acting in the capacity of a developer or speculative builder of a housing project. As a result, the owner or consultants retained by the owner will likely provide the engineering services, specify the brand names of materials and equipment, and administer payments to contractors, among other project responsibilities. B188–1996 is not coordinated for use with any other AIA standard form documents.

B201™–2007 (formerly B141™–1997 Part 2) Standard Form of Architect's Services: Design and Construction Contract Administration

B201–2007 replaces AIA Document B141–1997, Part 2. B201–2007 defines the architect's traditional scope of services for design and construction contract administration in a standard form that the owner and architect can modify to suit the needs of the project. The services set forth in B201–2007 parallel those set forth in AIA Document B101–2007: the traditional division of services into basic and additional services, with five phases of basic services. B201–2007 may be used in two ways: (1) incorporated into the owner-architect agreement as the architect's sole scope of services or in conjunction with other scope of services documents, or (2) attached to G802™–2007, Amendment to the Professional Services Agreement, to create a modification to an existing owner-architect agreement. B201–2007 is a scope of services document only and may not be used as a stand-alone owner-architect agreement.

B203™–2007 (formerly B203™–2005) Standard Form of Architect's Services: Site Evaluation and Planning

B203–2007 is intended for use where the architect provides the owner with services to assist in site selection for a project. Under this scope, the architect's services may include analysis of the owner's program and alternative sites, site utilization studies, and other analysis, such as planning and zoning requirements, site context, historic resources, utilities, environmental impact, and parking and circulation. B203–2007 may be used in two ways: (1) incorporated into the owner-architect agreement as the architect's sole scope of services or in conjunction with other scope of services documents, or (2) attached to G802™–2007, Amendment to the Professional Services Agreement, to create a modification to an existing owner-architect agreement. B203–2007 is a scope of services document only and may not be used as a stand-alone owner-architect agreement. B203–2007 was revised in 2007 to align, as applicable, with B101–2007.

B204™–2007 (formerly B204™–2004) Standard Form of Architect's Services: Value Analysis

B204–2007 establishes duties and responsibilities when the owner has employed a Value Analysis Consultant. This document provides the architect's services in three categories: Pre-Workshop Services, Workshop Services, and Post-Workshop Services. The services include presenting the project's goals and design rationale at the Value Analysis Workshop, reviewing and evaluating each Value Analysis Proposal, and preparing a Value Analysis Report for the owner that, among other things, advises the owner of the estimate of the cost of the work resulting from the implementation of the accepted Value Analysis Proposals. B204–2007 may be used in two ways: (1) incorporated into the owner-architect agreement as the architect's sole scope of services or in conjunction with other scope of services documents, or (2) attached to G802™–2007, Amendment to the Professional Services Agreement, to create a modification to an existing owner-architect agreement. B204–2007 is a scope of services document only and may not be used as a stand-alone owner-architect agreement. B204–2007 was revised in 2007 to align, as applicable, with B101–2007.

B205™–2007 (formerly B205™–2004) Standard Form of Architect's Services: Historic Preservation

B205–2007 establishes duties and responsibilities where the architect provides services for projects that are historically sensitive. The range of services the architect provides under this scope spans the life of the project and may require the architect to be responsible for preliminary surveys, applications for tax incentives, nominations for landmark status, analysis of historic finishes, and other services specific to historic preservation projects. B205–2007 may be used in two ways: (1) incorporated into the owner-architect agreement as the architect's sole scope of services or in conjunction with other scope of services documents, or (2) attached to G802™–2007, Amendment to the Professional Services Agreement, to create a modification to an existing owner-architect agreement. B205–2007 is a scope of services document only and may not be used as a stand-alone owner-architect agreement. B205–2007 was revised in 2007 to align, as applicable, with B101–2007.

B206™–2007 (formerly B206™–2004) Standard Form of Architect's Services: Security Evaluation and Planning

B206–2007 establishes duties and responsibilities where the architect provides services for projects that require greater security features and protection than would normally be incorporated into a building design. This scope requires the architect to identify and analyze the threats to a facility, survey the facility with respect to those threats, and prepare a Risk Assessment Report. Following the owner's approval of the Report, the architect prepares design documents and a Security Report. B206–2007 may be used in two ways: (1) incorporated into the owner-architect agreement as the architect's sole scope of services or in conjunction with other scope of services documents, or (2) attached to G802™–2007, Amendment to the Professional Services Agreement, to create a modification to an existing owner-architect agreement. B206–2007 is a scope of services document only and may not be used as a stand-alone owner-architect agreement. B206–2007 was revised in 2007 to align, as applicable, with B101–2007.

B209™–2007 (formerly B209™–2005) Standard Form of Architect's Services: Construction Phase Administration

B209–2007 establishes duties and responsibilities when an architect provides only Construction Phase services and the owner has retained another architect for design services. This scope requires the architect to perform the traditional contract administration services while design services are provided by another architect. B209–2007 may be used in two ways: (1) incorporated into the owner-architect agreement as the architect's sole scope of services or in conjunction with other scope of services documents, or (2) attached to G802™–2007, Amendment to the Professional Services Agreement, to create a modification to an existing owner-architect agreement. B209–2007 is a scope of services document only and may not be used as a stand-alone owner-architect agreement. B209–2007 was revised in 2007 to align, as applicable, with B101–2007.

B210™–2007 (formerly B210™–2004) Standard Form of Architect's Services: Facility Support Services

B210–2007 focuses attention on providing the owner with means and measures to ensure the proper function and maintenance of the building and site after final completion. This scope provides a menu of choices of services, including initial existing condition surveys of the building and its systems, evaluation of operating costs, and code compliance reviews. B210–2007 may be used in two ways: (1) incorporated into the owner-architect agreement as the architect's sole scope of services or in conjunction with other scope of services documents, or (2) attached to G802™–2007, Amendment to the Professional Services Agreement, to create a modification to an existing owner-architect agreement. B210–2007 is a scope of services document only and may not be used as a stand-alone owner-architect agreement. B210–2007 was revised in 2007 to align, as applicable, with B101–2007.

B211™–2007 (formerly B211™–2004) Standard Form of Architect's Services: Commissioning

B211–2007 requires that the architect, based on the owner's identification of systems to be commissioned, develop a Commissioning Plan, a Design Intent Document, and Commissioning Specifications. It also requires that the architect review the contractor's submittals and other documentation related to the systems to be commissioned, observe and document performance tests, train operators, and prepare a Final Commissioning Report. B211–2007 may be used in two ways: (1) incorporated into the owner-architect agreement as the architect's sole scope of services or in conjunction with other scope of services documents, or (2) attached to G802™–2007, Amendment to the Professional Services Agreement, to create a modification to an existing owner-architect agreement. B211–2007 is a scope of services document only and may not be used as a stand-alone owner-architect agreement. B211–2007 was revised in 2007 to align, as applicable, with B101–2007.

B214™–2007 (formerly B214™–2004) Standard Form of Architect's Services: LEED® Certification

B214–2007 establishes duties and responsibilities when the owner seeks certification from the U.S. Green Building Council's Leadership in Energy and Environmental Design (LEED). Among other things, the architect's services include conducting a predesign workshop where the LEED rating system will be reviewed and LEED points will be targeted, preparing a LEED Certification plan, monitoring the LEED Certification process, providing LEED specifications for inclusion in the contract documents and preparing a LEED Certification report detailing the LEED rating the project achieved. B214–2007 may be used in two ways: (1) incorporated into the owner-architect agreement as the architect's sole scope of services or in conjunction with other scope of services documents, or (2) attached to G802™–2007, Amendment to the Professional Services Agreement, to create a modification to an existing owner-architect agreement. B214–2007 is a scope of services document only and may not be used as a stand-alone owner-architect agreement. B214–2007 was revised in 2007 to align, as applicable, with B101–2007.

B252™–2007 (formerly B252™–2005) Standard Form of Architect's Services: Architectural Interior Design

B252–2007 establishes duties and responsibilities where the architect provides both architectural interior design services and design services for furniture, furnishings, and equipment (FF&E). The scope of services in B252–2007 is substantially similar to the services described in B152–2007. Unlike B152–2007, B252–2007 is a scope of services document only and may not be used as a stand-alone owner-architect agreement. B252–2007 may be used in two ways: (1) incorporated into the owner-architect agreement as the architect's sole scope of services or in conjunction with other scope of services documents, or (2) attached to G802™–2007, Amendment to the Professional Services Agreement, to create a modification to an existing owner-architect agreement. B252–2007 was revised in 2007 to align, as applicable, with B101–2007.

B253™–2007 (formerly B253™–2005) Standard Form of Architect's Services: Furniture, Furnishings, and Equipment Design

B253–2007 establishes duties and responsibilities where the architect provides design services for furniture, furnishings, and equipment (FF&E). The scope of services in B253–2007 is substantially similar to the services described in B153–2007. Unlike B153–2007, B253–2007 is a scope of services document only and may not be used as a stand-alone owner-architect agreement. B253–2007 may be used in two ways: (1) incorporated into the owner-architect agreement as the architect's sole scope of services or in conjunction with other scope of services documents, or (2) attached to G802™–2007, Amendment to the Professional Services Agreement, to create a modification to an existing owner-architect agreement. B253–2007 was revised in 2007 to align, as applicable, with B101–2007.

B352™–2000 Duties, Responsibilities, and Limitations of Authority of the Architect's Project Representative

When and if the owner wants additional project representation at the construction site on a full- or part-time basis, B352–2000 establishes the project representative's duties, responsibilities, and limitations of authority. The project representative is employed and supervised by the architect.

B503™–2007(formerly B511™–2001) Guide for Amendments to AIA Owner-Architect Agreements

B503–2007 is not an agreement, but is a guide containing model provisions for amending owner-architect agreements. Some provisions, such as a limitation of liability clause, further define or limit the scope of services and responsibilities. Other provisions introduce a different approach to a project, such as fast-track construction. In all cases, these provisions are provided because they deal with circumstances that are not typically included in other AIA standard form owner-architect agreements.

B727™–1988 Standard Form of Agreement Between Owner and Architect for Special Services

B727–1988 provides only the terms and conditions of the agreement between the owner and architect—the description of services is left entirely to the parties, and must be inserted in the agreement or attached in an exhibit. Otherwise, the terms and conditions are similar to those found in B151–1997. B727–1988 is often used for planning, feasibility studies, and other services that do not follow the phasing sequence of services set forth in B151–1997 and other AIA documents. If construction administration services are to be provided using B727–1988, which is not recommended, care must be taken to coordinate it with the appropriate general conditions of the contract for construction.

C101™–1993 (formerly C801™–1993) Joint Venture Agreement for Professional Services

This document is intended to be used by two or more parties to provide for their mutual rights and obligations in forming a joint venture. It is intended that the joint venture, once established, will enter into an agreement with the owner to provide professional services. The parties may be all architects, all engineers, a combination of architects and engineers, or another combination of professionals. The document provides a choice between two methods of joint venture operation. The Division of Compensation method assumes that services provided and the compensation received will be divided among the parties in the proportions agreed to at the outset of the project. Each party's profitability is then dependent on individual performance of pre-assigned tasks and is not directly tied to that of the other parties. The Division of Profit and Loss method is based on each party performing work and billing the joint venture at cost plus a nominal amount for overhead. The ultimate profit or loss of the joint venture is divided between or among the parties at completion of the project, based on their respective interests. C101–1993 was only renumbered in 2007; its content remains the same as in C801–1993.

C105™–2005 Standard Form of Agreement Between Architect and Consulting Architect

C105–2005 will be discontinued after May 31, 2009; C401™-2007, Standard Form of Agreement Between Architect and Consultant, may be used for the same purpose. C105–2005 is a standard form of agreement between the architect and another architect that provides services as a consultant. C105–2005 assumes and references a preexisting owner-architect agreement known as the Prime Agreement. C105–2005 does not describe a fixed scope of services for the consulting architect but instead provides a location in the agreement for inserting a description of those services. This document may be used with a variety of compensation methods, including multiple of direct personnel expense and stipulated sum.

C142™–1997 Abbreviated Standard Form of Agreement Between Architect and Consultant

C142–1997 will be discontinued after May 31, 2009. It is an abbreviated standard form of agreement between architect and consultant. This document may be used with a variety of compensation methods, including multiple of direct personnel expense and stipulated sum. C142–1997 is intended to be used with B141™–1997, Standard Form of Agreement Between Owner and Architect, or B151™–1997, Abbreviated Standard Form of Agreement Between Owner and Architect. Both B141–1997 and B151–1997 will be discontinued after May 31, 2009.

C401™–2007 (formerly C141™–1997) Standard Form of Agreement Between Architect and Consultant

C401–2007 is a standard form of agreement between the architect and the consultant providing services to the architect. C401–2007 is suitable for use with all types of consultants, including consulting architects. This document may be used with a variety of compensation methods. C401–2007 assumes and incorporates by reference a preexisting owner-architect agreement known as the Prime Agreement. B101–2007, B103–2007, B104–2007, B105–2007, and B152–2007 are the documents most frequently used to establish the Prime Agreement. C401–2007 was modified in 2007 to be shorter and more flexible by "flowing down" the provisions of the Prime Agreement, except as specifically stated in C401–2007.

C727™–1992 Standard Form of Agreement Between Architect and Consultant for Special Services

C727–1992 provides only the terms and conditions of the agreement between the architect and the consultant—the description of services is left entirely to the parties, and must be inserted in the agreement or attached in an exhibit. It is often used for planning, feasibility studies, postoccupancy studies, and other services that require specialized descriptions.

SMALL PROJECT FAMILY

A105™–2007 (formerly A105™–1993 and A205™–1993) Standard Form of Agreement Between Owner and Contractor for a Residential or Small Commercial Project

A105–2007 is a stand-alone agreement with its own general conditions; it replaces A105–1993 and A205–1993. A105–2007 is for use on a project that is modest in size and brief in duration, and where payment to the contractor is based on a stipulated sum (fixed price). For larger and more complex projects, other AIA agreements are more suitable, such as A107™–2007, Agreement Between Owner and Contractor for a Project of Limited Scope. A105–2007 and B105™–2007, Standard Form of Agreement Between Owner and Architect for a Residential or Small Commercial Project, comprise the Small Projects family of documents. Although A105–2007 and B105–2007 share some similarities with other agreements, the Small Projects family should not be used in tandem with agreements in other document families without careful side-by-side comparison of contents.

B105™–2007 (formerly B155™–1993) Standard Form of Agreement Between Owner and Architect for a Residential or Small Commercial Project

B105–2007 is a standard form of agreement between owner and architect intended for use on a residential or small commercial project that is modest in size and brief in duration. B105–2007 and AIA Document A105™–2007, Standard Form of Agreement Between Owner and Contractor for a Residential or Small Commercial Project, comprise the Small Projects family of documents. B105–2007 is intended for use with A105–2007, which it incorporates by reference. B105–2007 is extremely abbreviated and is formatted more informally than other AIA agreements. Although A105–2007 and B105–2007 share some similarities with other AIA agreements, the Small Projects family should not be used with other AIA document families without careful side-by-side comparison of contents.

CM ADVISER FAMILY

A101™CMa–1992 Standard Form of Agreement Between Owner and Contractor Where the Basis of Payment Is a Stipulated Sum, Construction Manager–Adviser Edition

A101CMa–1992 is a standard form of agreement between owner and contractor for use on projects where the basis of payment is a stipulated sum (fixed price), and where, in addition to the contractor and the architect, a construction manager assists the owner in an advisory capacity during design and construction. The document has been prepared for use with A201™CMa–1992, General Conditions of the Contract for Construction, Construction Manager-Adviser Edition. This integrated set of documents is appropriate for use on projects where the construction manager only serves in the capacity of an adviser to the owner, rather than as constructor (the latter relationship being represented in documents A121CMc–1991 and A131CMc–1991). A101CMa–1992 is suitable for projects where the cost of construction has been predetermined, either by bidding or by negotiation.

A201™CMa–1992 General Conditions of the Contract for Construction, Construction Manager–Adviser Edition

A201CMa–1992 sets forth the rights, responsibilities, and relationships of the owner, contractor, construction manager, and architect. A201CMa–1992 is adopted by reference in owner-architect, owner-contractor, and owner-construction manager agreements in the A201CMa family of documents. Under A201CMa–1992, the construction manager serves as an independent adviser to the owner, who enters into multiple contracts with prime trade contractors.

Caution: Do not use A201CMa–1992 in combination with agreements where the construction manager takes on the role of constructor, gives the owner a guaranteed maximum price, or contracts directly with those who supply labor and materials for the project, such as A121CMc–2003 or A131CMc–2003.

A511™CMa–1993 Guide for Supplementary Conditions, Construction Manager–Adviser Edition

Similar to A503–2007, A511CMa–1993 is a guide for amending or supplementing the general conditions document A201CMa–1992. A511CMa–1993 should only be employed, as should A201CMa–1992, on projects where the construction manager is serving in the capacity of adviser to the owner (as represented by the CMa document designation), and not in situations where the Construction Manager is also the constructor (CMc document-based relationships). Like A503–2007, this document contains suggested language for supplementary conditions, along with notes on appropriate usage.

B141™CMa–1992 Standard Form of Agreement Between Owner and Architect, Construction Manager–Adviser Edition

B141CMa–1992 is a standard form of agreement between owner and architect for use on building projects where construction management services are to be provided under a separate contract with the owner. It is coordinated with B801CMa–1992, an owner-construction manager-adviser agreement where the construction manager is an independent, professional adviser to the owner throughout the course of the project. Both B141CMa–1992 and B801CMa–1992 are based on the premise that one or more separate construction contractors will also contract with the owner. The owner-contractor agreement is jointly administered by the architect and the construction manager under A201™CMa–1992, General Conditions of the Contract for Construction, Construction Manager–Adviser Edition.

B801™CMa–1992 Standard Form of Agreement Between Owner and Construction Manager

B801CMa–1992 provides the agreement between the owner and the construction manager, a single entity who is separate and independent from the architect and the contractor, and who acts solely as an adviser (CMa) to the owner throughout the course of the project. B801CMa–1992 is coordinated for use with B141™CMa–1992, Standard Form of Agreement Between Owner and Architect, Construction Manager-Adviser Edition. Both B801CMa–1992 and B141CMa–1992 are based on the premise that there will be a separate, and possibly multiple, construction contractor(s) whose contracts with the owner will be jointly administered by the architect and the construction manager under A201CMa–1992. B801CMa–1992 is not coordinated with, and should not be used with, documents where the construction manager acts as the constructor for the project, such as A121CMc–1991 or A131CMc–1991.

G701™CMa–1992 Change Order, Construction Manager–Adviser Edition

G701CMa–1992 is for implementing changes in the work agreed to by the owner, contractor, construction manager adviser, and architect. Execution of a completed G701–2000 indicates agreement upon all the terms of the change, including any changes in the contract sum (or guaranteed maximum price) and contract time. It provides space for the signatures of the owner, contractor, construction manager adviser, and architect, and for a complete description of the change. The major difference between G701CMa–1992 and G701–2000 is that the signature of the construction manager adviser, along with those of the owner, architect, and contractor, is required to validate the change order.

G702™CMa–1992 Application and Certificate for Payment, Construction Manager–Adviser Edition

G702CMa–1992 serves the same purposes as G702–1992 except that this document expands responsibility for certification of payment to include both the architect and the construction manager. Similarly, both the architect and the construction manager may certify a different amount than that applied for, with each initialing the figures that have been changed and providing written explanation(s) accordingly. The standard form G703™–1992, Continuation Sheet, is appropriate for use with G702CMa–1992.

G704™CMa–1992 Certificate of Substantial Completion, Construction Manager–Adviser Edition

G704CMa–1992 serves the same purpose as G704–2000 except that this document expands responsibility for certification of substantial completion to include both the architect and the construction manager.

G714™CMa–1992 Construction Change Directive, Construction Manager-Adviser Edition

G714CMa–1992 serves the same purpose as G714–2007 except that this document expands responsibility for signing construction change directives to include both the architect and the construction manager.

G722™CMa–1992 Project Application and Project Certificate for Payment, Construction Manager-Adviser Edition, and G723™CMa–1992 Project Application Summary, Construction Manager-Adviser Edition

G722CMa–1992 is to be used in conjunction with G723™CMa–1992, Project Application Summary. These documents are designed to be used on a project where a construction manager is employed as an adviser to the owner, but not as a constructor, and where multiple contractors have separate, direct agreements with the owner. Each contractor submits separate G702CMa–1992 and G703CMa–1992, payment application forms to the construction manager-adviser, who collects and compiles them to complete G723CMa–1992. G723CMa–1992 serves as a summary of the contractors' applications with totals being transferred to the G722CMa–1992. The construction manager–adviser can then sign the G722CMa–1992, have it notarized, and submit it along with the G723CMa-1992 (to which all of the separate contractors' G702CMa–1992 forms are attached) to the architect. Both the architect and the construction manager must certify the payment amount.

CM CONSTRUCTOR FAMILY

A121™CMc–2003 Standard Form of Agreement Between Owner and Construction Manager Where the Construction Manager Is Also the Constructor (AGC Document 565)

A121CMc–2003 is intended for use on projects where a construction manager, in addition to serving as adviser to the owner, assumes financial responsibility for construction of the project. The construction manager provides the owner with a guaranteed maximum price proposal, which the owner may accept, reject, or negotiate. Upon the owner's acceptance of the proposal by execution of an amendment, the construction manager becomes contractually bound to provide labor and materials for the project. The document divides the construction manager's services into two phases: the preconstruction phase and the construction phase, portions of which may proceed concurrently in order to fast-track the process. A121CMc–2003 is coordinated for use with A201™–1997, General Conditions of the Contract for Construction, and B151™–1997, Standard Form of Agreement Between Owner and Architect.

A131™CMc–2003 Standard Form of Agreement Between Owner and Construction Manager Where the Construction Manager Is Also the Constructor and Where the Basis of Payment Is the Cost Plus a Fee and There Is No Guarantee of Cost (AGC Document 566)

Similar to A121CMc–1991, this construction manager-as-constructor agreement is intended for use when the owner seeks a construction manager who will take on responsibility for providing the means and methods of construction. However, in A131CMc–2003 the construction manager does not provide a guaranteed maximum price (GMP). A131CMc–2003 employs the cost-plus-a-fee method, wherein the owner can monitor cost through periodic review of a control estimate that is revised as the project proceeds. The agreement divides the construction manager's services into two phases: the preconstruction phase and the construction phase, portions of which may proceed concurrently in order to fast-track the process. A131CMc–2003 is coordinated for use with A201™–1997, General Conditions of the Contract for Construction, and B151™–1997, Standard Form of Agreement Between Owner and Architect.

INTERIORS FAMILY

A151™–2007 (formerly A175™ID–2003) Standard Form of Agreement Between Owner and Vendor for Furniture, Furnishings, and Equipment Where the Basis of Payment Is a Stipulated Sum

A151–2007 is intended for use as the contract between owner and vendor for furniture, furnishings, and equipment (FF&E) where the basis of payment is a stipulated sum (fixed price) agreed to at the time of contracting. A151–2007 adopts by reference and is intended for use with A251™–2007, General Conditions of the Contract for Furniture, Furnishings, and Equipment. It may be used in any arrangement between the owner and the contractor where the cost of FF&E has been determined in advance, either through bidding or negotiation.

A251™–2007 (formerly A275™ID–2003) General Conditions of the Contract for Furniture, Furnishings, and Equipment

A251–2007 provides general conditions for the A151™–2007, Standard Form Agreement Between Owner and Vendor for Furniture, Furnishings, and Equipment

Where the Basis of Payment Is a Stipulated Sum. A251–2007 sets forth the duties of the owner, architect, and vendor, just as A201™–2007, General Conditions of the Contract for Construction, does for building construction projects. Because the Uniform Commercial Code (UCC) governs the sale of goods and has been adopted in nearly every jurisdiction, A251–2007 recognizes the commercial standards set forth in Article 2 of the UCC, and uses certain standard UCC terms and definitions. A251–2007 was renumbered in 2007 and modified, as applicable, to coordinate with A201–2007.

A751™–2007 (formerly A775™ID–2003) Invitation and Instructions for Quotation for Furniture, Furnishings and Equipment

A751–2007 provides (1) the Invitation for Quotation for Furniture, Furnishings, and Equipment (FF&E) and (2) Instructions for Quotation for Furniture, Furnishings, and Equipment. These two documents define the owner's requirements for a vendor to provide a complete quotation for the work. The purchase of FF&E is governed by the UCC, and A751–2007 has been developed to coordinate with the provisions of the UCC.

B152™–2007 (formerly B171™ID–2003) Standard Form of Agreement Between Owner and Architect for Architectural Interior Design Services

B152–2007 is a standard form of agreement between the owner and architect for design services related to Furniture, Furnishings, and Equipment (FF&E) as well as to architectural interior design. B152–2007 divides the architect's services into eight phases: Programming, Pre-lease Analysis and Feasibility, Schematic Design, Design Development, Contract Documents, Bidding and Quotation, Construction Phase Services, and FF&E Contract Administration. B152–2007 was renumbered in 2007 and modified to align, as applicable, with B101–2007 and A201–2007. B152–2007 is intended for use in conjunction with A251™–2007, General Conditions of the Contract for Furniture, Furnishings and Equipment, and A201™–2007, General Conditions of the Contract for Construction, both of which it incorporates by reference.

B153™–2007 (formerly B175™ID–2003) Standard Form of Agreement Between Owner and Architect for Furniture, Furnishings, and Equipment Design Services

B153–2007 is a standard form of agreement between the owner and architect for design services related solely to Furniture, Furnishings, and Equipment (FF&E). B153–2007 divides the architect's services into six phases: Programming, Schematic Design, Design Development, Contract Documents, Quotation, and FF&E Contract Administration. B153–2007 was renumbered in 2007 and modified to align, as applicable, with B101–2007. B153–2007 is intended for use in conjunction with A251™–2007, General Conditions of the Contract for Furniture, Furnishings, and Equipment, which it incorporates by reference.

DESIGN/BUILD FAMILY

A141™–2004 Agreement Between Owner and Design-Builder

A141–2004 replaces A191–1996 and consists of the agreement and three exhibits: Exhibit A, Terms and Conditions; Exhibit B, Determination of the Cost of the Work; and Exhibit C, Insurance and Bonds. Exhibit B is not applicable if the parties select to use a Stipulated Sum. A141–2004 obligates the design-builder to execute fully the work required by the design-build documents, which include A141–2004 with its attached exhibits, the project criteria and the design-builder's proposal, including any revisions to those documents accepted by the owner, supplementary and other conditions, addenda, and modifications. The agreement requires the parties to select the payment type from three choices: (1) Stipulated Sum, (2) Cost of the Work Plus Design-Builder's Fee, and (3) Cost of the Work Plus Design-Builder's Fee with a Guaranteed Maximum Price. A141–2004 with its attached exhibits forms the nucleus of the design-build contract. Because A141–2004 includes its own terms and conditions, it does not use A201–1997.

A142™–2004 Agreement Between Design-Builder and Contractor

A142–2004 replaces A491–1996 and consists of the agreement and five exhibits: Exhibit A, Terms and Conditions; Exhibit B, Preconstruction Services; Exhibit C, Contractor's Scope of Work; Exhibit D, Determination of the Cost of the Work; and Exhibit E, Insurance and Bonds. Unlike B491–1996, A142–2004 does not rely on A201 for its general conditions of the contract. A142–2004 contains its own terms and conditions. A142-2004 obligates the contractor to perform the work in accordance with the contract documents, which include A142–2004 with its attached exhibits, supplementary and other conditions, drawings, specifications, addenda, and modifications. Like A141–2004, A142–2004 requires the parties to select the payment type from three choices: (1) Stipulated Sum, (2) Cost of the Work Plus Design-Builder's Fee, and (3) Cost of the Work Plus Design-Builder's Fee with a Guaranteed Maximum Price.

B142™–2004 Agreement Between Owner and Consultant Where the Owner Contemplates Using the Design-Build Method of Project Delivery

B142–2004 provides a standard form for the upfront services an owner may require when considering design-build delivery. The consultant, who may or may not be an architect or other design professional, may perform a wide-ranging array of services for the owner, including programming and planning, budgeting and cost estimating, project criteria development services, and many others, commencing with initial data gathering and continuing through to post occupancy. B142–2004 consists of the agreement portion and two exhibits, Exhibit A, Initial Information, and Exhibit B, Standard Form of Consultant's Services. Exhibit B provides a menu of briefly described services that the parties can select and augment to suit the needs of the project.

B143™–2004 Agreement Between Design-Builder and Architect

B143–2004 replaces B901–1996 and establishes the contractual relationship between the design-builder and its architect. B143–2004 consists of the Agreement, Exhibit A, Initial Information, and Exhibit B, Standard Form of Architect's Services. Exhibit B provides a menu of briefly described services that the parties can select and augment to suit the needs of the project.

G704/DB™–2004 Acknowledgment of Substantial Completion of a Design-Build Project

Because of the nature of design-build contracting, the project owner assumes many of the construction contract administration duties performed by the architect in a traditional project. Because there is not an architect to certify substantial completion, A141–2004 requires the owner to inspect the project to determine whether the work is substantially complete in accordance with the design-build documents and to acknowledge the date when it occurs. G704/DB–2004 is a variation of G704–2000 and provides a standard form for the owner to acknowledge the date of substantial completion.

DIGITAL PRACTICE FAMILY

C106™–2007 Digital Data Licensing Agreement

C106–2007 serves as a licensing agreement between two parties who otherwise have no existing licensing agreement for the use and transmission of digital data, including instruments of service. C106–2007 defines digital data as information, communications, drawings, or designs created or stored for a specific project in digital form. C106–2007 allows one party to (1) grant another party a limited nonexclusive license to use digital data on a specific project, (2) set forth procedures for transmitting the digital data, and (3) place restrictions on the license granted. In addition, C106–2007 allows the party transmitting digital data to collect a licensing fee for the recipient's use of the digital data.

E201™–2007 Digital Data Protocol Exhibit

E201–2007 is not a stand-alone document, but must be attached as an exhibit to an existing agreement, such as the B101™–2007, Standard Form of Agreement Between Owner and Architect, or A101™–2007, Agreement Between Owner and Contractor. Its purpose is to establish the procedures the parties agree to follow with respect to the transmission or exchange of digital data, including instruments of service. E201–2007 defines digital data as information, communications, drawings, or designs created or stored for a specific project in digital form. E201 does not create a separate license to use digital data, because AIA documents for design or construction, to which E201–2007 would be attached, already include those provisions. Parties not covered under such agreements should consider executing AIA Document C106™–2007, Digital Data Licensing Agreement.

INTERNATIONAL FAMILY

B161™–2002 (formerly B611™INT–2002) Standard Form of Agreement Between Client and Consultant for Use Where the Project Is Located Outside the United States

B161–2002 is designed to assist U.S. architects involved in projects based in foreign countries, where the U.S. architect is hired on a consulting basis for design services and the owner will retain a local architect in the foreign country. The document is intended to clarify the assumptions, roles, responsibilities, and obligations of the parties; to provide a clear, narrative description of services; and to facilitate, strengthen, and maintain the working and contractual relationship between the parties. Because of foreign practices, the term Owner has been replaced with Client throughout the document. Also, since it is assumed that the U.S. architect is not licensed to practice architecture in the foreign country where the project is located, the term Consultant is used throughout the document to refer to the U.S. architect. B161–2002 was only renumbered in 2007; its content remains the same as in B611INT–2002.

B162™–2002 (formerly B621™INT–2002) Abbreviated Standard Form of Agreement Between Client and Consultant for Use Where the Project Is Located Outside the United States

B162–2002 is an abbreviated version of B161™–2002, Standard Form of Agreement Between Client and Consultant. The document is designed to assist U.S. architects involved in projects based in foreign countries where the U.S. architect is hired on a consulting basis for design services and a local architect will be retained. The document is intended to clarify the assumptions, roles, responsibilities, and obligations of the parties; to provide a clear, narrative description of services; and to facilitate, strengthen, and maintain the working and contractual relationship between the parties. Because of foreign practices, the term Owner has been replaced with Client throughout the document. Also, since it is assumed that the U.S. architect is not licensed to practice architecture in the foreign country where the project is located, the term Consultant is used throughout the document to refer to the U.S. architect. B162–2002 was only renumbered in 2007; its content remains the same as in B621INT–2002.

CONTRACT ADMINISTRATION AND PROJECT MANAGEMENT FORMS

A305™–1986 Contractor's Qualification Statement

An owner preparing to request bids or to award a contract for a construction project often requires a means of verifying the background, references, work experience, and financial stability of any contractor being considered. These factors, along with the time frame for construction, are important for an owner to investigate. Using A305–1986, the contractor may provide a sworn, notarized statement and appropriate attachments to elaborate on important aspects of the contractor's qualifications.

A310™–1970 Bid Bond

This simple, one-page form establishes the maximum penal amount that may be due to the owner if the selected bidder fails to execute the contract and/or fails to provide any required performance and payment bonds.

A312™–1984 Performance Bond and Payment Bond

This form incorporates two bonds: one covering the contractor's performance, and the other covering the contractor's obligations to pay subcontractors and others for material and labor. In addition, A312–1984 obligates the surety to act responsively to the owner's requests for discussions aimed at anticipating or preventing a contractor's default.

B305™–1993 (formerly B431™–1993) Architect's Qualification Statement

B305–1993 is a standardized outline form on which the architect may enter information that a client may wish to review before selecting the architect. The owner may use B305–1993 as part of a Request for Proposal or as a final check on the architect's credentials. Under some circumstances, B305–1993 may be attached to the owner-architect agreement to show, as for example, the team of professionals and consultants expected to be employed on the project. B305–1993 was only renumbered in 2007; its content remains the same as in B431–1993.

D101™–1995 Methods of Calculating Areas and Volumes of Buildings

This document establishes definitions for methods of calculating the architectural area and volume of buildings. D101–1995 also covers interstitial space and office, retail, and residential areas.

D200™–1995 Project Checklist

The project checklist is a convenient listing of tasks a practitioner may perform on a given project. This checklist will assist the architect in recognizing required tasks and in locating the data necessary to fulfill assigned responsibilities. By providing space for notes on actions taken, assignment of tasks, and time frames for completion, D200–1995 may also serve as a permanent record of the owner's, contractor's, and architect's actions and decisions.

G601™–1994 Request for Proposal–Land Survey

G601–1994 allows owners to request proposals from a number of surveyors based on information deemed necessary by the owner and architect. G601–1994 allows owners to create a Request for Proposal through checking appropriate boxes and filling in project specifics, thus avoiding the costs associated with requesting unnecessary information. G601–1994 may be executed to form the agreement between the owner and the land surveyor once an understanding is reached.

G602™–1993 Request for Proposal–Geotechnical Services

Similar in structure and format to G601–1994, G602–1993 can form the agreement between the owner and the geotechnical engineer. It allows the owner to tailor the proposal request to address the specific needs of the project. In consultation with the architect, the owner establishes the parameters of service required and evaluates submissions based on criteria such as time, cost, and overall responsiveness to the terms set forth in the request for proposal. When an acceptable submission is selected, the owner signs the document in triplicate, returning one copy to the engineer and one to the architect, thus forming the agreement between owner and geotechnical engineer.

G612™–2001 Owner's Instructions to the Architect Regarding the Construction Contract, Insurance and Bonds, and Bidding Procedures

G612–2001 is a three-part questionnaire, drafted to elicit information from the owner regarding the nature of the construction contract. Part A relates to contracts, Part B relates to insurance and bonds, and Part C deals with bidding procedures. The order of the parts follows the project's chronological sequence to match the points in time when the information will be needed. Because many of the items relating to the contract will have some bearing on the development of construction documents, it is important to place Part A in the owner's hands at the earliest possible phase of the project. The owner's responses to Part A will lead to a selection of the appropriate delivery method and contract forms, including the general conditions. Part B naturally follows after selection of the general conditions because insurance and bonding information is dependent upon the type of general conditions chosen. Answers to Part C will follow as the contract documents are further developed.

G701™–2001 Change Order

G701–2001 is for implementing changes in the Work agreed to by the owner, contractor, and architect. Execution of a completed G701–2001 indicates agreement upon all the terms of the change, including any changes in the Contract Sum (or Guaranteed Maximum Price) and Contract Time. The form provides space for the signatures of the owner, architect, and contractor, and for a complete description of the change.

G702™–1992 Application and Certificate for Payment, and G703™–1992 Continuation Sheet

These two documents provide convenient and complete forms on which the contractor can apply for payment and the architect can certify that payment is due. The forms require the contractor to show the status of the contract sum to date, including the total dollar amount of the work completed and stored to date, the amount of retainage (if any), the total of previous payments, a summary of change orders, and the amount of current payment requested. G703–1992 breaks the contract sum into portions of the work in accordance with a schedule of values prepared by the contractor as required by the general conditions. (Note: The AIA does not publish a standard schedule of values form.) G702–1992 serves as both the contractor's application and the architect's certification. Its use can expedite payment and reduce the possibility of error. If the application is properly completed and acceptable to the architect, the architect's signature certifies to the owner that a payment in the amount indicated is due to the contractor. The form also allows the architect to certify an amount different than the amount applied for, with explanation provided by the architect.

G704™–2000 Certificate of Substantial Completion

G704–2000 is a standard form for recording the date of substantial completion of the work or a designated portion thereof. The contractor prepares a list of items to be completed or corrected, and the architect verifies and amends this list. If the architect finds that the work is substantially complete, the form is prepared for acceptance by the contractor and the owner, and the list of items to be completed or corrected is attached. In G704–2000, the parties agree on the time allowed for completion or correction of the items, the date when the owner will occupy the work or designated portion thereof, and a description of responsibilities for maintenance, heat, utilities, and insurance.

G705™–2001 (formerly G805™–2001) List of Subcontractors

G705–2001 is a form for listing subcontractors and others proposed to be employed on a project as required by the bidding documents. It is to be filled out by the contractor and returned to the architect for submission to the owner. G705–2001 was only renumbered in 2007; its content remains the same as in G805–2001.

G706™–1994 Contractor's Affidavit of Payment of Debts and Claims

The contractor submits this affidavit with the final request for payment, stating that all payrolls, bills for materials and equipment, and other indebtedness connected with the work for which the owner might be responsible has been paid or otherwise satisfied. G706–1994 requires the contractor to list any indebtedness or known claims in connection with the construction contract that have not been paid or otherwise satisfied. The contractor may also be required to furnish a lien bond or indemnity bond to protect the owner with respect to each exception.

G706A™–1994 Contractor's Affidavit of Release of Liens

G706A–1994 supports G706–1994 in the event that the owner requires a sworn statement of the contractor stating that all releases or waivers of liens have been received. In such event, it is normal for the contractor to submit G706–1994 and G706A-1994 along with attached releases or waivers of liens for the contractor, all subcontractors, and others who may have lien rights against the owner's property. The contractor is required to list any exceptions to the sworn statement provided in G706A–1994, and may be required to furnish to the owner a lien bond or indemnity bond to protect the owner with respect to such exceptions.

G707™–1994 Consent of Surety to Final Payment

This document is intended for use as a companion to G706™–1994, Contractor's Affidavit of Payment of Debts and Claims, on construction projects where the contractor is required to furnish a bond. By obtaining the surety's approval of final payment to the contractor and its agreement that final payment will not relieve the surety of any of its obligations, the owner may preserve its rights under the bond.

G707A™–1994 Consent of Surety to Final Reduction in or Partial Release of Retainage

This is a standard form for use when a surety company is involved and the owner-contractor agreement contains a clause whereby retainage is reduced during the course of the construction project. When duly executed, G707A–1994 assures the owner that such reduction or partial release of retainage does not relieve the surety of its obligations.

G709™–2001 Work Changes Proposal Request

This form is used to obtain price quotations required in the negotiation of change orders. G709–2001 is not a change order or a direction to proceed with the work. It is simply a request to the contractor for information related to a proposed change in the construction contract. G709–2001 provides a clear and concise means of initiating the process for changes in the Work.

G710™–1992 Architect's Supplemental Instructions

This form is used by the architect to issue additional instructions or interpretations or to order minor changes in the work. It is intended to assist the architect in performing its obligations as interpreter of the contract documents in accordance with the owner-architect agreement and the general conditions of the contract for construction. G710–1992 should not be used to change the contract sum or contract time. It is intended to help the architect perform its services with respect to minor changes not involving adjustment in the contract sum or contract time. Such minor changes are authorized under Section 7.4 of A201™–2007, General Conditions of the Contract for Construction.

G711™–1972 Architect's Field Report

The architect's project representative can use this standard form to maintain a concise record of site visits or, in the case of a full-time project representative, a daily log of construction activities.

G712™–1972 Shop Drawing and Sample Record

This is a standard form by which the architect can log and monitor shop drawings and samples. The form allows the architect to document receipt of the contractor's submittals, subsequent referrals of the submittals to the architect's consultants, action taken, and the date returned to the contractor. G712–1972 can also serve as a permanent record of the chronology of the submittal process.

G714™–2007 (formerly G714™–2001) Construction Change Directive

G714–2007 is a directive for changes in the work for use where the owner and contractor have not reached an agreement on proposed changes in the contract sum or contract time. G714–2007 was developed as a directive for changes in the work which, if not expeditiously implemented, might delay the project. Upon receipt of a completed G714–2007, the contractor must promptly proceed with the change in the work described therein.

G715™–1991 Supplemental Attachment for ACORD Certificate of Insurance 25-S (7/90)

This document is intended for use in adopting ACORD Form 25-S to certify the coverage required of contractors under A201™–2007, General Conditions of the Contract for Construction. Since the ACORD certificate does not have space to show all the coverages required in A201–2007, the Supplemental Attachment form should be completed, signed by the contractor's insurance representative, and attached to the ACORD certificate.

G716™–2004 Request for Information

G716–2004 provides a standard form for an owner, architect, and contractor to request further information from each other during construction. The form asks the requesting party to list the relevant drawing, specification, or submittal reviewed in attempting to find the information. Neither the request nor the response received provides authorization for work that increases the cost or time of the project.

G801™–2007 (formerly G605™–2000) Notification of Amendment to the Professional Services Agreement

G801–2007 is intended to be used by an architect when notifying an owner of a proposed amendment to the AIA owner-architect agreements, such as B101–2007.

G802™-2007 (formerly G606™-2000) Amendment to the Professional Services Agreement

G802–2007 is intended to be used by an architect when amending the professional services provisions in the AIA owner-architect agreements, such as B101–2007.

G803™–2007 (formerly G607™–2000) Amendment to the Consultant Services Agreement

G803–2007 is intended to be used by an architect or consultant when amending the professional services provisions in AIA architect-consultant agreement C401–2007.

G804™–2001 Register of Bid Documents

G804–2001 serves as a log for bid documents while they are in the possession of contractors, subcontractors, and suppliers during the bidding process. The form allows tracking by bidder of documents issued, deposits received, and documents and deposits returned. G804–2001 is particularly useful as a single point of reference when parties interested in the project call for information during the bidding process.

G806™–2001 Project Parameters Worksheet

G806–2001 is an administrative form intended to help maintain a single standard list of project parameters including project objectives, owner's program, project delivery method, legal parameters, and financial parameters.

G807™–2001 Project Team Directory

G807–2001 is used as a single point of reference for basic information about project team members including the owner, architect's consultants, contractor, and other entities. G807–2001 differs from AIA Document G808™–2001, Project Data, which contains only data about the project and project site.

G807–2001 should be carefully checked against the owner-architect agreement so that specific requirements as to personnel representing the owner and those involved with the architect in providing services are in conformance with the agreement.

G808™–2001 Project Data and G808™A–2001 Construction Classification Worksheet

G808–2001 is used for recording information about approvals and zoning and building code issues gathered in the course of providing professional services. G808–2001 should be completed piece by piece as a project progresses and periodically reviewed to ensure information relevance. The attached worksheet, G808A™–2001, Construction Classification Worksheet, can be used to supplement the G808–2001. G808A–2001 can help a design team work through the range of code compliance combinations available before choosing a final compliance strategy.

G809™–2001 Project Abstract

G809–2001 establishes a brief, uniform description of project data to be used in the tabulation of architect marketing information and firm statistics. The intent is to provide a single-sheet summary where information can be sorted, compiled, and summarized to present a firm's experience. Information compiled in G809–2001 can support planning for similar projects and answer questions pertaining to past work.

G810™–2001 Transmittal Letter

G810–2001 allows for the orderly flow of information between parties involved in the design and construction phase of a project. It serves as a written record of the exchange of project information and acts as a checklist reminding the sender to tell the recipient what exactly is being sent, how the material is being sent, and why it is being sent.

Appendix **A**

RESOURCES FOR INTERN ARCHITECTS

THE INTERN DEVELOPMENT PROGRAM

National Council of Architectural Registration Boards

Education as an architect typically begins in a school of architecture, but it does not end there. Training in architecture firms, continuing education, and professional practice further the educational process. Schools and firms offer many opportunities for acquiring knowledge and skills; however, the individual must take responsibility for planning his or her career as an architect to the fullest.

Governmental jurisdictions (states and territories of the United States) establish minimum registration requirements for legally practicing architecture in each jurisdiction. Currently, fifty-one of the fifty-four U.S. jurisdictions require participation in the NCARB Intern Development Program (IDP) for initial registration. Participation in IDP exposes architectural interns to the comprehensive training that is essential for competent practice.

IDP responds to an intern's professional development needs by providing useful resources that enhance day-to-day experience, and the IDP training requirement establishes levels of training in important areas of architectural practice. The IDP mentorship system gives interns access to advice and guidance from practicing architects. The IDP record-keeping system facilitates the documentation of internship activities, and the IDP supplementary education system provides a variety of learning resources designed to enrich training.

More information about the Intern Development Program, training requirements, and conditions regarding acceptability of an intern's training experience is available in the IDP Guidelines, which can be downloaded from the NCARB Web site at www.ncarb.org.

THE EMERGING PROFESSIONAL'S COMPANION

The American Institute of Architects and the National Council of Architectural Registration Boards

More architecture students each year are seeking internships before graduation, whether as a summer job or as part of their curriculum for credit. Individuals can begin to gain credit in IDP after the third year in a National Architectural Accrediting Board (NAAB)-accredited architecture program or preprofessional program accepted for direct entry to a NAAB-accredited professional degree program, or after the first year in a NAAB-accredited Master of Architecture program.

The AIA and NCARB offer the *Emerging Professional's Companion* (EPC) to students as a way to gain exposure to practice issues while still in school and to interns in the architecture field as a means of augmenting what they learn on the job. Students and interns can use the EPC in a number of ways:

Students can do the exercises independently or in groups for course credit. Interns can do the same for IDP credit.

Interns can choose sections of the EPC to learn more about training areas that are sometimes difficult for an intern to access in the office environment.

Students and interns can gain knowledge about nontraditional areas of practice by reviewing a list of expanded practice opportunities in Chapter 16 of the *Companion*, "Professional and Community Service." Interns can earn IDP credit for this review.

Students and interns can use the EPC to guide preparation of a personal portfolio of work they can use to advance professionally.

Each chapter of the EPC is aligned with an NCARB IDP Training Area to provide a seamless learning environment for the intern, as well as a well-rounded collection of exercises for any architecture professional. Users—whether intern, student, or young architect—can approach the EPC content at any point, choosing material of interest or a subject in which additional support is needed.

Beginner, intermediate, and advanced exercises and scenarios are available. Those who need help determining where to start can ask their supervisors or mentors to help them determine which level is appropriate.

The EPC chapters are designed to lead users through an in-depth look at each IDP training area. Each chapter begins with general information on the topic followed by self-paced exercises. Some of these are based on the narrative; some are evidence-based learning modules based on actual projects; and other sections are based on fictional scenarios that simulate experiences with clients, consultants, and other project team members.

It is no secret that an internship is the best way to gain the knowledge needed to become a licensed architect. But how does an individual ensure that an internship provides knowledge and experience sufficient to develop professional competence? And how can you manage your internship and your career on your own terms? The AIA and NCARB have developed the answer—the *Emerging Professional's Companion*, a powerful professional development tool that can help you navigate the path to obtaining an architectural license. This resource is available online at www.epcompanion.org. Log on, and take your career into your own hands.

Appendix **B**
ALLIED PROFESSIONAL ORGANIZATIONS

AIA-RELATED ORGANIZATIONS

The American Architectural Foundation (AAF)
1735 New York Avenue NW
Washington, DC 20006
(202) 626-7318
www.archfoundation.org/aaf/aaf/index.htm

AIA Trust
1735 New York Avenue NW
Washington, DC 20006
(202) 785-2324
www.theaiatrust.com

AIA/ACSA Council on Architectural Research
c/o Association of Collegiate Schools of Architecture
1735 New York Avenue NW
Washington, DC 20006
(202) 785-2324

Council of Architecture Component Executives (CACE)
1735 New York Avenue NW
Washington, DC 20006
(202) 626-7377

Society of Architectural Administrators (SAA)
1735 New York Avenue NW
Washington, DC 20006
(202) 626-7300

For the names of AIA state and regional components, call the AIA at (202) 626-7351 or (800) 242-3837 or visit www.aia.org and look for the components map.

COLLATERAL ORGANIZATIONS

The American Institute of Architecture Students (AIAS)
1735 New York Avenue NW
Washington, DC 20006
(202) 626-7472
Fax: (202) 626-7414
www.aias.org

Association of Collegiate Schools of Architecture (ACSA)
1735 New York Avenue NW
Washington, DC 20006
(202) 785-2324
Fax: (202) 628-0448
www.acsa-arch.org

National Architectural Accrediting Board (NAAB)
1735 New York Avenue NW
Washington, DC 20006
(202) 783-2007
Fax: (202) 783-2822
www.naab.org

National Council of Architectural Registration Boards (NCARB)
1801 K Street NW, Suite 1100
Washington, DC 20006
(202) 783-6500
Fax: (202) 783-0290
www.ncarb.org

OTHER PROFESSIONAL ORGANIZATIONS

Accreditation Board for Engineering and Technology (ABET)
111 Market Place, Suite 1050
Baltimore, MD 21202
(410) 347-7700
Fax: (410) 625-2238
www.abet.org

Acoustical Society of America (ASA)
2 Huntington Quadrangle, Suite 1N01
Melville, NY 11747-4502
(516) 576-2360
Fax: (516) 576-2377
http://asa.aip.org

Alliance to Save Energy (ASE)
1200 18th Street NW, Suite 900
Washington, DC 20036
(202) 857-0666
Fax: (202) 331-9588
www.ase.org

American Arbitration Association (AAA)
335 Madison Avenue, 10th Floor
New York, NY 10017-4605
(212) 716-5800
Fax: (212) 716-5905
www.adr.org

American Association of Engineering Societies (AAES)
1828 L Street NW, Suite 906
Washington, DC 20036
(202) 296-2237
Fax: (202) 296-1151
www.aaes.org

American Association of Homes and Services for the Aging (AAHSA)
2519 Connecticut Avenue NW
Washington, DC 20008
(202) 783-2242
Fax: (202) 783-2255
www.aahsa.org

American Association of Housing Educators (AAHE)
Illinois State University
Department of Family and Consumer Sciences
Normal, IL 61790-5060
(309) 438-5802
www.extension.iastate.edu/Pages/housing/aahe-links.html

American Bar Association (ABA)
321 North Clark Street
Chicago, IL 60610
(312) 988-5000
Service center: (800) 285-2221
www.abanet.org

American College of Healthcare Architects (ACHA)
P.O. Box 14548
Lenexa, KS 66285-4548
(913) 895-4604
Fax: (913) 895-4652
www.healtharchitects.org

American Congress on Surveying & Mapping (ACSM)
6 Montgomery Village Avenue, Suite 403
Gaithersburg, MD 20879
(240) 632-9716
Fax: (240) 632-1321
www.survmap.com

American Council for Construction Education (ACCE)
1717 North Loop 1604 East, Suite 320
San Antonio, TX 78232-1570
(210) 495-6161
Fax: (210) 495-6168
www.acce-hq.org

American Council for an Energy-Efficient Economy (ACEEE)
1001 Connecticut Avenue NW, Suite 801
Washington, DC 20036
(202) 429-8873
Fax: (202) 429-2248
www.aceee.org

American Council of Engineering Companies (ACEC)
1015 15th Street NW, Suite 802
Washington, DC 20005
(202) 347-7474
Fax: (202) 898-0068
www.acec.org

American Hospital Association (AHA)
1 North Franklin
Chicago, IL 60606-3421
(312) 422-3000
Fax: (312) 422-4796
www.aha.org

American Indian Council of Architects and Engineers (AICAE)
www.aicae.org

American Institute for Conservation of Historic & Artistic Works (AIC)
1717 K Street NW, Suite 200
Washington, DC 20006-5346
(202) 452-9545
Fax: (202) 452-9328
http://aic.stanford.edu

American Institute of Graphic Artists (AIGA)
164 Fifth Avenue
New York, NY 10010
(212) 807-1990
Fax: (212) 807-1799
www.aiga.org

American National Standards Institute (ANSI)
1819 L Street NW, 6th Floor
Washington, DC 20036
(202) 293-8020
Fax: (202) 293-9287
www.ansi.org

American Planning Association (APA)
122 S. Michigan Avenue, Suite 1600
Chicago, IL 60603-6107
(312) 431-9100
Fax: (312) 431-9985
www.planning.org

American Society of Architectural Illustrators (ASAI)
11756 W. Hopi Street
Avondale, AZ 85323
(623) 433-8782
Fax: (623) 444-7420
www.asai.org

American Society of Civil Engineers (ASCE)
1801 Alexander Bell Drive
Reston, VA 20191-4400
(703) 295-6300
(800) 548-2723
Fax: (703) 295-6222
www.asce.org

American Society for Engineering Education (ASEE)
1818 N Street NW, Suite 600
Washington, DC 20036-2479
(202) 331-3500
Fax: (202) 265-8504
www.asee.org

American Society of Golf Course Architects (ASGCA)
125 North Executive Drive, Suite 106
Brookfield, WI 53005
(262) 786-5960
Fax: (262) 786-5919
www.asgca.org

American Society of Heating, Refrigerating and Air-Conditioning Engineers (ASHRAE)
1791 Tullie Circle NE
Atlanta, GA 30329
(404) 636-8400
Fax: (404) 321-5478
www.ashrae.org

American Society of Interior Designers (ASID)
608 Massachusetts Avenue, NE
Washington, DC 20002-6006
(202) 546-3480
Fax: (202) 546-3240
www.asid.org

American Society of Landscape Architects (ASLA)
636 Eye Street NW
Washington, DC 20001-3736
(202) 898-2444
Fax: (202) 898-1185
www.asla.org

American Society of Mechanical Engineers (ASME)
3 Park Avenue
New York, NY 10016-5990
(800) 843-2763
www.asme.org

American Society for Quality (ASQ)
P.O. Box 3005
Milwaukee, WI 53201-3005
(800) 248-1946
Fax: (414) 272-1734
www.asq.org

American Society for Testing and Materials (ASTM) International
P.O. Box C700
(100 Barr Harbor Drive)
West Conshohocken, PA 19428-2959
(610) 832-9585
Fax: (610) 832-9555
www.astm.org

American Solar Energy Society (ASES)
2400 Central Avenue, Suite A
Boulder, CO 80301
(303) 443-3130
Fax: (303) 443-3212
www.ases.org

American Subcontractors Association (ASA)
1004 Duke Street
Alexandria, VA 22314
(703) 684-3450
Fax: (703) 836-3482
www.asaonline.com

Architects/Designers/Planners for
Social Responsibility (ADPSR)
National Forum
P.O. Box 9126
Berkeley, CA 94709
(510) 845-1000
www.adpsr.org

Architectural Research Centers
Consortium (ARCC)
c/o Walter Grondzik
School of Architecture
Florida A&M University
Tallahassee, FL 32307-4200
(850) 599-8782
Fax: (850) 599-3535
www.arccweb.org

Associated Builders and Contractors
(ABC)
4250 N. Fairfax Drive, 9th Floor
Arlington, VA 22203-1607
(703) 812-2000
www.abc.org

Associated General Contractors
(AGC) of America
2300 Wilson Boulevard, Suite 400
Arlington, VA 22201
(703) 548-3118
Fax: (703) 548-3119
www.agc.org

Associated Specialty Contractors, Inc.
(ASC)
3 Bethesda Metro Center, Suite 1100
Bethesda, MD 20814
www.assoc-spec-con.org

Association for Computer-Aided
Design in Architecture (ACADIA)
www.acadia.org

Association of Energy Engineers
(AEE)
4025 Pleasantdale Road, Suite 420
Atlanta, GA 30340
(770) 447-5083
Fax: (770) 446-3969
www.aeecenter.org

Association of Engineering Firms
Practicing in the Geosciences (ASFE)
8811 Colesville Road, Suite G106
Silver Spring, MD 20910
(301) 565-2733
Fax: (301) 589-2017
www.asfe.org

Association of Higher Education
Facilities Officers (APPA)
1643 Prince Street
Alexandria, VA 22314-2818
(703) 684-1446
Fax: (703) 549-2772
www.appa.org

Association for Preservation
Technology International (APT)
1224 Centre West, Suite 400B
Springfield, IL 62704
(217) 793-7874
Fax: (888) 723-4242
www.apti.org

Association of University Architects
(AUA)
www.auaweb.net

Building Owners and Managers
Association International (BOMA)
1201 New York Avenue NW, Suite 300
Washington, DC 20005
(202) 408-2662
Fax: (202) 371-0181
www.boma.org

Canadian Home Builders' Association
(CHBA)
150 Laurier Avenue West, Suite 500
Ottawa, ON K1P 5J4, Canada
(613) 230-3060
Fax: (613) 232-8214
www.chba.ca

Canadian Institute of Planners (CIP)
Institut Canadien des Urbanistes (ICU)
116 Albert Street, Suite 801
Ottawa, ON K1P 5G3, Canada
(613) 237-7526
Fax: (613) 237-7045
www.cip-icu.ca

Canadian Society of Landscape
Architecture (CSLA)
P.O. Box 13594
Ottawa, ON K2K 1X6, Canada
(613) 622-5520
Fax: (613) 622-5870
www.csla.ca

Canadian Standards Association (CSA)
5060 Spectrum Way
Mississauga, ON L4W 5N6, Canada
(416) 747-4000
Fax: (416) 747-2473
www.csa.ca

Construction Management
Association of America (CMAA)
7918 Jones Branch Drive, Suite 540
McLean, Virginia 22102
(703) 356-2622
Fax: (703) 356-6388
http://cmaanet.org

Construction Specifications Institute
(CSI)
99 Canal Center Plaza, Suite 300
Alexandria, VA 22314
(703) 684-0300
(800) 689-2900
Fax: (703) 684-0465
www.csinet.org

Construction Users Roundtable
(CURT)
4100 Executive Park Drive
Cincinnati, OH 45241
(513) 563-4131
Fax: (513) 733-9551
www.curt.org

CoreNet Global
260 Peachtree Street NW, Suite 1500
Atlanta, GA 30303
(404) 589-3200
Fax: (404) 589-3201
www.corenetglobal.org

Council of Educational Facility
Planners International (CEFPI)
9180 E. Desert Cove Drive, Suite 104
Scottsdale, AZ 85260-6231
(480) 391-0840
Fax: (480) 391-0940
www.cefpi.org

Council for Interior Design
Accreditation
(formerly Foundation for Interior Design
Education Research)
146 Monroe Center NW, Suite 1318
Grand Rapids, MI 49503-2822
(616) 458-0400
Fax: (616) 458-0460
www.accredit-id.org

Council of Landscape Architectural
Registration Boards (CLARB)
144 Church Street NW, Suite 201
Vienna, VA 22180
(703) 319-8380
www.clarb.org

Design-Build Institute of America (DBIA)
1100 H Street NW, Suite 500
Washington, DC 20005-5476
(202) 682-0110
Fax: (202) 682-5877
www.dbia.org

Edison Electric Institute (EEI)
701 Pennsylvania Avenue NW
Washington, DC 20004-2696
(202) 508-5000
www.eei.org

Electric Power Research Institute (EPRI)
3420 Hillview Avenue
Palo Alto, CA 94304
(650) 855-2000
Fax: (650) 855-2900
www.epri.com

Energy & Environmental Building Association
6520 Edenvale Boulevard, Suite 112
Eden Prairie, MN 55346
(952) 881-1098
Fax: (952) 881-2048
www.eeba.org

EnterpriseWorks/VITA
1825 Connecticut Avenue NW, Suite 630
Washington, DC 20009
(202) 293-4600
Fax: (202) 293-4598
www.enterpriseworks.org

Environmental Design Research Association (EDRA)
P.O. Box 7146
Edmond, OK 73083-7146
(405) 330-4863
Fax: (405) 330-4150
www.edra.org

Gas Technology Institute (GTI)
1700 South Mount Prospect Road
Des Plaines, IL 60018-1804
(847) 768-0500
Fax: (847) 768-0501
www.gastechnology.org

Heritage Canada Foundation (HCF)
5 Blackburn Avenue
Ottawa, ON K1N 8A2, Canada
(613) 237-1066
Fax: (613) 237-5987
www.heritagecanada.org

Illuminating Engineering Society of North America (IESNA)
120 Wall Street, 17th Floor
New York, NY 10005-4001
(212) 248-5000
Fax: (212) 248-5017
www.iesna.org

Industrial Designers Society of America (IDSA)
45195 Business Court, Suite 250
Dulles, VA 20166-6717
(703) 707-6000
www.idsa.org

Institute of Electrical and Electronics Engineers (IEEE)
3 Park Avenue, 17th Floor
New York, NY 10016-5997
(212) 419-7900
Fax: (212) 752-4929
www.ieee.org

Interior Design Educators Council (IDEC)
7150 Winton Drive, Suite 300
Indianapolis, IN 46268
(317) 328-4437
Fax: (317) 280-8527
www.idec.org

International Association of Lighting Designers (IALD)
Merchandise Mart, Suite 9-104
200 World Trade Center
Chicago, IL 60654
(312) 527-3677
Fax: (312) 527-3680
www.iald.org

International Code Council (ICC)
5203 Leesburg Pike, Suite 600
Falls Church, VA 22041-3401
(888) 422-7233
Fax: (703) 379-1546
www.iccsafe.org

International Council for Research and Innovation in Building and Construction (CIB)
P.O. 1837
3000 BV Rotterdam, The Netherlands
+31 10 411 0240
Fax: +31 10 433 4372
www.cibworld.nl

International Facility Management Association (IFMA)
1 E. Greenway Plaza, Suite 1100
Houston, TX 77046-0194
(713) 623-4362
Fax: (713) 623-6124
www.ifma.org

International Institute for Energy Conservation (IIEC)
10005 Leamoore Lane, #100
Vienna, VA 22181
(703) 281-7263
Fax: (703) 938-5153
www.iiec.org

International Interior Design Association (IIDA)
222 Merchandise Mart Plaza, Suite 1540
Chicago, IL 60654-1104
(312) 467-1950
Fax: (312) 467-0779
www.iida.org

International Union of Architects (UIA)
Union Internationale des Architects
51, rue Raynouard
75016 Paris, France
+33 1 45 24 3688
Fax: +33 1 45 24 0278
www.uia-architectes.org

Junior Engineering Technical Society (JETS)
1420 King Street, Suite 405
Alexandria, VA 22314-2794
(703) 548-5387
Fax: (703) 548-0769
www.jets.org

Lighting Research Center
Rensselaer Polytechnic Institute
21 Union St.
Troy, NY 12180
(518) 687-7100
Fax: (518) 687-7120
www.lrc.rpi.edu

National Association of Home Builders of the United States (NAHB)
1201 15th Street NW
Washington, DC 20005
(202) 266-8200 x0
Fax: (202) 266-8400
www.nahb.com

National Association of Housing and Redevelopment Officials (NAHRO)
630 Eye Street NW
Washington, DC 20001
(202) 289-3500
Fax: (202) 289-8181
www.nahro.org

National Association of State Facilities Administrators (NASFA)
P.O. Box 11910
Lexington, KY 40578-1910
(859) 244-8181
(859) 244-8001
www.nasfa.net

National Association of Surety Bond Producers (NASBP)
1828 L Street, NW, Suite 720
Washington, DC 20036-5104
(202) 686-3700
Fax: (202) 686-3656
www.nasbp.org

National Conference of State Historic Preservation Officers (NCSHPO)
444 North Capitol Street NW
Suite 342 Hall of the States
Washington, DC 20001-7572
(202) 624-5465
Fax: (202) 624-5419
www.ncshpo.org

National Conference of States on Building Codes and Standards (NCSBCS)
505 Huntmar Park Drive, Suite 210
Herndon, VA 20170
(703) 437-0100
(800) 362-2633
Fax: (703) 481-3596
www.ncsbcs.org

National Council of Acoustical Consultants (NCAC)
7150 Winton Drive, Suite 300
Indianapolis, IN 46268
(317) 328-0642
Fax: (317) 328-4629
www.ncac.com

National Council for Interior Design Qualification (NCIDQ)
1200 18th Street NW, Suite 1001
Washington, DC 20036-2506
(202) 721-0220
Fax: (202) 721-0221
www.ncidq.org

National Fire Protection Association (NFPA)
1 Batterymarch Park
Quincy, MA 02169-7471
(617) 770-3000
Fax: (617) 770-0700
www.nfpa.org

National Institute of Building Sciences (NIBS)
1090 Vermont Avenue NW, Suite 700
Washington, DC 20005-4905
(202) 289-7800
Fax: (202) 289-1092
www.nibs.org

National Organization of Minority Architects (NOMA)
c/o School of Architecture & Design
College of Engineering, Architecture & Computer Sciences
Howard University
2366 6th Street NW, Room 100
Washington, DC 20059
(202) 686-2780
www.noma.net

National Research Council Canada
1200 Montreal Road, Bldg. M-58
Ottawa, ON K1A 0R6, Canada
(613) 993-9101
Fax: (613) 952-9907
www.nrc-cnrc.gc.ca

National Society of Professional Engineers (NSPE)
1420 King Street
Alexandria, VA 22314
(703) 684-2800
Fax: (703) 836-4875
www.nspe.org

National Trust for Historic Preservation
1785 Massachusetts Avenue NW
Washington, DC 20036-2117
(202) 588-6000
Fax: (202) 588-6038
www.nationaltrust.org

Professional Photographers of America, Inc. (PPA)
229 Peachtree Street NE, Suite 2200
Atlanta, GA 30303
(404) 522-8600
(800) 786-6277
Fax: (404) 614-6400
www.ppa.com

Professional Services Management Association (PSMA)
99 Canal Center Plaza, Suite 330
Alexandria, VA 22314
(703) 739-0277
Fax: (703) 549-2498
www.psmanet.org

Project Management Institute (PMI)
Four Campus Boulevard
Newtown Square, PA 19073-3299
(610) 356-4600
Fax: (610) 356-4647
www.pmi.org

Smart Growth Network
Sustainable Communities Network
c/o CONCERN
P.O. Box 21301
Washington, DC 20009
www.smartgrowth.org

Society of Architectural Historians (SAH)
1365 North Astor Street
Chicago, IL 60610-2144
(312) 573-1365
Fax: (312) 573-1141
www.sah.org

Society for College and University Planning (SCUP)
339 E. Liberty, Suite 300
Ann Arbor, MI 48104
(734) 998-7832
Fax: (734) 998-6532
www.scup.org

Society for Design Administration (SDA)
5020 Clark Road, #134
Sarasota, FL 34233
(800) 711-8199
Fax: (941) 921-3465
www.sdadmin.org

Society for Environmental Graphic Design (SEGD)
1000 Vermont Avenue NW, Suite 400
Washington, DC 20005
(202) 638-5555
Fax: (202) 638-0891
www.segd.org

Society of Fire Protection Engineers (SFPE)
7315 Wisconsin Avenue, Suite 620E
Bethesda, MD 20814
(301) 718-2910
Fax: (301) 718-2242
www.sfpe.org

APPENDICES

Society for Marketing Professional Services (SMPS)
99 Canal Center Plaza, Suite 330
Alexandria, VA 22314
(800) 292-7677
Fax: (703) 549-2498
www.smps.org

Surety & Fidelity Association of America (SFAA)
1101 Connecticut Avenue NW, Suite 800
Washington, DC 20036
(202) 463-0600
Fax: (202) 463-0606
www.surety.org

Sustainable Buildings Industry Council (SBIC)
1112 16th Street NW, Suite 240
Washington, DC 20036
(202) 628-7400
Fax: (202) 393-5043
www.sbicouncil.org

Underwriters Laboratories, Inc. (UL)
333 Pfingsten Road
Northbrook, IL 60062-2096
(847) 272-8800
Fax: (847) 272-8129
www.ul.com

U.S. Metric Association, Inc. (USMA)
10245 Andasol Avenue
Northridge, CA 91325-1504
Voice or fax: (818) 363-5606
www.metric.org

U.S. National Committee of the International Council on Monuments and Sites (US/ICOMOS)
401 F Street NW, Room 331
Washington, DC 20001
(202) 842-1866
Fax: (202) 842-1861
www.icomos.org/usicomos

Urban Land Institute (ULI)
1025 Thomas Jefferson Street NW, Suite 500W
Washington, DC 20007
(202) 624-7000
(800) 321-5011
Fax: (202) 624-7140
www.uli.org

FEDERAL GOVERNMENT

Advisory Council on Historic Preservation
1100 Pennsylvania Avenue NW, Suite 809
Washington, DC 20004
(202) 606-8503
www.achp.gov

Americans with Disabilities Act Information Office
U.S. Department of Justice
950 Pennsylvania Avenue NW
Civil Rights Division
Disability Rights Section–NYAV
Washington, DC 20530
(202) 514-0301
(800) 514-0383 TTY
Fax: (202) 307-1198
www.usdoj.gov/crt/ada

Architectural and Transportation Barriers Compliance Board
United States Access Board
Office of Technical and Information Services
1331 F Street NW, Suite 1000
Washington, DC 20004-1111
(202) 272-0080
Fax: (202) 272-0081
www.access-board.gov

Board on Infrastructure and the Constructed Environment (BICE)
500 Fifth Street NW, W916
Washington, DC 20001
(202) 334-3376
Fax: (202) 334-3370
www.nationalacademies.org/bice

Department of Energy (DOE)
1000 Independence Avenue SW
Washington, DC 20585
(202) 586-5000
Fax: (202) 586-4403
www.energy.gov

Department of Health & Human Services (HHS)
Office for Facilities Management and Policy
Division of Real Property
Parklawn Building, Room 5B17
5600 Fishers Lane
Rockville, MD 20857
(301) 443-2265
www.hhs.gov/asam/ofmp

Department of Housing and Urban Development (HUD)
451 7th Street SW
Washington, DC 20410
(202) 708-1112
www.hud.gov

Department of Veterans Affairs
Office of Facilities Management
810 Vermont Avenue NW
Washington, DC 20420
www.va.gov/facmgt

Energy Efficiency and Renewable Energy (EERE)
Department of Energy
Office of the Assistant Secretary
Mail Stop EE-1
Washington, DC 20585
(202) 586-9220
www.eere.energy.gov

Environmental Protection Agency (EPA)
U.S. EPA/Office of Radiation and Indoor Air
Indoor Environments Division
1200 Pennsylvania Avenue NW
Mail Code 6609J
Washington, DC 20460
(202) 343-9370
Fax: (202) 343-2394
www.epa.gov

Federal Bureau of Prisons
Property & Construction Branch
320 First Street NW
Washington, DC 20534
(202) 307-0954
www.bop.gov

Federal Emergency Management Agency (FEMA)
500 C Street SW
Washington, DC 20472
(202) 566-1600
(800) 621-3362
www.fema.gov

General Services Administration (GSA)
1800 F Street NW
Washington, DC 20405
(202) 708-5334
www.gsa.gov

Green Building Council
1800 Massachusetts Avenue NW
Suite 300
Washington, DC 20036
(202) 828-7422
www.usgbc.org

National Center for Appropriate Technology (NCAT)
U.S. Department of Energy
P.O. Box 3838
(3040 Continental Drive)
Butte, MT 59702
(406) 404-4572
(800) 275-6228
Fax: (406) 494-2905
www.ncat.org

National Endowment for the Arts (NEA)
1100 Pennsylvania Avenue NW
Washington, DC 20506-0001
(202) 682-5400
www.arts.endow.gov

National Institute of Corrections
320 First Street N.W.
Washington, DC 20534
(800) 995-6423
Fax: (202) 307-3106
www.nicic.org

National Institute of Standards and Technology (NIST)
100 Bureau Drive, Stop 1070
Gaithersburg, MD 20899-1070
(301) 975-6478
www.nist.gov

National Renewable Energy Laboratory (NREL)
1617 Cole Boulevard
Golden, CO 80401-3393
(303) 275-3000
www.nrel.gov

National Technical Information Service (NTIS)
U.S. Department of Commerce
Technology Administration
5285 Port Royal Road
Springfield, VA 22161
(703) 605-6000
www.ntis.gov

Occupational Safety and Health Administration (OSHA)
U.S. Department of Labor
200 Constitution Avenue NW,
Suite 440
Washington, DC 20210
(800) 321-6742
www.osha.gov

Office of Scientific and Technical Information
Department of Energy
P.O. Box 62
Oak Ridge, TN 37831
(865) 576-1188
Fax: (865) 576-2865
www.osti.gov

TRADE PRESS

Architectural Record
Two Penn Plaza
New York, NY 10121-2298
(212) 904-2594
Fax: (212) 904-4256
www.architecturalrecord.com

Architecture
770 Broadway, 4th Floor
New York, NY 10003
(646) 654-5766
Fax: (646) 654-5817
www.architecturemag.com

Building Design & Construction
2000 Clearwater Drive
Oak Brook, IL 60523
(630) 288-8081
www.bdcnetwork.com

Construction Specifier
Construction Specifications Institute (CSI)
99 Canal Center Plaza, Suite 300
Alexandria, VA 22314
(703) 684-0300
(800) 689-2900
Fax: (703) 684-8436
www.csinet.org

CRIT: Journal of the AIAS
1735 New York Avenue NW
Washington, DC 20006-5292
(202) 626-7472
www.aias.org/crit_journal/
crit_journal.php

Engineering News-Record
Two Penn Plaza, 9th Floor
New York, NY 10120
(212) 904-6428
Fax: (212) 904-2820
www.enr.com

Journal of Architectural Education
Association of Collegiate Schools of Architecture
1735 New York Avenue NW
Washington, DC 20006
(202) 785-2324
Fax: (202) 628-0448
www.acsa-arch.org

APPENDICES

Appendix **C**

SCHOOLS OF ARCHITECTURE

Schools on this list have NAAB-accredited professional degree programs.

Andrews University
Division of Architecture
Berrien Springs, MI 49104-0450
(269) 471-6003
Fax: (269) 471-6261
www.andrews.edu/ARCH

University of Arizona
College of Architecture, Planning, and
Landscape Architecture
P.O. Box 210075
1040 North Olive Road
Tucson, AZ 85721
(520) 621-6751
Fax: (520) 621-8700
www.architecture.arizona.edu

Arizona State University
School of Architecture & Landscape
Architecture
College of Design
P.O. Box 871605
Tempe, AZ 85287-1605
(480) 965-3536
(480) 965-0968
http://design.asu.edu

University of Arkansas
School of Architecture
120 Vol Walker Hall
Fayetteville, AR 72701
(479) 575-4945
Fax: (479) 575-7099
http://architecture.uark.edu

**Auburn University School of
Architecture**
College of Architecture, Design and
Construction
202 Dudley Commons
Auburn, AL 36849-5313
(334) 844-4524
Fax: (334) 844-2735
www.cadc.auburn.edu

Ball State University
College of Architecture and Planning
Architecture Building 104
Muncie, IN 47306-0305
(765) 285-5861
Fax: (765) 285-3726
www.bsu.edu/cap

Boston Architectural Center
320 Newbury Street
Boston, MA 02115
(617) 262-5000
www.the-bac.edu

University of California, Berkeley
College of Environmental Design
Department of Architecture
232 Wurster Hall, MC #1800
Berkeley, CA 94720-1800
(510) 642-4942
Fax: (510) 643-5607
http://arch.ced.berkeley.edu

University of California, Los Angeles
Department of Architecture and Urban
Design
P.O. Box 951467
Los Angeles, CA 90095-1467
(310) 825-7857
Fax: (310) 825-8959
www.aud.ucla.edu

California College of the Arts
1111 Eighth Street
San Francisco, CA 94107-2247
415-703-9500
(800) 447-1278
Fax: (415-703-9524
Email: info@cca.edu
www.ccac-art.edu

**California Polytechnic State
University, San Luis Obispo**
College of Architecture and
Environmental Design
Building 05, Room 212
San Luis Obispo, CA 93407
(805) 756-1311
Fax: (805) 756-5986
www.caed.calpoly.edu/

**California State Polytechnic
University, Pomona**
College of Environmental Design
Department of Architecture
3801 West Temple Avenue, Building 7
Pomona, CA 91768-4048
(909) 869-2683
Fax: (909) 869-4331
www.csupomona.edu/~arc

Carnegie Mellon University
School of Architecture
201 College of Fine Arts
Pittsburgh, PA 15213
(412) 268-2354
Fax: (412) 268-7819
www.arc.cmu.edu

Catholic University of America
School of Architecture and Planning
Crough Center
620 Michigan Avenue NE
Washington, DC 20064
(202) 319-5188
Fax: (202) 319-5728
http://architecture.cua.edu

University of Cincinnati
School of Architecture and Interior
Design
College of Design, Architecture, Art, and
Planning
P.O. Box 210016
Cincinnati, OH 45221-0016
(513) 556-6426
Fax: (513) 556-1230
http://daap.uc.edu/said

City College of New York
City University of New York
School of Architecture, Urban Design,
and Landscape Architecture
160 Convent Avenue
New York, NY 10031
(212) 650-7118
Fax: (212) 650-6566
www1.ccny.cuny.edu/prospective/
architecture

Clemson University
College of Architecture, Arts,
and Humanities
145 Lee Hall
Clemson, SC 29634
(864) 656-3898
Fax: (864) 656-1810
www.clemson.edu/caah/architecture

**University of Colorado at Denver
and Health Sciences Center**
College of Architecture and Planning
Campus Box 126
P.O. Box 173364
Denver, CO 80217-3364
(303) 556-3382
Fax: (303) 556-3687
www.cudenver.edu/Academics/Colleges/
ArchitecturePlanning/Default.htm

Columbia University
Graduate School of Architecture,
Planning, and Preservation
1172 Amsterdam Avenue
New York, NY 10027
(212) 854-3414
Fax: (212) 864-0410
www.arch.columbia.edu

Cooper Union
Irwin S. Chanin School of Architecture
30 Cooper Square
New York, NY 10003
(212) 353-4220
http://archweb.cooper.edu

Cornell University
College of Architecture, Art,
and Planning
Department of Architecture
139 East Sibley Hall
Ithaca, NY 14853-2801
(607) 255-5236
Fax: (607) 255-0291
www.architecture.cornell.edu/index.htm

University of Detroit, Mercy
School of Architecture
4001 West McNichols Road
Detroit, MI 48221
(313) 993-1532
Fax: (313) 993-1512
http://architecture.udmercy.edu

Drexel University
Antoinette Westphal College of Media
Arts & Design
Department of Architecture
Nesbitt Hall
33rd and Market Streets
Philadelphia, PA 19104
(215) 895-2409
Fax: (215) 895-4921
www.drexel.edu/academics/comad

Drury College
Hammons School of Architecture
900 North Benton Avenue
Springfield, MI 65802
(417) 873-7288
Fax: (417) 873-7446
www.drury.edu/section/section.cfm?sid=48

**University of Florida College of
Design, Construction & Planning**
331 ARCH P.O. Box 115701
Gainesville, FL 32611-5701
(352) 392-4836
Fax: (352) 392-4606
www.dcp.ufl.edu

**Florida A&M University School of
Architecture**
1936 S. Martin Luther King Boulevard
Tallahassee, FL 32307
(850) 599-3244
Fax: (850) 599-3436
www.famusoa.net

Florida Atlantic University
School of Architecture
FAU/BCC Higher Education Complex
111 East Las Olas Boulevard
Fort Lauderdale, FL 33301
(954) 762-5654
Fax: (954) 762-5673
www.fau.edu/caupa/arch/index.html

Florida International University
School of Architecture
11200 SW 8th Street, PCA 272
Miami, FL 33199
(305) 348-3181
Fax: (305) 348-2650
www.fiu.edu/~soa

**Taliesin, the Frank Lloyd Wright
School of Architecture**
Taliesin West
P.O. Box 4430
Scottsdale, AZ 85261-4430
(480) 860-2700
Fax: (480) 860-8472
www.taliesin.edu

Georgia Institute of Technology
College of Architecture
247 4th Street
Atlanta, GA 30332-0155
(404) 894-3880
Fax: (404) 894-2678
www.arch.gatech.edu

Hampton University
Department of Architecture
Hampton, VA 23668
(757) 727-5440
Fax: (757) 728-6680
www.hamptonu.edu/academics/schools/
engineering/architecture/index.htm

**Harvard University Graduate School
of Design**
Department of Architecture
48 Quincy Street
Cambridge, MA 02138
(617) 495-4731
Fax: (617) 495-8916
www.gsd.harvard.edu

University of Hawaii at Manoa
School of Architecture
2410 Campus Road
Honolulu, HI 96822
(808) 956-7225
Fax: (808) 956-7778
http://web1.arch.hawaii.edu

University of Houston
Gerald D. Hines College of Architecture
122 College of Architecture Building
Houston, TX 77204-4000
(713) 743-2400
Fax: (713) 743-2358
www.arch.uh.edu

**Howard University College of
Engineering, Architecture, and
Computer Sciences**
School of Architecture and Design
2300 6th Street NW
Washington, DC 20059
(202) 806-7424
Fax: (202) 462-2158
www.howard.edu/ceacs

University of Idaho
Department of Architecture
AAS 207
Moscow, ID 83844-2451
(208) 885-6781
Fax: (208) 885-9428
www.class.uidaho.edu/arch

University of Illinois at Chicago
School of Architecture (MC 030)
845 West Harrison Street, Room 3100
Chicago, IL 60607
(312) 996-3335
Fax: (312) 413-4488
www.arch.uic.edu/index.php

**University of Illinois at
Urbana-Champaign**
College of Fine and Applied Arts
School of Architecture
611 Lorado Taft Drive, MC-621
Champaign, IL 61820
(217) 333-1330
Fax: (217) 244-2900
www.arch.uiuc.edu

Illinois Institute of Technology
College of Architecture
S. R. Crown Hall (CR005)
3360 South State Street
Chicago, IL 60616
(312) 567-3230
Fax: (312) 567-5820
www.iit.edu/~arch

**Iowa State University College
of Design**
Department of Architecture
156 College of Design
Ames, IA 50011-3093
(515) 294-4717
Fax: (515) 294-1440
www.design.iastate.edu/ARCH

University of Kansas
School of Architecture and Urban Design
1465 Jayhawk Blvd., 206 Marvin Hall
Lawrence, KS 66045-7614
(785) 864-3390
Fax: (785) 864-5185
www.saud.ku.edu

Kansas State University
College of Architecture, Planning,
and Design
115 Seaton Hall
Manhattan, KS 66506-2902
(913) 532-5950
Fax: (913) 532-6722
www.capd.ksu.edu

Kent State University
College of Architecture and
Environmental Design
200 Taylor Hall
Kent, OH 44242-0001
(330) 672-2917
Fax: (330) 672-3809
www.caed.kent.edu

**University of Kentucky College
of Design**
School of Architecture
117 Pence Hall
Lexington, KY 40506-0041
(859) 257-3030
Fax: (859) 323-1990
www.uky.edu/Design/architecture.htm

Lawrence Technological University
College of Architecture and Design
21000 West Ten Mile Road
Architecture Bldg., A116
Southfield, MI 48075-1058
(248) 204-2800
www.ltu.edu/architecture_and_design/
index.asp

University of Louisiana at Lafayette
School of Architecture and Design
P.O. Box 43850
Lafayette, LA 70504-0001
(337) 482-6224
Fax: (337) 482-5907
http://soad.louisiana.edu

**Louisiana State University College
of Art & Design**
School of Architecture
136 Atkinson Hall
Baton Rouge, LA 70803-5710
(225) 578-6885
Fax: (225) 578-2168
www.design.lsu.edu

Louisiana Tech University
School of Architecture
P.O. Box 3147
Ruston, LA 71270
(318) 257-2816
Fax: (318) 257-4687
www.latech.edu/tech/liberal-arts/
architecture/About.htm

University of Maryland
School of Architecture, Planning,
and Preservation
College Park, MD 20742
(301) 405-6284
Fax: (301) 314-9583
www.arch.umd.edu

Massachusetts Institute of Technology
Department of Architecture
77 Massachusetts Avenue, Room 7-337
Cambridge, MA 02139-2307
(617) 253-7791
Fax: (617) 253-8993
http://architecture.mit.edu

University of Miami
School of Architecture
1223 Dickson Drive
Coral Gables, FL 33146
(305) 284-3438
Fax: (305) 284-2999
www.arc.miami.edu

Miami University
Department of Architecture and Interior
Design
101 Alumni Hall
Oxford, OH 45056
(513) 529-7210
www.muohio.edu/architecture

University of Michigan
A. Alfred Taubman College of
Architecture and Urban Planning
2000 Bonisteel Boulevard, Room 2150
Ann Arbor, MI 48109-2069
(734) 764-1300
Fax: (734) 763-2322
www.caup.umich.edu

University of Minnesota
College of Architecture and Landscape
Design
89 Church Street, SE
Minneapolis, MN 55418
(612) 626-9068
Fax: (612) 625-7525
www.cala.umn.edu

**Mississippi State University College of
Architecture, Art & Design**
School of Architecture
Barr Avenue, 240 Giles Hall
P.O. Box AQ
Mississippi State, MS 39762
(662) 325-2202
Fax: (662) 325-8872
www.caad.msstate.edu/sarc

Montana State University
School of Architecture
P.O. Box 173760
Bozeman, MT 59717-3760
Fax: (406) 994-4256
www.arch.montana.edu

Institute of Architecture and Planning
Morgan State University
2201 Argonne Drive
Baltimore, MD 21251
(443) 885-3225
Fax: (410) 319-3786
www.morgan.edu/academics/
IAP/index.html

University of Nebraska-Lincoln
College of Architecture
210 Architecture Hall
Lincoln, NE 68588-0106
(402) 472-9212
Fax: (402) 472-3806
www.unl.edu/archcoll/index.html

University of Nevada, Las Vegas
School of Architecture
4505 Maryland Parkway
Box 454018
Las Vegas, NV 89154
(702) 895-3031
Fax: (702) 895-1119
www.unlv.edu/Colleges/Fine_Arts/
Architecture

New Jersey Institute of Technology
School of Architecture
University Heights
Newark, NJ 07102-1982
(973) 596-3080
Fax: (973) 596-8296
http://architecture.njit.edu

University of New Mexico
School of Architecture and Planning
2414 Central Avenue SE
MSC04 2530-1
Albuquerque, NM 87131-0001
(505) 277-2903
Fax: (505) 277-0076
http://saap.unm.edu

New York Institute of Technology
School of Architecture and Design
Northern Boulevard
Old Westbury, NY 11568-8000
(516) 686-7659
Fax: (516) 686-7921
http://iris.nyit.edu/architecture

New School of Architecture
and Design
1249 F Street
San Diego, CA 92101
(619) 235-4100
Fax: (619) 235-4651
www.newschoolarch.edu

University of North Carolina
at Charlotte
College of Architecture
9201 University City Boulevard
Charlotte, NC 28223
(704) 687-4841
www.coa.uncc.edu

North Carolina State University
College of Design
Department of Architecture
Campus Box 7701
Raleigh, NC 27695
(919) 515-8350
Fax: (919) 515-7330
www.ncsu.edu/design

North Dakota State University
Department of Architecture and
Landscape Architecture
P.O. Box 5285, SU Station
Fargo, ND 58105
(701) 231-8614
Fax: (701) 231-7342
www.ndsu.nodak.edu/arch

Norwich University
Division of Architecture and Art
158 Harmon Drive
Northfield, VT 05663
(800) 468-6679
www.norwich.edu

University of Notre Dame
School of Architecture
110 Bond Hall
Notre Dame, IN 46556
(219) 631-6137
Fax: (219) 631-8486
http://architecture.nd.edu

Ohio State University
Austin E. Knowlton School
of Architecture
275 West Woodruff Ave
Columbus, OH 43210-1138
(614) 292-1012
Fax: (614) 292-7106
http://knowlton.osu.edu

University of Oklahoma
Division of Architecture
830 Van Vleet Oval
Norman, OK 73019
(405) 325-3990
Fax: (405) 325-0108
http://arch.ou.edu

Oklahoma State University
School of Architecture
101 Architecture Building
Stillwater, OK 74078-5051
(405) 744-6043
Fax: (405) 744-6491
http://architecture.ceat.okstate.edu

University of Oregon
School of Architecture & Allied Arts
105 Lawrence Hall
Eugene, OR 97403
(541) 346-3631
Fax: (541) 346-3626
http://aaa.uoregon.edu

Parsons The New School for Design
Department of Architecture
25 East 13th Street
New York, NY 10011
(212) 229-8937
www2.parsons.edu/architecture/aidl/
homepage.html

University of Pennsylvania
Graduate School of Fine Arts
207 Meyerson Hall
Philadelphia, PA 19104-6311
(215) 898-5728
Fax: (215) 573-2192
www.design.upenn.edu/new/arch/
index.php

Pennsylvania State University College
of Arts and Architecture
Department of Architecture
121 Stuckeman Family Building
University Park, PA 16802
(814) 865-9535
Fax: (814) 865-3289
www.arch.psu.edu

Philadelphia University
School of Architecture and Design
School House Lane and Henry Avenue
Philadelphia, PA 19144-5497
(215) 951-2700
www.philau.edu/schools/add/index.htm

Polytechnic University of Puerto Rico
New School of Architecture
P.O. Box 192017
San Juan, PR 00919-2017
(787) 765-1465
Fax: (787) 767-0607
www.pupr.edu

Prairie View A&M University
School of Architecture
P.O. Box 4207
Prairie View, TX 77446-4207
(936) 857-2014
Fax: (936) 857-2350
www.pvamu.edu/pages/229.asp

Pratt Institute
School of Architecture
200 Willoughby Avenue
Brooklyn, NY 11205
(718) 399-4304
Fax: (718) 399-4315
www.pratt.edu/arch/index.html

Princeton University
School of Architecture
Princeton, NJ 08544-5264
(609) 258-3741
Fax: (609) 258-4740
www.princeton.edu/~soa

University of Puerto Rico
School of Architecture
P.O. Box 21909
San Juan, PR 00931-1909
(787) 250-8581
Fax: (787) 763-5377
www.estado.gobierno.pr/Juntas_
Examinadoras/Formularios/Arquitectos/
License_In_Training.pdf

Architecture Rensselaer
Rensselaer Polytechnic Institute
Greene Building
110 8th Street
Troy, NY 12180-3590
(518) 276-6466
www.arch.rpi.edu

Rhode Island School of Design
Department of Architecture
Two College Street
Providence, RI 02903-2784
(401) 454-6281
Fax: (401) 454-6299
www.risd.edu

Rice University
School of Architecture
MS-50 P.O. Box 1892
Houston, TX 77251-1892
(713) 348-4864
Fax: (713) 348-5277
www.arch.rice.edu

Roger Williams University
School of Architecture, Art, and
Historical Preservation
One Old Ferry Road
Bristol, RI 02809-2921
(401) 254-3605
www.rwu.edu/academics/schools/saahp

Savannah College of Art and Design
P.O. Box 2072
Savannah, GA 31402-2072
(912) 525-5100
(800) 869-7223
www.scad.edu

University of South Florida
School of Architecture and Community
Design
4202 E. Fowler Ave.
HMS 301
Tampa, FL 33620
(813) 974-4031
Fax: (813) 974-2557
www.arch.usf.edu

University of Southern California
School of Architecture
Watt Hall, Suite 204
Los Angeles, CA 90089-0291
(213) 740-2723
Fax: (213) 740-8884
www.usc.edu/dept/architecture

**Southern California Institute
of Architecture**
960 E. 3rd Street
Los Angeles, CA 90013
(213) 613-2200
Fax: (213) 613-2260
www.sciarc.edu

Southern Polytechnic State University
School of Architecture, Civil Engineering
Technology, and Construction
1100 S. Marietta Parkway
Marietta, GA 30060-2896
(678) 915-7253
Fax: (770) 528-5484
www.spsu.edu/home/academics/
architecture.html

**Southern University and A&M
College**
School of Architecture
201 Architecture West Building
Baton Rouge, LA 70813
(225) 771-3015
Fax: (225) 771-4709
http://susa.subr.edu

**State University of New York at
Buffalo**
School of Architecture and Planning
139 Hayes Hall
3435 Main Street
Buffalo, NY 14214-3087
(716) 829-3485 x114
www.ap.buffalo.edu

Syracuse University
School of Architecture
103 Slocum Hall
Syracuse, NY 13244-1250
(315) 443-2256
http://soa.syr.edu

Temple University
Tyler School of Art Architecture
Program
1947 N. 12th Street
Philadelphia, PA 19122
(215) 204-8813
www.temple.edu/architecture

University of Tennessee, Knoxville
College of Architecture and Design
1715 Volunteer Blvd.
Knoxville, TN 37996-2400
(865) 974-5267
Fax: (865) 974-0656
www.arch.utk.edu

University of Texas at Arlington
School of Architecture
P.O. Box 19108
Arlington, TX 76019-0108
(817) 272-2801
Fax: (817) 272-5098
www.uta.edu/architecture

University of Texas at Austin
School of Architecture
1 University Station B7500
Austin, TX 78712-0222
(512) 471-1922
Fax: (512) 471-0716
http://soa.utexas.edu

University of Texas at San Antonio
School of Architecture
501 W. Durango Boulevard
San Antonio, TX 78207
(210) 458-3010
Fax: (210) 458-3016
www.utsa.edu/architecture

Texas A&M University
College of Architecture
3137 TAMU
College Station, TX 77843-3137
(979) 845-1221
Fax: (979) 845-4491
http://archone.tamu.edu/College

Texas Tech University
College of Architecture
P.O. Box 42091
Lubbock, TX 79409-2091
(806) 742-3136
Fax: (806) 742-2855
www.arch.ttu.edu/Architecture

Tulane University
School of Architecture
New Orleans, LA 70118-3529
(504) 865-5389
Fax: (504) 862-8798
www.tulane.edu/~tsahome

Tuskegee University
College of Engineering, Architecture,
and Physical Sciences
Tuskegee, AL 36088
(334) 727-8356
Fax: (334) 727-8090
www.tuskegee.edu/Global/category.asp?
C=35010&nav=CcX8CqPB

University of Utah
College of Architecture & Planning
375 S. 1530 E., Room 235
Salt Lake City, UT 84112-0370
(801) 581-8254
Fax: (801) 581-8217
www.arch.utah.edu

University of Virginia
School of Architecture
Campbell Hall
P.O. Box 400122
Charlottesville, VA 22904-4122
(434) 924-3715
Fax: (434) 982-2678
www.arch.virginia.edu

**Virginia Polytechnic Institute
and State University**
College of Architecture & Urban Studies
202 Cowgill Hall (0205)
Blacksburg, VA 24061-0205
(540) 231-6416
Fax: (540) 231-9938
www.caus.vt.edu

University of Washington
Department of Architecture
P.O. Box 355720
Seattle, WA 98195-5720
(206) 543-4180
Fax: (206) 616-4992
http://depts.washington.edu/archdept

Washington State University
School of Architecture & Construction
Management
P.O. Box 642220
Pullman, WA 99164-2220
(509) 335-5539
www.arch.wsu.edu

Washington University in St. Louis
School of Architecture
Campus Box 1079
One Brookings Drive
St. Louis, MO 63130
(314) 935-6200
Fax: (314) 935-7656
www.arch.wustl.edu

Wentworth Institute of Technology
Department of Architecture
550 Huntington Avenue
Boston, MA 02115-5998
(617) 989-4450
www.wit.edu/arch

University of Wisconsin, Milwaukee
School of Architecture and Urban
Planning
P.O. Box 413
Milwaukee, WI 53211
(414) 229-4014
Fax: (414) 229-6976
www.uwm.edu/SARUP/index.html

Woodbury University
School of Architecture and Design
7500 Glenoaks Boulevard
Burbank, CA 91510-7846
(818) 767-0888
www.woodbury.edu

Yale University
Yale School of Architecture
180 York Street, 3rd Floor
New Haven, CT 06511
(203) 432-2288
Fax: (203) 432-7175
www.architecture.yale.edu

Appendix D

STATE REGISTRATION BOARDS

State of Alabama Board for Registration of Architects
770 Washington Avenue, Suite 150
Montgomery, AL 36130-4450
(334) 242-4179
Fax: (334) 242-4531
www.alarchbd.state.al.us

Alaska State Board of Registration for Architects, Engineers, and Land Surveyors
P.O. Box 110806
(333 Willoughby Ave., 9th Floor)
Juneau, AK 99811-0806
(907) 465-1676
Fax: (907) 465-2974
www.dced.state.ak.us/occ/pael.htm

Arizona State Board of Technical Registration
1110 W. Washington St., Suite 240
Phoenix, AZ 85007
(602) 364-4930
Fax: (602) 364-4931
www.btr.state.az.us

Arkansas State Board of Architects
101 East Capitol Street, Suite 110
Little Rock, AR 72201-3822
(501) 682-3171
Fax: (501) 682-3172
www.arkansas.gov/arch

California Architects Board
2420 Del Paso Road, Suite 105
Sacramento, CA 95834
(916) 574-7220
Fax: (916) 575-7283
www.cab.ca.gov

Colorado Board of Examiners of Architects
1560 Broadway, Suite 1350
Denver, CO 80202
(303) 894-7800
Fax: (303) 894-7790
www.dora.state.co.us/aes

Connecticut Department of Consumer Protection
Occupational and Professional Licensing Division
Architectural Licensing Board
165 Capitol Avenue
Hartford, CT 06106
(860) 713-6050
Fax: (860) 713-7243
www.ct.gov/dcp/cwp/view.asp?a=1624&q=273664&dcpNav_GID=1543

Board of Architects, Division of Professional Regulation
Delaware Department of State
861 Silver Lake Boulevard, Suite 203
Dover, DE 19904
(302) 739-4505
Fax: (302) 739-2711
http://dpr.delaware.gov/boards/architects/index.shtml

D.C. Department of Consumer and Regulatory Affairs
Government of the District of Columbia
941 North Capitol Street NE
Washington, D.C. 20002
(202) 442-4400
Fax: (202) 442-9445
www.dcra.dc.gov/dcra/site/default.asp

Florida Department of Business and Professional Regulation
Board of Architecture and Interior Design
1940 North Monroe Street
Tallahassee, FL 32399-0751
(850) 487-1395
www.myflorida.com/dbpr/pro/arch/arc_index.shtml

Georgia State Board of Architects
237 Coliseum Drive
Macon, GA 31217-3858
(478) 207-2440
Fax: (478) 207-1363
www.sos.state.ga.us/plb/architects

Guam Board of Registration for Engineers, Architects, and Land Surveyors
718 N. Marine Drive, Unit D, Suite 208
Upper Tumon, GU 96913
(671) 646-3138
Fax: (671) 649-9533
www.guam-peals.org/

Board of Engineers, Architects, Surveyors, and Landscape Architects
Professional and Vocational Licensing Division
Department of Commerce & Consumer Affairs
P.O. Box 3469
Honolulu, HI 96801
(808) 586-2702
Fax: (808) 586-2874
www.hawaii.gov/dcca/areas/pvl/boards/engineer

Idaho Bureau of Occupational Licenses
1109 Main Street, Suite 220
Boise, ID 83702-5642
(208) 334-3233
Fax: (208) 334-3945
www.ibol.idaho.gov/arc.htm

Illinois Department of Professional Regulation
320 W. Washington Street, 3rd Floor
Springfield, IL 62786
(217) 785-0800
Fax: (217) 782-7645
www.idfpr.com/dpr/who/archt.asp

State Board of Registration for Architects & Landscape Architects
Indiana Professional Licensing Agency
402 West Washington Street, Room W072
Indianapolis, IN 46204
(317) 234-3022
www.in.gov/pla/bandc/architects

Iowa Professional Licensing Division: Architects
1920 S.E. Hulsizer Road
Ankeny, IA 50021
(515) 281-5910
Fax: (515) 281-7411
www.state.ia.us/government/com/prof/
architect/home.html

Kansas State Board of Technical Professions
900 S.W. Jackson Street, Suite 507
Topeka, KS 66612-1257
(785) 296-3053
www.accesskansas.org/ksbtp

Kentucky Board of Architects
2624 Research Park Drive, Suite 101
Lexington, KY 40511
(859) 246-2069
Fax: (859) 246-2431
www.kybera.com

Louisiana Board of Architectural Examiners
9625 Fenway Avenue, Suite B
Baton Rouge, LA 70809
(225) 925-4802
Fax: (225) 925-4804
www.lastbdarchs.com

Maine Department of Professional and Financial Regulation
Office of Licensing & Registration
Board for Licensure of Architects,
Landscape Architects, & Interior
Designers
35 State House Station
Augusta, ME 04333-0035
(207) 624-8522
Fax: (207) 624-8637
www.state.me.us/pfr/olr/categories/
cat04.htm

Maryland State Board of Architects
Department of Labor, Licensing, and
Regulation
Division of Occupational and
Professional Licensing
500 North Calvert Street, Room 308
Baltimore, MD 21202-3651
(410) 230-6322
Fax: (410) 333-0021
www.dllr.state.md.us/license/occprof/
arc.html

Massachusetts Board of Registration of Architects
239 Causeway Street, Suite 500
Boston, MA 02114
(617) 727-3072
Fax: (617) 727-1627
www.mass.gov/dpl/boards/ar

Michigan State Board of Architects
P.O. Box 30018
Lansing, MI 48909
(517) 241-9253
Fax: (517) 241-9280
www.michigan.gov/cis/0,1607,7-154-
35299_35414_35452--,00.html

Minnesota Board of Architecture, Engineering, Land Surveying, Landscape Architecture, Geoscience, and Interior Design
85 East 7th Place, Suite 160
St. Paul, MN 55101
(651) 296-2388
Fax: (651) 297-5310
www.aelslagid.state.mn.us

Mississippi State Board of Architecture
2 Professional Parkway, #2B
Ridgeland, MS 39157
(601) 856-4652
Fax: (601) 856-1510
www.archbd.state.ms.us

Missouri State Board for Architects, Professional Engineers, Professional Land Surveyors, and Landscape Architects
3605 Missouri Boulevard, Suite 380
P.O. Box 184
Jefferson City, MO 65102-0184
(573) 751-0293
Fax: (573) 751-8046
http://pr.mo.gov/apelsla.asp

Montana Board of Architects
P.O. Box 200513
(301 South Park, Room 430)
Helena, MT 59620-0513
(406) 841-2300
Fax: (406) 841-2309
http://mt.gov/dli/bsd/license/bsd_boards/
arc_board/board_page.asp

Board of Professional Licensing
Northern Mariana Islands
P.O. Box 502078
Saipan, MP 96950
(670) 234-5897
Fax: (670) 234-6040

Nebraska Board of Engineers and Architects
215 Centennial Mall South, State 400
P.O. Box 95165
Lincoln, NE 68509-5165
(402) 471-2021
Fax: (402) 471-0787
www.ea.state.ne.us

Nevada State Board of Architecture, Interior Design, and Residential Design
2080 E. Flamingo Road, #120
Las Vegas, NV 89119
(702) 486-7300
Fax: (702) 486-7304
http://nsbaidrd.state.nv.us

New Hampshire Joint Board of Licensure and Certification
57 Regional Drive
Concord, NH 03301-8518
(603) 271-2219
Fax: (603) 271-6990
www.state.nh.us/jtboard/home.htm

New Jersey Board of Architects and Certified Landscape Architects
P.O. Box 45001
Newark, NJ 07101
(973) 504-6385
Fax: (973) 504-6458
www.state.nj.us/lps/ca/nonmedical/
architects.htm

New Mexico Board of Examiners for Architects
P.O. Box 509
Santa Fe, NM 87504
(505) 982-2869
Fax: (505) 982-8953
www.nmbea.org

New York State Education Department
Office of the Professions: Division of
Professional Licensing Services
Architecture Unit
89 Washington Avenue
Albany, NY 12234-1000
(518) 474-3817, ext. 250
Fax: (518) 402-5354
www.op.nysed.gov/arch.htm

North Carolina Board of Architecture
127 West Hargett Street, Suite 304
Raleigh, NC 27601
(919) 733-9544
Fax: (919) 733-1272
www.ncbarch.org

**North Dakota State Board
of Architecture**
P.O. Box 7370
Bismarck, ND 58507-7370
(701) 223-3540
www.ndsba.net

**State of Ohio Board of Examiners
of Architects**
77 S. High Street, 16th Floor
Columbus, OH 43215-6108
(614) 466-2316
Fax: (614) 644-9048
www.state.oh.us/arc

**Oklahoma Board of Architects
and Landscape Architects**
Landmark Towers
P.O. Box 53430
Oklahoma City, OK 73152
(405) 949-2383
Fax: (405) 949-1690
www.ok.gov/architects

Oregon Board of Architect Examiners
205 Liberty Street NE, Suite A
Salem, OR 97301
(503) 763-0662
Fax: (503) 364-0510
http://new.orbae.com

Pennsylvania Department of State
State Architects Licensure Board
P.O. Box 2649
Harrisburg, PA 17105-2649
(717) 783-3397
Fax: (717) 705-5540
www.dos.state.pa.us/bpoa/arcbd/
mainpage.htm

**Commonwealth of Puerto Rico
Department of State**
Board of Engineers, Architects, and Land
Surveyors
P.O. Box 9023271
San Juan, PR 00902-3271
(787) 722-4816
Fax: (787) 722-4818
www.estado.gobierno.pr

**State of Rhode Island Board of
Examination and Registration of
Architects**
Boards for Design Professionals
One Capitol Hill, 3rd Floor
Providence, RI 02908
(401) 222-2565
Fax: (401) 222-5744
www.bdp.state.ri.us

**South Carolina Department of Labor,
Licensing & Regulation**
Board of Architectural Examiners
P.O. Box 11419
Columbia, SC 29211-1419
(803) 896-4408
Fax: (803) 896-4410
www.llr.state.sc.us/POL/Architects

**South Dakota Board of Technical
Professions**
2040 W. Main Street, Suite 304
Rapid City, SD 57702-2447
(605) 394-2510
Fax: (605) 394-2509
www.state.sd.us/dol/boards/engineer

**Tennessee Division of Regulatory
Boards**
Architectural and Engineering Examiners
500 James Robertson Parkway
Nashville, TN 37243-1142
(615) 741-2241
Fax: (615) 532-9410
www.state.tn.us/commerce/boards/ae

Texas Board of Architectural Examiners
P.O. Box 12337
(333 Guadalupe, Suite 2-350)
Austin, TX 78711
(512) 305-9000
Fax: (512) 305-8900
www.tbae.state.tx.us

Utah Department of Commerce
Division of Occupational and
Professional Licensing
P.O. Box 146741
Salt Lake City, UT 84114-6741
(801) 530-6628
Fax: (801) 530-6511
www.dopl.utah.gov

Vermont State Board of Architects
26 Terrace Street, Drawer 09
Montpelier, VT 05609-1101
(802) 828-2363
Fax: (802) 828-2496
http://vtprofessionals.org/opr1/
architects

**Virgin Island Board of Architects,
Engineers, and Land Surveyors**
Department of Licensing and Consumer
Affairs
Golden Rock Shopping Center
Christiansted
St. Croix, VI 00820
(340) 773-2226
Fax: (340) 778-8250
www.dlca.gov.vi

**Virginia Board for Architects,
Professional Engineers, Land
Surveyors, Certified Interior
Designers, and Landscape Architects**
Department of Professional and
Occupational Regulation
3600 West Broad Street
Richmond, VA 23230-4917
(804) 367-8500
Fax: (804) 367-2475
www.dpor.virginia.gov/dporweb/
ape_main.cfm

Washington Department of Licensing
Board of Registration for Architects
P.O. Box 9045
Olympia, WA 98507-9045
(360) 664-1388
Fax: (360) 664-1495
www.dol.wa.gov/business/architects/
architectboard.html

West Virginia Board of Architects
P.O. Box 9125
Huntington, WV 25704-0125
(304) 528-5825
Fax: (304) 528-5826
www.wvbrdarch.org

**Wisconsin Bureau of Business
and Design Professions**
P.O. Box 8935
(1400 East Washington Avenue,
Room 173)
Madison, WI 53708-8935
(608) 266-2112
Fax: (608) 267-3816
http://drl.wi.gov/index.htm

**Wyoming Board of Architects and
Landscape Architects**
2020 Carey Avenue, Suite 201
Cheyenne, WY 82002
(307) 777-3628
Fax: (307) 777-3508
http://plboards.state.wy.us/architecture/
index.asp

Appendix E
GLOSSARY

This glossary includes general terms as well as those associated with legal, contractual, financial, and other business aspects of architecture practice.

Account: A tabular record of financial transactions related to a particular item or class of items; used to classify and record financial details of business transactions of the firm.

Account balance: The difference between the total debit entries and credit entries in a single account or class of accounts. If the debits exceed the credits, the balance is a debit balance; if the credits exceed the debits, the balance is a credit balance. When revenue and expense accounts are closed, the balance is brought to zero by equalizing debits and credits and transferring the excess to one of the balance sheet accounts.

Accounting period: The time that elapses between the preparation of financial statements.

Accounts payable: Money owed by the firm to vendors, consultants, or others for merchandise or services that have been provided to the firm on open account or short-term credit.

Accounts receivable: Money owed by clients to the firm for services rendered or for reimbursement of expenses. Accounts receivable are aged until they are collected or until it becomes apparent they will not be collectible, at which time they are written off.

Accrual accounting: A method of keeping accounting records in which revenue is recognized as having been earned when services are performed and expenses are recognized when incurred, without regard to when cash payments are received or made. See also *Cash accounting.*

Addendum (pl. addenda): A written or graphic instrument issued by the architect before execution of the construction contract that modifies or interprets the bidding documents by additions, deletions, clarifications, or corrections.

Additional services: Professional services that may, if authorized or confirmed in writing by the owner, be rendered by the architect in addition to the basic services identified in the owner-architect agreement.

Additive (or add) alternate: See *Alternate bid.*

Admonition: A private reprimand issued by a jurisdictional registration board (or other administrative agency) for violation of professional conduct rules in that jurisdiction, or by the AIA for violation of its Code of Ethics and Professional Conduct. See also *Censure.*

Advertisement for bids: Published public notice soliciting bids for a construction project or designated portion thereof, included as part of the bidding documents; most frequently used to conform to legal requirements pertaining to public projects and usually published in newspapers of general circulation in those political subdivisions from which the public funds are derived or in which the project is located.

Aged accounts receivable: Accounts receivable classified according to the length of time each invoice has been outstanding. The age analysis highlights which accounts are falling past due.

Agent: A person or entity who acts for or in place of another. See also *Attorney-in-fact.*

Agreement: (1) A meeting of minds; (2) legally enforceable obligations between two or several persons; (3) the document stating the terms of the contract between the parties, as between owner and architect, architect and consultants, or owner and contractor. Although "agreement" is a broader term, it is frequently used interchangeably with "contract" without any intended change in meaning. See also *Contract.*

Alliance: A specific and beneficial relationship between two or more entities to further the interests of those entities.

Allowance: See *Cash allowance, Contingency allowance.*

All-risk insurance: See *Causes of loss—special form.*

Alternate: A proposed possible change in the work described in the contract documents; provides the owner with an option to select between alternative materials, products, or systems or to add or delete portions of work.

Alternate bid: Amount stated in the bid to be added to or deducted from the amount of the base bid if the corresponding change in work, as described in the bidding documents, is accepted. An alternate bid resulting in an addition to the bidder's base bid is an additive (or "add") alternate, and an alternate bid resulting in a deduction from the base bid is a deductive ("deduct") alternate.

Alternative dispute resolution (ADR): A method of resolving disputes by means other than litigation, such as mediation, arbitration, mini-trial, or dispute review board.

Anti-indemnification statutes: Laws that invalidate contract clauses related to a party being indemnified or held harmless for damages or that limit the ways such contract clauses operate.

Antitrust: Laws to protect trade and commerce from unlawful restraints and monopolies or unfair business practices.

Application for payment: Contractor's certified request for payment for completed portions of the work and, if the contract so provides, for materials or equipment suitably stored pending their incorporation into the work.

Approved equal: Material, equipment, or method proposed by the contractor and approved by the architect for incorporation or use in the work as equivalent in essential attributes to the material, equipment, or method specified in the contract documents.

Arbitration: Method of dispute resolution in which an arbitrator or panel of arbitrators evaluates the merits of the positions of the respective parties and renders a decision.

Architect: Designation reserved, usually by law, for a person or organization professionally qualified and duly licensed to perform architecture services.

Architect of record: The architect licensed in the jurisdiction in which the project is located who prepares, seals, and signs the construction documents.

Architect-consultant agreement: Contract between an architect and another firm (e.g., engineer, specialist, another architect, or other consultant) for professional services.

As-built drawings: Drawings based on field measurements for an existing building. Generally, these drawings record only visible building elements. The level and detail of measurements included in the drawings will depend on how the drawings will be used. As-built drawings should not be confused with record drawings. See also *Record drawings*.

Asset: A resource owned by the firm, either tangible or intangible, on which a monetary value can be placed.

Associate (or associated) architect: An architect who has an arrangement with another architect to collaborate in the performance of services for a project or series of projects.

Attorney-in-fact: A person authorized to act for or on behalf of another person or entity to the extent usually prescribed in a written instrument known as a *power of attorney*.

Audit: A service performed by a certified public accountant attesting to the firm's statement of assets, liabilities, and capital, and the firm's financial transactions, during a fiscal period. The examination should be in enough detail to permit the auditor to state that the financial transactions are substantially correct and that they have been recorded following generally accepted accounting principles. The audit may also suggest improved or alternative procedures in accounting practices to increase efficiency, safeguard assets, or improve financial operations.

Average collection period: Accounts receivable divided by an average day's billings; the number of days on average between issuing an invoice and receiving payment.

Award: See *Contract award.*

Backlog: Dollar value of anticipated revenues from projects contracted but as yet unearned (i.e., the work is contracted but has not been performed). Backlog is reduced by the value of revenue earned and increased by the value of new commissions acquired in a period.

Bad debt: A debt owed to the firm that is uncollectible (e.g., losses on accounts receivable due to clients' failure to pay).

Balance sheet: A statement of the firm's financial condition as of a specific date. It is a statement of the balance between the assets accounts, on one hand, and the liabilities and net worth (owners' equity) accounts, on the other.

Bankruptcy: A state of insolvency in which the property of the debtor is placed under the control of a receiver or trustee in bankruptcy for the benefit of creditors.

Base bid: Amount of money stated in the bid as the sum for which the bidder offers to perform the work described in the bidding documents, exclusive of adjustments for alternate bids.

Basic services: The architect's services consisting of the phases described in the owner-architect agreement that are provided for basic compensation. AIA Document B101–2007, for example, includes a basic services package for schematic design, design development, construction documents, bidding or negotiation, and construction phase services. Distinguished from *additional services*.

Beneficial occupancy: Use of a project or portion thereof for the purpose intended.

Benefits, employee: Personnel benefits required by law (such as employment taxes and other statutory employee benefits) and by custom (such as insurance, sick leave, holidays, vacations, pensions, and similar contributions and benefits). Sometimes called "customary and mandatory benefits."

Best-value procurement: The evaluation and selection of construction and/or design services where total costs are considered along with other specialized qualification criteria.

Betterment: An improvement to a property that enhances its value more than mere replacement, maintenance, or repairs.

Bid: A complete and properly signed proposal, submitted in accordance with the bidding requirements, to perform the work or a designated portion thereof for the amount or amounts stipulated therein.

Bid bond: A form of bid security executed by the bidder as principal and by a surety to guarantee that the bidder will enter into a contract within a specified time and furnish any required bond. See also *Bid security*.

Bid date: See *Bid time*.

Bid form: A form prescribed by the bidding requirements to be completed, signed, and submitted as the bidder's bid.

Bid opening: The physical opening and tabulation of sealed bids following the time specified in the bidding requirements. This term is preferable to "bid letting."

Bid price: The amount stated in the bid.

Bid security: A deposit of cash, certified check, cashier's check, bank draft, stocks or bonds, money order, or bid bond submitted with a bid; provides that the bidder, if awarded the contract, will execute such contract in accordance with the requirements of the bidding documents.

Bid time: The date and hour established by the owner or the architect for the receipt of bids.

Bidder: A person or entity that submits a bid for a prime contract with the owner; in contrast to a sub-bidder, who submits a bid to a prime bidder.

Bidding documents: The documents required to bid or negotiate the construction contract, including the bidding requirements, contract forms, contract conditions, specifications, drawings, and addenda.

Bidding period: The calendar period beginning when bidding documents are issued and ending at the prescribed bid time.

Bidding requirements: Collectively, the advertisement or invitation to bid, instructions to bidders, sample forms, the bid form, and portions of addenda relating to bidding requirements.

Bill of quantities: See *Quantity survey*.

Bill of sale: A document executed by the seller or other transferor of property by which the transferor's ownership or other interest in the property is transferred to the buyer or other transferee.

Billable time: Time that is charged to projects (direct time) and is ultimately invoiced to the client. Time may be charged to projects but not be billable (i.e., the time is necessary to produce the services contracted but will not result in revenue).

Billing rate: The price per unit of time (hour, day, week) for staff (principal or employee) billed to a client for work under a contract for a project.

Bodily injury (insurance terminology): Physical injury, sickness, disease, or resulting death sustained by a person.

Bona fide bid: Bid submitted in good faith, complete, and in accordance with the bidding documents, and properly signed by a person legally authorized to sign such bid.

Bond: In suretyship, an obligation by which one party (surety or obligor) agrees to guarantee performance by another (principal) of a specified obligation for the benefit of a third person or entity (obligee). See also *Bid bond, Completion bond,* *Dual obligee bond, Fidelity bond, Payment bond, Performance bond, Statutory bond,* and *Supply bond*.

Bonus clause: A provision in the construction contract for additional payment to the contractor as a reward for completing the work prior to a stipulated date.

Book value: (1) The net amount at which an asset is carried on the books of the firm (e.g., a building would be carried at cost, plus improvements, minus depreciation); this may not resemble the market or intrinsic value of the item; (2) the owners' equity accounts, representing the net worth of the firm.

Bookkeeping: The procedures by which financial transactions are systematically analyzed, classified, and recorded in the firm's books of account.

Breach of contract: The failure, without legal justification, to fulfill an obligation required by contract. The breach of a contract can be intentional, inadvertent, or caused by the negligence of the party breaching the contract.

Breach of duty: A failure to perform an obligation created by law or by contract.

Break-even: (1) The point in dollars of revenue at which there is neither profit nor loss—that is, revenue equals fixed and variable costs; (2) in life cycle cost analysis, the point in time at which two mutually exclusive design alternatives have the same life cycle cost.

Break-even multiplier: The relevant factor by which an architect's direct personnel expense, or direct salary expense, is multiplied to determine compensation required to cover direct and indirect expenses—but not profit. See also *Multiplier*.

Brief: A written argument, usually prepared by a lawyer, setting forth facts, legal points, and authorities to persuade a court about the merits of or defenses against a claim.

Budget: The sum established as available for a given purpose. See also *Construction budget, Project budget,* and (for the architecture firm) *Internal project budget*.

Budgeting: (1) Forecasting future business activities of the firm, usually for fiscal periods or for specific projects in terms of revenues, expenses, and income (profit); (2) developing a plan for achieving future desired activities; (3) planning expenditures of time or money. These definitions can also be applied to budgeting construction or project costs or the firm's costs of providing professional services.

Builder's risk insurance: A specialized form of property insurance that provides coverage for loss or damage to the work during the course of construction.

Building code: See *Codes*.

Building information model: A digital three-dimensional representation of a building consisting of objects that simulate specific properties of actual building components.

Building information modeling (BIM): The use of virtual building information models to develop building design solutions and design documentation, and to analyze construction processes. See also *Building information model*.

Building inspector: See *Code enforcement official*.

Building permit: A permit issued by appropriate governmental authority allowing construction of a project in accordance with approved construction documents.

Burden: Another term for overhead or indirect expense. The efforts of the firm that directly produce revenue are "burdened" with or must carry the indirect expenses of the firm.

Burden of proof: The duty of a party to substantiate an allegation or issue in order to convince a trier of fact of the merits of the party's claim; necessary in order to prevail in a claim.

Business income coverage: Insurance protecting against financial loss during the time required to repair or replace property damaged or destroyed by an insured peril. (Also called loss-of-use coverage.)

Business plan: Plan that describes the strategic and tactical goals of a business entity. Strategic issues include mergers and acquisitions, geographic locations, research and development, market penetration, forecasts, new product introduction, and business integration. Tactical considerations include product and quantity information, head counts, subcontracting, logistics, and processes. Business plans form the basis for strategic facilities planning. See also *Strategic facilities plan*.

CAD (or CADD): See *Computer-aided design*.

Capital: (1) In the broadest sense, the value of total assets of the firm carried on the balance sheet; (2) in the narrowest sense, the net worth or value of owners' equity accounts; (3) typically, the firm's funding that is expected to be provided for periods beyond one year. Includes *equity and debt*.

Capital accounts: (1) In a partnership, the accounts showing each partner's equity in the firm as well as any transactions other than salary draws that they may have with the firm; (2) in a corporation, the accounts recording the shareholders' investment in the firm represented by three accounts: capital (common or preferred stock at par), paid-in capital (capital contributions in excess of the stated value, or par value, of the shares), and retained earnings.

Capital expenditure: An expense for fixed (long-term) assets such as land, buildings, furnishings, equipment, and automobiles.

Care, custody, or control (insurance terminology): A standard exclusion in liability insurance policies that provides that the liability insurance does not apply to damage to property over which the insured is for any purpose exercising physical control.

Cash accounting: A method of keeping accounting records in which revenue is not considered earned unless received in cash and expenses are not recognized unless disbursed in cash. See also *Accrual accounting*.

Cash allowance: An amount established in the contract documents for inclusion in the contract sum to cover the cost of prescribed items not specified in detail, with the provision that variations between such amount and the finally determined cost of the prescribed items will be reflected in change orders appropriately adjusting the contract sum.

Cash budget: A plan for cash that will be needed for future operations. Usually forecast monthly for several months ahead; the beginning cash balance, anticipated cash receipts, and anticipated cash disbursements are evaluated to determine timing and magnitude of cash surpluses and cash deficits.

Cash cycle: The use of cash to pay for salaries and other goods and services in delivering professional services (work in process), rendering to the client an invoice for the value of those services (accounts receivable), and collecting the invoice, which returns the value earned back into cash ready to be used again for payment of salaries, goods, and services.

Cash flow: The change in the firm's cash account during a given period. Positive cash flow (more cash received than disbursed) results in an increase in the cash account; conversely, negative cash flow decreases the cash account.

Cash flow statement: A statement prepared to analyze the sources and applications of a firm's cash during a given period.

Cash journals: The cash receipts journal and the cash disbursements journal. These are books of "original entry" because transactions are first recorded in them, in chronological order, as money is received or paid out.

Cash projection worksheet: A form on which cash at the beginning of a period is shown, together with estimated cash inflows and outflows during the period and the resulting cash balance at the end of the period.

Causes of loss—broad form: A method of writing a contract of insurance that specifies those perils that are covered. Sometimes referred to as "named perils insurance." See also *Causes of loss—special form*.

Causes of loss—special form: A form of insurance coverage that protects against losses arising from any cause other than specifically excluded perils; sometimes referred to as "all-risk insurance." See also *Causes of loss—broad form*.

Censure: A public reprimand issued by a jurisdictional registration board (or other administrative agency) for violation of professional conduct rules in that jurisdiction or by the AIA for violation of its Code of Ethics and Professional Conduct. See also *Admonition*.

Certificate for payment: A written statement from the architect to the owner confirming the amount of money due the contractor for work accomplished or materials and equipment suitably stored or both during a specified period.

Certificate of insurance: A document issued by an authorized representative of an insurance company stating the types, amounts, and effective dates of insurance for a designated insured.

Certificate of occupancy: Document issued by a governmental authority certifying that all or a designated portion of a building is approved for its designated use.

Certificate of substantial completion: A certificate prepared by the architect on the basis of an inspection (a) stating that the work or a designated portion thereof is substantially complete; (b) establishing the date of substantial completion; (c) stating the responsibilities of the owner and the contractor for security, maintenance, heat, utilities, damage to the work, and insurance; and (d) fixing the time within which the contractor shall complete the items listed therein.

Change order: An amendment to the construction contract signed by the owner, architect, and contractor authorizing a change in the work, an adjustment in the contract sum or the contract time, or both.

Change order request: A request by the contractor for implementing a change in the work that may change the contract sum, the contract period of performance, or both. See also *Proposal request.*

Charrette: The intense effort to complete an architectural project within a specified time or the time in which this work is done.

Chart of accounts: A list of accounts used by the firm in keeping its books, usually classified as assets, liabilities, owners' equity, revenue, and expense.

Civil action: A lawsuit in court seeking enforcement or protection of private rights.

Claim: A demand or assertion by a party to the contract who is seeking, as a matter of right, adjustment or interpretation of contract terms, payment of money, extension of time, or other relief with respect to the terms of the contract.

Claim expense: As defined in the insurance policy, the costs associated with the handling of a claim. This often includes defense attorney fees, investigation costs, and expert witnesses. The salaries of insurance company employees and direct expenses that they may incur in performing their duties are normally not included.

Claims-made policy: An insurance policy that provides coverage only (a) if the claim is first made during the term of the policy, and (b) if the services from which the claim arose were performed during the period specified by the policy.

Clarification drawing: A graphic interpretation of the drawings or other contract documents issued by the architect.

Clerk of the works: Variously used to refer to the owner's inspector or owner's site representative. The term is not in common use today.

Client: A person or entity being provided professional services by the architect. The client includes those who own or lease assets relevant to the services being provided and can include persons or entities that use, operate, and maintain those assets. In the contractual context, the term "owner" is used to signify the person or entity entering into the agreement with the architect of contractor. See also *Owner.*

Closed bidders list: See *Invited bidders.*

Closed specifications: Specifications stipulating the use of specific or proprietary products or processes without provision for substitution.

Code enforcement official: A representative of a governmental authority employed to inspect construction for compliance with applicable codes, regulations, ordinances, and permit requirements.

Codes: Government regulations, ordinances, or statutory requirements relating to building construction and occupancy, generally adopted and administered for the protection of public health, safety, and welfare.

Coinsurance: An insurance policy provision that requires the insured to carry insurance equal to a named percentage of the value of the property covered by the policy or suffer a penalty in the event of a loss. This penalty reduces the amount paid by the insurance company in direct proportion to the amount by which the property is underinsured.

Commercial general liability insurance: A broad form of liability insurance covering claims for bodily injury and property damage that combines, under one policy, coverage for business liability exposures (except those specifically excluded) and new and unknown hazards that may develop. Commercial general liability insurance automatically includes contractual liability coverage for certain types of contracts and personal injury coverage. Products liability, completed operations liability, and broader contractual liability coverage may be available on an optional basis. This policy may be written on either an occurrence form or a claims-made form. See also *Claims-made policy* and *Occurrence.*

Commissioning: A process for achieving, validating, and documenting that the performance of the completed building and its systems meet the design requirements. (Traditionally, "commissioning" has referred to the process by which the heating, ventilation, and air-conditioning systems of a building were tested and balanced according to established standards prior to acceptance by the building owner. However, the scope of commissioning is being broadened to encompass other systems.)

Comparative negligence: The proportional sharing of liability between a plaintiff and defendant for damages based on the percentage of negligence of each. Not all states allow a sharing of liability based on comparative negligence. See also *Contributory negligence*.

Compensation: (1) Payment for services rendered or products or materials furnished or delivered; (2) payment in satisfaction of claims for damages incurred; (3) salary, bonus, profit sharing, and other income received by a firm owner or employee.

Compensatory damages: Damages awarded to compensate a plaintiff for his or her injuries; includes direct out-of-pocket losses as well as compensation for pain and suffering.

Completed operations insurance: Liability insurance coverage for injuries to persons or damage to property occurring after an operation is completed (a) when all operations under the contract have been completed or abandoned, (b) when all operations at one project site are completed, or (c) when the portion of the work out of which the injury or damage arises has been put to its intended use by the person or organization for whom that portion of the work was done. Completed operations insurance does not apply to damage to the completed work itself.

Completion bond: Bond guaranteeing the lender that the project will be completed free of liens.

Completion date: See *Substantial completion*.

Computer-aided design (commonly abbreviated as CAD, or CADD for "computer-aided design and drafting"): A term applied to systems or techniques for design and drafting using integrated computer hardware and software systems to produce graphic images.

Conditions of the contract: Those portions of the contract documents that define the rights and responsibilities of the contracting parties and of others involved in the work. The conditions of the contract include general conditions, supplementary conditions, and other conditions.

Consent of surety: Written consent of the surety on a performance bond, payment bond, or both to changes in the contract, reductions in the contractor's retainage, transfer of final payment to the contractor, or waiver of notification of contract changes. The term is also used with respect to an extension of time in a bid bond.

Consequential loss: Loss not directly caused by damage to property but that may arise as a result of such damage (e.g., damage to other portions of a building or its contents due to roof leaks).

Construction budget: The sum established by the owner as available for construction of the project, including contingencies for bidding and for changes during construction. See also *Project budget*.

Construction change directive: A written order prepared by the architect and signed by the owner and architect that directs a change in the work and states a proposed basis for adjustment, if any, in the contract sum or contract time, or both.

Construction contract administration services: Services for the architect's general administration of the construction contract(s). This includes reviewing and certifying amounts due the contractor, approving the contractor's submittals, preparing change orders, making site visits to observe progress of the work, and conducting site inspections to determine dates of substantial completion and final completion.

Construction cost: As used for calculating the architect's compensation, or as a fixed limit in the owner-architect agreement, this is the total cost or estimated cost to the owner of all elements of the project designed or specified by the architect, including the cost at current market rates of labor and materials furnished by the owner and equipment specified, selected, designed, or specially provided for by the architect (plus a reasonable allowance for the contractor's overhead and profit). Construction cost also includes a reasonable allowance for contingencies for market conditions at the time of bidding and for changes in the work during construction; however, it doesn't include compensation of the architect and the architect's consultants or the costs of the land, rights-of-way, financing, or other costs that remain the responsibility of the owner.

Construction documents: Drawings and specifications prepared by the architect setting forth the requirements for the construction of the project.

Construction documents services: The architect's services in which the architect prepares the construction documents from the approved design development documents and assists the owner in the preparation of the bidding documents.

Construction management: Services provided to an owner to manage a project during the design phase, construction phase, or both. Such services may include advice on the time and cost consequences of design and construction decisions, scheduling, cost control, coordination of contract negotiations and awards, timely purchasing of critical materials and long-lead-time items, and coordination of construction activities.

Construction manager: An individual or entity that provides construction management services. This entity may remain as adviser (CMa) during construction or become the construction contractor (CMc).

Construction procurement services: Services in which the architect assists the owner in obtaining either competitive or negotiated proposals and assists the owner in awarding and preparing contracts for construction.

Consultant: A person or entity who provides advice or services.

Contingency allowance: A sum included in the construction budget and project budget to cover unpredictable or unforeseen items of work or changes in the work.

Contingent agreement: An agreement, generally between an owner and an architect, in which some portion of the architect's compensation is contingent upon some specially prescribed condition such as government approvals or the owner's success in obtaining funds for the project.

Contingent liability: Liability that is not absolute and fixed but dependent on the occurrence of some uncertain future event or the existence of an uncertain specified condition.

Contract: A legally enforceable agreement between two or several parties that creates an obligation to do or not to do a particular thing. It also refers to the document that describes the agreement of the parties with the terms and conditions, and which serves as evidence of the obligation. See also *Agreement*.

Contract award: A communication from an owner accepting a bid or negotiated proposal. An award creates legal obligations between parties.

Contract date: See *Date of agreement*.

Contract documents: The documents that form the legal agreement between the owner and the contractor. These include the agreement between owner and contractor; conditions of the contract (general, supplementary, and other conditions); drawings, specifications, and addenda issued prior to execution of the contract; other documents listed in the agreement; and modifications issued after execution of the contract.

Contract limit: (1) A limit line or perimeter line established on the drawings or elsewhere in the contract documents defining the physical boundaries of the site available to the contractor for construction; (2) a monetary limit established by contract.

Contract sum: The sum stated in the owner-contractor agreement that is the total amount payable by the owner to the contractor for the performance of the work under the contract documents.

Contract time: The period of time allotted in the contract documents for substantial completion of the work, including authorized adjustments thereto. If a number of days is specified, calendar or working days should be stipulated.

Contracting officer: The person designated as the official representative of the owner with specific authority to act on the owner's behalf in connection with a project.

Contractor: (1) One who enters into a contract; (2) in construction terminology, the person or entity responsible for performing the work under the contract for construction.

Contractor's affidavit: A certified statement of the contractor, properly notarized or otherwise subject to prosecution for perjury if false, relating to such items as payment of debts and claims, release of liens, or similar matters requiring specific evidence for the protection of the owner.

Contractor's design liability insurance: An insurance policy that covers contractors for claims alleging faulty design services, including design services performed by the contractor's in-house staff, by design firms hired as subcontractors, and by design firms in joint venture with the contractor.

Contractor's liability insurance: Insurance purchased and maintained by the contractor that insures the contractor for claims for property damage, bodily injury, or death.

Contractor's option: The provision of the contract documents under which the contractor may select certain specified materials, methods, or systems at the contractor's option without change in the contract sum.

Contractual liability: Liability assumed by a person or entity under a contract. Indemnification or hold-harmless clauses are examples of contractual liability.

Contribution: The extent to which revenues remaining after payment of direct expenses will offset the firm's indirect expenses and add to income (profit); may be expressed in dollars or as a percentage of revenue.

Contributory negligence: The plaintiff or claimant, by not exercising ordinary care, contributed to the injury; in some states, a plaintiff's contributory negligence will bar the plaintiff from recovering damages. See also *Comparative negligence*.

Copyright: Exclusive right to control the making of copies of a work of authorship, such as design plans or other architectural work, granted by federal statute to the author for a limited period of time.

Corporation: A legal entity organized under the laws of a particular jurisdiction. The entity has a legal identity separate from the stockholders, owners, managers, officers, directors, or employees of the enterprise. A corporation is "domestic" to the state of its incorporation and "foreign" to all other states.

Cost-based selection: The procurement of professional design services based solely on the cost for those services.

Cost-benefit analysis: An evaluation technique in which the total expected costs and the total expected benefits of one or more actions are compared in order to choose the most effective option.

Cost-plus-fee agreement: An agreement under which the contractor (in an agreement between owner and contractor) or the architect (in an agreement between owner and architect) is reimbursed for stipulated direct and indirect costs of performance of the agreement and, in addition, is paid a fee for services.

Counterclaim: An independent cause of action or demand made by a defendant against a plaintiff. This occurs when a defendant in a case files a claim against the plaintiff.

Covenant: A written, signed agreement between two or more parties pledging that something is done, shall be done, or shall not be done (e.g., a covenant not to sue).

Credit: (1) The right-hand entry of a double-entry bookkeeping system—abbreviated CR and distinguished from a debit; (2) the firm's reputation for solvency (ability to pay debts in a timely fashion), which enables the firm to purchase goods and services with time allowed for payment.

Critical path method (CPM): A scheduling method in which all events expected to occur and operations to be performed in completing a given process are rendered in a form permitting determination of the optimum sequence and duration of each operation.

Current assets: Cash or assets that are readily convertible into cash, usually within one year; examples include cash, accounts receivable, notes receivable, work in process, or unbilled revenue and short-term prepaid expenses. See also *Fixed assets.*

Current liability: See *Liabilities.*

Current ratio: Current assets divided by current liabilities; regarded as a measure of liquidity.

Customary and mandatory benefits: See *Benefits, employee.*

Daily billing rate: A rate established for billing for services of identified personnel on a per day basis.

Damages: The amount claimed or allowed as compensation for injuries sustained or property damaged through the wrongful acts, negligence, or breach of contract of another.

Date of agreement: The date an agreement is made or when it is effective. If not stated in the agreement, it is the date on which the agreement is signed by the last person or entity.

Date of commencement of the work: The date established in a notice to the contractor to proceed or, in the absence of such notice, the date of the contract for construction or such other date as may be established therein.

Date of substantial completion: See *Substantial completion.*

Debit: The left-hand entry of a double-entry bookkeeping system—abbreviated DR and distinguished from a credit. Debit entries decrease assets and increase liabilities and owner's equity. For every debit, there must be a corresponding credit or series of credits totaling the same amount.

Debt: An obligation of one party to pay money, goods, or services to another party as the result of some prior agreement. In an architecture firm, debt usually consists of

short-term debt (due within a year) and long-term debt (notes and mortgages).

Declaratory judgment: The order of a court that establishes the rights of parties on a question of law or on a contract.

Deductive (or deduct) alternate: See *Alternate bid.*

Default: Substantive failure to fulfill a material obligation under a contract.

Defective work: See *Nonconforming work.*

Deferred revenue: The value of revenue that has been billed but not yet earned.

Demurrage: A charge for time exceeding that allowed for loading, unloading, or removing goods shipped or delivered from a railroad car or similar vehicle or location.

Deposit for bidding documents: Monetary deposit required to obtain a set of bidding documents.

Deposition: Pretrial testimony in the form of oral questions and answers by a party or witness. Depositions are taken under oath and may be used during a trial or arbitration proceeding.

Depreciation: The reduction in value of a long-term (fixed) asset that occurs over a stated period of time known as the "useful life" of the asset, after which the asset retains only a salvage value. This reduction in value may result from lapse of time, obsolescence, deterioration, wear, or consumption and is recorded periodically as an expense to the firm. The amount of depreciation that may be taken as a deduction for tax purposes may have no relation to any actual decrease in value or usefulness; consequently, depreciation rates vary depending on whether they are being used for income tax purposes, other types of taxes, or management in planning capital expenditures or establishing credit.

Design development documents: Drawings and other documentation that fix and describe the size and character of the entire project with respect to architectural, structural, mechanical, and electrical systems; materials; and other elements as may be appropriate.

Design development services: Services in which the architect prepares the design development documents from the approved schematic design studies, for submission to the owner for the owner's approval.

Design-build: A method of project delivery in which the owner contracts directly with a single entity that is responsible for both design and construction services for a construction project.

Detail: A drawing, explanatory of another drawing, indicating in detail and at a larger scale the design, location, composition, and correlation of elements and materials.

Detailed estimate of construction cost: A forecast of construction cost prepared on the basis of a detailed analysis of materials and labor for all items of work, as distinguished from a preliminary estimate of construction cost based on current area, volume, or similar conceptual estimating techniques.

Direct expense: All items of expense directly incurred for or specifically attributable to a particular project, assignment, or task.

Direct personnel expense (DPE): Direct salaries of all the architect's personnel engaged on the project and the portion of the cost of their employee benefits related thereto.

Direct salary expense (DSE): Direct salaries of all the architect's personnel engaged on the project, excluding the cost of fringe benefits (payroll burden).

Discovery: The process by which parties or witnesses in a lawsuit are required before trial to disclose evidence that they possess in relation to issues in the lawsuit.

Dividend: In an ongoing corporation, a payment to shareholders out of net income (profits). Payment is in proportion to the number of shares held and is usually made either in cash or in stock.

Double-entry bookkeeping: A system of keeping books of an account in which there are always two entries, a debit and a credit, for every transaction.

DPE factor: See *Indirect expense factor.*

Draw: (1) The amount of cash that a proprietor or partner withdraws from the business. It can be considered the amount the proprietor or partner should earn for personal professional services to the firm on a weekly, semimonthly, or monthly basis. There may be an "added" draw made at the end of a fiscal period to distribute the balance of income (profits) earned by the business during the year; (2) a partial distribution of a construction loan to the borrower.

Drawings: Graphic and pictorial documents depicting the design, location, and dimensions of the elements of a project. Drawings generally include plans, elevations, sections, details, schedules, and diagrams. When the term is capitalized, it refers to the graphic and pictorial portions of the contract documents.

DSE factor: See *Indirect expense factor.*

Dual obligee bond: A bond in which two obligees are identified, either of whom may enforce the bonded obligation. An example is a performance bond furnished by a contractor in which the entity providing the financing is named as an obligee along with the owner.

Duty: An obligation imposed by law or by contract.

Earned revenue: Revenue for which services have been rendered by the architect and for which payment from the client may be rightfully claimed. Earned revenue may be unbilled, billed but uncollected, or billed and collected.

Earned surplus: Retained earnings, accumulated earnings, or retained income (profit) in a corporate accounting system;

part of the shareholders' equity, together with capital stock and paid-in capital.

Earnings per share: Net income (earnings) divided by the number of shares outstanding.

Easement: A legally created restriction on the unlimited use of all or part of one's land.

Employers' liability insurance: Insurance protection purchased by an employer to cover the employer against claims arising out of bodily injury to an employee who is not covered by a workers' compensation statute. This is usually provided on the same policy form as the employer's workers' compensation insurance.

Endorsement: A written amendment (sometimes called a "rider") that affects the declarations, insuring agreements, exclusions, or conditions of an insurance policy.

Entity: A person, partnership, corporation, estate, trustee, government unit, or other organization.

Environmental design professions: The professions collectively responsible for the design of the human physical environment, including architecture, urban planning, and similar environment-related professions.

Equity: Value of the firm's assets in excess of its liabilities; the total claims the owners would have to the value of the business if all assets were liquidated at the values shown on the balance sheet and all liabilities were paid as reflected on the balance sheet.

Equity capital: That portion of funding of the business supplied by the proprietor, partners, or shareholders; the balance of funds needed is borrowed and is furnished by creditors.

Erratum (pl. errata): Correction of a printing, typographical, or editorial error.

Errors and omissions insurance: See *Professional liability insurance.*

Estimate of construction cost: A forecast of construction cost. See also *Detailed estimate of construction cost.*

Estoppel: A legal bar that prevents a person from asserting a legal position because of his or her own conduct or for some other reason created by operation of law.

Ethics: See *Professional ethics.*

Excess liability insurance: A separate insurance policy that provides higher limits of liability than the coverage provided by a scheduled list of underlying insurance policies. The terms of the excess liability insurance are never broader than the underlying policy.

Exclusions: A list in an insurance policy or bond of losses, hazards, or circumstances not included within the scope of coverage of the policy or bond.

Execution of the contract (or agreement): (1) Performance of a contract or agreement according to its terms; (2) the acts of signing and delivering (to the parties) the document or documents constituting the contract or agreement.

Expenditure: A commitment by the firm to incur a cost on behalf of the firm. Capital expenditures result in the cost being capitalized—established as an asset. Expenditures that are not to be capitalized become expenses in the period in which they generate revenue.

Expense: (1) As a noun: in cash accounting, actual cash disbursements made for goods or services that do not result in the acquisition of an asset, distribution of profit, or reduction of a liability. In accrual accounting, expenses may be recognized when they are incurred without regard to the date of payment; (2) as a verb: to transfer an amount previously regarded as an asset (e.g., an account receivable) to an expense account or to the profit-and-loss account. The amount is said to be "expensed."

Expense-only claim: A claim that results only in claim expenses being incurred by the insurance company; no indemnity payment is made.

Expert witness: A witness who, by virtue of experience, training, skill, or knowledge of a particular field or subject, is recognized as qualified to render an informed opinion on matters relating to that field or subject.

Exposure: Estimate of the probability of loss from some hazard, contingency, or circumstance; also used to signify the estimate of an insurer's liability under a policy from any one loss or accident or group or class thereof.

Express warranty: An explicit affirmation of fact or promise. Any description of materials or equipment, or a sample or model, furnished by or agreed to by the warrantor can create an express warranty.

Extended coverage insurance: Property insurance that extends the perils covered beyond basic causes such as fire and lightning to include windstorm, hail, riot, civil commotion, explosion (except steam boiler), aircraft, vehicles, and smoke.

Extended reporting period: The time period beyond the expiration of the original policy term during which an insured may report claims from acts that occur within the original policy term and thereby obtain coverage for such claims.

Extra: A term sometimes used to denote an item of work involving additional cost.

Facility life cycle: The series of stages or increments through which a building facility passes during its lifetime. Stages can be structured in various ways. One example includes planning, entitlement, design, construction, move-in, use and operation, and disposal.

Facility planning: Planning for the long-term use of a building or buildings, which may include furnishings, equipment, operations, maintenance, renovation, expansion, and life cycle planning.

Faithful performance: Performance of contractual duties with reasonable skill and diligence.

Fast track: A process in which certain portions of the architect's design services overlap with construction activities in order to expedite the owner's occupancy of all or a portion of the project.

Feasibility study: A detailed investigation and analysis conducted to determine the financial, economic, technical, or other advisability of a proposed project.

Fee: A term used to denote the amount of compensation to be paid to a person who provides a specific service; sometimes used to denote compensation of any kind for services rendered. The fee may be the entire compensation or a portion thereof.

Fidelity bond: A surety bond that reimburses an obligee named in the bond for loss sustained by reason of the dishonest acts of an individual or entity covered by the conditions of the bond.

Final acceptance: The owner's acceptance of the work from the contractor upon final completion. The owner may sometimes accept a portion of the completed work.

Final completion: Term denoting that the work has been completed in accordance with the terms and conditions of the contract documents.

Final inspection: Final review of the construction by the architect to determine whether final completion has been achieved; performed prior to issuance of the final certificate for payment.

Final payment: Payment made by the owner to the contractor, upon issuance by the architect of the final certificate for payment, of the entire unpaid balance of the contract sum as adjusted by change orders.

Fiscal year: Any period of twelve consecutive months that is used as the basis for budgeting or for reporting financial activity. The period may coincide with the calendar year or it may begin on any day of the year and close on the last day of the succeeding twelve-month period.

Fixed assets: Assets of a tangible, physical, and relatively permanent nature (such as furniture, equipment, buildings, and automobiles) that are used in the operation of a business and that will not be consumed within one year. See also *Current assets*.

Fixed fee: Compensation for professional services or construction services on a lump-sum basis, not affected by project scope or other variables except as may be specifically designated.

Fixed limit of construction cost: The maximum construction cost established in the agreement between the owner and the architect.

Force account: Term used when work is ordered, often under urgent circumstances, to be performed by the contractor without prior agreement as to lump-sum or unit-price cost thereof and is to be billed at the cost of labor, material, and equipment, insurance, taxes, and so on, plus an agreed percentage for overhead and profit; sometimes used to describe work performed by the owner's own forces in a similar manner.

Fringe benefits: Benefits paid for by an employer on behalf of an employee in addition to direct compensation; frequently includes health care, retirement, and disability insurance.

Frivolous suit: A suit that is so totally without merit on its face as to show bad faith or other improper motive on the part of the plaintiff.

General conditions (of the contract for construction): That part of the contract documents that sets forth many of the rights, responsibilities, and relationships of the parties, particularly those provisions that are common to many construction projects.

General contract: (1) The contract between the owner and the contractor for construction of the entire work, which can be accomplished by the contractor with its own forces and through subcontractors; (2) under multiple prime contracting, a contract between the owner and a contractor for general construction that includes architectural and structural work.

General journal: In accounting, a book of original entry. Adjusting and closing entries and transactions that are not recorded in the cash journals or payroll journal are first recorded here.

General ledger: A book of accounts used in complete accounting systems. It is a book of "final entry," containing a summary of all transactions in separate accounts.

General requirements: Title of Division 01 of the specifications when MasterFormat is used.

Geotechnical investigation (or subsurface investigation): The boring and sampling process, together with associated laboratory tests, necessary to establish subsurface profiles and the relative strengths, compressibility, and other characteristics of the various strata encountered within depths likely to have an influence on the design of the building.

Goodwill: An asset, representing the excess of the value paid or to be paid for a firm over and above its net worth. It usually arises when a firm or an interest in a firm is purchased by a second firm for more than its book value. Goodwill is carried on the books of the purchasing firm as an asset, and its impairment value written off each year. Goodwill cannot be amortized for tax purposes.

Gross income from projects: Revenue remaining after direct (project) expenses are subtracted from project revenues.

Gross negligence: Failure to use even the slightest amount of care in a way that shows recklessness or willful disregard for the safety of others.

Guarantee: See *Warranty*.

Guaranteed maximum price (GMP): A sum established in an agreement between owner and contractor as the maximum compensation to be paid by the owner to the contractor for performing specified work on the basis of the cost of labor and materials plus overhead expenses and profit.

Hold harmless: See *Indemnification*.

Hourly billing rate: A rate established for billing for services of identified personnel on a per-hour basis.

Implied warranty: An affirmation of fact or promise imposed on a party by law, even without an express warranty, as a result of that party's relationship with another. See also *Express warranty*.

Incentive clause: A term used to describe savings that are shared proportionally in an agreed manner between an owner and a contractor and that are derived from the difference between the guaranteed maximum price and the actual cost of a project when the work is performed on the basis of cost plus a fee with a guaranteed maximum price. The terms of an incentive clause are normally included in the agreement between the owner and the contractor.

Income: Profits remaining after expenses have been subtracted from revenues.

Income statement: The basic operating financial statement showing the activity of the firm for the accounting period specified; shows revenues, expenses, and the resulting income (profit). Also called "profit-and-loss statement" or "revenue-and-expense statement."

Indemnification: A contractual obligation by which one person or entity agrees to reimburse another for loss or damage arising from specified liabilities.

Indemnification, implied: An indemnification that is implied by common law or statute rather than arising out of an express contract to provide indemnification.

Indemnify: To protect another against loss or damage or to promise compensation for loss or damage. The duty to indemnify may be created by rule of common law, by statute, or by contract. The party who is to be indemnified from loss or damage is the indemnitee; the party providing the indemnification is the indemnitor.

Indemnity payment: A payment to a third party by an insurance company and/or the insured in satisfaction of a claim made against the insured.

Indirect expense: An expense indirectly incurred and not directly related to a specific project. Also called "overhead expense."

Indirect expense allocation: The process of allocating or prorating to projects on some consistent basis the indirect expenses of the firm.

Indirect expense factor: The ratio of all indirect expenses to either direct salary expense (DSE) or direct personnel expense (DPE), depending on how the firm applies the expense of benefits in project accounting. The ratio can be expressed either as a percentage of DSE or DPE (e.g., 250 percent) or as a multiple of DSE or DPE (e.g., 2.50).

Initial decision maker: A person not a party to the agreement between the owner and the contractor who will render initial decisions on claims. (The appointment of the initial decision maker is optional in A201–2007, General Conditions of the Contract for Construction.)

Insolvency: Inability of the firm to meet (pay) financial obligations as they come due. The firm may have assets that exceed the value of its liabilities but be temporarily unable to meet maturing obligations because its assets cannot be easily converted into cash; or the firm may have liabilities greater than its assets, which may lead to bankruptcy.

Inspection: (1) The architect's examination of the work completed or in progress to determine its conformance with the requirements of the contract documents (distinguished from the more general observations made by the architect from time to time on visits to the site during the progress of the work); (2) examination of the work by a public official, owner's representative, or others.

Inspection list: A list of items of work to be completed or corrected by the contractor after substantial completion; sometimes referred to as a "punch list."

Instructions to bidders: Instructions contained in the bidding documents for preparing and submitting bids for a construction project or designated portion thereof.

Instruments of service: Drawings, specifications, and other documents prepared by the architect as part of providing services under the owner-architect agreement. Instruments of service may be in any medium, including electronic, and may encompass sketches, preliminary drawings, outline specifications, calculations, studies, analyses, models, and renderings.

Insurable interest: An insured party's interest in property or relation thereto of such nature that damage to the property will cause pecuniary loss to the insured. If an insured party does not have an insurable interest, the insurance agreement may be treated as an unlawful gambling transaction contrary to public policy.

Insured: The party under a liability policy to whom or on whose behalf benefits are payable.

Integrated practice: An approach to the planning, design, and construction of buildings that leverages early contributions of the expertise of all team participants in an environment of true collaboration and open information sharing. Building information modeling tools and technologies enable the realization of the greatest benefits of integrated practice. See also *Building information model* and *Building information modeling*.

Interest: An amount of money paid for the use of capital, usually expressed as a rate (a percentage). Simple interest is calculated on the principal amount borrowed; compound interest is calculated on the principal amount plus interest added from prior periods.

Intern: An individual in the process of satisfying a registration board's training requirements; includes graduates from recognized architecture programs, architecture students who acquire acceptable training prior to graduation, and other qualified individuals identified by a registration board.

Internal project budget: Resources allocated by a design firm for performance of its obligations with respect to a particular project.

Interoperability: The ability for software applications to exchange information directly through open industry standards. This capability supports effective collaboration between project participants.

Interrogatories: A set or series of formal written questions used to obtain information from a party before trial; a series of written questions exchanged between parties to a lawsuit, which must be answered under oath.

Investment credit: Federal tax legislation allowing businesses a specified percentage of new capital expenditures as credits against tax liabilities. The IRS defines rules for the percentages, applicability to various expenditures, and recapture in the event of early disposal of the asset before the end of its assumed useful life.

Invitation to bid: A portion of the bidding documents soliciting bids for a construction project.

Invited bidders: The bidders selected by the owner after review of their qualifications as the only persons or entities from whom bids will be received.

Invoice: A bill, usually itemized, received or sent for goods or services.

Job captain: A term frequently used for an individual within the architect's office responsible for preparation of the construction documents.

Job site: See *Site*.

Joinder: Uniting two or more elements into one, such as the joinder of parties as coplaintiffs or codefendants in a suit or as parties to an arbitration.

Joint and several liability: A legal concept under which defendants can be held both collectively and individually liable for all damages, regardless of their degree of fault.

Joint venture: A business relationship consisting of two or more persons or entities that has legal characteristics similar to those of a partnership.

Journal: Any book of original entry in accounting. A journal records financial transactions in the order in which they occur day to day. Periodically, the journal entries, which were entered randomly with regard to the accounts involved, are "posted" to the ledger. See also *Cash journals* and *Payroll journal*.

Judgment: The final decision of a court with respect to the rights of the parties in a suit. A summary judgment is a decision of a court before the actual trial, made in suits in which there are no disputes about material issues of fact.

Jury: (1) A committee for evaluating design work and, in connection with a design competition, for designating awards; (2) a panel convened by a court and sworn to give a verdict in a civil or criminal matter.

Labor and material payment bond: See *Payment bond.*

Latent defect: A defect in materials, equipment, or completed work that reasonably careful observation would not detect; distinguished from a patent defect, which would ordinarily be detected by reasonably careful observation.

Legal liability: An obligation that arises out of contract or by operation of law.

Letter form of agreement (or letter agreement): A letter stating all material terms of an agreement between addressor and addressee. When countersigned without change by the addressee the letter becomes a contract.

Letter of intent: A letter signifying an intention to enter into a formal agreement, usually setting forth the material terms of the proposed agreement.

Liabilities: Debts or obligations of the firm owed to others. They may be subdivided as current liabilities (due within one year) and long-term liabilities (due beyond one year). See also *Contingent liability.*

Liability insurance: A contract under which an insurance company agrees to protect a person or entity against claims arising from a real or alleged failure to fulfill an obligation or duty to a third party who is an incidental beneficiary. See also *Commercial general liability insurance; Completed operations insurance; Contractor's liability insurance; Employer's liability insurance; Owner's liability insurance; Professional liability insurance; Property damage insurance; Public liability insurance;* and *Special hazards insurance.*

Licensed architect: See *Architect.*

Licensed contractor: A person or entity authorized by governmental authority to engage in construction contracting for others.

Licensed engineer: See *Professional engineer.*

Lien: See *Mechanic's lien.*

Life cycle cost: The capital and operational cost of a construction item or system during the estimated useful life of the building.

Limit of liability: The maximum amount an insurance company is obligated to pay in case of loss.

Limitation of liability: Monetary limit of the legal liability of a person or entity to another based on an agreement or established by statute.

Line of credit: An agreement between a bank and a firm whereby the bank agrees to lend the firm funds up to a maximum amount. The firm may borrow, as needed, as much as it requires up to the maximum and pays interest only on the amount borrowed and outstanding.

Liquid assets: Items that have a readily ascertainable market value and can be relatively easily converted to cash without significant loss of value. Items such as cash, notes receivable, marketable securities, and certificates of deposit are typical liquid assets.

Liquidated damages: A sum established in a construction contract, usually as a fixed sum per day, as the predetermined measure of damages to be paid to the owner because of the contractor's failure to complete the work within a stipulated time; not enforceable as a penalty.

Liquidity: The ability to convert an asset into cash with relative speed and ease and without significant loss in value.

Long-term: Beyond one year (e.g., long-term liabilities are those liabilities or portions of liabilities that will come due beyond twelve months of the date of the statement).

Loss: Excess of expense over revenues during an accounting period.

Loss of use insurance: See *Business income coverage.*

Low bid: Bid stating the lowest price proposed by two or more bidders for performance of the work, including selected alternates, if any.

Lowest responsible bidder: Bidder who submits the lowest bona fide bid and is considered by the owner and the architect to be fully responsible and qualified to perform the work for which the bid is submitted.

Lowest responsive bid: The lowest bid that is responsive to and complies with the requirements of the bidding documents.

Lump-sum agreement: See *Stipulated sum agreement.*

Malpractice: Breach of a professional duty by one rendering professional services, where the breach is the proximate cause of injury, loss, or damage to another.

Margin: The degree of difference; in financial reporting, the profit margin is the difference between revenues and expenses. ("Margin" has a different meaning in the commodities and securities markets.)

MasterFormat™: A system for classifying building products and systems by materials and trades (e.g., concrete, masonry, thermal and moisture protection, etc.). See also *UniFormat.*

Mechanic's lien: A claim on real property, to be satisfied by sale of that property, created by statute in favor of a person supplying labor, materials, or services for nongovernmental improvements to that property for the value of labor, materials, or services supplied by the claimant. In some jurisdictions, an architect or engineer may be entitled to assert a mechanic's lien. Clear title to the property cannot be obtained until the claim is settled.

Mediation: Effort by an independent party to help others reach settlement of a controversy or claim. The mediator participates impartially in the proceedings, advising and consulting the various parties involved. A mediator cannot impose a settlement but can seek to guide the parties to achieve their own settlement voluntarily.

Memorandum of insurance: See *Certificate of insurance*.

Merger: The combination of two businesses in which one company survives and the other loses all or part of its identity. ("Consolidation" is the complete fusion of two companies to form one entirely new company. "Acquisition" is a general term used to indicate the combining of one business enterprise with another.)

Minor changes in the work: Changes in the construction work that do not involve an adjustment in the contract sum or an extension of the contract time and that are not inconsistent with the intent of the contract documents. Minor changes are effected by written order issued by the architect.

Modification (to the contract documents): (1) A written amendment to the contract signed by both parties; (2) a change order; (3) a construction change directive; (4) a written order for a minor change in the work issued by the architect.

Mortgage: A pledge of property to a creditor as security against a loan; the contract specifying the terms of the pledge to repay the loan. The lender or creditor of a note or loan secured by a mortgage is the mortgagee; the one who borrows on a note or loan secured with a mortgage is the mortgagor.

Moving average: A series of averages, each of which excludes the first unit of the preceding average and includes the next unit in the series. Used by some financial managers in calculating statistics or ratios such as average collection period.

Multiple of direct personnel expense (or DPE multiple): A method of compensation for professional services based on direct personnel expense multiplied by an agreed DPE factor to cover indirect expenses, other direct expense, and profit.

Multiple of direct salary expense (or DSE multiple): A method of compensation for professional services based on direct salary expense multiplied by an agreed DSE factor to cover the cost of payroll burden related to direct salary expense, indirect expenses, other direct expense, and profit.

Multiple prime contracts: Two or more separate owner-contractor contracts for work on a construction project (e.g., separate prime contracts might be for site work, general construction, mechanical, plumbing, electrical, etc.). See also *Prime contract*.

Multiplier: The relevant factor by which an architect's direct personnel expense, direct salary expense, or reimbursable expense is multiplied to determine compensation for professional services. See also *Break-even multiplier*.

Named insured: Any person or entity specifically designated for coverage by name in an insurance policy, as distinguished from others who, although unnamed, may be afforded coverage under some circumstances.

Negligence: Failure to exercise due care under the circumstances. Legal liability is imposed on a person or entity that is negligent when such negligence causes damage to some other person to whom the negligent actor owes a duty recognized by law.

Negligence per se: An act or omission regarded as negligence without argument or proof because it violates a standard of care defined by statute or is obviously contrary to common prudence.

Negligent act or omission: In law, an act or omission involving a failure to exercise due care.

Net: (1) As a noun, the amount remaining after some or all specified deductions. Net income is the income (profit) remaining after all expenses are deducted from revenue; value of an asset net of depreciation means the cost of the asset less the amount reserved for depreciation; (2) as a verb, to subtract one value from another to arrive at the net figure.

Net working capital: Current assets less current liabilities (this definition is used by some financial managers as "working capital").

Net worth: The value of the owners' equity (investment) in the firm—basically, book value (assets minus liabilities); in a proprietorship, the proprietor's capital account; in a partnership, the total of the partners' capital accounts; in a corporation, the total of capital stock (par value paid) plus paid-in capital (capital contributed in excess of par value) plus retained earnings.

Non-collusion affidavit: Statement by a bidder under oath that the bid was prepared without collusion of any kind.

Nonconforming work: Work that does not fulfill the requirements of the contract documents. Sometimes called "defective work."

Non-expense items: Expenditures affecting only the assets, liabilities, or net worth of the firm, including all those that cannot be charged to a reimbursable, direct, or indirect expense account. Most often these expenditures are for the purchase of a capital asset.

Notice to bidders: A notice informing prospective bidders of the opportunity to submit bids on a project and setting forth the procedures for doing so.

Notice to proceed: Written communication that may be issued by the owner to the contractor authorizing the contractor to proceed with the work and establishing the date for commencement of the work.

Observation of the work: That part of the architect's contract administration services in which the architect visits the site to become generally familiar with the progress and quality of the work completed to determine, in general, if the work observed is being performed in a manner indicating it will be in accordance with the contract documents when fully completed.

Occupancy permit: See *Certificate of occupancy.*

Occupational accident: Accident occurring in the course of one's employment and caused by inherent or related hazards.

Occurrence (insurance terminology): An accident (an unexpected and unintended event, identifiable as to time and place, resulting in bodily injury or property damage) or a continuous or repeated exposure to conditions that result in injury or damage.

Occurrence policy: An insurance policy that covers acts or omissions occurring during the policy term, regardless of when a claim against the insured is first asserted, even if the policy is no longer in existence; usually relates to general liability insurance. See also *Claims-made policy.*

Open bidding: Method of soliciting bids in which a public notice inviting bids is published and bids are accepted from all who submit them; most frequently used to conform to legal requirements pertaining to public projects and usually published in newspapers of general circulation in those political subdivisions from which the public funds are derived or where the project is located. See also *Invited bidders.*

Opening of bids: See *Bid opening.*

Or equal: See *Approved equal.*

Organizational expense: Expenses incurred in organizing a corporation (e.g., attorney's and accountant's fees, incorporation taxes and fees, printing of stock certificates). These expenses are accounted for as intangible assets and are amortized over a period of years because it is generally felt that benefits of the expenses are felt over several years.

Other conditions (of the contract for construction): See *Special conditions.*

Outline specifications: An abbreviated set of specification requirements normally included with schematic design or design development documents.

Outstanding stock: The total shares of a corporation fully paid for and held by shareholders.

Overhead expense: See *Indirect expense.*

Owner: A person or entity who retains services for building design and contracts for construction or acquisition of furniture, furnishings, and equipment; so called because this person or entity typically owns or is the lessee of the site or building premises.

Owner-architect agreement: A document that sets forth the contract between owner and architect for professional services.

Owner-contractor agreement: A document that sets forth the contract between owner and contractor for performance of the work for construction of the project or portion thereof.

Owner's and contractor's protective liability coverage: Third-party legal liability insurance coverage protecting a contractor or owner from claims arising from the construction process.

Owner's liability insurance: Insurance to protect the owner against claims arising from its ownership of property. See also *Commercial general liability insurance* and *Owner's and contractor's protective liability coverage.*

Owner's representative: The person designated as the official representative of the owner in connection with a project.

Paid-in capital: One of the owner's equity accounts, in a corporation, representing the amount of capital contributed by shareholders in excess of the stated par value. Also known as capital surplus.

Par value: The minimum dollar value that must be paid for capital stock issued by a corporation. The amount is fixed at the time of incorporation and remains the same regardless of the trading price of the stock. There is no necessary relation between the par value and the real value of the stock.

Parti: A scheme or concept for the design of a building.

Partial occupancy: Occupancy by the owner of a portion of a building facility or facilities prior to completion of the entire facility.

Partnership: An association in which two or more persons or entities conduct an enterprise as co-owners.

Patent defect: A defect in materials, equipment, or completed work that reasonably careful observation could have discovered. See also *Latent defect.*

Payment bond: A bond in which the contractor and the contractor's surety guarantee to the owner that the contractor will pay for labor and materials furnished for use in the performance of the contract. Persons entitled to the benefits of the bond are defined as claimants in the bond. A payment bond is sometimes referred to as a "labor and material payment bond."

Payment request: See *Application for payment.*

Payroll journal: A book of "original entry" similar to cash journals, used to record the details of the firm's payroll expenses.

Payroll taxes: Taxes, such as Social Security taxes, that are based on the payroll.

Payroll utilization: See *Utilization ratio.*

Penal sum: The amount named in a bond as the pecuniary limit of liability to be paid by a signatory thereto in the event the obligations are not performed.

Pension plan: A plan established and maintained by an employer for the benefit of the firm's employees by which contributions are systematically accumulated based on actuarial assumptions and invested during the employment of personnel; pension benefits are payable to its member employees over a period of years after retirement. Funding of a pension plan is not discretionary based on profits, as are profit-sharing plans. Pension plans are subject to regulatory control.

Percentage fee: Compensation based on a percentage of construction cost; applicable to either construction contracts or professional service agreements.

Performance: To carry out the obligations and duties set forth in a contract.

Performance bond: A bond in which the contractor and the contractor's surety guarantee to the owner that the work will be performed in accordance with the contract documents.

Permit: See *Building permit, Certificate of occupancy,* and *Zoning permit.*

Personal injury: Physical or mental injury to a human being.

Personal injury liability coverage: Personal injury insurance includes coverage for injuries or damage to others caused by specified actions of the insured, such as false arrest, malicious prosecution, willful detention or imprisonment, libel, slander, defamation of character, wrongful eviction, invasion of privacy, or wrongful entry. Occasionally the term "personal injury" will include bodily injury by definition in an insurance policy.

Petty cash: An amount of cash on hand for disbursements that are too small to justify the use of checks.

Phase (of professional services): An increment or stage of project development established by the architect for professional services.

Plan deposit: See *Deposit for bidding documents.*

Postoccupancy evaluation: An evaluation by an architect of the performance of a building. Application varies widely in scope, as an evaluation may take place at any time after the building is occupied and may address one or more aspects of the performance of a building.

Postoccupancy services: (1) Under traditional forms of agreement between owner and architect, services rendered by the architect after issuance of the final certificate for payment or, in the absence of a final certificate for payment, more than sixty days after the date of substantial completion of the work; (2) under designated services forms of agreement, services necessary to assist the owner in the use and occupancy of the facility.

Power of attorney: A document authorizing a person or entity to act as another's agent.

Preconstruction (design-build): Preliminary design and budgeting phases of a design-build project.

Predesign services: Services of the architect provided prior to the customary basic services, including services to assist the owner in establishing the program, financial and time requirements, and limitations for the project.

Preliminary design (design-build): Architect's services performed under the Part I agreement of a design-build project, including program review, preliminary program evaluation, review of alternative approaches to design and construction, and preliminary design documents.

Preliminary design documents (design-build): Preliminary design drawings, outline specifications, and other documents that fix and describe the size, quality, and character of a design-build project, including architectural, structural, mechanical, and electrical systems, as well as materials and such other elements of the project as may be appropriate.

Preliminary drawings: Drawings prepared during the early stages of the design of a project.

Premium: The amount paid by an insured for the coverage to be provided by the insurance company.

Prequalification of bidders: The process of investigating the qualifications of prospective bidders on the basis of their experience, availability, and capability for the contemplated project, and then approving qualified bidders.

Prime contract: A contract between owner and contractor for performance of the work or designated portion thereof. See also *Subcontract.*

Prime contractor: Any contractor on a project having a contract directly with the owner. See also *Subcontractor.*

Prime professional: Any person or entity having a contract directly with the owner for professional services.

Principal: In architecture firms, most often a proprietor or any individual who has an equity position in the firm (owns shares in a corporation or is a partner in a partnership). Sometimes limited to owners holding a certain percentage of the business; sometimes expanded to include anyone in a significant leadership role in the firm.

Principal-in-charge: The architect charged with the responsibility for the firm's services in connection with a given project.

Prior acts: See *Retroactive coverage.*

Privity: The direct relationship between two parties to a contract. Privity continues when certain subsequent parties succeed to the rights of a contract.

Pro bono services: Literally "for the good," referring to work or services performed without compensation.

Pro forma: Provided in advance in prescribed form. For example, a pro forma income statement is a projected or budgeted income statement (profit plan), which shows the effects of planned financial activity during a planning period as if the events had taken place as forecast. Pro formas are also commonly developed as part of real estate financial feasibility studies.

Pro rata: In proportion. For example, if three partners owned 30 percent, 30 percent, and 40 percent of a partnership and profits were distributed pro rata based on ownership, the profits would be distributed according to these percentages.

Product data: Illustrations, standard schedules, performance charts, instructions, brochures, diagrams, and other information furnished by the contractor to illustrate a material, product, or system for some portion of the work.

Product liability insurance: Insurance for liability imposed for damages caused by an occurrence arising out of goods or products manufactured, sold, handled, or distributed by the insured or others trading under the insured's name. Occurrence must occur after possession of the product has been relinquished to others and after the product has been removed from the possession of the insured.

Professional: A person who is deemed to have specialized knowledge and skills acquired through education and experience to be used in advising or providing services to others.

Professional adviser: (1) An architect engaged by the owner to direct a design competition for the selection of an architect; (2) in the NCARB Intern Development Program, a registered architect, usually outside the intern's firm, who meets periodically with the intern to discuss career objectives and review training progress.

Professional engineer: A designation reserved, usually by law, for a person professionally qualified and duly licensed to perform engineering services such as structural, mechanical, electrical, sanitary, civil, and so on.

Professional ethics: Statements of principles promulgated by professional societies or public agencies governing professional practice in order to guide members or licensees in their professional conduct.

Professional fee plus expenses: A method of compensation for professional services separating the services from identified costs for reimbursable expenses, consultant services, and similar items.

Professional fee: See *Fee.*

Professional liability insurance: Insurance coverage for the insured professional's legal liability for claims arising out of damages sustained by others allegedly as a result of negligent acts, errors, or omissions in the performance of professional services.

Professional sponsor: In the intern development program, an individual within the firm or organization who supervises the intern on a daily basis, regularly assesses the quality of his or her effort, and periodically certifies documentation of the intern's training activity.

Profit: Excess of revenues over expenses during an accounting period. In cash accounting, profit is the excess of cash received (revenue) over cash disbursements (expenses); in accrual accounting, profit is the excess of earned revenue (irrespective of when received) over accrued expenses (irrespective of when paid). Also called "income."

Profitability: The quality or state of being able to produce profits (income) from revenues generated in delivering the firm's services.

Profit margin: See *Margin.*

Profit-sharing plan: A mechanism for distributing a portion of the firm's profits to employees during or soon after the period in which they are earned (current profit-sharing plan) or to provide a later benefit to the employees (deferred profit-sharing plan). One of the prime purposes of a profit-sharing plan is to increase interest in current profitable performance since contributions are made only if there are profits.

Program (architectural or facilities): A written statement setting forth design objectives, constraints, and criteria for a project, including space requirements and relationships, flexibility and expandability, special equipment and systems, and site requirements.

Program management: The science and practice of managing large private and public projects.

Programming: The research and decision-making process that defines the problem to be solved by design.

Progress payments: Payments made periodically during progress of the work based upon the amount of work performed.

Progress schedule: A diagram, graph, or other pictorial or written schedule showing proposed or actual times of commencement and completion of the various elements of the work.

Project: A planned undertaking in which the architect provides a service or set of services to achieve a desired objective or set of objectives for the client. A project may or may not ultimately include construction work or result in the creation of physical space.

Project architect: See *Project manager.*

Project budget: The sum established by the owner as available for the entire project, which for building projects includes the budget for the cost of the work; land costs; costs of furniture, furnishings, and equipment; financing costs; compensation for professional services; costs of owner-furnished goods and services; contingency allowance; and similar established or estimated costs. See also *Construction budget* and *Internal project budget.*

Project checklist: A list used to record the actions taken by the architect, beginning before the agreement with the owner has been signed, continuing with the range of services to be provided to the owner. For building design and construction services, AIA Document D200–1995, Project Checklist, lists actions for predesign, design, and construction increments of work.

Project closeout: Requirements established in the contract documents for final inspection, submittal of necessary documentation, acceptance, and final payment on a construction project.

Project cost: Total cost of the project, including construction cost, professional compensation, land costs, furnishings and equipment, financing, and other charges.

Project delivery system: The method selected to allocate roles, responsibilities, risks, and rewards among the parties accomplishing the design, preparation of construction documents, construction, and management of a construction project.

Project expense: See *Direct expense.*

Project gross margin: The percentage of revenue using gross income from projects (profit after direct expenses have been deducted from revenues but before indirect expenses have been deducted).

Project liability insurance: Professional liability insurance providing coverage for claims arising out of a specific project as designated in the policy.

Project manager: (1) A term frequently used interchangeably with "project architect" to identify the individual designated to manage the firm's services related to a given project. Normally these services include administrative responsibilities as well as technical responsibilities. There also may be a designated principal-in-charge; (2) as to the contractor or construction manager, the term may refer to the individual designated by that entity to manage that entity's activities.

Project manual: The volume usually assembled for the construction work, which may include the bidding requirements, sample forms, conditions of the contract, and the specifications.

Project policy: A professional liability insurance policy written to provide coverage for claims arising out of a specific project designated in the policy.

Project representative: The architect's representative at the project site who assists in the administration of the construction contract.

Project revenues: The value received (or anticipated to be received) from the client for services rendered (or to be rendered). Excludes reimbursable revenues, which are offset by reimbursable expenses.

Project work plan: (1) A strategy by which the firm intends to produce a project on time, within the client's budget, and

within the firm's project budget; (2) the document spelling out the details of the strategy.

Property damage insurance: Insurance coverage for the insured's legal liability for claims for injury to or destruction of tangible property, including loss of use resulting therefrom, but usually not including coverage for injury to or destruction of property in the care, custody, or control of the insured.

Property insurance: Coverage for loss or damage to property. See also *Builder's risk insurance, Causes of loss—broad form, Causes of loss—special form, Extended coverage insurance,* and *Special hazards insurance.*

Proposal request: A document issued by the architect after contract award that may include drawings and other information used to solicit a proposal for a change in the work; sometimes called "request for a change" or "bulletin."

Proprietorship: A form of business organization that is owned entirely by one person.

Proximate cause: The cause of an injury or of damages that, in natural and continuous sequence, unbroken by any legally recognized intervening cause, produces the injury and without which the result would not have occurred. Existence of proximate cause involves both (a) causation in fact, i.e., that the wrongdoer actually produced an injury or damages, and (b) a public policy determination that the wrongdoer should be held responsible.

Public authority: Local, state, or federal government body having jurisdiction over the work or project.

Public liability insurance: Insurance covering liability of the insured for negligent acts resulting in bodily injury, disease, or death of persons other than employees of the insured and/or damage to property other than that owned by or within the care, custody, or control of the insured. See also *Commercial general liability insurance* and *Contractor's liability insurance.*

Punch list: See *Inspection list.*

Punitive damages: Damages in addition to proven loss (compensatory damages) that may be assessed against a defendant as punishment or as a deterrent to others.

Qualifications-based selection: The procurement of professional design services based on evaluating the qualifications of firms being considered. This approach is sometimes part of a two-step process that involves other criteria. See also *Best-value procurement* and *Cost-based selection.*

Qualified bid: A bid the bidder has conditioned or restricted in some manner.

Quantity survey: Detailed listing and quantities (bill of quantities) of all items of material and equipment necessary to construct a project.

Quotation: A contractor's or vendor's cost estimate for a given job or product. Sometimes shortened to "quote."

Reasonable care and skill: See *Standard of care.*

Record drawings: Construction drawings revised to show significant changes made during the construction process, usually based on marked-up prints, drawings, and other data furnished by the contractor to the architect. This term is preferable to *as-built drawings.*

Registered architect: See *Architect.*

Reimbursable expenses: Amounts expended for or on account of the project that, in accordance with the terms of the appropriate agreement, are to be reimbursed by the owner.

Reinsurance: An arrangement between two insurance companies whereby one assumes all or part of the risk of loss under the terms of a policy issued by the other.

Rejection of work (by the architect): The act of rejecting construction work that does not conform to the requirements of the contract documents.

Release of lien: An instrument executed by a person or entity supplying labor, materials, or professional services on a project that releases, in whole or in part, that person's or entity's mechanic's lien or right to assert a mechanic's lien against the project property.

Remedies: The legal means a party may have to obtain redress for a loss or injury or to prevent the occurrence of a loss or injury.

Request for payment: See *Application for payment.*

Request for qualifications: A document describing a project in enough detail so that potential providers of services or products can determine if they wish to compete. Building owners typically issue RFQs as part of a two-stage process in which an RFQ is followed by the issuance of an RFP.

Responsible bidder: See *Lowest responsible bidder.*

Restricted bid: See *Qualified bid.*

Restricted list of bidders: See *Invited bidders.*

Retainage: A sum withheld from the progress payments to the contractor and later paid in accordance with the terms of the agreement between owner and contractor.

Retained earnings: The portion of net income (income after income taxes) that is accumulated in a corporation and is not distributed as dividends.

Retroactive coverage: In an insurance policy, coverage for claims made during the policy period related to occurrences prior to the date of the policy; also referred to as "prior acts coverage." Sometimes the retroactive coverage commences at a specific date referred to as the "retroactive date," which is either the inception date of a claims-made policy or an agreed-upon date set earlier than the inception date.

Revenue: The value received from clients as a result of the firm rendering its services (operating revenues); the value received as capital gains from the sale of long-term (fixed) assets or from aspects of the business not central to the primary purpose, such as rents from rental properties or royalties from designs (non-operating revenues).

Risk: The probability of an unfavorable outcome.

Risk management: The strategies and processes used to minimize the probability and severity of an unfavorable outcome at the lowest long-term cost to an individual or organization.

Salary: Regular payments to staff for services; also used to designate the regular withdrawals by a proprietor or by partners to pay for the value of the professional services they render to the firm.

Samples: Physical examples that illustrate materials, equipment, or workmanship, and establish standards by which the work will be judged.

Schedule: (1) Of drawings: a supplemental list, usually in chart form, of a project system, subsystem, or portion thereof; (2) of specifications: a detailed written list included in the specifications; (3) of tasks and deadlines.

Schedule of values: A statement furnished by the contractor to the architect reflecting the portions of the contract sum allocated to the various portions of the work and used as the basis for reviewing the contractor's applications for payment. This term is preferable to "contractor's breakdown."

Schematic design: Services in which the architect consults with the owner to ascertain the requirements of the building project and prepares schematic design studies consisting of drawings and other documents illustrating the scale and relationships of the building components for approval by the owner. The architect also submits to the owner a preliminary estimate of construction cost based on current area, volume, or similar conceptual estimating techniques.

Schematic design documents: Drawings and other documents illustrating the scale and relationship of project components.

Seal: (1) An embossing device, stamp, or other device used by a design professional on drawings and specifications as evidence of registration in the state where the work is to be performed; (2) a device formerly consisting of an impression upon wax or paper, or a wafer, which is used in the execution of a formal legal document such as a deed or contract. The statute of limitations applicable to a contract under seal may be longer than for a contract not under seal.

Separate contract: One of several prime contracts for design or the construction of the project.

Separate contractor: A contractor on a construction project, other than the contractor identified in the agreement between owner and contractor, who has a contract with the owner.

Settlement: Voluntary agreement to resolve a claim. It is not necessarily an admission of liability.

Share: See *Stock.*

Shop drawings: Drawings, diagrams, schedules, and other data specially prepared for the work by the contractor or a subcontractor, sub-subcontractor, manufacturer, supplier, or distributor to illustrate some portion of the work.

Short-term (in financial management): Within one year; e.g., a short-term loan would come due within twelve months.

Site: Geographic location of the project, usually defined by legal boundary lines.

Site analysis services (of the architect): Services described in the schedule of designated services in some AIA documents necessary to establish site-related limitations and requirements for a building project.

Site observation: See *Observation of the work.*

Soil survey: See *Geotechnical investigation.*

Solvency: The ability of the firm to meet its financial obligations as they mature.

Sovereign immunity: A long-standing doctrine to the effect that government entities cannot be sued without their consent. Federal and state laws allow suits against government agencies under certain circumstances.

Special conditions: A section of the conditions of the contract, other than general conditions and supplementary conditions, that may be prepared to describe conditions applicable to a particular project.

Special hazards insurance: Insurance coverage for damage caused by additional perils or risks to be included in the property insurance (at the request of the contractor or at the option of the owner). Examples often included are sprinkler leakage, collapse, water damage, and coverage for materials in transit to the site or stored off the site.

Specifications: A part of the contract documents contained in the project manual consisting of written requirements for materials, equipment, construction systems, standards, and workmanship.

Staff leveling: The process by which needs for staff generated by project services are matched to available sources or staff in an attempt to minimize either the unmet demand for services or the underutilization of staff.

Standard form of agreement: A document setting forth in printed form the general provisions of an agreement, with spaces provided for insertion of specific data relating to a particular project.

Standard of care: Usually defined as what a reasonably prudent architect, in the same community at the same time, facing the same or similar circumstances would do. It is the measure by which behavior is judged in determining legal duties and rights.

Statement of account: A summary of outstanding invoices sometimes listed by number, date, and amount (rendered to but not paid by the client); total earned revenue, total paid, and total due are usually shown.

Statute of limitations: A statute specifying the period of time within which legal action must be brought for legal relief after an alleged injury or damage has occurred. The lengths of the periods vary from state to state and depend upon the type of legal action.

Statute of repose: A statute limiting the time within which an action may be brought, without relation to whether injury has yet occurred or been discovered. The time begins when a specific event occurs, such as substantial completion of a project, and the statute of repose may extinguish the remedy even before a cause of action has accrued.

Statutory bond: A bond, the form or content of which is prescribed by statute.

Stipulated sum agreement: Contract in which a specific amount is set forth as the total payment for performance of the contract. Also called "lump-sum agreement."

Stock: (1) The capital that a corporation raises through the sale of shares entitling the holder of the shares to rights of ownership; (2) the certificate evidencing ownership in a corporation.

Strategic facilities plan: Plan that integrates facilities into the organization's strategic business plan and forecasts the supply and demand for physical space, options for acquiring space, location of the space, and budgets and schedules. Strategic facilities plans are based on goals set in business plans. See also *Business plan.*

Strict liability: Liability without proof of negligence but based on one or more conditional requirements.

Sub-bidder: A person or entity who submits a bid to a bidder for materials or labor for a portion of the work.

Subcontract: Agreement between a prime contractor and a subcontractor for performance of a portion of the work at the site. See also *Prime contract.*

Subcontractor: A person or entity who has a direct contract with the contractor to perform any of the work at the site. See also *Prime contractor.*

Subpoena: A writ issued under the authority of a court or arbitrator to compel the appearance of a witness for deposition, trial, or arbitration hearing.

Subrogation: The substitution of one person for another with respect to legal rights such as a right of recovery. Subrogation occurs when a third person, such as an insurance company, has paid a debt of another or claim against another and succeeds to all legal rights that the debtor or person against whom the claim was asserted may have against other persons.

Substantial completion: The stage in the progress of the work when the work or designated portion thereof is sufficiently complete in accordance with the contract documents that the owner can occupy or use the work for its intended purpose.

Substitution: A material, product, or item of equipment in place of that specified.

Sub-subcontractor: A person or entity who has a direct or indirect contract with a subcontractor to perform any of the work at the site.

Subsurface investigation: See *Geotechnical investigation.*

Successful bidder: The bidder chosen by the owner for the award of a construction contract. Also called "selected bidder."

Successor: A person or entity who succeeds to a title, estate, or office.

Summary judgment: The decision of a court without hearing evidence, usually because the pleadings show no issue of fact.

Summons: A legal paper to be served on a person named as a defendant in a legal action notifying him or her to answer the complaint or be in default; also used to require nonparty witnesses to appear for depositions or at the trial or arbitration hearings.

Superintendent: The contractor's representative at the site who is responsible for continuous field supervision, coordination, completion of the work, and, unless another person is designated in writing by the contractor to the owner and the architect, for the prevention of accidents.

Supervision (during construction): Direction of the work by the contractor's personnel.

Supplementary conditions: A part of the contract documents that supplements and may also modify, change, add to, or delete provisions of the general conditions.

Supplier: A person or entity who supplies materials or equipment for the work, including that fabricated to a special design, but who does not perform labor at the site.

Supply bond: A bond by which a surety guarantees that a supplier will furnish goods or materials.

Surety: A person or entity who guarantees, in writing, the performance of an obligation by another.

Surety bond: See *Bond.*

Survey: (1) Mapping the boundary, topographic, and/or utility features of a site; (2) measuring an existing building; (3) analyzing a building for use of space; (4) determining owner's requirements for a project; (5) investigating and reporting required data for a project.

Sustainability: The concept of meeting present needs without compromising the ability of future generations to meet their own needs.

Sustainable design: Design that seeks to avoid depletion of energy, water, and raw material resources; prevent environmental degradation caused by facility and infrastructure development over their life cycle; and create environments that are livable, comfortable, and safe and that promote productivity.

Termination: The abrogation of a contract by one party, with notice to the other party; depending upon the terms of the contract, governing law, and the actual circumstances, such abrogation may or may not be within the rights of the terminating party.

Termination expenses: Expenses directly attributable to the termination of an agreement, including an amount allowing for compensation earned to the time of termination.

Testimony: Oral evidence given by a witness.

Third party: Someone other than the original parties involved in a contract, claim, or action.

Third-party beneficiary: Someone who is not a party to a contract but has a direct interest in some or all of the terms and conditions of the contract.

Time (as the essence of a construction contract): Time limits or periods stated in the contract. A provision in a construction contract that "time is of the essence of the contract" signifies that the parties consider punctual performance within the time limits or periods in the contract to be a material part of the performance, and failure to perform on time is a breach for which the injured party is entitled to damages in the amount of loss sustained.

Time of completion: Date established in the contract, by calendar date or by number of calendar or working days, for substantial completion of the work.

Time utilization: See *Utilization ratio.*

Timely completion: Completion of the work or designated portion thereof on or before the date required.

Timely notice: Notice given within time limits prescribed by contract or in sufficient time to allow the party receiving notice to take appropriate action.

Tort: A violation of a right created by operation of law; a private or civil wrong or injury.

Trade discount: The difference between the seller's list price and the purchaser's actual cost, excluding discounts for prompt payment.

Trial balance: A list of the debit and credit balances of accounts maintained in the general ledger. The purpose of the trial balance is to see if the total debit balances equal the total credit balances.

Turnkey: A construction process in which one party agrees to deliver to another party a fully completed project, ready for the other party's use and occupancy by "turning the key."

Umbrella liability insurance: Insurance providing coverage in an amount above existing liability policies and sometimes providing direct coverage for losses not insured under existing policies; frequently specified deductible amounts are required.

Unbilled revenue: Revenue that has been earned but for which the client has not been given an invoice. See also *Work in process*.

Unearned revenue: Backlog. Revenue from services the firm has a signed commitment to render but which the firm has not yet rendered.

Uniform Commercial Code (UCC): A model statute dealing with certain commercial transactions that has been adopted by every state except Louisiana. UCC provisions do not normally apply to professional services.

UniFormat™: A system for classifying building products and systems by functional subsystem (e.g., substructure, superstructure, exterior closure, etc.). See also *MasterFormat*.

Unit price: Amount stated in the bid as a price per unit of measurement for materials or services as described in the bidding documents or in the proposed contract documents.

Unit price contract: A contract based on acceptance and incorporation of unit price quotations for the various portions of the project.

Universal design: The design of building environments to be usable by all people, to the greatest extent possible, without the need for adaptation or specialized design.

Unjust enrichment: A legal concept that prevents a party from receiving a monetary benefit to which he or she is not entitled.

Upset price: See *Guaranteed maximum price*.

Utilization ratio: (1) Time utilization is a ratio of direct hours billed to projects to the total hours reported; (2) payroll utilization is the ratio of direct salary expense to total salary expense. Can be calculated for an individual, a group of individuals, or the entire firm.

Value analysis: An organized effort directed at analyzing systems, equipment, facilities, services, and supplies for the purpose of achieving essential functions at the lowest life cycle cost consistent with the required performance, reliability, quality, and safety. (Also referred to as "value management" or "value engineering.")

Value-enhanced design: The process of analyzing the elements of a building design in terms of its cost-effectiveness, including the proposed substitution of less expensive materials or systems for those initially suggested.

Vandalism and malicious mischief insurance: Insurance against loss or damage to the insured's property caused by willful and malicious damage or destruction.

Variance: (1) A limited waiver from the requirements of a zoning ordinance that may be granted because of special circumstances regarding the subject property; (2) an actual value less a budgeted or planned value.

Vicarious liability: Indirect liability imposed on a party resulting from the acts or omissions of another person or entity for whose conduct the party is responsible.

Vouchers: Forms of receipt or statements used to recognize the existence of an expense and to justify a cash outlay, serving as evidence of an obligation owed by the firm.

Waiver of lien: A document by which a person or entity who has or may have a right of mechanic's lien against the property of another relinquishes such right. See also *Release of lien*.

Waiver of subrogation: The relinquishment by an insured of the right of its insurance carrier to recover damages paid on behalf of the insured.

Warranty: Legally enforceable assurance of quality or performance of a product or work or of the duration of satisfactory performance.

Work (in the AIA documents): The construction and services required by the contract documents—whether completed or partially completed—including all labor, materials, equipment, and services provided or to be provided by the contractor to fulfill the contractor's obligations. The work may constitute the whole or a part of the project.

Work changes proposal request: A request, typically prepared by the architect, to obtain price quotations needed for negotiating changes in the contract for construction.

Work in process: Work the firm has under way for a client that is not far enough along to be billed. Work in process is a current asset and may be carried at cost or at the value of expected revenue, in which case it can also be called "unbilled revenue."

Workers' compensation insurance: Insurance covering the liability of an employer to employees for compensation and other benefits required by workers' compensation laws with respect to injury, sickness, disease, or death arising from their employment. Previously referred to as "workmen's compensation insurance."

Working capital: The minimum amount of liquid capital needed to maintain the flow of capital from cash to work in process (unbilled revenue) to accounts receivable and again to cash, plus an amount as contingency.

Working drawings: See *Drawings*.

Write off: The transfer of an amount previously regarded as an asset (e.g., an account receivable) to an expense account or to the profit-and-loss account.

Zoning: Local ordinances regulating the use and development of property through the use of standards for such things as minimum building setbacks, maximum heights, minimum open spaces, and so on.

Zoning permit: A permit issued by appropriate government authority authorizing land to be used for a specific purpose. Required prior to obtaining a building permit. See also *Building permit*.

Index

A

Absolute expectations, 458
Academic jargon, avoidance, 72
Access Board guidelines, DOJ adoption
  (absence), 556–557
Accessory use areas, 569
Accommodation units, 502
Account, 673
  balance, 673
  chart, 157, 677
  codes, usage, 480–481
  statement, 692
Accountants, financial statement selection, 162
Accounting
  codes, 158
  methods, 158–159
  original entity, book, 684
  period, 673
  records, 219
  software, 233
  systems, 156–158
Accounts payable, 673
Accounts receivable (receivables), 673
  aging report, sample, 487
  current asset, 169
  usage, 166
Accretion, 276
Accrual accounting, 673
  example, 160
Accrual method, accounting method, 159
Action item lists, usage, 470
Action item meeting report, 469
  sample, 446
Actual harm, result, 33
Actual net multiplier, usage, 154
Adaptable buildings, design, 312
Addenda (addendum), 427, 615, 673
  management, 430
Additional services, 673
  list, 245–246
Additive (add) alternate, 673
Adjudication, consideration, 489
Administrative expenses, 156
  inclusion, 157–158

Administrative rules/regulations, legal source, 31
Admonition, 9, 673
Advantage/Vision (financial management
  software), 164
Adversarial relationships, impact, 300
Advertisement for bids, 673
Advice, giving, 36
Aged accounts receivable, 673
Agency relationships, 34–36
Agenda
  development, 117
  effectiveness, 468–469
Agent, 673
Agreement, 673
  assessment, matrix, 190–191
  date, 680
  execution, 682
  letter form, 685
  modification, 584–585
  standard form, 692
  usage, sense, 578–584
Agricultural materials, usage (U.S. government
  promotion), 320
Air Quality Sciences, Inc., 321
Alliance, 673
Allied professional organizations, 657
Allied professionals
  contact, 135
  groups, connection, 25
Allowance, determination, 507
AllPlan (software), 231
Alterations, estimation, 509
Alternate, 673
  requirement, 507
Alternate bid, 673
Alternative construction detail, usage, 520–521
Alternative dispute resolution (ADR), 619, 673
American Architectural Foundation (AAF),
  formation, 26
American Architectural Manufacturers
  Association (AAMA), 408
American Bar Association (ABA),
  formation, 24
American Consulting Engineers Council,
  construction partnering endorsement,
  114

American Council of Engineer Companies
  (ACEC), professional liability insurance
  survey, 207
American Forest & Paper Association
  (AF&PA), 322
American Institute of Architects (AIA),
  655–656
  agreements, publication, 579
  AIA Commended Professional Liability
    Insurance, 203
  programs, 196, 207–208
  AIA Firm Survey (2006), 25
  AIA Legal Citator, 37
  AIA Member Benefits Guide, 27
  AIA Public Policies and Position Statements, 27
  AIA-related organizations, 657
  AIA Trust News, 203
  CAD Layer Guidelines, 224, 419
  canons, 46
  CM Adviser family, 643–645
  CM Constructor family, 645
  Code of Ethics, 8–9
    application/enforcement/amendment
      rules, 18
    publication (2004), 15–18
    usage, 46
  Code of Ethics and Professional Conduct, 46
  Committee on the Environment (COTE),
    305, 317
  conduct, rules, 46
  construction partnering endorsement, 113
  Contract Administration forms, 648–653
  Contract Documents, 28, 591, 632–633
    development, 622–625
    program (2007), 629–631
    synopses, 634–653
    usage, 631–632
  Design/Build family, 646–647
  Design Knowledge Community, 340
  Digital Practice family, 647–648
  Document A102-2007, 423
  Document A201-2007, 437, 524
  Document A131/CMc-2003, 424
  Document A201 Indemnity Clause, 601
  Document B101-2007, 244, 335, 496,
    578, 608

American Institute of Architects (AIA) (*continued*)
Document B103 (2007), 181
Document B141, 260, 628
Document D200-1995, 425, 524
Document G704-2000, 449
Document G710-1992, 444
Document G716-2004, 444
Documents, A201 family, 634–642
Documents Committee, 623–625
Documents Drafting Principles, 624–625
Documents program, 622
ethical standards, 46
founding, 23–24
honors/awards programs, 28–29
industry impact, 625–629
information, 27–29
Interiors family, 645–646
International family, 648
knowledge communities/resources, 28
lobbying, 28
MASTERSPEC® specification system, 229,
    402–403, 418
    continuing education, 421
    divisions/sections, 404–407
    editing assistance, 421
    naming conventions, 421
    Section 013300, 443
    supporting documents, 421
    tools, 420–422
    usage, 409
member benefits, 29
member participation, 27
National Convention and Design
    Exposition, 28
National Ethics Council, 9
    procedures, 9
owner-architect agreements, project phases,
    334–335
Owner-Architect Agreements (2007 Series),
    246–247
professional liability insurance survey, 207
professionals
    programs, 28
professionals, consortium, 29
programs, 27–29
Project Management forms, 648–653
Risk Management Committee, 196
Risk Management Resource Center, 185
Small Project family, 642–643
standard forms, benefits, 623–624
Trust
    benefits/services, 203
    creation, 194, 203
    programs, 194
    Small Firm Program, 208
American Iron and Steel Institute (AISI), 408
American National Standards Institute
    (ANSI), 408
American Society for Testing and Materials
    (ASTM), 408
    standards, 562–563
American Society of Association Executives
    (ASAE), coalition formation, 25
American Society of Civil Engineers
    (ASCE), establishment, 298
American Society of Heating, Refrigeration, and
    Air-Conditioning Engineers (ASHRAE),
    317, 408, 556
American Society of Landscape Architects, 24
Analytical classification, 221
Annualized method, 363
Anti-indemnification statutes, 674
Antitrust, 674
    concerns, 46–47
    principles, 46–47
Antitrust law, compliance, 14

Approved equal, 674
Arbitration, 674
    adversarial characteristic, 208–209
ArchiCAD (software), 231
Architect-consultant agreements, 606–608, 674
    BIM management issues, 608
    compensation issues, 607–608
    digital practice protocols, 608
    form, 606, 608
    legal rights/responsibilities, 606–607
    risks/rewards, 607
Architect-consultant relationships, 35–36,
    603–609
Architect-employee relationships, 35
Architect-Engineer Qualifications (Standard
    Form 330), 137
Architect-led CM, rewards, 384
Architect of record, 674
Architect Registration Examination (ARE), 47
Architects, 674
    activities, review (requirement), 47
    causality, 216
    claims, 174
        property damage/economic loss,
            involvement, 211
    client collaboration, increase, 284
    client selection
        criteria, 134
        process, 133–144
    concerns, 496–497
    conduct, 32
    construction manager role, 383
    construction phase activities, 436
    contractual language, agreement, 32
    coordination, importance, 609
    cost-based selection, 134–136
    decisions, restrictions, 466
    ethics standards, 7–9
    etymology, 297
    financial institution document, signing, 32
    indemnification, owner request, 587
    indemnities, consideration, 586–588
    information management, usage, 219–220
    initial decision maker, 215–216
    integrator role, 250
    law, relationship, 30
    leadership training, 62
    legal responsibility, 31–33
    liability concepts, consideration, 590
    meaning, 19
    performance standard, 497
    professional services, 495–496
        inclusion, 495
    promise, 32
    property insurance, 201
    provisions, 496
    relationships, maintenance, 144
    responsibility, 393–394, 606
        admission, 216–217
    RFQ questions, 577–578
    roles
        communication, 143
        multiplicity, 55
    services, 250–252
    specialization, evidence-based design
        requirement (absence), 291
    survey data, usage, 58
    team-building activities, 115–120
    team-building principles, 120
    title, usage (restriction), 45
    violation, 46
Architectural Computer Services, Inc.
    (ARCOM), 229
    Master Systems, 409
Architectural/construction information,
    395–397

Architectural design, programmer
    familiarity, 262
Architectural information, classification systems,
    220–223
Architectural program, 689
Architectural programming, 261
    team process, 263
    values, 260
    values identification, 263
Architectural projects, management, 459–477
    activities, 460
Architectural services/compensation, 249–259
Architectural works, copyright, 39
Architecture
    compensation, 249–259
    creativity/art (reduction), evidence-based
        design (impact), 291
    design/construction, integration (history), 297
    internal social structure, 5–6
    lessons, 286
    practice
        leadership concepts, relevance, 53
        penalties, 45
        software programs, 231–233
    practice, service leadership, 19–21
    profession, 2
        comparison, 4–6
    schools, 664
Architecture Engineering Construction/Facility
    Management (AEC/FM) community,
    standards, 233
Architecture Engineering Construction Owning
    Operating (AECOO) community,
    standards, 233
Architecture firm
    administration/support, 82
    assessment, matrix, 187
    atmosphere, selection, 78
    brand, action, 125
    budget, 127
    business
        design, archetypes, 103–104
        development/sales, 129–132
        licenses, application, 85
        opening, 87
        plan, preparation, 80–81
    business models
        elements, 105
        selection, 98–101
    capital, absence, 84
    challenge, 107–108
    claims
        experience, insurance premium factor, 198
        management, 217
        number, 211
    client base, identification, 127
    cold calls, usage, 132–133
    commercial space, rental, 84
    community contributors, usage, 100
    competition, identification, 126, 131
    competitors, 127
    consultants, usage, 82
    corporations, 90–95
        employee shares, 90
        income taxes, 91–92
        liabilities, 91
        ownership, change, 91
        ownership/control, 90–91
    cost/quality experts, usage, 100–101
    design, 80–81, 103–105
    driving force
        identification, 102
        impact, 103
    employees
        benefits, determination, 85
        dispute resolution, awareness, 210

ethical matters, 80
expert advice, obtaining, 83
expertise, 97–108
facilities, 82
FEIN, acquisition, 85
finances, management, 155
financial goals, meeting, 155
financial issues, 82
financial systems, selection, 86
firmwide profit, 169–170
focus, 101–103
full-service client partners, usage, 99
furniture/equipment needs, determination, 85
generalization strategy, 123
goals, identification, 124
identity, 97–108
　defining, 80
　selection, 103–104
image, creation, 86
incidents, management, 217
initiation, 76–87
　decision, 77–79
　timing, 79
innovators, usage, 99
insurance/benefits, 82
investment level, 83
IRA option, 85
leads, development, 131–132
legal/regulatory issues, 82
legal sculpture, 87–97
limitations, assessment, 176
limited liability companies, 96–97
　income taxes, 97
　liabilities, 96–97
　ownership, changes, 97
　ownership/control, 96
loan proposal, components, 83
market
　defining, challenge, 126
　identification, 123, 126, 127
　position, value, 125
　requirements, 126
　size/trends, 127
marketing, 82
　budget, determination, 127–128
　plan, 126–128
　strategy, development, 86
　strategy/planning, 121–133
marketing plan
　development, 127
message
　identification, 125
　transmission, determination, 125
mission, identification, 124, 127
name, branding importance, 125
networking, 130
objectives, 127
offering, identification, 126
office space, considerations, 84
operating model archetypes, 106–107
ownership, paths, 79
partner
　agreements, 78
　liability, 89
partnerships, 88–90
　agreement, 88–90
　income taxes, 89–90
pension plans, 96
perception, clarification, 125
positioning
　identification, 127
　statement, development, 126
professional registration, requirements, 89
profit, making, 155
profit-sharing plans, 96
project

definition, 131
　timing, 131
project management experts, usage, 100
project-type specialists, usage, 99
publicity, importance, 86
public relations, 82
quality assurance effort, checking
　(importance), 418
questions, 101
relationships, importance, 130
responsibilities, 127
risk assessment, 176
schedule, 127
self-identification, 122–123
SEP option, 85
shareholder agreements, 78
skills, requirement, 77–78
sole proprietorships, 88
　liability, 88
specialization strategy, 123
staffing, 82
　needs, identification, 81
start-up
　checklist, 82
　funding, acquisition, 81–83
　involvement, 79
　planning/decision making, 77
　tasks, 81–86
strategic evaluation, 176
strategic planning, 104
strategy, communication process, 124
strengths
　assessment, 176
　identification, 123
subchapter S corporation, 95
taxes
　accounting method, 95–96
　considerations, 95–96
　domestic production deduction, 95
　rates, 95
　tax year, 95
tax ID numbers, application, 85
technology plan, development, 225
threats, identification, 123
value position, assessment, 256–258
vision, identification, 123–124
weaknesses, identification, 123
work, quality, 103
Architecture services, 249–259
　compensation, calculation, 249–250
　marketing, 121–122
　value, recognition, 251–252
Archives, 220
　usage, 224
Area, graying, 544
Area methods, 502
Army Corps of Engineers, construction
　partnering development, 114
ARRIS (software), 231
Artlantis (software), 232
Arts, architecture (relationship), 4
As-built drawings, 674
Assets, 674
　heading, 157
　sale, income, 155
Assignment, 40
　consent, 595–596
Associate associated architect, 674
Associated General Contractors (AGC), 623
　construction partnering endorsement,
　113–114
　formation, 24
Associated professional firms, 611
Associations
　advocacy/lobbying, 25–26
　continuing education programs, offering, 25

emergence, 23–24
　function, 23
　funds, raising, 26
　uniqueness, 24
Athena® EcoCalculator for Assemblies, 316, 317
Athena® Impact Estimator for Buildings,
　316, 317
Athena Sustainable Materials Institute,
　reports, 329
Attorney-in-fact, 674
Audiences, defining, 124
Audit, 674
AutoCAD (software), 231
Average collection period, 674
　calculation, 169
Average revenue per day, calculation, 169
AXIUM (financial management software), 164

B

Backlog, 168, 674
Bad debt, 674
Balance sheet, 674
　example, 160
　usage, 159–160
Bankruptcy, 674
Bar charts, 491–492
Base bid, 674
Basic services, 674
　additional services, contrast, 244
　list, 244–245
Behavior
　code development, 277
　mapping, 277
　observation, 275–277
　traces, observation, 276
Behavioral theory, 52
Bentley Architecture (software), 231
Best-value procurement, 674
Betterment, 674
Biases, acknowledgment, 67
Bidders, 675
　instruction, 684
　instructions, 425–426
　legal/insurance consultants, usage, 431
　notice (notification), 428, 686
　prequalification, 424, 688
　questions, responses, 431
Bidding
　activities, 382
　assumptions, 423
　documents, 392, 675
　　deposit, 680
　　distribution, 427
　　errors/withdrawals/revocations, 428
　　issues, 425
　　preparation, 425
　period, 675
　phase, 245, 422–433
　preparation, steps, 423–427
　problems, avoidance, 429–431
　process, management/control, 427–429
　requirement, 392, 675
　results, 428
　strategies, 507–508
Bids, 674
　alternate, submission (requirement), 507
　bond, 428, 674
　construction documents, insufficiency (basis),
　　429–430
　contract aware, 428
　evaluation, 428
　form, 426, 675
　invitation, 684

Bids (*continued*)
    negotiation, 428
    opening, 675
    price, 675
    projects, construction cost control, 431–432
    receipt, 427–428
    rejection, 428
    security, 675
    time date, 675
    understanding, 429
Bids, advertisement, 425
BIFMA International, 321
Billable time, 675
Billing
    control, 483–486
    forecasting, 167
    requirements, 483–484
    usage, 258–259
    volume, insurance premium factor, 198
Billing rate, 675
    setting, 154
Bill of quantities, 690
Bill of sale, 675
Bio-based materials, promotion incentives,
        320–321
Bio-based sources, 320–321
Bioclimatic design, engagement, 307–309
Biological pollutants, presence, 309
Board for the Coordination of the Model Codes
        (BCMC), 559
Board of zoning appeals, 547
Bodily injury, 675
Bona fide bid, 675
Bond, 675
Bonus clause, 675
Bookkeeping, 675
Book value, 675
Bottlenecks, search, 414
Brainstorming, usage, 110
Branding, 124–125
Break-even, 675
    multiplier, 675
BricsCAD (software), 231
Brief, 675
BST (financial management software), 164
Budget, 675
    adherence information, 135
    architect evaluation, 495
    confirmation letter, sample, 511
    excess, prevention, 512
    monitoring, 480
    preparation, 127–128
    project manager control, 480–483
    redraw clause, 512
Budgeting, 675
    matrix, sample, 129
BuildersCAD (software), 231
Builder's risk insurance, 675
Building
    alternates/substitutions, usage, 430
    area (maximum), determination (formula),
        559–560
    climate, impact, 308
    codes, 554–568
        AIA policy, 555
        importance, 533
        practice issues, 565–566
    commissioning, 313
    complexity, increase, 299
    consensus, 624–625
    context, 331
    costs
        construction factors, 504
        design factors, 504
        factors, 504–505
        location factors, 504

    qualitative factors, 504
    time factors, 504
delivery, acceleration, 298
design, synthesis, 334
elements, UniFormat classification, 499–500
envelope design, 350
height/area
    allowance, 571
    determination, 559–560
industry, LEED (impact), 327–328
information model, 227, 675
    inclusion, 227
materials, usage, 304
occupancy classification, impact, 559
performance
    monitoring, 313
    testing/verification, 565
permit, 552–553676
processes, programmer familiarity, 262
product performance, calculation (sample), 325
projects, complexity, 240
sitework, UniFormat classification, 499–500
standards, 554–568
structure, inadequacy, 33
technology, 331
type, expertise/experience, 251
water/energy, usage, 304
Building for Environmental and Economic
        Sustainability (BEES®), 316
    software, 317
    tool, availability, 329
Building information modeling (BIM), 676
    author tools, 231–232
    benefits, 237–238
    example, 237–238
    management issues, 608
    opportunities, 238
    problems, 238
    project services, relationship, 248
    systems, usage, 228–229
    technology, 396–397, 410
        adoption, 235
    usage, 413–414
Building Officials and Code Administrators
        (BOCA), 555
Building Owners and Managers Association, 24
Built environment, sustainability (defining),
        304–305
Burden, 676
Burden of proof, 676
Business
    allocation, 47
    automobile liability, 201
    development/sales, 129–132
    functions, 219
    insurance, 201–202
    intelligence, 268
    interruption, insurance, 202
    model, elements, 105
    plan, 676
    planning, 145–146
        paths, 146
    practices, problems, 185
    ventures, revenue, 155
Business income coverage (loss-of-use coverage),
        676
Business overhead expense (BOE) disability
        benefits, 206

C

Canadian Standards Association (CSA), 322
Canvas X (software), 232
Capital, 676

accounts, 676
    expenditure, 676
        inclusion, 158
        planning, 155
    infusions, 155
Capital Facilities Information Handover Guide
        (CFIHG), 236
Care, 676
    professional standard, interpretation, 31–32
    standard, 473, 582–583, 692
        measurements, 32–33
        risk exposure, 589–590
Cars, usage (impact), 306
Cash
    accounting, 676
        example, 160
    allowance, 676
    budget, 676
        development, steps, 167
    budgeting, 166
    cycle, 676
        illustration, 166
    disbursements, forecasting, 167
    journals, 676
    management, 166–168
        techniques, 168
    receipts, amounts/timing (forecasting), 167
Cash flow, 676
    controls, 168
    projections, 166–167
    process, 167
    statement, 676
Cash method, accounting method, 158–159
Cash projection worksheet, 676
Causes of loss—special form (all-risk insurance),
        676
Censure, 676
Center for Health Design, evidence-based
        design publications, 292
Certifications, consideration, 596–597
Certified public accountants (CPAs), financial
        consultant selection, 162
Certified value specialist (CVS), usage, 343
Change order, 508, 615, 677
    request, 677
Changes, 584
    documentation, 489
    responses, 459
Charitable institutions, composition, 24
Charrette, 677
Chemical pollutants, presence, 309
Cities
    long-range plans, 535–537
    planning departments, consultants (usage), 537
    resource removal, 306
Citizen review boards/commissions, 547
Civil action, 677
Civil matters, 31
Claims, 508, 677
    expense, 677
    experience, 211–212
    frequency, stability, 212
    making, 216–218
    management, 217
    number, increase, 181
    professional liability, 200
    resolution, choice (making), 218
    substantial completion, relationship, 212
Claims-made policy, 677
Clarification drawing, 677
Class, 221
Classification, 221
    systems
        applications, 222–223
        uses, 222
Clerk of the works, 677

Client-evaluation checklist, usage, 488
Client-generated work scope, 251
Clients, 677
    administrative/accounting practices,
        understanding, 258
    architect qualifications, identification,
        138–139
    assessment, matrix, 187–188
    claims, origination, 211
    communication, 214
    competition, discussion (absence), 135
    consequences, project manager explanations,
        457–458
    cost-based selection, usage, 134
    decision making/approvals, 252
    decisions, evidence-based design (impact), 291
    discussion, architect objective, 135
    disputes, danger signals, 210–211
    ethical obligations, 16–17
    events, attendance, 66
    expectations
        clarification, 214
        project management, relationship, 457–458
        setting, 457–458
    expectations, management, 210–212
        contracts, usage, 210
    hidden agenda
        architecture firm, driving force
            (relationship), 102–103
        defining, 103
    homework, 268
    information, sources, 270–271
    invoices
        control, 476
        receiving, 484
    leads, development, 131–132
    legal recourse, 486
    list, assembly, 131
    needs
        consultation, 255
        understanding, 139
    objectives, monitoring, 474–475
    obligation, understanding, 37
    payment withholding, right (avoidance), 213
    plan usage, 136
    priorities, consultation, 255
    programming needs, 260–262
    project goals, establishment, 288
    quality, definition, 177
    questions, 135
    relationships, 466
        loyalty, 252
    research methods, 269
    selection, 176–178
    targeting, 131
    values
        expectations, understanding, 347–348
        research, 139
    year-end review, 477
Climate-based design, 308
Climate zone, strategies, 308–309
Closed-ended questions
    inclusion, 273–274
    results, analysis, 275
    results, presentation (sample), 275
Closed specifications, 677
Closeout checklist, 450
Clothing, issues, 70
Cluster development, 541
Cluster zoning, 539
CNA Insurance Companies, 208
Codes, 677
    analysis, 333
    appeals, 567–568
    checklists, 565
    development, participation, 568

enforcement, 566–568
    enforcement official, 677
    local adoption, 565–566
    standards, relationship, 561–563
Coinsurance, 677
Cold calls, usage, 132
Collaboration
    importance, 293–295
    inhibition, impact, 300
    occurrence, 294
Colleagues, ethical obligations, 18
Collections, 258–259
    agency, usage, 487
    pursuit, 484–486
Collective-bargaining agreements, usage, 204
Commentary, avoidance, 67
Commercial general liability insurance, 677
Commissioning, 677
Committee on the Environment (COTE), 304
Communication
    assumptions, challenge, 73
    basics, 64–66
    goals, 65
    importance, 215
    loop, team player role, 434
    management systems, 229–230
    open lines, maintenance, 214
    openness, IPD principle, 390
    plan, building process, 124–125
    problems, 185
    processes/procedures, refining, 115
    rules, 73
        understanding, 488–489
    skills
        development, 64–73
        improvement, 56–57, 62
Community
    board, approach, 551
    impact, 331
    planning
        controls, 533–554
        sustainability, importance, 539
    plans, preparation, 535–536
Comparability plan, 207
Comparative negligence, 678
Compensation, 678
    control, 483–486
    options, 253–255
    worksheet, sample, 257
Compensatory damages, 678
Competence, importance, 20
Competition, insurance premium factor, 198
Competitive bidding, 47
Competitor, boycott, 47
Completed operations insurance, 678
Completion bond, 678
Completion time, 693
Complexity, illustration, 298
Composite Panel Association, EPP
    specification, 320
Compound class, 221
Computer-aided design (CAD) (CADD),
    225, 678
    advances, 399–400
    automatic dimensioning, 399
    CAD-produced drawing sheets, filing
        convention (creation), 223
    data, exchange, 412
    layer guidelines, 401–402
    software programs, 231–233
    technology, usage, 400–401
Computer-aided drafting, 400
Computer hardware, advances, 225
Computerized financial systems, 162–164
    accounting functions, 163
    characteristics, 163–164

initiation, 162–163
    selection, 163
Computer programs, usage, 506
Computer technology, 225–236
    future, 236
Concepts, copyright exclusion, 38
Concurrency, 295–296
Concurrent engineering, feedback, 301
Conditions, documentation, 333
ConDoc Drawing System, 401, 410
Condos
    client consideration, 179
    litigation attorney, prevalence, 179
    problems, 179
Confidentiality
    ethics, 13
    provisions, 597
Conflict management, necessity, 209–210
Consequential damages, 589, 619–620
Consequential loss, 678
Conservation design, 541
Constant dollars, 358–360
Construction
    administration, three-way win, 450–451
    agreements, complexity, 36
    budget, 678
    CA activities, 441–451
    change directive, 614, 678
    changes
        client decision, documentation, 214
        client update, 214
        handling, procedures, 213–214
        options, analysis/presentation, 214
    claims litigation, increase, 423
    closeout, 508
    contingencies, 505
    contract administration (CA), 433–451, 495
        services, 678
    drawings, standards development, 401–402
    industry practice, consideration, 333
    managers, 678
        qualifications, 384
        roles, 383
    nonconformance, avoidance (steps), 518–519
    partnering, 113–115
    procurement services, 678
    procurement services, knowledge/skills
        requirement, 423
    progress payments, 508
    responsibility, absence, 599
    site, architect visit, 32
    supervision, 693
    sustainable actions, 315
    team, 432
    technology, 228
    type, code comparison, 570
Construction contracts, 612–621, 625–627
    change orders, 615
    commencement date, 617
    components, 613–616
    conditions, 614–615
    consequential damages, 619–620
    construction change directives, 615
    design-award-build project delivery method,
        usage, 613
    documents, 614
    drawings, 615
    final completion/payment, 619
    general conditions, 683
    GMP, 616–617
    liquidated damages, 620
    modifications, 616
    notice to proceed, 617
    payment basis, 615–617
    progress payments, 618
    project delivery method, impact, 612–613

Construction contracts (*continued*)
  project/work provision, 617
  provisions, 617–620
  retainage, 618
  schedule of values, 618
  specifications/addenda, 615
  statute of limitations/repose, 620
  stimulated sum, 616
  structure, decisions, 425
  subcontracts, 620–621
  substantial completion, 619
  sum, 617
  unit price, 617
  warranties, 619
  work, changes, 615
  work correction period, 619
Construction cost, 678
  analysis tools, detail, 227–228
  architect responsibility, 495–497
  attention, 498
  control, 508–509
  design objective, 501
  detailed estimate, 680–681
  estimate, 681
  fixed limit, 682
  information, programmer familiarity, 263
  management, 495–510
    organization, 509–510
    principles, 497–501
  monitoring/reporting, 501
  objectives, setting, 497–498
  peer reviews, usage, 432
  percentage, 254–255
  preconstruction services, 431–432
  preliminary estimate, 336
  program manager, usage, 432
  programming detail, 431
  regulatory agency/building department
    reviews, 432
  responsibility, 253
  targets, assignation, 499, 501
Construction documentation, 338, 391–419
  decisions, 411
  management, 410–419
  preparation, 412
  production management, features, 411
  purposes, 392
  RediCheck checklist, 416–417
  review/checking, 417–418
  sustainable actions, 314
  tools, 228
Construction documents, 410, 678
  alternates/substitutions, use, 430
  phase, 244–245
  services, 678
Construction-driven delivery schedules, 253
Construction management (CM), 626, 678
  approach, cost-of-work approach (contrast),
    414
  elements, 382
  negotiated contract, 424
  risks/rewards, 383–384
  services, marketing, 384
  services, providing, 613
    scope, factors (impact), 435
  usage, 381–384
Construction Manager as Adviser (CMa), 626
  projects, documents, 626
Construction Manager as Constructor
  (CMc), 626
  projects, documents, 627
Construction phase, 245
  activities, 382
  communications, 438
  completion/closeout, 449–450
  design, continuation, 338, 340

disputes, prevention, 214
  problem solving, 444–445
  relationships, maintenance, 434
Construction Specifications Institute
  (CSI), 26
  CSI Format for Construction Specifications, 221
  GreenFormat development, 329
  nomenclature/organizational standards,
    236
  punch list form, development, 527
Consultants, 678
  assessment, matrix, 191–192
  claims, 174
  client selection, risk, 183–184
  documents, coordination, 609
  insurance, usage, 183
  management, 474
  meeting, 439
  price competition, difficulty, 182
  selection, risk, 182–183, 184
  team report, sample, 480
  usage, 262
Consultation, seeking, 445
Consumer-directed plans, 203
Contact management software, 233
Content management software, 233
Context, design strategies, 307
Contextual infill, 548–549
Contingency
  allowance, 679
  application, 256
  inclusion, 498, 505
  structure, 253
Contingency theory, 52–53
Contingent agreement, 679
Contingent liability, 679
Continuing education, requirement, 48–49
Continuity, 296–297
  insurance premium factor, 198
Contract administration (CA), 433
  activities, preparation, 438–441
  services, agreement inclusion, 434
  team participants, roles, 434–438
Contracting officer, 679
Contractor, 679
  affidavit, 679
  application, error (detection), 33
  assessment, matrix, 192
  changes, initiation, 441
  cleaning, requirement, 529–530
  design liability insurance, 679
  disputes, mitigation, 212–216
  liability insurance, 679
  opinion, 679
  primary role, 437
  protective liability coverage, 687
  selection, risk, 184
  submittal schedule, 514
  warranty, provision, 437
Contracts, 679
  award, 428, 679
  breach, 675
    action, 33
    claim, 218
  changes, 489
    documentation, 489
  conditions, 392, 678
  documents, 679
    modification, 686
    selection, risk, 180
  execution, 682
  forms/supplements, 392
  issues, 583–584
  limit, 679
  risk, 180
  rules, establishment, 180

specificity, importance, 488
  sum, 679
  time, 679
Contractual framework, 334–341
Contractual liability, 679
  usage, 200
Contribution, 679
Contributory negligence, 679
Control, 676
Conversations, documentation, 470–471
Conveying systems, design decisions, 339
Coordination sessions, 468
Copying, infringement, 42
Copyright, 679
  application, 41
  author creation, 38
  concept, 37–38
  deposit submissions, guidelines, 41
  digital impact, 37–43
  exclusions, 38
  notice, 41
  origination, 38
  ownership, 38
  public policy, 43
  registration, 41
  subject matter, 38–39
  term, 40
Copyrighted material, publication, 39
Core values, clarification, 61
Corporation, 679
  comparison, 92–94
  legal entities, 90
Correspondence, rules, 470–472
Cost
  awareness, 136
  categories, 361–362
  consultants, usage, 497
  control, 501
  criterion, comparison (determination),
    134–135–135
  estimates
    architect evaluation, 495
    presentation, 506
  estimation provisions, 592–593
  indexes, 505
  information, sources, 505–506
  services, 497
Cost-based project, responses, 135–136
Cost-based selection, 679
Cost-benefit analysis, 679
Cost-motivated actions, impact, 519
Cost-plus-fee agreement, 616, 679–680
Cost plus fixed fee, usage, 254
Counsel, request, 36–37
Counterclaim, 680
Covenant, 680
Coverage, 200
Creative conflict, 458
Creativity, monopoly, 43
Credit, 680
  attribution, 10–11
  line, 685
Criminal matters, 31
Critical path method (CPM), 680
  usage, 492–494
Cultural barriers, crossing, 69–71
Cultural taboos, 70
Current assets (short-term assets), 680
  acquisition, 165
Current dollars, 358, 359
Current operating expenses, 157
Current ratio, 679
Custody, 676
Customer
  allocation, 47
  boycott, 47

D

Daily billing rate, 680
Damages, 680
  result, 33
Data analysis, 266–267
  skills, importance, 262
Databases, usage, 270
DataCAD (software), 231
Data gathering, unobtrusiveness, 277
Data-gathering process, 266
Debit, 680
Debt, 680
Declaratory judgment, 680
Deductive (deduct) alternate, 673
Deductives, requirement, 197
Default, 680
Deferred revenue, 680
Defined benefit plans, 207
Deliverables
  control, 213
  statement, 461
  written architectural program, 267
Deltek Vision (financial management software), 164
Demographic changes, impact, 534
Demurrage, 680
Dental insurance, 205
Deposition, 680
Depreciation, 680
Descriptive specifying, 404
Design
  activity, continuousness, 330
  analysis, involvement, 332–333
  changes, 415
    impact, 519
  client, importance, 332
  climate, impact, 331
  competitions, 47
    entry/usage, 138
  compromise, examples, 519—521
  concepts
    alternatives, evaluation, 334
    evolution, 334
    exploration, 290
  contingencies, 505
  contracts, 627–629
    multiplicity, impact, 435
  contractual framework, 334–341
  coordination, standard of care, 253
  cost, impact, 332
  cost estimation, 501–506
    area method, 502
    assemblies method, 502–503
    elemental methods, 502–503
    quantity survey method, 505
    single-unit rate method, 502
    subsystems method, 502–503
    volume method, 502
  decisions, 338
    list, 339–340
  development, 336, 338
    deliverables, 336
    documentation, 337–338
    documents, 680
    phase, 244
    services, 680
    sustainable actions, 314
  documentation, phase basis, 337–338
  external factors, 332
  factors, 330–332
  feedback, access, 227
  fees, delivery method (impact), 424
  goals, establishment, 334
  implementation phases, 338, 340

importance, 4
improvement, reduction (impact), 300
issues
  environmental aspects, pursuit, 289
  identification, 288–289
objective, 501
phase, 330–341
  construction phase, overlap, 295
precedents, 333
preeminence, 251
process, 332–334
  information (product), 21
professions, frustration, 98
project outcomes, connection, 286
public agency approvals, impact, 331
quality, maintenance, 510–521
regulatory constraints, 331
research
  implications, interpretation, 284–285
  logic, 285
review meetings, 63
schedule, impact, 332
services, expansion/integration offer, 250
site, impact, 331
software, advances, 225
stage, importance, 503
success, feedback (strategies), 313
team
  involvement, 430–431
  selection, risk, 182–183
technologies, 225–227
tools, 225–228
Design-bid-build delivery, usage, 300–301
Design-bid/negotiate-build
  projects, documents, 628
  usage, 625
Design-build, 680
  appeal, 385
  cost control, 432
  entities, 497
  firm, operation, 295
  market entry, 386–387
  projects
    delivery, 384–387
    documents, 627
    risk, 253
  risk factors, 385
  start-up considerations, 385–386
Design-Build Institute of America, 26, 302
Design Excellence Program, 137
Design-through-construction phase services, 243–244
Detail, 680
Dialogue, monologue (contrast), 69
Digital Project (software), 231
Dignity/integrity, ethical standard, 10
Direct expense, 681
  charge, 157
  usage, 155–156
Direct hire, 143–144
Direct personnel expense (DPE), 681
  multiple, 686
Direct salary expense (DSE), 681
  multiple, 686
  representation, 156
Disability benefits, 205–206
Discovery, 681
DISC Personal Profile System, 115
Discussions (recording), flip chart (usage), 117
Disputes, 508
  action, requirement, 212
  anticipation/prevention, 209–210
  avoidance, 218
  changes/delays, impact, 209
  communication, importance, 215
  documentation, importance, 215

follow-up actions, 218
management/avoidance, 208–218
mitigation techniques, attention, 213
potential, enhancement, 212
reduction, contracts (usage), 210
resolution strategy, 208–209
review board, usage, 216
Distractions, avoidance, 68
Dividend, 681
Documentary classification, 221
Documentation (documents)
  changes, impact, 512
  checklists, 475
  completion, 513
  coordination, 414–418
  importance, 215, 286
  ownership, 590–591
  reviews, project manager responsibility, 475
  rules, understanding, 488–489
Documentum (software), 233
DOE-2 (energy efficiency computer program), 315
Double-barreled questions, avoidance, 274
Double-entry bookkeeping, 681
Draw, 681
Drawings, 681
  coordination, 409
  documentation, 337–338
  elements, 399
  insurance coverage, 201
  integration, 410
  organization, 401
  production methods, 399–400
  review, 409–410
  scale/dimensions/targets, 398–399
  sequence, 397–398
  sheet formats, 397–398
  standards, 400–401
  usage, 335, 397–401
Dual obligee bond, 681
Durability, design, 312
Duty, 681
  breach, 675
Duty to defend, inclusion, 587–588

E

Earned revenue, 681
Earned surplus, 681
Earned value tracking chart, 483
Earnings per share, 681
Easement, 681
Ecological context, design, 307
Economic analysis
  period, 360
  principles, 357–362
Economic equivalence, 361
Economic factors, impact, 435
Economic formulas (present value), 359, 360
Economic performance, improvement, 249–250
Economic structure, architecture (placement), 5
ECOTECT (software), 231–232
Egan Report (UK Construction Task Force), 300
Ego, constraints, 67
Egress
  means, 560–561, 572–573
  times, 564
Electrical systems, design decisions, 340
Electronic data management (EDM), 400
Electronic files, 223–224
E-mail, business tool, 471
Email communication, 71
Embodied energy, report, 323
Emerging Professional's Companion (EPC), 655–656

Empathetic listening, 67–68
    frames of reference, 67–68
    keys, 67
Empathetic perspective, usage, 73
Employee
    benefits (customary and mandatory benefits),
        674
    replacement benefits, 205–206
    time records, tracking, 476
Employer, liability insurance, 681
Employer identification number (EIN),
        acquisition, 85
Employer-related insurance, 202–207
Employment practices liability insurance, 201
Endorsement, 681
End User License Agreement (EULA_, 631
Energy
    costs, increase, 332
    efficiency, evaluation (computer programs), 315
    reduction, strategies, 311
Energy-10™ (energy efficiency computer
        program), 315
Energy Star program (EPA), 316
Entity, 681
Enumerative classification, 221
Environment, building material-related impact,
        328
Environmental design professions, 681
Environmental impacts
    consideration, 319
    estimation, 325
Environmental LCA, 315–316
Environmentally friendly materials, usage
        (strategies), 312
Environmentally preferable building materials,
        usage, 311–312
Environmentally preferable products (EPPs)
    claims, 323
    construction process, 319
    definition, 318–319
        variation, 319
    FTC guidance, 319
    programs, green product basis, 319–320
    selection, 318–330
        guiding principles, 328–330
    standards
        approaches, variation, 326–327
        interim solution, 326–328
Environmental plans, 537
Envisioning, 279
    confidentiality, 279
    homogeneous groups, building, 279
    participants, identification, 279
    questions, sample, 279
    sessions
        guidelines, 279
        scheduling, 279
eQUEST® (energy efficiency computer
        program), 315
Equipment, design decisions, 340
Equity, 681
    capital, 681
    ethics definition, 7
Equivalence, example, 361
Erratum (errata), 681
Errors/omissions
    changes, 441
    elimination, 477
e-SPECS (InterSpec, Inc.), 409
    Linx™, 422
Estimates, detail, 431
Estimation approaches/systems, categories, 502
Estoppel, 681
Ethics
    definition, 7
    future, 14

levels, 13–14
    professional conduct, relationship, 6–14
    standards, 10
    violations, 10–12
Euclidean zoning, 538–540
Evidence, interpretation, 289–290
Evidence-based concepts, outcomes
        (hypothesis), 290
Evidence-based design, 281–292
    adoption, 292
    advantages, 291–292
    definition, 283
    hypothesis/measurement, commitment, 286
    impact, 283
    interest, increase, 283–285
    lessons, 286
    myths, debunking, 290–291
    practicing
        skills, 287
    practicing, weakness, 285
    process, 287–290
        list, 288
        product, contrast, 283–284
    rules/standards, 291
    steps, 288–290
    undertaking, 285–287
Excess liability insurance, 681
Excess liability policies, 201
Exclusions, 681
Exclusive rights
    authorized use, 40
    benefits, 40
    limitations, 42
    unauthorized use, 40
Executive sessions, 468
Exits, travel distance, 561
Expanded services, offering, 250
Expectations
    written word, relationship, 458
Expenditure, 682
Expense (expenses), 682
    cash coverage, 155
    classification, 157–158
    heading, 157
Expense-only claim, 682
Expert witness, 682
Exposure, 682
Express warranty, 682
Extended coverage insurance, 682
Extended reporting period, 682
eXtensible Markup Language (XML),
        usage, 234
Exterior closure, design decisions, 339
Externalities, 306
Extra, 682

F

Faceted classification, 221
Facilitation skills, learning, 62
Facility
    information, classification, 221
    life cycle, 682
    planning, 682
    procurement, LCC applications, 366
    program, 689
    space needs, identification (steps), 264
Facility performance evaluation (FPE), 279–280
    benefits, 280
    procedure, 280
    questions, sample, 280
    timing, variation, 280
Fairness, ethics definition, 7
Fair use, 42

Faithful performance, 682
Fast track, 682
Fast-track delivery schedules, 253
Feasibility study, 682
    usage, 136
Federal architect selection process, 137
Federal government, organizations, 662–663
Federal ID number (FEIN), acquisition, 85
Fees, 682
    disputes
        adjudication, consideration, 489
        prevention, 488–489
    mandatory schedule, 47
    multipliers, 254
    retaining, risk/response, 259
Fidelity bond, 682
    usage, 202
Final acceptance, 682
Final change order, 527
    omission, 523
Final completion, contractor requirement,
        527–528
Final entry, book, 683
Final inspection, 682
Final payment, 449, 682
Financial consultant, selection, 162
Financial health, maintenance, 165–173
Financial management software packages, 164
Financial management systems, 155–163
Financial planning, 145–154
    factors, 165–166
    process, streamlining, 152–154
Financial reports, 159–162
    usage, 162
Financial statements, reporting (frequency), 160
Financial strength, 168–170
Financial systems
    financial data entry, 230
Fire areas, identification, 569–570
Fire protection, 558–559
Fiscal year, 682
Fixed assets (long-term assets), 682
    acquisition, 165
Fixed expenses, reimbursement, 202
Fixed fees (stipulated sum fees), 682
    usage, 253
Flexible zoning, 539, 540
Floating zones, 541
Floor-area ratio (FAR), example, 541
Floor plan, obtaining, 277
Focus group sessions, 279
Force account, 683
Forest certification program, development, 322
Forest Stewardship Council (FSC), 322
    forest product certification, 329
Form-based zoning, 542–544
    purpose, 543
    secondary impacts, generation, 544
    variations, 544–545
Form VA, completion, 43–44
FormZ (software), 232
Foundation, design decisions, 339
4-D models, 227
401(k) plan
    characteristics, 206
Frames of reference, comparison, 68
Frequency questions, choices (quantification),
        274–275
Fringe benefits, 683
Frivolous suit, 683
Functional area method, 502
Function analysis, 346–347
    conducting, 344–345
Function logic diagram, 351
Function Pareto cost model, 352
Funds, sources/uses, 155–156

G

Gender differences, 68
General accounting, 158
General contract, 683
General expenses, 156
  inclusion, 157–158
General journal, 683
General ledger, 683
General project meetings, 468
General requirements, 683
Geographic location, insurance premium
  factor, 198
Geotechnical investigation (subsurface
  investigation), 683
Glossaries, usage, 66
Goal-based work plans, 60–61
  worksheet
    completion, steps, 60
    sample, 61
Goals
  defining, 56
  early definition, IPD principle, 390
  statement/partnering charter, writing, 115
Goodwill, 683
Google Desktop (software), 233
Government agencies, programming services
  (usage), 260–261
Graphic works, copyright, 38–39
Green Building Rating System (U.S. Green
  Building Council), 315
Green buildings
  building systems, 311
  evaluation tools, 315–317
  green products, usage, 318–319
  rating systems, 315–317
Greenguard Environmental Institute (GEI),
  321, 322
  product certification, 329
Green Label Plus, 321
Green Seal, standards, 329
GreenSpec® Directory, 329
Gross negligence, 683
Gross revenue per total employees, usefulness,
  169
Group meetings
  decision-making exercises, conducting,
    119–120
  facilitation, 118
    example, 118
  leadership, rotation, 117
  questions, addressing, 119
  strengthening, 117
Groups
  discussions, facilitation skills, 62
  dynamics, 343–344
  observation, 276–277
  sessions, usage, 266
Guaranteed maximum price (GMP), 616–617,
  683
Guided walk-throughs, 277–279
  form, sample, 278
Guidelines for Improving Practice" (Schinnerer),
  37

H

Harm, proximate cause, 33
Hazardous materials, responsibility (absence),
  599–600
Health, safety, or welfare (HSW)
  benefits, 48
  credit

MCE course qualification, 49
  state MCE requirements, relationship, 50
  subject areas, 49–50
Health and Community Design (FrankEngelke/
  Schmid), 292
Health care flexible spending amounts, 205
Health insurance, 203–205
  plans, 203
Health Insurance Portability and Accountability
  Act (HIPAA), 204
  protection, 205
Health maintenance organizations (HMOs)
  plans, 203
  usage, 204
Health reimbursement accounts (HRAs), 204
Health savings accounts (HSAs), 204
Healthy Building Network, 329
Heliodon, illustration, 316
Hierarchy, 221
Higher-risk project types, 178
Hold-harmless provision, 200, 583
Honesty, importance, 20
Hourly billing rate, 683
  usage, 254
Housing development, solutions, 553
Human comfort/strategies, understanding, 308
Human resources
  software, 233
  systems, usage, 230

I

Ideas
  alternatives, identification/evaluation, 345
  copyright exclusion, 38
  generation, 110
Illuminating Engineering Society (IES), 408
Immunities, 34
Implied indemnification, 693
Implied nonexclusive license, 591
Implied warranty, 683
Incentive clause, 683
Incentive zoning, 539, 540–542
Incidental use areas, 569
Incidents, management, 217
Inclusionary zoning, 539
Income, 693
  protection, 205–206
  statement, 683
    example, 161
    time utilization monitoring, 172
    usage, 159–160
Indemnification, 683
  obligations, triggers (identification), 586–587
  provisions, 583
Indemnities, 586–588
  clause, 601
  duty to defend inclusion, 587–588
Indemnity plans, 203
  rarity, 204
Independent postoccupancy evaluation, 287
Indirect expense, 683
  allocation, 683
  budgeting, 172
  factor, 683–684
    usage/calculation, 170
  identification, 156
Indirect salary expenses, usage, 170–171
Indirect time, monitoring, 481
Individual project planning, 152
Individual Retirement Account (IRA) plan
  setup, 207
  usage, 85
Indoor air, pollution, 309

Indoor athletic facilities, example, 265
Indoor environment creation, health
  quality, 309
  strategies, 309
Industrial Revolution, impact, 23–24, 303
Industry comments, attention, 625
Industry foundation classes (IFCs),
  233–234
Industry resources, 220
Inflation, impact, 358
Informant
  expert role, 269
  language, mirroring, 269
Information
  classification terminology, 221
  ethical obligation, 285
  exchange, deceleration (impact), 300
  gathering, 264–266, 344
  models, importance, 396
  needs, responses, 444
  relevance, possibilities, 289
  sources, variety (usage), 284
  storage/retrieval, 223–224
  surveys, 47
Information management, 218–224,
  472–473
  archives, 220
  business functions, 219
  importance, 224
  industry resources, 220
  project materials, 220
  systems, 229–230
    development, 220
Informing, communication goal, 65
Infringement, 40
  claims
    initiation, 43
    registration, requirement, 40
Infringing uses, 42
In-house cost estimator, usage, 510
Initial decision maker, 684
Innovation, collaboration (IPD principle), 390
Innovator archetype, business design model
  (sample), 105
Insolvency, 684
Inspection, 684
  list (punch list), 684
Inspector of record, 437
Inspiration, ability (importance), 20–21
Institute for Market Transformation to
  Sustainability, standards endorsement,
  328
Institute of Management and Administration
  (IOMA), cost management/control
  resource, 173
Instruction, communication goal, 65
Insurability issues, 199
Insurable interest, 684
Insurance, 598–599
  brokers/companies, selection, 195–196
  certificate, 677
  consultants, usage, 431
  costs, 197
  coverage, 194–208
    insurance premium factor, 199
    policy considerations, 195
  policy limits, 197
  simplicity, influence, 198
  split limits, 197
Insured, 684
Insurer, attributes, 195–196
Integrated Budget and Schedule Method
  (PlanTrax®), 479
Integrated design, 314
Integrated firms, construction/design (timing),
  295–296

Integrated practice, 684
  foundations, 293–297
    illustration, 294
  implementation, 302
  providers, impact, 301
  services, offering, 296
  support, 228
  traditional practice, contrast, 293–302
Integrated project delivery (IPD), 387–391
  benefits, 388–389
  change, achievement, 391
  principles, 389–391
  value propositions, 389
Integrated service providers, project delivery
    method usage, 295
Integrated services, offering, 250
Integration, benefits, 300–302
Intellectual property, 583
  digital impact, 37–43
  ethics, 13–14
  long-term access, 233
  public policy, 43
Interest, 684
  income, 155
  rate, discount rate (similarity), 358
Interest, showing, 67
Interior construction, design decisions, 339
Intern, 684
Internal budget tracking/management, 475–476
Internal project budget, 684
Intern architects, resources, 655
International Alliance for Interoperability (IAI),
    233–234, 236
International Building Code (IBC), 556, 564,
    568–573
  fire suppression threshold limits, 570
  fundamentals, 557–561
International Code Council (ICC), 555–557
  model codes, 566
  performance code, 563
International Conference of Building Officials
    (ICBO), 555
International Facility Management Association,
    24
International Fire Code (IFC), 556
  fundamentals, 557–561
International projects, estimation, 509
Intern Development Program (IDP), 655
  NCARB management, 47
Internet, usage, 139
Interoperability, 684
  NIST definition, 221
  open standards basis, 233
  usage, 230, 233–234
Interprofessional relationships, professional
    liability, 199
Interrogatories, 684
Interview
  focus, absence, 142
  guide, usage, 271
  guidelines, 269, 271–272
  objective, 266
  why questions, avoidance, 271
Interviewing
  clarification, request, 271
  effectiveness, 269–273
  restatement/summarization, 273
  silence, allowance, 271
  stories, invitation, 271
  usage, 265–266
Intranets, usage, 229–230
Investment credit, 684
Invitation letter, pretesting, 275
Invited bidders, 684
Invoice, 684
  control, 483–484

format
  percent complete, 486
  time/materials, 485
Invoicing
  advice, 476
  terms, 259

J

Jargon, avoidance, 70–71
Job captain, 684
Joinder, 684
Joint and several liability, 684
Joint ventures, 609–611, 684
  agreements, 611
  consideration, 36
  formation, reasons, 610
  process, 610–611
  professional liability, 199
Journal, 684
Judgment, 685
Jurisdictions, usage, 45–46
Jury, 685

K

Keynote-based drawings, 410
Keynote system, 401

L

Land use classifications, 548
Languages, learning, 65–66
Large group coverage, 205
Large-scale drawings, usage, 226
Latent defect, 685
Law
  legal concepts, 30–31
  practice, 36–37
Lawyers, financial consultant selection, 162
Leaders
  awareness, improvement, 59
  beliefs, 22
  blind spots, clarification, 60
  self-development, 22
  serving, challenge/difficulty, 52
  strengths, construction, 60
  understanding, 60
Leadership
  architect, concern (reasons), 51–64
  ascent, 43
  authenticity, 21–22
  basics, 54–55
  concepts, 52–55
  credibility, 20–21
  development, action learning, 63–64
  effectiveness, 21–22
  higher matters, 55
  performance descriptors, 53
  roles, 61
  skills, development, 51
  teams, 110
  training, 55–63
    aspects, 57
    participation, 55–56
    tools, 57–63
Leadership in Energy & Environmental Design
    (LEED), 389, 530
  certification, 283, 628
  Commercial Interiors program, 321
  Green Building Rating System (U.S. Green
    Building Council), 315

LEED Reference Guide, 310
  Rating System, impact, 327–328
Leads, development, 131–132
Learning, types, 56–57
Learning from Our Buildings (Federal Facilities
    Council publication), 281
Legal consultants, usage, 431
Legal/contractual information, 393–394
Legal counsel, necessity, 36
Legal duty, 33
Legal records, 219
Legal structures, legal attributes (comparison),
    92–94
Lender requirements, 595
Lessons learned meetings, 63
Letter agreement, 685
Letter of intent, 429, 578, 685
Level 5 leadership, 54
Liability (liabilities), 685
  heading, 157
  insurance, 685
  legal concept, 217
  limit, 685
    addition, 197
Licensed contractor, 685
Licensing, 40
Lien
  release, 691
  waiver, 694
Life cycle
  data, usage, 328
  knowledge management, impact, 297
  services, expansion, 297
  thinking, application, 328
Life cycle assessment (LCA), 315–316
  comprehensive approach, 323–326
  maturity, 326
  measurement, 316
  problems/limitations, 324
  results, interpretation, 325–326
  single-score approach, 325–326
  studies
    absence, 324
    results, usage, 326
Life cycle cost, 685
  calculations, example, 364
  model, 353
  quality, impact, 356–357
Life cycle costing (LCC), 347, 356–370
  analyses, accuracy requirements, 364–365
  applications, examples, 368–369
  data, sources, 366
  LCA contrast, 323–324
  procedures, 362–367
  study, 366
  worksheet, 370
Life insurance, 205
Lighting systems, design decisions, 340
Limitation of liability (LOL), 583, 685
  contractual provision, 181
Limited liability companies (LLCs), 96–97
  comparison, 92–94
  income taxes, 97
  liabilities, 96–97
  ownership, changes, 97
  ownership/control, 96
Limited medical plans, 203
  usage, 204
Liquid assets, 685
Liquidated damages, 620, 685
Liquidity, 685
  financial planning factor, 165
  maintenance, 165–166
Listening
  communication goal, 66–68
  devaluation, 66

marketing tool, 66
Literature
    search/review, usage, 264–265
    usage, 285
Litigation, number (increase), 181
Local identity, promotion (strategies), 306–307
Location Alphabet Time Category Hierarchy
        (LATCH) information organization, 220
Long-range planning, 534–537
Long-range plans, zoning ordinances
        (relationship), 536
Long-term, term usage, 685
Long-term client relationships, 252
Long-term disability benefits, 206
Long-term planning, 312–313
    strategies, 313
Long-term value, client expectation, 347
Loss, 685
    heading, 157
    inclusion, 158
Low bid, 685
Low chemical emissions, 321–322
Low embodied energy, 323–324
Lowest responsible bidder, 685
Lowest responsive bid, 685
Low-volume materials, concerns, 326

M

Maintenance manuals, usage, 528–529
Maintenance training, omission, 523
Malpractice, 685
Management
    consultants, financial consultant selection, 162
    information, 219
    reports, 160
Mandated QBS, 136–137
Mandatory continuing education (MCE), 48–49
    courses/providers, qualification determination,
        48
    credit, qualification, 48
    hours
        reporting, deadline, 48
        state requirements, 48
    state reciprocity, 48
    state variation, 48–49
    tracking/administration, identification, 48
Manual drafting, 399–400
Margin, 685
Marketing
    information, 219
    plan
        living document, 128
        sample, 128
    project manager involvement, 453
    relationships, importance, 122
    software, usage, 230
    strategy, 122–124
*Marketing Handbook for the Design & Construction
        Professional* (SMPS), 133
Marketplace forces, 298–300
Market position, value, 125
MasterFormat™, 224, 685
    information arrangement, 221
Master plan, usage, 136
Master specifications, 409
MASTERWORKS™ (software), 421–422
Materials
    green attributes, 319–323
    life cycle, environmental effects, 311
    usage
        incentives, 327
        phase, examination, 328
Material safety data sheets (MSDS), 530

Matrices
    completion, 186
    requests, importance, 136
Maxwell Render (software), 232
Maya (software), 232
McDonough Braungart Design Chemistry, 329
Mechanic, lien, 685–686
Mechanical systems, design decisions, 340
Media, insurance coverage, 202
Mediation, 686
Meetings
    management plan, 467–468
        example, 467
    schedule, 467
Members, resources (providing), 24–25
Membership
    suspension, 9
    termination, 9
Memoranda, usage, 470
M/E/P engineer, involvement, 461
Merger, 686
Message
    erosion, occurrence, 64–65
    focus, 68
Message systems, technology (impact), 230
Microsoft Office Project (software), 233, 494
Milestone charts, 491
Minimally processed materials, 322
Minimum profit targets, 256
Mission statements, 219
Mixed occupancy, 569
Modeling software programs, 232
Modification, 686
Money, loss, 202
Moonlighting, ethics, 14
Mortgage, 686
Motivation, usage, 111
Moving average, 686
Multiple-choice questions, scale (usage), 274
Multiple prime contracts, 686
Multiplier, 686
    calculation, 153–154
    usefulness, 173
Mutual understanding/trust, 115
    personality profiles, usage, 116
Myers-Briggs Type Indicator (MBTI), 115

N

Named insured, 686
Narrative meeting report, 469
National Association of Home Builders, 24
National Building Information Modeling
        Standard (NBIMS), 234
    development, 402
National Council of Architectural Registration
        Boards (NCARB), 655–656
    building code compliance, information, 554
    interns/architects, services (management), 47
National Electrical Code, 556
National Fire Protection Association (NFPA),
        408
    codes, specification-oriented/performance
        options, 557
    NFPA 13, 555, 562
    standards, regulatory characteristic, 562
National Institute for Standards and Technology
        (NIST), building performance valuation
        software, 565
National Institute of Building Sciences (NIBS),
        standard
    development, 234
    publication, 222
National Manufacturers Association, 25

National Renewable Energy Laboratory, 329
National Society of Professional Engineers
        (NSPE)
    formation, 24
    PEPP Professional Liability Committee,
        professional liability insurance survey, 207
Natural light, usage, 309
Natural materials, usage, 322
Natural resources, consideration, 317
Natural world, interdependence (recognition),
        304–305
Negligence, 686
    action, success, 33
    claim, 218
Negligence per se, 686
Negligent act/omission, 686
Negotiation
    activities, 382
    bidding, contrast, 423–424
    phase, 245, 422–433
    preparation, steps, 423–427
Neighborhood development, 545
Net, 686
Net DSE multiplier, usage, 151
Net multiplier
    calculation, 172
    usage, 154
Networking
    building, 130
Net working capital, 686
Net worth, 686
    heading, 157
NewForma Project Center (software), 233
Niche practice, establishment, 108–109
Nonbiased questions, writing, 274
Nonchargeable time, monitoring, 481
Non-collusion affidavit, 686
Nonconforming work, changes, 441
Nonconforming work (defective work), 686
Non-expense items, 686
Non-recourse provisions, 597–598
Nonreimbursable direct costs, 255
Nonrenewable energy sources, usage
        (minimization), 310–311
Non-standard agreements
    usage, 584
    usage, risk (architect identification), 180
Nonverbal communication, 70
Notes, taking, 67
Notice to proceed, 617, 686–687
    issuance, 439
    letter, sample, 440

O

Obligation, statements (rules), 12
Observation
    information-gathering technique, 266
Occupancy
    certificate, 677
    determination, 569
    structure classification, 558
    sustainable actions, 315
Occupational accident, 687
Occurrence, 687
    policy, 687
Off-gassing test chamber, 321
Office contents, insurance, 201
OmniClass Classification System, 222
OmniClass Construction Classification System
        (OCCS), 222, 224
    tables, 222
OmniClass tables, 223
One-on-one communication skills,
        improvement, 62

On-site observations, 459
Open access POS plans, 204
Open bidding, 687
Open-ended questions
    inclusion, 273–274
    information, 58
    responses, coding (sample), 276
    usage, 271
Operation manuals, usage, 528–529
Oral agreements, 578
    risk, 180
Organizational chart, programmer review,
        265–266
Organizational expense, 687
Organizational link, 111
Organization chart, clarity (absence), 142
Organization/content, 392–397
Organization/leadership, IPD principle, 390
Original entity, book, 676
Original work, copyright, 38
Outcome-based value pricing, 255
Outline specifications, 687
    usage, 336
Outstanding stock, 687
Overhead expense budget, 146
    sample, 150
Overhead expenses, 149, 156
Overhead management, 170–172
Overlay zoning, 539
Overruns, 483
Overtime, 483
Owner, 687
    agreements, 576–585
    board/committee representation, 579
    boiler-plate provisions, 595–599
    budget, designing, 584
    characteristics, 579–580
    concerns, 496–497
    decisions, cost basis, 134
    liability insurance, 687
    litigation, 580
    occupancy date, omission, 523
    personnel, demonstration/training, 529
    protective liability coverage, 687
    representative, 687
    responsibility, 394
Owner-architect agreements, 687
    effectiveness, 585
    usefulness, 251
Owner-architect relationships, 35
Owner-contractor agreements, 613, 614, 687
    form, 426
Owner-generated agreements, 247, 585–601
    concerns, 586–599
Owner-generation indemnification provision,
        consideration, 586
Owner-provided information, 600–601
Owner-retained consultants, 608–609
Ownership teams, 110
Owners 401(k) plan, 207

P

Paid-in capital, 687
Paper records, 223
Papers, insurance coverage, 202
Parametric objects, 227
Pareto cost model, 352
Parking, 549–550
Parti, 687
Partial occupancy, 687
Partner, professional registration requirements, 89
Partnership, 687
    comparison, 92–94

Par value, 687
Passive design, 308
Patent defect, 687
Pattern books, example, 543
Payment
    amounts, dispute, 594–595
    application, 447–448, 674
        processing, 447
    bond (labor and material payment bond),
        426, 687
    certificate, 677
    information, 448
    patterns, performance feedback, 259
    provisions, 594–595
    slowness, risk/response, 259
    terms, 259
Payroll
    burden, 156
    expenses, cash coverage, 155
    journal, 687
        original entity, book, 687
    taxes, 687
    utilization, 694
        ratio, 170
Peachtree Software (financial management
        software), 164
Peer review, 432
    forms, 287
    submission, 286–287
Penal sum, 688
Pension plan, 688
    characteristics, 206
Percentage-based contract, disadvantages,
        254–255
Percentage-based fee agreement, structure, 255
Percentage fee, 688
Percent-for-art programs, 43
Performance, 688
    appraisals, 63
    bond, 426, 688
    codes, 563–565
    levels, 49
    standard, 541
    zoning, 540
Performance specifying, 404
Permit, 688, 694
Personal commitment, ethics, 14
Personal financial advisers, financial consultant
        selection, 162
Personal injury, 688
    liability coverage, 688
Personality profiles, 60
Personal journal, value, 471–472
Personal projects, ethics, 14
Personal space, respect, 70
Personal vision statements, 61–62
Persuasion, communication goal, 65
Petty cash, 688
Pharos Project (Healthy Building Network), 329
Pictorial works, copyright, 38–39
Plane of connection, establishment, 67
Planned unit development (PUD), 539, 541
Planning
    commissions, role/authority, 535
    intensification, 390
    process, 146
        example, 536
    regulations, 567
    study, usage, 136
Plotting Guidelines (Tri-Service), 419
Plumbing codes, 567
Point-of-service (POS) plans, 203
    usage, 204
Point rating systems, 541
Political action committees (PACs), 26
Populations, study, 280

Porras, Jerry I., 108
Portable equipment, insurance coverage, 201
Positioning, 125–126
Post-construction
    evaluation, 477
    services, 244
Post-consumer recycled materials, 320
Postindustrial recycled materials, 320
Postoccupancy
    evaluation, 688
        comparisons, 313
    services, 531
    sustainable actions, 315
Postoccupany services, 688
Postproject review, 509
Power of attorney, 688
Practitioners
    lessons, 286
    project goals, listing, 288
Pre-bid conference, 427
Precautionary Principle, 310
Precedence diagram (CPM variation), 494
Preconstruction (design-build), 688
    activities, 382
    conference, 429
        agenda, sample, 440
        conducting, 439, 441
    services, 431–432
Pre-consumer recycled materials, 320
Predesign, sustainable actions, 314
Predesign services, 688
    usage, 243
Preferred provider organizations (PPOs) plans,
        203
    usage, 204
Preliminary design (design-build), 688
    documents, 688
Preliminary drawings, 688
Premium, 688
Prepaid expenses, inclusion, 158
Presentation
    advice, 68
    drawings, 226
Present worth, 359
    analysis, 363–364
Present-worth method, 362–363
Price escalation, 505
Price fixing, 46–47
Pricing strategy, 255–258
Primavera Project Planner (software),
        233, 494
Prime contract, 688
Prime contractor, 688
Prime professional, 688
Principal, 688
Principal-in-charge, 688
Private legal arrangements, legal source, 31
Privity, 688
    legal concept, change, 34
Proactive CA
    achievement, 434
    reactive CA, contrast, 434
Problem identification/analysis, 445
Pro bono service, 688
Procedural/administrative information, 394–395
Process
    complexity, 299
    jargon, avoidance, 72
    leadership, 143
Processes/procedures, improvement, 57, 62–63
Procurement, cost issues, 507–508
Product
    data, 689
    green attributes, 319–323
        differentiation, 328
    liability insurance, 689

models, AISC term, 413–414
substitutions, 442
Production
methods, selection, 412–414
planning, 411–414
elements, 412
importance, 414
scheduling/budgeting, 411–412
sequence, 413
Productivity
DSE management principle, 172
increase, BIM technology usage, 235
Professional, 689
Professional adviser, 689
Professional aspirations, ethical conduct
(contrast), 8
Professional conduct, 8–9
canons, 15–18
defining, 45
rules, 10, 45–46
Professional engineer, 689
Professional ethics, 689
defining, 14
Professional liability, 33–34
change, 34
coverage, 196–200
policy, 196
insurance premiums, establishment, 198–199
risk, impact, 195–196
Professional members, value (promotion), 25
Professional misconduct, defining, 45
Professional organizations, 657–662
participation, 23–27
Professional practice
regulation, 44–47
strengthening, 280–281
Professional Pricing Society (PPS), support/
resource, 259
Professional recognition
ethical standard, 10
rules, 12
Professional services
agreement, 246–247
phase, 688
Professional societies
definition, 24
roles, 24–26
Professional sponsor, 689
Professoin
autonomy, intention, 4
characteristics, 3–4
education, requirement, 3
entry requirements, establishment, 45
ethical obligations, 17
expertise/judgment, usage, 3
registration, 3
society, relationship, 6
traits, 4
Profit, 689
estimation, method, 151
heading, 157
loss, reimbursement, 202
plan, 146
establishment, 152–153
restatement, 153
sample, 151
usage, 150–151
planning, paths, 146
representation, 156
requirement, 151
target, 151
terms, addition, 256–258
Profitability, 689
client expectation, 347
financial planning factor, 165
requirement, 165

Profit-sharing plan, 689
characteristics, 206
Pro forma, 689
Program
analysis, 333
management, 689
manager, usage, 432
Programming, 689
client values, 263
constraints/opportunities, 264
data analysis, 266–267
detail, 431
equipment, 263
facility requirements, 264
information gathering, 264–266
preliminary studies, 261
process, 263–267
project goals, 264
skills, 262–263
usage, 260–267
user values, 263
Progress
payments, 618, 689
reporting, 476, 487
schedule, 689
Project, 689
accounting, 158
agreements, review, 439
archives, usage, 477
area, analysis, 307
assessment, matrix, 188–190
authority matrix, 438
budget, 350, 464, 581, 689
conceptual statement, 498
confirmation, 512
drafting, realism, 499
establishment, 498
maintenance, 511–513
budgeting/profitability, 63
CAD model, setup guidelines, 415
changes/delays, impact, 209
characteristics, 580–581
charges, 481
checklist, 690
choices, making, 180
CM conversion, 430
completion
data capture, 283
review alternatives, 483
complexity, experience, 139
conclusion, 476–477
construction, 290
characteristics, 581
control, 478–495
yardsticks/measurements/comparisons, 478
cost, 690
estimates, performing, 513
estimating, 513
cost-of-work-plus-a-fee contract bid, 430
course corrections, 487–490
database
development, 227
setup, 439
debriefing, 477
decision making, 466
description, client requirements, 461
difficulty, 178
directory, 463–464
update, 439
documentation, 290, 393
effort, project manager lead, 456
importance, 470–473
documents, review, 439
estimates, 350
estimating challenges, 509
execution, 212–213

expectations, 209
expenses
management, 172–173
usage, 155–156
facilitation, 466–470
feedback, 531
filing system, sample, 472
findings/implications, conflict, 285
gross income, 683
gross margin, 690
homework, 268
insurance
needs, 197
policy, 197
jurisdictional factors, 581–582
leadership capability, 252
liability insurance, 690
litigation history, 580
manual, contents, 392
materials, 220
meetings, 447
management, 466–468
report, 469–470
monitoring, 473–476
technique, 479
organization, 453, 460–465
chart, sample, 462
outcome, improvement, 519
owner contemplation, 464
participants, expectations, 32
passion, importance, 122
phase
documentation, 335
establishment, AIA owner-architect
agreement (usage), 334–335
plan, 464
planning, 453, 460–465
role, 606
policy, 690
preliminary schedule, 462
professional liability insurance, 200
profit goals, setting, 154
program
design information, 331
monitoring, 474
progress
monitoring, 453
report, sample, 482
record keeping, 451
records
documents, 528
preparation, 215
regulatory requirements, 464
reports, 481, 483
representative, 690
research, timing, 286–287
responsibility matrix, sample, 463
revenues, 690
right sizing, 312
risk, management, 184–185
schedules, 581
negotiation/development, 464
scheduling, example, 491–494
scope, 498
control, 501
fee, providing, 136
project manager monitoring, 478–480
selection, risk, 178–180
size, experience, 139
speed, 298
staffing, 453, 460–465
review, 464–465
status, 476
structure/organization, 602
submittals, checking, 479–480
success, steps, 248

Project (*continued*)
teams, 110
assessment, matrix, 193
continuity, 296
management, 466
type, experience (importance), 138
uniqueness, 284
value, 257
web sites, usage, 229
work plan, 690
Project at a Glance work plan, 461
Project closeout, 522–532, 690
architect responsibility, 525
contractor responsibility, 525
documentation, 522
implementation/enforcement, 525–526
owner responsibility, 525
problems, results, 523
procedures, decisions, 524
responsibilities, 525
expansion, 525
services, client expectation, 524
success, 522
Project delivery
approach, impact, 435
method, VA (relationship), 346
methods, 371–381
process, closeout integration,
523–528
sustainable actions, 314–315
system, 581–582, 690
Project design
characteristics, 581
meetings, 468
team agreements, 602–611
Project management
activities, 452–453
perspective, 454
risk management, 458–459
software, 233
list, 494
Project managers
advocates, role, 456
attitude, impact, 455
client appreciation, 455
communication, consistency, 457
design backgrounds, 454
effectiveness, 452–459
reasons, 455
lead, 455–456
motivation impact, 456
multiplicity, 454
origination, 454–455
personality/behavior, impact, 455
problem solving, 456
progress, monitoring, 456–457
role, 455–457
selection, risk, 182
technical backgrounds, 454
Project Resource Manual, The (CSI), 223–224,
402
Project services
comparison, 479
defining, 240–248
steps, 241–243
description, benefit, 240–241
project manager control, 478–480
specificity, defining, 250–251
types/categories, 243–244
Project-site dispute resolution methods, 215
Project-site dispute resolution techniques,
215–216
Property
damage insurance, 690
insurance, 690
maintenance issues, 566

Proposals
architecture firm, past experience
(comparison), 258
offers, 578
request, 690
Proprietary specifying, 408
Proprietorship, 690
Pro rata, 689
Prospective clients, research, 177
Prospects
homework, 268
information, sources, 270–271
Provisions, absence, 599–601
Proximate cause, 690
PSMJ Financial Statistics Survey (PSMJ), 173
Public, ethical obligations, 16
Public accountants, financial consultant
selection, 162
Public art/architecture, usage, 43
Public authority, 690
Public censure, 9
Public liability insurance, 690
Public transit system, implementation, 550
Punitive damages, 690

Q

Qualification-based interviews, 140–141
details, importance, 142
Qualification-based selection (QBS), 690
explanatory exhibits, 140
responses, 139–142
RFP response, 139
usage, 136–142
value-based selection, differences, 142–143
variation, 137
written proposal elements, 139–140
Qualifications
matrix, sample, 141
representation, accuracy, 11–12
request, 691
short list, determination, 142
Qualified bid, 690
Quality
improvement, BIM usage, 235
levels, 498
management, 474
project notebook, relationship, 490
model, 354–355
Quantitative questions, information, 58
Quantity survey, 690
method, 505
Questionnaires
brevity, 274
completion ease, 273
guidelines, 273–275
mutually exclusive answer choices, inclusion, 274
pretesting, 275
respondent interest, capture/holding, 273
responses
choices, 274
point scales, range, 274
simplicity, 275
usage, 266
Questions
answering, 282–283
measures, selection, 290
arrangement, 275
asking, 69
results, analysis, 275
Question types, 274
QuickBooks Pro (financial management
software), 164
Quotation, 690

R

Raw materials
construction requirements, 324
disposal/recycling/reuse, 324
manufacturing, 323–324
transportation, 324
usage, 324
Raw materials, extraction/harvesting, 323
Reasonable care, standard, 31–32
Record drawings, 691
Record product data submittals, marking, 528
Records, insurance coverage, 202
Recovered material, term (EPA usage), 320
Recycled content
programs, usage, 320
promotion, 320
RediCheck Associates, 418
Redline work sessions, 468
References, usage, 66
Regional/community identity, promotion, 305–307
Registration
board, empowerment, 45
statutes/regulations, 45
Regulatory environment, importance, 545
Reimbursable costs, 255
Reimbursable expenses, 691
categories, 156
control, 476
Reinsurance, 691
Relationships, breakdown, 185
Renewable energy, usage (maximization), 310–311
Renovation projects, impact, 435
Renovations, estimation, 509
Rents, income, 155
Request for information (RFI), 444
answers, 459
Request For Proposal (RFP), 462
cost/cost control questions, 135
experience requirements, 138
responses, 577–578
Research
design, linkage, 285
designers, education, 282–283
findings, designer interpretation, 284
questions
design issues, conversion, 289
information/evidence collection, 289
usage, cost, 291
Research/analysis, 267–281
knowledge, application, 2686
Reserves, inclusion, 505
Resource flows
environmental impact translation, 324–325
input/output, aggregation, 325–326
Resource flows, quantification, 323
Responsibility
admission, 216–217
allocation format, 604–605
matrix, 461
Restrictive specifying, 409
Retainage, 618691
Retained earnings, 691
Retirement benefits, 206–207
Retroactive coverage (prior acts coverage), 691
Retrocommissioning, 313
Revenue, 691
addition, 483
fund source, 155
heading, 157
projection, 145
example, 148
list, 147
projected income categories, 147
usage, 147

Revenues per employee, 169
Review times, allotment, 443
REVIT (software), 232
Rezoning, 546–547
Rhinoceros (software), 232
Risk, 691
    allocation, 624
    avoidance, 175
    elimination, 181
    exposure, 588–590
    factors, evaluation, 256
    identification/evaluation, 175
    model, 354
    planning, 175
    retention/reduction, 175
    transfer, 175
    understanding, 582–583
Risk assessment, pricing (relationship), 252–253
Risk assessment matrices
    analysis, 186
    assessment process, 186
    recommendation, 186–187
    response, 186
    summary assessment, 186
    usage, process, 186–190
Risk management, 691
    encouragement, 197
    initiation, 175
    methods, 175–176
    reasons, 174
    strategies, 174
    techniques, focus, 208
    usage, 207
Roofing, design decisions, 339

S

Safe Harbor 401(k) plan, 207
Salary, 691
Samples, 691
Sampling scheme, selection, 277
Schedule, 399, 691
    project manager control, 480–483
    providing, 135–136
Scheduling, 382
    advice, 464
    approaches, impact, 435
    importance, 333
    provisions, 591–592
Schematic design, 691
    approvals, necessity, 336
    documentation, 337–338
    documents, 691
    phase, 244
    services, addition, 336
    sustainable actions, 314
    usage, 335–336
Scholarly journals, peer review, 287
Scientific Certification Systems (SCS), 322
    third-party certification services, 329
Scientific classifications, 221
S corporation, comparison, 92–94
Sculptural works, copyright, 38–39
Seal, 691
SectionFormat™ Outline CSI/CSC, 407–408
Securities insurance, 202
Self, awareness (increase), 56
Senior manager, response control, 142
Separate contract, 691
Separate contractor, 691
Service Corps of Retired Executives (SCORE), 87
Services
    agreement, risks/responses, 259
    changes, 247–248

contract issues, 583–584
control, 213
diversification, 250
establishment, 605–606
identification, 248
instruments, 684
leadership definition, 22
methods/tools, uniqueness, 252
programming, cost, 261–262
provision, 591–595
    cost, estimation, 256
    explanation, 457
strategy, 255–258
    identification, 256
suspension, 489–490, 600
termination, 600
tracking, 473
types, insurance premium factor, 198
Settlement, 691
    issues, 200
Shared parking opportunities, usage, 550
Shop drawings, 691
Short-term, 692
Short-term investing, surpluses (usage), 166
Short-term value, client expectation, 347
Simple class, 221
SIMPLE 401(k) plan, characteristics, 206–207
Simplified Employee Pension (SEP) plan
    characteristics, 207
    usage, 85
Single-rate unit cost, 502
Site, 692
    analysis, 333
        services, 692
    design decisions, 339
    differences, sustainable design
        acknowledgment, 307
    footprint, example, 307
    plan, obtaining, 277
    suitability studies, 261
    visits, 445, 447
    work, bid, 430
SketchUp (software), 232
Small Business Administration (SBA),
    publications/financial assistance, 87
Small group coverage, 205
Smart Code zoning, 544
SMART(c) Consensus Sustainable Product
    Standards, market definitions/rating
    systems, 329
Social structure, architecture (placement), 5
Society for Design Administration (SDA),
    software program development, 25
Society for Marketing Professional Services
    (SMPS), 133
SoftCAD.3D Architecture (software), 232
Soil survey, 692
Sole proprietorships, comparison, 92–94
Solution options, evaluation, 445
Solvency, 692
    ability, 166
    financial planning factor, 165
Southern Building Code Congress International
    (SBCCI), 555
Sovereign immunity, 692
Space
    individual, observation, 276
    patterns, graphic presentation, 277
    size standards, knowledge (requirement),
        262
Special conditions, 692
Special hazards insurance, 692
Special projects, teams, 110
Specifications, 392, 615, 692
    coordination, 409
    design documentation, 338

integration, 410
method, 403–404
organization, 402–403
production, time (requirement), 412
production methods, 409–410
reference standards, usage, 408
review, 409–410
usage, 402–410
SpecText® (Construction Sciences Research
    Foundation, Inc.), 409
SPECWARE, 418, 421–422
Split limits, 197
Staff
    leveling, 692
    morale, improvement (BIM technology
        usage), 235
    schedule, sample, 465
    selection, risk, 182
Staffing
    expenses, 147–148
    needs, 462–463
    plan, 146
    sample, 149
Stakeholders
    cross-section, selection, 277
    invitation, 279
Standard agreements, 247
Standard fires, curves (increase), 562
Standard form of agreement, 692
Standard Practice for the Testing of Volatile
    Organic Emissions (California protocol),
    321–322
Standards, codes (relationship), 561–563
Standard State Zoning Enabling Act, 547–548
Standing neutral, setup, 216
State registration boards, 670
Statute of limitations, 620, 692
    impact, 34
Statute of repose, 620, 692
Statutes
    interpretations, 31
    legal source, 30
Statutes of repose, 34
Statutory bond, 692
Stipulated sum agreement (lump-sum
    agreement), 692
Stock, 692
Stored materials, usage, 447
Strategic facilities plan, 692
Strategic marketing, 132–133
Strategic parking plans, district scale
    creation, 550
Strategic plans, 219
Strategic value proposition, 348
Strict liability, 692
Strings, 398
Sub-bidder, 692
Subclass, 221
Subcontractor, 692
Subcontracts, 620–621
Subdivision plot, example, 534
Subdivision regulations, importance, 533
Submittals
    management, 442–444
    process, manipulation, 519–520
    review, 442–444, 459, 593–594
        process, architect management, 514
        process, management, 513–514
    schedule, contractor development, 513–514
    tracking, 443
Subpoena, 692
Subrogation, 692
    waiver, 694
Substantial completion, 448–449, 692–693
    certificate, 677
    contractor requirements, 526–527

Substantial similarity, infringement, 42
Substitution, 693
    control, 514–518
Substructure, design decisions, 339
Sub-subcontractor, 693
Successful bidder (selected bidder), 693
Summary assessment matrix, 193
Summary judgment, 693
Summons, 693
Superintendent, 693
Superstructure, design decisions, 339
Supplementary conditions, 693
Supplier, 693
Supply bond, 693
Surety, 693
    consent, 678
Survey, 693
    confidentiality, 273
    design, information gathering, 273–275
    introduction, inclusion, 273
    results, linkage, 58
    sample, selection, 273
    usage, 266
Sustainability, 693
    concerns, 322
    usage, 331
    World Commission on the Environment and
        Development definition, 305
Sustainable design, 693
    achievement, measures, 305–313
    collaboration, reliance, 314
    collective wisdom/feedback, usage, 313
    development patterns, relationship, 549
    documentation, 530
    opportunities, recognition, 305–306
        strategies, 305
    ordinance, establishment, 549
    regional/community identity, promotion,
        305–307
    usage, 303–318
Symbols/abbreviations, usage, 399
Synergy, importance, 110

T

Tangible medium, copyright fixation, 38
Tangible personal property/realty, exclusions, 40
Task order agreement, 137
Tax increment financing (TIF), 547
Taxonomies, 221
Team
    assignments, verification, 439
    communications, 235
    goals (clarification), written goals statement
        (usage), 116–117
    identification, 256
    members, information needs, 119
    organization, 461
    performance, assessment, 115–116
    roles/responsibilities, clarification, 119
    roundtable, 477
Team building, 110–120, 343
    experiences, 114
    myths/facts, 112–113
    practices, comparison, 113
    process, 113–115
Teamwork
    architectural challenges, 111–112
    challenges, 111–112
    ethics, problems, 111
    focus, 111
    groupthink, 111
    individual/loner focus, problem, 111
    leadership, ineffectiveness, 111

    myths/facts, 112–113
    negativity/passivity, 111
    performance slippage, 111
    power, 110–111
    problems, 111
    project ownership, problems, 112
Technical coordination, standard of care, 253
Technical drawings, coordination, 225
Technical jargon, avoidance, 72
Technical references, identification, 414
Technology, IPD principle, 390
Tech speak, avoidance, 70–71
Telephone systems, technology (impact), 230
Tenability, risk, 564
Termination, 693
    expenses, 693
Testimony, 693
Third party, 693
Third-party actions, 33–34
Third-party beneficiary, 693
Third-party legal liability, 200
Third-party project management, 253
3D computer modeling, 226
3D models, time (impact), 227
3ds Max (software), 232
360-degree performance surveys, 57–58
    sample, 59
Threshold inspector, 437
Thresholds, identification, 569–570
Time, 693
    analysis
        report, sample, 171
        time utilization monitoring, 172
    complexity, 299
    management agenda, construction, 60
    provisions, 591–592
    utilization, 694
        monitoring, 172
        ratio, 170
Timely completion, 693
Timely notice, 693
Title block, information, 397–398
Top Ten Green Projects award program, 305
Top Ten Measures of Sustainable Design,
    criteria, 305
Tort, 693
Trade associations, definition, 24
Trade discount, 693
Trade press, 663
Traditional neighborhood development, 545
Traditional project delivery
    approaches, 296
        expansion, 200
    cost, 300
    evolution, 297–298
    IPD, contrast, 388
Transactional/transformational leadership, 53–54
Transect System, diagram, 544
Transfer of development rights (TOD), 539
Transit-oriented development (TOD), 546
Transportation patterns/modes/design, 550
Trial balance, 693
TurboProject (software), 233
Turnkey, 693
2D CAD system, usage, 228
2D computer-aided drafting, 226
Two-dimensional depictions, public showing, 39
2030 Challenge program, 317

U

Umbrella liability insurance, 693
Umbrella liability policies, 201
Unbilled detail report, sample, 484

Unbilled revenue, 694
Uncertain credit, risk/response, 259
Understanding, source, 37
Underwriters Laboratories (UL), 408
    standards, 562
Undesirable client, recognition, 177–178
Unearned revenue, 694
UniFormat™, 224, 694
    usage, 221–222
Uniform Commercial Code (UCC), 694
Uniform Contract, industry acceptance, 623
Uniform Development Code (UDC), 541–542
Uniform Drawing System (CSI), 224, 397, 419
    development, 401
    information, organization method, 398
Uniform Plumbing and Mechanical Code,
    IAPMO publication, 567
Unit cost methods, 254
United Nations Earth Summit, environmental
    design issues, 304
Unit price, 617, 694
    contract, 694
    usage, 507
Universal design, 694
Unjust enrichment, 694
U.S. code documents, history, 555–557
U.S. Constitution, legal source, 30
U.S. Energy Information Administration,
    greenhouse emissions (tracking), 304
U.S. Environmental Protection Agency (EPA)
    environmental toolkit, 327–328
    publications, 318
U.S. Green Building Council, 26
    LEED, impact, 327–328
U.S. Life Cycle Inventory Database Project, 329
U.S. National CAD Standard (NCS), 222–223,
    397, 419–420
    benefits, 420
    development, 402
    NIBS publication, 236
    participation, opportunities, 420
    sheet identification system, 223–224
    Version 3.1, publication, 224
Usage, exclusive rights, 39–40
Users, research methods, 269
Utilization
    DSE management principle, 172
    ratio, 694

V

Value
    changes, development, 345
    competition, 12
    report, preparation, 345–346
    schedule, 508, 618, 691
Value analysis (VA), 694
    concept, 343
    example, 349–355
    methodology, 344–346
    practice opportunity, 349
    tools, 346–347
    training/certification, 348
    usage, 341–354
    value analysis-induced changes, 441–442
    value management, terms (difference), 342
Value-based concepts, 343
Value-based decision making, 342–344
Value-based project, responses, 143
Value-based RFP, response (leadership
    demonstration), 143
Value-based selection, 142–143
Value engineering (VE), 343
Value-enhanced design, 694
    concept, 343

Value management (VM), 343
Vandalism and malicious mischief insurance, 694
Variance, 694
  impact, 487–490
VectorWorks (software), 232
Verbal communication, 69–71
Vertical circulation, design decisions, 339
Vicarious liability, 694
Victor O. Schinnerer & Company
  risk management resource, 185
  Small Firm Program, 208
Virtual buildings
  design options, analysis, 227
  information modeling, 226–227
  modeling, uses, 234
  software programs, 231–233
Virtual design technology, 228
Vision, defining, 56
Vision care (insurance), 205
Visual Artists Rights Act (VARA), 43
Visualization
  software, 232
  tools, 225–228
Volatile organic compounds (VOCs), 321
  off-gassing, 321
Volume methods, 502
Voluntary QBS, 137–138
Vouchers, 694

W

Walk-throughs
  comments, recording, 278
  conducting, 277
  findings, summarization, 278
  photography, usage, 278
  questions, 278
Warranties, 582, 619
  copies, requirement, 529
Warranting, 32
Warranty, 694

Waste flow
  environmental impact translation, 324–325
  input/output, aggregation, 325–326
Waste removal, 206
  operations, 529–530
Water
  codes, 567
  conservation, 310, 550–551
  leakage, 551
Web resources, 270–271
Web site examination, 268
Web survey software, 275
Western Fire Chiefs Association (WFCA), 556
Window shading, impact, 308
Work, 694
  architect rejection, 691
  attainment, 12
  changes, management, 441–442
  changes proposal request, 694
  commencement date, 680
  correction period, 619
  cost, budget, 496–497
  facilitation, 453
  minor changes, 686
  observation, 687
  perspectives, archetypal perspective, 104
  plan, 460–464
  plan, customization, 251
  representation, 447–448
  samples, provision, 12
Workers, compensation insurance, 694
  usage, 202
Workers, compensation policy, rating, 202
Work flow
  management, software, 233
  routing, 229
Work for hire, 42
Working capital, 694
  architect understanding, 169
Work in process, 694
Work in progress, 166
Work-on-the-Boards, 25
Workplace interview guide, sample, 272
Work scope

changes, 252
  descriptions, customization, 251
  identification, 256
World Watch Institute, population/consumption estimates, 304
World Wide Web Consortium (W3C), 234
Write off, 694
Written communication, 71–73
  facts, usage, 71
  jargon, avoidance, 72
  language, vividness, 72
  puffery, avoidance, 72–73
  reading ease, 72
  simplicity, 71–72
  word power, control, 71–72
Written contract, usage, 213

Z

Zoning, 694
  analysis, 333
  boards/commissions, 547–548
  city/county planning commissions, 547
  commissions/boards, 535
  concepts, 538–545
  contextual infill, 548–549
  governing body, 547–548
  impact, 306
  innovations, 539
  long-range plans, 546
  ordinance/code, document, 534–535
  permit, 694
  regulations, 566
  regulatory tool, 535
  review factors, 548–552
  review process, 552–553
    locally specific review processes, 553
    planning staff review, 552
    purpose, 552
  role, importance, 533
  structural review, 552–553
  tools, 546–547
  variances, 546

About the CD-ROM

Contents of the CD-ROM

The CD-ROM contains samples of all AIA Contract Documents (in PDF format for Mac and PC computers) that were released through 2007.

System requirements for the sample AIA Contract Documents

Internet Explorer 6.0 or higher
Firefox 1.5 or higher
Safari 2.0 or higher
Adobe Acrobat Reader 6.0 or higher

To view the sample AIA Contract Documents

If the Autorun program does not automatically run, go to Start | Run and enter aia.htm. Insert the CD into the CD-ROM drive. From the table of contents listing, double click on a file name to launch that file using the Adobe Acrobat Reader. If you do not have the Adobe Acrobat Reader already installed on your computer, you can download the Reader for free from http://www.adobe.com.

For technical support

If you cannot find the answer to your question in the Help section on the CD-ROM, please contact us by phone or through online support.

For technical support, please visit the Wiley Customer Support Website at http://wiley.custhelp.com. This searchable knowledge base contains FAQs, installation notes, content updates, and more for many of our current products. It also enables you to contact a technical support representative directly if you do not find the answer to your question.

Or call 1-800-762-2974 (U.S.) and 1-317-572-3994 (international) from 8:00am to 8:00pm Eastern time, Monday through Friday.

To purchase AIA Contract Documents

AIA Contract Documents are available in electronic format, which allows users to digitally customize and create contract documents for all types and sizes of projects, and in print. For information about how to purchase AIA Contract Documents software or a list of distributors for paper documents, visit www.aia.org/docs_purchase or call 800-242-3837.

PLEASE READ THE FOLLOWING BEFORE OPENING THE SOFTWARE PACKAGE

By opening the package, you are agreeing to be bound by the following agreement:

To place additional orders or to request information about other Wiley products, visit www.wiley.com.